Cambridge International AS & A Level

Complete

Biology

Third Edition

Stephanie Fowler

Glenn and Susan Toole

Beverlyn Nathan
Padmajyothi Sripada

OXFORD
UNIVERSITY PRESS

Great Clarendon Street, Oxford, OX2 6DP, United Kingdom

Oxford University Press is a department of the University of Oxford.
It furthers the University's objective of excellence in research, scholarship, and education by publishing worldwide. Oxford is a registered trade mark of Oxford University Press in the UK and in certain other countries

This edition published in 2020
First edition published in 2013

British Library Cataloguing in Publication Data
Data available

978-1-38-200523-4

10 9 8 7

Paper used in the production of this book is a natural, recyclable product made from wood grown in sustainable forests. The manufacturing process conforms to the environmental regulations of the country of origin.

Printed and bound by CPI Group (UK) Ltd, Croydon, CR0 4YY

Acknowledgements

The publisher and author wish to thank Helen Braben for her insightful comments and thoughts on the syllabus and the development of this book. They also wish to thank Lynda Sharp and Frances Tan for writing the end-of-chapter exam-style questions.

The publisher and author would like to thank the following for permission to use photographs and other copyright material:

Cover: Pulsar Imagens/Alamy; pp2-3: Shutterstock; p9(t): Dr Gopal Murti/SPL; p9(b): Kevin & Betty Collins, Visuals Unlimited/SPL; p13(t): MARKA/Alamy; p13(c): Pascal Goetgheluck/SPL; p14(t): Ami Images/Science Photo Library (hereafter 'SPL'); p14(c): SPL; p14(b): Steve Gschmeissner/SPL; p15(l): Dr Jeremy Burgess/SPL; p15(r): Public Domain; p16: Steve Gschmeissner/SPL; p17(t): Science Source/SPL; p17(tc): Michael Abbey/SPL; p17(c, bc, b): Shutterstock; p20(c): Dennis Kunkel Microscopy/SPL; p20(b): Dr Kari Lounatmaa/SPL; p25: Ami Images/SPL; p26(t): Omikron/SPL; p26(b): Don W. Fawcett/SPL; p28: Power And Syred/SPL; p30(l): Microscape/SPL; p30(r): Cynthia Goldsmith; p50, 51: Shutterstock; p54: J.C. Revy, Ism/SPL; p60: Martyn F. Chillmaid/SPL; p62: imagebroker/Alamy; p95: Dr Yorgos Nikas/SPL; p96: Steve Gschmeissner/SPL; p97(tl, tr, bl, br): Pr. G Gimenez-Martin/SPL; p100: Christopher Tranter; p102(b): Scenics & Science/Alamy; p102(t): Alfred Pasieka/SPL; p124(l): Travelstock44/Image Professionals Gmbh/Alamy; p124(r): D. Hurst/Alamy; p126, p127: Dr Keith Wheeler/SPL; p128(b): Christopher Tranter; p128(t): Garry Delong/SPL; p129: Biophoto Associates/SPL; p131(t): Claude Nuridsany & Marie Perennou/SPL; p131(b): Dr David Furness, Keele University/SPL; p133(t): Dr Keith Wheeler/SPL; p133(b): J.C. Revy, ISM/SPL; p139: Peter Bond, EM Centre, University Of Plymouth/SPL; p140: Steve Hamblin/Alamy; p141(tr): Dr Keith Wheeler/SPL; p141(cr): Courtesy of the authors; p141(tl): John Clegg/SPL; p146(b): blickwinkel/Alamy; p146(t): John Clegg/SPL; p149(l): Steve Gschmeissner/SPL; p151: Dr. Gladden Willis, Visuals Unlimited/SPL; p154: National Cancer Institute/SPL; p155, 156: Steve Gschmeissner/SPL; p188: James Cavallini/Science Source/SPL; p166: SPL; p175: Alfred Pasieka/SPL; p178: Prof. P. Motta/Dept. Of Anatomy/University "La Sapienza", Rome/SPL; p179(b): Dr. John Sasner/UNH, Visuals Unlimited/SPL; p180: Dr. Gladden Willis, Visuals Unlimited/SPL; p181(l, r): Jose Calvo/SPL; p182: Shutterstock; p183: Biophoto Associates/SPL; p184(b): Dr. Gladden Willis, Visuals Unlimited/SPL; p184(t): Shutterstock; p186: Michael Abbey/SPL; p187: Eric Grave/SPL; p192: Alfred Pasieka/SPL; p196(t): CNRI/SPL; p196(b): Julio Etchart/Alamy; p197: Andrew McConnell/Alamy; p198(t): CNRI/

SPL; p198(b): Sinclair Stammers/SPL; p201: Jenny Matthews/Alamy; p203: John Durham/SPL; p204: Moredun Animal Health Ltd/SPL; p206: Biology Media/SPL; p209, 214: Steve Gschmeissner/SPL; p217(t): Dr Jeremy Burgess/SPL; p217(b), 219: Shutterstock; p221: ITAR-TASS News Agency/Alamy; p223: Robert Longuehaye, NIBSC/SPL; p223(l): blickwinkel/Alamy; p223(r): Eric Gevaert/Alamy; p226-227: Shutterstock; p243(r): CNRI/SPL; p243(l): Dennis Kunkel Microscopy/SPL; p244: Professors P. Motta & T. Naguro/SPL; p254(t): Jeff Rotman/SPL; p254(b): Sinclair Stammers/SPL; p257: Dr.Jeremy Burgess/SPL; p278(l): Science History Images/Alamy; p278(r): Shutterstock; p280: Mitsuaki Iwago/Minden/naturepl.com; p281(l): Konrad Wothe/Imagebroker/Alamy; p281(r): Mike Goldwater/Alamy; p285(l): Astrid & Hanns-Frieder Michler/SPL; p285(r): Science VU, Visuals Unlimited/SPL; p286: Prof. P. Motta/Dept. of Anatomy/University "La Sapienza", Rome/SPL; p288: Thomas Deerinck, NCMIR/SPL; p297: Steve Gschmeissner/SPL; p302: Saturn Stills/SPL; p303: SPL; p305: Dr Jeremy Burgess/SPL; p306: University of Edinburgh; p311, 313, 318: Steve Gschmeissner/SPL; p320: CNRI/SPL; p325: Astrid & Hanns-Frieder Michler/SPL; p326: Biology Media/SPL; p330(t): Shutterstock; p330(b): Noah Elhardt; p335: Dept. Of Clinical Cytogenetics, Addenbrookes Hospital/SPL; p336(t): Science Pictures Ltd/SPL; p336(b): Adrian T Sumner/SPL; p337(t): Adrian T Sumner/SPL; p337(b): Biophoto Associates/SPL; p352: SPL; p355(l): Rudmer Zwerver/123RF; p355(c, r): Vasiliy Koval/123RF; p356(t): FLPA/Alamy; p356(cl): Vasiliy Vishnevskiy/Alamy; p356(cr): Jan Kupracz/Alamy; p366: Virtual Class Biology, Faculty of Science, Radboud University, Nijmegen, Netherlands.; p368(t, c ,b), 381: Shutterstock; p382: Eye Of Science/SPL; p383(l, r): Michael W. Tweedie/SPL; p386(t): Shutterstock; p386(b): Ingo Schulz/imageBROKER/Alamy; p387: Peter Menzel/SPL; p388: Nigel Cattlin/Alamy; p389: Pierre BRYE/Alamy; p390(t): Shutterstock; p390(b): Science History Images/Alamy; p395(t): Shutterstock; p395(b): Juniors Bildarchiv GmbH/Alamy; p396(t): Shutterstock; p396(b): Scott Leslie/Nature Picture Library; p399(l): Photostock-Israel/Cultura/SPL; p399(r): Claudio Contreras/Nature Picture Library/SPL; p401(t): CNRI/SPL; p401(b): Eye Of Science/SPL; p402(t): Wim Van Egmond/SPL; p402(b): Veronique Leplat/SPL; p403(t): Glyn Ryland/Alamy; p403(c): John Bennet/Alamy; p404: Dennis Frates/Alamy; p405(t): Simon Fraser/SPL; p405(b): Geoffrey Morgan/Alamy; p409: Martyn F. Chillmaid/SPL; p414(t): Wayne Lawler/SPL; p414(b): Ivy Close Images/Alamy; p415: Julie Dermansky/SPL; p416, 417: Shutterstock; p418(t): Jonathan Dorey - China/Alamy; p418(b): blickwinkel/Schmidbauer/Alamy; p419: Matthew Oldfield/SPL; p420: Shutterstock; p422: Patrick Landmann/SPL; p424: Ron N Beths/Flickr; p429(l): Shutterstock; p429(r): louise Murray/SPL; p430: Philippe Psaila/SPL; p433: Dr Gopal Murti/SPL; p435: Pascal Goetgheluck/SPL; p437(b): Shutterstock; p437(t): Arno Massee/SPL; p438: James King-Holmes/SPL; p439: Medical School, University Of Newcastle Upon Tyne/Simon Fraser/SPL; p441: Lydie Naneix/123RF; p443: Mauro Fermariello/SPL; p447: Shutterstock; p448: Sara Tassan Mazzocco/123RF; p450: Nigel Cattlin/Alamy; p451(t): Paulo Oliveira/Alamy; p451(b): Shutterstock; p452: Scott Sinklier/Agstockusa/SPL.

Figure 5 on page 421: source published by the Royal Society, 2019, reprinted under the terms of the Creative Commons Attribution License (CC-BY 4.0)

Artwork by GreenGate Publishing Services, Aptara, and OUP.

Every effort has been made to contact copyright holders of material reproduced in this book. Any omissions will be rectified in subsequent printings if notice is given to the publisher.

This Student Book refers to the Cambridge International AS & A Level Biology (9700) Syllabus published by Cambridge Assessment International Education.

This work has been developed independently from and is not endorsed by or otherwise connected with Cambridge Assessment International Education.

Contents

Contents

Contents

Introduction

Complete Biology aims to make your study of biology successful and interesting. It has been written specifically to meet the requirements of the latest Cambridge International AS & A Level Biology syllabus 9700.

The book is divided into 19 chapters:

- Chapters 1–11 cover AS level.
- Chapters 12–19 cover A level.

Note that the contents list is your syllabus matching grid.

New ideas are presented in the book in a careful step-by-step manner to allow you to develop a firm understanding of concepts and ideas. Biology at this level will require you to describe and explain facts and processes in detail and with accuracy. The course is also about developing skills so that you can apply what you have learned.

Within each chapter of the book, the sections are set out in an easy-to-follow sequential approach. They can also be covered in an order that suits your learning or one that matches the scheme of work that your teacher is following.

New biological discoveries are made each day, which add to our knowledge and understanding of the world and make it a safer and healthier place to live. *Complete Biology* explores these discoveries in a way that not only provides the facts, but also considers the social, environmental, technological, ethical and economic implications which they present.

The layout of the book is designed to cover information in a clear way that is easy to access. Its features include:

- **Short, manageable sections** covering related concepts and biological facts.
- **Full-colour diagrams** to illustrate points made in the text. Labels and annotations are included so that these diagrams aid your understanding and improve clarity.
- **Colour photographs** to improve your understanding further and add realism to the information and ideas within the text.
- **Extensive use of bullet points** to produce lists of information that you will find easy to follow. They are useful for making your own learning and revision notes. They often have key introductory words that make your learning, and hence your revision, easier.
- **Frequent cross-referencing** to link different topics and provide you with a fully integrated understanding of biology as a whole.
- **Accessible language** so that you can focus more attention on learning the scientific terminology used. Where a term has been given that is less commonly used, an alternative term is also given in brackets to help your understanding.
- **Bold type** to emphasise key terms in the text. They also allow for quick reference when you are looking through the book. This should make your revision more effective.

- **Purple type** to highlight biological words that are not defined within a specific topic, but which can be found in the glossary. This allows you to easily access a full explanation of important biological terms used in the text.
- **Extension material** helps to widen your horizons and stimulate an interest in broader aspects of biology. Some will consolidate your understanding of the subject matter covered in that section.
- **Remember boxes** to give you useful advice about certain aspects of a topic and so aid your learning. They include reminders of important knowledge from other chapters, memory aids, helpful information, useful tips on answering examination questions.
- **Comprehensive glossary** to provide definitions of over 250 biological terms used throughout the book.
- **Summary tests** to provide a quick check on how well you have learnt and understood the factual content of each topic. Answers are provided at the back of the book.
- **Exam-style questions** to give you practice of the type of questions you can expect in the final examination. This will allow you to check your progress. Arranged at the end of each chapter, these questions test the full range of skills expected at AS and A Level, including application of knowledge, understanding, analysis, synthesis and evaluation. The questions cover mostly material in the same chapter but may sometimes include information from other chapters, largely earlier ones.
- **Additional practice questions** to consolidate learning.
- **Suggested answers to exam-style and practice questions** which indicate the possible type of responses that are likely to bring you credit in examinations. The answers are not exhaustive and there may be acceptable alternatives.

In the exam-style and practice questions sections at the end of the chapters, you will find the following icon:

In the Enhanced Online Student Book, this icon will launch additional digital resources to support your learning further. This content includes:

- **Worksheets** containing additional questions and practice
- **Interactive online quizzes**, including **multiple-choice** question practice

Visit **www.oxfordsecondary.com/bookshelf** to redeem your token code and access the Enhanced Online Student Book.

Answers to questions in this book and the syllabus matching grid are also available on the support website, which can be accessed via the URL or QR code: **www.oxfordsecondary.com/caie-al-complete-science**

Key concepts in Biology

In many textbooks, including **Complete Biology,** the subject of biology is broken down into small parts to help you understand its often complex elements. In reality, however, biology has just a few underlying principles that run through all aspects of the subject. These are known as **key concepts**. In learning each of the individual components of biology, it is possible to lose sight of these key concepts, or even to ignore them altogether. To do so would be a mistake, as an appreciation of the key concepts not only unifies biology but also aids your understanding of the subject.

Key concepts are essential principles, theories and ideas that help you to develop a deeper comprehension of biology and to make relevant links between different topics. They are, in effect, the foundations upon which the whole subject is based. An awareness of key concepts allows you to see biology, not as a set of isolated topics, but rather an interrelated and coherent whole. Once you have mastered the key concepts you will be able to use them to help you solve problems and to understand related biological material that is completely new to you.

There are a number of possible ways to divide up the key concepts in Biology. For the purposes of the Cambridge International AS and A Level Biology syllabus the six key concepts are:

- **Cells as the units of life** – As a biologist, it is important to understand that a cell is the basic unit of life, and understand the role that cells play in key processes in all living organisms.

- **Biochemical processes** – This key concept is about using biochemistry and molecular biology to explain important cell functions.

- **DNA, the molecule of heredity** – This key concept focuses on the role DNA plays in the continuity and evolution of life. It helps you to understand how mutations – a change in an organism's DNA – can bring about genetic variation, which are essential for evolution.

- **Natural selection** – Acting on genetic variation, natural selection is the key drive in evolution, including speciation. This is a key concept that explains the effects of genetic mutations on particular populations, as well as helping biologists to understand how populations can adapt to meet the demands of changing environments.

- **Organisms in their environment** – It is important to study the interactions of organisms with their biotic and abiotic environments, for it improves biologists' understanding of human impact on ecosystems, as well as to develop new strategies in biodiversity conservation, and to help with predicting future implications of changes in our environment.

- **Observation and experiment** – Observation, enquiry, experimentation and fieldwork are essential skills all biologists need, for it is through these processes that evidence from the different fields of biology is collected and analysed, in order that new models and theories can be developed and tested.

As these key concepts are the fundamental ideas upon which the subject of biology is based, they can be found, in some form or other, within every chapter of this book. To illustrate this, the table opposite provides one example of each key concept for each of the 19 chapters that relate to the Cambridge International AS and A Level Biology syllabus.

The table is for illustration purposes only. The content does not need to be learned, as key concepts will not be assessed as such. They will, however, help you to understand the syllabus as a whole and to make useful connections between different aspects of biology. They are something to keep at the back of your mind – a framework upon which to hang the various elements of the subject.

Each entry in the table is just a single example of that key concept in the particular chapter. There are many more possible examples, and those chosen have no particular significance.

We trust that you will enjoy using this book and find it interesting and informative. We hope that it will build upon the knowledge and skills that you have already acquired and so stimulate a further interest in biology that encourages you to pursue your study beyond this level. Above all, we hope it will contribute to your success in the AS and A Level examinations.

Stephanie Fowler

Chapter in Complete Biology	Key concept					
	Cells as the units of life	Biochemical processes	DNA, the molecule of heredity	Natural selection	Organisms in their environment	Observation and experiment
1 Cell structure	All organisms are composed of cells	Biochemical processes are carried out by cell organelles e.g. the Golgi body forms glycoproteins	DNA is contained within the nucleus and contains coded information for the synthesis of polypeptides at the ribosomes	Natural selection has determined the structure of cells and their organelles e.g. muscle cells with many mitochondria	Environment affects cells e.g. phagocytes are attracted to chemicals produced by non-self cells	Microscopy is used to investigate cell structure
2 Biological molecules	Cells are made up of biological molecules such as carbohydrates, lipids and proteins	Biochemical processes convert molecules into one another e.g. hydrolysis of starch to glucose	DNA is a complex biological molecule made up of a long chain of nucleotides	Natural selection has determined the structure of molecules for certain functions e.g. collagen for strength in tendons	Environment changes structure of molecules e.g. temperature can change the shape of globular proteins	Tests are used to identify biological molecules such as reducing sugars, starch, lipids and proteins
3 Enzymes	Cells produce enzymes to catalyse reactions inside and outside of them	Biochemical processes are controlled by enzymes e.g. lipase controls the breakdown of lipids to fatty acids and glycerol	The replication of DNA involves enzymes e.g. DNA polymerase	An organism will be selected for if a gene mutation results in an altered enzyme that improves the chance of survival	Environmental changes affect enzymes e.g. temperatures above 60°C fully denatures many enzymes	Experiments can be carried out to determine the effect of temperature and pH on enzyme action
4 Cell membranes and transport	Cell membranes control the movement of ions and molecules in and out of cells	Enzymes and carrier molecules can be located in membranes to allow biochemical processes to be carried out	DNA is contained within the nucleus by the nuclear envelope that surrounds it	The complex structure of cell membranes has evolved through natural selection	Cell membranes are the interface between cells and their environment and control the interchange of molecules between the two	Osmosis can be observed in experiments with potato cubes, beetroot and onion epidermis
5 The mitotic cell cycle	Diploid cells divide by mitosis to give diploid cells	During interphase of the cell cycle biochemical processes produce new cell organelles	DNA replication takes place during the S phase of interphase in the cell cycle	The process of meiosis produces variety in offspring which is essential to natural selection	Environmental factors, such as certain chemicals and radiation, can affect mitosis and lead to cancer	Mitosis can be observed through a microscope in stained preparations of cells
6 Nucleic acids and protein synthesis	Cells contain the organelles required for DNA replication and for protein synthesis e.g. ribosomes	Protein synthesis involves the biochemical processes of transcription and translation	The coded information in DNA is transcribed to produce mRNA that is translated into specific polypeptides	It is variation in DNA that determines the range of characteristics in organisms from which the best adapted are selected	Environmental factors such as UV radiation can cause mutations in DNA	The experiments of Meselsohn and Stahl showed that DNA replication was semi-conservative
7 Transport in plants	Cells called sieve tubes are specially adapted for sugar transport and xylem vessels for water transport	Biochemical processes are involved in the movement of sucrose into phloem sieve tubes	Different lengths of DNA, genes, are switched on or off to produce the different cells in xylem and phloem tissue	As a result of natural selection, xerophytes evolved to live in conditions where there is a limited supply of water	The rate of transpiration is affected by environmental factors like humidity, light and air movement	Sections of roots and stems can be made to investigate the distribution of plant tissues
8 Transport in mammals	Many different cell types are involved in animal transport e.g. red blood cells, endothelial cells and cardiac muscle	The formation of oxy-haemoglobin and carbamino-haemoglobin are the result of biochemical processes	DNA determines the structure of haemoglobin – a molecule adapted to transporting oxygen in blood	Native highlanders adapted to the transport of oxygen at low atmospheric oxygen partial pressures are the result of natural selection	The loading of haemoglobin with oxygen changes under different environmental conditions e.g. it is greater at low CO_2 concentrations	The heart rate before and after exercise, can be calculated by taking the pulse

Chapter in Complete Biology	Key concept					
	Cells as the units of life	Biochemical processes	DNA, the molecule of heredity	Natural selection	Organisms in their environment	Observation and experiment
9 Gas exchange	Specialised cells known as squamous epithelial are involved in gas exchange	Biochemical processes allow the production of mucus in the gas exchange system	In cystic fibosis, a gene mutation results in a thick mucus to be produced by goblet cells and mucous glands	Natural selection favours individuals living at high altitude if they have greater lung capacities	Environmental conditions such as air pollution and smoking affect the efficiency of gas exchange.	Using a microscope, the distribution in the gas exchange system of smooth muscle and elastic fibres can be investigated
10 Infectious diseases	Some prokaryotic cells cause disease e.g.the bacterium Vibrio cholerae causes cholera	Pathogens often cause disease by interfering with the normal biochemical processes of host cells	HIV synthesises a DNA copy of its genome to integrate into the DNA of the host cell	Natural selection of bacteria that produce penicillinase has led to antibiotic resistance	Environmental conditions determine the geographical distribution of vectors and so the diseases they spread e.g. Anopheles mosquitoes, and hence malaria, occurs in tropical/sub tropical areas	Antibiotic discs placed on bacterial lawns grown on agar can identify bacterial resistance
11 Immunity	White blood cells protect organisms from disease and memory cells are produced, which provide immunity from further infection	T killer cells produce proteins called perforins which make holes in cell surface membranes	DNA replication occurs in activated lymphocytes during clonal expansion	Immunity is a factor in selection. Organisms with immunity to a disease are more likely to survive to breed in the presence of that disease than those without	It is a response to the environment, e.g. exposure to a pathogen, that stimulates an immune response	Monoclonal antibodies immobilised on a test strip can be used in the detection of glucose in urine
12 Energy and respiration	Cells possess mitochondria which are essential for cellular respiration	The respiratory processes glycolysis and Krebs cycle are examples of biochemical pathways	The enzymes of glycolysis and Krebs cycle are coded for by DNA	Anaerobic organisms have evolved, through natural selection, respiratory pathways that enable them to release energy in the absence of molecular oxygen	The rate of cellular respiration is influenced by environmental conditions e.g. in most organisms it slows in low temperatures, cyanide can halt it altogether	A respirometer can be used to measure the rate of respiration in different environmental conditions
13 Photosynthesis	Photosynthesis takes place in palisade cells which possess the cell organelles, chloroplasts	The light-independent stage (Calvin cycle) of photosynthesis is a biochemical process	Chloroplasts contain their own DNA, separate from that in the nucleus	It is thought that chloroplasts evolved from a symbiotic relationship between a eukaryotic cell and a photosynthetic prokaryotic one	The rate of photosynthesis is determined by environmental factors such as light intensity and carbon dioxide concentration	The rate of photosynthesis under differing conditions can be measured using a photosynthometer
14 Homeostasis	Homeostatic processes are important in maintaining a constant internal environment in cells	The homeostatic control of blood sugar involves the biochemical inter-conversion of glucose and glycogen	Variations in certain genes (DNA) increase the likelihood of individuals developing diabetes	The evolution of complex organs that are involved in homeostatic mechanisms is a result of natural selection	Homeostasis allows organisms a degree of independence from changes to the external environment	Biosensors can be used to analyse the concentration of glucose in sample material
15 Control and coordination	Neurones are highly specialised cells adapted to carry nerve impulses	Cell signalling by glucagon is an example of a biochemical process	Huntington's disease is a degenerative disorder of the nervous system due to a single gene mutation.	Natural selection has led to the evolution of increasingly complex nervous systems	The nervous system allows organisms to respond to environmental stimuli	Experiments can be carried out to investigate stomatal opening and closure under different conditions

Chapter in Complete Biology	Cells as the units of life	Biochemical processes	DNA, the molecule of heredity	Key concept		
				Natural selection	Organisms in their environment	Observation and experiment
16 Inheritance	Meiosis is the means by which cells reduce the number of chromosomes from the diploid to haploid number, usually in the formation of gametes	Biochemical processes such as the production of β-galactosidase are controlled by groups of genes e.g. the lac operon	A gene is a length of DNA that codes for a particular polypeptide and alleles are different forms of a gene	Mutations of genes produce new varieties of offspring that, through the process of natural selection, may evolve into new species	The phenotype of an organism is the result of interaction between the genotype of an organism and its environment	Genetic experiments can be carried out to illustrate Mendel's Laws e.g. using fruit flies
17 Selection and evolution	Variation results from the random fusion of egg and sperm cells	Selective breeding can improve milk production in dairy cattle	Changes to the nucleotides in DNA give rise to mutations and lead to increased variety in organisms	Variation and overproduction of offspring are important factors in natural selection	The environment affects the expression of genes e.g. the effect of altitude on the size of genetically identical *Potentilla grandulosa* plants	Selective breeding (artifical selection) involves observation of offspring and identification of desirable features
18 Classification, biodiversity and conservation	The classification of organisms into the three domains (Bacteria, Archaea and Eukarya) is by cell type	Conservation techniques involve the process of in vitro fertilisation	Protecting endangered species is a means of preventing certain genes from being lost forever	Natural classification is based on the evolutionary relationships between organisms	Ecology is the study of the inter-relationships between organisms and their environment	Fieldwork involving a variety of techniques is essential to the study of ecology
19 Genetic technology	Plasmids from bacterial cells are the vectors used in gene technology	Reverse transcriptase and restriction endonucleases are important enzymes in the biochemical process in gene technology	Genetic technology involves the combining of DNA from two different organisms	Genetic technology can result in organisms with advantageous features that are more likely to be selected for e.g. herbicide resistant plants	Crop improvement through genetic modification can enable plants to better survive hostile environments e.g. tolerate dry conditions	Gel electrophoresis can be used to separate out DNA fragments

AS Level

This section of the book contains the material, including practical skills, that you will cover in the first year of the Cambridge International AS and A Level course (9700).

There are 11 chapters in the AS Level section:

Each chapter is matched to the syllabus, and is followed by exercises that will test your understanding and give you practice at tackling Cambridge examination questions.

1 Cell structure

1.1 The microscope in cell studies

a. Using a light microscope: an introduction

Units of length used in biology

The base unit of length used in the International System of Units (SI units) is the metre. A common decimal multiple of the metre is the kilometre and common decimal submultiples of the metre are the centimetre, millimetre, micrometre and nanometre. Table 1 summarises the units of length.

Table 1 *Units of length used in biology*

	Unit	Symbol	Scientific notation	As a number
longest	kilometre	km	10^3 m	1000 m
	metre	m	1 m	1 m
	centimetre	cm	10^{-2} m	0.01 m
	millimetre	mm	10^{-3} m	0.001 m
	micrometre	μm	10^{-6} m	0.000001 m
shortest	nanometre	nm	10^{-9} m	0.00000000 m

Units of length: a worked example

A blue whale, *Balaenoptera musculus*, can swim hundreds of kilometres to feeding grounds.

Blue whales can reach lengths of 25–30 m.

The layer of fat, known as blubber, found under the skin of the blue whale, varies in thickness from 5–30 cm.

The outer surface skin layer of the blue whale is about 1 mm thick.

A cell from the blue whale is about 10 μm in diameter.

The thickness of the cell surface membrane is about 7 nm.

You should be able to suggest appropriate units of length to use in different situations. For example, from the information given above, it would be reasonable to suggest that the diameter of a structure within the cell should be given in nanometres or micrometres, rather than mm, knowing that the diameter of the cell is 10 μm and the thickness of the membrane is 7 nm.

The compound light microscope

The compound light microscope (Figure 1), commonly called a light microscope, is the type of microscope that you will use when studying the structure of plant and animal cells.

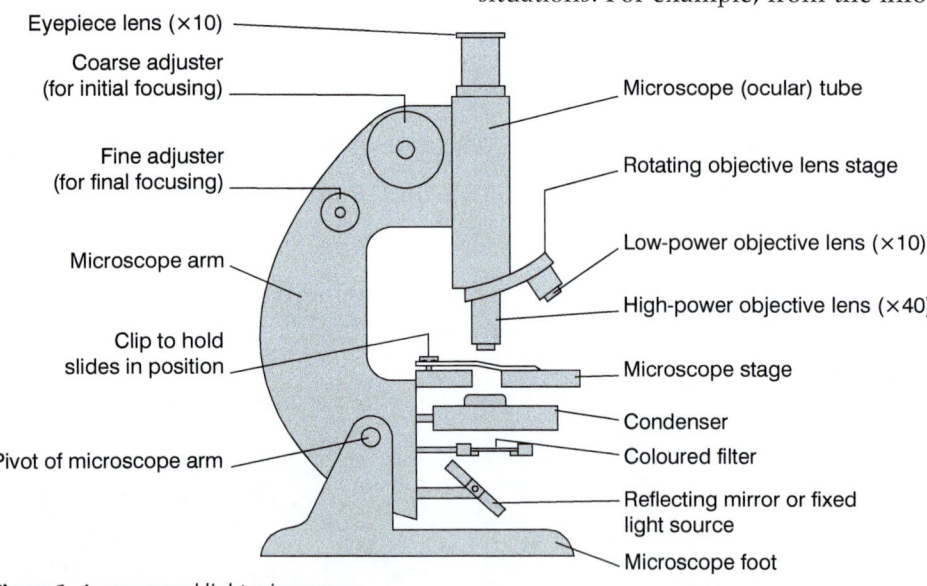

Eyepiece lens (×10)
Coarse adjuster (for initial focusing)
Fine adjuster (for final focusing)
Microscope arm
Clip to hold slides in position
Pivot of microscope arm
Microscope (ocular) tube
Rotating objective lens stage
Low-power objective lens (×10)
High-power objective lens (×40)
Microscope stage
Condenser
Coloured filter
Reflecting mirror or fixed light source
Microscope foot

Figure 1 *A compound light microscope*

The light microscope has three systems of lenses:

- The **condenser lens** can be adjusted in height to ensure that light from the reflecting mirror or fixed light source is focused on the specimen being examined. This allows the resolving power (see 1.1e) of the microscope to be used to its full effect.
- The **objective** and **eyepiece lenses** focus and enlarge the image, with the objective lens producing an initial magnified image of the specimen and the eyepiece lens further magnifying the image.

Table 2 Magnifications obtained using the low-power and high-power objective lenses

Image	Eyepiece lens	Objective lens	Final magnification
Low power	×10	×10	×100
High power	×10	×40	×400

Practical skill

Using the low-power and high-power objective lenses to view slides

To view a slide using the low-power (×10) objective lens:

- Turn the coarse adjuster knob so that there is maximum distance between the rotating objective lens stage and the microscope stage.
- Move the rotating objective lens so that the low-power objective lens 'clicks' into place.
- Place the slide on the microscope stage and, by looking from the side, turn the coarse adjuster knob so that the low-power lens is at its closest to the slide.
- Look down the eyepiece lens and turn the coarse adjuster knob slowly so that the low-power lens moves up away from the specimen and the specimen becomes in focus in the circular area of view.
- Move the slide on the stage until the area required is in the circular area of view (field of view) before using the clip to hold the slide in place.

To view a slide using the high-power (×40) objective lens, you must first view using the low-power objective lens:

- Follow steps above. Make sure that the specimen is in sharp focus and that the area you want to observe is in the centre of the field of view.
- Look from the side and slowly move the rotating objective lens so that the high-power objective lens 'clicks' into place. It should be very close but not touching the slide.
- Look down the eyepiece lens and, if focusing is still required, turn the fine adjuster knob slowly. Only half a turn in one direction or half a turn in the other direction should bring the specimen into sharp focus.

Summary test 1.1a

A unit of length which is stated as 10^{-9} m is known as a **(1)**, and has the symbol **(2)**. To convert this unit of length to a micrometre (µm), **(3)** by 1000. The base unit of length in the SI system is the **(4)**. A ×10 eyepiece lens used with a ×10 objective lens in a light microscope will produce an image with a magnification of **(5)**.

Practical skill

Using a magnifying glass

To use a magnifying glass, which is actually the simplest form of a light microscope, the specimen to be viewed should be kept on a firm surface and the magnifying glass should be held close to your eye. Move your head down, holding the magnifying glass, until the specimen is seen clearly enlarged and in focus.

Remember

You will use a microscope fitted with a ×10 eyepiece lens, a ×10 low-power lens and a ×40 high-power lens. The final **magnification** of the image that is obtained is the product of the eyepiece and objective lenses (Table 2).

Extension

Advances with light microscopes

There are now many different types of very sophisticated light microscope that can be quite large and cost as much as an electron microscope. In addition, they require considerable technical expertise in preparation and in handling.

Remember

Never use the fine focusing adjuster when you are only viewing the specimen on low power. Using the fine focusing adjuster for viewing on low power means that it will not be set correctly for focusing on high power.

These pages help you to:

- learn how to make temporary preparations of cellular material for viewing with the light microscope (1.1.1)

You will also:

- appreciate the importance of the microscope in cell studies

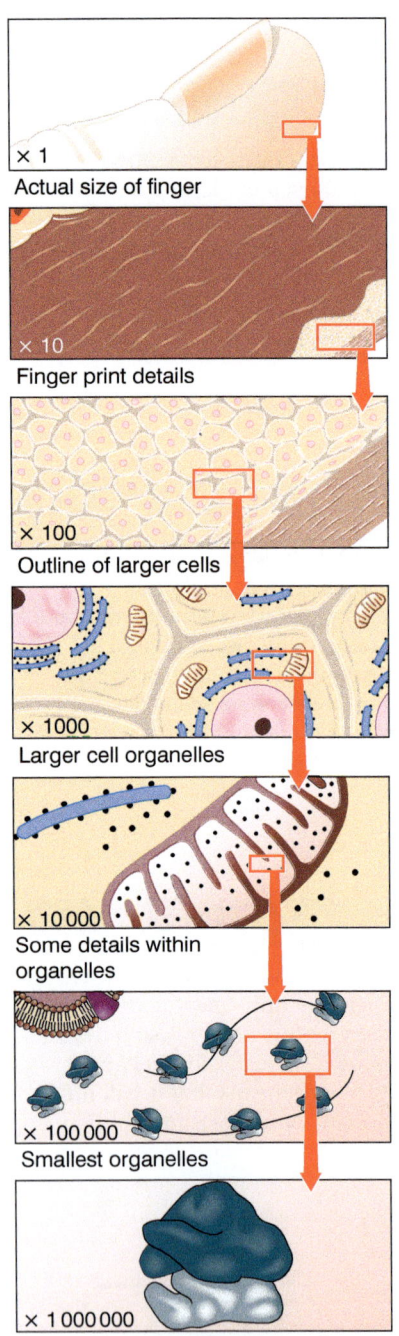

× 1
Actual size of finger

× 10
Finger print details

× 100
Outline of larger cells

× 1000
Larger cell organelles

× 10 000
Some details within organelles

× 100 000
Smallest organelles

× 1 000 000
Some detail of smallest organelles

Figure 1 *The effect of progressive magnification of a portion of human skin*

Making temporary preparations of cellular material for viewing with the light microscope

During your course you will develop your practical ability to manipulate apparatus and materials. This includes making your own microscope slides of **cellular material**, which can be viewed using a light microscope. These slides will not be permanent but will be temporary preparations. Some examples of the cellular material that can be used to make temporary preparations are summarised in Table 1.

Table 1 *Examples of cellular material that can be used to make temporary preparations*

Example of cellular material	Use
Onion epidermal tissue	To investigate plant cell structure seen using a light microscope (see 1.1c)
	To study changes that occur in plant cells placed in different water potentials (4.2c)
Sections of fruits or seeds	To observe the results of biochemical tests carried out on a microscopic scale to identify biological molecules (2.1b)
Garlic or onion root tip squashes	To observe different stages in the division of cells by mitosis (mitotic cell cycle) (5.2a)
Sections of stems or roots	To study the distribution of different tissue types, including the transport tissue, xylem and phloem (7.1a)

Extension

The importance of microscopes

Imagine the excitement early scientists must have felt when the first glass lenses, and then the compound light microscope, were developed, allowing the enlarged (magnified) images of cellular material to be seen. The extra detail revealed introduced a whole new world to the scientists. The quality of microscopes improved, but there were limits to the **subcellular detail** that could be seen. The development of the electron microscope meant that far higher magnifications were possible and the ability to see detail **(resolution)** was much greater (Figure 1). Previously unknown cell structures were discovered. With this knowledge of cell **ultrastructure**, scientists could improve their understanding of cell functioning. Thanks to microscopes, we now take it for granted that living organisms are composed of cells. Remember that this knowledge came from a series of developments and discoveries made over more than two centuries, and was not the result of a single piece of research.

Practical skill

Preparing a wet mount slide

The following describes a procedure to make a 'wet mount' preparation of epidermis (outer cell layer) from the scale leaf (leaf modified for storage) of an onion, *Allium cepa*. The procedure includes:

- a technique to place the coverslip over the epidermis so that no air bubbles are trapped.
- a technique to add a stain to the slide so that some cells are stained, while others are left unstained, to allow a comparison to be made.

Remember to carry out a risk assessment before you start.

Use a small square (approximately 1 × 1 cm) cut from an onion scale leaf.

Using fine forceps, peel off a piece of epidermal tissue, one cell thick, from the concave side (inner side) (Figure 2) and place onto the centre of a microscope slide.

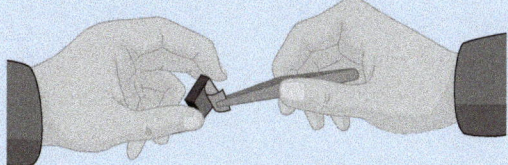

Figure 2 *Preparing the specimen*

Add a drop of water and use forceps or a mounted needle to help spread out the tissue to obtain a flat layer with no creases.

Place a coverslip at an angle to the slide and move it slowly towards the tissue until water runs under the edge of the slip. Use the forceps or a mounted needle to lower the coverslip onto the tissue at an angle to prevent air bubbles forming (Figure 3).

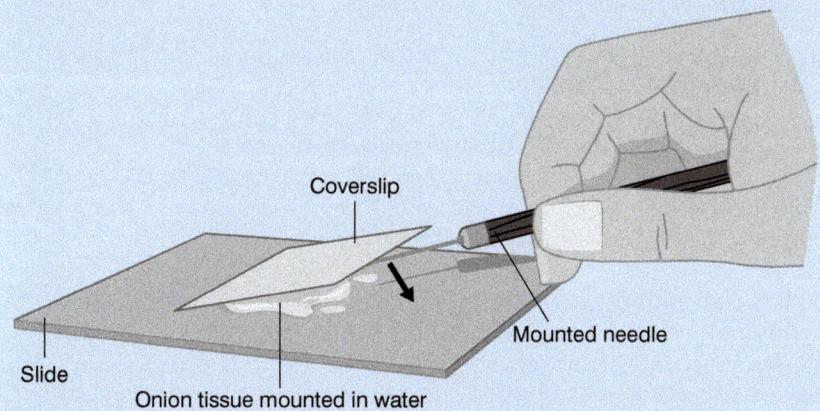

Coverslip
Mounted needle
Slide
Onion tissue mounted in water

Figure 3 *Mounting the specimen*

Add a drop of iodine solution to the microscope slide against one edge of the coverslip.

Place a piece of filter paper against the other side of the coverslip so that it soaks up some of the water and 'pulls' some of the iodine solution to stain a portion of the epidermis (this is known as 'irrigation').

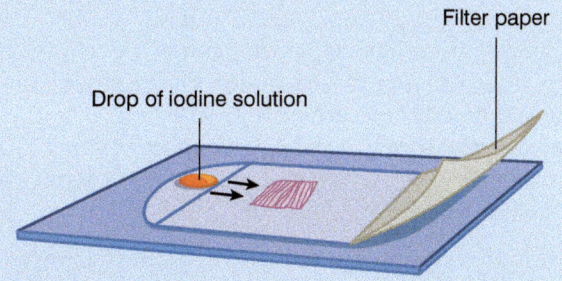

Filter paper
Drop of iodine solution

Figure 4 *Staining the specimen*

Carefully blot up any fluid on top of the coverslip before viewing using the microscope.

Note: if there are any air bubbles, they may be removed by gently tapping the coverslip with the other end of the mounted needle.

Practical skill

Obtaining a sample

It is usually important for the cellular material to be thin, often just a single layer of cells thick. Different techniques can be used to achieve this. For example:

- a single layer of onion epidermal cells can be peeled off using forceps
- single root tip cells can be obtained by placing pressure on the coverslip to spread out cells
- a section of a fruit, stem or root can be sliced by using a sharp single-sided razor or scalpel
- cellular material can be spread out across the microscope slide by using another glass slide.

However good a microscope is, it will only be effective if the cellular material to be viewed is properly prepared. This often involves the material being stained in some way to make the different parts of cells or different tissues more easily visible. A thin glass coverslip should always be placed over the cellular material on the microscope slide. This protects the microscope lens from damage and helps prevent cells from drying out.

Remember

You may be asked to draw some of the cells visible in a prepared slide or in a **photomicrograph**. Drawing skills are covered in 1.1c.

Summary test 1.1b

Microscope slides can be made for immediate viewing using the compound **(1)** microscope. These are not permanent slides and are only **(2)** preparations. They may or may not involve using **(3)** to help make cell structures or tissues more visible. The cellular material to be studied is placed on a glass microscope slide and a thin glass **(4)** is placed over the material. When making a slide of onion epidermis, a one-cell thick layer can be peeled off using **(5)**. The coverslip should not be dropped onto the microscope slide, but should be lowered at an angle to avoid **(6)** forming.

c. Drawing cells

Cell structures visible using the light microscope

Figures 1 and 2 show the cell structures visible using the light microscope in an animal cell and a plant cell. These are generalised diagrams and not drawn from actual cells. The cell structures are described in detail in 1.2b, 1.2c, 1.2d and 1.2e.

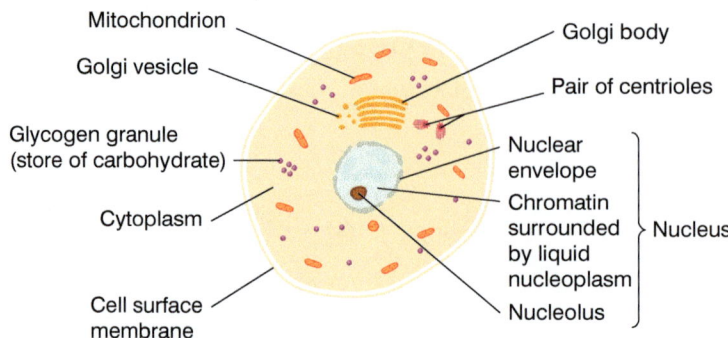

Figure 1 *Generalised animal cell as seen under a light microscope*

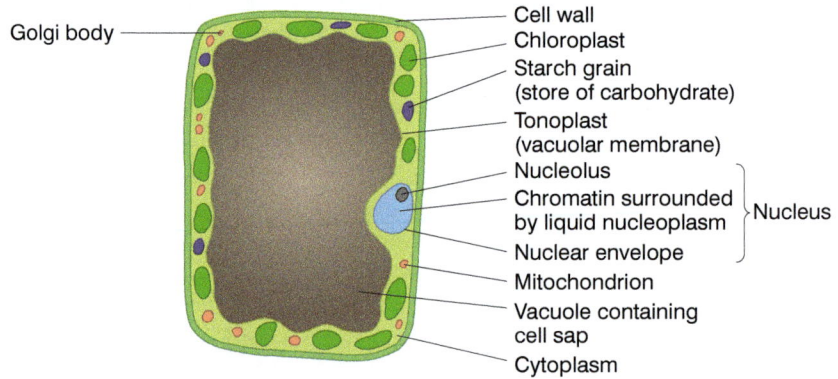

Figure 2 *Generalised plant cell as seen under a light microscope*

You may be familiar with the nucleus, cytoplasm, cell surface membrane and, additionally in plant cells, chloroplasts and the large permanent vacuole. The cell surface membrane of the animal cell and the vacuolar membrane, or tonoplast, of the plant cell are too thin to interfere with the light waves and so cannot be seen directly (see details on resolution in 1.1e). With the use of stains and with the contrast that is obtained, these structures can be observed indirectly.

To see all the structures that should be visible using a light microscope, such as the mitochondrion and Golgi body labelled in Figures 1 and 2, a very good quality microscope, that can achieve a magnification of about ×1500, is required. Golgi bodies in plant cells are much smaller than those in animal cells, and generally are only seen using certain preparation techniques. The centrioles of animal cells, important in cell division, are also difficult to distinguish, even with a good light microscope. No detail inside mitochondria and chloroplasts can be seen.

A photomicrograph of **epithelial cells** is shown in Figure 3. A swab of the inside of the human mouth has been taken and the cellular material has been smeared across a microscope slide using another slide, before adding the coverslip. The thin layer produced by the smear allows individual cells to be observed.

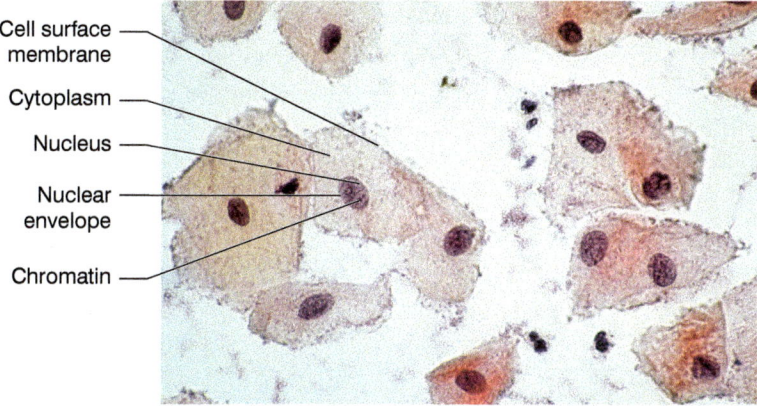

Cell surface membrane
Cytoplasm
Nucleus
Nuclear envelope
Chromatin

Figure 3 *A photomicrograph of animal cells (epithelial cells from the human mouth)*

Nucleoli, although present in the nuclei of the epithelial cells, cannot be seen clearly in Figure 3 (see 1.2b).

A photomicrograph of onion cell epidermis is shown in Figure 4. Figure 5 is a labelled drawing of three adjacent epidermal cells (cells next to each other).

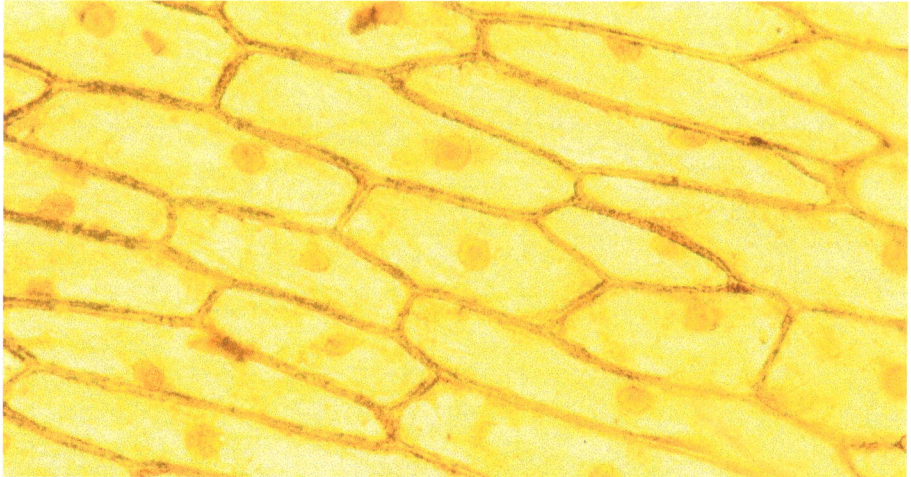

Figure 4 *A photomicrograph of plant cells (onion epidermis) stained with iodine solution*

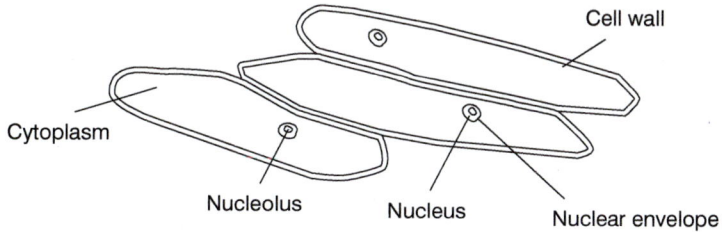

Cell wall
Cytoplasm
Nucleolus
Nucleus
Nuclear envelope

Figure 5 *A high-power drawing of onion epidermal cells*

d. Making measurements and calculating magnification of images

These pages help you to:

- understand how to make calculations of magnification, image size and actual size of cellular material being studied using the microscope (1.1.3)
- learn how to use the eyepiece graticule and stage micrometer to make measurements and give estimates of sizes (1.1.4)
- explain what is meant by magnification, with reference to the light and electron microscopes (1.1.5)

You will also:

- become more familiar with using the light microscope

Practical skill

Calibrating the eyepiece graticule

To calibrate an eyepiece graticule you need to use a special microscope slide called a stage micrometer. This slide also has a scale etched onto it. Usually the scale is 2 mm long and its smallest subdivisions are 0.01 mm (10 µm).

When the eyepiece graticule scale and the stage micrometer scales are lined up, as shown in Figure 1, the distance between the divisions on the eyepiece graticule can be calculated. For example, you can see in Figure 1:

- On the micrometer scale, 10 units are equivalent to 40 units on the graticule scale.
- Therefore, one unit on the micrometer scale equals 4 units on the graticule scale.
- As each unit on the micrometer scale is 10 µm, each unit on the graticule equals 10 ÷ 4 = 2.5 µm.

Parallax error occurs due to the apparent difference in position of an object when viewed from two different lines of sight. To avoid parallax error when reading a scale and pointer, the observer's eye and pointer must be in a perpendicular line to the plane of the scale.

Measuring cells

When using a light microscope, we can measure the size of cellular material such as cells and cell structures using an eyepiece graticule:

- The graticule is a glass disc, which is placed in the eyepiece of a microscope.
- A scale is etched on the disc.
- This scale is typically 10 mm long and is divided into 100 subdivisions (Figure 1).
- The scale is visible when looking down the eyepiece of the microscope.

The scale on the eyepiece graticule cannot be used directly to measure the size of objects under a microscope's objective lens because each objective lens magnifies to a different degree. The graticule must first be calibrated for a particular objective lens.

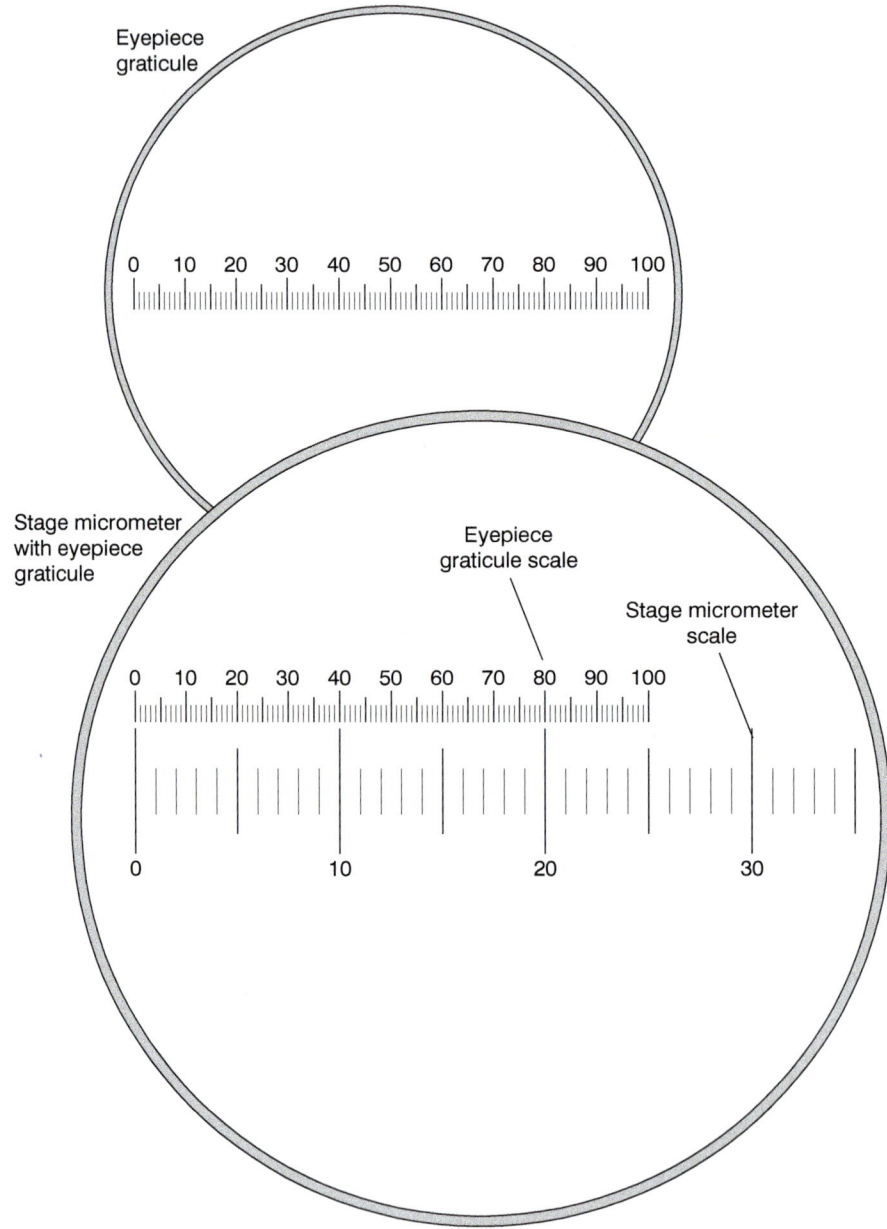

Figure 1 *An eyepiece graticule and how it is calibrated using a stage micrometer*

Magnification

Magnification, in microscopy, always means **enlargement** (making bigger). The numerical value of the magnification tells you the **number of times larger the image is than the actual size of the cellular material** (sometimes called the object).

Using the microscope, the cellular material being studied will appear larger than it is and the image in the photomicrograph from the light microscope or the electron micrograph from the electron microscope will show the enlarged view. Magnification beyond ×1500 with a light microscope does not provide any more detail, whereas using the electron microscope it is possible to obtain clear images at magnifications up to ×500 000.

Calculating magnification and actual size

If you are studying an image of cellular material, for example, onion epidermal cells, and you are told a dimension of a particular cell (for example, length, width or diameter), you can use a simple formula (Figure 2) to calculate the magnification used to produce the image.

If the magnification is stated, but the actual size is not known, the formula can be rearranged and used for the calculation (Figure 2).

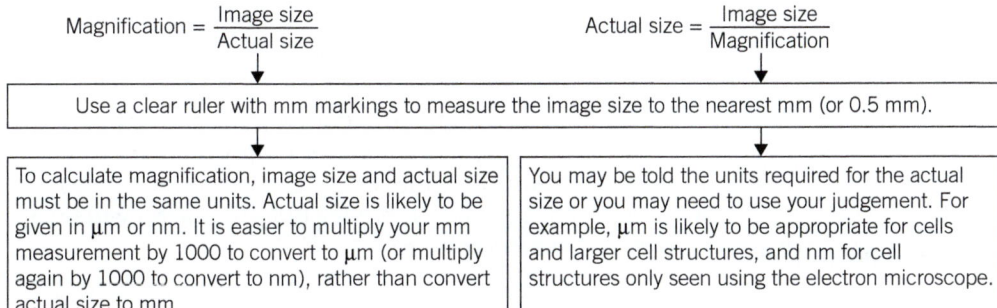

Figure 2 *How to calculate magnification and actual size*

A scale bar, if included, can be used to calculate the magnification of drawings, photomicrographs and electron micrographs. The scale bar shows the actual length it represents. In the example in Figure 3, the actual length is 2 μm. If the measured length of the scale bar is converted to micrometers to match the units for the actual length, then the magnification can be calculated using the formula shown in Figure 2.

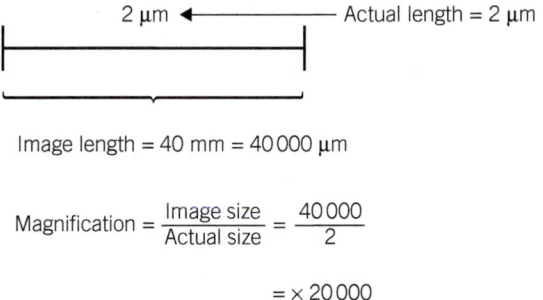

Figure 3 *Using a scale bar to calculate magnification*

Summary test 1.1d

To measure the size of an object under a **(1)** microscope we can use an **(2)** graticule and a stage **(3)**. Before we can use the graticule to measure the size of objects, it must first be **(4)**. An electron micrograph of a cell is magnified 5000 times. On the micrograph the nucleus measures 100 mm in diameter. The actual size of the nucleus is therefore **(5)** μm. A chloroplast that is 5 μm in diameter measures 15 mm in a drawing made of a plant cell seen under a light microscope. The magnification of this drawing is therefore **(6)** times.

These pages help you to:

- explain what is meant by resolution, with reference to the light and electron microscopes (1.1.5)
- understand the difference between magnification and resolution (1.1.5)

You will also:

- learn the main differences between the light microscope and the electron microscope
- understand the main differences between the transmission and scanning electron microscope and transmission and scanning electron micrographs

Resolution

Resolution is the ability to distinguish between two points. In microscopy, the resolution is the minimum distance apart that two objects can be in order for them to appear as separate items. The higher the resolution (resolving power), the clearer, sharper and more detailed is the image produced.

Comparing the resolution of the light microscope and the electron microscope

The shortest wavelength of visible light that our eyes can detect well is approximately 400 nm. The best resolution that can be obtained using a light microscope is approximately half this wavelength, 200 nm or 0.2 µm:

- any two objects which are 0.2 µm or more apart will be seen separately
- any objects closer than 0.2 µm will appear as a single item
- a cell structure that has dimensions smaller than 0.2 µm cannot be seen.

The electron microscope has a much higher resolution, up to 2000 times better, than the light microscope. This is because the wavelength of electrons is much shorter than the wavelength of light. Depending on the electron microscope used, resolution may vary between less than 0.1 nm and 30 nm.

Cell structures that are too small to be seen using a light microscope can be observed using an electron microscope. Note that, if specimens are viewed at the **same magnification**, the resolution achieved by an electron microscope is always much higher than that achieved by a light microscope.

The electron microscope

Electron microscopes use a fine beam of electrons focused onto the specimen. Because electrons are absorbed or deflected by the molecules in air, a near-vacuum has to be created within the chamber of an electron microscope in order for it to work effectively.

Heavy metal stains are used to stain the specimen to improve the contrast of the image obtained. Living material cannot therefore be viewed. Specimens must be carefully prepared to prevent damage and reduce **artefacts**, features that are not naturally present but produced during preparation of a section.

The two main types of electron microscope used in biology are the transmission electron microscope (TEM, Figure 2) and the scanning electron microscope (SEM, Figure 3).

For transmission electron microscopy, **very thin sections** of the specimen are required. Electrons penetrate and pass through different parts of the specimen to varying degrees. The electons that pass through the specimen hit a fluorescent

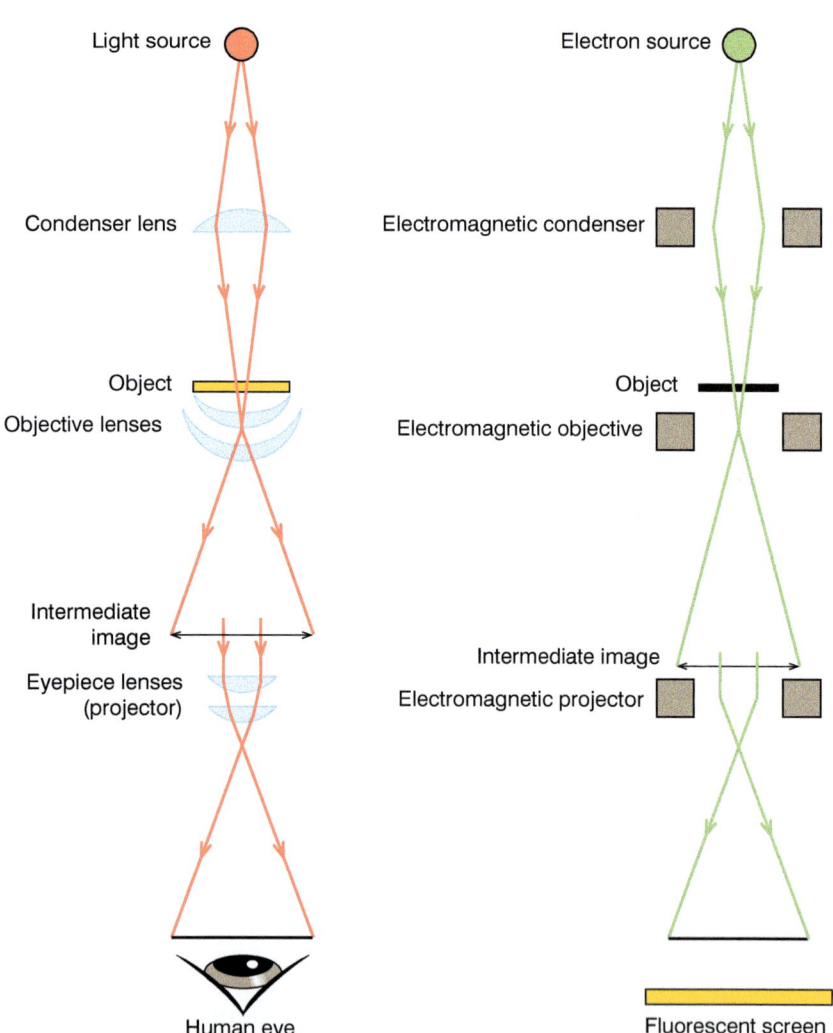

Figure 1 *Comparison of radiation pathways in light and electron microscopes*

screen producing an image. Alternatively, the image can be captured using a camera built into the microscope creating a transmission electron micrograph.

With scanning electron microscopy, the electron beam is directed over the surface of the specimen. Electrons are scattered by the different contours on the specimen allowing a three-dimensional image to be built up and viewed on a monitor, or in a scanning electron micrograph.

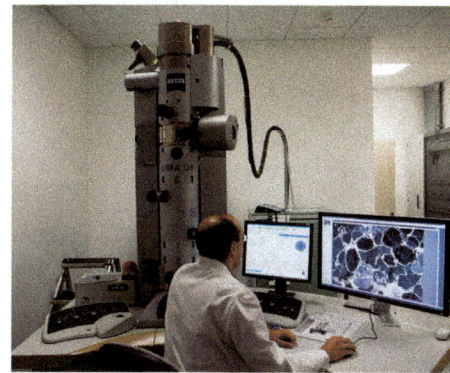

Figure 2 A transmission electron microscope

Electron micrographs

Images obtained using electron microscopes are called electron micrographs. If produced directly from the result of microscopy, electron micrographs are black and white. Examples of electron micrographs can be seen throughout this book. Notice that some have been coloured using a computer (false-colour electron micrographs). Table 1 compares features of transmission and scanning electron micrographs.

Table 1 *Differences between transmission and scanning electron micrographs*

Transmission electron micrograph	Scanning electron micrograph
Flat, two-dimensional (2D) image.	Three-dimensional (3D) image
Fine details of internal features visible	Shows surface contours (topography) only
Represents one plane of view (many sections and images are required to 'build up' a picture).	Provides a greater depth of area that will be acceptably sharp in one image.

Figure 3 A scanning electron microscope

Extension

More information about electron microscopy

'Electron guns' are used to produce the beam of negatively charged electrons by heating a tungsten filament. A high voltage accelerates the electrons: varying this can produce electrons of different wavelengths, so microscopes may differ in their resolving power. A condenser made from electromagnets focuses the electron beam onto the specimen. In the TEM, the electron beam can penetrate through the section. Different features of the specimen are composed of different proportions of chemical elements and vary in the ability to take up the heavy metal stains, which deflect electrons. The different degrees of penetration of electrons produce better contrast. Electrons may pass through some parts of the specimen directly and hit a section of the fluorescent viewing screen, which will appear bright. Other parts of the specimen may mainly absorb or reflect electrons and so sections of the screen appear darker.

In a scanning electron microscope, the electron beam scans backwards and forwards over the surface of the specimen. Electrons are bounced back, or secondary electrons are emitted (released) from the stained surface, and hit the screen. Depending on the surface contours, different intensities of reflected and released electrons hit the screen to give a three-dimensional image. With the correct preparation, images of internal surfaces within a cell can also be seen.

Remember

The scanning electron microscope has the highest depth of field. This is the distance between the nearest and furthest parts of the specimen that are acceptably sharp in one view. Generally, a higher magnification and resolution can be achieved with the transmission electron microscope than with the scanning electron microscope.

Summary test 1.1e

The relatively long wavelength of light means that a light microscope can only distinguish between two objects if they are **(1)** nm, or further, apart. With their **(2)** wavelengths, the beam of electrons in the electron microscope can distinguish two objects as close together as 0.1 **(3)**, so electron microscopes have a higher **(4)** than a light microscope. To allow the electrons to move across the chamber of the electron microscope, the **(5)** within it must be largely removed to create a **(6)**. Using the **(7)** electron microscope, a beam of electrons is passed backwards and forwards over the surface of the specimen to produce a **(8)** image showing surface contours. Very **(9)** sections need to be prepared for viewing with the **(10)** electron microscope, which allows fine details of the internal features of a cell to be observed.

Remember

The abbreviations TEM and SEM are used for transmission and scanning electron microscopes. You can also use them for transmission and scanning electron micrographs.

f. Images of cells and cell structures

These pages help you to:

- identify an image as a photomicrograph, a transmission electron micrograph or a scanning electron micrograph (useful for 1.1.2, 1.1.3 and 1.2.2)

You will also:

- consider the advantages and disadvantages of using a light microscope compared with using an electron microscope in biological studies

Figure 1 *Ciliated epithelium*

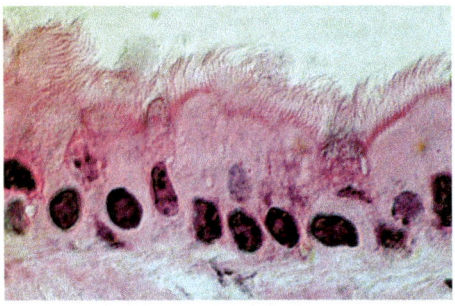

Figure 2 *Ciliated epithelium*

Figure 3 *Ciliated epithelium*

Photomicrograph, transmission electron micrograph or a scanning electron micrograph?

In 9.1b, you will learn about the ciliated epithelium lining the airways of the gas exchange system. Figures 1, 2 and 3 are images showing two types of cell that form part of ciliated epithelium. Ciliated epithelial cells have many hair-like structures, known as cilia, on their outer surface. Goblet cells have much smaller, finger-like projections of the cytoplasm known as microvilli on their outer surface. The structure and function of cilia and microvilli are covered in 1.2e.

The three images have a similar magnification, but each has been produced using a different type of microscope. Study each image and decide, which is the photomicrograph, which is the transmission electron micrograph and which is the scanning electron micrograph.

Each image gives different information. Figure 1 is a transmission electron micrograph. The thin section means the entire image is in focus. Internal cellular details are clear, and tiny microvilli can be seen on the surface of the goblet cells (see 9.1b). The image is two-dimensional, with no surface contours. The cilia appear to be in fragments because of the way the section was cut. The cilia appear as rigid structures: there is no impression of movement. The original black and white image has been coloured.

Figure 2 is a photomicrograph. The image has more blurring than Figures 1 and 3 and there is less detail of cell structure compared to Figure 1. The microvilli of the goblet cells cannot be seen. The less harsh preparation means that the cilia appear more natural and there is the impression of a wave-like motion. This is the actual image that would be viewed using the light microscope as the colours result from the stains used to highlight different cell features.

Figure 3 is a scanning electron micrograph. The surface contours are clearly shown and there is a three-dimensional appearance to the image. Although there is depth to the image, with whole cilia being visible, all the image is in sharp focus. The preparation of the specimen, as with Figure 1, makes the cilia appear as fairly rigid, bent structures. This image has also been coloured.

Comparing the light and electron microscopes: advantages and disadvantages

Although there are limitations with resolution and magnification, Table 1 shows that the light microscope has many advantages over the electron microscope. The use of the light microscope is still vital to improving our knowledge of the biological world, especially for viewing living tissue. The processes and changes over time in living cells, such as in cell division and in cell movement, can only be seen with the light microscope.

> **Remember**
>
> You should develop your ability to make comparisons. Comparison can include similarities as well as differences. Table 1 highlights differences between the two types of microscope.

Extension

Microscopes in biological studies – a historical view

The book *Micrographia* (1665) contained accurate, detailed drawings of specimens by the scientist Robert Hooke (Figure 4) using a light microscope he had made. He was the first person to describe the units that make up organisms as 'cells'. At about the same time, Anton van Leeuwenhoek, who used microscopes with single lenses, was making detailed observations and drawings of single-celled organisms.

After photography became popular in the nineteenth century, photomicrographs were also produced (Figure 5).

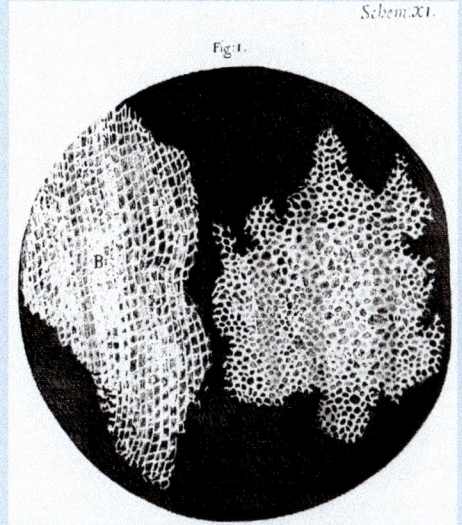

Figure 4 *Cork cells as drawn by the scientist Robert Hooke in 1665*

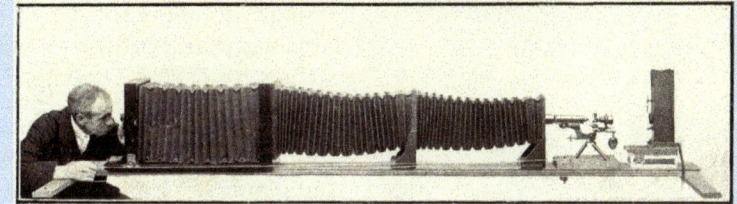

Figure 5 *Taking photomicrographs in the early nineteenth century*

In 1931, the scientist Ernst Ruska, aided by Maximilian Knoll, developed the first electron microscope. In 1933, Ruska built the first transmission electron microscope that produced a better image than a light microscope. Knoll built the first scanning electron microscope in 1935. The immense importance of Ruska's design and development of the first electron microscope was recognised when Ruska was jointly awarded the Nobel Prize in Physics 1986.

Table 1 *Comparing the light and electron microscopes: advantages and disadvantages*

Light microscope disadvantages	Electron microscope advantages
Limit of magnification up to ×1500	Magnifications of more than ×500 000 possible
Low resolution	High resolution
The depth of field is restricted	Greater depth of field possible with the scanning electron microscope
Light microscope advantages	**Electron microscope disadvantages**
Living and dead material can be observed	Only dead material can be observed (vacuum used)
Natural colour of the material can be observed	All images are in black and white, or artificially coloured
Material rarely distorted by preparation (less risk of artefacts)	Preparation of material may distort it (greater risk of artefacts)
Preparation of material is relatively quick and simple, requiring only a little expertise	Preparation of material is lengthy and requires considerable expertise and sometimes complex equipment
Small and portable – can be used almost anywhere	Large and must be operated in special rooms, away from magnetic fields
Cheap to purchase and operate	Expensive to purchase and operate

Summary test 1.1f

Using a microscope, the magnification of an object is how many times **(1)** the image is when compared to the object, whereas the **(2)** of a microscope is the ability to distinguish between two separate points. At a magnification of ×400, images in electron **(3)** compared with photomicrographs will appear sharper and will contain more **(4)** of cellular structure. Living cells can only be viewed using the **(5)** microscope. The preparation involved using the electron microscope is more likely to distort biological material and lead to **(6)**, which may mistakenly be thought of as part of the actual cellular structure.

Cells as basic units of living organisms
a. An introduction to cells

These pages help you to:

- understand that all living organisms are composed of one or more cells (1.2 Introduction)
- understand there are two fundamental (basic) types of cell, eukaryotic and prokaryotic (1.2.5 Introduction)

You will also:

- understand the key concept that a cell is the basic unit of life
- know what is meant by an organelle
- become familiar with cell theory

Extension

Unicellular or multicellular?

The distinction between unicellular and multicellular is not always clear. For example, a filamentous (chain-like) form or a colonial (clumped together) form may look like a multicellular organism, but on closer observation, it consists of many unicellular organisms joined together, with each cell performing all the metabolic reactions necessary for its own survival.

The cell

There are many different kinds, or species, of living organisms on this planet. The one thing they all have in common is that the basic unit of their structural and functional organisation is the cell: it is the basic unit of life.

Cells are necessary because the biochemical reactions of life processes, such as respiration (Chapter 12) and photosynthesis (Chapter 13), require molecules to come into contact with each other. Keeping the required molecules within the boundary of a cell surface membrane, rather than letting them disperse freely throughout the organism, allows them to react more effectively. In addition, each cell surface membrane can control, to some extent, which molecules enter or are excluded from the cell (4.1b). This allows different cells to carry out different functions.

Unicellular and multicellular organisms

Some living organisms are unicellular, made of a single cell. All the chemical reactions and processes necessary for life must be carried out within this cell. The sum of these chemical reactions and processes is known as **metabolism**.

Multicellular organisms are made of many cells. Cells can become specialised to perform a particular function, such as the cells that carry out photosynthesis in plants or the cells that form muscle tissue in animals. Collectively, all the metabolic needs of the organism are provided by this division of labour. Look for examples of cell specialisation and division of labour throughout this book.

Eukaryotic and prokaryotic cells

There are two fundamental cell types, **eukaryotic** and **prokaryotic**. Eukaryotic organisms, or eukaryotes, have cells with a true nucleus ('eu' = true, 'karyote' = nucleus). This means that the genetic material is enclosed by a nuclear envelope (Figures 1 and 2 in 1.2b). Prokaryotic organisms, or prokaryotes, have cells that do not have a true nucleus ('pro' = before). The genetic material lies free in the cytoplasm and is not enclosed by a nuclear envelope (Figure 2 in 1.2f). These two cell types are compared in 1.2f.

Extension

Table 1 summarises cell type and cell organisation in the main groups of organism that you will come across in this book. In this chapter, you will learn about cell structure in bacteria, plants and animals. In 18.1b, you will learn more about the classification of living organisms.

Table 1 *The main organism groups: cell type and unicellular / multicellular*

Organism group	Cell type		Unicellular or multicellular	
	Eukaryotic	Prokaryotic	Unicellular	Multicellular
Archaea		✓	✓	
Bacteria		✓	✓	
Protoctist	✓		✓	✓
Fungi	✓		✓	✓
Plant	✓			✓
Animal	✓			✓

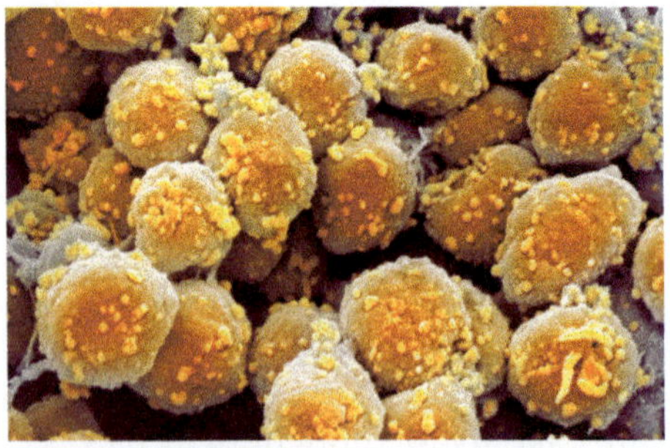

Figure 1 *Scanning electon micrograph of a group of archaean cells*

Organisation in the eukaryotic cell

The cell surface membrane surrounds the cell. Within this is the nucleus and the cytoplasm. The cytoplasm is a watery material with a jelly-like consistency. The three main components of cytoplasm are cytosol, organelles (except the nucleus) and inclusions. Cytosol is the fluid component of cytoplasm. It is mainly composed of water and water-soluble molecules. Some of the cell's enzyme-catalysed reactions take place in the cytosol.

An organelle is a cell structure that performs a particular function in the cell. Many organelles form compartments and are membrane bound, most with a single membrane and some with a double membrane. There are a few organelles that are non-membrane bound and can perform their function without the need to be surrounded by a membrane.

Inclusions are cell structures that are necessary for the overall functioning of the cell, but are not active and usually consist of one type of large molecule. Examples of inclusions are pigments and molecules used as long-term energy stores, such as glycogen and starch.

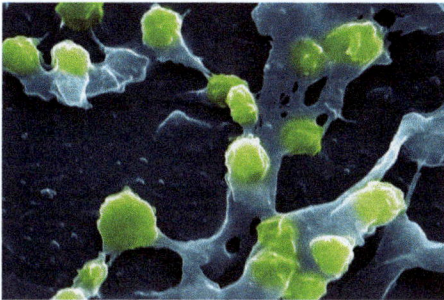

Figure 2 An example of a bacterium

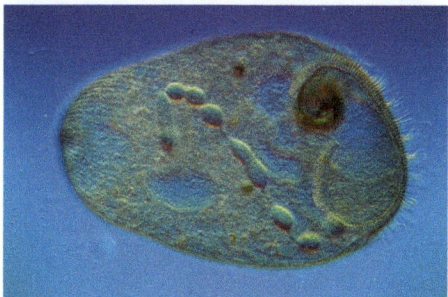

Figure 3 An example of a protoctist

Extension

The cell theory

Observations of cell structure and function by early microscopists, such as Hooke and van Leeuwenhoek, led to the development of cell theory by Matthias Schleiden (1838), Theodor Schwann (1839) and later Rudolph Virchow (1855). The theory has developed as further discoveries have been made.

The ideas in the modern cell theory include:

- The cell is the basic living structural unit of all organisms and all organisms are made of one or more cells (see Chapter 1).
- Every cell is the product of a pre-existing cell: cells arise by cell division from other cells and not spontaneously (see Chapters 5 and 16).
- Biochemical reactions take place within cells (see Chapters 2, 3, 12 and 13).
- Cells contain the genetic material of an organism, which is passed from parent cells to daughter cells (see Chapters 6 and 16).

The features of cell theory are **not** shared by viruses. They are not made of cells. Some scientists prefer to refer to them as infectious agents rather than microorganisms.

Figure 4 An example of a fungus

Figure 5 An example of a plant

Extension

The extracellular matrix, essential for the functioning of cells

Plant and animal cells are surrounded by an extracellular matrix (ECM) composed of large biological molecules released (secreted) by cells. The ECM can be closely associated with cells or form the general area between cells. Its composition differs for different cell types. The cell wall of plant cells, composed mainly of cellulose (1.2e), is an ECM. Collagen fibres (2.3c) and elastic fibres are found as part of the ECM in the walls of arteries and veins (8.1b).

Summary test 1.2a

Cells are the basic **(1)** of living organisms. Plants and animals are composed of many cells and so are termed **(2)**, whereas bacteria are made of only a single cell and are **(3)**. There is division of **(4)** in plants and animals, so that cells can be **(5)** to perform a particular function and collectively carry out all the functions of life. The cells of plants and animals have a true nucleus and are termed **(6)** cells, whereas the cells of bacteria are **(7)** and their genetic material is not surrounded by a **(8)**.

Figure 6 An example of an animal

These pages help you to:

- recognise organelles and other cell structures present in a plant cell and in an animal cell (1.2.1)
- describe drawings of typical plants and animal cells (1.2.2)
- compare the structure of a plant cell and an animal cell (1.2.3)

You will also:

- learn the cell structures present only in plant cells and only in animal cells

The structure of plant and animal cells

Each plant and animal cell can be regarded as a metabolic compartment designed to perform a particular function. Each cell type has an internal structure suited to its function. The plant and animal cell shown in Figures 1 and 2 are generalised, representing a combination of many different types of cell. Details of the structure and function of these cell structures is covered in the rest of this chapter.

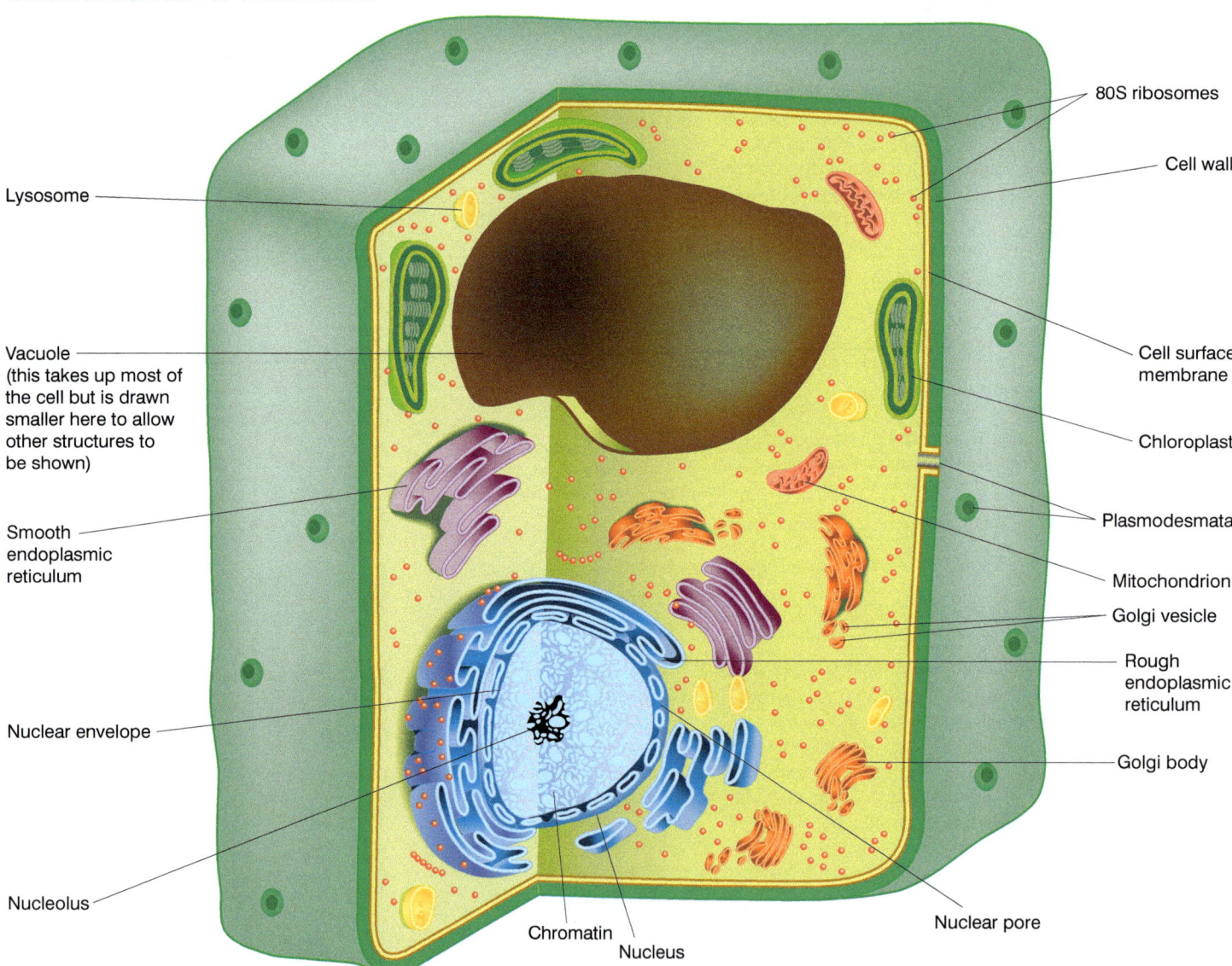

Figure 1 *The structure of a plant cell*

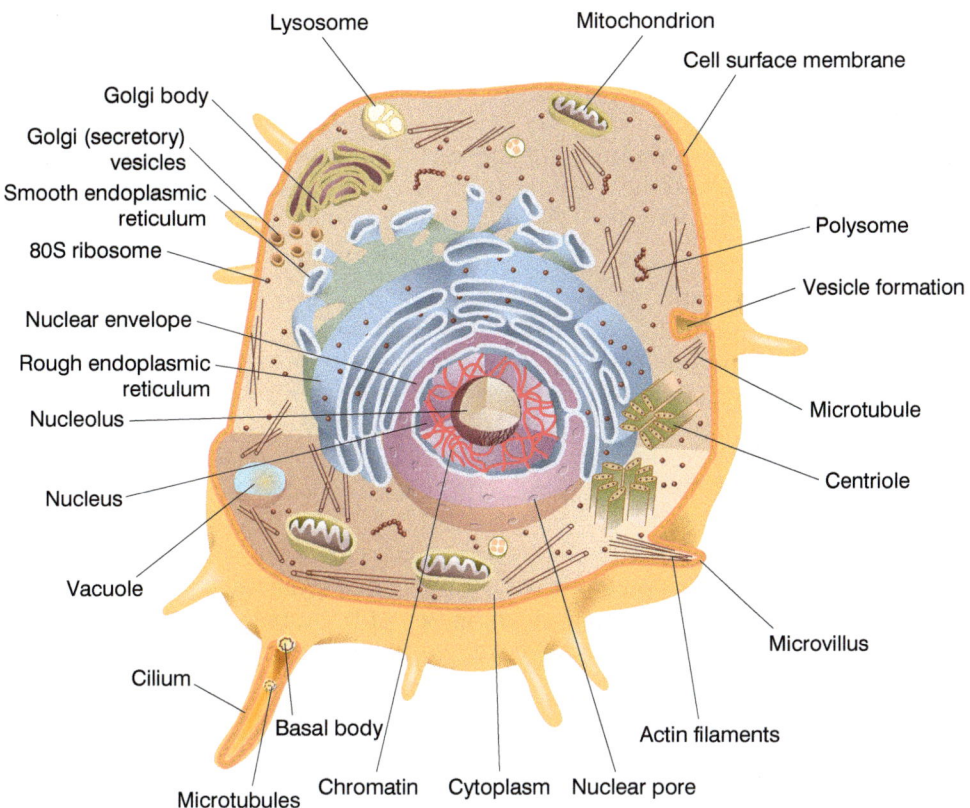

Lysosome
Mitochondrion
Cell surface membrane
Golgi body
Golgi (secretory) vesicles
Smooth endoplasmic reticulum
80S ribosome
Polysome
Vesicle formation
Nuclear envelope
Rough endoplasmic reticulum
Nucleolus
Microtubule
Nucleus
Centriole
Vacuole
Microvillus
Cilium
Basal body
Actin filaments
Microtubules
Chromatin
Cytoplasm
Nuclear pore

Figure 2 *The structure of an animal cell*

Remember

Using the light microscope, very few cell structures are visible. The diagrams of the plant cell and animal cell here include all the additional structures that are visible using the electron microscope. You should practise identifying these cell structures in diagrams, photomicrographs and electron micrographs of actual cell types. Only some of the structures shown will be present and in different cells there may be different proportions of organelles, such as mitochondria, Golgi bodies and endoplasmic reticulum. This depends on the function of the cell.

Remember

Most cells have a single nucleus, but some have many nuclei and are known as multinucleate.

Remember

Plant cells only	**Animal cells only**
• cell wall	• centrioles
• chloroplasts	• cilia
• plasmodesmata	• microvilli
• large permanent vacuole	• glycogen granules
• starch grains and granules	

Table 1 *Differences between the structures of plant and animal cells*

Plant cells	**Animal cells**
Cellulose cell wall present (in addition to the cell surface membrane)	Cell wall absent – only a cell surface membrane surrounds the cell
Plasmodesmata present	No cell wall and therefore no plasmodesmata
Chloroplasts present in large numbers to carry out photosynthesis	Chloroplasts absent
Mature cells normally have a large single, central permanent vacuole filled with cell sap which is surrounded by a vacuolar membrane (tonoplast)	Temporary vacuoles, if present, are small and scattered throughout the cell
Centrioles absent in higher plants	Centrioles present
Cilia absent in higher plants	Cilia may be present
Microvilli absent	Microvilli may be present
Starch grains (or smaller starch granules) used for carbohydrate storage	Glycogen granules used for carbohydrate storage
Cytoplasm normally confined to a thin layer at the edge of the cell because of vacuole	Cytoplasm present throughout the cell
Nucleus at the edge of the cell	Nucleus anywhere in the cell, but often central
Golgi bodies smaller and greater in number	One or a few Golgi bodies, generally larger

Summary test 1.2b

Using an electron microscope, it is possible to observe rough and **(1)** endoplasmic reticulum in plant and animal cells. Some animal cells have cilia, constructed from **(2)**. Animal cells may also have projections known as **(3)**. As animal cells do not photosynthesise, they do not have **(4)**. Starch grains are carbohydrate stores found in plant cells. Animal cells store carbohydrate as **(5)** granules. Passing through the cell wall of plant cells, there are cell structures known as **(6)**, which are not present in animal cells.

These pages help you to:

- recognise the nucleus, with its nuclear envelope and nucleolus (1.2.1)
- recognise a mitochondrion and a chloroplast (1.2.1)
- outline the structure and functions of these cell structures (1.2.1)
- learn that the molecule ATP is used by cells for energy-requiring processes (1.2.4)

You will also:

- become familiar with the role of mitochondria in respiration (for Chapter 12) and chloroplasts in photosynthesis (for Chapter 13)

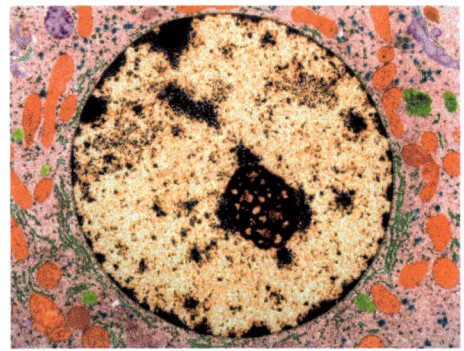

Figure 1 *Colourised transmission electron micrograph of liver cell nucleus*

Figure 2 *Coloured transmission electron micrograph of chloroplasts showing thylakoids (yellow) stacked to form grana. The black spots are oil droplets (× 10 000)*

The nucleus

The nucleus is the most prominent feature of a eukaryotic cell when viewed under the microscope. It may vary in shape, size and position from cell to cell. Usually spherical and between 10 and 20 μm in diameter, the nucleus has a number of parts:

- The **nuclear envelope** is a double membrane that surrounds the nucleus. Its outer membrane is continuous with the endoplasmic reticulum of the cell and often has ribosomes on its surface. It controls the entry and exit of materials in and out of the nucleus and contains the reactions taking place within it.
- **Nuclear pores** allow the passage of large molecules such as messenger RNA (mRNA) out of the nucleus but are too small to allow DNA to leave. There are typically around 3000 pores in each nucleus, each being 40–100 nm in diameter.
- **Chromatin** is the diffuse, thread-like form that chromosomes take up when the cell is not dividing. When the cell divides, the chromatin condenses into chromosomes (5.1a). Chromatin is composed of DNA, the genetic material of the cell, complexed with proteins known as histone proteins. The fluid surrounding chromatin is known as nucleoplasm.
- The **nucleolus** is a small spherical region (there may be more than one) that manufactures ribosomal RNA (rRNA) and assembles the subunits of the ribosomes.

As well as producing ribosomal subunits, the nucleus has other functions:

- It contains genes (units of inheritance), which are lengths of DNA along a chromosome. The coded information for the production of proteins is contained in the sequence of nucleotides that comprise a gene (6.2a). This information is carried in the form of mRNA (which exits the nucleus).
- It controls protein synthesis (through the production of mRNA) by switching genes on or off (6.2b, 16.3b).
- It is the location for DNA replication before a cell divides (5.1a).
- With its envelope, the nucleus protects the DNA from the rest of the cell; for example, protection from cytoplasmic enzymes.

Chloroplasts

The **function of chloroplasts** is photosynthesis (Chapter 13). Chloroplasts are found in plant cells and other eukaryotic cells that photosynthesise. They are flat discs, usually 3–10 μm in diameter and 1 μm thick (Figure 3).

- The **chloroplast envelope** is a double membrane. It controls the entry and exit of substances.
- The **grana** (singular granum) are structures that look like a pile of coins. Each is made up of a stack of flattened sacs called thylakoids, or lamellae (Figure 3). The thylakoid membranes contain chlorophyll molecules, which absorb light energy in the first, or light-dependent, stage of photosynthesis and produce ATP.
- The **stroma** is a colourless, gelatinous (jelly-like) matrix. This contains the enzymes necessary for the light-independent stage of photosynthesis (Chapter 13), in which complex organic molecules are produced, using the ATP made in the first stage. Oil droplets (lipid globules) are present. There is also a small circular DNA molecule and 70S ribosomes, which allow some chloroplast proteins to be made (13.1b).
- **Starch grains** act as temporary stores of the carbohydrate that is produced during photosynthesis.

Mitochondria

The **function** of mitochondria is aerobic respiration (Chapter 12). They supply energy to the cell because they synthesise (produce) ATP molecules from carbohydrates and other respiratory substrates (for example, fatty acids in a process known as beta-oxidation).

Present in all but a few eukaryotic cells, mitochondria (Figure 4) are usually rod-shaped, 1–7 μm in length and 0.5–1.0 μm in diameter. A single mitochondrion is made up of a number of parts:

- **A double membrane** around the organelle that controls the entry and exit of substances.
- **Cristae** are infoldings of the inner membrane, some of which extend across most of the width of the mitochondrion. They contain enzymes and other molecules involved in aerobic respiration. The cristae provide a large surface area for a stage of aerobic respiration known as oxidative phosphorylation, which results in the synthesis of ATP molecules (Chapter 12). ATP is used for energy-requiring processes. The size and the number of cristae increase in cells that have a high level of metabolic activity and therefore need a good supply of ATP. These include muscle and liver cells.
- The **matrix** is a viscous (thick) fluid containing enzymes involved in the Krebs cycle, a stage of aerobic respiration. Small circular molecules of DNA, mitochondrial DNA (mtDNA), and 70S ribosomes are also found in the matrix. This means that mitochondria are able to produce some of their own proteins.

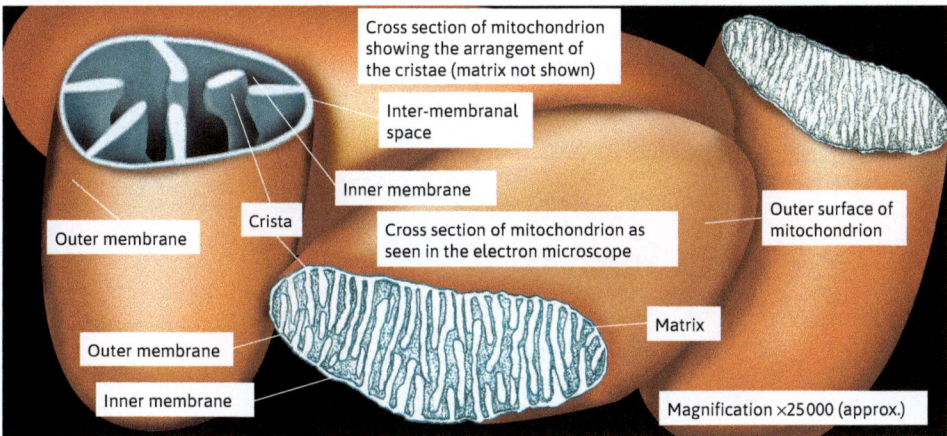

Figure 4 Mitochondria

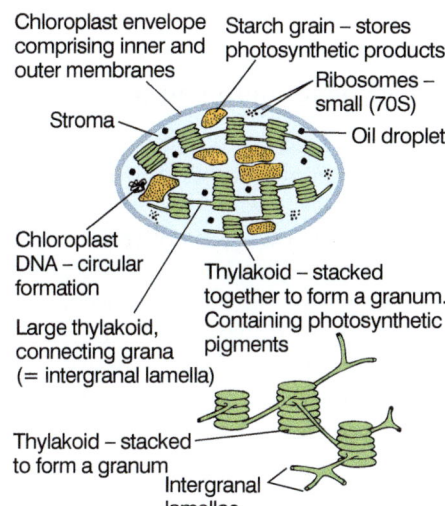

Figure 3 Structure of chloroplasts

Chloroplast envelope comprising inner and outer membranes

Starch grain – stores photosynthetic products

Stroma

Ribosomes – small (70S)

Oil droplet

Chloroplast DNA – circular formation

Thylakoid – stacked together to form a granum. Containing photosynthetic pigments

Large thylakoid, connecting grana (= intergranal lamella)

Thylakoid – stacked to form a granum

Intergranal lamellae

Extension

Adenosine triphosphate (ATP)

ATP, synthesised in respiration, is the universal energy currency of the cell (Chapter 12). ATP molecules provide the source of energy for many reactions and processes, such as building large molecules from small ones, muscle contraction, active transport and the secretion of cell products.

Extension

Grana and thylakoids

There are typically 50 grana in a chloroplast, and each is made up of up to 100 thylakoids. The stacked arrangement maximises the number of chlorophyll molecules that can be contained in the chloroplast for light absorption.

Summary test 1.2c

The nucleus is surrounded by a double membrane called the **(1)**. The genetic material, **(2)**, cannot leave the nucleus as it is too large to pass through the **(3)**. Within the nucleus is a small spherical body called the **(4)** that manufactures **(5)** RNA and assembles the subunits of **(6)**. Chloroplasts are the organelles of **(7)**. They contain structures that look like a stack of coins. These are called **(8)** and contain **(9)** molecules. Mitochondria are the sites for the two stages of **(10)** respiration. The enzymes for these processes are found either in the **(11)** or are located in the **(12)** membrane, especially in infoldings called **(13)**.

These pages help you to:

- recognise smooth and rough endoplasmic reticulum (SER and RER) (1.2.1)
- recognise a Golgi body and lysosomes (1.2.1)
- outline the structure and functions of these cell structures (1.2.1)
- learn that there are two main types of ribosome, 70S and 80S (1.2.1)

You will also:

- understand the relationship between the nucleus, endoplasmic reticulum, the Golgi body, Golgi vesicles and lysosomes

Endoplasmic reticulum

The endoplasmic reticulum (ER) is an elaborate, extensive, three-dimensional system of sheet-like membranes spreading through the cytoplasm of cells. ER comprises a network of tubules and flattened sacs enclosed by single membranes. There are two types of ER: rough endoplasmic reticulum and smooth endoplasmic reticulum (see Figures 1 and 2).

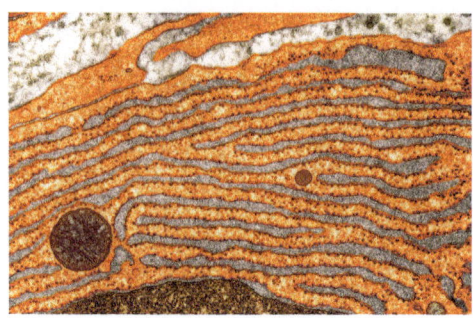

Figure 1 *Colourised transmission electron micrograph of rough endoplasmic reticulum*

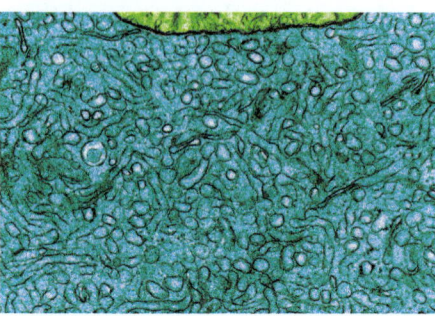

Figure 2 *Colourised transmission electron micrograph of smooth endoplasmic reticulum*

Rough endoplasmic reticulum (RER)

Rough endoplasmic reticulum (RER) has 80S ribosomes on the outer surfaces of the membranes (the surface facing the cytoplasm/cytosol). RER looks like flattened sacs known as cisternae (Figure 3) and often appears layered or more organised than smooth endoplasmic reticulum. The outer nuclear membrane is continuous with RER.

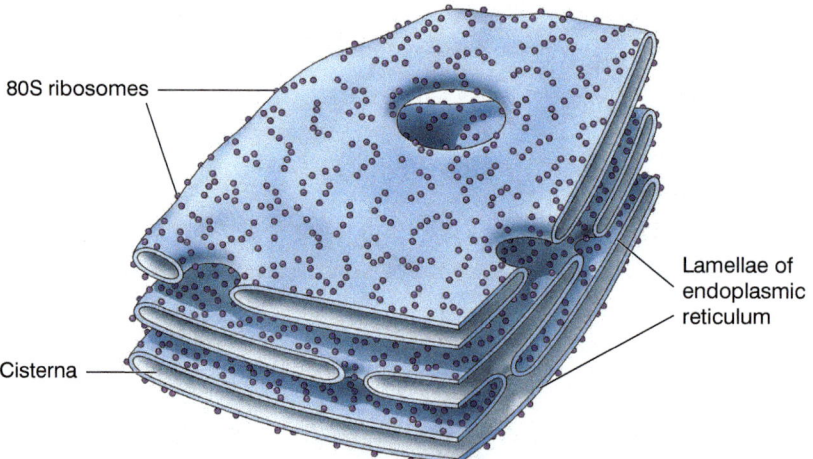

Figure 3 *Structure of rough endoplasmic reticulum*

Functions of RER:

- Provides a large surface area for the attachment of ribosomes and synthesis of polypeptides (proteins). The polypeptides pass through into the lumen of RER.
- Provides a space (lumen of RER) for the modification of proteins (see detail of modification in the Golgi body).
- Provides a pathway for the transport of proteins throughout the cell.
- Forms transport vesicles, small membrane-bound sacs that transport proteins to the Golgi body for further processing.

> **Remember**
>
> In your research, you may also see the Golgi body written as the Golgi complex or Golgi apparatus.

> **Remember**
>
> A newly formed chain of amino acids is often termed a polypeptide rather than a protein. A newly formed polypeptide (or protein) needs to be processed further to become a functioning protein.

Smooth endoplasmic reticulum (SER)

Smooth endoplasmic reticulum (SER) lacks ribosomes and is more tubular in appearance than RER. SER often appears to be more disorganised than RER and is spread throughout the cell, rather than appearing in layers.

Functions of SER:

- provides a compartment (lumen of SER) for the synthesis of lipids, including cholesterol, and their storage and transport
- forms transport vesicles that transport lipids to the Golgi body for further processing.

The extent of the endoplasmic reticulum network and the proportion of SER to RER varies according to the needs of the cell. For example, cells that are specialised to manufacture and secrete (release) large quantities of protein have a very extensive and well-developed RER. Examples of this are liver cells that secrete blood plasma proteins (8.1d) and plasma cells that secrete antibodies (11.1b).

Ribosomes

Ribosomes are small spherical structures found in all cells. They may occur in the cytoplasm or be associated with the RER. There are two types:

- 80S ribosomes are found in eukaryotic cells and are approximately 22 nm in diameter.
- 70S ribosomes are found in prokaryotic cells (1.2f) and in the mitochondria and chloroplasts of eukaryotic cells (1.2c). They are slightly smaller (17 nm) than 80S ribosomes.

Each ribosome has two subunits – a large and a small (Figure 4) – each of which contains ribosomal RNA and protein. Despite their small size, they occur in such vast numbers that they can account for up to 25% of the dry mass of a cell. Ribosomes are the sites of protein synthesis in the cell (6.2c).

Golgi body

The Golgi body occurs in most eukaryotic cells. It consists of a stack of membranes which make up flattened sacs, or cisternae, and associated hollow vesicles (Figure 5). Often the stack of cisternae has a curved appearance.

The proteins arriving from the RER or SER are passed through the Golgi body in strict sequence, starting at one 'face' (cis) of the complex and finishing at the other 'face' (trans). The Golgi processes these molecules, modifying them so that they will function correctly in their final destination. It also 'labels' them, so they can be sorted and sent to their correct destinations. Once sorted, the modified proteins and lipids are packaged into Golgi vesicles, which are regularly pinched off from the ends of the Golgi cisternae (Figure 5).

Remember

When asked to name a cell structure, write out the full name, for example, *rough endoplasmic reticulum*. If writing a more extended response, name the cell structure and put the abbreviation in brackets after: *rough endoplasmic reticulum (RER)*. You can then use the abbreviation in the rest of the response.

Extension

Other functions of SER

SER has other functions in some specialised tissues, for example the synthesis of steroid hormones in endocrine tissue and the breakdown of glycogen in liver cells to release glucose. In liver cells, SER is also used to detoxify some harmful chemicals, such as toxic metabolic waste, harmful drugs and excess alcohol.

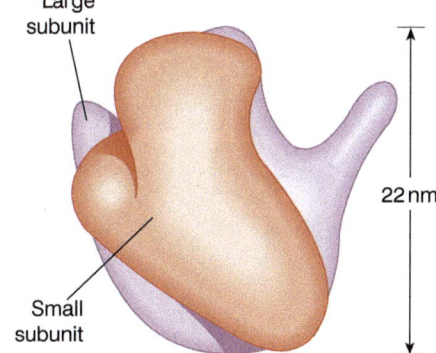

Figure 4 *Structure of an 80S ribosome*

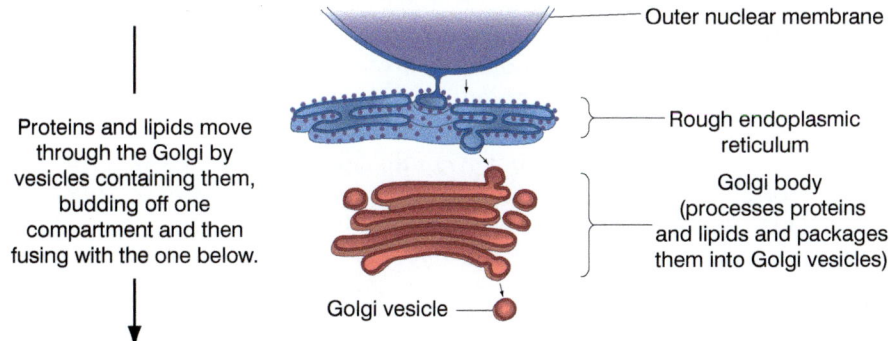

Figure 5 *The Golgi body and its relationship to the nucleus, ER and lysosomes (the exact details of how this functions is not yet known)*

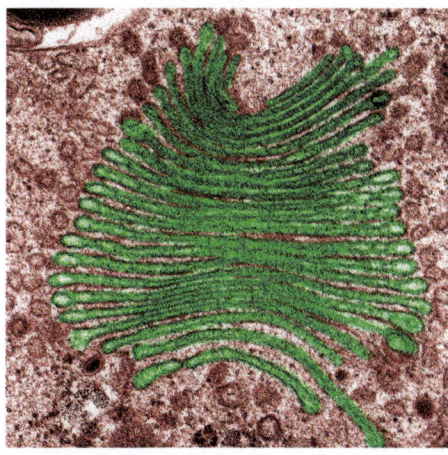

Figure 6 *Colourised transmission electron micrograph of Golgi body (green) (×6000)*

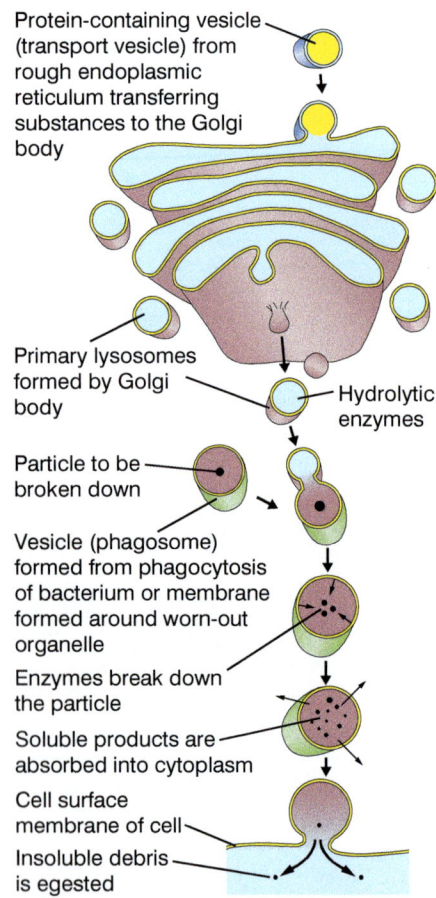

Protein-containing vesicle (transport vesicle) from rough endoplasmic reticulum transferring substances to the Golgi body

Primary lysosomes formed by Golgi body

Hydrolytic enzymes

Particle to be broken down

Vesicle (phagosome) formed from phagocytosis of bacterium or membrane formed around worn-out organelle

Enzymes break down the particle

Soluble products are absorbed into cytoplasm

Cell surface membrane of cell

Insoluble debris is egested

Figure 7 *The formation and functioning of a lysosome*

Functions of the Golgi body include:

- modification and final processing of proteins and lipids
- packaging of proteins or lipids, forming Golgi vesicles
- formation of primary lysosomes.

Examples of protein modification include:

- adding non-protein components, for example, glycosylation is the addition of a carbohydrate portion to make a glycoprotein (4.1b)
- folding of proteins into their final three-dimensional conformation (shape)
- joining together polypeptides to make a functioning protein (2.3b).

(Note that protein modification can also occur within RER.)

Golgi vesicles can be moved towards the cell surface membrane along microtubules (1.2e). Some vesicles fuse with the membrane and release their contents to become part of the cell surface membrane, while others fuse and release their contents to the external environment (see exocytosis in 4.2f).

Lysosomes

Lysosomes are spherical organelles bound by a single membrane that protects the rest of the cell from up to 50 different acid hydrolases contained within them. These are hydrolytic enzymes, such as proteases, lipases and nucleases that work at a pH of about 5. The enzymes are not active until the lysosome fuses with another membrane-bound sac containing the material that needs to be broken down.

Some membrane-bound sacs are formed within a cell, for example a membrane surrounding a damaged or old organelle. Others, known as phagosomes or phagocytic vacuoles, are formed when the cell surface membrane invaginates (folds in) to enclose bacterial or other foreign material to destroy it (Figure 7). Some cells (phagocytes) specialise in engulfing bacteria or other foreign material to destroy them (see 4.2f and 11.1a).

Lysosomes vary greatly in size, from 50 nm to over 700 nm.

Functions of lysosomes include:

- digestion (breakdown) of old or worn-out organelles (autophagy) such as mitochondria, allowing re-use of chemicals by the cell
- digestion of bacteria, other foreign material, or cell debris that have been taken into the cell in phagosomes
- digestion of cells after they have died (autolysis)
- release of hydrolytic enzymes to the outside of the cell to destroy material around the cell.

Summary test 1.2d

Rough endoplasmic reticulum has **(1)** on its **(2)** surface so that proteins can be synthesised. Within the **(3)** of RER, proteins can be modified or transported to other areas. Smooth endoplasmic reticulum functions to synthesise **(4)**. SER has a more **(5)** appearance, whereas RER appears as flattened sacs known as **(6)**. Transport **(7)** move proteins to the **(8)** body where they can be **(9)** and packaged into **(10)**. Powerful digestive enzymes known as **(11)** are contained within **(12)**. These function to **(13)** material such as ingested bacteria or old or damaged **(14)**.

Cell surface membrane

The cell surface membrane defines the cell and encloses the cell contents (see Figure 3 in 1.1c). It is a phospholipid bilayer containing proteins (4.1a). Its phospholipid bilayer means that it can prevent the entry or exit of some substances based on their size and solubility in lipids. The presence of proteins allows some substances that are soluble in water to pass through. For these reasons, it is described as partially permeable.

Functions of the cell surface membrane:

- It is the boundary, and forms a barrier, between the cell cytoplasm and the external environment, including protecting the cell from harmful substances.
- It controls movement of substances into or out of the cell.
- It is important in cell recognition, and has molecules on its surface that are recognised by other cells.
- It has receptor sites which bind specific hormones, neurotransmitters and other cell signalling molecules
- It has components that attach to one another and so help cells to form **tissues** by cell-to-cell adhesion.
- It can contain enzymes to catalyse specific reactions.

Microvilli (animal cells only)

In some animal cells, such as those lining the small intestine, the cell surface membrane extends outwards to form many tiny projections, approximately 1 μm long, called microvilli (Figure 1). Using the light microscope, the densely packed microvilli can only be seen as a blurred edge, known as a brush border.

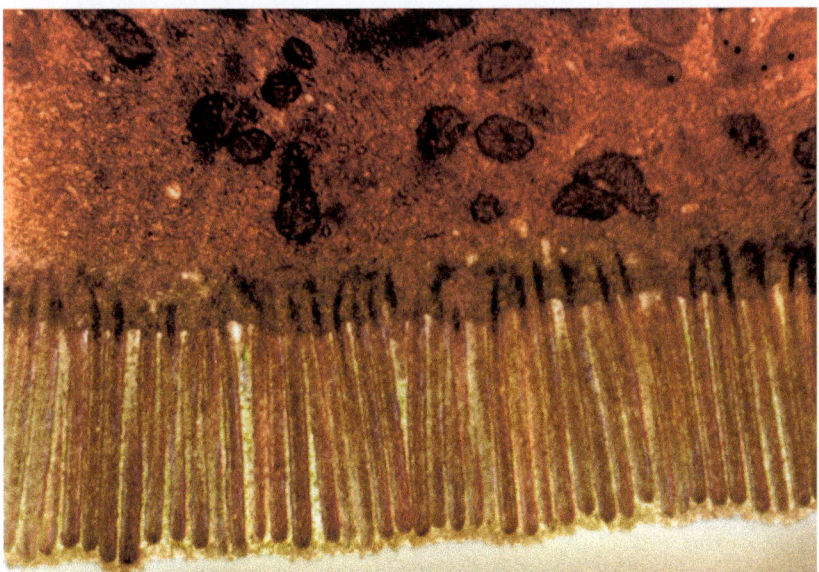

Figure 1 *Intestinal microvilli*

Microvilli vastly increase the surface area over which absorption or secretion can take place.

> **Remember**
>
> When you look at a group of animal cells under a light microscope, you cannot see the cell surface membrane because it is too thin to be observed. What you see is the boundary between cells.

Cilia (animal cells only)

Cilia are hair-like structures that extend from a basal body (Figure 2 in 1.2b) at the surface of some animal cells. They are covered in cell surface membrane and are constructed from microtubules. In cross section, a '9 + 2' microtubule arrangement can be seen (Figure 2). They are motile (can move) and have a whip-like movement. Each ciliated cell has many cilia that are able to move in a synchronised manner (synchronous rhythm). The cilia function to move substances across the surface of cells, such as mucus in the respiratory airways. Their wave-like action also helps to move the egg cell and sperm in the fallopian tubes.

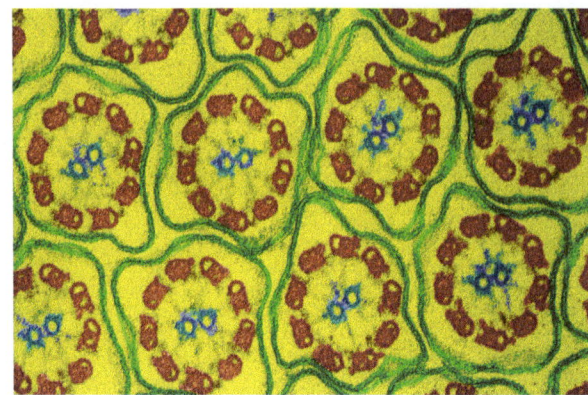

Figure 2 Cilia

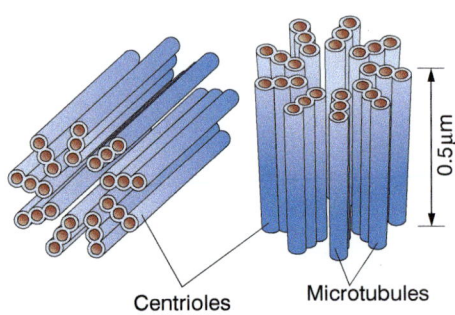

Centrioles   Microtubules

Figure 3 Centrioles

Centrioles and microtubules

Centrioles are found in almost all animal cells, as well as in the cells of some algae and fungi, but not in the cells of higher plants. They are hollow cylinders 0.5 µm in length and 0.2 µm in diameter made up of nine sets of three microtubules (Figures 3). There are two centrioles in an animal cell and they lie at right angles to one another near to the nucleus (Figure 4). Microtubules are composed of a globular protein called tubulin.

Functions of centrioles and microtubules:

- The centrioles have a role in organising microtubules to form the spindle fibres during nuclear division (5.2).
- The basal body of a cilium is a modified centriole, responsible for organising microtubules to form the cilium.
- In addition to forming spindle fibres, microtubules form part of the cytoskeleton, the internal 'skeleton' of the cell that provides support and gives shape to the cell.
- Microtubules serve as a scaffold for the movement and positioning of organelles within the cell, including transport and Golgi vesicles.

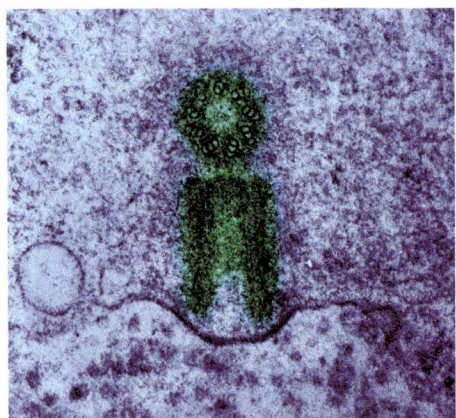

Figure 4 Colourised transmission electron micrograph of two centrioles in transverse (top) and longitudinal (bottom) section

Cell wall (plant cells only)

Characteristic of all plant cells, the cell wall consists of cellulose microfibrils which contain the polysaccharide cellulose (2.2c) embedded in a matrix. Cellulose microfibrils have considerable strength and so contribute to the overall strength of the cell wall. The cell wall also contains other polysaccharides such as hemicellulose and pectin.

A thin layer, called the middle lamella, between adjacent cell walls cements adjacent cells together.

The functions of the cell wall are to:

- provide mechanical strength in order to prevent the cell bursting (cell lysis) under turgor pressure, the pressure created by the osmotic entry of water (4.2c)
- give mechanical strength to the plant as a whole
- allow water to pass along it and so contribute to the movement of water through the plant.

Plasmodesmata (plant cells only)

Small thin cytoplasmic strands called **plasmodesmata** are present crossing through cell walls. The channels through which they pass are lined with cell surface membrane. These connect the cytoplasm of adjacent cells for cell communication and allow substances to pass between them without having to pass through the cell wall or cell surface membrane. They form part of the symplast pathway (7.2a) by which water moves through plants. Mineral ions, dissolved solutes and cell signalling molecules also pass between cells via the plasmodesmata. A plasmodesma can be described as simple (a single channel) or complex (branched channelling).

Large permanent vacuole (plant cells only)

Plant cells have a large permanent vacuole that is surrounded by a membrane called the tonoplast and contains a fluid known as cell sap. The functions of the vacuole are: to store water, ions, sugars and pigments; push chloroplasts to the edge of the cell for photosynthesis; and give turgidity to the cell to help support the plant. It can also serve as a store of waste substances. Hydrolytic enzymes have also been found in vacuoles. These break down waste metabolic products.

Tonoplast (plant cells only)

This is the vacuolar membrane. It has the same basic structure as the cell surface membrane. It serves as a barrier between the contents of the vacuole and the cytoplasm and, like the cell surface membrane, has some control over the substances that enter or leave the vacuole.

Extension

The vacuole, lysosomes and plant cells

Lysosomes are common in animal cells, but there is some debate about the existence of lysosomes in plant cells. The large permanent vacuoles of plant cells contain hydrolytic enzymes and may be described as having lysosomal functions, so possibly some plant cells do not require lysosomes because their vacuole performs the same function. However, membrane-bound vesicles containing hydrolytic enzymes have been found in some plant cells, so it could be argued that these are lysosomes – some scientists have called these lytic organelles.

Summary test 1.2e

The cell surface membrane of a cell is a **(1)** between the cell and the external environment. It is **(2)** permeable. Extensions known as **(3)** increase the surface area for **(4)** or secretion. In cross section, cilia have a **(5)** microtubule arrangement. In animal cells, there is a total of **(6)** centrioles. These are important in forming **(7)** fibres during nuclear division. The vacuolar membrane is also known as the **(8)**. **(9)** are cytoplasmic strands that pass from one plant cell to the next through the cell walls. The cellulose in plant cell walls provides strength and prevents bursting, or **(10)**.

These pages help you to:

- outline key structural features of a prokaryotic cell as found in a typical bacterium (1.2.5)
- understand that there are no organelles surrounded by double membranes in prokaryotes (1.2.5)
- compare the structure of a bacterial cell (as an example of a prokaryote) with the structure of a eukaryotic cell (for example, a typical plant or animal cell) (1.2.6)
- understand that viruses are non-cellular structures (1.2.7)
- outline the structure of viruses (1.2.7)

You will also:

- consolidate your knowledge that plants and animals are multicellular organisms, bacteria are unicellular organisms and that viruses are non-cellular
- be able to explain why viruses are non-cellular organisms

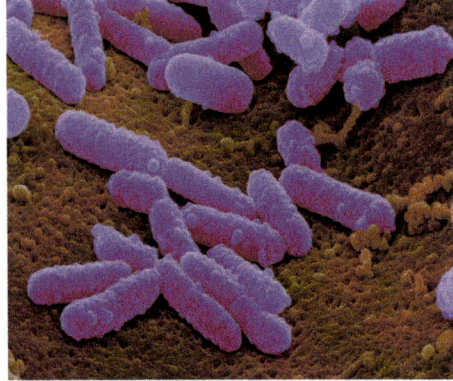

Figure 1 *Colourised scanning electron micrograph of a colony of the rod-shaped bacterium,* Escherichia coli

Remember

'Naked DNA' refers to DNA that lacks associated protein, while 'free DNA' refers to DNA that is not confined to the nucleus.

Introduction

Although there is a huge variety of cells in terms of size, shape and function (see 1.2a), each cell belongs to one of two basic groups: prokaryotes and eukaryotes.

Both cell types have a cell surface membrane, DNA as their genetic material, cytoplasm and ribosomes. The functions of these are the same in both types.

The differences between prokaryotic and eukaryotic cells are listed in Table 1.

Table 1 *Differences between prokaryotic and eukaryotic cells*

Prokaryotic cells	Eukaryotic cells
No true nucleus or nuclear envelope (so DNA is free in the cytoplasm)	Distinct nucleus, with a nuclear envelope (so DNA is enclosed)
No nucleolus	Nucleolus is present
DNA is not associated with histone proteins (naked DNA)	DNA is associated with histone proteins to form chromosomes
Circular (closed loop) DNA	Linear DNA
Cell wall made of peptidoglycan (murein)	Where present, cell wall is made mostly of cellulose (plants) or chitin (fungi)
No double membrane bounded organelles	Double membrane bounded organelles such as mitochondria and chloroplasts (e.g. in plant cells) are present
Ribosomes are 70S, smaller	Ribosomes are 80S, larger
Plasmids may be present	No plasmids present
Flagella (if present) lack internal 9 + 2 microtubule arrangement	Flagella, where present, have a 9 + 2 internal microtubule arrangement
No endoplasmic reticulum or associated Golgi body and lysosomes	Endoplasmic reticulum present along with Golgi body and lysosomes

Structure of a typical bacterial cell, an example of a prokaryotic cell

Bacteria are normally in the range 0.1–5.0 μm in length. Their cellular structure is relatively simple (Figures 1 and 2). All bacteria have a cell wall which is made up of peptidoglycan (murein), a polysaccharide cross-linked by peptide molecules.

The cytoplasm of bacterial cells contains 70S ribosomes, the sites of protein synthesis. They are smaller and have a slightly different structure to the 80S ribosomes of eukaryotes.

The genetic material in bacteria is usually circular (double-stranded) DNA. Although there are proteins present, DNA is not complexed with histone proteins. Separate from this, and not necessary for growth and metabolism, are smaller circular molecules of DNA called plasmids. These can replicate independently and may contain genes that give the bacterium an advantage, for example, produce enzymes to give resistance to chemicals such as **antibiotics**. Plasmids are used extensively as vectors (carriers of genetic information) in genetic engineering (19.1c).

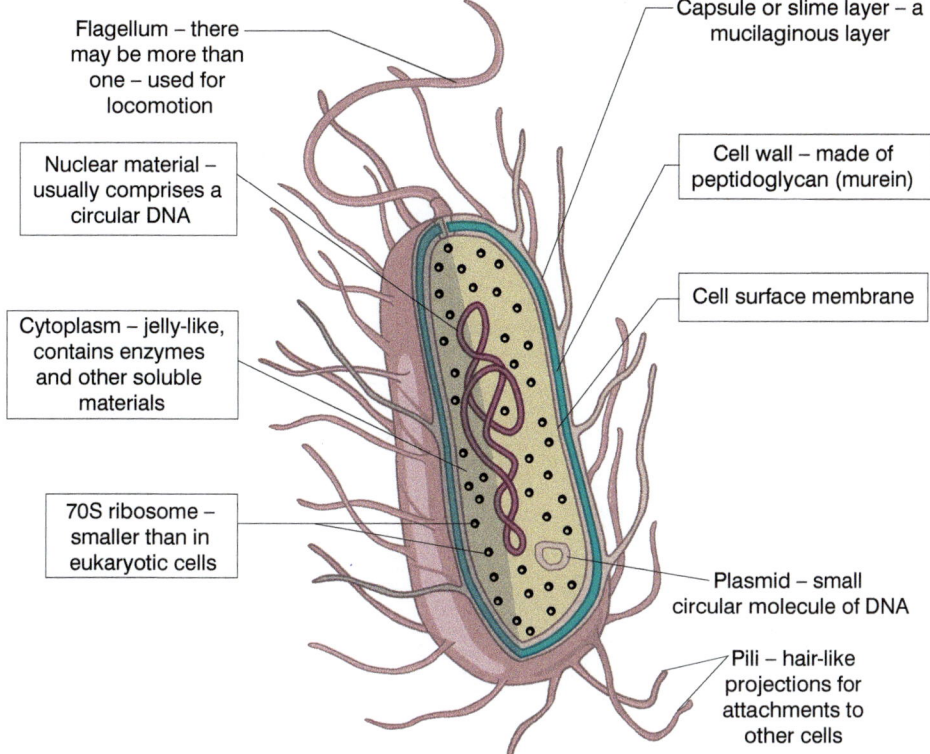

Flagellum – there may be more than one – used for locomotion

Nuclear material – usually comprises a circular DNA

Cytoplasm – jelly-like, contains enzymes and other soluble materials

70S ribosome – smaller than in eukaryotic cells

Capsule or slime layer – a mucilaginous layer

Cell wall – made of peptidoglycan (murein)

Cell surface membrane

Plasmid – small circular molecule of DNA

Pili – hair-like projections for attachments to other cells

Figure 2 *Structure of a generalised bacterial cell. Structures labelled in boxes occur in all bacteria whereas the others occur only in certain species*

Viruses

Viruses (Figures 3 and 4) are generally smaller than bacteria, most ranging in size from 5 to 300 nm. They are not made of cells and have no cell organelles. They can be described as non-cellular (or acellular). They are made up of a protective protein coat known as a capsid, which gives a particular shape to the virus. The capsid is made of repeating protein subunits known as capsomeres. It contains glycoproteins, which bind to receptor sites on host cells. The capsid surrounds a nucleic acid core of either DNA or RNA. A virus does not have DNA **and** RNA. The nucleic acid codes for proteins that allow the virus to complete a successful life cycle using a host cell. The complete virus particle is termed a virion.

Some viruses have an outer phospholipid envelope that is derived from their host cell. This gives the virus a more flexible shape and, in addition to being another protective layer, can help the virus attach to host cells for infection.

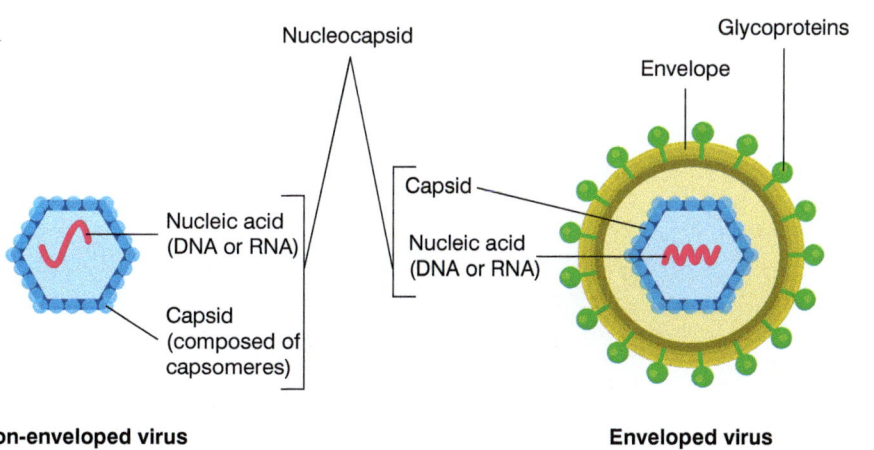

Nucleocapsid

Nucleic acid (DNA or RNA)

Capsid (composed of capsomeres)

Glycoproteins

Envelope

Capsid

Nucleic acid (DNA or RNA)

Non-enveloped virus

Enveloped virus

Figure 3 *Enveloped and non-enveloped viruses*

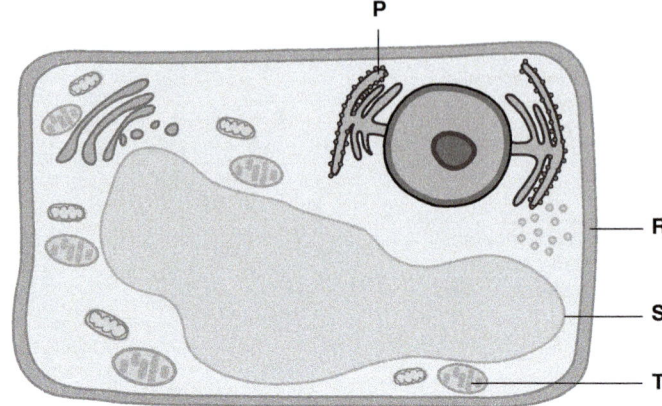

(Launch additional digital resources for the chapter)

1 Exam-style questions

1 Plant cells are stained and then viewed through a light microscope.

Which structures would be clearly visible at a magnification of ×400?

A mitochondria cristae

B lysosomes

C nucleoli

D ribosomes

(1 mark)

2 a Figure 1 shows a transmission electron micrograph of a cell from the pancreas of a rat.

Figure 1

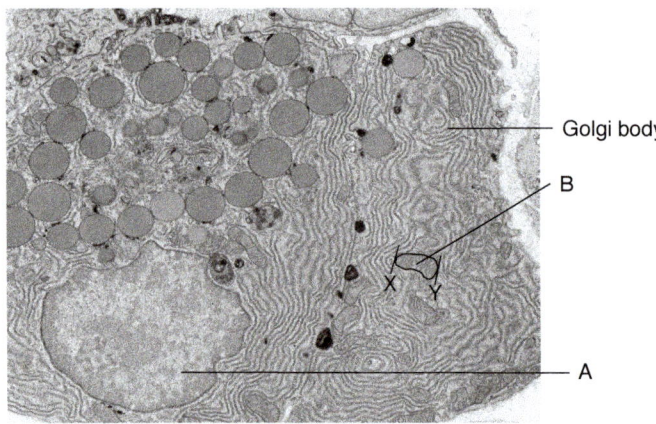

Identify the structures labelled **A** and **B**.   *(3 marks)*

b Outline the function of the Golgi body in the secretion of proteins, such as the enzyme lipase, from the cells of the pancreas.   *(3 marks)*

c It is important to use both light microscopes and electron microscopes, when investigating how cell organelles carry out various functions within a cell.

Suggest **two** advantages of using light microscopes and **two** advantages of using electron microscopes to investigate how organelles/structures carry out their particular function.   *(4 marks)*

d The magnification in Figure 1 is ×1500.

Calculate the actual diameter of the organelle labelled B. Give your answer in micrometres to the nearest whole number. Show your working including the formula that you will use for your calculation.   *(3 marks)*

(Total 13 marks)

3 a Figure 2 shows the structure of a typical cell from a leaf (not all to scale).

Figure 2

i Identify cell structures **P**, **R**, **S** and **T and** state one function for each structure in Table 1.

Table 1

Cell structure	Name of cell structure	Function
P		protein synthesis
R		
S		controls what enters/leaves the vacuole
T	chloroplast	

(5 marks)

ii The cell shown in Figure 2 is a eukaryotic cell.

State how the structure of a eukaryotic cell differs from a prokaryotic cell.   *(3 marks)*

b Figure 3 shows the virus responsible for causing the infectious disease influenza.

Figure 3

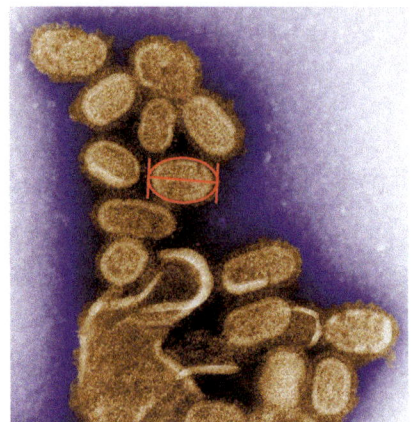

i State two structural features shown by the virus in Figure 3 that are commonly found in other viruses. *(2 marks)*

ii The length of the virus shown in Figure 3 is 150 nm.

Calculate the magnification to the nearest whole number. State the formula that you will use for your calculation and show your working. *(3 marks)*

c The tobacco mosaic virus is a common plant virus that spreads rapidly through an infected plant.

Suggest how these viruses are able to pass from one plant cell to the next without crossing membranes. *(1 mark)*

(Total 14 marks)

1 Practice questions

4 The table below lists some features of cells. For the letter in each box, write down one of the following: 'present' if the feature always occurs, 'absent' if it never occurs and 'sometimes' if it occurs in some cells but not others.

Feature	Prokaryotic cell	Eukaryotic cell
nuclear envelope	A	B
cell wall	C	D
flagellum	E	F
ribosomes	G	H
plasmid	I	J
cell surface membrane	K	L
mitochondria	M	N

5 a Distinguish between magnification and resolution.

b An organelle that is 5 µm in diameter appears under a microscope to have a diameter of 1 mm. How many times has the organelle been magnified?

c A ribosome is 25 nm in diameter. If viewed under an electron microscope that magnified it 400 000 times, what would the diameter of the ribosome appear to be in millimetres?

d At a magnification of 12 000 times, a structure appears to be 6 mm long. What is its actual length?

e Why is the electron microscope able to resolve objects better than the light microscope?

f Why do specimens have to be kept in a near-vacuum in order to be viewed effectively using an electron microscope?

g Of the following list of biological structures: plant cell (100 µm); DNA molecule (2 nm); virus (100 nm); actin molecule (3.5 nm) and a bacterium (1 µm) which ones can, in theory, be resolved by:
i a light microscope
ii a transmission electron microscope
iii a scanning electron microscope?

h Suggest why, in practice, the theoretical resolution of an electron microscope cannot always be achieved.

6 a Ribosomes are important in which process?

b In each of the following, name the organelle being referred to.
i Possesses structures called cristae; **(ii)** Contains chromatin; **(iii)** Synthesises glycoproteins; **(iv)** Digests worn-out organelles.

c The following list names a type of cell and a brief description of its role. Suggest in each case two organelles that might be numerous and/or well developed in that cell.
i A sperm cell swims a considerable distance and when it reaches an egg releases enzymes to digest a path.
ii A type of white blood cell engulfs and digests foreign material.
iii Cells lining a kidney tubule reabsorb soluble substances against a concentration gradient.
iv Liver cells manufacture proteins and lipids at a rapid rate.

7 The drawing in the figure has been made from an electron micrograph of a cell lining the human intestine.

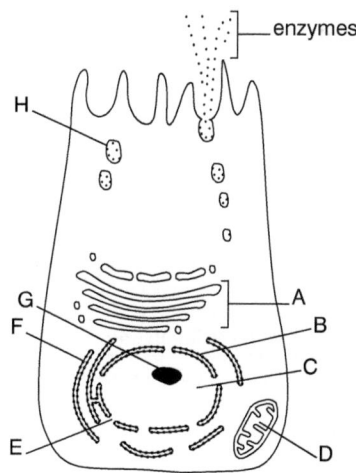

a Give the names of the structures labelled **A–H**.

b Give the letter of the structure that best fits the following descriptions:
i Produces ATP molecules
ii Manufactures ribosomal RNA
iii Possesses structures called cristae
iv Produce the enzymes shown being released from the cell.

31

2 Biological molecules

2.1 Testing for biological molecules

a. An introduction to biological molecules

These pages help you to:

- define the terms monomer, polymer and macromolecule (2.2.2)
- understand the role of covalent bonds in joining smaller molecules together to form polymers (2.2.3)

You will also:

- learn what is meant by atoms and isotopes and ions, to help your understanding of biological molecules
- understand the difference between oxidation and reduction reactions
- learn the difference between covalent bonding, ionic bonding and hydrogen bonding
- understand the difference between anabolism and catabolism

Biological molecules are particular groups of chemicals that are found in living organisms. A good understanding of biological molecules is necessary for **molecular biology** and for **biochemistry**. All molecules, whether biological or not, are made up of units called atoms.

> ### Extension
>
> **Atoms, isotopes and ions**
>
> Atoms are the smallest units of a chemical **element** that can exist independently. An atom comprises a nucleus that contains particles called protons (positively charged) and neutrons (the hydrogen atom is the only exception as it has no neutrons). Neutrons have the same mass as protons but no electrical charge. Tiny particles called electrons (negatively charged) orbit in fixed shells around the nucleus but a long way from it. They have such a small mass that their contribution to the overall mass of the atom is negligible. Their number determines the chemical properties of an atom.
>
> In an atom, the number of protons and electrons is the same so there is no overall charge. The **mass number** of an atom is the total number of protons and neutrons in a given atom. The atomic structure of three common elements is given in Figure 1.
>
> Isotopes of an element have the same number of protons and the same chemical properties but a different number of neutrons and a different mass. Isotopes, especially radioactive ones, are very useful in biology for tracing the route of certain elements in biological processes and for dating fossils.
>
> An ion is an atom or a molecule that has a charge. When an atom loses an electron, it becomes a positively charged ion (e.g. a hydrogen ion, H^+). When an atom gains an electron, it becomes negatively charged (e.g. a chloride ion Cl^-). More than one electron may be lost or received (e.g. Ca^{2+}). Ions may be made up of more than one type of atom (e.g. SO_4^{2-}).

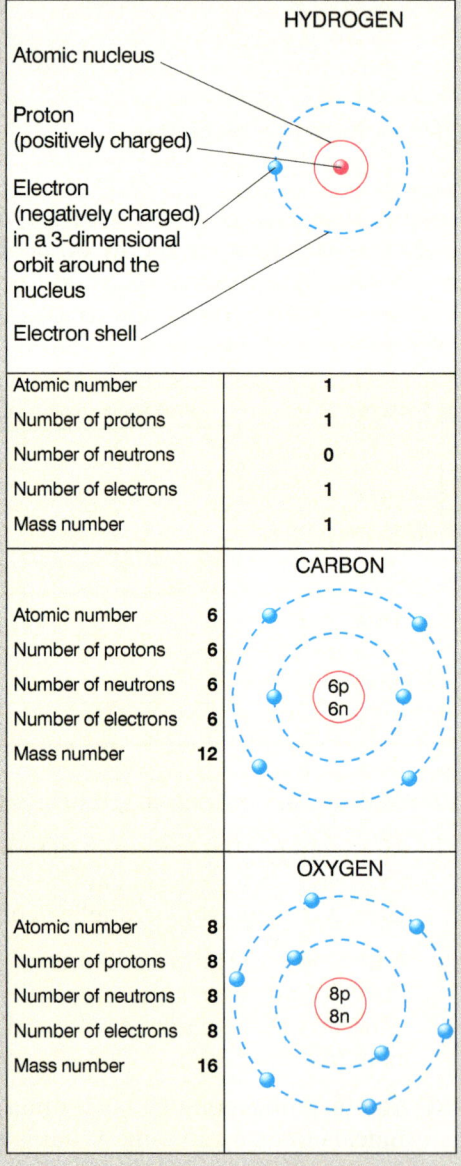

Figure 1 *Atomic structure of three commonly occurring elements*

> ### Remember
>
> The loss of an electron from an atom or molecule is called **oxidation**.
>
> The receiving of an electron from an atom or molecule is called **reduction**.
>
> To avoid confusing the two terms oxidation and reduction, simply look at the first vowel in each of the key words in the table below:
>
> | Process | Oxidation | Reduction |
> |---|---|---|
> | Change of electrons in atoms | **L**oses | **R**eceives |
> | Atom becomes | **O**xidised | **R**educed |
> | Ion produced | **P**ositive | **N**egative |
> | First vowel | **o** | **e** |
>
> A useful acronym is OIL RIG – Oxidation Is Loss, Reduction Is Gain.

Bonding and the formation of molecules

Atoms may combine with each other in a number of ways:

- **Covalent bonding** – atoms share a pair of electrons in their outer shells. As a result the outer shell of both atoms is filled and a more stable compound, called a **molecule**, is formed. Examples of covalent bonds are the glycosidic bonds that form in carbohydrates (2.2b), ester bonds in lipids (2.3d), peptide and disulfide bonds in proteins (2.3a) and phosphodiester bonds in nucleic acids (Chapter 6).
- **Ionic bonding** – ions with opposite charges attract one another. This electrostatic attraction is known as an ionic bond. For example the positively charged sodium Na^+ and negatively charged chloride Cl^- form an ionic bond to make sodium chloride. Ionic bonds are weaker than covalent bonds.
- **Hydrogen bonding** – occurs when a weak attractive force occurs between an electronegative atom of one molecule and a hydrogen of another molecule that is bonded to an electronegative atom. This electronegative atom has a tendency to attract electrons, so giving the hydrogen atom a slightly positive charge. It is due to hydrogen bonding that water molecules tend to stick together.

Polar and non-polar molecules

In some molecules with covalent bonds, one atom slightly attracts the shared electrons towards its nucleus, so that, even though the molecule has no overall charge, one atom has a slightly negative charge (δ^-) and the other a slightly positive charge (δ^+). The molecule is said to be a polar molecule. Water is a polar molecule (2.4a). Polar molecules are attracted to water and can be described as hydrophilic ('water-loving'). Where there is an equal sharing of electrons in a covalent bond, the molecule is said to be non-polar and can be described as hydrophobic ('water-hating').

Macromolecules, monomers and polymers

A macromolecule is a large molecule composed of many atoms. One macromolecule could contain a thousand or more atoms. This means that macromolecules have a high molecular mass. However, there is not an agreed definition of how large a molecule must be to be called a macromolecule.

A **polymer** is composed of similar repeating subunits known as **monomers**. A polymer is a macromolecule, but not all macromolecules are polymers. For example, lipids (2.2b) can be considered macromolecules but they are not polymers as they are not composed of repeating smaller molecules (subunits). Polymers are formed by a process called polymerisation.

The monomers of a polymer are usually based on carbon. Many polymers, such as polythene and polyesters, are industrially produced. Others, like polysaccharides, polypeptides and polynucleotides, are made naturally by living organisms. The basic subunit of a polysaccharide is a monosaccharide (2.2b and c), e.g. glucose. Polynucleotides are formed from mononucleotide subunits (6.1a). Amino acids are the monomers of polypeptides (2.3a).

Condensation and hydrolysis reactions

In polymerisation in living organisms, each time a new subunit is attached a molecule of water is formed. Reactions that produce water in this way are termed **condensation reactions**. Therefore the formation of a polypeptide from amino acids and that of the polysaccharide starch from the monosaccharide glucose are both condensation reactions.

Polymers can be broken down through the addition of water. Water molecules break down the bonds that link the subunits of a polymer, thereby splitting the molecule into its constituent parts. This type of reaction is called **hydrolysis** ('hydro' = water; 'lysis' = splitting). Thus polypeptides can be hydrolysed into amino acids, and starch can be hydrolysed into glucose.

Metabolism

All the chemical processes that take place in living organisms are collectively called metabolism. Metabolism can be divided into two parts:

- **Anabolism** – an energy-requiring process in which small molecules (e.g. amino acids) are combined to make larger ones (e.g. polypeptides). The condensation reactions that build polymers from basic subunits, e.g. polypeptides formed from amino acids, are examples of anabolic reactions.
- **Catabolism** – chemical reactions involving the release of energy in the breakdown of larger molecules into smaller ones. The hydrolysis reactions that split polymers into their basic subunits, e.g. polypeptides being split into amino acids, are examples of catabolic reactions.

Summary test 2.1a

Polysaccharides and lipids are examples of large molecules, or (**1**). Lipids are not polymers as they are not composed of many similar repeating (**2**), whereas polysaccharides are polymers. A (**3**) is composed of a chain of amino acids joined by strong (**4**) bonds in (**5**) reactions. Water is a product of these reactions. The type of metabolic reaction where larger molecules are built from small molecules is known as (**6**). When a polymer is broken down, (**7**) reactions occur where (**8**) molecules are used to break bonds.

b. Reducing and non-reducing sugars, starch, lipids and proteins

These pages help you to:

- learn the Benedict's test for reducing sugars (2.1.1)
- describe a semi-quantitative Benedict's test (2.1.2)
- prepare a test for non-reducing sugars, using acid hydrolysis and Benedict's solution (2.1.3)
- remember the iodine test for starch (2.1.1)
- remember the emulsion test for lipids (2.1.1)
- remember the biuret test for proteins (2.1.1)

You will also:

- appreciate the need for control experiments

The biochemical tests described here can be used to identify different types of biological molecules, but they cannot identify specific molecules. Table 1 is a summary of the tests that you will carry out.

Table 1 *Summary of tests for identifying biological molecules*

Test for	Reagent or reagents used	Temperature	Positive result
Reducing sugars	Benedict's solution	95°C	Change from clear blue to coloured precipitate
Non-reducing sugars	Benedict's solution dilute hydrochloric acid sodium hydrogen carbonate	95°C	Remains blue on first testing; coloured precipitate obtained when tested again after hydrolysis
Starch	iodine solution	Room temperature	Change from orange/brown to blue-black colour
Lipids	ethanol (alcohol) water	Room temperature	Change from clear mixture to milky (cloudy) emulsion
Protein	Biuret reagent	Room temperature	Change from pale blue to lilac/purple colour

Remember

Each time you carry out a practical, you will need to consider any risks and take the appropriate precautions. It is essential to be able to prepare a risk assessment for any practical activity.

Remember

To confirm that a reducing sugar is present when you obtain a positive result, carry out a control experiment using distilled water in place of the test solution. This should show that no change occurs with Benedict's solution alone and prove that it is the test solution that causes the change.

Table 2 *Benedict's test – visual results*

Concentration of reducing sugar	Colour of solution or precipitate
None	Blue
Very low	Green
Low	Yellow
Medium	Brown
High	Red

Practical skills

Tests for reducing and non-reducing sugars

All monosaccharides and most disaccharides are reducing sugars. The test for a reducing sugar is known as the **Benedict's test**. When a reducing sugar is heated with an alkaline solution of copper(II) sulfate (Benedict's reagent) it forms an insoluble precipitate of copper(I) oxide. The colour of the precipitate changes from green through yellow, orange and brown to deep red, depending on the quantity of reducing sugar present (see Table 2). The disaccharide sucrose is a non-reducing sugar. A non-reducing sugar can be identified by first hydrolysing with a dilute acid and then detecting the resulting reducing sugars using the Benedict's test. The process is as follows.

- Heat a sample with Benedict's reagent in a water bath. If there is no change (solution remains blue), then no reducing sugar is present.
- Heat a fresh sample in a water bath for five minutes with dilute hydrochloric acid to hydrolyse the non-reducing sugar, then neutralise with sodium hydrogencarbonate and allow to cool.
- Re-test the resulting solution by heating in a water bath with Benedict's reagent, which will now turn yellow/brown/red due to the reducing sugars made from hydrolysis of the non-reducing sugar.

Semi-quantitative nature of the Benedict's test

Table 2 shows the relationship between the concentration of reducing sugar and the colour of the solution and precipitate formed during the Benedict's test. The differences in colour mean that the test can be used to give **semi-quantitative** results, i.e. it can be used to estimate the approximate concentration of reducing sugar in a sample.

First, a range of colour standards is produced by preparing a series of glucose solutions of known concentration. An excess of Benedict's reagent is added to test tubes containing an equal volume of each. They are then heated for the same length of time before being cooled to room temperature. An equal volume of an unknown sample is then treated in the same way and the colour compared with that of the colour standards. Use a piece of white card placed behind the tubes to make the colours easier to see. The test is not fully quantitative because you cannot be sure of the actual concentration of the unknown sample. You can only match it up to the colour standards. If you judge that it is in between two colour standards, you may suggest a value in between the two known concentrations, but this is not an accurate result.

A further extension of this experiment would be to carry out the reducing sugar test and then to filter the suspensions. The precipitate can then be dried and weighed. The greater the mass of precipitate, the more reducing sugar is present. Alternatively, the filtrate can be placed in a colorimeter (see 3.1c) – the more intense the blue colour the less concentrated the reducing sugar. Remember that the precipitate in the colour standards you prepare will settle to the bottom of the test tube over time. You may need to gently swirl the tube to re-mix the contents before making a colour comparison with your unknown.

Test for starch

Starch is easily detected by its ability to turn the iodine in potassium iodide solution from an orange/yellow colour to blue-black. The colouration is due to the iodine molecules becoming fixed in the centre of the helix of each starch molecule (Figure 2). It is important that this test is carried out at room temperature (or below), as high temperatures cause the starch helix to unwind, releasing the iodine, which then returns to its usual yellow colour.

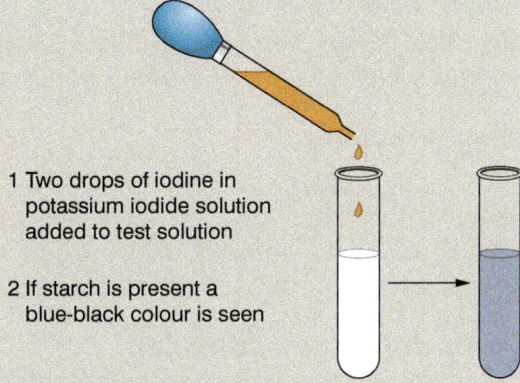

1 Two drops of iodine in potassium iodide solution added to test solution

2 If starch is present a blue-black colour is seen

Figure 1 *Test for starch*

Test for lipids

The test for lipids is known as the **emulsion test** and is carried out as follows.

- Take a completely dry and grease-free test tube.
- Add about 2 cm³ of the sample being tested and add 5 cm³ of ethanol.
- Shake the tube thoroughly to dissolve any lipid in the sample.
- Add 5 cm³ of water and shake gently.
- A cloudy-white colour indicates the presence of a lipid.
- As a control, repeat the procedures using water instead of the sample; the final solution should remain clear.

Iodine molecule in the centre of the amylose helix. Amylose is one of the two polymers that make up a starch molecule (see 2.2b)

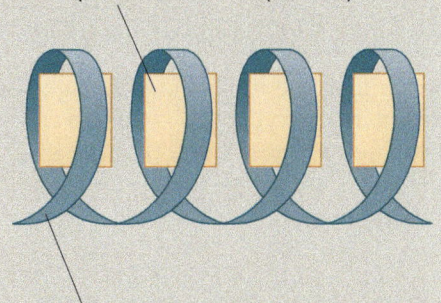

Amylose helix formed by α-glucose molecules (6 per turn of helix). The dimensions of the centre are just sufficient to fit iodine molecules within it

Figure 2 *Amylose – iodine staining reaction*

The cloudy colour is due to any lipid in the sample being finely dispersed in the water to form an emulsion. Light passing through this emulsion is refracted as it passes from oil droplets to water droplets, making it appear cloudy.

Test for proteins

The most reliable protein test is the **biuret test**, which detects peptide links.

- To a sample of the test solution, add an equal volume of prepared biuret reagent (potassium hydroxide and copper(II) sulfate solution) and mix gently.
- A change from a clear blue colour to a lilac or purple (or sometimes a pink) indicates the presence of peptide bonds and hence a protein. If no protein is present, the solution remains blue.
- A control should be carried out by performing the above stages, but with water replacing the sample under test.

Summary test 2.1b

The starch test uses **(1)** solution. A positive result is a change from an **(2)** to a **(3)** colour. If a solution contains **(4)**, it must first be heated with Benedict's solution to check for a negative result and then, using a fresh sample, heat with dilute **(5)**, neutralise and test again with Benedict's solution. This should give a coloured **(6)**. If colour standards are used when carrying out a reducing sugar test, then **(7)** results can be obtained: the exact concentration of the solution cannot be determined. The protein test uses **(8)** reagent. A positive result is a **(9)** colour. To test for lipids, the sample can be dissolved in **(10)** and mixed thoroughly. When water is added a milky **(11)** is formed if lipid is present.

Carbohydrates and lipids
a. Monosaccharides and disaccharides

Table 1 Types of monosaccharide

Formula	Name	Examples
$C_3H_6O_3$ (n = 3)	Triose	Glyceraldehyde
$C_5H_{10}O_5$ (n = 5)	Pentose	Ribose Deoxyribose
$C_6H_{12}O_6$ (n = 6)	Hexose	Glucose, Fructose, Galactose

Table 2 Types of disaccharide

glucose	+	glucose	=	maltose
glucose	+	fructose	=	sucrose
glucose	+	galactose	=	lactose

Introduction

As the word suggests, carbohydrates are carbon molecules (carbo) combined with water (hydrate); their general formula is $C_x(H_2O)_y$. The simple sugars, monosaccharides, are monomers of disaccharides and polysaccharides. The type of covalent bond that forms between the monosaccharide monomers is a glycosidic bond.

- Disaccharides are composed of two monosaccharides joined by a single glycosidic bond.
- Polysaccharides are composed of more than two monosaccharides, with glycosidic bonds connecting adjacent monosaccharides. Polysaccharides are macromolecules, with some composed of many thousands of monosaccharides.

Monosaccharides

Monosaccharides are sweet-tasting, soluble substances that have the general formula $(CH_2O)_n$. While 'n' can be any number from 3 to 7, the three most common groups of monosaccharides are trioses, pentoses and hexoses (tri-, pent- and hex- refer to the number of carbon atoms in the molecule), shown in Table 1.

Structure of monosaccharides

Perhaps the best-known monosaccharide is **glucose**. This molecule is a hexose (6-carbon) sugar and has the formula $C_6H_{12}O_6$. However, the atoms of carbon, hydrogen and oxygen can be arranged in many different ways. Although the molecular arrangement is often shown as a straight chain for convenience, the atoms actually form a ring which can take a number of forms, as shown in Figure 1. Different molecular structures are given different names, e.g. glucose, fructose and galactose, and further differences are shown by a letter before the name of the molecule, e.g. α-glucose, β-glucose. You will see from Figure 1 that the hydroxyl group —OH on carbon atom 1 is at the bottom of the ring in α-glucose and at the top of the ring in β-glucose. Although some of these differences are small, they often give the resulting molecules very different properties. All monosaccharides are reducing sugars.

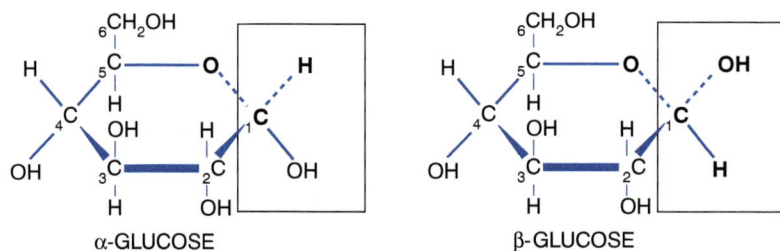

α-GLUCOSE   β-GLUCOSE

Figure 1 Molecular arrangement of α-glucose and β-glucose. In the straight chain form, carbon atoms forming the backbone are numbered 1 to 6. The same numbers are used in the ring forms.

Disaccharides

When two monosaccharides are joined by a glycosidic bond, a **disaccharide** is formed. As Table 2 shows, the two monosaccharides that combine can be the same or different. When they join, a molecule of water is removed and the reaction is therefore called a **condensation reaction**. The disaccharide maltose is produced in a condensation reaction between two α-glucose molecules. Maltose has reactive groups for the reduction reaction with

(a) Formation of glycosidic bond by removal of water (condensation reaction)

(b) Breaking of glycosidic bond by addition of water (hydrolysis reaction)

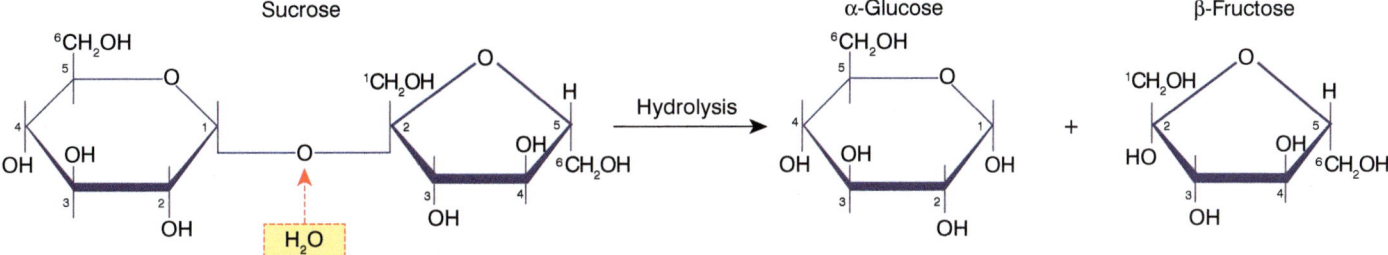

Figure 2 *Formation and breaking of glycosidic bond (some carbon and hydrogen atoms have been omitted for simplicity)*

Benedict's solution and so is a reducing sugar. In the formation of sucrose, the glycosidic bond is between carbon atom 1 of α-glucose and carbon atom 2 of β-fructose. It is known as a 1,2-glycosidic bond. Figure 2 illustrates the formation and breaking of a 1,2-glycosidic bond.

When water is added to a disaccharide under suitable conditions, it breaks the glycosidic bond into its constituent monosaccharides. This is called **hydrolysis** (breaking a bond using water). Sucrose cannot react with Benedict's so is a non-reducing sugar. During hydrolysis by boiling with acid, the glycosidic bond is broken to release fructose and glucose, which are both reducing sugars.

In a cell, the hydrolysis of sucrose occurs rapidly in the presence of the appropriate enzyme (sucrase). Without an enzyme, the breakdown would be very slow.

Roles of monosaccharides and disaccharides

Monosaccharides function as respiratory substrates that are broken down to produce **ATP**. They are particularly useful because they have a large number of C—H groups and these can be easily oxidised, yielding a lot of energy. Disaccharides are easily broken down to provide monosaccharides. Sucrose is the main sugar transported in plants as it is less reactive than glucose and is less likely to take part in reactions while it is transported.

> **Remember**
>
> Condensation is the **giving out** of water in reactions while hydrolysis is the **taking in** of water to break bonds and separate molecules in reactions.

Summary test 2.2a

Monosaccharides are the **(1)** of disaccharides and polysaccharides. Glucose is a 6C sugar so is a **(2)** sugar. When a **(3)** reaction occurs between glucose and **(4)**, the disaccharide sucrose is formed. Two α-glucose molecules form the disaccharide **(5)**, which, like all monosaccharides, is a **(6)** sugar. Sucrose is a **(7)** sugar. Breaking the **(8)** bond in sucrose using water is known as **(9)**.

These pages help you to:

- understand that polysaccharides are formed by condensation reactions and are broken down by hydrolysis reactions (2.2.5 and 2.2.6)
- understand that the polysaccharide starch is composed of two polymers, amylose and amylopectin (2.2.7)
- describe the molecular structure of amylose and amylopectin (2.2.7)
- describe the molecular structure of the polysaccharide glycogen (2.2.7)
- relate the structures of starch and glycogen to their functions in living organisms (2.2.7)

You will also:

- understand how starch from different sources can produce different results when the starch test is carried out

Starch and glycogen are examples of **polysaccharides**. Polysaccharides are polymers, formed from combining together many monosaccharide units. The monosaccharides are joined by glycosidic bonds that are formed by **condensation reactions**. The resulting chain may vary in length and be branched and folded in various ways. All these features affect the properties of the polysaccharide that is formed. As polysaccharides are very large molecules (**macromolecules**), they are insoluble – a feature which suits them for storage. When they are **hydrolysed**, polysaccharides break down into monosaccharides or disaccharides. Some polysaccharides, such as cellulose (2.2c), are not used for storage, but give structural support to plant cells.

Starch

Starch is a polysaccharide found in many parts of a plant in the form of small granules, or grains, e.g. starch grains in chloroplasts. Especially large amounts occur in seeds and storage organs such as potato tubers. It forms an important component of food and is the major energy source in most diets. Apart from the starch produced for eating, it is extracted from plants across the world for other purposes. These include wallpaper pastes, paper coatings, textiles, paints, cosmetics and medicines. Starch is a mixture of two polymers of α-glucose, amylose and amylopectin.

- **Amylose** is composed of between 200 and 5000 glucose units, which are joined in a straight chain by α-1,4-glycosidic bonds. This chain is then wound into a tight helix which makes the molecule more compact and therefore it can be stored more efficiently as it takes up less space.

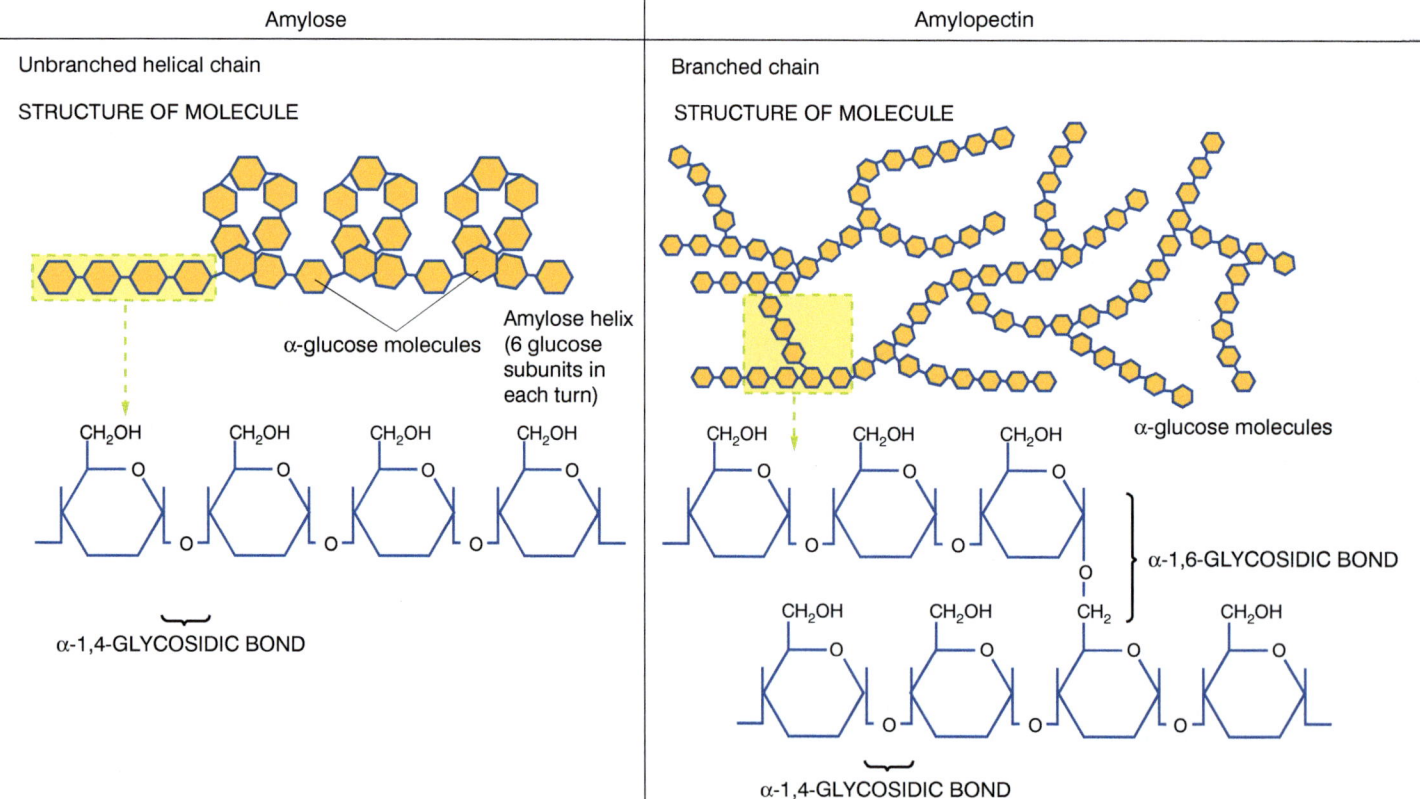

Figure 1 *Comparison of amylose and amylopectin*

- **Amylopectin** is made up of between 5000 and 100 000 α-glucose units joined to each other by α-1,4- and α-1,6-glycosidic bonds.

A comparison of amylose and amylopectin is given in Figure 1. About 80% of starch is amylopectin and the remaining 20% is amylose. These relative proportions can vary slightly depending on the source of the starch. The main role of starch is for energy storage, something it is especially suited for because:

- It is insoluble and therefore does not have any **osmotic** effects within cells, i.e. it does not affect the water potential of the cell.
- Being insoluble, it does not diffuse out of cells.
- Amylose is a helical molecule and is compact, so a lot of it can be stored in a small space.
- Amylopectin is branched and so has many free ends that amylase, the enzyme that catalyses the hydrolysis of starch, can work on simultaneously, meaning that glucose monomers are rapidly released.
- When hydrolysed it forms glucose, which is easily transported and readily used in respiration to provide ATP.

Starch is never found in animal cells. Instead a similar polysaccharide, called **glycogen**, serves the same role.

Glycogen

Glycogen is very similar in structure to amylopectin but has shorter chains and is more highly branched (see Figure 2). It is the major carbohydrate storage product of animals and it is stored as small granules, mainly in the muscles and the liver. Its structure suits it for storage for the same reasons as those given for starch, except that it is more highly branched than starch and so has more ends that can be simultaneously acted on by enzymes. It is therefore more rapidly broken down to release energy quickly when the animal needs it.

Extension

The proportions of amylopectin and amylose in starch

Different starches can produce different colours when tested with iodine in potassium iodide solution, varying from black to red/purple. This is because they have different proportions of amylose to amylopectin. Because iodine molecules become trapped inside the helix created by amylose, a starch with a high proportion of amylose will produce a more intense blue-black colour. Some cereals have very little amylose and give a weak positive result. Some genetically engineered barley starches may have 50–80% amylose and will give a very intense blue-black colour on testing.

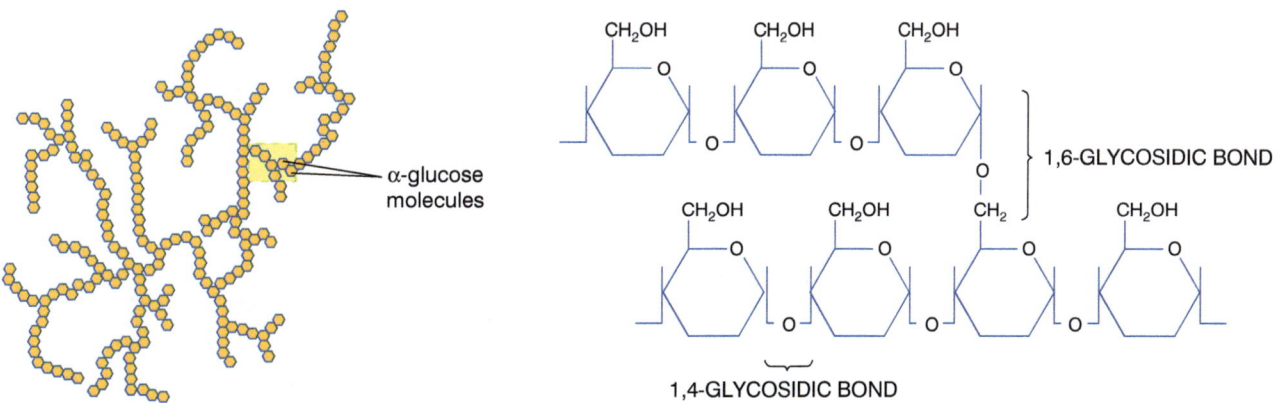

Figure 2 *Glycogen*

Summary test 2.2b

Starch and glycogen are polymers of **(1)** glucose joined by **(2)** bonds. Starch is composed of two polymers, **(3)**, which is a **(4)** shape, and amylopectin. Starch granules are not found in **(5)** cells. Starch functions as a store of **(6)** and does not affect the water potential of cells because it is **(7)**. Glycogen is more highly **(8)** than amylopectin but both have α-1,4- and **(9)** glycosidic bonds. Liver and **(10)** cells have large stores of glycogen. The structure of starch and glycogen is suited to their function as energy stores as the molecules do not take up much space and are very **(11)**.

2.2 c. The polysaccharide cellulose

These pages help you to:

- describe the molecular structure of the polysaccharide cellulose (2.2.8)
- understand how the arrangement of cellulose molecules contributes to the function of cell walls (2.2.8)

You will also:

- learn more about the structure of the cell wall

Cellulose is a polysaccharide that makes up around 50% of all organic carbon and is therefore the most abundant organic molecule on Earth.

Structure of cellulose

Cellulose differs from starch and glycogen in one major respect – it is made of monomers of β-glucose rather than α-glucose. This seemingly small variation produces fundamental differences in the structure and function of this polysaccharide. The main reason for this is that, in the β-glucose units, the positions of the —H group and the —OH group on carbon atom 1 are reversed (Figure 1). In β-glucose, the —OH group is above, rather than below, the ring. This means that, in order for β-1,4-glycosidic bonds to form, each β-glucose molecule must be rotated by 180° compared to its neighbour. The result is that carbon atom 6 (the one forming part of the —CH_2OH group) on each β-glucose molecule alternates between being above and below the chain (Figure 1). Rather than forming a coiled chain like starch, cellulose has straight, unbranched chains. These run parallel to one another, allowing hydrogen bonds (2.1a) to form cross-linkages between adjacent chains. While each individual hydrogen bond adds very little to the strength of the molecule, the sheer overall number of them makes a considerable contribution to strengthening cellulose and making it the valuable structural material it is. The arrangement of β-glucose chains in a cellulose molecule is shown in Figure 2.

Portion of cellulose molecule

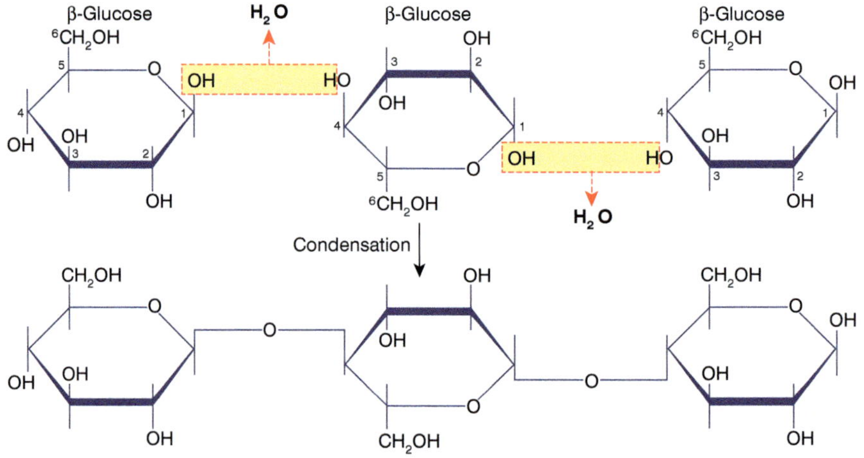

Figure 1 *Formation of β-1,4-glycosidic bonds between three β-glucose molecules (some carbon and hydrogen atoms have been omitted for simplicity)*

The cellulose chain has adjacent glucose molecules rotated by 180°. This allows hydrogen bonds to be formed between the hydroxyl (—OH) groups on adjacent parallel chains which help to give cellulose its structural stability.

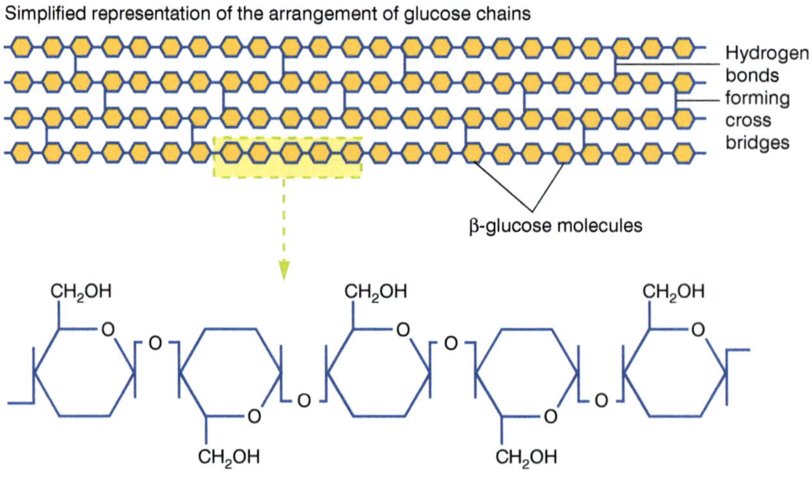

Figure 2 *Structure of the cellulose molecule*

The cellulose molecules are grouped together to form microfibrils which, in turn, are arranged in parallel groups called fibres. With many —OH groups, cellulose can form hydrogen bonds with water and so the molecule is hydrophilic ('water loving'). However, due to the large size of the molecules, cellulose is insoluble. Within a microfibril, the individual linear cellulose molecules start and end in different places so that they overlap. This contributes to the strength of the microfibril. The cellulose fibres are laid down at different angles, further increasing their overall strength.

Functions of cellulose

Cellulose frequently makes up between 20% and 50% of plant cell walls. It is, however, not part of the living cell but rather a non-living covering that encases the protoplast within. The cellulose cell wall is therefore freely permeable, allowing materials to access the cell surface membrane. It also allows the movement of water along the cell walls of adjacent cells (7.2a). Cellulose performs a mainly structural role by providing rigidity to the plant cell wall, which prevents the cell from bursting as water enters it by osmosis. The cellulose cell wall exerts an inward pressure that stops any further influx of water. As a result, living plant cells are turgid and push against one another, making herbaceous parts of the plant semi-rigid. This is especially important in maintaining stems and leaves in a turgid state so that they can provide the maximum surface area for photosynthesis.

Comparison of cellulose and other carbohydrates

Table 1 compares cellulose with the other polysaccharides, amylose, amylopectin and glycogen.

Table 1 Comparison of the polysaccharides amylose, amylopectin, glycogen and cellulose

Characteristic	Amylose	Amylopectin	Glycogen	Cellulose
Found in	Plants	Plants	Animals and fungi	Plants
Found as	Grains (in starch)	Grains (in starch)	Tiny granules	Fibres
Function	Energy store	Energy store	Energy store	Structural support
Basic monomer unit	α-glucose	α-glucose	α-glucose	β-glucose
Type of bond between monomer units	α-1,4-glycosidic	α-1,4 and α-1,6-glycosidic	α-1,4 and α-1,6-glycosidic	β-1,4-glycosidic
Type of chain	Unbranched and helical (coiled)	Branched, but less highly branched than glycogen	Short and highly branched	Long, unbranched straight chains with no coiling

Summary test 2.2c

Cellulose is made up of (1) monomers joined together by (2) links. It forms straight, unbranched chains that run parallel to each other and are cross-linked by (3). These cellulose molecules are then grouped together to form (4), which in turn are grouped into fibres. Cellulose performs a (5) function in plants by giving a plant cell rigidity. Cellulose is (6) as it can form hydrogen bonds with water. However it is (7) in water, which suits it for its structural role.

Extension

More about cellulose

Cellulose is difficult to digest. It is therefore not a useful food for animals, which rarely produce cellulose-digesting enzymes. Some animals get round this by forming mutualistic relationships with cellulose-digesting microorganisms in their intestines. The structural strength of cellulose has been made use of by humans. Cotton and rayon used in fabrics are largely cellulose. Cellophane used in packaging and celluloid used in photographic films are also derived from cellulose. Paper is perhaps the best-known cellulose product.

Extension

Other cell wall components

Cellulose is the main component of the cell wall, but the overall strength of the wall is due to the presence of other components such as hemicellulose and pectin. Together these form a strong, meshwork of fibres. The large spaces in the wall mean that water can flow quite freely and the wall is permeable to most substances.

Remember

Benedict's solution does not react with polysaccharides. A negative result will be obtained, that is, the colour remains clear blue after heating with the solution.

Cellulose does not react with iodine in potassium iodide solution, as it does not have a helical structure to complex with iodine. The highly compact and branched glycogen molecule forms a granule with an overall spherical shape and some iodine may get trapped but a blue-black colour is not obtained.

Lipids make up a varied and diverse group of substances that share the following characteristics:

- They contain carbon, hydrogen and oxygen.
- The proportion of oxygen to carbon and hydrogen is smaller than in carbohydrates.
- They are non-polar, hydrophobic molecules (2.1a) and so are insoluble in water.
- They are soluble in organic solvents such as alcohols.

The main groups of lipids are **triglycerides (fats and oils)** and **phospholipids**. Other forms include waxes, steroids and cholesterol.

Triglycerides (fats and oils)

There is no fundamental chemical difference between a fat and an oil. Fats are solid at room temperature (10–20 °C), whereas oils are liquid. Triglycerides are so called because they have three (tri) fatty acids combined with glycerol (glyceride). Each fatty acid forms an **ester bond** with glycerol in a **condensation reaction** (Figure 1). Hydrolysis of a triglyceride therefore produces glycerol and three fatty acids.

The structure of triglycerides related to their functions

- Triglycerides have a high ratio of energy-storing carbon–hydrogen bonds to carbon atoms and are therefore an excellent source of energy. They therefore supply many hydrogens for the reduction of NAD, a molecule involved in the production of ATP (12.2b and 12.2c).
- Triglycerides have low mass to volume ratio making them good storage molecules because much energy can be stored in a small volume. This is especially beneficial to animals, as it reduces the mass they have to carry as they move around.
- Being large, non-polar molecules, triglycerides are insoluble in water. As a result their storage does not affect the **water potential** of cells.
- As they have a high ratio of hydrogen to oxygen atoms, triglycerides release water when oxidised and therefore provide an important source of water, especially for organisms living in dry deserts.

The three fatty acids may all be the same, thereby forming a simple triglyceride, or they may be different, in which case a mixed triglyceride is produced. In either case each fatty acid is joined to the glycerol in a condensation reaction.

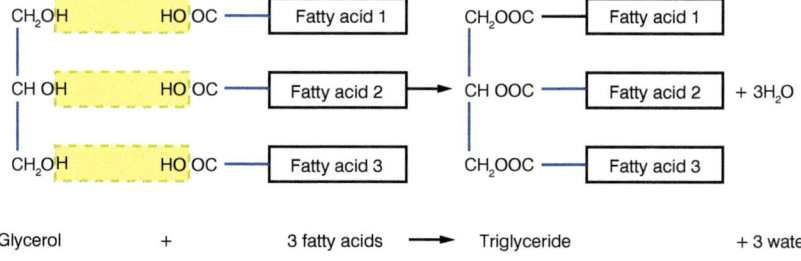

Figure 1 *Formation of a triglyceride*

Fatty acids

As the glycerol molecule in all triglycerides is the same, the differences in the properties of different fats and oils come from variations in the fatty acids. There are over 70 fatty acids and all have a carboxyl (—COOH) group with a hydrocarbon chain attached. This chain may have no double bonds and is then described as **saturated**, because all the carbon atoms are linked to the maximum possible number of hydrogen atoms, i.e. they are saturated with hydrogen atoms. If there is a single double bond, it is **mono-unsaturated**; if more than one double bond is present, it is **polyunsaturated** (Figure 2). The kinked shape of polyunsaturated fatty acids means that the molecules don't fit as closely together. The effect of this is that the intermolecular interactions are weaker and unsaturated fatty acids therefore have a lower melting point.

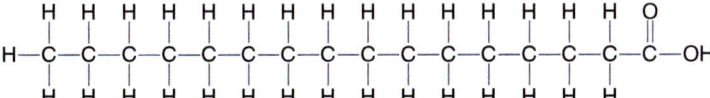

Palmitic acid: a saturated fatty acid. There are no double bonds in the hydrocarbon chain and this produces a linear chain

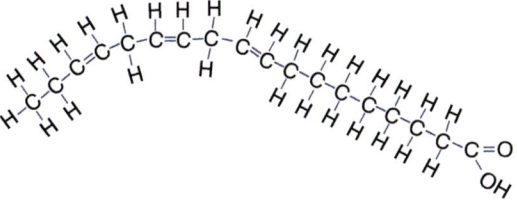

Linoleic acid: a polyunsaturated fatty acid, with two double bonds in the hydrocarbon chain. The double bonds produce a slight 'kink' in the fatty acid chain

Figure 2 Examples of a saturated and unsaturated fatty acid molecule

Phospholipids

Phospholipids are similar to lipids except that one of the fatty acid molecules is replaced by a phosphate molecule (Figure 3). Whereas fatty acid molecules repel water (are **hydrophobic**), phosphate molecules attract water (are **hydrophilic**).

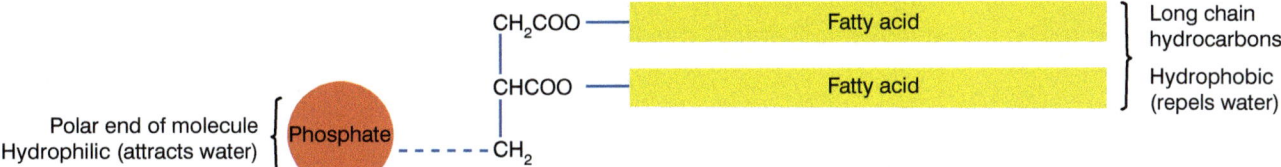

Figure 3 Structure of a phospholipid

Remember

Phospholipids are important components of cell surface membranes. Both the inside of a cell and the environment outside are watery, and the phospholipids in cell surface membranes form a double layer, with the hydrophilic heads of the molecules pointing into either the watery environment outside the membrane or the watery medium inside the cell. The hydrophobic tails point into the middle of the membrane to form a hydrophobic core (Figure 4). This **bilayer** arrangement makes cell surface membranes fluid and easily crossed by lipid-soluble substances. There is more detail about the role of phospholipids in cell surface membranes in 4.1a and 4.1b.

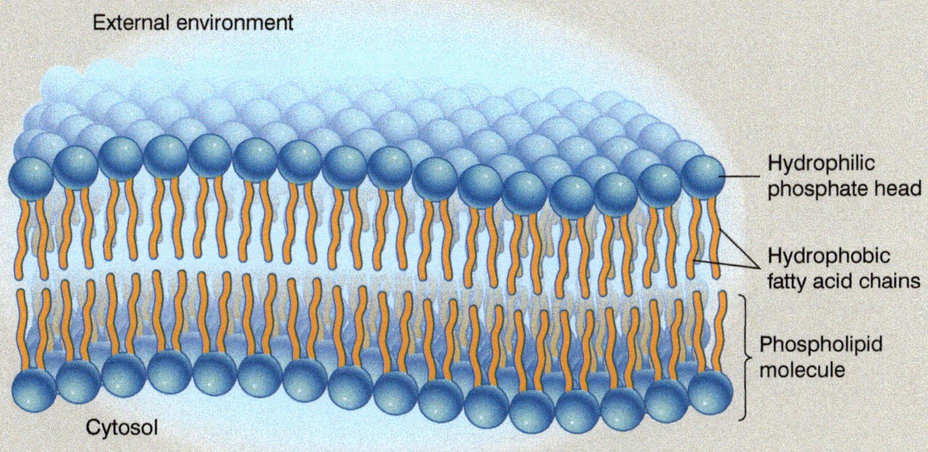

External environment

Hydrophilic phosphate head

Hydrophobic fatty acid chains

Phospholipid molecule

Cytosol

Figure 4 The bilayer arrangement of phospholipids in a cell membrane

Summary test 2.2d

Fats and oils make up a group of lipids called **(1)** which when hydrolysed form **(2)** and fatty acids. A fatty acid with more than one double bond is called **(3)**. In a phospholipid the number of fatty acids is **(4)**; these are called **(5)** because they repel water. Triglycerides have a high ratio of carbon to **(6)** atoms and so are an excellent source of **(7)**.

These pages help you to:

- describe and draw the general structure of an amino acid (2.3.1)
- describe and draw the formation and breakage of a peptide bond (2.3.1)
- understand what is meant by primary structure of proteins (2.3.2)

You will also:

- understand that the primary structure of proteins is determined by information stored in DNA

Amino acids are the monomers that combine to make up proteins. Around 100 amino acids have been identified, of which 20 occur naturally in proteins.

Structure of an amino acid

Every amino acid has a central carbon atom to which are attached four different chemical groups:

- **amino group** (—NH$_2$) – a basic group from which part of the name amino acid is derived
- **carboxyl group** (—COOH) – an acid group which gives the amino acid the rest of its name
- **hydrogen atom** (—H)
- **R-group** – a variety of different chemical groups ranging from a single hydrogen atom, as in glycine, to a double ring structure, as in tyrosine. Each amino acid has a different R-group, or side chain.

The general structure of an amino acid is shown in Figures 1 and 2.

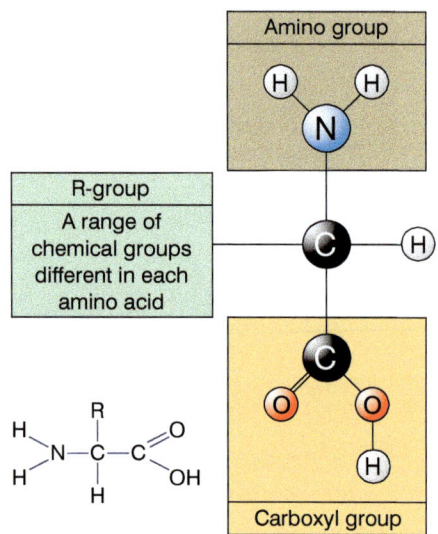

Figure 1 *General structure of an amino acid*

> ### Extension
>
> As the carboxyl group is acidic and the amino group is basic, an amino acid is both an acid and a base – it is said to be **amphoteric**. Amphoteric compounds act as **buffer** solutions in that they resist the tendency to alter their pH, despite the addition of acids or bases. This property is important in cells because it helps them maintain the stable pH that is necessary for the efficient functioning of enzymes.

Formation and breakage of a peptide bond

Figure 2 shows how amino acid monomers can combine to form a **dipeptide** by the removal of a water molecule in a condensation reaction (2.1a). The water is made by combining an —OH from the carboxyl group of one amino acid with an —H from the amino group of another amino acid. The two amino acids then become linked by a new **covalent bond** between the carbon atom of one amino acid and the nitrogen atom of the other. The peptide bond of a dipeptide can be broken by hydrolysis (the addition of water – see also 2.1a) to give its two constituent amino acids.

> ### Extension
>
> Plants can manufacture all the amino acids they need by combining nitrates, which they absorb from the soil, with various carbohydrates that they make during photosynthesis. Animals, however, need to obtain some amino acids from their food. These are called **essential amino acids**. The remaining amino acids, called non-essential amino acids, can be manufactured from the essential ones if they are not provided in adequate amounts in the diet. In humans, nine amino acids are considered essential.

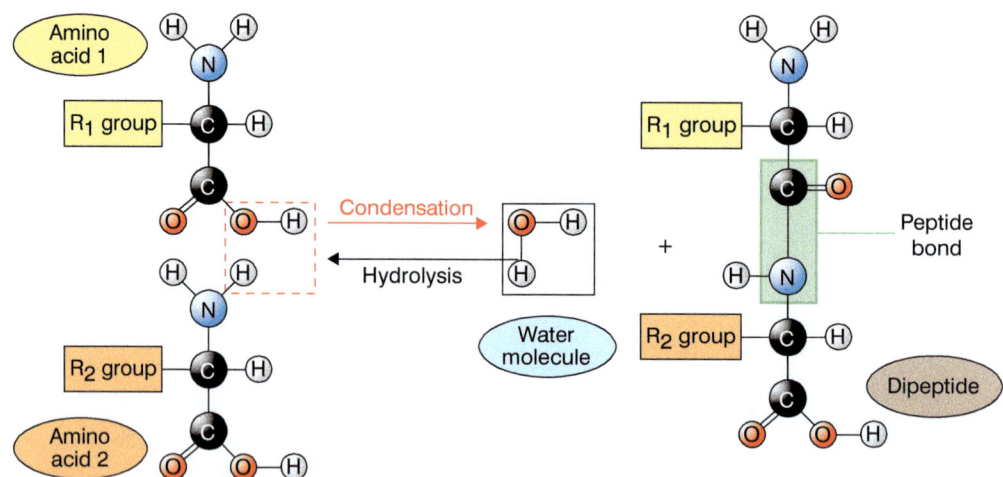

Figure 2 *Formation of a peptide bond*

The primary structure of proteins

Through a series of condensation reactions, many amino acid monomers can be joined together in a process called **polymerisation**. The resulting chain of many hundreds of amino acids is called a **polypeptide**. The sequence of amino acids in a polypeptide chain forms the **primary structure** of any protein. If the amino acid sequence is known, then the primary structure also includes the number of amino acids in the final polypeptide chain. The amino acid sequence is not random but is determined by the genetic information, a sequence of nucleotides, stored in DNA (see 6.2a and 6.2c).

The secondary structure of proteins

The linked amino acids that make up a polypeptide possess both —NH and —C=O groups on either side of every peptide bond. Both these groups are polar, i.e. their **electrons** are unevenly distributed. As a result, the hydrogen of the —NH group has an overall positive charge while the O of the —C=O group has an overall negative charge. These two groups therefore readily form hydrogen bonds. This causes sections of the polypeptide chain to form one of two regular three-dimensional shapes that have a repeating pattern:

- **α-helix** – the polypeptide chain is coiled into a spiral shape. The hydrogen bonding occurs in a regular pattern between every fourth amino acid.
- **β-pleated sheet** – regions of the polypeptide chain that lie side-by-side are linked by hydrogen bonds to give parallel sheets. The regions of chain can run in the same direction to give parallel β-pleated sheets or in opposite directions to give anti-parallel β-pleated sheets.

Figure 3 illustrates these two basic types of protein structure. Some areas of the protein do not have the regular arrangement shown by alpha helices and beta-pleated sheets and form what is termed a random coil. Different proteins have differences in the extent of the alpha helices and beta-pleated sheets formed.

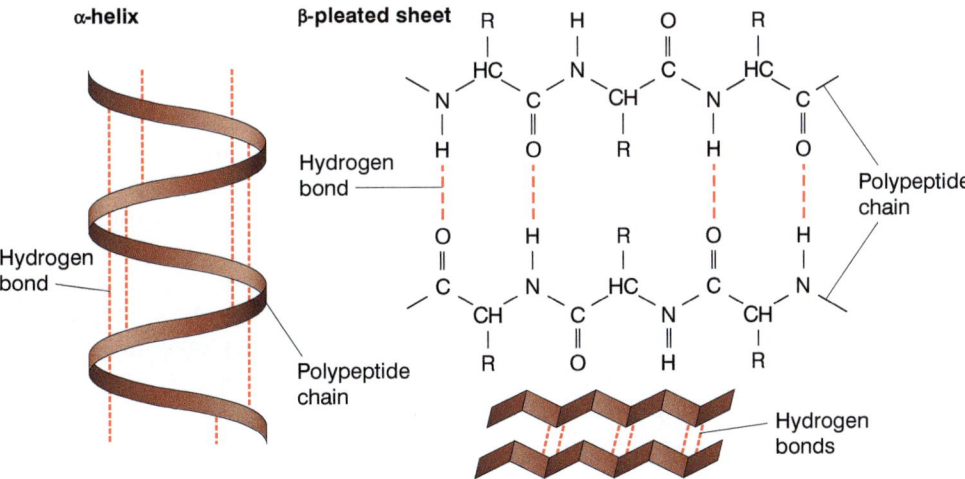

Figure 3 *Structure of the α-helix and the β-pleated sheet – note that R-groups are not involved in protein secondary structure*

Summary test 2.3a

Amino acids always contain an acid carboxyl group, which has the chemical formula **(1)**, as well as a basic group called an **(2)** group. Amino acids therefore have both acidic and basic properties and are said to be **(3)**. Any two amino acids can combine in a **(4)** reaction to form a **(5)** bond between them. Many amino acids can combine to form a polypeptide chain and the sequence of amino acids is known as the **(6)** structure. Secondary structure is a result of **(7)** bonding between amino acids. The two main shapes of secondary structure are the **(8)**, which is spiral-shaped, and the **(9)**.

b. Protein structure

- understand what is meant by the tertiary and quaternary structure of proteins (2.3.2)
- describe the types of interaction (hydrogen, ionic, disulfide bonds and hydrophobic interactions) that hold these molecules in shape (2.3.3)

You will also:

- understand how a protein can be denatured

Proteins are macromolecules. While the types of carbohydrates and lipids of all organisms are relatively few and very similar, their proteins are numerous (estimated to be up to two million types in humans) and differ from species to species. Proteins can consist of fewer than a hundred amino acids to more than 34 000 amino acids. The shape of any one type of protein molecule differs from that of other proteins. As the amino acids of which they are made differ only in their R-groups, it is these that determine the shape, and therefore the functions, of a protein. We have already seen in 2.3a how the primary and secondary structures of a protein are determined. We shall now see how these structures are moulded into the tertiary and quaternary structures that make up a protein's final shape, or **conformation**.

Tertiary structure of proteins

The polypeptide chain, which may already have sections of secondary structure (alpha helixes and beta-pleated sheets), undergoes further folding and coiling to give the complex, and often unique, three-dimensional structure of each protein (Figure 2). This is known as the tertiary structure and is the result of four possible types of bonds that can arise between the R-groups (side chains) of each amino acid. The interactions between R-groups, in order of relative strength, are:

- **Disulfide bridges** – found between sulfur atoms in the molecules of the amino acid cysteine. They are **covalent bonds** and, as such, form very strong links which make the tertiary protein structure very stable.
- **Ionic bonds** – occur between any carboxyl and amino groups that have not been involved in forming peptide bonds. These groups ionise to give —NH$_3$+ and —COO$^-$ groups, which then form electrostatic bonds due to their mutual attraction. These bonds are weaker than disulfide bridges and can be broken by changes in pH.
- **Hydrogen bonds** – result from the attraction between the electronegative oxygen atoms on the —CO groups and the electropositive H atoms on either the —OH or —NH groups. Although they are individually weaker than ionic bonds, their large number makes them an important factor in maintaining the tertiary structure of a protein. Note that they are not the same hydrogen bonds as with secondary structure.
- **Hydrophobic interactions** – formed between amino acids that contain non-polar R-groups which repel water. As a result they may fold or twist the polypeptide chain as they take up a position towards the centre of the protein, further away from the watery medium outside.

Figure 1 illustrates how each of these bonds is formed.

Quaternary structure of proteins

A protein with quaternary structure is composed of more than one polypeptide chain. There may also be non-protein (prosthetic) groups associated with the molecules (Figure 2). An example of quaternary structure is illustrated by the proteins haemoglobin and collagen (2.3c).

(a) **Disulfide bridges** – *covalent bond between R-groups of cysteine amino acids*

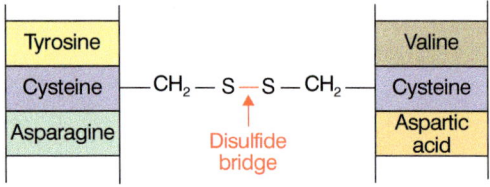

(b) **Ionic bonds** – *between NH$_3$+ and COO$^-$ ions on basic amino acids such as asparagine and acid ones such as aspartic acid*

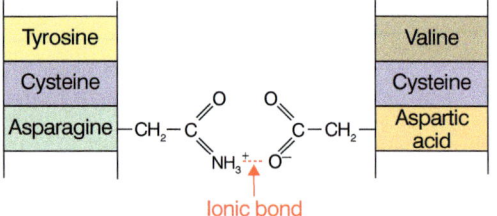

(c) **Hydrophobic interactions** – *between non-polar R-groups such as those on the amino acids tyrosine and valine*

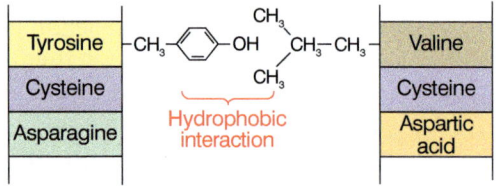

(d) **Hydrogen bonds** – *between electronegative oxygen atoms on CO groups and electropositive H atoms on NH groups*

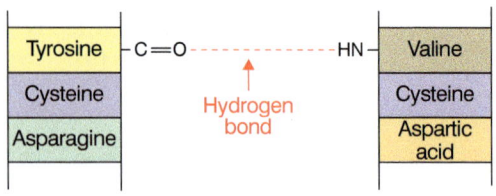

Figure 1 *Types of bond that determine the shape of a protein*

(a) *The primary structure of a protein is the sequence of amino acids found in its polypeptide chains. This sequence determines its properties and shape. Following the discovery of the amino acid sequence of the hormone insulin by Frederick Sanger in 1954, the primary structure of many other proteins is now known.*

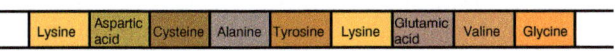

(b) *The secondary structure is the shape which the polypeptide chain forms as a result of bonding between the hydrogens of the amino group and the oxygens of the carboxyl group. This may be an alpha-helix or a beta-pleated sheet.*

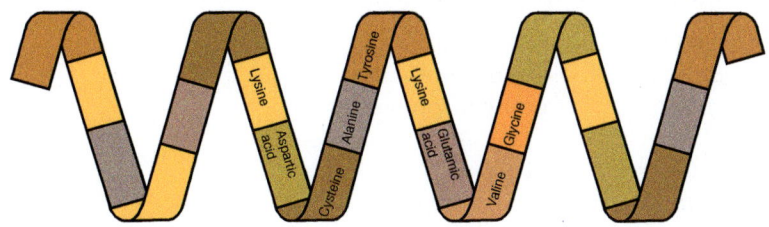

(c) *The tertiary structure is due to the coiling and folding of the polypeptide chain into a specific three-dimensional structure. All four types of interaction between R-groups contribute to the maintenance of the tertiary structure.*

The tertiary structure is held in shape by all four types of interaction

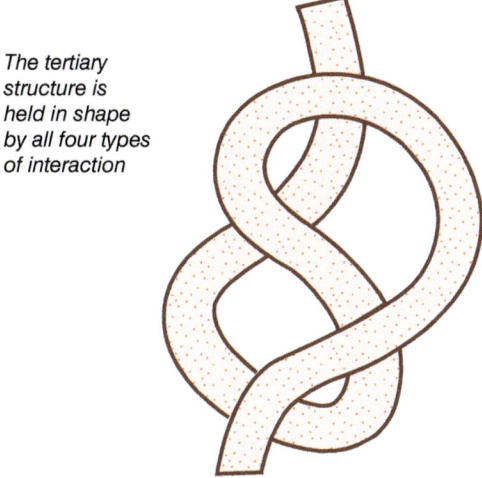

(d) *The quaternary structure arises from the combination of a number of different polypeptide chains and associated non-protein (prosthetic) groups into a large, complex protein molecule.*

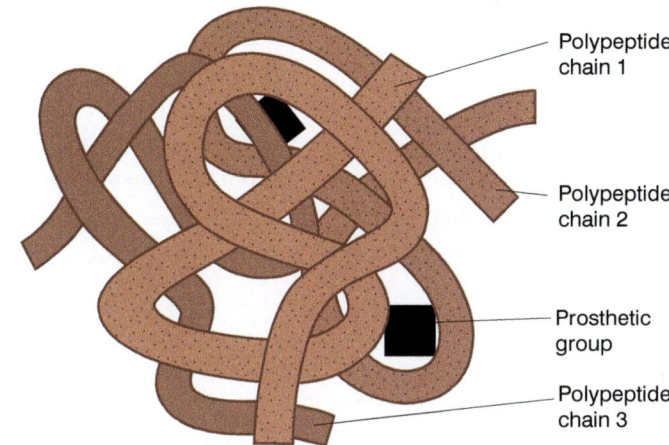

Polypeptide chain 1

Polypeptide chain 2

Prosthetic group

Polypeptide chain 3

Figure 2 *Structure of proteins*

Summary test 2.3b

The primary structure of proteins is determined by the sequence of **(1)** which make up the **(2)** chain. The secondary structure results from coiling or folding of the chain due to **(3)** formed between the —NH of one amino acid and the **(4)** group of another **(5)**. Four types of bond between R-groups cause further twisting and folding of the chain. The first of these bonds arises between **(6)** atoms in cysteine molecules and is called **(7)**. The second type is called **(8)** and results from electrostatic forces between carboxyl and amino groups on the R-groups of amino acids. Thirdly there are forces due to amino acid R-groups which repel water and these are called **(9)**. The fourth type of bond is the hydrogen bond. The quaternary structure of proteins results from a number of chains combining, sometimes also incorporating non-protein groups known as **(10)** groups.

These pages help you to:

- learn that globular proteins are generally soluble and fibrous proteins are generally insoluble (2.3.4)
- describe the structure of haemoglobin as an example of a globular protein (2.3.5)
- relate the structure of haemoglobin to its function (2.3.6)
- describe the structure of a molecule of collagen as an example of a fibrous protein (2.3.7)
- understand how collagen molecules are arranged to form a collagen fibre (2.3.7)
- relate the structure of collagen molecules and fibres to their function (2.3.8)

You will also:

- learn the main differences between a globular and a fibrous protein
- learn that most types of collagen have collagen molecules grouped to form collagen fibrils, that are arranged to form collagen fibres

Proteins perform many different roles in living organisms. In one form or another they are essential for the efficient functioning of every characteristic of life. A protein's conformation (shape) is dependent on the spatial arrangement of the bonds and atoms within the molecule (the molecular configuration). The role of a protein is determined by this 3-dimensional arrangment. There are of two basic types.

- **Fibrous proteins**, such as collagen and keratin, generally have structural functions.
- **Globular proteins**, such as enzymes, haemoglobin, antibodies and insulin, generally carry out physiological roles (metabolic functions).

Table 1 lists the differences between fibrous and globular proteins.

Table 1 *Comparison of fibrous and globular proteins*

Fibrous proteins	Globular proteins
Repetitive regular sequences of amino acids	Irregular amino acid sequences
Actual sequences may vary slightly between two examples of the same protein	Sequence highly specific and never varies between two examples of the same protein
Polypeptide chains form long parallel strands	Polypeptide chains folded into a spherical shape
Length of chain may vary in two examples of the same protein	Length always identical in two examples of the same protein
Stable structure	Relatively unstable structure
Insoluble	Generally water soluble – forms **colloidal** suspensions
Support and structural functions	Metabolic functions
Examples include keratin (found in skin, nails and hair) and collagen	Examples include all enzymes, some hormones (e.g. insulin), antibodies and haemoglobin

The globular protein haemoglobin

The sequence of amino acids in globular proteins is more varied than in fibrous proteins. They form a compact spherical structure. One example of a globular protein is haemoglobin (Figure 1). This is an oxygen-carrying respiratory pigment found in most animal groups. Its ability to transport oxygen is related to its structural features, which in adult humans include the following:

- It has a quaternary structure of four polypeptide chains, two identical α-globin polypeptides of 141 amino acids each, and two identical β-globin polypeptides of 146 amino acids each.
- Each polypeptide chain is folded into a compact shape and all four are linked together to form an almost spherical haemoglobin molecule.
- Hydrophobic interactions (2.3b) between amino acids with non-polar (hydrophobic) R-groups within the haemoglobin molecule help to maintain its precise shape – an important factor in its ability to carry oxygen.
- Amino acids with hydrophilic R-groups in the molecule tend to orient themselves to point outwards. This enables haemoglobin to be soluble and mix more readily with a watery medium (the cytoplasm of the red blood cell).
- Associated with each polypeptide is a haem group – which contains a ferrous (Fe^{2+}) ion. Non-protein groups such as this are called **prosthetic groups** and they form an important and integral part of the protein molecule.
- Each Fe^{2+} ion can combine with a single oxygen molecule (O_2), making a total of four O_2 molecules that can be carried by a single haemoglobin molecule in humans.

Four polypeptide chains make up the haemoglobin molecule. Each molecule contains 574 amino acids

Each chain is attached to a haem group that can combine with oxygen

Figure 1 *Quaternary structure of a haemoglobin molecule*

When haemoglobin combines with oxygen it forms a molecule called **oxyhaemoglobin** and changes colour from purple to bright red.

Globular proteins such as haemoglobin and enzymes have a very specific shape. Even slight changes to their structure can make such molecules far less efficient at carrying out their functions. In the case of haemoglobin a slight alteration in shape as a result of a mutation in one of the genes coding for the globin chains (see sickle cell anaemia in 16.2i), makes it far less able to transport oxygen.

The fibrous protein collagen

Fibrous proteins tend to form long chains which run parallel to one another. These chains are linked by cross-bridges and so form very stable molecules. One example is **collagen**, a protein found in tissues requiring physical strength, e.g. **tendons**, walls of blood vessels, bone and the fibres that hold teeth in place. There are a number of different types of collagen. Collagen is extremely strong and stable. It has a very high tensile strength and so is able to withstand immense pulling forces without stretching. At the same time it is flexible, so that, while the collagen in a tendon transmits the pull of a muscle to the bone without stretching, it can still bend around a joint as it flexes during movement. The ability of collagen to do this is the result of the following features of its structure.

- Its primary structure is largely a repeat of the amino acid sequence glycine–proline–alanine, which forms an unbranched polypeptide chain.
- The collagen molecule is made up of three such polypeptide chains wound in a triple helix that is held together by hydrogen bonds between the peptide bond NH of a glycine and a peptide C=O (carbonyl) group of amino acids in the adjacent polypeptide.
- As every third amino acid is the relatively small and compact glycine molecule, the triple helix produced is very tightly wound. Larger amino acids would produce a more loosely wound, and therefore less strong, triple helix.
- The triple-stranded molecules run parallel to others, and in most types of collagen these form even stronger units called fibrils, with fibrils forming collagen fibres.
- The collagen molecules in the collagen fibrils or fibres are held together by cross-linkages formed by covalent bonds between lysine amino acids of adjacent molecules. This adds greater strength and stability to the structure.
- The points where one collagen molecule ends and the next begins are spread throughout the structure. If they were all joined together in the same region this would be a weak point and therefore prone to breaking under tension.

The structure of collagen is illustrated in Figure 2.

Summary test 2.3c

Proteins are of two basic types: fibrous proteins such as collagen and **(1)** proteins such as the respiratory pigment haemoglobin. Proteins like actin found in muscle have a structural function and are therefore examples of a **(2)** protein. Collagen is a fibrous protein with a commonly repeating amino acid sequence of **(3)**. It is found in structures such as **(4),** which attach muscle to bone, where its properties of **(5)**, and **(6)** suit it to its role. A single haemoglobin molecule is made up of polypeptides, which total **(7)** in number. Each polypeptide contains a **(8)** group that contains a single **(9)** ion, to which can be attached a single oxygen molecule.

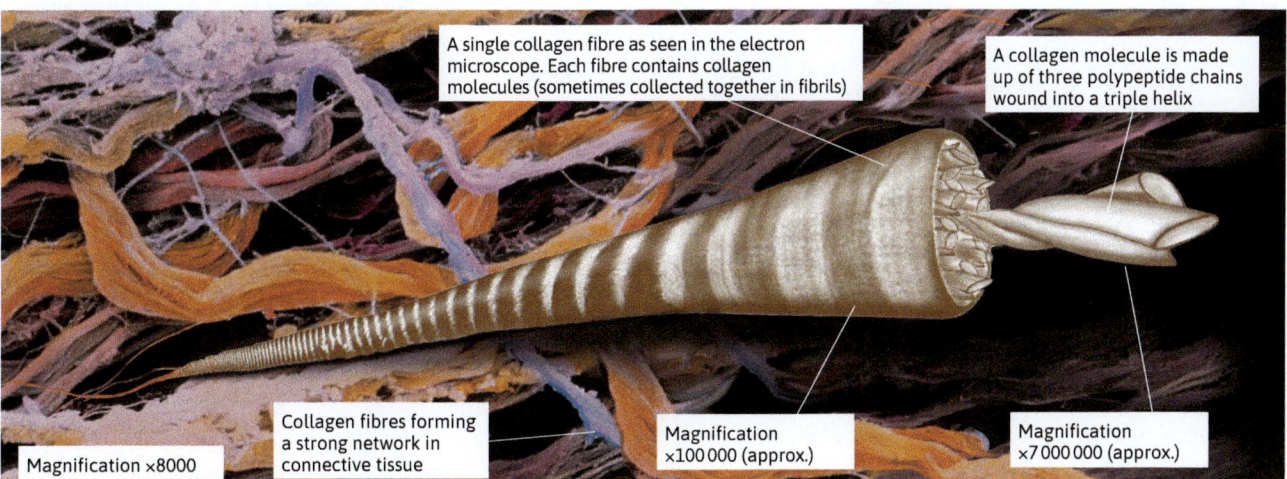

A single collagen fibre as seen in the electron microscope. Each fibre contains collagen molecules (sometimes collected together in fibrils)

A collagen molecule is made up of three polypeptide chains wound into a triple helix

Collagen fibres forming a strong network in connective tissue

Magnification ×8000

Magnification ×100 000 (approx.)

Magnification ×7 000 000 (approx.)

Figure 2 *Fine structure of the fibrous protein collagen*

Properties of water
a. The role of water in living organisms

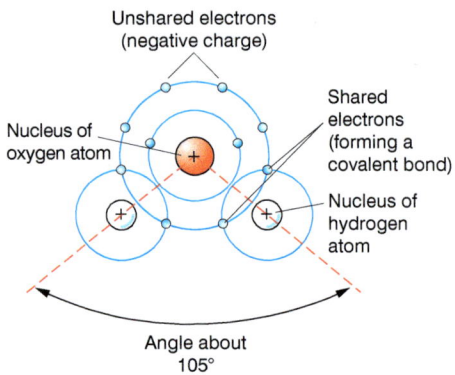

Figure 1 *A water molecule*

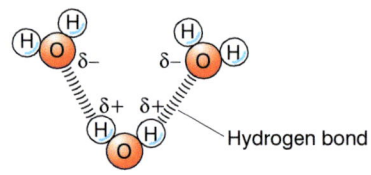

Figure 2 *Water molecules showing hydrogen bonding*

Although water is the most abundant liquid on Earth, it is certainly no ordinary molecule. Its unusual properties are due to its dipolar nature and the subsequent hydrogen bonding that this allows.

The dipolar water molecule

A water molecule is made up of two atoms of hydrogen and one of oxygen as shown in Figure 1. The atoms form a triangular shape. Although the molecule has no overall charge, the distribution of negatively charged electrons is uneven because the oxygen atom pulls them away from the hydrogen atoms. The oxygen atom therefore has a slight negative charge (δ^-), while the hydrogen atoms have a slight positive one (δ^+). In other words, the water molecule has both positive and negative poles and is therefore described as **dipolar**.

Water and hydrogen bonding

Different poles attract, and therefore the positive pole of one water molecule is attracted to the negative pole of another water molecule. The attractive force between these opposite charges is called a **hydrogen bond** (Figure 2). Although each bond is fairly weak (about one-tenth as strong as a **covalent bond**), together they form important forces that cause the water molecules to stick together (**cohesion**), giving water its unusual properties.

Specific heat capacity

As water molecules are cohesive (sticky) it takes more energy (heat) to separate them than would be needed if they did not bond to one another. For this reason the boiling point of water is higher than expected. Without its hydrogen bonding, water would be a gas (water vapour) at the temperatures commonly found on Earth and life as we know it would not exist. For the same reason, it takes more energy to heat a given mass of water, i.e. water has a high **specific heat capacity**. The high specific heat capacity is an important property for organisms that live in water, buffering against sudden temperature variations, helping to regulate temperature and avoid extremes. It is also very important for the internal cellular environment in helping to maintain a constant internal environment.

Extension

Cohesion and surface tension in water

Water molecules at the surface of a body of water tend to be pulled back into the body of water rather than escaping from it. This force is called **surface tension** and means that the water surface acts like a skin and is strong enough to support small organisms such as pond skaters (Figure 3).

The density of water

Most substances are at their least dense when a gas and at their most dense when a solid, with the liquid phase having an intermediate density. Water is different. Water is actually less dense in the form of ice than when it is a liquid. This property is crucial to the survival of aquatic organisms as it means that ponds, lakes, etc. freeze from the top down rather than from the bottom up. The ice formed at the top then acts as an insulating layer that delays the freezing of the water beneath it. Large bodies of water almost never freeze completely, allowing their inhabitants to survive.

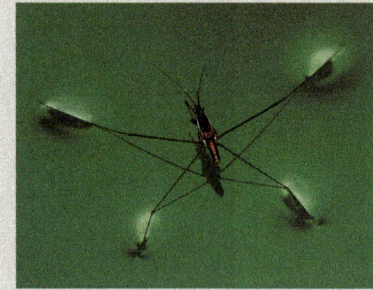

Figure 3 *Due to surface tension, pond skaters walk on water*

Latent heat of vaporisation

Hydrogen bonding between water molecules means that it requires a lot of energy to evaporate one gram of water. The energy is called the **latent heat of vaporisation** so water is described as having a high latent heat of vaporisation. Evaporation of water such as sweat in mammals is therefore a very effective means of cooling because body heat is used to evaporate the water. Similarly, the evaporation of water from the surfaces of mesophyll cells within the leaves of a plant cools the plant, when the external temperature is high.

Solvent action

The dipolar nature of the water molecule means that other polar molecules and ions readily dissolve in water. As a result, water is a very good solvent and a wide range of substances dissolve in it. This property means that water is used for:

* transport, e.g. sugars in blood and phloem
* removal of wastes, e.g. ammonia, urea
* secretions, e.g. digestive juices, tears
* the environment in which enzyme reactions take place.

Figure 4 *Evaporation of water during sweating helps to maintain body temperature*

Extension

The importance of water to living organisms

Water is the main constituent of all organisms – up to 98% of a jellyfish is water and mammals are typically 65% water. Water is also where life on Earth began and it is the environment in which many species still live. It is important for other reasons too. In this book you will meet examples of the importance of water to living organisms. These include the following.

Water in metabolism
* Water is used to break down many complex molecules by **hydrolysis**, e.g. proteins to amino acids.
* Chemical reactions take place in an aqueous medium, for example, the cytosol of cells, the matrix of mitochondria and the stroma of chloroplasts.
* Water is a major raw material in photosynthesis.

Water as a solvent
The importance of water as a solvent was discussed above.

Water giving support
Water is not easily compressed and therefore is used in:

* the hydrostatic skeleton of animals such as earthworms
* the amniotic fluid to support the fetus
* creating the turgor pressure of leaf cells that contribute to the support of leaves.

Other important features of water
* Its evaporation cools organisms and allows them to control their temperature.
* In plants, it is involved in cell elongation and expansion.

Water as an environment for living organisms
* Water acts as a buffer against sudden temperature variations, making the aquatic environment a temperature-stable one.
* Large bodies of water almost never freeze completely, allowing living organisms to survive.
* Water is transparent and therefore aquatic plants can photosynthesise.
* Water is a dense medium and so provides support for organisms which therefore require less supporting tissue than on land.

Summary test 2.4a

A water molecule is said to be **(1)** because it has a positive and a negative pole as a result of the uneven distribution of **(2)** within it. This creates attractive forces called **(3)** between water molecules, causing them to stick together. This stickiness of water means that it takes more energy to heat a given mass of water. Water therefore has a high **(4)**. Hydrogen bonding between water molecules means that it requires a lot of energy to evaporate one gram of water. This energy is called the **(5)**.

(🗐   **Launch additional digital resources for the chapter**)

2 Exam-style questions

1 In some foods, saturated fats have been removed and replaced with unsaturated fats.

State which property of the fats will have changed.

A Their molecules will fit together less closely.

B Their solubility in water will decrease.

C They will have fewer double bonds in their molecules.

D They will remain solid at room temperature.

(1 mark)

2 Starch is a polysaccharide made of two components, amylose and amylopectin.

a i Describe how the structure of amylose differs from the structure of amylopectin.   *(2 marks)*

  ii Explain why it is better to store carbohydrates in the form of starch rather than glucose.   *(3 marks)*

b Glucose can be added to starch to make the molecule larger.

Figure 1 shows part of a starch molecule in detail.

Figure 1

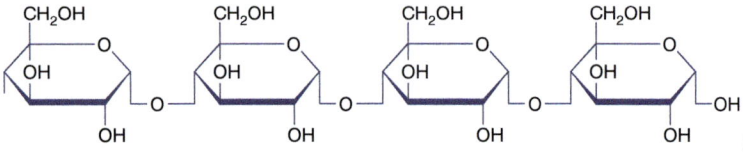

Sketch an annotated diagram to explain how a glucose molecule can be added to the free end of the starch molecule shown in Figure 1.   *(3 marks)*

(Total 8 marks)

3 a Lactose is a sugar found in milk. Figure 2 shows the breakdown of a molecule of lactose.

  i Identify the bond indicated by W.   *(1 mark)*

  ii This reaction involves the addition of water. Identify this type of reaction.   *(1 mark)*

  iii Give three ways in which water is used within an animal other than taking part in breakdown reactions.   *(3 marks)*

Figure 2

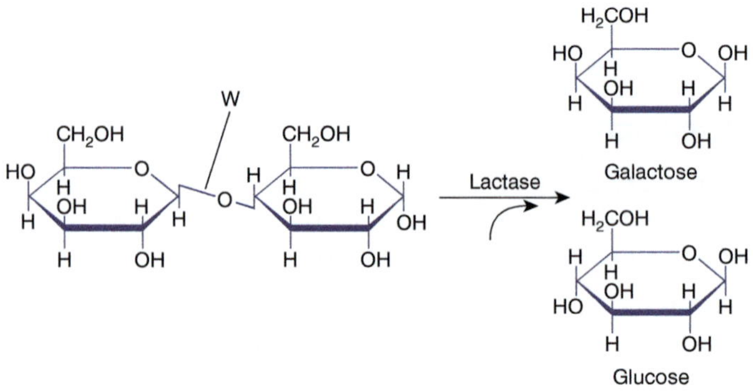

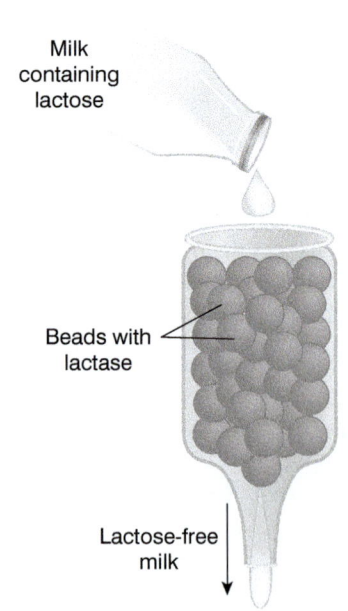

b The reaction shown in Figure 2 is catalysed by the enzyme lactase.

Enzymes are globular proteins which all have a primary, secondary and tertiary structure. State what is meant by:

  i a primary structure   *(1 mark)*

  ii a tertiary structure   *(2 marks)*

c Lactose is a non-reducing sugar. Some people are lactose intolerant, which means that they are unable to digest lactose. This causes abdominal pain and other side effects.
Lactase can be immobilised on sodium alginate beads. When milk is poured over the beads, the lactase breaks the lactose down. The milk that is produced is lactose free. Figure 3 outlines this process.

Figure 3

Explain how you could determine whether any lactose has been broken down in the lactose-free milk.

(3 marks)

(Total 11 marks)

2 Practice questions

4 The figure below represents a phospholipid molecule.

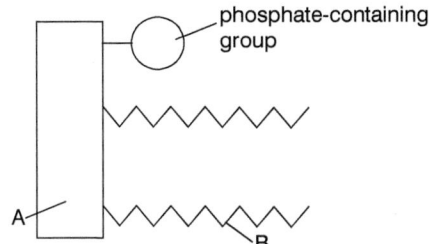

a Give the names of the structures labelled **A** and **B**.

b State how the structures **A** and **B** differ in the way they react to water.

c Which chemical elements are found in fats?

d What is meant by a 'saturated' fatty acid?

e A 200 g portion of chips (French fries) from a restaurant was found to contain 19.2 g of fat. The same mass of chips from a frozen oven-ready portion was found to contain 11.6 g of fat. When broken down, fat releases $38 \, kJ \, g^{-1}$. How much more energy is released from a portion of chips from a restaurant compared to an oven-ready portion? Show your working.

5 The figure below represents a polypeptide made up of seven amino acids, **A–G**.

a What is the chemical formula of the group represented by the box?

b Name the type of bond that links one amino acid to another.

c What is the type of reaction that links amino acids together called?

d Name the test that is used to test for proteins.

e Protein molecules are held together by a combination of the following: peptide bonds, hydrogen bonds, ionic bonds, disulfide bonds, hydrophobic interactions. Which one or more of these bonds:
  i maintain the primary structure of a protein
  ii maintain the secondary structure of a protein
  iii maintain the tertiary structure of a protein
  iv are individually the two strongest?

6 The figure below shows eight biological molecules **A–H**.

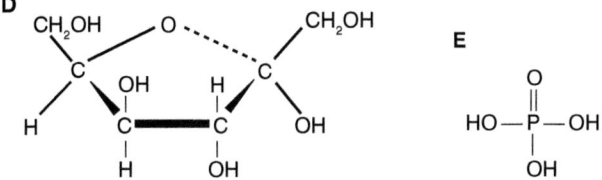

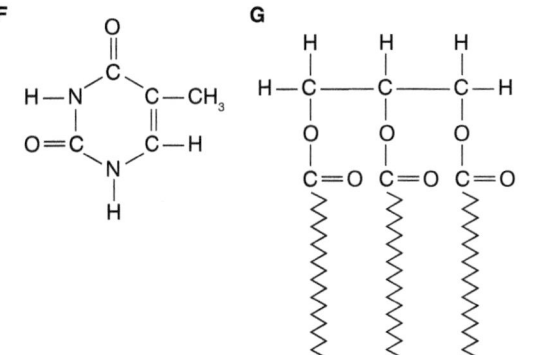

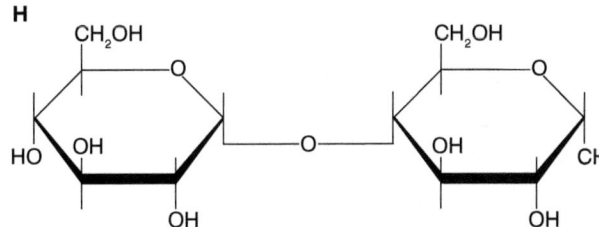

For each of the following give the letter(s) of one or more molecules that fits the description in each case.

a A triglyceride

b A disaccharide

c Can be polymerised to make a protein

d An inorganic molecule

e Has hydrophilic and hydrophobic portions

f An amino acid that can form disulfide bonds

g Is insoluble in water and stores energy in organisms

h A reducing sugar

3.1 Mode of action of enzymes

a. Enzyme structure and mechanism of action

Enzymes are globular proteins that catalyse metabolic reactions. A catalyst alters the rate of a chemical reaction, but at the end of the reaction is unchanged and can be used again. This means that enzymes are effective in tiny quantities. Enzymes do not make a reaction happen; they simply speed up ones that already occur, sometimes by a factor of many millions. All enzymes are synthesised within the cell. Intracellular enzymes remain within the cell to catalyse metabolic reactions. Extracellular enzymes are secreted from, and act outside, the cell.

Enzyme structure

As globular proteins, enzymes have an overall spherical shape (Figure 1), determined by their sequence of amino acids (2.3c). Despite their large size, enzyme molecules only have a small region that is functional. This is known as the **active site**. Only a few amino acids make up this active site. The active site forms a hollow depression within the much larger enzyme molecule. The substrate molecule is held within the active site by bonds, such as hydrogen bonds, that temporarily form between the R-groups of the amino acids of the active site and groups on the substrate molecule. This structure is known as the **enzyme–substrate complex**. Figure 2 shows part of an enzyme molecule during enzyme–substrate complex formation (the substrate can be described as being in a transition state):

- Amino acids 20 and 21 form temporary hydrogen bonds with the substrate molecule at the binding site of the active site.
- The area of the active site that is directly involved in the reaction is composed of amino acids 7, 8, 36 and 37 (the catalytic site).
- Amino acids 2 and 42 are not part of the active site but play an essential role in helping to maintain the shape of the active site. There are R-group interactions between these and amino acids 6 and 38.

These pages help you to:

- describe enzymes as globular proteins (3.1.1)
- understand that enzymes catalyse reactions (3.1.1)
- explain the difference between intracellular and extracellular enzymes (3.1.1)
- understand the mode of action of enzymes by considering the role of the active site, enzyme–substrate complex and lowering activation energy (3.1.2)
- understand the difference between the lock and key hypothesis of enzyme action and the induced-fit hypothesis (3.1.2)

You will also:

- begin to appreciate the importance of enzymes for living organisms
- be able to explain terms associated with enzyme structure and mechanism of action

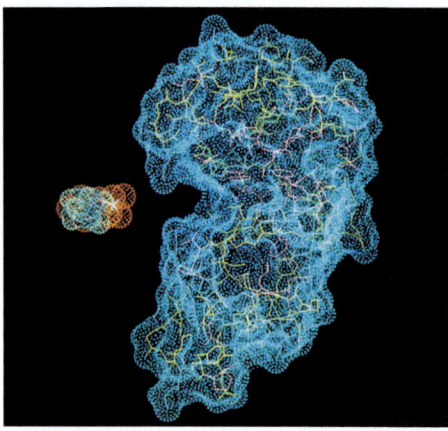

Figure 1 *The ribonuclease A enzyme and its substrate close to the enzyme's active site*

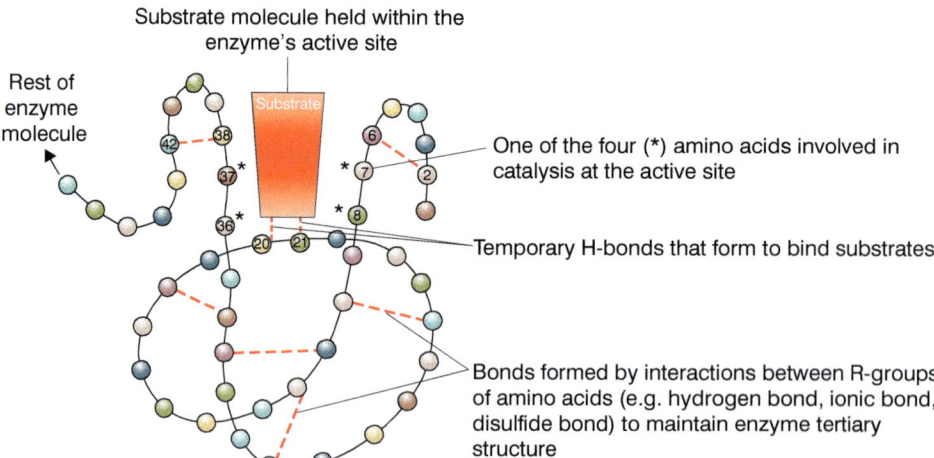

Substrate molecule held within the enzyme's active site

Rest of enzyme molecule

One of the four (*) amino acids involved in catalysis at the active site

Temporary H-bonds that form to bind substrates

Bonds formed by interactions between R-groups of amino acids (e.g. hydrogen bond, ionic bond, disulfide bond) to maintain enzyme tertiary structure

Figure 2 *Section of an enzyme molecule during the formation of an enzyme–substrate complex*

Changes to amino acids in the active site or in amino acids maintaining the shape of the active site can lead to loss of the specific three-dimensional shape of the active site and reduce or prevent catalysis.

How enzymes work

(a) The lock and key hypothesis

In one sense, enzymes work in the same way as a key operates a lock: each key has a very specific shape which, on the whole, fits and operates only one lock. In the same way, a substrate only fits into the active site of one particular enzyme. Enzymes are therefore **specific** in the reactions that they catalyse. The shape of the substrate (key) is complementary to the shape of the active site of the enzyme (lock). This is known as the **lock and key hypothesis**. It attempts to explain the specificity of enzymes. Figure 3 shows how two different substrates have a complementary shape to regions within the active site. The enzyme–substrate complex results in one product molecule (see Extension).

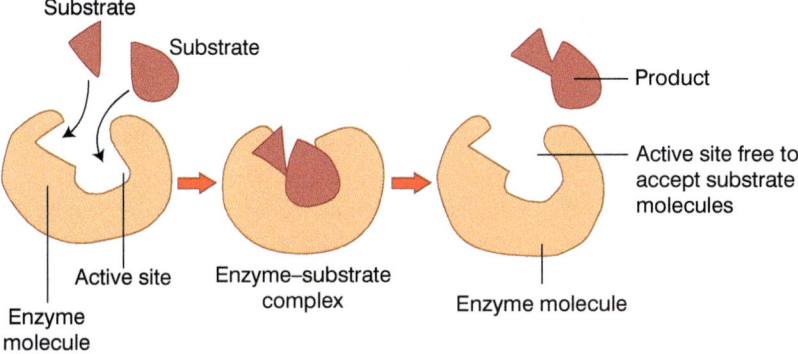

Figure 3 *The lock and key mechanism of enzyme action*

(b) The induced-fit hypothesis

In practice, rather than being a rigid lock, the active site of the enzyme is flexible and changes its form slightly to fit the shape of the substrate. This means that the substrate fits better into the active site. This is the **induced-fit hypothesis** of enzyme action because the shape of the substrate and active site become fully complementary.

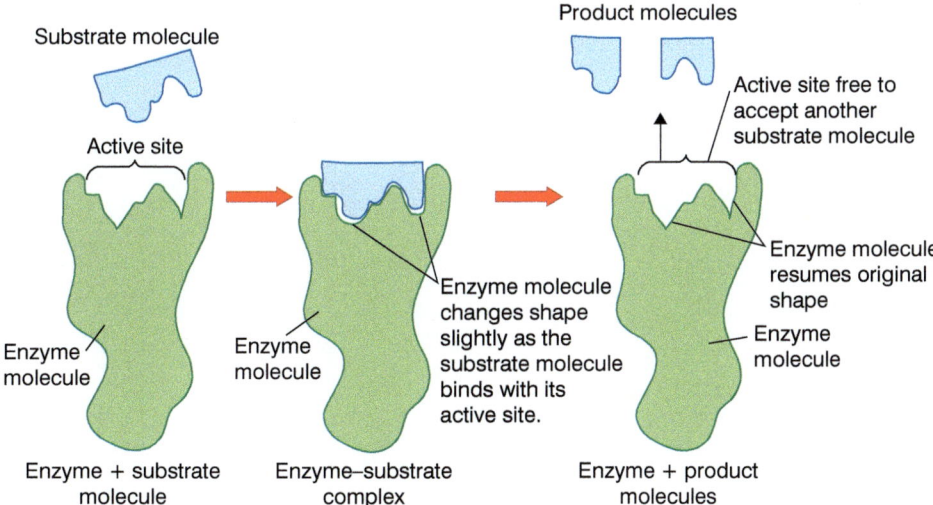

Figure 4 *Induced-fit mechanism of enzyme action*

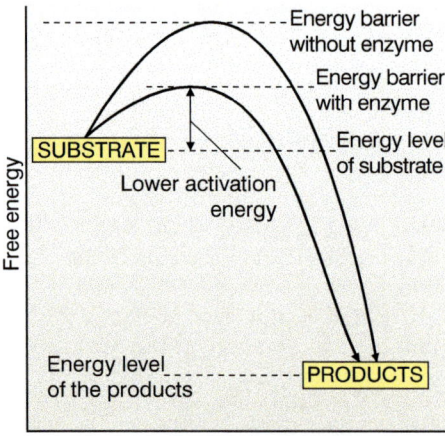

Figure 5 *How enzymes lower activation energy*

Enzymes and activation energy

Consider a typical chemical reaction:

$$2H_2O_2 \rightarrow 2H_2O + O_2$$

hydrogen peroxide   water   oxygen
(substrate)   (products)

Catalase is an enzyme found in living tissue. It decomposes hydrogen peroxide, a toxic waste product of metabolic reactions. For such a reaction to occur naturally, the energy of the products must be less than that of the substrates. Such reactions, however, need an initial boost of energy to get them kick-started. This is known as the **activation energy**. In other words, there is an energy hill, or barrier, which must be overcome before the reaction can proceed. Enzymes lower this activation energy level so that the reaction can happen more rapidly (Figure 5).

Summary test 3.1a

Enzymes act as biological **(1)**. They are **(2)** proteins that have a specific shape within which there is a functional portion known as the **(3)**. Enzymes lower the **(4)** of a reaction, allowing it to proceed at a lower temperature than it would normally. In an enzyme-controlled reaction, the general term for the substance on which the enzyme acts is **(5)** and the substances formed at the end of the reaction are known as the **(6)**. The enzyme molecule and the substance it acts on fit together very precisely, giving rise to the name **(7)** hypothesis of enzyme action. In practice, most enzymes have active sites that change shape slightly and so mould around the shape of their substrates. This is called the **(8)** hypothesis of enzyme action.

Extension

How enzymes lower activation energy

Supplying heat energy will increase the rate of a slow reaction because the proportion of molecules that have activation energy will increase. This is not possible in cells as protein denaturation will occur. Using the active site, enzymes help to *lower* the activation energy required. Ways that this can be achieved are: holding the substrates close together for easier bond formation; exposing bonds; holding a substrate to slightly strain bonds to be broken; providing a hydrophobic region for a reaction involving non-polar substrates; transfer of electrons.

b. Investigating the progress of enzyme-catalysed reactions

Before considering how different factors affect enzymes, it is worth bearing in mind that, for an enzyme to work, it must:

- come into physical contact with its substrate
- have an **active site** which fits the substrate.

Almost all factors that influence the rate at which an enzyme works do so by affecting one or both of the above two features. In order to investigate how enzymes are affected by various factors we need to be able to measure the reactions they catalyse.

Measuring enzyme-catalysed reactions

To measure the progress of an enzyme-catalysed reaction we usually measure its time-course, i.e. how long it takes for a particular event to run its course. The two 'events' most frequently measured are:

- **the formation of products** of the reaction, e.g. the volume of oxygen produced when catalase acts on hydrogen peroxide (Figure 1)

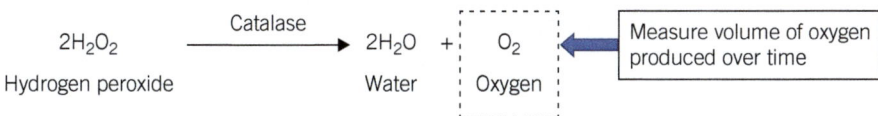

- **the disappearance of the substrate**, e.g. the reduction in concentration of starch when it is acted upon by amylase (Figure 2).

An experiment to determine the activity of an enzyme is known as an enzyme assay.

Although the graphs in Figures 1 and 2 differ, the explanation for their shapes is the same:

- At first there is a lot of substrate (hydrogen peroxide/starch) but no product (water and oxygen/maltose).
- It is very easy for substrate molecules to come into contact with the empty active sites on the enzyme molecules.
- All enzyme active sites are filled and the substrate is rapidly broken down into its products.
- The quantity of substrate decreases as it is broken down, resulting in an increase in the quantity of product.
- As the reaction proceeds, there is less and less substrate and more and more product.
- The product produced per unit time decreases as there are fewer substrate molecules and so some active sites may not be filled at any one moment.
- The rate of reaction continues to slow as the substrate concentration decreases.
- The graphs flatten out because all the substrate has been used up and so no new product can be produced.

These pages help you to:

- learn how to investigate the progress of enzyme-catalysed reactions (3.1.3)
- understand that the rate of an enzyme-catalysed reaction can be calculated by measuring rate of product formation or rate of substrate formation (3.1.3)

You will also:

- understand the difference between independent and dependent variables
- understand what is meant by standardised variables
- understand what is meant by a control

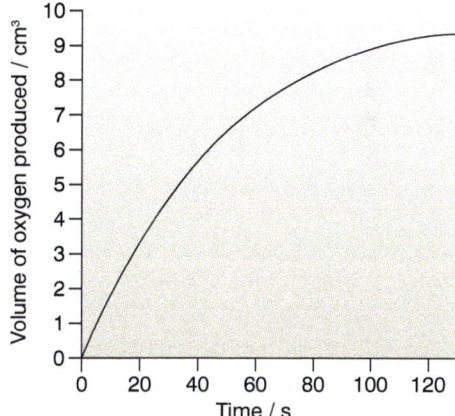

Figure 1 *Measurement of the formation of oxygen due to the action of catalase on hydrogen peroxide*

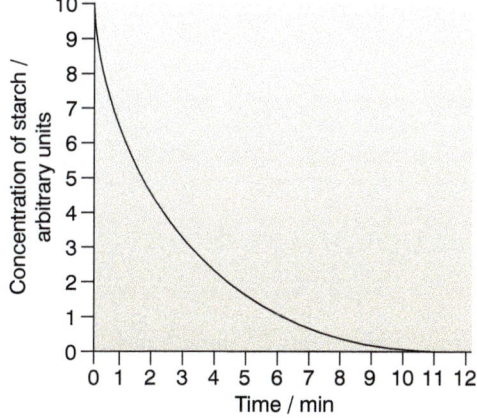

Figure 2 *Measurement of the disappearance of starch due to the action of amylase*

Remember

As an enzyme-catalysed reaction proceeds, substrate molecules are used up. The enzyme will only be able to work at its maximum rate in the initial stage of the reaction when there are most substrate molecules. For this reason, the initial rate of reaction for an enzyme is frequently calculated. Figure 1 (on previous page) shows that the curve is almost a straight line until approximately 30 seconds, so the initial rate can be calculated using the gradient of this straight line. After this time, the rate slows down.

Practical skill

Following the progress of a catalase-controlled reaction

Figure 3 shows one method to measure the volume of oxygen produced over time. Hydrogen peroxide solution, the substrate, and catalase solution, the enzyme, are mixed together at time 0 and the volume of oxygen produced is recorded at set time intervals.

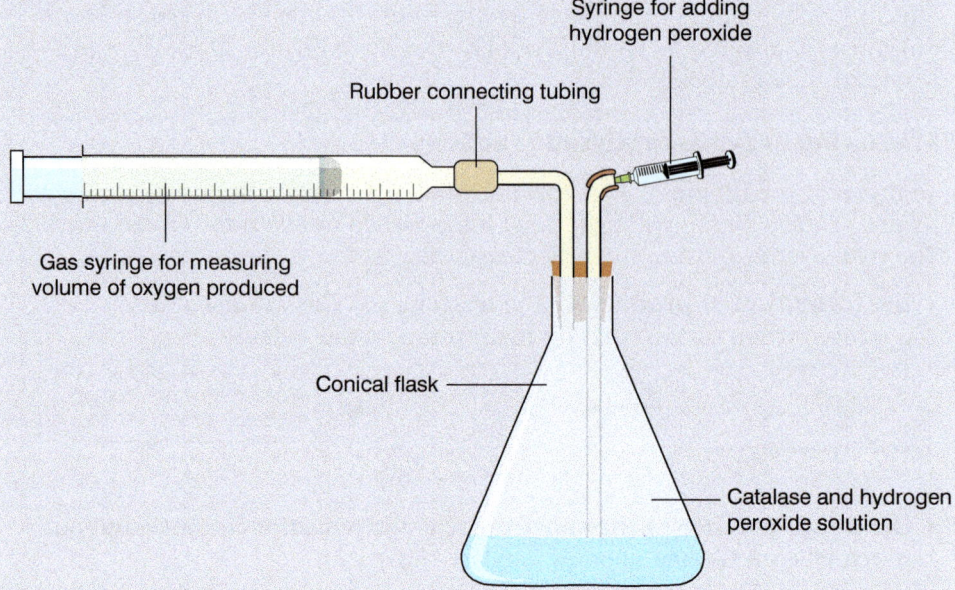

Figure 3 *Measuring the volume of oxygen given off over time in a catalase-controlled reaction*

Variables

In this experiment:

The **independent variable** is time. On a graph, this is on the *x*-axis. This is the variable that is controlled by you. In this example, you would decide appropriate and regular time intervals for recording the volume of oxygen given off. For example, the volume of oxygen given off every 10 or 20 seconds is recorded for 120 seconds. Note that there should be at least 5 readings.

The **dependent variable**, the volume of oxygen given off, is the variable that is affected by the independent variable. It is on the *y*-axis of a graph. Figure 3 shows that a gas syringe can be used to collect oxygen. Another method is to collect the gas under water, with the oxygen displacing water in a graduated cylinder.

Standardised variables are other variables that may have an effect on the results and need to be controlled. For example, in this experiment it is important to standardise temperature as this has a large effect on enzyme action (see 3.2a). The hydrogen peroxide solution and catalase solution should be at the standardised temperature before they are mixed, and the conical flask should be kept at the same temperature throughout the experiment. It is also important when repeating experiments to use the same temperature and the same volume and concentration of enzyme solution and substrate solution as the first experiment.

Controls

A control run should also be conducted and the results compared to the experimental results. This ensures that it is only the action of catalase that allows oxygen to be released and that no other variable is acting.

Here, the same quantity of boiled (denatured) enzyme should confirm that no oxygen is produced. In reality, adding the hydrogen peroxide solution at time 0 will cause some displacement of air in the conical flask. The control will show how much air is displaced and this can be taken into account when the results are analysed.

Practical skill

Following the progress of an amylase-controlled reaction

A simple way to follow the progress of the breakdown of starch by amylase is to use iodine in potassium iodide (I in KI) solution. Colour changes over time reflect the decrease in starch (substrate) that is occurring owing to its hydrolysis by the enzyme. Testing samples of the reaction mixture will result in a change from a blue-black colour at time 0 seconds to the orange colour of I in KI solution (when all starch has been used up). This is the end point.

On a small scale, a spotting tile can be used:

- Using a dropper, add one drop of I in KI solution to each well of the tile.
- At time 0 seconds (that is, when the enzyme and substrate solutions are mixed), remove a small sample of the reaction mixture to add to the first well.
- Mix gently with the end of the dropper and record the colour.
- Repeat the sampling at regular time intervals (for example every 20 seconds).
- Record the time when the end point has been reached.

You will need to judge the end point of the reaction. A reference well can be prepared with one drop of I in KI solution and the same quantity of water as the sample quantity. This acts as the mixture after full hydrolysis of substrate. Alternatively, you can continue for two more samples after you think an end point has been reached and check that there is no further colour change.

As there are no numerical quantity measurements of the loss of substrate over time, the time taken (t) for the reaction to reach the end point can be used to calculate a rate of reaction. The shorter the time, the faster the rate. The rate can be calculated by using the formula 1/t.

For example, a reaction that takes 120 seconds to reach an end point will be 1/120 = 0.008.

A reaction that takes 40 seconds to reach an end point will be 1/40 = 0.025, which is a faster rate of reaction.

The standardised variables for this experiment are the same as those for the catalase experiment. In addition, the same quantity of the sample mixture should be taken and observations made immediately after adding the sample.

Summary test 3.1b

We can measure the progress of an enzyme-catalysed reaction by measuring its **(1)**. This is usually done by measuring either the **(2)** of the substrate or the formation of the **(3)**. For example, in the case of the enzyme amylase, we could either measure the rate at which **(4)** is produced or the rate at which **(5)** is used up. To follow the progress of a reaction catalysed by the enzyme catalase, the volume of oxygen produced by the breakdown of **(6)** can be measured. This is the **(7)** variable. A graph can be drawn of total volume of oxygen produced on the y-axis and **(8)** on the x-axis. The steepest part of the graph is in the first 30 seconds and by using the change in volume over time, an **(9)** rate of reaction can be calculated. In a reaction involving the hydrolysis of starch by the enzyme **(10)**, the colour change that occurs when testing samples at regular time intervals with **(11)** solution can be observed and the time to reach an **(12)** can be recorded.

c. Using a colorimeter

These pages help you to:

- learn how to use a colorimeter to measure the progress of enzyme-catalysed reactions (3.1.4)

You will also:

- have an understanding of how colorimeters work
- see how to apply the main ideas to the example of starch hydrolysis by amylase
- understand how colorimeter measurements can be converted to concentrations

Understanding the colorimeter

A colorimeter is a light-sensitive piece of equipment that gives a quantitative measurement for a coloured solution.

The solution is placed into a small container, known as a cuvette, that typically holds 3 or 4 cm³ of solution. The cuvette is clear on two opposite sides and frosted (translucent) on the other two sides (Figure 1).

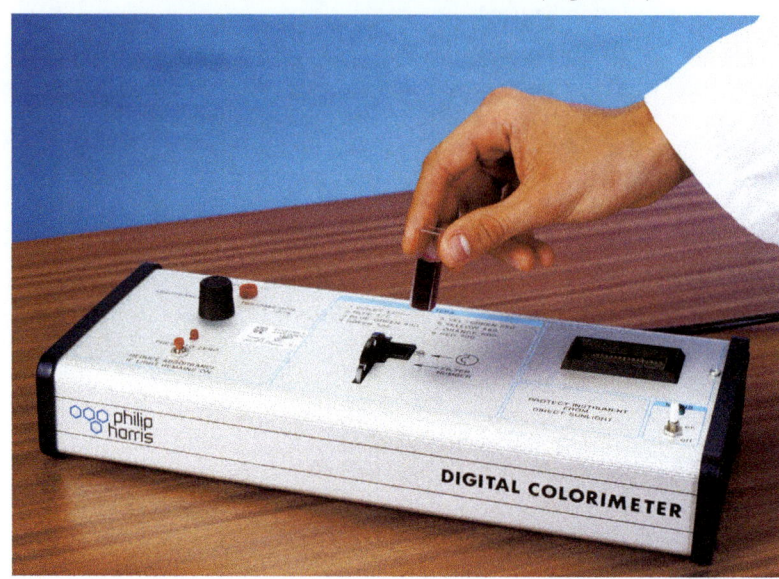

Figure 1 *A colorimeter and a cuvette*

The cuvette is placed into the sample well of a colorimeter and a beam of light is aimed through the clear sides of the cuvette. Some light is absorbed by the solution and the rest of the light is transmitted through the solution. The light reaches a sensor and a numerical reading is obtained:

- a transmission value is given as a percentage transmission or
- an absorbance value is given in absorbance units (au).

Different colour intensities, or colour shades, give different readings (Figure 2) that can be compared.

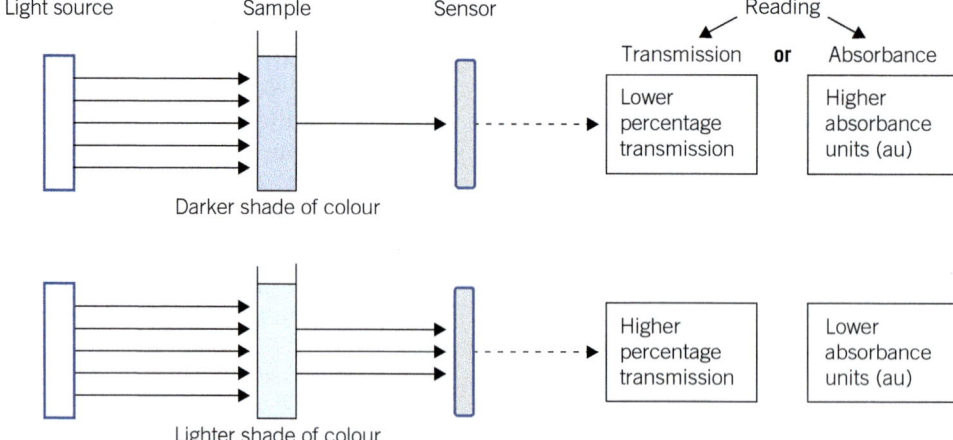

Figure 2 *Using a colorimeter to compare sample solutions of two different intensities of colour*

A particular wavelength of light is used. This is achieved by using LEDs or a coloured filter. Some colorimeters have a slot to add a filter, others incorporate a rotating wheel of coloured filters. To produce the most accurate results, the wavelength that is absorbed best by the coloured solution is chosen as this makes it easier to detect small differences in colour change.

The colorimeter is calibrated (standardised) using a reference, or blank, solution in a cuvette. This may be distilled water. Using this reference solution, the transmission is set as 100% (and the absorbance is set as 0 au) as the baseline reading.

The transmittance or absorbance readings of the sample solution can be taken visually. Alternatively, readings can be recorded by downloading to a computer, or the data can be sent to a phone, tablet or laptop.

Using the colorimeter to measure an enzyme-catalysed reaction involving a colour change

A simple way to follow the progress of the breakdown of starch by amylase is to use iodine in potassium iodide (I in KI) solution. Colour changes over time reflect the decrease in starch (substrate) that is occurring owing to its hydrolysis by the enzyme. The reaction mixture changes from a blue-black colour at time 0 to the orange colour of I in KI solution (when all starch has been used up). This is the end point.

A sample of reaction mixture removed at time 0, when added to a cuvette containing I in KI solution, gives the darkest blue-black colour. This produces the highest absorbance reading.

At the end of the reaction, all of the starch is hydrolysed to reducing sugars. A sample taken at the end of the reaction produces a pale orange colour (the colour of the I in KI in the cuvette) and has the lowest absorbance reading. Samples taken at set time intervals during the reaction show a decrease in the absorbance readings.

A graph can be plotted of absorbance (*y*-axis) against time (*x*-axis) to show the progress of the reaction.

Summary test 3.1c

A **(1)** is a piece of equipment that is sensitive to light and can be used to provide a **(2)** measurement for a coloured solution. The sample solution to be tested is added to a small container known as a **(3)**. This is placed in the sample well and the quantity of light that passes through the sample is detected by a **(4)**. A reading of percentage **(5)** is obtained. The result can also be obtained as the quantity of light that is **(6)** by the sample.

Remember

Carry out a trial to determine an appropriate concentration of I in KI solution to use in the cuvettes. If the concentration is too high, a reading cannot be obtained as the blue-black colour would be too intense.

Extension

Preparing a calibration curve to determine concentrations

It is possible to determine the concentration of starch in a sample cuvette by preparing a calibration curve.

You can use the colorimeter to obtain absorbance readings for known concentrations of starch solution. Plot a graph of absorbance (*y*-axis) against concentration of starch (*x*-axis) and draw in the calibration curve. This means that the absorbance readings obtained during the experiment can be converted directly to starch concentration.

Remember

A digitally controlled water bath can be used to allow the amylase and starch solutions to equilibrate to the reaction temperature (e.g. 30°C) before they are mixed together.

These pages help you to:

- understand how to investigate the effects of temperature and pH on enzyme-catalysed reactions (3.2.1)
- explain why changing temperature or pH will affect an enzyme catalysed reaction (3.2.1)

You will also:

- appreciate the importance of standardising variables
- be able to make decisions relating to measurement and observations
- be able to interpret and explain results

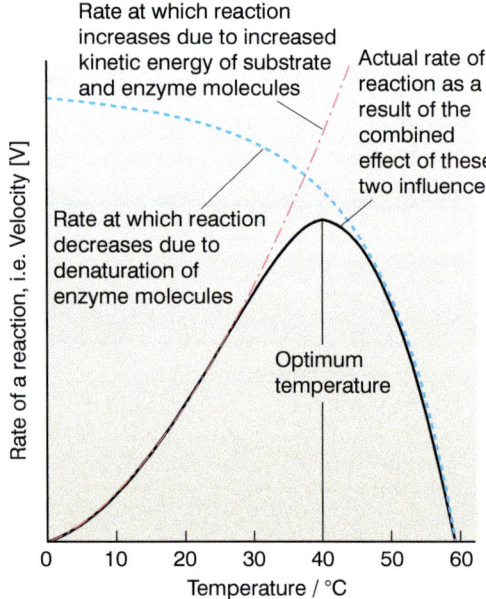

Figure 1 *Effect of temperature on the rate of an enzyme-controlled reaction*

Figure 2 *Bacteria (red) growing in this hot spring in New Zealand are not killed, and their enzymes are not denatured, at temperatures in excess of 80°C*

Effect of temperature on enzymes

A rise in temperature increases the **kinetic energy** of molecules, which therefore move around more rapidly and collide with one another more often. In an enzyme-catalysed reaction, this means that the enzyme and substrate molecules come together more often in a given time, so that the rate of reaction is increased. Shown on a graph, this is a rising curve. However, the temperature rise also increases the energy of the atoms that make up the enzyme molecule. Its atoms begin to vibrate and cause bonds to break, with weaker bonds such as hydrogen bonds, breaking first. Gradually, the shape of the active site is changed. At first, the substrate fits less easily into the active site slowing the rate of reaction. For many human enzymes, this may begin at temperatures of around 45°C. At some point, usually around 60°C, the tertiary structure of the enzyme and shape of the active site is so changed that it stops working altogether. It is said to be **denatured**. Shown on a graph, the rate of this reaction follows a falling curve. The actual effect of temperature on the rate of an enzyme reaction is a combination of these two factors, increased kinetic energy of molecules and denaturation of the enzyme (Figure 1). The optimum working temperature differs from enzyme to enzyme. Some work best at around 10°C, while others continue to work well at 80°C (Figure 2). Each enzyme in the human body has a different optimum working temperature. Our body temperatures have, however, evolved to be 37°C because:

- Although higher body temperatures would increase the metabolic rate slightly, the advantages are offset by the additional energy (food) that would be needed to maintain the higher temperature.
- Proteins other than enzymes may be denatured at higher temperatures.
- At higher temperatures, any further rise in temperature, e.g. during illness, might denature the enzymes.

Denaturing enzymes using high temperatures prevents spoilage (breakdown) of food materials. This is the basis for heating food before canning or bottling it and for blanching vegetables before freezing.

Effect of pH on enzymes

The pH of a solution is a measure of its hydrogen ion concentration. Each enzyme has an optimum pH, i.e. a pH at which it works fastest (Figure 3). At a pH lower or higher than this optimum, the activity of the enzyme will decrease. Small changes in the pH can affect some of the amino acids in the active site that are involved in catalysis. These have R-groups that, at a specific pH, can act as proton donors or acceptors (ionisable R-groups) in a reaction, so small changes in pH may affect the efficiency of catalysis. Large changes in the pH, or hydrogen ion concentration, can cause hydrogen bonds and ionic bonds to become disrupted and break. This can lead to a change in the shape of the active site because these bonds are important in maintaining the tertiary structure of the enzyme, including its active site. A slight change in the active site shape may allow the enzyme to function, but less effectively. At extremes of pH, denaturation occurs and as a result, the substrate can no longer become attached to the active site and the enzyme–substrate complex cannot be formed. This is why foods can be preserved in vinegar: the low pH denatures the enzymes that would otherwise cause the food to break down. Decreasing or increasing the pH from the optimum can also affect the transfer of electrons that may occur during catalysis. Changes to the substrate may also occur. Solutions, known as **buffer solutions**, can be used to prevent fluctuations in pH.

Making decisions in investigations

The effect of temperature on the action of catalase

You have been asked to determine the optimum temperature of the enzyme catalase at its optimum pH of 7. The optimum is stated to be between 30°C and 40°C.

The apparatus is set up for you and you have been instructed to transfer 2 cm³ of buffered enzyme solution to a test tube containing the substrate. You have a choice of a 50 cm³ beaker, a 10 cm³ measuring cylinder and a 5 cm³ syringe to use for this.

You are supplied with buffer solutions from pH 4 to 8.

The initial rate of reaction can be determined by the volume of oxygen given off in the first 30 seconds collected in a gas syringe connected to a delivery tube. The other end of the delivery tube passes through a bung that will be placed into the test tube after enzyme is added.

Example of a decision you may need to make	Decision made, with reasons
Choosing the appropriate chemicals to use	Use buffer solution at pH 7, as this is the optimum pH for catalase
Choosing the correct apparatus to use	Use the 5 cm³ syringe, as this has the smallest graduations and so is the most precise apparatus
Identifying the independent variable	Temperature, as this is the variable that is to be changed
Identifying the dependent variable	Volume of oxygen given off, as this is being affected by the temperature change
How to change the independent variable	Use a digitally controlled water bath, as it can be set at the desired temperatures
Range and spacing to be used for the independent variable and the number of values at which the dependent variable is to be recorded	• Range between 30°C and 40°C, as this covers the given range and you are limited for time (ideally 28°C and 42°C if time allows) • Take measurements, at 2°C intervals to pinpoint more accurately the optimum temperature (a minimum of five measurements)
How frequently the dependent variable should be measured	Take readings of oxygen volume every 5 seconds for 30 seconds to allow a graph to be drawn for calculation of initial rate of reaction
Whether the experiment should be repeated	Repeat each temperature three times to obtain means and to detect any anomalous results
Which variables it is possible to standardise	At each temperature use: same volumes of substrate; same volumes of enzyme solution; same volumes of buffer solution to add to the enzyme to maintain pH, as these are factors that affect enzyme action
Whether a control should be carried out	Use the same quantity of boiled (denatured) enzyme (and with all other variables kept constant) to ensure that it is only the enzyme action that allows oxygen to be released and no other variable is acting

The effect of pH on the action of catalase

In this experiment, many of the decisions made for investigating the effect of temperature will be the same. However, the independent variable is pH. Temperature must be constant, but pH needs to be altered using buffers. You can check the pH of a solution by using a pH probe and meter or by using universal indicator paper.

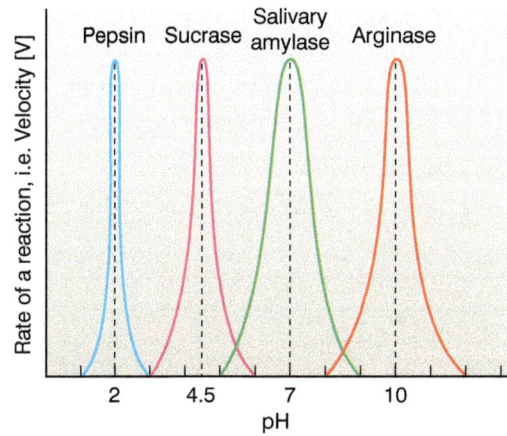

Figure 3 *Effect of pH on the rate of an enzyme-controlled reaction*

Summary test 3.2a

If the temperature is increased, the rate of enzyme action will **(1)** up to a point at which its molecular structure is disrupted and the shape of its **(2)** is altered so that the substrate no longer fits it. At this point the enzyme is said to be **(3)**. Many human enzymes have an optimum working temperature of **(4)**. Enzymes also have an optimum pH at which they operate. Some, like pepsin, work fastest at a pH of **(5)** while others, such as **(6)**, function fastest in neutral conditions.

Changing the pH changes the concentration of **(7)**. This will affect hydrogen and **(8)** bonds between amino acids and can affect the **(9)** of the active site so that the enzyme is prevented from operating at its maximum rate. The ability to transfer **(10)** to catalyse the reaction may also be hindered.

These pages help you to:

- understand how to investigate and explain the effects of enzyme concentration and substrate concentration on enzyme-catalysed reactions (3.2.1)
- understand what is meant by V_{max} and K_m and how to derive K_m from V_{max} (3.2.2)

You will also:

- be able to interpret and explain results
- identify sources of error
- suggest improvements to your investigations

In addition to external factors, such as temperature and pH, substrate and enzyme concentrations affect the rate of enzyme-catalysed reactions. An enzyme reaction is always most rapid at first because the enzyme and substrate molecules can freely collide with one another. As the reaction proceeds, substrate molecules decrease in concentration and there are fewer successful collisions between the molecules. The rate of reaction therefore slows.

Effect of enzyme concentration on the rate of reaction

Once an **active site** of an enzyme has acted on its substrate, it is free to repeat the procedure on another substrate molecule. This means that enzymes are not used up in the reaction and therefore work efficiently at very low concentrations. In some cases, a single enzyme molecule can act on millions of substrate molecules in one minute.

As long as there is an excess of substrate, an increase in the quantity of enzyme leads to a proportionate increase in the rate of reaction. A graph of the rate of reaction against enzyme concentration will initially show a proportionate increase (straight line). This is because there is more substrate than active sites. If we increase the enzyme concentration, more substrate will be acted upon and the rate of reaction will increase. If, however, the substrate is limiting, i.e. there is not sufficient to supply all the enzyme's active sites at one time, then any increase in enzyme concentration will have no effect on the rate of reaction. The rate of reaction will therefore stabilise at a constant level, i.e. the graph will level off. This is because the available substrate is already being used as rapidly as it can be by the existing enzyme molecules. These events are summarised in Figure 1.

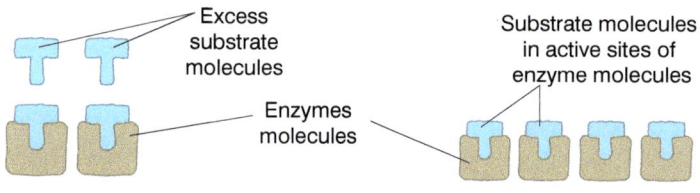

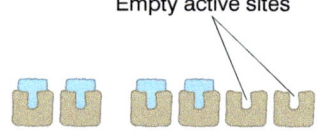

Low enzyme concentration

There are too few enzyme molecules to allow all substrate molecules to find an active site at one time. In this example the rate of reaction is therefore only half the maximum possible for the number of substrate molecules available.

Intermediate enzyme concentration

With twice as many enzyme molecules available, all the substrate molecules can occupy an active site at the same time. The rate of reaction has doubled to its maximum because all active site are filled.

High enzyme concentration

An increase in the number of enzyme molecules present has no effect as there will not be enough substrate to fill all the available active sites. There is no increase in the rate of reaction.

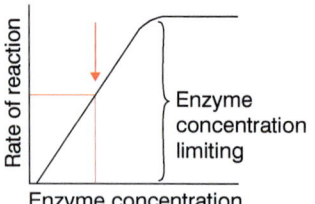

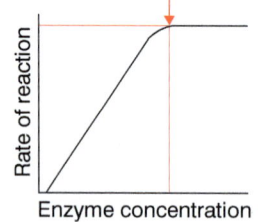

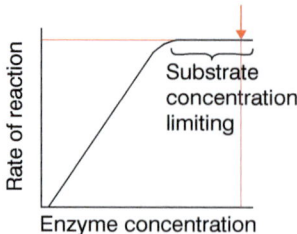

Figure 1 *Effect of enzyme concentration on the rate of enzyme action*

Effects of substrate concentration on the rate of enzyme action

If the concentration of enzyme is fixed at a constant level and substrate concentration is increased, the rate of reaction increases in proportion to the increase in substrate concentration. If a higher concentration of substrate is used, the active sites become fully occupied. They are said to be fully saturated at the point where they are all working as fast as they can. The rate of reaction is at its maximum (V_{max}). After that, the addition of more substrate will have no effect on the rate of reaction. In other words, when the substrate is in excess the rate of reaction levels off. A summary of the effect of substrate concentration on the rate of enzyme action is given in Figure 2.

Remember

The active site and the substrate are not the same, any more than a lock and key are the same. The correct term is **complementary**.

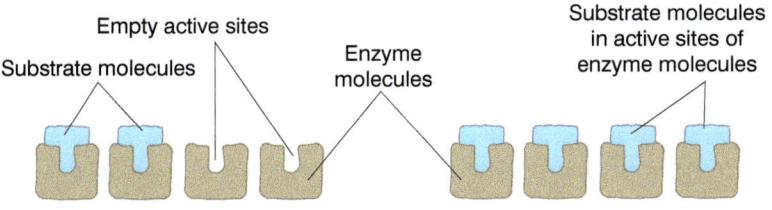

Low substrate concentration | **Intermediate substrate concentration** | **High substrate concentration**

There are too few substrate molecules to occupy all the available active sites in this example. The rate of reaction is therefore only half the maximum possible for the number of enzyme molecules available.

With twice as many substrate molecules available in this example, all the active sites are occupied at one time. The rate of reaction has doubled to its maximum because all the active sites are filled.

A higher concentration of substrate has no effect as all active sites are already occupied at one time. There is no increase in the rate of reaction.

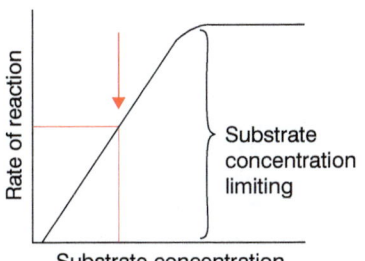

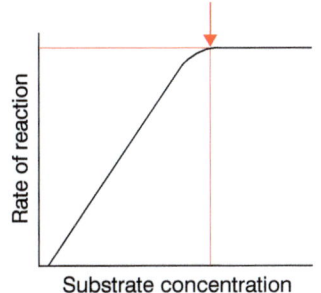

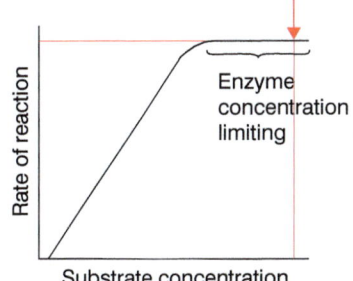

Remember

The Michaelis–Menten constant is a substrate concentration.

Figure 2 *Effect of substrate concentration on the rate of enzyme action*

Maximum rate of reaction and the Michaelis–Menten constant

The Michaelis–Menten constant (K_m) is the substrate concentration needed for an enzyme reaction to proceed at half of its maximum rate (Figure 3). The constant is the same for any one enzyme but varies for different enzymes. It gives a measure of how easily an enzyme reacts with its substrate. In other words, it measures the affinity of an enzyme for its substrate.

For example, consider two enzymes, **X** and **Y**:

- Enzyme **X** has a higher K_m than enzyme **Y**.
- So, enzyme **X** has a lower affinity for its substrate than enzyme **Y**.
- This means that enzyme **X** needs a higher concentration of substrate to reach V_{max}.

The Michaelis–Menten constant can therefore be used to compare the efficiency of different enzymes for their substrates (see also 3.2d).

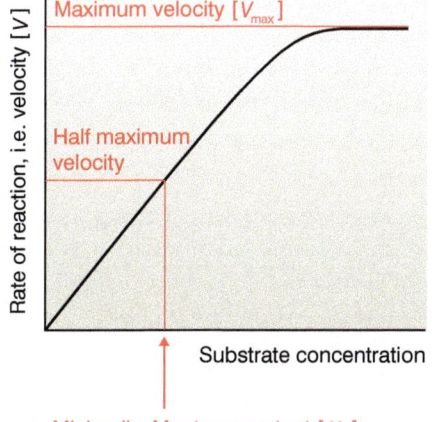

Figure 3 *The relationship between V_{max} and K_m*

Summary test 3.2b

Enzymes work fastest at the start of a process and this is called the **(1)**. As the enzyme concentration increases, the rate of reaction **(2)**, provided there is excess substrate. The graph may later 'tail off' if the concentration of substrate is limited because not all the **(3)** of the enzyme molecules are filled. If the substrate concentration of an enzyme-controlled reaction is halved then the rate of reaction will be **(4)**, but when the substrate is in excess the rate of reaction will **(5)**. A higher **(6)** constant for enzyme X compared to enzyme Y tells us that enzyme Y has a higher **(7)** for its substrate.

These pages help you to:

- understand the difference between competitive and non-competitive inhibitors (3.2.1)
- explain the effects of reversible inhibitors on enzyme activity (3.2.3)

You will also:

- appreciate the importance of inhibitors in allowing the cell to function efficiently
- consider how to investigate the effect of inhibitors on the rate of reaction of an enzyme

Enzyme inhibitors are substances that directly or indirectly interfere with the functioning of the **active site** of an enzyme and so reduce enzyme activity. Most inhibitors only make temporary attachments to the active site. These are called **reversible inhibitors** and are of two types:

- **competitive** (active site directed) – inhibitor binds to the active site of the enzyme
- **non-competitive** (non-active site directed) – inhibitor binds to the enzyme at a position other than the active site.

Competitive inhibitors

Competitive inhibitors have a molecular shape that is similar to that of the substrate, and are therefore complementary to the shape of the active site of an enzyme. They can bind to the active site instead of the substrate, and so compete with the substrate for the available active sites (Figure 1). It is the difference between the concentration of the inhibitor and the concentration of the substrate that determines the effect this has on enzyme activity: if the substrate concentration is increased, the effect of the inhibitor is reduced. The inhibitor is not permanently bound to the active site and so, when it leaves, another molecule can take its place. This could be a substrate or inhibitor molecule, depending on how much of each type is present. Sooner or later, all the substrate molecules will find an active site, but the greater the concentration of inhibitor, the longer this will take.

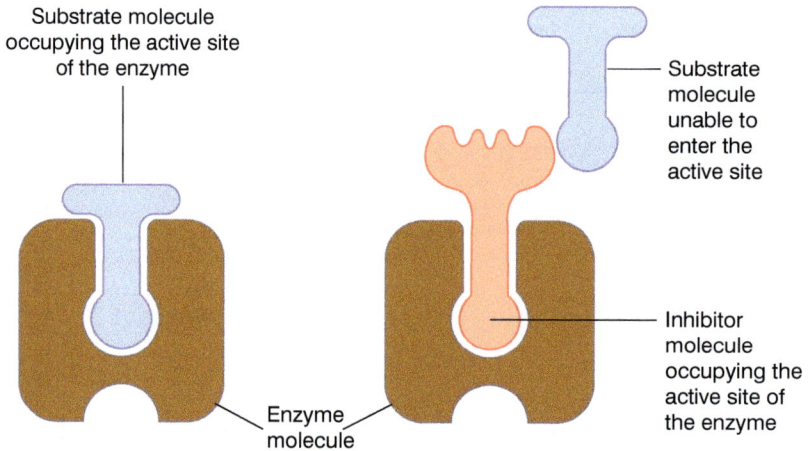

Figure 1 *Competitive inhibition*

Non-competitive inhibitors

Non-competitive inhibitors attach themselves to the enzyme at a binding site which is not the active site. This is known as the **allosteric site** (allosteric = 'at another place'). Upon attaching to the enzyme, the inhibitor alters the shape of the enzyme's active site in such a way that substrate molecules can no longer occupy it, and so the enzyme cannot function (Figure 2). As the substrate and the inhibitor are not competing for the same site, an increase in substrate concentration does not decrease the effect of the inhibitor (Figure 3).

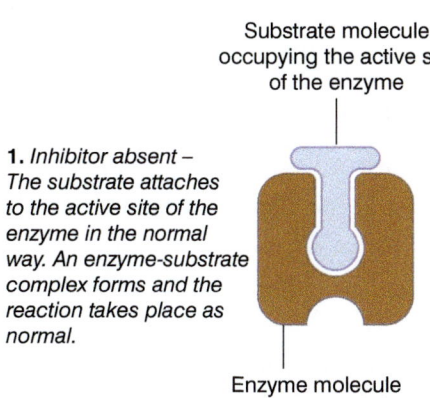

1. *Inhibitor absent – The substrate attaches to the active site of the enzyme in the normal way. An enzyme-substrate complex forms and the reaction takes place as normal.*

Substrate molecule occupying the active site of the enzyme

Enzyme molecule

2. *Inhibitor present – The inhibitor prevents the normal enzyme–substrate complex being formed. The reaction rate is reduced.*

In this example, the substrate molecule cannot enter the active site because the the active site has changed shape. This means that it is no longer complementary to the shape of the substrate. In some cases, the substrate may be able to enter the active site but the changes are too great to allow binding or catalysis to occur.

Enzyme molecule shape is changed due to presence of the inhibitor molecule, changing the shape of the active site

Inhibitor molecule attached to enzyme molecule

Figure 2 *Non-competitive inhibition*

Investigating the effect of inhibitors

The rate of reaction of the enzyme needs to be determined over a range of substrates, with and without the presence of an inhibitor at each substrate concentration. The main variables that need to be standardised are: temperature, enzyme concentration, volume of enzyme solution, volume of substrate solution and pH. The quantity of inhibitor (concentration and volume) also needs to be standardised.

How the presence of inhibitors affects V_{max} and K_m

Competitive inhibition

- At higher substrate concentrations, the effect of a competitive inhibitor decreases and V_{max} is reached.
- K_m increases (Figure 4).
- The enzyme has a lower affinity for its substrate.

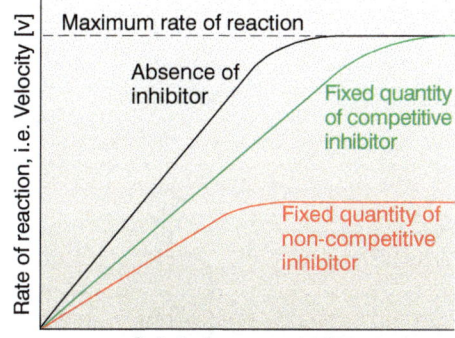

Figure 3 *Comparison of competitive and non-competitive inhibition on the rate of an enzyme-controlled reaction at different substrate concentrations*

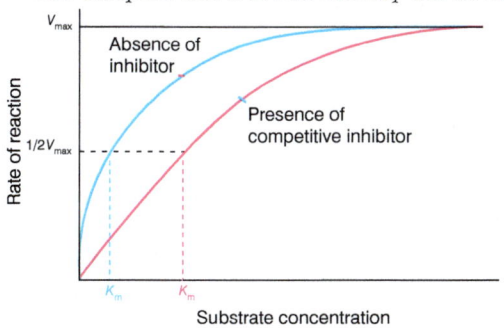

Figure 4 *The effect of competitive inhibition on V_{max} and K_m*

Non-competitive inhibition

- The effect of a non-competitive inhibitor remains the same and V_{max} is not reached.
- K_m remains the same (Figure 5).
- The enzyme has the same affinity for its substrate.

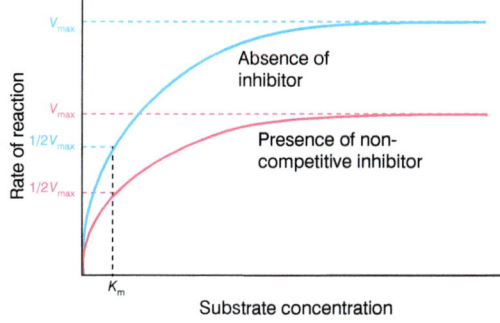

Figure 5 *The effect of non-competitive inhibition on V_{max} and K_m*

Summary test 3.2c

In competitive inhibition, the inhibitor has a similar shape to the **(1)**. This allows it to fit into the active site of the enzyme, preventing the formation of an **(2)**. Increasing the substrate concentration decreases the inhibition and **(3)** is reached. K_m is increased, showing that the enzyme has less **(4)** for its substrate. In non-competitive inhibition, the inhibitor does not bind to the active site but to the **(5)**, causing the **(6)** of the active site to change. The active site is no longer **(7)** in shape to the shape of the substrate, and catalysis cannot occur.

d. Immobilised enzymes

These pages help you to:

- understand how to investigate the difference in activity between an enzyme that is immobilised in alginate and the same enzyme free in solution (3.2.4)
- state the advantages of using immobilised enzymes rather than enzymes free in solution (3.2.4)

You will also:

- improve your ability to describe and interpret graphical results

Enzymes are used in a wide range of industrial processes, including the production of foods, agrochemicals and drugs. In many cases, the enzyme and substrate are mixed together to form a product. This is then extracted and the rest of the mixture, including the enzyme, is discarded. Enzymes are costly to produce so this is both wasteful and expensive. As enzymes are not used up in reactions, keeping them for future use clearly has a cost benefit. One way of doing this is to immobilise the enzymes so that they can be retained rather than discarded.

One method of immobilising enzymes is to trap them in small alginate beads. This is carried out in a laboratory as follows.

- The enzyme to be immobilised is mixed with a solution of sodium alginate.
- Tiny droplets of this mixture are added to a solution of calcium chloride, one at a time using a syringe.
- A reaction takes place between the sodium alginate–enzyme mixture and the calcium, causing calcium ions to replace sodium ions.
- As a result of this reaction, jelly-like beads are formed in which the enzyme is trapped.

To catalyse reactions, the beads are packed into a long column in a vessel and the substrate is poured in at the top. As the substrate enters the beads, it is converted to the product by the enzymes immobilised in the beads. Although the process cannot continue indefinitely, as impurities accumulate, it can proceed for a considerable time without renewing the enzyme (Figure 1).

Advantages of using immobilised enzymes or cells

There are a number of advantages to immobilising enzymes or cells.

- With enzyme immobilisation, the enzyme can be used repeatedly as it is not lost in the process, making it more economic, especially where the enzyme is expensive.
- Enzymes are vulnerable to changes in temperature and pH. The beads in which they are trapped can buffer them against these changes.
- The immobilised enzymes and cells, being held in place, cannot contaminate the substance being made, which leads to a purer product.
- With whole cell immobilisation, a number of enzymes can act together at the same time in a single process.
- Downstream processing (the steps needed to obtain a purified, high quality product) is easier. This is because very little, or no enzyme is lost from the reaction vessel.
- The shelf-life of the enzyme is longer because it is less vulnerable to extremes of pH and temperature.
- The protection given by the matrix to higher temperatures means that the reaction can proceed at higher temperatures to give greater productivity.
- The process can be carried out on a continuous basis as enzyme does not need to be continually recovered from the product mixture.

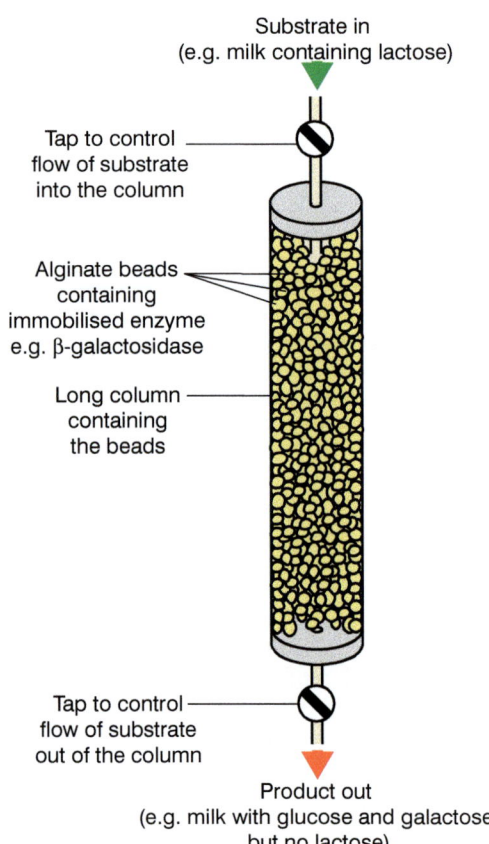

Figure 1 *Using immobilised enzymes to produce lactose-free milk*

Practical skills

Improving the productivity of an immobilised enzyme

The experimental set-up shown in Figure 1 can be used to determine the conditions that give the highest rate of product formation. One factor should be investigated at a time, with all other conditions kept constant. Examples of factors that can be varied: temperature, substrate concentration, enzyme concentration, pH, size of bead, rate of flow of substrate through the column.

Investigating the difference in activity between an immobilised enzyme and an enzyme free in solution

The optimum temperature or the optimum pH for an enzyme that has been immobilised is not always the same as those for the enzyme when it is free in solution.

When comparing the rate of reactions of an immobilised enzyme and the enzyme free in solution at different temperatures, pH or substrate concentrations, remember that all factors other than the one being investigated should be kept constant (standardised variables).

Once you have obtained your raw data, it is helpful to construct one graph that contains the results for both, for easier comparison. Remember that *comparing* means that you need to look for similarities as well as differences.

For temperature or pH, compare:

- the optimum for the immobilised enzyme with the enzyme free in solution
- the pattern that is shown as temperature (or pH) increases (look at the overall shape of the curves)
- any differences in the level of activity shown at each temperature (or pH) tested
- any differences in the steepness of the curve 'before' the optimum and 'after the optimum'.

For substrate concentration compare:

- the maximum velocity, V_{max} and the Michaelis–Menten constant, K_m
- the steepness of the increase up to the V_{max}.

Summary test 3.2d

To immobilise an enzyme in beads, the enzyme solution is mixed with sodium **(1)** and the mixture is placed into a **(2)** to make small drops that can be added to a solution of **(3)**. Advantages of using immobilised enzymes include: the product is not **(4)** by enzyme; the enzyme can be recovered and **(5)**; the enzyme is more tolerant to changes in **(6)** and temperature; **(7)** processing is easier.

Extension

An example of the commercial use of immobilised enzymes is in the manufacture of lactose-free milk for people with lactose intolerance. In this case the immobilised enzyme is β-galactosidase. Milk contains the sugar lactose which is the cause of the discomfort experienced by lactose-intolerant individuals. To produce lactose-free milk, the milk is passed over the immobilised β-galactosidase which catalyses the hydrolysis of lactose to glucose and galactose. Figure 1 illustrates the process.

You can check specifically for the presence of glucose using test strips known as glucose dipsticks:

- Test the lactose at the start of the experiment to confirm that there is no glucose
- Test the product mixture to confirm that hydrolysis has taken place.

Remember

In a cell, an enzyme with a low K_m will have a high affinity to its substrate. Even if the substrate concentration in the cell varies, it will not have a great effect on enzyme activity as the enzyme is likely to be saturated with substrate at low concentrations. This means that there will be a fairly constant rate of product formation even if substrate concentrations change.

This concept can be applied to the commercial use of enzymes, including immobilised enzymes. The substrate concentration is less important if using an enzyme with a lower K_m. An enzyme with a higher K_m will show a more varied rate of product formation as the substrate concentration varies, which means that this factor must be carefully controlled to give a constant, high output.

Launch additional digital resources for the chapter

3 Exam-style questions

1   Phosphatases are a group of enzymes that catalyse the removal of phosphate groups from organic compounds.

A group of students investigated the effect of substrate concentration on the initial rate of the reaction catalysed by phosphatase 1. The results are shown in Figure 1.

Figure 1

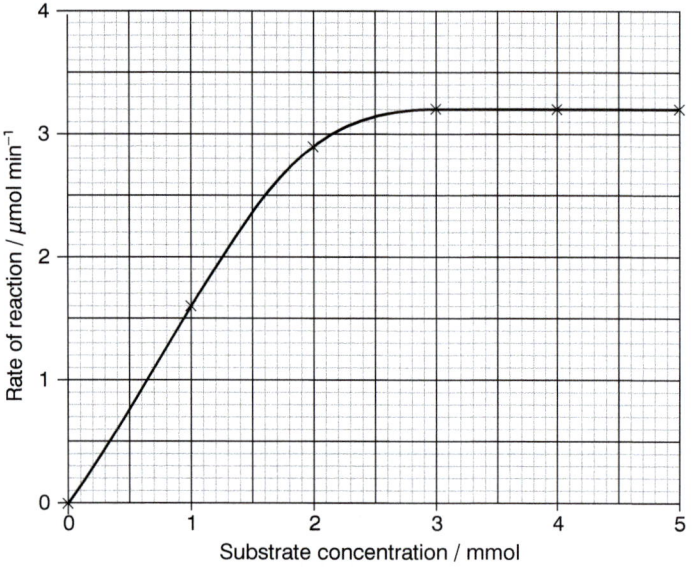

a   Explain the results shown in Figure 1.   *(5 marks)*

b   i   State the lowest substrate concentration to give the maximum rate of reaction, V_{max}.   *(1 mark)*

    ii   Determine the Michaelis–Menten constant, K_m.   *(1 mark)*

c   The students repeated the investigation, but added glycine, a competitive inhibitor of phosphatase 1, to each reaction mixture.

    i   Sketch a curve on Figure 1 to show the expected results.   *(2 marks)*

    ii   Explain the effect that glycine has on the action of phosphatase 1.   *(2 marks)*

(Total 11 marks)

2   A student carried out an investigation into the digestion of triglycerides using lipase.

A volume of 20 cm³ of vegetable oil, adjusted to pH 8.0, was added to a test tube, which was then put in a water bath at 40 °C for 5 minutes.

A 2 cm³ volume of lipase solution was incubated at the same temperature in a separate test tube before being added to the vegetable oil.

The initial pH of the reaction mixture was measured using a pH meter. The pH was recorded at 5-minute intervals for 60 minutes.

a   State why the lipase solution was incubated separately before being added to the vegetable oil.   *(1 mark)*

b   Suggest why the vegetable oil was adjusted to pH 8.0 before the lipase was added.   *(1 mark)*

Figure 2 shows the results of the investigation.

Figure 2

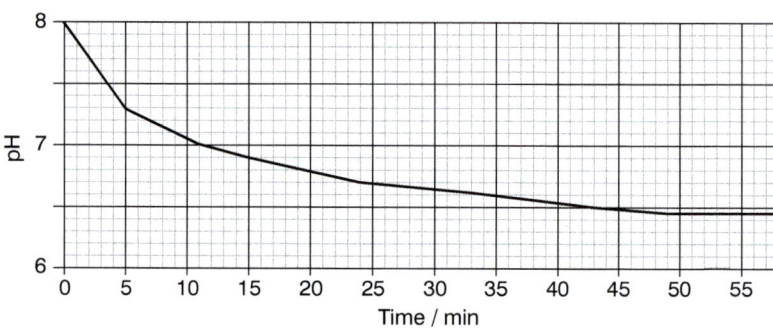

c   With reference to Figure 2, describe and explain the results of the investigation.   *(5 marks)*

d   Lysozyme A is an enzyme found in human tears and saliva. It hydrolyses the β-1,4 glycosidic bonds present in compounds found in bacterial cell walls.

Lysozyme uses the induced fit mechanism.

Explain the mode of action of an enzyme that uses the induced fit mechanism.   *(4 marks)*

e   Each molecule of lysozyme consists of a single polypeptide. In a variant lysozyme, a mutation has caused a single amino acid, phenylalanine, to be replaced by the amino acid isoleucine. Variant lysozyme is less active than normal lysozyme and has also been linked to a disease called renal amyloidosis, where protein fibrils are deposited in the kidneys.

Suggest how the difference in one amino acid is responsible for the lower activity of variant lysozyme compared with normal lysozyme. *(2 marks)*

(Total 13 marks)

3 Practice questions

3 Enzymes can function at a wide range of temperatures. Shrimps that live in Arctic waters have enzymes that function best around 4 °C and are denatured at around 15 °C. By contrast, bacteria that live in hot springs have enzymes that function best at 95 °C and continue to operate effectively above 100 °C. These bacteria are called thermophilic (heat-loving) bacteria.

Enzyme X is produced by thermophilic bacteria and hydrolyses many proteins, including haemoglobin and egg albumin.

Enzyme Y is found in the stomach of young mammals, where it acts on a single soluble protein found in milk, causing it to coagulate (clot).

a i From the descriptions, comment on the differences in the specificity of the two enzymes.
ii Enzymes X and Y are each used for different commercial purposes. Suggest what this might be in each case.
iii Suggest a possible purpose of enzyme Y in the mammalian stomach.
iv Use the information about the two enzymes to suggest a possible difference in the type of bonding found in the tertiary structure of each. Explain your reasoning.

b An experiment was carried out with enzyme X in which the time taken for it to fully hydolyse 5 g of its protein substrate was measured at different temperatures. The following data were obtained:

Temperature/°C	Time for hydrolysis of protein/min	Rate of reaction $\frac{1}{time}$
15	5.8	
25	3.4	
35	1.7	
45	0.7	
55	0.6	
65	0.9	
75	7.1	

i Calculate the values for 1/time for each of the temperatures.
ii Sketch a graph that shows the effect of temperature on the rate of reaction of enzyme X.
iii State the optimum temperature for the action of enzyme X.
iv Suggest how you might determine this optimum temperature more precisely.

4 a Explain why enzymes function less well at lower temperatures.

b Explain how high temperatures may prevent enzymes from functioning at all.

c Enzymes produced by microorganisms are responsible for spoiling food. Using this fact and your knowledge of enzymes, suggest why the following procedures are carried out:
i Food is heated to a high temperature before being canned.
ii Some foods, such as onions, are preserved in vinegar.

d The figure below represents an enzyme and its substrate. Of the other four molecules shown, one is a competitive inhibitor and one is a non-competitive inhibitor of the enzyme.

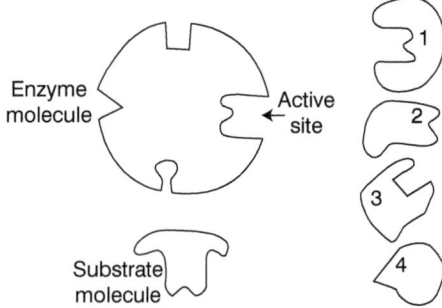

i State the number of the molecule that is a competitive inhibitor.
ii State the number of the molecule that is a non-competitive inhibitor.

4 Cell membranes and transport

4.1 Fluid mosaic membranes

a. The fluid mosaic model of membrane structure

These pages help you to:

- describe the fluid mosaic model of membrane structure (4.1.1)
- explain how hydrophobic and hydrophilic interactions account for the phospholipid bilayer (4.1.1)
- describe the arrangement of cholesterol, glycolipids and glycoproteins in cell surface membranes (4.1.2)

You will also:

- consolidate your understanding about the role of the cell surface membrane

All membranes around and within cells (including those around and within cell organelles) have the same basic structure. The cell surface membrane is the membrane that surrounds cells. It is the boundary between the cell cytoplasm and the environment. It interacts with chemical signals arriving from other areas and, to a great extent, controls the movement of substances in and out of the cell. To understand how the cell surface membrane functions, we need first to look in more detail at the molecules that form its structure – phospholipids, proteins, cholesterol, glycolipids and glycoproteins.

Phospholipids

The molecular structure of a phospholipid is described in 2.2d and shown in Figure 1. A phospholipid is made up of:

- **a hydrophilic phosphate 'head'**, which is attracted to water but not to lipid
- **two fatty acid hydrophobic 'tails'**, which are repelled by water but mix readily with lipid.

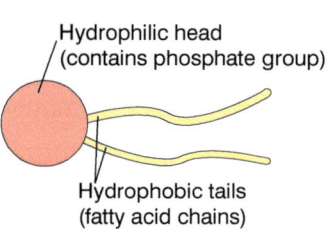

Hydrophilic head
(contains phosphate group)

Hydrophobic tails
(fatty acid chains)

Figure 1 *Structure of a phospholipid*

This means that when phospholipid molecules are placed in water they take up positions that place the hydrophilic heads as close to the water as possible, and the hydrophobic tails as far away from the water as possible. The phospholipids in the cell surface membrane form a bilayer (Figure 2), which has:

- one layer of phospholipids with their hydrophilic heads pointing inwards (attracted by the water in the cell cytoplasm)
- the other layer of phospholipids with their hydrophilic heads pointing outwards (attracted by the watery environment which surrounds all cells)
- the hydrophobic tails of both phospholipid layers pointing into the centre of the membrane – repelled by the water on both sides and forming a hydrophobic core.

Phospholipids can move within their own layer.

Glycolipids

Glycolipids are made up of a carbohydrate portion, that is hydrophilic, covalently bonded with a lipid tail that is hydrophobic and located in the hydrophobic core of the bilayer. The carbohydrate portion extends from the phospholipid bilayer into the watery environment outside the cell.

Extension

A monolayer of phospholipids

When phospholipids are added to water, a single layer, or monolayer, of phospholipids is formed. The phosphate heads are held in the water and the fatty acid tails project away from the water, facing up into the air above.

Extension

Phospholipids can 'flip' between layers

On occasion, phospholipids in one layer of the bilayer may 'flip' to the other side. For example, when new phospholipids are added to the cytosol side of the membrane, they may flip to the external surface side to equalise the quantity of phospholipids in the membrane.

Proteins

The proteins of the cell surface membrane are arranged more randomly than the regular pattern of phospholipids. They are scattered within the bilayer. Some move within the bilayer and some are anchored in one location, held by fibres in the cytoplasm of the cell. Proteins are associated with the phospholipid bilayer in two main ways:

- **Extrinsic (peripheral) proteins** occur on both surfaces of the bilayer but never extend completely across it.
- **Intrinsic (integral) proteins** may have regions embedded in the bilayer from one side to the other. Some are **channel proteins**, which form open water-filled tubes to allow water-soluble ions to diffuse across the membrane. Some are **carrier proteins** that bind to molecules such as glucose and amino acids, then change shape in order to move these molecules across the membrane. Proteins have regions of amino acids with hydrophobic R-groups. These hydrophobic regions of the protein are repelled by the aqueous environment and face the internal hydrophobic core of the phospholipid bilayer. Regions of the protein that face the aqueous external or internal cellular environment have amino acids with hydrophilic R-groups.

Glycoproteins

Carbohydrate chains are attached to many proteins on the outer surface of the cell membrane.

Cholesterol

Cholesterol molecules occur within the phospholipid bilayer. A cholesterol molecule is a complex lipid that has a hydrophilic portion and a hydrophobic portion. The hydrophobic portion of the cholesterol molecule is embedded in the hydrophobic region of the bilayer. Cholesterol molecules also interact with the fatty acid tails of the phospholipid molecules.

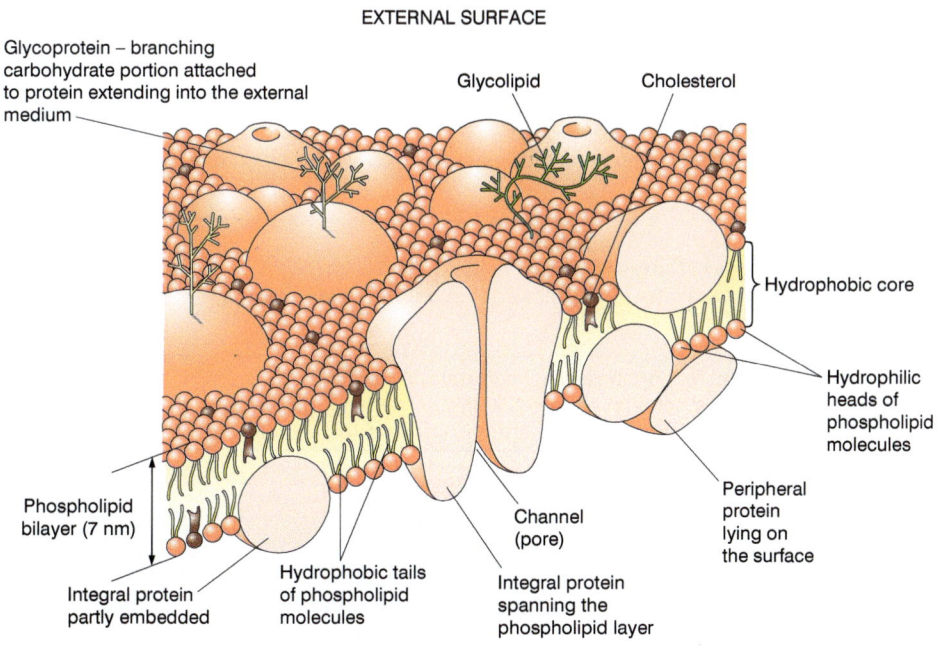

Figure 2 Structure of the cell surface membrane

Extension

Membrane potentials
There is an unequal concentration of ions across a cell surface membrane. This means that there is a potential difference (difference in voltage) between the inside of a cell and the outside, known as a membrane potential. This varies for different cell types. The potential difference is shown as a negative value, for example −10mV, meaning that the outside of the cell is more positive than the inside of the cell. In 15.1d, you will learn about changes to membrane potential that occur during the conduction of a nerve impulse.

Remember

The arrangement shown in Figure 2 is known as the **fluid mosaic model** for the following reasons:

- **fluid** because the individual phospholipid and protein molecules can move relative to one another. This gives the membrane a flexible structure that is constantly changing in shape.
- **mosaic** because the proteins that occur in the phospholipid bilayer vary in shape, size and pattern (scattered) in the same way as the tiles in a mosaic. The fluid mosaic model was first proposed by Singer and Nicolson in 1972.

Summary test 4.1.a

The cell surface (plasma) membrane is made up of five main types of molecules. Phospholipid molecules form a **(1)** in which their **(2)** heads point both inwards towards the cell cytoplasm and outwards towards the external environment. The **(3)** tails of the phospholipids point into the centre of the membrane. Within the phospholipid layer are both **(4)** proteins that span the complete membrane or are partly embedded in it and **(5)** proteins that occur on the membrane surface. The remaining types of molecules within a cell surface membrane are **(6)**, **(7)** and **(8)**.

Introduction

Table 1 is a summary of the roles of the components of the cell surface membrane (see also Figure 1).

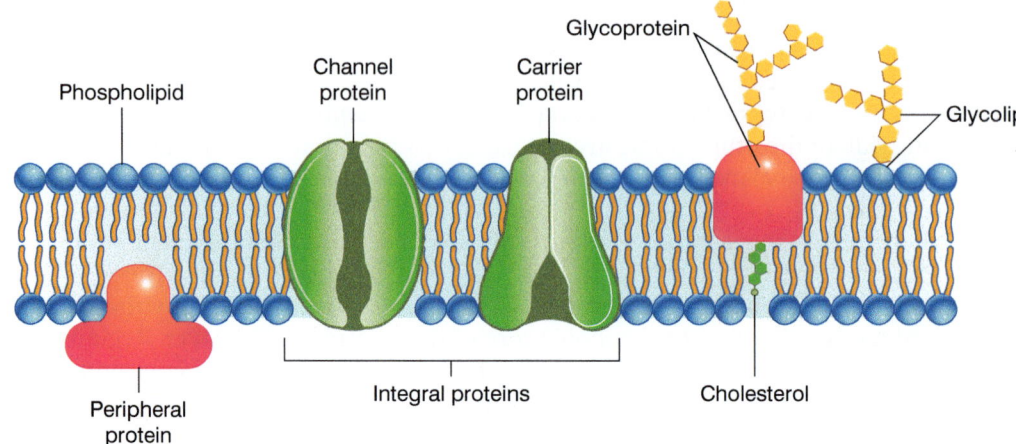

Figure 1

Table 1 *Summary of functions of the components of the cell surface membrane*

Proteins

- provide structural support
- act as **carrier proteins** transporting water soluble substances such as small polar substances and ions
- form **channel proteins** to transport water soluble substances, such as small polar substances and ions
- function as enzymes
- help cells attach to one another (cell-to-cell adhesion) and so form tissues
- act as cell surface receptors for cell signalling molecules

Phospholipids

- form a bilayer that encloses and protects cell contents
- move within the bilayer to give the membrane fluidity
- (as part of the bilayer) allow lipid-soluble substances to enter and leave the cell
- (as part of the bilayer) prevent water-soluble substances entering and leaving the cell

Cholesterol

- reduces lateral movement of phospholipids
- regulates membrane fluidity depending on temperature
- prevents passage of dissolved polar molecules and ions across the membrane

Glycolipids

- act as antigens for cell-to-cell recognition
- help maintain stability of the membrane
- help cells attach to one another (cell-to-cell adhesion) and so form tissues

Glycoproteins

- act as recognition sites for hormones and neurotransmitters
- help cells attach to one another (cell-to-cell adhesion) and so form tissues
- act as antigens for cell-to-cell recognition (proteins can also act as antigens)

Movement of substances across the membrane

Phospholipids

The importance of the structure of an individual phospholipid molecule can only be appreciated when you consider its role as part of the phospholipid bilayer. The hydrophobic core that is created by the fatty acid tails of the phospholipids in the bilayer allows many substances to cross the membrane. Small, lipid soluble (non-polar, hydrophobic) substances and respiratory gases (oxygen and carbon dioxide) can pass easily across the membrane. The bilayer is permeable to these substances. Water molecules, because of their very small size, are able to pass across the phospholipid bilayer.

The phospholipid bilayer is largely impermeable to small polar molecules. Although there may be small gaps between the phospholipids that are moving within their own monolayer, hydrophobic interactions in the hydrophobic core generally prevent water-soluble substances from crossing the bilayer directly, and so very few of these substances pass through.

The phospholipid bilayer is impermeable to ions (charged particles).

Cholesterol

Cholesterol molecules have a small hydrophilic portion located in the phosphate head region of the bilayer and a longer hydrophobic tail that interacts with the fatty acid tails of the phospholipid molecules. This means that cholesterol molecules play an important role in preventing the movement of dissolved ions and polar molecules across the bilayer.

Membrane transport proteins: channel and carrier proteins

Membrane transport proteins are integral proteins that have regions of amino acids with hydrophilic R-groups. Polar substances (such as glucose and amino acids) and ions are water-soluble (hydrophilic) and can pass across the membrane via these transport proteins. As outlined in 4.1a, there are two main types of transport protein, channel proteins and carrier proteins. These can be composed of one or more polypeptides.

Channel proteins have a hydrophilic, water-filled pore allowing the movement of water-soluble substances across the membrane. Many are **ion channels**. A large proportion of these are selective, with a narrow channel that only allows a particular ion through. Others are nonselective, with wider channels. The conformation of most ion channels can change slightly, allowing them to 'open' or 'close' to control the movement of ions. These are known as gated channel proteins. They are activated to open or close in response to a physical change (mechanically-gated), a change in membrane potential (voltage-gated) or the binding of a chemical messenger or ligand (ligand-gated).

Aquaporins are channel proteins that allow large quantities of water molecules to pass through.

Carrier proteins also help to transport ions and polar molecules across the membrane, but do not have a hydrophilic channel. They are specific to a particular molecule or ion. The molecule or ion on one side of the membrane fits into a specific binding site on the carrier protein. A slight conformational (shape) change in the

protein occurs so that the binding site becomes exposed to the other side of the membrane and the molecule or ion is released.

> **Remember**
>
> The cell surface membrane can be described as partially permeable. It is selective in the substances that pass across. Large molecules are not able to pass through the membrane. Only small non-polar molecules pass easily across the hydrophobic core of the phospholipid bilayer. Carrier and many channel proteins are very specific in the water-soluble substances that are transported.

Membrane fluidity

Cholesterol

- Cholesterol regulates the fluidity of membranes. It also adds stability to the membrane.
- Cholesterol molecules prevent close packing of phospholipids when temperatures decrease to help keep the membrane fluid. This means they increase fluidity in cold temperatures. When temperatures increase, they can prevent excessive movement of phospholipids and so act to decrease fluidity.

Saturated and unsaturated fatty acid tails of phospholipids

- The fatty acid tails of phospholipids can be saturated or unsaturated. In 2.2d, you learned that unsaturated fatty acids have hydrocarbon chains that have one or more double bonds. In phospholipids, these produce 'kinks' in the tails (which differ depending on the type of unsaturated fatty acid present). These kinks help to keep the membrane fluid as they prevent phospholipids from packing very closely to each other.

Fatty acid tails and hydrophobic interactions

- Another feature of the phospholipid bilayer is that the hydrocarbon chains of the fatty acids interact with each other. Shorter chains interact less and the phospholipids are less closely packed making the membrane more fluid.
- Hydrophobic interactions of the fatty acid tails contribute to membrane stability.

Phospholipid composition

- Membranes that have a high proportion of phospholipids with short fatty acid chains and that have unsaturated fatty acids with a high degree of bending (owing to the kinks) will be very fluid and flexible.

> **Remember**
>
> Cholesterol is not found in plant cell membranes. Plant sterols are membrane components that function in a similar way, and have the same roles, as cholesterol.

Varying proportions of cholesterol

- An increase in the proportion of cholesterol molecules makes the membrane less fluid.

Temperature

- An increase in temperature increases the fluidity of membranes. The increase in kinetic energy will increase the movement of molecules. Temperature is not a main factor when considering membrane fluidity in mammalian cells because they are in a constant temperature environment. However, unicellular organisms can vary their membrane composition in response to a changing external environment. A high temperature will affect tertiary and quaternary protein structure and very high temperatures can denature proteins and prevent them functioning. Microorganisms that live in high-temperature environments have heat-stable proteins in their membranes.

Cell signalling

Cell signalling is the process by which cells interact with their environment and with the cells around them. The main stages are as follows:

1 Synthesis and release of specific chemicals

   Particular cells synthesise and secrete (release) specific cell signalling molecules. Cell signalling molecules are examples of ligands, molecules that bind to other biological molecules. Many cell signalling molecules are glycoproteins or proteins.

2 Transport of ligands to target cells

   Cell signalling molecules are transported in the blood circulatory system. In the capillary network, they pass into the fluid surrounding body cells (tissue fluid). Only some body cells, known as target cells, respond to the presence of the cell signalling molecules. In plants, cell signalling molecules can be transported within phloem sap or move from cell to cell via plasmodesmata, or through the cell walls of cells.

3 Binding of ligands to cell surface receptors on target cells

   Target cells have membrane proteins that act as receptors for cell signalling molecules. Each type of cell signalling molecule only binds to a receptor that has a complementary shape, making cell signalling very specific.

4 Response by target cells

   The binding of a ligand to its specific receptor triggers events to occur within the target cell that eventually lead to the desired response.

Cell recognition

Some membrane proteins, glycoproteins and glycolipids are important in cell recognition. These molecules act as 'markers' on the surface of cells so that the cells of the immune system can identify the cells as 'self'. In this way, the immune system cells do not respond to their presence. The molecules are known as self-antigens.

If the cells are transferred into another organisms that has its own set of self-antigens, then the antigens will be considered foreign (non-self) and the cells will be destroyed in an immune response (see Chapter 11).

Remember

The binding of a ligand to a receptor on a target cell does not cause an immediate, direct response. 14.1g details the events that occur within a target cell in response to the binding of a hormone, glucagon.

Extension

The glycocalyx

In some animal cells, glycolipids and glycoproteins form part of an external surface known as the glycocalyx. The glycocalyx, in addition to having a role in cell recognition and cell-to-cell adhesion, can strengthen, protect and provide stability to the cell surface membrane.

Summary test 4.1b

Phospholipids form a (1) that encloses the cell contents and prevents the passage of polar molecules and (2) (charged particles). This is because the fatty acid tails form a (3) core region. (4)-soluble substances are transported across with the help of channel and (5) proteins. (6) molecules regulate the fluidity of membranes. The fluididty of a membrane is increased with an increase in the proportions of phospholipids with (7) fatty acid chains. Proteins, (8) and glycolipids can act as self-antigens and are important in cell (9). In cell signalling, cell signalling molecules, also termed (10), are released from cells and bind to cell surface (11) on (12) cells where events are triggered to produce a response.

Movement into and out of cells
a. Simple diffusion and facilitated diffusion

The movement of material into and out of cells occurs in a number of ways, some of which require energy **(active transport)** and some of which do not **(passive transport)**. Simple diffusion and **facilitated diffusion** are examples of passive transport.

Explanation of simple diffusion

As all movement requires energy, it is possibly confusing to describe **diffusion** as passive transport. What is meant by passive, in this sense, is that the energy comes from the natural, inbuilt motion **(kinetic energy)** of particles, rather than ATP from respiration. To help understand diffusion and other passive forms of transport it is necessary to understand that:

- all particles are constantly in motion due to the kinetic energy that they possess
- this motion is random, with no set pattern to the way the particles move around
- particles are constantly bouncing off one another as well as other objects, e.g. the sides of a vessel in which they are contained.

Given those facts, Figure 1 shows how particles concentrated together in part of a closed vessel become evenly distributed throughout the vessel, due to diffusion. Diffusion is therefore defined as *the net movement of molecules or ions from a region where they are more highly concentrated to one where their concentration is lower*.

These pages help you to:

- describe and explain the processes of simple diffusion and facilitated diffusion (4.2.1)

You will also:

- learn about Fick's Law

1. *If 10 particles occupying the left-hand side of a closed vessel are in random motion, they will collide with each other and the sides of the vessel. Some particles from the left-hand side move to the right, but initially there are no available particles to move in the opposite direction, so the movement is in one direction only. There is a large concentration gradient and diffusion is rapid.*

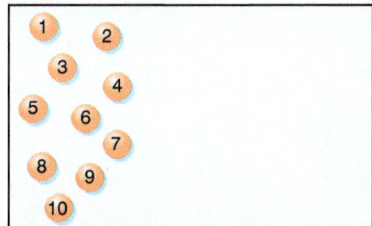

2. *After a short time the particles (still in random motion) have spread themselves more evenly. Particles can now move from right to left as well as from left to right. However, with a higher concentration of particles (7 particles) on the left than on the right (3 particles), there is a greater probability of a particle moving to the right than in the reverse direction There is a smaller concentration gradient and diffusion is slower.*

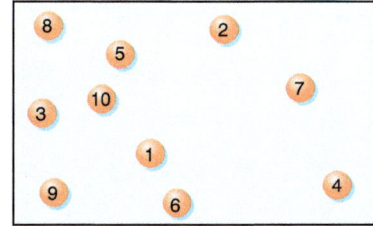

3. *Some time later, the particles will be evenly distributed throughout the vessel and the concentrations will be equal on each side. The system is in equilibrium. However, the particles are not static but remain in random motion. With equal concentrations on each side, the probability of a particle moving from left to right is equal to the probability of one moving in the opposite direction. There is no concentration gradient and no net diffusion.*

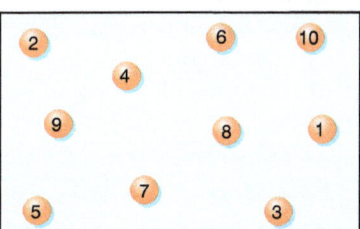

4. *At a later stage, the particles remain evenly distributed and will continue to do so. Although the number of particles on each side remains the same, individual particles are continuously changing position. This situation is called* **dynamic equilibrium**.

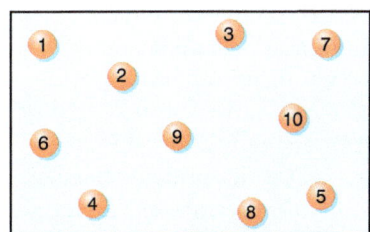

Figure 1 *Diffusion*

Rate of diffusion

A number of factors affect the rate at which molecules or ions diffuse. These include:

- **The concentration gradient** – the greater the difference in concentration between two regions of molecules or ions, the faster the rate of diffusion.
- **The area over which diffusion takes place** – the larger the area, the faster the rate of diffusion.
- **The distance over which diffusion occurs** – the shorter the distance, the faster the rate of diffusion.

Facilitated diffusion

Facilitated diffusion is a passive process relying only on the kinetic energy of the diffusing molecules. Like diffusion, it occurs along a concentration gradient, but it differs in that it occurs at specific locations in the membrane where there are channel and carrier proteins. These proteins allow the diffusion of water-soluble substances, including ions, across the membrane, avoiding the hydrophobic core of the phospholipid bilayer.

Many ion channels are selective. By having a channel with a specific shape, they allow one specific ion through. Although some ion channels remain open, most are closed until the ion is present, at which point they open allowing diffusion to occur (see 4.1b).

An alternative form of facilitated diffusion involves **carrier proteins** which also span the membrane. When a particular molecule specific to the protein is present it binds with the protein at a specific binding point, causing the protein to change shape (conformational change) in such a way that the molecule is released to the other side of the membrane (Figure 2). Again, energy from ATP is not used, and the molecules move from a region where they are highly concentrated to one of lower concentration, using only the kinetic energy of the molecules themselves.

Summary test 4.2a

Diffusion is the net movement of molecules or ions from where they are in a **(1)** concentration to a region where their concentration is **(2)**. The energy for this movement comes from the **(3)** energy of the molecules themselves and the process is therefore said to be a **(4)** one. If the area over which diffusion takes place is made smaller, its rate becomes **(5)**. If the concentration gradient is reduced, the rate becomes **(6)** and if the distance over which diffusion takes place is made shorter, its rate becomes **(7)**. Facilitated diffusion involves membrane transport proteins known as **(8)** proteins and carrier proteins. These proteins are selective and generally only allow one type of molecule or **(9)** to pass across. Carrier proteins have a specific **(10)** to which the molecule attaches and undergo a change in shape known as a **(11)** change, releasing the molecule on the other side of the cell surface membrane.

Extension

Fick's Law

The relationship between the concentration gradient, the surface area and the diffusion distance is expressed in **Fick's Law**, which states:

Diffusion is proportional to:

$$\frac{\text{surface area} \times \text{difference in concentration}}{\text{length of diffusion path}}$$

Although Fick's Law gives a good guide to the rate of diffusion, it is not wholly applicable to the movement of substances across membranes, because diffusion is also affected by:

- **the nature of the cell surface membrane** – its composition and number of carrier and channel proteins
- **the size and nature of the diffusing molecule** – for example:
  - small molecules diffuse faster than large ones
  - fat-soluble molecules such as glycerol diffuse faster than water-soluble ones such as glucose.

Surface area to volume ratio

As a shape such as a cube becomes larger, its volume increases at a greater rate than its surface area. In other words, the cube's surface area to volume ratio becomes smaller. This is illustrated with specific examples in 4.2e.

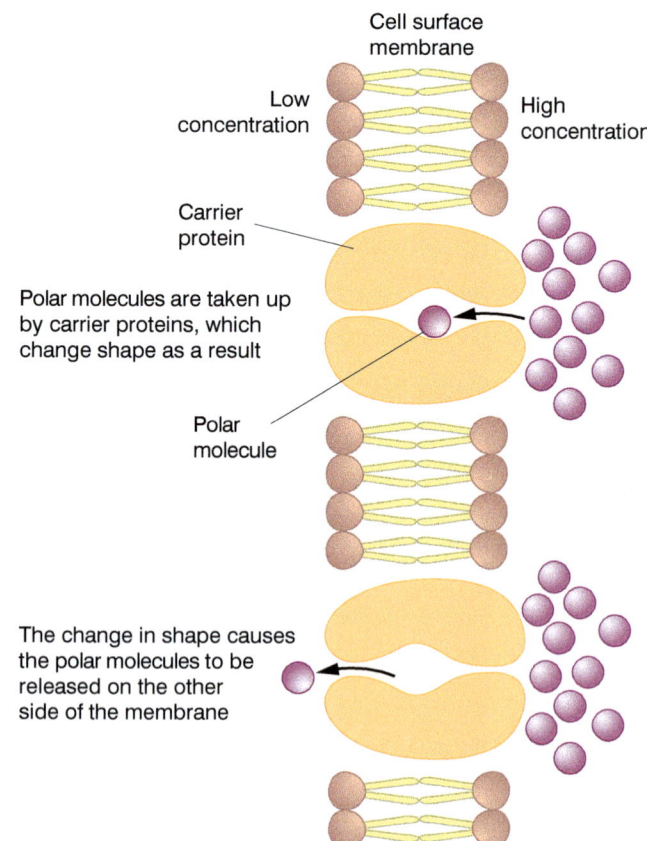

Figure 2 *Facilitated diffusion of a polar molecule involving carrier proteins*

b. Osmosis and water potential

Osmosis is a passive form of transport involving only water molecules. It is defined as *the passage of water from a region where it has a higher water potential to a region where it has a lower water potential, through a partially permeable membrane.* Cell surface membranes and other membranes, such as those surrounding organelles, are **partially (selectively) permeable**, i.e. they are permeable to water molecules and certain solute molecules but not to many other molecules. A **solute** is any substance that is dissolved in a **solvent**, e.g. glucose in water. The solute and the solvent together form a **solution**.

Explanation of osmosis

Consider the hypothetical situation in Figure 1, in which a partially permeable membrane separates two solutions.

- The solution on the left has more free water molecules while the solution on the right has fewer free water molecules.
- Both the solute and water molecules are in random motion due to their kinetic energy.
- The partially permeable membrane, however, only allows water molecules across it and not solute molecules.
- Solute molecules are unable to cross membranes because they are too large or they cannot cross the phospholipid bilayer as there are no specific carrier proteins to allow them through.
- The water molecules move from the left-hand side, which has the higher water potential, to the right-hand side, which has the lower water potential, i.e. down a water potential gradient.
- At the point where the water potentials on either side of the membrane are equal, a dynamic equilibrium is established and there is no **net** movement of water.

Remember

While diffusion can be the movement of any molecule, osmosis is the movement of water molecules only.

These pages help you to:

- describe and explain the process of osmosis (4.2.1)
- understand what is meant by water potential (4.2.2)

You will also:

- learn more about the factors that can affect water potential

Extension

There are many examples throughout this book where you can consider the functions of membranes that occur within cells. Table 1 outlines some functions.

Table 1 *Functions of membranes within cells*

- Control the entry and exit of materials in discrete organelles such as mitochondria and chloroplasts
- Isolate organelles so that specific metabolic reactions can take place within them
- Provide an internal transport system, e.g. endoplasmic reticulum
- Isolate enzymes that might damage the cell, e.g. lysosomes
- Provide surfaces on which processes can occur, e.g. protein synthesis using ribosomes on rough endoplasmic reticulum

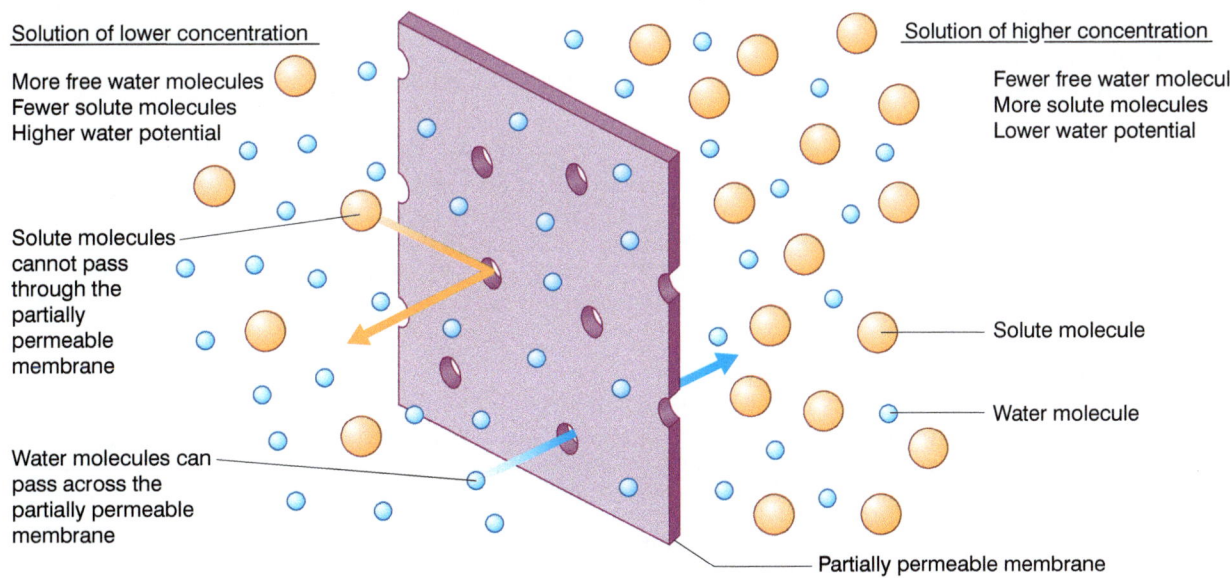

Solution of lower concentration

More free water molecules
Fewer solute molecules
Higher water potential

Solute molecules cannot pass through the partially permeable membrane

Water molecules can pass across the partially permeable membrane

Solution of higher concentration

Fewer free water molecules
More solute molecules
Lower water potential

Solute molecule

Water molecule

Partially permeable membrane

Figure 1 *Osmosis (Note: free water refers to water molecules that are available to move freely, for example those that are not interacting with solutes or other substances)*

Key

xkPa water potential of cell

➡ direction of water movment

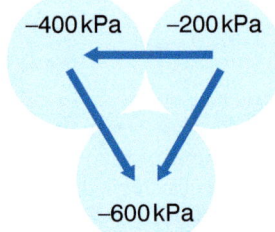

Water moves from higher water potential to lower water potential. The highest water potential is zero.

Figure 2 *Movement of water between cells down a water potential gradient*

Summary test 4.2b

Osmosis is the passage of **(1)** from a region where there is a higher water potential to a region where there is a lower water potential through a **(2)** membrane. Water potential is the **(3)** created by water molecules and its value for pure water is **(4)**. The addition of a solute to water makes its water potential **(5)**. If solution A has a water potential of −20 kPa and solution B has a water potential of −30 kPa, water will move into solution **(6)**. Osmosis does not require energy supplied by ATP, so it is a **(7)** process.

Water potential

Water potential is represented by the Greek letter psi (Ψ), and is measured in units of pressure, usually kilopascals (kPa). It is the pressure created by water molecules. Under standard conditions of temperature and pressure (25 °C and 100 kPa), pure water is said to have a water potential of zero. It follows that:

- the addition of a solute to pure water lowers its water potential
- the water potential of a solution (water + solute) must always be less than zero, i.e. a negative value
- the more solute that is added (i.e. the more concentrated a solution), the lower (more negative) its water potential
- water moves by osmosis from a region of higher (less negative) water potential (e.g. −10 kPa) to one of lower (more negative) water potential (e.g. −20 kPa). An example of how water moves between cells of different water potentials is shown in Figure 2.

c. Osmosis and cells

In 4.2b we looked at what osmosis is and why it occurs. We now need to turn our attention to how it affects living cells. Due to the structural differences between plant and animal cells, osmosis affects them in different ways.

Osmosis and animal cells

Animal cells, such as red blood cells, contain a variety of solutes dissolved in their watery cytoplasm. If a red blood cell is placed in pure water, water will move in by osmosis because the cytoplasm has a lower water potential. Cell surface membranes are very thin (7 nm) and, although they are flexible, they cannot stretch to any great extent. The cell surface membrane will therefore break, bursting the cell and releasing its contents – an event known as **lysis**. To prevent this happening, animal cells are normally surrounded by a liquid which has the same water potential as the cells. For example, normally the blood plasma and red blood cells have the same water potential. If a red blood cell is placed in a solution with a lower water potential than its own, water leaves by osmosis and the cell shrinks, causing its shape to shrivel (Figure 1).

These pages help you to:

- explain the movement of water between cells and solutions in terms of water potential (4.2.6)
- explain the different effects of the movement of water on plant cells and animal cells (4.2.6)
- outline how to investigate osmosis using plant tissue (4.2.2)

You will also:

- be able to compare the different effects of movement of water between plant and animal cells

Water potential (Ψ) of external solution compared to cell solution	Higher (less negative)	Equal	Lower (more negative)
Net movement of water	Enters cell	No net movement	Leaves cell
State of cell	Swells and bursts	No change	Shrinks
	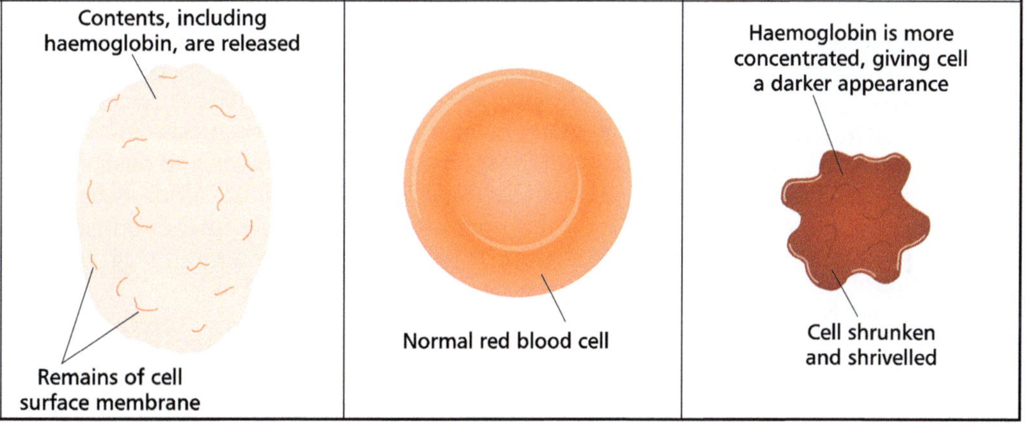 Contents, including haemoglobin, are released / Remains of cell surface membrane	Normal red blood cell	Haemoglobin is more concentrated, giving cell a darker appearance / Cell shrunken and shrivelled

Figure 1 *Summary of osmosis in an animal cell, e.g. a red blood cell*

Osmosis and plant cells

When studying osmosis in plant cells, the term **protoplast** is sometimes used. The **protoplast** is the plant cell without the cell wall, that is, the cell surface membrane and the cell contents, including the large permanent vacuole containing cell sap.

Like animal cells, plant cells also contain a variety of solutes, largely dissolved in the water of the large cell vacuole that each possesses. When placed in pure water, water moves in by osmosis because of their lower (more negative) water potential. Indeed, plant cells are normally permanently bathed in almost pure water, which is constantly absorbed by the plant's roots (7.2a).

Remember

- Pure water has a water potential (Ψ) of zero.
- Solute makes the water potential lower (more negative).
- Water always moves from a higher (less negative) water potential to a lower (more negative) one.

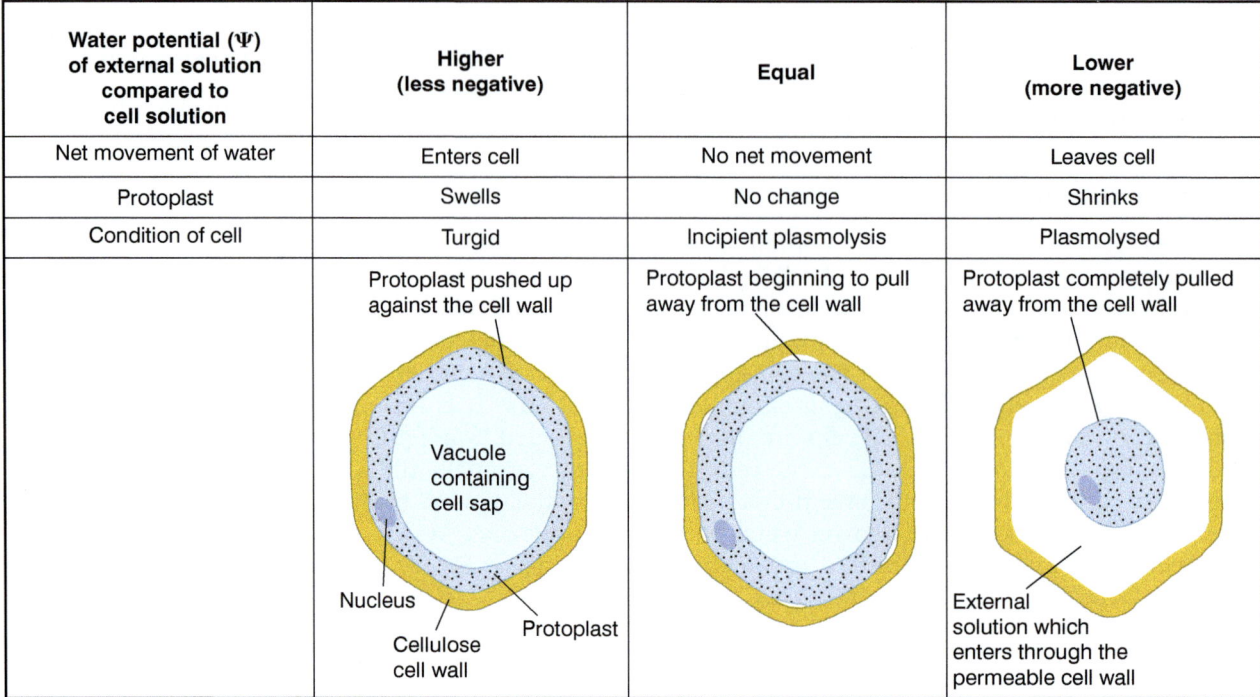

Water potential (Ψ) of external solution compared to cell solution	Higher (less negative)	Equal	Lower (more negative)
Net movement of water	Enters cell	No net movement	Leaves cell
Protoplast	Swells	No change	Shrinks
Condition of cell	Turgid	Incipient plasmolysis	Plasmolysed

Figure 2 *Summary of osmosis in a plant cell*

Practical skill

Observing plasmolysis

Using the method for making a temporary preparation of onion epidermis described in 1.1b, you can observe the changes that occur when a plant cell is immersed in a solution with a lower water potential. Use epidermis from a red onion: the vacuole of red onion epidermal cells contains red pigments (anthocyanins) and it is easier to see changes occurring.

Irrigate your prepared slide with 1.0 mol dm³ sodium chloride solution. The water potential of this solution is much lower than the water potential inside the cell. By irrigating the slide, you will be able to see the cells fully turgid before they come in contact with the sodium chloride solution and can then observe the cell surface membrane peeling away from the cell wall and the protoplast shrinking as water leaves the vacuole and cell by osmosis. Notice that the cell wall is fully permeable to the sodium chloride solution: the space between the cell wall and the shrinking protoplast is not air but sodium chloride solution.

So why don't the cells burst? The answer lies in the cellulose cell wall which surrounds every plant cell. How then does it work?

- The cellulose fibres of the cell wall have great tensile strength. The fibres are laid down in layers, with different layers at different angles to contribute to the overall strength and rigidity of the cell wall.
- Water entering a plant cell by osmosis enters the vacuole, which increases in size and causes the protoplast to swell and push against the cellulose cell wall.
- Because the cell wall is capable of only very limited extension, a pressure builds up on it that resists the further entry of water.
- Because it prevents more water entering, this pressure increases the water potential of the cell.
- In this situation, the protoplast of the cell is pushed against the cell wall and the cell is said to be turgid.

If the same plant cell is placed in a solution with a lower water potential than its own, water leaves by osmosis. The volume of the vacuole and hence the cell decreases. A stage is reached where the protoplast no longer presses on the cellulose cell wall. At this point the cell is said to be at **incipient plasmolysis**. Further loss of water causes the cell to shrink further and the cell surface membrane to begin to peel away from the cell wall. This condition is called plasmolysis. Figure 2 summarises osmosis in plant cells.

Summary test 4.2c

A red blood cell will burst if placed in a solution which has a **(1)** water potential than itself. To prevent this, animal cells such as red blood cells are normally surrounded by a solution that has the same **(2)** as themselves. A plant cell placed in pure water takes in water by **(3)**, causing the living contents, called the **(4)**, to swell. This creates a pressure on the **(5)**. This pressure prevents water entering and therefore makes the water potential **(6)**. If a plant cell is placed in a solution with a lower water potential than itself, the cell contents shrink away from the cell wall, a process called **(7)**.

Estimating the water potential of plant tissue

If plant tissue is placed into a solution that has the same water potential, then there will be no net movement of water into or out of the cells. This means that there will be no change in the mass of the tissue.

One method to estimate the water potential tissue is outlined below:

1 Prepare six different concentrations of sucrose solution, 0.0, 0.2, 0.4, 0.6, 0.8, 1.0 mol dm⁻³. Place equal volumes of each solution into six small beakers.

2 Cut six small cubes of potato of equal size and use filter or blotting paper to remove surface water.

3 Weigh one potato cube, record the mass and place it into the first beaker of sucrose solution.

4 Repeat step 3, placing one potato cube in each beaker.

5 After 30 minutes, remove the potato cubes, remove the surface solution and reweigh the cubes.

6 Calculate the percentage change in mass of each potato cube:

$$\text{Percentage change in mass} = \frac{\text{final mass} - \text{initial mass}}{\text{initial mass}} \times 100$$

7 Construct a graph of the percentage change in mass (*y* axis) against the concentration of the sucrose solution/mol dm⁻³ (*x* axis).

8 The point where the curve or line crosses the *x* axis is the concentration of sucrose solution where there is no change of mass (no net gain or loss of mass). This is the molarity (concentration) of sucrose solution that has the same water potential as the potato tuber cells. This molarity (mol dm⁻³) can be converted to a water potential (kPa) by looking up the value in conversion tables. Alternatively, conversion tables can be used to convert the different concentrations of sucrose solution to water potentials, and these can be used for the *x* axis.

This is an outline method. To develop your skills in planning investigations, refer back to 3.2a to consider the extra information you would add, including a risk assessment, to make this a detailed set of instructions that could be followed successfully and safely.

Investigating simple diffusion and osmosis using dialysis tubing

Dialysis (or Visking) tubing is artificial membrane tubing that can be used for investigations of osmosis and simple diffusion. The tubing is manufactured with pores of a particular diameter, for example, large enough for glucose molecules to pass through but too small for sucrose, proteins or starch molecules to pass through.

Osmosis

To show osmosis, sucrose solution containing food colouring is added to a section of dialysis tubing. The molecules in the food colouring are also too large to pass through the pores of the tubing. The tubing is tied at one end and a syringe is used to add the sucrose solution. The other end of the tubing is tied around a bung with a capillary tube inserted. The outside of the tubing is rinsed with distilled water to remove any sucrose solution. Then the tube is placed in a beaker of distilled water. Figure 1 (on page 84) summarises this simple investigation.

These pages help you to:

- describe how to estimate the water potential of the plant tissues by investigating the effects of immersing the tissues in solutions of different water potentials (4.2.5)
- describe how to investigate simple diffusion and osmosis using dialysis tubing (4.2.2)

You will also:

- develop planning skills

Remember

Calculating percentage changes allows us to make valid comparisons. In the method to estimate water potential, two potato cubes may be slightly different masses at the start of the experiment. Stating that one cube increased by 5 g and another by 8 g is raw data only and does not show the proportionate change in mass of each. The 5 g may be an increase from an initial 20 g cube, so will be a 25% increase, whereas the 8 g increase may be on a 40 g cube, so only a 20% increase.

Remember

If the balance used to weigh the potato cubes is not calibrated (for example, all readings are 0.5 g higher than the true mass of the cubes), then all results are shifted in the same direction. Repeating the experiment using the same balance will still produce the same **systematic error**. The student will not know the error has occurred and should have planned to use a calibrated balance to increase accuracy in the results.

The results may vary because of **random errors**. For example, by using different potatoes to cut the cubes. If a ruler and knife are used to obtain the potato cubes, it is not possible to cut exactly the same size cubes. Some ways to minimise random errors: increase precision by using callipers to measure, a scalpel to cut cubes, use the same potato for all cubes, repeating the experiment to calculate means.

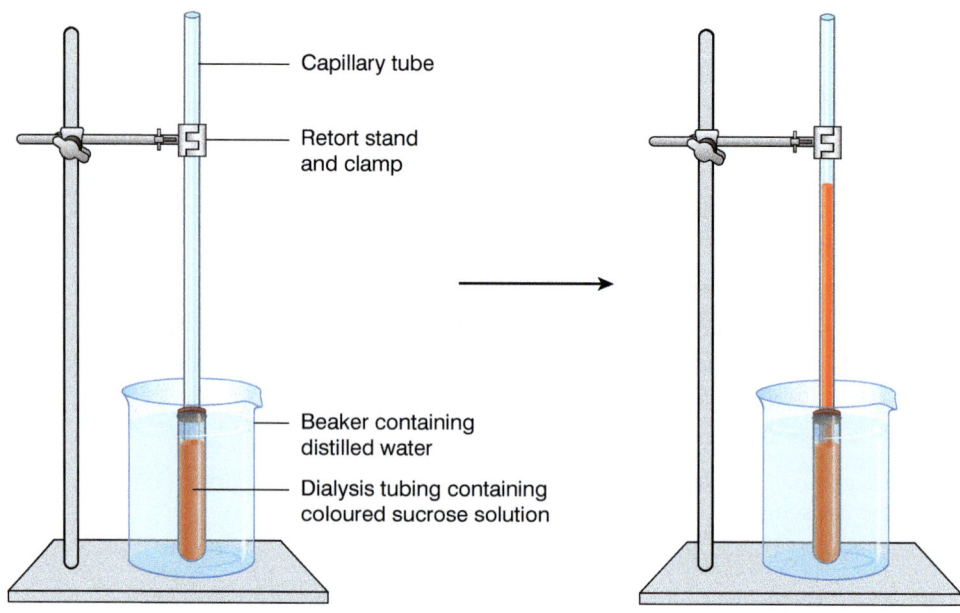

Figure 1 *Investigating osmosis using dialysis tubing*

The solution in the tubing has a lower water potential than the external solution (water, with water potential of zero). Water moves into the tubing by osmosis down the water potential gradient and, over time, this causes the dialysis tubing to swell; the increase in volume in the tubing pushes solution up the capillary tube.

Diffusion

Diffusion can also be investigated using dialysis tubing; for example, by adding a mixture of glucose and starch to a section of tubing tied at the end, tying the top and placing it in a beaker of distilled water (Figure 2).

- Water in the external medium enters the dialysis tubing by osmosis down the water potential gradient.
- Glucose molecules diffuse out of the tubing down the concentration gradient into the external medium.
- Glucose molecules and water molecules are small enough to pass through the pores of the dialysis tubing.
- Starch molecules are too large to leave the tubing.
- There are more water molecules entering the mixture in the tubing than glucose molecules leaving, so the tubing swells (and is of a greater mass than at the start of the investigation).

The presence of glucose inside and outside the tubing is confirmed using samples heated with Benedict's solution (2.1b). Alternatively, test strips specific for glucose can be used (see 3.2d Extension).

The presence of starch inside the tubing and the absence of starch in the external solution is confirmed using iodine solution (2.1b).

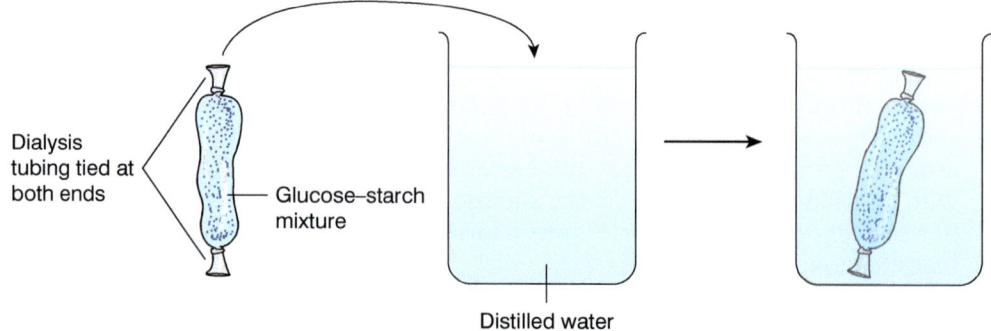

Figure 2 *Investigating diffusion using dialysis tubing*

Improving your practical work

Accuracy

Accuracy is the closeness of agreement between your measurement and the 'true' (correct) measurement. Your measurement is an estimate of the true measurement.

You should aim for a set of accurate results as they will be close to the true results and will improve the validity and reliability of the conclusions that you draw.

Precision

How closely your measurements agree when you repeat an experiment is an indication of precision. Precise measurements do not mean accurate measurements. Choosing the correct apparatus or techniques to make measurements can improve precision.

Error

The difference between your results and the true results is known as 'error'. Error is a combination of two main components, systematic error and random error.

Systematic errors cause all your results to be shifted in the same way so that all your results are either overestimated or underestimated. Repeating the experiment will still give the same shift in the results from the true values. You may not know that a systematic error has occurred because they may not affect the trend in the results.

With random errors, your results vary in an unpredictable way and affect the trend in the results. Here, repeating an experiment gives more measurements and calculating a mean helps to make the results closer to the true results (as some may be overestimates, whereas others may be underestimates). Chance variation that occurs with random errors cannot always be explained.

An error is an inaccuracy in measurement – it is not a mistake that you have made when carrying out the experiment.

Uncertainty

There is always some uncertainty in the measurements you obtain. Results are commonly shown with a degree of uncertainly. For example, you have measured the length of a potato cube as 36 mm. Your ruler has markings every 1 mm and you can be sure that the measurement is more than 35.5 mm but less than 36.5 mm. You record your measurement as 36 ± 0.5 mm, to show the range within which you think the true measurement lies.

Reliability

The more you can do to minimise errors and uncertainty, the more reliable your results become. This means that the conclusions you make are more valid. One way to help improve reliability is to carry out more repeats of the experiment or investigation.

Validity

When you are successful at measuring the intended dependent variable, your results are said to be valid. The results can then be reliably used for conclusions to be drawn. Factors that may limit the validity of results should be identified in planning investigations and where possible, should be standardised (controlled). Identifying factors that cannot be (or are not) standardised will help you to make judgements about the validity of your results.

These pages help you to:

- calculate surface areas and volumes of simple three-dimensional shapes (4.2.3)
- understand the relationship between size and surface area to volume ratios (4.2.3)
- describe how to investigate simple diffusion using agar (4.2.2)
- describe how to investigate the effect of changing surface area to volume ratio on diffusion using agar blocks of different sizes (4.2.4)

You will also:

- have a better understanding of terminology used in practical work
- understand how to improve the validity of your results when carrying out practical work

Example

In an experiment to estimate the water potential of potato tissue, a student used a balance to weigh cubes of potato (measured using a ruler and cut using a knife). The balance had not been calibrated correctly by the technician and all readings were 0.5 g higher than the true mass of the cubes.

All the masses will be overestimates: they will appear to be a higher mass than their true value. This is an example of a systematic error as all results are shifted in the same direction and repeating the experiment using the same miscalibrated balance will still produce the same systematic error. The student may not be aware of the miscalibration.

In an experiment such as this, random errors could be present because it is not possible to cut cubes to exactly the same size, or the potato cubes could have been cut from different potatoes.

A more accurate set of results could be obtained by:

- minimising systematic error by using a correctly calibrated balance
- minimising random errors by, for example:
  - using callipers to measure and a scalpel to cut cubes – to increase precision
  - cutting the cubes from the same potato – to increase precision
  - repeating the experiment to calculate means.

Practical skill

Calculating surface areas and volumes of simple three-dimensional shapes

Cuboids

A cuboid is a three-dimensional shape that has six faces, like a cube, but the faces are not all of equal dimensions. Figure 1 shows two different cuboids. Notice that, even though they have the same surface area, the volumes, and hence the SA:V are different.

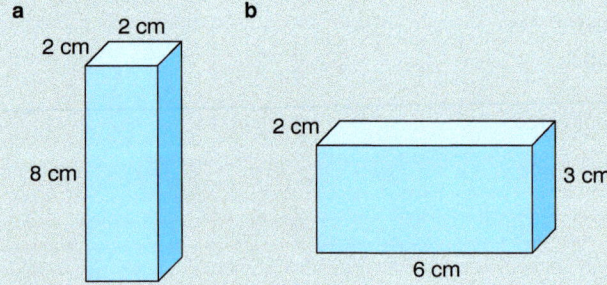

Figure 1 Cuboids

Surface area for cuboid **a:**
two sides measure 2 × 2 cm = 4 (× 2) = 8 cm²
four sides measure 8 × 2 cm = 16 (× 4) = 64 cm²
$$\text{Total SA} = 72 \text{ cm}^2$$
Volume for cuboid **a:** 8 × 2 × 2 = 32 cm³

$$\text{SA:V} = \frac{72}{32} = 2.25{:}1$$

Surface area for cuboid **b:**
two sides measure 2 × 3 cm = 6 (× 2) = 12 cm²
two sides measure 6 × 2 cm = 12 (× 2) = 24 cm²
two sides measure 6 × 3 cm = 18 (× 2) = 36 cm²
$$\text{Total SA} = 72 \text{ cm}^2$$
Volume for cuboid **b:** 6 × 3 × 2 = 36 cm³

$$\text{SA:V} = \frac{72}{36} = 2{:}1$$

Cylinders

The surface area of a cylinder $= 2\pi r^2 + 2\pi r h$

The volume of a cylinder $= \pi r^2 h$

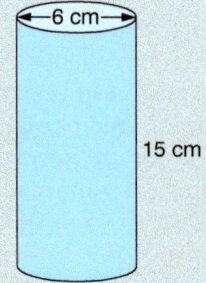

Surface area $= (2 \times \pi \times 3^2) + (2 \times \pi \times 3 \times 15)$ cm²
$= 56.6 + 282.7$ cm²
$= 339.3$ cm²
Volume $= \pi \times 3^2 \times 15$ cm³
$= 424.1$ cm³
SA:V = 0.8:1

Practical skill

Investigating simple diffusion using agar blocks with different surface area to volume ratios.

Agar blocks containing a pH indicator can be prepared to investigate diffusion.

Cubes of different dimensions are cut from agar blocks containing a pH indicator. The indicator changes colour as dilute hydrochloric acid diffuses into the cube, so it is possible to 'see' diffusion occurring and to make comparisons between the different-sized cubes. The time taken for each cube to change colour completely can be timed to give an end point. In practice, judging an end point is very difficult (and is an example of a random error).

To make a quantitative comparison, the surface area to volume ratio (SA:V) of the cubes needs to be calculated. Table 1 shows the SA:V for 6 cubes of different dimensions.

Table 1 *How the surface area to volume ratio gets smaller as an object becomes larger*

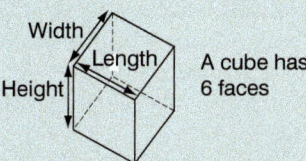

Length of edge of a cube/cm	Surface area of whole cube (area of one face × 6)/cm²	Volume of cube (length × width × height)/cm³	Ratio of surface area to volume (surface area ÷ volume)
1	1 × 6 = 6	1 × 1 × 1 = 1	$\frac{6}{1}$ = 6.0:1
2	4 × 6 = 24	2 × 2 × 2 = 8	$\frac{24}{8}$ = 3.0:1
3	9 × 6 = 54	3 × 3 × 3 = 27	$\frac{54}{27}$ = 2.0:1
4	16 × 6 = 96	4 × 4 × 4 = 64	$\frac{96}{64}$ = 1.5:1
5	25 × 6 = 150	5 × 5 × 5 = 125	$\frac{150}{125}$ = 1.2:1
6	36 × 6 = 216	6 × 6 × 6 = 216	$\frac{216}{216}$ = 1.0:1

- As the cubes increase in size from 1 × 1 × 1 cm to 6 × 6 × 6 cm, the SA:V decreases from 6:1 to 1:1.

- Although the surface area of the largest cube is 36 times larger than the smallest cube, there is *less* surface area for each unit of volume in the larger cube.

- It will take a longer time for the largest cube to change colour completely than the smallest cube.

- If the cubes represent living organisms, this means that essential molecules such as oxygen and glucose will take much longer to diffuse to the 'centre' of the largest organism than the smallest organism.

Remember

Practise calculations of surface area and volumes of cuboids and cylinders. You can make up your own dimensions, and then check if your final calculated values are correct by using formulae functions on a calculator or on the internet.

If you find it difficult to remember the formula for the surface area of a cylinder, then try to recall your knowledge of the formulae for surface area of a circle, A = πr^2 and the circumference of a circle, C = $2\pi r$.

The ends of the cylinder are two circles, so SA = $2 \times \pi r^2$.

If a cylinder is cut lengthways a rectangle would be obtained. This means that the surface area is the circumference of the circle × height of the cylinder (*h*), so SA = $2\pi r \times h$.

Therefore, the total area of the cylinder is $2\pi r^2 + 2\pi r h$.

Summary test 4.2e

In an investigation into the effect of surface area to volume ratios (SA:V) on **(1)**, a student cut different sized agar cubes containing a **(2)** indicator. The cubes were immersed in dilute **(3)**. The larger cube took a **(4)** time to change colour completely because it had a smaller **(5)**. To improve the **(6)** of the results, the student repeated the investigation three times. In this investigation, **(7)** errors could have occurred as a result of the methods used to measure and cut the cubes. To calculate the **(8)** of a cylinder, the formula $\pi r^2 h$ can be used. The formula to calculate the surface area of a cylinder is $2\pi r^2 +$ **(9)**.

These pages help you to:

- describe and explain the process of active transport (4.2.1)
- describe and explain the processes of endocytosis and exocytosis (4.2.1)

You will also:

- be able to compare different mechanisms of transport across cell surface membranes

Remember

Active transport and facilitated diffusion both use carrier proteins but while facilitated diffusion occurs down a concentration gradient, active transport occurs against a concentration gradient. This means that facilitated diffusion does not require metabolic energy, while active transport does. The metabolic energy is provided in the form of ATP.

Active transport is the *movement of molecules or ions across the cell surface membrane into or out of a cell from a region of lower concentration to a region of higher concentration using energy and carrier molecules.*

The main features of active transport are:

- Metabolic energy supplied by ATP is needed.
- Materials are moved against a concentration gradient (i.e. from a lower to a higher concentration).
- Carrier protein molecules, which act as 'pumps', are involved.
- The protein molecules undergo a change in shape (conformational change).
- The process is very selective, with specific substances being transported.

Some cells need greater quantities of a particular molecule or ion than they can take up by passive mechanisms of transport. They therefore need to use active transport to take up the ions. For example, the concentration of mineral ions in the soil solution is so low that root hair cells of plants need to use active transport to take up most of their required ions, such as nitrate and phosphate ions. In the lumen of the intestine, glucose is actively transported into intestinal epithelial cells. It would be wasteful to take up glucose by facilitated diffusion because, after a meal, only part of the glucose produced as a result of digestion would be absorbed.

Mechanism of active transport

An example of active transport of an ion is described below:

- The carrier proteins span the cell surface membrane and accept the ions to be transported on one side of it.
- The ions bind to specific binding sites on the inside of the carrier protein.
- On the cytosol side of the cell surface membrane, ATP binds to the carrier protein causing ATP to split into ADP and Pi (inorganic phosphate). As a result, the protein molecule changes shape and opens to the opposite side of the membrane.
- The ions are then released to the other side of the membrane.
- Inorganic phosphate is released from the protein (ADP and Pi can be re-used to produce ATP molecules in respiration, Chapter 12).
- This causes the protein to return to its original shape, ready for the process to be repeated.

These events are illustrated in Figure 1.

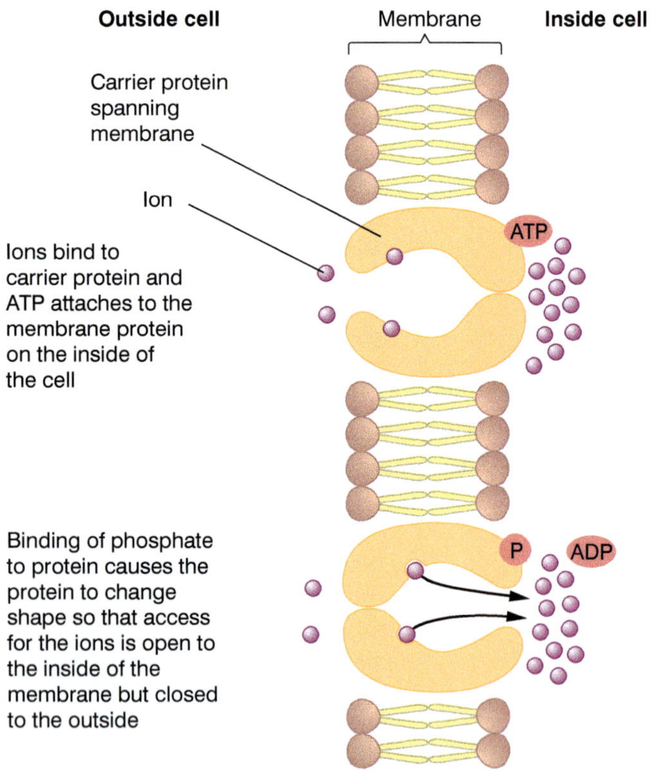

One kind of active transport involves the ion moving into a cell at the same time as a different one is being removed from it. One example of this is the **sodium–potassium pump**.

In the sodium–potassium pump, sodium ions are actively removed from the cell while potassium ions are actively taken in from the surroundings. This process is essential to a number of important processes in organisms including the creation of a nerve impulse.

Outside cell   Membrane   **Inside cell**

Carrier protein spanning membrane

Ion

Ions bind to carrier protein and ATP attaches to the membrane protein on the inside of the cell

ATP

Binding of phosphate to protein causes the protein to change shape so that access for the ions is open to the inside of the membrane but closed to the outside

P   ADP

Figure 1 *Active transport*

Requirements for active transport

Certain conditions are necessary if a cell is to carry out active transport effectively. These include:

- the presence of numerous mitochondria
- a ready supply of ATP
- a high rate of respiration.

Clearly, any factor that affects the rate of respiration will affect active transport, and therefore higher temperatures up to an optimum, or an increased supply of oxygen, will increase the rate of active transport. Lower temperatures, less oxygen or the presence of respiratory inhibitors, such as cyanide, will slow the rate of active transport.

Bulk transport across the cell surface membrane

The two forms of bulk movement require ATP (Figure 2).

Endocytosis

Endocytosis is the bulk movement of material into a cell by active means. It takes two forms:

- Phagocytosis involves the invagination (folding in of itself) of the cell surface membrane to form a cup-shaped depression in which large particles or even whole organisms are contained. The depression is then pinched off to the inside of the cell, forming a vesicle. When the vesicle pinches off, the two areas of cell surface membrane meet and fuse so that the membrane remains intact. In unicellular (single-celled) organisms such as *Amoeba* sp., phagocytosis is used as a method of feeding. A few specialised cells in higher organisms also carry out phagocytosis (see 11.1a).
- **Pinocytosis** is very similar to phagocytosis, except that the vesicles formed are smaller. Pinocytosis is often used for the uptake of liquids.

Exocytosis

Exocytosis is the bulk movement of material out of the cell. It is the reverse of phagocytosis and pinocytosis. Vesicles, budded off from a Golgi body within the cell, move towards the cell surface membrane along microtubules (1.2d and e). They fuse with the cell surface membrane and their contents are expelled into the medium outside. In higher organisms, exocytosis is used to release hormones, e.g. insulin, from the cells that manufacture them.

> **Remember**
>
> Carrier proteins for active transport are also found in the membranes within cells, such as the tonoplast of the vacuole and the membranes of chloroplasts and mitochondria.

> **Remember**
>
> Table 1 compares transport mechanisms across membranes.

Table 1 *Comparison of different forms of transport*

Process	Occurs against a concentration gradient	Needs ATP to supply energy	May use carrier molecules
Simple diffusion	No	No	No
Facilitated diffusion	No	No	Yes
Osmosis	No	No	No
Active transport	Yes	Yes	Yes

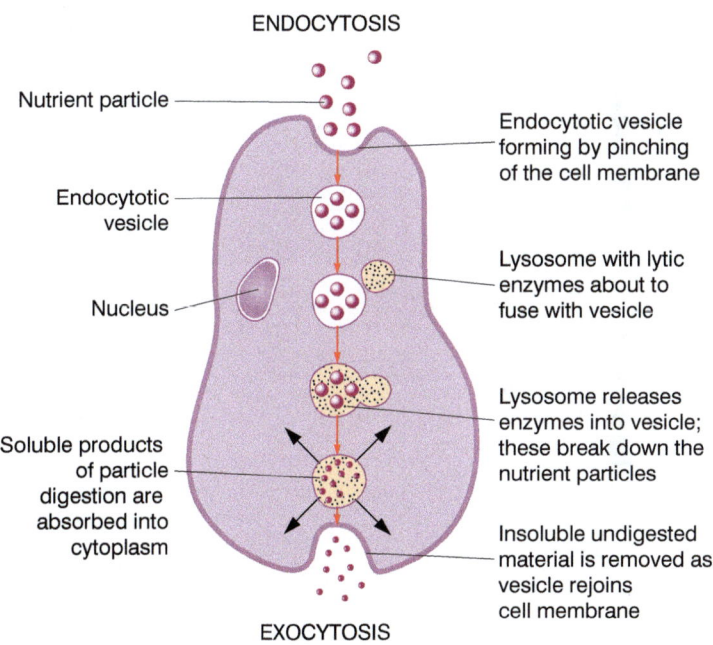

Figure 2 *Example of endocytosis and exocytosis*

ENDOCYTOSIS

- Nutrient particle
- Endocytotic vesicle
- Nucleus
- Soluble products of particle digestion are absorbed into cytoplasm

- Endocytotic vesicle forming by pinching of the cell membrane
- Lysosome with lytic enzymes about to fuse with vesicle
- Lysosome releases enzymes into vesicle; these break down the nutrient particles
- Insoluble undigested material is removed as vesicle rejoins cell membrane

EXOCYTOSIS

Summary test 4.2f

Active transport occurs **(1)** a concentration gradient. It requires energy supplied by **(2)** and cells exhibiting active transport therefore have numerous **(3)** and a high **(4)** rate. The bulk movement of molecules and particles across the cell surface membrane is called **(5)**. Where this movement is into the cell, it is called **(6)**. Where this movement is out of the cell, it is called **(7)**. The invagination of a cell surface membrane to ingest particles and form a vesicle is known as **(8)**, whereas the invagination of the membrane to ingest liquids and form a vesicle is known as **(9)**.

4 Exam-style and practice questions

(📖 **Launch additional digital resources for the chapter**)

4 Exam-style questions

1 State what happens to an animal cell when it is placed in a solution with a less negative water potential.

  A It loses solutes to the solution and swells.

  B It loses water by osmosis and shrinks.

  C It takes in solutes and swells.

  D It takes in water by osmosis and bursts. *(1 mark)*

2 Figure 1 shows a diagram of a cell surface (plasma) membrane.

Figure 1

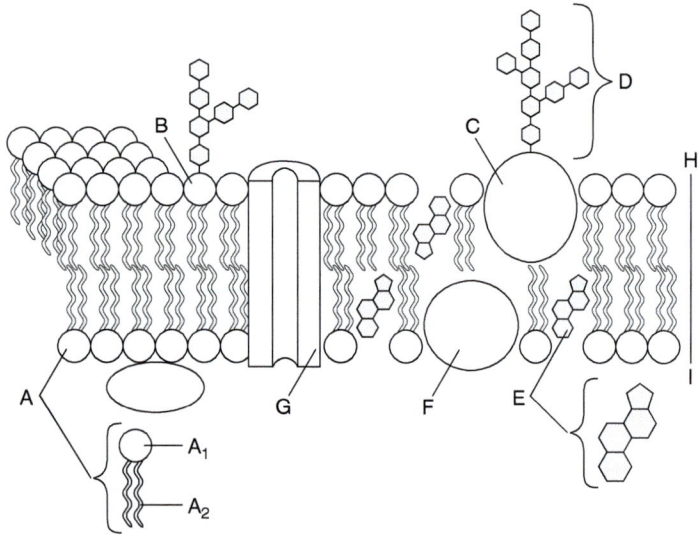

  a Identify the following parts of the membrane shown in Figure 1.

  i A_1

  ii A_2

  iii E

  iv G *(4 marks)*

  b Outline the functions of the following components of the cell surface membrane.

  i C

  ii E

  iii G *(3 marks)*

  c State the width of the membrane shown in Figure 1.
  (1 mark)

  d The structure of the membrane shown in Figure 1 is known as a 'fluid mosaic'.

  Explain why 'fluid mosaic' is a suitable name to use to describe membrane structure. *(3 marks)*

  e Lipid soluble molecules such as vitamins A and D can be absorbed from the lumen of the small intestine by simple diffusion. Water-soluble vitamins such as vitamins B and C are absorbed by facilitated diffusion.

  i Explain the difference between simple and facilitated diffusion. *(1 mark)*

  ii State why two methods of diffusion are needed for vitamins A and C. *(2 marks)*

  (Total 14 marks)

3 **a** A student carried out an investigation, looking at the effect of temperature on beetroot tissue. Beetroot cells contain dark red pigment called betalain stored inside their vacuoles.

  The student:

  • removed the skin from the beetroot

  • cut the beetroot tissue into 27 cubes of the same size

  • washed the cubes thoroughly in distilled water

  • placed 3 cubes into each of 9 test tubes containing distilled water at 9 different temperatures.

  After 20 minutes, samples of the water were removed and placed in a colorimeter to measure the absorption of light. The higher the absorption of light, the more betalain is present in the water.

  The results are shown in Figure 2.

Figure 2

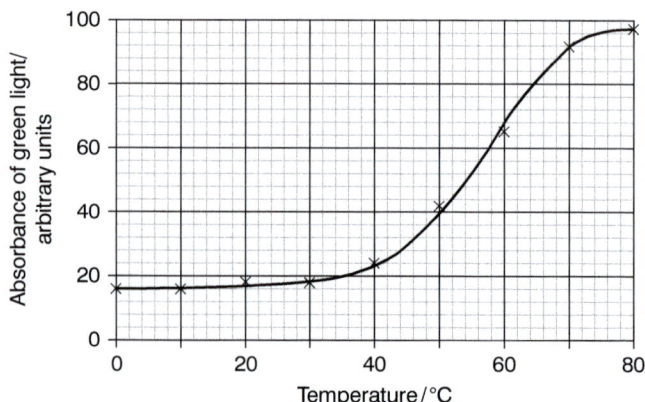

i Describe the student's results. *(3 marks)*

ii Explain the effect of increasing temperature on the beetroot tissue. *(3 marks)*

b Substances can move into and out of cells through cell surface membranes.

Sodium ion pumps are found in many cell surface membranes and their function is to remove sodium ions from the cell. This maintains a higher concentration of sodium ions outside of the cell than inside.

Figure 3 shows the movement of sodium ions across a cell surface membrane.

Figure 3

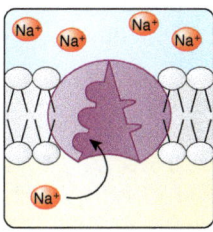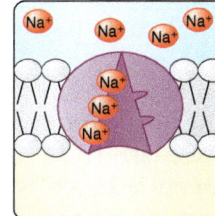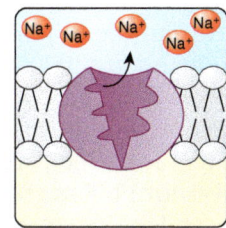

i Identify and describe the process by which sodium ions move across the membrane. *(3 marks)*

ii Explain why the sodium pump would not be able to pump calcium ions out of the cell. *(2 marks)*

(Total 11 marks)

4 Practice questions

4 Glucose must be taken into cells so that it can be used as a substrate for respiration.

a Glucose molecules mostly diffuse into cells through the carrier proteins that span the phospholipid bilayer. Why do they not pass easily through the phospholipid bilayer?

b State **two** changes to the structure of cell surface membranes that would increase the rate at which glucose diffuses into a cell.

c State four factors that may affect the rate at which a substance may diffuse across a cell surface membrane.

5 a What is meant by a partially permeable membrane?

b Under standard conditions of pressure and temperature, what is the water potential of pure water?

c Four cells have the following water potentials:

Cell A = −200 kPa   Cell C = −100 kPa

Cell B = −250 kPa   Cell D = −150 kPa.

In what order could the cells be placed for water to pass from one cell to the next if arranged in a line?

6 a Explain why an animal cell placed in pure water bursts, while a plant cell placed in pure water does not.

b Plant cells that have a water potential of −600 kPa are placed in solutions of different water potentials. State in each of the following cases whether, after 10 minutes, the cells would be turgid, plasmolysed or at incipient plasmolysis.

Solution A = −400 kPa   Solution C = −900 kPa

Solution B = −600 kPa   Solution D = pure water

c If an animal cell with a water potential of −700 kPa was placed in each of the solutions, in which solutions is it likely to burst?

7 a State one similarity and one difference between active transport and facilitated diffusion.

b The presence of many mitochondria is typical of cells that carry out active transport. Explain why this is so.

c In the making of urine, glucose is initially lost from the blood but is then reabsorbed back into it by cells in the kidneys. Explain why it is important that this reabsorption occurs by active transport rather than diffusion.

5.1 Replication and division of nuclei and cells

a. Chromosome structure and the mitotic cell cycle

The cells that make up organisms always arise from existing cells by the process of division. This occurs in two main stages:

- **Nuclear division** is the process by which the nucleus divides. There are two types of nuclear division:
  - **Mitosis**, results in two daughter nuclei having the same number of chromosomes as the parent nucleus. The nuclei formed are normally genetically identical to the parent one. If the parent nucleus has two complete sets of chromosomes (diploid), then each daughter nucleus contains two complete sets (diploid).
  - **Meiosis**, results in four daughter nuclei having half the number of chromosomes as the parent nucleus. The nuclei formed have a genetic composition different from the parent one (see 16.1a, 16.1b, 16.1c).
- **Cytokinesis (cell division)** follows nuclear division, and is the process by which the whole cell divides and the cytoplasm is shared out between the new cells.

The mitotic cell cycle

Cells do not divide continuously, but undergo a regular cycle of division separated by periods of cell growth. This is known as the **cell cycle** (Figure 1) and has three main stages:

- **Interphase** – occupies most of the cell cycle, and is sometimes known as the resting phase, because no division takes place. In one sense, this could hardly

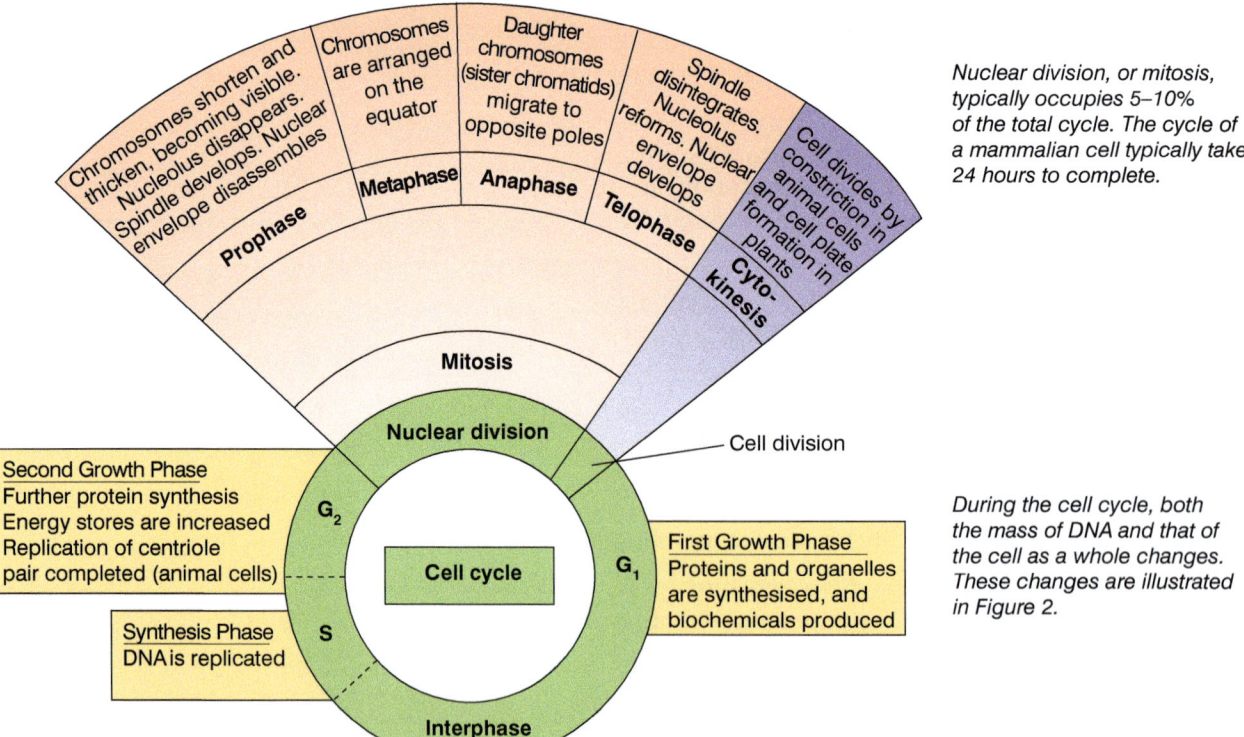

Nuclear division, or mitosis, typically occupies 5–10% of the total cycle. The cycle of a mammalian cell typically takes 24 hours to complete.

During the cell cycle, both the mass of DNA and that of the cell as a whole changes. These changes are illustrated in Figure 2.

Figure 1 *The cell cycle (Note: the length of a typical cell cycle varies between different species; within a species, it can vary greatly with different cell types)*

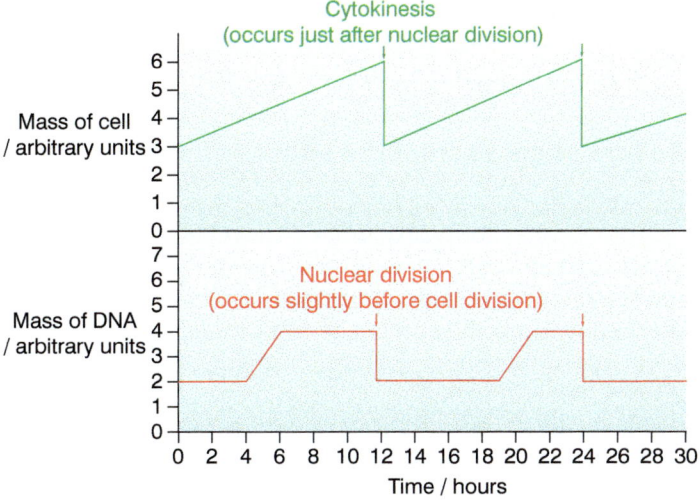

Figure 2 *Variations in the mass of a diploid cell and DNA within it during two cell cycles*

be further from the truth, as interphase is a period of intense chemical activity, divided into three parts:

- **First growth (G_1) phase**, when the cell is synthesising proteins required for cell growth, including enzymes. At this time, there is a great quantity of messenger RNA (mRNA) for polypeptide synthesis at the ribosomes (see transcription and translation in Chapter 6). More cell organelles are also synthesised in the G_1 phase.
- **Synthesis (S) phase**, when DNA is replicated. Following replication, each interphase chromosome is now composed of two structures (the sister chromatids that can be seen in mitosis), each containing identical molecules of DNA.
- **Second growth (G_2) phase**, when the cell continues to grow, mitochondria divide and there is a further increase in the quantity of other organelles ready for cell division. There is intensive preparation for mitosis. By the end of the G_2 phase, there is a large enough store of microtubules for the formation of the spindle. In animal cells, the pair of centrioles (see 1.2e) complete their replication (started earlier in interphase) so that there are now two pairs of centrioles.
- **Mitosis**, which is subdivided into prophase, metaphase, anaphase and telophase and results in nuclear division to produce two nuclei.
- **Cytokinesis**, when the cell divides into two and cytoplasm, organelles and other cell structures are shared out between the two new daughter cells. Each cell has its own nucleus.

Chromosome structure

Chromosomes have a characteristic shape, occur in pairs in diploid cells and carry the hereditary (genetic) material of the cell. Chromosomes are only visible as discrete structures when a cell is dividing. The rest of the time, they consist of widely spread areas of darkly staining material called **chromatin**. When they are first visible, chromosomes appear as long, thin threads around 50 μm long. They are made up of two genetically identical sister **chromatids**, joined at a point called the **centromere** (Figure 3 and Figure 4).

Chromosomes are made up mainly of:

- **proteins** (70%), mostly in the form of highly basic (alkaline) proteins known as **histone** proteins.
- **deoxyribonucleic acid** – DNA (15%).

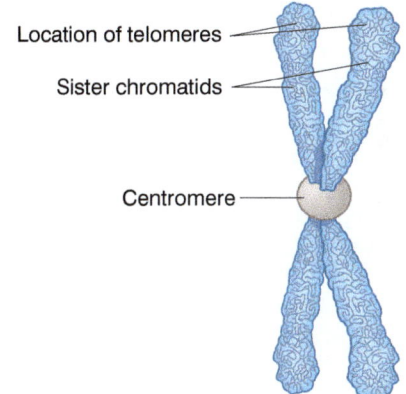

Figure 3 *Structure of a chromosome during the prophase and metaphase stages of mitosis*

Remember

You should be able to draw a chromosome, such as Figure 3, and label your drawing to show the parts of the chromosome.

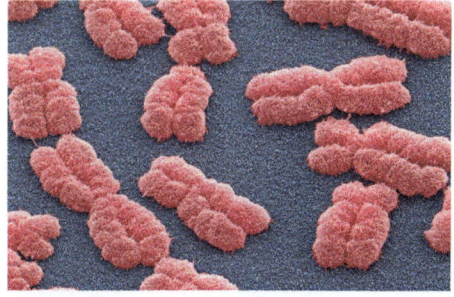

Figure 4 *Colourised scanning electron micrograph of a group of human chromosomes*

To fit in, the considerable length of DNA found in each cell (around 2 metres in humans) is highly coiled and folded. This DNA is held in position by histone proteins. The DNA and histones together form a complex known as **chromatin**.

Telomeres prevent the loss of genes from the ends of chromosomes

At the ends of each chromosome there is a region, called the telomere, where a sequence of **nucleotide bases** is repeated many times. This repeated sequence acts as a protection for genes further along the chromosome and does not contain genetic information. When cells divide, the enzymes that replicate DNA are unable to continue to work to the end of the DNA molecules in each of the chromosomes. As a result some genetic material is missing from the end of the new chromosomes. The lost genetic material is part of the telomere repeated base sequence. This means that the genes located near the ends of the chromosomes, which contain vital genetic information, are protected and are not lost. After repeated cell divisions, the telomeres are used up and the cell dies. The length of telomeres therefore determines the life span of cells. Cells that keep the ability to divide by mitosis have a mechanism to add more bases to the ends of the chromosomes. This helps to slow down the shortening of chromosome ends and allows the cell to carry out many mitotic cell cycles.

Nucleosomes

The chromatin has a beaded appearance due to the presence of nucleosomes (Figure 5). A nucleosome consists of a portion of DNA which is 146 base pairs in length and wrapped around eight histone molecules.

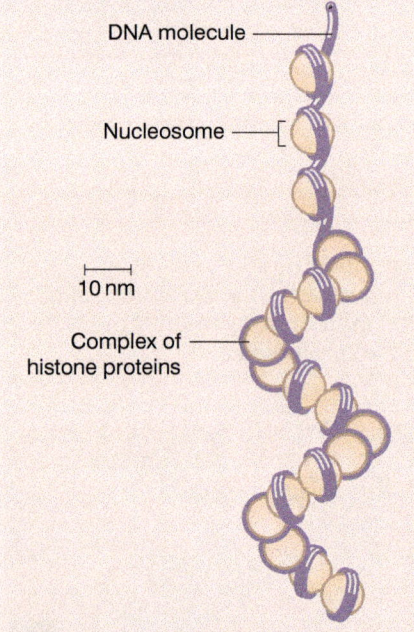

DNA molecule

Nucleosome

10 nm

Complex of histone proteins

Figure 5 *Structure of a chromosome*

More about telomeres

Telomeres prevents chromosome ends from degrading and from sticking to other chromosome ends. In cells that are actively dividing, the enzyme telomerase catalyses the addition of the repeating sequence of bases. In cells that are not dividing, telomerase is only present in very low concentrations or is not detectable. Cancer cells make more telomerase so the telomeres do not shorten and the cells do not die. Scientists are researching into whether telomerase could be used in humans to allow our cells to live longer and therefore increase our life span. One problem would be that the use of telomerase could increase the risk of cancer.

Karytotypes

For convenience, and to make them easier to study, photographs of chromosomes are cut out and pasted into a logical format where they are arranged in their pairs, by size, and given numbers to identify them. This organisation, showing the full diploid set of chromosomes, is known as a karyotype.

Summary test 5.1a

A chromosome during the prophase stage of mitosis is composed of two genetically identical (**1**), joined at a (**2**). Chromosomes contain DNA complexed with (**3**) proteins. At the ends of the chromosomes are (**4**). These allow continued replication of the cell as they prevent the loss of (**5**) and help to stop chromosome ends from (**6**). The interphase stage of the mitotic (**7**) follows on from (**8**), when cytoplasm and (**9**) are shared out to the two new daughter cells. The phase during interphase when DNA is replicated is known as the (**10**). Protein synthesis and growth occurs during the (**11**) phases. Mitosis consists of (**12**) main stages.

Mitosis produces daughter cells that are genetically identical to the parent cells. There are certain processes in living organisms that require new cells to be genetically identical.

Let us look at each in turn to see why mitosis is essential.

Growth of multicellular organisms

When two **haploid** cells (e.g. a sperm and an ovum) fuse together to form a diploid cell (e.g. a zygote), this cell has all the genetic information needed to form the new organism. The cell first divides a number of times to give a group of genetically identical cells like those shown in Figure 1. This is growth by increase in cell numbers. Although all cells have a complete set of genetic information, only part of it is expressed in any one cell. Depending on which part is expressed, cells change (differentiate) to give groups of specialised cells, e.g. muscle or epithelium in animals, xylem or phloem in plants. Cells formed by mitosis must all be genetically identical so that no genetic information is lost and the newly formed cells can become specialised with their particular structure and function.

Cell replacement

All cells have a limited life span and so die naturally at some stage. Other cells may become damaged and cell death is triggered. These cells need to be replaced if the organism is to continue to function normally. Examples include red blood cells (lifespan of only 120 days) and the cells of the lining of the airways in the gas exchange system. The renewal of cells by mitosis takes place constantly during an organism's lifetime.

Repair of tissues

If cells in a tissue are damaged or destroyed in some way, it is important that they are replaced as rapidly as possible. The replacement cells need to have an identical structure and function to the ones that have been damaged for the tissue to function effectively.

> **Remember**
>
> When tissues are damaged, many cells need to be replaced by mitosis so that the tissue is repaired. Mitosis is the division of cells and is **not** a process that repairs cells.

Asexual reproduction

Mitosis is the means by which certain organisms carry out asexual reproduction. It produces offspring that are genetically identical (assuming no **mutations**) to their parents and to each other. This has one main advantage. Because they have been able to survive, grow and produce offspring, the parents must be well adapted to the environmental conditions in which they currently live. By producing genetically identical offspring they can be sure that these too will survive as long as conditions do not change.

Asexual reproduction is a relatively rapid form of reproduction and so large numbers can be quickly built up and the local area colonised. Plants can gain a competitive advantage, especially for light, by this means. In plants, a variety of forms of vegetative propagation are used. For example, the rhizome is a modified stem that grows under the soil level and a new genetically identical plant can grow from this stem. Other examples are plants that grow from horizontal underground stems produced by grasses and strawberry plant runners. In eukaryotic, unicellular organisms, mitosis *is* asexual reproduction,

These pages help you to:

- explain the importance of mitosis in the production of genetically identical daughter cells (5.1.2)
- outline the role of stem cells in cell replacement and tissue repair by mitosis (5.1.5)
- explain how uncontrolled cell division can result in the formation of a tumour (5.1.6)

You will also:

- understand the difference between a tumour cell and a tumour
- know that tumour cells can be malignant (cancerous) or benign (non-cancerous)
- understand the difference between adult and embryonic stem cells

> **Remember**
>
> Although mitosis results in the production of two genetically identical cells, the cells are not completely identical because during cytokinesis the cytoplasm and organelles may not be shared out exactly equally.

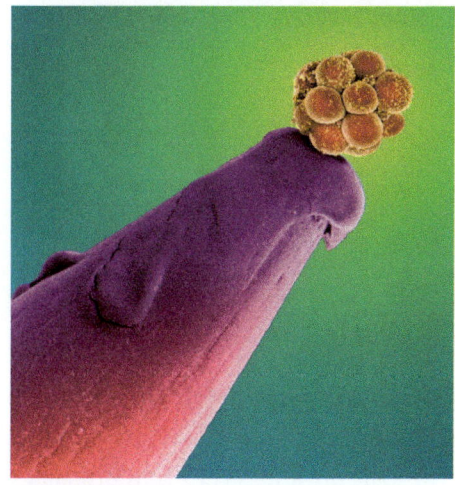

Figure 1 *Colourised scanning electron micrograph of a 3-day-old human embryo at the 16 cell stage on the top of a pin. The cells are produced mitotically from the zygote and are genetically identical.*

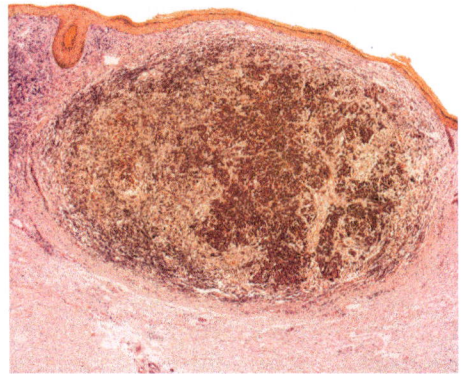

Figure 2 *This cancerous tissue in the skin is produced by the uncontrolled mitotic growth of skin cells.*

Extension

Malignant and benign tumours

Cells of malignant tumours often have a faster rate of division than cells of benign tumours. When some malignant tumour cells get carried in the bloodstream they can infiltrate (invade) other healthy tissues and form secondary tumours (metastatic tumours). Benign tumours grow in a contained area (are encapsulated) and do not infiltrate surrounding tissue.

with a single 'parent' producing two genetically identical unicellular organisms. Mitosis is also the basis of natural and artificial **cloning**.

Stem cells and the significance of mitosis

Adult stem cells are **undifferentiated**, continuously dividing cells that occur in animal tissues. They are found, for example, in the inner lining of the small intestine, in the skin, in the lining of the gas exchange system and also in the bone marrow, which produces red and white blood cells. The genetically identical undifferentiated daughter cells that are produced can produce more adult stem cells. When necessary, a daughter cell can differentiate and become specialised for a specific role, serving as a replacement for cells that are damaged. A set of genes is switched on that causes the cell to function in the same way as all the other cells of that tissue type.

Adult stem cells are not completely undifferentiated: they can only develop into the cell type or types in the region they are located. For example, stem cells in the lining of the airways can only differentiate into the cells of the airways and not into blood cells. The stem cells can divide repeatedly for many divisions but cannot divide indefinitely.

In addition to the adult stem cells found in mature organisms, stem cells also occur at the earliest stage of the development of an embryo, before the cells have differentiated. These are called embryonic stem cells. These cells can divide an infinite number of times. They can also differentiate into any of the tissue types found in the body. This is important because stem cells can be used to treat a variety of genetic disorders, such as the blood diseases thalassaemia and sickle cell anaemia. Research on the use of stem cells to replace tissues that have been damaged by injury or disease, for example, in replacing heart tissue damaged by a heart attack, is ongoing.

Mitosis and tumour formation

Damage to the genes that regulate mitosis and the cell cycle can lead to uncontrolled cell division. Genes involved in growth, proto-oncogenes, can mutate and become oncogenes which cause the cell to continue to grow and divide. Genes that help to regulate cell division, **tumour suppressor genes**, can switch off as a result of a mutation. Checkpoints that control mitosis do not function correctly in tumour cells. The cells do not undergo programmed cell death (apoptosis) and can live indefinitely. The cells become less differentiated with each division and lose their ability to function properly. As a consequence, a group of abnormal cells, called a **tumour**, develops and continues to expand in size as new cells are formed. Healthy cells stop growing when they come into contact with another cell, a phenomenon known as contact inhibition. Tumour cells do not show contact inhibition, which explains why tumours continue to increase in size. Tumours can develop in any organ of the body, but are most commonly found in the lungs, prostate (male), breast and ovaries (female), large intestine, stomach, oesophagus and pancreas. Some tumours are cancerous (malignant) (Figure 2) while others are non-cancerous (benign). Uncontrolled cell division in plants may also lead to the formation of a tumour.

Summary test 5.1b

Mitosis produces cells that are genetically identical unless a **(1)** occurs. Mitosis is important in replacing cells that die naturally, especially **(2)** cells that only have a life span of 120 days. Other processes in which mitosis is important include **(3)**, **(4)** and **(5)**. Mitosis replaces undifferentiated dividing cells, called **(6)**, that occur in adult animal tissues. Damage may occur to the genes that regulate mitosis and the cell cycle. This can lead to uncontrolled cell division and as a consequence a group of abnormal cells, called a **(7)**, develops and continues to expand in size.

Chromosome behaviour in mitosis
a. Mitosis in plant and animal cells, and cytokinesis

Mitosis is the process of nuclear and cell division that results in two daughter cells. Each daughter cell has a nucleus that is genetically identical to the nucleus of the parent cell (except in the rare event of a **mutation**). The chromosome number and type of **chromosomes** in each cell is the same as the parent cell. Before mitosis there is always a period in the cell cycle during which the cell is not dividing. This period is called **interphase**. Although mitosis is a continuous process, it can be divided into four stages:

- **Prophase** – chromosomes become visible and the nuclear envelope disassembles.
- **Metaphase** – chromosomes arrange themselves at the equator (metaphase plate) of the cell.
- **Anaphase** – **sister chromatids** (daughter chromosomes) move to opposite poles.
- **Telophase** – the nuclear envelope reforms.

The different stages are shown in Figure 1 and illustrated in Figure 2 (over the page).

Prophase

The chromosomes first become visible as long thin threads, which later shorten and thicken. This is known as chromosome condensation and during this time the DNA molecule within each chromatid coils and supercoils. In animal cells the two pairs of centrioles separate and each pair moves to opposite poles. From each pair of centrioles, **microtubules** develop and form spindle fibres which span the cell from pole to pole. Collectively, these microtubules are called the **spindle apparatus** (or spindle). The nucleolus disappears and the nuclear envelope disassembles (breaks up into vesicles), leaving the chromosomes free in the cytoplasm of the cell. These chromosomes, which are dispersed at random, become attached by their centromeres to microtubules of spindle fibres and are moved towards the equator of the cell towards the end of prophase.

Metaphase

The spindle is fully formed and the chromosomes are arranged at the spindle equator. They remain attached to microtubules of spindle fibres at their centromere and the sister chromatids of each chromosome remain attached to each other.

Anaphase

The centromeres divide into two and the spindle fibres joined to each contract, causing the sister chromatids to separate and move to opposite poles of the cell. The chromatids, which are now known as daughter chromosomes, move rapidly to their respective poles. Energy for the process is provided by mitochondria, which gather around the spindle fibres. If cells are treated with chemicals that destroy the spindle, the chromosomes remain at the equator, unable to reach the poles.

Telophase

The daughter chromosomes reach their respective poles and become longer and thinner, finally disappearing altogether, leaving only widely spread **chromatin**. The spindle disassembles, the nuclear envelope reassembles (vesicles formed in prophase fuse together) and the nucleolus re-forms. Two separate nuclei can be seen. Cytokinesis frequently begins before the end of telophase.

These pages help you to:

- learn the names and the correct sequence of the main stages of mitosis: prophase, metaphase, anaphase and telophase (5.2.1)
- describe the behaviour of chromosomes in plant and animal cells during the mitotic cell cycle (5.2.1)
- describe the associated behaviour of the nuclear envelope, the cell surface membrane and the spindle during the mitotic cell cycle (5.2.1)
- interpret photomicrographs, diagrams and microscope slides of cells in different stages of the mitotic cell cycle and identify the main stages of mitosis (5.2.2)

You will also:

- learn about the centrosome and the microtubule organising centre (MTOC)
- learn about the kinetochore

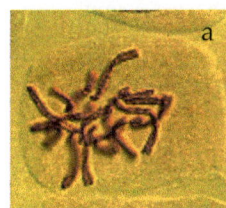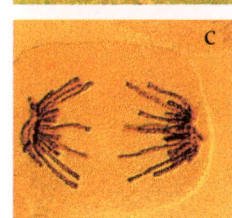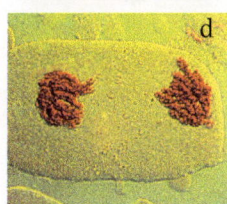

Figure 1 *The main stages of mitosis: a) prophase, b) metaphase, c) anaphase and d) telophase*

Remember

The replication of DNA takes place during interphase before the nucleus and cell divide.

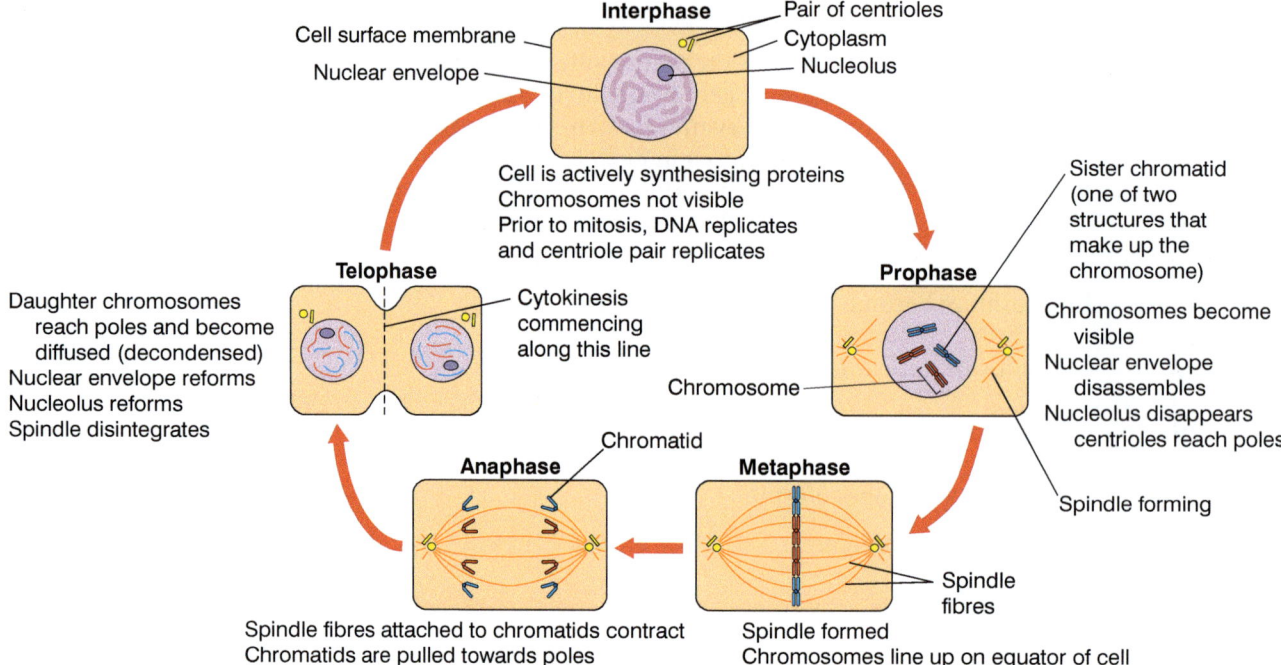

Figure 2 *Outline summary of stages of mitosis in an animal cell*

The kinetochore

The kinetochore is the protein complex where microtubules of the spindle, kinetochore microtubules, attach to the centromere during prophase and metaphase. During anaphase, the kinetochore maintains the attachment of the kinetochore microtubules, so that movement of the daughter chromosomes (sister chromatids) to their opposite poles can be achieved.

In animal cells, the pair of centrioles is replicated before the start of mitosis. The centrosome is the area containing the centrioles and associated proteins. During prophase, the centrosome divides so that each centriole pair moves to the opposite poles of the cell and the spindle apparatus forms. Animal cells that have the centrioles removed can still form a spindle, but not always with successful results. Plant cells do not have centrioles but do have microtubule organising centres (MTOCs) that perform the same role as the centrosome in animal cells.

Cytokinesis

In animal cells, cytokinesis begins when a cleavage furrow forms (Figure 2) and the cytoplasm constricts to pinch the cell into two new cells. Cell organelles are shared out between the two cells. Each cell has its own nucleus with the same number and type of chromosomes as the original parent cell.

Cytokinesis in plant cells involves the division of the cytoplasm and the sharing of organelles. A cleavage furrow does not form. Instead, vesicles from the Golgi body bring materials to form a cell plate across the equator of the parent cell from the centre outwards and then cellulose is laid down on this plate to form the cell wall.

Differences between nuclear and cell division in plant and animal cells

In plants, mitosis occurs in a specialised tissue known as meristematic tissue. Plant meristems occur in the growing regions, for example in root and shoot tips and in the cambium of stems and roots (7.1b). In animals, stem cells are able to divide by mitosis. Stem cells occur where there is a requirement for growth, tissue repair and cell replacement (5.1b).

Summary test 5.2a

The stage when a cell is not dividing is called **(1)**. The first stage of mitosis is called **(2)**. During this stage in animal cells, each pair of cylindrical structures, called **(3)**, move to the opposite **(4)** of the cell. Thin structures called microtubules develop and form the spindle fibres that span the cell and together form the **(5)**. Towards the end of this stage, the **(6)** disassembles and the **(7)** disappears. During the second stage, called **(8)**, the chromosomes arrange themselves at the **(9)**. In the third stage, called **(10)**, the **(11)** of each chromosome divides into two and the microtubules attached to each pull the individual **(12)** to opposite ends of the cell. In the final stage, known as **(13)**, the nuclear envelope and nucleolus reform and chromosomes become longer and thinner to form chromatin.

Developing practical skills

Table 1 shows the skills you should aim to develop during your course. Information about experimental work and working with the microscope is also included.

You may be asked to make your own slide and to make observations. This can be a straightforward exercise or may involve a comparison with another slide or a photomicrograph.

The same skills are required as for carrying out investigations.

These pages help you to:

- interpret microscope slides of cells in different stages of the mitotic cell cycle and identify the main stages of mitosis (5.2.2)

You will also:

- have a better understanding of how to improve your practical skills
- have a better understanding of what is expected of you when you carry out practical assessments

Table 1 *Practical skills to develop*

Skill	Breakdown of skills	Further notes on experimental work	Further notes on microscope work
Manipulation, measurement and observation	Measuring and observing	The aim is to increase precision and accuracy (4.2a).	Decide how to use the microscope to view and observe specimens. The set-up will differ, e.g. plan diagram = low power; cells = high power.
			Use your knowledge to identify the correct tissues and make decisions about how to produce drawings.
			Decide how to stain and make a slide (see example of a root tip squash preparation).
			Decide how to calibrate an eyepiece graticule using a stage micrometer and how to obtain actual sizes.
			Decide how to make estimates of numbers (of cells or organelles).
	Collecting data and making observations	To give you the best chance of obtaining an accurate set of results: • follow instructions precisely • handle apparatus and chemicals with care (assess the risk of the procedure) and with expertise • be accurate when making observations and measurements • if you recognise that you have an anomalous result during an experiment, repeat the procedure to obtain a new measurement and disregard the anomalous result.	You should be able to make observations by drawing plan diagrams and individual cells. Other data could include estimates of dimensions or relative sizes by using a calibrated eyepiece graticule or scale bar or magnification. You should be able to make observations of features within cells and should be able to compare the observable features of two specimens.
Presentation of data and observations	Recording data and observations	Measurements and observations need to be written down or recorded in a table. This is raw (unprocessed) data that can then be further organised when the experiment is finished.	The detail that you observe should be recorded: this includes drawing details.
	Displaying calculations and reasoning	When you have been asked to calculate or to handle data, show the steps involved and be clear why you have carried out those steps.	Show the steps involved in calibration of the eyepiece or in calculating sizes and magnification. You may be asked to: calculate the total number of a feature in the field of view; calculate a mean; determine a ratio. You should know how to use the correct number of significant figures.
	Laying out data and observations	Raw data, whether numerical values (including calculated values) or descriptive observations, should be organised in such a way that it is easier to analyse and to draw conclusions. For example, this may be achieved by construction of a graph or production of a table or chart.	You should become skilled at producing diagrams. If asked to make comparisons, you should be able to organise your observations to show similarities and/or differences.

Analysis, conclusions and evaluation	Interpreting data and observations	Interpreting the organised numerical data or observations is an important step to being able to draw the correct conclusions from your results.	Being able to calibrate the eyepiece graticule scale, determine actual sizes and magnifications, and calculate numbers in a field of view are all examples of interpreting data.
		You need to make sense of the data you have collected. This may involve: removal of anomalous results; calculations; extraction of data; describing patterns and trends.	An awareness of sources of error will help you to arrive at the correct answers.
			The ability to make comparisons of observable features is also an example of interpretation.
		You should be able to identify sources of error, evaluate the effect of the standardised variables and give quantitative information about uncertainty in measurements.	
	Drawing conclusions	You will need to use knowledge and understanding of the relevant syllabus topics as well as the results to be able to draw valid conclusions.	You will need to use knowledge and understanding of the relevant syllabus topics to draw valid conclusions about the specimens you observe.
	Suggesting improvements	You should be able to consider the investigation that you have carried out and think of ways to limit errors and increase the accuracy of the set of results.	You should suggest ways to limit errors and increase the accuracy of the observations, e.g. using precise methods for measuring or collecting replicate data to calculate a mean.
		You should also be able to think about how you would alter the investigation to improve confidence in your results.	

Observing mitosis in prepared slides

Allium cepa (onion), *Allium sativum* (garlic) and *Vicia faba* (broad bean) are commonly used for these preparations as their roots grow quickly and the number of chromosomes per cell (*Allium cepa/sativum* = 16; *Vicia faba* = 12) is low enough to see individual chromosomes.

The slides will generally be of sections from root tips. The root tip has a meristematic region where mitosis occurs. In a prepared slide of a complete root tip, you will see that at the very end there are protective cells forming the root cap and there are no cells in stages of mitosis. Further back from the root tip are cells that are elongating and differentiating (for example, into xylem and phloem tissue). In a prepared slide of a root tip squash, pressure has been placed on the glass cover slip placed over the slide and the cells in stages of mitosis will be spread out. Root cap cells will appear to be 'rounded' and vary in size (most are larger than meristematic cells).

A stain is used that is taken up by DNA so that chromosomes will be more easily visible when viewed using the light microscope.

Observing on low power

This allows you to find cells and gain an idea where there may be cells in stages of mitosis so that you can adjust the position of the microscope slide on the microscope stage. The cells you want to see using high power must be in the very centre of your field of view before changing to the high power objective lens. Figure 1 shows the area where there will be the greatest density of cells in stages of mitosis in a complete root tip.

Observing on high power

Using the high power objective lens, you can observe individual cells in stages of mitosis. Carefully move the slide a very small distance to find suitable cells in stages of mitosis that you can draw or describe.

Figure 1 *A photomicrograph of the root tip. Cells further back from the root tip have completed mitosis and may look elongated.*

Making high power drawings of cells in stages of mitosis

In a root tip squash, the cells will not be arranged in an orderly fashion as in a prepared slide of a root tip. You need to use your knowledge to identify the cells in the stages you have been asked to draw.

Follow instructions about:

- the number of cells to draw – *do not* draw extra cells
- which stages of mitosis to draw – *do not* draw additional stages
- adding labels and/or annotations (further descriptive notes) – *do not* add if they are not required.

When labelling:

- use ruled label lines
- *do not* use arrow heads
- *do not* let label lines cross.

When drawing individual cells:

- use sharp, continuous lines – *do not* draw sketchy lines
- *do not* shade in the nucleus or the chromosomes
- draw chromosomes in correct proportion to the size of the cell
- for late prophase, metaphase, anaphase and early telophase, where chromosomes (or daughter chromosomes) are visible:
  - try to draw each chromosome – *do not* draw one large shape (or two if anaphase and early telophase) with only one outline containing all the chromosomes
  - try to count how many chromosomes there are and match this in your diagram – *do not* draw a tangled mass
- for early prophase and late telophase, the chromosomes could be drawn together as one mass
- only draw what is visible – a textbook diagram, for example drawing centromeres or spindle fibres, *will not gain credit*
- make good use of the available space but *do not* let labels overlap printed text or go too close to the margins of the paper.

Estimating dimensions of cells or chromosomes

If you are asked for dimensions of cells or chromosomes that you have drawn, then this can be determined using the eyepiece graticule scale. If, for example, you are asked for the dimensions of cells undergoing mitosis, then you should measure a number of cells and calculate the mean. Remember:

- to calibrate the eyepiece graticule scale using the stage micrometer using the high power objective lens (the same lens as used for viewing)
- to adjust the position of the slide and/or rotate the eyepiece lens so that you can align the edge of the cell or the chromosome with the eyepiece graticule scale.

Remember

You may be asked to use the light microscope or images to make calculations. If you are not told how many significant figures to use for a calculated value, then use the same number of significant figures as the value in the data that has the least number (smallest number) of significant figures, or at most one more than this.

Summary test 5.2b

Mitosis can be observed in the **(1)** area of a root tip. Using the correct stain allows chromosomes to be seen more easily, because the **(2)** they contain takes up the stain. At the very end of the root tip are non-dividing cells known as **(3)** cells. In the area of cell division there will also be cells in the **(4)** stage of the cell cycle, which is not a stage of mitosis. To observe and draw individual cells in stages of mitosis, the high-power **(5)** should be used after observing on low power. After drawing and labelling cells, you may be asked to add notes to the labels – these are known as **(6)**. Draw chromosomes in the correct **(7)** to the size of the cell. Do not include structures that you cannot see using a light microscope, such as **(8)**. To estimate dimensions of cells, use a calibrated **(9)**.

Launch additional digital resources for the chapter

5 Exam-style questions

1 Identify the event that occurs in the formation of a tumour.

A contact inhibition

B oncogene forms from proto-oncogene

C programmed cell death (apoptosis)

D tumour suppressor gene switches on

(1 mark)

2 Vinblastine is a chemical used in the treatment of cancer. It causes all mitotic cells to stop dividing at metaphase.

Identify the statements that suggest how this chemical might work.

   1 stops sister chromatids migrating to opposite poles

   2 prevents replication of the centrioles

   3 inhibits chromatin condensing in the nucleus

A 1, 2 and 3

B 2 only

C 1 and 3 only

D 1 only

(1 mark)

3 Figure 1 is a photomicrograph of a root tip of onion, *Allium cepa*, showing cells in stages of mitosis.

Figure 1

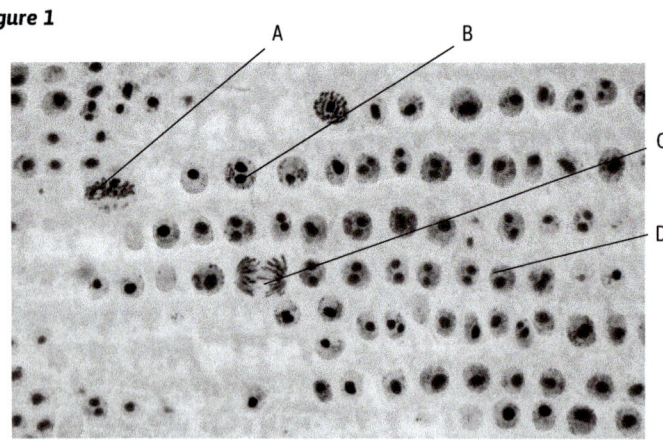

a Identify the stages of mitosis shown in the cells labelled A, B and C. *(3 marks)*

b The cell labelled D is in interphase. Interphase is sometimes described as a 'resting stage'.

Explain why 'resting stage' is not a suitable term for cells in interphase. *(2 marks)*

c Mitosis is important in producing more cells for plant growth.

Describe **three other** ways in which mitosis is important in plants. *(3 marks)*

(Total 8 marks)

4 a Figure 2 shows a chromosome during late prophase of mitosis.

Figure 2

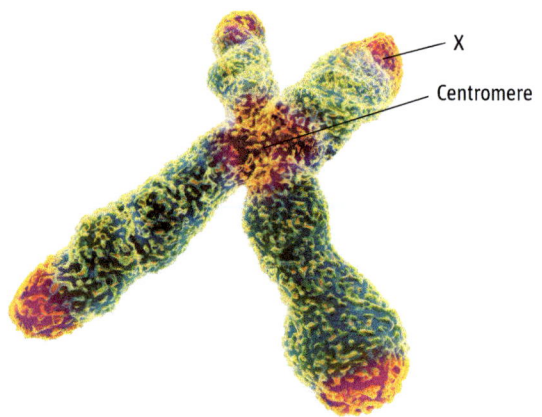

   i State the name **and** function of the region of the chromosome labelled **X**. *(2 marks)*

   ii State **three** differences between the chromosome shown in Figure 2 and a chromosome at late anaphase. *(3 marks)*

b During mitosis, the centromere attaches to spindle fibres. Describe the role of spindle fibres during mitosis. *(2 marks)*

c One of the functions of a plant hormone known as cytokinin is to act as a cell-signalling molecule and promote cytokinesis.

Suggest how cytokinin acts as a cell-signalling molecule. *(3 marks)*

(Total 10 marks)

5 Practice questions

5 **a** What is the function of the protein found in chromosomes?

b How is the considerable length of a DNA molecule compacted into a chromosome?

6 Mitosis is a continuous process. When mitosis is viewed under a microscope, the observer only gets a snapshot of the process at one moment in time. In this snapshot, the number of cells at each stage of mitosis is proportional to the time each cell spends undergoing that stage. Table 1 shows the number of cells at each stage of mitosis during one observation.

Table 1

Stage	Number of cells
Interphase	890
Prophase	73
Metaphase	20
Anaphase	9
Telophase	8

a If one complete cycle takes 20 hours, how many minutes were spent in metaphase? Show your working.

b In what percentage of cells would the chromosomes have been visible? Show your working.

7 Cancer is a group of diseases which results from uncontrolled growth and division of cells. As a consequence, a group of abnormal cells, called a tumour, develops and continues to expand in size.

The treatment of cancer often involves blocking some part of the cell cycle with drugs. In this way the cell cycle is disrupted and cell division, and hence cancer growth, ceases.

The problem with such drugs is that they also disrupt the cell cycle of normal cells. However, the drugs are more effective against rapidly dividing cells. As cancer cells have a particularly fast rate of division, they are damaged to a greater degree than normal cells.

The graph below shows the effect of a chemotherapy drug that kills dividing cells. It was given to a person with cancer once every three weeks starting at time 0.

The graph plots the changes in the number of healthy cells and cancer cells in a tissue over the treatment period of 12 weeks.

Figure 3 Changes in the number of healthy cells and cancer cells in a tissue during a chemotherapy treatment of 12 weeks

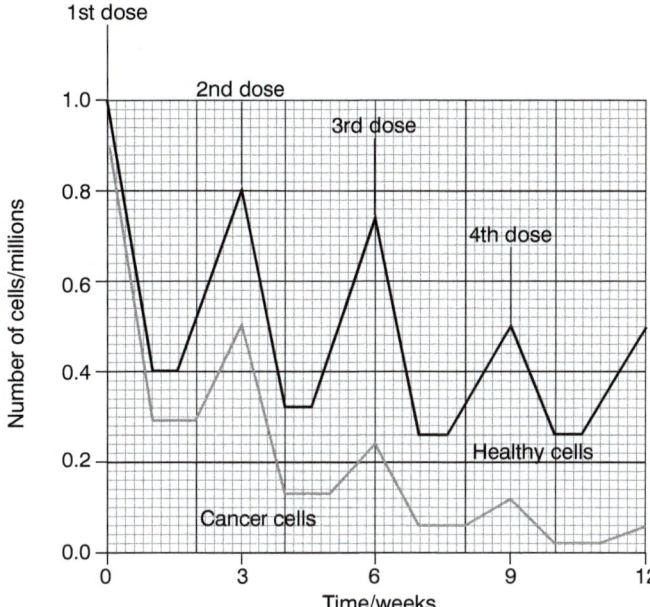

a How many fewer healthy cells were there after three weeks compared to the start of the treatment?

b What percentage of the original number of healthy cells were still present at 12 weeks?

c How many times greater is the number of healthy cells compared to the number of cancer cells after 12 weeks?

d Give a reason for the lower number of cancer cells compared to healthy cells at 12 weeks.

e Describe two differences between the effect of the drug on cancer cells compared with healthy cells throughout the treatment.

f Use the graph to explain why chemotherapy drugs have to be given a number of times if they are to be effective in treating cancer.

6 Nucleic acids and protein synthesis

6.1 Structure of nucleic acids and replication of DNA

a. Nucleotides and ribonucleic acid (RNA)

Nucleotides are the basic units which make up a group of the most important chemicals in all organisms – the **nucleic acids** – of which the best known are:

- **ribonucleic acid (RNA)**
- **deoxyribonucleic acid (DNA)**.

Nucleotide structure

Individual nucleotides are made up of three components (Figure 1):

- **a pentose (5C) sugar**, of which there are two types: ribose and deoxyribose (representative shape is a pentagon)
- **a phosphate group** (representative shape is a circle)
- **a nitrogenous organic base**, of which five different forms are found in nucleic acids. These are divided into two groups:
  - **pyrimidines**, which are made up of a single six-sided ring, include **cytosine**, **thymine** and **uracil**
  - **purines**, which are made up of a six-sided ring joined to a five-sided one. The two examples found in nucleic acids are **adenine** and **guanine**.

The pentose sugar, phosphate group and organic base are combined, as a result of **condensation reactions**, to give a **nucleotide**. Two nucleotides may, in turn, be combined to form a **dinucleotide** as a result of a condensation reaction between the pentose sugar of one nucleotide and the phosphate group of another. The strong covalent bond formed is called a **phosphodiester bond**. Continued linking of nucleotides in this way forms a **polynucleotide**, such as RNA (Figure 2).

Ribonucleic acid (RNA) structure

Ribonucleic acid (RNA) is a polymer made up of repeating nucleotide sub-units. It forms a single strand in which the pentose sugar is always **ribose** and the organic bases are adenine, guanine, cytosine and uracil (Figure 2). There are three types of RNA, all of which are important in protein synthesis:

- **ribosomal RNA (rRNA)**
- **transfer RNA (tRNA)**
- **messenger RNA (mRNA)**.

These pages help you to:

- describe the structure of the nucleotides in RNA and DNA (6.1.1)
- describe the structure of the phosphorylated nucleotide ATP (6.1.1)
- learn that bases adenine and guanine are purines with a double ring structure, and that the bases cytosine, thymine and uracil are pyrimidines with a single ring structure (6.1.2)
- learn that nucleotides are linked by phosphodiester bonds (6.1.3)
- describe the structure of messenger RNA (mRNA) (6.1.5)

You will also:

- learn about ribosomal RNA (rRNA) and transfer RNA (tRNA)

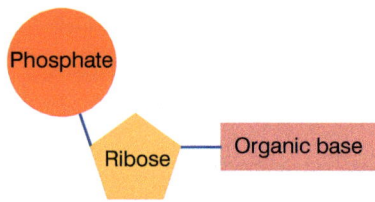

Figure 1 *Generalised structure of an RNA nucleotide*

Extension

The phosphate group in RNA and DNA is involved in the phosphodiester bond (linkage). In a single nucleotide, the phosphate group is attached to the 5' carbon of the pentose sugar, ribose or deoxyribose (see Figures 1 and 4) by a phosphoester bond. The same phosphate group is used to bond (by a phosphoester bond) to the 3' carbon of the pentose sugar of the next nucleotide, so forming the complete phosphodiester bond.

Extension

Ribosomal RNA and transfer RNA

Ribosomal RNA (rRNA) is a large molecule that is complexed with proteins to form the subunits of ribosomes. It has a sequence of organic bases which is very similar in organisms within the same kingdom (18.2b).

Transfer RNA (tRNA) is a relatively small molecule which is made up of around 80 nucleotides. It makes up 10–15% of the total RNA in a cell. Although there are at least 20 types of tRNA, each carrying a different amino acid, they are in fact very similar (see Figure 1 in 6.2c).

Messenger RNA (mRNA)

An mRNA molecule:

- is a single-stranded molecule
- is composed of a chain of thousands of RNA nucleotides
  - each nucleotide is composed of a phosphate group, a ribose sugar and one of four bases: cytosine, uracil, adenine or guanine
  - each RNA nucleotide is joined to the next by a condensation reaction to form a ribose (sugar)–phosphate backbone (Figure 2)
  - the bond between adjacent RNA nucleotides is a strong covalent bond known as a phosphodiester bond (see Extension on previous page and also 6.1b).

The base sequence of an mRNA molecule is determined by the sequence of bases in a length of DNA (gene) in a process called transcription. Different genes have different sequence lengths. The extent of modification of RNA following transcription partly determines the final length of the mRNA molecule produced. Once formed, mRNA leaves the nucleus via pores in the nuclear envelope and enters the cytoplasm, where it associates with the ribosomes. There it acts as a template for protein synthesis. Its structure is suited to this function because it possesses the correct sequence of triplets that allow the production of specific polypeptides. It is usually broken down quickly and normally exists only for as long as it is needed to manufacture a given protein. mRNA molecules are made in the nucleus and carry out their function in the cytoplasm.

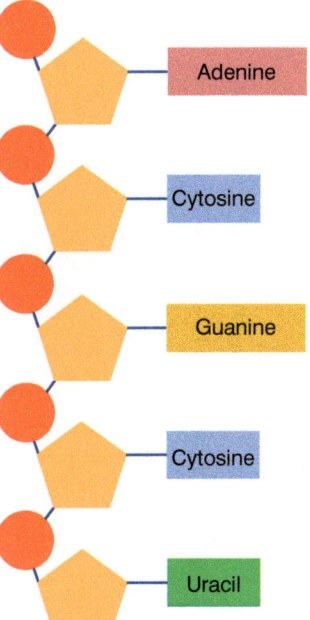

Figure 2 *Section of an RNA polynucleotide*

Adenosine triphosphate (ATP)

ATP is a phosphorylated nucleotide made up of an adenine molecule, a ribose molecule and three phosphate molecules. It is the universal energy currency of all cells. The structure of an ATP molecule is shown in Figure 3.

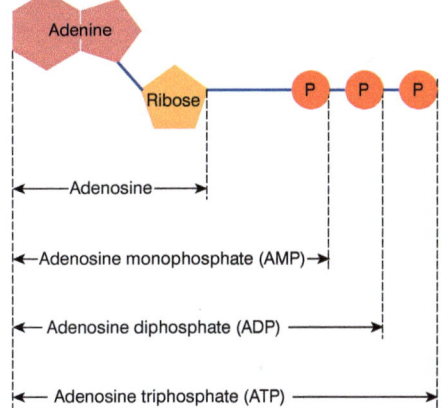

Figure 3 *Structure of ATP*

Extension

Structural formulae for ribose and deoxyribose

Figure 4 shows the difference between the two pentose sugars ribose and deoxyribose. You do not need to learn these, but by studying the structures you will notice that deoxyribose only has a hydrogen atom on carbon number 2 of the molecule, rather than a hydroxyl (OH) group. This explains 'deoxy'. Each carbon is numbered, 1' to 5'.

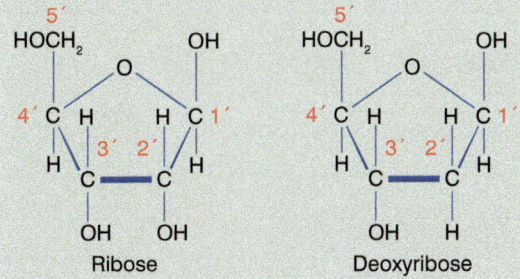

Figure 4 *Ribose and deoxyribose*

Summary test 6.1a

Nucleotides are organic compounds that contain the elements carbon, hydrogen, oxygen, **(1)** and **(2)**. A nucleotide contains a **(3)** sugar, which has **(4)** carbon atoms and has two forms: **(5)** and **(6)**. It also contains one of five organic bases, which fall into two groups. Those with a six-carbon ring only are called **(7)** and exist in three forms: thymine, **(8)** and **(9)**. Those of the second group, called **(10)**, have a six-sided ring joined to a **(11)**-sided ring; there are two such molecules: **(12)** and **(13)**. Ribonucleic acid, which never has the organic base **(14)**, exists in three forms. The form that has a similar sequence of organic bases in all living organisms is called **(15)**; the form that has a sequence of three bases called an anticodon is **(16)**; and the remaining form, upon which proteins are formed, is **(17)**.

These pages help you to:

- describe the structure of a DNA molecule as a double helix (6.1.3)
- understand the importance of complementary base pairing between the 5' to 3' strand and the 3' to 5' strand (antiparallel strands) in a DNA molecule (6.1.3)
- state the differences in hydrogen bonding between C–G and A–T base pairs (6.1.3)

You will also:

- consider the differences between RNA and DNA

Deoxyribonucleic acid (DNA) is made up of two **nucleotide polymer** strands. In DNA, the pentose sugar is **deoxyribose** and the organic bases are adenine, guanine, cytosine and thymine. Each of the two polynucleotide strands is extremely long, and they are wound around one another to form a double helix. The differences between ribonucleic acid (RNA) and DNA are listed in Table 1.

DNA structure

The basic structure of DNA is shown in Figure 1.

- For each strand of the DNA double helix, the deoxyribose sugars and phosphates alternate to form a strong sugar–phosphate backbone.
- The backbone has a 'direction'. One end of the sugar backbone is designated 5' and the other 3'. These refer to the carbon atoms of the deoxyribose sugars at either end of the strand (Figure 1).
- The two strands are antiparallel. They are the same distance apart but one strand runs in a 5' to 3' direction and the other in a 3' to 5' direction.
- The strands are held together by hydrogen bonding between precise pairings of the bases.
- The two strands are always the same distance apart from each other because of the base pairs between the two strands.
- Each base pair consists of a purine and a pyrimidine, so that all the base pairs are the same length.
  - Adenine (A) always pairs with thymine (T) by means of two **hydrogen bonds**.
  - Guanine (G) always pairs with cytosine (C) by means of three hydrogen bonds.
- The precise pairing of bases is known as complementary base pairing.
- Three hydrogen bonds between G and C mean that this is a slightly stronger pairing than between A and T.

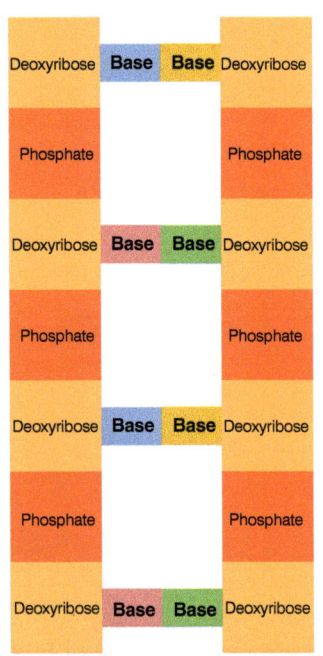

Simplified structure

Alternating phosphate and deoxyribose molecules make up the sugar–phosphate backbones and pairs of organic bases hold the two together.

Figure 1 *Basic structure of DNA*

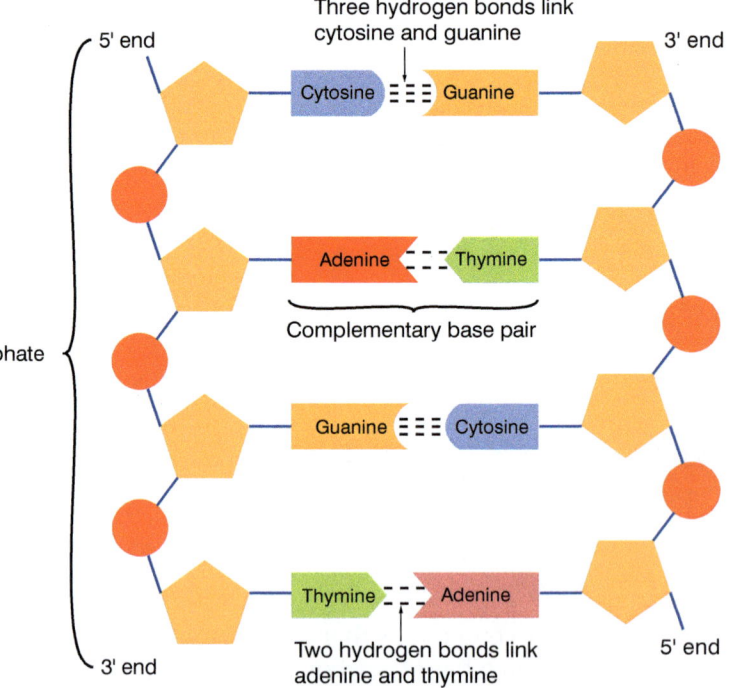

Molecular arrangement

Note the base pairings are always cytosine–guanine and adenine–thymine. This allows the two strands to be the same distance apart along the length of the molecule. Note that the sugar–phosphate backbones 'run' in the opposite direction to each other (i.e. are antiparallel).

Remember

It follows that, in DNA, the quantity of adenine is equal to the quantity of thymine, and similarly, the quantity of guanine is equal to the quantity of cytosine. However, the ratio of adenine and thymine to guanine and cytosine varies from species to species.

The structure of DNA is a **double helix** (Figures 2 and 3). The sugar–phosphate backbones form the overall structural backbone of the DNA molecule. For each complete turn of the double helix, there are 10 base pairs (Figure 2).

The DNA molecule functions in a number of ways:

- It passes from generation to generation without change. Although a hydrogen bond is a weak bond, the sum total of all the hydrogen bonds holding together the two strands of DNA, and the strong sugar–phosphate backbone, results in a very stable molecule.
- The hydrogen bonds can be separated during replication (6.1c) to form **messenger RNA** during protein synthesis (6.2b).
- It is an extremely large molecule and it therefore carries an immense amount of genetic information in the sequence of nucleotides.
- By having the base pairs within the helical cylinder of the sugar–phosphate backbone, the genetic information is largely protected from being corrupted by outside chemical and physical forces.

Table 1 *Differences between RNA and DNA*

RNA	DNA
Single polynucleotide strand (chain)	Double polynucleotide chain (double helix)
Smaller molecular mass (20 000–2 000 000)	Larger molecular mass (100 000–150 000 000)
Pentose sugar is ribose	Pentose sugar is deoxyribose
Organic bases present are adenine, guanine, cytosine and uracil	Organic bases present are adenine, guanine, cytosine and thymine
Ratio of adenine to uracil and the ratio of cytosine to guanine varies	Ratio of adenine to thymine and the ratio of cytosine to guanine is one
Manufactured in the nucleus but found throughout the cell	Found mostly in the nucleus with some present in mitochondria and chloroplasts
Amount varies from cell to cell (and within a cell according to metabolic activity)	Amount is constant for all cells of a species (except gametes and spores)
Chemically less stable	Chemically very stable
Three basic forms: messenger, transfer and ribosomal RNA	Only one basic form, but with an almost infinite variety within that form

Summary test 6.1b

DNA is made up of a **(1)** sugar called **(2)**. This forms a structure, with the sugar and **(3)** groups forming the backbone and the organic bases making up the base pairs. These organic bases are always the same pairings: thymine is always paired with **(4)**, while guanine is always paired with **(5)**. The two backbones run in opposite directions, i.e. they are **(6)**, and are twisted around one another to form a **(7)** shape.

Extension

The importance of DNA

In 1953, James Watson and Francis Crick determined the structure of DNA, building on crucial work by Rosalind Franklin and Maurice Wilkins on X-ray diffraction patterns of DNA.

This led to many major developments in biology. DNA as the molecule of heredity is a key concept. The Key Concepts table at the beginning of this book shows examples of how each chapter relates to DNA. The information in Chapter 19 particularly shows how our knowledge of DNA has been applied to the important field of genetic technology.

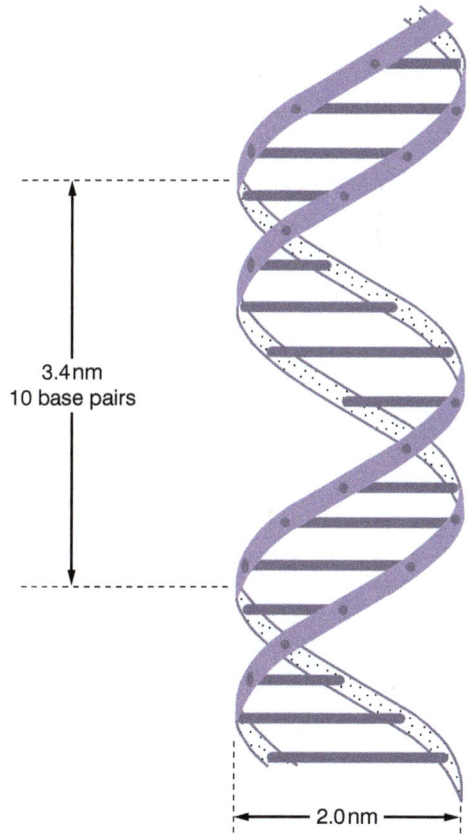

3.4 nm
10 base pairs

2.0 nm

Figure 2 *The DNA double helix structure*

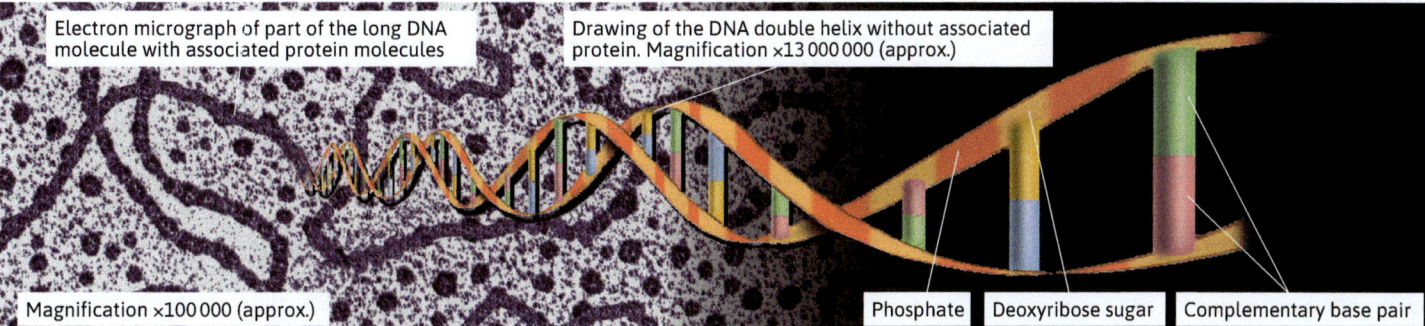

Electron micrograph of part of the long DNA molecule with associated protein molecules

Drawing of the DNA double helix without associated protein. Magnification ×13 000 000 (approx.)

Magnification ×100 000 (approx.)

Phosphate | Deoxyribose sugar | Complementary base pair

Figure 3 *Deoxyribonucleic acid*

These pages help you to:

- describe the semi-conservative replication of DNA during the S phase of the cell cycle (6.1.4)
- understand the roles of DNA polymerase and DNA ligase in semi-conservative replication (6.1.4)
- learn that DNA polymerase adds nucleotides only in a 5' to 3' direction (6.1.4)
- describe and explain the differences between leading strand and lagging strand replication (6.1.4)

You will also:

- read about other proteins involved in replication

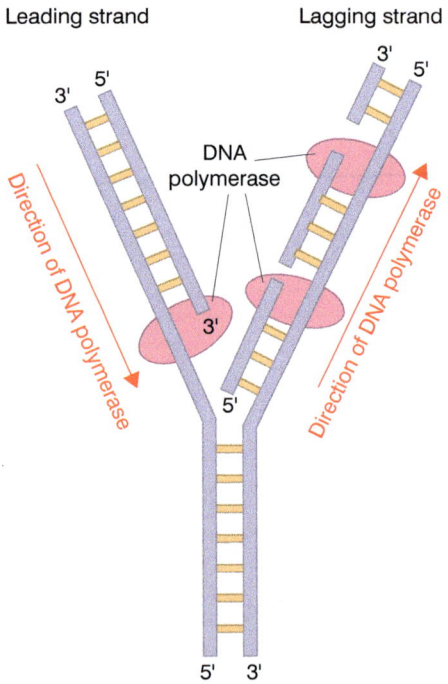

Leading strand   Lagging strand

DNA polymerase

Direction of DNA polymerase

Direction of DNA polymerase

DNA polymerase synthesises DNA which is complementary to both strands. It works in the 5'→3' direction of the new strand. As the DNA molecule is antiparallel, the DNA polymerase makes new DNA on the leading strand as a continuous process in the direction of the replication fork. On the lagging strand it makes small sections simultaneously in the opposite direction. These sections are later joined by the enzyme DNA ligase.

Figure 1 *DNA replication fork showing the action of DNA polymerase*

DNA is the molecule of heredity and the genetic information it holds is passed from parent cell to daughter cell and from generation to generation. We have only to look at identical twins to see just how perfectly the 3.2 billion base pairs of DNA in the **human genome** can be copied. The process of **DNA replication** is clearly very precise. How then is it achieved?

> **Remember**
>
> When smaller molecules are built up into larger ones, energy is required. When larger molecules are broken down into smaller ones, energy is released.

Semi-conservative replication

The Watson–Crick model of DNA structure (6.1b) explains how DNA can produce exact copies of itself. The **hydrogen bonds** linking the base pairs of DNA break and the two strands of the double helix separate. Each exposed strand then acts as a template to which free DNA **nucleotides** bind by complementary base pairing. These nucleotides have been activated by having two phosphate molecules added to them to make them more reactive. Adjacent activated nucleotides are joined together one nucleotide at a time to form the new strand. This results in two DNA molecules that are identical to each other and to the original DNA molecule (Figure 2). Each of the new DNA molecules contains one of the original parental DNA strands – and one newly synthesised strand. The process is therefore termed **semi-conservative replication**. It takes place during interphase in the cell cycle (5.1a).

This complex process can be summarised as follows:

- **Opening up and unwinding the DNA double helix** – an enzyme (**DNA helicase**) breaks the hydrogen bonds between the complementary base pairs of the two parental strands of DNA, and the double helix unwinds. This occurs at a number of points, called replication origins, which form **replication forks** (Figure 1). Both strands are exposed, each of which acts as a template for the synthesis of a complementary new strand.

- **Assembling the leading strand** – one strand of DNA is made by **DNA polymerase** in a continuous process that occurs in the same direction (5'→3') as the replication fork is moving.

- **Assembling the lagging strand** – the other strand of the DNA is antiparallel (6.1b) and runs in the 3'→5' direction. DNA polymerase can only work in the 5'→3' direction. Therefore short sections of complementary DNA, known as **Okazaki fragments**, are made simultaneously in the 5'→3' direction. These are then linked together using the enzyme DNA ligase to form phosphodiester bonds. Ligase only functions on the lagging strand as it is only this strand that has Okazaki fragments.

- **Removing wrongly coded DNA** – errors occasionally occur during replication, such as an incorrect nucleotide being added to the elongating polynucleotide chain (causing a mismatch of base pairs). DNA polymerase checks for mismatch errors (DNA proofreading) and repairs them as it assembles the new DNA strand. Proofreading is highly accurate but on rare occasions the errors are not corrected. This may lead to mutations, which are the basis for genetic variation.

> **Remember**
>
> DNA polymerase can only:
> - add DNA nucleotides to extend a chain and cannot start a chain
> - synthesise new polynucleotide chains in the 5' to 3' direction, so the enzyme works in a 3' to 5' direction on the template strand of DNA.

1. A representative portion of DNA involved in replication

2. DNA double helix unwinds at the replication fork as DNA helicase breaks hydrogen bonds between the two strands, each acting as a template strand. Free activated DNA nucleotides are available for the replication process

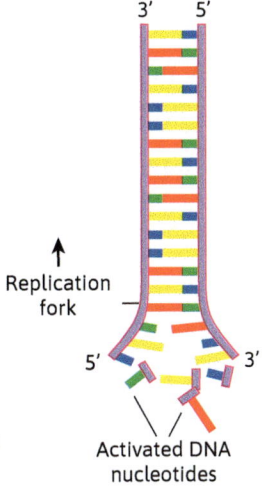

Replication fork

Activated DNA nucleotides

3. DNA helicase continues to separate strands at the moving replication fork. DNA polymerase catalyses the synthesis of the leading and lagging strands by the step-wise addition of complementary DNA nucleotides (each releases two phosphates)

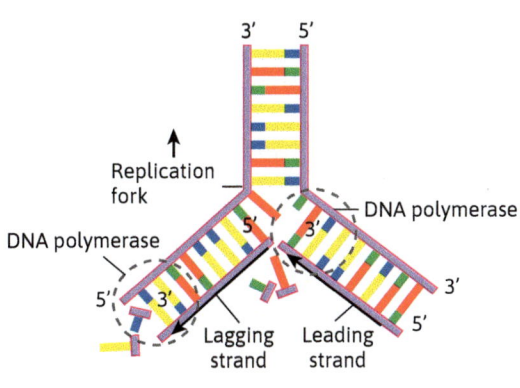

Replication fork

DNA polymerase

DNA polymerase

Lagging strand

Leading strand

4. The leading strand is synthesised as a continuous polynucleotide chain. The lagging strand is synthesised in short fragments (Okazaki fragments). DNA ligase joins the Okazaki fragments to produce a continuous lagging strand

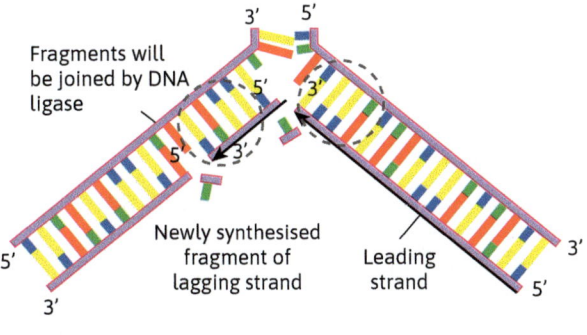

Fragments will be joined by DNA ligase

Newly synthesised fragment of lagging strand

Leading strand

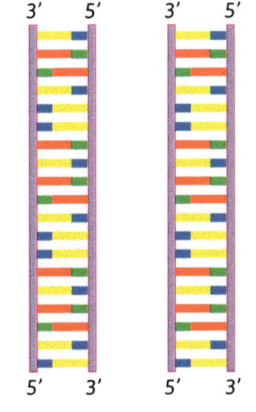

5. The process occurs along the length of the entire DNA molecule. The result is two genetically identical DNA molecules, each comprising one original (parental) strand and one newly synthesised strand, hence semi-conservative DNA replication

Figure 2 The semi-conservative replication of DNA

Extension

Other proteins involved in DNA replication

Topoisomerase solves the problem of tension and twisting that is caused by unwinding the double helix. This enzyme temporarily causes a break in one strand to release tension and rejoins it after unwinding has occurred.

RNA primase catalyses the synthesis of short lengths of RNA, RNA primers, on the DNA strand to allow DNA polymerase to begin polynucleotide synthesis. The lengths of RNA are replaced by DNA nucleotides before replication completes.

Single-strand DNA-binding proteins bind to DNA after unwinding to help keep the strands apart and to protect them until the replication process is complete.

Extension

Replication bubbles

DNA replication in eukaryotic cells would take far too long if replication began at one end and continued all the way to the other end of the DNA molecule. In a eukaryotic cell, there are many origins of replication, with many sections of DNA unwound and being replicated at the same time. The 'open' sections along the DNA molecule are termed replication bubbles. In a prokaryotic cell, there is far less DNA and there is only one origin of replication on the circular molecule. Here, each strand is continuously copied, with DNA polymerase moving in opposite directions.

Summary test 6.1c

Semi-conservative replication involves the separation of the two **(1)** strands that make up the DNA molecule. First, the double helix is opened up by an enzyme that breaks the **(2)** bonds between the strands. The points where the helix splits are called **(3)**. One new strand of DNA is made using the enzyme **(4)**, which adds nucleotides with bases that are **(5)** to the bases on the original parent strand in a continuous process. This strand is the **(6)** strand. The enzyme only works in one direction, so on the other strand, DNA is synthesised in short sections known as **(7)**. This strand is known as the **(8)**. The sections are then joined together by the enzyme **(9)**. As the new DNA contains one original strand and one newly synthesised strand, the process is known as **(10)** replication.

d. Extension: Evidence for semi-conservative DNA replication

These extension pages help you to:

- understand the experimental work carried out by Meselson and Stahl that provided evidence for the semi-conservative replication of DNA

You will also:

- appreciate that scientists build on the work carried out by other scientists

When James Watson and Francis Crick deduced the structure of DNA in 1953 with the help of Rosalind Franklin's diffraction studies, they remarked in their paper *'It has not escaped our notice that the specific pairing we have postulated immediately suggests a possible copying mechanism for the genetic material'*.

Their idea, namely the semi-conservative method, was, however, only one of three possible mechanisms that needed to be scientifically tested before a definite conclusion could be drawn.

Possible mechanisms of DNA replication

In 1953, the three most feasible explanations for how DNA might replicate were as follows.

- **The conservative model** suggested that the parental DNA remained intact and that a separate daughter DNA copy was built up from new molecules of deoxyribose, phosphate and organic bases. Of the two molecules present, one would be made of entirely new material while the other would be entirely original material (Figure 1).
- **The semi-conservative model** proposed that the DNA molecule split into two separate strands, each of which then replicated its mirror image (i.e. the missing half). Each of the two new molecules would therefore have one strand of new material and one strand of original material (Figure 1).
- **The dispersive model** predicted that parental DNA would be broken down and the **nucleotides** replicated before being dispersed randomly throughout the new molecules. The new molecules would contain both new and original material but this would be randomly distributed and not necessarily with equal amounts of old and new material in each molecule.

The experiments of Meselson and Stahl

In 1958, Matthew Meselson and Franklin Stahl of the California Institute of Technology evaluated the three proposed mechanisms of DNA replication. If we look at Figure 1, we can see that the distribution of the 'old' DNA after replication is different in each of the three cases. To find out which mechanism was correct was therefore easy, in theory at least – simply label the old DNA in some way and then look at how it was distributed after replication. Meselson and Stahl achieved this in a neat and elegant experiment using the **isotope** heavy ^{15}N nitrogen. Their work can be summarised as follows.

- Cells of the gut bacterium *Escherichia coli* were grown on a medium containing a nitrogen source made up of the common form of nitrogen ^{14}N. This sample acted as the first control.
- Some bacterial cells were transferred to a medium where the nitrogen (in the form of ammonium chloride) was of the heavier isotope of nitrogen (^{15}N).
- The bacteria were grown, during which time the nitrogen they needed to make new DNA came from the growth medium and was therefore of the ^{15}N type. The resultant DNA was therefore heavier than that formed by the bacteria grown on the medium with ^{14}N. This was the second control.
- After many generations, the DNA of the cells was almost exclusively of the heavy type.
- Samples of the 'heavy DNA' bacteria were then transferred to a medium in which the nitrogen source (ammonium chloride) was of the light (^{14}N) type.
- The bacteria were grown just long enough for the cells to divide once (20–50 minutes, depending on temperature).

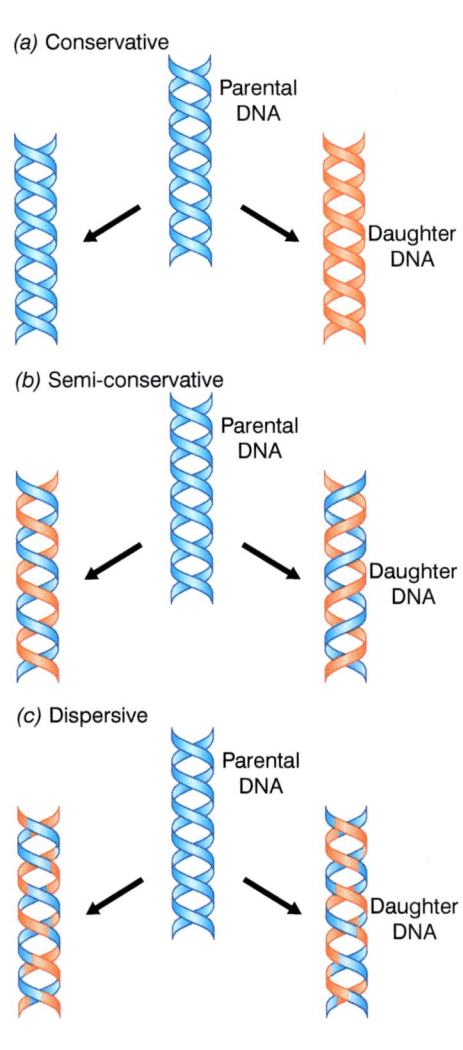

(a) Conservative

Parental DNA

Daughter DNA

(b) Semi-conservative

Parental DNA

Daughter DNA

(c) Dispersive

Parental DNA

Daughter DNA

■ = original (parental DNA) ■ = new DNA

Figure 1 *Possible methods of DNA replication*

- A sample was removed and the DNA of the bacterial cells was extracted and placed in a solution of caesium chloride and centrifuged.
- Because the caesium atom is heavy, it sinks towards the bottom of the tube during **centrifugation** and a density gradient is established in the tube.
- DNA molecules sink in the gradient until they reach a level where their density equals that of the caesium chloride. They then 'float' at this level in the tube.
- The DNA containing ^{15}N is denser than that containing ^{14}N and therefore sinks to a lower level in the tube.

- After one generation in the ^{14}N medium, bacteria were found to have produced DNA with a density mid-way between that of the light (^{14}N) DNA and the heavy (^{15}N) DNA. This meant that one strand of each molecule of this DNA contained ^{14}N while the other strand contained ^{15}N.
- An extract of bacteria was taken after two generations and treated in the same way. Two bands were formed – one with the density of light DNA (indicating it contained only nitrogen of the ^{14}N type) and one of intermediate density (half ^{14}N and half ^{15}N).
- After three generations, there was three times as much DNA in the 'light' band than in the 'intermediate' band.

All these results are consistent with the semi-conservative theory of DNA replication. These experiments and the results are illustrated in Figure 2.

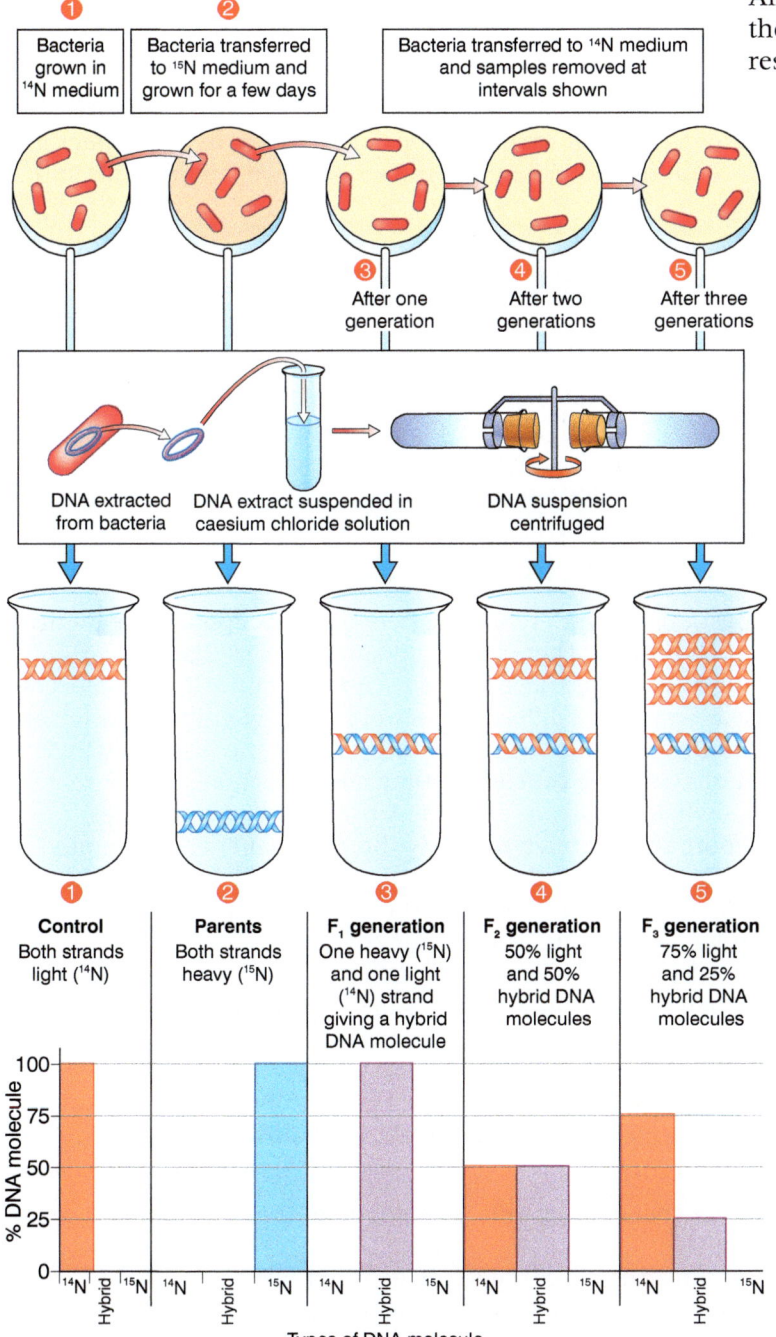

Summary test 6.1d

In experiments to explain DNA replication, Meselson and Stahl used two forms of nitrogen: light nitrogen, written as **(1)** and heavy nitrogen, written as **(2)**. Heavy nitrogen is an **(3)** of light nitrogen. Some bacteria were grown only in light nitrogen, others only in heavy nitrogen. These were the **(4)** experiments. Some bacteria grown in heavy nitrogen were transferred to a medium containing light nitrogen and left to divide once. A sample of the bacteria produced was then placed in a solution of caesium chloride and then **(5)**. The DNA of these bacteria had an intermediate density showing that they had hybrid DNA made up of half heavy and half light nitrogen. After a second division, the next generation produced two types of DNA molecule, a **(6)** and a **(7)**. After three generations there were two types of DNA molecule, 75% were of the **(8)** DNA and 25% of the **(9)** DNA. These results support the **(10)** theory of DNA replication.

Figure 2 *Summary of Meselson–Stahl experiments on the semi-conservative replication of DNA*

111

Protein synthesis
a. The gene and the genetic code of a protein

These pages help you to:

- understand that a gene is a sequence of nucleotides that forms part of a DNA molecule (6.2.1)
- understand that a gene codes for a polypeptide (6.2.1)
- describe the principle of the universal genetic code (6.2.2)
- outline the features of the genetic code (6.2.2)

You will also:

- understand what is meant by the central dogma

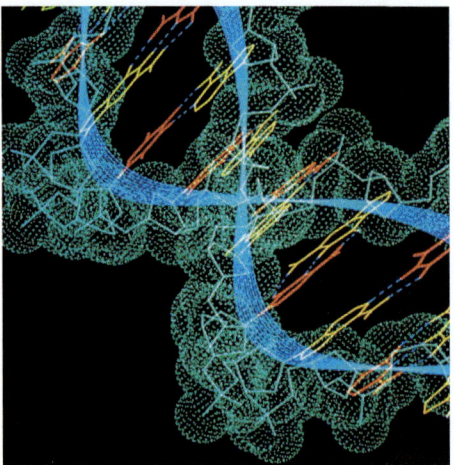

Figure 1 *Computer representation of part of a DNA molecule*

Remember

An mRNA codon is a sequence of three adjacent nucleotides in mRNA that codes for an amino acid, with the exception of STOP codons, which do not code for an amino acid.

Remember

A genetic code that contains T (thymine) is based on DNA triplets. You need to check whether this code represents the transcribed strand OR the non-transcribed strand. Using a genetic code based on mRNA **codons** (contains U, uracil) avoids this confusion. For example, for Cys (cysteine amino acid):

mRNA codon = UGU; DNA triplet, transcribed strand = ACA; DNA triplet, non-transcribed strand = TGT

Once the structure of DNA had been discovered, and it had been established that it was the means by which genetic information was passed from generation to generation, scientists puzzled as to exactly how DNA determined the features of organisms. Although there are only four nucleotide bases in DNA, the considerable length of a DNA molecule means that there is an almost unlimited variety of combinations of these bases. Different sequences can represent different pieces of genetic information. The capacity to store information is large. For example, there is an estimated 3.2 billion (3.2×10^9) base pairs contained in the human genome.

What is a gene?

DNA carries coded information. This information allows the cell to produce polypeptide chains, and so form proteins, many of which are enzymes.

A polypeptide is coded for by a gene. The coded information to synthesise a particular polypeptide is in the form of a particular sequence of nucleotides in the DNA molecule, and this will determine the sequence of amino acids in the polypeptide.

In molecular terms, a gene can be described as a section of a DNA molecule containing a sequence of nucleotides (and hence bases) that codes for a polypeptide.

Enzymes are proteins. As enzymes control chemical reactions, they are responsible for an organism's development and activities. In other words, genes, along with environmental factors, determine the nature and development of all organisms. So how exactly does a sequence of DNA nucleotides determine a sequence of amino acids?

The genetic code is based on triplets of bases

Proteins show almost infinite variety. This variety depends upon the sequence of amino acids in each protein. There are just 20 amino acids that regularly occur in proteins, and each must have its own sequence of nucleotide bases on the DNA. As there are only four different bases (adenine, guanine, cytosine and thymine) present in DNA, if each coded for a different amino acid, only four different combinations could be coded for. Using a pair of bases, 16 different codes are possible – which is still not enough. A triplet of bases produces 64 combinations, more than enough to satisfy the requirements of 20 amino acids. This is called the **genetic code**. In eukaryotes, in the length of DNA corresponding to a gene, there are coding portions known as exons and non-coding portions known as **introns**. The genetic code is used only for exons. As it is the triplets of mRNA bases that are translated into the correct sequence of amino acids, the genetic code is often given as mRNA codons.

Features of the genetic code
Experimental work has revealed the following features of the genetic code. In each case, the codon referred to is the triplet of bases found on mRNA (see Table 1).

- Two amino acids are coded for by only a single triplet, e.g. tryptophan is coded only by UGG.
- The remaining amino acids are coded for by between two and six codons each, e.g. leucine has six – UUA, UUG, CUU, CUC, CUA and CUG.
- The codon is always read in the 5' → 3' direction.
- The code is a **degenerate code**, because most amino acids are coded for by more than one triplet.

Extension

The central dogma

Scientists rapidly extended their knowledge of DNA after the discovery of the structure of the molecule (Figure 1). The role of DNA as the molecule of heredity was widely accepted. Experimentation and observation, a key concept in biology, allowed scientists to discover how DNA could replicate faithfully to allow information to pass from generation to generation and how the information in DNA could result in the production of proteins. This is summarised in what has become known as the central dogma of biology, which outlines the flow of information from the key molecule, DNA. The three main processes to consider in the central dogma are outlined here:

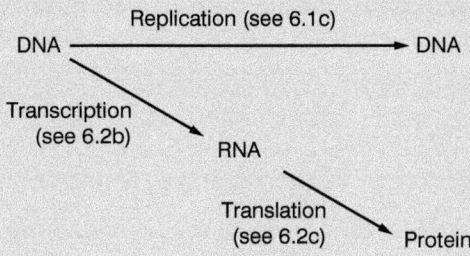

- The start of a sequence is always the codon AUG. This codes for the amino acid methionine (met). If this first methionine molecule does not form part of the final polypeptide, it is later removed.
- Three codons, UAA, UAG and UGA, do not code for any amino acid. These are called **STOP codons** and mark the end of a polypeptide chain.
- The genetic code is **non-overlapping**, i.e. each base in the sequence is read only once: six bases numbered 123456 are read as triplets 123 and 456, rather than as triplets 123, 234, 345, 456. Non-overlapping codes need more bases but are less likely to be affected by error. Some viruses, with limited amounts of DNA, use overlapping codes, but this is extremely rare.
- The code is **universal**, i.e. with a few minor exceptions, each triplet codes for the same amino acid in all organisms.

Summary test 6.2a

The sequence of nucleotides that determines the amino acid sequence of a polypeptide is called a **(1)**. Each amino acid in the sequence is coded for by a total of **(2)** nucleotide bases on a DNA molecule. The complementary sequence of these bases on a messenger RNA molecule is called a **(3)**. An immense variety of proteins can be made in an organism because the length of DNA in each cell is very large. In humans it totals **(4)** base pairs. Most amino acids have more than one codon and the genetic code is therefore described as **(5)**. Each base sequence is read only once and the code is therefore said to be **(6)**. Three codons do not correspond to an amino acid. These are called **(7)** codons. Using a genetic code table, we can find that the sequence UAU on mRNA codes for the amino acid named **(8)**. The two base sequences on the template strand of DNA that could give rise to this same amino acid are **(9)** and **(10)**.

Table 1 *The genetic code*
The base sequences shown are those on mRNA. A codon is made up of three nucleotide bases read in the sequence shown. For example, UGC codes for the amino acid Cys (cysteine). The first letter (U) is in the 'first position' column, the second letter (G) is in the 'second position' column and the third letter (C) is in the 'third position' column. Each of the 20 amino acids is represented by a three-letter abbreviation.

First position	Second position				Third position
	U	C	A	G	
U	Phe	Ser	Tyr	Cys	U
	Phe	Ser	Tyr	Cys	C
	Leu	Ser	STOP	STOP	A
	Leu	Ser	STOP	Trp	G
C	Leu	Pro	His	Arg	U
	Leu	Pro	His	Arg	C
	Leu	Pro	Gln	Arg	A
	Leu	Pro	Gln	Arg	G
A	Ile	Thr	Asn	Ser	U
	Ile	Thr	Asn	Ser	C
	Ile	Thr	Lys	Arg	A
	Met	Thr	Lys	Arg	G
G	Val	Ala	Asp	Gly	U
	Val	Ala	Asp	Gly	C
	Val	Ala	Glu	Gly	A
	Val	Ala	Glu	Gly	G

Remember

You do not need to know the full names of all the 20 amino acids, but you should be able to recognise that the three-letter abbreviations represent amino acids.

Remember

The sequence of nucleotides on the mRNA strand is a complementary copy of the sequence of bases on the DNA template (transcribed) strand. For example, the mRNA codon GUC for the amino acid valine (val) will have been copied from the DNA triplet CAG.

These pages help you to:

- describe how the information in DNA is used during transcription to produce an RNA molecule, the primary transcript, which is then modified to produce messenger RNA (mRNA) (6.2.3 and 6.2.5)
- explain the difference between the transcribed or template strand and the non-transcribed strand of DNA (6.2.4)
- understand the role of RNA polymerase in transcription (6.2.3)
- understand that an intron is a non-coding sequence of DNA and an exon is a coding sequence (6.2.5)
- explain how mRNA is produced in eukaryotes (6.2.5)

You will also:

- understand how more than one polypeptide can be produced from a single gene

Remember

An enzyme that adds nucleotides to an elongating polynucleotide chain is a polymerase.

If DNA nucleotides are added, as in semi-conservative replication (6.1c), then the enzyme is **DNA polymerase**.

If RNA nucleotides are added, as in transcription described on these pages, the enzyme is **RNA polymerase**.

Extension

Producing many RNA transcripts in a short time

Because only the active section of DNA is unwound during transcription, the RNA molecule formed does not remain attached to the entire DNA template (transcribed) strand. This means that while transcription is continuing further along the length of DNA, another RNA polymerase can attach to the promoter region and begin transcribing the template strand.

Proteins, especially enzymes, are essential to all aspects of life. Every organism needs to make its own, sometimes unique, proteins. Each cell is capable of making any and every protein from just 20 amino acids. Exactly which proteins it manufactures depends on the instructions that are provided, at any given time, by the DNA in the cell's nucleus.

DNA cannot leave the nucleus. It is too large to pass through the nuclear pores and by remaining in the nucleus it is protected from the rest of the cell. This means that the genetic information in a gene, carried by the sequence of bases in the DNA, must be copied so that the copy can leave the nucleus. The copy, or transcript, of the gene is mRNA.

The process of copying is known as **transcription**. At the ribosome, mRNA is used to produce a polypeptide chain in a process known as **translation**.

Transcription – production of the primary transcript (RNA)

Transcription (Figure 1) is the process of making a molecule of RNA, the primary transcript, using one strand of the section of DNA as a template. This strand is known as the transcribed strand or the template strand. The strand that is **not** copied and does **not** play a part in transcription can be termed the non-transcribed strand.

The primary transcript is modified in the nucleus to form mRNA (6.1a) in a process known as post-transcriptional modification.

This mRNA then carries the information out of the nucleus to the ribosomes, in the cytoplasm, that are the site of protein synthesis. The process is as follows.

Initiation
- RNA polymerase enzyme attaches to a region of DNA known as the promoter. The promoter is close to the section of DNA that is to be transcribed (see 16.3a).
- The DNA molecule in the region of attachment of RNA polymerase unwinds and hydrogen bonds between the two strands are broken.

Elongation
- The strands continue to separate as RNA polymerase moves along the DNA. As the hydrogen bonds between complementary bases are broken, this exposes the nucleotides on the template strand.
- The nucleotide bases on the DNA **template strand** pair with their complementary RNA nucleotides from the pool that is present in the nucleus. As RNA polymerase moves along the strand the correct RNA nucleotide base is aligned opposite its complementary DNA base and is joined to its neighbouring nucleotide by a phosphodiester bond.
- In this way, an exposed guanine base on the DNA is temporarily linked by hydrogen bonds to the cytosine base of a free activated RNA nucleotide. Similarly, cytosine links to guanine, and thymine links to adenine. The exception is adenine, which links to uracil rather than thymine.
- As the RNA polymerase adds the nucleotides one at a time to build a strand of primary transcript RNA, the DNA strands rejoin behind it. This rejoining allows the newly synthesised sections of the RNA molecule to be released from the DNA template strand. As a result, only around 12 base pairs on the DNA are exposed at any one time.

Termination
- When the RNA polymerase reaches a particular sequence of bases known as a termination sequence, it detaches, and the production of the primary RNA transcript is then complete. This single-stranded transcript represents a copy of

the gene on the DNA, so the length of the RNA molecule formed is the same length as the gene.

Processing of primary transcript RNA to form mRNA – post-transcriptional modification

Before leaving the nucleus, the primary transcript RNA produced during transcription is modified as follows:

- A guanine nucleotide is added to the 5' end of the primary transcript RNA. This 'cap' is used to set off the process of translation when the mRNA reaches a ribosome. This process can occur before the release of the primary transcript from the DNA template.
- Around 100 adenine nucleotides are added to the other end of the RNA. It is thought that this 'tail' may prevent the breakdown of the mRNA in the cytoplasm by nucleases because mRNA without a 'tail' is rapidly destroyed.
- DNA is made up of sections called exons that are coding sequences for polypeptides and sections called introns that are non-coding sequences. These intervening introns would interfere with the synthesis of a polypeptide. In the primary transcript RNA of **eukaryotic cells**, the base sequences corresponding to the introns are removed and the functional exons are joined together in a process called **splicing**. This process is shown in Figure 2.

As there is almost always removal of introns from a primary transcript, the mRNA molecule formed is shorter than the primary transcript and the gene that has been transcribed.

Once the introns have been removed, the remaining exon sections can be rejoined in a variety of different combinations. This means that a single section of DNA (gene) can code for up to a number of proteins, depending on the order in which the exons are recombined. The final result of post-transcriptional modification is a molecule of mRNA.

The mRNA molecules are too large to diffuse out of the nucleus and so, having been processed, they leave via a nuclear pore. Once in the cytoplasm they attach to ribosomes for the next stage of protein synthesis, translation.

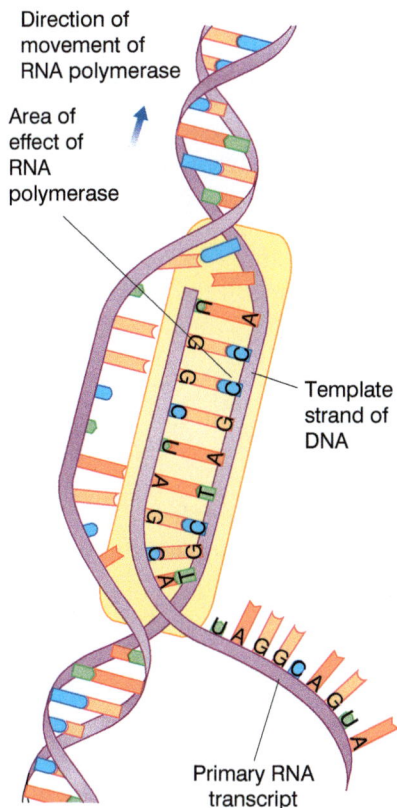

Direction of movement of RNA polymerase

Area of effect of RNA polymerase

Template strand of DNA

Primary RNA transcript

Figure 1 *Summary of transcription*

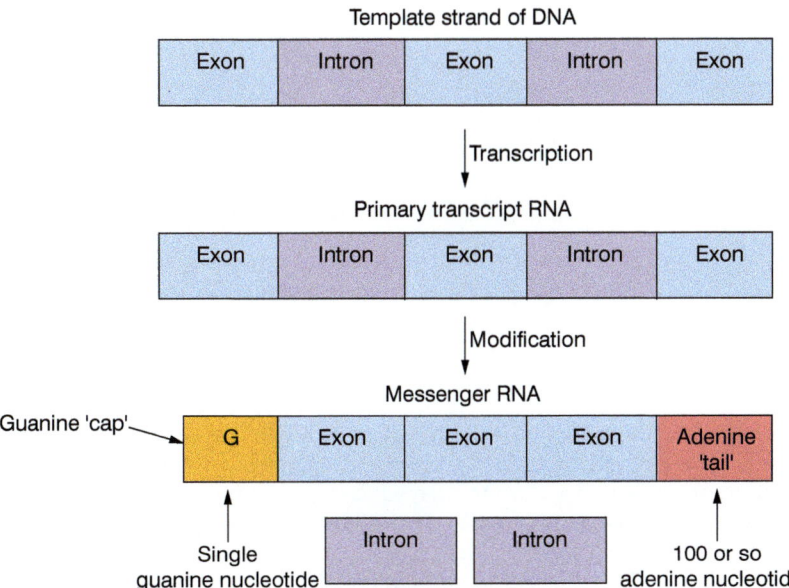

Figure 2 *Processing of primary transcript RNA to form mRNA*

Summary test 6.2b

In transcription, a complementary copy of only one strand of DNA, the **(1)** strand, is produced to form an RNA molecule known as a **(2)**. This goes through modification in the nucleus to form **(3)**. In the initiation stage, the enzyme **(4)** attaches to the DNA and breaks **(5)** bonds between the complementary DNA strands as it moves along the strand of DNA. In the elongation stage, the enzyme adds free **(6)** RNA nucleotides one at a time. These form temporary base pairs with the bases on the DNA strand, for example the RNA base **(7)** pairs with the DNA base adenine and cytosine pairs with the DNA base **(8)**. The RNA molecule formed is **(9)**-stranded. One example of post-translational modification is the addition of a modified **(10)** to the 5' end of the RNA to form a 'cap'. Another is the addition of a protective 'tail' composed of repeating **(11)** nucleotides. In the process of splicing, non-coding sequences known as **(12)** are removed and the remaining coding sequences known as **(13)** are joined. The **(14)** molecule formed leaves the nucleus via a **(15)**.

These pages help you to:

- describe how the information in DNA is used during translation to construct polypeptides (6.2.3 and 6.2.5)
- describe the role of mRNA and the ribosome in the process of translation (6.2.3)
- understand the roles of codons, transfer RNA (tRNA) and anticodons in translation (6.2.3)

You will also:

- learn some examples of post-translational modification

Translation is the process by which the messenger RNA from the nucleus of a cell forms a polypeptide; the sequence of nucleotide bases along the length of mRNA is used to produce the sequence of amino acids in the polypeptide. The process begins with the activation of the amino acids that will make up the polypeptide.

Amino acid activation

The amino acids present in cells must first be **activated** before they can be assembled into a polypeptide. This occurs in two steps:

- The amino acid first forms an intermediate with **ATP**. Much of the energy provided by ATP is conserved for peptide bond formation later.
- The intermediate then combines with transfer RNA to form an amino acid–tRNA complex called **amino-acyl tRNA** (Figure 1). The reaction is controlled by the enzyme amino-acyl tRNA synthetase.

Although the basic structure of tRNA is always the same, a sequence of three bases on the anticodon loop varies. Each anticodon sequence is complementary to a particular mRNA codon sequence. At the other end of the tRNA molecule there is always the sequence of bases adenine–cytosine–cytosine, and it is to this end that the amino acid attaches (Figure 2). The tRNA anticodon sequence determines which amino acid is attached to the tRNA molecule.

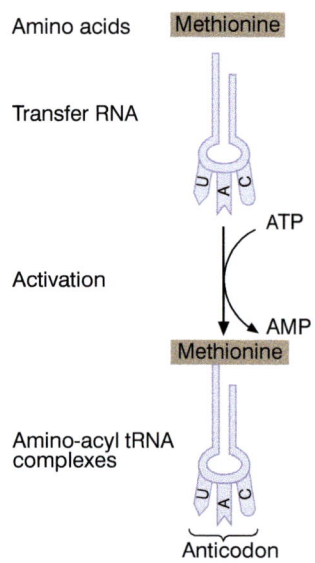
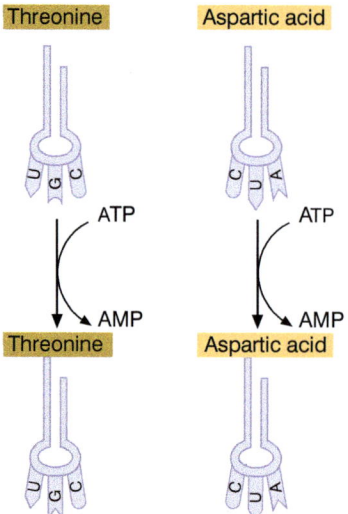

Figure 1 *Amino acid activation*

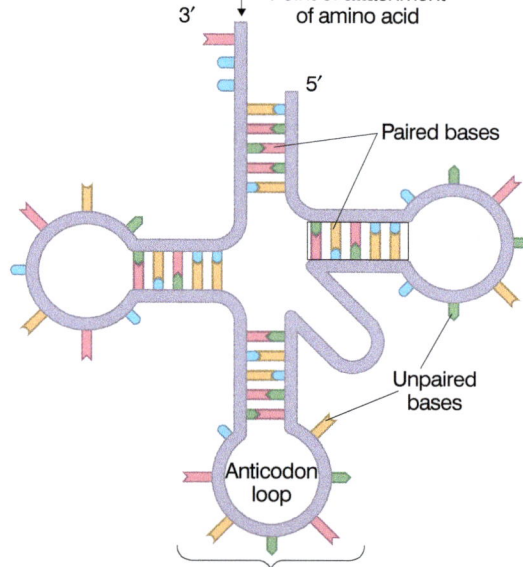

The three bases forming the anticodon: base pairing between an anticodon and a complementary mRNA codon occurs during translation

Figure 2 *Clover-leaf structure of tRNA*

Remember

The genetic code in 6.2a shows that 61 codons code for 20 different amino acids (64 codons in total, three of which are STOP codons). This means that there must be at least 20 different tRNA molecules. As there is more than one codon for most amino acids, cells can have tRNA molecules with different anticodons to attach to a particular amino acid. For example, for the amino acid Ser, the possible mRNA codons are UCU and UCC. This means that two different tRNAs can bind Ser, one with tranticodon AGA and the other with AGG.

Starting polypeptide construction

- The small subunit of the ribosome becomes attached to one end of the mRNA molecule (5' end). The large and small subunit of the ribosome come together to hold the mRNA molecule in place (Figure 3).
- The starting point for translation on the mRNA is normally the triplet of bases **(codon)** AUG (AUG is often known as the START codon).
- There are three attachment points on the large ribosomal subunit for tRNA. These are known as the exit site (E-site), the peptidyl site (P-site) and the aminoacyl site (A-site).
- The amino-acyl tRNA molecule with the anticodon sequence of UAC (also known as tRNA$^{(Met)}$) moves to the ribosome and attaches to the P-site so that it pairs up with the AUG sequence on the mRNA by complementary base pairing (Figure 4).
- As the tRNA which pairs with the AUG sequence on the mRNA always carries the amino acid methionine, polypeptides initially have methionine as the first amino acid.
- However, if this methionine molecule does not make up part of the finished polypeptide, it is removed at the end of the synthesis.

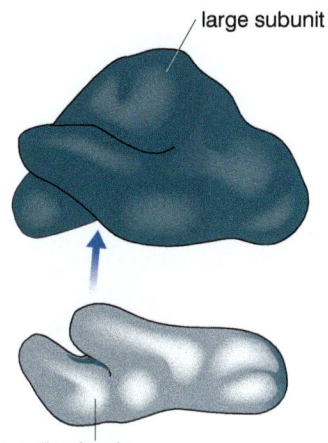

Figure 3 *Structure of a ribosome. The smaller subunit fits into a depression on the surface of the larger one*

> ### Remember
>
> The sequence of bases of an anticodon is the same as the sequence of bases on the triplet of the DNA template (transcribed) strand, with the exception that uracil replaces thymine.
>
> Example: DNA template strand triplet = GTC
>
> mRNA codon that is transcribed = CAG
>
> tRNA anticodon that binds with mRNA codon = GUC

Making the polypeptide

A polypeptide is made as follows:

- A second activated tRNA molecule binds to the ribosome adjacent to tRNA$^{(Met)}$ in the A-site and the anticodon binds to the complementary mRNA codon.
- This brings the two amino acids carried by the tRNA molecules close together.
- By means of an enzyme, the two amino acids on the tRNA are joined by a peptide bond.
- The ribosome moves on to the third codon in the sequence on the mRNA, so that the amino acids on the second and third tRNA molecules can be linked.
- As this happens, the first tRNA is released from its amino acid (methionine) and briefly occupies the E-site on the ribosome before being released into the cytoplasm to collect another methionine molecule from the amino acid pool in the cell.
- The process continues in this way, with up to 15 amino acids being linked each second, until a complete polypeptide chain is built up.
- Up to 50 ribosomes can pass immediately behind the first, so that many identical polypeptides can be made at the same time (Figure 5 on page 118). A group of ribosomes acting in this way is known as a **polysome**.
- The process continues until the ribosome reaches a **STOP codon**. These are UGA, UAG and UAA, and do not attract a tRNA. At this point, therefore, the ribosome, mRNA and the last tRNA molecule all separate and the polypeptide chain is complete.
- The ribosomal subunits separate. Subunits will come together in the presence of another mRNA to start translation and so will become cytoplasmic ribosomes or will bind to the rough endoplasmic reticulum.

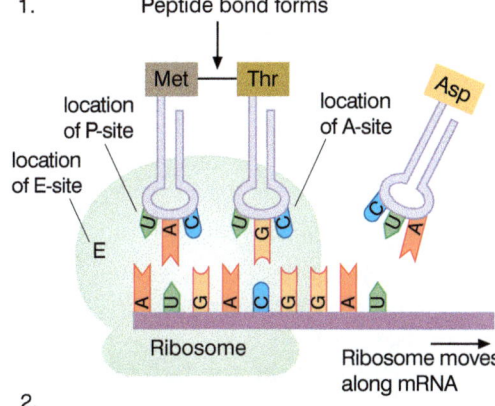

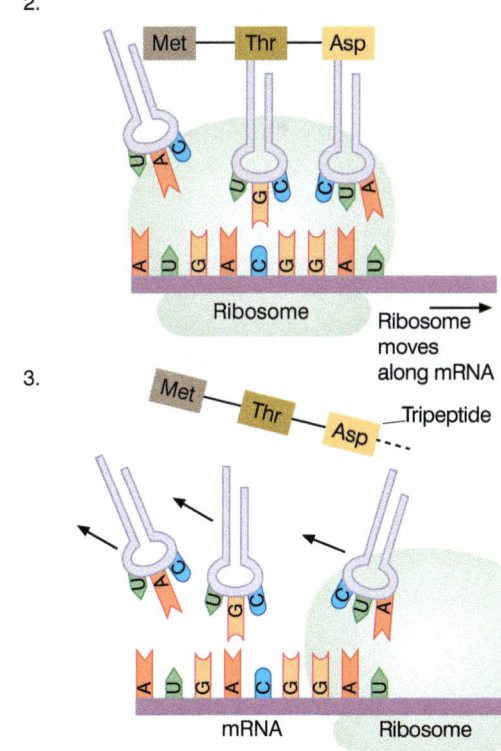

Figure 4 *Translation*

117

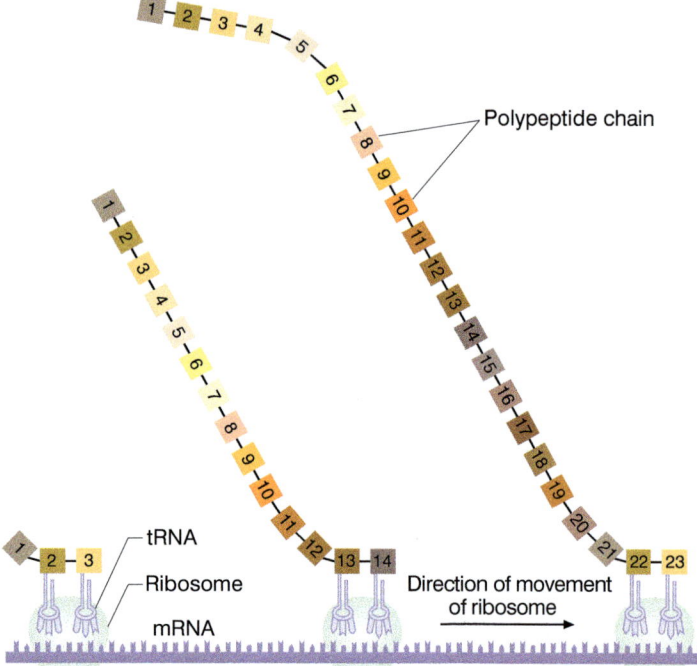

Figure 5 *Polypeptide formation*

Assembling the protein – post-translational modification

Sometimes a single chain folds or coils into its tertiary conformation to become a functional protein. Often, a number of polypeptides are linked to give a functional protein (quaternary structure). Other examples of post-translational modification that may occur, apart from removal of the first amino acid, methionine, are: addition of non-protein units, such as carbohydrates (glycosylation) to form glycoproteins, or lipids to form lipoproteins; modification of the structure of some amino acids, for example in a collagen polypeptide some of the proline amino acids are modified to form hydroxyproline to help the stability of the collagen molecule.

Summary test 6.2c

The formation of a polypeptide from the sequence of bases on messenger RNA is known as **(1)**. It begins with the addition of **(2)** to amino acids, in a process known as activation. These amino acids then combine with transfer RNA to form a complex called **(3)**. To form the polypeptide, a **(4)** becomes attached to the mRNA molecule. Two tRNAs attach to the ribosome so that the **(5)** of each tRNA binds to its mRNA codon. This brings the amino acids close together for **(6)** bond formation. The **(4)** moves along the mRNA three bases at a time and the process repeats to form the polypeptide chain. The process stops when a **(7)** codon is reached.

Extension

Structural formulae of the purine and pyrimidine bases

Figure 6 shows the structural formulae for the purine and pyrimidine bases. You do not need to learn these, but by observing their structure you can see that the purines are 'longer' than the pyrimidines. This means that only a purine–pyrimidine pairing system along the length of a DNA molecule will produce parallel strands (see 6.1b and 6.2b).

This pairing system occurs:

- with DNA nucleotides (A-T, G-C) in DNA replication
- with DNA nucleotides and RNA nucleotides (A-U, G-C, T-A, C-G) in DNA transcription
- with RNA nucleotides (A-U, G-C) in mRNA codon to tRNA anticodon binding during translation

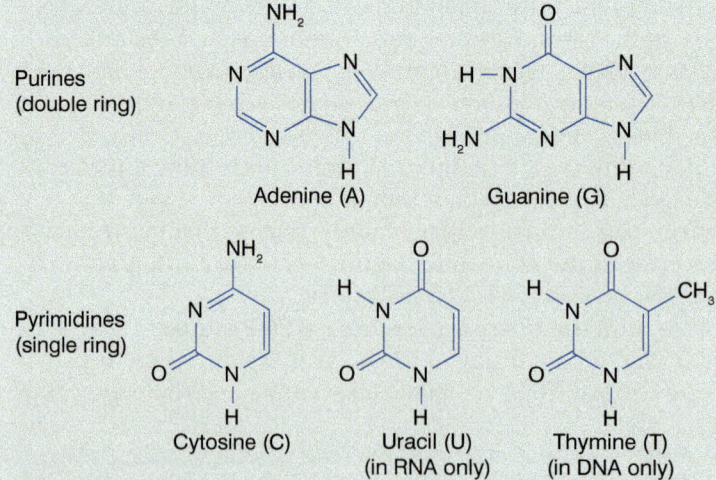

Figure 6 *Purine and pyrimidine bases*

Mutations

A mutation is a change in the sequence of nucleotide bases of DNA. This change may alter a codon, causing it to code for a different amino acid. This may result in a different polypeptide and a different primary structure in a protein. In turn this may result in a different tertiary structure of the protein.

If this protein is an enzyme it could mean a change in shape of the active site. The substrate may no longer fit the active site, preventing the enzyme from functioning. If the alteration to the codon produces a STOP codon, then the polypeptide may be shortened and the final protein may be non-functional.

Mutations occurring in body cells will not be passed on to the next generation. Those occurring during the formation of gametes may, however, be inherited, often producing sudden and distinct differences between individuals.

Insertions

A gene mutation by insertion occurs when one or more extra nucleotides are added into the normal sequence of nucleotides in a DNA molecule. In transcription, this sequence is copied to form mRNA. The nucleotides are 'read' in threes (triplet code) when they are translated into a sequence of amino acids (6.2c). The insertion of an extra base can completely alter the sequence of amino acids from the point of mutation onwards. This means that the primary structure is altered and this will affect the secondary and tertiary protein structure.

As a result of the inserted nucleotide, every triplet of bases that follows the insertion is altered by one nucleotide. This type of mutation, where the whole 'reading frame' is changed, is called a **frame shift**. The frame shift may alter the nucleotide sequence so that a STOP codon is created and the polypeptide chain that results will be shorter (premature chain termination). In many cases, the cell will not recognise the altered or shortened polypeptide chain produced and so there is no further processing to produce a functioning protein. As polypeptides are components of enzymes, this often means that the enzyme cannot be made. The complete biochemical pathway that involves the missing enzyme stops, with potentially fatal consequences for the organism.

Insertions of more than one nucleotide are also possible. Where there is an insertion of three nucleotides there will be a change at the site of insertion but the sequence of amino acids following this will be the same. Even so, a change such as this can greatly alter the tertiary structure of the protein formed.

Deletions

A gene mutation by deletion occurs when one or more nucleotides are lost from the normal DNA sequence. Again, this causes a frame shift that results in a completely different sequence of amino acids in the polypeptide from that originally coded for. Deletions of three (or multiples of three) nucleotides result in the loss of one (or more) amino acids from the chain, with the rest of the chain having the same sequence. Enzymes are often not produced, or do not function properly, with major consequences for the organism.

These pages help you to:

- learn that a gene mutation is a change in the sequence of base pairs in a DNA molecule that may result in an altered polypeptide (6.2.6)
- explain that a gene mutation is a result of substitution, deletion or insertion of nucleotides in DNA (6.2.7)
- outline how a substitution, deletion or insertion mutation may affect the polypeptide produced (6.2.7)

You will also:

- understand the difference between gene mutations and chromosome mutations

Remember

Changes in the structure or number of whole chromosomes are called **chromosome mutations**, whereas changes to DNA that affect a single locus and therefore produce a different allele of a gene are called **gene mutations** or **point mutations**.

Extension

One missing amino acid

One of the most common mutations associated with the genetic disorder cystic fibrosis is a deletion of three nucleotides. This causes the loss of one amino acid, phenylalanine, from the polypeptide chain formed, resulting in a defective membrane channel protein. In cystic fibrosis (see 19.2b) the individual produces mucus that is stickier than usual. As a result, the lungs become congested with this stickier mucus, leading to reduced gaseous exchange. The mucus often blocks the pancreatic ducts as well.

Figure 1 shows the effect of an insertion and deletion mutation on an amino acid sequence.

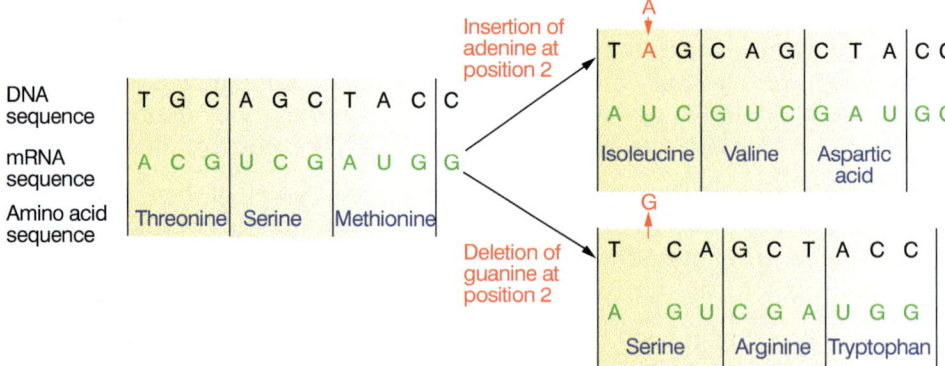

Figure 1 *Effect of insertion and deletion mutations on amino acid sequence*

Substitutions

If a nucleotide in a DNA molecule is replaced by another that has a different base, the type of mutation is known as a substitution. Depending on which new base substitutes for the original one, there are three possible consequences. For example, if we take the triplet of bases in the DNA template strand guanine–thymine–cytosine (GTC) that codes for the amino acid glutamine, a change to a single base could result in one of the following:

- **A nonsense mutation** occurs if the base change results in the formation of one of the three STOP codons that mark the end of a polypeptide chain (see 6.2a). For example if the first base, guanine, is substituted by adenine, then GTC becomes ATC. The triplet ATC codes for one of the three STOP codons on mRNA. As a result the production of the polypeptide would be stopped prematurely. The final protein would be shortened and the protein could not perform its usual function or be degraded (broken down) in the cytoplasm.

- **A mis-sense mutation** occurs when the base change results in a different amino acid being coded for. In our example, if the final base, cytosine, is substituted by guanine, then GTC becomes GTG. The amino acid histidine is coded for by GTG and this then replaces the original amino acid, glutamine. The polypeptide produced as a consequence will be different. How important this change proves to be will depend upon the precise role of the original amino acid. If it is important in forming the bonds that determine the three-dimensional shape of the final protein, then the protein may not function. For example, if the protein is an enzyme, it may no longer have an active site that is complementary to its substrate molecule and so will not catalyse a reaction. The amino acid that is substituted is likely to have less of an effect on the tertiary structure of a protein if the nature of the R-groups are the same (see 2.3b). For example, threonine and serine both have polar R-groups. It is possible that replacing serine with threonine may allow the protein to keep a very similar tertiary structure and have partial function. If tyrosine, with a hydrophobic R-group, replaces serine then it is likely the tertiary structure of the protein will be greatly altered.

- **A silent mutation** is one in which the substitution results in a different base occurring in a DNA triplet but one that still codes for the same amino acid. The final polypeptide produced is identical to the original and no effects are apparent. For instance, if the final base in our example is replaced by thymine then GTC becomes GTT. However, as both these triplets code for glutamine, there is no change to the polypeptide produced. Examples of all three types of substitution mutation are given in Table 1.

Table 1 *Different types of substitution mutation*

	Usual triplet of DNA bases	Nonsense mutation	Mis-sense mutation	Silent mutation
Sequence of bases in DNA non-template strand	CAG	TAG	CAC	CAA
Sequence of bases in DNA template strand	GTC	ATC	GTG	GTT
Sequence of bases in mRNA	CAG	UAG	CAC	CAA
Amino acid in polypeptide	glutamine	stop codon	histidine	glutamine

Extension

Mutagens
Mutagens are agents that increase the natural mutation rate. These agents include:

- Chemicals such as dinitrogen oxide and mustard gas that may directly alter the structure of DNA or interfere with transcription. Hydroxylamine, for example, causes cytosine to pair with adenine rather than guanine. Benzopyrene, a constituent of tobacco smoke, is a powerful mutagen that inactivates the tumour suppressor gene p53 and so leads to cancer (5.1b).

- High energy radiation, e.g. α particles, β particles and neutrons as well as short wavelength ionising radiation such as X-rays and ultraviolet light. These forms of radiation can disrupt the structure of DNA.

Extension

Chromosome mutations
Chromosome mutations can take a number of forms:

- **Changes in whole sets of chromosomes** occur when organisms have three or more sets of chromosomes rather than the usual two. This condition is called **polyploidy** and occurs mostly in plants.

- **Changes in the number of individual chromosomes**. Sometimes individual chromosomes fail to segregate during the anaphase stage of meiosis (see 16.1b). This is known as **non-disjunction** and results in an organism having one or more additional chromosomes. This is called polysomy. Where **polysomy** in humans occurs with the larger chromosomes, the developmental defects are so severe that infants with them die within a few months. The smaller autosomes (chromosomes that are not the sex chromosomes), such as numbers 13, 15, 18, 21 and 22, can however be present as three copies and the individual may survive for some time; in the case of chromosomes 21 and 22 they usually survive to adulthood. An example of a non-disjunction in humans is **Down syndrome**.

Summary test 6.2d

Genes may exist in two or more different forms called **(1)**. Gene mutations arise through a change to a sequence of **(2)** that make up a gene. They take a number of forms. If the original base sequence was GGCTAGATC, then the types of mutation in the following cases would be: GGCTACGATC = **(3)**, GCCTAGATC = **(4)**, GGCTAGTTC = **(5)**, GGCTAGAC = **(6)**, GGCTAGATCC = **(7)**. The type of mutation known as substitution takes three forms depending on the consequences of the change. If the mutation results in a different amino acid being coded for, it is called a **(8)** mutation, if the same amino acid is coded for it is a **(9)** mutation. If one of the three stop codons is formed, it is known as a **(10)** mutation.

6 Exam-style and practice questions

(Launch additional digital resources for the chapter)

6 Exam-style questions

1 DNA was extracted from the muscle of a fruit fly and a human nerve cell.

State how the DNA molecules differed.

A in the ratio of adenine to thymine

B in the sequence of the nucleotides

C in the type of pentose sugar

D in the types of nucleotide *(1 mark)*

2 In an experiment a piece of double-stranded DNA containing 12 000 nucleotides coding for a specific polypeptide is transcribed and translated. The DNA did not contain any introns.

State the total number of amino acids in this polypeptide.

A 1000

B 2000

C 4000

D 6000 *(1 mark)*

3 a Figure 1 shows part of a molecule of DNA.

Figure 1

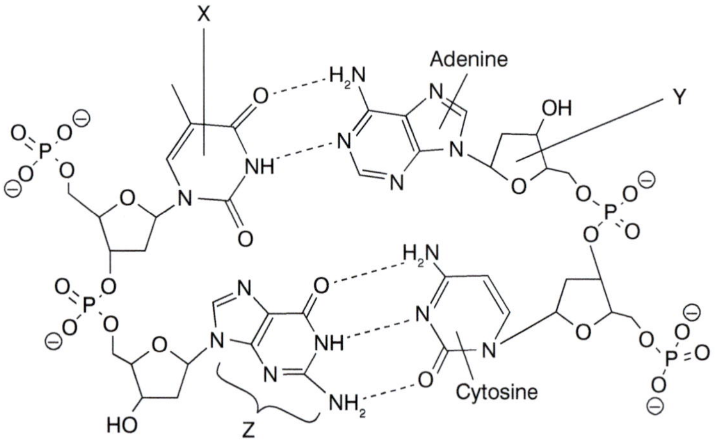

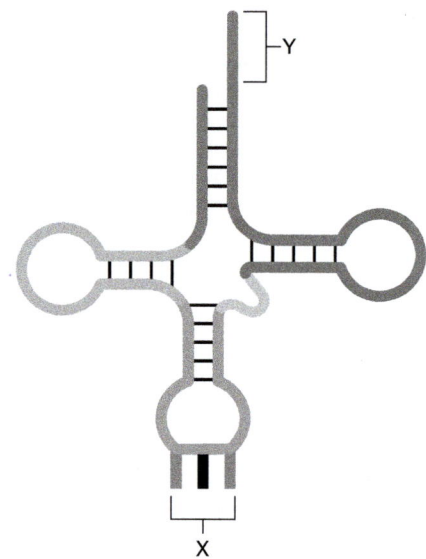

   i Identify the bonds shown by the dashed lines. *(1 mark)*

  ii Identify the parts labelled X, Y and Z. *(3 marks)*

b In Table 1, identify **three** ways in which the structure of DNA differs from the structure of mRNA.

Table 1

DNA	mRNA

(3 marks)

c During the mitotic cell cycle, DNA replicates by semi-conservative replication.

   i Name the stage during the cell cycle when DNA replication takes place. *(1 mark)*

  ii Explain why DNA replication is described as semi-conservative. *(2 marks)*

(Total 10 marks)

4 a Figure 2 is a diagram of a molecule of tRNA.

Figure 2

   i State the function of region Y. *(1 mark)*

  ii State the name of region X **and** explain the role of region X in translation. *(3 marks)*

b tRNA molecules are synthesised inside the nucleus of eukaryotic cells in the same way as RNA transcripts are produced.

Outline the process by which tRNA molecules are synthesised in the nucleus. *(3 marks)*

(Total 7 marks)

6 Practice questions

5 a What are the three basic components of a nucleotide?

b In terms of the structure of the DNA molecule, explain why the base pairings are not adenine with guanine and thymine with cytosine.

c The bases on one strand of DNA are TGGAGACT. What is the base sequence on the other strand?

d If 19.9% of the base pairs in human DNA is guanine, what percentage of human DNA is thymine? Show your reasoning.

6 A section of DNA has the following sequence of bases along it: TACGCTCCGCTGTAC.

All of the bases are part of the code for amino acids. The first base in the sequence is the start of the code.

a How many amino acids does the section of DNA code for?

b Two of the amino acids coded for will be the same. Which two?

c Explain how a length of mRNA containing 10 codons that all have a different base sequence can produce a polypeptide chain containing only six different amino acids.

d Explain how a change in one base along a DNA molecule might result in an enzyme becoming non-functional.

7 a Describe the role of RNA polymerase in the elongation stage of transcription.

b State how RNA polymerase causes the strands of the DNA molecule to separate.

c Why is splicing of primary transcript (RNA) necessary?

d A sequence of bases along the template strand of DNA is ATGCAAGTCCAG.
  i What is the sequence of bases on a messenger RNA molecule that has been transcribed from this part of the DNA molecule?
  ii How many amino acids does the sequence code for?

e A gene is made up of 756 base pairs. The mRNA that is transcribed from this gene is only 524 nucleotides long. Explain why there is this difference.

8 a Explain why the genetic code is described as:
  i universal
  ii degenerate
  iii non-overlapping.

b State three ways in which the molecular structure of RNA differs from DNA.

c Distinguish between a codon and an anticodon.

d Explain why:
  i DNA needs to be chemically very stable
  ii mRNA needs to be easily broken down (chemically unstable).

9 The table below lists some amino acids and the codon for each amino acid found on mRNA. The strand of DNA against which mRNA is transcribed is called the template strand.

Amino acid	Codon
Tyrosine	UAC
Serine	AGU
Aspartic acid	GAC
Glutamine	GAG
Histidine	CAU
Leucine	CUA
Alanine	GCA
Lysine	AAA
Proline	CCU
Glycine	GGC

a Using the table, state the:
  i tRNA anticodon for histidine
  ii triplet on the DNA template strand that codes for serine.

b Name the amino acid coded by the tRNA anticodon GAU.

c A sequence of bases on the template strand of DNA is CTCCGTGGAATGCGT. List the sequence of amino acids that would appear in a polypeptide coded for by this DNA.

d The sequence of amino acids in a section of polypeptide is histidine, proline, aspartic acid, leucine. List the sequence of bases on the DNA template strand that codes for this polypeptide section.

10a Name the cell organelle involved in translation.

b A codon found on a section of messenger RNA has the sequence of bases AUC. List the sequence of bases found on:
  i the transfer RNA anticodon that attaches to this codon
  ii the template strand of DNA that formed the mRNA codon.

c Describe the role of tRNA in the process of translation.

d A strand of mRNA has 64 codons but the protein produced from it has only 63 amino acids. Suggest a reason for this difference.

123

Transport in plants

7.1 Structure of transport tissues

a. Plant anatomy: roots, stems and leaves

These pages help you to:

- become familiar with the distribution of xylem and phloem in transverse sections of stems, roots and leaves of herbaceous dicotyledonous plants (7.1.2)

You will also:

- understand what is meant by the terms herbaceous and dicotyledon
- understand why plants need transport systems
- become familiar with the main parts of a plant

Introduction: the need for a transport system in plants

Plants are multicellular organisms that show a division of labour (1.2a).

The photosynthetic organs of the plant, the leaves, are the source of essential organic products made as a result of photosynthesis. These products are termed assimilates, or photosynthates. Assimilates need to be transported to other regions of the plant, such as the growing regions in root and stem tips, and maturing leaves.

Roots are the organs that take up water and mineral ions from the soil and these need to reach all parts of the plant. When you consider the delivery of water and mineral ions to the leaves of the tallest trees, the distances involved are great (Figure 1).

Osmosis (4.2b) and diffusion (4.2a) are two transport mechanisms that can be used in plants for short distance transport. When longer distances are involved, it would take a long time for water, mineral ions and organic compounds to reach their destination by these transport mechanisms and the requirements of the plant would not be supported. Therefore, a transport system is needed in plants.

Features of plant transport systems

Transport in plants requires specialised transport tissue known collectively as **vascular tissue**. Phloem tissue and xylem tissue are the two types of plant vascular tissue that are present in roots and stems. In leaves, the vascular tissue is located in a network of leaf veins (Figure 2).

Figure 2 *The veins of a leaf form a network that allows material to be transported to and from its cells*

- Xylem tissue functions to transport water and mineral ions from the roots to the stems and leaves (7.2a and 7.2b).
- Phloem tissue functions to transport assimilates from places of synthesis, such as the leaves, to places where they are required, such as the roots and buds (7.2d).

Xylem tissue and phloem tissue contain more than one cell type. There are cells that form the tubular transport vessels and cells that function to support the transport vessels, either providing mechanical or physiological support. These cell types are discussed in 7.1d and 7.1e.

Other features of plant transport systems include:

- long distance, bulk transport involving mass flow
- transport tissue distributed so that all cells can receive the required water, mineral ions and organic compounds
- a transport medium, phloem sap or xylem sap, which is based on water to transport dissolved substances
- movement of the transport medium using pressure differences.

Unlike transport in mammals, the respiratory gases oxygen and carbon dioxide are not transported in vascular tissue. Also, transport is unidirectional, with a starting point and a destination (in contrast to the circulatory system in mammals).

Figure 1 *Giant redwoods can transport water to a height of 100 m without the expenditure of metabolic energy*

The distribution of vascular tissues in dicotyledonous plants

Figure 3 shows the distribution of xylem tissue and phloem tissue in dicotyledonous plants. The two tissues occur together throughout the plant, sometimes with associated tissues, such as **sclerenchyma fibres**, to form distinct areas, known as **vascular bundles**.

You can see that the location of the vascular bundles in the root, stem and leaf differs greatly. The distribution of these tissues and details of the histology of roots, stems and leaves are discussed in 7.1b and 7.1c.

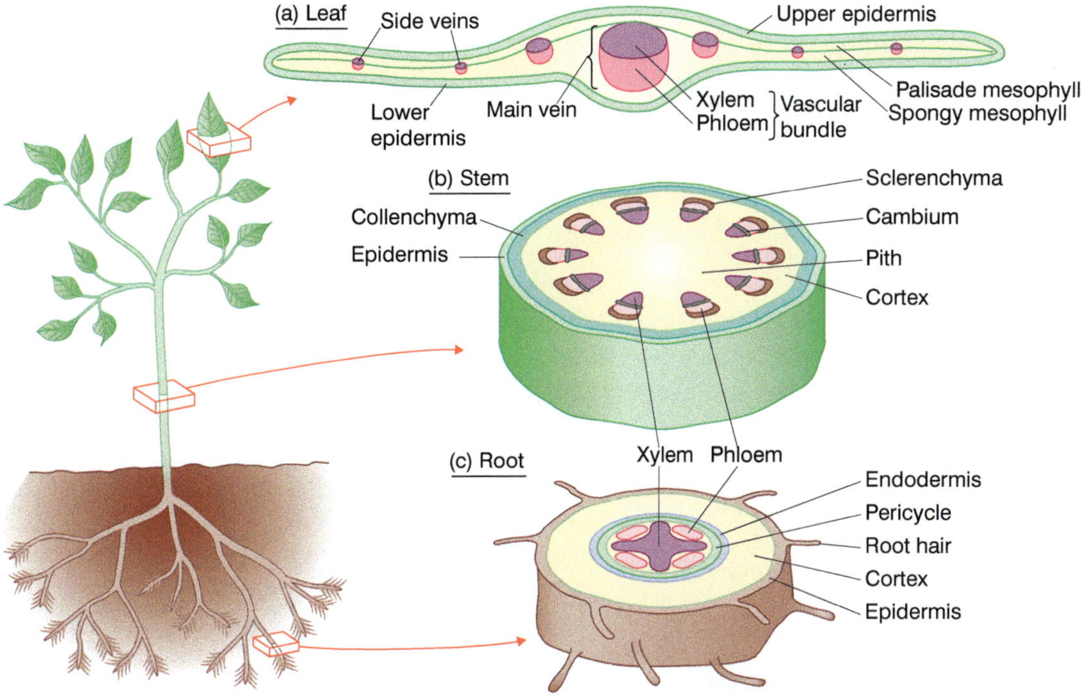

Figure 3 Distribution of vascular tissues in dicotyledonous plants

Herbaceous dicotyledonous plants

Herbaceous plants are plants that have stems that are soft and non-woody, including plants that have a life-cycle that only last a year (annuals). Plants that are long lived may be herbaceous or woody.

Dicotyledons are flowering plants, either woody or herbaceous, that have developed from seeds that have two embryonic leaves (seed leaves or **cotyledons**). They have leaves that have a network of veins, and in stems their vascular tissue is arranged in bundles and in a ring pattern.

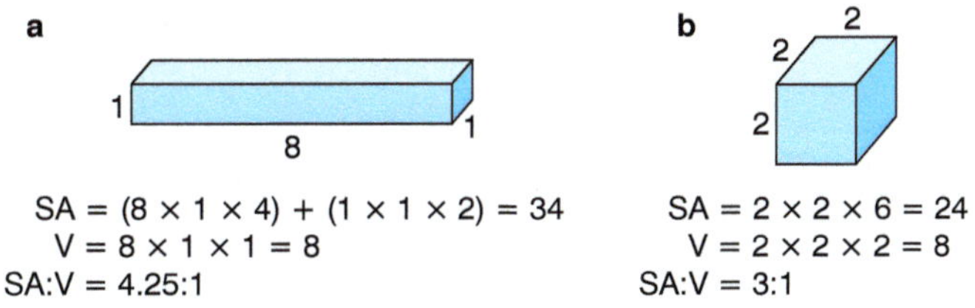

a

SA = (8 × 1 × 4) + (1 × 1 × 2) = 34
V = 8 × 1 × 1 = 8
SA:V = 4.25:1

b

SA = 2 × 2 × 6 = 24
V = 2 × 2 × 2 = 8
SA:V = 3:1

Figure 4 How SA:V changes when shape changes

We have seen that as size increases, the surface area to volume ratio (SA:V) decreases (4.2e). For the same volume, it is possible for an organism to have a different SA:V by having a different body shape. Consider the leaves of a plant. These need to absorb sunlight and take in carbon dioxide for photosynthesis. Figure 4 illustrates how, for the same volume, plant leaves have evolved to maximise SA:V. This principle can also be applied to the extensive root system of plants – a larger SA:V allows a proportionately larger quantity of water and mineral ions to be taken up.

Summary test 7.1a

The main role of xylem tissue is the transport of **(1)** and mineral ions from the **(2)** to the stem and leaves. The organic products of photosynthesis, the **(3)**, are produced in the leaves and transported to other parts of the plant in the **(4)**. The two types of transport, or **(5)** tissue, are located together in the root, stem and leaves. In the **(6)**, these bundles are located in a **(7)**. A herbaceous dicotyledonous plant is non-**(8)** and the seed has two **(9)**.

Extension

Monocotyledons

Monocotyledons are herbaceous flowering plants that have only one embryonic leaf in their seeds. Their leaves have parallel veins and in stems their vascular tissue is arranged in bundles scattered around the stem. Grasses are monocotyledons.

Extension

More about plant requirements

In addition to transport systems, plants have other adaptations to support their requirements. For example, they have a body form (morphology) that helps to increase their surface area to volume ratio so that plant cells in the different organs of the plant are not far from an external surface. The leaves have specialised structures, stomata, that allow gas exchange to occur. Stomata are found on the stems of herbaceous plants. In woody plants, similar structures known as lenticels are present for gas exchange. There are air spaces within the plant to allow rapid diffusion of gases. Plants also do not move and have a lower requirement than animals for oxygen for respiration and ATP production. In leaves, some of the oxygen produced as waste from photosynthesis is used in respiration.

These pages help you to:

- draw plan diagrams of transverse sections (TS) of stems and roots of herbaceous dicotyledonous plants from microscope slides and photomicrographs (7.1.1)
- describe the distribution of xylem and phloem in transverse sections of stems and roots of herbaceous dicotyledonous plants (7.1.2)

You will also:

- be able to relate the structure of a root hair cell to its function
- learn about parenchyma, sclerenchyma and collenchyma

The structure of stem and roots

Stems and roots are organs. These organs contain different tissues, each of which has a particular function.

Figures 1, 2, 3 and 4 show the distribution of the vascular bundles containing phloem tissue and xylem tissue in stems and roots.

The outermost layer of the stem and root is the epidermis. The epidermis is a protective layer of cells that has a thin waxy coating known as the cuticle on its external surface. The cuticle, which is waterproof, is absent in the areas of the root that absorb water from the soil.

Much of the stem and root contains living, undifferentiated (not specialised) cells known as parenchyma cells that function as a packing tissue, filling in the 'spaces', and as a storage tissue. These are roughly spherical or isodiametric (equal diameter in all directions) cells with thin cellulose cell walls and large vacuoles. The cortex of stems and roots, and the pith of stems, is composed of parenchyma cells. Some parenchyma cells have chloroplasts.

Extension

Providing support

There are different mechanical stresses on roots, stems and leaves. Above the soil level, the plant needs to cope with the effects of the wind. Some plants can grow to a very large size and there must be support for this. Vascular tissue, xylem in particular, provides important strength and support for the plant and turgid parenchyma cells packed close together offer hydrostatic support.

Collenchyma and sclerenchyma are tissues specialised for support: collenchyma is a tissue composed of living cells whereas sclerenchyma is composed mainly of dead cells.

Collenchyma tissue is commonly found as a layer directly beneath the outer epidermis. The cells have cellulose cell walls that have an uneven thickening and the walls also contain the polysaccharide pectin: these walls are strong and the packing of cells gives great strength. Collenchyma cells are adapted for areas of growth as their walls are able to stretch.

There are two distinct groups of sclerenchyma cells: sclereids and fibres. Their walls are very thick and many of them have lignin in addition to cellulose. Sclerenchyma tissue is very important for support and strength in areas that are no longer elongating (as dead cells they cannot stretch like collenchyma cells). Fibres are long cells, whereas sclereids are shorter and of varying shapes.

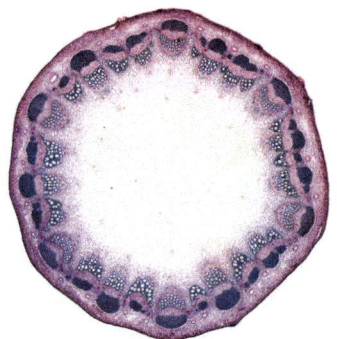

Figure 1 *Transverse section (TS) dicotyledonous stem*

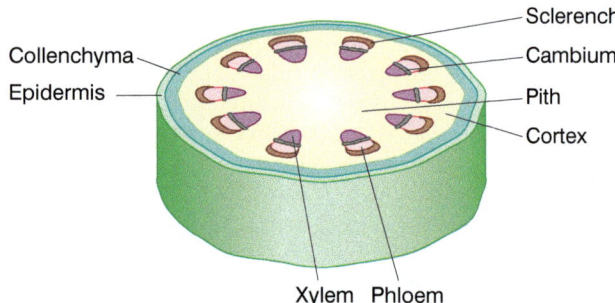

Collenchyma
Epidermis
Sclerenchyma
Cambium
Pith
Cortex
Xylem   Phloem

Figure 2 *Distribution of vascular tissues in the stem*

Distribution of vascular tissue in a stem

The xylem and phloem in a dicotyledonous stem form vascular bundles that are arranged towards the outside of the stem (Figures 1 and 2). The reason for this is that the vascular bundles, together with associated sclerenchyma fibres, provide support in herbaceous stems as well as transport material. The main forces acting on stems are lateral ones caused by the action of wind on them. Such forces are best resisted by an outer cylinder of supporting tissue. Hence the vascular bundles form a non-continuous ring towards the edge of the stem, nearer to the epidermis (Figures 1 and 2). Being non-continuous, this ring of supporting tissues allows the stem to be flexible and to bend in the wind. Within the vascular bundles, the xylem is to the inside of the stem (towards the centre of the stem) and the phloem towards the outside (towards the epidermal layer). Between the two is a thin layer of cells forming a tissue known as **cambium**. Cambium is meristematic tissue (5.2a). The cells are able to divide by mitosis to produce cells that can differentiate to form new xylem to the inside and new phloem to the outside.

Distribution of vascular tissue in a root

The vascular tissue in the root of a dicotyledonous plant (Figures 3 and 4) is situated centrally rather than towards the outer edge, as in a stem. This is because roots are subject only to pulling forces. Vertical forces are better resisted by a central column of supporting tissues, such as xylem, rather than an outer cylinder of tissue. The xylem is typically arranged in a single star-shaped block of tissue at the centre of the root, with the phloem situated in separate groups between each of the points of the star-shaped xylem. Around both is the **pericycle** and **endodermis**, more details of which are given in 7.2a.

Root hair cells

The section of the root shown in Figure 4 is from a young area of root. The epidermis in this region, known as the piliferous layer, has many root hair cells.

A root hair cell (Figure 5) is a modified epidermal cell. The cell has a large vacuole and a long cytoplasmic extension projecting into the soil environment, providing a large surface area for water and mineral ion uptake. The root hair is very delicate and the cell does not live for long. As the root grows, new root hair cells nearer to the tip are formed to replace old ones.

Other structural adaptations of a root hair cell include:

- no waxy cuticle, with a thin cellulose cell wall
- many aquaporins (channel proteins for water uptake) in the cell surface membrane
- many mitochondria to provide ATP for the active uptake of mineral ions.

Figure 3 TS dicotyledonous root

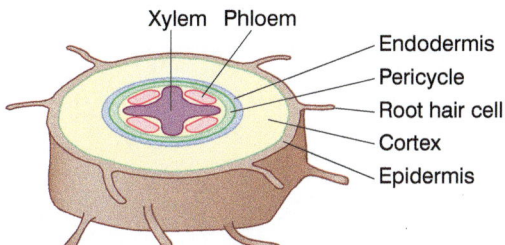

Figure 4 Distribution of vascular tissues in the root

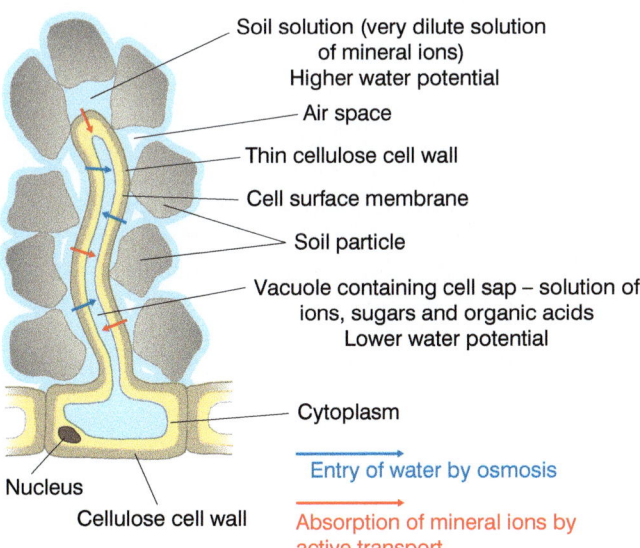

Figure 5 Absorption of water and mineral ions by a root hair cell

Practical skill

Drawing plan diagrams of transverse sections of stems and roots

Figures 6 and 7 show plan diagrams drawn from transverse sections of a stem and a root.

Notice that individual cells are not drawn. This is because a plan diagram is a drawing that shows the distribution of tissues in a section. These have been labelled. They also show the proportions of the different tissues.

Annotations can also be added if required. These include descriptions of shape, size and colour (for example, differences in staining).

You will learn more about drawing plan diagrams on page 130 in 7.1c.

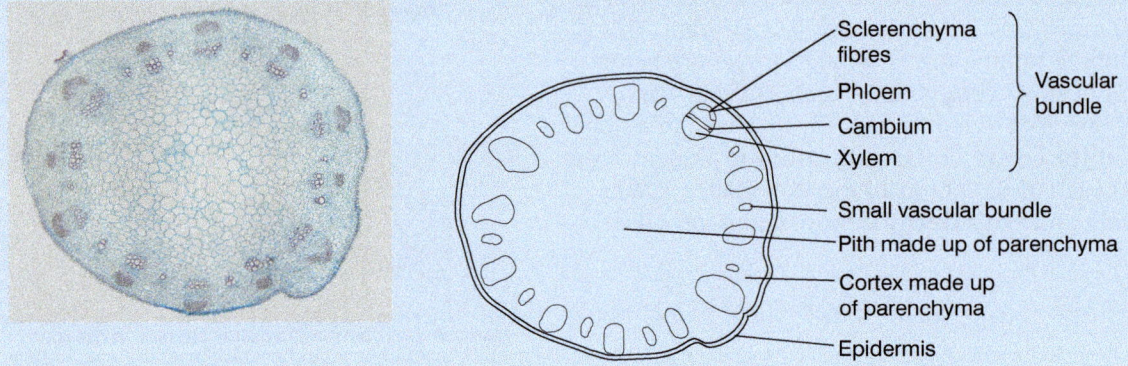

Figure 6 *Low power plan diagram (right) of the tissues shown in photograph (left) of a TS through a dicotyledonous stem*

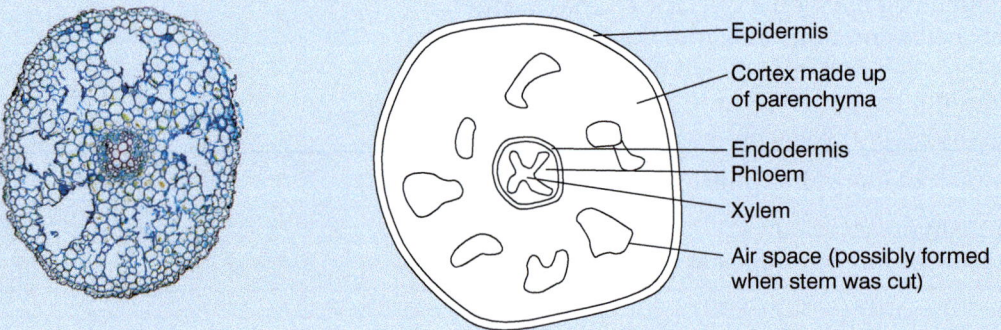

Figure 7 *Low power plan diagram (right) of the tissues shown in photograph (left) of a TS through a dicotyledonous root*

Summary test 7.1b

Stems and roots are **(1)**, because they are made of different tissues. The outer layer is a tissue known as the **(2)**, which has an outer waterproof **(3)**. Undifferentiated cells with large vacuoles form **(4)** tissue, which serves as a packing tissue and has a role in **(5)** and providing hydrostatic support. When observing transverse sections, in the root, the vascular bundle is located **(6)**, with the **(7)** tissue frequently in a 3- or 5-point star shape and the **(8)** tissue between each of the points.

Distribution of vascular tissues in a leaf

The leaf of the plant is the organ of photosynthesis. Figure 2 shows a transverse section of a dicotyledonous leaf. The distribution of the vascular tissue is in more than one location in this section. The vascular tissues in a **dicotyledonous** leaf form a network of tiny vascular bundles throughout the blade, or **lamina**, of the leaf. These vascular bundles form a series of **side veins** that run parallel with one another. These side veins then merge into a central **main vein**, also known as the midrib (Figure 1). The main vein runs along the centre of the leaf, increasing in diameter towards the petiole, or leaf stalk. Within each vein, or vascular bundle, there is an area of xylem towards the upper surface of the leaf and an area of phloem towards the lower surface. This arrangement is shown in the section through the leaf shown in Figure 2. As the phloem is on the lower surface, it follows that in the transition from leaf stalk to stem, the phloem tissue will be nearer to the periphery (edge) of the stem and the xylem nearer to the centre (7.1b).

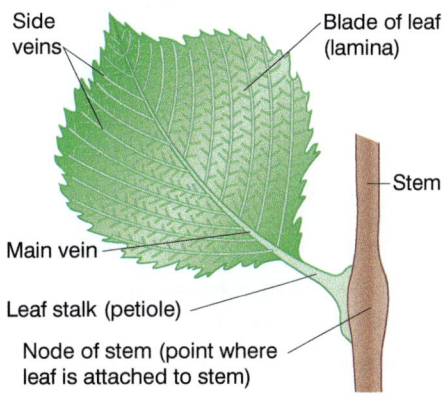

Figure 1 Leaf of a dicotyledonous plant, e.g. elm, showing arrangement of veins

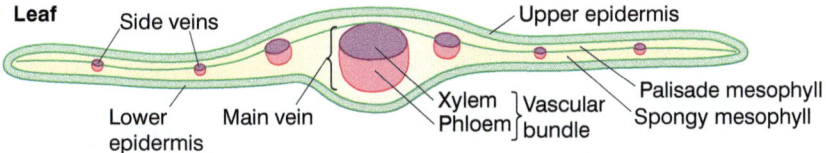

Figure 2 Distribution of vascular tissues in dicotyledonous plants

Leaf structure

The different tissues shown in Figures 2 and 3 carry out different functions:

- The **epidermis** is composed of colourless cells, allowing light to enter the leaf. It protects the leaf. There are specialised epidermal cells, mainly on the lower epidermis, known as guard cells. These cells enclose pores known as stomata (see 14.2a). The exchange of gases takes place through stomata: carbon dioxide is needed during the day for photosynthesis and oxygen is needed during the day and night for respiration. Most water vapour is lost from the plant through the stomata (7.2b). The outer surface of the epidermis is covered with a waxy cuticle to help minimise water loss.
- The **palisade mesophyll** is the main tissue that carries out photosynthesis.
- The **spongy mesophyll** is loosely packed so provides large air spaces between cells (intercellular air spaces) for efficient diffusion of gases. Spongy mesophyll cells can photosynthesise (but have fewer chloroplasts than palisade cells) and store starch.
- The **phloem** transports organic materials away from the leaf.
- The **xylem** transports water and ions into the leaf.
- **Parenchyma, collenchyma** and **sclerenchyma** are present in different proportions in the region of the veins of leaves. Veins frequently have a ring of parenchyma cells around them and collenchyma and sclerenchyma provide support.

These pages help you to:

- draw plan diagrams of transverse sections of leaves of herbaceous dicotyledonous plants from microscope slides and photomicrographs (7.1.1)
- describe the distribution of xylem and phloem in transverse sections of leaves of herbaceous dicotyledonous plants (7.1.2)

You will also:

- be able to describe the structure of a palisade mesophyll cell and relate the structure to its function in photosynthesis

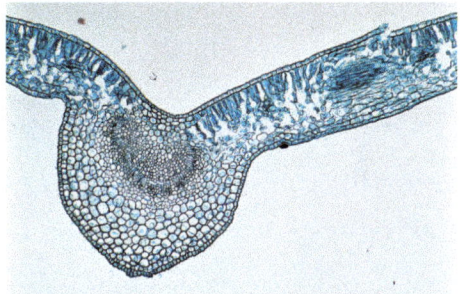

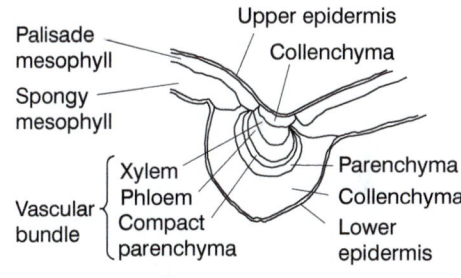

Figure 3 Low power plan diagram (bottom) of the tissues shown in the photograph (top) of a TS through the main vein of a dicotyledonous leaf

Remember

When you observe slides of plant tissue, the common stains used can highlight different tissues. For example, tissue containing cells with lignified walls, such as xylem and sclerenchyma, commonly stain pink or red, whereas tissue containing cells that only have cellulose in their walls commonly stain blue or green.

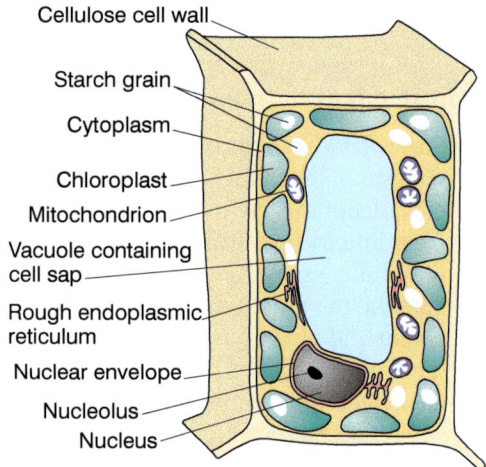

Cellulose cell wall

Starch grain

Cytoplasm

Chloroplast

Mitochondrion

Vacuole containing
cell sap

Rough endoplasmic
reticulum

Nuclear envelope

Nucleolus

Nucleus

Figure 4 *Palisade mesophyll cell*

Extension

Structure to function – the palisade mesophyll cell

Using your knowledge of cell structure, you should be able to give an account of how a palisade mesophyll cell (Figure 4) has a structure that is adapted to its function as a photosynthetic cell.

Palisade mesophyll cells are adapted to carry out photosynthesis because they:

- are closely packed and thin-walled to absorb maximum light
- are arranged vertically so there are fewer cross walls that could filter out the light
- are packed with numerous chloroplasts that move within the cells and are arranged in the best positions to collect the maximum quantity of light
- have a large vacuole that pushes the cytoplasm and chloroplasts to the edge of the cells, allowing them to absorb maximum light and leave a short diffusion pathway for carbon dioxide
- have a large surface area and moist, thin walls for rapid diffusion of gases.

Practical skill

Drawing plan diagrams from microscope slides and photomicrographs

If you follow some simple 'rules' about drawing plan diagrams, then these become relatively straightforward to produce. A plan diagram using the low power objective lens of the microscope or from a photomicrograph often takes less time than drawing cells visible under high power.

Instructions	Comment
Use a sharp pencil	Before you start, round off a sharpened pencil slightly so that the pointed end does not break off.
Make lines clear	Do not allow your pencil to become blunt and produce a thickened line.
Use continuous lines	The lines should not be broken or appear sketchy.
Do not show individual cells	Do not be tempted to add these to try and make your diagram look more interesting.
Only show tissues	You can do this by giving an outline of the tissue areas or layers.
When drawing outlines of different tissues, make the proportions realistic	With a photomicrograph, use a ruler, or lightly draw over with a large-squared grid to get the proportions correct. With a prepared slide, use the eyepiece graticule to gauge proportions.
Use the available space	Make sure you leave enough room for labels if you have been told to include these.
Do not shade or colour in the final diagram	Unless you are asked to do so to highlight a particular area.
Add labels and/or annotations only if instructed to do so	Annotations are additional notes that show observations that you have not included in your diagram (e.g. to describe colour or intensity of staining or give further information about a feature).
Use a ruler for label lines	Remember label lines should not be crossed and should not have arrow heads.

Summary test 7.1c

The vascular tissue in **(1)** leaves forms a network of vascular bundles throughout the leaf **(2)**. There is one main central **(3)** and from this there are many **(4)**. In a transverse section (TS) of a leaf, the outer protective tissue is the **(5)**. The loosely packed tissue is **(6)** and these provide large **(7)** for rapid diffusion of gases. The main photosynthetic tissue is **(8)**. The **(9)** tissue in the vascular bundles is nearer to the upper surface of the leaf.

d. Xylem vessel elements

Xylem is the main water-conducting tissue in vascular plants. It also transports mineral ions dissolved in the water, to form xylem sap, and provides support for plants. Xylem vessels are formed from xylem vessel elements.

Structure of xylem vessel elements

Xylem vessel elements vary in structure, depending on the type and amount of thickening of their cell walls, but are all hollow and elongated. As they mature their walls become impregnated with lignin, which causes them to die because the cells are unable to obtain water. The end walls break down, causing the cells to form a continuous tube, known as a xylem vessel. (The word 'element' is sometimes used rather than 'cell' because a cell is a living structure, whereas mature xylem vessels are dead.) Sometimes the lignin forms rings (annular thickening) around the vessel; in other cases it forms a spiral or a network (reticulate thickening), see Figure 3. This arrangement is better than a continuous thickening, because it allows elongation of the vessels as the plant grows. There are areas of the lignified wall where lignin is absent. These non-lignified regions are called **pits** (Figure 5, page 132). They are not completely open as there is still a cellulose cell wall across them – it is just that the wall is not lignified at these points. Pits allow for lateral (sideways) movement of water. In angiosperms (flowering plants), xylem vessels are the structures through which the vast majority of water is transported. As water is a universal solvent, it is the ideal medium in which to dissolve mineral ions for transport from the roots to the cells in the stem and leaves of the plant.

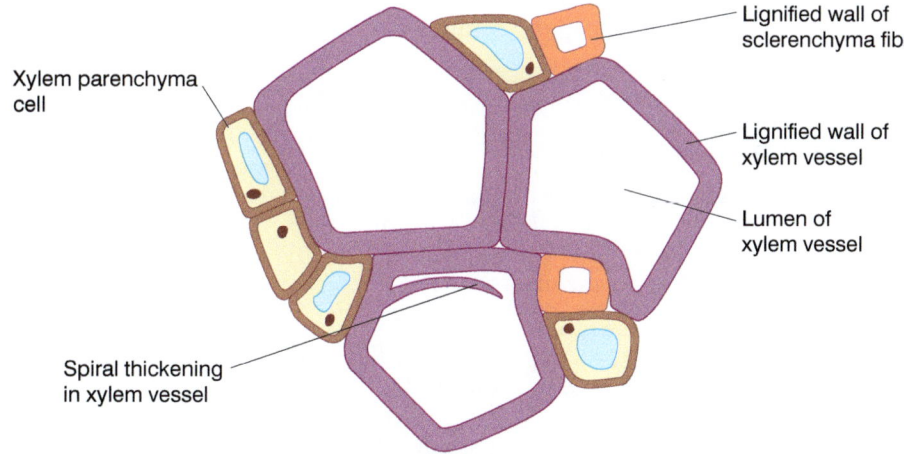

Xylem parenchyma cell

Lignified wall of sclerenchyma fibre

Lignified wall of xylem vessel

Lumen of xylem vessel

Spiral thickening in xylem vessel

Figure 4 *Xylem in TS as seen using a light microscope*

Practical skill

Drawing xylem vessel elements

Figures 2 and 4 show transverse sections of xylem vessel elements and surrounding cells. If asked to produce a high power drawing of xylem vessel elements, then you should not include xylem parenchyma or sclerenchyma fibres. Make sure that the walls appear thick and if possible use the eyepiece graticule to give you the correct proportion of wall thickness to lumen diameter. Remember that the lumen of the xylem vessel element has no contents and can be annotated as hollow. The cell wall of the xylem vessel element is lignified, but remember that it contains cellulose impregnated with lignin. There is no cell surface membrane and pits are too small in diameter to be seen.

If drawing xylem vessel elements in longitudinal section (LS), such as those in Figure 1, remember to add a label line exactly to the spiral or ring to label the lignin – a label line in between can be mistaken for the hollow lumen.

These pages help you to:

- draw and label xylem vessel elements from microscope slides, photomicrographs and electron micrographs (7.1.3)
- relate the structure of xylem vessel elements to their functions (7.1.4)

You will also:

- learn about other cell types in xylem tissue

Figure 1 *Xylem in LS as seen using a light microscope*

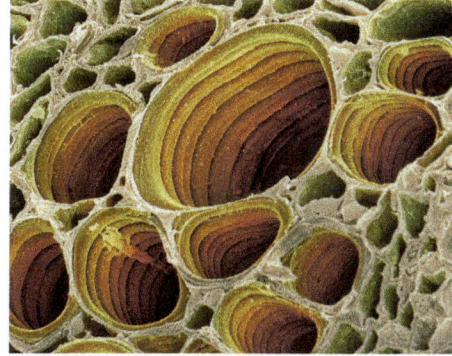

Figure 2 *Leaf of tobacco showing xylem vessels (SEM) (×500 approx.)*

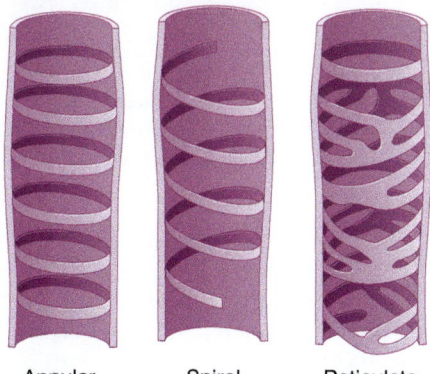

Annular Spiral Reticulate

Figure 3 *Types of thickening in xylem vessels*

131

Extension

Xylem fibres (Figure 4, page 132)

Xylem fibres are elongated sclerenchyma cells with walls that are thickened with lignin to provide support.

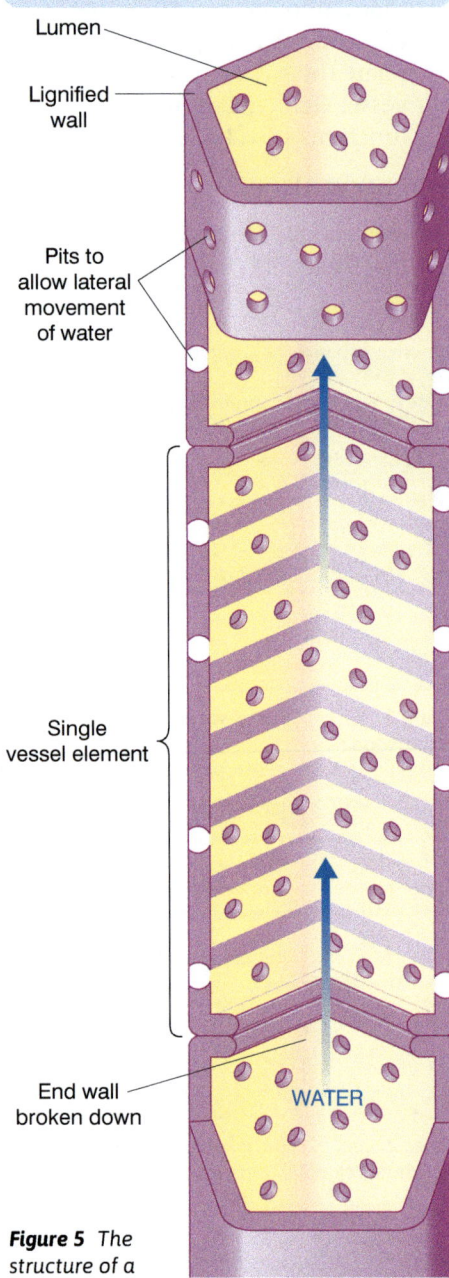

Figure 5 *The structure of a xylem vessel*

Labels on figure:
- Lumen
- Lignified wall
- Pits to allow lateral movement of water
- Single vessel element
- End wall broken down
- WATER
- Vessel

Extension

Lignin

Lignin is a biological polymer that is the main component of wood in woody plants. By providing mechanical strength to the cell walls of sclerenchyma, xylem vessel elements and xylem tracheids, it gives strength and support to the whole plant.

Structure of xylem vessel elements related to function

The structure of xylem vessel elements is well suited to their function in the transport of water and mineral ions:

- The cells are long and arranged end to end to form a continuous tube.
- The cell dies when mature, which means that:
  - the cell is hollow with no cytoplasmic contents and no nucleus to minimise the resistance to flow of xylem sap (water and mineral ions) and allow a larger volume of water per unit time to be transported
  - the end walls break down to produce a continuous tube with no resistance to flow between cells.
- Cellulose cell walls are thickened with lignin, known as secondary thickening, which:
  - makes them more rigid and therefore less likely to collapse inwards under the tension created by transpiration pull (7.2b)
  - is a largely hydrophobic compound, so that the mature xylem vessel wall is waterproof to prevent water escaping.
- Lignin is deposited over time, and in maturing xylem, different types of lignin thickening can be seen. Annular, reticulate and spiral thickening (Figure 3) allow xylem vessels to elongate during growth.
- In mature xylem vessel elements, there are pits throughout the cells. These can occur in pairs to connect adjacent xylem vessel elements and can supply surrounding cells with water. If tiny air bubbles occur in one xylem vessel and movement of water is hindered, water can detour this area by passing through the pit to the adjacent xylem vessel.
- Cellulose walls increase the **adhesion** of water molecules, which helps to resist the effects of gravity and keep the column of water moving up (7.2b).

Extension

Other cell types in xylem tissue

- **Xylem parenchyma** is composed of unspecialised cells that act as packing tissue around the other components of the xylem. They are roughly spherical in shape, but when they are turgid they press upon and flatten each other in places. In this way they provide hydrostatic support.

- **Tracheids** have a similar structure to vessels, except they are longer and thinner, and have tapering ends. They, too, are thickened with lignin and therefore die when mature. As with vessels, the end walls break down, and their side walls possess pits which allow lateral movement of water between adjacent cells. Tracheids are found in all plants and are the main water-conducting tissue in ferns and conifers. Like xylem vessel elements, tracheids function to transport water and dissolved ions and provide support to the plant.

Summary test 7.1d

Xylem vessel elements are joined end to end to form tubes known as xylem **(1)**. The walls of xylem vessel elements are thickened with a substance called **(2)**, which forms different patterns of thickening, such as **(3)**, **(4)** and **(5)** in young xylem. Water moves through the central cavity, called the **(6)**, of the xylem elements but can move sideways between adjacent elements through structures called **(7)**. Also found within the xylem is supporting tissue, called **(8)**. Xylem vessel elements are suited to the function as they are **(9)** cells joined end to end to form a **(10)**. The cells are dead, which means that they are **(11)**, with no **(12)** and nucleus. The **(13)** are broken down. These features minimise **(14)** to flow. The **(15)** walls prevent water loss and prevent **(16)** of the xylem vessel elements.

Phloem is the main transport tissue of organic material in vascular plants. It carries organic material such as sugars, amino acids and plant hormones from leaves and storage organs, known as sources, to other parts of the plant, known as sinks. These organic compounds, together with some mineral ions, are carried dissolved in water to form a fluid known as phloem sap.

Structure of phloem

Phloem is composed of a number of cell types:

- **Sieve tube elements** are elongated cells that are joined end to end to form long tubes, as shown in Figures 1 and 3a. The cells are living and retain a thin layer of cytoplasm under their cell surface membrane (peripheral cytoplasm), which lies against the cellulose cell wall. In the cytoplasm are mitochondria and a modified form of endoplasmic reticulum (rough and smooth endoplasmic reticulum are not present). However, unlike most cells, there is no nucleus or Golgi body and there are no ribosomes. These are broken down in order to have fewer cell structures within the sieve tubes and so reduce resistance to the flow of liquid within them. The end walls of the sieve tubes are perforated by large pores, 2–6 μm in diameter. These perforated end walls are called **sieve plates (**Figure 2 and Figure 4 on page 134). The central space within the sieve tube is called the **lumen**.

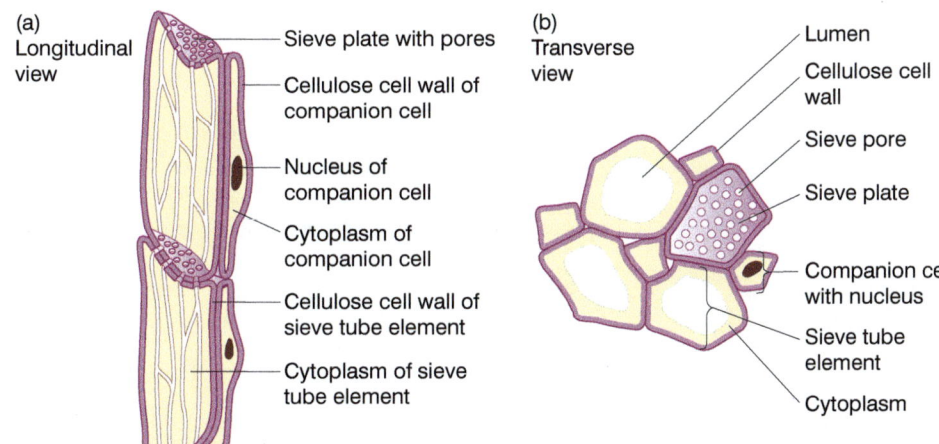

(a) Longitudinal view — Sieve plate with pores — Cellulose cell wall of companion cell — Nucleus of companion cell — Cytoplasm of companion cell — Cellulose cell wall of sieve tube element — Cytoplasm of sieve tube element

(b) Transverse view — Lumen — Cellulose cell wall — Sieve pore — Sieve plate — Companion cell with nucleus — Sieve tube element — Cytoplasm

Figure 3 Phloem as seen under a light microscope

> **Remember**
>
> Although there is some endoplasmic reticulum in a phloem sieve tube element, there is no rough or smooth endoplasmic reticulum.

These pages help you to:

- draw and label phloem sieve tube elements and companion cells from microscope slides, photomicrographs and electron micrographs (7.1.3)
- relate the structure of phloem sieve tube elements and companion cells to their functions (7.1.4)

You will also:

- learn about other cell types in phloem tissue

Figure 1 Phloem sieve tube as seen under a light microscope (×400 approx.)

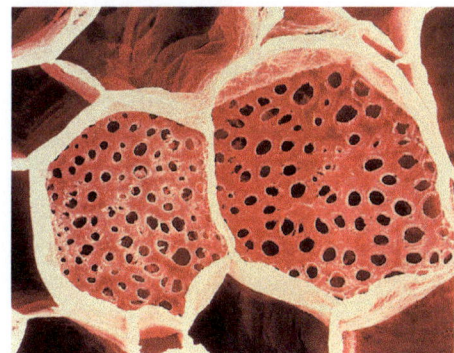

Figure 2 Colourised scanning electron micrograph of sieve plates

- **Companion cells** are always associated with phloem sieve tube elements (Figure 3 on page 133 and Figure 4) and both come from the same cell division. As the sieve tube elements lack structures such as a nucleus, ribosomes and Golgi body, they are unable to carry out many of the metabolic processes essential for their survival. The companion cells are the site of these processes. With all the required organelles, dense cytoplasm and thin cellulose cell wall, they perform the metabolic activities for both themselves and the sieve tube elements. In the areas where assimilates are loaded or unloaded there are many plasmodesmata (Figure 4) between the companion cell and the phloem sieve tube element. In other areas where there are fewer plasmodesmata (to maintain pressure gradients; see 7.2d) the companion cell is likely to use specific membrane carrier proteins for the lateral transfer of materials. At the tips of veins in the leaf, companion cells have very folded cell walls and cell surface membranes. These special types of companion cells are called **transfer cells** and their large surface area increases the rate of transfer of sucrose into the sieve tube elements.

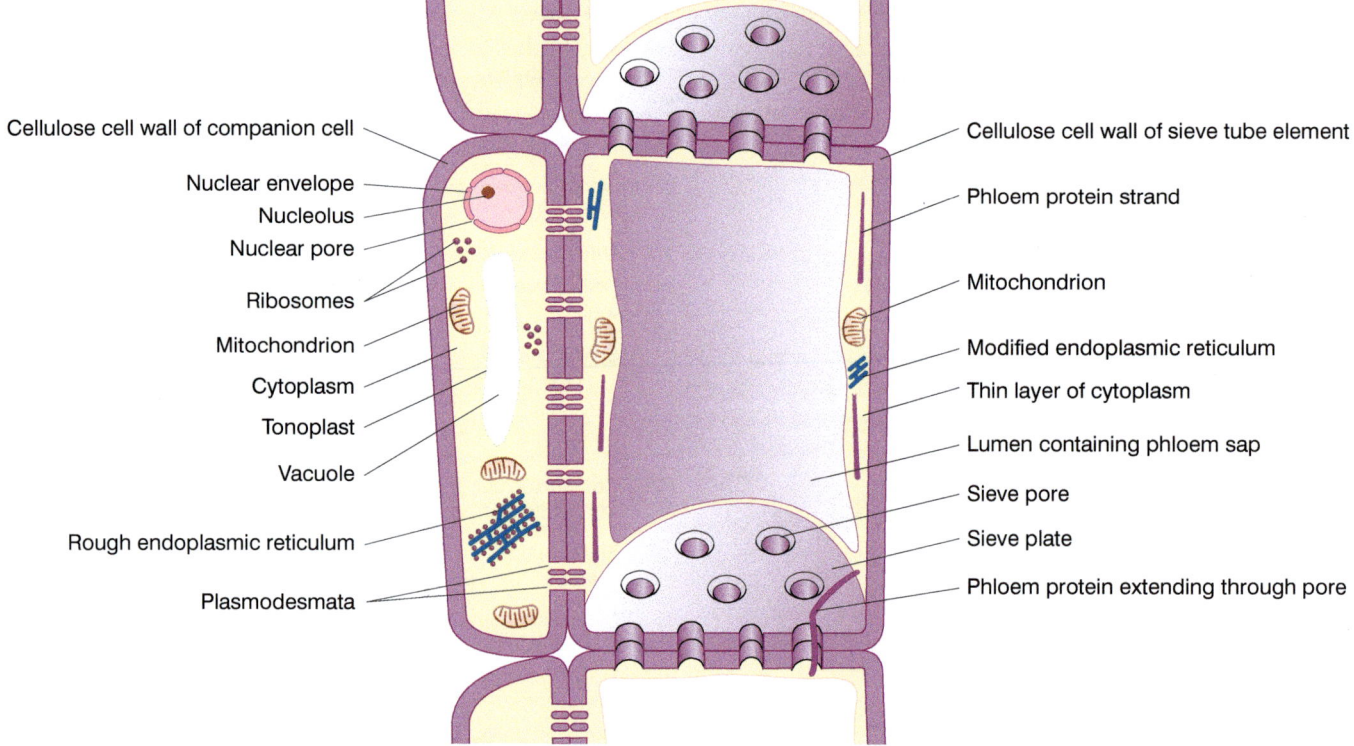

Cellulose cell wall of companion cell

Nuclear envelope

Nucleolus

Nuclear pore

Ribosomes

Mitochondrion

Cytoplasm

Tonoplast

Vacuole

Rough endoplasmic reticulum

Plasmodesmata

Cellulose cell wall of sieve tube element

Phloem protein strand

Mitochondrion

Modified endoplasmic reticulum

Thin layer of cytoplasm

Lumen containing phloem sap

Sieve pore

Sieve plate

Phloem protein extending through pore

Figure 4 *Sieve tube element and companion cell structure as shown by using an electron microscope*

Remember

A companion cell serves to transfer assimilates such as sucrose to or from a phloem sieve tube element. It is not the conducting cell transporting assimilates from a source to a sink.

Structure of phloem sieve tube elements and companion cells related to function

The structure of sieve tubes has evolved to suit their function of transporting organic materials in solution. Also, the structure of companion cells is suited to their function in physiologically supporting phloem sieve tube elements and in transferring assimilates to and from the sieve tubes.

- Sieve tube elements are elongated and arranged end to end to form a continuous phloem sieve tube.
- The nucleus and many of the organelles are located in the companion cells, leaving the lumen of the sieve tube elements more open so reducing resistance to the flow of phloem sap.
- Sieve plates are perforated with sieve pores, reducing resistance to liquid flow.
- Sieve plates hold the walls of sieve tube elements together and prevent them from bursting.
- The walls contain cellulose microfibrils that run around the cells, giving strength and preventing the tubes bursting under pressure.
- The walls are thin to allow easy entry of water at the source, which helps to build up pressure.
- Companion cells have many mitochondria to release the ATP needed for translocation of organic materials.
- Plasmodesmata in the areas of loading and unloading allow easy movement of substances to and from companion cells.
- Phloem proteins are a variety of different proteins that are thought to have a role in defence against pathogens and in sealing wounds.

Practical skill

Drawing phloem sieve tube elements and companion cells

In a prepared slide of a transverse section of phloem tissue, phloem sieve tube elements can be identified by having thinner walls proportionate to their lumen, compared to xylem vessel elements (also if stains have been used, the xylem vessel walls are commonly stained red). You can also look for an area where there is an obvious sieve plate.

You should draw cells touching each other, and, unless told otherwise, show the smaller companion cells or any parenchyma cells adjacent to the sieve tube elements.

In longitudinal section (LS), phloem sieve tube elements appear as elongate, individual cells joined end to end and separated by cross walls. These walls are in fact sieve plates with sieve pores (it is not always possible to see sieve pores if the plate is horizontal in the cut section). Companion cells appear much narrower adjacent to phloem sieve tubes.

A phloem sieve tube element is a living cell, but remember it does not have a nucleus or a large central vacuole. If you observe a dark spot in a phloem sieve tube cell in a prepared slide, then it is not a nucleus and is likely to be a speck of dust or an artefact on the slide. If you observe a cell of a smaller diameter than the others, it is likely to be a companion cell.

Extension

Other cell types in phloem tissue

Sclerenchyma fibres and/or sclereids and parenchyma cells can be found associated with phloem sieve tube elements and companion cells.

Summary test 7.1e

Phloem sieve tube elements transport organic materials such as (1) and (2) from the leaves and (3) regions to other parts of the plant. They are made up of two main cell types. The sieve tube elements form long, vertical tubes. Each element has perforated end walls called (4). The pores within them have strands of (5) running through them. To reduce resistance to flow of phloem sap, sieve tube elements lack important structures found in other cells. These include (6), (7) and (8). Associated with sieve tube elements are cells that carry out the metabolic activities of sieve tube elements. These cells are called (9) and, in the areas of loading and unloading of assimilates, transfer materials to and from sieve tube elements via connecting strands of cytoplasm known as (10).

Transport mechanisms
a. Transport of water from the root to the xylem

These pages help you to:

- state that some mineral ions can be transported within plants dissolved in water (7.2.1)
- describe the transport of water from the soil to the xylem through the apoplast and symplast pathways (7.2.2)
- understand the importance of the endodermis, Casparian strip and suberin in the transport of water across the root (7.2.2)

You will also:

- understand how mineral ions are transported into root hair cells
- learn more about aquaporins

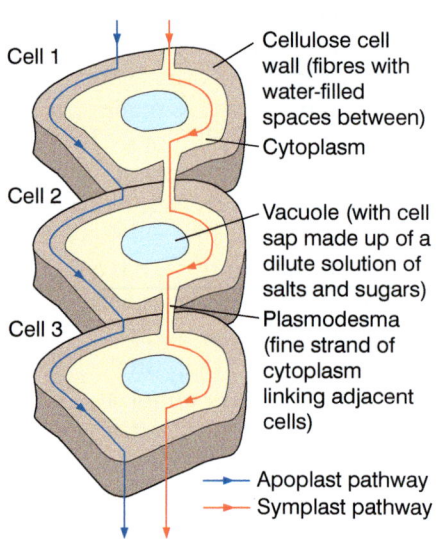

Cell 1

Cell 2

Cell 3

- Cellulose cell wall (fibres with water-filled spaces between)
- Cytoplasm
- Vacuole (with cell sap made up of a dilute solution of salts and sugars)
- Plasmodesma (fine strand of cytoplasm linking adjacent cells)

→ Apoplast pathway
→ Symplast pathway

Figure 1 *Apoplast and symplast pathway across the root cortex*

Extension

Aquaporins

As water passes across the cortex of the root, some water molecules will enter the cells from the apoplast pathway and vice versa. Specialised protein channels called **aquaporins** (4.1b) span the cell surface membranes. These water channels allow water molecules to pass from cell to cell. This can help to maximise the volume of water that enters the xylem. They are also present in the tonoplast of the vacuole. It is known that cells are able to increase and decrease the number of aquaporins in their cell surface membranes so that this might be one way to control the movement of water across the root. The cell surface membranes of root hair cells also have aquaporins.

In 7.1b we saw how root hair cells are adapted to their role of absorbing water and mineral **ions**. These cells take up water, which then passes across the root cortex into the water-conducting tissue of the plant, the xylem. This, in turn, carries it up the stem to the aerial parts of the plant. The general structure of roots and stems is covered in 7.1b.

Uptake of water by root hairs

The root hairs of root hair cells extend into the spaces around soil particles. In damp conditions they are surrounded by a soil solution which contains small quantities of mineral ions, but which is mostly water and therefore has a very high **water potential** – only slightly less than zero. By contrast, the root hair cells, and other cells of the root, have sugars, amino acids and mineral ions dissolved within them. These cells therefore have a much lower water potential. As a result, water moves into the epidermal cell by osmosis, crossing the cell surface membrane and entering the cytoplasm, or moves into the cell wall of the epidermal cell down the water potential gradient.

Water then continues its journey across the root cortex in two ways, as shown in Figures 1 and 2:

- the **apoplast pathway**
- the **symplast pathway**.

The apoplast pathway

The first part of the apoplast pathway involves the movement of water from the cell walls of the root hair cells, across the cortex to the endodermis (Figure 2). As water is drawn into endodermal cells, it pulls more water along behind it, due to the cohesive properties of the water molecules. This creates a tension that draws water along the cell walls of the cells of the root cortex (cortical cells) and the fluid-filled spaces between the cortical cells (intercellular spaces). The mesh-like structure of the cellulose cell walls of the cortical cells has many water-filled spaces and so there is little or no resistance to this pull of water along the cell walls. The apoplast route can be described as a non-living pathway as water does not cross cell surface membranes and does not enter the cytoplasm of cells.

The symplast pathway

This takes place across the cytoplasm of the cortical cells as a result of differences in the water potential between cells. Water moves from one cell to the next cell through plasmodesmata, down the water potential gradient. Plasmodesmata are strands of cytoplasm that directly connect one cell to the adjacent cell so that water can take a cytoplasmic route across the cortex.

- Water entering the root hair cell by osmosis (4.2b and 4.2c) makes its water potential higher.
- The root hair cell now has a higher water potential than the adjacent cortical cell.
- Water therefore moves from the root hair cell to the cortical cells via the plasmodesmata, down the water potential gradient.
- This first cortical cell now has a higher water potential than the cell nearer to the centre of the root.
- Water therefore moves into this neighbouring cortical cell via plasmodesmata down the water potential gradient.

- This second cortical cell now has a higher water potential than the next cell nearer to the centre of the root, and so water moves from the second to the third cell via plasmodesmata down the water potential gradient.
- At the same time, this loss of water from the first cortical cell lowers its water potential, causing more water to enter it from the root hair cell.
- In this way, a water potential gradient is set up across all the cells of the cortex, which carries water along the cytoplasm from the root hair cell to the endodermis, surrounding the central xylem.
- In its passage through a cell, water can also enter and exit the vacuole, but as it has to cross the tonoplast, the vacuolar membrane, this will involve osmosis.

The presence of plasmodesmata between adjacent cells means that water passes through cell walls without having to cross the cell surface membranes. The passage of water in the symplast pathway is slower than in the apoplast pathway as the cytoplasm and organelles within cells present a greater obstruction to flow.

Passage of water into the xylem

Water reaching the endodermis by the apoplast pathway finds its further progress along the cell wall prevented by the waterproof band of **suberin** that makes up the **Casparian strip** in endodermal cells (Figure 2). At this point, water must enter (by osmosis) the living protoplast of the cell, where it joins water in the cytoplasm that has reached there by the symplast pathway. Water leaving the endodermis passes across a layer of parenchyma cells known as the pericyle and on entering the xylem it takes the apoplastic, non-living pathway. Overall, there is a water potential gradient between the soil solution and the xylem of the root.

Movement of mineral ions across the root

Mineral ions are in a very low concentration in the soil solution so the bulk of the uptake into the root hair cell is against the concentration gradient. Specific membrane proteins are present in the cell surface membrane for active uptake. Mineral ions that enter the root, both in the apoplast and symplast, are dissolved in water and so can move passively in solution as water moves across the cortex. Dissolved ions in the apoplast pathway, on reaching the endodermis, must also enter the endodermal cell to continue across the pericycle and enter the xylem. The presence of mineral ions helps to lower the water potential in the root xylem.

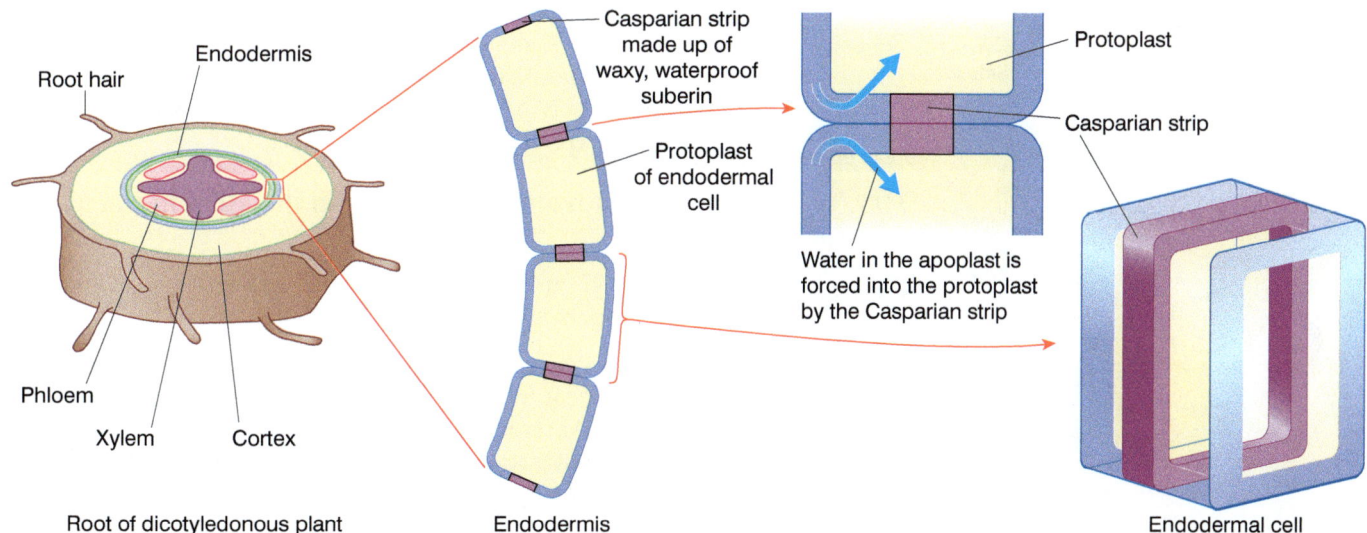

Figure 2 *Movement of water across the endodermis*

Summary test 7.2a

The uptake of water from the soil solution involves specialised epidermal cells known as **(1)**. This water is taken up because these cells have a **(2)** water potential than the soil solution that surrounds them. Water now passes into the cortical cells of the root in two ways: through the water-filled spaces of the cellulose cell wall, a route called the **(3)** pathway; and through the cytoplasm alone, a route called the **(4)** pathway, in which water crosses the cell walls through strands of cytoplasm called **(5)**. Around the vascular tissue at the centre of the root is a one-cell-thick ring of cells, called the **(6)**, the cell walls of which are impregnated with a band called the **(7)**, which is made up of the waxy, waterproof substance called **(8)**. Water from all pathways is now forced through the living portion, or **(9)**, of the endodermal cells. The entry of **(10)** ions into the xylem **(11)** the water potential. Water enters the xylem down the water potential gradient.

b. Movement of water in the xylem

These pages help you to:

- understand the importance of lignin and cellulose in xylem vessel walls (7.2.2)
- explain how hydrogen bonding of water molecules is involved with movement of water in the xylem by cohesion-tension in transpiration pull and by adhesion to cellulose in cell walls (7.2.4)
- explain that transpiration involves the evaporation of water from the internal surfaces of leaves followed by diffusion of water vapour to the atmosphere (7.2.3)

You will also:

- revise your knowledge of hydrogen bonding of water molecules

The main force that pulls water up the stem of a plant is the evaporation of water vapour from surfaces of the spongy mesophyll cells of leaves into the air spaces, from where the water vapour diffuses out to the atmosphere through open stomata. The loss of water vapour from the aerial parts of a plant (mostly the leaves) is termed transpiration. It is therefore logical to begin this topic from the point where water molecules evaporate from spongy mesophyll cells and diffuse through the tiny pores, called **stomata**, on the surface of a leaf.

Movement of water across the leaf

The humidity of the atmosphere is usually less than that of the sub-stomatal air space and so, provided that the stomata are open, water vapour diffuses out of the air spaces into the surrounding air, which has a lower water potential. Water vapour lost from the air spaces is replaced by water evaporating from the cell walls of the surrounding **spongy mesophyll** cells, so that the air spaces tend to be saturated. By closing stomatal pores, plants can control water loss. Water evaporating from the cell walls of spongy mesophyll cells is replaced by water reaching them from the xylem by either the apoplast or symplast pathway (7.2a). In the case of the symplast pathway, the water movement occurs because, once the spongy mesophyll cells have lost water to the sub-stomatal air space, they have a lower (more negative) **water potential**. Water therefore enters from the adjacent cells. The loss of water from these adjacent cells causes them to have a lower (more negative) water potential and so they, in turn, take in water from their neighbours. In this way, a water potential gradient is established that pulls water from the xylem, across the leaf mesophyll, and finally out into the atmosphere. These events are summarised in Figures 1 and 3. Figure 2 shows the loosely packed spongy mesophyll cells with the large intercellular air spaces.

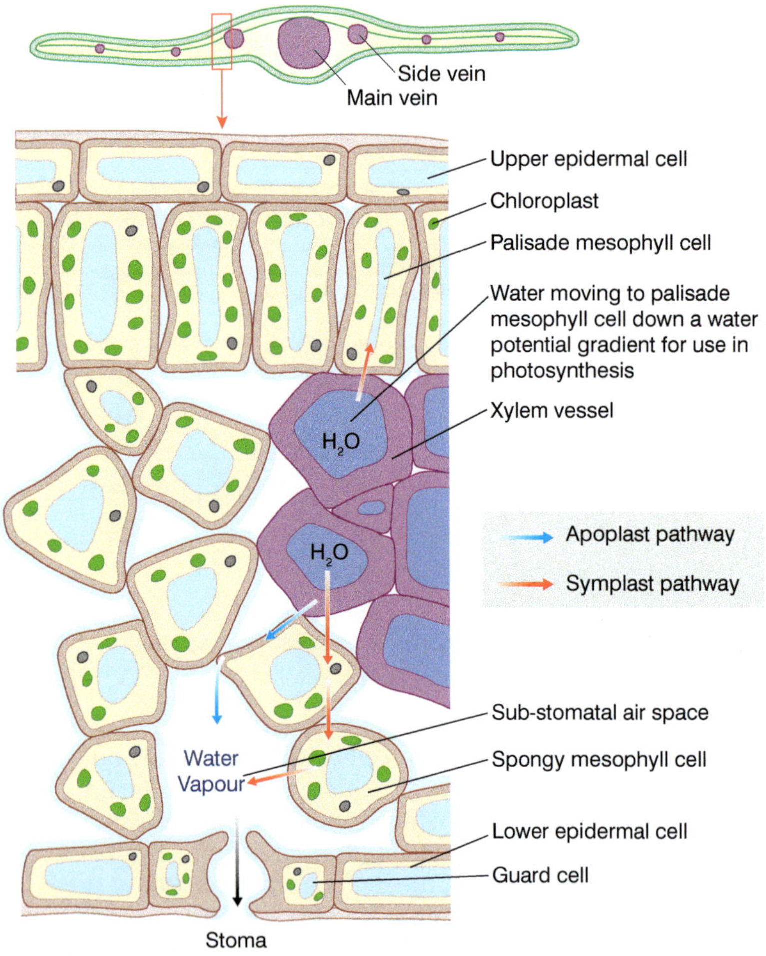

Movement of water up the stem in the xylem

The main mechanism by which water moves up the xylem is known as the **cohesion-tension theory**. It operates as follows:

- Water evaporates from spongy mesophyll cells due to heat from the sun, leading to transpiration.
- Water molecules form **hydrogen bonds** between one another and hence tend to stick together – this is known as **cohesion.**
- Water forms a continuous, unbroken column across the mesophyll cells and down the xylem. This is known as the transpiration stream.
- As water evaporates from mesophyll cells in the leaf into the sub-stomatal air space, more molecules of water are drawn up behind it as a result of this cohesion.

Upper epidermal cell
Chloroplast
Palisade mesophyll cell
Water moving to palisade mesophyll cell down a water potential gradient for use in photosynthesis
Xylem vessel

H_2O
H_2O

→ Apoplast pathway
→ Symplast pathway

Side vein
Main vein

Sub-stomatal air space
Spongy mesophyll cell
Lower epidermal cell
Guard cell

Water Vapour

Stoma

Figure 1 *Movement of water across a leaf*

> **Remember**
>
> Cohesion is the attraction of the *same* type of molecules for one another. In other words, it is the ability of molecules (in this case water molecules) to stick to one another.

- A column of water is hence pulled up the xylem as a result of transpiration. This is called the **transpiration pull**.
- The transpiration pull puts the xylem under **tension**, i.e. there is a negative pressure within the xylem – hence the name cohesion-tension theory (Figure 3).

Extension

Evidence for the cohesion-tension theory

Evidence for the cohesion-tension theory includes:

- The change which occurs in the diameter of trees according to the rate of transpiration. During the day, when transpiration is at its greatest, there is more tension (more negative pressure) in the xylem. This causes the trunk to shrink in diameter. This is because the inward pull on the xylem vessels slightly reduces their diameter. At night, when transpiration is at its lowest, there is less tension in the xylem and so the diameter of the trunk increases.
- When a xylem vessel is broken, water does not leak out, which would be the case if it were under pressure, but rather air is pulled in, which is consistent with it being under tension.

The cellulose lining of the xylem vessels is hydrophilic. Lignin, although mainly a hydrophobic molecule, has some hydrophilic groups. Adhesion of water molecules to the cellulose lining and to the hydrophilic groups in lignin in the xylem wall also help to keep the column of water from collapsing and moving up the xylem by the cohesion-tension mechanism. This adhesion is due to hydrogen bonding that occurs between water molecules and cellulose molecules, as well as to the hydrophilic groups of lignin.

The tension that is created by transpiration pull will tend to create an inward pull on xylem vessel walls. Lignin plays a very important role in preventing the inward collapse of the vessels.

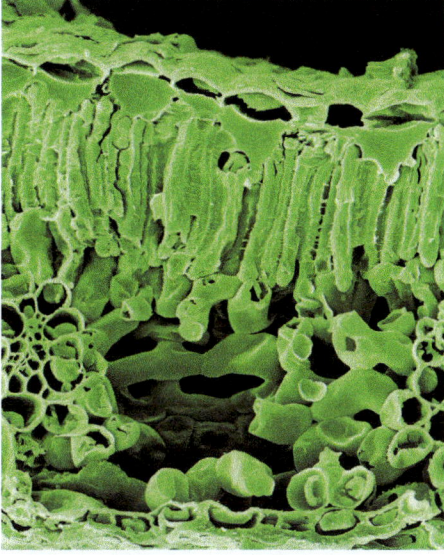

Figure 2 *Colourised scanning electron micrograph of a leaf showing palisade mesophyll above and spongy mesophyll below. Water evaporates from the cell walls of the spongy mesophyll cells into the large air spaces between the cells.*

Summary test 7.2b

Water **(1)** from the surfaces of spongy mesophyll to the intercellular air spaces in the plant leaf. This water vapour then diffuses through pores called **(2)** in the epidermis of the leaf, each of which is surrounded by a pair of **(3)**. The spongy mesophyll cells have a **(4)** water potential and so draw water from adjacent cells. In this way, a **(5)** gradient is set up that draws water from the xylem. Water is pulled up the xylem because water molecules stick together – a phenomenon called **(6)**. The attraction of water molecules to the **(7)** lining of the xylem vessel is known as **(8)**.

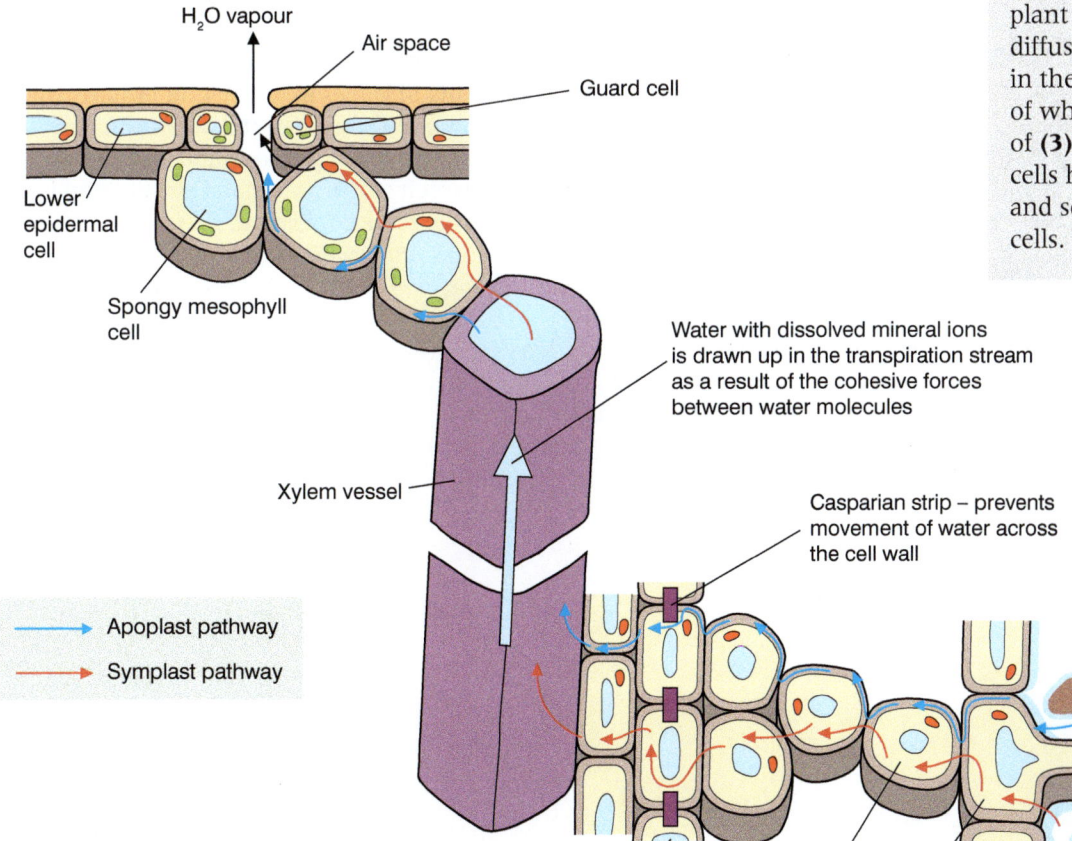

Figure 3 *Summary of water transport through a plant*

These pages help you to:

- understand how the leaves of xerophytic plants are adapted to reduce water loss by transpiration (7.2.5)
- make annotated drawings of transverse sections of leaves from xerophytic plants to show how they are adapted to reduce water loss (7.2.5)
- consolidate knowledge that transpiration involves the evaporation of water from the internal surfaces of leaves followed by diffusion of water vapour to the atmosphere (7.2.3)

You will also:

- be able to compare the leaves of xerophytic plants with the leaves of plants that do not need to conserve water
- learn more about transpiration

Xerophytes (xero = 'dry', phyte = 'plant') are plants that are structurally and physiologically adapted to living in areas where their water losses due to **transpiration** (7.2b) may be higher than their water uptake. Without these adaptations, individual plant cells would become plasmolysed (4.2c) to the point that recovery would not be possible and these plants would become desiccated (dry out) and die.

> **Remember**
>
> Transpiration is the loss of water vapour from the aerial parts of the plants, particularly the leaves. It occurs mainly as a result of the diffusion of water vapour out of the leaf through open stomata.
>
> The water vapour is present as a result of evaporation from the internal surfaces of the leaves, mainly the saturated cell walls of the spongy mesophyll cells.

Xerophytic adaptations of leaves that reduce transpiration

One way of surviving in habitats with an unfavourable water balance is to reduce the rate at which water vapour can be lost through transpiration. As most transpiration occurs through the leaves, mainly through the stomata (and with some loss through the cuticle, known as cuticular transpiration), these organs have the most modification. Examples include:

- **Having a thick cuticle.** Although the waxy cuticle on leaves forms a waterproofing barrier, up to 10% of water loss can still occur by this route. The thicker the cuticle is, the less water vapour can escape by this means. Some xerophytes that live in very dry environments have a cuticle that is as thick as the diameter of the epidermal cell that they are covering. Many plants, such as *Agave* sp (Figure 1), have thick cuticles to reduce water vapour loss.
- **Curling up of leaves.** Most leaves have their **stomata** largely, or entirely, located on the lower epidermis. The curling of leaves in a way that protects this lower epidermis from the outside helps to trap a region of still air within the curled leaf. This region becomes saturated with water vapour and so there is only a very slight water potential gradient between the sub-stomatal air space and the outside, and so transpiration is considerably reduced. Esparto grass is an example of a plant with curled leaves. Plants such as *Ammophila* (marram grass) (Figure 2), which grows on sand dunes, roll their leaves when transpiration rates are high, e.g. in hot or windy conditions.
- **Having trichomes (hairs) on leaves.** A thick layer of hair on leaves, especially on the lower epidermis, traps moist air next to the leaf surface. The water potential gradient between the inside and the outside of the leaves is reduced and therefore less water vapour is lost by transpiration. *Nerium oleander* (oleander) has this modification (Figure 3).

Figure 1 *Agave has leaves with a thick waxy cuticle to reduce water loss*

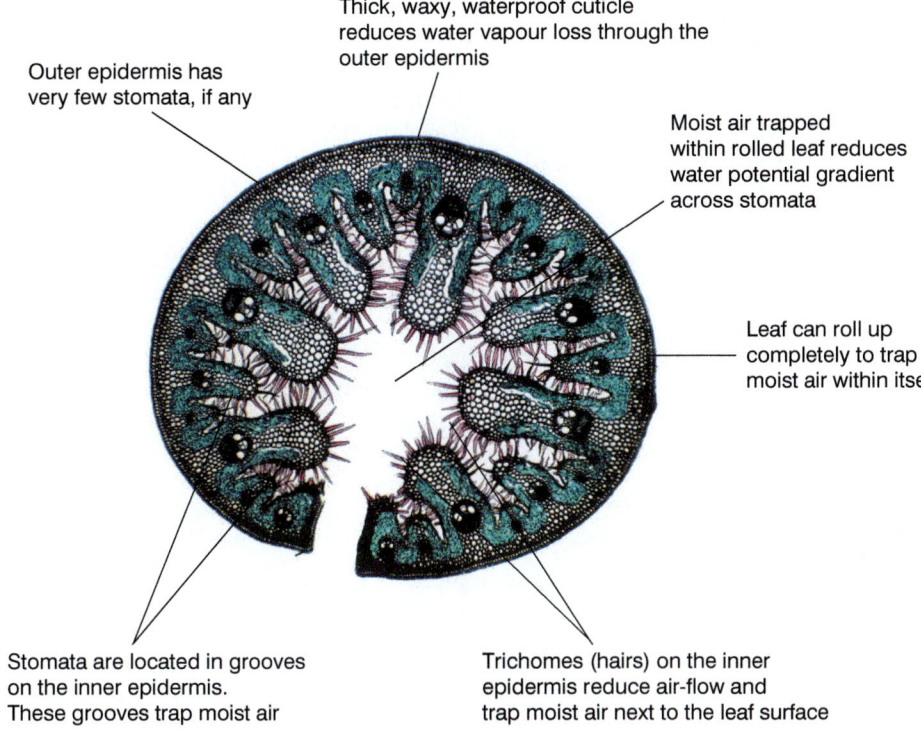

Thick, waxy, waterproof cuticle reduces water vapour loss through the outer epidermis

Outer epidermis has very few stomata, if any

Moist air trapped within rolled leaf reduces water potential gradient across stomata

Leaf can roll up completely to trap moist air within itself

Stomata are located in grooves on the inner epidermis. These grooves trap moist air

Trichomes (hairs) on the inner epidermis reduce air-flow and trap moist air next to the leaf surface

Figure 2 *Xerophytic modifications of the leaf of marram grass*

Figure 3 *Transverse section through a leaf of Nerium oleander showing pits containing hairs on the underside. The stomata are located in these pits. Both pits and hairs help to trap water vapour and reduce transpiration*

- **Having stomata in pits or grooves.** These again trap moist air next to the leaf and reduce the water potential gradient. Examples of plants using this mechanism include *N. oleander* (oleander).
- **Having sunken stomata.** In some plants, such as shrubs of the genus *Hakea*, the stomata are located just below the surface of the epidermis, so they are not directly exposed to air movements.
- **Having needle-like leaves.** By having leaves that are small and roughly circular in cross-section (Figure 4), as in conifers e.g. *Pinus sylvestris* (Scot's pine), rather than ones that are broad and flat, the rate of water loss can be considerably reduced. This reduction in surface area must always be balanced against the need for a sufficient area for photosynthesis to meet the needs of the plant.

Figure 4 *Conifers such as this have needle-like leaves to reduce the surface area to volume ratio and reduce water loss*

Extension

More about transpiration

Transpiration is the unavoidable result of plants having leaves adapted for photosynthesis. Stomata open during daylight hours to allow carbon dioxide to enter for photosynthesis. They close at night to reduce water loss by transpiration.

However, transpiration is also essential as it brings water up from the roots to:

- supply the cells of the leaf with water and mineral ions
- supply water as a reactant, for example in photosynthesis
- maintain turgor in the cells to support the leaf
- supply water for phloem sap to allow assimilates to be transported to other areas of the plant (7.2d).

Evaporation of water from the internal surfaces requires heat energy and has a cooling effect on the plant (2.4a).

Remember

When explaining adaptations of xerophytic plants to reduce water loss, relate these adaptations to a decrease in transpiration rate by reducing (making less steep) the water potential gradient between the sub-stomatal air space and the external atmosphere.

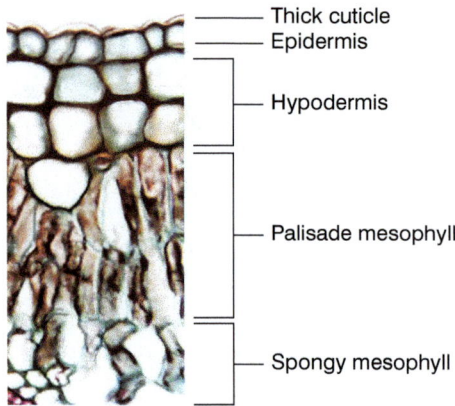

Thick cuticle
Epidermis

Hypodermis

Palisade mesophyll

Spongy mesophyll

Figure 5 *Transverse section through the upper epidermis region of the leaf of* N. oleander

- **Closing stomata when transpiration rates are very high.** Some xerophytes can close stomata during the hottest parts of the day. Some plants, called C4 plants, use a modified form of photosynthesis that makes more efficient use of carbon dioxide, and so this closure of stomata does not greatly affect rates of photosynthesis. Other plants produce a plant hormone, **abscisic acid**, in response to the stress of dehydration and this causes the stomata to close. The mechanism of how stomata open and close is explained in 14.2a.
- **Multi-layered epidermis.** Having many epidermal layers will reduce water loss through the cuticle because this increases the distance for diffusion of water vapour from the intercellular air spaces. One or more layers of cells between the epidermis and the palisade mesophyll is also known as the hypodermis. *N. oleander* has a multilayered lower and upper epidermis. Figure 5 shows a hypodermis of two layers of cells in *N. oleander*. In addition, some xerophytes may have epidermal cells and cells below the epidermis that have cell walls impregnated with cutin.

Extension

The different habitats of xerophytic plants

Xerophytes are typically thought of as desert plants, showing a whole range of adaptations to cope with hot, dry conditions. However, similar adaptations may also be seen in plants found in sand dunes or other dry, windy places where rainfall is high and temperature relatively low. These adaptations are essential because the rainfall quickly drains away through the sand and out of the reach of the roots, making it difficult for these plants to obtain water. At the same time, coastal areas where sand dunes typically occur have salty soils and this lowers the **water potential** of the soil solution, reducing the water potential gradient between the soil solution and the root hair cells. Water uptake by **osmosis** is therefore very slow. Many halophytes (plants adapted to live in saline habitats, like salt marshes) can also be described as xerophytic plants as they have adaptations to cope with a physiological lack of water. In addition, coastal regions are exposed to greater wind speeds, which increase transpiration rates. Plants living in cold regions often have difficulty obtaining water because it is frozen in the soil for much of the year. These plants also show xerophytic modifications to enable them to survive. There are therefore many habitats where plants show structural and physiological modifications designed to increase water uptake, store water and reduce transpiration. These modifications are called xerophytic features.

Practical skill

Making annotated drawings of transverse sections of leaves from xerophytic plants

You may be asked to produce a high powered drawing of a few cells (see advice in 1.1c) or a low power drawing of a plan diagram (see advice in 7.1c).

Remember that the cuticle is a separate, continuous, transparent layer on the surface of the epidermis. Trichomes should be shown in proportion to the dimensions of the epidermal cell (width and length) and should not be a single line.

Annotations are additional notes that can be added to support your observations, for example:
- thick waxy cuticle/waxy cuticle one-quarter thickness of diameter of epidermal cell/transparent thick waxy cuticle
- long/short/dense covering of trichomes
- thick walls for collenchyma cells (of hypodermis); some xerophytes also have sclerenchyma and these will appear empty, with very thick (lignified) walls
- thick walls for epidermal cells.

If you are asked to annotate your drawing with notes to explain how the features you have shown are xerophytic adaptations, then explain in terms of:
- reducing water potential gradients between the saturated sub-stomatal air spaces and the external atmosphere, e.g. for trichomes, sunken stomata or stomata in grooves or pits, curled or rolled leaves
- increasing distance for diffusion of water vapour from the saturated intercellular air spaces, e.g. for thick walled cells at the epidermis or below the epidermis, and for the cuticle
- maintaining volume of leaf but reducing surface area exposed for water vapour loss, e.g. for needle-shaped leaves.

Summary test 7.2c

Xerophytes are plants adapted to living in areas where transpiration rates may be higher than water uptake. In addition to hot and cold deserts, xerophytes can be found in other habitats such as **(1)** or **(2)**. The leaves of xerophytic plants show adaptations to reduce water loss. These include having a thick, waxy **(3)** or closing stomata when transpiration rates are high. Increasing humidity around stomata is an effective way of reducing transpiration and three methods by which leaves achieve this are **(4)**, **(5)** and **(6)**.

d. Phloem tissue and the transport of assimilates

Cells can use the glucose produced by photosynthesis to synthesise many other organic compounds required by the plant, such as other carbohydrates, including starch and cellulose, amino acids and plant hormones.

If a synthesised product, an assimilate, needs to be moved to another location in the plant, then it is transported in the phloem sieve tubes. The leaves are not the only place assimilates are synthesised. For example, starch stores in a root might be converted to sugars for transport to growing leaves. Sites of synthesis are known as sources.

Locations in the plant that require assimilates are known as sinks. These include highly metabolic areas such as the growing regions (buds, root tips and shoot tips, flowers) and locations that function as storage areas (roots and underground stems). As sinks can be anywhere in a plant – sometimes above and sometimes below the source – the **translocation** of molecules in phloem can be in either direction, transported in separate sieve tubes. The phloem transports assimilates, such as sucrose and amino acids as well as plant hormones and inorganic **ions**, such as potassium, chloride, phosphate and magnesium ions. These organic compounds and mineral ions are transported dissolved in water. This highly concentrated solution is known as phloem sap.

Mechanism of translocation

Substances are transported in the phloem (7.1e), but the rate of movement is too fast to be explained by diffusion. The mass flow theory explains the mechanism of how translocation (movement from one location to another) of assimilates is achieved. It can be divided into three phases, summarised in Figures 1 and 2 (over the page).

Transfer of sucrose into sieve tube elements from photosynthesising tissue.

One way that many plants appear to load sucrose into phloem sieve tubes is by a process known as apoplastic loading:

- Sucrose is manufactured from the products of photosynthesis in cells with chloroplasts.
- Hydrogen ions (protons) are actively pumped from companion cells into the apoplast (cell walls and spaces between cells) using ATP.
- The hydrogen ion concentration builds up and these hydrogen ions (protons) then flow down a concentration gradient through carrier proteins (facilitated diffusion) back into the companion cells.
- Sucrose molecules are transported along with the hydrogen ions (protons) in a process known as **cotransport**. The carrier proteins are therefore also known as cotransporter proteins. This movement is against the concentration gradient for sucrose and is powered by the flow of protons back into the companion cell.
- Sucrose molecules then move by simple diffusion through the plasmodesmata from the companion cell into the phloem sieve tube element.

These pages help you to:

- learn that some mineral ions and organic compounds can be transported within plants dissolved in water (7.2.1)
- learn that assimilates dissolved in water, such as sucrose and amino acids, move from sources to sinks in phloem sieve tubes (7.2.6)
- explain how companion cells transfer assimilates to phloem sieve tubes, including the roles of proton pumps and cotransporter proteins (7.2.7)
- explain mass flow in phloem sieve tubes down a hydrostatic pressure gradient from source to sink (7.2.8)

You will also:

- consider evidence that translocation of organic molecules occurs in phloem

Remember

At any one time phloem sap can be moving in different directions in different sieve tubes.

Movement of phloem sap in sieve tube elements from source to sink

'Mass flow' is the bulk movement of a substance through a given channel or area in a specified time. Mass flow of sucrose and other assimilates through sieve tube elements takes place as follows:

- The loading of sucrose into the sieve tubes is as described above. It is sometimes termed active loading, as ATP is required to pump out hydrogen ions in order for cotransport of sucrose to occur.
- This causes the sieve tubes to have a lower (more negative) water potential.
- As the xylem has a much higher (less negative) water potential (see 7.2b), water moves from the xylem into the sieve tubes by osmosis, creating a high hydrostatic pressure within them.
- At the sink, sucrose leaves the phloem sieve tubes to move into the destination cells where it is needed.
- This increases the water potential of the phloem sap and water leaves the phloem sieve tubes to follow sucrose osmotically or to return to adjacent xylem vessel elements.
- The hydrostatic pressure of the sieve tubes in this region is therefore low.
- As a result of water entering the sieve tube elements at the source and leaving at the sink, there is a high hydrostatic pressure at the source and a low one at the sink.
- There is therefore a mass flow of sucrose solution down this hydrostatic pressure gradient in the sieve tubes from a higher hydrostatic pressure at the source to a lower hydrostatic pressure at the sink.

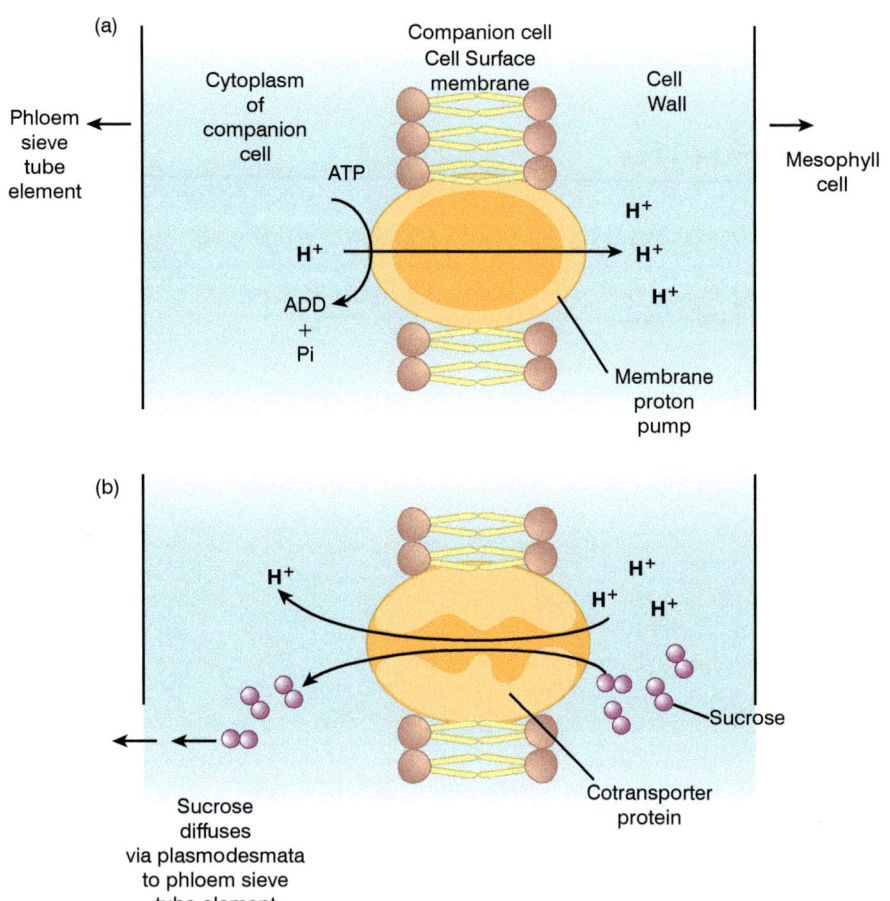

Figure 1 *A summary of the role of the companion cell in the transfer of sucrose to a phloem sieve tube element. In (a), protons are pumped out to the apoplast from the companion cell, building up a proton gradient. In (b), protons are passing back into the companion cell by facilitated diffusion, sucrose molecules are cotransported.*

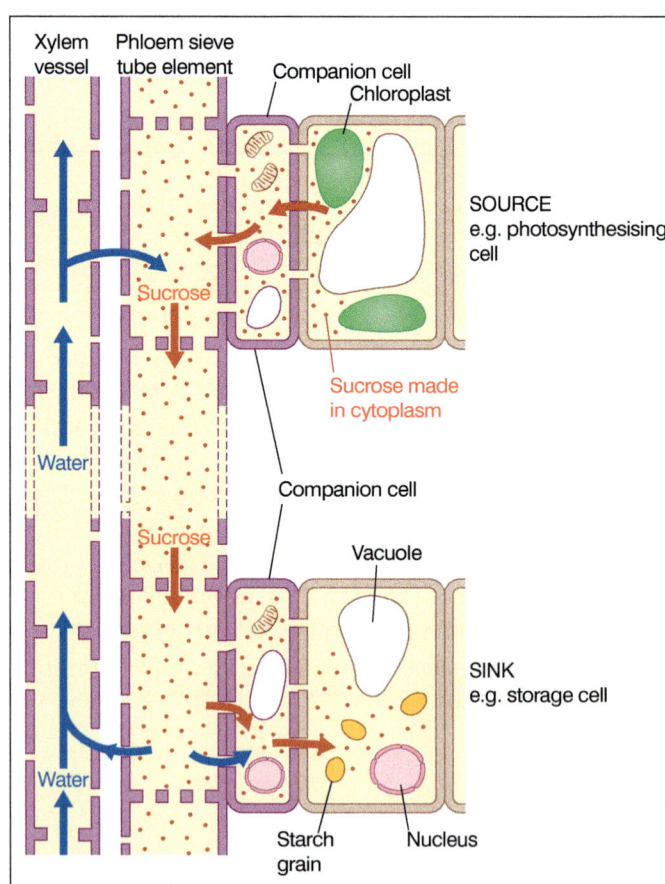

Figure 2 *Movement of sucrose from source to sink through the phloem of a plant*

Transfer of sucrose from the sieve tube elements into storage or other sink cells. Research into unloading of assimilates has shown that sucrose can pass into companion cells by diffusion from phloem sieve tubes or can directly pass into sink cells. Where the sucrose is rapidly used up, for example, converted to glucose for respiration or starch for storage, diffusion of sucrose into the destination cell is favoured. Where the destination cell has a higher concentration of sucrose, for example if it stores sucrose, active uptake into the cell can occur.

Extension

Evidence that translocation of organic molecules occurs in phloem

- When phloem is cut, a solution of organic molecules (sap) is exuded.
- Plants provided with radioactive carbon dioxide can be shown to have radioactively labelled carbon in phloem after a short time.
- Aphids which have pierced the phloem with their needle-like mouthparts can be used to extract the contents of the sieve tubes. This shows diurnal (daily) variations in the sucrose content of leaves that are reflected by similar trends a little later in the sucrose content of the phloem (Figure 3).
- The removal of a ring of phloem from around the whole circumference of a stem leads to the accumulation of sugars above the ring and their disappearance from below it.

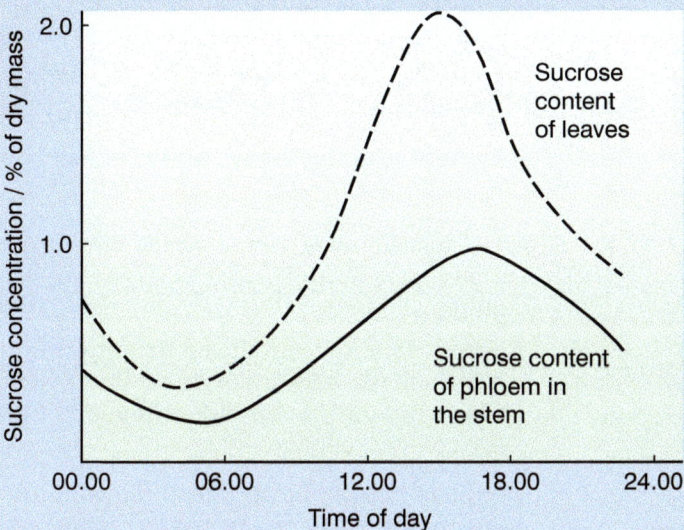

Figure 3 *Diurnal variation in sucrose content of leaves and phloem*

Summary test 7.2d

Transport of sucrose in plants occurs in the tissue called **(1)**, from places where it is produced, known as **(2)**, to places where it is used up or stored, called **(3)**. One theory of how it is translocated is called the **(4)** theory. Initially hydrogen ions are pumped out of the **(5)** into the **(6)**. As hydrogen ions flow back into the cell, sucrose molecules are also transported in through **(7)** proteins. The sucrose molecules then diffuse into the phloem sieve tube. The contents of the sieve tubes now have a **(8)** water potential due to this sucrose. Water therefore moves into them from the nearby **(9)** tissue that has a **(10)** water potential. The opposite occurs in those cells (sinks) using up sucrose, and water therefore leaves them by the process of **(11)**. Water entering at the sources and leaving at the sinks creates a **(12)** pressure gradient that causes the mass flow of sucrose solution along the phloem.

Launch additional digital resources for the chapter

7 Exam-style questions

1 Figure 1 is a photomicrograph showing a transverse section through a leaf.

State which features of a xerophytic leaf are visible in this section. Feature options are as follows:

Figure 1

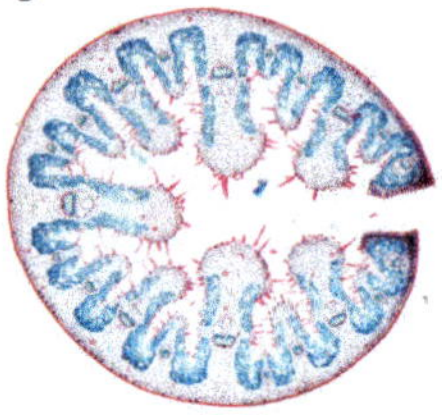

1 thick cuticle
2 small surface area to volume
3 sunken stomata
4 trichomes

A 1, 3 and 4 only   C 1, 2 and 4 only
B 2 and 4 only   D 1, 2, 3 and 4   *(1 mark)*

2 Figure 2 shows some adjacent cells from the root of a plant. Identify which of the following shows the symplastic pathway of water movement. *(1 mark)*

Figure 2

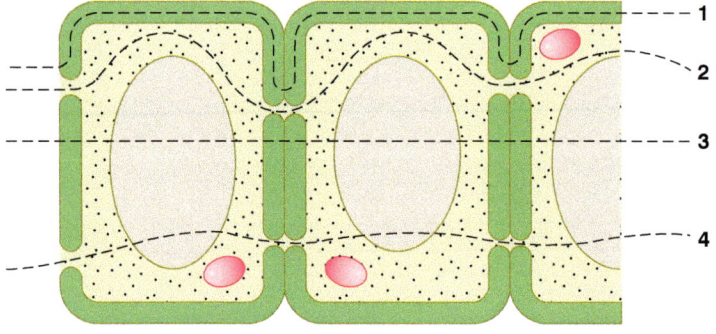

A 1 and 3 only
B 2 and 4 only
C 2 and 3 only
D 1, 3 and 4 only

3 a Define *transpiration*.   *(1 mark)*

b Explain how water is lost from the leaves of a plant.

(2 marks)

c The main mechanism by which water moves up the xylem is known as the cohesion-tension theory. Outline this theory.   *(5 marks)*

d Name two substances in the structure of xylem cells that water molecules adhere to.   *(2 marks)*

(Total 10 marks)

4 a Figure 3 is a photomicrograph of a section through the stem of maize plant, *Zea mays*, showing a vascular bundle.

Figure 3

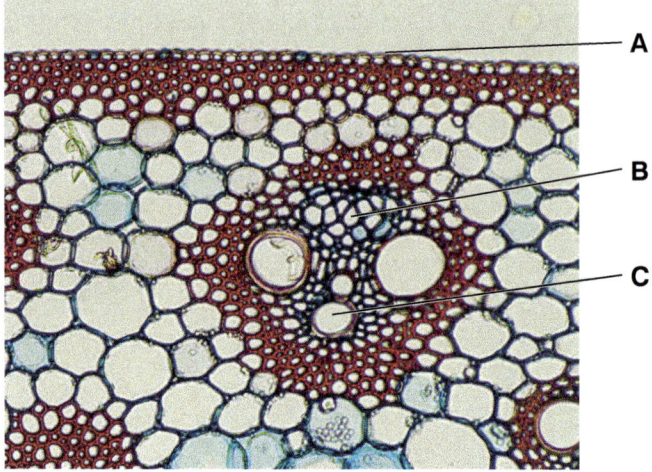

Identify structures **A**, **B**, and **C** in Figure 3.

(3 marks)

b Vascular bundles contain meristematic tissues. These have a similar role to the stem cells found in animals.

Some of the cells produced by mitosis in these meristematic cells differentiate into xylem vessel elements. During this differentiation, the structure of the cell wall changes.

Explain how the structure of the walls of xylem vessel elements are adapted to their functions.

(3 marks)

c Meristematic regions in the plant can sometimes be described as strong sinks.
   i State what is meant by a *sink*.   *(1 mark)*
   ii Suggest what is meant by a **strong** sink.   *(1 mark)*

d Describe **and** explain how sucrose is loaded into phloem sieve tubes.   *(4 marks)*

(Total 12 marks)

7 Practice questions

5 a Give two reasons why plants growing on sand dunes in temperate regions need to have xerophytic features even though there is plentiful rainfall.

b Explain in terms of water potential why salt marsh plants have difficulty absorbing water despite having plenty around their roots.

c Why do plants in cold regions 'have difficulty obtaining water from the soil for much of the year'?

d Plants living in cold regions often reduce water loss by having needle-like leaves with a small surface area to volume ratio. This reduces the surface area available to capture light for photosynthesis. Photosynthesis is, in part, an enzyme-controlled process. Suggest a reason why a smaller leaf area does not limit the rate of photosynthesis in the way it would for plants in warmer climates.

6 Figure 4 shows the rate of water flow up a tree and the diameter of the tree trunk over a 24-hour period.

a At what time of day is the transpiration rate greatest? Explain your answer.

b Describe the changes in the rate of flow of water during the 24-hour period.

c Explain in terms of the cohesion-tension theory the changes in the rate of flow of water during the 24-hour period.

d Explain the changes in the diameter of the tree trunk over the 24-hour period.

e If the tree were sprayed with ammonium sulfamate, a herbicide that kills living cells, the rate of water flow would be unchanged for some time. Explain why.

Figure 4

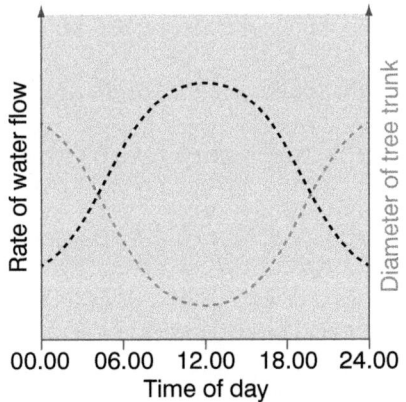

7 State the term used to match descriptions (i) to (x).
i The name of the highly concentrated solution that is transported in vascular tissue from source to sink.
ii The name of the theory used to describe the bulk movement of assimilates from source to sink.
iii The ring of tissue surrounding the central vascular bundle in the root, the cells of which have a Casparian strip.
iv The macromolecule that is the main component of the Casparian strip.
v The name of the pathway where water moves within cell walls and the spaces between cells to pass from cell to cell.
vi The area of the root containing parenchyma cells across which water moves from the epidermis to the xylem.
vii A modified epidermal cell with a long cytoplasm extension to increase surface area for water absorption.
viii The name of the cells that enclose a stoma.
ix The process where water vapour is lost from the aerial parts of a plant.
x The hair-like outgrowths from leaf epidermal cells that help to trap a layer of moist air.

Transport in mammals

The circulatory system

a. The mammalian circulatory system: structure and function of capillaries

These pages help you to:

- describe the mammalian circulatory system as a closed double circulation consisting of a heart, blood and blood vessels (8.1.1)
- list the different types of blood vessel in the mammalian circulatory system: arteries, arterioles, capillaries, venules and veins (8.1.1)
- describe the functions of the main blood vessels, the pulmonary artery and pulmonary vein of the pulmonary circulation and the aorta and vena cava of the systemic circulation (8.1.2)
- recognise capillaries from microscope slides, photomicrographs and electron micrographs (8.1.3)
- explain how the structure of capillaries is related to their function (8.1.4)

You will also:

- understand why mammals need a transport system
- have an overview of the mammalian circulatory system

Remember

The **a**orta is an **a**rtery and the **v**ena cavae are **v**eins.

The circulatory system of mammals

Mammals can be described as having a closed double circulation.

- In a closed system, blood is contained within blood vessels and the heart.
- In double circulation, blood passes twice through the heart in each complete circuit of the body.

Types of blood vessel:

- **Arteries** carry blood away from the heart.
- **Arterioles** branch off arteries and pass blood to capillaries.
- **Capillaries** are the smallest vessels, serving body cells and linking arterioles (and arteries) to venules (and veins).
- **Venules** collect blood from capillaries and pass blood to veins.
- **Veins** carry blood towards the heart.

In mammals, the blood loses pressure as it passes through the capillaries of the lungs. It is therefore returned to the heart to boost its pressure and ensure its rapid circulation to the tissues and organs of the body. Therefore, the complete circuit of the body that blood takes is divided into the pulmonary circulation and the systemic circulation.

In the pulmonary circulation:

- deoxygenated blood leaves the heart in the **pulmonary artery**, which branches to take blood to the left and right lungs
- blood becomes oxygenated in the pulmonary capillaries in the alveoli of the lungs
- oxygenated blood returns to the heart from the left and right lungs in the **pulmonary veins**.

In the systemic circulation:

- oxygenated blood leaves the heart in the main artery, the **aorta**, to take blood to the body tissues and organs
- oxygen, glucose and other essential supplies are delivered to body cells served by capillaries
- deoxygenated blood returns to the heart in the main veins, **the superior and inferior vena cavae**.

Remember

Branching off an artery, arterioles get increasingly smaller towards the capillary network, and venules get increasingly larger away from the network. For each type of blood vessel, a range of diameters exist. For example, the smallest artery in the body will have a smaller diameter than the largest arteriole. So, although arterioles are generally smaller than arteries, it is more precise to state that an arteriole has a smaller diameter than the artery from which it is branching. Similarly, venules are generally smaller than veins, and a venule delivers blood to a vein, which is of a larger diameter.

Capillary structure related to function

Figure 1 shows the structure of a capillary (see also Figure 2 in 8.1b). The function of capillaries is to exchange substances, such as oxygen, carbon dioxide and glucose, between the blood and the cells of the body. These substances pass into a fluid, known as tissue fluid, surrounding the capillaries and the body cells. The structure of capillaries is related to their function as follows:

- **Their walls consist only of endothelium,** making them extremely thin (one cell thick). This allows for rapid diffusion of useful substances, such as oxygen and glucose, between the blood and the cells, due to the short distance over which diffusion takes place.
- **They are numerous and highly branched** to form capillary networks. This provides a large surface area for diffusion.
- **They have a narrow diameter** and so can reach all body tissues, which means that no cell is far from a capillary.
- **Their lumen is so narrow** – around 7 μm in diameter – that red blood cells are squeezed flat against the side of a capillary (Figures 1 and 2). This brings them even closer (as little as 1 μm) to the cells to which they supply oxygen. In the pulmonary capillaries, this reduces the diffusion distance between the air in the alveoli and the red blood cell to allow oxygen to reach the haemoglobin within the cells.
- **In many capillary networks, the capillaries have spaces between endothelial cells** (known as fenestrations or endothelial pores) which allow white blood cells to escape in order to combat infections within tissues. Also, this means that components of blood or of the tissue fluid surrounding cells do not have to pass through the endothelial cells. This can speed up the delivery or collection of materials, although they still have to cross the basement membrane, which can act as a selective layer. The degree to which material can escape from capillaries through the endothelial pores varies from tissue to tissue, being greatest in the kidney and least in the brain, where the capillaries have no endothelial pores and all substances have to pass through the endothelial cells.

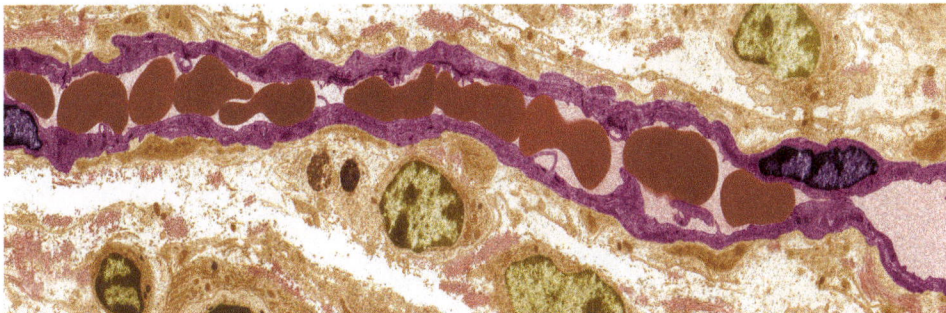

Figure 1 Colourised transmission electron micrograph of a longitudinal section (LS) of a capillary

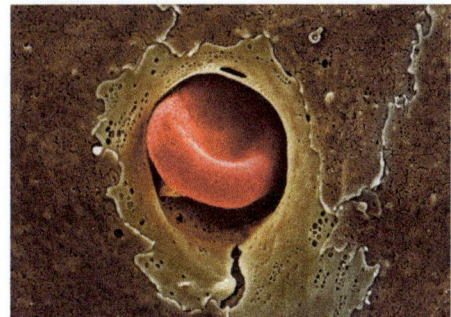

Figure 2 Colourised scanning electron micrograph of blood capillary with a red blood cell

Identifying capillaries in images

You may need to identify the type of blood vessel shown in a highly magnified image or you may need to identify a capillary within an image at a slightly lower magnification. There are some features to look for to help your identification:

- Look for a red blood cell – in transverse section you should only see one red blood cell because the diameter of the cells is approximately the same as the lumen diameter of the capillary (Figure 2).
- Look for a blood vessel wall that is a single layer of cells. Remember that there is a basement membrane around the outside of the wall.
- Look for a nucleus in a cell that appears to have a wider diameter than that of the cell, so it bulges out (see Figure 1).

Extension

The main arteries and veins of the mammalian circulatory system

Figure 3 is a simplified summary of the mammalian circulatory system. It also shows the two smaller circuits, the pulmonary and systemic circulations. The pulmonary arteries and pulmonary veins are not the only arteries and veins going to and from the lungs. The lungs are also served by the systemic system. A branch of the aorta takes oxygenated blood to supply the tissues of the lungs that are not directly involved in gas exchange. Deoxygenated blood from these areas leaves the lungs in veins towards the heart.

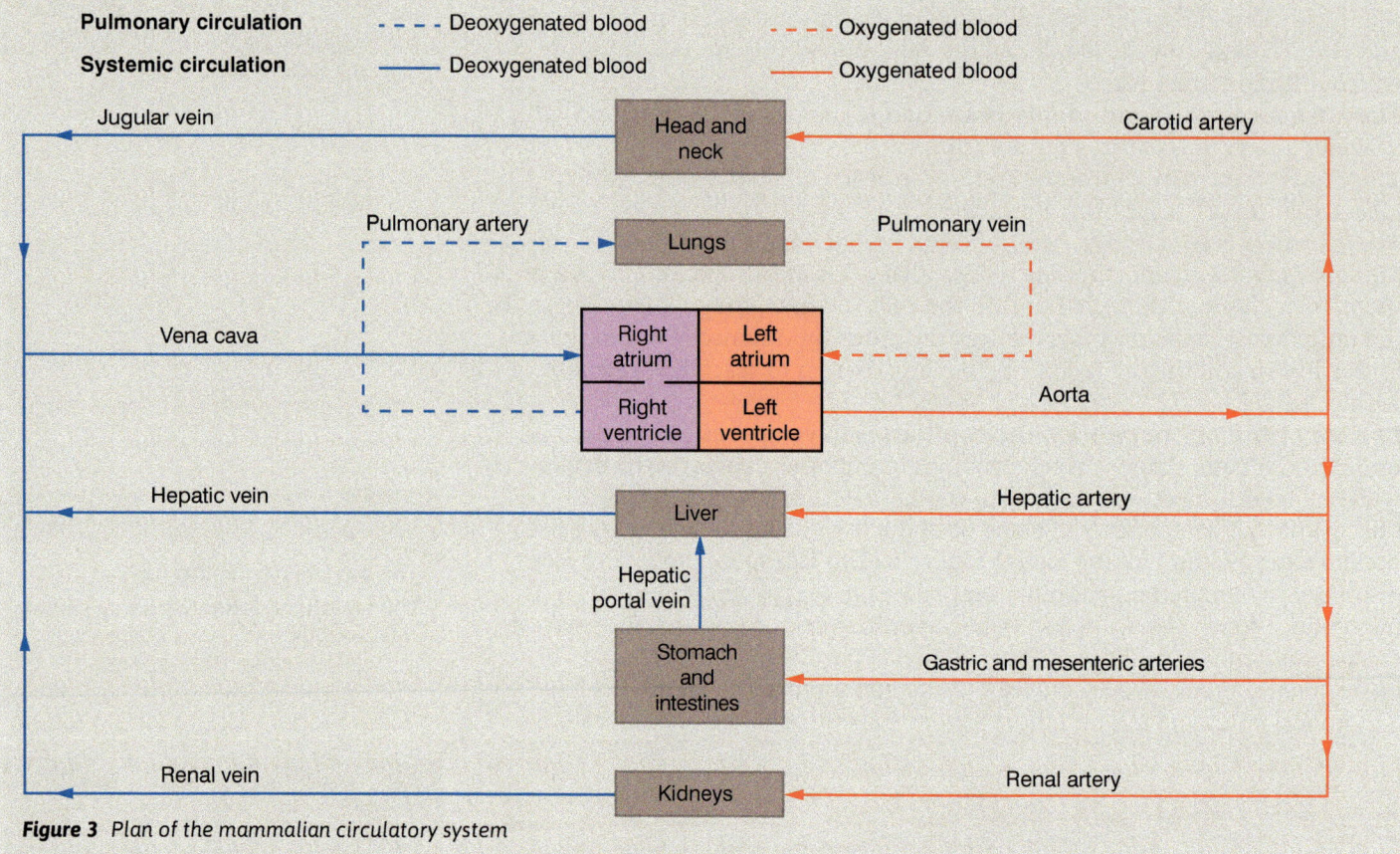

Figure 3 *Plan of the mammalian circulatory system*

Summary test 8.1a

The mammalian circulatory system is described as a closed **(1)** circulation. If blood takes one complete circuit round the entire body, it passes through the **(2)** twice and travels in two different circulations, the pulmonary circulation and the **(3)** circulation. In a closed circulation, blood is kept within **(4)**, of which there are five kinds: arteries, **(5)**, **(6)**, veins and capillaries. The capillary wall is also known as the **(7)** and consists of flattened cells so that there is only a short **(8)** distance to reach body cells. The diameter of a capillary lumen is about the same size as the diameter of a **(9)** cell. The **(10)** is the artery leaving the heart to the body and contains **(11)** blood. The pulmonary vein brings blood from the **(12)** to the heart.

The basic structure of arteries and veins

The walls of arteries and veins have the same basic structure. There are three main layers:

- The **tunica intima** (the lining layer) is a single layer of endothelial cells attached to a basement membrane (see 8.1a). This inner layer is the protective barrier between the blood and the rest of the blood vessel wall. It provides a smooth surface for blood flow. To the outside of the tunica intima in larger arteries is a thin layer known as the internal elastic lamina, which contains elastic fibres and a small amount of collagen. In some arteries it is very easily seen as a wavy layer.
- The **tunica media** (the middle layer) contains elastic fibres (mainly composed of the protein elastin) and smooth muscle. Depending on the type of blood vessel, the proportion of smooth muscle and elastic fibres varies greatly. To the outside of the tunica media in larger arteries, separating it from the tunica adventitia, is an external elastic lamina.
- The **tunica adventitia** (the outer layer, also known as the tunica externa) is composed mainly of collagen fibres with some elastic fibres. The thickness of this layer can vary greatly but it is usually thinner than the tunica media.

Figure 1 is a photomicrograph showing an artery and a vein.

The structure of arterioles and venules

Arterioles have a tunica intima with an internal elastic lamina, a tunica media with only a few layers of smooth muscle cells and a thin tunica adventitia.

Small venules are similar to capillaries in that they do not have a tunica media or tunica adventitia. The walls of these venules appear as a single layer of endothelial cells. However, their diameter (and hence lumen) is four or five times wider than capillaries. In a capillary, one or two endothelial cells can wrap round to form a section of the blood vessel wall, but in venules, in any one section, the wall is composed of several joined endothelial cells and several red blood cells can fit in at once. In larger venules there is also one or two layers of smooth muscle cells.

These pages help you to:

- recognise arteries and veins from microscope slides, photomicrographs and electron micrographs (8.1.3)
- make plan diagrams of arteries and veins in transverse section (TS) and longitudinal section (LS) (8.1.3)
- explain how the structure of arteries and veins is related to their function (8.1.4)
- understand how the differences in the structure of muscular and elastic arteries are explained by their different functions (8.1.4)

You will also:

- be able to compare arteries, veins and capillaries

> **Remember**
>
> Elastic fibres allow stretch and recoil.
>
> Smooth muscle contracts and relaxes.

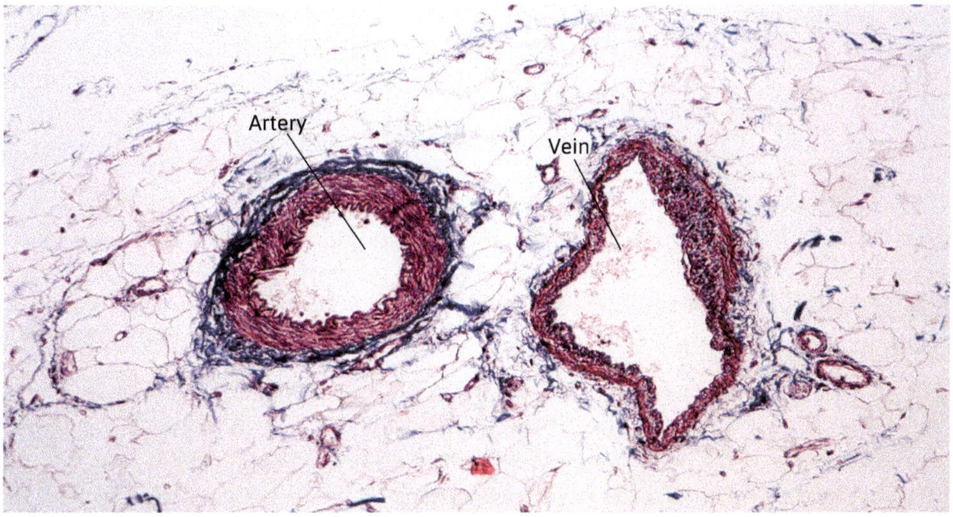

Figure 1 *TS artery (thick-walled vessel on the left) and TS vein (thin-walled vessel on the right) as viewed using a light microscope.*

> **Remember**
>
> Blood vessels have a generally similar structure, but the exact details are different. Arterioles may share some structural features with arteries, and venules may share some structural features with veins, but each type has its own specialised structures. Also, for each type of blood vessel, the exact structure will differ according to the size of the vessel and the where it is located in the body.

Figure 2 includes an outline summary of differences in the structure of arteries, veins and capillaries. The drawings and plan diagrams shown in Figure 2 illustrate the structural differences (drawing plan diagrams is covered in 7.1c).

Artery structure related to function

Figure 2 illustrates the structure of an artery. Arteries function in transporting blood rapidly, under high hydrostatic pressure, from the heart to the tissues. Their structure is related to this function in the following ways:

- **The tunica media is relatively thick** so that the artery is well adapted to withstand the high pressure of the blood flowing within it. In the arteries close to the heart, such as the aorta and pulmonary arteries, there is a high proportion of elastic fibres and relatively little smooth muscle. These arteries are known as **elastic arteries**. This is for two main reasons. Firstly, when blood is forced into the arteries following contraction of the ventricles (8.3b), it creates a **pulse** of very high pressure. The elastic wall allows the arteries to expand rather than rupture (burst) under this pressure. Secondly, it is important that blood pressure in arteries is kept high if blood is to reach the extremities of the body. When the elastic wall is stretched by the pressure within it, it springs back in the same way as a stretched elastic band. This **recoil action** creates another surge of pressure that carries blood forwards in a series of pulses and helps to maintain the blood pressure and the flow of blood forwards when the heart relaxes. In arteries further away from the heart, the tunica media is comparatively thinner than the tunica media of elastic arteries, there are far fewer elastic fibres and a much higher proportion of smooth muscle. These arteries are known as **muscular arteries**. The flow of blood is less pulse-like but does not smooth out completely until it reaches the smallest arteries. Smooth muscle contraction of the muscular arteries is controlled and helps to keep blood moving forward as well as allowing different quantities of blood to be distributed to different locations according to needs. When the smooth muscle contracts, this causes the vessels to constrict, narrowing the diameter of the lumen and allowing the regulation of blood flow to the tissues.
- **The tunica adventia, with its collagen fibres, provides a tough outer layer.** This outer layer also contains some elastic fibres to allow for stretching as blood flows through.
- **The overall thickness of the wall is large**. This again helps prevent arteries bursting under pressure. Arteries have a relatively small lumen in proportion to the thickness of the wall.
- **There are no valves** (except where the pulmonary artery and aorta leave the heart) because blood is under constant high pressure due to the heart pumping blood into the arteries. It therefore tends not to flow backwards.
- **Larger arteries have their own blood supply, the vasa vasorum**. Diffusion through from the blood is not enough to supply the metabolic needs of larger arteries. The vasa vasorum is part of the tunica adventitia.

Figure 2 *Comparison of arteries, veins and capillaries*

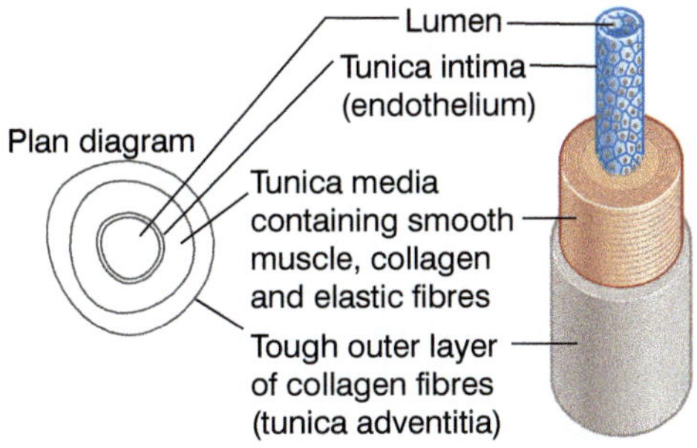

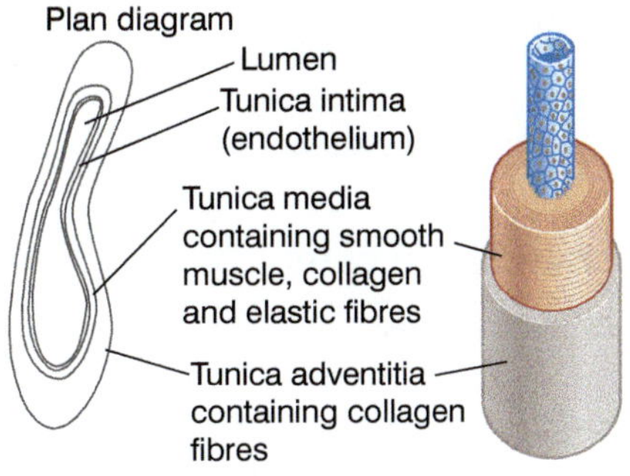

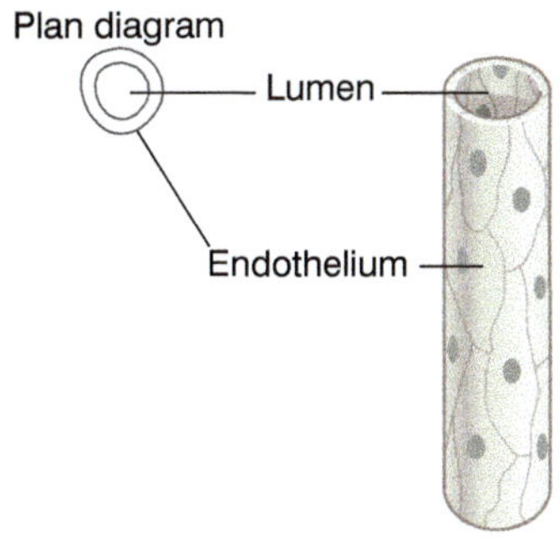

Artery	Vein	Capillary
Thick wall	Thin wall	Wall one cell layer thick
Tunica media with higher proportions of smooth muscle and elastic fibres than veins	Smaller proportion of smooth muscle and elastic fibres in tunica media	No elastic tissue
Small **lumen** relative to thickness of wall	Large lumen relative to thickness of wall	Very large lumen relative to thickness of wall
Lumen appears rounded (circular) or oval in transverse sections	Lumen irregular in transverse section, appearing collapsed	Lumen circular in cross-section
Valves in aorta and pulmonary artery only	Valves throughout all veins	No valves
Transports blood from the heart	Transports blood to heart	Links arteries to veins
Oxygenated blood except in pulmonary artery	Deoxygenated blood except in pulmonary vein	Blood changes from oxygenated to deoxygenated
Blood under high pressure (10–16 kPa)	Blood under low pressure (1 kPa)	Blood pressure reducing (4–1 kPa)
Blood moves in pulses	No pulses	No pulses
Blood flows rapidly	Blood flows slowly	Blood flow slowing

Vein structure related to function

Figure 2 illustrates the structure of a vein. Veins function in transporting blood, under low pressure, from the tissues to the heart. Their structure is related to this function in the following ways:

- **The tunica media is thin** as the low pressure of the blood will not cause them to burst. There are very few elastic fibres because they do not need to stretch and recoil and there is less smooth muscle because veins carry blood away from tissues and therefore their constriction and dilation cannot control the flow of blood to the tissues. The smooth muscle can contract and relax to cope with changes in blood volumes.
- **The tunica adventitia, with its collagen fibres, provides a tough outer layer** in order to prevent the veins bursting – more from external physical forces (they are nearer the skin surface than arteries) than from the blood pressure within them. In larger veins there is also a small amount of smooth muscle.
- **The overall thickness of the wall is small** because there is no need for a thick wall as the pressure within the veins is too low to create any risk of bursting. It also allows them to be flattened easily, aiding the flow of blood within them. The lumen is relatively large compared to the thickness of the wall.
- **There are semi-lunar valves throughout** (in all but the largest veins) to ensure that blood does not flow backwards, which it might otherwise do because the pressure is so low. When the muscles of the body contract during movement, veins are compressed, pressurising the blood within them. The valves ensure that this pressure directs the blood in one direction only – towards the heart.

Summary test 8.1b

Arteries and veins share the same basic structure. The outer layer of the walls, the **(1)**, contains mainly **(2)** and some elastic fibres to help protect the blood vessel from bursting. The inner lining is the **(3)** composed of a single layer of **(4)** cells. The tunica media is thicker in **(5)** than in **(6)**. It contains **(7)** muscle and elastic fibres. An example of an elastic artery is the **(8)**. Unlike arteries, veins have **(9)** at intervals to prevent blood flowing backwards. The type of blood vessel containing blood at the lowest blood pressure is the **(10)**.

c. Structure and functions of red and white blood cells

These pages help you to:

- recognise and draw red blood cells, monocytes, neutrophils and lymphocytes from microscope slides, photomicrographs and electron micrographs (8.1.5)

You will also:

- read about other cell types found in blood
- become familiar with the roles of the different blood cells

Blood is the medium by which materials are transported between different parts of the body. Humans have between 4 dm³ and 6 dm³ of blood. It is made up of a liquid – the **plasma** (55%) and three types of cells (45%) – **red cells**, **white cells** and **platelets** (small cells involved in blood clotting; see Figure 2). You will learn more about plasma in 8.1d.

Red blood cells

Red blood cells are biconcave discs, i.e. they are like a doughnut with a hole that does not quite go all the way through (Figure 1). Around 7–8 μm in diameter, there are 5 million in each mm³ of blood and each lives for around 120 days. This means that, in adult humans, to maintain their numbers, the bone marrow of certain bones (cranium, sternum, vertebrae and ribs) needs to make over 2 million red blood cells each second. These red blood cells are unusual in having no nucleus, and other organelles such as mitochondria, endoplasmic reticulum or Golgi body when mature – a feature which, although it gives them a shorter life span, makes them more efficient in their role of transporting oxygen because, without the nucleus and other organelles:

- they are much thinner in the middle and so form a biconcave shape which gives them a larger surface area to volume ratio
- they can more easily change shape, allowing them to be flattened against the capillary walls, reducing the distance across which diffusion takes place, and so increasing the rate of diffusion (4.2a)
- there is more room for the pigment **haemoglobin**, which carries oxygen.

It is the pigment **haemoglobin** that gives red blood cells their characteristic colour. The structure of haemoglobin is illustrated in 2.3c and its role in oxygen transport is described in 8.2a and 8.2b.

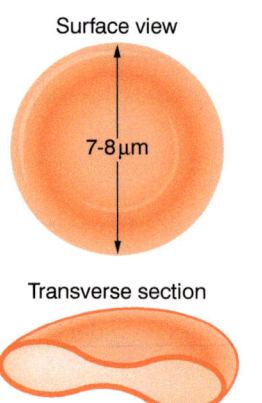

Surface view

7-8 μm

Transverse section

Figure 1 *Red blood cell*

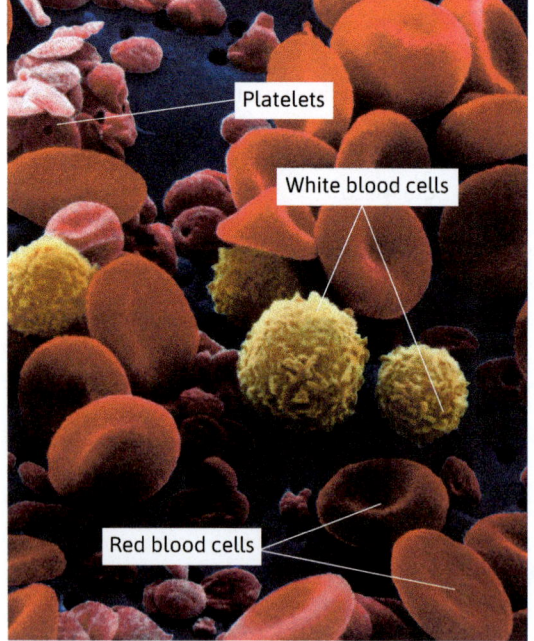

Platelets

White blood cells

Red blood cells

Figure 2 *Colourised scanning electron micrograph of blood showing red cells (red), white cells (yellow) and platelets (pink)*

Practical and observation skill

Recognising and drawing red blood cells in prepared slides and images

There are a number of features that can help you recognise and identify red blood cells in a prepared slide or in an image:

- Look for uniformly rounded cells (see Figure 2).
- Look for evidence of the biconcave shape, for example an indentation or shadow in the centre (do not mistake this for a large nucleus).
- Look for uniform cytoplasm, because there are no structures inside, only haemoglobin (they will not have a granular appearance).
- Look for uniform size and size relative to other blood cells – red blood cells are generally smaller in diameter than white blood cells and are approximately the same size as other red blood cells.
- Red blood cells do not take up the same stains as white blood cells.
- Red blood cells may be collected together in a pile or stack known as a rouleau.

Remember to draw the red blood cells in proportion to white blood cells. The indentation caused by the biconcave area can be drawn as a fainter circle inside the cell.

White blood cells

White blood cells exist in a variety of forms, three of which are shown in Figure 4. They all contain a nucleus. When a sample of blood is viewed using a light microscope, some of the white blood cells have a spherical shape and a large, compact spherical nucleus. These are known as lymphocytes. Other white blood cells, known as neutrophils, have a less regular shape and a lobed nucleus. Larger cells known as monocytes, also with an irregular shape, have a large, kidney-shaped nucleus. These cells mature into cells with a granular cytoplasm and are known as macrophages. Unlike red blood cells, white blood cells can pass through the gaps in the capillary endothelium into the fluid that surrounds the cells of tissues. Made in the marrow of the limb bones, the white blood cells function to protect the body against infection. These cells form part of the body's immune system. When the body responds to foreign cells or material, an immune response occurs.

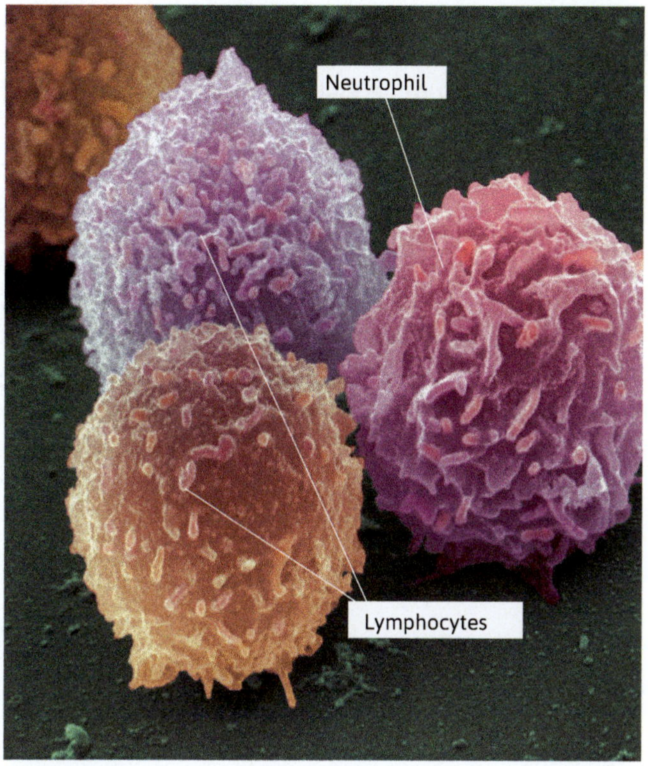

In terms of their function, the cells can be divided into two groups.

- **Phagocytes**, such as neutrophils and macrophages, remove microorganisms, other foreign material and dead cells by the process of phagocytosis (4.2f and 11.1a). Phagocytosis is non-specific and occurs whatever the infection.
- **Lymphocytes**, such as B- and T-lymphocytes, act against disease-causing microorganisms (pathogens). B-lymphocytes are white blood cells that secrete **antibodies** that immobilise pathogens and make them ready for phagocytes to engulf.

There are different kinds of T-lymphocytes. Some secrete cell-signalling molecules to stimulate further responses against foreign cells and others directly kill cells. More about these processes can be found in Chapter 11. Each type of lymphocyte acts against one particular pathogen, i.e. they are specific. They can provide long-term immunity to future infections.

Figure 3 *Colourised scanning electron micrograph of white blood cells. The most common white blood cell in blood is the neutrophil*

Remember

There is only one type of red blood cell, but there are a number of different types of white blood cell.

Extension

Other terms for red blood cells and white blood cells

You may come across other terms used to describe red and white blood cells (you do not need to remember these).

A red blood cell is also known as an erythrocyte or a red corpuscle.

A white blood cell is also known as a leucocyte or a white corpuscle.

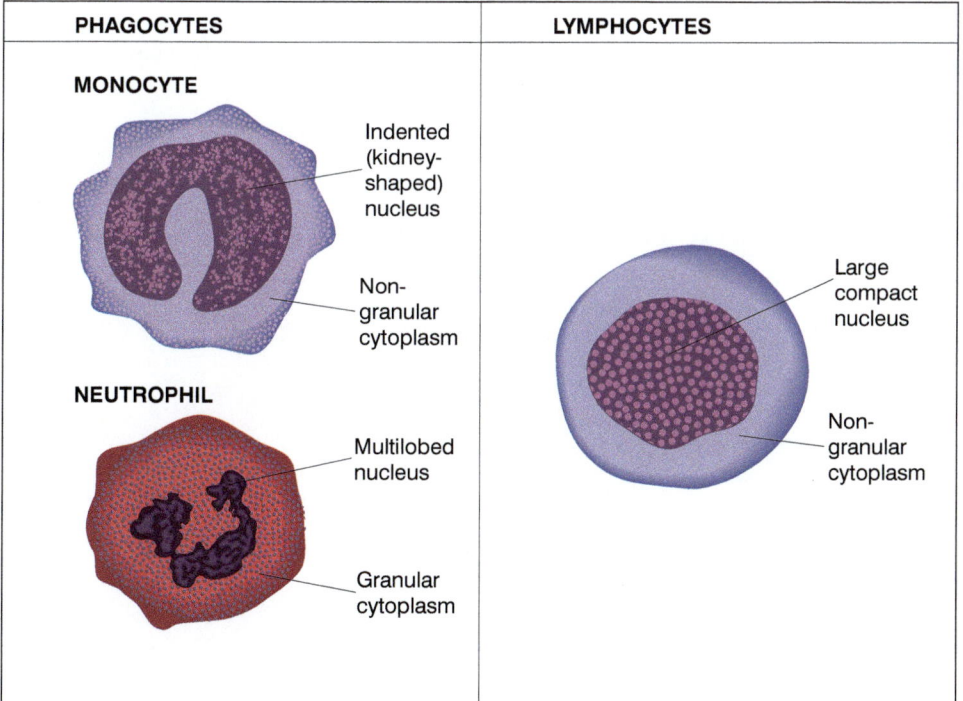

Figure 4 *Three types of white blood cell*

Practical and observation skill

Identifying and drawing white blood cells in microscope slides and images

Figure 5 shows red blood cells, lymphocytes, neutrophils and monocytes (plus two other cell types that you do not have to identify – see **Extension**).

Remember to draw cells in proportion to each other and to show the differences in the size and shape of the nuclei of the white blood cells and in the nature of their cytoplasm (with or without granules – see **Extension**).

Lymphocytes are spherical cells (see Figure 3 on page 155) that have a spherical nucleus that almost fills the cell. They have a non-granular cytoplasm. Inactive lymphocytes are just larger than red blood cells, whereas activated lymphocytes are considerably larger. You cannot see a difference between B-lymphocytes and T-lymphocytes.

Monocytes are large cells that are roughly spherical in shape (Figure 4 on page 155), with a non-granular cytoplasm and a kidney-shaped nucleus. They are larger and less numerous than neutrophils. These cells are commonly seen in blood, only migrating into tissues to develop into macrophages.

Macrophages are large phagocytes with a large kidney-shaped (bean-shaped) nucleus and a cytoplasm that looks granular. They are rarely seen in blood slides.

Neutrophils are the most common white blood cells in blood. They are roughly spherical and have a distinctive lobed nucleus.

Extension

Granulocytes and agranulocytes

White blood cells can be divided into two main types according to their morphology (form):

Granulocytes have a cytoplasm that appears granular.

Neutrophils and macrophages are granulocytes and most of their granules are lysosomes (remember that these cells are phagocytes). You will learn about these in Chapter 11.

Basophils are involved in immune responses to parasites and can also release chemicals to increase blood flow to sites of infection in an inflammation response (Chapter 11). They are not commonly seen in blood slides.

Eosinophils are large granulocytes that are active against multicellular parasites such as parasitic worms and are also important in allergic responses. They are rarely seen in blood slides as they migrate into tissues to carry out their role. They have a cytoplasm that stains red/pink and have a large bi-lobed nucleus.

Agranulocytes have a cytoplasm that is non-granular.

Monocytes and lymphocytes are agranular.

Summary test 8.1c

Blood is made up of a watery liquid called **(1)**, in which lie a variety of cells. The most numerous are the **(2)**, which are biconcave discs about **(3)** in diameter. They live for about **(4)** and contain a red pigment called **(5)** that carries **(6)**. A second type of cell is the **(7)**, which has a variety of forms. Those that engulf bacteria are called **(8)**, examples of which are a cell type with a large kidney-shaped nucleus, called a **(9)**, and a cell type which is smaller and with a **(10)** nucleus, called a **(11)**. Monocytes are large cells with no granules in their cytoplasm and a **(12)** nucleus. Spherical cells with no granules in their cytoplasm and a large **(13)** nucleus are known as lymphocytes. In a blood slide, the most numerous white blood cells are likely to be the **(14)**.

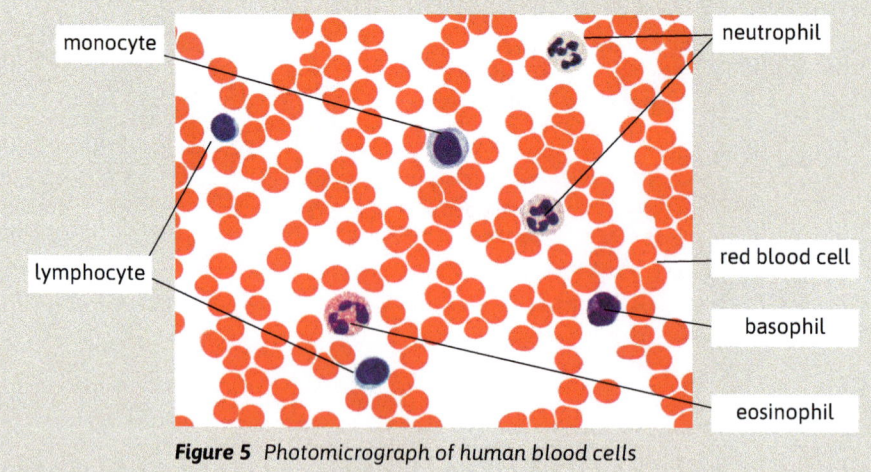

Figure 5 *Photomicrograph of human blood cells*

d. Blood plasma, tissue fluid and the role of water in transport

Blood supplies nutrients to the tissues of the body via tiny blood vessels called capillaries. These cannot serve every single cell directly, and the final stage of the delivery of nutrients, such as glucose and amino acids, of oxygen and of molecules such as cell signalling molecules is made in solution in a liquid that bathes the tissues – **tissue fluid**. This fluid also transfers waste substances produced by body cells to the blood.

Tissue fluid is formed from blood plasma.

The plasma

Blood plasma is 90% water and 10% chemicals, which are either dissolved or suspended in it. The function of the plasma is to transport these chemicals from where they are produced or absorbed to the cells that use or excrete them. These chemicals include:

- **nutrients**, e.g. dissolved glucose, amino acids and vitamins
- **waste products**, e.g. **urea**
- **mineral ions**, e.g. calcium, iron
- **hormones**, e.g. insulin, adrenaline
- **plasma proteins**, e.g. fibrinogen, prothrombin, albumin
- **respiratory gases**, e.g. oxygen, carbon dioxide.

Between them, these chemicals make the plasma slightly alkaline – around pH 7.4. The removal from the plasma of the clotting proteins prothrombin and fibrinogen results in a liquid called **serum**, which does not clot.

The functions of tissue fluid

Like plasma, the main component of tissue fluid is water. The wide range of dissolved substances found in this fluid has been filtered from blood plasma or transported out of body cells. Tissue fluid is the means by which materials are exchanged between blood and cells and it bathes all cells of the body.

Tissue fluid:

- supplies dissolved glucose, amino acids, mineral ions and other essential nutrients to body cells for their metabolic processes
- provides cells with oxygen for aerobic respiration
- transfers carbon dioxide and other waste substances produced by body cells to plasma
- provides an aqueous environment (of the same water potential) for body cells
- provides a medium for the movement of macrophages within body tissues to defend against infection.

These pages help you to:

- understand that plasma is the fluid component of blood and is the source of tissue fluid (8.1.6 and 8.1.7)
- understand that water is the main component of blood and tissue fluid (8.1.6)
- relate the properties of water to its role in transport in mammals (8.1.6)
- describe the formation of tissue fluid in a capillary network (8.1.7)
- state the functions of tissue fluid (8.1.7)

You will also:

- learn about the lymphatic system

> **Remember**
>
> Exchange between blood and cells does not take place at arteries or veins, only at capillaries.

Extension

Return of tissue fluid to the circulatory system

As the blood passes through the capillary network, its hydrostatic pressure becomes lower than that of the tissue fluid.

The large plasma proteins remaining in the capillary help to lower the water potential, so water has a tendency to move back into the plasma by osmosis. There is an overall negative pressure of 1.5 kPa drawing tissue fluid back into the capillaries. Not all the tissue fluid can return to the capillaries; the remainder drains into blind-ended (closed at one end) vessels called lymph capillaries that merge into larger vessels, forming a network known as the lymphatic system around the body. The lymph vessels drain their contents back into the blood stream, into the large veins leading to the heart.

At points along the lymph vessels are a series of **lymph nodes**, which produce and store lymphocytes.

Lymph is a liquid that resembles the tissue fluid that drains back into the blood circulatory system, but will also contain lymphocytes. In the ileum (small intestine) droplets of fat are passed into lymph, giving it a milky appearance.

Formation of tissue fluid

Blood pumped by the heart passes along arteries, then the narrower arterioles and, finally, the even narrower capillaries. By this time the pressure of blood, known as the **hydrostatic pressure**, is around 4.8 kPa at the arterial end of the capillaries, which causes fluid to move out of the blood. The outward pressure is, however, opposed by two other forces:

- hydrostatic pressure of the tissue fluid outside the capillaries, which resists outward movement of liquid
- the lower water potential of the blood (due to plasma proteins) that causes water to move back into the capillaries.

The combined effect of all these forces is to create an overall pressure of 1.7 kPa, which pushes fluid out of the capillaries at the arterial end. This pressure is only enough to force small molecules, such as dissolved glucose and amino acids (and oxygen that has diffused out of red blood cells), out of the capillaries, leaving red blood cells and proteins in the blood. This type of filtration under pressure is called **ultrafiltration**. Some white blood cells may also leave the plasma. The loss of the tissue fluid reduces the pressure in the capillaries and so, by the time the blood has reached the venous end of the network, its hydrostatic pressure is less than that of the tissue fluid outside it. Figure 1 summarises the formation of tissue fluid. Notice that the blood leaving the capillary network has lost most of its oxygen and nutrients to the body cells, and it has gained carbon dioxide and other excretory waste. If the body cells are secretory cells, for example of cell-signalling molecules, then these substances will have been transferred into the blood plasma for delivery to target tissues.

The extent to which the substances in plasma move through the endothelial pores compared to the endothelial cells (by simple or facilitated diffusion or osmosis, for water) will vary depending on the tissue. Remember that there are some capillaries with no endothelial pores. For those capillaries with endothelial pores, much of the tissue fluid is formed by filtration through these gaps.

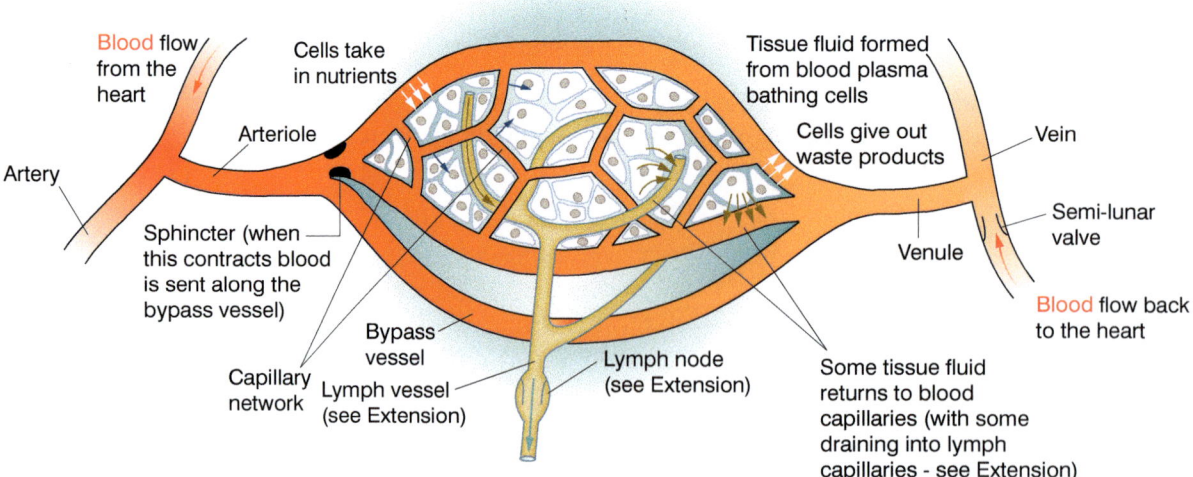

Figure 1 *Formation and return of tissue fluid*

The role of water in transport

Bulk transport in mammals would not be possible without water as the main component of plasma and of blood. Two important properties of water that help it carry out its role in transport are its solvent action and its high specific heat capacity.

In 2.4a, we looked at the dipolar nature of water and the role of water as a solvent. Many of the essential nutrients required by cells for their metabolic needs are ions or polar molecules, and these are easily able to dissolve in plasma, with water as the solvent. Urea, produced by cells of the liver, is a waste product from the breakdown of excess amino acids. This needs to be transported, dissolved in plasma, to the kidneys for excretion (14.1b). Carbon dioxide is transported, mainly as dissolved hydrogen carbonate ions (see 8.2b), from body cells to the lungs for excretion. Lipid molecules cannot dissolve in water but can be transported within spherical complexes known as lipoproteins: these have a hydrophilic exterior that dissolves in plasma.

A high specific heat capacity (see 2.4a) is an extremely important property of water for the thermal stability of blood and of tissue fluid. Blood, with its high water content, resists changes in temperature and so helps to keep the external environment of cells at a constant temperature. This is essential for the efficient functioning of enzymes.

Tissue fluid is formed from the **(1)** due to the **(2)** pressure at the **(3)** end of the capillary network. Although other forces oppose the formation of tissue fluid, there is still sufficient pressure to force water and small molecules out of the blood, but not red blood cells and large molecules such as plasma proteins. This process is called **(4)**. Plasma is approximately **(5)** water. Water is a good **(6)** because many of the essential molecules and ions that are needed by cells can **(7)** in it. Waste substances such as **(8)**, made in the liver, are transported in plasma. Blood does not change its temperature easily because it has a **(9)**.

Transport of oxygen and carbon dioxide

8.2 a. Haemoglobin and the oxygen dissociation curve

These pages help you to:

- outline the role of red blood cells in transporting oxygen (8.2.1)
- describe the role of haemoglobin in transporting oxygen (8.2.1)
- describe and explain the oxygen dissociation curve of adult haemoglobin (8.2.4)
- explain the importance of the oxygen dissociation curve at partial pressures of oxygen in the lungs and in respiring tissues (8.2.5)

You will also:

- consolidate your knowledge of the structure of the haemoglobin molecule

Remember

A molecule of haemoglobin has a quaternary protein structure, with two α-globin and two β-globin polypeptide chains, each with an iron-containing haem group (2.3c). Each haem group can bind one oxygen molecule.

Extension

Why is haemoglobin contained in red blood cells?

Haemoglobin (Figure 1) has a molar mass of $65\,000\ \mathrm{g\,mol^{-1}}$. As such, it could be lost from the body during ultrafiltration in the kidneys (14.1d). It is therefore contained within the red blood cells that carry it around the body, separated from the plasma. It is not a plasma protein because it is contained within red blood cells. A single cell can carry approximately 250 000 000 haemoglobin molecules and collectively this gives the cell its red colour. This becomes a brighter red in the presence of oxyhaemoglobin.

Introduction

As organisms evolved, they became more complex and, in many cases, much larger. The demand for oxygen increased as the metabolic rates increased. Specialised gas exchange surfaces, such as alveoli in the lungs (9.1c), developed to meet this need and a mechanism to transport the oxygen from these surfaces to the cells requiring it had to be developed. Even with blood vessels and a heart to pump the blood around them, transporting oxygen dissolved in plasma is not enough to satisfy the needs of respiring tissues. Organisms evolved specialised cells, red blood cells, which could be packed with molecules specialised to take up oxygen from the gas exchange surface, transport it and release it to respiring tissues. These molecules are called **respiratory pigments**, the best known of which is **haemoglobin**.

Haemoglobin

Haemoglobin is a large globular protein that functions to carry oxygen and carbon dioxide within red blood cells. Its structure is described in 2.3c. One oxygen molecule can combine with each of its four haem groups to form oxyhaemoglobin. Each red blood cell has many millions of haemoglobin molecules, which means that a large quantity of oxygen can be transported by a single red blood cell.

To be efficient, haemoglobin must:

- readily associate with oxygen at the gas exchange surface (loading)
- readily dissociate from oxygen at those tissues requiring it (unloading).

These two requirements may appear contradictory, but are achieved by the remarkable property of haemoglobin changing its affinity for (ability to bind to) oxygen in different concentrations of oxygen and carbon dioxide (Table 1). The changing affinity of haemoglobin for oxygen in different concentrations of carbon dioxide is known as the Bohr effect and is explained in 8.2b.

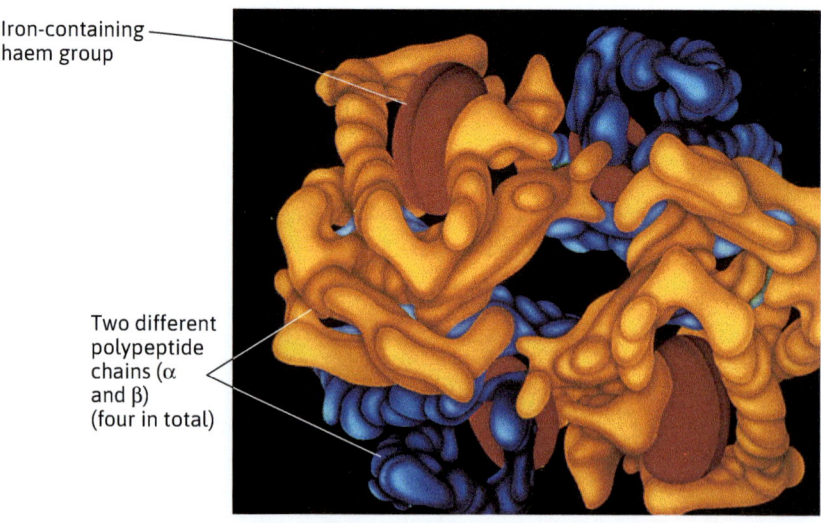

Iron-containing haem group

Two different polypeptide chains (α and β) (four in total)

Figure 1 *Computer graphic representation of a haemoglobin molecule showing two pairs of polypeptide chains (orange and blue) associated with the haem groups (red)*

Table 1 *Affinity of haemoglobin for oxygen under different conditions*

Region of body	Oxygen partial pressure (concentration)	Carbon dioxide partial pressure (concentration)	Affinity of haemoglobin for oxygen	Result
Gas exchange surface	High	Low	High	Oxygen is loaded
Respiring tissues	Low	High	Low	Oxygen is unloaded

Oxygen dissociation curves

The relationship between partial pressure of oxygen and the percentage saturation of haemoglobin with oxygen is shown by the **oxygen dissociation curve**. You will see from this curve, which is shown in Figure 2, that haemoglobin does not load or unload oxygen evenly. The explanation of the shape of the oxygen dissociation curve in terms of loading oxygen is as follows:

- The shape of the haemoglobin molecule makes it difficult for the first oxygen molecule to bind to one of the haem groups on its four polypeptide chains because they interact closely. Therefore at low oxygen concentrations, little oxygen binds to haemoglobin. The gradient of the curve is not very steep initially.
- The binding of this first oxygen molecule changes the quaternary structure of the haemoglobin molecule. This causes it to change shape and makes it easier for another haem group (on another polypeptide chain) to bind an oxygen molecule. This is known as an allosteric effect.
- As a consequence of the allosteric effect, it takes a smaller increase in the partial pressure of oxygen to bind the second oxygen molecule than it did to bind the first one. This is known as **positive cooperativity**, because binding of the first molecule makes binding of the second easier, and so on. The gradient of the curve steepens.
- At high oxygen concentrations most, but not all, of the haemoglobin molecules are completely loaded with oxygen molecules and the gradient of the curve reduces and begins to level off (plateau). There is never completely 100% saturation as, with the majority of binding sites occupied, it is less likely that a single oxygen molecule will find an empty site to bind to.

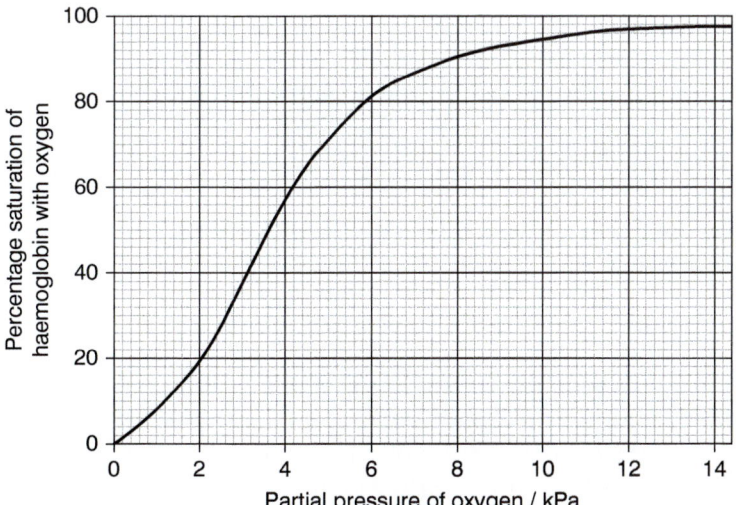

Figure 2 *The oxygen dissociation curve of adult human haemoglobin*

Extension

Measuring oxygen concentration
The quantity of a gas that is present in a mixture of gases is measured by the pressure it contributes to the total pressure of the gas mixture. This is known as the **partial pressure** of the gas and, in the case of oxygen, is written as $p\mathrm{O}_2$. It is also known as **oxygen tension** and is measured in the usual unit for pressure, namely kilopascals (kPa). Atmospheric pressure at sea level is approximately 100 kPa. As oxygen makes up 21% of the atmosphere, its partial pressure at sea level is approximately 21 kPa.

Remember

In Figure 2, partial pressure values around 13.3 kPa (range 12 to 14 kPa) represent those pressures found in the alveolar tissues in the lungs. Haemoglobin associates readily with oxygen to form oxyhaemoglobin. Using Figure 2, it can be seen that when haemoglobin arrives in tissues (with a partial partial pressure of oxygen around 2 to 6 kPa), the affinity of haemoglobin for oxygen will decrease and oxygen will begin to dissociate from oxyhaemoglobin. This releases oxygen to the tissues (see also p162).

Extension

Oxygen dissociation curves
There are many different oxygen dissociation curves because:

- there are a number of different respiratory pigments
- haemoglobin exists in a number of different forms
- the behaviour of each pigment changes under different conditions, for example with a change in pH, temperature or at altitude.

Remember

Use of abbreviation – Hb

Hb is commonly used as an abbreviation for haemoglobin. As a haemoglobin molecule has four haem groups, each of which carries an oxygen molecule (O_2), you may see the abbreviation for oxyhaemoglobin shown as Hb_4O_8. Notice that this abbreviation does **not** mean four haemoglobin molecules.

Remember

The oxygen dissociation curve is constructed from the results of laboratory experiments where the percentage saturation of haemoglobin with oxygen is measured at different partial pressures of oxygen (pO_2), in standard conditions of temperature and carbon dioxide concentration.

It is most useful to be able to interpret the curve in the upper range of pO_2, which represents the conditions in the lungs, and in the lower range of pO_2 representing the conditions in the respiring tissues.

Extension

Carbon monoxide

Haemoglobin has an affinity for carbon monoxide some 250 times greater than for oxygen – a feature which makes carbon monoxide potentially lethal. Carbon monoxide permanently binds to haemoglobin to form carboxyhemoglobin, and so prevents oxygen molecules being loaded. As carbon monoxide is found in fumes from the burning of fuels and in tobacco smoke, both reduce the oxygen-carrying capacity of the blood because haemoglobin is less saturated with oxygen.

Oxygen transport in the body

The shape of the curve helps to explain the events that occur:

- in the lungs, where haemoglobin associates with oxygen (loading) to carry it in the form of oxyhaemoglobin to respiring tissues
- in respiring tissues, where the reverse occurs and oxygen dissociates (unloads) from oxyhaemoglobin.

In the lungs

A fully saturated haemoglobin molecule has an oxygen molecule bound to all four of its iron ions in each haem group. For this to occur, haemoglobin must be in an environment where the oxygen partial pressure is high, such as in the alveolar capillaries in the lungs (9.1c). These pressures are typically 13.3 kPa, and range from 12 to 14 kPa.

You can see in Figure 2, at the range of pO_2 found in the lungs, the curve plateaus (flattens out) and the percentage saturation of haemoglobin with oxygen in this range is 98%. This means that practically all haemoglobin molecules are carrying the maximum number of oxygen molecules. Haemoglobin is described as having a high affinity for oxygen at higher partial pressures of oxygen.

Very little oxygen is dissociated from this oxyhaemoglobin as the blood passes from the lungs to the tissues.

In respiring tissues

There is considerable variation in partial pressures of oxygen (pO_2) in different tissues of the body, but typically pressures range from about 2 kPa to 6 kPa. For any one tissue, pO_2 will be lower when the tissue is active compared to the pO_2 of resting tissue.

In resting tissues, for example at pO_2 5 kPa, you can see from Figure 2 on page 162 that oxyhaemoglobin will release some oxygen to the respiring tissues, as the percentage saturation has decreased to approximately 70%. Haemoglobin has a lower affinity for oxygen compared to its affinity in the lungs.

There is a steep decrease in the curve as pO_2 decreases further from 5 kPa. This shows that only a small decrease in pO_2 will cause a large difference in the quantity of oxygen that dissociates from oxyhaemoglobin. As we will see in 8.2b, the affinity of haemoglobin for oxygen changes with changing concentrations of carbon dioxide.

Although it is relatively easy for the first three oxygen molecules to dissociate as the partial pressure of oxygen decreases, it is much harder for the final molecule to dissociate so that percentage saturation of haemoglobin never reaches 0%.

Summary test 8.2a

Haemoglobin in humans is an example of a **(1)**. Haemoglobin is found in cells known as **(2)**. A single haemoglobin molecule possesses a total of **(3)** haem groups, each of which possesses a single atom of **(4)**. The 'globin' part of the molecule comprises four **(5)**. Each haemoglobin molecule can carry a total of **(6)** molecules of oxygen. The amount of oxygen present in a mixture of gases is known as the oxygen **(7)** and the graph of the relationship between this and the quantity of oxygen taken up by haemoglobin is called the **(8)**. The binding of successive oxygen molecules to haemoglobin can be described as an **(9)** effect, with the **(10)** oxygen molecule being most difficult to bind. In partial pressures found in respiring tissues, a small change in pressure results in a **(11)** decrease in percentage **(12)** of haemoglobin with oxygen. At these pressures, the **(13)** of haemoglobin for oxygen is low.

b. The role of red blood cells in transporting carbon dioxide

The carbon dioxide produced by respiratory tissues must be carried back to the gas exchange surface for removal from the body because its accumulation (build-up) is harmful. This carbon dioxide is, however, essential to the efficient dissociation of oxygen from **oxyhaemoglobin** to the tissues. This is the **Bohr effect**, named after the person who discovered it in 1904, Christian Bohr.

The Bohr effect

Haemoglobin has a reduced affinity for (ability to bind to) oxygen in the presence of carbon dioxide. The greater the concentration of carbon dioxide, or the higher the pCO_2, the more readily it releases its oxygen. This is the Bohr effect, and explains the differing behaviour of haemoglobin in different regions of the body and in the same region of the body under different conditions.

- At the gas exchange surface (e.g. lungs), the concentration of carbon dioxide is lower than in the respiratory tissues because it diffuses across the exchange surface and is expelled from the organism. Haemoglobin's affinity for oxygen is increased. Together with the high concentration of oxygen in the lungs this means that haemoglobin readily binds oxygen.
- In the respiratory tissues (e.g. muscles), the concentration of carbon dioxide is higher in the blood because of its production during respiration. The affinity of haemoglobin for oxygen is reduced. Together with the low concentration of oxygen in the muscles this means that oxygen readily dissociates from oxyhaemoglobin. During exercise, even more carbon dioxide is produced and this increases the concentration in the blood. This shifts the oxygen dissociation curve to the right (Figure 1) so that more oxygen is released from haemoglobin (the percentage saturation of haemoglobin with oxygen is decreased). Oxygen is supplied more readily to meet extra energy demands due to exercise.

The Bohr effect is a consequence of the acidic nature of dissolved carbon dioxide: it forms hydrogen ions and hydrogencarbonate ions. It is the hydrogen ions that lower the pH and the affinity of haemoglobin for oxygen (see pages 164 and 165). Low pH caused by other chemicals, e.g. lactate, therefore also reduces haemoglobin's affinity for oxygen in the same way.

The Bohr effect is very important in allowing the body to respond and adjust to the changing conditions that occur in respiring tissue:

- Higher activity needs more oxygen for aerobic respiration.
- A higher rate of respiration produces more carbon dioxide that passes into tissue fluid.
- A higher concentration of carbon dioxide in the area causes more oxygen to dissociate from oxyhaemoglobin.

As an example, consider the curves on Figure 1 for carbon dioxide concentrations of 5.3 kPa and 10.8 kPa. At a partial pressure of oxygen in respiring tissues of 5 kPa (*x*-axis), the percentage saturation of haemoglobin with oxygen in the tissue when it is at a lower activity (5.3 kPa curve) will be approaching 65%. If the tissue is very actively respiring and releasing large quantities of carbon dioxide (10.8 kPa curve), the percentage saturation of haemoglobin with oxygen is now only approximately 45%. More oxygen has dissociated from haemoglobin to satisfy the respiratory demands of the tissue.

These pages help you to:

- outline the role of red blood cells and plasma in the transport of carbon dioxide (8.2.1 and 8.2.3)
- describe the events that occur when carbon dioxide enters red blood cells, including the formation of haemoglobinic acid and carbaminohaemoglobin (8.2.1)
- understand the role of carbonic anhydrase and haemoglobin in the transport of carbon dioxide (8.2.1)
- describe the chloride shift and explain its importance (8.2.2)
- describe the Bohr effect and explain its importance (8.2.6)

You will also:

- learn about the transport protein involved in the chloride shift

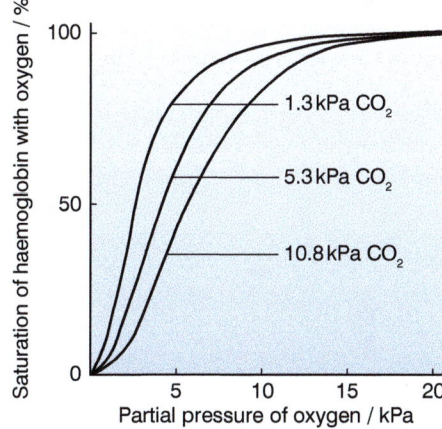

Figure 1 The Bohr effect: how the oxygen dissociation curve changes with different partial pressures of carbon dioxide (pCO_2)

Transport of carbon dioxide

Around 5% of carbon dioxide is carried from the tissues to the gas exchange surface in solution in blood plasma. The transport of the remaining 95% involves haemoglobin. The carbon dioxide is transported in two ways:

- **In combination with haemoglobin** – carbon dioxide can combine with amino groups in the protein part of the haemoglobin molecule:

$$Hb-N\begin{array}{c}H\\[2pt]\\H\end{array} \;+\; CO_2 \;\rightleftharpoons\; Hb-N\begin{array}{c}H\\[2pt]\\COO^-\end{array} \;+\; H^+$$

haemoglobin carbon dioxide carbaminohaemoglobin hydrogen ions

About 10% of the total carbon dioxide is carried in this way.

- **As hydrogencarbonate ions** – 85% of the total carbon dioxide is transported in this form. The carbon dioxide combines with water to form carbonic acid, which then dissociates (splits) into hydrogen ions (H^+) and hydrogencarbonate ions (HCO_3^-). The reaction is catalysed by the enzyme carbonic anhydrase and is summarised as:

$$H_2O \;+\; CO_2 \;\xrightarrow[\text{anhydrase}]{\text{carbonic}}\; H_2CO_3 \;\longrightarrow\; H^+ \;+\; HCO_3^-$$

water carbon dioxide carbonic acid hydrogen ion hydrogencarbonate ion

This reaction takes place in red blood cells. The hydrogencarbonate ions diffuse out of the red blood cell. The cell compensates for this loss of negatively charged ions in a process known as the **chloride shift**. A membrane transport protein known as an anion exchanger is involved: as a hydrogencarbonate ion diffuses out of the cell through the exchanger, a chloride ion diffuses in through the same protein. In this way, there is no change in overall charge in the cell. The hydrogen ions produced from the dissociation of carbonic acid combine with haemoglobin to form **haemoglobinic acid** and so cause it to release its oxygen, which diffuses out of the cell into the plasma, to then enter the tissue fluid and diffuse into respiring cells. In this way, haemoglobin acts as a **buffer**, helping to keep the pH of the blood around 7.4. The transport of carbon dioxide is summarised in Figure 2.

When the blood arrives in the alveolar capillaries in the lungs, the events shown in Figure 2 are reversed, and haemoglobin is able to bind oxygen to form oxyhaemoglobin.

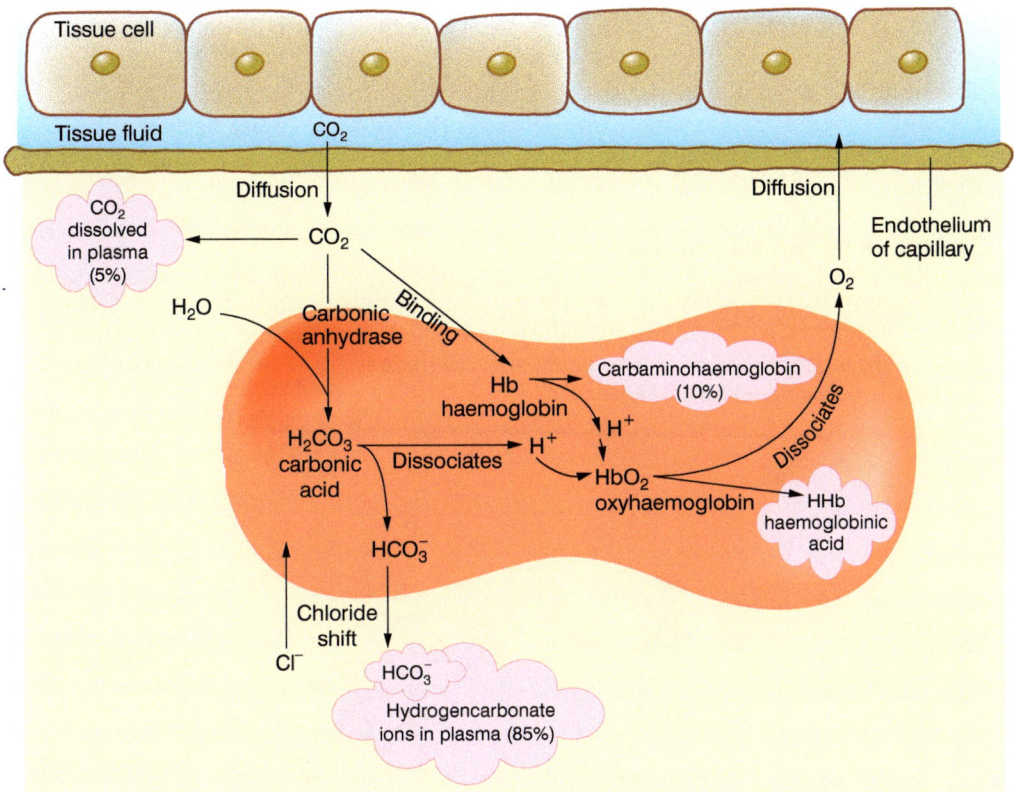

Figure 2 *Transport of carbon dioxide*

Remember

The events outlined in Figure 2 refer to the respiring tissue. In the lungs, the reverse occurs in the red blood cell:

- Hydrogencarbonate ions diffuse in, chloride ions diffuse out.
- Hydrogen ions are released from haemoglobin and combine with hydrogencarbonate ions to form carbonic acid.
- Carbonic acid, catalysed by carbonic anhydrase, produces carbon dioxide and water.
- Carbaminohaemoglobin is converted to haemoglobin and releases carbon dioxide.
- Carbon dioxide diffuses out of the red blood cell.
- Haemoglobin is free to bind to oxygen.

Summary test 8.2b

Carbon dioxide produced by tissues during the process of (1) is transported to the gas exchange surface in three ways. Firstly, it combines with haemoglobin in red blood cells to form (2) and (3) ions; this accounts for about (4)% of the total carbon dioxide carried. Secondly, around (5)% is transported in solution in the (6). The remaining (7)% is carried in the form of (8), which are formed from the dissociation of (9), which has been formed from carbon dioxide and water in a reaction catalysed by the enzyme (10). One product of this reaction is hydrogen ions, which then combine with haemoglobin to form (11), which acts as a (12) by helping to keep the blood pH around neutral. The affinity of haemoglobin for oxygen is reduced in the presence of carbon dioxide. This change is known as the (13).

The heart

a. The internal and external structure of the heart

These pages help you to:

- describe the internal structure of the heart (8.3.1)
- describe the external structure of the heart (8.3.1)
- understand that there are differences in the thickness of the walls of the atria and ventricles and the left ventricle and right ventricle (8.3.2)

You will also:

- learn about cardiac muscle

Remember

Atria are linked to **V**eins, and **A**rteries are linked to **V**entricles. In other words, **A** and **V** always go together.

The heart is a muscular organ that operates continuously and tirelessly throughout the life of an organism. Lying in the thoracic cavity between the two lungs, the heart is made up of a unique type of muscle called cardiac muscle.

Structure of the human heart

The human heart is really two separate pumps lying side-by-side, divided by a septum (Figure 1). The left-hand pump deals with oxygenated blood from the lungs, while the right-hand one deals with deoxygenated blood from the body. Each pump has two chambers.

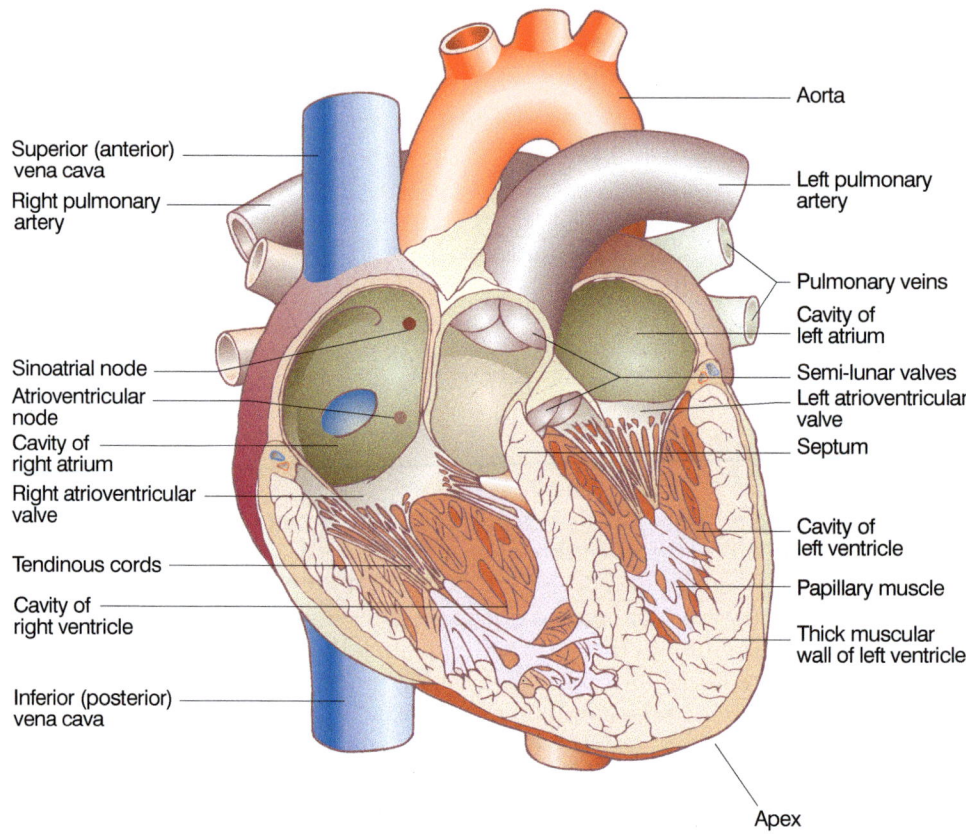

Figure 1 *Vertical section through the human heart*

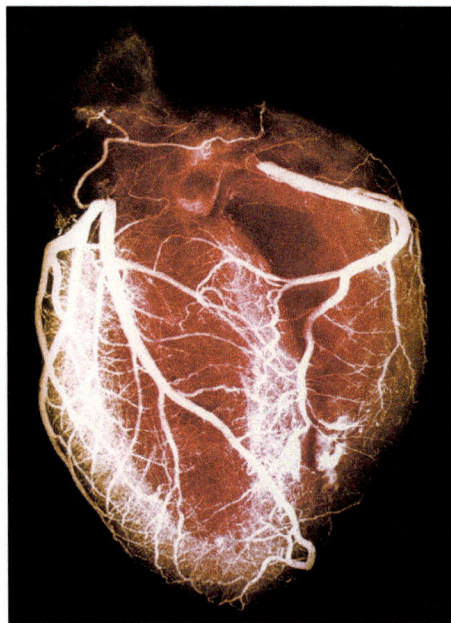

Figure 2 *X-ray of the heart showing coronary arteries which have been injected with an X-ray opaque dye*

Extension

Structure of cardiac muscle

The wall of the heart is almost entirely made up from a special type of muscle called cardiac muscle. **Cardiac muscle** is capable of rhythmic contraction and relaxation over a long period without fatigue. It is not under voluntary control like striated muscle. It appears striped under a light microscope and is made up of the proteins **actin** and **myosin**. The molecular mechanism of contraction is also the same as that of striated muscle (body muscle) (15.1h) and both have many mitochondria to supply **ATP**. Cardiac muscle is made up of short fibres – the fibres interconnect so that when muscle contraction has been stimulated, all the fibres act as one unit.

- **The atrium** is thin-walled and when the muscle walls are relaxed, it expands as it collects blood. There is very little resistance to blood flow as blood passes only a very short distance into the ventricles, so less cardiac muscle is required when the atrial walls contract.
- **The ventricle** has a much thicker muscular wall as it has to pump blood some distance, either to the lungs or the rest of the body. The walls of the blood vessels present a resistance to the blood flowing through them. This means more cardiac muscle is required to generate a force to overcome this resistance and allow blood to reach its destination.

As the right ventricle pumps blood at low pressure to the lungs, which are only a short distance away, it has a thinner muscular wall than the left ventricle because there is very little resistance to blood flow in the pulmonary circulation (circulation to the lungs). The left ventricle, in contrast, has a thick muscular wall, enabling it to contract forcefully to create a high pressure to overcome the greater resistance in the systemic circulation (circulation to the rest of the body) and pump blood to the extremities of the body, a distance of about 1.5 m. Although the two sides of the heart are separate pumps and there is no mixing of the blood in each after birth, they still pump in time with each other: both atria contract together, followed by both ventricles contracting together, pumping the same volume of blood.

Between the atrium and ventricle are valves that prevent the backflow of blood into the atria when the ventricles contract. There are two sets of valves.

- **Left atrioventricular (bicuspid) valves** are formed of two cup-shaped flaps on the left side of the heart.
- **Right atrioventricular (tricuspid) valves** are formed of three cup-shaped flaps on the right side of the heart.

To prevent these valves turning inside out under pressure, they are attached to special pillars of muscle (papillary muscles) on the heart wall by fibres called the tendinous cords (chordae tendinae). Each of the four chambers of the heart is served by large blood vessels that carry blood into or away from the heart. Vessels connecting the heart to the lungs are called **pulmonary** vessels. The vessels connected to the four chambers are as follows.

- **The aorta** is connected to the left ventricle and carries oxygenated blood to all parts of the body.
- **The vena cava** is connected to the right atrium and brings deoxygenated blood back from the tissues of the body.
- **The pulmonary artery** is connected to the right ventricle and carries deoxygenated blood to the lungs. Unusually for an artery, it carries deoxygenated blood.
- **The pulmonary vein** is connected to the left atrium and brings oxygenated blood back from the lungs. Unusually for a vein, it carries oxygenated blood.

Although oxygenated blood passes through the left side of the heart in vast quantities, the heart does not use this oxygen to meet its own great respiratory needs. Instead, the heart muscle is supplied by its own blood vessels, called the **coronary arteries** (Figure 2), which branch off the aorta shortly after it leaves the heart.

The structure of the heart and its associated blood vessels is shown in Figures 1 and 3.

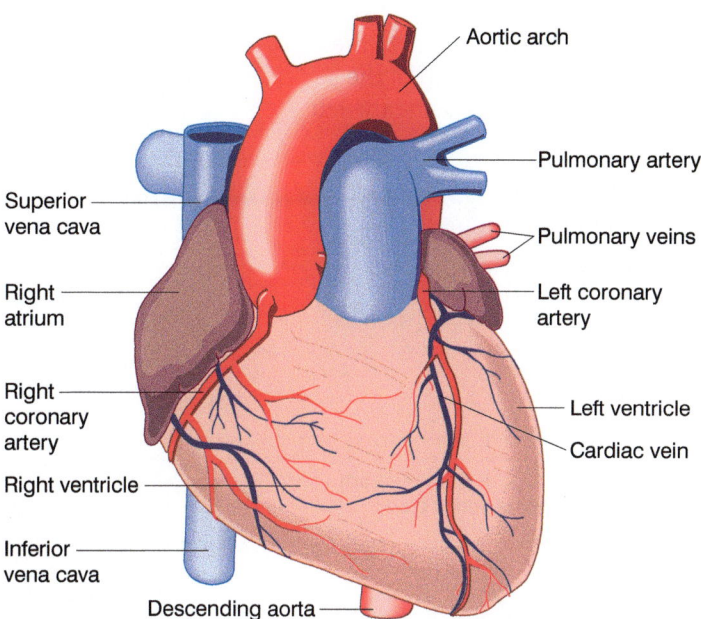

Figure 3 *External appearance of the human heart showing the blood supply to the heart muscle*

Extension

Supplying the cardiac muscle with oxygen

Blockage of the coronary arteries, e.g. by a blood clot, leads to **myocardial infarction**, or **heart attack**, because an area of the heart muscle is deprived of oxygen and so dies, leaving scar tissue.

Summary test 8.3a

The mammalian heart is made up of four chambers: a pair of thin-walled chambers called **(1)** and a pair of thick muscular ones called **(2)**. Between the chambers on the left side of the heart are the **(3)** valves, while those on the right side are called **(4)** valves. Blood from the lungs passes to the heart by the **(5)** and into the chamber called the **(6)**; it leaves the heart via the vessel called the **(7)**.

b. The cardiac cycle

The heart carries out a sequence of events that is repeated in humans around 70 times each minute when at rest. This is known as the **cardiac cycle**. There are two basic components to the beating of the heart – contraction, or **systole**, and relaxation, or **diastole**. Systole occurs separately in the ventricles and the atria and is therefore described in two phases but, for some of the time, diastole takes place at the same time in all chambers of the heart and is therefore treated as a single phase in the account below. The cardiac cycle is illustrated in Figure 1.

Diastole (relaxation of the heart)

Blood returns to the atria of the heart through the pulmonary vein (from the lungs) and the vena cava (from the body) and the atria begin to fill. As the ventricles relax, the pressure within them becomes lower than the pressure in the atria and the atrioventricular valves open, allowing the blood to pass into the ventricles. The cardiac muscle of both the atria and ventricles is relaxed at this stage. The relaxation of the ventricles' cardiac muscle causes them to recoil and reduces the pressure within the ventricles. This causes the pressure to be lower than that in the aorta and the pulmonary artery, and so the semi-lunar valves in the aorta and the pulmonary artery close.

1.

Blood enters atria and ventricles from pulmonary veins and venae cavae

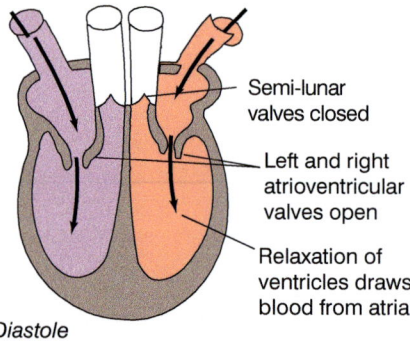

Semi-lunar valves closed

Left and right atrioventricular valves open

Relaxation of ventricles draws blood from atria

Diastole
Atria are relaxed and fill with blood. Ventricles are also relaxed.

2.

Atria contract to push remaining blood into ventricles

Semi-lunar valves closed

Left and right atrioventricular valves open

Blood pumped from atria to ventricles

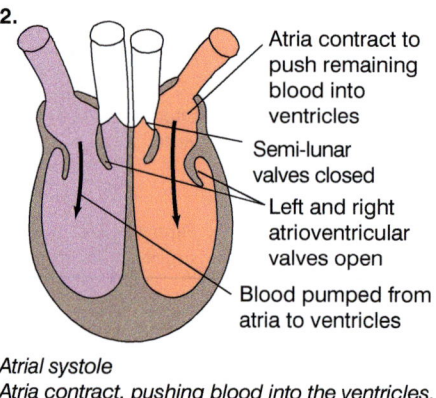

Atrial systole
Atria contract, pushing blood into the ventricles. Ventricles remain relaxed.

3.

Blood pumped into pulmonary arteries and the aorta

Semi-lunar valves open

Left and right atrioventricular valves closed

Ventricles contract

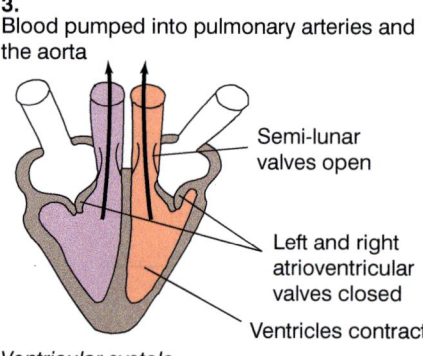

Ventricular systole
Atria relax. Ventricles contract, pushing blood away from heart through pulmonary arteries and the aorta.

Figure 1 *The cardiac cycle*

Atrial systole (contraction of the atria)

The contraction of the atrial walls forces the remaining blood into the ventricles from the atria. The blood pressure is slightly higher than at diastole. During this stage, the cardiac muscle of the ventricle walls remains relaxed (ventricular diastole).

Ventricular systole (contraction of the ventricles)

After a short delay, the walls of the ventricles contract simultaneously. This increases the blood pressure within them, forcing shut the atrioventricular valves and preventing backflow of blood into the atria. With the atrioventricular valves closed, the pressure in the ventricles rises. Once it is higher than that in the aorta and pulmonary artery, the semi-lunar valves open and blood is forced from the ventricles through the semi-lunar valves into these vessels. 8.3c provides more information on the changes in volume and blood pressure in the heart.

Valves in the control of blood flow

It is important to keep blood flowing in the right direction through the heart and around the body. This is achieved mainly by the pressure created by the heart muscle. Blood, as with all liquids and gases, will always move from a region of higher pressure to one of lower pressure. There are, however, situations within the circulatory system when pressure differences would result in blood flowing in the opposite direction. Here, valves are used to prevent any unwanted backflow of blood. Valves in the cardiovascular system are designed so that they open whenever the difference in blood pressure either side of them favours the movement of blood in the desired direction. When pressure differences are reversed, i.e. when blood flows in the opposite direction to that which is desirable, the valves are designed to close. Examples of such valves include:

- **The atrioventricular valves** between the left atrium and ventricle (bicuspid valves) and the right atrium and ventricle (tricuspid valves). These prevent backflow of blood when contraction of the ventricles means that ventricular pressure exceeds atrial pressure. Closure of these valves ensures that, when the ventricles contract, blood within them moves to the aorta and pulmonary arteries rather than back to the atria.
- **The semi-lunar valves** in the aorta and pulmonary arteries. These prevent backflow of blood into the ventricles at the beginning of ventricular diastole, when the pressure in the ventricles has started to decrease and the elastic walls of the arteries recoil (8.1b). This produces a greater pressure in the arteries than in the ventricles.
- **Pocket (semi-lunar) valves** in veins, which occur throughout the venous system. These ensure that when the veins are squeezed, e.g. when body muscles contract, blood flows back to the heart rather than away from it.

The design of all these valves is basically the same. They are made up of a number of flaps of tough, but flexible, fibrous tissue, which are cusp-shaped, i.e. like deep saucers or bowls. When pressure is greater on the convex side of these cusps, rather than on the concave side, they move apart to let blood pass between the cusps. However, when pressure is greater on the concave side than on the convex side, blood collects within the 'bowl' of the cusps, pushing them together to form a tight fit that prevents the passage of blood (Figure 2). So great are the pressures created within the ventricles of the heart that the atrioventricular valves are at risk of becoming inverted. To prevent this, the valves have string-like tendons called the chordae tendinae (tendinous cords) that are attached to pillars of muscle in the ventricle wall. These are known as papillary muscles.

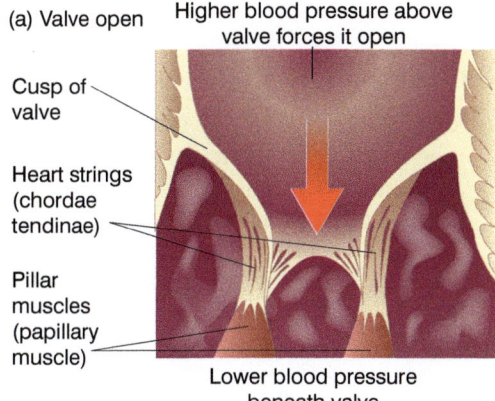

(a) Valve open — Higher blood pressure above valve forces it open

Cusp of valve

Heart strings (chordae tendinae)

Pillar muscles (papillary muscle)

Lower blood pressure beneath valve

(b) Valve closed

Lower blood pressure cannot open valve

Cusps of valves fit closely together

Higher blood pressure beneath valve forces it closed

Figure 2 *Action of valves*

Remember

The thickness of cardiac muscle in each chamber of the heart indicates the force that can be generated by the muscle to move blood onwards.

Contraction of the thin walls of the atria generates a small force to push blood into the ventricles. There is very little resistance to overcome in moving the short distance into the ventricles.

Contraction of the thick walls of the left ventricle generates enough force for blood to reach the furthest parts of the body. The surfaces of the blood vessel walls present friction to the passage of blood and so there is considerable resistance to overcome. The less thick (but thicker than atria) walls of the right ventricle generate less force when they contract, but this is enough to send the blood the shorter distance to the lungs and makes sure that the pressure is not too great to damage the fragile alveolar capillaries.

Remember

Although the left ventricle has a thicker wall than the right ventricle, their internal volumes are the same.

Summary test 8.3b

In humans the cardiac cycle repeats itself about **(1)** times each minute when the heart is at rest. The phase of the cycle when the atria and ventricles are relaxed is called **(2)**. When the atria contract during the phase called **(3)**, the remaining blood in them is pushed past the **(4)** valves into the chambers called **(5)**. Contraction of these chambers forces open the **(6)** valves and pushes blood into the **(7)**, which then goes to the lungs, and the **(8)**, which supplies blood to the rest of the body.

These pages help you to:

- explain the roles of the sinoatrial node, the atrioventricular node and the Purkyne tissue in the cardiac cycle (8.3.4)

You will also:

- be introduced to electrocardiograms

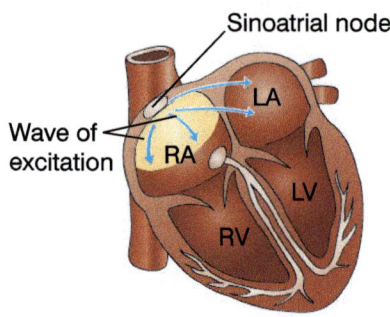

a Wave of excitation spreads out from the sinoatrial node

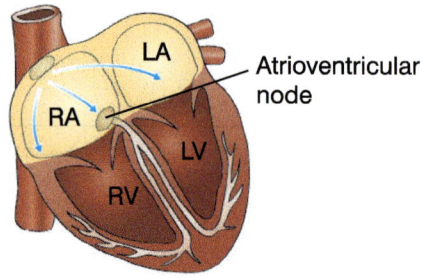

b Wave of excitation spreads across both atria causing them to contract and reaches the atrioventricular node

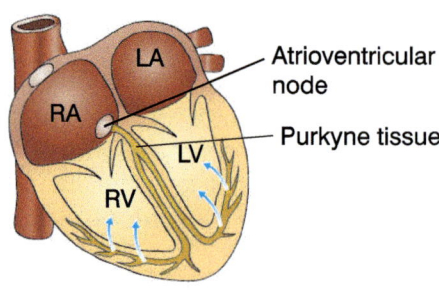

c Atrioventricular node passes a wave of excitation down the septum along the Purkyne fibres to the apex, and up through the ventricle walls, causing the ventricles to contract

Figure 1 *Control of the cardiac cycle*

For the heart to function efficiently, there must be careful control of the sequence of events that takes place during the **cardiac cycle**.

How is the cardiac cycle controlled?

Cardiac muscle is **myogenic**, i.e. its contraction is initiated from within the muscle itself, rather than by nervous impulses from outside (neurogenic), as is the case with other muscle. Within the wall of the right atrium of the heart is a distinct group of cells known as the **sinoatrial node (SAN)**. It is from here that the initial stimulus for contraction originates. The sinoatrial node has a basic rhythm of stimulation that determines the beat of the heart. For this reason it is often referred to as the **pacemaker**. The sequence of events (Figure 1) is as follows.

- A wave of excitation spreads out from the sinoatrial node across the walls of both atria, causing them to contract at the same time.
- A fibrous ring of non-conductive tissue (atrioventricular septum) prevents the wave crossing to the ventricles and this prevents the walls of the atria and ventricles contracting at the same time.
- The wave of excitation is allowed to pass through a second group of cells called the **atrioventricular node (AVN)**, which lies in the septum between the atria.
- The atrioventricular node, after a short delay of 0.1–0.2 seconds to ensure the ventricles contract after the atria and not at the same time, passes a wave of excitation between the ventricles along a series of specialised muscle fibres called the **Purkyne tissue**.
- The Purkyne tissue conducts the wave very rapidly through the septum to the base of the ventricles to allow near instantaneous stimulation of cardiac muscle.
- The wave of excitation is released from the Purkyne tissue, and passes more slowly across the cardiac muscle causing the ventricles to contract, from the apex of the heart towards the aorta and pulmonary artery.

Table 1 summarises the roles of the SAN, AVN and Purkyne tissue in the control of the cardiac cycle.

Table 1 *Summary of the roles of the SAN, AVN and Purkyne tissue*

Heart structure	Role
SAN	- acts as a pacemaker and initiates the heart beat (the cardiac cycle) - sends out impulses (waves of excitation) that spread across the atria and bring about atrial contraction, so causing the atria to contract at the same time - sends out impulses at regular intervals to produce a rhythmic contraction of the heart

AVN	- acts to relay (pass on) impulses generated by the SAN down the septum to the Purkyne tissue (via the Bundle of His)
	- delays the impulse (by approximately 0.1 s) arriving from the SAN to:
	  - give time for the atria to empty and the ventricles to fill with blood
	  - prevent the ventricles from contracting at the same time as the atria

Purkyne tissue	- pass the impulse down the septum to the base of the ventricle walls and then upwards - to make sure that the ventricles contract from the apex upwards - to make sure the ventricles contract at the same time

Extension

Pressure and volume changes of the heart

Mammals have a closed, double circulatory system, i.e. blood is kept within blood vessels and this allows the pressure within them to be maintained and regulated. Figure 2 shows the pressure within blood vessels. Blood pressure varies between a maximum (systolic blood pressure) when the ventricles contract and a minimum (diastolic blood pressure) when the heart is relaxed. In humans it is normally 16 kPa (120 mmHg) (systolic) and 10.7 kPa (80 mmHg) (diastolic). Figure 3 illustrates the pressure and volume changes that take place in the heart during a typical cardiac cycle.

Blood pressure / kPa
20
15
10
5
0
Arteries
Capillaries
Veins
Arterioles
Venules

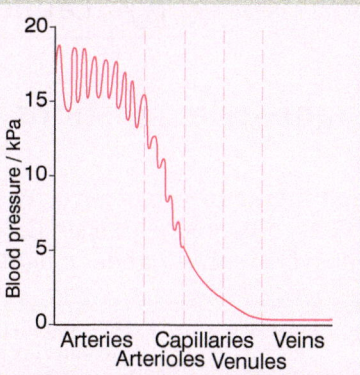

Figure 2 *Blood pressure in arteries, capillaries and veins*

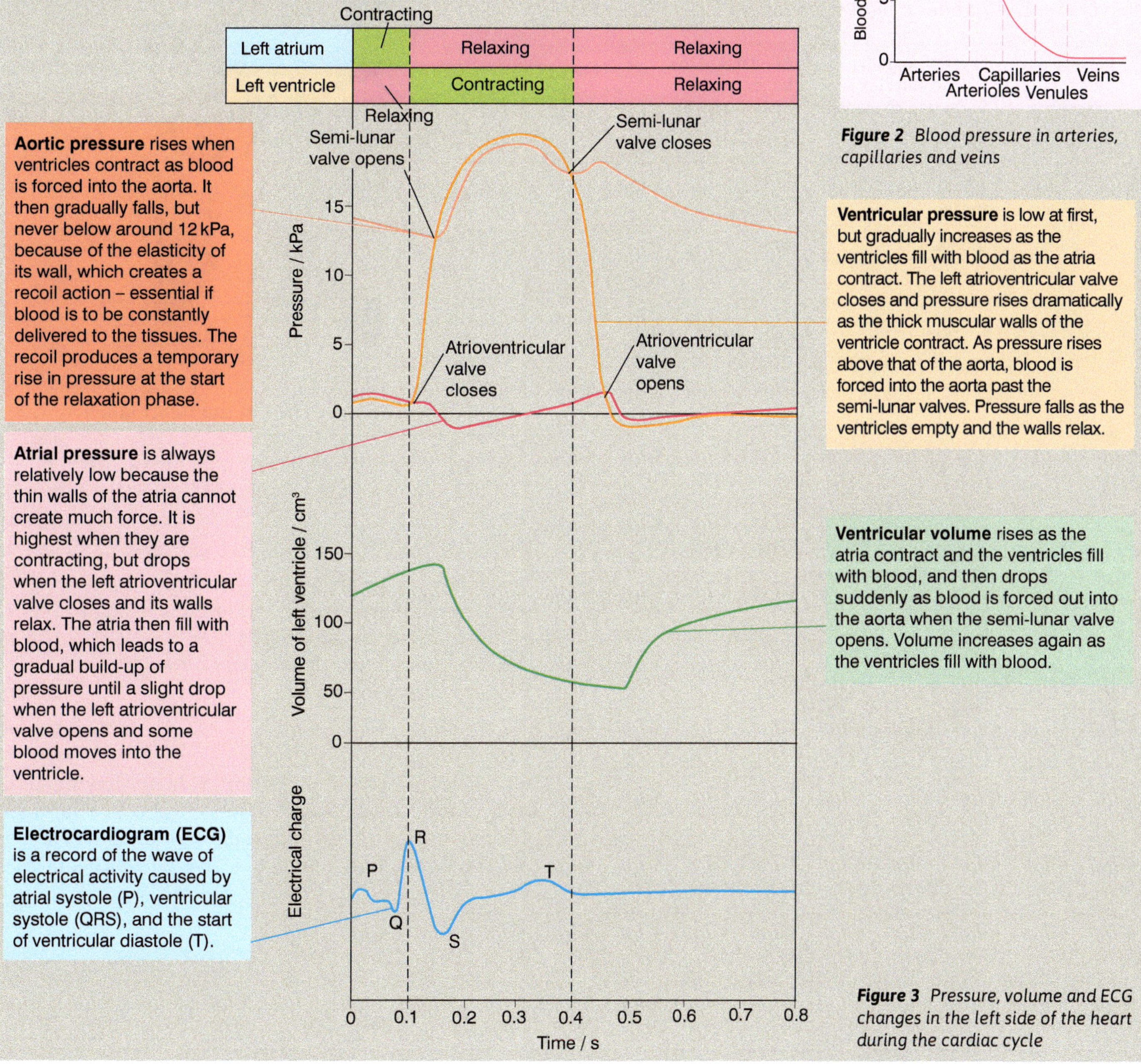

Contracting
Left atrium
Relaxing
Relaxing
Left ventricle
Contracting
Relaxing
Relaxing
Semi-lunar valve opens
Semi-lunar valve closes
Atrioventricular valve closes
Atrioventricular valve opens
Pressure / kPa
15
10
5
0
Volume of left ventricle / cm³
150
100
50
0
Electrical charge
P
Q
R
S
T
0
0.1
0.2
0.3
0.4
0.5
0.6
0.7
0.8
Time / s
Aortic pressure rises when ventricles contract as blood is forced into the aorta. It then gradually falls, but never below around 12 kPa, because of the elasticity of its wall, which creates a recoil action – essential if blood is to be constantly delivered to the tissues. The recoil produces a temporary rise in pressure at the start of the relaxation phase.
Atrial pressure is always relatively low because the thin walls of the atria cannot create much force. It is highest when they are contracting, but drops when the left atrioventricular valve closes and its walls relax. The atria then fill with blood, which leads to a gradual build-up of pressure until a slight drop when the left atrioventricular valve opens and some blood moves into the ventricle.
Electrocardiogram (ECG) is a record of the wave of electrical activity caused by atrial systole (P), ventricular systole (QRS), and the start of ventricular diastole (T).
Ventricular pressure is low at first, but gradually increases as the ventricles fill with blood as the atria contract. The left atrioventricular valve closes and pressure rises dramatically as the thick muscular walls of the ventricle contract. As pressure rises above that of the aorta, blood is forced into the aorta past the semi-lunar valves. Pressure falls as the ventricles empty and the walls relax.
Ventricular volume rises as the atria contract and the ventricles fill with blood, and then drops suddenly as blood is forced out into the aorta when the semi-lunar valve opens. Volume increases again as the ventricles fill with blood.

Figure 3 *Pressure, volume and ECG changes in the left side of the heart during the cardiac cycle*

Summary test 8.3c

The mammalian heart beat is initiated from within the heart muscle itself, which is therefore termed **(1)**. The pacemaker of the heart is the **(2)**, which lies in the wall of the chamber called the **(3)**. A wave of excitation causes both **(4)** to contract. The wave is picked up by another group of specialised cells, called the **(5)**, which in turn passes it down to the apex of the ventricles and out into the muscle via small branches of specialised muscle fibres called **(6)**.

Launch additional digital resources for the chapter

8 Exam-style questions

1 Identify the row that correctly shows the structure of a vein compared with a similar-sized artery seen in transverse section under a light microscope.

	Shape in cross section	Layer of smooth muscle and elastic fibres (tunica media)	Diameter of the lumen (hollow space)
A	circular	thicker	narrower
B	circular	thinner	wider
C	irregular	thicker	narrower
D	irregular	thinner	wider

(1 mark)

2 Red blood cells transport oxygen from the lungs to the body tissues. Figure 1 is a diagram of a red blood cell.

Figure 1

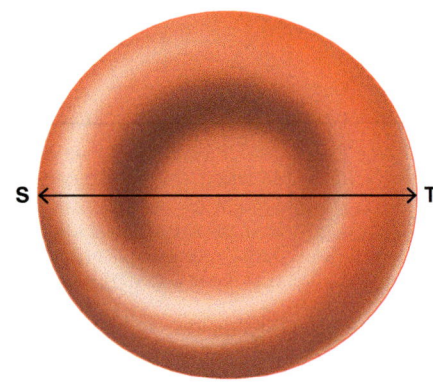

Magnification × 6000

a Calculate the actual diameter of the red blood cell along the line S-T. Show your working and give your answer to the nearest micrometre. *(3 marks)*

b Explain how the structure of red blood cells is suited to their function of transporting oxygen to body tissues. *(3 marks)*

c Red blood cells in circulation are metabolically active but only live for about 120 days. During this time, some important enzymes are gradually broken down and this may contribute to the death of the cell. Explain why the red blood cell is not able to replace important enzymes that have been broken down. *(2 marks)*

(Total 8 marks)

3 Figure 2 is a diagram of a vertical section through a healthy mammalian heart.

Figure 2

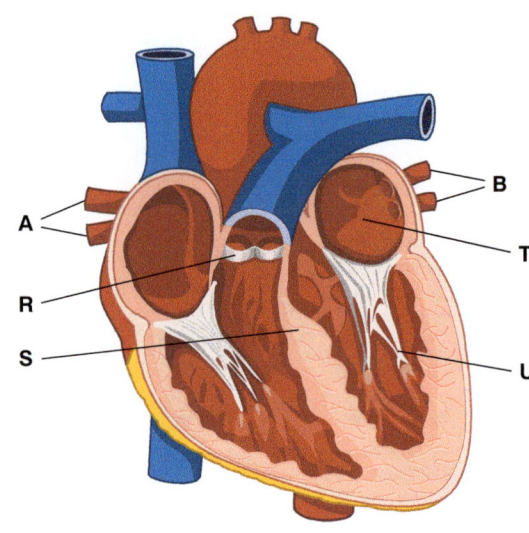

a i Identify the structures of the heart labelled R, S, T and U. *(4 marks)*

   ii State two ways in which the **composition** of blood entering **A** is different to blood entering **B**. *(2 marks)*

b Explain how the following structural features of a capillary are related to its function.

   i The capillary wall is composed of a single layer of squamous epithelial cells. *(1 mark)*

   ii The diameter of the capillary lumen is approximately 8 µm. *(2 marks)*

(Total 9 marks)

4 Haemoglobin plays an important role in carrying oxygen and carbon dioxide. Figure 3 shows a summary of some of the events that occur as blood enters a capillary located in an area of actively respiring cells.

Figure 3

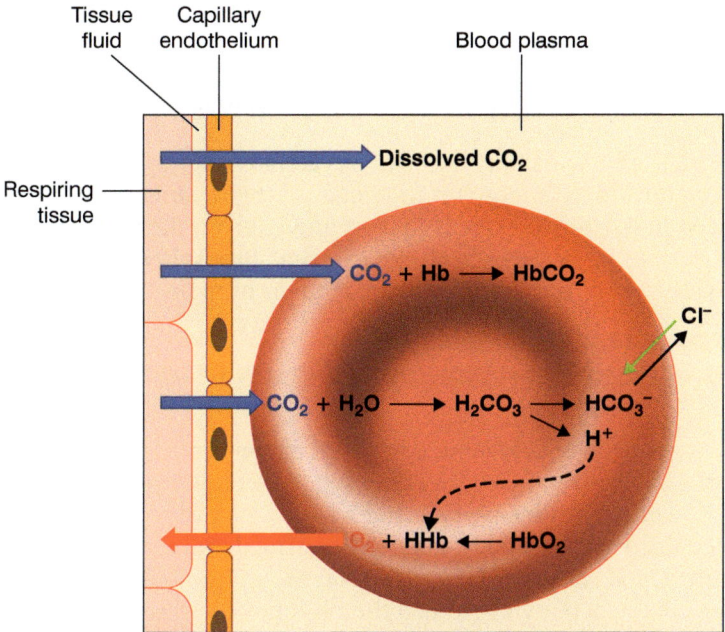

Tissue fluid | Capillary endothelium | Blood plasma
Respiring tissue

a Describe and explain how carbon dioxide (CO_2), chloride ions (Cl^-) and hydrogen ions (H^+) play a role in the unloading of oxygen from haemoglobin.
(5 marks)

b Figure 4 shows the effect of increasing the carbon dioxide concentration on the oxygen haemoglobin dissociation curve.

Figure 4

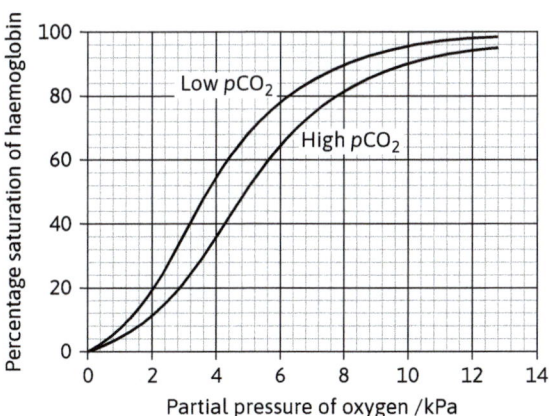

i Determine the percentage saturation of haemoglobin at both low and high partial pressures of carbon dioxide when the partial pressure of oxygen is 4 kPA. *(1 mark)*

ii Name the effect of increasing carbon dioxide concentration on the oxygen dissociation curve. *(1 mark)*

iii The percentage saturation of haemoglobin with oxygen decreases as the partial pressure of carbon dioxide increases.

Explain the importance of the effect of carbon dioxide on haemoglobin, as shown in Figure 4.
(3 marks)

(Total 10 marks)

8 Practice questions

5 The lugworm is an organism that spends almost all its life in a U-shaped burrow made on muddy seashores. Most of the time it is covered by sea water, which it circulates through its burrow. Oxygen diffuses into the lugworm's blood from the water and it uses haemoglobin to transport oxygen to its tissues. Figure 5 shows the oxygen dissociation curve of lugworm haemoglobin compared to that of adult human haemoglobin.

Figure 5

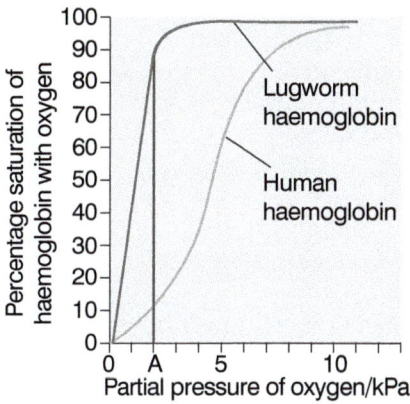

a In Figure 5, line A is drawn at a partial pressure of oxygen of 2 kPa. This is the partial pressure of oxygen found in lugworm burrows after the sea no longer covers them. Using figures from the graph, suggest why a lugworm can survive at these concentrations of oxygen while a human could not.

b Using the graphs in Figure 5, explain how the lugworm is able to obtain sufficient oxygen from an environment that contains so little.

c Haemoglobin usually loads oxygen less readily when the concentration of carbon dioxide is high (the Bohr effect). The haemoglobin of lugworms does not exhibit this effect. Explain why to do so could be harmful.

d Suggest a reason why lugworms are not found higher up the seashore.

e Llamas are animals that live at high altitudes. At these altitudes the atmospheric pressure is lower and so the partial pressure of oxygen is also lower. It is therefore difficult to load haemoglobin with oxygen. Suggest where the oxygen dissociation curve of llama haemoglobin is shifted to, relative to human haemoglobin.

9.1 The gas exchange system

a. The structure of the human gas exchange system

All **aerobic** organisms require a constant supply of oxygen in order to produce **ATP** during respiration and supply energy for the needs of the organism. The carbon dioxide produced in the process needs to be removed from the body. The volume of oxygen that has to be taken in from the external atmosphere and the volume of carbon dioxide that must be removed are large in humans because:

- they are relatively large multicellular organisms
- as mammals, they maintain a constant body temperature and therefore have high metabolic and respiratory rates.

Humans have evolved a gas exchange system, composed of a group of specialised organs and tissues working together to ensure efficient gas exchange between the air and the blood. The gas exchange surfaces are within a pair of organs, the lungs, which are located deep within the thorax. Air is warmed and moistened before it reaches the lungs, and so loss of heat and water are minimised. The lungs are supported and protected by a bony box called the rib cage. The ribs can be moved by the muscles between them, called the intercostal muscles. This enables the lungs to be ventilated so that the air within them is constantly changed.

The gross structure of the gas exchange system

The gross structure describes the detail that you can see with the naked eye, without the help of magnifying lenses or microscopes.

The gas exchange system is a collection of organs and tissues, specialised for gas exchange. Figure 1 shows that a single tube, the trachea, branches into two bronchi. Air that enters the upper part of the trachea has already passed through a number of important structures so that it has been filtered to remove large particles, moistened and warmed (see Extension on page 176).

Each bronchus enters a lung. Notice that the right lung refers to the organ as it is situated in the body, and so it appears on the left-hand side of Figure 1. Figure 1 shows the right lung cut open vertically to expose the other gross structures. The lungs are lobed structures, with the right lung having three lobes and the left lung only two.

Each bronchus divides further into smaller bronchi, which branch into smaller bronchioles. These branch out to form increasingly smaller bronchioles to end up at the alveoli. The Extension provides some more detail about the fine structures at the end of the bronchiole pathway.

If you have good eyesight, it is theoretically possible to see some larger alveoli. However, out of the body, alveoli would collapse if not filled with air. A magnifying lens is needed to see the tiny alveolar pulmonary capillaries, so these would not be included as part of the gross structure of the gas exchange system.

Extension

Reaching the gas exchange surface

The gas exchange system functions to deliver and take away air and to carry out gas exchange. The small terminal bronchioles branch into smaller structures, known as the respiratory bronchioles, which are at the start of the gas exchange area. Alveolar ducts end in alveolar sacs that are composed of many alveoli.

Distribution of cells and tissues within the trachea, bronchi, bronchioles and alveoli

The **trachea** is a flexible airway that is supported by pieces of **cartilage** (Figure 1). These pieces of cartilage do not form complete rings, but are C-shaped. This allows the adjacent oesophagus to expand without obstruction when food passes along it on its way to the stomach. The wall of the trachea is made up of **smooth muscle** and elastic fibres, and in the gap created by the C-shaped cartilage rings there is also smooth muscle and elastic fibres. The trachea is lined with **ciliated epithelium** which is composed of ciliated epithelial cells and **goblet cells**. In cross section, the epithelial lining looks layered, but it is actually a single layer of ciliated columnar (column-shaped) epithelial cells attached to a basement membrane (Figure 2).

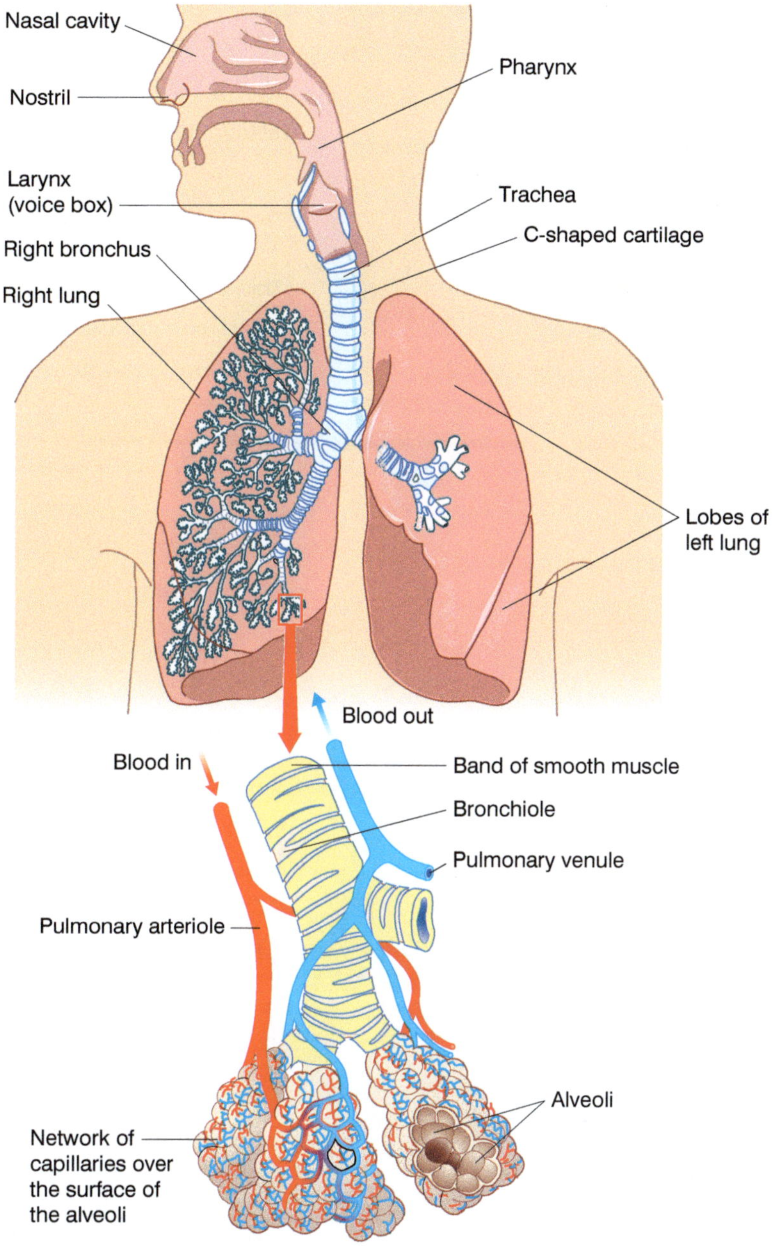

The bronchi

The structure of the bronchi is similar to that of the trachea, only they are smaller in diameter. They too are supported by cartilage, but these are irregular plates of cartilage, not C-shaped rings and the quantity of cartilage plates decreases as the larger bronchi branch into smaller bronchi. They have walls of smooth muscle and elastic fibres. The ciliated epithelium is a single layer of ciliated columnar cells and goblet cells. In cross section, this lining looks folded (convoluted).

The bronchioles

There is a transition between the smaller bronchi and the bronchioles. These structures are less than 1mm in diameter. No cartilage is visible in cross sections of bronchioles, but there are areas of smooth muscle, and elastic fibres are present. The walls of the bronchioles are thinner than the bronchi and the layer of ciliated epithelium appears more infolded. The ciliated epithelium consists of ciliated columnar cells and a few goblet cells. Approaching the alveoli, there will be no goblet cells and the epithelial cells become more cuboidal and have no cilia.

Alveoli

At the end of the gas exchange system are groups of alveoli (Figure 1) which are tiny hollow sacs. The wall of the alveolus contains a few cells that secrete surfactant (see Extension on the following page) but most of the wall is composed of a layer of large, thin, flattened cells known as **squamous epithelium**. These are the cells that function in gas exchange. The wall of the alveolus contains elastic fibres. Each alveolus is surrounded by a network of **blood capillaries**. These are extremely closely located near the wall of the alveolus (9.1c).

Figure 1 *Human gas exchange system showing positions of trachea, bronchi and bronchioles as well as the arrangement of blood vessels and alveoli in the lungs*

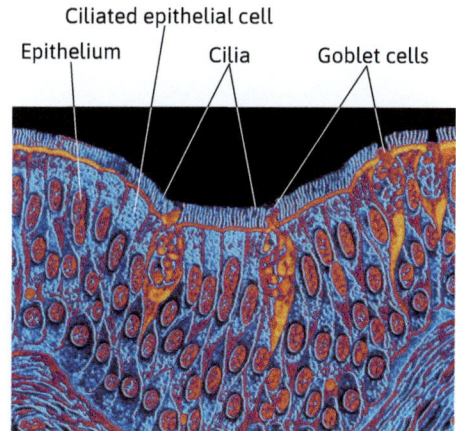

Figure 2 *Ciliated epithelium of human trachea showing goblet cells*

175

Table 1 shows the distribution of cartilage, elastic fibres, smooth muscle and ciliated epithelium in the gas exchange system. The table also shows the distribution of goblet cells (which form part of ciliated epithelium).

Table 1 *Distribution of tissues within the human gas exchange system*

Structure	Features				
	Cartilage	Ciliated epithelium	Elastic fibres	Goblet cells	Smooth muscle
Trachea	present	present	present	present	present
Bronchus	present	present	present	present	present
Bronchiole	absent	present	present	present (but becoming fewer)	present
Alveolus	absent	absent	present	absent	absent

Summary test 9.1a

Air enters the body through the mouth or nose and enters the trachea, which is supported by **(1)** shaped pieces of cartilage. The trachea branches into two bronchi. The trachea and bronchi are lined with epithelium, which produces mucus from **(2)** cells. This mucus is sticky and traps **(3)** and **(4)** present in the air. The mucus is moved towards the mouth by **(5)**, present on the epithelium. The bronchi, in turn, divide to form **(6)**, which can constrict when the **(7)** they contain contracts. **(8)** are present throughout the system and allow expansion without overstretching.

Functions of tissues within the gas exchange system

- **Cartilage** is a rigid, but flexible supporting material containing a high proportion of collagen fibres (2.3c). The incomplete rings of cartilage in the trachea and plates of cartilage in the bronchus (see Figure 1 in 9.1a) support the airways, keeping them in an open position. In this way, it prevents the trachea and bronchi from collapsing when the air pressure inside them is lowered when breathing in. In the trachea, the arrangement of incomplete cartilage rings, with spaces in between, provides flexibility so that it allows the trachea to bend and extend – essential when bending or stretching the neck as a whole.

- **Smooth muscle** is tissue which is capable of contraction, but which is not under voluntary control. Smooth muscle contraction is not necessary for normal ventilation. In the trachea, the smooth muscle located between the ends of the C-shape of the cartilage rings can contract to constrict the airway, helping to force air out, for example in coughing. Similarly, smooth muscle contraction in the bronchi will constrict airways. This will help to expel air more forcefully. Contraction of the rings of smooth muscle around the bronchioles (see Figure 1 in 9.1a) causes them to constrict, narrowing the lumen diameter of the airway. In this way, the flow of air to and from the alveoli can be restricted and therefore controlled.

- **Elastic fibres** are present throughout the gas exchange system and provide flexibility during ventilation. Elastic fibres, just as in the walls of the blood vessels (8.1b), are mainly composed of the protein elastin. The ability to stretch is needed when the airways expand, but the elastic nature of the tissue means that overstretching is prevented, and the ability to recoil helps to move air out of the system.

- Ciliated epithelium is a tissue composed of two cell types, ciliated epithelial cells and goblet cells.
  - **Ciliated epithelial cells** have hair-like organelles called cilia on one surface (Figure 1 over the page). These cilia move in a synchronised (coordinated) manner. In any one area, the cilia move in rhythm, with an effective power stroke which wafts (moves) the layer of mucus in one direction and a recovery stroke where the cilia roll back along the cell surface to the starting position. In this way, the cilia transport mucus containing trapped microorganisms, **allergens** and dust upwards towards the pharynx. Once at the pharynx, the mucus passes down the oesophagus to the stomach, usually unnoticed. Here the acid conditions kill any bacteria not destroyed by the macrophages that are present in the gas exchange system.
  - **Goblet cells** are so called because they have long, thin stems and rounded tops, resembling a wine goblet in shape (Figure 1 over the page; also see 1.1f and 9.1a). They also produce mucus to line the epithelial surface. There are many microvilli (1.2e and Figure 1) on the secretory surface of the goblet cell to increase the surface area over which the release of mucus can take place.

These pages help you to:

- describe the functions in the gas exchange system of cartilage, smooth muscle and elastic fibres (9.1.6)
- describe the functions of ciliated epithelial cells, goblet cells and mucous glands in the gas exchange system (9.1.5)

You will also:

- become familiar with the roles of macrophages in the gas exchange system

Extension

The role of macrophages

The phagocytic white blood cells, macrophages that are present in the lung tissue, engulf bacteria and other particles trapped in the mucus. Alveolar macrophages are present in the alveolar area to engulf any foreign particles or organisms that have not been trapped by mucus. In this way the risk of lung infections is reduced.

Microvilli on goblet cells   Cilia

Figure 1 *False-colour SEM of epithelium of the trachea showing ciliated epithelium (×3570)*

Maintaining the health of the gas exchange system

Air that is inhaled can contain harmful particulates as well as fungal spores and infectious bacteria and viruses. To keep the gas exchange system healthy, these foreign particles must be removed and in particular, infectious organisms must be prevented from infecting the cells of the airways. Pathogens must also be prevented from passing across the thin epithelial layer of the alveolus and entering the blood stream.

The body has evolved a very efficient first line of defence to protect from damage and infection: a sticky substance to trap foreign particles and a mechanism to move this substance away from the alveolar area and up out of the airways. Two tissues of the gas exchange system that are involved in this simple but very effective defence mechanism are the ciliated epithelium lining the airways and the mucous glands, located in the walls of the trachea and bronchi, close to the epithelial layer.

Mucous glands and the goblet cells of the ciliated epithelium produce and secrete the sticky substance, mucus. The mucus forms a thin layer covering the ciliated epithelium. Mucus acts as a barrier, preventing pathogens entering cells. Its thickness increases during infection to increase the distance between pathogens and body cells. Because mucus is sticky, bacteria, other pathogens, allergens such as pollen and dust particles are trapped in it as the air that contains them moves along these airways. As described, the cilia then waft the mucus away from the alveoli and other gas exchange structures up to the pharynx for removal. This helps to remove the potential for infection and helps to reduce the threat of allergic responses, so maintaining the health of the airways.

Summary test 9.1b

The trachea and the **(1)** have **(2)** for support of the airways. When smooth muscle **(3)** it narrows the lumen of the airway. In the **(4)** this helps regulate the airflow into and out of the alveoli. Goblet cells and the cells of **(5)** secrete mucus, which is a **(6)** substance that traps foreign particles. The layer of mucus is moved up and out of the gas exchange system by the action of **(7)**.

The alveoli are the site of gas exchange in mammals. They are tiny hollow sacs, each with a diameter of between 100 μm and 300 μm. Each lung of an adult human contains around 300 million alveoli giving them a surface area of around 70 m². This is about half the area of a tennis court. Each alveolus is lined with squamous epithelium and together with the thin basement membrane and small amount of connective tissue containing the elastic fibres, they form the wall of the alveolus, or alveolar wall. As each cell is only between 0.1 μm and 0.5 μm thick, the alveolar wall is very thin. The external appearance of a group of alveoli is shown in Figure 1.

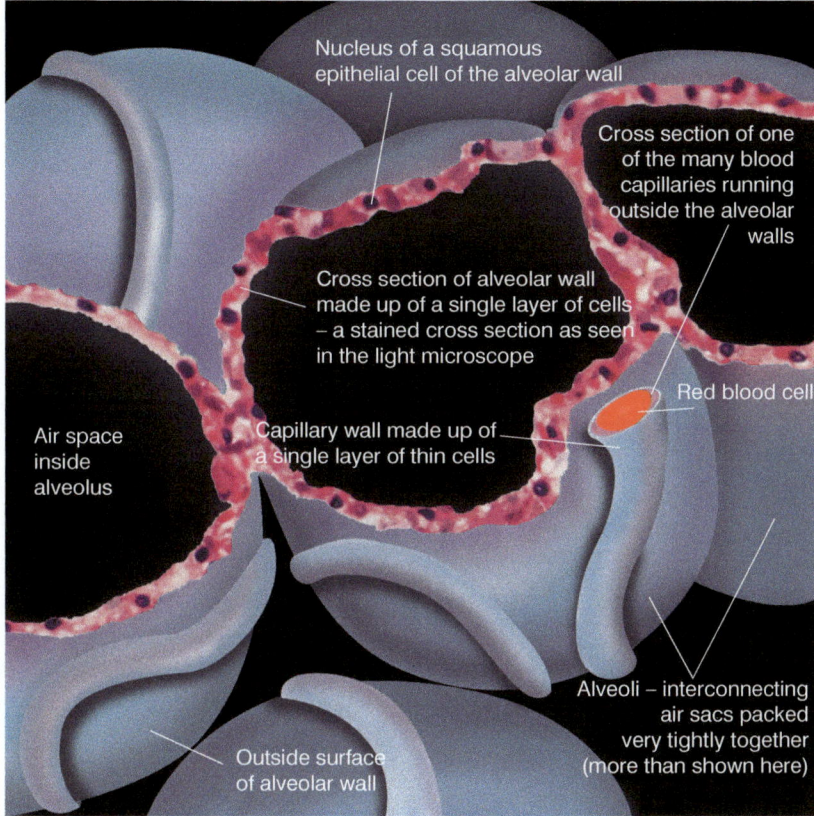

Nucleus of a squamous epithelial cell of the alveolar wall

Cross section of one of the many blood capillaries running outside the alveolar walls

Cross section of alveolar wall made up of a single layer of cells – a stained cross section as seen in the light microscope

Red blood cell

Air space inside alveolus

Capillary wall made up of a single layer of thin cells

Alveoli – interconnecting air sacs packed very tightly together (more than shown here)

Outside surface of alveolar wall

Figure 1 *External appearance of a group of alveoli*

Gas exchange between the alveoli and blood

Diffusion of gases between the alveoli and the blood is very rapid because:

- the walls of both alveoli and capillaries are very thin (Figure 2) and therefore the distance over which diffusion takes place is very short
- alveoli and pulmonary capillaries have a very large total surface area
- red blood cells are slowed as they pass through pulmonary capillaries, allowing more time for diffusion: generally the capillary is slightly narrower in diameter than a red blood cell, meaning that the cell has to squeeze through
- the distance between alveolar air and red blood cells is reduced as the red blood cells are flattened against the capillary walls: there is enough time as the red blood cell squeezes through the capillary for oxygen molecules to diffuse through to all haemoglobin molecules
- breathing movements constantly ventilate the lungs, and the action of the heart constantly circulates blood around alveoli. Together, these ensure that a steep concentration gradient of the gases to be exchanged is maintained.

These pages help you to:

- describe the functions in the gas exchange system of elastic fibres and squamous epithelium (9.1.6)
- describe gas exchange between air in the alveoli and blood in the capillaries (9.1.7)
- recognise squamous epithelium of alveoli and capillaries in microscope slides, photomicrographs and electron micrographs (9.1.3)

You will also:

- make connections with the information you have learned about the transport of oxygen and carbon dioxide

Remember

The diffusion pathway is short because the alveoli have only a single layer of epithelial cells and the pulmonary blood capillaries have only a single layer of endothelial cells.

Remember

A scanning electron micrograph (SEM) shows surface contours, as in the image shown in Figure 2. Here, the darker, relatively 'spherical' regions are the alveolar spaces that would contain alveolar air. In the lighter regions, the alveolar walls separating individual alveoli are not distinguishable from alveolar capillaries, and the very thin connective tissue, that are present.

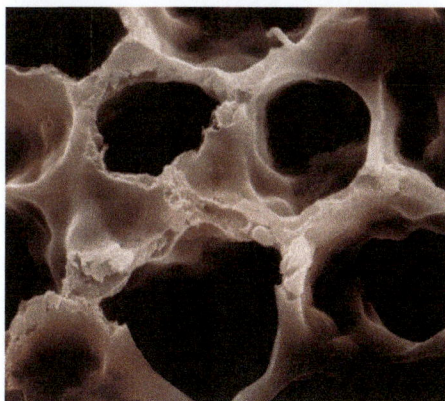

Figure 2 *Colourised scanning electron micrograph of human lung showing thin-walled alveoli*

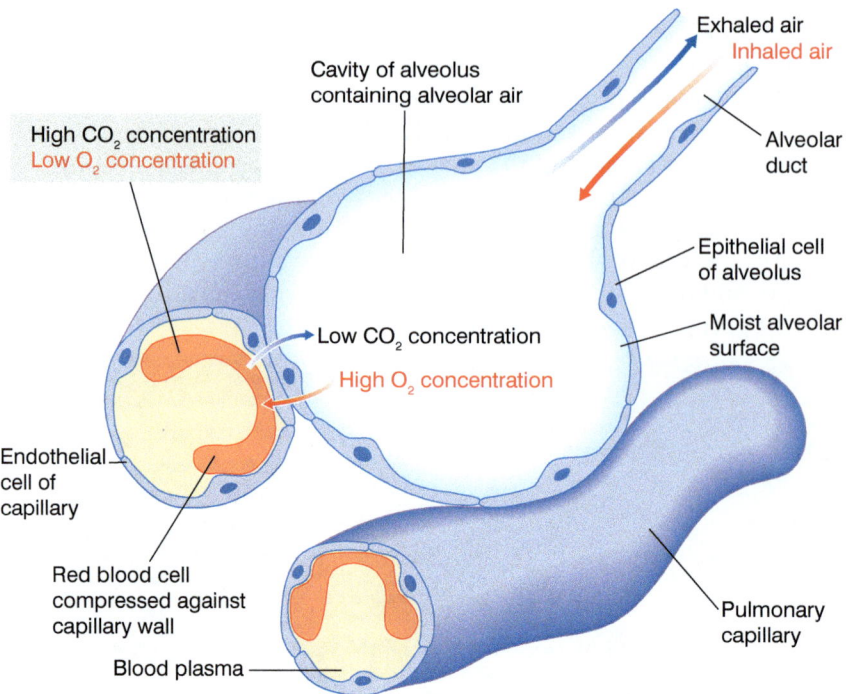

Figure 3 labels:
- Exhaled air
- Inhaled air
- Cavity of alveolus containing alveolar air
- High CO_2 concentration
- Low O_2 concentration
- Alveolar duct
- Epithelial cell of alveolus
- Low CO_2 concentration
- High O_2 concentration
- Moist alveolar surface
- Endothelial cell of capillary
- Red blood cell compressed against capillary wall
- Pulmonary capillary
- Blood plasma

Figure 3 *Diffusion of gases in an alveolus*

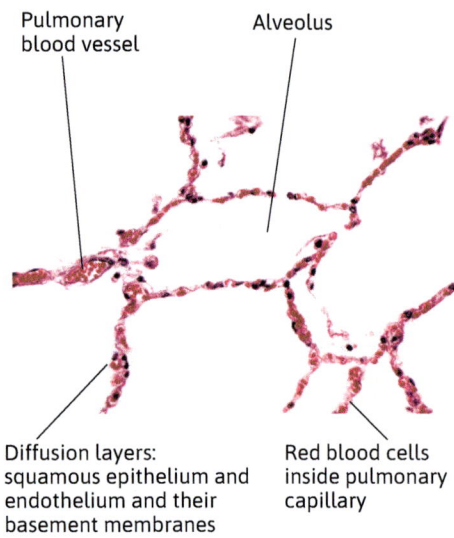

Figure 4 labels:
- Pulmonary blood vessel
- Alveolus
- Diffusion layers: squamous epithelium and endothelium and their basement membranes
- Red blood cells inside pulmonary capillary

Figure 4 *Squamous epithelium and its capillaries. The pulmonary blood vessel labelled is likely to be a pulmonary venule or arteriole rather than a capillary as a number of red blood cells can fit in the diameter of this vessel.*

Minimising the distance for diffusion

The distance for diffusion is minimised because the pulmonary capillary is very close to the alveolar wall. There are very few layers for the respiratory gases to pass through (Figures 3 and 4). For example, an oxygen molecule will pass:

- from alveolar air through the thin squamous epithelial cell
- through the basement membrane of the epithelium
- through the basement membrane of the endothelium of the capillary
- through the thin endothelial cell of the capillary wall into the blood plasma
- (and almost directly) through the cell surface membrane of the red blood cell to bind to haemoglobin.

Carbon dioxide diffuses in the opposite direction from the blood into the alveolus.

We have already seen how oxygen and carbon dioxide are transported in the blood in 8.2a and 8.2b. The information on these pages begins the journey for oxygen molecules and ends the journey for carbon dioxide molecules.

The function of elastic fibres and squamous epithelium

Elastic fibres are present in the walls of the alveoli. Their flexibility means that, when the alveoli expand during inhalation, the elastic fibres stretch but will not overstretch and so prevent bursting. Their ability to recoil will force air out of the alveoli for exhalation.

Squamous epithelium is a single layer of cells on a basement membrane. The cells have a structure ideally suited to their function as a gas exchange surface as they are extremely flat to minimise the distance for diffusion of the respiratory gases. Each cell has a small nucleus and a lot of cytoplasm. In addition, squamous epithelial cells are joined closely together and act as a barrier to defend against the entry of pathogens into the blood stream.

Figure 4 shows squamous epithelium and its capillaries. Notice that at this magnification, it is not possible to see two separate layers of cells, although it is possible to see red blood cells.

d. Identifying cells, tissues and organs in the gas exchange system

Goblet cells and ciliated epithelial cells

Figure 1 shows the two cell types that comprise ciliated epithelium, goblet cells and ciliated epithelial cells. Just below the ciliated epithelium there are elastic fibres.

The goblet cells do not have cilia and have a cup or goblet shape, very different to the columnar shape of the ciliated epithelial cell.

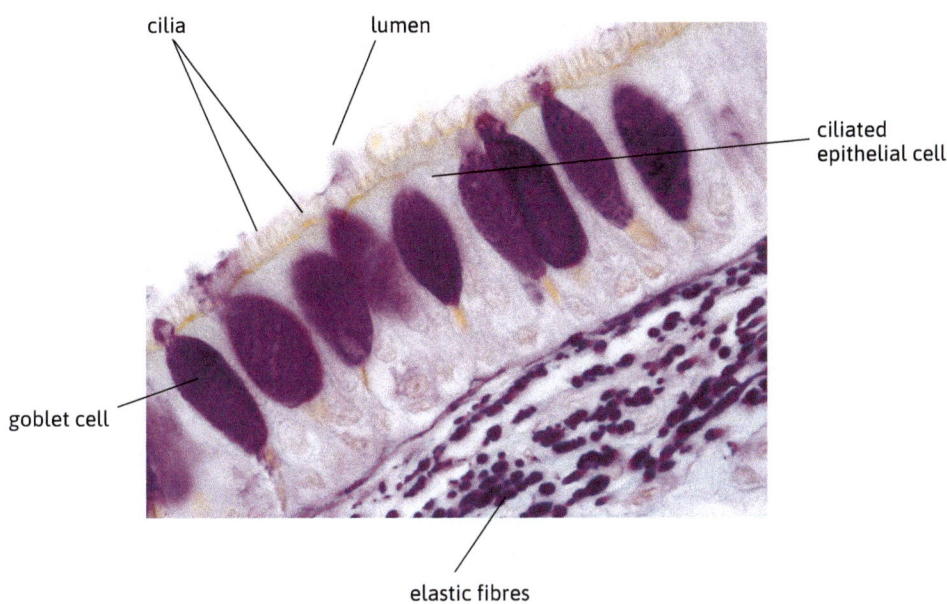

Figure 1 *High-power photomicrograph of ciliated epithelium and elastic fibres (in the trachea)*

Cartilage and smooth muscle tissue

In a low-power section or image, cartilage is easily visible (see Figures 2 and 3). In colour images, cartilage may have a different colour or shade to other tissues when using stains, and in a black and white image, it may appear a different shade of grey. On high power (Figure 1), you will be able to see many circular/oval structures. Each of these is a space in which two or a few cells are located. Cartilage does not have any blood vessels within it.

Figures 2, 3, 4 and 5 show the location and features of smooth muscle tissue. In the trachea it is more easily seen between the ends of the cartilage ring and a band around the cartilage. In the bronchus, it can be seen between the cartilage plates. In the bronchioles there is no cartilage and there is a ring of smooth muscle that will appear in sections as areas of muscle tissue just under the inner layer of the wall.

These pages help you to:

- recognise cartilage, ciliated epithelium, goblet cells and smooth muscle in microscope slides, photomicrographs and electron micrographs (9.1.3)
- recognise trachea, bronchi, bronchioles and alveoli in microscope slides, photomicrographs and electron micrographs (9.1.4)
- make plan diagrams of transverse sections of the walls of the trachea and bronchus (9.1.4)

You will also:

- be able to draw a plan diagram of a bronchiole and adjacent blood vessel
- consider how to prepare to draw diagrams in timed conditions

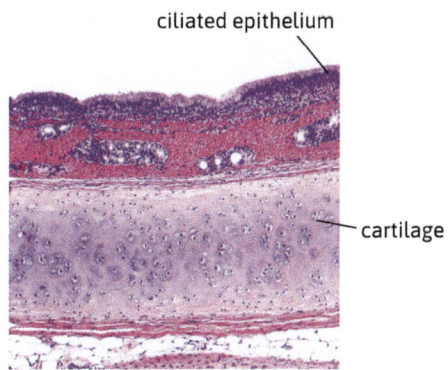

Figure 2 *Photomicrograph of a section through the wall of the trachea, showing cartilage*

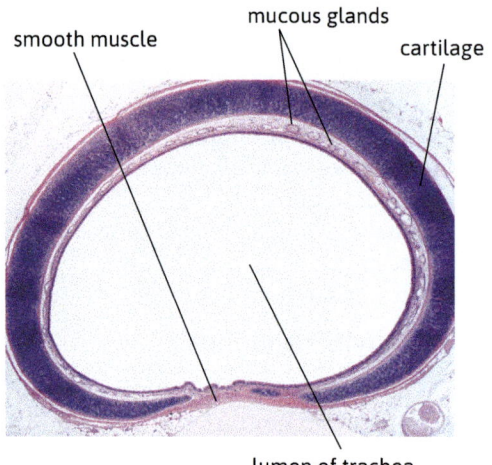

Figure 3 *Photomicrograph of a section through the trachea*

The trachea

Figures 2 and 3 are sections through the trachea. In Figure 2, a small area of the trachea wall is visible as the image is more greatly magnified. To identify the trachea:

- The most prominent feature visible is the incomplete ring of cartilage, clearly showing a C-shaped structure that dominates the section.
- The lumen of the trachea is large and there are no infoldings (convolutions) on the lining of the lumen.
- In the gap at the ends of the incomplete ring is a wide section of smooth muscle; this section of smooth muscle is called the trachealis muscle.
- There are many mucous glands between the cartilage and the ciliated epithelial layer.
- There is a clear epithelial layer: the surface of the layer facing the lumen may look slightly blurred, owing to the presence of cilia.
- The epithelial layer has the mistaken appearance of being 'multilayered'.

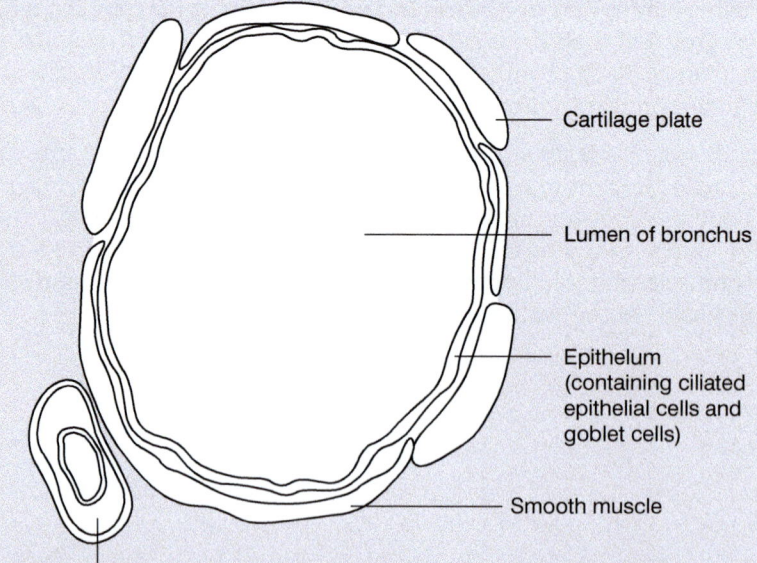

Figure 4 *Plan diagram of a section through the bronchus (practice drawing your own plan diagram of a section through a bronchus using Figure 1 on page 184)*

The bronchus

A section through a bronchus has some of the features seen in the trachea, and some features shown in the bronchioles. Remember that the two main bronchi divide into smaller bronchi, so in one low-power section, there may be more than one bronchus visible. Figure 4 shows a plan diagram of a section through a bronchus and a pulmonary blood vessel.

The bronchiole and surrounding alveoli

In Figure 5, you can see that the diameter of the smallest bronchioles can be similar to the diameter of an alveolus. The cilia on the surface of the ciliated epithelium are not visible, but their presence is indicated by the blurred edge to the lumen.

Although some of the alveoli look complete in Figure 5, some look joined to other alveoli to form bigger spaces. This is because of the section that was taken to prepare the slide.

There are different types of bronchiole and they will show considerable variation in transverse section, such as in the thickness of the surrounding smooth muscle and how convoluted (wavy) the lining of the lumen is. Figure 6 is a low-power plan diagram showing a transverse section through a different, larger bronchiole, two alveoli and one blood vessel. To identify the bronchiole:

- look for a roughly circular structure appearing between alveoli
- check that the lumen appears clear (blood vessels would show patches that are red blood cells)
- check that there are no obvious plates of cartilage surrounding
- looked for a fairly convoluted (wavy) inner lining
- looked for a fairly continuous layer of smooth muscle surrounding.

In this plan diagram (Figure 6), there is a 'circular' structure that is obviously a very small blood vessel, and this could be a pulmonary arteriole or pulmonary venule.

If asked to provide dimensions, then with a prepared slide you will be able to use an eyepiece graticule, calibrated using a stage micrometer to make these estimates. If provided with a photomicrograph, a scale bar or magnification would be given so that the necessary measurement(s) can be collected and the calculation made.

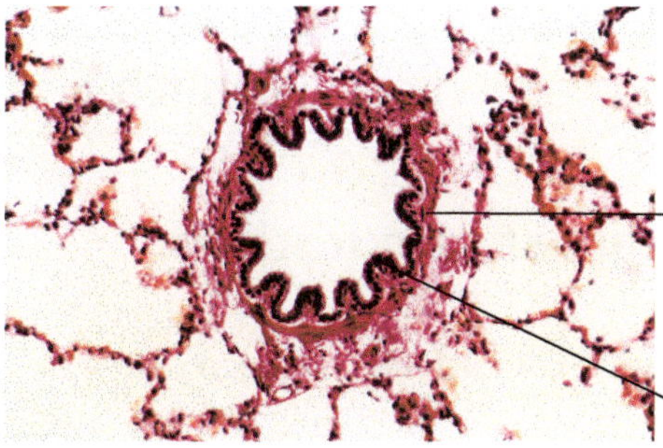

Figure 5 *Photomicrograph of a bronchiole and surrounding alveoli*

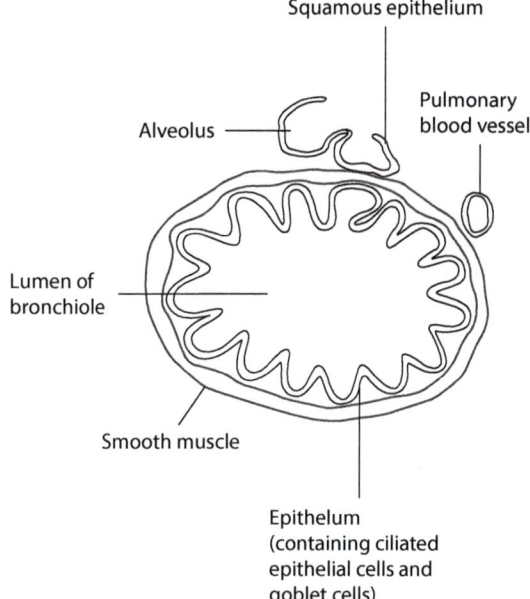

Figure 6 *Plan diagram of a section through a bronchiole and two alveoli*

Remember

Using your drawing skills in timed conditions requires preparation.

It is helpful to re-read instructions so that you are confident that you know what to do:

- Are you producing a low-power plan diagram to show the distribution and proportions of tissues or a high-power drawing of cells?
- How many cells are you required to draw?
- Do you need to label your diagram with the names of cell structures or the names of tissue layers?
- Do you need to add annotations, scales or a magnification?

Try and practise working to a time limit when you are drawing plan diagrams or diagrams of cells, so that in timed conditions, you can:

- think clearly
- work calmly
- finish the drawing so that you have time to add labels and annotations
- leave yourself enough time to check your observations.

Summary test 9.1d

The structures of the gas exchange system that may have a similar diameter as alveoli are the **(1)**. These do not have any **(2)**, unlike the trachea and the **(3)**. The gas exchange structure that has the most wavy inner lining is the **(4)**. All structures except **(5)** have a ciliated epithelium. Within the epithelium there are cells without cilia known as **(6)**.

┌───┐
│ 🗐 **Launch additional digital resources for the chapter** │
└───┘

9 Exam-style questions

1 During gas exchange, oxygen diffuses through a number of layers to reach a red blood cell. Four layers are listed below in alphabetical order.

   1 basement membrane of endothelium
   2 basement membrane of squamous epithelium
   3 endothelium
   4 squamous epithelium

Which is the correct sequence of layers through which oxygen diffuses from the alveolar air to reach the red blood cell? *(1 mark)*

   A 1, 3, 2, 4
   B 2, 4, 3, 1
   C 4, 2, 1, 3
   D 3, 1, 4, 2

2 A student was asked to describe the differences between four microscope slides of sections taken from different parts of the gas exchange system.

   slide 1 not present: cartilage, glands, goblet cells, smooth muscle
           present: squamous epithelial cells

   slide 2 not present: cartilage, glands
           present: few goblet cells, ciliated epithelial cells, smooth muscle

   slide 3 present: plates of cartilage, glands, goblet cells, ciliated epithelial cells, smooth muscle

   slide 4 present: incomplete cartilage rings, glands, goblet cells, ciliated epithelial cells, smooth muscle

Which is the correct identification of the parts of the gas exchange system? *(1 mark)*

	slide 1	slide 2	slide 3	slide 4
A	bronchiole	alveolus	trachea	bronchus
B	alveolus	bronchiole	bronchus	trachea
C	bronchus	trachea	bronchiole	alveolus
D	alveolus	trachea	bronchiole	bronchus

3 Figure 1 is a photomicrograph of a section of a bronchus and surrounding tissue.

Figure 1

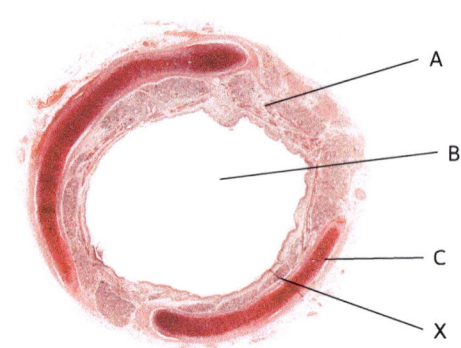

  a **i** Identify the structures labelled **A, B** and **C** shown in Figure 1. *(3 marks)*
      ii State one feature of the section, visible in Figure 1, which indicates that this is not a section of a bronchiole. *(1 mark)*
     iii Some pathogens can enter the human body through the gas exchange system.
        The cells in the area labelled **X** in Figure 1 are adapted for defence against pathogens.
        Name these cells and describe how they work together to defend against pathogens which enter the gas exchange system *(4 marks)*

(Total 8 marks)

4 **a** Figure 2 is a photomicrograph showing normal healthy lung tissue consisting of alveoli and associated capillaries.

Figure 2

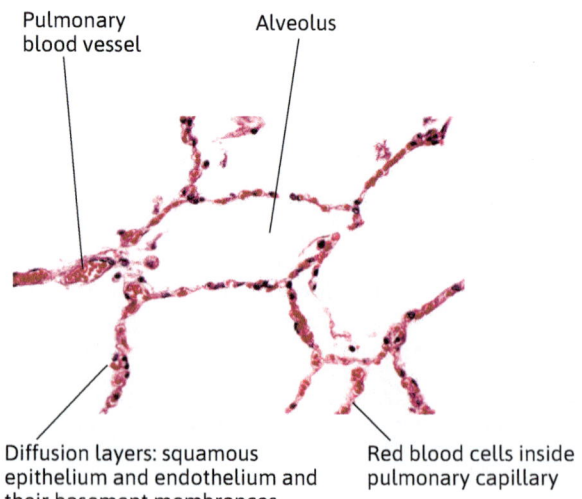

Pulmonary blood vessel   Alveolus

Diffusion layers: squamous epithelium and endothelium and their basement membranes   Red blood cells inside pulmonary capillary

i Explain how the structure of an alveolar cell, such as those as found in Figure 2, is adapted to its function. *(2 marks)*

ii Some alveolar cells secrete pulmonary surfactant into the watery fluid that lines the alveolus. The surfactant reduces the surface tension of the fluid so that the alveolus does not collapse. Pulmonary surfactant is a mixture of phospholipids and proteins. The phospholipids form a monolayer on the surface of the fluid. Explain how phospholipids interact with water to form a monolayer on the surface of the fluid. *(2 marks)*

(Total 4 marks)

9 Practice questions

5 a A prepared slide of a section through a bronchus can also include alveolar tissue and bronchioles. Explain why a section through a trachea will not include alveolar tissue and bronchioles.

b Rearrange the gas exchange structures in the list below to show the correct sequence air takes from the external atmosphere to the gas exchange surface.

External atmosphere
Bronchiole
Alveolus
Bronchus
Trachea
Gas exchange surface

c The list below names some structures of the gas exchange system.

alveolus   bronchus   trachea   bronchiole

Name the structure of the gas exchange system that matches each of the following descriptions:

i Has irregular plates of cartilage
ii Is the gas exchange surface
iii Has ciliated epithelium with very few goblet cells
iv Is composed of tightly connected squamous epithelial cells
v Has no ciliated epithelium

d i Describe how the properties of smooth muscle and elastic fibres can help to move air out of the lungs.

ii State one other function of elastic fibres.

6 a State and explain three differences in the composition of blood in a pulmonary vein compared to a pulmonary artery.

b Explain why, even though inhaled air may contain disease-causing microorganisms, a healthy person does not become ill with a respiratory infection.

10.1 Infectious diseases

a. Pathogens and infectious disease

The human body as a host

The human body is an ideal habitat for many microorganisms. It provides a warm environment of constant temperature and near-neutral pH, with a ready supply of nutrients and mechanisms for removing waste. Not surprising, then, that our bodies are colonised by a variety of microorganisms. Most cause us no harm and many are beneficial to our health. However, some can harm our **health**. In this chapter, you will learn about some microorganisms that cause **disease**.

Pathogens

The term pathogen is usually used to describe disease-causing microorganisms (microscopic organisms). There are four different types of pathogen:

- disease-causing bacteria
- disease-causing fungi
- viruses
- microscopic disease-causing protoctists.

Table 1 outlines the four diseases that you will learn about in this chapter.

Table 1 *A summary of four diseases of humans caused by pathogens*

Name of disease	Name of pathogen (causative organism)	Type of pathogen	Type of cell
Cholera	*Vibrio cholerae* (Figure 1)	bacterium	prokaryotic
Tuberculosis (TB)	*Mycobacterium tuberculosis* (Figure 2) and *Mycobacterium bovis*	bacterium	prokaryotic
HIV/AIDS	human immunodeficiency virus (HIV)	virus	not cellular (akaryotic)
Malaria	*Plasmodium falciparum* *Plasmodium malariae* *Plasmodium ovale* *Plasmodium vivax*	protoctist	eukaryotic

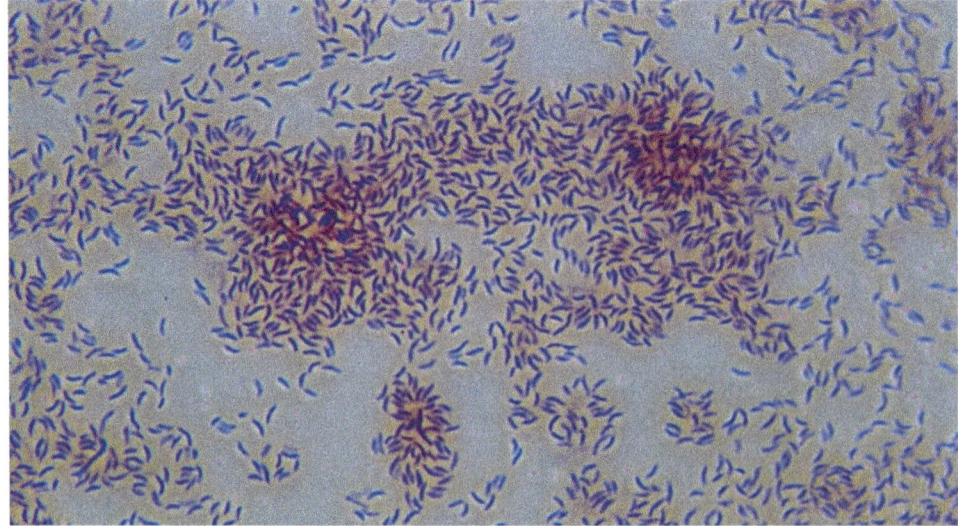

Figure 1 *Photomicrograph of* Vibrio cholerae *bacteria, the pathogen causing cholera (magnification x800 at 6x9 cm size)*

These pages help you to:

- understand what is meant by an infectious disease, including the terms pathogen and transmissible (10.1.1)
- learn the names and types of pathogen causing cholera, malaria, tuberculosis (TB) and HIV/AIDS (10.1.2)

You will also:

- use your knowledge of prokaryotes and viruses
- become familiar with the protoctist kingdom
- understand the difference between health and disease
- be introduced to some useful terminology
- understand what is meant by transmissible
- understand how to write a species name

Extension

Parasites and pathogens

There is no universal definition of a parasite or a pathogen. A parasite is an organism that benefits by living in or on a host organism, while causing harm to the host. A parasite can spend some or all of its life cycle living in or on the host. The term parasite is commonly used to describe larger organisms, such as pararasitic worms and insects (animal parasites), and microscopic eukaryotes of the kingdom Protoctista (Chapter 18). Examples of these include the organisms that cause trypanosomiasis (sleeping sickness) and malaria. A microscopic parasite, such as those covered in this chapter, is commonly known as a pathogen. *Plasmodium* spp. that cause malaria are microscopic protoctists. It is not unusual for the terms 'parasite' and 'pathogen' to be used when referring to *Plasmodium*.

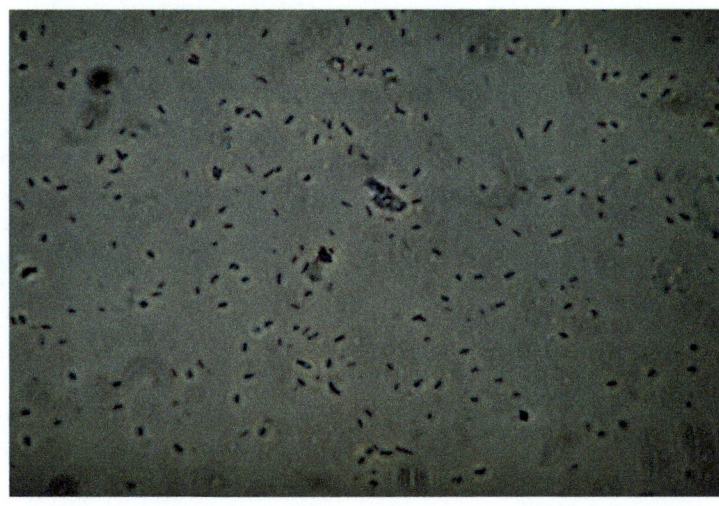

Figure 2 *Photomicrograph of Mycobacterium tuberculosis bacteria, the pathogen causing TB (magnification x330 at 35 mm size)*

You will see in Table 1 that the bacteria and the protoctists are given a name composed of two parts. Each one is the full species name. The first word, with a capitalised first letter, tells us the group, or genus, to which the species belongs. Table 1 gives two examples of bacterial species belonging to the genus *Mycobacterium* that cause tuberculosis (TB) in humans. The table also lists the four main species of the genus *Plasmodium* that cause malaria. The second word, with a lower case first letter, tells us the actual species to which an organism belongs. All organisms in a species share a common set of characteristics and will have DNA that is more similar (almost identical) to each other than to members of another species. In 18.1a, you will learn about different ways to define a species. Notice that the genus and species are written in italics.

Infectious diseases

Infectious diseases are diseases caused by pathogens. All infectious diseases are transmissible. A transmissible disease is one in which the pathogen is transferred from an infected individual to an individual who does not have the disease. Some diseases are not transmitted from an infected person but from another animal that is infected with the pathogen.

If a person is infected by a pathogen, it means that the organism has gained entry to the tissues or cells of a person's body. Here, the pathogen reproduces (or replicates in the case of viruses) increasing the population size of the pathogen. Frequently, the activity of the pathogen causes symptoms of the disease and the person becomes ill.

A carrier is a person who is infected by a pathogen but does not feel ill or have any symptoms of disease. This can be a person who has been ill with the disease and has made a recovery, but still has a reservoir of the pathogen in their body.

Each of the diseases listed in Table 1 has a different mode of transmission.

Presenting and comparing health statistics

When making comparisons between the numbers of deaths due to a disease in one population and another, it can be misleading simply to state the number of people affected or who die. This is because it takes no account of the total numbers in each population. Population A may have twice as many people affected by a disease as population B, but if population A is 10 times larger than population B, then the proportion of individuals affected is actually much lower. For this reason, health statistics are usually expressed as the number of deaths, or people affected, per 100 000 of the population.

Summary test 10.1a

A disease-causing microorganism is also known as a **(1)**. The different types of disease-causing microorganism include bacteria, **(2)**, **(3)** and fungi. The organism that causes the disease cholera is a **(4)** and the species name of the organism is **(5)**. There are four species of *Plasmodium* that commonly cause **(6)**. The cells of *Plasmodium* are **(7)**, unlike the prokaryotic cells of *Mycobacterium bovis*, one of the species of bacteria that cause the infectious disease **(8)**. HIV/AIDS is caused by a **(9)**.

These pages help you to:

- explain the different ways that HIV is transmitted (10.1.3)
- discuss the biological, social and economic factors related to the prevention of HIV transmission and the control of HIV/AIDS (10.1.4)

You will also:

- revisit viral structure
- be able to interpret some health statistics
- have a basic understanding of how HIV infects body cells

Extension

HIV is a retrovirus

Retroviruses differ from other RNA viruses by having an enzyme (reverse transcriptase) that synthesises DNA from their RNA. This DNA can integrate into the genome (DNA) of the host cells that they infect. Here, they can remain inactive (dormant) for many years. Once activated, they replicate by making RNA copies of their DNA and other viral parts, destroying the host cell when they leave to infect other cells (see Extension: HIV in the body)

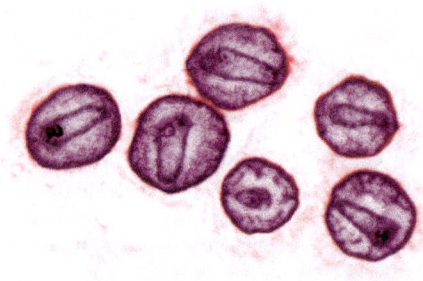

Figure 2 Colourised transmission electron micrograph of the human immunodeficiency virus (HIV)

HIV/AIDS is caused by the **human immunodeficiency virus (HIV)**, a roughly spherical enveloped virus, with RNA as its genetic material (Figures 1 and 2). Unlike many other infectious diseases, HIV/AIDS is a relative newcomer, having first been diagnosed in 1981, when it was known as AIDS (acquired immune deficiency syndrome). The virus infects T-lymphocytes, cells of the immune system (see Extension and 11.1c) and may be dormant for a number of years. This means a person living with HIV may not have any symptoms for some time. Without treatment, the virus will eventually become active, leading to a weakened immune system. This makes the person susceptible to pathogens that would normally be destroyed by the immune system. The illnesses that result are known as opportunistic infections, and can be fatal. This collection of illnesses is known as the disease HIV/AIDS. In many countries, tuberculosis (TB) is one of the most common opportunistic diseases.

Table 1 shows regional statistics for 2018; Figure 3 shows how the number of deaths from HIV/AIDS have changed in the time period from 1990 to 2017. Despite the enormous advances that have been made in the fight against the disease, HIV/AIDS is still the leading cause of death from infectious disease in many countries.

There are two main type of the virus, HIV-1 and HIV-2. HIV-1 is most common globally.

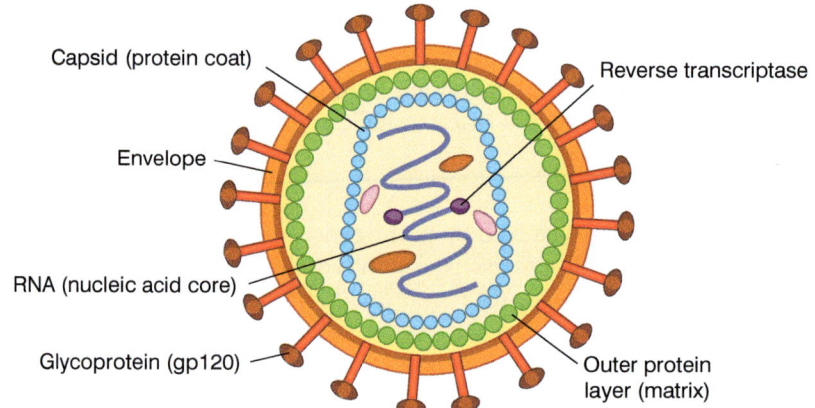

Figure 1 Structure of human immunodeficiency virus

Causes and means of transmission

Once infected with HIV, an individual is said to be living with HIV, or is **HIV positive**, a condition which lasts throughout life. The virus can remain dormant for 10 years or longer. During this time, an HIV-positive person does not show any symptoms but can act as a carrier, often not knowing that they could be spreading the virus. This is one of the biggest problems with trying to control the HIV/AIDS **pandemic**.

The virus can be detected in virtually all body fluids of a person living with HIV. However, since it is only in blood, semen or vaginal fluid that its concentration is high, the virus is usually spread through one of these fluids. The main modes of transmission of HIV are:

- sexual contact, mainly sexual intercourse, where semen or vaginal fluid containing the virus is transmitted
- transfer of contaminated blood from one person to another
  - during a blood transfusion, although many countries now have routine blood screening
  - when drug-abusers share a hypodermic needle

- mother to child transmission
  - across the placenta (uncommon)
  - during birth
  - in breast milk during breastfeeding.

An infected person has such a low presence of HIV in the faeces, urine, sweat, saliva and tears that contact with these does not present a risk. The virus quickly dies outside the human body, and therefore even blood, semen and vaginal secretions must be transferred directly.

Table 1 *Regional statistics for HIV 2018 (Source: UNAIDS)*

Region	Number of people living with HIV	Number of new HIV infections	Number of AIDS-related deaths	Number of people accessing treatment
Eastern and southern Africa	20 600 000	800 000	310 000	13 800 000
Asia and the Pacific	5 900 000	310 000	200 000	3 200 000
Western and central Africa	5 000 000	280 000	160 000	2 600 000
Latin America	1 900 000	100 000	35 000	1 200 000
The Caribbean	340 000	16 000	6700	187 000
Middle East and North Africa	240 000	20 000	8400	78 800
Eastern Europe and central Asia	1 700 000	150 000	38 000	648 000
Western and Central Europe and North America	2 200 000	68 000	13 000	1 700 000
Global totals	37 900 000	1 700 000	770 000	23 300 000

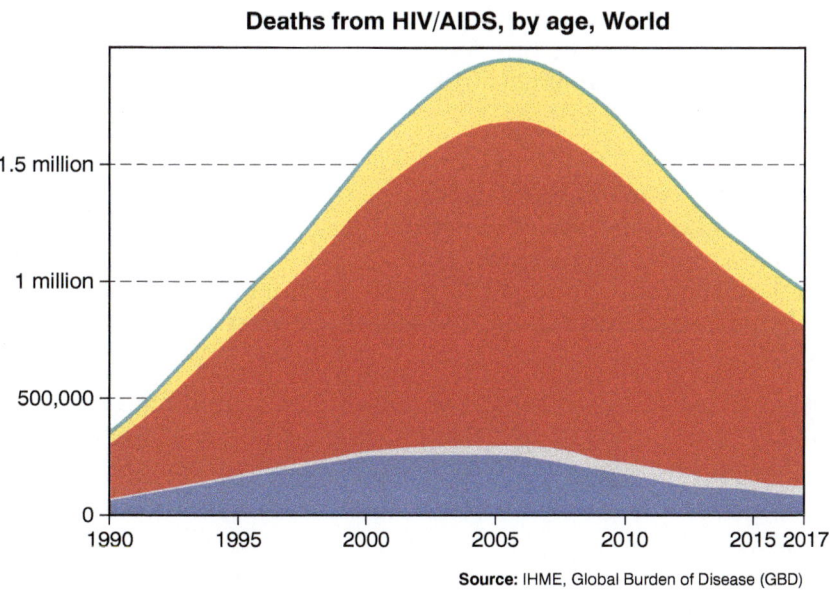

Deaths from HIV/AIDS, by age, World

Source: IHME, Global Burden of Disease (GBD)

- 70+ years
- 50–69 years
- 15–49 years
- 5–14 years
- Under 5 years

Figure 3 *Number of deaths from HIV/AIDS from 1990 to 2017*

Extension

HIV in the body

Having entered the blood, HIV infects white blood cells, such as T-helper cells (11.1c), as well as macrophages and brain cells, to which the virus readily binds using the glycoprotein gp120 'spikes' (Figure 1). HIV has an outer envelope containing sections of host cell surface membrane that it takes with it when it is released from a host cell. These sections of membrane readily fuse with the cell surface membrane of certain white blood cells, allowing it to easily gain entry to a new host cell. Because it has host cell surface membrane on its surface, it is not recognised as 'foreign' and so does not stimulate an immune response from the **lymphocytes** in the blood. Replication of the virus is controlled and it frequently becomes dormant. It is months or years later that the dormant virus replicates, so that it is a number of years before HIV/AIDS develops. When the virus becomes active, the number of T-cells decreases, increasing the chance of infection by other pathogens (opportunist pathogens). This can lead to a person having a number of different diseases, collectively known as HIV/AIDS.

Antiretroviral therapy (ART)

ART involves the use of combinations of three or more antiretroviral medicines, or antiretrovirals (ARVs). There are two types of ARV that prevent viral DNA from being synthesised so that it cannot integrate into the host cell DNA. Another type of ARV prevents a newly-released virus from maturing so that it cannot infect other host cells. Newer ARV types include medicines that prevent the virus from entering host cells or prevent viral DNA from integrating into the host cell DNA.

The aim of ART is to suppress viral replication to help prevent progression to HIV/AIDS. Another indicator of successful ART is an undetectable level of the virus in the blood. People can be regularly checked to see if their drug regimen (treatment plan) is still effective, and if not, a new combination of ARVs can be considered.

The economic impact of HIV/AIDS

HIV/AIDS is far more common in sub-Saharan Africa than elsewhere. Because people living with HIV/AIDS are more prone to other infections, the number of cases (**prevalence**) of the disease in Africa is especially significant because it also has the highest number of new cases (**incidence**) of other diseases, such as cholera and malaria. Also the rise in TB cases worldwide (10.1c) has been linked to an increase in the number of HIV/AIDS cases. This has a very harmful effect on the economy of African countries and other developing countries that have a high number of cases of HIV/AIDS because:

- HIV/AIDS mostly affects people aged 20–40 years and this is usually the most economically productive group of people of any population.
- Scarce financial resources have to be spent on prevention and control measures and on medical treatment for those who are ill. Medication for some of the diseases related to HIV/AIDS is expensive.

Prevention and control

There is, as yet, no cure for HIV/AIDS. A lot of effort has gone into developing a vaccine but progress is being hindered by the rapid rate at which HIV mutates, the fact that HIV conceals itself within the lymphocyte and the risk that a vaccine from attenuated (weakened) HIV could still lead to the virus replicating within cells.

Recent trials have shown some success. A large-scale vaccine trial, the HVTN 702 study, is being carried out, and will report results in 2023. It is hoped that this vaccine will reduce the risk of HIV infection by at least 50%.

Antiretroviral therapy

Antiretroviral therapy (ART) is an effective treatment for a person living with HIV, particularly if it is begun soon after infection. It involves taking a combination of drugs, each of which has a different action against the virus. In many people who have been treated the virus has remained dormant. In some, the virus is undetectable in tests. This does not mean the person is cured, but it does mean that they have a minimal risk of transmitting the virus. ART has been very successful in:

- reducing the transmission of HIV to uninfected people
- reducing mother to child transmission during birth and breast feeding
- reducing the number of people living with HIV that go on to develop HIV/AIDS (**morbidity rates** have decreased)
- increasing the chance that a person living with HIV can live a normal lifespan
- reducing the number of deaths from HIV/AIDS (**mortality** rates have decreased).

Figure 3 (page 189) shows a decrease in the number of deaths from HIV/AIDS from 2005. In the same period of time, the proportion of people living with HIV that receive ART has increased. This is due partly to a dramatic decrease in the cost of ART.

The drugs do have side effects, and regular reviews are required to make sure that the drug regimen (treatment plan) is still having an effect. Some people need to switch to a different combination of drugs. Without a cure or a vaccine available at present, preventive measures remain the best means of trying to control the disease. Such measures include:

- **Advising mothers living with HIV/AIDS to avoid breastfeeding** their babies. This must however be balanced against the benefits of breastfeeding.

- **Contact tracing** to avoid the spread of HIV: anyone who is found to be HIV positive is asked to contact others who he/she might have infected, e.g. sexual partners, so that they may be tested and treated as necessary.
- **Needle-exchange schemes** for drug-abusers who can exchange used needles for new ones so that needle-sharing becomes unnecessary.
- **Screening of blood from donors** now occurs routinely in many countries and it is heat treated to kill HIV so that the risk to haemophiliacs and others using blood products is almost zero in developed countries.
- **HIV testing for individuals** at particular risk, e.g. injecting drug-abusers, sex-workers, people who have had unprotected sexual contact with someone who they know is HIV-positive. Early diagnosis means early treatment with ART. This benefits the individual in reducing the risk of developing HIV/AIDS and benefits society in helping to prevent the spread of the virus. There are a number of tests used to detect the presence of HIV in the body. The most common is a blood test that can detect antibodies produced against the virus (known as the ELISA test; see 11.2a).
- **Using condoms** or femidoms for all forms of sexual contact. These act as a physical barrier and prevent the mixing of body fluids.
- **Education** is very important and involves informing the population of the risks and how to minimise them. For example, education about the benefits of using condoms and how to use condoms is a major part of education about HIV. Other education involves teaching about mother to child transmission, the importance of using sterile needles, and the need to arrange early testing and to keep up with the ART regimen. Many people are still unwilling to seek diagnosis or treatment for fear of rejection by their community, so education also involves the wider task of encouraging communities to work together positively to prevent the spread of the disease.

Summary test 10.1b

A person living with HIV is **(1)** but does not necessarily have HIV/AIDS. HIV/AIDS is actually a collection of **(2)** infections that occur when the virus becomes active and the person's **(3)** system is weakened. The full name for HIV is **(4)**. There is no cure for the disease, but **(5)** is a very effective treatment to reduce the risk of developing HIV/AIDS and in reducing **(6)** of the virus to uninfected people. Common ways of passing on the virus to uninfected people are: **(7)**, **(8)** and **(9)**.

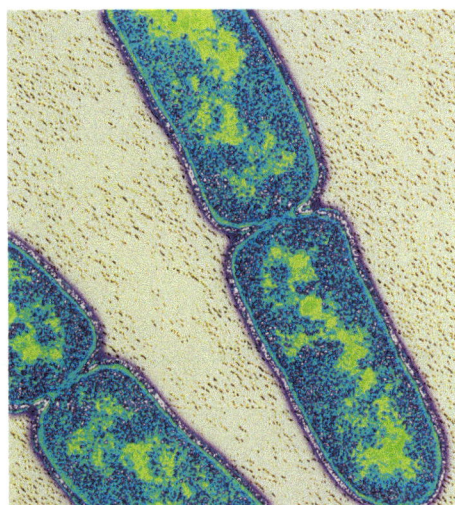

Figure 1 *Transmission electron micrograph of two pairs of recently divided* Mycobacterium tuberculosis, *the bacteria that causes tuberculosis*

Tuberculosis (TB) is an infectious disease that can affect any part of the body. It is usually found in the lungs because these are the first site of infection, causing persistent (continued) coughing, shortness of breath, tiredness, loss of weight, loss of appetite, fever and sweating. It is estimated that about a third of the population of the world is infected with the bacterium and it is the infectious disease that kills most people worldwide. Every country of the world has cases of TB and in many countries the disease is **endemic** (always present).

TB is caused by one of two rod-shaped bacteria: *Mycobacterium tuberculosis* or *Mycobacterium bovis* (Figure 1, and Figure 2 in 10.1a).

People who are infected with *Mycobacterium* form two groups which differ **epidemiologically**.

- Most (approximately 90–95%) do not suffer any symptoms and the infection is controlled by the body's immune system. These individuals cannot pass on the pathogen and so do not contribute to the spread of disease while the bacterium remains dormant or inactive, a condition known as latent TB. The inactive bacteria may, however, be activated, often after many years, especially when the person's immune system is weakened by other infections, or by HIV/AIDS.
- Approximately 5–10% of people infected by the pathogen develop the disease (primary active TB) because the bacteria overcome the body's defences, causing the symptoms listed above. These individuals can transmit the pathogen and so the disease can be spread to uninfected people. Young children, who have an immune system that is still developing, and people who have a weak immune system are most at risk of developing active TB.

Despite its **prevalence** (number of cases) around the world, it is not all that easy to contract TB compared to many other infectious diseases. It is spread through the air by **droplet infection** when infected individuals cough, sneeze, laugh or even just talk and uninfected individuals breathe in airborne droplets containing the bacterium. However, it normally takes close contact with an infected person over a period of time, rather than a casual meeting in the street, to transmit the bacteria. TB is therefore usually spread between family members, close friends or work colleagues, especially in crowded and poorly ventilated conditions. TB can also be spread from cows to humans because *M. bovis* also infects cattle. Meat and especially milk from infected cattle may contain the bacterium. This means that dairy products made from contaminated milk also are a source of the pathogen.

Some groups are at greater risk of contracting (becoming ill from) TB. These include people who:

- are in close contact over long periods with infected individuals, e.g. living, and especially sleeping, in over-crowded conditions
- are infected with HIV/AIDS and have a lowered immunity as a result of the infection
- have other medical conditions that make the body less able to resist the disease, e.g. diabetes, lung disease such as silicosis
- are undergoing treatment with immuno-suppressant drugs (e.g. following transplant surgery)
- are malnourished (do not have a balanced diet)
- are working or living in long-term care facilities where relatively large numbers of people live close together, e.g. old people's homes, care homes, hospitals and prisons

- are alcoholic, injecting drug-users and/or homeless
- live in regions or countries where there is a high number of infected cattle and milk is not pasteurised (heat-treated).

Extension

TB and antibiotic treatment

Poorly managed TB treatment and prevention programmes lead to incomplete treatment of TB or the wrong dose or drug being given. Many people do not finish their course of antibiotics as they feel better some time before they are actually cured.

Drug-resistant forms of *Mycobacterium* have developed throughout the world, largely as the result of incomplete treatment. If a person is infected with a rifampicin-resistant strain of *Mycobacterium*, this will seriously affect the treatment of TB as it is normally an effective first line antibiotic. This means a different strategy for treatment, and a much longer treatment time. More detail about antibiotic resistance is provided in 10.2a.

Remember

All TB prevention and control measures are aimed at breaking the transmission cycle of the disease. This means finding ways to stop the bacterium passing from infected people or cattle to uninfected people.

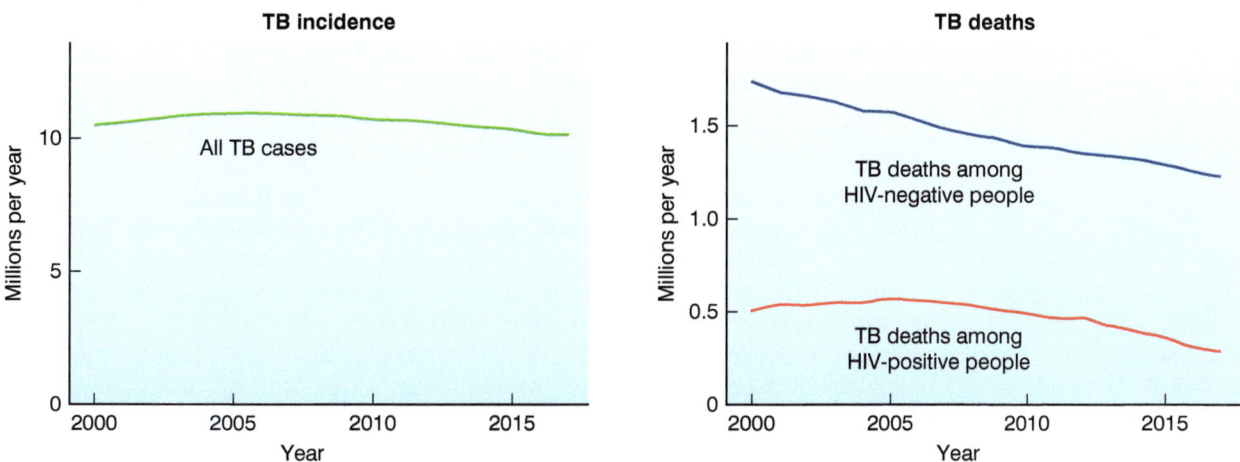

Figure 2 *Estimated number of new cases of TB and deaths from TB for the period 2000-2017*

Prevention and control

Vaccination

The main biological measure to prevent a person developing TB is **vaccination**. Children can be tested for their **immunity** to TB. Vaccination of those individuals who are already immune is unnecessary and dangerous. Those without immunity are given the **Bacillus Calmette–Guérin (BCG) vaccine**. This is an attenuated (weakened) strain of *M. bovis*, the organism that causes bovine TB. While this form of mass **immunisation** has been the major reason for the fall in cases of TB in many countries, improved social conditions have also played a part (Figure 2).

Antibiotic treatment

Another biological means of controlling the spread of TB involves a standard treatment where the two most effective drugs, isoniazid and rifampicin are taken daily for six months (or longer if required). In addition, in the first two months of the treatment, two other antibiotics (such as pyrazinamide and ethambutol) are also taken daily. If the *Mycobacterium* is a strain that is resistant to one of the antibiotics, taking a combination will help to make sure that the bacteria are destroyed.

Extension

Why mass vaccination has not eradicated TB

Vaccination has not eradicated TB because in some people, particularly those over 35, the immune system does not respond to the vaccine, or does not respond well, so the person has no, or limited, protection from the disease.

However, the vaccine is still 80% effective in preventing TB for 15 years. Many countries, particularly in Africa and Asia, have a national vaccination programme. Other countries have a policy of vaccinating groups of people at higher risk of the disease.

Remember

Even though governments may be able to get some financial aid, the overall cost of these prevention and control measures is enormous, particularly in the low income countries where the number of cases of the disease is high. Here, there is a financial burden on health care for those who are ill. Many people with HIV/AIDS develop TB, and so there are also the same economic strains as those outlined in 10.1b: reduced workforce will decrease productivity and reduce income gained by governments on tax paid by workers.

Summary test 10.1c

Tuberculosis (TB) is caused by two types of bacterium. The one found only in humans is **(1)** while the other, called **(2)**, is found in humans and cattle. The disease is mainly transmitted through the **(3)** by droplet infection. An infected person breathes out the pathogen in droplets and this is passed on when an uninfected person **(4)** the air. Most people infected with the bacterium have **(5)** TB and do not pass on the pathogen. Certain groups of people are more at risk, including those living in **(6)** conditions, those who are malnourished, and those whose immune systems are weakened by medicine and diseases like silicosis or who are **(7)**. It can be prevented by the **(8)** vaccine and can be treated by drugs. One problem with the drugs is that they need to be taken for **(9)** months and many people fail to complete the treatment, leading to **(10)** strains of the bacteria that cause TB.

One problem with all drug treatments for TB is the long period over which the drugs must be taken. When individuals are ill, they willingly take the drugs as they are keen to recover. After a number of months, the patients feel better because a large proportion of the bacterial population has been killed. Some people consider themselves cured and stop taking the drugs. This is almost the worst course of action because the few bacteria that remain are those that are least susceptible to the drug. These survive, leaving a reservoir (source) of bacteria in the body, which can multiply and so increase the chance of mutations occurring. This may result in resistance in some bacteria to one or more of the first-line antibiotics. When the symptoms of TB occur again and antibiotics are prescribed, there is less chance of effective treatment. The presence of antibiotics is a selection pressure: those bacteria with resistance are more likely to survive (see 10.2a).

End TB strategy

In 2014, 194 countries agreed to take part in the 'End TB Strategy', a scheme that incorporated and improved on an earlier strategy. The strategy requires political commitment from the government of each member country and covers biological, social and economic factors for preventing the spread of the disease, and for curing people with the disease. Features of the End TB Strategy include:

- testing for the presence of *Mycobacterium* in people suspected of having TB and screening for TB in high risk groups to allow early diagnosis of the disease. This allows earlier treatment and cure. People who have close contact with infectious individuals are considered part of the high risk group and making contact with these people for testing is known as contact tracing. The most common test that was used involved trained technicians looking at samples of sputum under a microscope to identify the bacterium. Only half the number of cases could be detected this way. Growing cultures to test for antibiotic resistance takes many weeks, so diagnosis for this took a long time. There is now an increasing use of the rapid test Xpert MTB/RIF®, which is able to analyse DNA and detect *Mycobacterium* and drug resistance with an extremely high success rate.
- providing treatment to all people with TB and giving support to make sure that the correct doses are taken and the course of treatment is completed
- monitoring and recording of each patient's treatment
- giving antibiotics to people with latent TB as a prevention treatment
- planning and managing treatment for people who are also infected with HIV
- better education about how TB is spread and how antibiotic resistance develops, particularly the need to complete all courses of drugs
- more and better housing, leading to less over-crowding
- improved health facilities and treatments, including more effective drugs
- vaccination programmes
- better nutrition to ensure that immune systems are not weakened by poor diet.

Preventing transmission from cattle

Another biological control method is the pasteurisation (heat treatment) of milk, which kills any *M. bovis* present. Cattle herds are also regularly checked by veterinary surgeons for any sign of TB or the bacterium causing it.

The extent to which a pathogen is able to cause disease or cause damage is known as **virulence**. To be considered a pathogen, a microorganism must:

- gain entry to the host
- colonise the tissues of the host
- resist the defences of the host
- cause damage to the host's tissues.

One such pathogen causes the disease known as cholera. The pathogen causing cholera is a curved, rod-shaped bacterium named *Vibrio cholerae*, which has a **flagellum** at one end (Figure 1 over the page).

V. cholerae is a very virulent organism. It can gain entry to the host easily as the host cells line the intestine. It does not take long to colonise the intestine, typically 2–3 days for symptoms to appear, but a person can become ill just a few hours after infection.

As cholera is an intestinal disease, it is more difficult for the immune system to act on the pathogen. A toxin, known as choleragen, is produced by the bacterium. This causes damage to the host epithelial cells and leads to illness. Water and mineral ions are lost from the cells to the gut lumen and are not reabsorbed. This causes very watery diarrhoea. Without treatment, the resulting dehydration can be fatal, especially for infants.

Transmission

Transmission Cholera is transmitted by ingestion of water and, more rarely, food, that has been contaminated with faecal material containing the pathogen. The route of transmission is known as the faecal–oral route. Such contamination can be caused when:

- drinking water is not properly purified (Figure 2 over the page) and the water is contaminated with the pathogen
- untreated contaminated sewage leaks into water-courses

Extension

Worldwide importance

There have been several **pandemics** of cholera. The last one began in 1961 in Indonesia and spread rapidly to Bangladesh (1963), India (1964), the USSR, Iran and Iraq (1965–66). In 1970 it reached West Africa – an area which had not experienced a cholera outbreak for more than a century. It has now become **endemic** to much of the continent of Africa. Cholera spread rapidly around the world, reaching Latin America in 1991 (from where it had also been absent for over 100 years). It has now spread throughout South America.

The strain of *Vibrio* initially responsible for the present pandemic is serogroup 01 and is of the variety called 'El Tor'. In 1992, however, a new strain, serogroup 0139 'Bengal', emerged in Bangladesh and has been responsible for more recent outbreaks of the disease. There is evidence that 'Bengal' is more **virulent** than 'El Tor'.

Globally, cholera is of great importance, affecting 3–5 million people and killing an estimated 120 000 people each year. In some areas fatality rates may exceed 20% of those contracting the disease; with proper treatment, this should not go above 1%. In 2011, there were nearly 600 000 cases reported to the World Health Organization (WHO) from 56 countries. The worst affected continent is Africa.

These pages help you to:

- explain the different ways that cholera is transmitted (10.1.3)
- discuss the biological, social and economic factors that need to be considered in the prevention and control of cholera (10.1.4)

You will also:

- learn more about how the pathogen causes the symptoms of cholera
- read an account of a cholera outbreak in Yemen

Extension

The flagellum

A flagellum allows *Vibrio cholerae* to move. This has been linked to the virulence of the bacterium. Experiments on small mammals have shown the mutant strains of *V. cholerae* that are non-motile are less able to bind to host cells and less able to colonise the host.

Remember

Contaminated water indicates that water contains the pathogen, *V. cholerae*.

Dirty or polluted water is **not** the same as contaminated water and these terms should not be used when describing water containing *V. cholerae*.

Extension

Serotypes

There are many different types of *V. cholerae*. These types, known as serotypes, have different sets of surface antigens (surface proteins). Only two main serotypes are linked to cholera: *V. cholerae* O1, which has been the cause of pandemics and major **epidemics**, and *V. cholerae* O139.

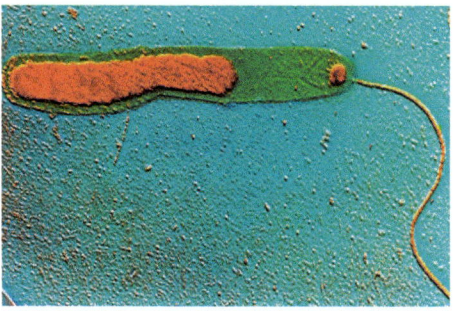

Figure 1 *Colourised scanning electron micrograph of Vibrio cholerae – the bacterium causing cholera*

Figure 2 *Cholera is most easily transmitted where there is a lack of treated water and where it is difficult to practise good hygiene*

- food to be eaten is washed in contaminated water, or contaminated by carriers who do not practise good hygiene when preparing food
- organisms, especially shellfish, feed on untreated contaminated sewage released into rivers or the sea, and these are consumed by humans
- contaminated human faeces are used as a fertiliser for food plants
- flies who have fed on contaminated faeces land on uncovered food.

Up to 75% of those with cholera have few if any symptoms. Consequently, they act as carriers, not knowing that they are spreading the disease to uninfected people. For transmission, the pathogen has to gain entry to the body of the uninfected person. In cholera, it is simply a matter of the uninfected person drinking contaminated water or eating contaminated food.

Prevention and control

To prevent the transmission of cholera, it is clearly necessary to prevent faecal matter containing *V. cholerae* from contaminating food and water. This can be achieved by:

- making sure that water supplies are clean, uncontaminated and treated, e.g. treatment with chlorine or boiling for at least a minute
- proper sewage treatment. New sewage treatment plants should be installed downstream of water treatment plants. In temporary camps, latrines should be provided or there should be a method to contain contaminated sewage for safe disposal. People should be discouraged from defecating near rivers used for washing
- discourage swimming or washing in rivers downstream of sewage outlets
- personal hygiene, e.g. washing hands thoroughly after using the toilet
- food hygiene, e.g. wearing gloves when handling food, washing food in treated water, cooking food thoroughly and covering food so that flies cannot land
- providing rapid treatment to minimise the length of time that a person is producing contaminated faeces
- educating people about how the pathogen is spread.

Oral rehydration solution (ORS) is used to treat most cases of cholera. It is a solution containing glucose and salts. In more severe cases it is possible to give the rehydration intravenously (directly into a vein). In severe cases, the use of antibiotics has been successful in helping people to recover more quickly from the disease.

Oral cholera vaccines (OCV) have been used successfully, particularly in mass vaccinations, to slow down or prevent the spread of cholera. The vaccine, which contains killed whole cells of *Vibrio*, is given in two doses. Although immunity against the disease lasts only for 3–5 years, spread can be minimised during an **outbreak**. This is because there are more people that are protected and so there is a smaller pool of people who will become ill and produce contaminated faeces.

In developing countries, as the population of cities grows rapidly, there is often not enough money or resources to provide the necessary infrastructure. As a result, there may be no treated water supply or sewerage system. Housing may be of a poor standard, with no running water or toilet facilities. Without the means to cook, food such as shellfish may be eaten raw, increasing the risk of contracting cholera. Cholera outbreaks frequently occur or worsen following natural disasters, such as earthquakes, or because of war, because:

- services such as water supply and sewage disposal are disrupted
- health services are overstretched
- residents are made homeless
- fleeing refugees spread the disease to neighbouring areas.

It is clearly not possible to build water treatment plants and sewerage systems and to re-house millions of people overnight. The main prevention method, in the short term, therefore has to be **vaccination**.

Cholera is an easily treatable disease. Up to 80% of sufferers can be successfully treated by replacing the lost fluids through oral rehydration therapy (see Extension). Apart from the social advantages of controlling cholera by providing better sanitation and housing with piped, treated water and flush toilets, there are economic ones too. In countries where the disease is endemic, the poor health of workers means that economic output is reduced. Tourism suffers because people are afraid of catching cholera and even food exports are hit because countries do not want to risk importing contaminated produce. Eradication of cholera would reverse these economic disadvantages.

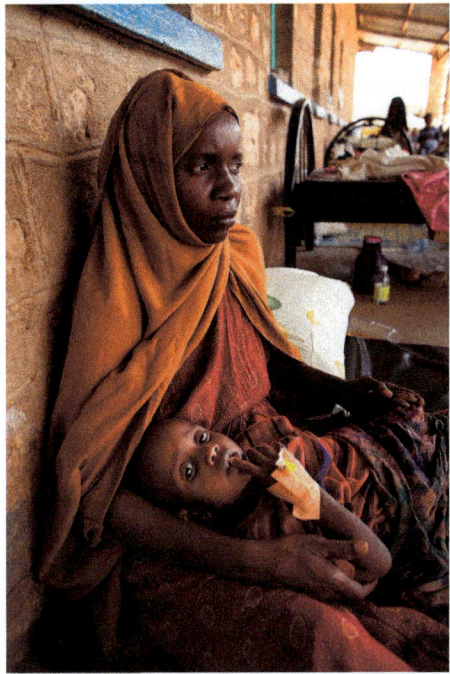

Figure 3 *A mother looks after her baby who is suffering from cholera. Infants are particularly at risk of dehydration if they are not able to access rehydration therapy*

Extension

Cholera, natural disasters and wars
Some of the worst cholera outbreaks occur during times of war or following natural disasters. This is often due to a lack of sanitation when water treatment plants and sewage treatment plants are destroyed, and when houses are destroyed so that there is a lack of flush toilets and piped drinking water. During these times it is easy for drinking water to become contaminated with raw sewage. There may be a drain on public health facilities and hospitals are unable to cope with the increased demands on their resources. Power cuts can mean that treatment plants cannot operate continually. Health centres that can provide oral rehydration may be destroyed and it may be difficult for non-governmental organisations to set up emergency centres to treat people quickly. This means that people are infected for a longer time, increasing the chance of spread of the disease. Poverty and an inability to transport food owing to wars leads to malnutrition, which means that the immune systems of many people are low and there is greater chance of becoming ill.

Summary test 10.1d

Cholera is a disease caused by the bacterium known as (**1**). The pathogen is transmitted by a (**2**) route. An infected person will pass out contaminated (**3**) and if this contaminates (**4**) or food to be eaten, then the pathogen will gain entry into the uninfected person. The immediate treatment for cholera is a simple solution of (**5**) and salts, and is known as (**6**). To prevent spread of the disease, mass (**7**) can be carried out. An individual can protect themselves by practising good (**8**), such as washing hands thoroughly, particularly after going to the toilet, and washing food in (**9**) water. In times of war or natural disaster, (**10**) can be mixed with drinking water.

These pages help you to:

- explain the different ways that malaria is transmitted (10.1.3)
- discuss the biological, social and economic factors that need to be considered in the prevention and control of malaria (10.1.4)

You will also:

- extend your knowledge of antigens

Most microorganisms that cause disease in humans are prokaryotes (1.2f) but a few are **eukaryotes**. One example of a disease caused by a eukaryotic **parasite (pathogen)** is malaria. It affects the liver, red blood cells and brain, causing pain, shivering, sweating and anaemia.

> **Extension**
>
> **Health statistics for 2017**
> Health statistics reported for 2017 by WHO estimated a total of 219 million cases of malaria worldwide, with India and ten countries in sub-Saharan Africa representing approximately 70% of these cases. Globally, there were 435 000 deaths from malaria in 2017.

Malaria is caused by parasites of the **protoctist** genus *Plasmodium*. Four species of *Plasmodium* can produce the disease in various forms: *P. falciparum*, *P. vivax*, *P. ovale* and *P. malariae*. Of these, *Plasmodium falciparum* is the most widespread and dangerous. It has two hosts: humans, and mosquitoes belonging to the genus *Anopheles*. Of the 380 or so species of *Anopheles*, 60 are capable of transmitting malaria to humans. Organisms such as *Anopheles* mosquitoes that transfer a parasite to its main (primary) host are known as **vectors**.

Transmission

Plasmodium has a complex life cycle, with stages within both its insect and human hosts. In humans, the pathogen spends some of its time within red blood cells (Figure 1) and within cells of the liver, as well as spending part of its life cycle in the blood plasma.

Transmission occurs when an infected person is bitten by a female *Anopheles* mosquito. Human blood is a good source of protein for development of the eggs of the insect. The insect sucks up blood containing *Plasmodium* when it is taking a blood meal (Figure 2).

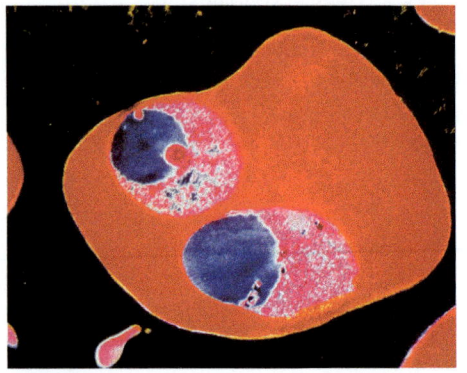

Figure 1 *Colourised transmission electron micrograph of two cells of the malarial parasite* Plasmodium *within a red blood cell*

The insect is a vector as it is not harmed by the pathogen. The pathogen migrates from the gut to the salivary glands. When the female *Anopheles* takes another blood meal, this time from an uninfected person, *Plasmodium* is injected into the person with an anticoagulant from the salivary gland. The anticoagulant prevents the human blood from clotting and so allows the mosquito to suck the blood up with her needle-like mouthparts.

Prevention and control

Malaria is largely confined to the tropics and sub-tropics because:

- Tropical climates provide the best breeding and living conditions for the *Anopheles* mosquito.
- *Plasmodium* needs temperatures in excess of 20 °C to complete its life cycle within the mosquito.
- The mosquito life cycle requires areas of still water and these are more common in the wetter tropics.

In deciding how to control malaria we need to look at the three living organisms involved in its spread:

- humans, who are highly mobile and spread the disease far and wide
- mosquitoes, which are highly mobile as flying adults but more or less stationary as larvae and pupae

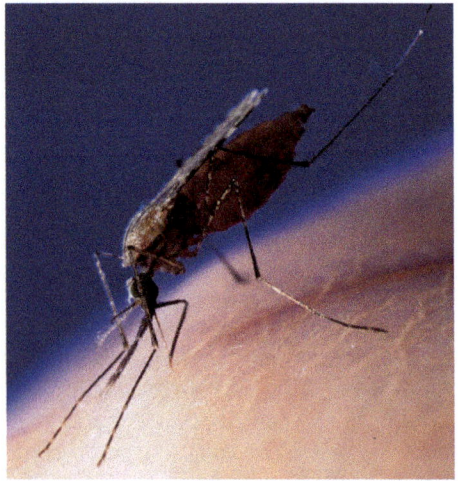

Figure 2 *A female* Anopheles *mosquito, the vector of the disease malaria, feeding on human blood*

- *Plasmodium*, which has developed resistance to drugs and adapts genetically to new situations.

The effective prevention and control of malaria needs to be aimed at all three of these biological factors:

- **Control of mosquitoes** – through reducing their populations by:
  - draining marshes and other areas of water where the mosquitoes lay their eggs and the larvae develop
  - introducing fish, which consume mosquito larvae, into marshes, ponds, etc. (biological control). However, these fish may also eat beneficial aquatic life
  - spraying freshwater areas with a parasite that kills mosquito larvae but is harmless to other wildlife (biological control)
  - spraying freshwater areas with insecticides to kill mosquito larvae (chemical control). These insecticides often kill beneficial aquatic organisms as well and may accumulate in food chains, harming other wildlife and even humans
  - spraying oil over freshwater areas to prevent the mosquito larvae breathing the air they need to survive (chemical control).
- **Control by humans** – through avoiding being bitten by mosquitoes by:
  - keeping doors and windows closed as far as possible
  - using insect repellents on the skin
  - wearing clothing that covers most, if not all, of the skin
  - sleeping under insecticide-treated bed nets to prevent the mosquito from reaching the human host
  - spraying the walls and ceilings of homes with an insecticide that will remain effective for some time (indoor residual spraying).
- **Control of *Plasmodium***
  - for *P. falciparum* malaria, especially where there are problems of resistance, WHO recommends using ACT (artemisinin-based combination therapy). This involves using a combination of drugs that have different effects
  - protect those not yet affected, by taking preventative (prophylactic) drugs, such as chloroquine, doxycycline, mefloquine, or tovaquone/proguanil. For different areas of the world, different prophylactic drugs are recommended, depending on the species of *Plasmodium* that presents the greatest risk, and whether the pathogen in that area has developed resistance to the drug. The drug needs to be taken before exposure to *Plasmodium* and continued after potential exposure.

The social and economic consequences of malaria are huge. Prevention and control of malaria is still proving difficult. Some of the reasons for this include the following:

- poor education and a failure to follow preventative measures properly
- wars and political unrest preventing governments and health authorities carrying out anti-malarial measures
- migrants, both political and economic, spreading the disease to previously unaffected areas
- poverty in affected countries leaving few resources for medical treatments or education about how to prevent the spread of the disease
- ease of movement, e.g. air travel, spreading the disease globally
- mosquitoes breeding in untreated water, e.g. puddles
- insecticide resistance in mosquitoes
- banning of certain insecticides, e.g. DDT
- drug resistance in *Plasmodium*
- **global warming** increasing the breeding range and life-span of *Anopheles* mosquitoes
- no vaccine being available.

Extension

Malaria treatment and disease recurrence

If the correct drugs are used and the treatment regimen (correct dose for the correct length of time) is followed, there is a good chance that a person can be cured of malaria. However, some people who have been infected with *P. vivax* or *P. ovale* appear to recover, but can have one or more relapses of the disease after months or years. This is because the pathogen can remain dormant in the liver and can become active again to cause symptoms. There are also cases where the pathogen is resistant to the drug used to treat the disease so the person continues to have symptoms even with treatment. In these cases, a different drug needs to be given. Also, in areas where there is a high rate of malaria cases, such as in Africa, it is common for a person to have the disease a number of times. This is particularly the case for young children, who have not had time to build up enough immunity to the disease. People who travel from low risk countries to high risk countries, can get malaria even if they have been previously cured of the disease. Any immunity gained from one infection may not give protection as different areas may have different species of *Plasmodium* or may have different strains of the same species, or the immunity gained is only partial.

Extension

Plasmodium knowlesi

In 2004, attention was drawn to *Plasmodium knowlesi* as a cause of malaria in humans. Before then, infection of humans by this species was considered to be rare, but with further research and more reports of cases, it is now acccepted that *P. knowlesi* is a fifth species of *Plasmodium* that causes malaria in humans. It is mainly found in Southeast Asia.

Summary test 10.1e

Malaria is caused by four species of the genus *Plasmodium*. *Plasmodium* belongs to the group **(1)** and it has two hosts: humans, and mosquitoes belonging to the genus **(2)**. As mosquitoes spread the disease to the main host, humans, they are called a **(3)**. *Plasmodium* is passed to a female mosquito when it takes a **(4)** meal. When the mosquito injects **(5)** into an uninfected person when it next feeds, the pathogen is transmitted. Control of mosquitoes can help prevent malaria. This is carried out by draining marshes, where the **(6)** stage of the mosquito lives, or by spraying chemical agents such as **(7)** or **(8)** on the water to kill them or using biological methods like **(9)** or **(10)** to have the same effect. Humans can help to avoid being bitten by mosquitoes by using **(11)** to cover them when sleeping or putting **(12)** on the skin to discourage them. IRS, or **(13)** is also recommended. **(14)** drugs such as atovaquone/proguanil may be used to prevent contracting malaria when visiting a country where it is endemic.

Extension

The life cycle of *Plasmodium*

The life cycle of *Plasmodium* can be summarised as follows.

- After mating, the female *Anopheles* mosquito requires a meal of blood in order for her eggs to mature. The eggs are later laid in water.
- When biting a human to obtain blood, the female mosquito injects saliva to prevent the blood clotting and blocking her needle-like mouthparts.
- If the saliva contains *Plasmodium*, this enters the human blood system and is carried to the liver.
- In the liver, *Plasmodium* multiplies to produce massive numbers that are released into the blood.
- These enter red blood cells (Figure 1), multiply and form gametes which are released into the blood plasma.
- When another female mosquito bites an infected human, these gametes are sucked up, along with the blood (Figure 2).
- The gametes fuse to form a zygote that develops into a cyst on the wall of the mosquito's stomach.
- The cyst releases *Plasmodium* cells which migrate to the salivary gland, ready to be injected into a human next time the mosquito feeds on blood.

Difficulties with developing a malarial vaccine

For years scientists have sought an effective vaccine to control malaria. In 2014, there was an announcement that a vaccine had been developed that, during trials, appeared to be effective in providing immunity to children against the disease. The RTS,S vaccine has now been approved for the malaria vaccine implementation programme (MVIP). This is a large-scale pilot programme where the vaccine is given to young children in selected areas of three African countries as part of their routine immunisation programme. It is the only vaccine that has been shown to give some protection against malaria.

The development of a vaccine against malaria has been very difficult. Reasons for this include:

- *Plasmodium* is a eukaryotic organism and therefore has many genes which can code for a wide variety of surface **antigens**.
- It has many stages in its life cycle within humans, each one having different surface antigens.
- *Plasmodium* also lives inside red blood cells and cells of the liver. Surrounded by the membrane of the host cells, it does not cause an immune response from the lymphocytes of the body's immune system (**antigenic concealment**). Equally, any antibodies present in the blood cannot work against the stages of *Plasmodium* that occur within cells.
- Different species of *Plasmodium* have different antigens (species-specific antigens).

Antibiotics are substances produced by microorganisms that destroy other microorganisms or inhibit their growth. Some of these we are able to use as therapeutic drugs. Using knowledge of the molecular structure and mode of action of these antibiotics, semi-synthetic antibiotics have also been developed. These are antibiotics that have been produced as a result of chemically modifying the natural antibiotic. The semi-synthetic antibiotic may have, for example, an improved efficacy (effectiveness) compared to the natural antibiotic, or may be more effective against a particular pathogen, or may produce fewer side effects. There are also some antibiotics that are completely synthetic.

Alexander Fleming discovered the first antibiotic, penicillin, in 1928, but it was not until the 1940s that large-scale production of penicillin began. Let us consider how penicillin works and look at the causes and effects of **antibiotic resistance.**

How the antibiotic penicillin works

Penicillin works by preventing bacteria from making normal cell walls. In bacterial cells, as in plant cells, the entry of water by osmosis (4.2b) down the water potential gradient does not cause osmotic lysis (bursting) because of the wall that surrounds all bacterial cells. This wall is made of **peptidoglycan (murein)**, a tough material that is not easily stretched. As water enters the cell by osmosis, it expands and pushes against the cell wall. Being relatively inelastic, the cell wall resists expansion and so prevents further entry of water.

The peptidoglycans of bacterial cell walls are polymers, long molecules made of a mixture of amino acids and sugars. These polymers are held together by short peptide molecules that form cross-linkages between them. As a bacterium develops its cell wall, it secretes enzymes known as **autolysins**. These break down areas of the cell wall forming tiny holes. The holes allow the cell wall to stretch as it grows and they are normally filled in as new peptidoglycan chains form across them. Penicillin inhibits enzymes, known as transpeptidases, required for the assembly of the peptide cross-linkages in the new bacterial cell walls. It enters the active site of the enzyme and binds permanently. This means that penicillin prevents the formation of the cross-linkages. This weakens the walls, making them unable to withstand pressure. As water enters naturally by osmosis, the cell bursts and the bacterium dies. Penicillin is therefore only effective when bacteria are growing.

Why antibiotics do not affect viruses

Viruses, unlike bacteria, are not affected by antibiotics. There are a number of reasons for this, including:

- Viruses do not have their own metabolism but rather use that of their host cells. Antibiotics that work by disrupting metabolism are therefore not effective on a virus.
- Viruses are extremely simple with very few structures of their own, as they use those of the host cell to carry out their replication. Antibiotics that target cellular organelles are again not effective.
- Viruses have a protein coat rather than a peptidoglycan (murein) cell wall. There are therefore no sites for antibiotics like penicillin to work on.
- Viruses live inside the cells of their host, out of reach of antibiotics.

These pages help you to:

- outline how penicillin acts on bacteria (10.2.1)
- explain why antibiotics do not affect viruses (10.2.1)
- consider the consequences of antibiotic resistance (10.2.2)
- discuss the steps that can be taken to reduce the impact of antibiotic resistance (10.2.2)

You will also:

- learn about how antibiotic resistance develops
- learn about different forms of tuberculosis in terms of antibiotic resistance
- understand that a strain is not a species

Remember

Penicillin prevents the last step in bacterial cell wall synthesis by preventing the formation of cross-links between peptidoglycan chains. It does this by inhibiting the bacterial transpeptidase enzyme that catalyses the formation of the cross-links. If the chains are not held together, the cell wall is too weak to prevent osmotic lysis.

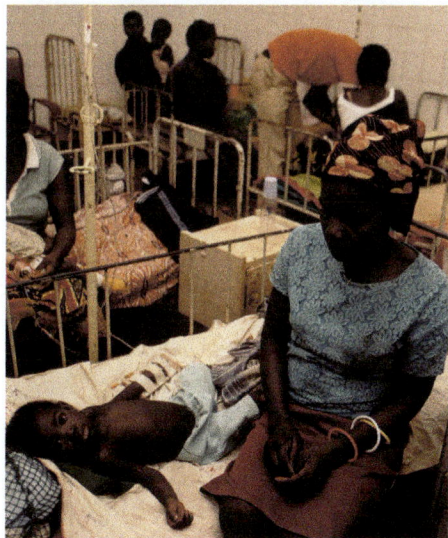

Figure 1 *The use of antibiotics is common in hospitals and increases the chance of resistance developing in bacteria*

Remember

Bacteria only have one copy of a gene. If a mutation occurs in a gene, then that bacterium has a new allele for that gene.

Remember

A bacterial strain is a sub-type of that particular species of bacterium, it is not a new species.

Extension

DR-TB, MDR-TB and XDR-TB

Antibiotics are essential in the treatment of TB. Resistance to rifampicin is common and the disease is known as drug resistant tuberculosis (DR-TB). Multidrug-resistant TB (MDR-TB) is becoming more common (resistance to two first-line antibiotics, rifampicin and isoniazid), but is still treatable. Extensively drug-resistant (XDR-TB) is rare: the bacteria have resistance to at least four antimicrobial drugs (three first-line drugs and at least one second-line drug) used for treatment. Some people do not respond to the remaining second-line drugs as they are not very effective.

Remember

Antibiotic resistance is not just a problem when treating humans for a bacterial disease. Veterinary practitioners and farmers use antibiotics to treat livestock for infectious diseases. In addition, there is the danger of transfer of antibiotic-resistant bacteria from farm animals to humans.

Remember

Resistance is the result of a chance mutation. This is a rare event. If it was a common event it is unlikely that any antibiotics would still be effective in treating disease.

Antibiotic resistance

Shortly after the discovery of antibiotics it became clear that the effectiveness of some of them was reduced. It was found that some populations of bacteria had developed resistance to antibiotics, such as penicillin. The resistance was due to a chance mutation within the bacteria.

Extension

Mutations and antibiotic resistance

We saw in 6.2d that a mutation is a change in the sequence of nucleotides in DNA that results in a new allele (form of a gene). With antibiotic resistance, the new allele will code for a protein that, in some way, will give the bacterium resistance against the antibiotic.

In the case of resistance to penicillin, a person who has not taken their full course of antibiotics for an infection may leave a reservoir of bacteria in their body. A mutation in one of the bacteria left in the body will result in the bacterium being able to make an enzyme, penicillinase. If the person becomes ill again, the penicillinase will break down penicillin when it is prescribed to combat the infection. This means that the person will not be cured of the disease.

A mutation that leads to the production of penicillinase is an advantage when the bacterium is in the presence of penicillin because the penicillin will kill all the normal bacteria without penicillinase, but not the mutant type. Only the mutant individual will survive and divide. This means that all bacteria produced from this survivor will be of the mutant type and have the gene coding for penicillinase. In this way, antibiotic resistance is passed from one generation to the next – **vertical gene transmission**. The resistant form is selected for rather than the non-resistant form when exposed to penicillin. These penicillin-resistant bacteria gradually form the largest part of the population. The frequency of the **allele** for penicillin resistance increases in the population. This has serious consequences when treating individuals for bacterial infections for which the best treatment is penicillin. A different, possibly less effective antibiotic will need to be used. We now know of many pathogenic species of bacteria as having strains that are resistant to one or more of the limited number of antibiotics available to us. Research for new natural antibiotics, and research and development of semi-synthetic and synthetic antibiotics, is very time consuming and costly. A new antibiotic needs to be trialled extensively before it is licenced for use and it is a matter of many years, rather than many months, before a new antimicrobial drug will be ready for use.

The allele for antibiotic resistance can be carried on **plasmids** (1.2f). These plasmids can be transferred to bacteria of the same species that do not have the plasmid or into other bacterial species – **horizontal gene transmission**. Horizontal gene transmission can lead to certain bacteria accumulating DNA that gives them resistance to a range of antibiotics (Figure 2). These are the so-called multi-drug resistant bacteria ('superbugs'). Two examples of superbugs are the bacteria causing chlolera, *V. cholerae* (10.1d), and TB, *M. tuberculosis* (10.1c).

If second-line drugs need to be used, they are less effective and the treatment takes longer. Not only is this more costly and more difficult for healthcare workers to manage, there is less chance that a person can make a recovery from the disease.

Antibiotic resistance is a threat to public health in all countries of the world. A major concern is that there will be no treatment for common bacterial diseases and mortality rates from these diseases will increase.

In terms of additional strain to health services and loss of productivity for the country, the economic effect to governments of antibiotic resistance is immense, particularly for low- and middle-income countries.

New mutations that give bacteria resistance to antibiotics occur randomly all the time. However, the more we use antibiotics the greater the chance that the mutant strain of the bacterial species will gain an advantage over the original strain. In time and with continued use of the antibiotic, there is a greater chance that the antibiotic-resistant strain will be the most common form of the species. Unfortunately, overuse and incorrect use of antibiotics is widespread, and antibiotic resistance is a major global health problem.

Reducing the impact of antibiotic resistance

Certain steps can be taken to reduce the impact of antibiotic resistance.

- Limit antibiotic treatments to cases where they are essential rather than to treat minor illnesses with symptoms that are not serious or are short-lived.
- Encourage patients to always complete the course of antibiotics as prescribed. If a person takes the correct antibiotic dose for the correct number of days, the whole population of the pathogenic bacteria will be eliminated. However, if a person feels better and stops taking the antibiotic, this leaves a reservoir of bacteria in the body that will increase in population size and can make the person ill again.
- Make sure that the most effective antibiotic is prescribed (narrow spectrum or broad spectrum).
- Try to prevent patients building up a supply of unused antibiotics from previous prescriptions and then using them later in smaller doses than they should.
- Control and limit use of antibiotics in farming to the treatment of only the most serious bacterial infections.
- Improve awareness of the issues caused by 'overuse' of antibiotics.
- Hold back certain antibiotics for future use when others have been made ineffective by resistance.
- Use other antibacterial compounds that are less likely to cause problems of resistance.
- Record and report patterns of antibiotic resistance.
- Quarantine (isolate) people that have drug-resistant infections to break the transmission cycle of the resistant bacteria.
- Improve prevention and control measures to reduce the spread of infection, e.g. vaccination programmes.

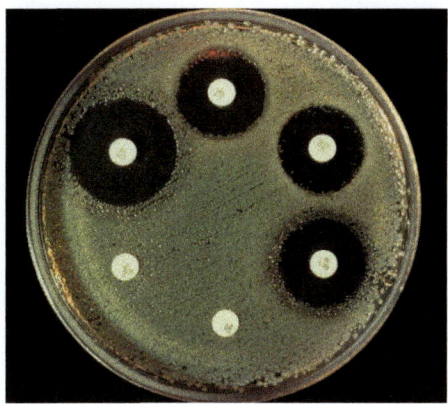

Figure 2 *Antibiotic resistance in Escherichia coli. The six white discs, each possessing a different antibiotic, were placed on a Petri dish with a growing culture of E. coli. Around four of the discs there is a lack of bacterial growth (inhibition zone), indicating that the bacterium is sensitive to these antibiotics. The growth of the bacterium around the two other discs is unaffected, however, indicating that it is resistant to these antibiotics.*

Summary test 10.2a

Young bacterial cells produce enzymes called **(1)** which make holes in their cell walls to allow the walls to **(2)** as they grow. These holes are normally covered over by chains of **(3)** molecules but penicillin can prevent this by inhibiting **(4)** that help to synthesise the **(5)** cross-links between these molecules. As a result, the wall is weakened and water entering the cell causes it to burst – a process called **(6)**. Resistance to penicillin is due to certain bacteria developing the ability to produce an enzyme called **(7)**. This happened suddenly as a result of a **(8)**. The gene for this enzyme is found on circular portions of DNA called **(9)** which can be inherited by each succeeding generation in a process known as **(10)**. These portions of DNA can also be transferred to other bacteria of the same or different species. This transfer is known as **(11)**.

Launch additional digital resources for the chapter

10 Exam-style questions

1 What could cause an outbreak of malaria in an area where it was previously under control?

1 movement of population due to war

2 malarial parasites became resistant to antimalarial drugs

3 mosquitoes became resistant to insecticides

A 1, 2 and 3   **B** 1 and 3 only
C 2 and 3 only   **D** 1 and 2 only

2 What do the causative agents of HIV / AIDS, malaria and cholera have in common?

Table 1

	they have a cell surface membrane	they have genes	they have ribosomes	they respire
A	✓	✓	✓	✓
B	✓	✗	✗	✓
C	✗	✓	✗	✓
D	✗	✓	✗	✗

key

✓ present in each causative agent

✗ not present in each causative agent

3 a Tuberculosis (TB) is an infectious disease. Name the bacterium that is the pathogen of tuberculosis (TB). *(1 mark)*

b Describe how TB is transmitted. *(2 marks)*

c Streptomycin was the first antibiotic used to treat TB in 1945.

Streptomycin works by binding to the smaller subunit of 70S ribosomes.

This binding leads to a frameshift mutation in mRNA, resulting in death of the bacterial cells.

i Suggest how a frameshift mutation in mRNA leads to the death of the bacterial cells. *(2 marks)*

ii Bacteria and humans both have ribosomes. Suggest why streptomycin does **not** affect human cells. *(1 mark)*

iii During the first few years after the introduction of streptomycin treatment, an increasing number of the TB bacteria developed resistance to streptomycin. Outline how this happened. *(4 marks)*

d The antibiotic rifampicin was introduced as an alternative to streptomycin.

Other drugs such as isoniazid are also used in the treatment of TB.

Some bacteria are now resistant to both of these drugs. These bacteria are known as multi-drug resistant (MDR) bacteria.

Outline the steps that can be taken to reduce the impact of drug resistance in bacteria. *(3 marks)*

e Explain why antibiotics can be used to treat bacterial infections and not viral infections. *(2 marks)*

(Total 15 marks)

4 Figure 1 is a scanning electron micrograph of the bacterium that causes cholera, *Vibrio cholerae*.

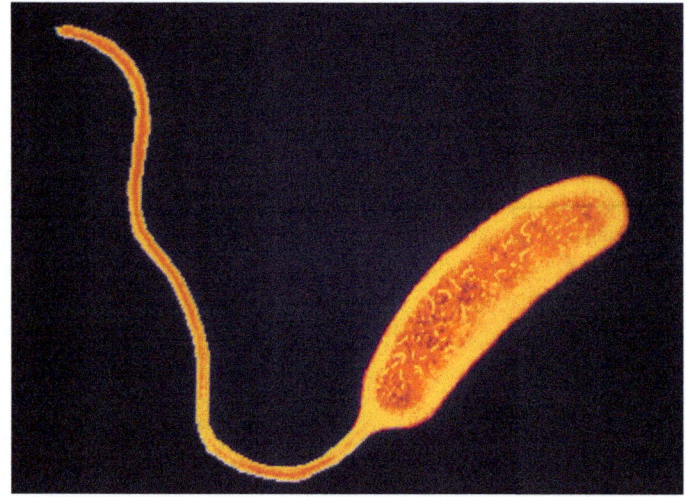

Figure 1

The bacterium affects epithelial cells lining the small intestine. The organism does not enter the cell but the toxin it releases can enter and cause damage. Large quantities of chloride ions and sodium ions are lost from the cell, leading to the production of watery diarrhoea. This can be severe and lead to death.

a i Explain how a loss of chloride ions and sodium ions from the intestinal epithelial cell causes watery diarrhoea. *(3 marks)*

ii Describe how cholera is transmitted from an infected person to an uninfected person. *(2 marks)*

b Table 1 shows the statistics for cholera reported to the World Health Organization (WHO) in four countries in 2018:

Table 1

Country	Number of cases	Deaths	Fatality rate %
Angola	828	43	
Nigeria	12173	288	
Thailand	8	0	0.0
United States of America	11	0	0.0

   i Calculate the cholera fatality rates in both Angola and Nigeria for 2018. Show your working. *(2 marks)*

   ii Apart from the differences in populations of these four countries, suggest explanations for the differences shown in Table 1. *(4 marks)*

(Total 11 marks)

10 Practice questions

4 a Cholera is transmitted by food and water that is contaminated with faecal matter. Suggest three measures that might be used to limit the spread of the disease.

   b Suggest a reason why, in countries where cholera is common, babies who are breast-fed are affected by cholera far less often than babies who are bottle-fed.

   c Suggest how inhibiting the development of a flagellum in the bacterium that causes cholera might prevent the disease.

   d Suggest a reason why injecting antibiotics into the blood can be effective in killing the cholera bacterium while the same antibiotic taken orally (by mouth) is not.

5 a Suggest what is meant by a natural antibiotic.

   b Some antibiotics prevent the synthesis of cross-links in bacterial cell walls. Explain how this may lead to the death of a bacterium.

   c Explain why antibiotic resistance is more likely to develop the more antibiotics are used.

   d Explain why patients with tuberculosis would be more likely to not finish a course of antibiotics than patients with other diseases.

   e Suggest why strains of bacteria that are resistant to many antibiotics are more likely to arise in hospitals.

6 Below is a list of four infectious diseases:
   P HIV/AIDS
   Q Malaria
   R Tuberculosis
   S Cholera

For each of the following statements give the letter corresponding to those diseases to which the statement refers. There may be more than one letter for each answer, and each letter may be used once, more than once or not at all.

   a Antibiotics are used in its control.

   b A vector is involved in its transmission.

   c It is spread through the air.

   d It has been controlled by vaccination for many years.

   e Treatment involves oral rehydration therapy.

   f The organism causing the disease is a prokaryote.

   g Infected persons are prone to opportunistic infections.

   h It occurs particularly where there is no proper treatment of sewage.

   i Symptoms include a persistent cough.

   j It is caused by a pathogen.

   k The pathogen can remain dormant in the host, but can still be transmitted to an uninfected person.

11.1 The immune system

a. The mode of action of phagocytes

Introduction

We have seen in Chapter 10 some examples of infectious diseases and the damage they can do. Tens of millions of humans die each year from such infections. Many more survive and others appear never to be affected in the first place. Why then are there these differences? Any disease is, in effect, a battle between the **pathogen** and the various defences of the body. Much depends on the overall state of health of an individual, and in particular, whether the immune system, which is specialised for defence against disease, is functioning efficiently. This is the system of the body that is specialised for defence against disease. Some groups of people are more at risk of serious illness or death from a disease because their immune system is weaker:

- very young children (maturing immune system)
- elderly people (aging immune system)
- people who have had transplants and are on immunosuppressant drugs to avoid rejection
- people who have a disease of the immune system as in HIV/AIDS
- malnourished individuals who have a low-protein diet.

The human body has a range of defences to protect itself from infection. There is a first line of defence to prevent the entry of pathogens, and if this is not successful, a second line of defence can be used: the immune system.

Immunity

If a person is able to resist the effects of a pathogen and does not become ill, then the person is said to be immune to the disease that the pathogen can cause. At birth, the body has a range of defences that give non-specific immunity. These are:

- general first-line defence mechanisms (see Extension)
- second-line defence mechanisms that involve cells of the immune system known as phagocytes (Figure 1 and also see 8.1c).

These defence mechanisms are targeted at all pathogens and are not selective.

If a pathogen is able to avoid all of the non-specific defence mechanisms, then the body needs to rely on other second-line specific response mechanisms. These involve cells of the immune system that are highly specific to the pathogen that has infected the body: the B-lymphocytes and the T-lymphocytes (see 8.1c). We will consider specific immunity later in this chapter. The aim of the second line of defence is to:

- neutralise any toxins produced by the pathogen
- prevent the pathogen multiplying
- kill the pathogen
- remove any remains of the pathogen.

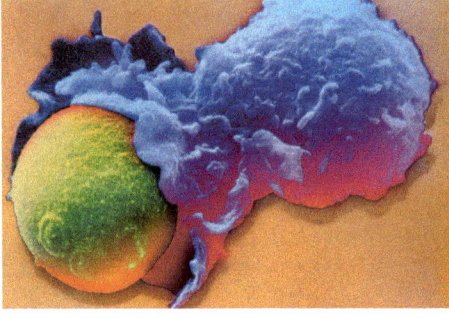

Figure 1 *Colourised scanning electron micrograph of a phagocyte engulfing a yeast cell by phagocytosis*

Antigens and the concept of self and non-self

Before second-line defences can respond, the pathogen needs to be recognised by the cells of the immune system.

An antigen is any substance that is recognised as **non-self** (foreign) by the immune system and which provokes (stimulates) an immune response. This involves the production of a specific antibody against the antigen. The sequence of events that lead to the production of antibodies is described in 11.1b.

Antigens are molecules with a high molecular weight and most are proteins, although glycoproteins and polysaccharides can also act as antigens.

The proteins are found, for example, on:

- the cell surface membranes (see 4.1b) of protoctists such as *Plasmodium* (10.1a and 10.1e)
- the surface of bacteria, such as the cell wall, flagellum and pili (1.2f)
- the protein coat or envelope of viruses (1.2f)
- the cell surface membrane of diseased cells, such as cancer cells (5.1b) or cells infected with a virus.

B-lymphocytes and T-lymphocytes must be able to distinguish the body's own cells, or **self,** from those that are non-self (foreign). If they could not do this, the lymphocytes would also act on body cells. Antigens on the surface of a person's body cells are known as self-antigens (see 4.1b) because their own lymphocytes are not activated by their presence. Non-self antigens are those on the surface of foreign material or cells and these will provoke a response by the lymphocytes.

Phagocytosis

Phagocytosis is the process by which large particles are taken up by cells, in the form of vacuoles (vesicles) formed from the cell surface membrane (see 4.2f and Figure 1). In the blood and other body tissues, two types of white blood cell that carry out phagocytosis are **macrophages** and **neutrophils** (8.1c). These cells are known as **phagocytes** and are produced in the marrow of the long bones. Phagocytes are very efficient at removing potentially harmful foreign invaders from the body and play an important role in limiting the increase in population size of pathogens and in trying to prevent the spread of the pathogen in the body. If they are not able to eliminate pathogens by their own actions, then they help to minimise infection so that there is time for the specific immune response to occur. The process of phagocytosis by a neutrophil is shown in Figure 2 and is summarised as follows:

- A series of reactions causes plasma proteins, known as complement proteins, to become attached to the surface of the bacterium.
- Complement proteins and any chemical products of the bacterium act as attractants, causing neutrophils to move towards the bacterium. The proteins act as opsonins, molecules that enhance (increase) phagocytosis.
- Neutrophils attach themselves by receptors to the opsonins on the surface of the bacterium.
- Neutrophils engulf the bacterium to form a vesicle, known as a **phagosome** or phagocytic vacuole.
- Lysosomes (1.2d) move towards the phagosome and fuse with it releasing their enzymes into the phagosome.
- The hydrolytic enzymes within the lysosomes break down the bacterium into smaller, soluble material.
- The soluble products from the breakdown of the bacterium are absorbed into the cytoplasm of the neutrophils and waste products are released from the cell.

The neutrophil can also interact directly and engulf the bacterial cell as it has receptors that can recognise particular patterns of molecules on the surface of the bacterial cells.

1. The neutrophil is attracted to the bacterium by chemoattractants

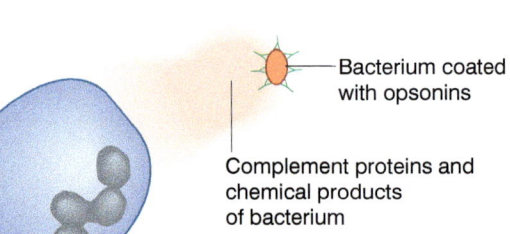

Bacterium coated with opsonins

Complement proteins and chemical products of bacterium

Neutrophil

2. The neutrophil binds to the bacterium

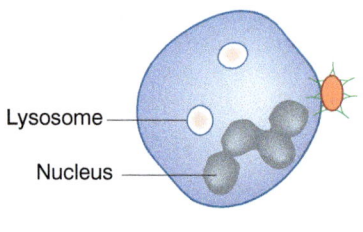

Lysosome

Nucleus

3. Lysosomes within the neutrophil migrate towards the phagosome formed by pseudopodia engulfing the bacterium

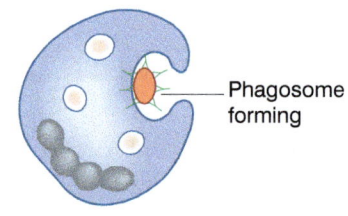

Phagosome forming

4. The lysosomes release their hydrolytic enzymes into the phagosome, where they break down the bacterium

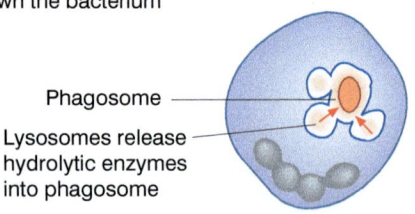

Phagosome

Lysosomes release hydrolytic enzymes into phagosome

5. The breakdown products of the bacterium are absorbed by the neutrophil or are released from the cell

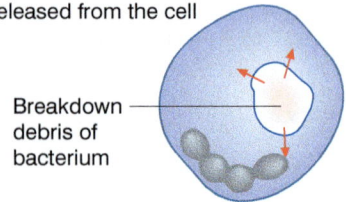

Breakdown debris of bacterium

Figure 2 *Summary of phagocytosis of a bacterium by a neutrophil*

b. B-lymphocytes and the immune response

As we saw in 11.1a, the non-specific response to infection is rapid and phagocytes carry out phagocytosis whatever the infection. The specific immune response to a non-self antigen, for example an antigen on the surface of a pathogen, or a toxin released by a pathogen, is much slower and a person may show symptoms of the disease. If the body has not encountered the antigen before, the combined responses of the B-lymphocytes and T-lymphocytes is known as the primary immune response. The result of this is destruction of the pathogen (or toxin) and recovery from infection.

An important part of the response is also to provide immunity if the same pathogen is encountered again. This is known as the secondary immune response (11.1c), and is rapid enough to prevent the person from becoming ill again from the same disease.

The two types of lymphocyte each has its own response:

- B-lymphocytes (B cells) – humoral immunity (involves antibodies which are present in body fluids or 'humours')
- T-lymphocytes (T cells) – cell-mediated immunity (involves cells).

The role of B-lymphocytes in the immune reponse

There are many different types of B-lymphocytes, and each type produces a different antibody which responds to one specific antigen. However, until a primary immune response occurs, there are only a few cells of each type.

Each B-lymphocyte needs to recognise its own specific antigen if it is to become active and produce antibody. This is achieved through the presence on the cell surface membrane of bound antibody molecules that act as receptors (4.1b): each is known as a B-cell antigen receptor, or B-cell receptor (BCR).

Antigen recognition and binding to B-cell receptors activates the B-lymphocyte. The antigen could be a protein on the surface of a pathogen or could be a toxin released by a pathogen. The activated B-lymphocyte grows rapidly, then a number of mitotic divisions (5.2a) occurs to form a population of genetically identical cells, known as a clone. The process is called clonal expansion. At the end of clonal expansion, the cells produced develop into either plasma cells (Figure 1) or memory B-cells. The specific B-lymphocytes and plasma cells, and the antibodies produced, together with the production of memory cells are all features of the **primary immune response**.

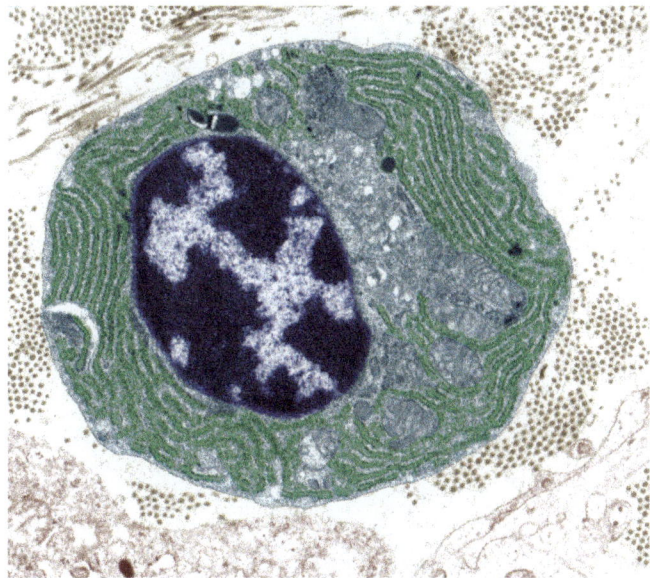

Figure 1 *Colourised transmission electron micrograph of a plasma cell*

These pages help you to:

- describe the sequence of events occurring during a primary immune response that results in the production of antibody and memory cells (11.1.3)
- understand the roles of macrophages, B-lymphocytes, plasma cells and T-helper cells (11.1.3)
- explain the role of memory cells in the secondary immune response and in long-term immunity (11.1.4)

You will also:

- learn about polyclonal activation

Polyclonal activation

In practice, a typical pathogen, e.g. *Mycobacterium tuberculosis*, has many different proteins on its surface, all of which act as antigens. Pathogens, such as the bacterium that causes tetanus, also produce toxins, each of which will act as an antigen. Therefore many different B-lymphocytes make **clones**, each of which produces its own type of antibody. This is known as **polyclonal activation**.

Plasma cells and antibodies

Plasma cells (Figure 1 on page 209) synthesise and secrete (release) antibodies specific to the antigen that triggered the B-lymphocyte response. The cells have a structure suited to their function of producing large quantities of antibody molecules, which are glycoproteins. There is extensive RER for polypeptide production and extensive Golgi body for final processing of the antibody. There is also a large nucleus, as transcription of the genes for the polypeptide antibodies is occurring, and many mitochondria for amino acid activation for translation. The plasma cells survive only a few days, but each can make around 2000 antibodies every second. The antibody molecule, which is soluble in blood and tissue fluid, has two sites with a complementary shape to the specific antigen. On binding, an antibody–antigen complex is formed and this facilitates (makes easier) phagocytosis and destruction by macrophages (see 11.1a).

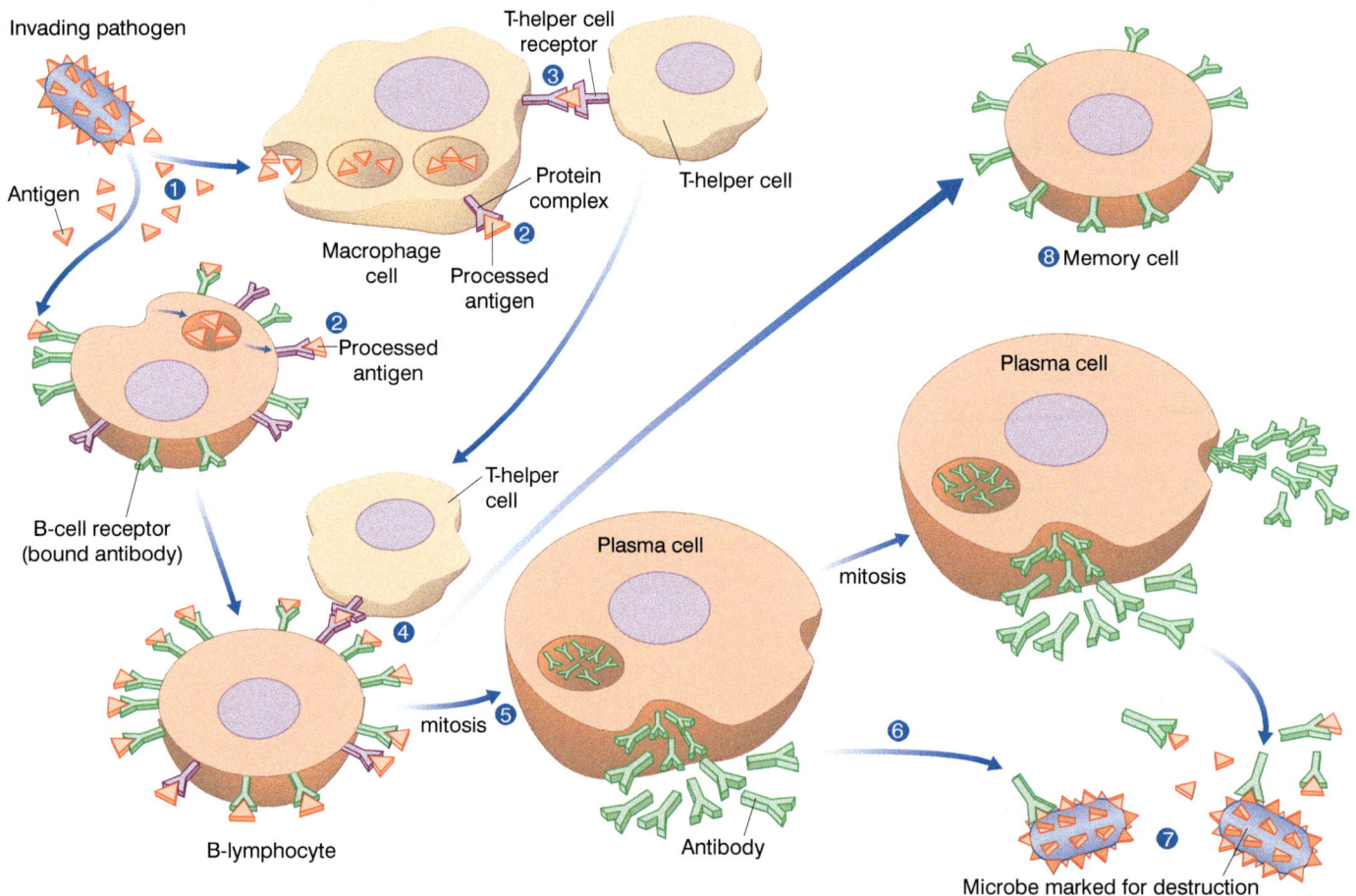

1. Invading pathogen has antigens that are taken up by macrophages by phagocytosis. Antigen bound to B-cell receptors activates the B-lymphocyte. Antigens can be taken into the cell for processing.

2. Both the macrophage cells and the B-lymphocytes process and present the antigens.

3. A T-helper cell attaches to the processed antigen on the antigen-presenting cell and becomes activated, making it capable of interacting with B-lymphocytes.

4. T-helper cells attach to antigens on the surface of the B-lymphocyte.

5. A clone of plasma cells are produced as a result of clonal expansion.

6. The cloned plasma cells produce antibodies that exactly fit antigens on the pathogen's surface.

7. The antibodies attach to antigens on the pathogen, forming antibody–antigen complexes and resulting in the destruction of the pathogen (see 11.2a) (= **primary immune response**).

8. A clone of memory B-cells are produced as a result of clonal expansion. The memory cells survive for long periods. Future invasions by the same pathogen lead to a secondary immune response, which involves rapid division of memory cells, some of which develop into plasma cells that produce antibodies. The process is then repeated from stage 6.

Figure 2 *Summary of the role of B-lymphocytes, T-helper lymphocytes and macrophages in the immune response (humoral immunity)*

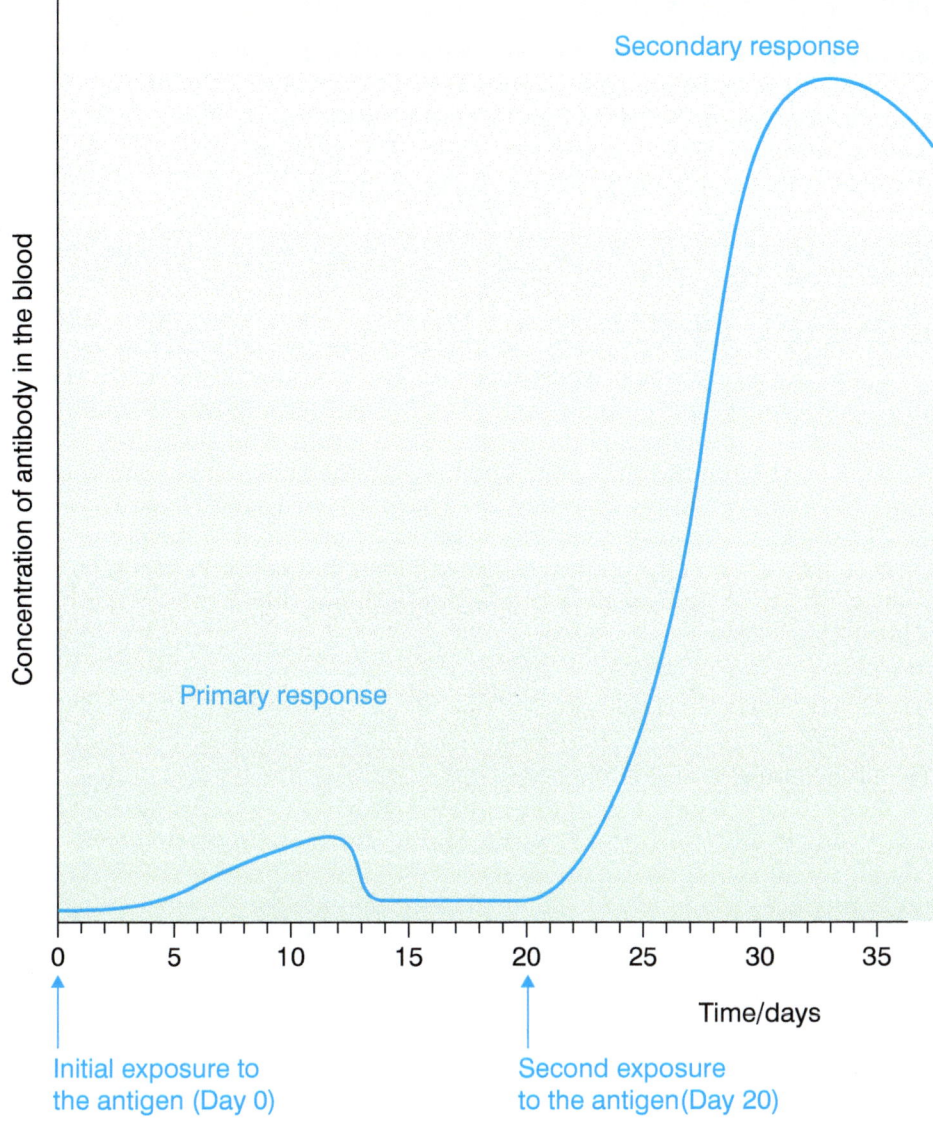

Figure 3 *Primary and secondary responses to an antigen*

Antigen-presenting cells

Although B-lymphocyte activation occurs when there is direct binding to an antigen (e.g. on a pathogen), as shown in Figure 2 (step 1), the B-lymphocyte can also be activated by binding to the antigen presented on a macrophage (not shown on Figure 2).

Macrophages are often the first cells to come across pathogens and destroy them following phagocytosis. The macrophages can process antigens (step 2) to form a complex with specific cell surface proteins so that the antigen is exposed on the surface of the cell. The macrophage is acting as an antigen-presenting cell or APC.

Figure 2 (step 2) shows that the B-lymphocyte is also able to process and present antigens.

A type of T-lymphocyte known as a T-helper cell (11.1c) can interact with a macrophage that is an APC (step 3). This stimulates the T-helper cell to bind to the B-lymphocyte (step 4) and improve the B-lymphocyte response. Other ways that the T-helper cell responds are discussed in 11.1c.

Extension

Why we keep having colds

The way that memory cells function explains why most of us only develop infectious diseases such as chickenpox once during our life. The pathogens causing each of these diseases are of a single type and so are quickly identified by the memory cells when they invade the body on subsequent occasions. Cold viruses, by contrast, have over 100 different strains, which are constantly changing. New infections are therefore highly unlikely to be the same as a previous one. With no specific memory cells to stimulate antibody production, we have to wait for our slower, less intense, primary response to overcome the infection – during which time we suffer a sore throat and runny nose.

Memory cells and the secondary immune response

Memory B-cells live considerably longer than plasma cells – often for decades. These memory cells do not produce antibodies directly, but rather remain in the circulation (blood, tissue fluid, lymph and lymph nodes) until they come across the same antigen at some future date. As a result of clonal expansion there is a greater number of specific cells present in the body so the chances of coming across the antigen more quickly than the first time are increased. When they do so, they rapidly divide and develop into plasma cells and more memory B-cells. The plasma cells produce the antibodies needed to destroy the pathogens, while the new memory cells circulate and are ready for a further infection at some time in the future. In this way, memory cells provide long-term immunity against the original infection. This is known as the **secondary immune response**. It is both more rapid and of greater intensity than the primary immune response and the pathogens are destroyed before they have a chance to multiply and cause any harm to the body. This means the person may not even know that they have been infected again. Figure 3 on page 212 shows the relative quantities of antibody produced in the primary and secondary immune responses. Notice in Figure 3, that in the secondary response, the curve is much steeper and reaches a much higher level than in the primary response.

Summary test 11.1b

The **(1)** response describes the events that occur the first time an antigen on the surface of a pathogen is encountered. B-lymphocytes can be **(2)** by direct contact with the non-self antigen or by contact with **(3)** that have engulfed pathogens and can act as **(4)** cells. The B-lymphocytes carry out **(5)** to produce a clone of cells. Some of these cells are **(6)** cells that secrete **(7)**. These molecules form **(8)** complexes and cause the destruction of the pathogen. Some cells become longer-lived **(9)** cells and give us **(10)** from illness when the pathogen invades again, by carrying out a fast **(11)** response.

T-lymphocytes and cell-mediated immunity

While B-lymphocytes respond to non-self (foreign) cells and the foreign products, e.g. toxins, that they produce, T-lymphocytes respond to an organism's own cells that have been invaded by non-self material, e.g. a virus, a bacterium or a **cancer** cell. They also respond to transplanted material, which is genetically different. How then can T-lymphocytes distinguish these invader cells from normal ones? It is made possible because:

- macrophage cells that have previously engulfed a pathogen before it has infected a host cell and broken it down, present some of the proteins produced on their own outer surface
- body cells invaded by a virus also present some of the viral proteins on their own cell surface membrane
- cancer cells display non-self proteins on their cell surface membranes.

The non-self materials on the surface of all these cells act as non-self **antigens** and therefore the term **antigen-presenting cells** is used to describe them (11.1b). Figure 1 summarises how T-lymphocytes respond to a viral infection.

These pages help you to:

- describe the sequence of events occurring during a primary immune response that results in the production of T-helper cells, T-killer cells and memory cells (11.1.3)
- understand the roles of macrophages, T-helper cells and T-killer cells in the primary immune response of T-lymphocytes (11.1.3)

You will also:

- learn about T-suppressor cells
- understand why transplanted organs are rejected

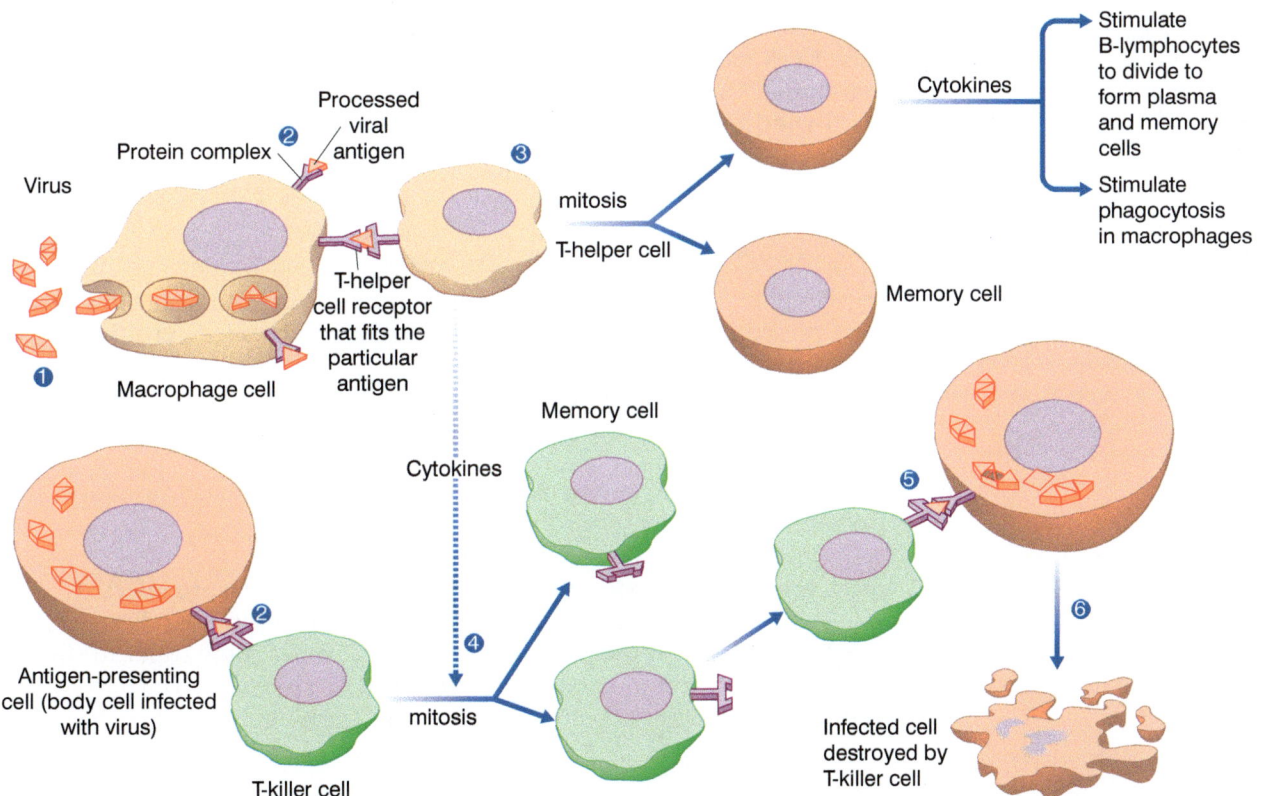

1. Viruses both invade body cells and are taken in during phagocytosis by macrophage cells.
2. Both the body cells and the macrophage cells process the viruses and present antigen for recognition by and binding to specific T-lymphocytes.
3. A T-helper cell attaches to the antigen on the surface of the macrophage cells and is stimulated to divide by mitosis (clonal expansion). Some of the new T-helper cells

develop into memory cells that survive for long periods and respond immediately to any new infection by the same virus. Other T-helper cells produce cytokines that stimulate B lymphocytes and macrophage cells.
4. The cytokines also cause T-killer cells to divide by mitosis. Some of these T-killer cells form memory cells that survive and respond immediately to any new infections by the same virus.

5. Other T-killer cells attach to any body cell presenting the viral antigen (i.e. those that are infected by the virus).
6. The attached T-killer cells produce perforins to make holes in the cell membrane and so destroy the cell, together with the viruses it contains.

Figure 1 *Summary of the role of T-lymphocytes in the immune response (cell-mediated immunity)*

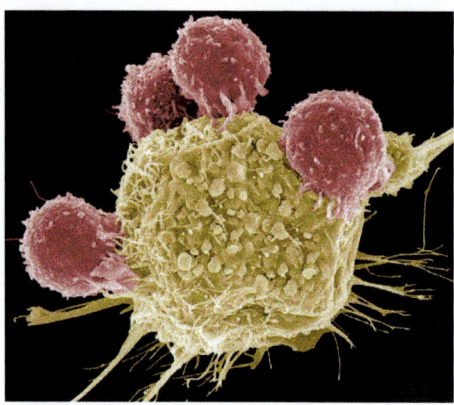

Figure 2 *Colourised scanning electron micrograph of lymphocytes (pink) attached to a cancer cell*

There are many different versions of the two main types of T-lymphocytes in the body, each of which has a different receptor protein on its surface. Although there are many similarities, the T-cell receptors are distinctly different to B-cell receptors. T-cell receptors can only bind to antigens presented on the surface of a body cell (rather than ones that are within body fluids). This type of response is called **cell-mediated immunity**.

Types of T-lymphocytes

There are two main types of T-lymphocyte:

- **T-helper cells**, which play a key role in immunity. When they attach to an antigen-presenting cell, T-helper cells secrete chemicals called **cytokines**. These cytokines:
  - stimulate macrophages to engulf pathogens and dead, infected host cells by phagocytosis. They are so effective that they are also called angry macrophages
  - stimulate B-lymphocytes to divide and develop into antibody-producing plasma cells (see 11.1b)
  - activate T-killer cells (T-cytotoxic cells).
- **T-killer cells (T-cytotoxic cells)**, which kill body cells that are infected by non-self (foreign) material. They kill by making holes in the cell surface membrane using proteins called **perforins**. These holes allow water to rush into the cell, causing it to burst. As viruses need living cells in which to reproduce, this sacrifice of body cells prevents viruses multiplying.

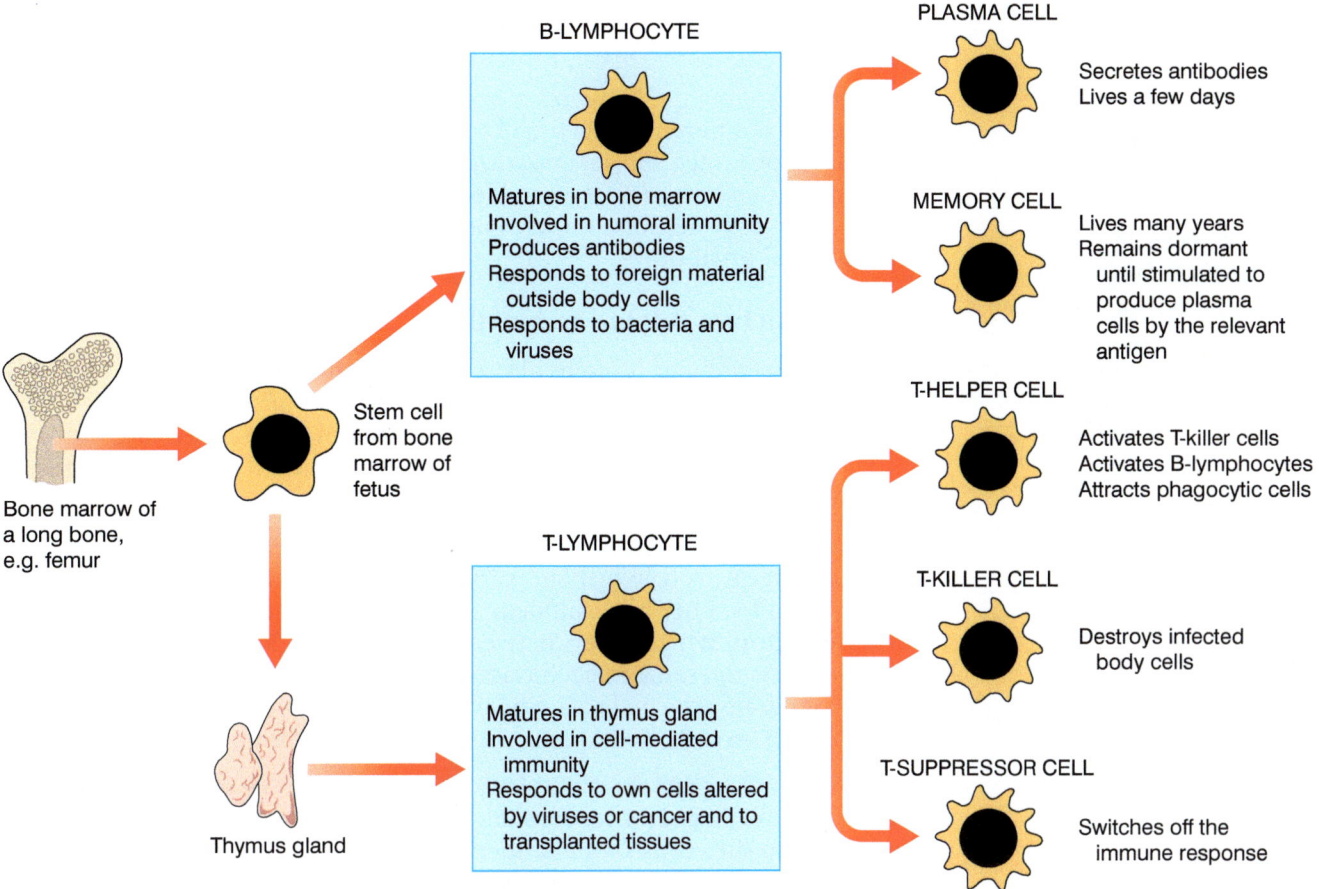

Figure 3 *The origin and roles of lymphocytes in immunity*

Both T-helper cells and T-killer cells produce their own type of **memory cells**, which circulate in the blood ready to respond to future invasions by the same pathogen. Figure 3 summarises the origin and roles of lymphocytes in immunity.

Summary test 11.1c

T-lymphocytes respond to body cells which have been infected by pathogens such as **(1)**. This type of response is called **(2)** immunity. There are a number of different types of T-lymphocytes. One type, called **(3)** cells, secretes chemicals called **(4)**, which stimulate **(5)** to engulf pathogens by **(6)** and also stimulate **(7)** to divide to form antibody-producing cells called **(8)** cells. They also stimulate another type of T-lymphocyte called **(9)** cells, which destroy pathogens.

Antibodies and vaccination
11.2
a. Antibodies and monoclonal antibodies

These pages help you to:

- relate the molecular structure of antibodies to their functions (11.2.1)
- learn the main stages in the hybridoma method for the production of monoclonal antibodies (11.2.2)
- outline the principles of using monoclonal antibodies in the diagnosis of disease (11.2.3)
- outline the principles of using monoclonal antibodies in the treatment of disease (11.2.3)

You will also:

- understand why monoclonal antibodies are important and can be used in targeted therapies

---

Remember

A B-cell receptor is an antibody molecule that is located on the cell surface membrane of a B-lymphocyte. The end of the Fc region of the antibody has a structure that allows it to remain within the hydrophobic core of the phospholipid bilayer. The antibody that is released into the circulation is fully soluble.

A pathogen invading the body has many hundreds of different antigens on its surface. Each different antigen will trigger clonal expansion in different specific B-lymphocytes and so a mixture of different antibodies is produced (polyclonal antibodies). It is of great medical benefit to produce a single type of antibody from just one clone rather than a mixture of them. These are known as **monoclonal antibodies**.

Antibody structure related to function

Antibodies are globular proteins also known as **immunoglobulins (Ig)**. An extremely large variety of antibodies is possible because they are proteins – molecules that occur in an almost infinite number of forms. There are five different classes of antibody that all share the same basic structure (Figure 1).

Antibodies are Y-shaped molecules made up of four polypeptide chains, two identical long chains called **heavy chains** and two identical shorter chains called **light chains**. A heavy chain pairs with a light chain (Figure 1). The chains are held together by disulfide bonds (2.3b). Each chain is divided into a **variable region**, which differs between different antibodies and a **constant region**, which is the same in each class of antibody. Antibodies also have some carbohydrate attached to the heavy chain and so can also be called glycoproteins. The carbohydrate portions differ in different antibodies.

The Fab section contains the variable regions of the four chains, where the two **antigen binding sites** are located, and a section of constant region. The antigen binding sites consist of a sequence of amino acids that form a specific three-dimensional shape which binds precisely to a single type of antigen.

The hinge region shown in Figure 1 is a flexible area that allows slight movement of the molecule when binding antigens.

The Fc section of the antibody contains most of the constant regions of the heavy chains only. When an antibody–antigen complex has formed, the end of the Fc region can bind to Fc receptors on phagocytes making phagocytosis of pathogens easier (see 11.1b).

The variable region differs with each antibody. It has a shape which exactly fits an antigen. Each antibody therefore can bind to two antigens.

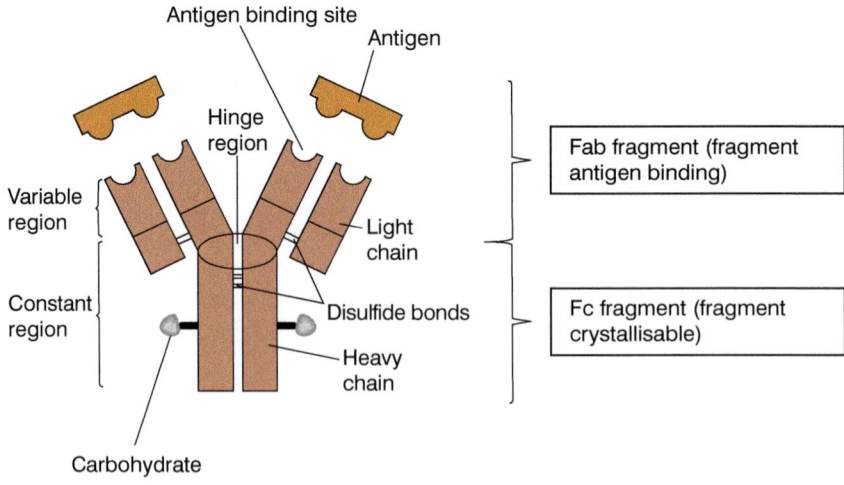

Figure 1 *Structure of an antibody molecule*

An antibody molecule can bind to an antigen on one pathogen and the same type of antigen on another pathogen. A pathogen can have a number of antigens, each of which is bound by an antibody. This leads to clumping of pathogens and so makes phagocytosis by macrophages easier.

Antibodies may also bind to a virus to prevent it entering a cell, or bind to a toxin to neutralise it.

Producing monoclonal antibodies

The production of monoclonal antibodies has long been recognised as useful. The problem had always been that B-lymphocytes are short-lived in culture and only divide inside a living body.

The production of monoclonal antibody outlined below is based on the method devised by the two scientists, Milstein and Köhler (see Extension). The method has since been refined to optimise production of different monoclonal antibodies and to improve their effectiveness. With genetic technology, we now have monoclonal antibodies that can be described as fully human products.

- A mouse is exposed to non-self material that carries the antigen against which an antibody is required.
- The different B-lymphocytes within the mouse produce a mixture of antibodies (polyclonal antibodies) and the cells are extracted from the spleen of the mouse.
- To enable these B-lymphocytes to divide outside the body, they are mixed with cells that divide readily outside the body, e.g. cells from a cancer tumour known as myeloma cells.
- A fusogen (a detergent such as polyethylene glycol) is added to the mixture to allow the cell surface membranes of both types of cell to fuse together. These fused cells are called **hybridoma** cells (Figure 2).
- The hybridoma cells are separated out and each single cell is grown into a group of genetically identical cells from the single ancestor hybridoma cell (clone). Each clone is tested to see if it is producing the required antibody.
- Any group producing the required antibody is grown on a large scale and the antibodies extracted from the growing medium.
- As these antibodies come from cells cloned from a hybridoma cell, they are monoclonal antibodies (collectively termed monoclonal antibody).
- As a mouse was used as the host organism to produce the B-lymphocytes, the monoclonal antibodies produced have to be modified to make them like human cells before they can be used – a process called **humanisation**.

Use of monoclonal antibodies in diagnosing disease

Monoclonal antibodies are a very valuable tool in diagnosing disease, with many different diagnostic products based on them. The monoclonal antibodies are highly specific for a single type of antigen so detection is very precise. They are used for the diagnosis of infectious diseases where they produce a much more rapid result than conventional methods of diagnosis. One of the most common diagnostic tests is a technique called ELISA. This technique can be used on samples to identify pathogens directly by their specific antigens. Successful binding of monoclonal antibody to specific antigens on the pathogen is detected. In indirect ELISA, monoclonal antibody is used that can bind to the antibodies produced against a non-self antigen of a pathogen (for example, in the detection of *Mycobacterium tuberculosis* and HIV). The test can distinguish between different strains of the same pathogens. They are important in diagnosing certain cancers (Figure 3). For example, men with prostate cancer often produce more of a protein called prostate specific antigen (PSA) and unusually high levels of this in the blood can be detected using monoclonal antibody. This can lead to an early diagnosis.

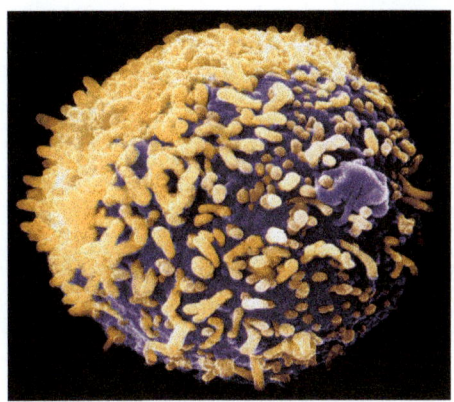

Figure 2 *Colourised scanning electron micrograph of a hybridoma cell used to produce monoclonal antibodies*

Figure 3 *Technician testing for cancer by adding monoclonal antibodies to human tissue samples*

Monoclonal antibodies can also be tagged, for example with a fluorescent dye, and be used to detect the location of diseased cells that have non-self antigens displayed on their surface.

Use of monoclonal antibodies in treatment of disease

As antibodies are very specific to particular proteins (antigens), monoclonal antibodies can be used to target specific substances and specific cells. One type of cell they can target is cancer cells. Monoclonal antibodies can be used to treat cancer in a number of ways. By far the most successful is direct monoclonal antibody therapy.

- Monoclonal antibodies are produced that are specific to an antigen on cancer cells.
- The person with cancer is treated with these monoclonal antibodies.
- The antibodies attach to the receptors on the cancer cells.
- They then block the chemical signals that stimulate the cells' uncontrolled growth.

An example is herceptin, a monoclonal antibody used to treat breast cancer. The advantage of direct monoclonal antibody therapy is that since the antibodies are not toxic, they lead to fewer side effects than other forms of therapy.

Another method, called indirect monoclonal antibody therapy, involves attaching a radioactive or cytotoxic drug (a drug that kills cells) to the monoclonal antibody. When the antibody attaches to the cancer cells, the cells are killed. In a variation on this treatment, drugs can be given in two stages:

- In stage 1, a monoclonal antibody is chemically linked to an enzyme and the antibody–enzyme complex is given to the patient and attaches itself to the surface of the cancer cells.
- In stage 2, the patient is given an inactive form of a cytotoxic drug. This drug is activated by the enzyme. As the enzyme is attached to the monoclonal antibody, and this is only found on the cancer cell, only these cells, and not the rest of the body cells, are killed by the drug.

For obvious reasons, monoclonal antibodies used in this way are referred to as 'magic bullets' and can be used in smaller doses because they are targeted on specific sites. Using them in smaller doses is not only cheaper but also reduces any side effects the drug might have. Binding of monoclonal antibody to a diseased cell may also stimulate immune system cells, for example, stimulating phagocytosis of the diseased cell by macrophages.

Some infectious diseases, such as ebola, rabies and tetanus, have been treated with specific monoclonal antibody to help add to the natural immune response. Phagocytosis by macrophages is stimulated by binding of the monoclonal antibody to the non-self antigens.

Remember

Antibodies can act as opsonins – molecules that facilitate phagocytosis by phagocytes

Summary test 11.2a

Monoclonal antibodies are produced by fusing a **(1)** lymphocyte with a cancer cell to form a **(2)** cell. These cells are allowed to divide to form a **(3)** of identical cells, which produce one type of antibody. Monoclonal antibodies are valuable in **(4)** and treating diseases. In the treatment of cancer they can be used to directly stop cancer cells dividing as in the case of **(5)** used to treat breast cancer. Alternatively, they can be used to deliver either a radioactive or a **(6)** drug to cancer cells. An antibody molecule is a **(7)** protein composed of two **(8)** and two **(9)** chains held together by **(10)**. The two antigen binding sites are located in the **(11)** fragment, which contains the **(12)** regions of the chains. The **(13)** region is flexible for binding antigen. The Fc region binds to Fc receptors on **(14)** and this makes the process of **(15)** easier.

Immunity is the ability of an organism to resist becoming ill after being infected by a pathogen. No symptoms of disease are experienced. Immunity does not mean preventing entry of the pathogen to the body. It means that the immune system can react quickly to the presence of the pathogen so that it does not cause enough harm for symptoms to occur. The destruction of the pathogen is so rapid that there is not enough time for numbers to build up and to spread to others.

Types of immunity

- **Natural immunity** is immunity which is either inherited, or acquired as part of normal life processes, e.g. as a result of having had a disease.
- **Artificial immunity** is immunity acquired as a result of the deliberate exposure of the body to **antibodies** or **antigens** in non-natural circumstances (situations), e.g. **vaccination** (Figure 1).

Both natural and artificial immunity may be passively or actively acquired.

- **Passive immunity** is immunity acquired from the introduction of antibodies from another source, rather than one's own immune system. It is generally short-lived.
- **Active immunity** is immunity resulting from the activities of an individual's own immune system, rather than an outside source. It is generally long-lasting.

Passive immunity

- **Natural passive immunity** occurs when an individual receives antibodies from their mother. Antibodies may cross the placenta to a fetus, or may be in the mother's milk during suckling (breast feeding in humans).
- **Artificial passive immunity** occurs when antibodies from another source are injected. The source could be antibodies harvested from another individual or from monoclonal antibody production. This treatment is commonly given to prevent disease from occurring when a person is suspected of having been infected by a pathogen.

Passive immunity is short-lived as only antibody is given and there is no opportunity for memory cell formation.

The antibodies will only last for a few months and will not give protection after this time. Figure 2 (see next page) shows the changes in antibody concentration over time with passive and active immunity.

Active immunity

- **Natural active immunity** results from an individual becoming infected with a disease under normal circumstances. The body produces its own antibodies, and may continue to do so for many years. It is for this reason that many people suffer diseases such as chickenpox only once in a lifetime. The immunity results from the activities of memory cells (11.1b).
- **Artificial active immunity** forms the basis of immunisation. It involves inducing an immune response in an individual, without them having the symptoms of the disease. This is achieved by introducing the appropriate disease antigens into the body, either by injection or by mouth. The process is called **vaccination,** and the material introduced is called **vaccine**. The immune response to the antigen means that memory cells are produced to give long-term protection. Invasion by the actual pathogen for the first time will be treated as a secondary immune response rather than a primary immune response. There are four forms of vaccine (see 11.2c).

These pages help you to:

- understand and describe the differences between active immunity and passive immunity and between natural immunity and artificial immunity (11.2.4)
- explain how long-term immunity can be gained as a result of the stimulation of immune responses from exposure to antigens in vaccines (11.2.5)
- explain how vaccination programmes can help to control the spread of infectious diseases (11.2.6)

You will also:

- understand what is meant by immunity
- understand the importance of immunity in children

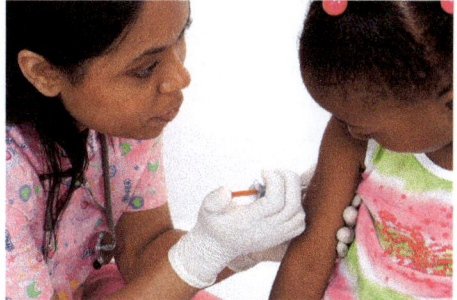

Figure 1 *Vaccination programmes for children have considerably reduced deaths from infectious diseases*

Remember

Artificial passive immunity should prevent infectious disease so that a person does not become ill.

Giving antibodies to a person who is already ill is not providing them with passive immunity, it is a form of treatment of disease (see treatment of disease using monoclonal antibodies in 11.2a).

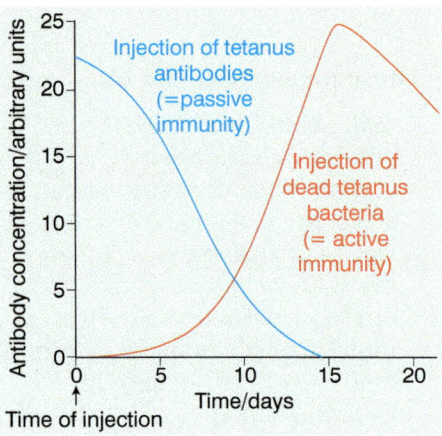

Figure 2 *Graph showing the concentration of tetanus antibodies, over time, with active and passive immunity*

Remember

Immunity may be naturally acquired (obtained) or artificially induced (caused). The process of artificially inducing immunity is known as **immunisation**.

Summary test 11.2b

Where immunity is acquired naturally, it is referred to as **(1)** immunity. It may also be acquired from the introduction of antibodies from someone else or another source rather than an individual's own immune system, in which case it is said to be **(2)** immunity. Where immunity is given by deliberately exposing the body to antibodies, it is known as artificial immunity. Artificial active immunity forms the basis of immunisation, where antigens are introduced into the body as part of the process known as **(3)**. Of the various forms of immunity, the full name of each of the following examples is: via the placenta as a fetus, called **(4)** immunity; injecting microorganisms weakened by heat treatment, called **(5)** immunity; and injecting antibodies, such as those from the tetanus bacterium, called **(6)** immunity.

Vaccination and the immune response

The response to the antigen in the vaccine is a primary immune response, with the activation of lymphocytes leading to production of antibody and long-lived memory cells. The rapid secondary immune response occurs on invasion by the actual pathogen. This time there are many more specific lymphocytes present as memory cells, so activation of a greater proportion of these than the primary immune response will lead to a steeper increase in the concentration of antibody and a far higher level.

Immunity in children

As most immunity has to be acquired, either naturally or artificially, it follows that children, and especially newborn babies, are particularly at risk from infection. It takes many years for an individual to build up immunity to a wide variety of diseases. Why then is it that deaths from infections in young humans are not as common as might be expected? There are a number of reasons:

- Even before birth, a fetus has immunity to certain diseases. This is because the placenta allows some antibodies, e.g. anti-measles ones to pass across from the mother's circulation into the circulation of the fetus (natural passive immunity). This immunity only lasts for a short period after birth – in the case of measles for around four months.
- The milk formed by the mother during the first few days after birth contains antibodies. This early breast milk, called **colostrum**, has a high concentration of antibodies belonging to the class Immunoglobulin A (IgA). These antibodies both remain in the intestines and are absorbed into the blood providing temporary immunity to a variety of pathogens both inside the intestines and within the body (natural passive immunity). Breast milk produced after this time contains a lower concentration of antibodies.
- In many countries there are programmes of vaccination designed to artificially induce immunity at the most appropriate stage of a child's development.

Table 1 *Summary of different types of immunity*

	Natural Acquired naturally, not deliberately	Artificial Acquired deliberately by exposure to antibody or antigen
Passive Results from the introduction of antibodies from another source, rather than one's own immune system (no immune response) Short-lived but immediate protection	Antibodies pass from mother • to fetus via placenta • to baby during suckling	Antibodies from a different source (monoclonal antibody or another individual) are injected
Active Results from the activities of an individual's own immune system and immune response occurs Long-lasting but takes time	Antibodies acquired as a result of a previous infection producing B-lymphocyte memory cells, which are reactivated on the second infection T-lymphocyte memory cells are also present and reactivated	Antigens are injected or given orally as a vaccine. They induce the body to produce its own antibodies to the pathogen. Memory cells are also formed. Vaccine may contain • dead pathogen • attenuated pathogen • genetically engineered antigens

There are many different types of vaccination programme:

- It can be a goverment-organised schedule for individuals throughout childhood and teenage years. The aim is to give children protection from the most common (and often most harmful) infectious diseases that they are likely to come across throughout their lives.
- It can be a programme designed for a particular group of people that are considered to be at risk of a particular disease, such as people living in overcrowded areas where tuberculosis is a problem, or in regions of a country where a disease is endemic.
- It can form an emergency response to an outbreak of a particular disease that threatens to spread, such as a cholera outbreak following a natural disaster or war, or a measles outbreak in a country where not enough people have been vaccinated to prevent spread of the disease.

Using vaccination programmes to control the spread of disease

Vaccination is a very effective method to prevent the transmission cycle of a disease. The more people that are vaccinated against a particular disease, the less likely the disease will spread. This is because a vaccinated person is highly likely to be immune to the disease and will not pass on the pathogen to an uninfected person. A vulnerable (at risk) person who does not have immunity who is surrounded by those that do, is unlikely to have the disease. In addition, a small outbreak of the disease is unlikely to have any effect and will quickly die out. This concept is known as herd immunity and involves:

- vaccination of a large group of people
- resistance to becoming ill by infection from a pathogen (immunity)
- avoidance of spread of disease
- protection of people who do not have immunity.

The aim of a vaccination programme is to get 100% of the targeted group of people to have the vaccine. Some people do not respond to vaccines, so will not be immune. Others will have a weak response and still be at risk, for example people who are malnourished. Of all of the vaccinations given, only 95% might be effective, that is only 95% of the people receiving the vaccine will be immune. In practice, it is not possible to vaccinate 100% of a targeted group, so the aim is to vaccinate as many people as possible and reach a target percentage that has been calculated as the threshold value to prevent spread. This value is calculated by considering a number of factors, such as:

- some infectious diseases are easily transmitted
- some infectious diseases affect certain age groups more than others
- some vaccines are less effective than others.

A disease such as measles requires a very high percentage of the population to be effectively immunised, and so the calculated value is 93–95% of the population need to be vaccinated to prevent spread. However, for those who have two doses of the MMR (measle, mumps, rubella) vaccine, up to 99% will be protected from measles.

Vaccination for the control of the spread of disease is also effective because most vaccines will provide protection for many years. Some may require repeated, or booster, vaccine doses. These make sure that numbers of specific memory cells remains high.

These pages help you to:

- explain how vaccination programmes can help to control the spread of infectious diseases (11.2.6)

You will also:

- learn about the success of the vaccination programme against smallpox
- read about the different types of vaccine available

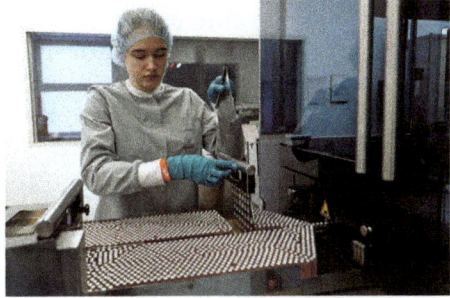

Figure 1 *The production of new vaccines is a highly technological process requiring an extremely high standard of hygiene*

Remember

A vaccine is the preparation containing the non-self antigen in one form or another that will provoke an immune response in the person to be protected against disease. The aim of a vaccine is to give immunity to a particular infectious disease.

Vaccination is the treatment given using vaccines that aims to prevent a person from becoming ill from an infectious disease.

For general protection, vaccination programmes are designed to give protection against particular diseases at the correct time of an individual's life. Vaccines against the whole range of diseases on a public health schedule cannot all be given all at once and it makes sense to protect the most vulnerable age group and so maximise the prevention of spread. The programme begins with babies who have vaccinations against diseases at which there is the greatest risk (see Extension). At the appropriate times through childhood and as young adults other vaccines and booster doses are given. For example, meningococcal disease is more likely to spread between older teenagers and young adults, so a vaccine for this is given in the teenage years. Elderly people are at risk from shingles (*Herpes zoster*) and have this vaccine later in life.

Features of a successful vaccination programme

To be effective, a programme of vaccination depends upon:

- **A suitable vaccine** being economically available and enough of the vaccine being available to immunise all of the vulnerable (at risk) population.
- **Few, if any, side effects** from vaccination. Unpleasant side effects may discourage individuals in the population from being vaccinated.
- **The mechanisms to produce, store and transport the vaccine**. This normally involves technologically advanced equipment (Figure 1 on page 221), hygienic conditions and refrigerated transport. Many vaccines are not thermostable and require storage conditions that will prevent them degrading. Freeze-dried vaccines have good thermostability.
- **The means of administering (giving) the vaccine properly at the appropriate time**. This involves training staff, at different centres, to be able to give the vaccine in the correct way and at the right time.
- **The ability to vaccinate the vast majority (all, if possible) of the vulnerable population**. This is best done at one time so that the transmission of the **pathogen** is interrupted because for a certain period there are no individuals in the population with the disease (herd immunity).

Why vaccination does not eliminate a disease

Even where these criteria for successful vaccination are met, it can still prove extremely difficult to eradicate a disease. The reasons for this include:

- Vaccination fails to induce immunity in certain individuals, e.g. ones with defective immune systems that do not produce the necessary **clones** of B- and T-lymphocytes (11.1b and 11.1c) or ones whose diet lacks protein (malnourished).
- Individuals may develop the disease immediately after vaccination, but before their immunity levels are high enough to fight it. These individuals may harbour the pathogen and reinfect others.

Extension

Types of vaccine

Although you do not need to know the different types of vaccine, it is useful to aid your understanding of the immune response by considering how vaccines help to give immunity.

Dead microorganisms or parts of microorganisms

Pathogenic bacteria that have been grown in culture are killed by heat or by chemicals. Similarly, viruses can be cultured in host tissue in culture and inactivated. The whole organism or parts of the organism can be used. There is no chance of causing illness. They will be unable to replicate in the body. However they are able to cause an immune response and bring about immunity to the disease as the non-self antigens are still present. The immune response may not be as strong as with living microorganisms, and for some pathogens no immune response will occur so this type of vaccine is not appropriate. As they will not replicate in the body fewer specific lymphocytes may come across them to become activated and a proportion may be destroyed by phagocytosis by phagocytes.

Living attenuated strains of microorganism

Living microorganisms are treated in some way so that they do not cause symptoms of disease, for example, they are made weaker by culturing for many generations, or are heat-treated or chemicals are used to make them non-pathogenic. Sometimes a non-pathogenic strain can be used that still has the non-self antigens that will provoke an immune response. Although harmless, they stimulate a strong response by the body's immune system as they are able to increase in numbers and a higher proportion of specific lymphocytes will be activated to form memory cells.

Toxoids

These are modified toxins. The toxins are chemicals released by pathogenic organisms and it is these that cause the symptoms of disease rather than the actual organism. The toxins are harvested from a culture and are made harmless by heat or chemical treatment. It is the modified toxin, or toxoid that is the antigen that stimulates the immune response.

Genetically engineered antigens of microorganisms

Genes coding for antigens can be transferred from the genome of the pathogen into a host organism. The genetically engineered host organisms can be cultured on a large scale in fermenters and large quantities of the antigen can be separated and purified for use in a vaccine.

Some vaccines given today against a particular pathogen contain more than one type of preparation in a single vaccine. For some pathogens, there is a choice of which type of vaccine to use. It is becoming increasingly common to give a single injection containing vaccine preparations for more than one pathogen, for example about 100 countries give the '6-in-one' vaccine to babies. This is for protection against diptheria, hepatitis B, haemophilus influenza type b, polio, tetanus and pertussis (whooping cough). The MMR injection contains preparations against measles, mumps and rubella (German measles).

- The disease-causing agent (pathogen) may mutate frequently, so that its **antigens** change suddenly (antigenic shift) as opposed to gradually (antigenic drift). This means that vaccines suddenly become ineffective as the **antibodies** they induce the immune system to produce no longer recognise the new antigens on the pathogen. This happens with the influenza virus, which changes its antigens frequently.
- There may be so many varieties of a particular pathogen that it is all but impossible to develop a vaccine that is effective against them all. The common cold has over 100 types, for example.
- There are, as yet, no established vaccines against pathogens that are **eukaryotes**. However, the vaccination programme against malaria, which is being trialled in some countries in Africa (see 10.1e) is a recent major achievement and there are hopes that this will be extended to other areas.
- Certain pathogens 'hide away' from the body's immune system, either by concealing themselves inside cells, or by living in places out of reach (antigenic concealment), such as within the intestines, e.g. the cholera pathogen (10.1d).
- Some pathogens suppress the body's immune system, so stimulating it through vaccination is ineffective, e.g. human immunodeficiency virus (10.1b).
- Some vaccines require booster (repeated) doses for full immunity and some people may not have these, e.g. living in remote areas and not being able to get to health centres, being displaced because of war or natural disaster.
- There may be objections to vaccination for religious, ethical or medical reasons. For example, concerns over the Measles, Mumps and Rubella (MMR) triple vaccine led a number of parents to opt for separate vaccinations for their children, or to avoid vaccination altogether. Here, education and informative advertising is important in helping parents make choices (Figure 2).

Figure 2 *Posters promoting child vaccination programmes are used to encourage parents to have their children immunised*

Extension

Smallpox – the last Jenneration!

The first ever vaccinations were carried out by Edward Jenner in 1794, against smallpox, and this very same disease was the first to be completely eradicated from the world, by the same process, in 1977. Some of the reasons for the success of the vaccination programme included:

- There was a simple, safe, easily stored vaccine against smallpox.
- The smallpox vaccine was easily and economically produced and simply administered.
- As a live vaccine, it was especially effective in producing immunity.
- The smallpox virus did not mutate or change its antigens and so the vaccine was always effective and the same vaccine could be used anywhere across the globe.
- The lethal nature of the disease (up to 30% of the victims died) encouraged people to be involved in the vaccination programme.
- There was a concerted worldwide vaccination programme, coordinated by the World Health Organization.

Summary test 11.2c

A vaccination programme aims to give individuals **(1)** against an infectious disease. If enough people are vaccinated then spread of disease is prevented or limited by an effect known as **(2)**. One feature of a successful vaccination programme is a vaccine that has few **(3)** so that individuals are not discouraged from taking part in the programme. A vaccine that is **(4)** is thermostable and is likely to last longer. Mass vaccination programmes may be required as an emergency measure, for example **(5)**. Not everyone that has a vaccination will have an immune response. For example, a person who is **(6)** and who does not get enough protein in their diet. Some vaccination programmes require repeated doses of vaccine, or **(7)**.

Launch additional digital resources for the chapter

11 Exam-style questions

1 Which set of descriptions relates to antibodies (immunoglobulins) during a normal immune response? *(1 mark)*

	bound to cell surface membrane of B-lymphocytes	circulating free dissolved in blood plasma	bound to antigen and attached to Fc receptor on phagocyte	attached to T-cell antigen receptor
A	x	✓	X	✓
B	✓	✓	✓	X
C	X	X	✓	✓
D	✓	✓	X	X

2 a Figure 1 shows the structure of an antibody molecule.

Figure 1

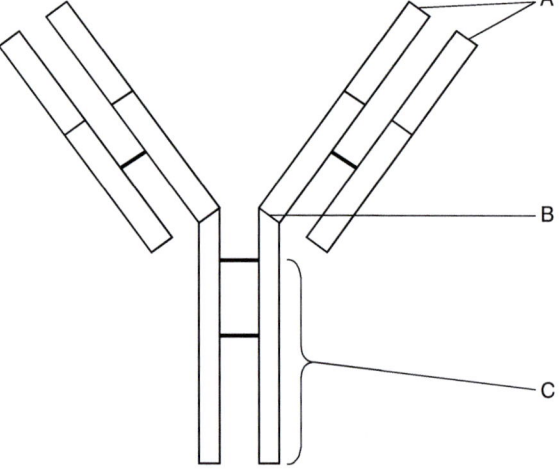

   i   Name the parts of the antibody molecule labelled **A**, **B** and **C**. *(3 marks)*

   ii Explain how you know the antibody molecule shown in Figure 1 has a quaternary structure. *(1 mark)*

b Monoclonal antibodies (MAbs) are used both in diagnosis and in treatment of disease.

   i   Outline how monoclonal antibodies are produced. *(4 marks)*

   ii Monoclonal antibodies can be designed to bind to a protein on diseased cells, so causing their destruction by cells of the person's immune system. An example of this type of monoclonal antibody is Mabthera (rituximab), used in the treatment of the cancer chronic lymphocytic leukaemia (CLL). Suggest how the binding of monoclonal antibody, such as Mabthera, to cancer cells causes their destruction by cells of the person's immune system. *(4 marks)*

   (Total 12 marks)

3 Globally, measles is an important disease that mainly affects children. Many deaths from measles occur in children under five years of age.

a Young children worldwide are routinely vaccinated against measles and other infectious diseases. Explain how vaccination can control infectious diseases. *(3 marks)*

b Figure 2 is a graph from the World Health Organization (WHO) showing the global annual reported cases of measles as well as the percentage of children vaccinated against measles over 39 years from 1980 to 2018.

   • The number of new cases are the numbers of reported new cases of measles worldwide (in millions) in the given year.

   • The percentage immunisation coverage represents children under one year of age who have been given at least one dose of the vaccine against measles in the given year.

Vaccination is known to protect populations against infectious diseases. Some of the data in Figure 2 supports this statement. Describe the data that supports this statement **and** comment on the data that does **not** support this statement. *(4 marks)*

   (Total 7 marks)

Figure 2

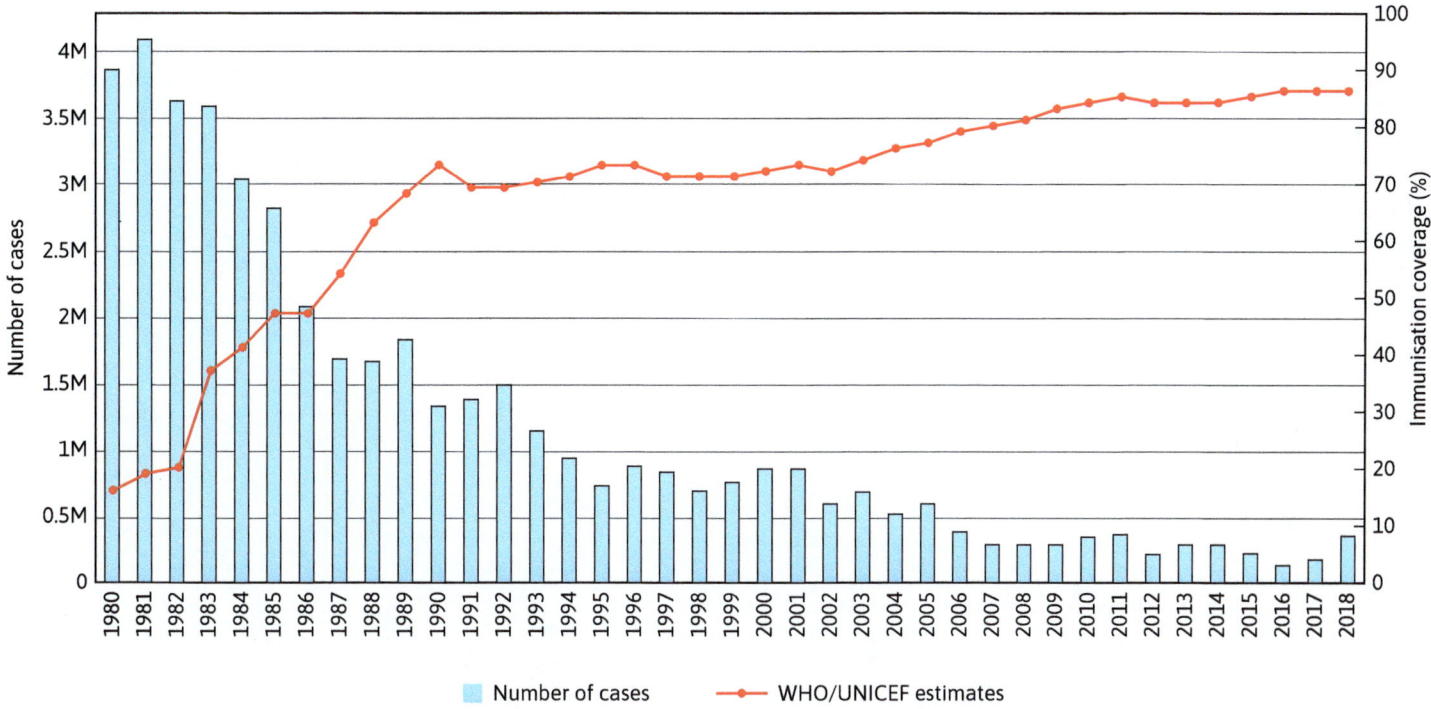

Number of cases ● WHO/UNICEF estimates

11 Practice questions

4 a State two differences between a specific and a non-specific defence mechanism.

b Distinguish between self antigens and non-self antigens.

c Explain why, after a pathogen gains entry to the body, it is often a number of days before the body's immune system begins to control it.

5 a Explain why the secondary immune response is much more rapid than the primary one.

b Name the two main cell types that carry out phagocytosis.

c Describe how the structure of a plasma cell is suited to its function.

d Suggest why proteins, rather than carbohydrates or fats, have evolved as the molecules of which antibodies are made.

6 a State what is meant by an antigen.

b State two similarities of T-lymphocytes and B-lymphocytes.

c Name two types of T-lymphocyte.

7 a Place the statements **A** to **E** in the correct sequence.

A B-lymphocytes are activated.

B Plasma cells secrete antibodies.

C Antigens are presented.

D Macrophages engulf pathogens and process antigens.

E Clonal expansion occurs.

b Describe the structure of an antibody molecule.

8 Figure 3 below shows part of the process occurring in an immune response.

Figure 3

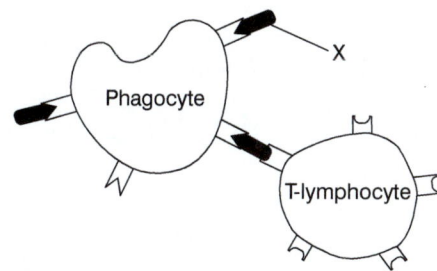

a What is the name of the structure labelled X?

b Give an alternative name for the cell labelled phagocyte.

c State the type of T-lymphocyte shown in Figure 3.

d This type of T-lymphocyte divides by mitosis to form long-lasting cells. Name these long-lasting cells.

e The T-lymphocytes secretes chemicals called cytokines. State two effects of cytokines.

9 a Immunity is the ability of organisms to resist infection. It can be divided into two types – active and passive. Distinguish between active and passive immunity.

b Many diseases can be controlled through vaccination programmes to achieve herd immunity. Explain what is meant by herd immunity.

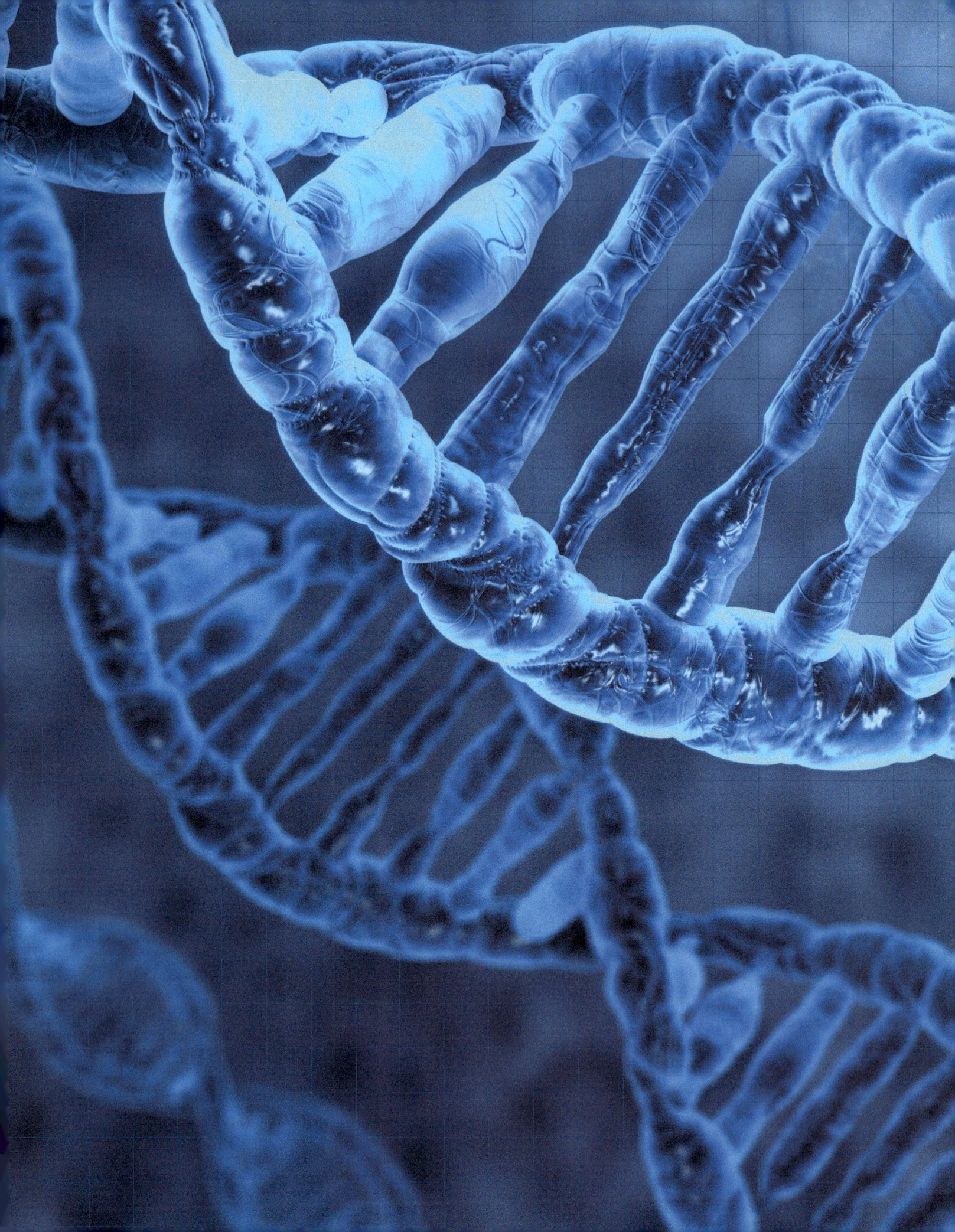

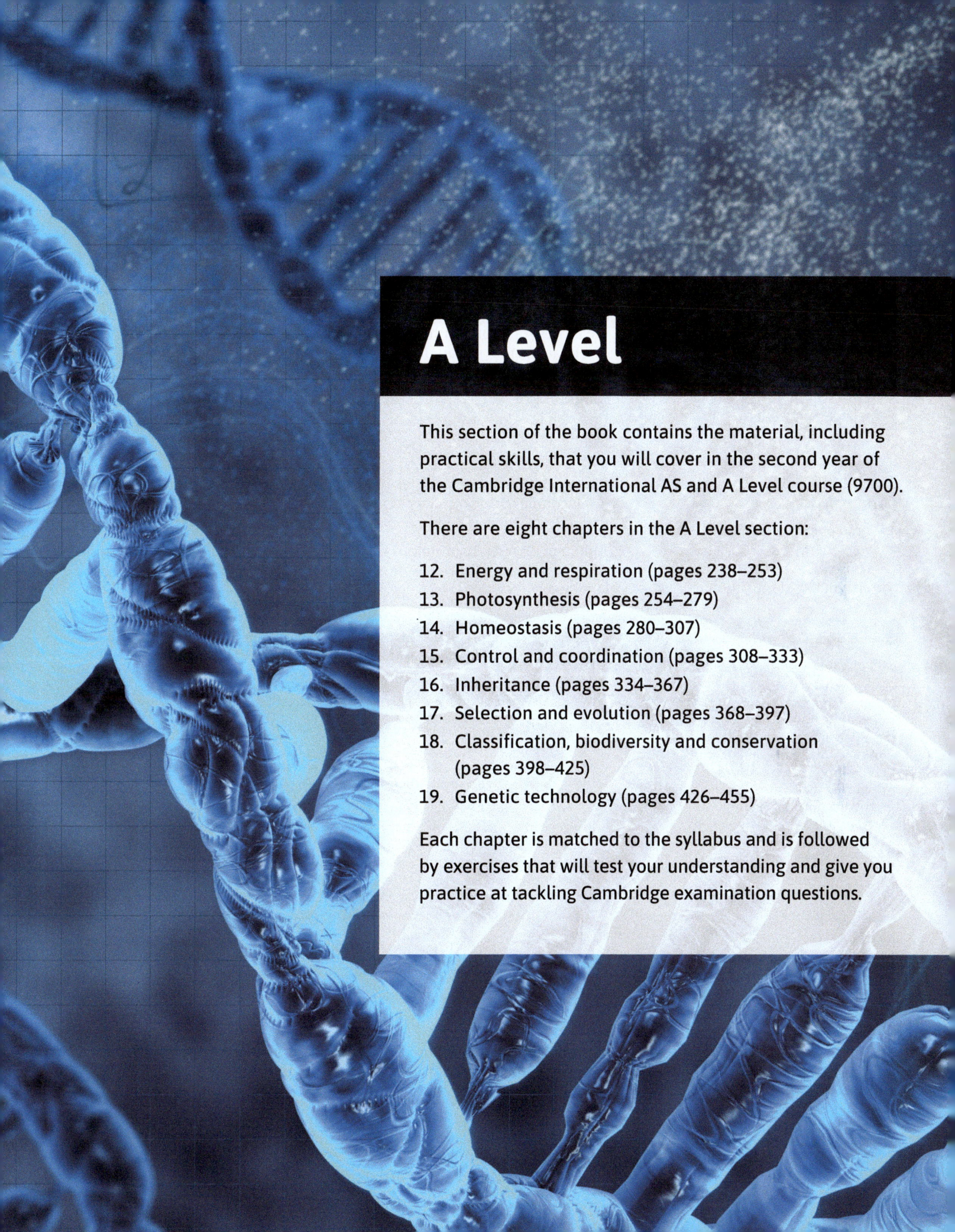

A Level

This section of the book contains the material, including practical skills, that you will cover in the second year of the Cambridge International AS and A Level course (9700).

There are eight chapters in the A Level section:

Each chapter is matched to the syllabus and is followed by exercises that will test your understanding and give you practice at tackling Cambridge examination questions.

12.1 | Energy

a. The need for energy

The flow of energy through living systems

All living organisms require energy in order to remain alive. The input of energy to the Earth is solar energy from the Sun. However, only some organisms, known as photoautotrophs, can make use of this energy to synthesise (produce) complex organic biological compounds from carbon dioxide and water through the process of photosynthesis (Chapter 13). Plants, some protoctists (1.2a and 18.1b) and some prokaryotes are photosynthetic organisms.

Heterotrophs are not able to convert light energy to chemical energy. They rely completely on autotrophs to carry out this conversion and supply them with the complex organic molecules that they will use as a source of energy for their metabolic needs.

Respiration is a process that occurs in all organisms. This is the process that breaks down the complex organic molecules to release energy for the production of the molecule adenosine triphosphate or ATP. It is this molecule that all cells need as an immediate source of energy to perform useful work.

Although there is an enormous variety of life on Earth, all living organisms use ATP as their energy currency, and for this reason it is known as the universal energy currency.

These pages help you to:

- explain why living organisms need energy, including reference to active transport, movement and anabolic reactions (12.1.1)
- understand that living organisms need energy for DNA replication and protein synthesis, and that these processes involve anabolic reactions (12.1.1)
- understand that ATP is the universal energy currency (12.1.2)

You will also:

- understand what is meant by free energy
- consolidate understanding of enzymes and activation energy

Extension

Chemoautotrophs

Some prokaryotes are chemoautotrophs. They use carbon dioxide as their carbon source to synthesise organic compounds and the source of energy for this comes from a chemical reaction involving inorganic substances such as hydrogen sulfide, ammonia or ferrous iron. Chemoautotrophs have been found in the most extreme environments, such as deep-sea vents and acidic hot springs.

Extension

What is energy?

Energy, which is measured in joules (J), is defined as 'the ability to do work'. It cannot be created or destroyed. It can be considered to exist in two states:

- **Kinetic energy** is the energy of motion. Moving objects perform work by making other objects move.
- **Potential energy** is stored energy. An object that is not moving may still have the capacity to do so and therefore possesses potential energy.

When one form of energy is converted to another some is lost as heat and is no longer available to do useful work. Energy that is available to do work under conditions of constant temperature and pressure is called **free energy**. If the products of a reaction contain more energy than the reactants and free energy must be supplied to make the reaction happen, it is known as an **endergonic (endothermic) reaction**. Reactions in which the products have less energy than the reactants and therefore energy is released, are known as **exergonic (exothermic) reactions**.

Remember

All the reactions that take place within organisms are collectively known as **metabolism**. These reactions are of two types:

- **Anabolism** is the build up of larger, more complex molecules from smaller, simpler ones – a process requiring energy.
- **Catabolism** is the breakdown of complex molecules into simpler ones, with the release of energy.

Activation energy

Before any chemical reaction can proceed it must be initially activated, i.e. its energy must be increased. The energy required is called the **activation energy**. Catalysts, such as enzymes, lower this activation energy (3.1a) and enable reactions to take place more rapidly and/or at lower temperatures. These events are summarised in Figure 1.

Respiration is a process that involves a sequence of reactions that are each catalysed by a specific enzyme. Without the presence of these enzymes and their ability to lower activation energy, the cell would not be able to produce enough ATP for its metabolic needs.

Why do organisms need energy?

The energy provided by ATP is needed for many different processes. These include:

- **Anabolic reactions** in which smaller, more simple molecules are built up into larger, more complex ones (see also 2.1a). For example:
  - During DNA replication: Unwinding the DNA double helix to obtain template strands requires energy. Energy is also required to produce the activated free DNA nucleotides that are then used to form the new polynucleotide strand. The energy released when the additional phosphates are removed is used to form phosphodiester bonds, catalysed by DNA polymerase.
  - For protein synthesis: A large proportion of a cell's energy supply is used up in protein synthesis (6.2c). Here, ATP is used for charging amino acids before they are brought to the ribosome by tRNA molecules (tRNA aminoacylation). The energy is required for the condensation reactions that occur when amino acids are joined by peptide bonds at the ribosome.
  - For the synthesis of other macromolecules: The synthesis of other macromolecules requires energy provided by ATP, such as the synthesis of RNA polynucleotides, polysaccharide synthesis from monosaccharides and the synthesis of lipids.

- **Movement** both within an organism and of the organism itself:
  - **Muscle contraction** (15.1j) requires energy to allow the protein filaments of striated muscle, actin and myosin, to slide past one another to cause the shortening of the overall length of muscle fibres. Contraction of cardiac muscle of the heart ventricles allows blood to flow round the body; and contraction of skeletal muscle allows organisms to move.
  - **Movement of cilia and flagella** needs energy. We have seen that the synchronous movement of cilia in the airways of the gas exchange system moves a layer of mucus towards the top of the trachea (9.1b). Many bacterial cells, including *Vibrio cholerae*, have a flagellum that allows the cell to move in aquatic environments.
  - **Movement of vesicles** along microtubules within the cell, for example in moving Golgi vesicles to the cell surface membrane for exocytosis of secretory products, requires energy.
  - **Organisation of microtubules** to form the spindle in mitosis and in meiosis is an energy-requiring process.
- **Active transport** of ions and molecules against a concentration gradient across membranes, such as the cell surface membrane and the tonoplast. This is an essential role, as every cell must maintain a precise ionic concentration. A membrane protein, Na^+/K^+-ATPase (the **sodium–potassium pump**), is an enzyme that can hydrolyse ATP to release energy to pump 3 sodium ions out of a cell and 2 potassium ions into a cell. Although all cells have sodium–potassium pumps in their cell surface membranes, they are particularly important in neurones and nerve cells to conduct impulses (15.1d).
- **Maintenance, repair and division** of cells and the organelles within them.
- **Maintenance of body temperature** in birds and mammals. These organisms are **endothermic** and need energy to replace that lost as heat to the surrounding environment.

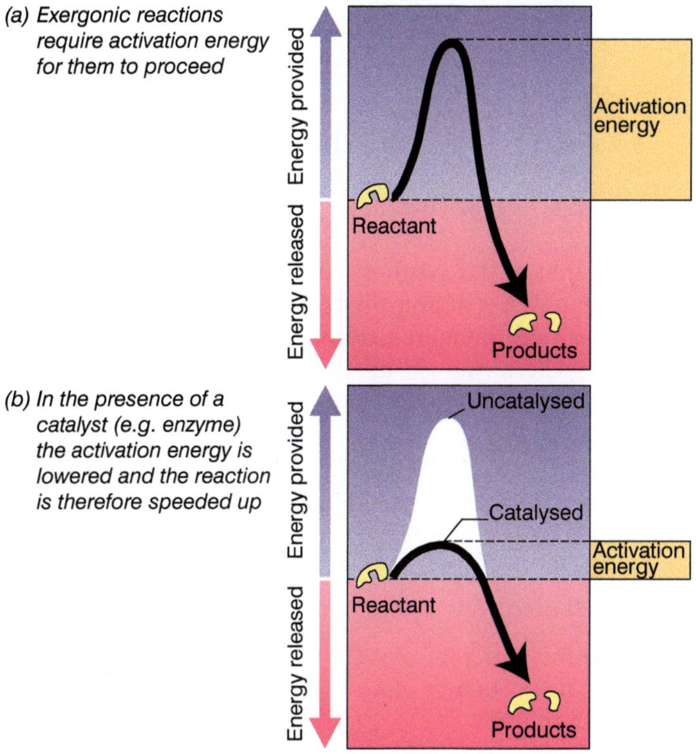

(a) Exergonic reactions require activation energy for them to proceed

(b) In the presence of a catalyst (e.g. enzyme) the activation energy is lowered and the reaction is therefore speeded up

Figure 1 *Effects of catalysts on activation energy*

Summary test 12.1a

Energy is defined as the ability to do **(1)**. The energy of motion is known as **(2)** energy, whereas **(3)** energy is stored energy. Living organisms need energy for many reasons, including **(4)** reactions in which simple molecules are built up into complex ones and the movement of material by **(5)** against a concentration gradient. Living organisms also use energy for movement and the maintenance of **(6)** in birds and mammals. Before a chemical reaction can take place energy must be provided; this is known as **(7)** energy. The process that converts **(8)** energy from the Sun into chemical energy and results in the synthesis of complex **(9)** molecules is known as **(10)**. When these molecules are broken down in the process of **(11)**, energy is released to synthesise **(12)** molecules for use by the cell.

These pages help you to:

- describe the features of ATP that make it suitable as the universal energy currency (12.1.2)
- learn that ATP is synthesised by the transfer of phosphate in substrate-linked reactions and by chemiosmosis in membranes of mitochondria and chloroplasts (12.1.3)
- explain the relative energy values of carbohydrate, lipid and protein as respiratory substrates (12.1.4)

You will also:

- revise the structure of ATP
- revise the structure of a mitochondrion

Structure of adenosine triphosphate (ATP)

The ATP molecule (Figure 1) is a phosphorylated nucleotide and it has three parts:

- **Adenine** – a nitrogen-containing organic base belonging to the group called purines.
- **Ribose** – a sugar molecule with a 5-carbon ring structure (pentose sugar) that acts as the backbone to which the other parts are attached.
- **Phosphates** – a chain of three phosphate groups.

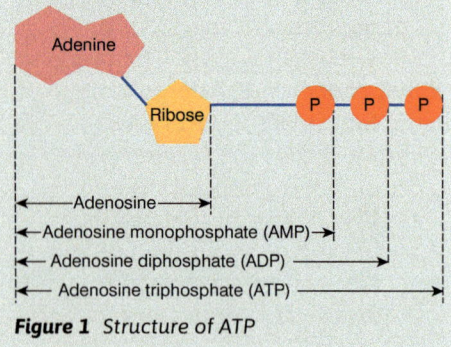

Figure 1 *Structure of ATP*

ATP as the universal energy currency

ATP functions as an energy transfer molecule, and almost every energy-requiring process in cells uses ATP. It is used by all organisms in all cells. Some of the features that help to explain why ATP is suitable as the universal energy currency include:

- it is always present in cells as a product of respiration
- a one-step reaction provides an immediate source of energy (see below)
- it is easily hydrolysed to release a relatively large quantity of energy (see below)
- a constant supply of ATP is possible as it is recycled from ADP, which is easily phosphorylated (see Figure 2)
- it is a relatively small molecule that can move around the cell with ease
- it is a water-soluble molecule so it can take part in metabolic reactions
- the quantity of energy released and the efficiency of recycling ATP means that the needs of the cell can be satisfied.

It is the three phosphate groups that are the key to how ATP is the energy currency of the cell. Each one is very negatively charged and so they repel one another. This makes the **covalent bonds** that link them rather unstable. These unstable covalent bonds have a low activation energy, which means they are easily broken. When they do break they release a considerable quantity of energy – $30.5\,kJ\,mol^{-1}$ for each of the first two phosphates removed and $14.2\,kJ\,mol^{-1}$ for the removal of the final phosphate. The terminal phosphate is removed according to the enzyme-catalysed reversible equation:

$$\underset{\substack{\text{adenosine}\\\text{triphosphate}}}{\text{ATP}} + \underset{\text{water}}{\text{H}_2\text{O}} \rightleftharpoons \underset{\substack{\text{adenosine}\\\text{diphosphate}}}{\text{ADP}} + \underset{\substack{\text{inorganic}\\\text{phosphate}}}{\text{P}_i} + \underset{\text{energy}}{30.5\,\text{kJ}}$$

Synthesis of ATP

The conversion of ATP to ADP is a reversible reaction (Figure 2) and therefore energy can be used to add an inorganic phosphate to ADP to re-form ATP. Although a cell will have a high turnover (use) rate of ATP, it is rapidly re-formed from ADP and inorganic phosphate (Pi). This means that cells do not need to store large quantities of ATP, but rather just maintain a few seconds' supply (see Extension). The interconversion rate of ATP and ADP is phenomenal. Although there are only around 50 g of ATP in the human body at any point in time, it is thought that, even at rest, a single human uses 65 kg of ATP in a 24-hour period. This means that, on average, a single ATP molecule undergoes around 1300 cycles of synthesis and **hydrolysis** each day. ATP is produced during photosynthesis as well as during respiration. Light energy cannot directly be used to produce complex organic molecules, so ATP is synthesised and can be used as an energy source for the production of these molecules.

As the synthesis of ATP from ADP involves the addition of a phosphate molecule, it is a **phosphorylation** reaction. This phosphorylation occurs in two main ways: substrate-linked phosphorylation and chemiosmosis.

Substrate-linked phosphorylation

This involves the transfer of phosphate groups from donor molecules to ADP to make ATP. The glycolysis stage of respiration (12.2a) in aerobic and in anaerobic conditions produces ATP in this way. Also, in aerobic conditions, substrate-linked phosphorylation occurs within the matrix of the mitochondrion (12.2b). These phosphorylation reactions are catalysed by enzymes.

Chemiosmosis

This involves the build up of an electrochemical gradient across a membrane. In **chemiosmosis** involving ATP production, the electrochemical gradient (see Remember box) is produced by accumulating (building up) protons (hydrogen ions). The force that is generated by the gradient is known as a proton motive force. The protons flood through a membrane protein known as the ATP synthase complex and this drives the synthesis of ATP from ADP and inorganic phosphate. This ATP is formed using a diffusion force that resembles osmosis, which is why the process is called chemiosmosis. Chemiosmosis produces the ATP needed in:

- **Photophosphorylation** that takes place in grana of the chloroplasts during photosynthesis (13.1e).
- **Oxidative phosphorylation** that takes place on the inner mitochondrial membranes of most eukaryotic cells, and the cell surface membrane of prokaryotes (e.g. bacteria). Figure 3 shows the location of the ATP synthase complexes in a mitochondrion (see 12.2c for more detail on chemiosmosis).

Respiratory pathways

Figure 4 is a summary of respiratory pathways. Notice that in respiration in anaerobic conditions, ATP is only produced by substrate-linked phosphorylation in glycolysis. The pyruvate produced is further metabolised to

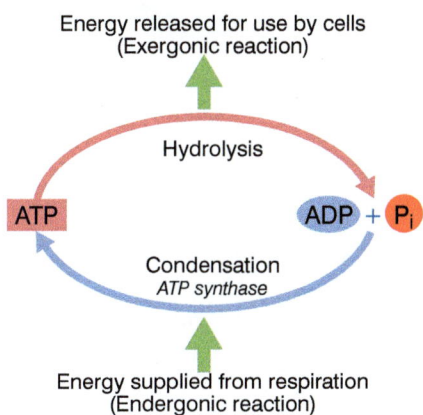

Figure 2 *ATP cycle*

> ### Remember
>
> When there is a difference in concentration of an ion either side of a membrane, there is a a difference in electrical charge as well as a difference in solute concentration – the gradient that builds up is known as an electrochemical gradient.

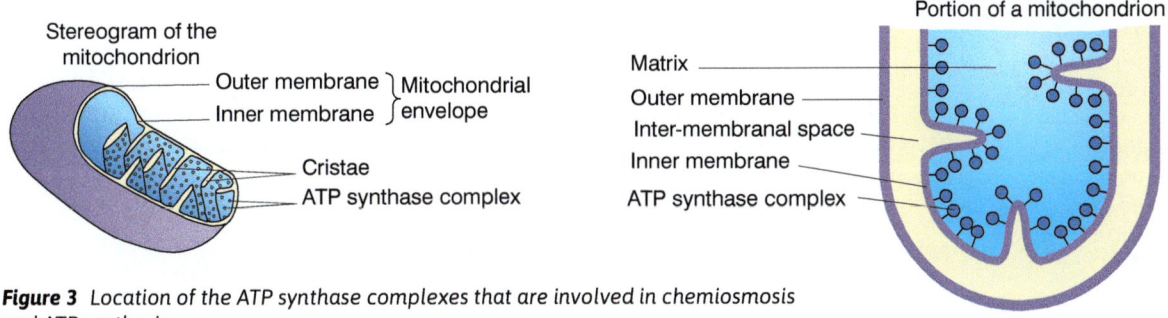

Figure 3 *Location of the ATP synthase complexes that are involved in chemiosmosis and ATP synthesis*

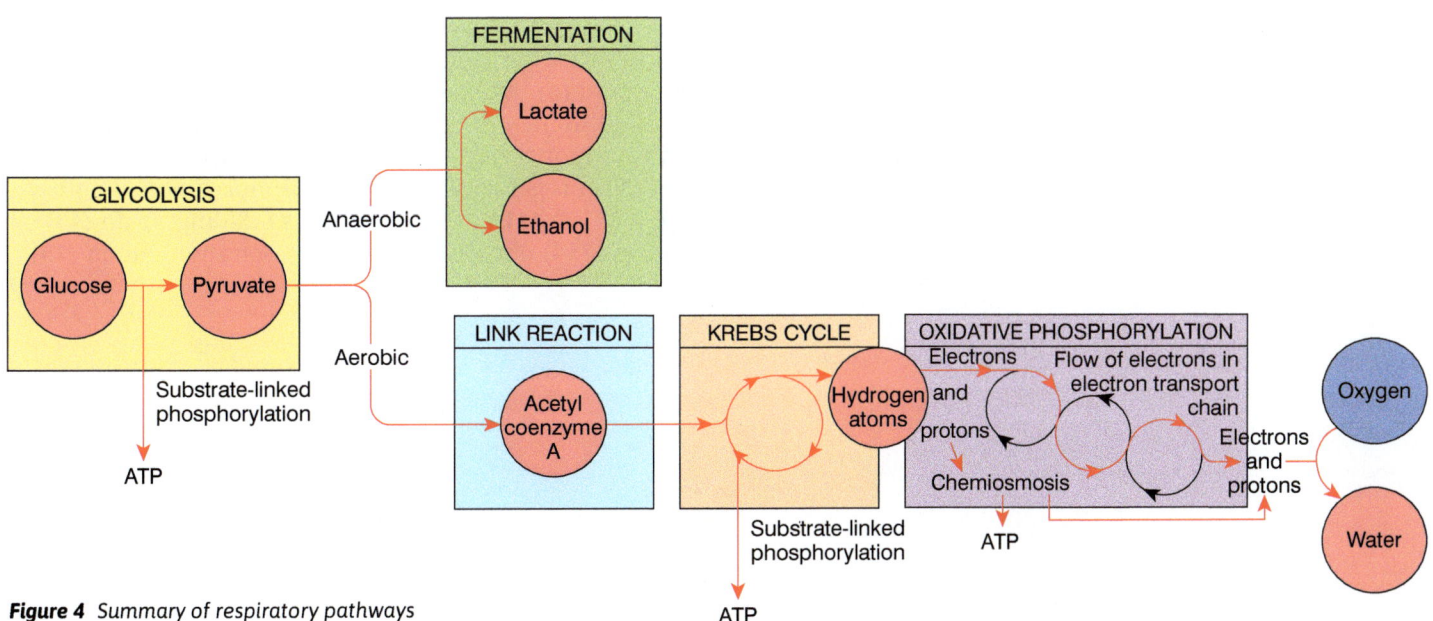

Figure 4 *Summary of respiratory pathways*

Remember

In aerobic respiration, the majority of the ATP synthesised is in the oxidative phosphorylation stage (12.2c). In 12.1b we saw that the energy to synthesise ATP molecules from ADP and Pi comes from the flow of protons (hydrogen ions) in chemiosmosis. The source of these are hydrogen atoms (Figure 4 on page 231) from respiratory substrates such as glucose, fatty acids (from lipids) and amino acids (from proteins). Because of the presence of the hydrocarbon chains (see 2.2d), lipids have a far higher proportion of hydrogens that can be donated for chemiosmosis than carbohydrates.

Extension

Proteins as respiratory substrates

Because proteins are being synthesised in the cell continually, it is cost efficient for an organism to use a pool of amino acids within a cell for protein synthesis rather than direct them into the process of respiration. However, excess amino acids can be used for respiration by organisms. There are also examples, particularly in seed germination, where proteins are broken down to use as respiratory substrates. In humans, the breakdown of structural protein, such as muscle, for use in respiration is often associated with times of starvation or malnutrition. However in endurance sports, there may be protein breakdown to supply energy when glucose and glycogen supplies have been used up and fat stores have been mobilised and used.

lactate in mammalian tissue and to ethanol (and carbon dioxide) in yeast, but no additional ATP is synthesised (see 12.2e).

Energy yields from respiratory substrates

Carbohydrates, lipids and protein can all be respiratory substrates. Glycogen stores in animals and starch stores in plants are broken down to release glucose for respiration. Lipids can be broken down to fatty acids and glycerol for use in respiration. Lipids contain relatively more C–H bonds than an equivalent mass of carbohydrate, so they release more hydrogen atoms for the electron transport chain and chemiosmosis. Lipids release more than twice as much energy ($39.4 \, kJ \, g^{-1}$) than the same mass of carbohydrate ($15.8 \, kJ \, g^{-1}$). Excess amino acids, or amino acids from protein breakdown, can be respired after the removal of the amino groups (NH_2). Although the energy yield depends on the exact composition of each protein, they normally yield around $17.0 \, kJ \, g^{-1}$, slightly more energy than carbohydrates. Normally a cell will use amino acids to synthesise proteins required by the cell.

Glycerol and fatty acids, and different amino acids, enter at different points in the respiratory pathway.

Role of ATP

ATP is **not** a good long-term energy store. Fats, and carbohydrates such as glycogen, serve this purpose far better. ATP can only be considered as a very short-term energy store and it is better described as the **immediate energy source** of a cell. We have seen in 12.1a why energy is needed by living organisms and have seen some specific examples of the use of ATP in the cell. In the first stage of respiration, glycolysis (12.2a), we will see how ATP is used to activate glucose so that the process can begin. There is an additional advantage to this step: in phosphorylating glucose, the concentration gradient between the inside of the cell and the external tissue fluid becomes steeper and this means that the cell always has a ready supply of glucose.

Summary test 12.1b

The immediate source of energy for a cell is ATP, or **(1)**. ATP can be called the **(2)** energy currency of the cell. ATP is an ideal molecule as it is easily **(3)** to release energy: the energy that is released when ADP is formed is **(4)** kJ mol⁻¹, ATP can move easily around the cell and can take part in reactions because it is **(5)** and **(6)**. ATP has a high **(7)** rate but the reaction to form ATP is **(8)** and rapid so the cell does not need to **(9)** large quantities of the molecule. When **(10)** groups are transferred to ADP from a donor molecule to synthesise ATP, this is known as **(11)** phosphorylation. Another main way to synthesise ATP is by **(12)**, which involves building up an **(13)** gradient. This occurs during **(14)** phosphorylation in respiration and in **(15)** in photosynthesis.

c. Measurement of respiration and respiratory quotients

Respiratory quotients

The **respiratory quotient (RQ)** is a measure of the ratio of the number of molecules of carbon dioxide given out by an organism to the number of molecules of oxygen consumed in respiration, over a given period:

$$RQ = \frac{\text{number of molecules of } CO_2 \text{ given out}}{\text{number of molecules of } O_2 \text{ taken in}}$$

When carrying out practical work, we can use the following formula:

$$RQ = \frac{\text{volume of } CO_2 \text{ given out}}{\text{volume of } O_2 \text{ taken in}}$$

Different RQs give an indication of the type of substrate being respired. For example, a typical sugar such as glucose is oxidised according to the following equation:

$$C_6H_{12}O_6 + 6O_2 \longrightarrow 6CO_2 + 6H_2O$$

The RQ is therefore: $\frac{6CO_2}{6O_2} = 1.0$

Lipids, however, have less oxygen relative to carbon and hydrogen. A greater volume of oxygen is therefore required to oxidise a lipid completely and their RQs are therefore lower than those of carbohydrates:

$$C_{18}H_{36}O_2 + 26O_2 \longrightarrow 18CO_2 + 18H_2O$$
stearic acid
(fatty acid)

The RQ is therefore: $\frac{18CO_2}{26O_2} = 0.7$

Proteins have a very varied structure depending on the number and types of each amino acid in the protein molecule. Their RQs are therefore equally varied but most have values around 0.9.

The usefulness of RQs in determining the substrate being respired is limited because:

- substances are rarely completely oxidised and partial oxidation gives a different value

- organisms rarely, if ever, respire a single food substance and the RQ therefore reflects the proportions of the different substrates being respired.

Most resting animals have an RQ of between 0.8 and 0.9 (Figure 1). Although these values would suggest that protein was being respired, it is likely that these values are due to a mixture of carbohydrate (1.0), lipid (0.7) and excess amino acids (approx. 0.9) being respired.

In anaerobic respiration, carbon dioxide is produced but no oxygen is taken in. If only anaerobic respiration takes place, then the RQ will be infinity. Where there is a mixture of aerobic and anaerobic respiration, RQ values are greater than 1.0. Some of these various values and their explanations are shown in Table 1, which shows the RQ of germinating seeds.

Table 1 *Showing the RQ values of germinating seeds*

Time	RQ	Possible explanations
Seeds soaked in water	7.2	With little dissolved oxygen in water, respiration is a mixture of aerobic (≤1.0) and anaerobic (infinity)
After 14 hours in soil	1.5	As oxygen becomes available, the amount of aerobic respiration (≤1.0) increases, whereas anaerobic respiration (infinity) decreases
After 48 hours in soil	0.7	A mixture of lipids (0.7) and carbohydrate (1.0) from the stores in the seed is being respired. The conversion of stored lipid to carbohydrate is also taking place
After 14 days	1.0	The leaves have emerged and photosynthesis is producing carbohydrate (1.0), which is being respired

Figure 1 *Most resting animals such as this Mediterranean tree frog and lioness have an RQ between 0.8 and 0.9 by respiring a mixture of fat and carbohydrate*

Practical skill

Using respirometers to determine RQs

The volume of oxygen taken in, and the volume of carbon dioxide given out, in respiration can be determined using the same apparatus. Measurements can be taken using a simple respirometer, such as the one shown in Figure 2.

It consists of two identical chambers – an experimental one containing the respiring organisms, such as germinating seeds, woodlice or blowfly larvae, and a control one containing an equal volume of non-respiring material such as glass beads. The two chambers are connected by a U-shaped manometer tube that contains a coloured fluid. This type of respirometer is sometimes referred to as a **differential respirometer** because it has a built-in control chamber that makes sure that any fluctuation in temperature or pressure affects both sides of the manometer equally and so they cancel each other out. An equal volume of some carbon dioxide-absorbing material such as soda-lime is added to each chamber.

A simple respirometer is used to determine RQ as follows:

Experiment 1

- The apparatus is left in the water bath for 5 minutes to allow it to reach a steady temperature (equilibrate).
- Screw clips A and B are open to allow air exchange.
- After 5 minutes, the screw clips are closed and the timer is started (0 min).
- Adjustments are made to the volume of air in chamber A using the syringe to level out the height of the manometer fluid.
- As the germinating seeds respire in chamber B, oxygen is taken in and the carbon dioxide that is given off is absorbed by the soda-lime, reducing the overall volume of gases in the chamber.
- This causes the level of the manometer fluid to go up on the side of chamber B and to go down on the side of chamber A.

After a set time, the volume of oxygen taken up is determined in one of two ways:

- We can calculate the volume using the equation:

$$\text{volume} = \pi r^2 h$$

  (where h is the distance moved by the liquid in the manometer and r is the internal radius of the manometer tube).
- We can simply measure on the calibrated syringe the volume of air needed to equalise the levels in the manometer tubes.

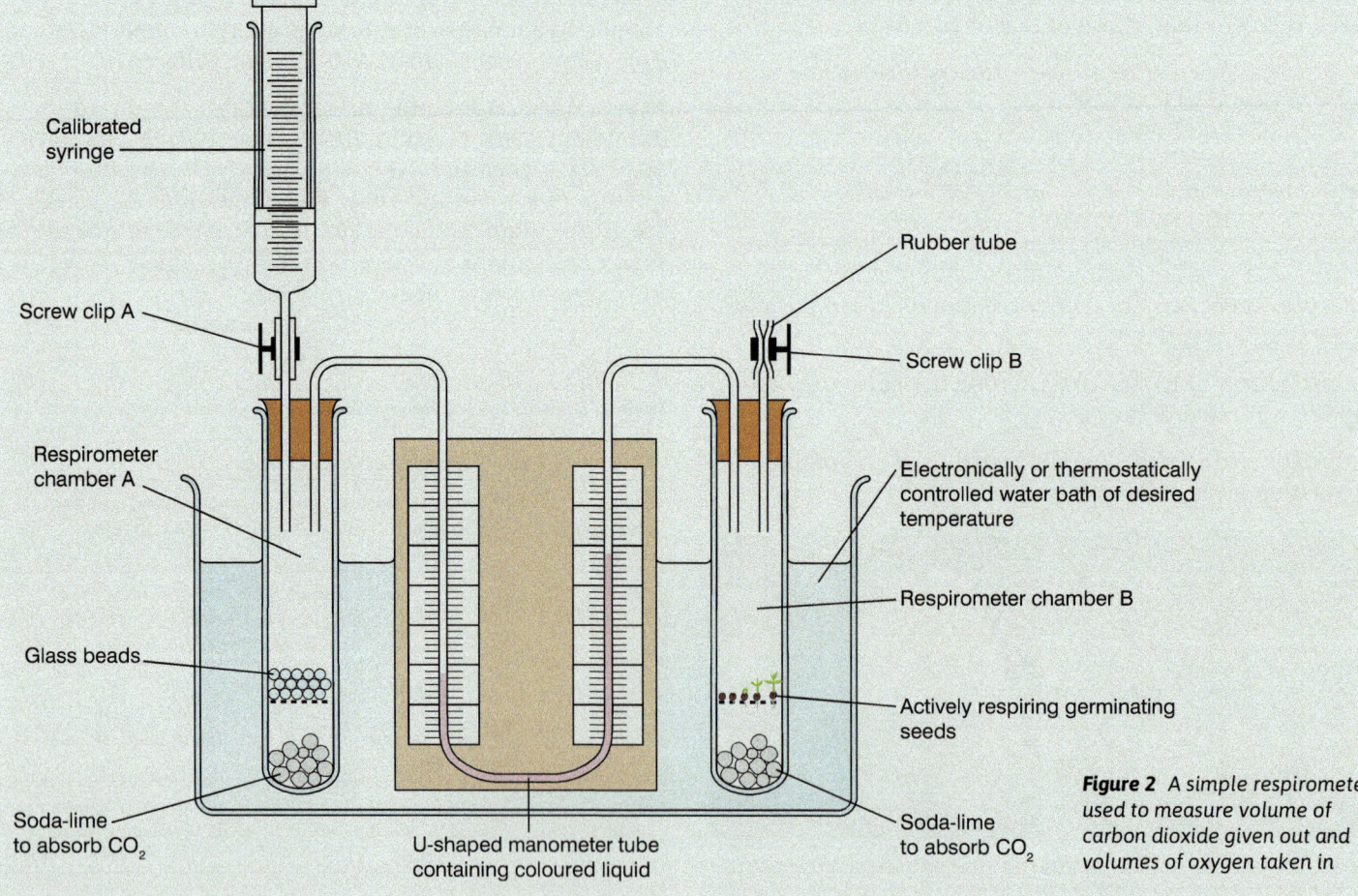

Figure 2 A simple respirometer used to measure volume of carbon dioxide given out and volumes of oxygen taken in

Practical skill

Experiment 2

To measure the volume of carbon dioxide given out, the procedure is repeated without soda-lime. After the same set time, the change in volume from the start of the experiment is measured. The difference between this and the change in the first experiment is calculated. This represents the volume of carbon dioxide given out.

Worked example A:

Experiment 1:   the height of the manometer fluid increased by 8 units = 8 units of oxygen absorbed

Experiment 2:   the height of the manometer fluid remained the same = 0 units

Difference between Experiment 1 and 2 = 8 units of carbon dioxide given out

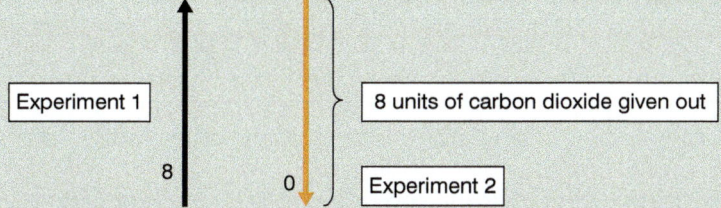

$RQ = \dfrac{8}{8} = 1$ (carbohydrate is likely to be the respiratory substrate)

Worked example B:

Experiment 1:   the height of the manometer fluid increased by 8 units = 8 units of oxygen absorbed

Experiment 2:   the height of the manometer fluid increased by 2 units

Difference between Experiment 1 and 2 = 6 units of carbon dioxide given out

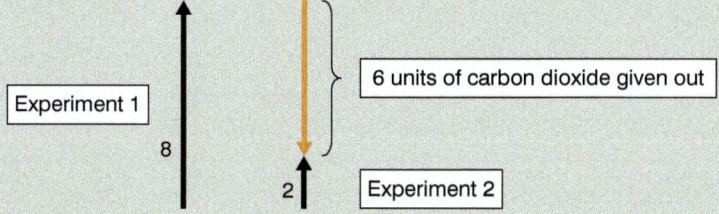

$RQ = \dfrac{6}{8} = 0.75$ (possibly mixture of lipids and carbohydrates are respiratory substrates)

Worked example C:

Experiment 1:   the height of the manometer fluid increased by 8 units = 8 units of oxygen absorbed

Experiment 2:   the height of the manometer fluid decreased by 2 units = –2 units

Difference between Experiment 1 and 2 = –2 to + 8 = 10 units of carbon dioxide given out

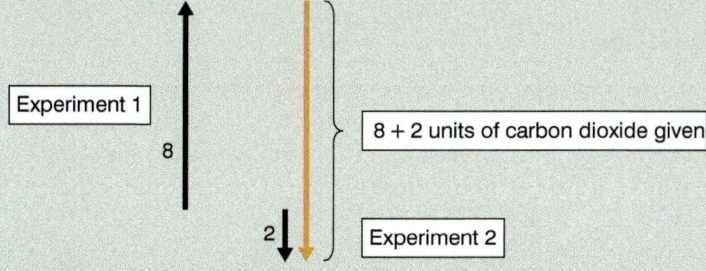

$RQ = \dfrac{10}{6} = 1.7$ (mix of aerobic and anaerobic respiration)

Summary test 12.1c

A **(1)** can be used to measure the volume of oxygen taken in over a given **(2)**. To absorb carbon dioxide, **(3)** is used. The procedure is repeated without **(3)** to determine the volume of carbon dioxide given out. The **(4)** of the number of molecules of carbon dioxide given out to the number of molecules of oxygen taken in is known as the **(5)**. For glucose, this is **(6)**, and for lipids is usually **(7)**. A value greater than 1 indicates that there is some **(8)** occurring.

Cellular respiration (also just called 'respiration') is the process by which the energy in food is converted into the energy for an organism to do biological work. Glucose is the main respiratory substrate and the overall equation for the process in aerobic conditions is:

$$C_6H_{12}O_6 \quad + \quad 6O_2 \quad \rightarrow \quad 6CO_2 \quad + \quad 6H_2O \quad + \quad \text{energy}$$

glucose   oxygen   carbon dioxide   water

Overview of respiration

Respiration in aerobic conditions can be divided into four stages:

- **Glycolysis** – an enzyme-controlled pathway in which one molecule of 6-carbon glucose is converted into two 3-carbon pyruvate molecules.
- **Link reaction (pyruvate oxidation)** – the 3-carbon pyruvate molecule is converted into carbon dioxide and a 2-carbon molecule called acetyl coenzyme A.
- **Krebs cycle** – the introduction of acetyl coenzyme A into a cycle of eight enzyme-catalysed reactions that yield reduced coenzymes NAD and FAD and some ATP.
- **Oxidative phosphorylation (electron transport system)** – oxidation of reduced NAD and FAD as part of an electron transport chain and ATP synthesis by chemiosmosis. Oxygen is required as a final electron acceptor and water is produced.

Respiration in anaerobic conditions involves glycolysis but not the other three stages described above. In mammalian tissue, lactate is produced from the pyruvate formed at the end of glycolysis in a one-step reaction. In yeast cells, a two-step reaction results in the production of carbon dioxide and ethanol.

Table 1 shows where each stage of respiration occurs within the cell.

Table 1 *Location within the cell of stages of respiration in aerobic and anaerobic conditions*

Conditions	Stage	Location in the cell
anaerobic	glycolysis	cytoplasm
	fermentation	
aerobic	glycolysis	cytoplasm
	link reaction	matrix of mitochondrion
	Krebs cycle	
	oxidative phosphorylation	cristae/inner membrane of mitochondrion

Coenzymes in respiration

A coenzyme is a small, organic, non-protein molecule that is not permanently attached to an enzyme, but is needed for the enzyme to catalyse a reaction. The coenzyme is changed during the reaction, and is important in carrying and transferring electrons, protons or chemical groups between molecules. The coenzyme is recycled so that it can take part in the reaction again. We will come across three coenzymes in this chapter:

- nicotinamide adenine dinucleotide (NAD^+), which carries hydrogen atoms
- flavine adenine dinucleotide (FAD), which carries hydrogen atoms
- coenzyme A (coA), which carries acetyl groups.

NAD

Each NAD molecule in a cell exists in a form in which it has lost an electron, i.e. it is oxidised and therefore exists as NAD⁺. It is essential for the production of small quantities of ATP in glycolysis and much larger quantities of ATP in oxidative phosphorylation (12.2c). As it acts as a carrier of hydrogen atoms that have been removed from substrates by dehydrogenase enzymes, NAD⁺ carries protons and electrons.

In the reaction catalysed by dehydrogenases, two hydrogen atoms are removed and dissociate into hydrogen ions (protons) and electrons, which are taken up by NAD⁺:

$$NAD^+ + 2H^+ + 2e^- \rightarrow \text{reduced NAD (NADH + H}^+)$$

The reduced NAD is re-oxidised, when the hydrogen atom is transferred to a new molecule, by the reversal of the above process, to re-form NAD⁺.

Glycolysis

Glycolysis occurs in the cytoplasm of all cells of multicellular organisms and in many unicellular organisms and is the process by which a hexose (6-carbon) sugar, usually glucose, is converted into two molecules of the 3-carbon molecule, pyruvate. Although there are 10 smaller enzyme-controlled reactions in glycolysis, these can be conveniently grouped into four stages (Figure 1):

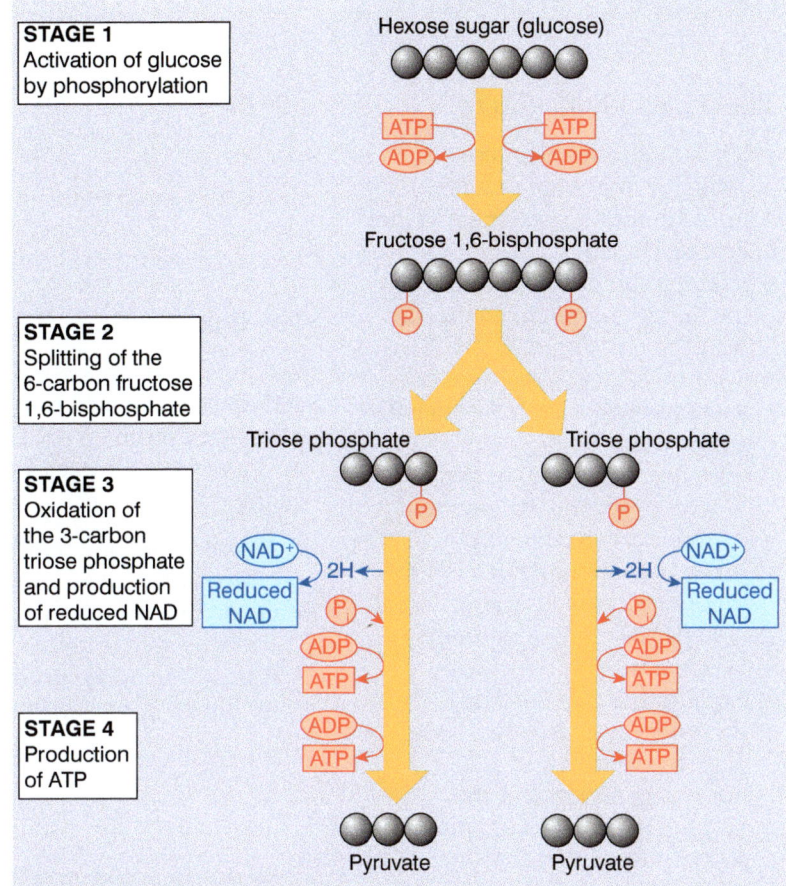

Figure 1 *Summary of glycolysis*

- **Activation of glucose by phosphorylation**. Before glycolysis can proceed, glucose must first be made more reactive by the addition of two phosphate groups = **phosphorylation**. The phosphates come from the **hydrolysis** of two ATP molecules to ADP. This provides the energy to activate glucose (**activation energy**) and also prevents glucose from being transported across the cell surface membrane and out of the cell. In a two-step process glucose is converted to fructose 1,6-bisphosphate.
- **Splitting of the fructose 1,6-bisphosphate.** This is then split into two 3-carbon molecules known as triose phosphate.
- **Oxidation of triose phosphate**. Hydrogen is removed from each of the two triose phosphate molecules and transferred to NAD⁺ to form reduced NAD.
- **The production of ATP**. Four enzyme reactions convert each triose phosphate (TP) into another 3-carbon molecule called pyruvate. In the process, for each TP formed two molecules of ATP are formed from ADP.

The overall yield from one glucose molecule undergoing glycolysis is therefore:

- two molecules of ATP (a net increase – four molecules of ATP are produced, but two were used up in activating glucose)
- two molecules of reduced NAD (with the potential to produce more ATP)
- two molecules of pyruvate.

Remember

For each molecule of glucose at the start of glycolysis, two molecules of triose phosphate are produced. Each triose phosphate to pyruvate conversion results in two molecules of ATP and one molecule of reduced NAD. So for one glucose molecule, these quantities should be doubled: four ATPs and two reduced NADs. In terms of ATP production, there is a **net** quantity of two ATPs from glycolysis.

Summary test 12.2a

Glycolysis occurs in the **(1)** of cells and begins with the activation of the respiratory substrate, the hexose sugar called **(2)**. This activation involves the addition of two **(3)** groups provided by two molecules of **(4)**. The molecule formed is known as **(5)**, which is then split into two molecules called **(6)**. The third stage involves the oxidation of these molecules by the removal of **(7)**, which is transferred to a carrier called **(8)**. The final stage is the production of the 3-carbon molecule **(9)**, which also results in the formation of two molecules of **(10)**.

These pages help you to:

- learn that when oxygen is available, pyruvate enters mitochondria to take part in the link reaction (12.2.3)
- describe the link reaction, including the role of coenzyme A in the transfer of acetyl (2C) groups (12.2.4)
- learn the Krebs cycle, to include an outline of:
  - oxaloacetate (4C) as the acceptor of the 2C fragment from acetyl coenzyme A
  - the formation of citrate (6C)
  - conversion in a series of small steps back to oxaloacetate (12.2.5)
- explain that reactions in the Krebs cycle involve decarboxylation and dehydrogenation and the reduction of the coenzymes NAD and FAD (12.2.6)

You will also:

- learn more about acetyl coenzyme A, NAD and FAD as coenzymes
- learn about enzyme complexes

Remember

Pyruvate is produced in the cytoplasm but is actively transported into the matrix of the mitochondrion when oxygen is present, so that it can take part in the link reaction.

The link reaction involves a number of enzyme-controlled steps. During the link reaction:

- decarboxylation occurs: carbon dioxide is removed from 3C pyruvate
- oxidation and reduction occurs: reduced NAD is produced
- a coenzyme, coenzyme A, carries a 2C acetyl group to the next stage, the Krebs cycle.

The pyruvate molecules produced during **glycolysis** possess potential energy that can only be released in a process called the **Krebs cycle**. Before they can enter the Krebs cycle, these pyruvate molecules must first be oxidised in a procedure known as the **link reaction**. In **eukaryotic cells** both the Krebs cycle and the link reaction take place exclusively inside mitochondria and these will only occur if oxygen is available.

The link reaction

The pyruvate molecules produced in the cytoplasm during glycolysis are actively transported into the matrix of mitochondria. Here pyruvate undergoes a complex series of oxidation-reduction reactions that are catalysed by a multienzyme complex (see Extension). During these reactions the following changes take place:

- A carbon dioxide molecule is removed (decarboxylation) from each pyruvate molecule by means of the enzyme pyruvate decarboxylase.
- Oxidation of pyruvate results in the reduction of NAD to form reduced NAD (later used to produce ATP).
- A 2-carbon acetyl group combines with coenzyme A (CoA) (see 12.2a) to produce a 2-carbon compound called **acetyl coenzyme A**.

The overall equation can be summarised as:

$$\text{pyruvate} + NAD^+ + CoA \rightarrow \text{acetyl CoA} + \text{reduced NAD} + CO_2$$

Extension

Enzyme complex – pyruvate dehydrogenase

The oxidation of pyruvate to acetyl coenzyme A in the link reaction involves a complex series of steps with three intermediate stages. The reaction is catalysed by a multienzyme complex called pyruvate dehydrogenase. This is one of the largest enzyme complexes in organisms, consisting of 60 sub-units. Enzyme complexes like this occur frequently in organisms and are made up of individual enzymes organised in sequence so that the product of one enzyme acts as the substrate for the next enzyme in the chain. This arrangement is more efficient because, rather than depending upon a chance meeting of enzyme and substrate as would be the case if the enzymes floated freely around, the substrate is not released but rather 'handed on' to the next enzyme in the biochemical sequence.

Extension

The importance of acetyl coenzyme A

Coenzyme A is made up of vitamin B5, the organic base adenine and the sugar ribose. It carries the acetyl group made from pyruvate into the Krebs cycle in the form of acetyl coenzyme A. Most molecules that are used by living organisms for energy are made into acetyl coenzyme A before entering the Krebs cycle. Most carbohydrates and fatty acids can be metabolised into acetyl coenzyme A to release energy. In the case of fats, these are first hydrolysed into glycerol and fatty acids. The glycerol can then be converted into triose phosphate that can be broken down during glycolysis, while the fatty acids are progressively broken down in the matrix of the mitochondria into 2-carbon fragments that are converted into acetyl coenzyme A. The reverse is also true, namely that excess carbohydrate can be made into fats via acetyl coenzyme A, making it a pivotal molecule in the interconversion of major substances in eukaryotic cells.

Krebs cycle

The Krebs cycle was named after the biochemist, Hans Krebs, who worked out its sequence in 1937. It involves a series of eight small enzyme-catalysed steps that take place in the matrix of mitochondria. Its events are shown in Figure 1 and can be summarised as:

- The 2-carbon acetyl coenzyme A from the link reaction transfers the acetyl group to a 4-carbon acceptor molecule, oxaloacetate, to produce a 6-carbon molecule, citrate.
- This 6-carbon molecule (citrate) is decarboxylated (loses CO_2) and dehydrogenated (loses hydrogen – in this case two hydrogens) to give a 5-carbon compound, carbon dioxide and reduced NAD.
- Further decarboxylation and dehydrogenation reactions produce a 4-carbon molecule (oxaloacetate), carbon dioxide, reduced NAD and reduced FAD and a single molecule of ATP (see Extension) produced as a result of substrate-linked phosphorylation (12.1b).
- The 4-carbon molecule (oxaloacetate) can now combine with a new molecule of acetyl coenzyme A to begin the cycle again.

For each molecule of pyruvate, the link reaction and Krebs cycle therefore produces:

- four molecules of reduced NAD
- one molecule of reduced FAD
- one molecule of ATP
- three molecules of carbon dioxide.

As two pyruvate molecules are produced for each original glucose molecule, these quantities must be doubled when the yields from a single glucose molecule are being calculated.

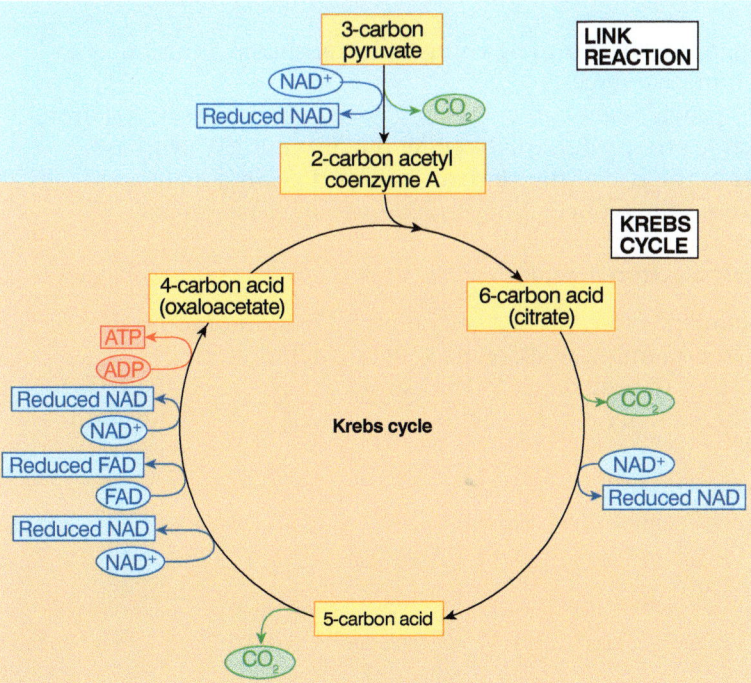

Figure 1 *Summary of link reaction and Krebs cycle – intermediate enzyme-controlled steps are not included*

The significance of the Krebs cycle

The Krebs cycle performs an important role in biochemistry for four reasons:

- It breaks down macromolecules into simpler ones; pyruvate is broken down into carbon dioxide.
- It produces hydrogen atoms that are carried by NAD and FAD to the electron transport chain for oxidative phosphorylation (12.2c) and the production of ATP by chemiosmosis (12.1b and 12.2c), which provides metabolic energy for the cell.
- It regenerates the starter material (oxaloacetate), which would otherwise be completely used up.
- It is a source of intermediate compounds used by cells in the manufacture of other important substances such as fatty acids, amino acids and chlorophyll.

These pages help you to:

- understand the sequence of events that occur during oxidative phosphorylation that result in the synthesis of ATP and give an account of
  - the splitting of hydrogen atoms into protons and energetic electrons that release energy as they pass through the electron transport chain
  - oxygen acting as the final electron acceptor to form water
  - the use of the released energy to transfer protons across the inner mitochondrial membrane
  - the return of protons by facilitated diffusion through ATP synthase to the mitochondrial matrix providing energy for ATP synthesis (12.2.8)
- use diagrams to describe the relationship between the structure and function of mitochondria (12.2.9)

You will also:

- understand what is meant by redox reactions
- learn about uncoupling proteins
- understand how cyanide acts as a respiratory inhibitor

Remember

ATP synthesis by chemiosmosis relies on the oxidation of NAD and FAD at the inner mitochondrial membrane. The energetic electrons that release energy in the electron transport chain come from the splitting of the hydrogen atoms that these coenzymes have carried. It is this energy which is used to pump protons to form the electrochemical gradient.

So far in the process of respiration, we have seen how glucose is converted to pyruvate in **glycolysis** and how the 3-carbon pyruvate is converted to the 2-carbon acetyl coenzyme A (link reaction) so that it can enter into the **Krebs cycle**. The carbon dioxide that is produced in the link reaction and Krebs cycle is a waste product (see Remember box). The hydrogen atoms, or more precisely the **electrons** they contain, carried by reduced coenzymes NAD and FAD, are valuable as a potential source of energy. **Oxidative phosphorylation** (Figure 1) is the final stage in aerobic respiration and it is during this stage that most ATP molecules are synthesised.

The process of oxidative phosphorylation

Figure 1 is a summary of oxidative phosphorylation. The numbers appearing on the diagram correspond to the text descriptions numbered 1 to 8.

1 reduced NAD (from the link reaction and Krebs cycle) and reduced FAD (from the Krebs cycle) carry hydrogen atoms to carriers of the electron transport chain of the inner mitochondrial membrane (Figure 1)
   - reduced NAD from glycolysis may be used in other reactions
2 oxidation of NAD and FAD releases hydrogen atoms, which split into protons (hydrogen ions or H^+) and energetic electrons
   - oxidised NAD and FAD can be recycled
3 energetic electrons pass along the carriers (the electron transport chain), each one being at a lower energy level
4 as the energetic electrons flow down the electron transport chain, energy is released, and this is used to pump protons across the inner membrane into the intermembrane space
   - three of the electron carriers are large complexes spanning the membrane that can also act as proton pumps
5 protons accumulate in the intermembrane space (Figure 1) and a proton motive force is generated by the electrochemical gradient that is built up
   - the gradient builds up because the inner membrane is mostly impermeable to protons
6 protons flow through the ATP synthase complex by facilitated diffusion as a result of the proton motive force
7 the flow of protons provides enough energy to drive the synthesis of ATP from ADP and P_i (inorganic phosphate), catalysed by the enzyme ATP synthase
8 the electron carrier at the end of the electron transport chain donates electrons to oxygen – it catalyses the reduction of oxygen (gain of electrons and protons) to form water
   - oxygen is the final electron acceptor.

The ATP synthase complex shown in Figure 2 allows diffusion of protons through it from the intermembrane space, as well as catalysing the phosphorylation reaction to produce ATP. The part of the complex that has the ATP synthase (enzyme) activity is the head of the complex that extends into the matrix.

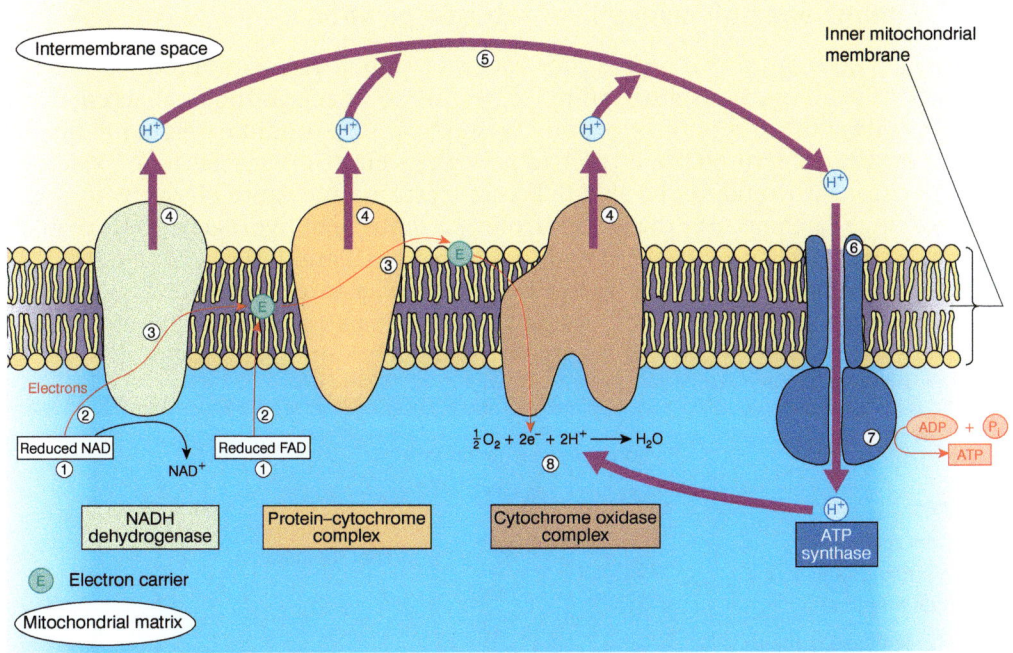

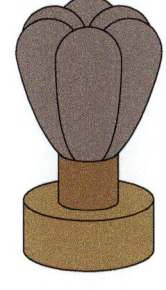

Figure 2 *ATP synthase complex*

Figure 1 *Summary of oxidative phosphorylation (note: you are not expected to remember the names of the electron carriers)*

Remember

NAD becomes reduced when it gains a hydrogen atom (so it is also gaining electrons).

Reduced NAD is oxidised when it releases a hydrogen atom (and hence electrons) to the carrier of the inner membrane.

A carrier is reduced when it accepts electrons, and becomes oxidised when it donates electrons to the next carrier.

Oxidation and reduction always take place together and we call such reactions **redox** reactions (**red**uction and **ox**idation). An oxidoreductase enzyme catalyses a redox reaction.

The flow of electrons through the electron transport chain involves a series of redox reactions. Carriers in the electron transport chain are oxidoreductases.

Extension

Stalked particles

The stalks and head pieces of the ATP synthase complexes could be seen using the electron microscope a long time before scientists knew what they were. The complexes were commonly known as stalked particles and this term is sometimes still used.

Extension

The energy released by the oxidation of one NAD is enough to drive the synthesis of approximately 2.5 ATP molecules.

As the hydrogen atom of reduced FAD enters the electron transport chain at a lower energy level, fewer ATP molecules (1.5) are synthesised for each hydrogen atom from reduced FAD.

Reduced NAD produced in glycolysis cannot pass directly across the inner membrane, but uses a 'shuttle' (transporting) mechanism to pass its energetic electrons to the electron transport mechanism. Depending on the mechanism used, there can be an energy cost to this and so less ATP is synthesised as a result.

Remember

NAD^+ and FAD are coenzymes. They function to transfer hydrogen atoms to the cristae of the inner mitochondrial membrane for the final stage of aerobic respiration, oxidative phosphorylation. So that the Krebs cycle can continue, the hydrogen atoms must be released to allow the coenzymes to be recycled.

Extension

The effect of cyanide as a respiratory inhibitor

Most people are aware that cyanide is a very potent poison that is potentially fatal. It has such a harmful effect because it is an inhibitor of the final dehydrogenase enzyme in the electron transport chain, cytochrome oxidase. This enzyme catalyses the reduction of oxygen to form water. The effect of cyanide is the same as having no oxygen. The only ATP that is synthesised is that made in glycolysis, which for most cells would not be enough for the needs of the cell. Cells and tissues would soon stop functioning.

Summary test 12.2c

In oxidative phosphorylation, reduced **(1)** and reduced FAD transfer hydrogen **(2)** to the carriers in the **(3)** mitochondrial membrane. **(4)** electrons flow down the **(5)** and this releases **(6)** to pump protons into the **(7)**. A proton **(8)** builds up. Protons move through the **(9)** and this provides **(10)** for the enzyme-catalysed **(11)** of ADP to produce ATP. **(12)** acts as the **(13)** electron acceptor and together with protons, forms **(14)**.

The importance of oxygen in aerobic respiration

Oxygen does not play a part in the process of aerobic respiration until the last stage of oxidative phosphorylation (see Figure 3). It acts as the final acceptor of electrons at the end of the electron transport chain. Without oxygen, the final electron carrier would not be able to pass on its electrons and become oxidised. This means it would not be able to accept electrons and cause electrons to back up along the chain. Hydrogen ions from the splitting of hydrogen atoms would not be pumped into the space, and so reduced NAD and FAD arriving at the inner membrane would not be oxidised. This has a 'knock-on' effect because the coenzymes are then not recycled back to take part in the link reaction and Krebs cycle. Pyruvate would not enter the mitochondrion and the process of aerobic respiration would come to a halt.

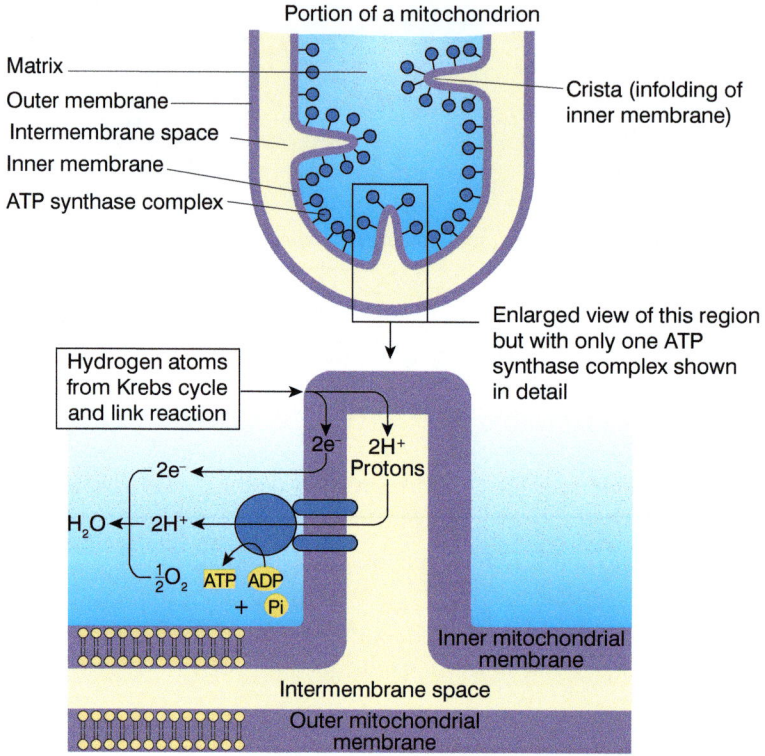

Figure 3 *Outline of oxidative phosphorylation showing oxygen as the final electron acceptor and the formation of water*

Extension

Uncoupling proteins

The inner mitochondrial membrane also has channel proteins known as uncoupling proteins (UCP) that, under controlled conditions, can allow protons to pass through by facilitated diffusion back to the matrix instead of flowing back through the ATP synthase complex. The proton gradient is used to generate heat and not ATP – the electron transport chain has been uncoupled from the synthesis of ATP. So far, five different uncoupling proteins have been identified in mammals. The first UCP to be discovered was in brown adipose tissue. This tissue is important in some mammals for generating heat during hibernation.

Some of the herbicides that are considered potentially hazardous to human health contain 2,4-dinitrophenol. This can act as a UCP and cause uncoupling of oxidative phosphorylation.

All eukaryotes have mitochondria (Figure 1). As mitochondria play such a vital role in respiration and the provision of energy to the cell, it is hardly surprising that, in multicellular organisms that show division of labour, they occur in greater numbers in metabolically active cells, such as those involved in movement (e.g. muscle cells and sperm cells), or active transport (e.g. root hair cells and intestinal epithelial cells). Cells that synthesise proteins for secretion, such as plasma cells that synthesise and release antibodies (11.1b) and liver cells that synthesise plasma proteins, also have a high density of mitochondria in their cytoplasm. Figure 2 is a transmission electron micrograph of a liver cell (hepatocyte). In this one very thin section, you can see large numbers of mitochondria. This contrasts with the mammalian red blood cell, which is metabolically relatively inactive and has no mitochondria.

The structure and function of mitochondria

Mitochondria are often seen as rod-shaped organelles, but they are flexible and can change shape. They are between $1\,\mu m$ and $10\,\mu m$ in diameter, and are found in all but a few eukaryotic cells. The mitochondrial envelope is a double membrane, a smooth outer mitochondrial membrane and an inner one that is folded into extensions called **cristae** (Figure 1, and Figure 4 on page 244). The inner space, or **matrix**, of the mitochondrion consists of a viscous (gel-like) fluid that contains 70S ribosomes, circular DNA enzymes, coenzymes, organic molecules of the Krebs cycle, lipids and other solutes (Figure 3).

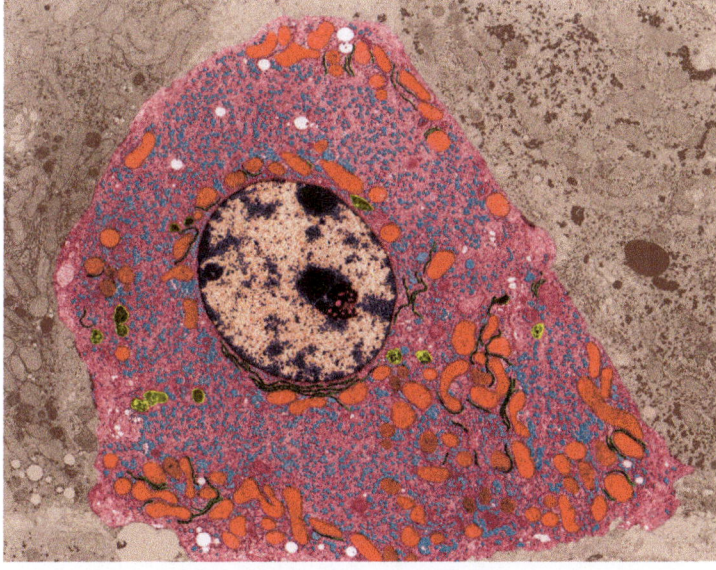

Figure 2 Colourised transmission electron micrograph of a liver cell (hepatocyte) showing numerous mitochondria (red)

These pages help you to:

- use diagrams and electron micrographs to describe the relationship between the structure and function of mitochondria (12.2.9)

You will also:

- understand why different cell types have a different number of mitochondria
- understand why some eukaryotes have underdeveloped mitochondria

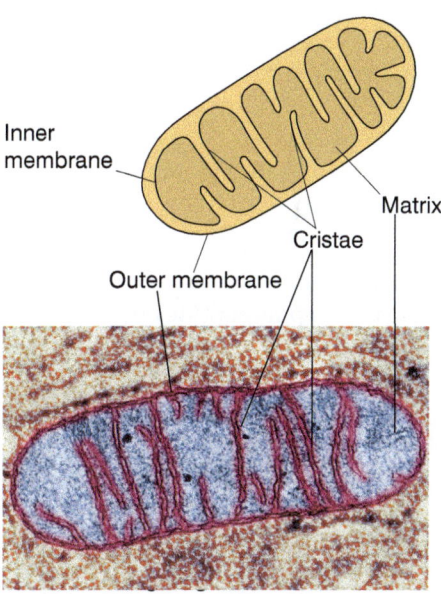

Figure 1 The basic structure of a mitochondrion (top); colourised transmission electron micrograph (TEM) of a mitochondrion (bottom)

Extension

Eukaryotes without mitochondria?

There are some unicellular organisms that have very rudimentary (undeveloped) mitochondria. These organisms all live in low-oxygen environments, so have little need for the organelles, and can obtain enough ATP from oxidation of respiratory substrates in the cytoplasm. In 2016, the first eukaryotes without mitochondria were discovered. These organisms belonged to a group (genus) known as *Monocercomonoides*. These are unicellular organisms living harmlessly in the gut of vertebrates, where the oxygen concentration is extremely low. A genome analysis showed that they did not have any genes associated with mitochondria. It is not the case that their ancestors did not have mitochondria, more an example of how the organisms have adapted by losing an organelle that had very little useful function to the life of the cell.

Mitochondria (Figures 1, 3 and 4) are the sites of the link reaction, Krebs cycle and **oxidative phosphorylation**. More specifically:

- **The inner folded membrane (cristae)** has attached to it the membrane carriers involved in the electron transport chain and therefore allows oxidative phosphorylation to take place. It provides a large surface area where the ATP synthase complexes and the electron carriers involved in oxidative phosphorylation are located (12.2c). As they are held in a membrane, there is an ordered and close arrangement of the carriers, which is essential for the flow of electrons in the electron transport chain. The inner membrane is also essential to allow an electrochemical gradient to build up for chemiosmosis to occur (12.1b). In metabolically active cells, the mitochondria have more densely packed cristae to provide an even greater surface area.
- **The ATP synthase** complexes located in the membrane of the cristae contain ATP synthase for the synthesis of ATP by the chemiosmosis method (12.1b and Figures 2 and 3 in 12.2c).
- **The matrix** has the enzymes needed for the link reaction and Krebs cycle (12.2b) and provides an aqueous environment for these processes to occur. In addition, the energy required to synthesise ATP results from the hydrogen ion (pH) gradient that exists between the matrix and intermembrane space.

70S ribosomes

Some of the polypeptides of the membrane complexes involved in oxidative phosphorylation are synthesised by the mitochondrial ribosomes.

Mitochondrial DNA

The closed circular mitochondrial DNA contains genes that code for some of the polypeptides of the membrane complexes of oxidative phosphorylation. There are also genes coding for rRNA and for tRNA.

Differences between the inner and outer mitochondrial membrane

The inner and outer mitochondrial membranes share the same fluid mosaic structure, but the composition of their components varies and this affects the permeability of the membranes. The outer mitochondrial membrane is much more permeable than the inner membrane. The impermeability of the inner membrane means that the electrochemical gradient can build up during chemiosmosis. The protons can mainly move back to the matrix through the specific ATP synthase complexes. Without this, ATP would not be synthesised. The relative impermeability of the inner membrane also means that the matrix is a compartment specialised for reactions such as those in the link reaction and Krebs cycle and has only the enzymes and substrates for its own metabolic reactions.

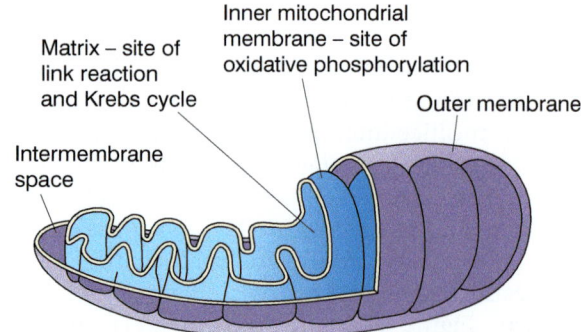

Figure 3 *Structure of a mitochondrion*

Figure 4 *Colourised scanning electron micrograph of a mitochondrion*

Proton gradients mainly build up within cristae, which are infoldings only of the inner membrane. This means that the area enclosing the protons is composed of impermeable inner membrane. In addition, there is a very steep electrochemical gradient such that protons will flow towards the matrix. As such, even though the outer membrane is more permeable than the inner membrane, there will not be a great loss of protons out of the mitochondrion through the outer membrane.

Summary test 12.2d

The mitochondrial **(1)** consists of a smooth outer membrane and an inner membrane with infoldings known as **(2)**. These increase the **(3)** for the final stage of aerobic respiration and contain the electron carriers for the **(4)**. Protons flow though a large membrane complex, which has the enzyme **(5)** for ATP synthesis. The inner mitochondrial membrane is impermeable to **(6)** and this helps the build up of the **(7)** gradient for ATP synthesis in **(8)**. The **(9)** is a viscous fluid that contains the **(10)** and substrates for the **(11)** cycle.

We saw in 12.2c that oxygen is needed to maintain the flow of energetic electrons down the electron transport chain and drive the production of ATP. What happens if oxygen is temporarily or permanently unavailable to a tissue or a whole organism?

In the absence of oxygen, the link reaction, the Krebs cycle and **oxidative phosphorylation** cannot take place, leaving only the **anaerobic** process of glycolysis as a potential source of ATP. For glycolysis to continue, its products of pyruvate and hydrogen must be constantly removed. In particular, the hydrogen must be released from the reduced **NAD** in order to regenerate NAD^+. Without this, the already tiny supply of NAD^+ in cells will be entirely converted to reduced NAD, leaving no NAD^+ to take up newly produced hydrogen from glycolysis. Glycolysis will then stop. The regeneration of NAD^+ is achieved by the pyruvate molecule from glycolysis accepting the hydrogen from reduced NAD in a process called fermentation.

In eukaryotic cells there are two main types of fermentation: alcoholic fermentation and lactate fermentation (Figure 1).

Alcoholic fermentation

Alcoholic fermentation occurs in certain bacteria and fungi (e.g. yeast) as well as in some cells of higher plants, e.g. root cells under waterlogged conditions.

The pyruvate molecule formed at the end of glycolysis first loses a molecule of carbon dioxide (decarboxylation) to form ethanal.

$$CH_3COCOOH \longrightarrow CH_3CHO + CO_2$$

pyruvate   ethanal   carbon dioxide

These pages help you to:

- outline respiration in anaerobic conditions in yeast cells: ethanol fermentation (12.2.10)
- outline respiration in anaerobic conditions in mammals: lactate fermentation (12.2.10)
- explain why the energy yield from respiration in aerobic conditions is much greater than the energy yield from respiration in anaerobic conditions (12.2.11)
- explain how rice is adapted to grow with its roots submerged in water by referring to the development of aerenchyma in roots, ethanol fermentation in roots and faster growth of stems (12.2.12)

You will also:

- learn that the liver is involved in processing lactate

The ethanal accepts hydrogen from reduced NAD to produce ethanol. The summary equation for this is:

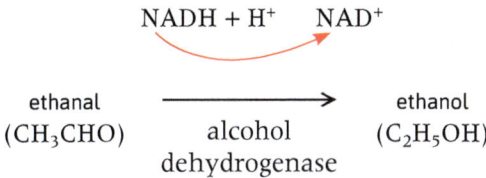

ethanal $\xrightarrow{\text{alcohol dehydrogenase}}$ ethanol
(CH_3CHO) (C_2H_5OH)

The overall equation using glucose as the starting point is:

$$C_6H_{12}O_6 \longrightarrow 2C_2H_5OH + 2CO_2$$

glucose   ethanol   carbon dioxide

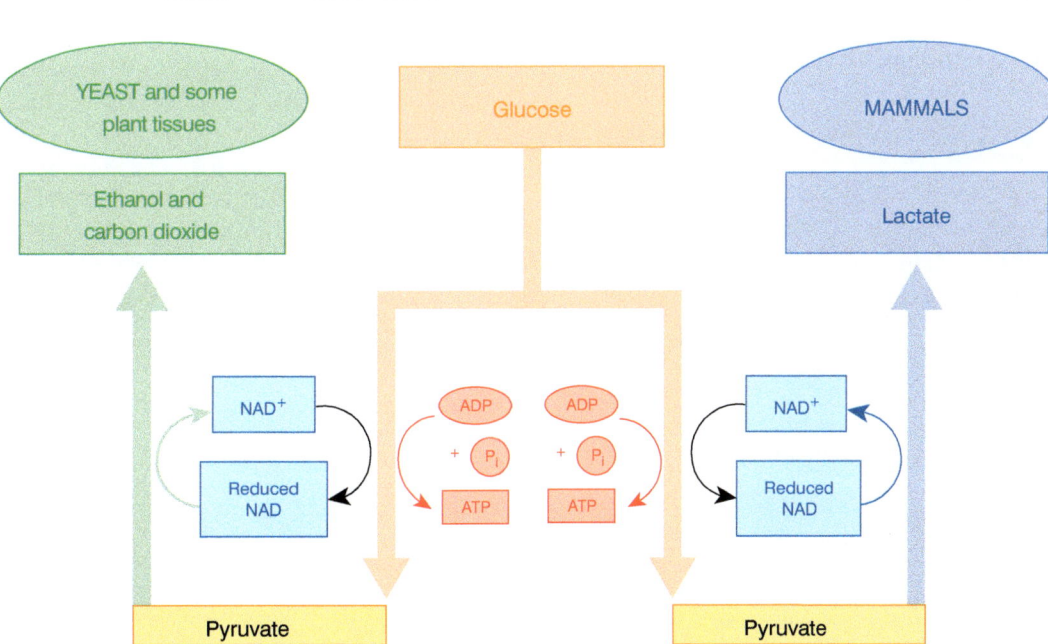

Figure 1 *How the NAD^+ needed for glycolysis is regenerated during fermentation in yeast and mammals*

Alcoholic fermentation in yeast has been exploited by humans for thousands of years, in both the brewing and baking industries. In brewing, ethanol is the important product. Yeast is grown in anaerobic conditions in which it ferments natural carbohydrates in plant products such as grapes (wine production) or barley seeds (beer production) into ethanol. The ethanol produced kills the yeast cells that make it when its concentration reaches around 15%. In baking, the carbon dioxide produced is used to help bread rise.

Adaptation of rice to anaerobic conditions

When soils are flooded or are waterlogged, the concentration of oxygen in the soil soon decreases and creates conditions where there is very little, or no, oxygen. If plant tissues are to survive submerged in water, there needs to be a way to receive oxygen from other areas of the plant that are not submerged. Alternatively, the submerged tissues, which now have to respire in anaerobic conditions, must either remove or show tolerance to the ethanol that is produced. This ethanol is normally toxic when it builds up. The cereal crop, rice, *Oryza sativa*, is a grass that is commonly grown in fields that are flooded with water. Rice has a number of adaptive features that allows it to grow with its roots submerged in water.

- The stems and roots have many air spaces between the cells, which allow oxygen to diffuse from aerial parts not submerged and allow the cells in the root tissue to respire aerobically. This type of tissue is called **aerenchyma**.
- The ridges created by the veins of the leaves can trap air, which will allow some oxygen to enter the plant.
- If the roots remain short of oxygen, they respire anaerobically and tolerate the build up of ethanol. They also produce an abundance of the enzyme alcohol dehydrogenase, which breaks the ethanol down.
- Some varieties of rice have a higher rate of anaerobic respiration to increase the rate of ATP production.

- Some varieties of rice that can grow in deep water have a very high rate of stem growth so that there is always part of the plant that is not submerged. The rate of elongation of the stem when the rice plant is partially submerged can be up to 25 cm a day. The low concentrations of oxygen and high concentrations of carbon dioxide lead to the production of ethene (ethylene), which stimulates elongation.
- If the whole plant is submerged for a short time, rice seeds that have formed will also be under water. The cells of the embryo in the seed are tolerant to the high concentrations of ethanol that build up as a result of anaerobic respiration.

Lactate fermentation

Lactate fermentation occurs in mammals as a means of overcoming a temporary shortage of oxygen. Clearly, such a mechanism has considerable survival value, for example for a baby mammal in the period immediately after birth or an animal living in water where the concentration of oxygen fluctuates. However, lactate fermentation occurs most commonly in muscles as a result of strenuous exercise. In these conditions oxygen may be used up more rapidly than it can be supplied and therefore an **oxygen deficit** occurs. It may be essential, however, that the muscles continue to work despite the lack of oxygen – for example if the organism is fleeing from a predator. In the absence of oxygen, each pyruvate molecule produced takes up the two hydrogen atoms from glycolysis to form lactate as shown below:

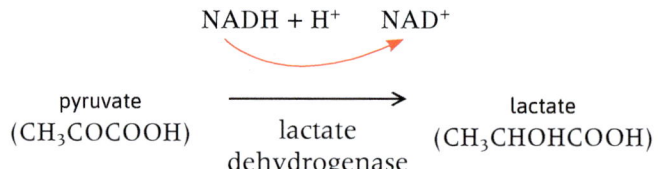

Energy yields in aerobic and anaerobic conditions

Respiration in aerobic conditions produces a much larger energy yield than respiration in anaerobic conditions.

Glycolysis occurs in both types of respiration. For each glucose molecule, there is a net gain of 2 ATP molecules. These are produced by substrate-linked phosphorylation. As each ATP molecule releases 30.5 kJ mol^{-1} on hydrolysis, this is a total yield of 61.0 kJ mol^{-1}.

In anaerobic conditions, glycolysis is the only stage that produces ATP. The conversion of pyruvate to lactate in mammals or ethanol in yeast does not release any of the potential energy of the molecule for ATP synthesis. So, for each glucose molecule, a total of only 2 ATP molecules is produced.

When oxygen is available, pyruvate can enter the mitochondrion and the three extra stages of aerobic respiration can proceed. This means for each glucose molecule:

- glycolysis results in a net gain of 2 ATP molecules
- two more ATP molecules are produced in the Krebs cycle by substrate-linked phosphorylation
- reduced NAD and reduced FAD are used in oxidative phosphorylation to produce many more molecules of ATP.

Extension

Efficiency of respiration

The theoretical maximum energy yield for the complete breakdown of a glucose molecule is much higher than the energy yield that is obtained in the ATP molecules produced in respiration. Respiration in aerobic conditions is approximately 33% efficient, whereas respiration in anaerobic conditions is only approximately 2% efficient. The heat energy that is lost during respiration can be used by organisms to heat the body, but all heat energy is eventually lost to the environment.

Summary test 12.2e

In respiration in anaerobic conditions, there is only a net gain of **(1)** ATP molecules for each molecule of glucose. In mammals, pyruvate is converted to **(2)** in a one-step reaction catalysed by **(3)**. In yeast, **(4)** fermentation occurs. This is a two-step process, where **(5)** and **(6)** are produced in the first reaction and ethanol is the final product. The conversions from pyruvate needs to occur so that **(7)** is regenerated for glycolysis. More ATP is produced in aerobic respiration, from substrate-linked phosphorylation in the **(8)** cycle and from oxidative phosphorylation. Rice plants are **(9)** to grow with their roots submerged in water. The roots and stems have large air spaces known as **(10)** to allow **(11)** to diffuse from the stem to the roots. Some varieties have a high rate of **(12)**, which is stimulated by the production of **(13)**. The cells of the root can respire by **(14)**.

These pages help you to:

- describe how redox indicators, such as DCPIP and methylene blue, can be used to investigate the effect of temperature and substrate concentration on the rate of respiration of yeast (12.2.13)
- describe how simple respirometers can be used to determine the effect of temperature on the rate of respiration (12.2.14)

You will also:

- develop your practical skills in planning investigations

Practical skill

Planning

Once you have developed most of the practical skills required for a practical assessment, you are well on your way to becoming skilled at the design and planning of investigations.

There are two main tasks for planning: defining the problem and devising methods. Tables 1 and 2 provide further detail of some of the skills you can develop within these skills.

Table 1 *Planning skills: Defining the problem*

Use the information provided to decide on the aim of the experiment/investigation that needs to be planned.	The information may be a reminder of subject matter that you have covered, or be unfamiliar information related to known subject matter.
Use your knowledge and understanding of topics studied to be able to predict the likely outcome of the experiment/investigation.	This can be used to justify your prediction.
Produce a relevant prediction or a hypothesis that can be tested.	This may be a written statement or a sketch graph to show the expected results.
Identify variables: • the independent variable or variables • the dependent variable • the key variables that must be standardised (controlled).	For the key variables, you should decide on the **main** variables that may affect the results of the investigation. If a variable is likely to only have a minimal effect, then it does not need to be included.

Table 2 *Planning skills: Methods*

Describe how to • vary the independent variable • measure the independent and dependent variables • standardise key variables.	State the apparatus and other materials to be used, give concentrations where necessary. Think about the most accurate and precise methods to use: • take account of precision in measuring, e.g. quantities, temperature, distances • decide on appropriate number of significant figures for measurements • give a step-by-step description, e.g. of how to make up solutions (serial or proportional dilution), how to set up apparatus, how to collect measurements.
Describe any control experiments that need to be carried out.	
Describe, in a sequence of steps, the procedure to be carried out.	Another person should be able to carry out the experiment and need no further explanation.
Describe how to assess the quality of results.	Refer to ways to explain anomalous results and consider whether using standard deviation, standard error and/or 95% confidence intervals can be used to assess the validity of results.
Produce a simple risk assessment.	Consider the severity of any hazards and the probability that a problem could occur. Describe how to minimise these potential problems.

The experiments outlined here show how you can apply some of these planning skills to investigations into the rate of respiration of organisms.

Using redox indicators to investigate the rate of respiration of yeast

We have seen how redox reactions are involved in respiration. If yeast is actively respiring, reduced NAD will be produced during glycolysis and, when oxygen is available, it is also produced during the link reaction and Krebs cycle. In practical investigations, we can use redox indicators to model NAD so that a rate of respiration can be estimated.

Methylene blue and DCPIP are redox indicators that accept and donate electrons. They are blue when oxidised and colourless when reduced:

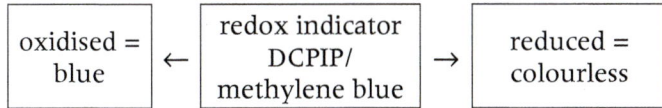

As respiration proceeds hydrogen atoms (and hence electrons) will be transferred to an oxidised redox indicator so that it becomes reduced. If we use DCPIP or methylene blue, this means that there will be a colour change from blue to colourless.

We can time how long it takes for this colour change to occur to obtain an estimate of the rate of respiration of yeast.

Using redox indicators to investigate the effect of temperature and substrate concentration on the rate of respiration of yeast in anaerobic conditions

Figure 1 shows a simple experimental set-up to measure the rate of respiration of yeast in anaerobic conditions. The apparatus could be used to investigate the effect of temperature or the effect of substrate concentration.

Temperature
In planning an investigation where temperature is the independent variable, there are a number of things you can consider.

Making a prediction:

- think about enzyme-controlled reactions
- remember that the rate of reaction will increase as temperatures increases, until a point where the enzyme denatures
- remember that the redox indicator is accepting hydrogen atoms (and hence electrons) produced in respiration
- understand that the longer it takes to change colour the slower the rate of respiration.

Varying and measuring the independent variable:

- using a controlled water bath (e.g. digital/electronic) to maintain temperatures
- use at least five different temperatures
- use a suitable range of temperatures
- using a thermometer to check temperatures.

Measuring the dependent variable:

- decide on what to measure, e.g. time to reach an end point
- decide what to use to measure the time for the colour change to occur, e.g. digital stopwatch
- decide how to measure an end point, e.g. when to judge a complete change from blue to colourless by comparing with a control with no methylene blue.

Key variables to standardise:

- glucose solution of a standard concentration, e.g. 1%
- standard mass of yeast in a standard volume of glucose solution to make up the yeast suspension

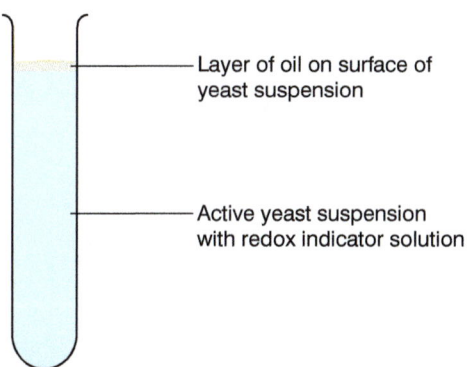

Figure 1 *Investigating rate of respiration in yeast using redox indicators*

- same concentration of redox indicator
- same volume of redox indicator added to the yeast suspension
- mixing suspension and indicator (e.g. stir with glass rod, three times)
- same depth of oil on surface of suspension.

Procedure:

- glucose solution prepared, then boiled and cooled, to remove any oxygen
- adding yeast to prepare suspension
- measuring out the correct quantity of yeast suspension into test-tube (using syringe of appropriate size)
- preparing standard to compare colour changes
- checking temperature of water bath
- equilibrating at the chosen temperature for set time in the water bath
- addition of correct quantity of redox indicator solution (using syringe of the appropriate size)
- adding oil to surface
- timing how long it takes to change from blue to colourless (using the standard to compare)
- repeats (replicates) at the same temperature, at least three, to calculate means.

Describe the control, e.g. boiled yeast suspension to show that colour does not change if no respiration is occurring.

Explain that the same procedure should be carried out at each of the chosen temperatures.

Risk assessment: low hazard activity but the redox indicator (and yeast suspension) could be hazardous to eyes.

Handling results: the mean rate of respiration at each temperature can be calculated as $1/t$. A graph can be constructed: y-axis = rate/$1/t$ and x-axis = temperature/°C.

Substrate concentration

To plan an experiment to investigate the effect of substrate concentration on the rate of respiration of yeast, exactly the same procedure as above can be used except:

- temperature now becomes a standardised variable
- the concentration of glucose solution now becomes the independent variable:
  - decide on at least five different concentrations
  - choose an appropriate range of concentrations.

After calculating rates, a graph can be drawn of rate against substrate concentration.

Investigation to determine the effect of temperature on the rate of respiration

The rate of respiration in an organism can be determined either by measuring the volume of oxygen taken in or the volume of carbon dioxide produced. The measurements can be made using simple respirometers, such as in Figure 2 or Figure 2 in 12.1c.

The main points to consider when planning the method:
- the independent variable is temperature
  - choose at least five different temperatures
  - choose an appropriate range of temperatures
  - alter temperature using a controlled water bath (e.g. digital/electronic)
  - check the temperature using a thermometer
  - allow organisms to equilibrate at each temperature
  - use the same organisms at each temperature.

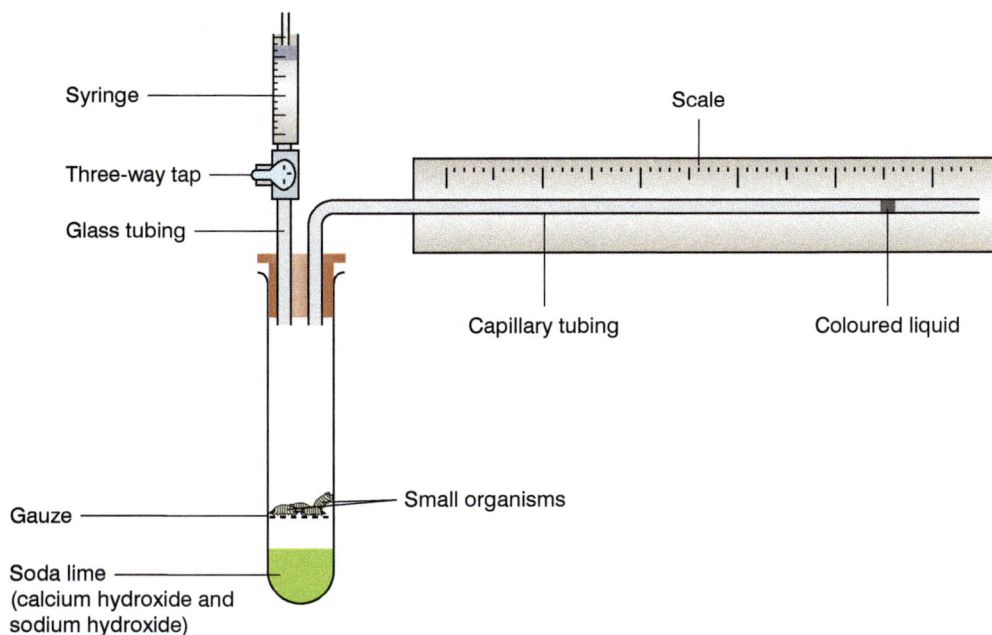

Syringe

Three-way tap

Glass tubing

Gauze

Soda lime
(calcium hydroxide and
sodium hydroxide)

Scale

Capillary tubing

Coloured liquid

Small organisms

Figure 2 *Simple respirometer without a control chamber (for the quantity of oxygen taken in, a scale reading can be taken, or the volume calculated using $\pi r^2 h$)*

- the dependent variable is the volume of oxygen taken in:
  - see 12.1c for details of how to calculate the volume (this is actual volume) *OR* take a scale reading (not an actual volume in mm^3 or cm^3, but units on the scale bar)
  - take readings at set time intervals, for example 0, 5, 10, 15, 20 minutes
  - repeat each temperature three times to obtain means
- risk assessment: low hazard experiment.

Taking measurements at set time intervals allows us to see if the rate of respiration changes over time, for example, if the decrease in oxygen in the chamber is affecting respiration rate. If this is so, then the rate can be calculated where the values produce a straight line in the earlier part of the experiment. The rate should be calculated using the same time after the start of the experiment for each temperature. Remember that the rate is volume of oxygen taken in per unit time (e.g. $cm^3\ min^{-1}$). A graph can be constructed using the calculated rates : y-axis = rate of respiration/$cm^3\ min^{-1}$ and x-axis = temperature/°C.

Experimental design usually involves carrying out pilot (trial) experiments, particularly when it is difficult to judge how many organisms to use and how long to time for to be able to measure a change in the level of manometer fluid.

The respirometer shown in Figure 2 does not take account of fluctuations in temperature or pressure so will produce less accurate results than a differential respirometer. For this respirometer, a separate control experiment is needed. This is the same set-up containing glass beads of the same mass as the experimental organisms. Any change in the level of the manometer fluid can be taken into account when calculating the volume of oxygen taken in by the organisms.

Summary test 12.2f

When carrying out an experiment using a redox indicator to investigate the rate of respiration of yeast at different temperatures, the yeast suspension must also contain **(1)** as a respiratory substrate. A redox indicator such as **(2)** or **(3)** can be used. The indicator changes from a **(4)** colour when it is oxidised to **(5)** when it is **(6)**. The rate can be calculated as **(7)**. Temperature can be changed using a **(8)**. To investigate the effect of substrate concentration, a key variable to standardise is **(9)**. The independent variable is **(10)** and the dependent variable is **(11)**. A **(12)** can be used to measure rates of respiration by measuring the volume of oxygen taken in or the volume of carbon dioxide given out in a set time period.

$$\boxed{\text{📄 Launch additional digital resources for the chapter}}$$

12 Exam-style questions

1 Figure 1 represents an ATP molecule.

Figure 1

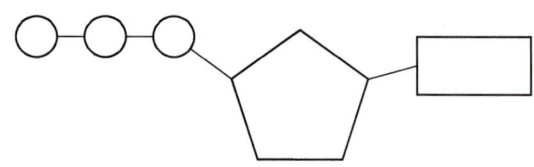

a On Figure 1, use label lines and letters to label each of the following parts:

   A – the nitrogenous base adenine
   P – phosphate   *(2 marks)*

b Name **one** location in the mitochondrion where ATP is produced.   *(1 mark)*

c Describe why ATP is considered the energy currency in all organisms.   *(2 marks)*

d Outline the events that allow chemiosmosis to occur in the mitochondrion **and** explain how these lead to the synthesis of ATP.   *(6 marks)*

(Total 11 marks)

2 Figure 2 shows the experimental set-up for a simple respirometer.

Figure 2

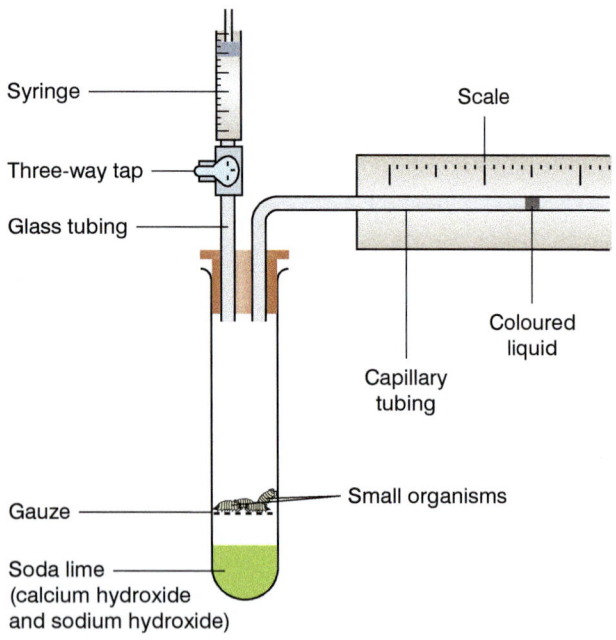

Syringe

Three-way tap

Glass tubing

Scale

Coloured liquid

Capillary tubing

Small organisms

Gauze

Soda lime (calcium hydroxide and sodium hydroxide)

A student used the experimental set-up shown in Figure 2 to carry out an investigation to compare the respiratory quotient (RQ) values of blowfly larvae and germinating seeds.

The experiment was first carried out using blowfly larvae.

The experiment was repeated using the blowfly larvae, but the soda lime was replaced with water.

The student then repeated these experiments using germinating seeds. The mass of the seeds was the same as the mass of blowfly larvae.

In all experiments, the distance moved by the coloured liquid after 15 minutes was recorded. All other variables were standardised. Table 2 shows the results obtained.

Table 2

Organism	Distance moved by coloured liquid / mm	
	with soda lime	with no soda lime (water)
Blowfly larvae	8	2
Germinating seeds	7	–2

The student calculated RQ using the formula:

$$RQ = \frac{a - b}{a}$$

a = distance moved by coloured liquid towards the tube with soda lime
b = distance moved by coloured liquid towards the tube without soda lime

a Explain why a negative value for distance moved by the coloured liquid was obtained for germinating seeds in the experimental set-up without soda lime.   *(1 mark)*

b With reference to Table 2, calculate the RQ for both the blowfly larvae and germinating seeds. Give your answer to 2 decimal places.   *(2 marks)*

c Suggest and explain what the RQ values indicate for the blowfly larvae **and** the germinating seeds.   *(4 marks)*

d Define *respiratory quotient (RQ)*.   *(1 mark)*

(Total 8 marks)

12 Practice questions

Incubated with	Complete homogenate		Nuclei only		Ribosomes only		Mitochondria only		Remaining cytoplasm only	
	Carbon dioxide	Lactate	Carbon dioxide	Lactate	Carbon dioxide	Lactate	Carbon dioxide	Lactate	Carbon dioxide	Lactate
Glucose	✓	✓	✗	✗	✗	✗	✗	✗	✗	✓
Pyruvate	✓	✓	✗	✗	✗	✗	✓	✗	✗	✓
Glucose + cyanide	✗	✓	✗	✗	✗	✗	✗	✗	✗	✓
Pyruvate + cyanide	✗	✓	✗	✗	✗	✗	✗	✗	✗	✓

3 Cyanide is a non-competitive inhibitor of an enzyme in the electron transport chain. It therefore prevents the transfer of electrons along this chain. To determine where in the cell some of the respiratory pathways take place, scientists carried out the following experiment involving cyanide.

Mammalian liver cells were broken up (homogenised) and a sample of whole homogenate was removed. The remaining homogenate was placed in a centrifuge. A centrifuge can be spun at different speeds to allow different fractions of homogenised cells to be collected. At slower speeds, heavier particles can be obtained from the bottom of the tube (sediment). The rest can be transferred to another tube and spun at a faster speed and the process continued until all fractions are obtained.

Portions containing only nuclei, ribosomes, mitochondria and the remaining cytoplasm were separated out. Samples of each portion, and of the complete homogenate, were incubated as follows:

- with glucose
- with pyruvate
- with glucose and cyanide
- with pyruvate and cyanide.

After incubation the presence or absence of carbon dioxide and lactate in each sample was recorded. The results are shown in the table above in which ✓ = present and ✗ = absent.

a Briefly describe how the different portions of the homogenate might have been separated out by centrifuging.

b From the results of this experiment, name **two** organelles that appear not to be involved in respiration. Explain your answer.

c i In which cell organelle would you expect to find the enzymes of the Krebs cycle?
ii Explain how the results in the table support your answer.

d Which portion of the homogenate contains the enzymes that convert pyruvate into lactate?

e Explain why lactate production occurs in the presence of cyanide but carbon dioxide production does not.

f Explain why, in samples incubated with glucose, carbon dioxide can be produced by the complete homogenate when none of the separate portions can do so.

g If glucose is incubated with cytoplasm from yeast cells, which **two** products would be formed?

h Which **three** of the following are likely to be rich in mitochondria: xylem vessel, liver cell, mature red blood cell, intestinal epithelial cell, muscle cell?

4 In an investigation into respiration in yeast, three test tubes were set up as follows:

Tube A	Tube B	Tube C
2 cm³ yeast suspension	2 cm³ distilled water	2 cm³ yeast suspension
2 cm³ glucose solution	2 cm³ glucose solution	2 cm³ distilled water
1 cm³ DCPIP	1 cm³ DCPIP	1 cm³ DCPIP

All three tubes were incubated at a temperature of 30 °C. The colour of each tube was recorded at the start of the experiment and after 5 and 15 minutes. The results are shown in the table below:

Time/mins	Colour of tube contents		
	Tube A	Tube B	Tube C
0	blue	blue	blue
5	colourless	blue	blue
15	colourless	blue	pale blue

a Tube B acts as a control. Explain why this control was necessary in this investigation.

b Using your knowledge of respiration, suggest an explanation for the colour change after 15 minutes in:
i tube A
ii tube C.

c How might the results in tube A after 15 minutes have been different if the experiment had been carried out at 60 °C? Explain your answer.

d After 20 minutes the contents of tube A were mixed with air by shaking it vigorously, turning the DCPIP back to a blue colour. Suggest a reason for this.

13.1 Photosynthesis as an energy transfer process

a. Two main stages of photosynthesis

These pages help you to:

- understand that the two main stages of photosynthesis are the light-dependent stage and the light-independent stage (Calvin cycle) (13.1.2)
- explain that energy transferred as ATP and reduced NADP from the light-dependent stage is used during the light-independent stage to produce complex organic molecules (13.1.2)

You will also:

- learn the overall equation for photosynthesis
- learn about types of photosynthetic organism other than green plants

Humans, along with almost every other living organism, owe their very existence to photosynthesis. The energy we use, whether from the food we respire or from the wood, coal, oil or gas that we burn in our homes, has been captured from sunlight by photosynthesis. Photosynthesis also produces the oxygen we breathe by releasing it from water molecules.

> **Extension**
>
> **Plants are not the only photosynthetic organisms**
>
> Unicellular and multicellular algae (including seaweeds) are photosynthetic protoctists. Figure 1 shows an aquatic forest of seaweeds known as giant kelp. They are a major source of food for heterotrophs and oxygenate the water for aquatic organisms. Some prokaryotes are also able to photosynthesise. Figure 2 shows the unicellular alga, *Chlorella*, the organisms used by Calvin in his famous 'lollipop' experiments to work out the Calvin cycle of the light-dependent stage of photosynthesis (13.1f).

An outline of photosynthesis

The overall equation for photosynthesis is:

$$6CO_2 \ + \ 6H_2O \ + \ \text{energy} \ \rightarrow \ C_6H_{12}O_6 \ + \ 6O_2$$

carbon dioxide   water   light   glucose   oxygen

Although the details are different, overall, photosynthesis is the reverse of aerobic respiration. In photosynthesis, oxygen is a waste product and carbon dioxide is needed.

The carbon dioxide produced as a waste product of respiration can be used during the day for photosynthesis. Some of the oxygen produced by photosynthesis during the day can be used by the plant for respiration. However, generally during the day the rate of photosynthesis exceeds (is higher than) that of respiration and oxygen diffuses out of the leaf through the open stomata.

Photosynthesis is a process in which the light energy, by a series of steps, is converted into chemical energy. There are two main stages in photosynthesis, the light-dependent stage and the light-independent stage. The overall equation above does not show us where in the process carbon dioxide is needed and where oxygen is produced. Figure 3 provides an overview of photosynthesis, showing the two main stages. You can see that oxygen is given off in the light-dependent stage and carbon dioxide is used in the light-independent stage.

> **Extension**
>
> **Autotrophic and heterotrophic nutrition**
>
> As we saw in 12.1a, autotrophs and heterotrophs have very different ways of obtaining the energy that they need for metabolic processes. **Nutrition** describes the process by which living organisms obtain this energy. The type of nutrition shown by photosynthetic organisms, such as plants, is autotrophic nutrition. All organisms that cannot build up complex organic compounds from simpler inorganic molecules show heterotrophic nutrition.

Figure 1

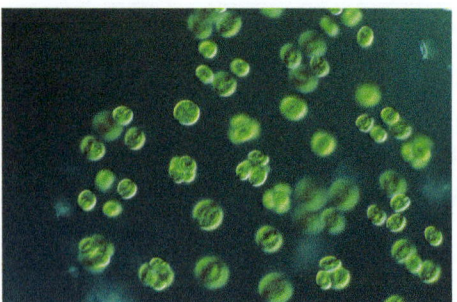

Figure 2

- **The light-dependent stage** is a process in which light energy is captured by chloroplast pigments such as chlorophyll, carotene and xanthophyll. An electron flow is created by the effect of light on chlorophyll, known as photoactivation. Photoactivation also causes water to split (**photolysis**) into hydrogen ions and oxygen. The useful products of the light-dependent stage are ATP from chemiosmosis, and reduced NADP.
- **The light-independent stage**, in which carbon dioxide is reduced to produce sugars and other organic molecules using the reduced NADP and ATP from the light-dependent stage.

The names of the two stages reflect the requirement for light for the reactions to proceed. The light-dependent stage absorbs light energy so that it can be converted to chemical energy and transferred as ATP and reduced NADP. The light-independent stage does not have any reactions that require light, but the reactions cannot proceed without ATP and reduced NADP. This means that this stage cannot occur in the dark (see Extension box in 13.1f).

ATP and NADP

So far, we have considered how the synthesis of ATP during respiration is used to provide energy to the cell for its metabolic needs. ATP is also synthesised during the light-dependent stage of photosynthesis by chemiosmosis. The energy to produce an electrochemical gradient to drive ATP synthesis comes from light and not from reduced coenzymes. Hydrolysis of ATP in the Calvin cycle in the light-independent stage provides energy for the cycle to continue and so produce sugars. The ADP and P_i (inorganic phosphate) produced can be recycled in the light-dependent stage.

NADP, nicotinamide adenine dinucleotide phosphate, is a coenzyme that, like coenzymes NAD and FAD, can take part in redox reactions. In the light-dependent stage, it accepts electrons and protons to become reduced. The reducing power of reduced NADP is essential for the light-independent stage and once oxidised during this stage it can be recycled.

Remember

In plants:

- photosynthesis occurs during daylight hours **only**
- respiration continues throughout the **day** and **night**.

Extension

A more accurate overall equation for photosynthesis

Experiments using radioactive **isotopes** show that all the oxygen produced ($6O_2$) comes from water molecules and not the carbon dioxide molecules. However, the $6H_2O$ in the equation only provides six oxygen atoms, rather than the 12 produced. What happens in practice is that 12 water molecules are used to produce the oxygen, and the hydrogens from the water are used to reduce the carbon dioxide and produce six water molecules. The equation for photosynthesis is therefore more accurately represented by the equation:

$$6CO_2 + 12H_2O + energy \rightarrow C_6H_{12}O_6 + 6O_2 + 6H_2O$$

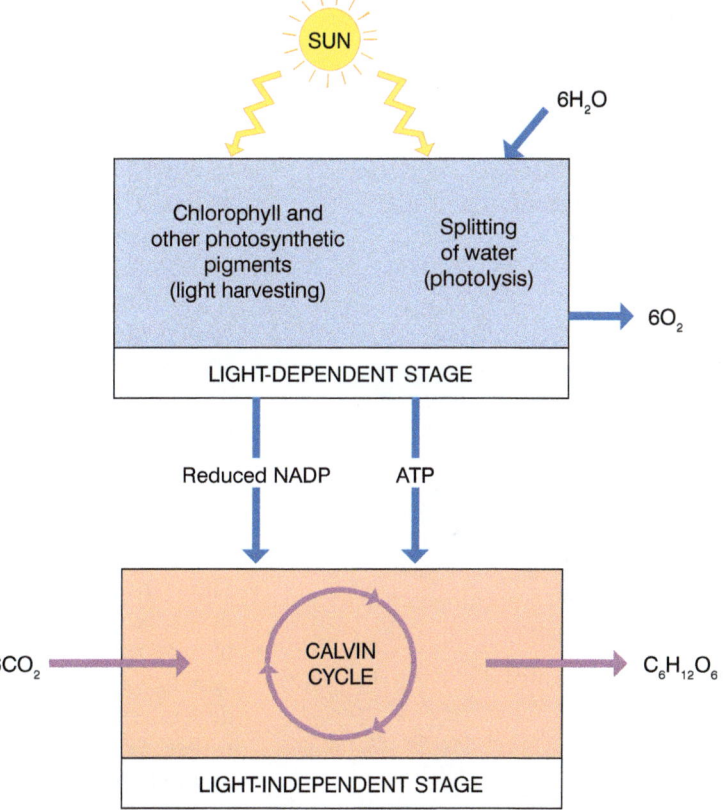

Figure 3 *Overview of photosynthesis*

Summary test 13.1a

Glucose, which has a molecular formula of **(1)**, is synthesised in photosynthesis using **(2)**, water and **(3)** energy. The first stage of photosynthesis is the **(4)** stage, where ATP and **(5)**, which is a **(6)**, are synthesised for the second stage. During the first stage, water is split and **(7)** is given off as a waste product. This can be used in the process of **(8)**. The second stage of photosynthesis is called the **(9)** stage. Here, **(10)** is reduced to produce sugars and other organic molecules.

These pages help you to:

- describe the relationship between the structure of chloroplasts, as shown in diagrams and electron micrographs, and their function (13.1.1)
- understand that thylakoids occur in stacks called grana and that thylakoids consist of the thylakoid membranes and thylakoid spaces (13.1.3)
- understand that within a chloroplast, the thylakoids are the site of the light-dependent stage and the stroma is the site of the light-independent stage of photosynthesis (13.1.3)

You will also:

- revise the structure of the leaf and the palisade mesophyll cell
- be able to relate these structures to their functions

Extension

Structure of the leaf

Leaves are adapted to bring together the three raw materials of photosynthesis (water, carbon dioxide and light) and remove its products (oxygen and glucose). These adaptations include:

- a large surface area that collects as much sunlight as possible
- a thin lamina (leaf blade), to keep the diffusion distance short
- a transparent cuticle and epidermis that let light through to the photosynthetic palisade cells
- numerous stomata for gaseous exchange that open and close in response to changes in light intensity
- many air spaces, especially in the spongy mesophyll, to allow diffusion of carbon dioxide and water vapour
- a network of vascular tissue made up of xylem that brings water to the leaf cells and phloem that carries away the sugars produced in photosynthesis.

The leaf is the main photosynthetic organ of the plant. Within the leaf, photosynthesis occurs in the cells of the palisade and spongy mesophyll tissues. In these cells, the organelles where photosynthesis takes place are the chloroplasts (Figure 1).

Structure and role of chloroplasts in photosynthesis

Photosynthesis takes place within cell organelles called **chloroplasts**, the structure of which is shown in Figure 2(d). These vary in shape and size but are typically disc-shaped, 3–10 µm long and 1 µm in diameter. They are surrounded by a double membrane called the **chloroplast envelope**. The inner membrane is highly selective in what it allows to enter and leave the chloroplast. Inside the chloroplast envelope are two distinct regions: the grana, where the light-dependent stage of photosynthesis occurs and the stroma, which is the site of the light-independent stage. Each granum is composed of thylakoids. The grana, with their thylakoids, and the stroma are well suited to their different functions.

- A **thylakoid** is a membrane-bound disc-shaped structure (Figure 2(e)). Within the thylakoid membranes are the light-absorbing chloroplast pigments, which are held by a network of membrane proteins in a structured arrangement to form complexes called photosystems I and II. This arrangement maximises light absorption. The thylakoid membranes enclose a fluid-filled lumen called the thylakoid space. This is where protons accumulate in the chemiosmosis process (12.1b). The membranes contain electron carriers and many ATP synthase complexes for ATP synthesis by chemiosmosis. They are relatively impermeable to protons to allow an electrochemical gradient to build up.
- A **granum** is a stack of up to 100 thylakoids (Figure 2(d)). The total quantity of thylakoid membranes in all the grana in a chloroplast provides an extremely large surface area for the attachment of the chloroplast pigments, electron carriers, enzymes and ATP synthase complexes that carry out the light-dependent stage. A granum offers a compact arrangement of thylakoids to maximise light absorption in the space available.
- **Intergranal lamellae** are tubular extensions that connect thylakoids of adjacent grana. They have mostly photosytem I complexes and also have ATP synthase complexes.
- The **stroma** is a fluid that has all the enzymes needed to carry out the reactions of the light-independent stage. It is colourless to allow light to reach the photosynthetic pigments. The stroma surrounds the grana and intergranal lamellae so provides easy access for ATP and reduced NADP from the light-dependent stage and for resulting ADP, P_i and oxidised NADP to be available for re-use. Within the stroma are a number of other structures such as starch grains and lipid droplets. Small, circular loops of DNA and 70S ribosomes are also present. Genes in chloroplast DNA code for some of the polypeptides needed in the chloroplast. The ribosomes are the sites of synthesis of these polypeptides.

Remember

Palisade mesophyll cells (Figure 2(c)) are adapted to carry out photosynthesis because they:

- are closely packed and thin-walled to absorb maximum light
- are arranged vertically so there are fewer cross walls that could filter out the light
- are packed with numerous chloroplasts that move within the cells to collect the maximum quantity of light
- have a large vacuole that pushes chloroplasts to the edge of the cell allowing them to absorb maximum light and reduce distance for the diffusion in of carbon dioxide
- have a large surface area and moist, thin walls for rapid diffusion of gases.

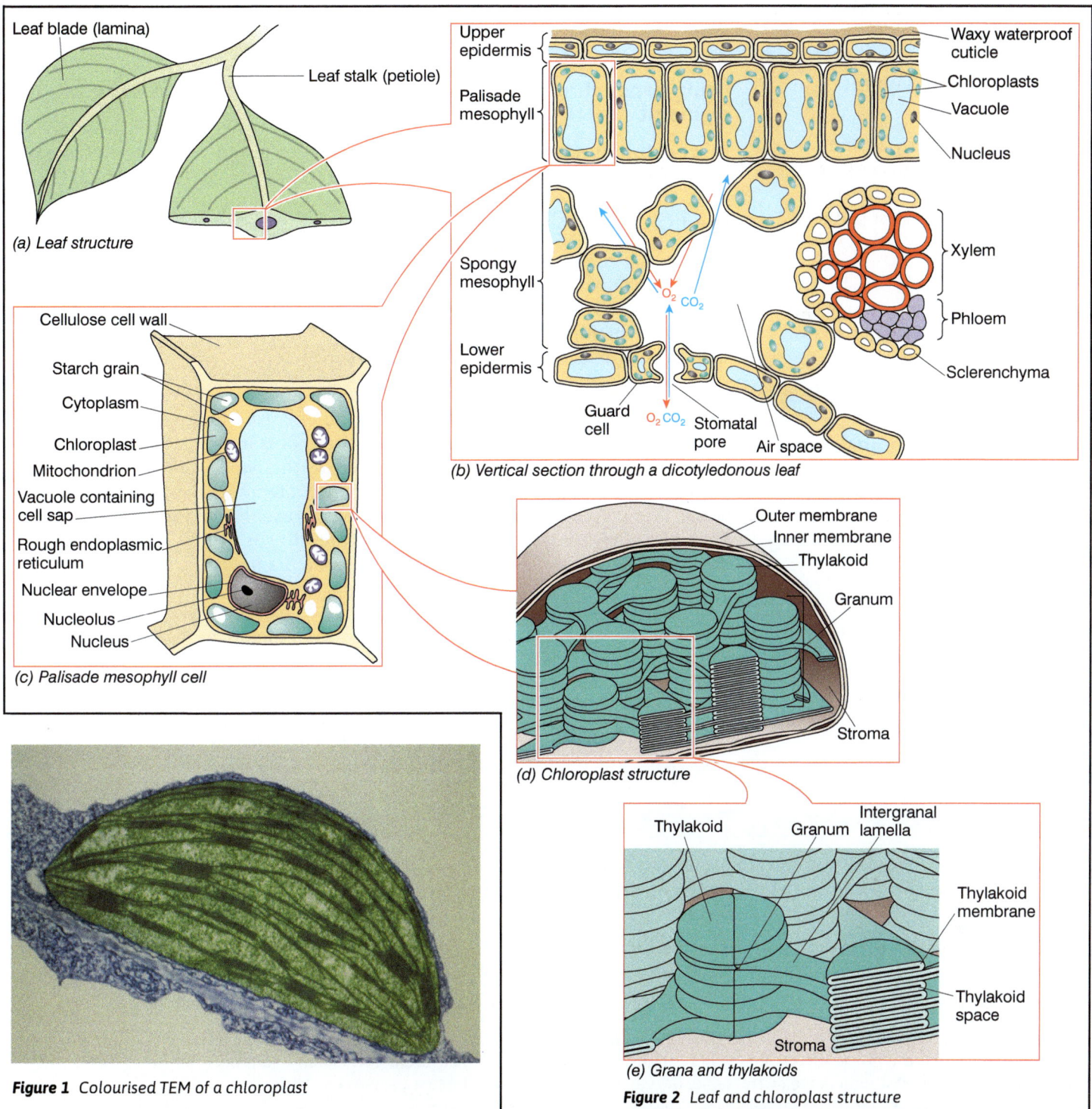

(a) Leaf structure

Leaf blade (lamina)

Leaf stalk (petiole)

Upper epidermis

Palisade mesophyll

Waxy waterproof cuticle

Chloroplasts

Vacuole

Nucleus

Spongy mesophyll

Lower epidermis

O₂ CO₂

Xylem

Phloem

Sclerenchyma

Guard cell

O₂ CO₂ Stomatal pore

Air space

(b) Vertical section through a dicotyledonous leaf

Cellulose cell wall

Starch grain

Cytoplasm

Chloroplast

Mitochondrion

Vacuole containing cell sap

Rough endoplasmic reticulum

Nuclear envelope

Nucleolus

Nucleus

(c) Palisade mesophyll cell

Outer membrane

Inner membrane

Thylakoid

Granum

Stroma

(d) Chloroplast structure

Figure 1 Colourised TEM of a chloroplast

Thylakoid

Granum

Intergranal lamella

Thylakoid membrane

Thylakoid space

Stroma

(e) Grana and thylakoids

Figure 2 Leaf and chloroplast structure

Summary test 13.1b

Leaves are the main site of photosynthesis, which occurs mainly in their **(1)** cells. They have numerous **(2)** that allow exchange of gases between themselves and the air around them and a network of veins made up of the tissue called **(3)** that brings water into the leaf and the tissue called **(4)** that carries away **(5)** produced in photosynthesis. Chloroplasts are the organelles that carry out photosynthesis. They are surrounded by a double membrane or **(6)** and possess both **(7)** and **(8)** that enable them to make their own proteins. Inside, there is a fluid-filled lumen called the **(9)** that has all the enzymes needed for the **(10)** reaction and also contains other structures like **(11)** grains and oil droplets. The fluid surrounds disc-like structures called **(12)** that are stacked in groups of up to 100 to form structures called **(13)** where the **(14)** reaction of photosynthesis takes place. The membranes of these structures are adapted for their function as they are the location for enzymes, chloroplast **(15)**, electron **(16)** and **(17)** complexes.

These pages help you to:

- describe and use chromatography to separate chloroplast pigments (13.1.6)
- describe how to use R_f values to identify chloroplast pigments (13.1.6)

You will also:

- improve your practical skills in planning investigations

Extension

Why do the pigments separate out in paper chromatography?

The chromatography paper has water bound to the cellulose fibres (water phase), and the pigments have different solubilities in the water. They are also retarded (held back) by the cellulose fibres to different extents as they move up the paper. Each pigment has a different solubility in the solvent: the more soluble the pigment, the further it will move up the paper with the solvent.

Using paper chromatography to separate and identify chloroplast pigments

Paper **chromatography** is a technique that can be used to separate and identify chloroplast pigments in a mixture. The most common chloroplast pigments in plants are: chlorophyll *a*, chlorophyll *b*, carotenes and xanthophylls (see 13.1d).

A solution containing a mixture of chloroplast pigments is obtained by placing pieces of leaf tissue in a mortar containing a small quantity of sand and solvent, and grinding with a pestle. A concentrated drop of the solution is prepared on a strip of chromatography paper (a special type of filter paper). The location of the spot, the origin, is marked (usually with a pencil line).

In ascending chromatography, the strip is placed vertically in a jar containing a small quantity of a different solvent to the one used to prepare the mixture. The end of the strip is in the solvent but the spot is located above its surface level. The solvent (the moving phase) ascends the paper (the stationary phase), running past the spot and carrying the pigments as it moves up the paper. The strip is removed before the solvent reaches the top of the paper. The point the solvent reaches is marked (the solvent front). After the paper has dried the positions that the different pigments have reached are marked.

The R_f (retention factor) value is calculated as:

$$\frac{\text{distance travelled by the pigment from the origin (baseline)}}{\text{distance travelled by the solvent front from the origin (baseline)}}$$

Each pigment has a specific R_f value in a particular solvent, and so the calculated values can be compared to known R_f values to identify the different pigments.

Practical skill

Planning an investigation using paper chromatography to identify and compare chloroplast pigments

You have been asked to plan an investigation to compare the chloroplast pigments in two different species of plant, **S** and **T**. Species **S** is a green-leaved plant and species **T** is a red-leaved plant.

You have been provided with solutions of the mixtures of chloroplast pigments of each species and have been given a set of R_f reference values of known chloroplast pigments so that you can compare the experimental R_f values obtained against these.

You have also been given details about the chemicals to use to make up the solvent used for the procedure.

When planning experiments the aim is to minimise error and to obtain results as close to the true values as possible. You should also have confidence that the procedure planned will result in precision in taking measurements. When you repeat the experiment, you should expect your measurements to be the same, or only vary slightly from the first experiment.

Knowledge and understanding required

- What is meant by a chloroplast pigment
- What is meant by an R_f value
- How to calculate R_f values
- It is also useful to understand the principles behind paper chromatography (see Extension).

Prediction

You will know that different chloroplast pigments will separate out using paper chromatography.

Although there are main chloroplast pigments that both species are likely to have, the red leaves of species **T** suggest that there will also be differences.

Variables

Make it clear that you know what the different variables are:

- independent variable = the species of plant
- dependent variable = the distance moved by the pigment
- variables to be standardised:
  - solvent used for the chromatography run (remember the paper is placed in the solvent so that it can move up the paper to meet the origin)
  - pH of solvent
  - temperature for the chromatography run
  - chromatography paper used
  - size of chromatography paper strip used
- two separate strips, one for each/one wider strip to run both at once:
  - volume of chromatography mixture applied
- give details, e.g. repeated spotting and drying, fixed number of spots:
  - distance moved by the solvent front (the solvent should not run off the end of the paper and should go far enough to be able to separate out the pigments in the mixture)
  - equipment used.

Procedure

Produce a step-by-step account, including apparatus to be used and taking account of precision: Give details of:

- preparation of solvent
- preparation of chromatography paper strip (dimensions)
- marking of solvent line
- spotting of mixture
- chromatography run so that the solvent front moves to near the top of the strip
- marking of solvent front
- collection of data.

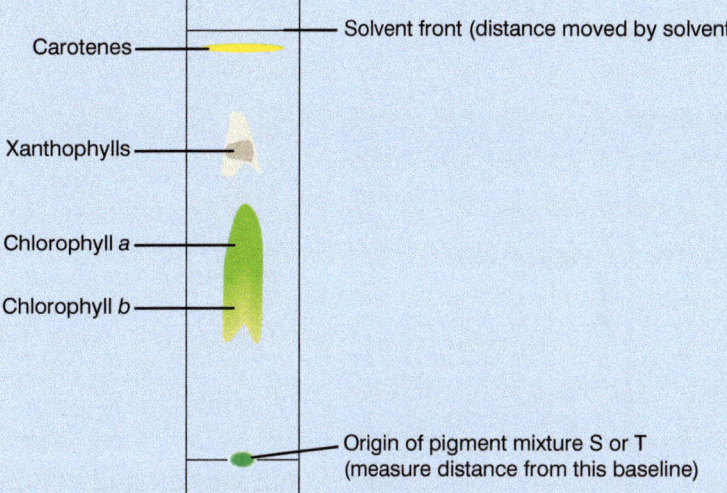

Carotenes — Solvent front (distance moved by solvent)

Xanthophylls —

Chlorophyll *a* —

Chlorophyll *b* —

Origin of pigment mixture S or T (measure distance from this baseline)

Figure 1 *Results of a paper chromatogram*

Collection of data

Figure 1 shows the results of a paper chromatogram with the most common pigments.

- Describe how to measure the distance moved by the chloroplast pigment and solvent front:
  - e.g. measure to the centre of the spot because some of the spots will be drawn out into larger areas OR measure to the top and to the bottom of the area and calculate the centre
  - state the equipment you will use to measure the distance (consider precision).
- State how many times (e.g. three) the chromatography should be repeated for each chloroplast mixture (replicates).

Results

Consider what to do with anomalous results. A larger number of replicates will allow anomalous results to be more easily detected.

Use the formula:

$$R_f = \frac{\text{distance travelled by the pigment from the origin (baseline)}}{\text{distance travelled by the solvent front from the origin (baseline)}}$$

If a large number of replicate results have been obtained, the standard deviation of the R_f values can be calculated for each pigment to provide a measure of precision of the procedure. For how to calculate the standard deviation, see 17.1c.

Compare results for **S** and **T**, using the reference values provided to identify the pigments.

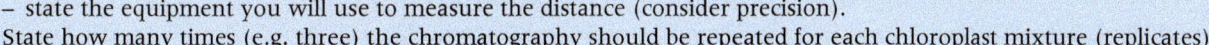

Summary test 13.1c

Chloroplast pigments in a mixture can be separated out using paper **(1)**. A concentrated spot of the mixture is built up on an origin line on the paper and a **(2)** moves up the paper to separate out the pigments. The pigment type that moves the furthest from the origin is **(3)**. The point where the solvent reaches is known as the **(4)**. The distance of this from the origin is measured. The **(5)** by each pigment from the origin is measured and the **(6)** value for each is calculated. This is compared to **(7)** values to identify each pigment.

These pages help you to:

- describe the role of chloroplast pigments (chlorophyll *a*, chlorophyll *b*, carotene and xanthophyll) in light absorption in thylakoids (13.1.4)
- interpret absorption spectra of chloroplast pigments and action spectra for photosynthesis (13.1.5)

You will also:

- become familiar with the general structure of chlorophylls, carotenes and xanthophylls
- understand that carotenes and xanthophylls are carotenoids

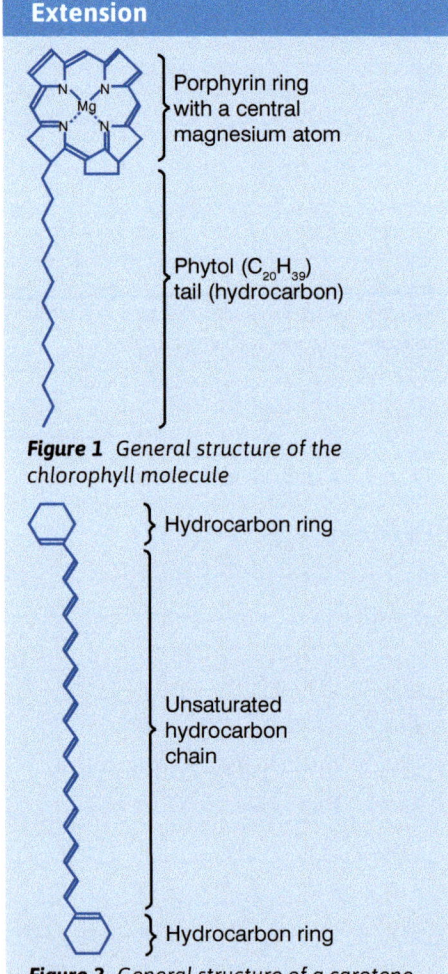

Extension

Figure 1 *General structure of the chlorophyll molecule*

Porphyrin ring with a central magnesium atom

Phytol ($C_{20}H_{39}$) tail (hydrocarbon)

Hydrocarbon ring

Unsaturated hydrocarbon chain

Hydrocarbon ring

Figure 2 *General structure of a carotene and xanthophyll molecule*

There are a number of pigments found in chloroplasts that act together to capture the light necessary for photosynthesis. The three most important groups of these pigments are the **chlorophylls**, **carotene** and **xanthophyll** (see Extension). Photosynthetic organisms are able to synthesise the pigments they need to carry out photosynthesis. Although all these organisms have chlorophyll *a*, there can be variation in the types and proportions of other photosynthetic pigments.

Chlorophyll

Chlorophyll is not a single substance, but rather a group of similar green pigments of which chlorophyll *a*, the most important photosynthetic pigment, and chlorophyll *b* are the most common. These pigments strongly absorb light in the blue and red wavelengths of the spectrum (Figure 3). Photoactivation of chlorophyll involves chlorophyll *a*. Chlorophylls are made up of a complex ring called a **porphyrin** ring, which has the same basic structure as the 'haem' group of the blood pigment **haemoglobin** but at its centre there is a magnesium atom (Figure 1).

Carotene and xanthophyll

Carotene and xanthophyll have a basic structure comprising two small rings linked by a long hydrocarbon chain (Figure 2). They range in colour from pale yellow, through orange to red. The greater the number of double bonds in the hydrocarbon chain, the deeper the colour. Carotene and xanthophyll are known as **accessory pigments** because they are not directly involved in the **light-dependent stage** of photosynthesis. Instead they absorb light wavelengths that are not efficiently absorbed by chlorophyll *a* and pass the energy they capture to chlorophyll *a* for use in the light-dependent stage.

Absorption and action spectra

Radiant energy comes in discrete packages called quanta. A single quantum of light is called a **photon**. Light also has a wave nature and so forms part of the electromagnetic spectrum. Visible light is made up of different wavelengths. The shorter the wavelength the greater the quantity of energy it possesses. A pigment, such as one of the chlorophylls, will absorb some wavelengths of light more than others. If the quantity of light it absorbs at each wavelength is plotted on a graph, we obtain what is called the **absorption spectrum**. The absorption spectra for chlorophyll *a*, chlorophyll *b* and carotene are shown in Figure 3.

We can also plot the effectiveness of different wavelengths of light in bringing about photosynthesis. This is called the **action spectrum** and shows that wavelengths around blue (450 nm) and red (650 nm) light are most effective in bringing about photosynthesis (Figure 3).

These two spectra are shown in Figure 3 and can be seen to follow a similar pattern, suggesting that the pigments are responsible for absorbing the light used in photosynthesis. If one pigment only is responsible for absorbing light for photosynthesis, then the absorption spectrum of that pigment would match closely the action spectrum.

If a pigment whose function is unknown is tested for its absorption spectrum, and the pigment has a peak absorption at 550 nm, then we can deduce that it does not function in absorbing light for photosynthesis.

Notice that chlorophylls *a* and *b* do not absorb much light in the green wavelengths and reflect most of this light. This explains why chlorophyll, and the chloroplasts in which they are located, appear green.

We can see in Figure 3 that carotene has a different absorption spectrum to chlorophylls *a* and *b*: this is an advantage as it extends the range of light wavelengths where light absorption can occur. For example, at wavelengths of approximately 450 nm, carotene has an absorption peak where chlorophyll *a* and *b* have a lower absorption. Carotene is also able to absorb light further into the green wavelengths than the chlorophylls.

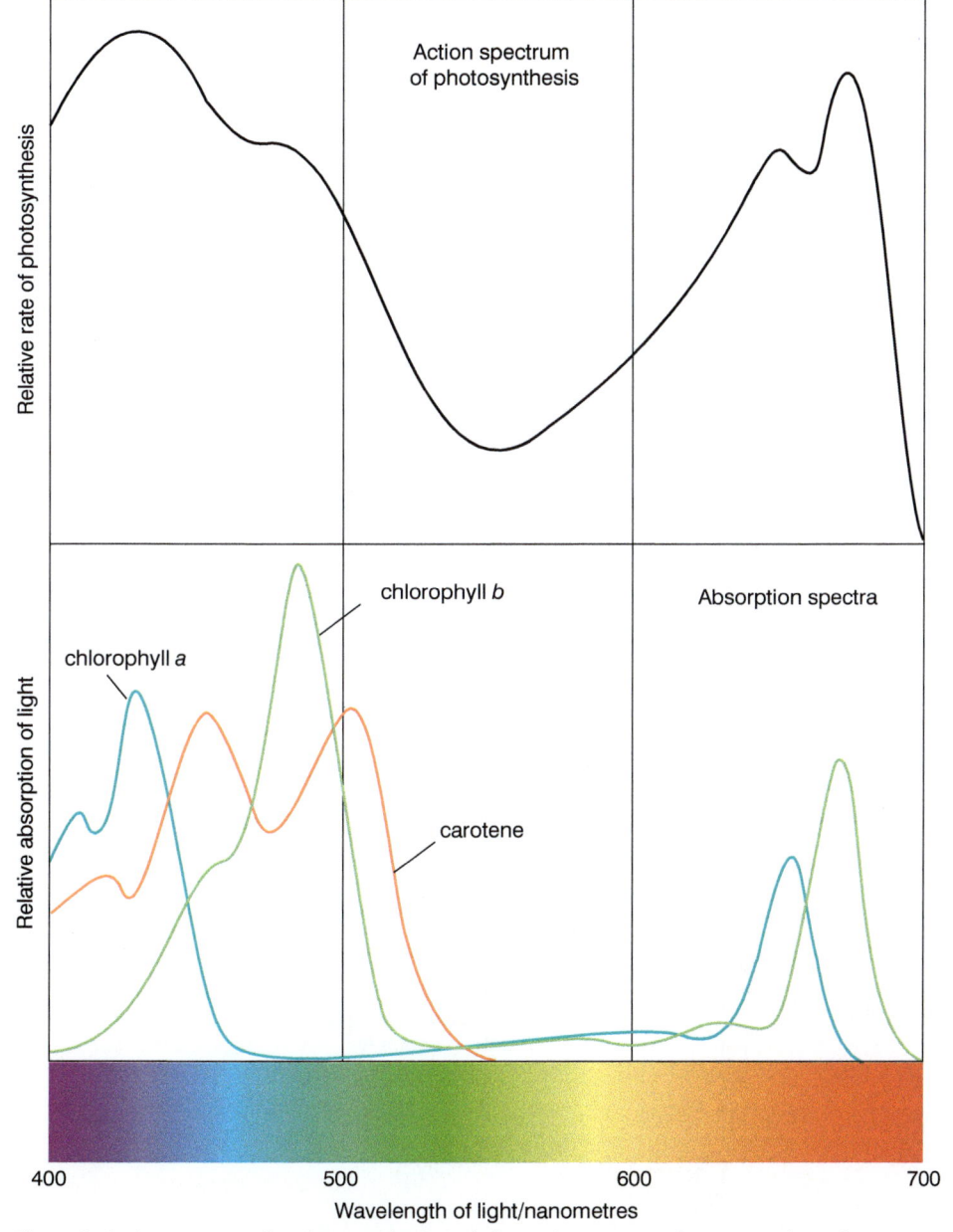

Figure 3 *Action spectrum for photosynthesis and absorption spectra of common plant pigments*

> ### Remember
>
> An absorption spectrum shows the absorption of different wavelengths of light by chloroplast pigments. Each pigment has its own pattern of absorption.
>
> An action spectrum shows the rate of photosynthesis at different wavelengths of light and results from the combined effect of the chloroplast pigments involved.

Remember

Chlorophyll *a* molecules that form part of the antenna complex absorb light energy and transfer this as an excitation energy to the reaction centre chlorophyll *a* molecules (special pair).

The reaction centre chlorophyll *a* molecules are the only pigments in the photosystem that emit excited electrons to pass to the electron transport chain. They have different peak absorptions of light to the antenna complex chlorophyll *a* molecules.

Summary test 13.1d

As part of the structure of their poryphyrin ring, chlorophylls *a* and *b* have a **(1)** atom. Two other common types of chloroplast pigment are **(2)** and **(3)**. Each photosystem has a reaction centre of two special chlorophyll *a* molecules, known as the **(4)**. An antenna complex is composed of **(5)** pigments. These pigments transfer **(6)** from light absorption to the reaction centre. Photosystems I and II differ in the light absorption peak of their reaction centres: this is **(7)** nm for photosystem I and **(8)** nm for photosystem II.

Light absorption

In 1932, plant physiologists Emerson and Arnold discovered that it took hundreds of chlorophyll molecules to produce a single molecule of oxygen. This led them to conclude that light for photosynthesis, rather than being absorbed by independent pigment molecules, is captured by groups of molecules. These groups are now known as **photosystems** and are located in the photosynthetic membranes (thylakoids and intergranal lamellae). They operate as follows:

- Each photosystem is a collection of photosynthetic pigments and associated proteins.
- One particular pair of chlorophyll *a* molecules, known as the primary pigments or the special pair, acts as a **reaction centre** for each photosystem.
- Surrounding the reaction centre are groups of pigment molecules that absorb light energy (photons). The pigment molecules are known as accessory pigments and can consist of chlorophyll *a* and *b*, carotene and xanthophyll molecules.
- These molecules form an **antenna complex**. They are held tightly together by proteins that act as a framework holding the pigment molecules in the best positions to allow energy to be transferred between them.
- The photon absorbed by an accessory pigment creates an excitation energy that is passed along a chain of pigment molecules to the reaction centre chlorophylls.
- Energy from many pigment molecules in an antenna complex is funnelled in this way to the reaction centre.
- Energy from one photon excites an electron in each of the primary pigment molecules (the 'special pair') of the reaction centre. These electrons play an important part in the light-dependent stage (13.1e).
- Close to the primary pigment molecules in the reaction centre is a molecule known as the primary electon acceptor.

Figure 4 illustrates the role of photosystems in light harvesting.

There are two different photosystems involved in photosynthesis:

- **Photosystem I (PSI)** has a reaction centre with a light absorption peak of 700 nm and is therefore known as P700.
- **Photosystem II (PSII)** has a reaction centre with a light absorption peak of 680 nm and is therefore known as P680.

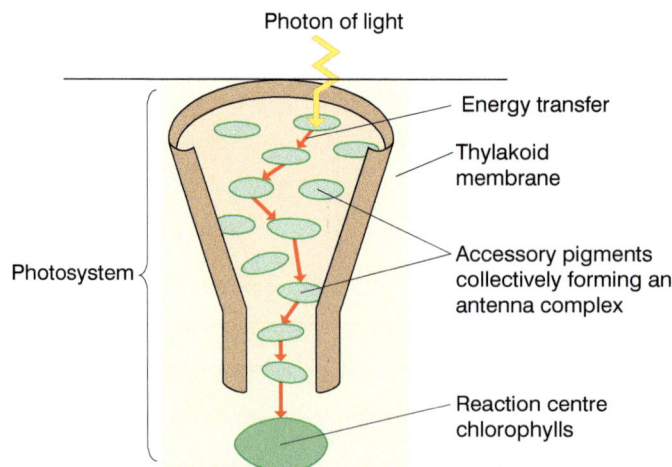

Figure 4 *Light harvesting system*

e. The light-dependent stage

The light-dependent stage of photosynthesis takes place in the thylakoids of the chloroplasts. It involves the absorption of light energy that is used for two purposes:

- To add an inorganic phosphate molecule to ADP, to make **ATP**. As this process of phosphorylation is brought about by light it is known as **photophosphorylation**.
- To split water into protons, electrons and oxygen. As the splitting is caused by light, it is known as **photolysis**.

The light-dependent stage consists of two separate processes, non-cyclic photophosphorylation and cyclic photophosphorylation.

- Non-cyclic photophosphorylation results in the production of ATP and reduced NADP for the light-independent stage of photosynthesis. Oxygen is a waste product.
- Cyclic photophosphorylation results in the production of ATP.

Photoactivation of chlorophyll and ATP synthesis

When light is passed to the reaction centre chlorophyll molecules, in photosystem I (PSI) or in photosystem II (PSII), a pair of electrons is raised to a higher energy level. This is known as the photoactivation of chlorophyll. These electrons are said to be in an **excited state** and are taken up by a molecule that is an **electron carrier** known as the **primary electron acceptor**.

The energetic electrons are now passed along a number of electron carriers in a series of redox reactions (12.2c). Each new carrier is at a slightly lower energy level than the previous one, and so the electrons lose energy at each stage. This energy is used to pump hydrogen ions (protons) across the thylakoid membrane into the thylakoid space (lumen). The photolysis of water, which is described in more detail on page 264, releases hydrogen ions (protons) to the thylakoid lumen, where they contribute to the build-up of the proton gradient.

ATP is produced as a result of chemiosmosis, with an accumulation of protons resulting in an electrochemical gradient (see also 12.1b and 12.2c). Protons that build up in the thylakoid space flow through the ATP synthase complex of the thylakoid membrane by facilitated diffusion to the stroma, providing the energy to combine inorganic phosphate with ADP to form ATP. This process is called photophosphorylation, as it requires light (not oxygen as in oxidative phosphorylation).

Cyclic photophosphorylation

Cyclic photophosphorylation uses only photosystem I. Photoactivation of the reaction centre chlorophyll *a* molecules results in the emitted energetic electrons being taken up by an electron acceptor and simply passed back to the same chlorophyll molecule via a sequence of electron carriers in the electron transport chain, i.e. they are recycled. While this does not produce any reduced NADP, it does generate enough energy to combine inorganic phosphate with ADP. The ATP so produced is then used in the light-independent stage (13.1f). This stage requires a higher proportion of ATP molecules than reduced NADP (3:2) so cyclic photophosphorylation provides the additional ATP needed. Cyclic photophosphorylation is summarised in Figure 1.

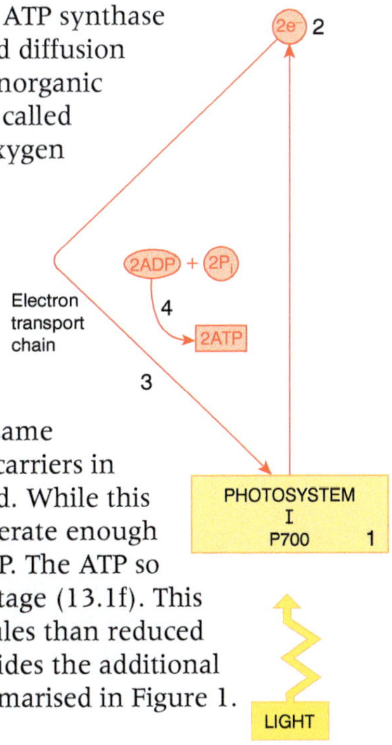

These pages help you to:

- learn that cyclic photophosphorylation and non-cyclic photophosphorylation occur during the light-dependent stage of photosynthesis (13.1.7)
- understand that photoactivation of chlorophyll occurs in photosystem I (PSI) and photosystem II (PSII) (13.1.8 and 13.1.9)
- explain that, in cyclic photophosphorylation, only PSI is involved and ATP is synthesised (13.1.8)
- explain that non-cyclic photophosphorylation involves PSI and PSII and results in the production of ATP and reduced NADP (13.1.9)
- understand that in non-cyclic photophosphorylation the oxygen-evolving complex catalyses the photolysis of water (13.1.9)
- describe how the flow of energetic electrons in the electron transport chain leads to the synthesis of ATP by chemiosmosis, including the build-up of a proton gradient in the thylakoid space and the return to the stroma of the protons though ATP synthase (13.1.10)

You will also:

- be able to compare cyclic and non-cyclic photophosphorylation
- read about the enhancement effect

Figure 1 *Summary of cyclic phosphorylation: (1) Light absorbed by PSI is used to excite electrons in the reaction centre chlorophyll a molecules. (2) Energetic electrons emitted are accepted by an electron acceptor. (3) Electrons flow down an electron transport chain to replace those lost from PSI. (4) Electron flow down energy levels in the electron transport chain leads to ATP synthesis*

Non-cyclic photophosphorylation

The overall process of non-cyclic photophosphorylation, outlined in Figure 2, involves a number of different events and uses both photosystem I (PSI) and photosystem II (PSII). For convenience, we can break down the process into sections. In each section, the numbered descriptions correspond to the numbers in the summary in Figure 3.

Photoactivation of chlorophyll

This is a process where light energy causes the excitation of electrons in chlorophyll molecules, resulting in them becoming temporarily raised to a higher energy level:

1 Light energy is absorbed by chloroplast pigments in photosystem II (PSII) and photosystem I (PSI).
2 Excitation energy is passed to the reaction centre chlorophyll *a* molecules of PSII and PSI. A pair of excited electrons are emitted from the reaction centre chlorophyll *a* molecules, which are now oxidised and cannot function until the electrons are replaced (see Extension).
3 The emitted electrons are raised to a higher energy level (energetic electrons) and are accepted by primary electron acceptors, which becomes reduced. The electron acceptors are different for PSII and PSI.

Photolysis of water

The splitting of water by photolysis is a direct consequence of the photoactivation of chlorophyll. It occurs only in photosystem II, which is associated with an enzyme known as the **oxygen-evolving complex** (OEC) (note that photolysis is shown apart from PSII in Figure 3 for convenience only). The reaction catalysed by the OEC is:

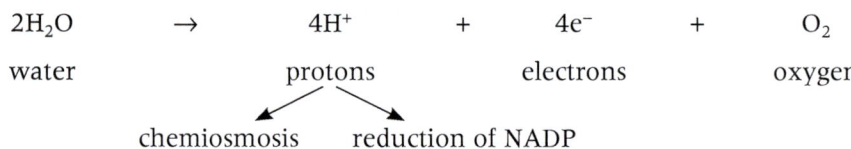

$$2H_2O \rightarrow 4H^+ + 4e^- + O_2$$

water   protons   electrons   oxygen

chemiosmosis   reduction of NADP

The oxygen by-product is either used in respiration or diffuses out of the leaf as a waste product of photosynthesis.

4 The absorption of light in PII leads to photolysis of water.
5 The electrons that have been lost from PII are replaced by electrons from the photolysis of water.

The electron transport chain and the synthesis of ATP (see page 263 and 12.1b).

6 The energetic electrons from PSII are passed along a sequence of electron carriers in the electron transport chain. The energy released by electron flow down energy levels is used in the synthesis of ATP by chemiosmosis.
7 At the end of the electron transport chain the electrons replace those lost from PSI (as a result of photoactivation of chlorophyll).

Reduction of coenzyme NADP⁺

8 The energetic electrons from PSI are passed by their primary electron acceptor to reduce NADP⁺ (NADPH + H⁺) in a reaction catalysed by NADP reductase. Protons from the photolysis of water are used in the reduction.

Table 1 *Comparison of cyclic and non-cyclic photophosphorylation*

	Cyclic	Non-cyclic
Electrons returned to chlorophyll molecule directly	Yes	No
Photosystems involved	I	I and II
Photolysis of water involved	No	Yes
Products	ATP	ATP, Reduced NADP + oxygen

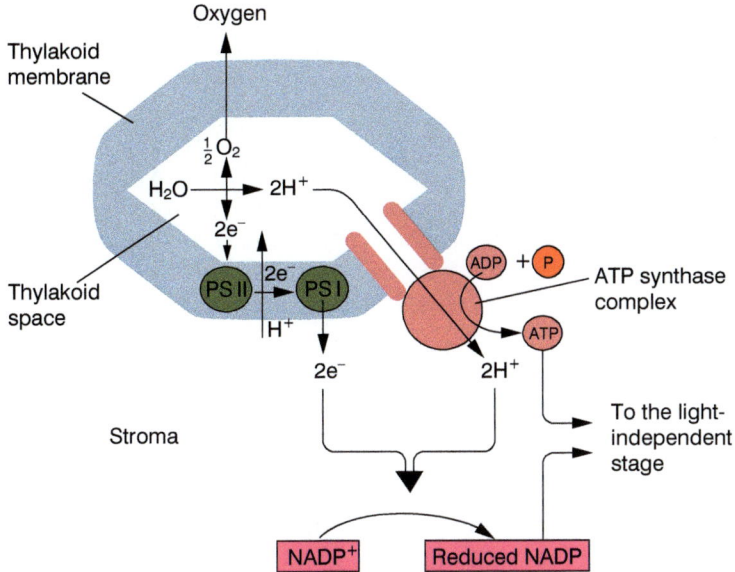

Figure 2 *Outline of non-cyclic photophosphorylation*

Table 1 compares cyclic and non-cyclic photophosphorylation.

The Z-scheme

The events occurring in non-cyclic photophosphorylation are summarised in Figure 3, which illustrates the zig-zag energy levels of the electrons. As the diagram resembles a Z on its side, the complete process is called the Z-scheme.

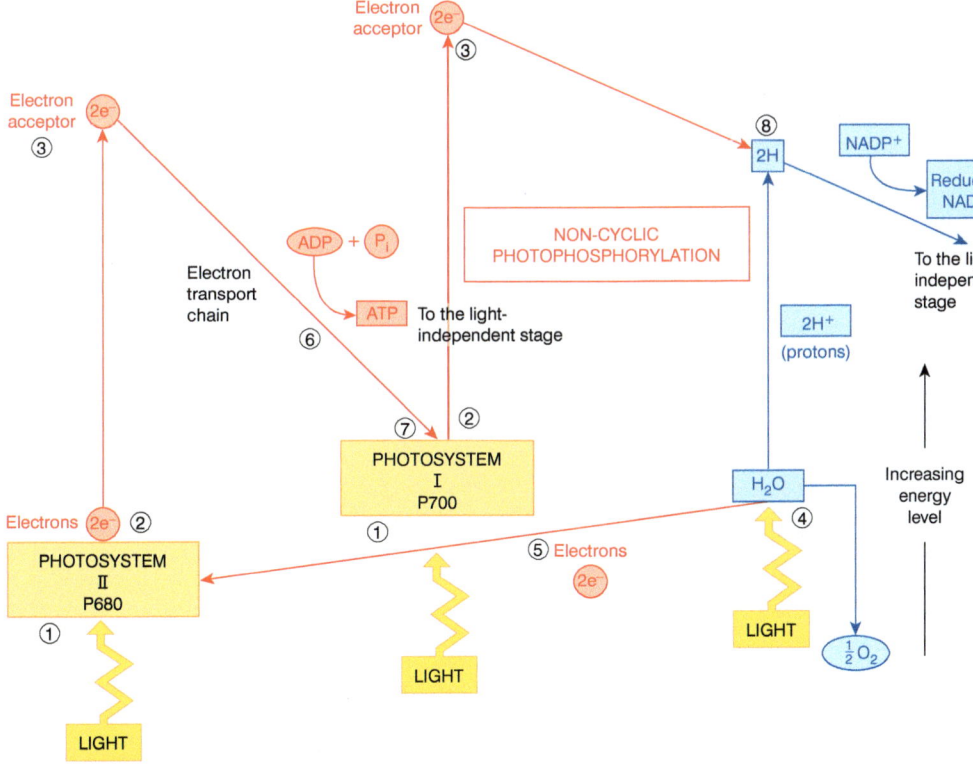

Figure 3 *Summary of the light-dependent stage of photosynthesis*

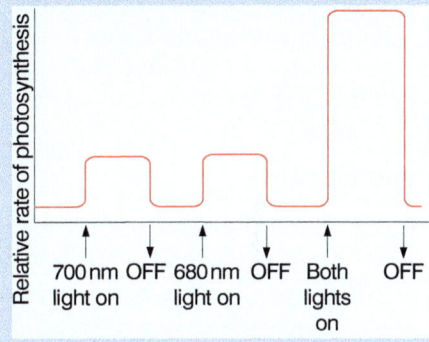

These pages help you to:

- understand that, in the Calvin cycle, ribulose bisphosphate (RuBP) combines with carbon dioxide in a reaction catalysed by rubisco, with the production of glycerate-3-phosphate (GP) (13.1.11)
- understand that the ATP and reduced NADP from the light-dependent stage are used to reduce GP to triose phosphate (TP) (13.1.11)
- understand that ATP is used to regenerate RuBP from TP (13.1.11)
- outline that GP is used to produce some amino acids and TP is used to produce carbohydrates, lipids and amino acids (13.1.12)

You will also:

- read about the work of Calvin, Benson and Bassham
- learn more about rubisco

The products of the light-dependent stage of photosynthesis, namely ATP and reduced NADP (NADPH + H$^+$) are used to reduce carbon dioxide in the second part of photosynthesis. Unlike the first stage, this stage does not require light directly and is therefore called the **light-independent stage**. In practice, it requires the products of the light-dependent stage and so rapidly stops when light is absent. The light-independent stage takes place in the **stroma** of the chloroplasts. The details of this stage were worked out by Melvin Calvin and his co-workers (see Extension). The process is therefore often known as the **Calvin cycle**.

The Calvin cycle

In the following account of the Calvin cycle, the numbered stages are shown in Figure 1. Each step in the Calvin cycle is enzyme controlled.

1. Carbon dioxide from the atmosphere diffuses into the leaf through **stomata** and dissolves in water around the walls of the **palisade** cells. It then diffuses through the cell surface membrane, cytoplasm and chloroplast envelope into the stroma of the chloroplast.
2. In the stroma, the carbon dioxide combines with the five-carbon compound **ribulose bisphosphate (RuBP)** using the enzyme **ribulose bisphosphate carboxylase (rubisco)**, to form an unstable six-carbon compound.
3. The unstable six-carbon compound immediately breaks down into two molecules of the three-carbon **glycerate 3-phosphate (GP)**.

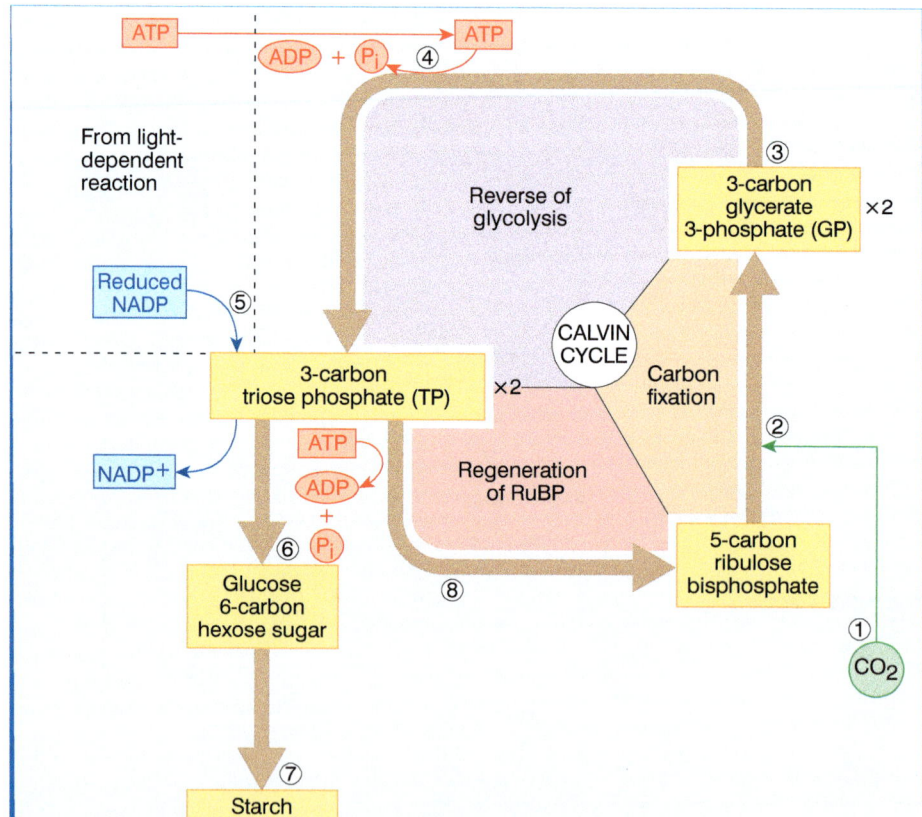

Figure 1 *Summary of the light-independent stage of photosynthesis*

4. Using one of the ATP molecules from the light-dependent stage, the GP (glycerate 3-phosphate) is converted into a three-carbon sugar **triose phosphate (TP)**.

5. Reduced NADP from the light-dependent stage provides hydrogen for the reduction of GP to TP (glycerate-3-phosphate to triose phosphate).

6. Triose phosphate molecules combine in pairs to form six-carbon (hexose) sugars such as glucose and fructose.

7. The six-carbon sugars can be **polymerised** into starch.

8. Five out of every six triose phosphate molecules produced are used to regenerate RuBP using the remainder of the ATP from the light-dependent stage as the source of energy.

Each complete Calvin cycle fixes one carbon dioxide molecule and produces two TPs. Six carbon dioxide molecules are used for the synthesis of one glucose molecule, so for six complete cycles 12 TPs are produced. Two of these are used to synthesise one glucose molecule, which leaves 10 TPs to regenerate the six RuBPs needed for the cycle to continue:

$$10 \times 3C \text{ TPs} = 30 \text{ carbons}$$
$$6 \times 5C \text{ RuBPs} = 30 \text{ carbons}$$

Formation of other substances for use by the plant

Plants, like other organisms, are made up of a range of complex organic molecules. The bulk of these are carbohydrates, lipids and proteins. Unlike animals and other **heterotrophic** organisms, plants cannot obtain these substances by taking them in from the outside. They must synthesise them from the various compounds of the Calvin cycle.

- Carbohydrates, e.g. sucrose (the carbohydrate which is transported in the phloem) are made by combining the two hexose sugars, glucose and fructose.
- Starch (the storage carbohydrate) and cellulose (the essential component of cell walls) are made by polymerising glucose in different ways.
- Lipids are made up of glycerol and fatty acids. Plants make glycerol from triose phosphate and fatty acids from glycerate 3-phosphate (GP). Lipids are used in plant cells for storage and to form phospholipids in their cell membranes.
- Proteins are made up of amino acids. Some amino acids can be produced from GP and some from TP. These can be used for the synthesis of other amino acids in proteins. Proteins are important components of cell membranes and all enzymes are proteins.

Summary test 13.1f

The light-independent stage is also known as the **(1)** cycle after the person who determined its biochemical sequence. In the process, carbon dioxide combines with a five-carbon compound called **(2)** to form a six-carbon intermediate that immediately splits into two molecules of **(3)**. By the addition of **(4)** and **(5)** formed in the **(6)** stage, each of the molecules is then converted into a **(7)** molecule. Six 'turns' of the cycle are required for the formation of one **(8)** molecule. This can be polymerised to form **(9)**, which can be stored. Other organic products from this molecule are **(10)** and amino acids. The five-carbon compound is **(11)** from TP. **(12)** is needed for this stage of the cycle. Some amino acids can also be made from **(13)**.

These pages help you to:

- understand that light intensity, carbon dioxide concentration and temperature are examples of limiting factors of photosynthesis (13.2.1)
- explain the effects of changes in light intensity, carbon dioxide concentration and temperature on the rate of photosynthesis (13.2.2)

You will also:

- see how knowledge of limiting factors can help increase crop yields in glasshouses

Remember

The law of limiting factors can therefore be expressed as: **At any given moment, the rate of a physiological process is limited by the one factor which is at its least favourable value, and by that factor alone.**

Before we consider some of the factors affecting photosynthesis, it is necessary to understand the **concept of limiting factors**.

Limiting factors

In any complex process such as photosynthesis, the factors that affect its rate all operate simultaneously. However, the rate of the process at any given moment is **not** affected by a combination of all the factors, but rather by just one – the one whose level is at the least favourable value. This factor is called the **limiting factor** because it alone limits the rate at which the process can take place. However much the levels of the other factors change, they do not alter the rate of the process.

To take the example of light intensity limiting the rate of photosynthesis:

- In complete darkness, it is the absence of light alone that prevents photosynthesis occurring.
- No matter how much we raise or lower the temperature or change the concentration of carbon dioxide, there will be no photosynthesis. Light, or rather the absence of it, is the factor determining the rate of photosynthesis at that moment.
- If we provide light, however, the rate of photosynthesis will increase.
- As we add more light, the more the rate increases. This does not continue indefinitely, however, because there comes a point at which further increases in light intensity have no effect on the rate of photosynthesis.
- At this point some other factor, such as the concentration of carbon dioxide, is in short supply and is now the limiting factor so, only an increase in its level will increase the rate of photosynthesis.
- Again, at some point further increases in carbon dioxide levels will fail to have any effect.
- At this point a different factor, e.g. temperature, is the limiting factor and only an alteration in its level will affect the rate of photosynthesis.

These events are shown in Figure 1.

Effect of light intensity on the rate of photosynthesis

The absorption of light in photosynthesis leads to the production of ATP and reduced NADP. A decrease in light intensity will decrease the quantity of these products and lead to a lower rate of glucose production in the Calvin cycle of the light-independent stage, so a lower rate of carbon dioxide uptake is measured. Additionally, less water is required as a source of electrons to replace those lost in PSII, so less oxygen is produced.

When light is the limiting factor, the rate of photosynthesis is directly proportional to light intensity. The rate of photosynthesis is usually measured in two ways:

- the volume of oxygen produced by a plant
- the volume of carbon dioxide taken up by a plant.

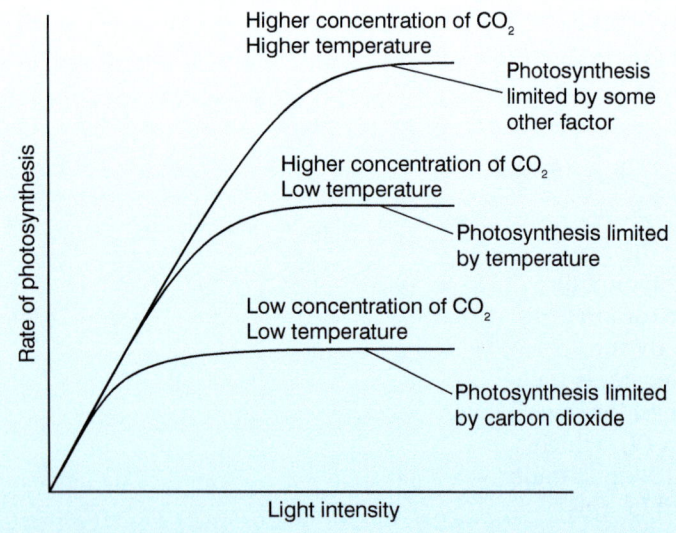

Figure 1 *Concept of limiting factors as illustrated by the effects of levels of different conditions on the rate of photosynthesis. Before the curves begin to level off, light intensity is a limiting factor*

As light intensity is increased, the volume of oxygen produced and carbon dioxide absorbed due to photosynthesis will increase to a point at which it is exactly balanced by the oxygen absorbed and carbon dioxide produced by respiration. At this point there will be no net exchange of gases into or out of the plant. This is known as the **light compensation point**. Further increases in light intensity will cause a proportional increase in the rate of photosynthesis and increasing volumes of oxygen will be given off and carbon dioxide taken up. A point will be reached at which further increases in light intensity will have no effect on photosynthesis. At this point some other factor such as carbon dioxide concentration or temperature is limiting the reaction. These events are shown in Figure 2.

Effect of carbon dioxide concentration on the rate of photosynthesis

Carbon dioxide is present in the atmosphere at a concentration of around 0.04%. This level continues to increase as the result of human activities such as burning fossil fuels and the clearing of rain forests. It is still one of the rarest gases present and is often the factor that limits the rate of photosynthesis under normal conditions. The optimum concentration of carbon dioxide for a consistently high rate of photosynthesis is 0.1%. Figures 1 and 2 illustrate the effect of increased carbon dioxide levels on photosynthesis.

Effect of temperature on the rate of photosynthesis

Provided that other factors are not limiting, the rate of photosynthesis increases in direct proportion to the temperature. This is because the process involves enzyme-catalysed reactions. Between the temperatures of 0°C and 25°C the rate of photosynthesis is approximately doubled for each 10°C rise in temperature. Above the optimum temperature of 25°C the rate levels off and then declines – largely as a result of enzyme **denaturation**. Each reaction in the Calvin cycle is catalysed by an enzyme and so temperature will affect the rate at which the light-independent stage proceeds. In the light-dependent stage, the oxygen-evolving complex involved in the photolysis of water and NADP reductase, which catalyses the reduction of NADP, are also affected by temperature.

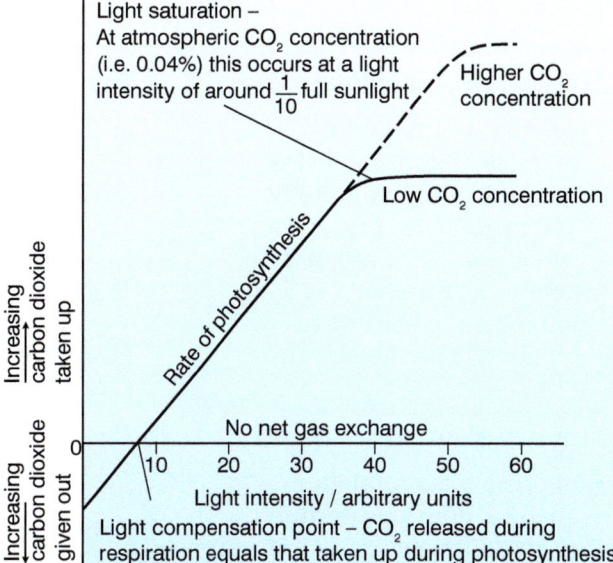

Figure 2 *Graph showing the effect of light intensity on the rate of photosynthesis as measured by the quantity of CO_2 exchange*

Extension

Increasing crop yields in glasshouses

Food production depends on photosynthesis. As the rate of photosynthesis is determined by the factor that is in shortest supply (limiting factor) it follows that there is commercial value in determining which factor is limiting photosynthesis at any one time. By supplying more of this factor, photosynthesis, and hence food production, can be increased.

Scientists are able to predict the effect of altering limiting factors and advise crop growers of the optimum conditions to create for the best crop yield. In enclosed environments such as glasshouses, it is relatively easy to control the conditions and optimise the environment for the best crop yield. Growers of some glasshouse crops like tomatoes enrich the air in the glasshouses with more carbon dioxide to provide higher yields.

In practice different plants have different optimum conditions and too high a level of a particular factor may reduce yield or kill the plant altogether. It is also uneconomic and wasteful to use energy to raise temperature or to increase carbon dioxide concentrations or light intensity if this does not produce a significantly increased yield. Precise control of the environment can be brought about in ways ranging from totally manual control to the use of advanced computerised systems.

Summary test 13.2a

At any given moment the rate of a physiological process is restricted by the one factor that is at its least favourable value. This is known as the **(1)**. The rate of photosynthesis can be measured by calculating the volume of **(2)** taken up or the volume of **(3)** produced by a plant. The light intensity at which there is no net exchange of gases into or out of the plant is known as the **(4)**. Carbon dioxide concentration affects the rate of photosynthesis. Normally present in the atmosphere at a proportion of **(5)**%, the optimum for a consistently high rate of photosynthesis is **(6)**%. As light intensity increases, the rate of photosynthesis increases **(7)** because **(8)** is the limiting factor. The rate increases at a decreasing rate and then **(9)** at higher light intensities because another factor becomes limiting.

Practical skill

Investigating the rate of the light-dependent stage of photosynthesis using isolated chloroplasts

We can use the method that Hill developed to investigate the effect of light wavelength and of light intensity on the rate of photosynthesis using a redox indicator, such as DCPIP or methylene blue (12.2f). The investigations using isolated chloroplasts are, in fact, measuring the rate of the light-dependent stage of photosynthesis because there is no carbon dioxide supplied to the chloroplast for the Calvin cycle of the light-independent stage to proceed.

A suspension medium for chloroplasts:

- is buffered so that it is at the correct pH for reactions to proceed
- is of the same water potential so that there is no net movement of water by osmosis, and therefore no shrinking or swelling (or lysis) of the organelles
- must be kept cold (in the refrigerator) until required for the experiments to prevent any damage to the chloroplasts (more specifically the thylakoid membranes) or to the enzymes needed for the light-dependent stage.

The Hill Reaction

In 1937, Robert Hill discovered that oxygen was given off from a suspension of isolated chloroplasts when they were illuminated. As there was no source of carbon dioxide in the suspension medium, this confirmed that the oxygen from photosynthesis came from water and not from carbon dioxide. The investigation he designed to show this used a redox indicator as an artificial electron acceptor. This is known as the Hill reaction.

Planning an investigation into the effect of light wavelength on the rate of photosynthesis

There are a number of considerations in planning an investigation into the effect of light wavelength on the rate of photosynthesis:

Knowledge and understanding required to plan the investigation

- **Redox indicators.** In the reactions of photosynthesis, DCPIP can accept electrons. This is accompanied by a colour change:

Chloroplast suspension is green. Therefore, the addition of DCPIP to a suspension of chloroplasts will give a blue-green colour rather than a blue colour. If electrons are accepted by the DCPIP, the colour that will be seen in the suspension is the original green colour (as the DCPIP is now colourless).
- **The light-dependent stage.** We know that, in nature, the final electron acceptor in non-cyclic photophosphorylation is the coenzyme NADP. Reduced NADP is required in the Calvin cycle in the light-independent stage. If non-cyclic photophosphorylation is occurring, this means that DCPIP can take the place of NADP in accepting the electrons, and so becomes reduced.
- **The action spectrum.** We have seen that different wavelengths of light will produce different rates of photosynthesis, so it is reasonable to deduce that the rate of formation of reduced NADP is affected by the wavelength of light.

Prediction

From your knowledge and understanding, you can deduce that:

- The chloroplast suspension is green and when blue DCPIP is added, the mixture will be blue-green.
- When the mixture is illuminated in the presence of DCPIP, the DCPIP will become colourless and so the mixture will become green again (Figure 1 on page 272).

You can predict that:

Particular wavelengths of light will cause the mixture to become green at a faster rate than other wavelengths (that is, a faster rate of photosynthesis) and that wavelengths at the orange/red and purple/blue end of the spectrum will become green at a faster rate than wavelengths in the green part of the spectrum.

Although you cannot predict numerical values for rate, you may also give a prediction by producing a sketch graph to show the pattern of the curve you would expect to observe (see 13.1d, the action spectrum):

- y-axis = rate/ $1/t$
- x-axis = wavelength of light/nm

Variables

Give details of the variables:

Independent variable. This is the factor that will have the effect on the rate of photosynthesis, which you can plan to control, the specific wavelength of light:

- state which colours (and hence wavelengths) are to be used
- e.g. use different coloured filters between the light source and the test mixture (each providing a specific wavelength of light).

Dependent variable. The time taken from first illumination for the mixture to become green, that is, the time taken for DCPIP to become colourless – you will need to decide how to judge this end point (e.g. colour standard, see below).

Variables to be standardised:

- volume of chloroplast suspension-DCPIP mixture (test mixture)
- background colour used to judge colour change, e.g. use a white tile or white piece of card
- intensity of light
  - e.g. distance of light source from mixture
  - e.g. light source shining from same angle
  - check filters allow the same intensity of light through
- temperature
- equipment used.

Control

You need to be sure that the DCPIP solution does not become colourless independently of the chloroplasts, so a suggested control could be to have only DCPIP solution and to check that this does not change colour from blue throughout the experiment.

Another control is to keep the same quantity of test mixture in the dark.

Procedure

Produce a step-by-step account, including apparatus to be used and taking account of precision. Give details of:

- handling the chloroplast suspension
- preparation of a colour standard to check for the original green colour (i.e. when DCPIP is colourless) – use chloroplast suspension without DCPIP
- addition of DCPIP solution to the suspension to obtain the test mixture with the blue-green start colour:
  - e.g. a standardised drop, one drop at a time, gently swirling to mix
  - test mixture to be kept in the dark, e.g. covered with foil, until needed
- light source
  - details of angle and distance of light source
  - where filter is placed, e.g. attached to lamp/directly in front of reaction mixture
  - light switched off until ready
- removal of chloroplast suspension–DCPIP mixture:
  - all volumes required measured using apparatus with precision, e.g. sizes of syringes/graduated droppers
  - container to be used to contain the test mixture, e.g. centrifuge tube/ capillary tube/cuvette/small specimen jar/small test-tube
  - describe a method to ensure fast transfer, i.e. from the dark to the start of timing.

Collection of data

- Give details of timing how long it takes for the test mixture to reach the colour standard:
  - manual/digital, stop clock or stop watch (aim for precision)
  - state to what precision timing should occur, e.g. to one decimal place
  - describe how to start the clock at the same time as turning on the light.
- Describe how to judge the end colour with accuracy and precision.
- State how many times the experiment should be repeated for each wavelength (at least three replicates).

Risk assessment

State the risk associated with the experiment. This is a low hazard experiment.

The chloroplast suspension mixture will stain clothes.

A statement of risk needs to be accompanied by a description of how to minimise risk, e.g. wear a laboratory coat and protective goggles.

Results

State what you would do with anomalous results.

State the calculations to be carried out and what can be done with the results, for example:

- mean times for each wavelength for mixture to reach the colour standard
- rate of reduction of DCPIP, e.g. rate = $100/t$ or $1000/t$ (t = seconds).
- plot values onto graph (see Prediction).

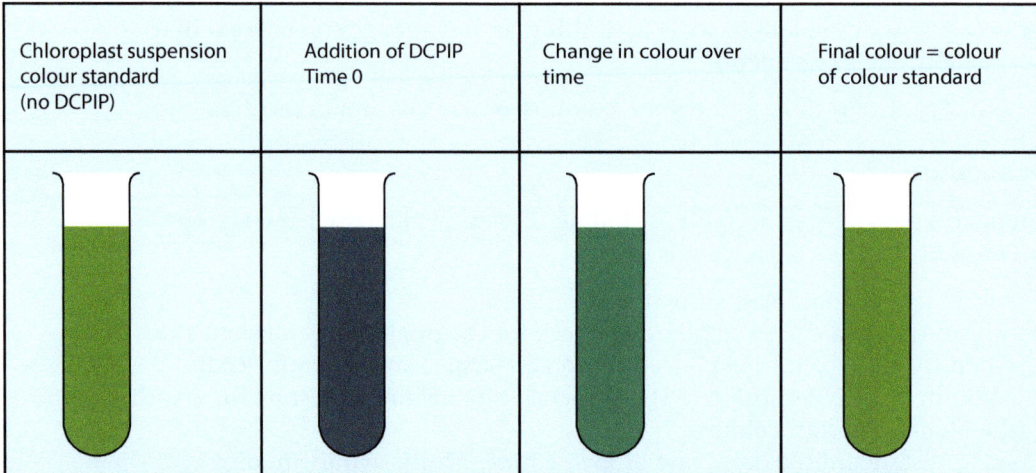

Chloroplast suspension colour standard (no DCPIP)	Addition of DCPIP Time 0	Change in colour over time	Final colour = colour of colour standard

Figure 1 *Colour changes occurring in a chloroplast suspension containing DCPIP*

The effect of light intensity on the rate of photosynthesis

Here the same investigation is carried out, but instead of changing the wavelength of light used, the light intensity can be varied by changing the distance of the light source from the test mixture of chloroplast suspension and DCPIP (light intensity is proportional to $1/\text{distance}^2$, so can be calculated). Alternatively, a light source that can have the voltage adjusted (dimmer knob) can be used (with light intensity measured by a light meter).

Practical skill

Analysis, conclusions and evaluation

For analysis, you need to become skilled at dealing with data. An overall aim of experiments and investigations is to draw valid conclusions using this analysed data. Evaluation involves making reasoned judgements about the quality of the data and the validity of the conclusions.

Dealing with data

If you are given data from experimental work you should be able to:

- Use tables and graphs to show the key points in quantitative (numerical) data
- Construct graphs (*y*-axis = dependent variable and *x*-axis = independent variable) and where relevant include confidence limit error bars or standard error bars.
- Decide which calculations to carry out, including the correct statistical test (if relevant), and then carry them out
  - this makes data easier to interpret, helps to increase the validity of conclusions drawn and can help in the evaluation of the experiment
  - calculations include means, percentages, rates of change and statistical tests
  - state a null hypothesis for a statistical test (see 16.2h and 17.1d)
  - calculations can compare data, e.g. percentage gain or loss.
- Use values of standard deviation or standard error, or graphs with standard error bars, to decide whether differences in mean values could be statistically significant.
- Recognise whether data is qualitative or quantitative:
  - recognise the difference between categoric (nominal) and ordered (ordinal) data.

Conclusions

To draw conclusions from results, you need to apply your knowledge and understanding to the analysed data.

- Summarise the main conclusions and give biological explanations of your conclusions.
- Refer to key points of the raw data and the processed data, e.g. from graphs and from the results of statistical tests.
- Make a statement as to whether a hypothesis is supported or not, discussing the extent to which the experimental data (results and analysis) strongly supports the hypothesis (strengths of evidence) or does not support (weaknesses of the evidence). The result of a statistical test is an important factor to include in the discussion.
- Use the conclusions you have drawn to make further predictions and hypotheses.

Evaluation

For evaluation, you need to make judgements about the accuracy of the results (how close they are to the 'true' results) and the quality of the experimental procedure used to obtain the results – the precision.

- Identify values in a table or graph that appear anomalous (e.g. check whether any do not appear to fit the trend), suggest possible explanations for them and suggest how to deal with them.
  - For example, one anomalous result in a set of repeat results may be excluded when calculating means. This may have been a random error of measurement.
  - For example, if all replicate results are similar, the mean when plotted on a graph may appear anomalous. You may decide a systematic error had occurred and so exclude this value when adding a curve of best fit.
- Revisit experimental design and comment on:
  - the number of repeats (replicates) carried out to minimise random errors
  - the range of values chosen for the independent variable and the intervals between measurements
  - the method used to measure the dependent variable
  - the apparatus or equipment used
  - the extent to which variables were controlled.
- Make judgements about the validity of the investigation and the extent to which the results and their analysis can be used to test the hypothesis.
  - explain how much confidence can be put in the conclusion made
  - suggest improvements to the investigation that will help increase confidence in the results.

Remember

Standard deviation is a measure of the variation in a sample that has an approximately normal distribution, i.e. how spread out values are from the mean. The wider the spread from the mean, the larger the standard deviation. 17.1c has more information about standard deviation and its calculation.

Standard error is calculated from the standard deviation, and is a measure of how close the sample mean is to the actual population mean.

The 95% confidence intervals are calculated from the standard error. These are a range of values within which, with 95% probability, the actual population mean occurs.

You do not have to learn the formulae to calculate these values as they will be provided for you.

Summary test 13.2b

Whole chloroplast suspensions can carry out the **(1)** stage of photosynthesis. DCPIP or **(2)** can be used as a **(3)** indicator to measure the rate of photosynthesis. The indicator is an artificial **(4)** acceptor and the actual acceptor in photosynthesis is the coenzyme **(5)**. When DCPIP is added to the chloroplast suspension, a **(6)** colour results. The time taken for this colour to change to **(7)** is recorded to calculate rate. Different **(8)** and **(9)** of light will result in different rates of photosynthesis.

These pages help you to:

- carry out investigations using whole plants, including aquatic plants, to determine the effects of light intensity, carbon dioxide concentration and temperature on the rate of photosynthesis (13.2.4)

You will also:

- get more practice at planning investigations

Measuring photosynthesis

The rate of photosynthesis is usually found by measuring the volume of oxygen produced by an aquatic plant such as *Elodea* (commonly known as waterweed or pondweed).

The following account outlines how the rate of photosynthesis at different light intensities can be measured.

- The apparatus, known as an **Audus photosynthometer**, is set up as in Figure 1, taking care not to introduce any air bubbles into it and checking that the apparatus is completely air-tight.
- An electronic or digital water bath is used to maintain a constant temperature throughout the experiment and should be adjusted as necessary.
- Potassium or sodium hydrogencarbonate solution can be used around the plant to provide a source of carbon dioxide – especially important if the experiment is to extend over a long period.
- A source of light that can have its voltage adjusted to change its intensity, is arranged close to the apparatus, which is kept in a dark room to prevent other light (which may vary in intensity) falling on the plant. If a controlled metal-sided water bath is used, the source of light needs to be arranged so that it is placed above the apparatus and can shine down onto the plant.
- The apparatus is kept in the dark for two hours to prevent photosynthesis and allow oxygen already produced by the plant to disperse.
- The light source is switched on and a stop clock started.
- Oxygen produced by the plant during photosynthesis collects in the funnel end of the capillary tube above the plant.
- After 30 minutes this oxygen is drawn up the capillary tube by gently withdrawing the syringe until its volume can be measured on the scale. This can be done directly (if the scale is calibrated in mm³) or, if the scale is not calibrated, calculated using the formula $\pi r^2 h$ (where r is the internal radius of the tube and h is the length of the column of oxygen collected).
- The gas is drawn up into the syringe, which is then pushed in again before the process is repeated at the same light intensity four or five times and the mean volume of oxygen produced per hour is calculated.
- The apparatus is left in the dark for two hours before the procedure is repeated with the light source set at a different light intensity. The actual light intensity can be measured by a light meter placed in the same position relative to the light source as the plant was during the experiment.
- An alternative method of varying the light intensity is to change the distance of the light source relative to the plant. The light intensity is inversely proportional to the square of the distance from the plant to the light source, i.e. doubling the distance apart reduces the light intensity by a quarter.

The experiment can be modified to measure the effect of other factors on the rate of photosynthesis as follows:

- **Temperature** – the temperature of the water bath can be varied and the rates of photosynthesis compared.
- **Carbon dioxide concentration** – different concentrations of potassium or sodium hydrogencarbonate can be used to compare the rate of photosynthesis at different carbon dioxide concentrations.

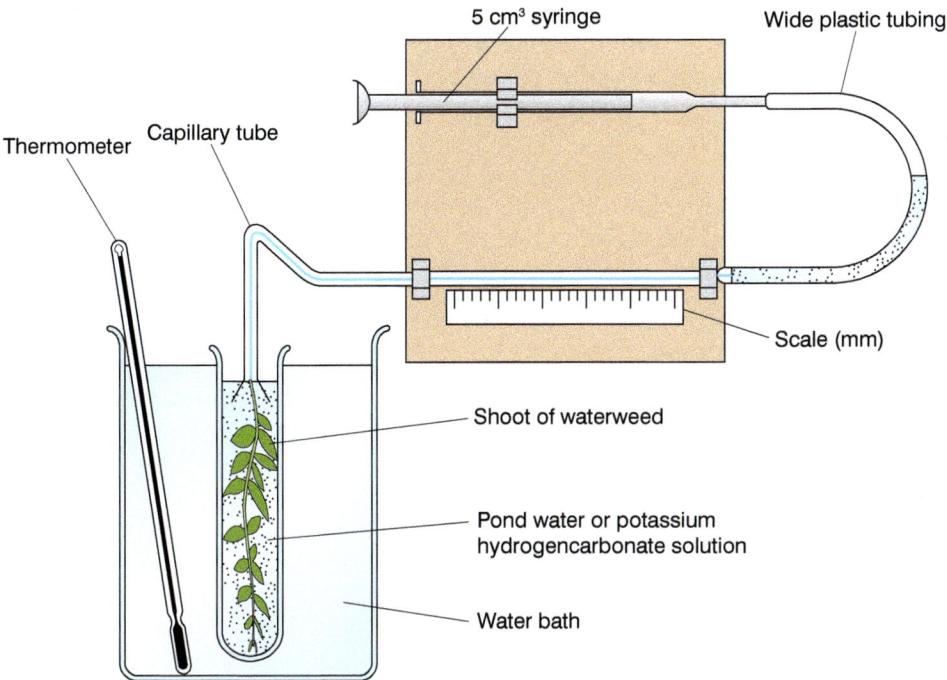

Figure 1 *Apparatus used to measure the rate of photosynthesis under various conditions*

Extension

Measuring volumes of carbon dioxide taken up or oxygen produced

Simple practical investigations measuring carbon dioxide uptake or oxygen produced do not provide an absolute measure of the rate of photosynthesis. This is because:

- some of the oxygen produced in photosynthesis is used in cellular respiration and so never leaves the plant and therefore cannot be measured
- in experiments involving aquatic organisms, dissolved oxygen, nitrogen and other gases are often released from the leaf and surrounding water and become included in the gas volume measured
- some carbon dioxide from cellular respiration is used up in photosynthesis and therefore the volume taken up from the atmosphere is less than that actually used in photosynthesis.

Summary test 13.2c

It is easier to measure the rate of photosynthesis using an **(1)** plant and measuring the volume of **(2)** given off in a set **(3)**. The apparatus that can be used is called a **(4)**. Changing the **(5)** of the light source from the plant changes light intensity, which is calculated as **(6)**. Carbon dioxide concentration can be changed by using different concentrations of **(7)**.

Practical skill

Planning an investigation into the factors affecting the rate of photosynthesis

Sometimes, when planning investigations, we are limited by the apparatus available. Figure 2 shows a very simple experimental set-up to investigate the rate of photosynthesis in an aquatic plant.

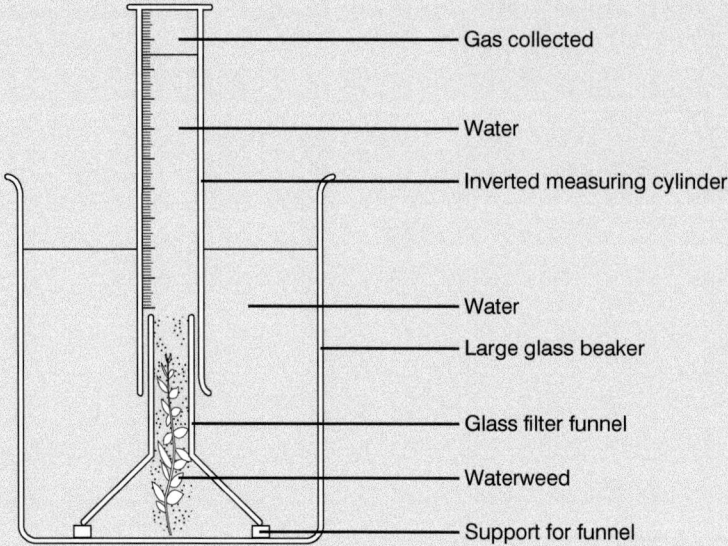

- Gas collected
- Water
- Inverted measuring cylinder
- Water
- Large glass beaker
- Glass filter funnel
- Waterweed
- Support for funnel

Figure 2 *Experimental set-up for investigating the rate of photosynthesis*

The following are points to consider when designing a plan to investigate the effect of light intensity, temperature or carbon dioxide concentration on the rate of photosynthesis of an aquatic plant, using the apparatus in Figure 2.

Prediction

The following are some predictions that could be made:

- There will be a linear increase in the rate of photosynthesis as the light intensity/temperature/carbon dioxide concentration increases.
- The rate of increase will slow down and then plateau as light intensity/temperature/carbon dioxide concentration increases further.

For light intensity and temperature:
- At very high light intensity/temperature, the rate of photosynthesis will show a steep decrease.

These predictions can be supported by knowledge of photosynthesis and limiting factors. For example, at the point where the increase in rate slows down and plateaus, it can be suggested that one or both of the other two factors will start to become limiting. Other supporting biological knowledge can include:

Light intensity:

- Increasing light intensity will increase the rate of the light-dependent stage.
- At very high light intensity, chlorophyll can be damaged.

Temperature:

- Temperature affects the rate of enzyme-catalysed reactions and enzymes are involved in both the light-dependent and light-independent stages.
- At very high temperatures enzymes will denature, so reactions will stop.

Carbon dioxide concentration:

- Increasing carbon dioxide concentration will increase carbon fixation and so increase the rate of the light-independent stage.

For these investigations predictions can include a sketch graph, with the independent variable on the x-axis and the dependent variable on the y-axis.

Variables

Independent variable.

- Light intensity: light source at different distances (at least five) from the beaker (light intensity is proportional to $1/distance^2$), arranged so that whole plant is illuminated (or a light source that can be dimmed).
- Temperature: beaker inside electronically/digitally controlled water bath, set for a range of temperatures (at least five) and checked with a thermometer. If no water baths are available, the temperature of the room can be changed with a thermostat, or a warming plate placed under the apparatus and the water stirred regularly.
- Carbon dioxide concentration: prepare different concentrations of sodium hydrogencarbonate solution (at least five) to replace the water in the beaker.

It is possible to vary two of the factors, e.g. carbon dioxide concentration at two different temperatures.

Dependent variable.

- This could be as simple as counting bubbles given off into a test tube (assuming all bubbles are of the same size).
- Use an inverted measuring cylinder – this has graduations so the volume can be determined (remember the cylinder is upside down).
- Use tubing attached to a gas syringe.

Standardised variables.

- Depending on which factor is the independent variable, the other two main factors must be standardised:
  - Light intensity – keep the light source at a constant distance from the lamp and use an LED lamp or fluorescent lamp to minimise temperature changes.
  - Temperature – maintain water bath at 25°C.
  - Carbon dioxide concentration – use the pond water, or if the rate is too slow to measure, use a standard concentration of sodium hydrogen carbonate solution.
- Waterweed mass/volume/age.
- Equipment used.

Procedure

Produce a step-by-step account, including apparatus to be used and taking account of precision. Give details of:

- setting up the apparatus
- preparing waterweed, e.g. cutting off sections under water just before the experiment
- how to prepare solutions of sodium hydrogen carbonate (if relevant)
- equilibration times, e.g. if changing temperatures, or if carrying out the experiment at a set temperature
- collection of data.

Risk assessment

This is a low hazard investigation.

Collection of data

- Give details of the timer used to measure the specified times for the collection of oxygen: manual/digital, stop clock or stop watch (aim for precision).
- Describe how to collect the volume of oxygen with accuracy and precision.
- State how many times the experiment should be repeated (replicates) to obtain means.

Results

- State what you would do with anomalous results.
- State calculations that could be carried out, for example:
  - mean volumes of oxygen evolved
  - rate of photosynthesis (e.g. $cm^3 min^{-1}$).
- Consider the quality of results by further calculations (e.g. standard error).
- Describe the graph to be constructed, e.g. rate (y-axis) against independent variable (x-axis).

Launch additional digital resources for the chapter

13 Exam-style questions

1 Figure 1 is an electron micrograph showing a chloroplast. It is the site of both light-dependent and light-independent stages.

Figure 1

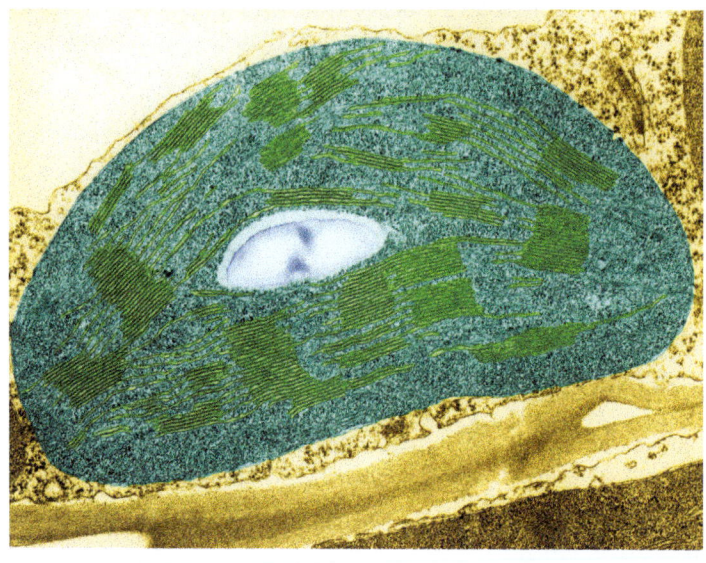

a On Figure 1, use label lines and letters to label where:

L – the light-dependent stage occurs
D – the light-independent stage occurs *(2 marks)*

b Figure 2 outlines the relationship between light-dependent and light-independent stages.

Figure 2

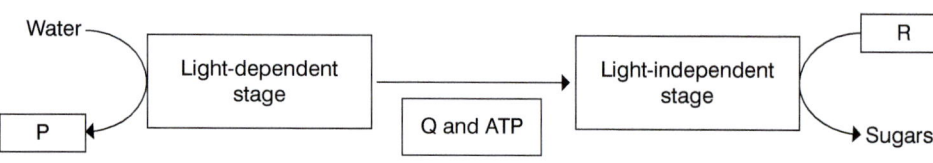

i Name compounds **P**, **Q** and **R**. *(3 marks)*
ii Describe how **P** is produced. *(2 marks)*
iii Outline the stages of the light-independent stage that lead to the formation of sugars from **R**. *(6 marks)*

(Total 13 marks)

2 Figure 3 shows leaves of a sugar maple tree, *Acer saccharum*. In summer, the leaves are green whereas, in autumn, the leaves change from green to various shades of yellow, orange and red.

Figure 3

A student wanted to compare the composition of leaf pigments in summer leaves and autumn leaves.

Samples of green summer leaves were collected in summer and samples of green, yellow, orange and red leaves were collected in autumn.

a i Outline the method by which the leaf pigments present in the leaves could be separated and identified. *(4 marks)*
ii State **two** variables, other than mass of leaves, that would need to be standardised in this investigation. *(2 marks)*

Figure 4 shows one of the chromatograms obtained by the student.

Figure 4

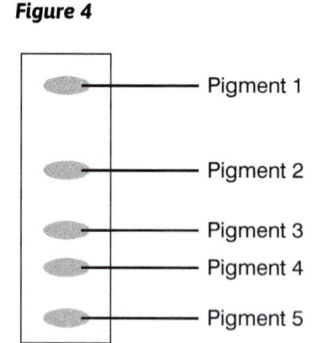

Pigment 1
Pigment 2
Pigment 3
Pigment 4
Pigment 5

Table 1 shows the results obtained for all leaf samples. A tick (✓) is placed where the pigment is present and a cross (✗) if the pigment is absent.

Table 1

Leaf sample colour	Pigment 1	Pigment 2	Pigment 3	Pigment 4	Pigment 5
green (summer)	✓	✓	✓	✓	✗
green (autumn)	✓	✓	✓	✓	✓
yellow	✓	✓	✗	✗	✓
orange	✓	✓	✗	✗	✓
red	✗	✗	✗	✗	✓

b i Identify which of the pigments would most likely be chlorophyll(s). *(1 mark)*

  ii Suggest and explain why leaves collected in autumn still appear green while other leaf pigments are present. *(3 marks)*

c Figure 5 shows the absorption spectra of extracts from green and yellow leaves from the same sugar maple tree in autumn.

Figure 5

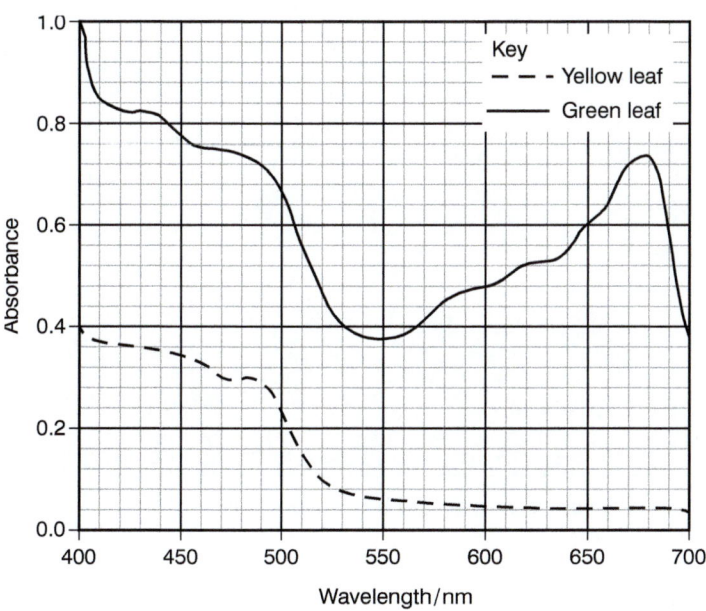

With reference to Figure 5 and the results in Table 1,

  i compare the absorption spectra of the extracts from green and yellow leaves. *(3 marks)*

  ii comment on **and** explain the shape of the absorption spectra for both leaf extracts. *(3 marks)*

(Total 16 marks)

13 Practice questions

3 Figure 5 shows the results of an experiment to measure the effect of different light intensities on the rate of photosynthesis under different conditions.

Figure 6

1 0.1% carbon dioxide at 25 °C

2 0.04% carbon dioxide at 35 °C

3 0.04% carbon dioxide at 25 °C

4 0.04% carbon dioxide at 15 °C

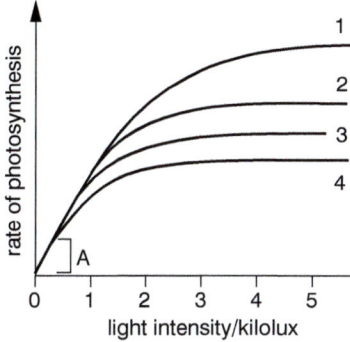

a State one measurement that could be taken to determine the rate of photosynthesis in this experiment.

b Name the factor that is limiting the rate of photosynthesis over the region marked A on the graph. Explain your answer.

c In the spring, a commercial grower of tomatoes keeps her glasshouses at 25 °C and at a carbon dioxide concentration of 0.04%. The light intensity is 4 kilolux at this time of year. Using the graph, predict whether the tomato plants would grow more if the carbon dioxide level was raised to 0.1% or if the temperature were increased to 35 °C. Explain your answer.

d Why is there no point in the grower heating her glasshouses on a dull day?

e Using your knowledge of the light-independent stage, explain why, at 25 °C, raising the level of carbon dioxide from 0.04% to 0.1% increases the concentration of glucose produced.

14.1 Homeostasis in mammals

a. The importance and principles of homeostasis

As species of organisms evolved from simple, unicellular organisms into complex, multicellular ones, these multicellular organisms evolved so that different groups of cells became different tissues, each specialised to perform a particular function. With specialisation in one function came the loss of the ability of cells to perform other functions, and this made the cells dependent on each other. This has resulted in the division of labour that is seen in tissues, organs and organ systems in more complex multicellular organisms. These different functional systems must be coordinated if they are to perform efficiently.

There are two coordination systems in most multicellular animals: nervous and endocrine. The nervous system allows rapid communication between specific parts of an organism (Figure 1). The endocrine system usually provides a slower, less specific form of communication. Both systems need to work together. The increased complexity of multicellular organisms meant the development of an internal environment at the same time. This internal environment is made up of extracellular fluids that bathe each cell, supplying nutrients and removing wastes. By maintaining this fluid at levels which suit the cells, the cells are protected from the changes that affect the external environment and so give the organism a degree of independence.

Figure 1 *The skills involved in this cheetah catching its gazelle prey require highly efficient coordination of many of its body systems*

What is homeostasis?

Homeostasis is the maintenance of a constant internal environment, generally using negative feedback mechanisms. It involves maintaining the chemical make-up, volume and other features of blood and tissue fluid of organisms within narrow limits, sometimes called **normal ranges**. It makes sure that the cells of the body are in an environment that meets their needs and allows them to function normally despite external changes. There are continuous fluctuations brought about by variations in internal and external conditions. These changes, however, occur around a **set point**. Homeostasis is the ability to return to that set point and so maintain organisms in a balanced equilibrium (Figure 2).

Figure 2 *Homeostasis allows animals such as these penguins in the Antarctic (left) and these camels in the desert (right) to survive in extreme environments*

The importance of homeostasis

Homeostasis is essential for the proper functioning of organisms because:

- The enzymes that control the biochemical reactions within cells, and other proteins such as membrane channel proteins, are sensitive to changes in pH and temperature (3.2a). Any change to these factors reduces the efficiency of enzymes or may even prevent them working altogether, e.g. may **denature** them. Changes to membrane proteins may mean that substances cannot be transported into or out of cells.
- Changes to the water potential of the blood and tissue fluids may cause cells to shrink and expand (even to bursting point) owing to water leaving or entering by **osmosis** (4.2b and 4.2c). In both situations the cells cannot operate normally.
- Biochemical reactions in organisms are in a state of dynamic equilibrium between the forward and reverse reactions. Changes to the environment of cells can upset this equilibrium to the harm of the organism.
- Organisms with the ability to maintain a constant internal environment are more independent of the external environment. They have a wider geographical range and therefore have a greater chance of finding food, shelter, etc. Mammals, for example, with their ability to maintain a constant temperature, are found in most habitats from hot, arid deserts to the cold, frozen poles.
- Maintaining a constant concentration of glucose in the blood means that an organism can release energy needed for various activities at a constant rate.

> **Remember**
>
> Examples of external stimuli are: light intensity, chemicals, temperature, sound, touch, pressure and gravity. Most internal stimuli are related to changes in blood and tissue fluid, and include: temperature, water potential, carbon dioxide concentration, glucose concentration and blood pressure.

Control mechanisms and feedback

The control of any self-regulating system involves a number of different components:

- **internal and external stimuli** – any factor that is detected and causes a response is a stimulus
- **the set point** – the desired level at which the system operates, with only small fluctuations from this point
- **receptors** – these detect internal and external stimuli and pass information to a control centre of any deviation from the set point
- **control centre** – this receives and coordinates information from one or more receptors and sends instructions in the form of nerve impuses (electrical messages) or hormones (chemical messages) to the relevant effectors
- **effectors** – these are often muscles or glands that bring about the necessary change needed to return the system to the set point.
- **negative feedback mechanisms** – once the effectors have returned a system back to a set point, the receptors detect this and inform the control centre that action is no longer necessary. Any change away from the set point will be detected by the receptors and the control centre will once again coordinate corrective action so that the system returns to the set point.

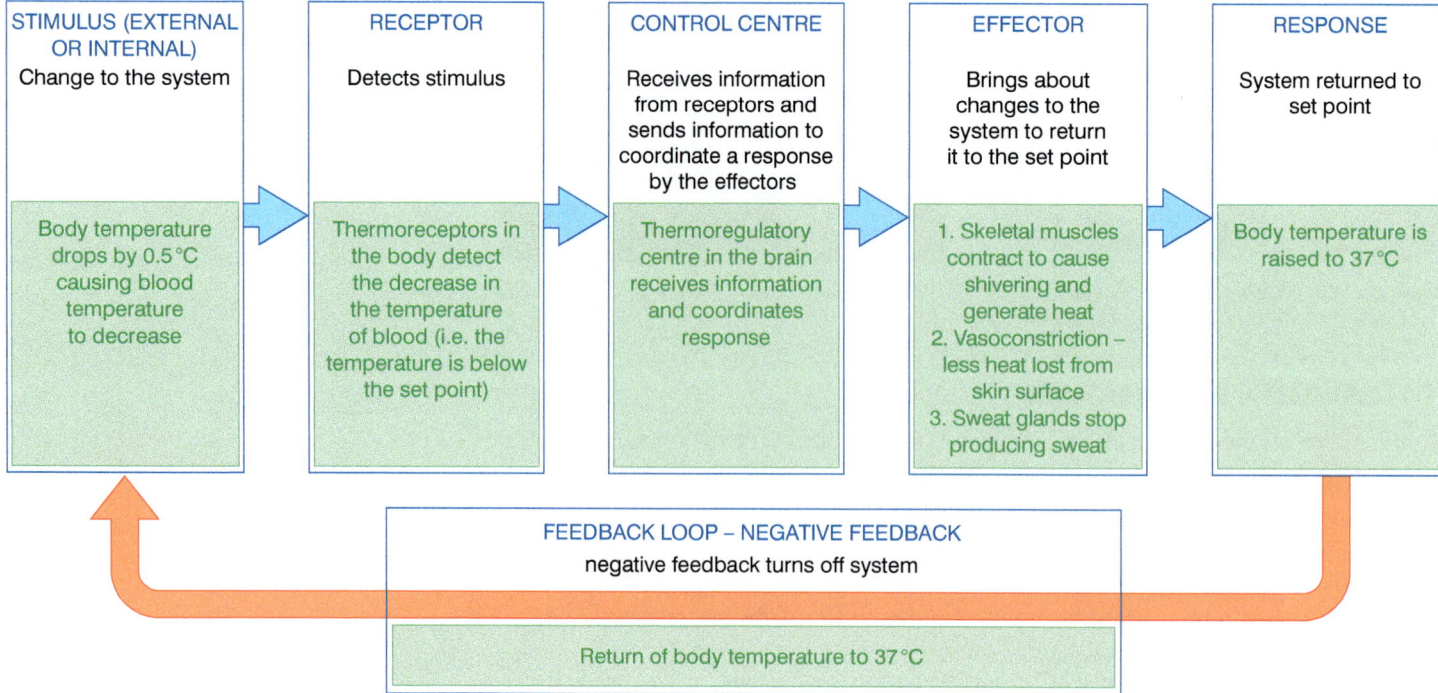

Figure 3 *Components of a typical coordination system*

Figure 3 shows the relationship between these stages using the homeostatic mechanism of thermoregulation, the control of body temperature, as an example. Later in this chapter, osmoregulation and the control of blood glucose concentration will be covered.

Coordination of control mechanisms

Systems normally have many receptors and effectors. It is important to ensure that the information provided by receptors is analysed by the control centre before action is taken. Receiving information from a number of sources allows a better degree of control. Although the nervous system and endocrine system are both coordination systems, they have very different ways of operating. However, it is often necessary for the two systems to interact to achieve homeostasis and allow the body to function efficiently. A comparison of the two systems is covered in 15.1a. In the same way, the control centre must coordinate the action of the effectors so that they operate together. Most systems, including biological ones, use **negative feedback**, i.e. the information fed back turns the system off. We shall see examples of negative feedback in the following topics.

The kidney functions as an organ of excretion and has a homeostatic role in the regulation of the composition of blood and tissue fluid. **Excretion** is the removal of the waste products that have been produced as a result of metabolic reactions or are in excess of needs and cannot be stored. These waste products, if allowed to build up, are toxic (harmful) to cells.

> **Remember**
>
> Excretion is distinct from **elimination (egestion)**, which is the removal of substances such as dietary fibre that have never been involved in the metabolic activities of cells.

Urea as the nitrogenous excretory produce of mammals

Urea ($CO(NH_2)_2$) is used as the nitrogenous excretory product of organisms that have some access to water, but not in large volumes, e.g. animals living on land, such as mammals. The amino acids that are absorbed in the small intestine as a result of protein digestion are transported in the blood to the liver. Amino acids that are in excess of the requirements of the body cannot be stored because the nitrogen-containing amino group is toxic to cells. In the liver cells, or hepatocytes, of mammals, amino groups (NH_2) are removed from the amino acids in a process called **deamination** and made into ammonia, which is converted into urea.

Urea, which is also toxic to cells, is fairly soluble in water and can be transported dissolved in blood plasma to the kidneys for excretion.

Structure of the mammalian kidney

In mammals there are two kidneys found at the back of the abdominal cavity, one on each side of the spinal cord (Figure 1).

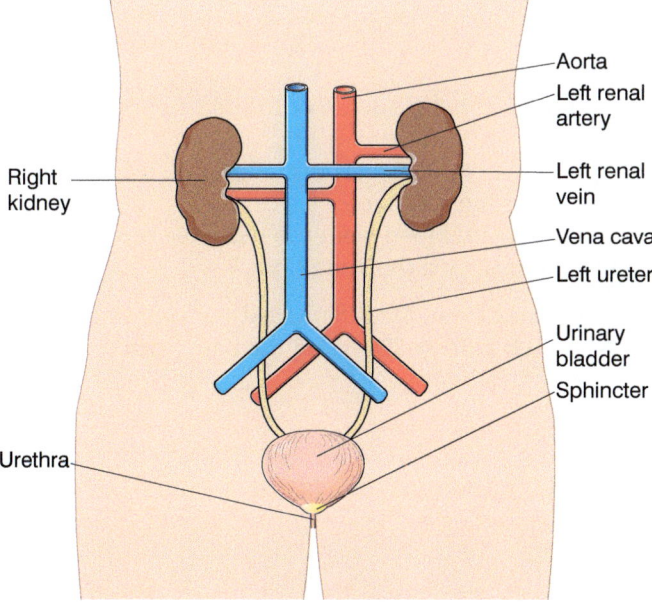

Figure 1 *Position of the kidneys in humans*

These pages help you to:

- learn that urea is produced in the liver from the deamination of excess amino acids (14.1.3)
- describe the structure of the human kidney, limited to fibrous capsule, cortex, medulla, renal pelvis, ureter and branches of the renal artery and renal vein (14.1.4)

You will also:

- learn more about other excretory products and the formation of urea

> **Extension**
>
> **Urea and other excretory substances**
>
> **Ammonia (NH_3)** is the easiest product to form from the amino groups (NH_2) produced when amino acids are oxidised. Its production requires no **ATP** and it is very soluble in water and so is easily dissolved and washed out of the body. It is, however, extremely poisonous – 800 times more so than carbon dioxide. Only organisms such as freshwater fish with access to large volumes of water are able to use ammonia as their nitrogenous excretory product. In mammals, the ammonia is converted to urea in a pathway called the **ornithine cycle**. The conversion, in addition to needing ATP, uses carbon dioxide and water. Urea requires less water for its excretion than ammonia but is still fairly toxic. The remainder of the amino acid is not wasted because it can be respired to produce ATP.
>
> **Uric acid** is almost insoluble in water and cannot diffuse into cells, making it hardly poisonous at all. However, it takes seven ATP molecules to produce it. As almost no water is needed for its removal, it is used by organisms living in very dry conditions. As it is low in mass when stored it is also used by flying organisms. Animals such as birds and reptiles that lay eggs have an additional reason for using it to remove their nitrogenous waste. As the young develop within the egg, their wastes cannot be removed and so anything more toxic than uric acid would kill them.
>
> Carbon dioxide and water, needed in the production of urea, are also excretory products. They are waste products of aerobic respiration (Chapter 12). An adult human produces about 500 dm³ of carbon dioxide and 400 cm³ of water each day as a result of respiration.
>
> Other excretory products include bile pigments and mineral salts.

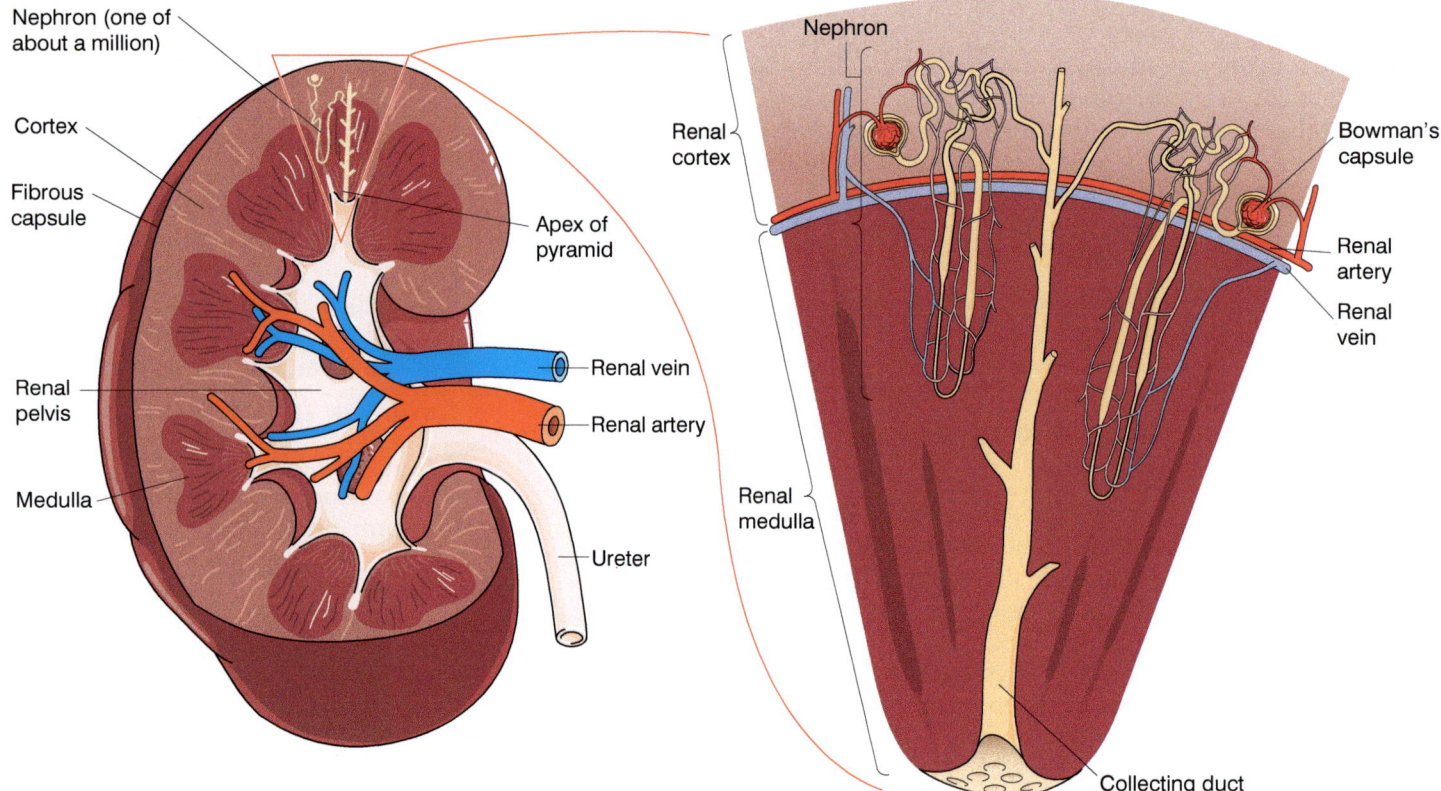

Figure 2 *Detailed structure of mammalian kidney showing the position of two of the million or more nephrons in each kidney*

Summary test 14.1b

The removal of metabolic waste products from the body is known as **(1)**. **(2)** is the main nitrogenous waste product of mammals. This is produced by the removal of the **(3)** groups from excess **(4)** that are not able to be stored because they are **(5)** to cells. This soluble waste product is made in the cells of the **(6)** and is transported to the kidneys for removal. The mammalian kidney is surrounded by a protective **(7)** and in cross section is seen to be made up of a lighter coloured outer region called the **(8)** and a darker inner region called the **(9)**. These regions are made up of around a million tubular structures called **(10)**. Blood is brought to the kidney by the vessel called the **(11)**, and urine leaves it via a tube called the **(12)**.

In humans each kidney is usually surrounded by fat that gives it some physical protection. Weighing only 150 g each, they filter your blood plasma every 22 minutes of your life. A section through the kidney (Figure 2) shows it is made up of the:

- **fibrous capsule** – a thin but tough outer layer of connective tissue, that protects the kidney
- **cortex** – a lighter coloured outer region made up of **Bowman's capsules**, convoluted tubules and blood vessels
- **medulla** – a darker coloured inner region made up of **loops of Henlé**, collecting ducts and blood vessels
- **renal pelvis** – a funnel-shaped cavity that collects urine into the ureter
- **ureter** – a tube that carries urine to the bladder
- **renal artery** – supplies the kidney with blood from the heart via the aorta
- **renal vein** – returns blood to the heart via the vena cava.

A microscopic examination of the cortex and medulla reveals around one million tiny tubular structures in each kidney. These are the basic structural and functional units of the kidney – the **nephrons**.

The nephron is the functional unit of the kidney. It is a narrow tube, closed at one end, with two twisted regions separated by a long hairpin loop. Each nephron is made up of a:

- **Bowman's (renal) capsule** – the closed end at the start of the nephron. It is cup-shaped and contains within it a mass of blood capillaries known as the glomerulus (Figures 1 and 4). Its inner layer is made up of specialised cells called **podocytes**.
- **Proximal (first) convoluted tubule** – a series of loops surrounded by blood capillaries. Its walls are made of cuboidal epithelial cells with microvilli (Figure 1, and Figure 4 on page 286).
- **Loop of Henlé** – a long, hairpin loop that extends from the cortex into the medulla of the kidney and back again. It is surrounded by blood capillaries (Figure 2).
- **Distal (second) convoluted tubule** – a series of loops surrounded by blood capillaries. Its walls are made of cuboidal epithelial cells, but it is surrounded by fewer capillaries than the proximal tubule.
- **Collecting duct** – a tube into which a number of distal convoluted tubules empty. It is lined by cuboidal epithelial cells and becomes increasingly wide as it empties into the pelvis of the kidney.

Associated with each nephron are a number of blood vessels (Figure 3 on page 286):

- **afferent arteriole** – a tiny vessel that is a branch of the renal artery and supplies the nephron with blood. The afferent arteriole enters the Bowman's capsule of the nephron where it forms the
- **glomerulus** – a many-branched knot of capillaries (Figure 4) from which fluid is forced out of the blood. The glomerular capillaries recombine to form the
- **efferent arteriole** – a tiny vessel that leaves the renal capsule. It has a smaller diameter than the afferent arteriole, which causes an increase in blood pressure within the glomerulus. The efferent arteriole carries blood away from the Bowman's capsule and later branches to form the
- **peritubular capillaries** – a concentrated network of capillaries that surrounds the proximal convoluted tubule, the loop of Henlé and the distal convoluted tubule and from where they reabsorb mineral salts, glucose and water. The peritubular capillaries merge together into venules (8.1b) that in turn merge together to form the renal vein.

These pages help you to:

- Identify, in diagrams, photomicrographs and electron micrographs, the parts of a nephron and its associated blood vessels and structures (14.1.5)

You will also:

- be able to describe the main features of the parts of a nephron

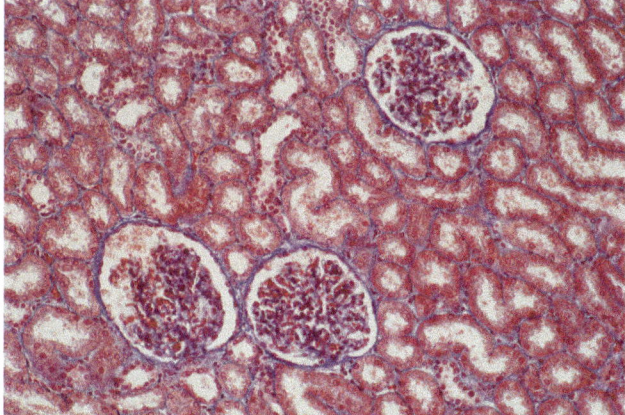

Figure 1 *Photomicrograph of cortex of human kidney. There are three glomeruli: each glomerulus appears as a mass of blood capillaries surrounded by a clear space – the lumen of the Bowman's capsule. The background shows sections through convoluted tubules. There are many that appear in tranverse (cross) section, with those appearing longer (e.g. central, lower centre and lower right of the image) in longitudinal section.*

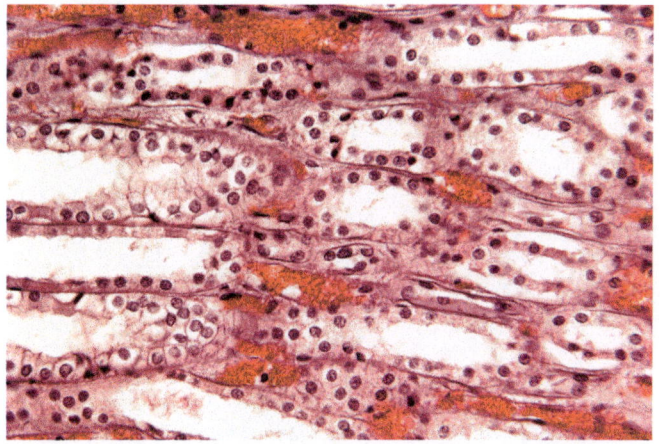

Figure 2 *Photomicrograph of medulla of human kidney showing loops of Henlé. Around them are blood capillaries containing red blood cells (red).*

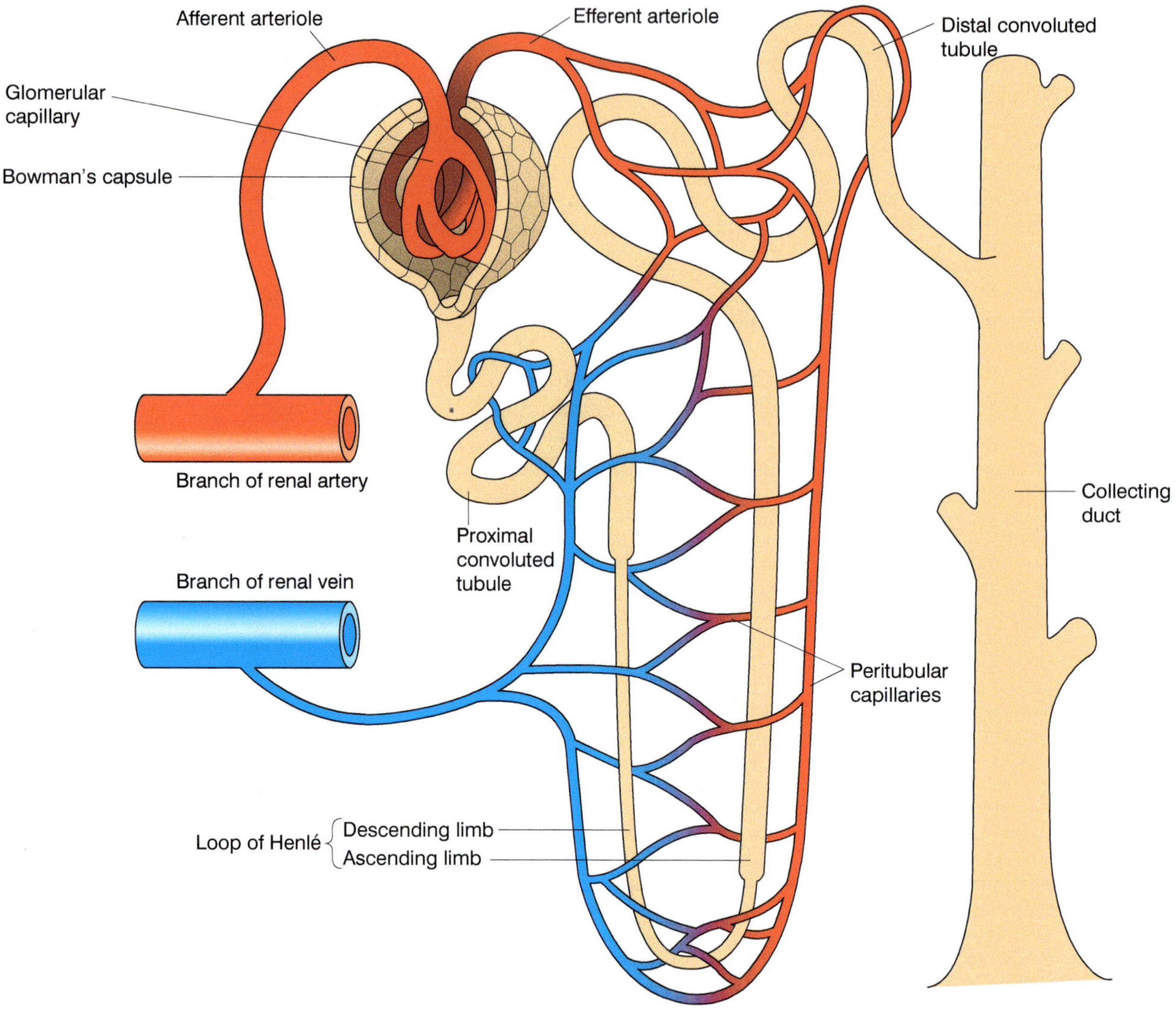

Afferent arteriole

Efferent arteriole

Distal convoluted tubule

Glomerular capillary

Bowman's capsule

Branch of renal artery

Proximal convoluted tubule

Branch of renal vein

Collecting duct

Peritubular capillaries

Loop of Henlé { Descending limb
Ascending limb

Figure 3 *Regions of the nephron and associated blood vessels*

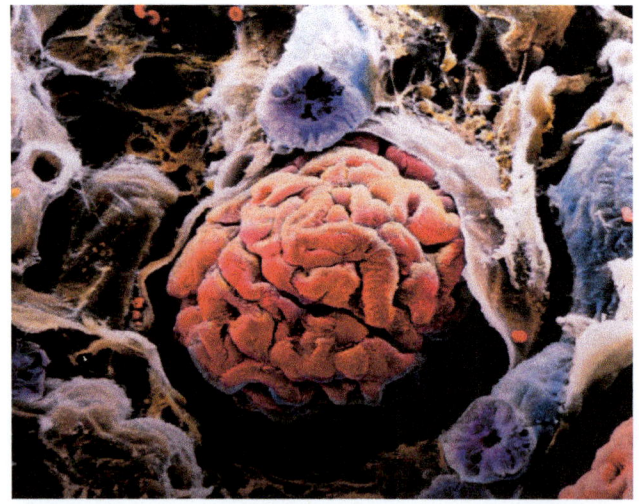

Figure 4 *Colourised scanning electron micrograph of a glomerulus (centre) surrounded by the Bowman's capsule, seen as a white-brown membrane at centre right. Part of the proximal convoluted tubule is seen, coloured blue.*

Summary test 14.1c

The nephron is the structural unit of the kidney. It comprises a cup-shaped structure called the **(1)** that contains a knot of blood vessels called the **(2)** which receives its blood from a vessel called the **(3)** arteriole. The inner wall of this cup-shaped structure is lined with specialised cells called **(4)** and from it extends the first, or **(5)**, convoluted tubule whose walls are lined with **(6)** epithelial cells that have **(7)** to increase their surface area. The next region of the nephron is a hairpin loop called the **(8)** which then leads onto the second, or **(9)**, convoluted tubule. This in turn leads onto the **(10)** which empties into the renal pelvis. Around much of the nephron is a dense network of blood vessels called the **(11)** capillaries.

The function of the kidney in regulating the composition of blood is carried out by the nephrons in a series of stages – ultrafiltration, selective reabsorption and the reabsorption of water and minerals. Ultrafiltration is the stage that occurs in the Bowman's capsule of the nephron, and selective reabosption takes place in the proximal convoluted tubule. After leaving the proximal convoluted tubule, the filtrate passes through the loop of Henlé and the distal convoluted tubule to enter the collecting duct. By the time the filtrate reaches the end of this duct, urine is formed. On these pages, we will see how ultrafiltration and selective reabsorption contribute to the formation of urine.

Ultrafiltration

Blood enters the kidney through the renal artery, which branches frequently to give around one million tiny arterioles, each of which enters a **Bowman's capsule** of a nephron. This is called the **afferent arteriole** and it divides to give a complex of capillaries known as the **glomerulus**. The glomerular capillaries later merge to form the **efferent arteriole**, which then sub-divides again into capillaries (the peritubular capillaries), which wind their way around the various tubules of the nephron before combining to form the renal vein (see Extension). The walls of the glomerular capillaries are made up of endothelial cells with endothelial pores between them. The high position of the kidneys in the abdomen means that the renal arteries, which branch off from the aorta close to the heart, carry blood at high hydrostatic pressure. As the diameter of the afferent arteriole is greater than that of the efferent arteriole, there is an additional build up of hydrostatic pressure within the glomerulus. As a result, water and many other small substances are squeezed out of the capillary to form the **glomerular filtrate**.

This filtration under pressure is known as ultrafiltration.

Red blood cells and large plasma proteins are too large to leave the capillaries.

To leave the capillaries and enter the Bowman's capsule, the filtrate must pass across:

- the endothelium of the capillary
- the basement membrane of the epithelial layer of the Bowman's capsule
- the actual layer of epithelial cells of the Bowman's capsule.

To reduce the effect of these barriers preventing the formation of the filtrate, the capillary endothelium and the epithelial layer of the Bowman's capsule have adaptations:

- The inner layer of the Bowman's capsule is made up of highly specialised cells called **podocytes** (Figure 2 on page 288). These cells, which are illustrated in Figure 1 on page 288, are lifted off the surface membrane on little 'feet' ('podo' = feet). This means that the podocytes are no barrier and so this allows filtrate to pass beneath them and through gaps between their branches. Filtrate passes between these cells rather than through them.
- The endothelium of the glomerular capillaries has endothelial pores up to 100 nm wide between its cells (Figure 1). Again, fluid can therefore pass between, rather than through, these cells.

These pages help you to:

- describe and explain the formation of glomerular filtrate by ultrafiltration in the Bowman's capsule and selective reabsorption in the proximal convoluted tubule as stages in the formation of urine in the nephron (14.1.6)
- relate the detailed structure of the Bowman's capsule and proximal convoluted tubule to their functions in the formation of urine (14.1.7)

You will also:

- learn more about the glomerulus

Extension

The glomerulus – a unique capillary bed

In mammals, the glomerulus is the only capillary bed in which an arteriole (the afferent arteriole) supplies it with blood and an arteriole (the efferent arteriole) also drains blood away. In all other mammalian capillary beds it is a venule that drains away the blood. Why then do we not make life simpler and call the efferent arteriole a venule? The reason is that the efferent arteriole later divides up into a second capillary bed – the peritubular capillaries – and these are drained by a venule. In any case, the structure of the wall is that of an arteriole and not a venule. The glomerular capillaries need to merge into an efferent arteriole because this increases the hydrostatic pressure within the glomerulus and allows ultrafiltration to occur.

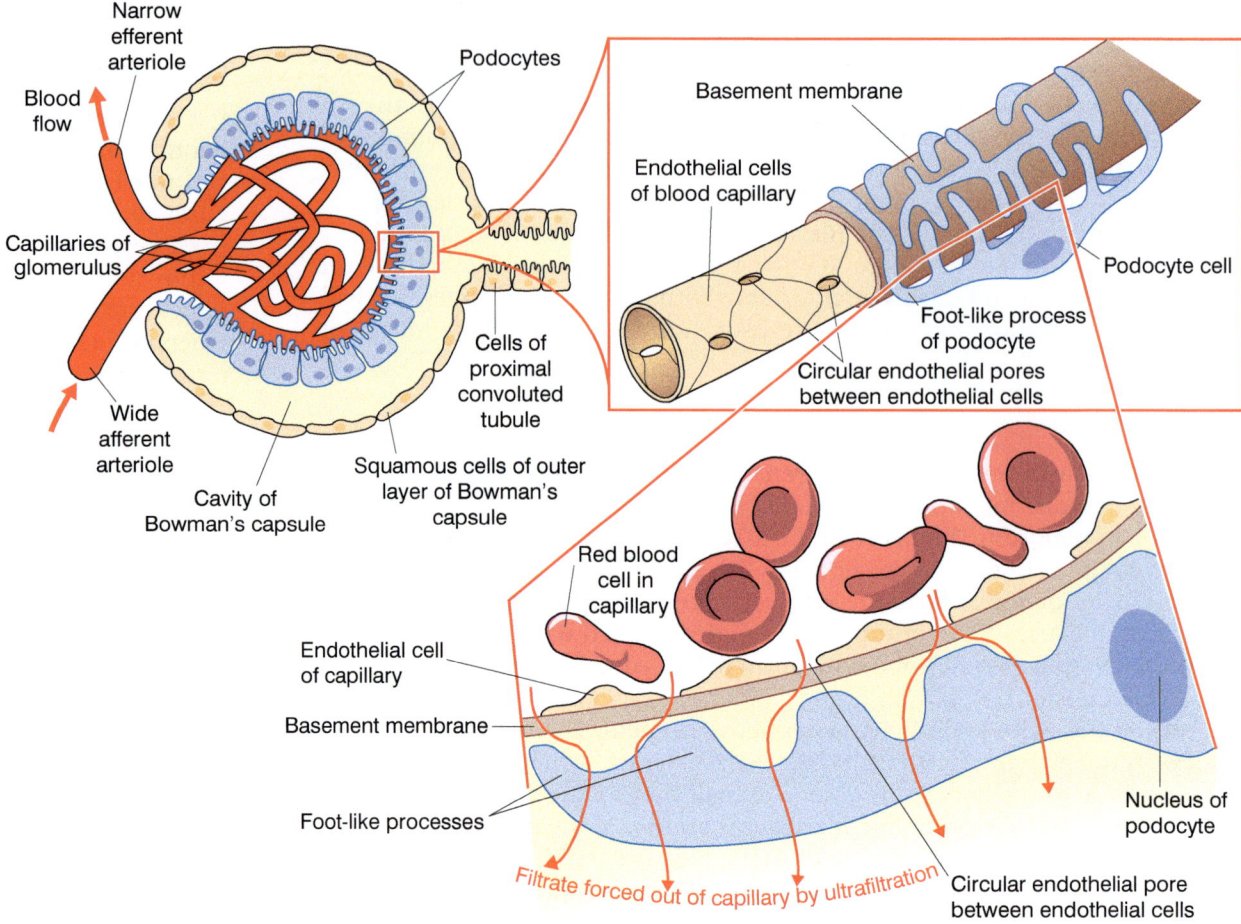

Figure 1 *Podocyte and ultrafiltration*

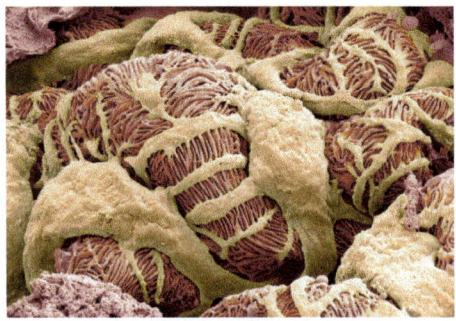

Figure 2 *Colourised scanning electron micrograph of podocyte cells around a glomerulus in a human kidney*

This means that it is the basement membrane that is the true filter, and it is this membrane that allows only substances of approximately 68 000 to 70 000 MM through to form the glomerular filtrate.

The hydrostatic pressure of the fluid in the Bowman's capsule space (the **intracapsular pressure**) and (because water is leaving) the low water potential of the blood in the glomerulus have an opposing effect on ultrafiltration. This means that not all the plasma will pass through into the glomerular filtrate. After ultrafiltration, the blood that leaves in the efferent arteriole is of a lower pressure, reduced volume, and lower water potential.

The glomerular filtrate contains water, glucose, amino acids, mineral ions and urea. Many of the substances in the 125 cm³ of filtrate passing out of blood each minute are extremely useful to the body and need to be reabsorbed.

Selective reabsorption

In the proximal convoluted tubule nearly 85% of the filtrate is reabsorbed back into the blood. Why then, you may ask, allow it to leave the blood in the first place? Ultrafiltration operates on the basis of size of molecule: all below 68 000 to 70 000 MM are removed. Some are wastes, but most are useful.

About 180 dm³ of water enters the nephrons each day. Of this volume, only about 1 dm³ leaves the body as urine. Eighty-five per cent of the reabsorption of water occurs in the proximal convoluted tubule.

In addition to water, glucose, amino acids and most mineral ions need to be reabsorbed. The transfer of these substances from the lumen of the proximal convoluted tubule to the blood within the peritubular capillaries involves active and passive transport. The process is as follows:

- Sodium ions (Na$^+$) are actively transported out of the proximal convoluted tubule cells using a sodium–potassium pump. This lowers the concentration within the cell.
- Na$^+$ ions pass from the tissue fluid into the peritubular capillary to be carried away.
- Sodium ions in the glomerular filtrate in the lumen now move into the cells through specific cotransporter proteins by facilitated diffusion. Glucose is cotransported from the lumen into the cells against its gradient.
- To balance the movement of positively charged sodium ions (Na$^+$), chloride ions (Cl$^-$), which are negatively charged, move into the tubule cells from the lumen and into the capillaries passively.
- Water follows osmotically down the water potential gradient that is created.
- The concentration of the molecules that have been cotransported into the cells of the proximal convoluted tubule builds up and this allows their facilitated diffusion (through specific membrane carrier proteins) out of the cells into the tissue fluid. They then diffuse into the capillaries. As a result, all the glucose, amino acids, chloride ions and most other valuable molecules are reabsorbed as well as water.
- Overall, approximately 50% of the urea in the glomerular filtrate leaves the lumen passively out of the tubule and passes into the tissue fluid to be reabsorbed into the blood.

Adaptation of proximal convoluted tubule cells to their function

The cells of the proximal convoluted tubule are cuboidal epithelial cells. Figure 3 shows that the cell surface membrane of the cell facing the lumen (apical membrane) of the tubule has many microvilli. This provides a large surface area for reabsorption and also means that there are many cotransporter proteins present for the uptake of sodium ions, glucose and amino acids. At this end, adjacent cells are joined closely by tight junctions to allow reabsorption to be selective. At the other (basal) surface of the cell, there is a folded basal membrane with many transport proteins for the facilitated diffusion of glucose, amino acids and ions and for ATP-requiring sodium–potassium pumps. The cytoplasm of the proximal convoluted cell contains many mitochondria to provide ATP for active transport.

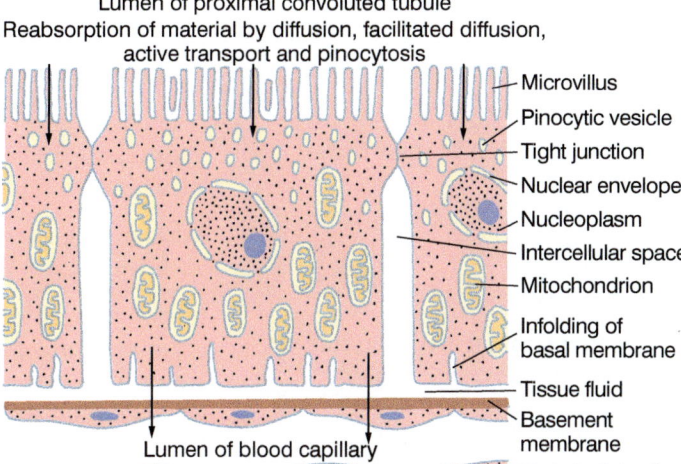

Lumen of proximal convoluted tubule
Reabsorption of material by diffusion, facilitated diffusion, active transport and pinocytosis

- Microvillus
- Pinocytic vesicle
- Tight junction
- Nuclear envelope
- Nucleoplasm
- Intercellular space
- Mitochondrion
- Infolding of basal membrane
- Tissue fluid
- Basement membrane
- Endothelial cell

Lumen of blood capillary

Figure 3 Details of cells from the wall of the proximal convoluted tubule

Remember

The sodium–potassium pump is a membrane carrier protein. Three sodium ions are actively removed from the cell while two potassium ions are actively taken into the cell from the tissue fluid.

The Na$^+$/glucose cotransporter protein is a membrane protein that tranports sodium ions down the gradient (facilitated diffusion) while cotransporting glucose against its gradient. There are other cotransport proteins for the cotransport of Na$^+$ and amino acids.

Extension

Pinocytosis in the proximal convoluted tubule

Some of the glomerular filtrate contains valuable small proteins and other molecules too large to pass across the membranes of the proximal convoluted tubule cells using transport proteins. These molecules can pass out of the filtrate by pinocytosis.

Summary test 14.1d

Pressure filtration, or **(1)** occurs in the **(2)** located in the Bowman's capsule. The **(3)** arteriole associated with the capsule has a smaller diameter than the **(4)** arteriole, which helps increase the hydrostatic pressure of the blood and form **(5)** filtrate. Water and small molecules, including waste **(6)** pass into the cavity of the capsule and then into the **(7)**, where the process of **(8)** occurs. **(9)** ions cotransport glucose and amino acids out of the lumen into the epithelial cells lining the lumen. Glucose and amino acids leave the cells by **(10)** and enter the **(11)** capillaries. To create a **(12)** for cotransport, at the basal end of the cells, sodium ions are actively transported out of the cell using a **(13)** pump. The cells have many **(14)** to provide energy for this and also have many **(15)** at the apical surface for reabsorption.

These pages help you to:

- explain the importance of osmoregulation in mammals (14.1.1)
- understand what is meant by osmoregulation (14.1.8)

You will also:

- become familiar with the role of the distal convoluted tubule
- become familiar with other functions of the kidney

Osmoregulation

One of the homeostatic mechanisms of mammals is osmoregulation, the maintenance of a constant water potential of the blood and of the tissue fluid surrounding cells. The kidney plays an important role in osmoregulation.

Maintaining a constant water potential involves balancing the volume of blood with the concentration of mineral ions and other solutes it contains.

If the water potential of blood was too high and not controlled, water would enter cells and cause swelling and ultimately cell lysis (bursting). When the water potential becomes higher than the set point, the permeability of the distal convoluted tubule and collecting duct can be changed so that the walls become impermeable to water and so more is passed out in the urine that is formed. A higher volume of more dilute urine is produced.

If the water potential of the blood was too low, water would move out of cells by osmosis. This would have damaging effects on cellular metabolism. When the water potential becomes lower than the set point, the walls of the tubule and collecting duct become permeable, so the kidney functions to conserve as much water as possible. This means that the minimum of water is released to allow the excretion of urea. The volume of urine formed is low and its concentration is very high. More detail about how the kidney plays a role in osmoregulation is in 14.1f.

The quantity of water and salts we take in varies from day to day, as does the quantity we lose. Table 1 shows the daily balance between loss and gain of salts and water for a typical human. The blood, however, needs to have a constant volume of water and concentration of salts to avoid osmotic disruption to cells. The **homeostatic** control of water and solute concentrations in the blood is achieved by hormones that act on the distal (second) convoluted tubule and the collecting duct.

Remember

Changes in the water content of the filtrate as it passes through the nephron will cause a change in the relative concentration of the solutes remaining in the fluid.

Table 1 Daily water and salt balance in a typical human

WATER				
Volume of water / cm^3 day^{-1}				
Water gain		**Water loss**		
Diet	2300	Urine	1500	
Metabolism, e.g. respiration	200	Expired air	400	
		Evaporation from skin	350	
		Faeces	150	
		Sweat	100	
TOTAL	2500	TOTAL	2500	
SALT				
Mass of salt / g day^{-1}				
Salt gain		**Salt loss**		
Diet	10.50	Urine	10.00	
		Faeces	0.25	
		Sweat	0.25	
TOTAL	10.50	TOTAL	10.50	

The loop of Henlé is responsible for creating the conditions in the surrounding interstitial (tissue) fluid that lead to the reabsorption of water from the distal convoluted tubule and the collecting duct. This results in concentrating the urine so that it has a lower **water potential** than the blood (see 14.1f).

Changes occurring in the filtrate

As we have seen, the glomerular filtrate that is formed in the Bowman's capsule contains useful substances, including water, and waste substances, including urea and any water that is in excess of needs. Almost all the glucose and amino acids are reabsorbed in the proximal convoluted tubule, together with a large proportion of mineral ions and water. Some urea also leaves the filtrate in the proximal convoluted tubule. In the descending limb of the loop of Henlé, more water is reabsorbed. A small proportion of the sodium and chloride ions from the interstitial fluid also moves back into the peritubular capillaries.

During its passage from the Bowman's capsule, through the proximal convoluted tubule and the loop of Henlé, the water potential of the filtrate continually changes. This is due to:

- water reabsorption in the proximal convoluted tubule and loop of Henlé
- reabsorption of solutes, including urea, in the proximal convoluted tubule
- loss of sodium ions and chloride ions in the loop of Henlé.

Most of the water from the filtrate arriving at the distal convoluted tubule has been reabsorbed. It is in the distal convoluted tubule and in the collecting ducts that homeostatic regulation of the water content of the filtrate occurs. The final product is urine. We will see in 14.1f how the water content of the filtrate is varied to make sure that the water potential of blood remains constant.

From the Extension, summarising the function of the kidneys, you can see that the kidney has other functions in addition to osmoregulation and excretion.

Extension

The distal (second) convoluted tubule

The main role of the distal tubule is to make final adjustments to the water and salts that are reabsorbed and to control the pH of the blood by selecting which ions to reabsorb.

Extension

The functions of the kidneys

- Regulating the composition of the blood and maintaining a constant water potential by:
  - Maintaining a constant volume of water
  - Removing wastes such as urea
  - Maintaining a constant concentration of mineral ions and other substances
  - Maintaining a constant blood pH
- Regulating blood pressure
- Maintaining the body's calcium level
- Stimulating the production of red blood cells

Summary test 14.1e

The maintenance of a constant water potential of the blood is known as **(1)**. The kidney helps to keep a constant **(2)** of blood as well as regulating the concentration of dissolved **(3)**. Almost all the **(4)** and amino acids leave the filtrate in the proximal convoluted tubule. After its passage through the **(5)** and distal convoluted tubule, the filtrate enters the **(6)**. The surrounding interstitial fluid has a **(7)** water potential than the filtrate. This is due to the presence of **(8)** ions and **(9)** ions.

f. Osmoregulation and water reabsorption in the collecting ducts

These pages help you to:

- describe the roles of the hypothalamus, posterior pituitary gland, antidiuretic hormone (ADH), aquaporins and collecting ducts in osmoregulation (14.1.8)

You will also:

- read about how antidiuretic hormone got its name
- learn about the role of the loop of Henlé in reabsorbing water and creating a concentration gradient in the interstitial fluid in the medulla

Extension

The naming of antidiuretic hormone

The name antidiuretic hormone (ADH) may, at first, seem unusual. However, it describes its function precisely. **Diuresis** is the production of large volumes of dilute urine. It is a symptom of a disease called **diabetes insipidus** (so called because the urine from sufferers did not taste sweet!). The disease was successfully treated with pituitary extract. Therefore it was suggested that a hormone existed that was given the name 'antidiuretic hormone'. As the effect of ADH is to increase the permeability of collecting ducts so that more water is reabsorbed into the blood, it causes the production of small volumes of concentrated urine.

This is the opposite of diuresis – hence the name **anti**diuretic hormone.

The importance of the interstitial fluid

As a result of facilitated diffusion and active transport by cells in the ascending limb of the loop of Henlé, sodium and chloride ions are concentrated in the interstitial fluid surrounding the distal convoluted tubule and the collecting duct. There is a gradient of water potential within this interstitial region, with the highest water potential in the cortex and outer medulla region, and the lowest in the inner medulla, the region closest to the renal pelvis (see 14.1e for further details). Some urea passes out of the filtrate in the collecting duct into the interstitial region, so further increasing the concentration of solutes and decreasing the water potential. At all points, the interstitial fluid has a lower water potential than the filtrate passing down the collecting duct.

This feature is essential in osmoregulation as it provides the correct environment for the osmotic flow of water out of the distal convoluted tubule and the collecting duct. However, for homeostatic regulation, the loss of water from the tubule and collecting duct must also be controlled.

Regulation of the water potential of the blood

The **water potential** of the blood is determined by the balance of water and salts within it. A rise in solute concentration lowers its water potential. This may be caused by:

- too little water being consumed
- much sweating occurring
- large amounts of salt being taken in (ingested).

The body responds to this decrease in water potential as follows:

- Sensory cells called **osmoreceptors** in the **hypothalamus** of the brain detect the decrease in water potential.
- It is thought that, when the water potential of the blood decreases below a set point, water is lost from these osmoreceptor cells by osmosis.
- Owing to this water loss the osmoreceptor cells shrink, a change that stimulates the neurosecretory cells in the hypothalamus to produce a hormone called **antidiuretic hormone (ADH)**. The osmoreceptor cells are very sensitive and only a small loss of water can stimulate a response.
- ADH passes along the neurones (nerve cells) to the posterior **pituitary gland**, from where it is secreted into the tissue fluid and passes into the capillaries.
- ADH passes in the blood to the kidney, where it increases the permeability to water of the cell surface membrane of the cells that make up the walls of the distal (second) convoluted tubule and the collecting duct.
- ADH molecules bind to complementary receptors on the cell surface membrane of these cells activating a second messenger system within the cell (cyclic AMP – 14.1g). This results in the activation of a protein kinase, an enzyme that adds phosphate groups to other proteins to activate them.
- This phosphorylation cascade causes vesicles within the cell to move to, and fuse with, its cell surface membrane. These vesicles contain aquaporins.
- ADH binding also leads to an increase in transcription of the gene coding for the aquaporin protein, increasing the number of available aquaporins.
- When the vesicles fuse with the cell surface membrane, the number of aquaporins in the membrane increases greatly, making the cell surface membrane much more permeable to water.

- ADH binding also leads to an increase in membrane transport proteins for urea, so that the collecting duct becomes more permeable to urea and some will leave the filtrate to further decrease the water potential of the interstitial fluid.
- The combined effect is that more water leaves the collecting duct by osmosis down a water potential gradient into the interstitial fluid that has a lower water potential (more concentrated) and then re-enters the blood.
- As the reabsorbed water came from the blood in the first place, this will not, in itself, increase the water potential of the blood, but merely prevent it from decreasing any further. Therefore there are osmoreceptors that stimulate a thirst response, to encourage the individual to seek out and drink more water.
- The osmoreceptors in the hypothalamus detect the increase in water potential and ADH secretion from the posterior pituitary is reduced.
- The decrease in ADH concentration in the blood will lead to a decreased permeability of the collecting duct to water and urea so that the permeability returns to its former state. This is an example of homeostasis and the principle of negative feedback (14.1a).

A decrease in the solute concentration of the blood increases its water potential. This may be caused:

- by large volumes of water being consumed
- by salts used in metabolism or excreted not being replaced in the diet.

The body responds to this increase in water potential as follows:

- The osmoreceptors in the hypothalamus detect the increase in water potential (slight swelling owing to water movement in by osmosis) and inhibits release of ADH from the posterior pituitary gland.
- This decreases the permeability of the collecting ducts to water and urea (some aquaporins are removed from the cell surface membrane).
- Less water is reabsorbed back into the blood from the collecting duct.
- More dilute urine is produced and the water potential of the blood decreases.
- When the water potential of the blood has returned to normal, the osmoreceptors in the hypothalamus cause the posterior pituitary to increase its release of ADH back to normal (= negative feedback).

These events are summarised in Figure 1.

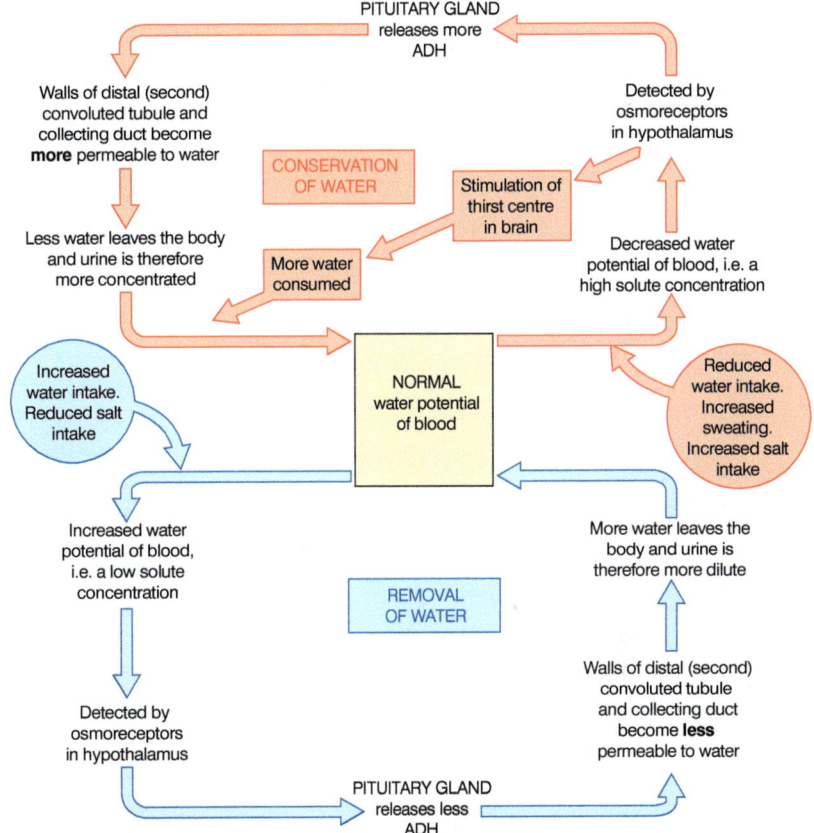

Figure 1 *Regulation of water potential of the blood by antidiuretic hormone (ADH)*

Summary test 14.1f

Despite daily fluctuations in water and salt intake, the water potential of the blood remains relatively constant as a result of **(1)** control achieved by the **(2)** hormone (ADH) that acts on the distal convoluted tubule and **(3)**. If too little water or too much salt is consumed, or if **(4)** is excessive, the water potential of the blood will **(5)**. In response to this, osmoreceptors in the **(6)** of the brain detect the change and produce ADH that passes to the **(7)** gland from where it is secreted. ADH passes via the **(8)** to the kidney where it increases the **(9)** of the distal convoluted tubule and collecting duct to water and **(10)**. As a result more water is reabsorbed and enters the blood. Osmoreceptors also stimulate a **(11)** response and so more water is drunk and the water potential of the blood therefore **(12)**. When the water potential returns to normal, the osmoreceptors detect this and ADH production is reduced to normal – an example of the principle of **(13)**.

Extension

The loop of Henlé

The loop of Henlé acts as a counter-current multiplier. To understand how this works it is necessary to consider the following sequence of events using Figure 2, to which the numbers refer.

1. As the filtrate arrives in the descending limb of the loop from the proximal convoluted tubule, water leaves by osmosis down the water potential gradient. The cells lining the tubule in the descending limb have many aquaporins in their cell surface membranes (4.1b).
2. At the hairpin turn of the loop in the inner medulla, the filtrate now has very little water and the water potential is low compared to the surrounding fluid. The filtrate has a high concentration of sodium ions, which move out by facilitated diffusion. Some chloride ions also move out. This gradually increases the water potential of the filtrate as it moves up the ascending limb.
3. Sodium ions and some chloride ions are now actively pumped out of the ascending limb. Water cannot leave the ascending limb so the water potential in the interstitial fluid remains lower than the water potential in the filtrate arriving at the descending limb.

Counter-current multiplier

Having the two limbs side-by-side allows a counter-current flow of filtrate (flow in opposite directions). This maximises the reabsorption of water and minimises the quantity of ATP that is needed for active transport of ions into the interstitial fluid. The gradient of ion concentration in the interstitial fluid means that at any one point, there is always a lower water potential in the fluid than in the filtrate in the descending limb.

The concentration of the urine produced is directly related to the length of the loop of Henlé. It is short in mammals whose **habitats** are in or by water (e.g. beavers) and long in those whose habitats are dry regions (e.g. kangaroo rat).

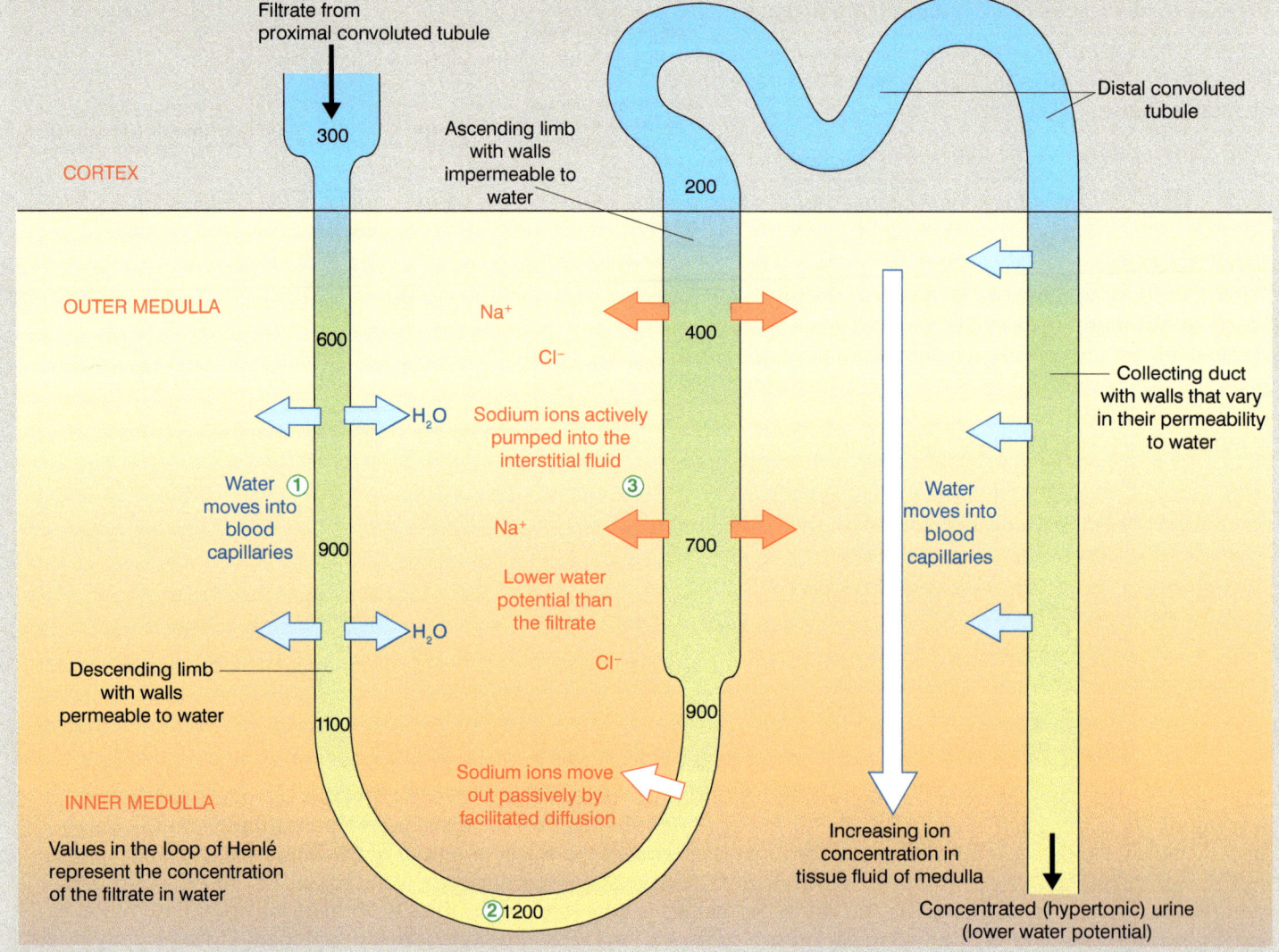

Figure 2 *Counter-current multiplier of the loop of Henlé*

Mammals possess two main coordinating systems – the nervous system that communicates rapidly, and the endocrine system that usually does so more slowly. Both systems interact in order to maintain a constant internal environment, at the same time being responsive to a varying external environment. Both systems also use chemical messengers – the endocrine system exclusively so, and the nervous system through the use of **neurotransmitters** in chemical **synapses**.

Hormones

A hormone is a regulating chemical produced and secreted by an endocrine gland and is carried in the blood to the cells, tissues or organ on which it acts – known as the **target cell (target tissue, target organ)** – that have complementary receptors on their cell surface membranes, or their internal membranes, or free in the cytoplasm. All body cells may be bathed in tissue fluid that contains a range of hormones, but only those with the specific receptors will respond. Hormones may differ chemically from one another, but they share many common characteristics. Some hormones have their action at the cell surface and other hormones are able to enter the cell to have an effect.

Hormones are examples of cell signalling molecules (4.1b). They are:

- effective in very small quantities, and some have widespread and permanent effects
- normally relatively small molecules
- often proteins or peptides (short chains of amino acids joined by peptide bonds), although some are **steroids**
- transported by the blood system
- produced by endocrine glands.

Endocrine glands

A gland is a group of cells that produce a particular substance or substances by a mechanism known as **secretion**.

Endocrine glands are ductless glands that secrete hormones directly into the tissue fluid to pass into the blood for transport round the body.

Endocrine glands may be discrete organs such as the thyroid gland, or groups of cells within other organs, such as the **islets of Langerhans** in the pancreas.

These pages help you to:

- understand and describe the principles of cell signalling using the example of the control of blood glucose concentration by glucagon: conformational change of receptor on binding hormone; G-protein activation stimulating adenylyl cyclase; formation of the second messenger, cyclic AMP (cAMP), which activates protein kinase A to initiate an enzyme cascade (14.1.9)
- understand how the cell signal amplifies the response and results in a large quantity of phosphorylated enzymes (14.1.9)

You will also:

- learn about the pancreas as an example of an organ that is an exocrine and an endocrine gland

Extension

Adrenaline

The hormone **adrenaline,** also known as the 'fight or flight' hormone, acts to prepare the body for more intense physical activity. It is produced in the adrenal glands that are located on top of the kidneys. One of the effects of adrenaline is to act on liver cells and trigger the breakdown of glycogen to glucose. The glucose that is released into the blood stream is needed for the increase in muscle activity. The mechanism of hormone action on the liver cells is similar to that of glucagon and also involves the cAMP second messenger system (described on page 296). Adrenaline is an example of a cell signalling molecule that has a variety of different target tissues.

Cell signalling and the hormone glucagon

Cell signalling involves:

- release of the cell-signalling molecules
- transport of the cell-signalling molecules to the target cells or target tissues
- binding of the cell-signalling molecules (ligands) to receptors on or in the target cell
- ligand binding triggering a specific response by the cell.

An example of cell signalling involves the peptide hormone glucagon.

The mechanism of hormone action involving glucagon is called the **cyclic AMP second messenger system**. Glucagon stimulates liver cells leading to the conversion of glycogen to glucose. Glucagon, together with the hormone insulin, is responsible for the homeostatic control of blood glucose concentration (14.1h).

The process involving glucagon, shown in Figure 1, is outlined below.

1. Glucagon is produced and secreted by the alpha cells of the pancreas (see Extension) in response to a low blood glucose concentration.
2. Glucagon is transported in the blood stream to reach its target cells, the cells of the liver.
3. The glucagon binds to its complementary receptor on the cell surface membrane of a liver cell. The glucagon receptor is an example of a G-protein-coupled receptor.
4. Ligand (glucagon) binding causes the receptor to undergo a conformation change (it changes shape) and this activates a membrane protein, termed a G protein.
5. The activated G protein activates another membrane protein, an enzyme called adenylyl cyclase.
6. The activated enzyme converts ATP to cyclic AMP (cAMP). cAMP is known as the second messenger as it has been triggered by the first messenger, the hormone glucagon, and sets off a cascade of reactions within the cell.
7. cAMP binds to and activates protein kinase A. Protein kinases are enzymes that catalyse the phosphorylation of other proteins, including enzymes.
8. This initiates an enzyme cascade in which enzymes are activated by phosphorylation. This amplifies the first signal as one enzyme molecule can catalyse the phosphorylation of many other enzyme molecules. The last enzyme in the chain catalyses the breakdown of glycogen to glucose. This is the specific response of the cell to binding by the cell-signalling molecule, glucagon.

The glucose diffuses out of the liver cell and into the blood, through protein carriers called transporter proteins.

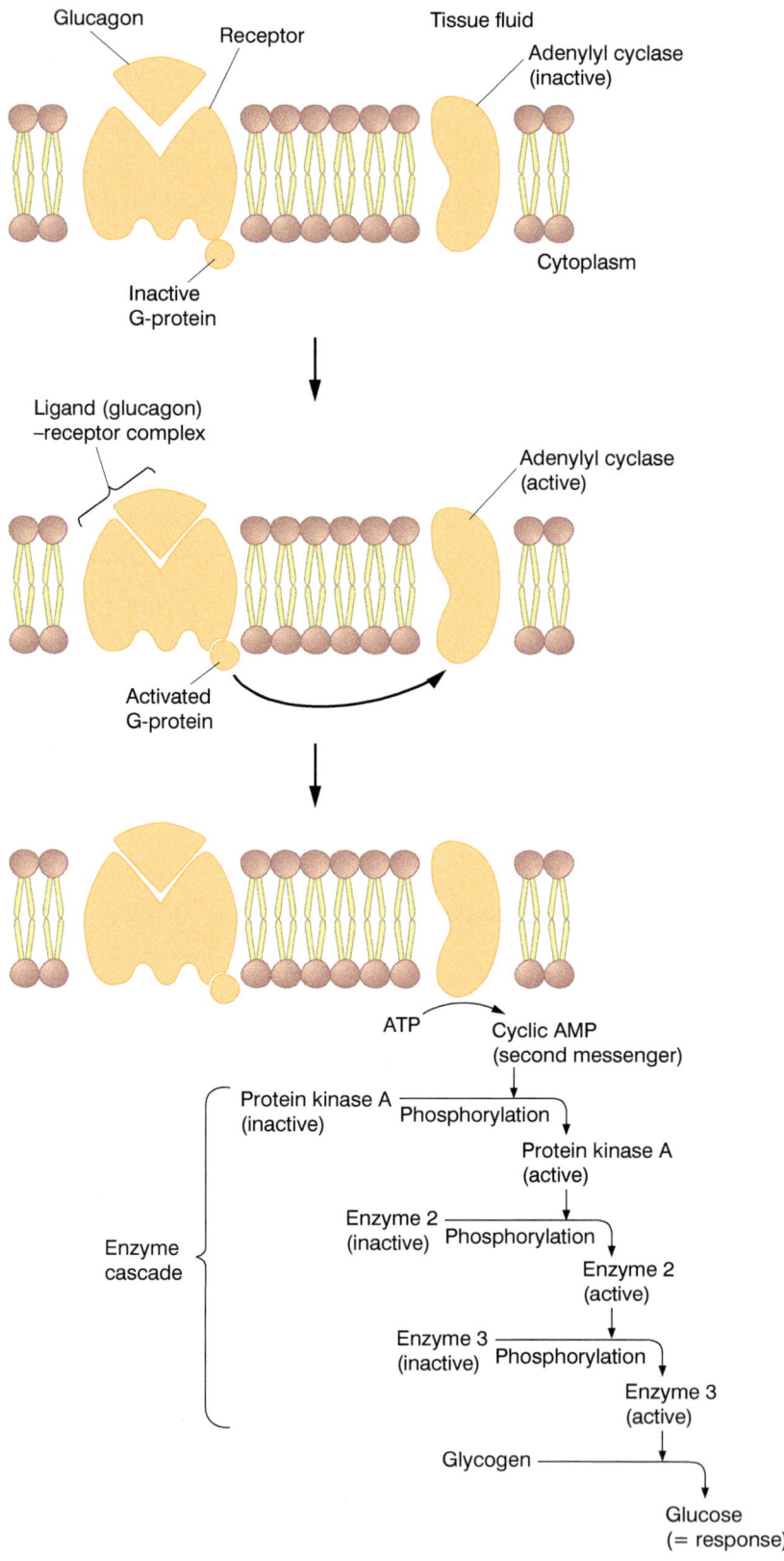

Figure 1 *Second messenger mechanism of hormone action*

Extension

The pancreas: an exocrine and an endocrine gland

The pancreas is a large, pale coloured gland that is situated in the upper abdomen, behind the stomach. It is an exocrine gland as it secretes pancreatic juice, which contains digestive enzymes. Pancreatic juice passes along the pancreatic duct to enter the duodenum of the small intestine. Exocrine glands contain cells that secrete substances into a duct (tube) that carries the substance to its site of action.

* It is also an **endocrine gland** because it produces the hormones **insulin** and **glucagon**, which pass directly into the tissue fluid to enter the blood capillaries that pass through it. The endocrine areas of the pancreas are ductless.

The groups of endocrine cells known as **islets of Langerhans** are of two types:

* the larger **α cells** that produce the hormone glucagon
* the smaller **β cells** that produce the hormone insulin.

Figure 2 shows the cellular structure of part of the pancreas. Both types of cells are rich in secretory vesicles and their role in controlling blood glucose concentrations is the subject of 14.1g.

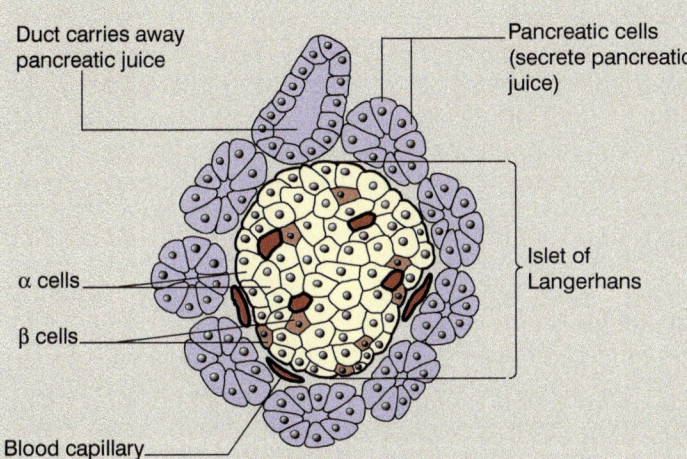

Figure 2 *Section through the pancreas showing an islet of Langerhans*

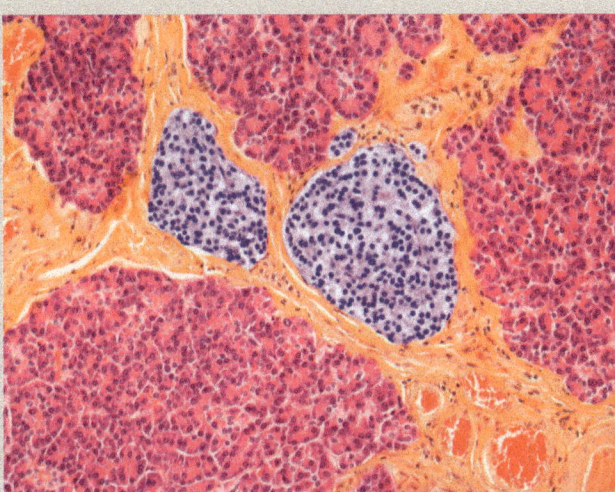

Figure 3 *Photomicrograph of the pancreas showing two islets of Langerhans (centre) containing α cells and β cells. Around the islets are the exocrine pancreatic cells.*

Summary test 14.1g

Hormones are produced by endocrine glands and are carried by **(1)** to the cell, tissue or organ on which they act, called the **(2)** cell/organ. Hormones may have widespread and **(3)** effects. They are usually proteins or peptides, although some are **(4)**. Not all cells respond to a particular hormone as they do not have the **(5)** receptors. The pancreas is an exocrine and an endocrine gland, producing the hormone **(6)** from β cells found in the groups of endocrine cells called the **(7)**. Another type of cell, called **(8)** cells produce the hormone glucagon. This binds to a glucagon receptor, which is an example of a type of receptor known as a **(9)**. Binding causes a **(10)** change and activates a **(11)**. This in turn activates a membrane enzyme known as **(12)** to cause the conversion of ATP to **(13)**, termed a **(14)** messenger. This activates the enzyme known as **(15)**, which initiates an **(16)**. There is an **(17)** of the signal so that the result is the activation of many enzymes by **(18)**. The response of the liver cell is the conversion of **(19)** to **(20)**.

These pages help you to:

- explain how negative feedback control mechanisms regulate blood glucose concentration, with reference to the effects of insulin on muscle cells and liver cells and the effect of glucagon on liver cells (14.1.10)

You will also:

- understand more about blood glucose concentrations
- understand the difference between Type I and Type II diabetes
- learn about other hormones that increase blood glucose concentration

Glucose is the main substrate for respiration, providing the source of energy for almost all organisms. It is therefore essential that the blood of mammals contains a relatively constant concentration of glucose for respiration. If it falls too low, the energy supply in cells will be too low and the cells will die – brain cells are especially sensitive in this respect because they can only respire glucose. If the concentration rises too high, it decreases the water potential of the blood and creates osmotic problems that can cause dehydration and be equally dangerous. Homeostatic control of blood glucose concentration is therefore essential.

Blood glucose and variations in its concentration

The normal concentration of blood glucose is 90–100 mg in each 100 cm^3 of blood (5.0–5.6 mmol dm^{-3}). There are three sources of blood glucose:

- **Directly from the diet** as glucose from the breakdown of other carbohydrates such as starch, maltose, lactose and sucrose.
- **Breakdown of glycogen (glycogenolysis)** from the stores in the liver and muscle cells. A normal liver contains 75–100 g of glycogen, made by converting excess glucose from the diet in a process called glycogenesis.
- **Gluconeogenesis** is the production of new glucose, i.e. from sources other than carbohydrate. The liver, for example, can make glucose from glycerol and amino acids.

Animals may not eat continuously and as their diet varies, their intake of glucose fluctuates. Likewise, glucose is used up at different rates depending on the level of mental and physical activity. With changes in the supply and demand of glucose the concentration of glucose in the blood fluctuates. Two main hormones, insulin and glucagon, operate to maintain a constant blood glucose concentration.

Insulin and the β cells of the pancreas

We saw in 14.1g that in the pancreas there are groups of special cells known as the islets of Langerhans. These cells are of two types: larger alpha (α) cells and smaller beta (β) cells. The β cells detect and respond to a rise in blood glucose concentration by secreting the hormone **insulin** directly into the blood. Insulin is a globular protein made up of 51 amino acids (Figure 1).

Almost all body cells (but not red blood cells) have **glycoprotein** receptors on their membranes that bind with insulin molecules. In blood glucose regulation, the two main types of target cells are those of the liver and the skeletal (striated) muscles. Binding of insulin triggers reactions within cells that result in one or more specific responses. These responses cause a lowering of blood glucose concentration:

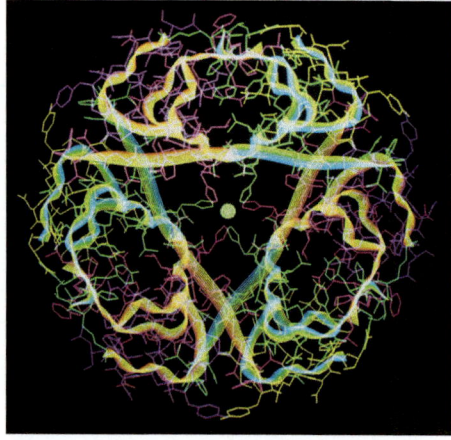

Figure 1 *Molecular graphic of an insulin molecule. Insulin is made up of 51 amino acids arranged in two chains (shown here as yellow and green ribbons) held together by disulfide bridges*

- Cellular respiratory rate is increased, using up more glucose.
- The rate of conversion of glucose into glycogen (glycogenesis) is increased in the cells of the liver and muscles, so that the concentration gradient between the tissue fluid and the cytoplasm remains steep for glucose uptake.
- In muscle cells, the permeability to glucose increases. Specific transport proteins, known as GLUT4 transporters, are held within vesicles that fuse with the cell surface membrane to add extra transporters for the uptake of glucose into the cell. This does not occur in liver cells as they have other specific glucose transporters that are continually present in their membranes, and so are always readily permeable to glucose.
- The rate of conversion of glucose to fat in **adipose tissue** is increased.

The effect of these processes is to remove glucose from the blood and return its concentration to normal. This lowering of the blood glucose concentration causes the β cells to reduce their secretion of insulin (= **negative feedback**) so that the concentration of glucose remains at or close to the set point of 90–100 mg in each 100 cm³ of blood.

Extension

Normal blood glucose concentrations and diabetes (diabetes mellitus)

The stated value of 90–100 mg in 100 cm³ of blood is for a healthy adult who has not eaten for 8 hours (fasting). The normal range is 79–110 mg in 100 cm³ of blood (4.4–6.1 mmol dm⁻³). However, a healthy adult may have a set value and a normal range that differs from these standard values. When the blood glucose concentrations are outside a normal range, homeostatic mechanisms operate to return the blood glucose to the set point. People with Type I diabetes cannot produce insulin. People with Type II diabetes show insulin resistance: insulin is produced and may bind to receptors but for some reason it does not have an effect. In both conditions, the body cannot keep the concentration of blood glucose within narrow limits.

Glucagon and the α cells of the pancreas

The α cells of the islets of Langerhans respond to a fall in blood glucose by secreting the hormone glucagon directly into the blood. Only the cells of the liver have receptors that bind to glucagon, so only liver cells respond, (see 14.1g) by activating the enzyme phosphorylase, which converts glycogen to glucose, and by increasing the conversion of amino acids and glycerol into glucose (= **gluconeogenesis**).

The overall effect is therefore to increase the quantity of glucose in the blood and return it to its normal concentration. This increase in the blood glucose concentration causes the α cells to reduce the secretion of glucagon (= negative feedback).

Hormone interaction in regulating blood sugar

The two hormones, insulin and glucagon, act in opposite directions. Insulin lowers blood glucose concentration, whereas glucagon increases it. The two hormones are said to act **antagonistically**. The system is self-regulating because the concentration of glucose in the blood determines the quantity of insulin and glucagon released. In this way the interaction of these two hormones allows highly sensitive control of the blood glucose concentration. The concentration of glucose is, however, not constant, but fluctuates around a set point. This is because of the way negative feedback mechanisms work. Only when the blood glucose concentration falls below the set point is insulin secretion reduced (negative feedback), leading to a rise in blood glucose. In the same way, only when the concentration exceeds the set point glucagon secretion is reduced (negative feedback), causing a fall in the blood glucose concentration. The control of blood glucose concentration is summarised in Figure 2 (page 300). Normally, an uncontrolled increase in blood glucose concentration occurs shortly after eating a meal that contains carbohydrates. A decrease in blood glucose concentration below the normal range may occur, for example, during intense physical activity. In both situations, the homeostatic control using negative feedback mechanisms returns the concentration back to the set point.

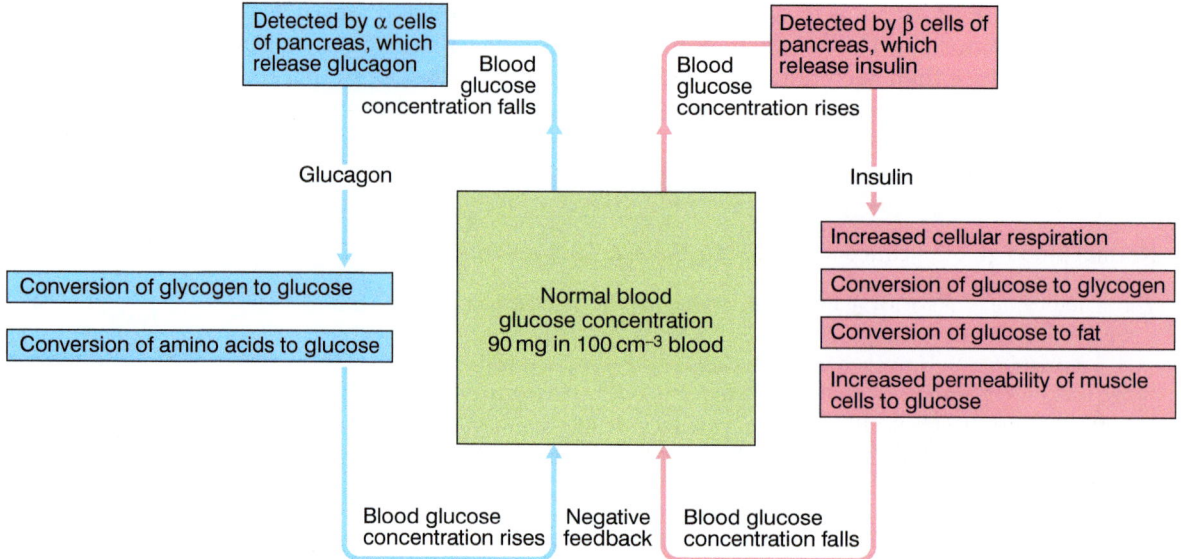

Figure 2 *Summary of regulation of blood glucose*

Remember

Glucagon and insulin act as cell signalling molecules. On binding with their specific receptors, reactions are triggered within the target cells that lead to a response. Cell signalling molecules do not take part in the reactions within the cell.

Extension

Other hormones that can increase blood glucose concentration

At times of excitement or stress, adrenaline release causes the breakdown of glycogen in the liver, raising the blood glucose concentration (see also 14.1g). If the glycogen supplies in the liver are used up, the adrenal glands produce the hormone **cortisol**, which causes the liver to convert amino acids and glycerol into glucose. Growth hormone can also increase blood glucose concentrations.

Summary test 14.1h

Glucose is the main **(1)**. It is important that blood glucose concentration is maintained at **(2)** mg in each 100 cm³ of blood by **(3)**, because if it falls too low the energy supply of cells will be too low. The cells of the **(4)** are especially sensitive to low blood glucose concentrations. If it rises too high **(5)** problems occur that may cause dehydration. Blood glucose is formed directly from **(6)** in the diet or from the breakdown of **(7)**, which is stored in the cells of the liver and **(8)**. The liver can also increase blood glucose levels by making glucose from other sources such as glycerol and **(9)** in a process known as **(10)**. Blood glucose is used up when it is absorbed into cells, converted into fat or **(11)** for storage or is used up during **(12)** by cells. To maintain a constant concentration of blood glucose the pancreas acts as an **(13)** gland in producing two hormones from clusters of cells within it called **(14)**. The β cells are **(15)** in size and produce the hormone **(16)**, which causes the blood glucose concentration to **(17)**. The α cells produce the hormone **(18)**, which has the opposite effect. The two hormones are therefore said to act **(19)**. The hormone produced by the β cells leads to an increase in the permeability to glucose of **(20)** cells by the addition of **(21)** to the cell surface membrane. The hormone also increases the rates of **(22)** and **(23)** in the target cells so that a **(24)** gradient for glucose uptake is maintained.

i. Test strips and biosensors to measure glucose concentrations

Biosensors are devices that use immobilised biological molecules, such as enzymes or antibodies, or biological systems, such as whole cells, to detect a specific chemical and in most cases, measure the concentration of the chemical. In its simplest form, a biosensor can be a test strip (dipstick), but commonly biosensors are now taken to mean those devices that are coupled with microelectronics so that results are rapid, the measurements are extremely accurate, and the chemical can be detected in very small quantities.

Detecting glucose in blood and urine

As explained in 14.1h it is important for healthy functioning that blood glucose concentrations remain at or around a normal concentration of 90 mg in 100 cm^{-3} blood. If concentrations rise too high, glucose is excreted in the urine.

Simple test strips or more complex biosensors are frequently used by people with diabetes (see Extension in 14.1h) to measure the concentration of glucose in the blood or urine. For people with Type I diabetes (a lack of insulin) a check of glucose concentration will help to inform them if they need to adjust their insulin doses. Health care professionals routinely use test strips as a quick and reliable method to detect the abnormal presence of glucose in urine.

The method of detection of glucose makes use of immobilised enzymes (see 3.2d). For both test strips and biosensors the same enzymes can be used:

- glucose oxidase catalyses the conversion of glucose to gluconic acid and hydrogen peroxide

$$\text{Glucose} + O_2 \xrightarrow{\text{Glucose oxidase}} \text{gluconic acid} + H_2O_2$$

- peroxidase catalyses the breakdown of hydrogen peroxide to water and oxygen

$$2H_2O_2 \xrightarrow{\text{Peroxidase}} 2H_2O + O_2$$

Test strips to detect glucose

Glucose test strips are a convenient way to detect glucose in a sample of urine.

They involve a colour change, which could be a change in the intensity of colour, to give a semi-quantitative measure of glucose concentration. The colour change can be compared to a coloured standards chart and an estimate of concentration of glucose can be obtained (Figure 1). The test strips are highly specific and detect only glucose.

To obtain a colour change, a colourless hydrogen donor is used to react with the oxygen released in the peroxidase reaction shown above. The hydrogen donor acts as a chromogen, changing colour by being oxidised by the oxygen that is given off.

$$H_2O_2 + DH_2 \xrightarrow{\text{Peroxidase}} 2H_2O + D$$

hydrogen donor   coloured
(colourless)   compound

These pages help you to:

- explain the principles of operation of test strips and biosensors for measuring the concentration of glucose in blood and urine, with reference to glucose oxidase and peroxidase enzymes (14.1.11)

You will also:

- learn how people are able to self-monitor blood glucose concentrations

The dipstick is a thin strip of absorbent paper (some test strips are a thin strip of plastic with a paper pad stuck on at one end). At the test end of the strip the chromogen and the enzymes glucose oxidase and peroxidase are added. A thin cellulose membrane covers the area so that only small molecules such as glucose can enter the test area. The end of the dipstick is dipped into the urine sample and after a set time any colour change can be compared to the chart. If glucose is present in the urine, the action of the two enzymes will result in a colour change.

Testing for the presence of glucose using test strips produces semi-quantitative results. The true concentration of glucose present in urine can be estimated using the colour standards chart. In Figure 1, the light green colour obtained on the test strip can be matched to approximately the concentration of $14 \, \text{mmol} \, \text{dm}^{-3}$, but this is not an exact colour match and is likely to be lower than this. It is less closely matched to the colour standard shown for the concentration of glucose at $5.5 \, \text{mmol} \, \text{dm}^{-3}$.

Urine test strips do not need to provide accurate results for glucose concentration: they only need to indicate to doctors that the kidney is excreting glucose in the urine and that this is not a normal result for a healthy person. Normally, almost all the glucose is reabsorbed into the blood during selective reabsorption in the proximal convoluted tubule of the nephron (14.1d). The results will indicate that further investigation is needed.

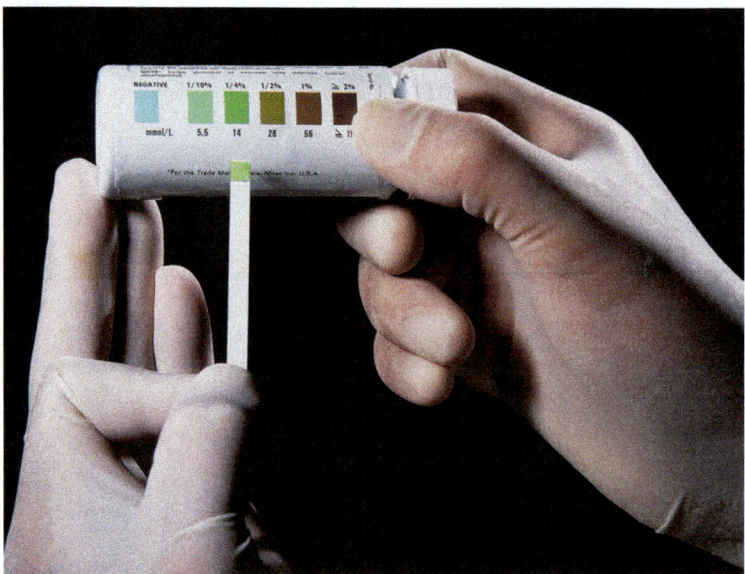

Figure 1 *The Diastix™ test for glucose carried out on the urine of a person with diabetes. A positive result for glucose is seen. People with diabetes lack the hormone insulin, or have an insensitivity to the presence of insulin. Insulin is the hormone that leads to a lowering of blood glucose concentration. The results here indicate that the person has a raised blood glucose concentration, as glucose has been excreted in the urine.*

Biosensors to detect glucose

Biosensors are extremely sensitive and accurate. As glucose oxidase is a highly specific enzyme, biosensors used to detect glucose in blood samples are insensitive to other chemicals present. They can also be re-used, so are cost effective and also have the advantage of being small and portable so that they can be carried by a person and used at any time.

In a glucose biosensor, the enzymes glucose oxidase is immobilised onto an inert supporting material to form a biological recognition layer. The layer is separated from the blood sample by a partially permeable membrane that only allows small molecules such as glucose to diffuse through. Glucose molecules present in the blood will bind to the active sites of the glucose oxidase enzymes and the reaction results in the production of gluconic acid and hydrogen peroxide, as shown on page 301.

The next part of the biosensor detects that a reaction has occurred and converts this into an electric current. This conversion is carried out by a transducer. In some biosensors the decrease in oxygen can be detected by a platinum oxygen electrode. In others, the production of hydrogen ions (from the gluconic acid produced) can be detected.

The final part of the biosensor is the amplification of the electrical signal and the production of a digital reading (Figure 2). The reading is proportional to the reaction that has occurred (for example, proportional to the decrease in oxygen, or the increase in hydrogen ions) so it is proportional to the concentration of glucose in the sample.

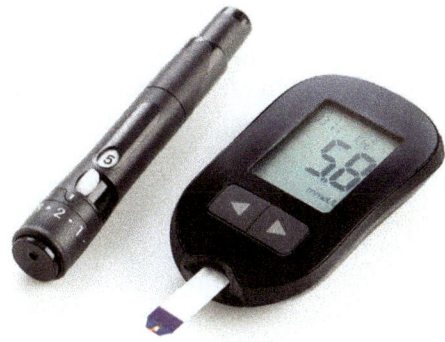

Figure 2 *Portable blood glucose testing kit. On the left is a spring-loaded pin that is used to prick a finger to obtain a drop of blood. This is transferred to the white test probe, which is placed into the glucose meter to give a digital readout.*

Extension

Daily checks of blood glucose concentrations

Portable biosensors are commonly used by people with diabetes to self-monitor their blood glucose concentrations. These involve using disposable test strips onto which a small drop of blood is placed. The test strip is placed into a biosensor (glucometer or glucose meter) to obtain a reading. This method involves pricking a finger to obtain the small drop of blood. Some glucose meters connect directly to smart phones to give a rapid reading and the measurements can be recorded and stored for later reference.

Apart from the inconvenience and pain (from finger-pricking), the finger-pricking method does not provide continuous monitoring of blood glucose concentrations. Implantable biosensors are being developed that would allow continuous monitoring. If coupled with insulin pumps, they could also deliver insulin at the appropriate times.

Summary test 14.1i

The methods to detect glucose in samples of blood and urine involve reacting glucose with **(1)** using the enzyme **(2)** to produce **(3)** and hydrogen peroxide. When testing a sample of urine, a simple **(4)** (dipstick) can be used. The reaction between hydrogen peroxide and a colourless **(5)**, catalysed by a **(6)** enzyme, will give a coloured compound. The colour can be compared to a chart to give a **(7)** estimate of glucose concentration. Portable **(8)** known as glucose meters can provide accurate **(9)** glucose concentrations. Here the enzyme catalysing the reaction with glucose is **(10)** onto an inert supporting material to form a **(11)**. Glucose **(12)** through a partially permeable membrane to reach the enzyme.

Plants, as well as animals, have homeostatic mechanisms to ensure that they maintain a constant level of essential materials for their needs. The regulation of carbon dioxide uptake by diffusion and water loss by transpiration is achieved by controlling the opening and closure of structures called **stomata**.

Guard cells and stomata

Stomata are minute pores that occur mainly on the leaves, especially the lower epidermis (underside). Each stoma (singular) is surrounded by a pair of special, kidney-shaped cells called **guard cells**. When a stoma is open, these cells surround a small opening a few micrometres wide called the **stomatal pore** (Figure 3). Unlike other epidermal cells, guard cells have chloroplasts and dense cytoplasm. The inner cell walls of the guard cells are thicker and less elastic than the outer ones. Any increase in the volume of the guard cells, for example due to the osmotic intake of water, causes the outer wall to bend more than the inner wall and so widen the stomatal pore. To 'close' the stoma completely, the reverse occurs. In this way they can control the rate of gaseous exchange. Figure 1 shows the structure of guard cells and the differences between an open and a closed stoma.

The mechanism of stomatal opening

Stomata open and close in response to certain stimuli. For example, they usually open in the light and close in the dark. A suggested mechanism for the opening and closing of stomata is as follows (see Figure 2).

- a particular stimulus such as light activates ATP synthase, an enzyme that increases the production of ATP by the chloroplasts in the guard cells
- these chloroplasts only have photosystem I (13.1e) and no Calvin cycle enzymes, so ATP is produced in cyclic photophosphorylation but not used up in the Calvin cycle
- this ATP is available to provide more energy for the active transport of protons (H^+) out of guard cells using cell surface membrane proton pumps
- the reduced H^+ concentration and increased negative charge inside the guard cell causes potassium channels in the membrane of these cells to open
- potassium ions (K^+) now diffuse into the guard cells down an electrochemical gradient. To maintain a balance, chloride ions also enter the guard cells
- these K^+ lower the water potential of the guard cells and so water enters them by osmosis down a water potential gradient. There are numerous aquaporins in the cell surface membranes of the guard cell for water movement
- the extra water causes the guard cells to become more turgid and to swell
- the thinner outer and thicker inner walls of the guard cells means that when they swell they bend outwards, and so widen the stomatal aperture.

The daily rhythm of stomatal opening and closure

Plants have a daily rhythm of opening and closing their stomata, so that they can balance the need for carbon dioxide and the need to conserve water.

During daylight hours, a plant carries out photosynthesis. This needs more carbon dioxide than is supplied by respiration and so carbon dioxide diffuses in from the atmosphere through open stomata. The concentration gradient between the outer atmosphere and the intercellular air spaces within the leaf is maintained because carbon dioxide is taken up and used by the photosynthetic

a *Stoma closed*

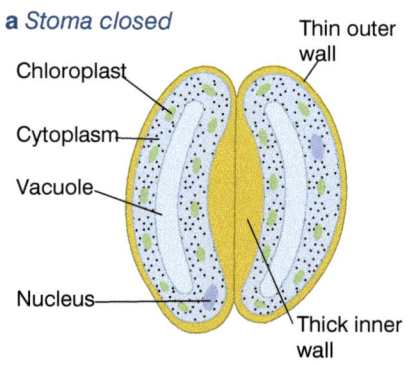

Chloroplast

Cytoplasm

Vacuole

Nucleus

Thin outer wall

Thick inner wall

b *Stoma open*

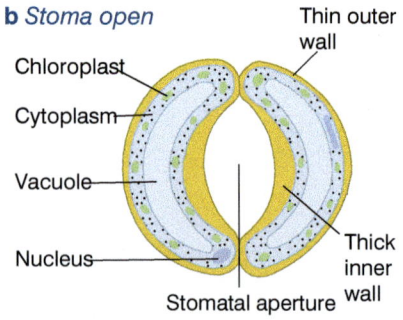

Chloroplast

Cytoplasm

Vacuole

Nucleus

Thin outer wall

Thick inner wall

Stomatal aperture

Figure 1 *Surface view of a stoma closed and open*

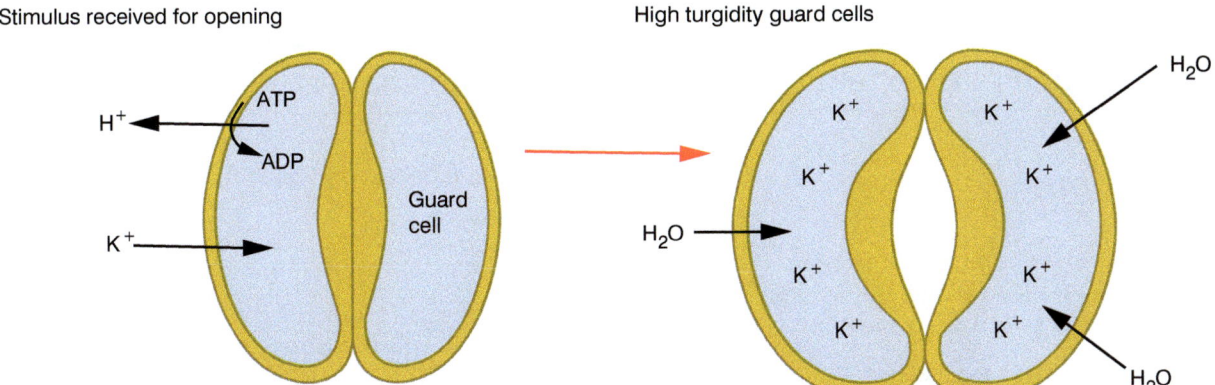

Stimulus received for opening

High turgidity guard cells

Figure 2 *Mechanism of stomatal opening*

palisade and spongy mesophyll cells. The consequence of open stomata is water loss by transpiration. During the day, water vapour diffuses out to the atmosphere through open stomata down a water potential gradient (7.2b). At night, photosynthesis stops and the stomata close as there is no need for carbon dioxide. This minimises water loss by stomatal transpiration.

During the day, if light intensity, temperature or air currents (wind) are too high, stomata respond by closing. This means that excessive water loss by transpiration is prevented and photosynthesis is temporarily prevented. During the day, stomata may also respond to heavy cloud cover (low light intensity) by temporarily closing, as the rate of photosynthesis is so low that it is better to conserve water during this time. Some plants also show a 'midday closure', for example some plants that go through a drought season may close their stomata at the time of day when the transpiration rate would be highest, to conserve water.

Role of abscisic acid in the closing of stomata

Abscisic acid (ABA) is sometimes referred to as the 'stress hormone' and has been shown to increase in concentration up to 40 times during drought conditions. This increase causes the closure of **stomata** when water loss by transpiration (7.2b) needs to be reduced. The response is rapid, as it needs to be if the plant is to survive, with stomata closing within a minute or two of ABA being applied. The speed of this reaction rules out a mechanism involving regulating the expression of a **gene**. One suggested mechanism of how ABA operates is as follows.

- Abscisic acid is secreted in response to drought stress and combines with specific receptors on the cell surface membrane of **guard cells**.
- Binding of ABA increases the concentration of calcium ions in the guard cells (more enters from outside and some is released from intracellular stores).
- The calcium ions act as a **second messenger** by altering potassium channels in the cell surface membrane in a way that causes potassium ions (K^+) to diffuse from the guard cells to the surrounding epidermal cells.
- ABA may also inhibit the action of the proton pump that moves H^+ out of the guard cells (and so reduces K^+ movement into the cell).
- The solute concentration in the guard cells is therefore reduced and their water potential becomes higher than in the epidermal cells.
- Water therefore leaves by osmosis, so the volume of the guard cells decreases, they become less turgid and therefore the stomatal pore closes.

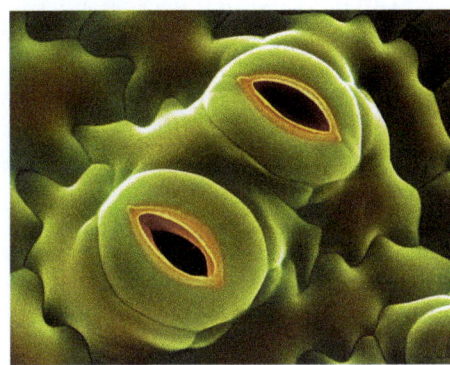

Figure 3 *Colourised scanning electron micrograph of open stomata on a tobacco leaf*

14 Exam-style questions

1 The liver has a vital role in carbohydrate and protein metabolism. It converts excess glucose and amino acids into products which are either stored or excreted.

   a Outline how liver cells metabolise excess amino acids. *(4 marks)*

   b Liver cells convert excess glucose into glycogen which is stored in liver cells. When blood glucose concentration falls below normal levels, glycogen can be converted back to glucose by initiating a cell-signalling pathway shown in Figure 1.

Figure 1

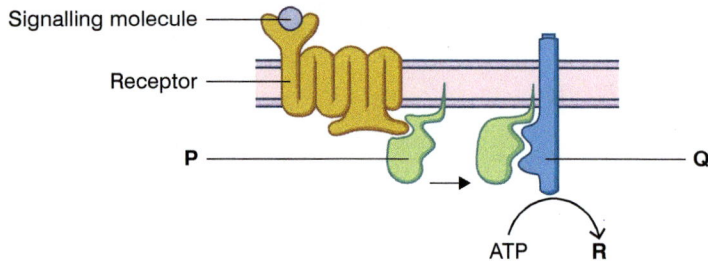

   i Name the signalling molecule in Figure 1. *(1 mark)*

   ii Identify molecules **P** and **Q**. *(2 marks)*

   iii Explain the role of **R** in causing the conversion of glycogen back to glucose. *(3 marks)*

(Total 10 marks)

2 Figure 2 is a transmission electron micrograph showing a section of part of the cortex region of the kidney (renal cortex).

Figure 2

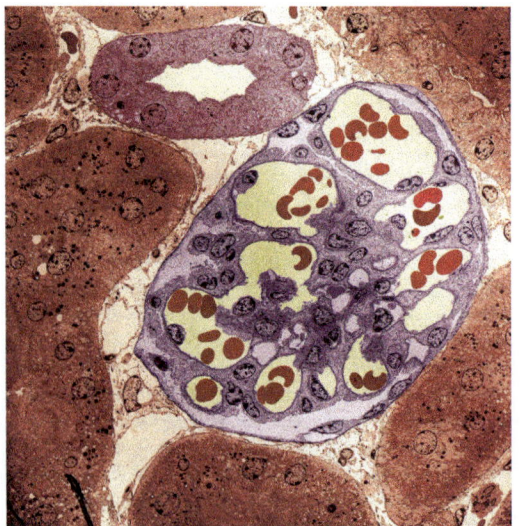

   a On the figure, label each of the following parts:

     G – the glomerulus

     P – the proximal convoluted tubule *(2 marks)*

   b When blood passes through the glomerulus, some of its contents pass into the Bowman's capsule, forming the glomerular filtrate.

     i Name the process by which the glomerular filtrate is formed. *(1 mark)*

     ii Explain how the structure of the glomerulus is adapted to its role in the process you have named in **i**. *(4 marks)*

The glomerular filtrate then passes through the proximal convoluted tubule where selection reabsorption occurs. Normally all glucose in the glomerular filtrate is reabsorbed back into the blood.

   c Describe how glucose is reabsorbed into the blood from the proximal convoluted tubule. *(5 marks)*

   d In some unusual conditions, unabsorbed glucose will continue to pass through the kidney tubules and is eventually excreted in urine.

Some people have a medical condition which is characterised by a high concentration of glucose in the urine. The concentration of glucose in urine can be estimated with a glucose test strip.

Outline the principles of glucose test strips for estimating the concentration of glucose in urine. *(6 marks)*

(Total 18 marks)

14 Practice questions

3 Figure 3 below shows some of the homeostatic changes that occur as a result of water being lost from the blood due to sweating.

Figure 3

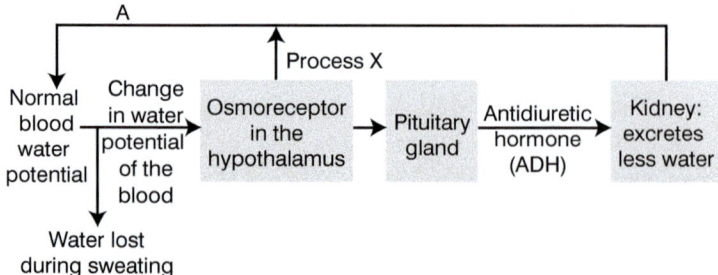

a Describe the change in water potential that occurs in the blood as a result of sweating.

b Which of the structures shown on Figure 3 acts as:
  i a receptor
  ii an effector?

c Describe how ADH gets from the pituitary gland to the kidney.

d The kidney conserves the water that is already in the blood. Given that the water potential of the blood returns to its normal level prior to sweating, suggest what is happening in process X.

e State as precisely as possible what mechanism is shown by the line labelled A.

4 An experiment was carried out with two groups of people. Group X had a condition known as Type I diabetes while group Y did not (control group). Every 15 minutes blood samples were taken from all members of both groups and the mean levels of insulin, glucagon and glucose were calculated. After an hour, every person was given a glucose drink. The results are shown in Figure 4 below.

Figure 4

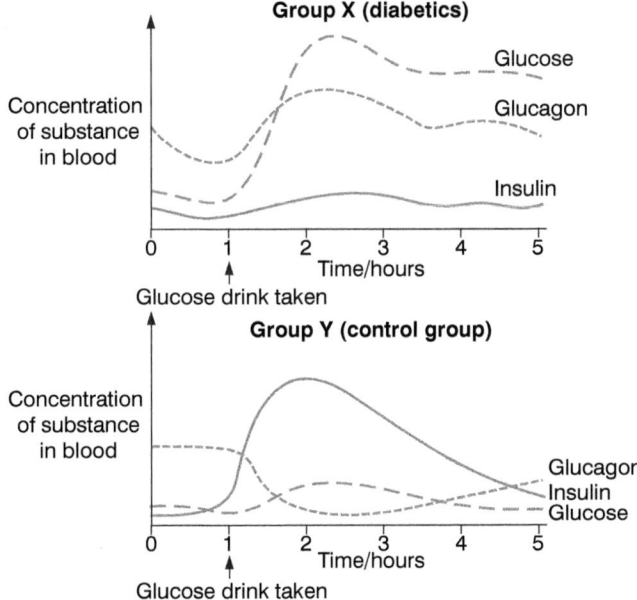

a Name a hormone that is involved in regulating blood glucose levels.

b State two differences between groups X and Y in the way insulin secretion responds to the drinking of glucose.

c Suggest a reason why the glucose concentration falls in both groups during the first hour.

d Using information from the graphs, explain the changes in the blood glucose concentration in group Y after the glucose is drunk.

e Explain the difference in blood glucose concentration in group X compared to group Y.

f Suggest what might happen to the blood glucose concentration of group X if they had no food intake over the next 24 hours.

5 Figure 5 is a diagram of the surface of a leaf showing a stoma with its guard cells and the surrounding epidermal cells.

Figure 5

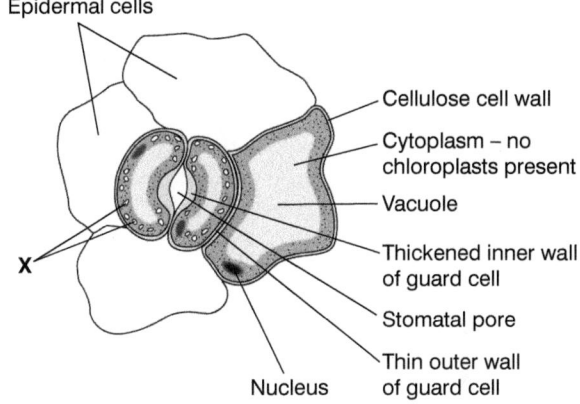

a Name the structures labelled X.

b Explain the importance of guard cells having inner and outer walls of different thicknesses.

c Stomata usually open in the light. During the process of opening:

  i What is the name of the enzyme that is activated by light?
  ii What is the name of the ion that is moved into the guard cells?
  iii By what process does this ion enter guard cells?
  iv Describe the relative water potential of the guard cells and the epidermal cells when a stoma is open.
  v State how the volume of the guard cells changes when a stoma is opening.

d Abscisic acid (ABA) causes stomata to close.

  i Where **exactly** does abscisic acid bind?
  ii Name the ion whose concentration increases in guard cells in response to this binding.
  iii This ion acts as a secondary messenger, which in turn causes another ion to move out of the guard cells. What is the name of this second ion and by what process does it move out?

15.1 Control and coordination in mammals

a. The endocrine system and the nervous system

These pages help you to:

- describe the features of the endocrine system with reference to the hormones ADH, glucagon and insulin (15.1.1)
- compare the features of the nervous system and the endocrine system (15.1.2)

You will also:

- learn about nervous organisation
- see where the main endocrine glands are located

The endocrine system and the nervous system are the two different coordination systems of the body. They are responsible for the regulation and control of body systems and of behaviour. Homeostasis involves both systems, which frequently work together to coordinate responses to stimuli.

Stimulus and response

The ability to react to **stimuli** (14.1a) is a basic characteristic of all living organisms. The stimuli may occur internally or externally and they lead to a **response** from the organism. The ability to respond to a stimulus increases the chances of survival for an organism. For example, to be able to detect and move away from harmful stimuli such as predators, extremes of temperature and pH, or to detect and move towards a source of food, clearly aids survival.

Those organisms that survive have a greater chance of raising offspring and of passing their **alleles** to the next generation. There is always, therefore, a **selection** pressure favouring organisms with better responses.

In the nervous system, stimuli are received by sensory **receptors** (15.1c) and the response is carried out by **effectors**, such as muscle (15.1j) and glands, including some endocrine glands. Receptors and effectors are often some distance apart and a form of communication is therefore needed between them if the organism is to respond effectively. This communication is electrical and uses nerve impulses, which are rapid and allow a fast response. The impulses travel along nerve cells, neurones, to reach their destination effector. If the effector is an endocrine gland, the destination target cells may also be some distance away. The form of communication is chemical and is slower as it uses hormones that travel in the blood stream. Further differences between the endocrine and nervous system are given in Table 1.

Table 1 Differences between the endocrine and nervous systems

Feature	Endocrine system	Nervous system
Communication	Chemical, involving cell signalling molecules known as hormones	Electrical, involving flow of ions across membranes to generate nerve impulses
Mode of transmission	Blood, in the circulatory system	Along axons (nerve fibres) of neurones (nerve cells)
Speed of transmission	Relatively slow, slower than nerve impulse conduction	Fast, faster than hormonal transmission
Parts of the body that respond (destinations)	Hormones travel to all parts of the body, but only target cells, tissues or organs respond	Nerve impulses travel to specific parts of the body
Response	Response is slower and can be long-lasting	Response is rapid and short-lived
Areas of body affected by response	Effects can be widespread	Effects are more localised
Duration of effect (how long the effect lasts)	Effect is longer and may be permanent (irreversible)	Effect is shorter and is temporary (reversible)

Although the main method of communication in the nervous system is electrical (using nerve impulses), there is also some chemical communication. This occurs at the locations where two neurones meet, known as synapses. There is a physical gap between the two neurones. Where the gap is very small, electrical transmission occurs. However, for many synapses, cell signalling molecules known as neurotransmitters are used to communicate between neurones to allow the impulses to proceed (see 15.1g).

The nervous system allows rapid, short-lived responses to stimuli that have an immediate and reversible effect. This contrasts with the endocrine system, where response time is more varied and where the effects of these responses can vary from fairly short term to permanent, such as the changes that occur in growth and during sexual development.

The endocrine system

The endocrine system consists of endocrine glands (Figure 1), and their secretions, hormones (14.1g). The glands are ductless and the secretions pass into the surrounding tissue fluid to move directly into the blood stream for transport round the body. At any one time, the blood will be transporting a range of different hormones and in the capillary networks, the cells will be bathed in tissue fluid containing these hormones, but only certain cells will be affected by each of the different hormones.

Endocrine glands in the body

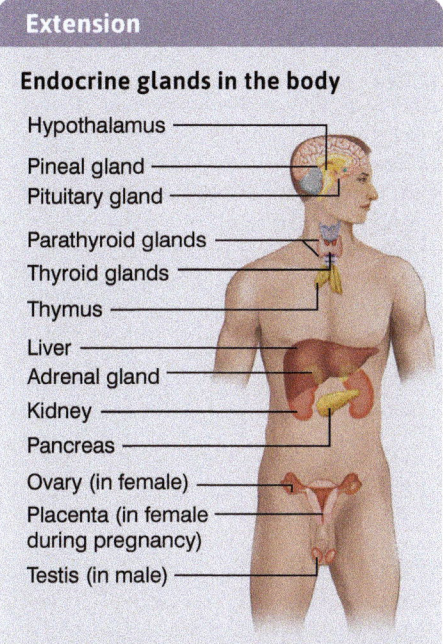

Hypothalamus
Pineal gland
Pituitary gland
Parathyroid glands
Thyroid glands
Thymus
Liver
Adrenal gland
Kidney
Pancreas
Ovary (in female)
Placenta (in female during pregnancy)
Testis (in male)

Figure 1 *Location of endocrine glands and organs with endocrine glandular tissue*

Extension

Nervous organisation

As animal species became more complex and the number of receptors and effectors increased, it became more efficient to link each receptor and effector to a central control centre.

The nervous system has two major divisions: the **central nervous system** (CNS), which is made up of the brain and spinal cord, and the **peripheral nervous system** (PNS), which is made up of pairs of nerves that originate from either the brain or the spinal cord.

The peripheral nervous system is divided into:

- **The sensory (afferent) nervous system**, which carries nerve impulses towards the central nervous system.
- **The motor (efferent) nervous system**, which carries nerve impulses away from the central nervous system.

The motor nervous system can be further sub-divided into:

- **The somatic nervous system**, which carries nerve impulses to skeletal muscles and is under voluntary control.
- **The autonomic nervous system**, which carries nerve impulses to glands, **smooth muscle** and **cardiac muscle** and is not under voluntary control, i.e. it is involuntary.

A summary of nervous organisation is given in Figure 2 and the way its components interact is shown in Figure 3.

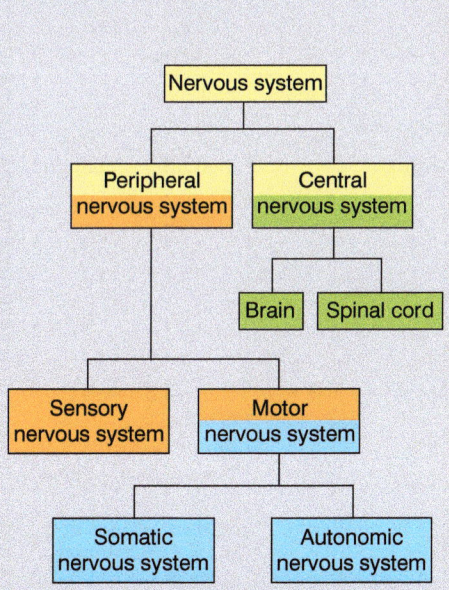

Figure 2 *Nervous organisation*

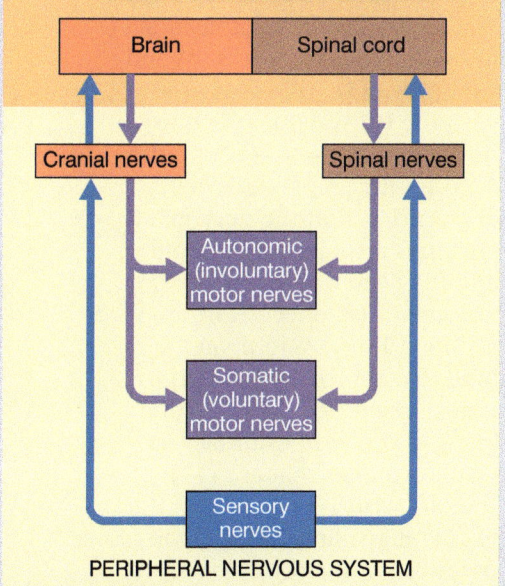

Figure 3 *Interaction between components of the nervous system*

Summary test 15.1a

A stimulus is any factor that is detected and produces a **(1)**. In the nervous system, a stimulus is received by a **(2)** and the response is carried out by an **(3)**. The method of communication in the nervous system is **(4)** and uses nerve **(5)**. This contrasts with the **(6)** system, which uses hormones and so is a **(7)** method of communication. Another difference is that the nervous system is responsible for rapid and **(8)**-lived responses that do not have a **(9)** effect. Hormones act on **(10)** cells and tissues and bind to complementary **(11)** to trigger responses. ADH, insulin and glucagon are examples of **(12)** hormones that are **(13)** soluble. ADH is produced in the **(14)** and insulin and glucagon are produced in the **(15)**. Endocrine glands are **(16)** and their secretions are passed directly into the blood.

The cells that respond to the hormone are known as target cells and they are identified by having specific receptors that have a complementary shape for binding the hormone (ligand–receptor binding, 4.1b). Some hormones, such as those involved in growth, development and the metabolic rate within cells (e.g. thyroid hormones and growth hormone) have widespread action and target cells are located throughout the body. Others, such as those shown in Table 2, mainly affect specific tissues and organs.

The response time within the target cells varies depending on the range of reactions triggered. For example, the response is slower if the hormone acts to switch on genes to express proteins, rather than just involving an enzyme cascade.

Table 2 illustrates some features of the endocrine system using three hormones from Chapter 14 as examples: antidiuretic hormone (ADH); insulin; and glucagon. These are peptide hormones, made of short chains of amino acids. They are water soluble and so pass across the cell surface membrane of the secretory cell by exocytosis and can travel in the blood dissolved in plasma. As they are peptides, they bind to specific receptors on the cell surface membranes of their target cells.

Table 2 *Some features of the endocrine system illustrated by the three hormones, ADH, insulin and glucagon*

Hormone	ADH	Insulin	Glucagon
Endocrine gland and secretory cells	Synthesised by the neurosecretory cells of the hypothalamus and released from the posterior pituitary gland	Synthesised by the β cells of the Islets of Langerhans of the pancreas	Synthesised by the α cells of the Islets of Langerhans of the pancreas
Nature of hormone	Peptide	Peptide	Peptide
Release from cells	Exocytosis	Exocytosis	Exocytosis
Transport in blood	Dissolved in plasma	Dissolved in plasma	Dissolved in plasma
Main target cells, tissues or organs	Cells of the collecting duct and distal convoluted tubule (DCT) of nephrons of the kidney	Liver cells Skeletal muscle Adipose tissue	Liver cells
Location of receptor in target cell	Cell surface membrane	Cell surface membrane	Cell surface membrane
Response	Increase in aquaporins in cell surface membrane	Increased permeability of muscle cells to glucose Increased rate of respiration of glucose Increased glycogenesis	Increased glycogenolysis Increased gluconeogenesis
Effect of response	Increased permeability of collecting duct and DCT to water More water removed from urine resulting in lower volume and more concentrated urine Reversible	Decrease in blood glucose concentration Reversible	Increase in blood glucose concentration Reversible
Homeostatic mechanism	Osmoregulation	Control of blood glucose concentration	Control of blood glucose concentration

In the nervous system, nerve impulses are transmitted within nerve cells, known as neurones. Each neurone has a nerve fibre, or axon, that carries the impulses. Bundles of nerve fibres are contained within structures known as nerves (see Extension).

The structure of neurones

Neurones are specialised cells adapted to rapidly carry electrochemical changes called nerve impulses from one part of the body to another. The different types of cell in the nervous system need to communicate with each other. Synapses between nerve cells occur where an impulse carried by one nerve cell needs to be passed onto another nerve cell (see 15.1f). Mammalian neurones are made up of:

- **A cell body** – contains a nucleus, mitochondria and large amounts of rough endoplasmic reticulum grouped to form **Nissl's granules**. These are associated with the production of proteins and neurotransmitters.
- **Dendrons** – small extensions of the cell body that sub-divide into smaller branched fibres called dendrites (Figure 1) that carry nerve impulses towards the cell body.
- **Axon** – a single long fibre that carries nerve impulses away from the cell body (the dendron of the sensory neurone is sometimes also termed a peripheral or afferent axon). Axons that transmit nerve impulses between the central nervous system and the furthest parts of the body are very long. The structure of a typical neurone is illustrated in Figure 2.

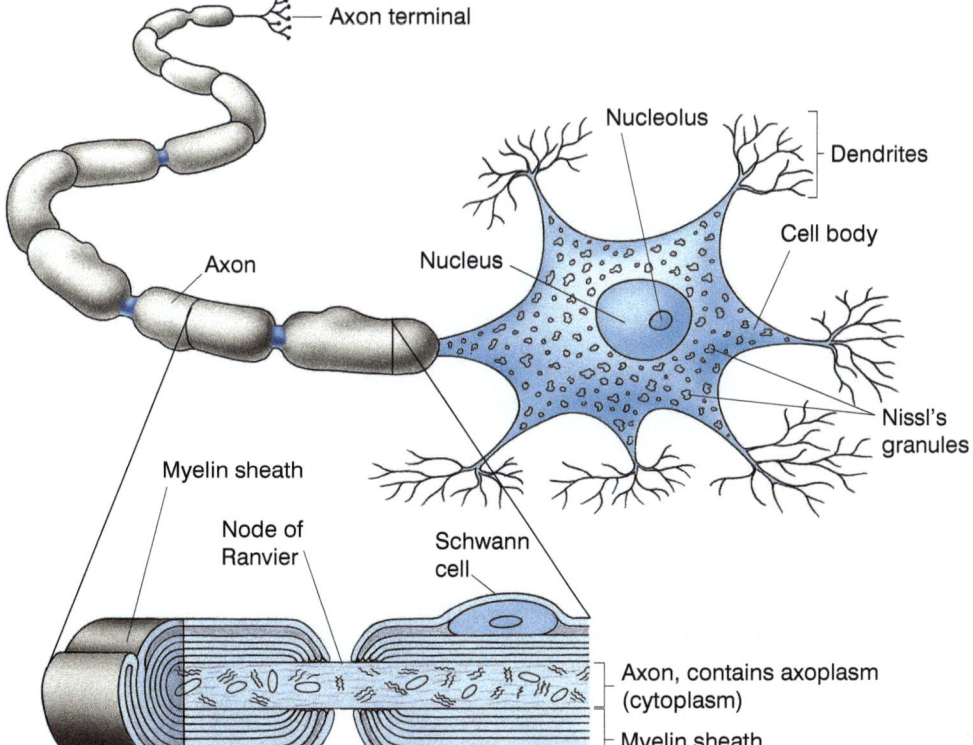

Figure 2 Motor (effector) neurone

These pages help you to:

- describe the structure and function of a sensory neurone and a motor neurone (15.1.3)
- understand that intermediate neurones connect sensory neurones and motor neurones (15.1.3)

You will also:

- see how neurones function together in a spinal reflex arc

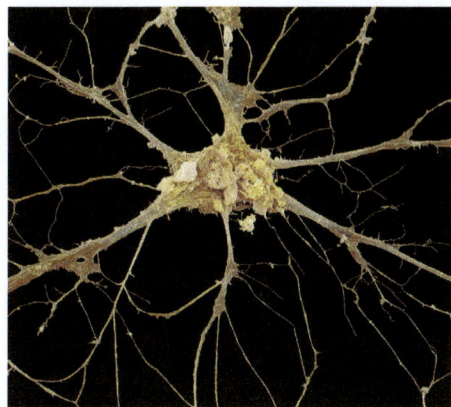

Figure 1 Scanning electron micrograph of neurone with cell body at its centre and dendrites radiating from it

Extension

Nerves

Most nerves are mixed nerves, containing nerve fibres of both motor and sensory neurones. There are some nerves that contain motor neurones only or sensory neurones only.

Individual nerve fibres are surrounded by a thin layer of connective tissue so are protected and separated from other nerve fibres. Each bundle of nerve fibres is surrounded by connective tissue within a nerve.

Nerves do not contain the cell bodies of the neurones. The cell bodies of motor neurones are located within the central nervous system and those of sensory neurones occur in swellings called ganglia in the peripheral nervous system (see also the Extension in 15.1a).

SENSORY NEURONE   MOTOR NEURONE

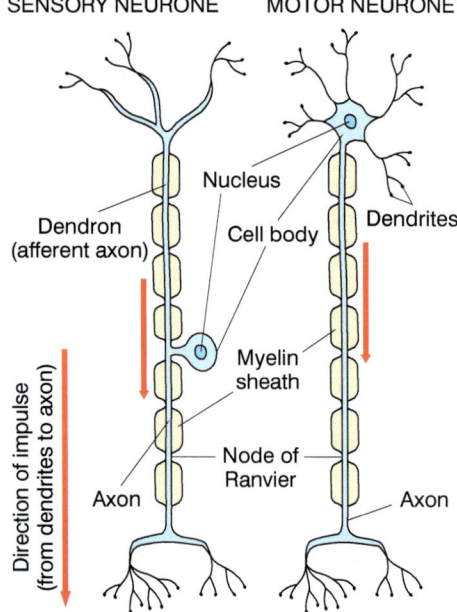

INTERMEDIATE NEURONE

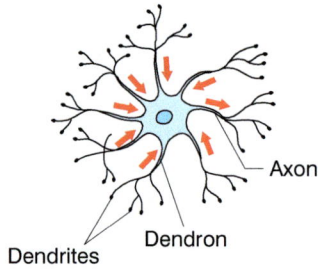

Figure 3 *Types of neurone*

Summary test 15.1b

The nucleus of a neurone is located in the **(1)**, which also contains many clusters of RER known as **(2)**. The long nerve fibre that carries impulses is also known as the **(3)**. In some neurones this is surrounded by a fatty covering called a **(4)**, produced by **(5)** cells. The very fine fibres that carry impulses towards the part of the neurone that contains the nucleus are known as **(6)**. A sensory neurone carries impulses from **(7)** to the **(8)** system. A **(9)** neurone carries impulses from the central nervous system to effectors, such as **(10)** and glands. **(11)** neurones transmit impulses between the other two types of neurone.

Many axons are surrounded by **Schwann cells**, which protect and provide insulation, remove cell debris by endocytosis (phagocytosis) and play a part in nerve regeneration. These Schwann cells wrap themselves around the axon many times, so that layers of their membranes build up around the axon. These membranes are rich in a lipid known as **myelin** and so form a covering to the axon called the **myelin sheath**. The space between adjacent Schwann cells lacks myelin, forming gaps 2–3 μm long, called **nodes of Ranvier**, which occur every 1–3 mm in humans. Neurones with a myelin sheath are called **myelinated neurones** and transmit nerve impulses faster than neurones without the myelin sheath (unmyelinated neurones) (15.1e).

Neurones can be classified according to their function:

- **Sensory neurones** transmit nerve impulses from a receptor to the central nervous system, and connect with an intermediate or motor neurone. They have one afferent axon (dendron) that brings the impulse towards the cell body and one axon that carries it away from the cell body.
- **Intermediate neurones (relay neurones)** transmit impulses between neurones, e.g. from sensory to motor neurones. They have numerous short processes (extensions).
- **Motor neurones (effector neurones)** transmit nerve impulses from a relay or sensory neurone to an effector such as a gland or a muscle. They have a long axon and many short dendrites.

The three different types of neurone are illustrated in Figure 3 and an example of how each of these cell types function is given in the Extension box.

Extension

A spinal reflex

An involuntary response to a stimulus is called a **reflex**. The pathway of neurones is a **reflex arc**, the simplest of which involves only a sensory and a motor neurone. Others involve an intermediate neurone. A **spinal reflex** involves the spinal cord (Figure 4). An example of a withdrawal reflex:

- **stimulus** – heat from touching the hot object
- **sensory receptor** – temperature receptors stimulate the transmission of nerve impulses in sensory neurones
- **sensory neurone** – impulses pass to the spinal cord
- **intermediate neurone** – links the sensory neurone via synapses to the motor neurone
- **motor (effector) neurone** – transmits impulses away from the spinal cord to the biceps muscle in the forearm
- **effector** – the biceps muscle of the forearm is stimulated to respond by contracting
- **effect of response** – the hand is raised away from the hot object.

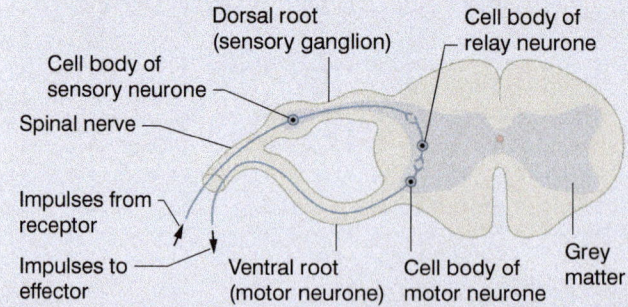

Figure 4 *Detail of reflex arc in the spinal cord of the central nervous system*

c. Sensory receptor cells

The central nervous system receives sensory information from its internal and external environment through a variety of sensory receptors that detect different types of stimuli. These sensory receptors include structures that are part of sensory neurones and sensory receptor cells. Sensory receptor cells are often found within sense organs. Each type of sensory receptor cell functions to detect a specific stimulus. It then stimulates the transmission of impulses in a sensory neurone. In this way, the information about the type and strength of the stimulus passes to the central nervous system. **Sensory perception** involves making sense of the information from the sensory receptors. This is largely a function of the brain (see Extension). In this topic we shall look at how chemoreceptors in taste buds act as sensory receptor cells.

The role of chemoreceptor cells of human taste buds as sensory receptor cells

Taste buds are onion-shaped structures located in the epithelium of the tongue (Figure 1). Within each taste bud there are 50–100 chemoreceptor cells that detect the presence of chemicals associated with taste. Chemoreceptor cells are thought to detect the chemicals associated with five tastes – salt, sour, bitter, sweet and savoury (also called umami).

These pages help you to:

- outline the role of sensory receptor cells in detecting stimuli and stimulating the transmission of impulses in sensory neurones (15.1.4)
- describe the sequence of events occurring in a chemoreceptor cell in a human taste bud that results in an action potential in a sensory neurone (15.1.5)

You will also:

- see how the different components of the nervous system are inter-related

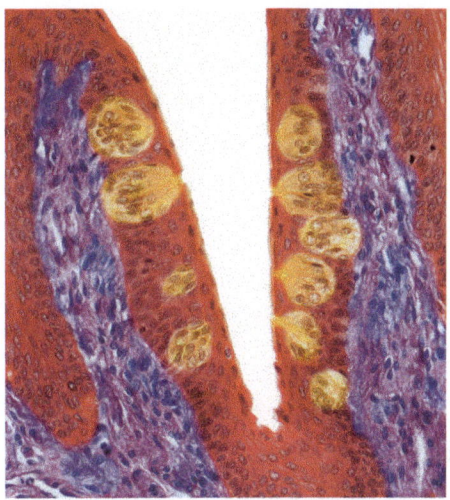

Figure 1 *Photomicrograph of the tongue, showing taste buds (yellow). Each taste bud contains chemoreceptor cells*

Extension

The role of sensory receptors as part of the nervous system

Figure 2 shows how sensory receptors are a functional part of the nervous system.

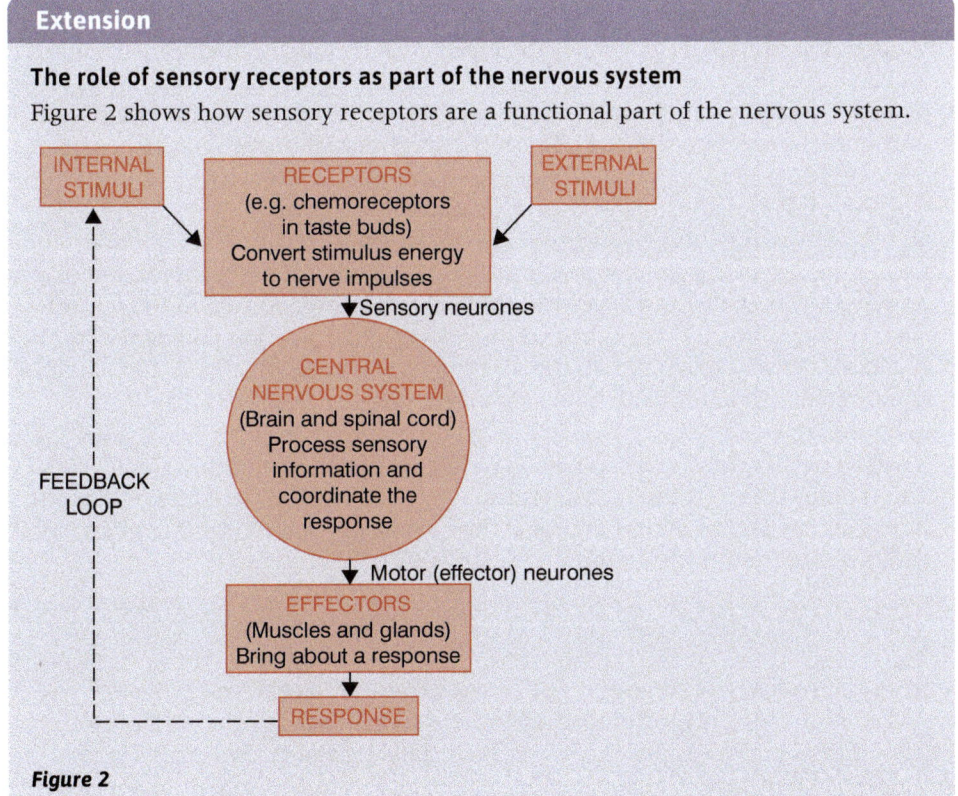

Figure 2

Remember

The term sensory receptor is used to describe a part of a nerve cell that detects stimuli or a specialised sensory receptor cell. It is sometimes shortened to 'receptor'.

The term 'receptor' is also used to describe a protein or glycoprotein, commonly located as a membrane protein in the cell surface membrane, that binds cell signalling molecules (ligands) such as hormones.

a Taste bud

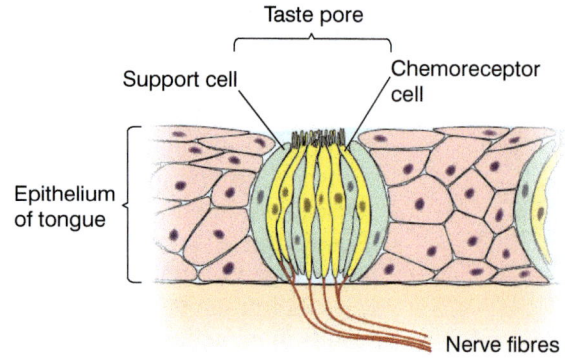

b Single chemoreceptor cell

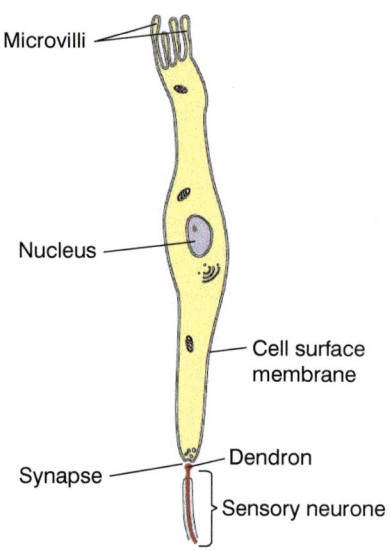

Figure 3 *Structure of a taste bud and chemoreceptor cell*

The structure of a taste bud and a chemoreceptor cell are shown in Figure 3. Each chemoreceptor cell has microvilli that project up through an opening at the top of the taste bud, called the taste pore. The microvilli provide a large surface area to allow chemicals dissolved in saliva to contact the chemoreceptor cell.

As with all sensory receptors, taste chemoreceptor cells:

- **are specific to a single type of stimulus** – in this case to dissolved chemicals only
- **act as transducers** – they convert the energy of the stimulus into a receptor potential, which is a change in the potential difference that exists across the membrane of the chemoreceptor cell (15.1d). Different types of chemoreceptor may have a slightly different sequence of events occurring when a stimulus is present. For some, the chemical binds to a specific membrane receptor, whereas for others the chemical enters the cell through specific membrane transport proteins. For example for a salty taste, the cell surface membrane of the microvilli have ion channel proteins through which sodium ions (Na^+) enter. Whichever mechanism, the events lead to a change in the cell surface membrane (depolarisation) to create the receptor potential. Calcium ion channels open and calcium ions (Ca^{2+}) enter. These cause vesicles containing a chemical transmitter, known as a neurotransmitter, to move to and fuse with the chemoreceptor membrane so that the neurotransmitter is released from the end of the chemoreceptor that forms a synapse with a sensory neurone (Figure 3(b)). The stronger the stimulus, the greater the receptor potential and the more chemical transmitter is released (15.1g).
- **produce a generator potential** – as a result of the release of the chemical transmitter (neurotransmitter), the receptor potential of the chemoreceptor cell may be enough to create a generator potential in the sensory neurone with which it synapses (in very close contact).
- **give an all-or-nothing response** – the greater the intensity of the stimulus, the greater the size of the generator potential. If the generator potential reaches or exceeds the set **threshold level**, an action potential is generated in the sensory neurone. Anything less than the threshold level, and no action potential is generated. Anything more than the threshold level, and the same action potential is generated, regardless of by how much the level is exceeded (15.1d).
- **become adapted** – if exposed to a steady stimulus over a period of time, there is a slow decline in the frequency of generator potentials produced and so action potentials in the sensory neurone become less frequent and eventually stop. This is adaptation and prevents the nervous system becoming overloaded with unimportant information.

Summary test 15.1c

Sensory receptors are cells and parts of sensory neurones that respond to different stimuli. Making sense of the information provided by sensory receptors is called sensory **(1)**. Chemoreceptor cells of taste buds respond to the stimulus of **(2)**, converting the energy of the stimulus into a **(3)** potential – as such they act as **(4)**. In turn a **(5)** potential is set up in the attached associated sensory neurone. If this potential equals or exceeds a threshold level, then an **(6)** is produced, which is the same regardless of how much the threshold level is exceeded. This is known as an **(7)** response. Different chemoreceptor cells are **(8)** to only one type of stimulus. For example when a salty taste is the stimulus, **(9)** ions enter through **(10)** located in the area with many extensions of the cell membrane known as **(11)**. This causes the membrane to **(12)**. The influx (entry) of **(13)** ions that follows causes **(14)** containing chemical transmitters to move to and fuse with the membrane near to the **(15)** neurone and release the chemical transmitter, also known as a **(16)**.

d. The nerve impulse

A nerve impulse may be defined as a self-propagating wave of electrical excitation that travels along the surface of the axon membrane. It is a temporary reversal of the electrical potential difference across the axon membrane. This reversal is between a state called the **resting potential** and another called the **action potential**.

Resting potential

The movement of sodium ions (Na$^+$) and potassium ions (K$^+$) across the axon membrane is controlled in a number of ways:

- The phospholipid bilayer of the axon cell surface membrane is impermeable to Na$^+$ and K$^+$.
- Voltage-gated channels specific to Na$^+$ or K$^+$ can be opened to allow the specific ion across or closed to prevent movement of that ion. During the resting potential, the voltage-gated channels remain closed.
- A different type of channel protein, 'leak' channels, remain open for facilitated diffusion, and there are more of these for K$^+$ than Na$^+$. During the resting potential many more K$^+$ diffuse out than Na$^+$ diffuse into the axon cytoplasm. The membrane is far more permeable to K$^+$ (100 times more).
- The **sodium–potassium pump** (12.1a) actively transports two K$^+$ ions into the axon for every three Na$^+$ ions pumped out of it.

As a result of these various controls, the inside of an axon is negatively charged relative to the outside. This is known as the **resting potential** and is in the range –50 to –90 millivolts (mV), but is usually –65 mV. In this condition the axon is said to be **polarised.** This potential difference is achieved because:

- More Na$^+$ is pumped out than K$^+$ in.
- More K$^+$ diffuses out through the leak channels than Na$^+$ in (very few).
- There are large, negatively charged proteins present within the cytoplasm of the axon.
- There are more Na$^+$ outside in the tissue fluid than K$^+$.
- There are more K$^+$ inside the axon than outside.
- Both ions will have a tendency to diffuse down the chemical concentration gradient, but the membrane is relatively impermeable to Na$^+$ compared to K$^+$ owing to the different quantities of specific leak channels present. This means very few Na$^+$ will be able to enter the axon.
- To counteract some of the movement out of K$^+$, the negatively charged proteins **(anions)** will attract K$^+$ and the overall positive charge outside the membrane will repel the ion.
- An equilibrium is established where there is no net movement of ions and where the tendency for K$^+$ to move down the chemical gradient is balanced by the force of the electrical gradient.

These events are summarised in Figure 1.

These pages help you to:

- learn about the changes that occur to the membrane potential of neurones by describing and explaining:
  - how the resting potential of membranes is maintained (15.1.6)
  - the events occurring during an action potential (15.1.6)
- describe and explain how the resting potential is restored during the refractory period (15.1.6)
- explain the importance of the refractory period in determining the frequency of impulses (15.1.8)

You will also:

- consolidate your understanding of the sodium–potassium pump and ion channel proteins

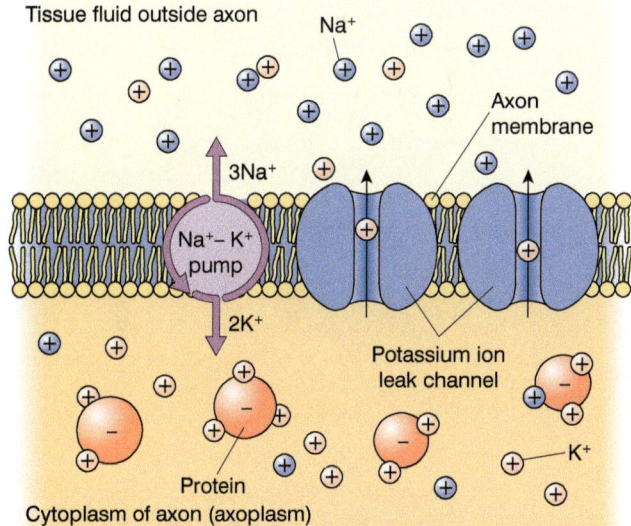

Figure 1 *Distribution of ions at resting potential. Voltage-gated channels remain closed and are not illustrated here. The membrane has very few Na$^+$ leak channels*

Remember

Nerve impulses are described as **all or nothing** responses. There is a certain level of stimulus, called the **threshold value**, which triggers an impulse. Below the threshold value no impulse is generated. The action potential is the same regardless of how much the stimulus is above the threshold value.

The action potential

The energy conversion that occurs when a stimulus is received by a receptor leads to a temporary reversal of the charges on the axon membrane (15.1c). As a result, the negative charge of −65 mV inside the membrane becomes a positive charge of around +40 mV. This is known as the **action potential**, and in this condition the membrane is said to be **depolarised**. This depolarisation involves the **voltage-gated** channels. The sequence of events is described below and the numbers relate to the stages shown in Figure 2.

1. At resting potential some potassium ion channels (leak channels) are open but the potassium voltage-gated and sodium voltage-gated channels are closed.

2. As a result of the stimulus some voltage-gated sodium channels in the axon membrane open and therefore sodium ions diffuse in through the channels along their electrochemical gradient. Being positively charged, they begin the reversal in the potential difference across the membrane and the membrane depolarises. Voltage-gated potassium channels remain closed.

3. As sodium ions enter, so more voltage-gated sodium channels open, causing an even greater influx of sodium ions. This is an example of positive feedback (14.1a). An action potential will only occur if the membrane depolarises enough to allow the remaining voltage-gated sodium channels to open. This is known as the threshold potential and occurs at around −50 mV (approximately −5 to −15 mV less negative than the resting potential).

4. Once the action potential of around +40 mV has been established (depolarisation has occurred), the voltage gates on sodium channels close (so further influx of sodium is prevented) and the voltage gates on the potassium channels begin to open.

5. With some voltage-gated potassium channels now open this causes the other voltage-gated channels to open and more potassium ions diffuse out, causing repolarisation of the axon membrane.

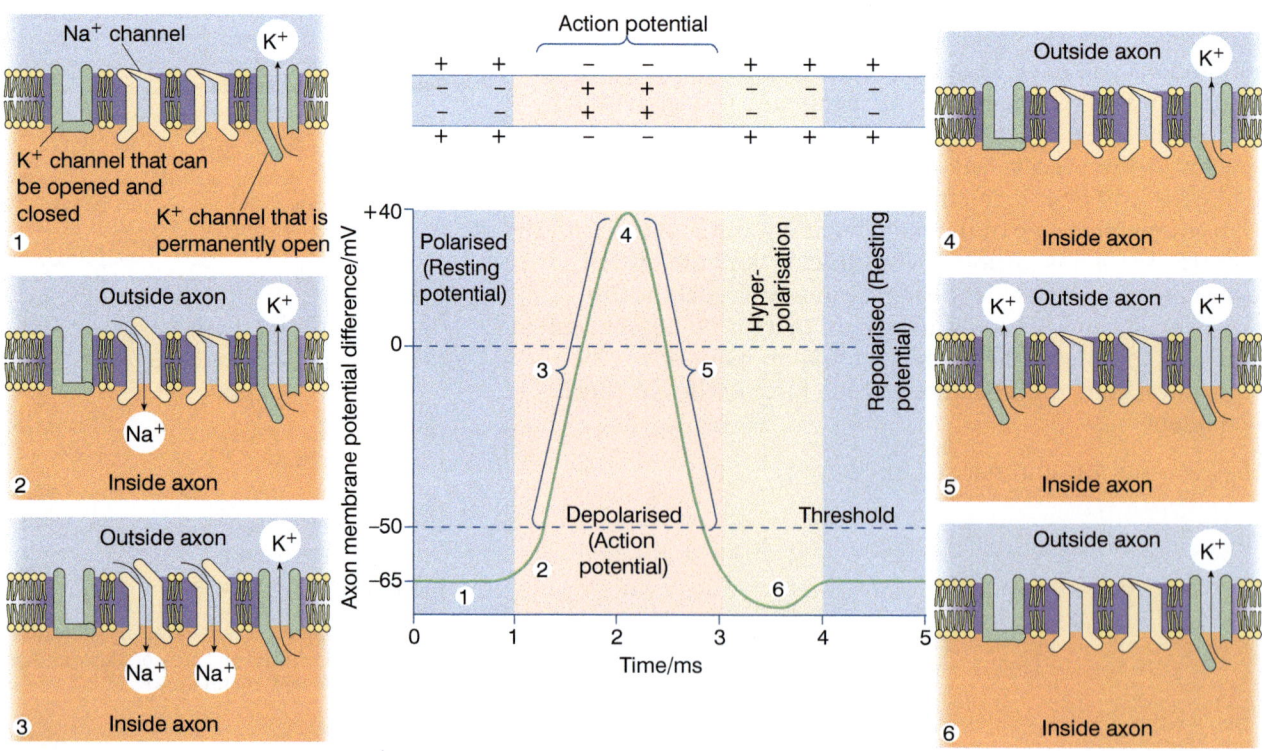

Figure 2 *The action potential*

6. The outward movement of these potassium ions and the slight delay in the closing of the gates causes the temporary overshoot of the electrical gradient, with the inside of the axon being more negative (relative to the outside) than usual. This is called **hyperpolarisation**. The gates on the potassium channels now close and the activities of the sodium–potassium pumps cause sodium ions to be pumped out and potassium ions in, once again. The axon membrane returns to a resting potential and the axon is said to be **repolarised**.

7. Although the resting potential is restored, the action of the sodium–potassium pump is needed to restore the original resting state and pump Na^+ out and K^+ in. The sodium–potassium pump works continuously throughout the action potential.

The term action potential simply means that the axon membrane is transmitting a nerve impulse, whereas resting potential means that it is not.

The refractory period

Once an action potential has been created in any region of an axon, there is a period afterwards when inward movement of sodium ions is prevented because the sodium **voltage-gated channels** are closed and temporarily inactivated. It takes time for all the channels to become activated again. This is known as the **refractory period**. At first, another action potential cannot be generated. After this, it is possible to generate another action potential but a higher threshold value must be reached. The refractory period is made up of two portions (Figure 3):

- **In the absolute refractory** period, no new impulses can be passed, however intense the stimulus. There is a neurone excitability of zero.
- **In the relative refractory** period, a new impulse may be propagated provided the stimulus exceeds the normal threshold value. The degree to which it needs to exceed the threshold value becomes less over the period. There is an increase in neurone excitability. At normal resting excitability the voltage-gated channels are returned to their resting potential state – closed but in an active (ready) state.

The refractory period serves two purposes:

- The action potential cannot be propagated in the region that is refractory, i.e. it can only move in a forward direction. This prevents the action potential from spreading out in both directions.
- Because a new action potential cannot be formed immediately behind the first one, it ensures that action potentials are separated from one another and therefore limits the number of action potentials that can pass along an axon in a given time, i.e. it determines their frequency.

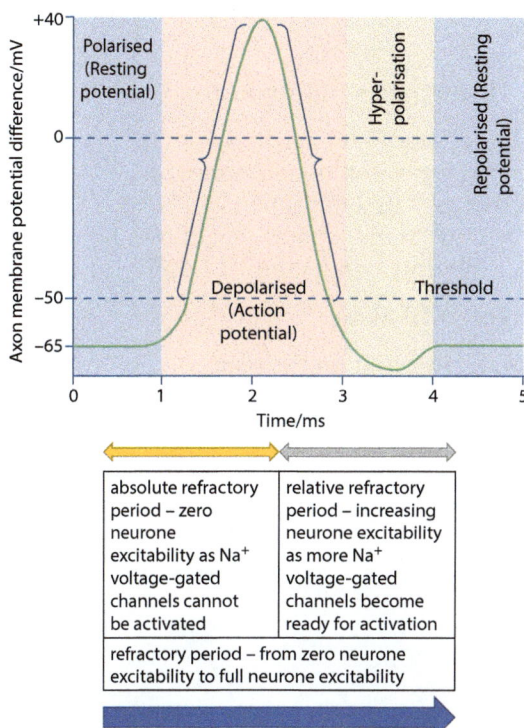

Figure 3 The refractory period

absolute refractory period – zero neurone excitability as Na$^+$ voltage-gated channels cannot be activated	relative refractory period – increasing neurone excitability as more Na$^+$ voltage-gated channels become ready for activation
refractory period – from zero neurone excitability to full neurone excitability	

Remember

The graph showing an action potential describes the flow of ions across a small section of the axon membrane. It shows how the potential difference across the membrane changes over time in response to that section of membrane being stimulated. Notice that the changes occur rapidly as the time is in milliseconds. As we will see in 15.1e, an action potential leads to the adjacent section of membrane becoming depolarised, and so an action potential is generated in the next section. This continues along the axon and can be described as a wave of depolarisation.

Summary test 15.1d

A nerve impulse is the result of a temporary reversal of (1) potential difference across the axon membrane. At resting potential the potential difference is in the range (2) millivolts but is usually around (3) millivolts. In this condition the axon is said to be (4) with the outside being (5) charged relative to the inside. During an action potential, the charges are reversed with a potential difference of (6) millivolts and the membrane is said to be (7). During the rising phase of the action potential (8) voltage-gated channels open and the ions flood into the axon. During the falling phase, these channels close and (9) voltage-gated channels open. During the action potential there is a time when a new action potential cannot be generated and this is known as the (10) refractory period. After this, during the (11) refractory period, an action potential can be generated if the (12) exceeds the normal value. The refractory period determines the (13) of action potentials.

These pages help you to:

- describe and explain the rapid transmission of an impulse in a myelinated neurone (15.1.8)
- understand what is meant by saltatory conduction (15.1.8)

You will also:

- learn about local circuits and impulse conduction in unmyelinated neurones

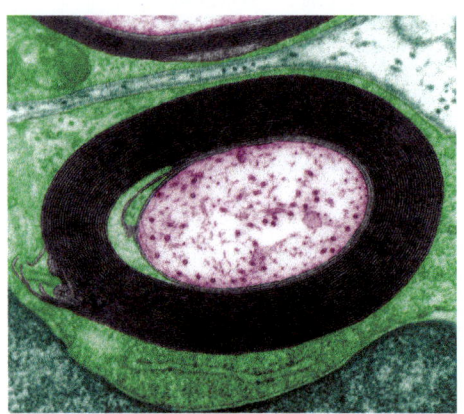

Figure 1 *Colourised transmission electron micrograph of a section through a myelinated neuron. A myelin sheath (black) surrounds the axon (purple). The myelin sheath is surrounded by the Schwann cell (green)*

Summary test 15.1e

In **(1)** neurones, there is a myelin sheath formed by **(2)** cells that wraps around the axon and **(3)** it so that **(4)** of the axon membrane can only occur at the nodes of **(5)**. Longer **(6)** are set up and the action potentials move by **(7)** conduction and jump from node to node to increase the speed of **(8)** of nerve impulses.

As one region of the axon produces an action potential and becomes depolarised, it acts as a stimulus for the **depolarisation** of the next region of the axon. This reversal of electrical charge is reproduced and action potentials are generated along the axon membrane. As one action potential triggers the next, the previous region of the membrane returns to its **resting potential**, i.e. it is repolarised. The size of the action potential remains the same from one end of the axon to the other. Strictly speaking, nothing physically 'moves' from place to place along the **axon** of the neurone, but rather the reversal of electrical charge is reproduced at different points along the axon membrane.

Transmission of a nerve impulse in a myelinated neurone

During an action potential, the movement in of sodium ions will lead to some passive movement of ions (current) within the axon. This is enough to begin depolarisation of the adjacent section of membrane. The positively charged ions have a tendency to repel each other and move towards the less positively charged region. A similar situation happens when the ions have moved out of the axon into the surrounding fluid.

These events set up what is known as a local circuit current. In myelinated neurones, longer local circuit currents are set up. This is because the Schwann cells wrap around axons to form a fatty sheath of myelin (Figure 1) and this acts as an electrical insulator, preventing action potentials from forming. At intervals of 1–3 mm there are breaks in this insulatory myelin, called **nodes of Ranvier**, where there is a high concentration of voltage-gated ion channels and sodium–potassium pumps (15.1d). Action potentials can only occur at these points. Local circuits are now longer as they occur only between adjacent nodes of Ranvier and the action potentials in effect 'jump' from node to node in a process known as **saltatory conduction** (Figure 2) so an impulse passes along a myelinated neurone faster than an unmyelinated one. Fewer action potentials generated for the same length of axon will mean a faster transmission speed for a myelinated axon than an unmyelinated axon, up to 100 to 120 m s^{-1}.

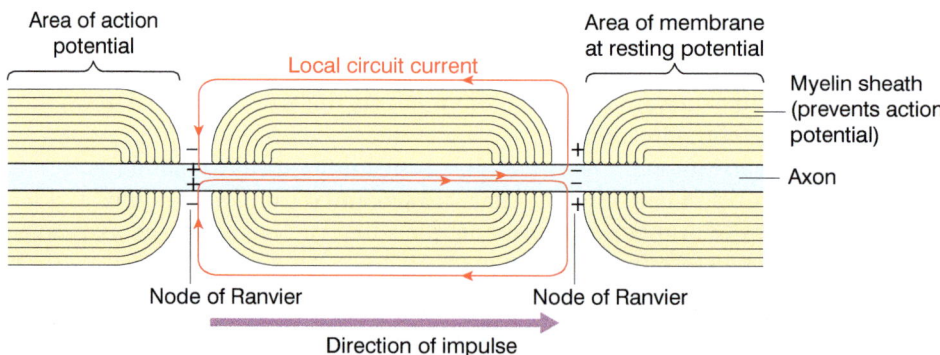

Figure 2 *Propagation of an impulse along a myelinated neurone. Action potentials are produced only at nodes of Ranvier. Depolarisation jumps from node to node – saltatory conduction (Latin 'saltare' = to jump). An action potential is occurring at the node of Ranvier on the left – the next action potential will occur in the node presently at resting potential (on the right)*

Extension

Transmission of the nerve impulse in an unmyelinated neurone

Figure 3 shows how an impulse is transmitted in an unmyelinated neurone by setting up local circuit currents.

☐ Polarised ☐ Depolarised ☐ Repolarised

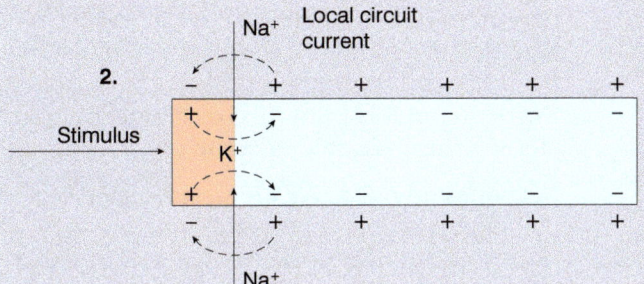

1. At resting potential the concentration of sodium ions outside the axon membrane is high relative to the inside, whereas that of the potassium ions is high inside the membrane relative to the outside. The overall concentration of positive ions is, however, greater on the outside, making this positive compared with the inside. The axon membrane is polarised. In a Mexican wave analogy, this is equivalent to all the people in the whole stadium being seated, i.e. at rest.

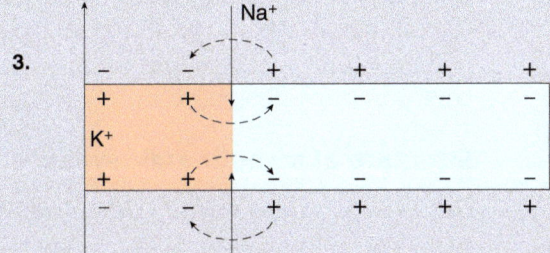

2. A stimulus causes the sodium voltage-gated channels to open leading to a sudden influx of sodium ions and hence a reversal of charge on the axon membrane making the inside positive. This is the action potential and the membrane is depolarised. In our analogy, a vertical line of people are stimulated into action and stand up and wave their arms.

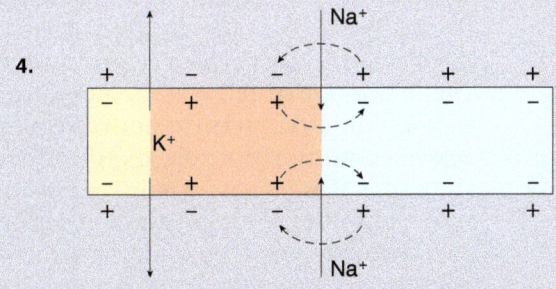

3. The local circuit currents set up by the influx of sodium ions cause the opening of sodium voltage-gated channels a little further along the axon. The resulting influx of sodium ions in this region causes depolarisation. Behind this new region of depolarisation, the sodium voltage-gated channels close and the potassium ones open. Potassium ions begin to leave the axon along their electrochemical gradient. The sight of the person next to them standing and waving stimulates the person in the adjacent seat to stand and wave. A new vertical line of people stands and waves, while the original line of people begin to sit down again.

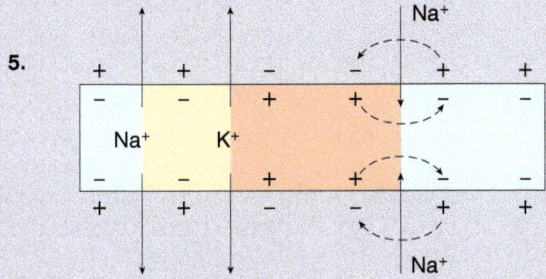

4. The action potential (depolarisation) is propagated in the same way further along the axon. The outward movement of the potassium ions has continued to the extent that the axon membrane behind the action potential has returned to its original charged state (positive outside, negative inside), i.e. it has been repolarised. The second line of people standing and waving stimulates the third line of people to do the same. Meanwhile, the first line have now returned to their original positions as they are now sitting down.

5. Repolarisation of the axon allows sodium ions to be actively transported out and potassium ions to be actively transported in, once again returning the axon to its resting potential in readiness for a new stimulus if it comes. The people who have just sat down settle back in their seats and readjust themselves ready to repeat the process should they be stimulated to do so again.

Figure 3 *Propagation of an impulse along an unmyelinated neurone – compare this to saltatory conduction in a myelinated neurone*

These pages help you to:

- describe the structure of a cholinergic synapse (15.1.9)

You will also:

- understand how transmission at the synapse is in one direction only
- read about functions of synapses

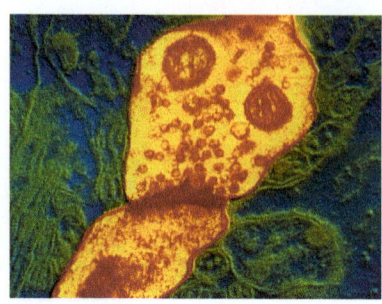

Figure 1 *Transmission electron micrograph of synapse. The synaptic cleft between the two neurones (centre) appears deep red. The cell above the cleft has many small vesicles (red-yellow spheres) containing neurotransmitter, whereas the two larger spheres above the vesicles are mitochondria*

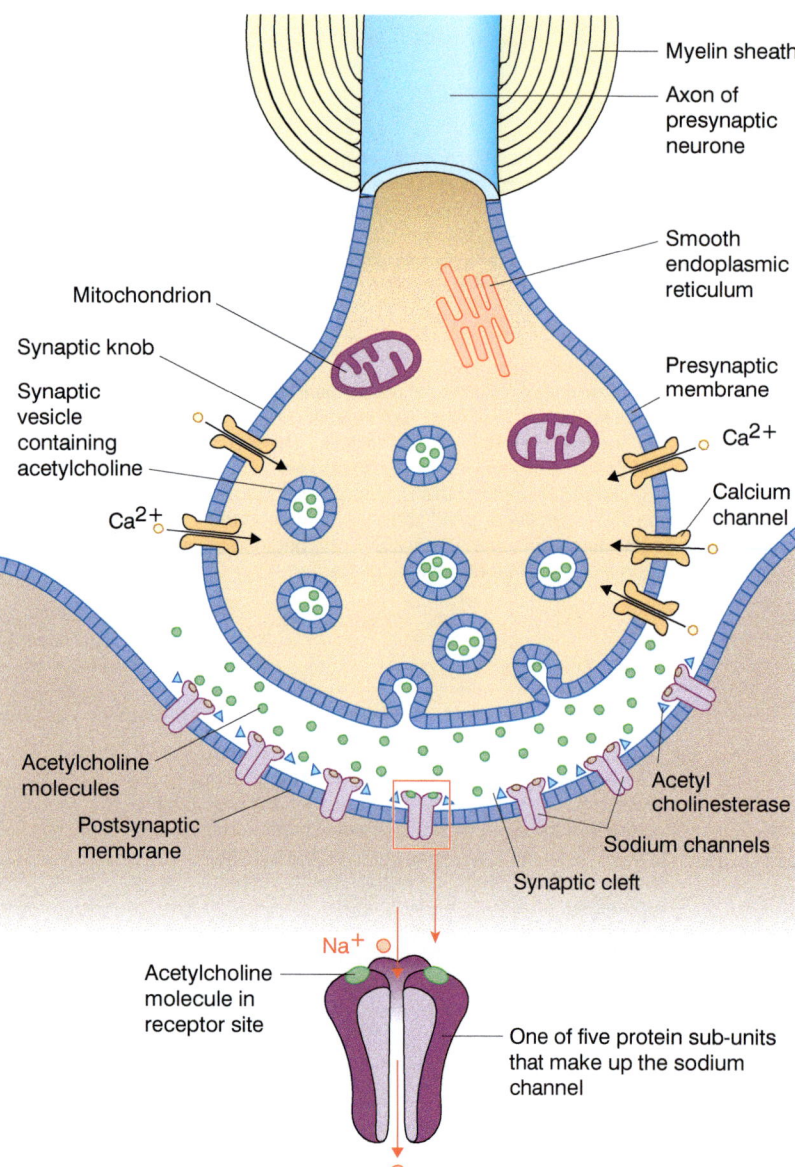

Figure 2 *Structure of a cholinergic synapse*

A synapse is the point where the **axon** of one **neurone** connects with the **dendrite** of another or with an effector. Synapses are important in linking different neurones together and therefore coordinating activities. Synapses convey impulses from one neurone to the next and it is from this basic function that all the others are able to occur (see Extension).

Neurones do not make physical contact, but the axon terminals of one neurone are very closely positioned to the dendrites of the next neurone so that transmission of the impulse is efficient. There are some synapses where the two neurones are so close that electrical transmission is possible, but for most synapses chemical transmission occurs.

Structure of a cholinergic synapse

Chemical synapses transmit impulses from one neurone to the next by means of chemicals known as **neurotransmitters**. In a cholinergic synapse, the neurotransmitter is **acetylcholine**. Neurones are separated by a small gap called the **synaptic cleft** which is 20–30 nm wide. The neurone that releases the neurotransmitter is called the **presynaptic neurone** and it has a swollen portion of axon, the **synaptic knob**, at its end. This possesses many mitochondria, large quantities of endoplasmic reticulum and **synaptic vesicles** containing the neurotransmitter which, once released from the vesicles by **exocytosis**, diffuses across to the postsynaptic neurone. There are ligand-gated sodium channels (4.1b) on the postsynaptic membrane. Each of these has two receptor sites for the acetylcholine molecule. Very close to these channels are membrane-bound enzyme molecules known as acetylcholinesterase (see 15.1g). The structure of a chemical synapse is shown in Figure 2.

Unidirectional (one-way) transmission

The structure of synapses shows that the impulses can only pass from the presynaptic neurone to the postsynaptic neurone and not the other way round. This is because only the presynaptic neurone has vesicles containing the neurotransmitter and only the postsynaptic membrane has receptors for the neurotransmitter. Any action potential arriving at the postsynaptic neurone would simply stop at this point.

Extension

How many synapses are there in the human brain

A recent estimate for the number of neurones present in the human brain is 86 billion. Estimates for the number of synapses in the brain vary considerably, and it has been suggested that on average, there are 1000 synapses for each neurone.

Summary test 15.1f

Synapses connect the axon of one neurone with the **(1)** of another. The two parts are separated by a gap called the synaptic **(2)** that is around **(3)** nm wide. One neurone, called the **(4)** neurone, releases a chemical messenger known generally as a **(5)**, of which acetylcholine is an example. These messengers are stored within small sacs called **(6)** and, once released, diffuse across to receptor molecules on the **(7)** neurone. Synapses perform a number of functions, all of which derive from their ability to transmit impulses between one neurone and the next. They are **(8)**, as they only allow impulses to pass in one direction across them.

Extension

Other functions of synapses

- **Act as junctions** – allowing nerve impulses to diverge and converge. In divergence a single impulse along one neurone can be conveyed to a number of different neurones at a synapse (Figure 3a). This allows a single stimulus to create a number of simultaneous (all at the same time) responses. In convergence, a number of impulses can be combined into a single impulse (Figure 3b). This occurs in the retina of the eye, for example.
- **Filter out low level stimuli** such as the background noise of traffic or machinery. The stimulus produces low frequency impulses that cause the release of only small quantities of neurotransmitter at the synapse. This is insufficient to create a new impulse in the postsynaptic neurone and so there is no response. The absence of a response is rarely, if ever, harmful.
- **Summation** – low frequency impulses that do not produce enough neurotransmitter to trigger a new action potential in the postsynaptic neurone can be made to do so by a process called **summation**. This needs a build up of neurotransmitter in the synapse by one of two methods:
  spatial – where a number of different presynaptic neurones together release enough neurotransmitter to trigger a new action potential
  temporal – where a single presynaptic neurone releases neurotransmitter many times over a short period. If the total amount of neurotransmitter exceeds the **threshold value** of the postsynaptic neurone, then a new action potential is triggered.
- **Prevent overstimulation and fatigue** – where a stimulus is powerful and prolonged, the high frequency of impulses in the presynaptic neurone leads to the release of considerable amounts of neurotransmitter. In these circumstances the release of neurotransmitter stops, together with any response to the stimulus. The synapse is said to be **fatigued**. The purpose of such a response is to prevent overstimulation, which might otherwise damage an effector.
- **Involved in memory and learning** – it is thought that synapses have a role in the brain in allowing organisms to recall events and learn to recognise individuals.
- **Inhibition** – on the postsynaptic membrane of some synapses, the protein channels carrying chloride ions (Cl^-) can be made to open. This leads to an inward diffusion of chloride ions making the inside of the postsynaptic membrane even more negative than when it is at resting potential. This is called hyperpolarisation and makes it less likely that a new action potential will be created. For this reason these synapses are called inhibitory synapses.

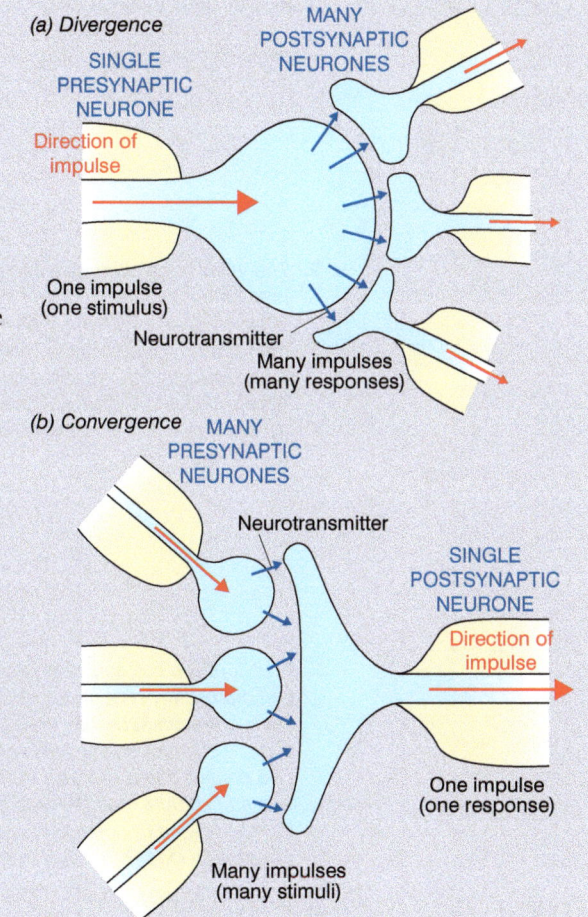

Figure 3 *Divergence and convergence at synapses*

These pages help you to:

- explain how a cholinergic synapse functions, including the role of calcium ions (15.1.9)

You will also:

- review exocytosis and ligand-gated channels
- learn more about synaptic vesicles

Figure 1 shows transmission across a chemical synapse that involves the neurotransmitter acetylcholine.

Extension

Synaptic vesicles

Within the vesicle membrane there are membrane proteins that actively transport resynthesised acetycholine into empty vesicles. These vesicles will then move towards the presynaptic membrane ready for exocytosis. It has been shown that, if calcium ions are not present, neurotransmitter will not be released when depolarisation of the membrane occurs. This shows that the calcium ions trigger fusion of the vesicles with the presynaptic membrane and release of the neurotransmitter into the synaptic cleft. It is known that calcium ions bind to proteins in the presynaptic membrane and to proteins in the vesicle membrane to trigger fusion and release of transmitter.

---

1. The arrival of an action potential at the end of the presynaptic neurone causes depolarisation of the presynaptic membrane. Voltage-gated calcium channels open and calcium ions (Ca^{2+}) enter the synaptic knob down their concentration gradient. Synaptic vesicles containing acetycholine are at the presynaptic membrane ready to release the neurotransmitter.

2. The influx of calcium ions into the presynaptic neurone causes synaptic vesicles to fuse with the presynaptic membrane, so releasing acetylcholine by exocytosis into the synaptic cleft. Acetylcholine diffuses across the synaptic cleft to the postsynaptic neurone.

3. Acetylcholine molecules bind with complementary receptor sites on two of the five protein sub-units that make up each sodium channel on the postsynaptic membrane. This causes the sodium channels to open, allowing sodium ions (Na^+) to diffuse in rapidly down a concentration gradient (potassium ions (K^+) are also able to enter).

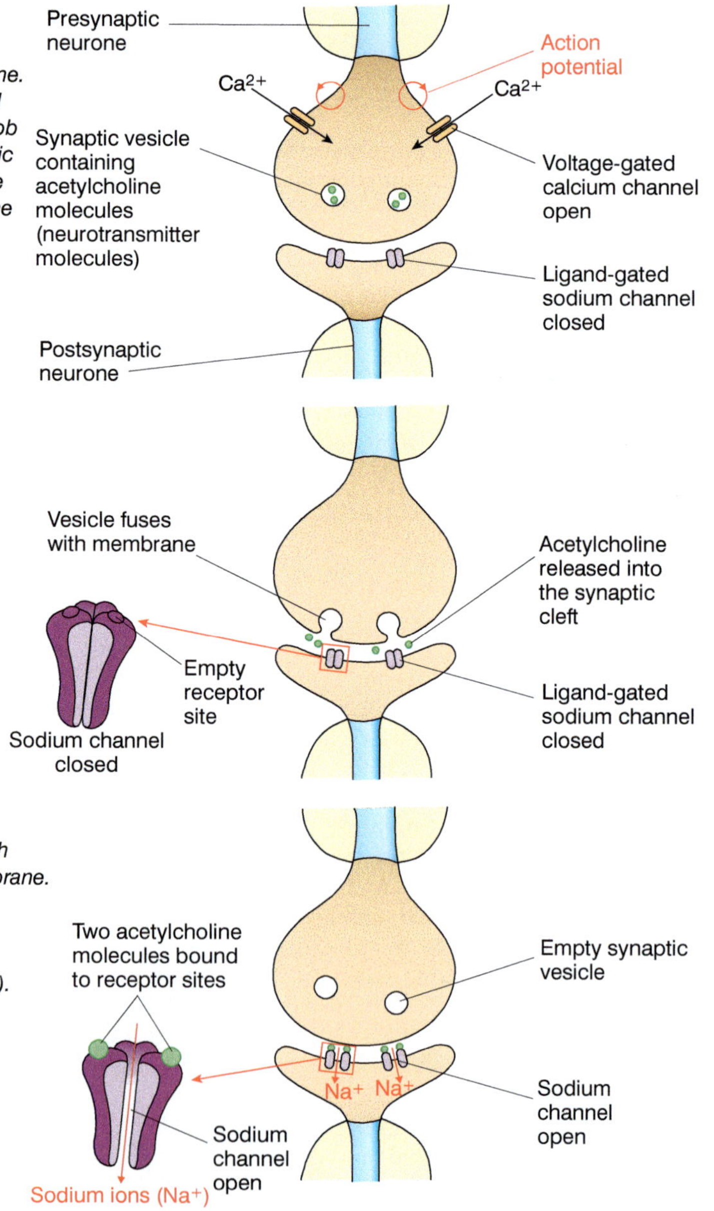

Figure 1 *Mechanism of transmission across a cholinergic synapse*

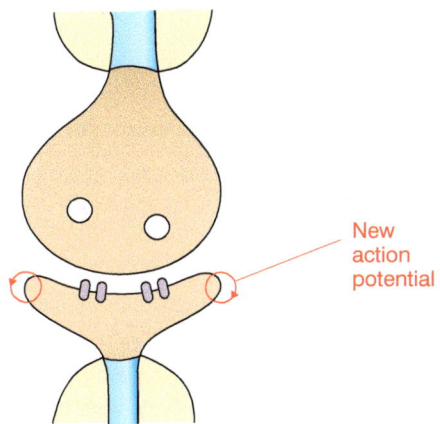

4. The influx of sodium ions generates an **excitatory postsynaptic potential (EPSP)** in the postsynaptic neurone. If enough EPSPs are generated in quick succession (one after the other) to reach the threshold, then an action potential is generated in the postsynaptic neurone.

New action potential

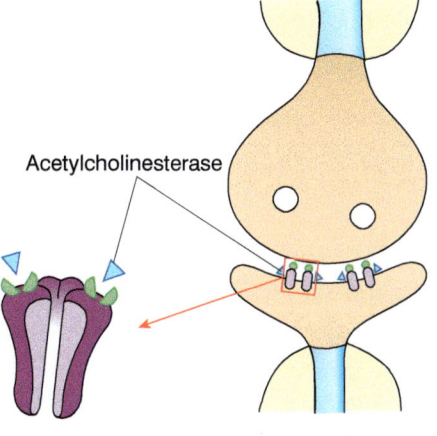

Acetylcholinesterase

5. The enzyme acetylcholinesterase hydrolyses acetylcholine into choline and acetate, which diffuse back across the synaptic cleft into the presynaptic neurone (= **recycling**).

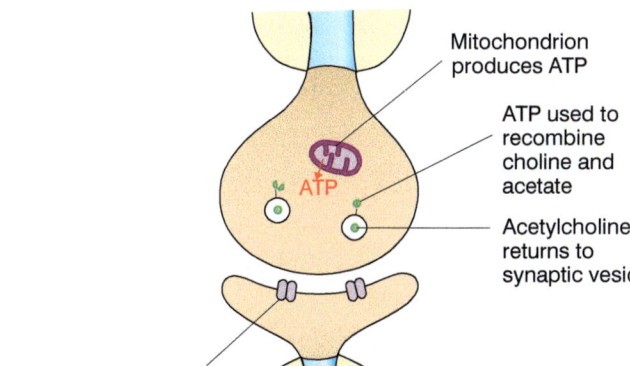

Mitochondrion produces ATP

ATP used to recombine choline and acetate

ATP

Acetylcholine returns to synaptic vesicle

Sodium channel closed

6. ATP released by mitochondria is used to drive recombination of choline and acetate into acetylcholine. This is stored in synaptic vesicles for future use. Sodium channels close in the absence of acetylcholine in the receptor sites.

Summary test 15.1g

When an action potential arrives at the end of the presynaptic neurone, **(1)** ions enter the synaptic knob. These ions cause **(2)** to fuse with the presynaptic membrane so releasing acetylcholine, by the process of **(3)**, into the **(4)**. Channels on the postsynaptic neurone have receptor sites to which acetylcholine binds, causing them to open and allowing **(5)** ions to move in by the process of **(6)**. The influx of these ions generates an **(7)** potential. If these are generated in rapid succession, then an **(8)** is generated for the impulse to continue.

These pages help you to:

- describe the ultrastructure of striated muscle with reference to sarcomere structure using electron micrographs and diagrams (15.1.11)
- describe the roles of neuromuscular junctions in stimulating contraction in striated muscle (15.1.10)

You will also:

- understand how myofibrils are arranged in muscle fibres, and how these are arranged in muscle

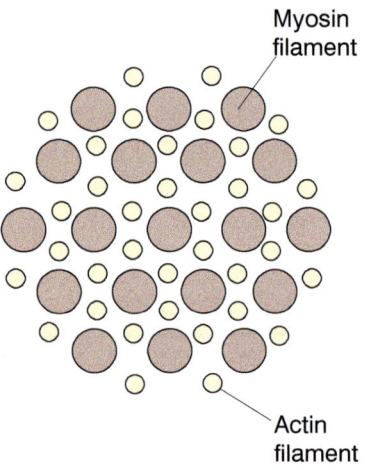

Figure 2 *Transverse section through part of a myofibril, showing the arrangement of actin and myosin filaments*

Muscles are effector organs that respond to nervous stimulation by contracting and so bring about movement. **Striated muscle** makes up the bulk of body muscle in vertebrates. It is attached to bone by tendons and acts under voluntary, conscious control.

A rope is made up of millions of separate threads, which grouped together in a rope, can support a mass of hundreds of tonnes. Individual muscles are made up of thousands of muscle fibres, bundled in groups, and running parallel to the length of the muscle. Each muscle fibre is a multinucleate (many nuclei) cell containing many parallel myofibrils (see Figure 1). Early in development, separate muscle cells fuse to give a single muscle fibre. This fusion allows the muscle to contract efficiently and gives the muscle overall strength. The cell surface membrane of a muscle fibre is also known as the sarcolemma. Surrounding the myofibrils is the muscle fibre cytoplasm, known as **sarcoplasm**, containing a large concentration of mitochondria and endoplasmic reticulum.

Microscopic structure of striated muscle

We can see from Figure 1 that each muscle fibre is made up of myofibrils. Myofibrils are made up of two types of protein filament, the arrangement of which is shown in Figure 2:

- **actin**, which is thinner and consists of two strands twisted around one another
- **myosin**, which is thicker and consists of long rod-shaped fibres with bulbous heads that project to the side.

Electron microscope studies provided detail of the ultrastructure of myofibrils (Figure 1 in 15.1i). Myofibrils appear striated (striped) due to their alternating light-coloured and dark-coloured bands. The light bands are called **isotropic bands (I-bands)**. They appear lighter because the actin and myosin filaments do not overlap in this region. The dark bands are called **anisotropic bands (A-bands)**. They appear darker because the actin and myosin filaments overlap in this region.

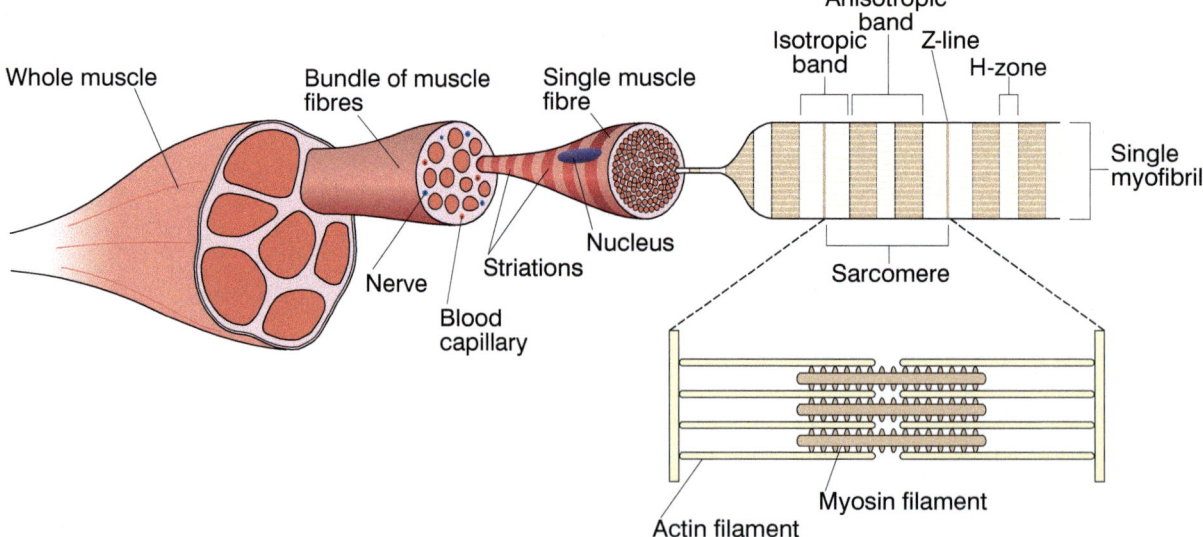

Figure 1 *The gross and microscopic structure of striated muscle*

At the centre of each A-band is a lighter coloured region called the **H-zone**. There is a thin line known as the M-line at the centre of this zone which contains proteins that anchor the myosin filaments (not shown in Figure 1). At the centre of each I-band is a line called the **Z-line**. The Z-line is composed of proteins that anchor the actin filaments. The area between adjacent Z-lines is called a **sarcomere**. When a muscle contracts, these sarcomeres shorten and the pattern of light and dark bands changes.

Two other important proteins are found in muscle:

- **tropomyosin**, which forms a fibrous strand around the actin filament
- **troponin**, a globular protein involved in muscle contraction.

The neuromuscular junction

The neuromuscular junction is the point at which a motor neurone meets a striated muscle fibre and is an example of a synapse. As rapid muscle contraction is frequently essential for survival, there are many neuromuscular junctions spread throughout the muscle (Figure 3). This is to ensure that contraction of a muscle is rapid and powerful when it is simultaneously stimulated by action potentials. All muscle fibres supplied by a single motor neurone act together as a single functional unit and are known as a **motor unit**. This arrangement gives control over the force that the muscle exerts. If only slight force is needed, only a few units are stimulated. If a greater force is required, a larger number of units are stimulated.

When a nerve impulse arrives at the synaptic knob of the axon terminal, the presynaptic membrane of the motor neurone depolarises. Voltage-gated calcium channels open and calcium ions diffuse in to cause the synaptic vesicles to fuse with the presynaptic membrane and release acetylcholine. The acetylcholine diffuses to the postsynaptic membrane (sarcolemma) and binds to the receptors on the ligand-gated sodium channels. The opening of the channels causes sodium ions to enter the muscle fibre, depolarising the membrane. The description of how this leads to the contraction of the muscle is given in 15.1i.

The acetylcholine is broken down by acetylcholinesterase so that the muscle is not over-stimulated. The resulting choline and acetate diffuse back into the neurone, where they are recombined to form acetylcholine using energy provided by the mitochondria found there.

The structure of a neuromuscular junction is shown in Figure 4.

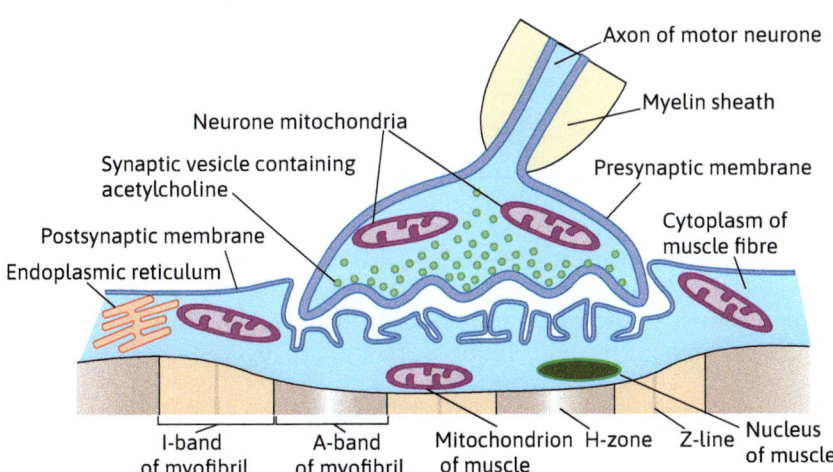

Figure 4 *The neuromuscular junction (also known as a motor end plate)*

Labels on Figure 4:
- Axon of motor neurone
- Myelin sheath
- Presynaptic membrane
- Cytoplasm of muscle fibre
- Neurone mitochondria
- Synaptic vesicle containing acetylcholine
- Postsynaptic membrane
- Endoplasmic reticulum
- I-band of myofibril
- A-band of myofibril
- Mitochondrion of muscle
- H-zone
- Z-line
- Nucleus of muscle

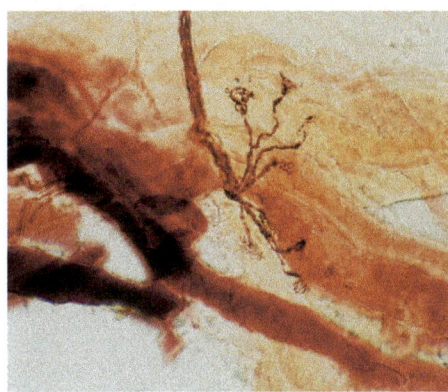

Figure 3 *Photomicrograph of axon terminals of a motor neurone with neuromuscular junctions*

Summary test 15.1h

A single striated muscle cell is known as a **(1)**. It is **(2)** (has many nuclei) and contains many parallel myofibrils that have two main types of **(3)** filament, **(4)** and myosin. The functional unit of the myofibril is the **(5)**, which is the unit between two **(6)**-lines. The lighter bands are called **(7)**-bands and the darker bands are the **(8)**-bands. The synapse between a synaptic knob of a **(9)** axon terminal and a striated muscle cell is called a **(10)**. Depolarisation of the presynaptic membrane causes release of **(11)** into the synaptic cleft and this leads to depolarisation of the **(12)**, which leads to contraction of the muscle cell.

These pages help you to:

- understand how the visible changes that occur in the sarcomere help to explain the sliding filament model of muscular contraction (15.1.12)

You will also:

- learn more about the four proteins involved in muscle contraction

Having looked at the structure of striated muscle in 15.1h, let us turn our attention to how exactly the arrangement of the various proteins brings about contraction of the muscle fibre. The process involves the actin and myosin filaments sliding past one another and is therefore called the **sliding filament model.**

Evidence for the sliding filament model of muscular contraction

In 15.1h, we saw that myofibrils appear darker in colour where actin and myosin filaments overlap and lighter where they do not (Figure 1). If the sliding filament mechanism is correct, then there will be more overlap of actin and myosin in a contracted muscle than in a relaxed one. Look at Figure 2. You will see that during muscular contraction the following changes occur to a **sarcomere**:

- the I-band becomes narrower
- the Z-lines move closer together (in other words, the sarcomere shortens)
- the H-zone becomes narrower.

The A-band remains the same width. As the width of this band is determined by the length of the myosin filaments, it follows that the myosin filaments have not become shorter.

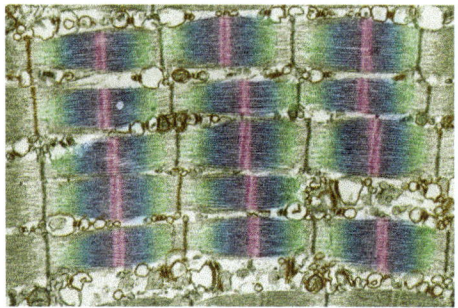

Figure 1 *Transmission electron micrograph of a section of a striated muscle fibre*

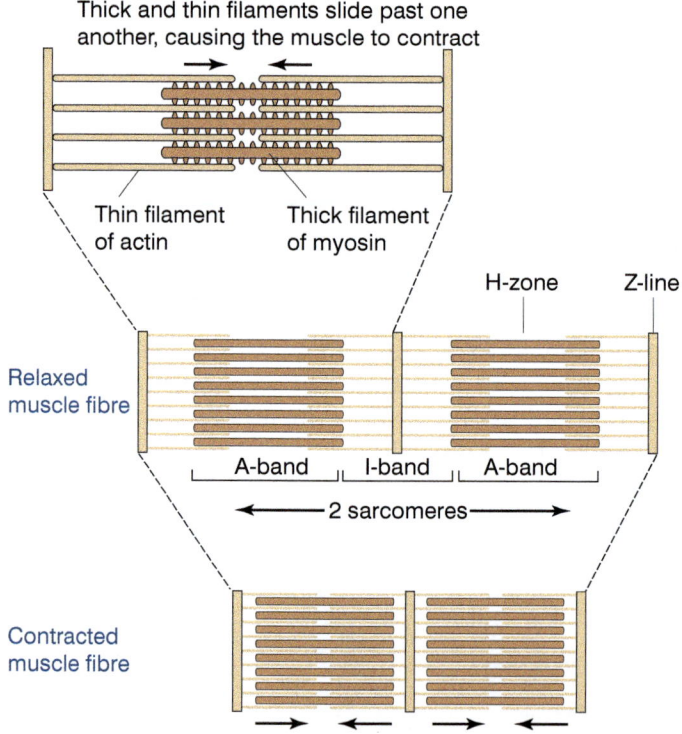

Figure 2 *Comparison of two sarcomeres in a relaxed and a contracted muscle*

Before we look at how the sliding filament mechanism works, let us take a closer look at the four main proteins involved in the process.

- **Myosin** (see Figure 3): each myosin filament is made up of several hundred myosin molecules. Each myosin molecule has a quaternary structure composed of six polypeptide chains. The molecule has a globular 'head' section and a long 'tail' region. The myosin heads play an essential role in the sliding filament mechanism. The heads are able to attach to actin filaments to form cross-bridges. They also have ATPase activity so are able to bind ATP molecules and catalyse their hydrolysis to provide energy for contraction.

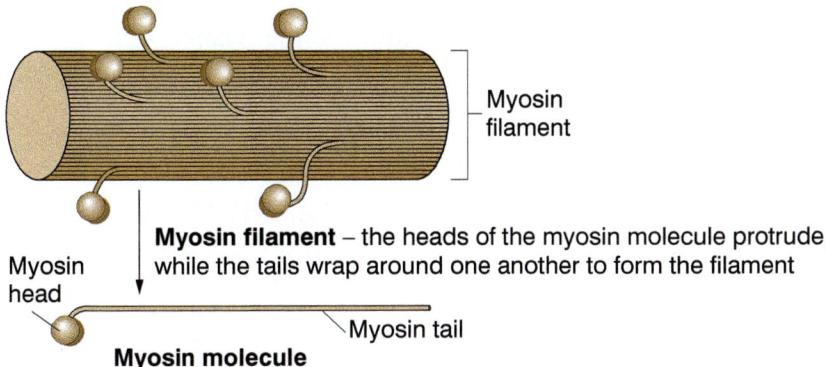

Myosin filament – the heads of the myosin molecule protrude, while the tails wrap around one another to form the filament

Figure 3 *Structure of the myosin filament*

- **Actin** is a globular protein whose molecules polymerise (join together) to form long helical chains and form an actin filament.
- **Tropomyosin** is a protein that binds to actin. Each molecule is composed of two long polypeptide chains coiled around each other.
- **Troponin** is a globular protein attached to tropomyosin to form a troponin–tropomyosin complex.

The arrangement of the actin filaments, troponin and tropomyosin is shown in Figure 4.

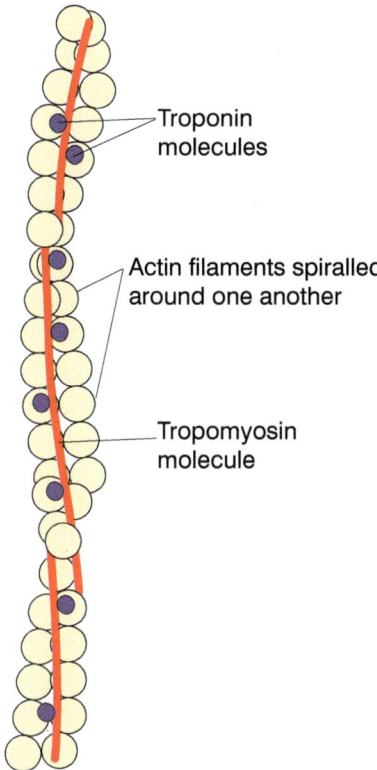

Figure 4 *The relationship of tropomyosin, troponin and actin filaments*

The sliding filament mechanism of muscle contraction

The hypothesis that actin and myosin filaments slide past one another during muscle contraction is supported by the changes in the band pattern on myofibrils. The next question that scientists had to answer was: by what mechanism do the filaments slide past one another? Clues to the answer lie in the shape of the various proteins involved.

To summarise: the bulbous heads of the myosin filaments form cross-bridges with actin filaments. They do this by attaching themselves to binding sites on the actin filaments, and then flexing (bending) in unison, pulling the actin filaments along the myosin filaments. They then become detached and, using ATP as a source of energy, return to their original angle and reattach themselves further along the actin filament. This process is repeated up to 100 times a second. The procedure is similar to the way a ratchet operates.

15.1j describes the sliding filament of muscle contraction in detail. The process is continuous but for ease of understanding has been divided into muscle stimulation, contraction and relaxation.

Remember

The action of the myosin heads is similar to the rowing action of rowers in a boat. The oars (myosin heads) are dipped into the water, flexed as the rowers pull on them, removed from the water and then dipped back into the water further along. The rowers work in unison and the boat and water move relative to one another.

Summary test 15.1i

In a sarcomere during muscular contraction, the (1) remains the same width because this is the length of the (2) filaments. However, the Z-lines get closer together because the thin (3) filaments slide over the thick filaments. Each myosin molecule has a bulbous (4) and a long tail. The tails wrap around each other to form a myosin (5). An actin filament is made of many molecules of actin, which is a (6) protein. Tropomyosin is a long protein that binds to (7). Attached to tropomyosin is another protein known as (8).

These pages help you to:

- describe the roles of transverse system tubules and sarcoplasmic reticulum in stimulating contraction in striated muscle (15.1.10)
- explain the sliding filament model of muscular contraction, including the roles of troponin, tropomyosin, calcium ions and ATP (15.1.12)

You will also:

- understand how sarcomere contraction results in muscle contraction

---

Remember

An action potential is the result of depolarisation of part of a membrane. The spread of the action potential across the muscle can be referred to as a 'wave of depolarisation'.

Remember

The hydrolysis of ATP releases energy and produces ADP and inorganic phosphate (P_i). For simplicity, this account just refers to ADP as the product.

Muscle stimulation

- An **action potential** reaches many **neuromuscular junctions** simultaneously, causing calcium channels to open and calcium **ions** to move into the synaptic knob.
- The calcium ions cause synaptic vesicles to fuse with the presynaptic membrane and release their acetylcholine into the synaptic cleft.
- Acetylcholine diffuses across the synaptic cleft and binds with receptors on the postsynaptic membrane, causing it to depolarise.

Muscle contraction

Muscle contraction occurs when the individual muscle fibres contract at the same time. Within the muscle fibres, myofibril contraction is occurring. The account here describes the sliding filament model and explains the events occurring in one section of the myofibril, at the level of the sarcomeres. The interaction between the four proteins involved in sarcomere contraction is illustrated in Figure 2.

- The action potential travels deep into the muscle fibre through a network of tubules called **transverse system tubules** (T-tubules) that branch throughout the cytoplasm of the muscle fibre (sarcoplasm); see Figure 1.
- The tubules are in contact with the endoplasmic reticulum of the muscle, known as the **sarcoplasmic reticulum**, which has actively taken up calcium ions from the sarcoplasm.
- The action potential opens the calcium channels on the endoplasmic reticulum and calcium ions flood into the sarcoplasm down a diffusion gradient.
- Some calcium ions attach to troponin and cause the troponin–tropomyosin complex to change shape, which displaces the tropomyosin molecules that were blocking the actin binding sites (stages 1 and 2).
- Before binding occurs, the ATPase of the myosin head has catalysed the hydrolysis of an ATP molecule, leaving ADP attached. The myosin head is in a ready (high-energy) state.
- Exposing the actin binding sites now allows the myosin heads to bind to the actin filament and form an actomyosin cross-bridge (stage 3).
- Once attached to the actin filament, the myosin heads, which are in a high-energy state, change their angle, pulling the actin filament along as they do so (power stroke) and releasing a molecule of ADP (stage 4).
  - An ATP molecule attaches to each myosin head, causing it to become detached from the actin filament (stage 5).
  - ATPase activity of the myosin head catalyses the hydolysis of ATP to ADP (stage 6). The myosin head can become extended again ready to bind to the next actin binding site.
  - The myosin head, once more with an attached ADP molecule, then reattaches itself further along the actin filament and the cycle is repeated as long as nervous stimulation of the muscle continues (stage 7).

Muscle relaxation

- When nervous stimulation stops, calcium ions are actively transported back into the sarcoplasmic reticulum through membrane calcium pumps.
- This reabsorption of the calcium ions allows tropomyosin to block the actin filament again.
- Myosin heads are now unable to bind to actin filaments and contraction stops, i.e. the muscle fibre relaxes.

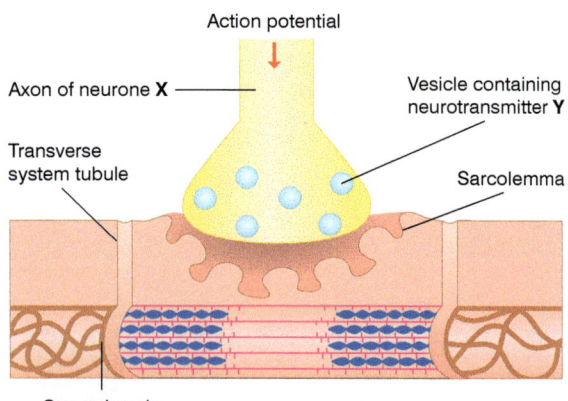

Figure 1 *A neuromuscular junction showing infoldings of the sarcolemma, known as transverse system tubules. These extend into the muscle fibre, making close contact with the sarcoplasmic reticulum*

1 Tropomyosin molecule prevents myosin head from attaching to the binding site on the actin molecule.

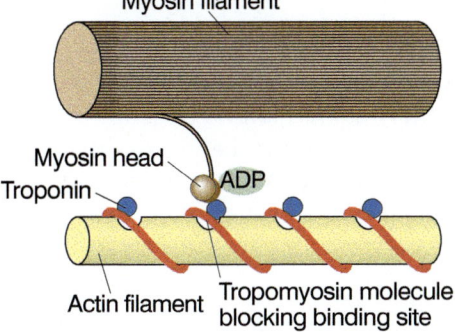

5 ATP molecule fixes to myosin head, causing it to detach from the actin filament.

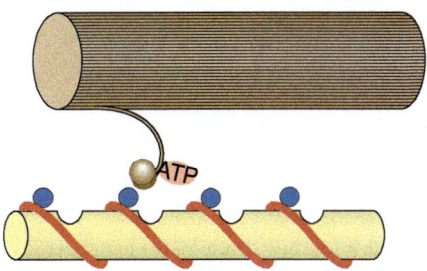

2 Calcium ions released from the endoplasmic reticulum bind with troponin and cause the tropomyosin molecule to be displaced from the binding sites on the actin molecule.

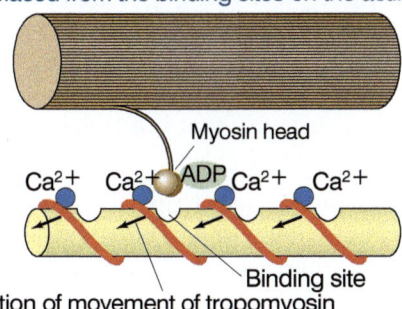

6 Hydrolysis of ATP to ADP by ATPase provides the energy for the myosin head to resume its normal position.

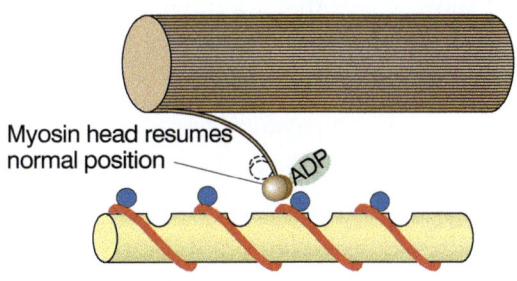

3 Myosin head now attaches to the binding site on the actin filament.

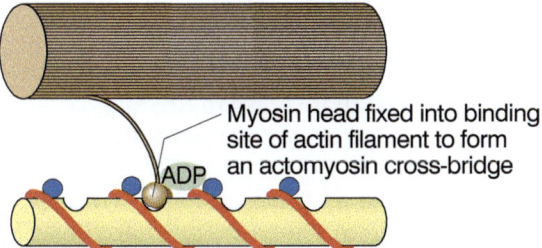

7 Head of myosin reattaches to a binding site further along the actin filament and the cycle is repeated.

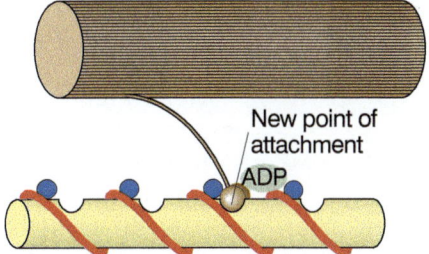

4 The myosin head can use the energy provided by the earlier hydrolysis of ATP for a power stroke. Head of myosin changes angle (tilts) during the power stroke, moving the actin filament along as it does so. The ADP molecule is released.

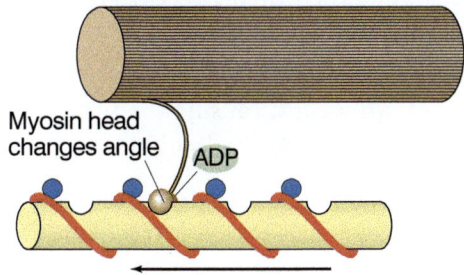

Figure 2 *Sliding filament model of muscle contraction (showing only one myosin head throughout)*

Summary test 15.1j

Before an action potential is generated in the muscle fibre, calcium ions are **(1)** into the endoplasmic reticulum from the cytoplasm, also called the **(2)**. Depolarisation of the **(3)** membrane of the synaptic knob at the **(4)** junction leads to the release of **(5)** and the generation of an action potential in the sarcolemma. This travels deep into a network of tubules called **(6)** tubules. These tubules are connected to the endoplasmic reticulum of the muscle, which is called the **(7)**. Some of the calcium ions from the endoplasmic reticulum attach to a protein molecule called **(8)**, which changes shape and causes the displacement of a molecule called **(9)** from the actin filament. This displacement allows the head of a **(10)** molecule to attach to the actin filament and to change the angle of its head and so pull the actin filament along. The molecule detaches from the actin filament when a molecule of **(11)** attaches to it.

Control and coordination in plants
a. The Venus fly trap, auxins, and gibberellins

These pages help you to:

- describe the rapid response of the Venus fly trap to stimulation of hairs on the lobes of modified leaves (15.2.1)
- explain how the closure of the trap of the Venus fly trap plant is achieved (15.2.1)
- understand the role of auxin in stimulating proton pumping to acidify cell walls, and so allow elongation growth (15.2.2)
- describe the role of gibberellin in the germination of barley (15.2.3)

You will also:

- learn more about gibberellins

Figure 1 *Venus fly trap*

Figure 2 *Trigger hairs on leaf lobes of the Venus fly trap plant*

Remember

Expansins are proteins, but are not enzymes.

The Venus fly trap, *Dionaea muscipula*, is a plant that can capture insects. It can generate an action potential, which is a more rapid method of communication than hormones, and so results in a fast response. Control and coordination involving plant hormones, such as stem elongation and germination, are slower processes.

Response of a Venus fly trap

The Venus fly trap lives in a boggy habitat with few nutrients. In order to obtain nutrients such as nitrogen, needed for growth, it has to capture and digest small insects. The plant has modified leaves, and each leaf has two lobes that are hinged along a midrib. The lobes have three or more hairs known as trigger hairs, which are part of specialised hair cells that can act as sensory receptors. When an insect lands on the specialised leaf of the Venus fly trap, the two lobes of the leaf that are usually convex suddenly become concave, snapping shut and so trapping the insect in the cavity that is formed (Figure 1). One explanation for this rapid response is as follows.

- The mechanical stimulus of the insect touching trigger hairs (Figure 2) on the lobes causes depolarisation and generates an action potential. The trigger hair cells (sensory receptors) act as transducers and convert mechanical energy to electrical energy.
- The action potential passes to the lower cells of the midrib, known as hinge cells. It requires at least two hairs to be triggered in quick succession (within approximately 15–20 seconds) to cause a response.
- This causes proton (H^+) pumps to move protons out of the hinge cells and into the cell wall spaces between the cells. This may be in response to **auxin**, the concentration of which has been observed to increase in the hinge cells.
- The increased acidity dissolves the calcium pectate that holds the cell walls together.
- The loss of protons from the hinge cells makes them more negative, and so positively charged ions such as calcium ions are attracted into the cells, decreasing their water potential.
- There is now a water potential gradient that causes water to enter the cells by osmosis. As the cell walls are much less rigid and more flexible, the cells rapidly expand, causing the lobes of the leaf to become concave, closing together and trapping the insect. The closure of the trap occurs extremely quickly, about 100 ms after the stimulus has been applied, making sure that the plant catches its prey.

Alternative theories involve loss of turgor in other cells, causing the response. There is some experimental evidence for each, so it may be that both mechanisms are involved.

Role of auxins in elongation growth

Auxins are a group of chemical substances of which indoleacetic acid (IAA) is the most common. The transport of auxin is in one direction, away from the tip of shoots and roots where it is produced. Auxin has a number of effects on plant cells, including altering the state of the cell wall so that permanent elongation of the cells can occur. This is only effective on young cell walls before they have developed greater rigidity through secondary thickening. The proposed explanation of how auxin has a role in this elongation growth is called the **acid growth hypothesis**.

- Auxin binds to receptors in the cell surface membranes of plant cells.
- This causes transport proteins (ATPases) in the cell surface membrane to actively transport protons (hydrogen ions) from the cytoplasm into spaces in the cell wall.
- The protons cause the fluid-filled spaces in the cell wall to become more acidic (lower the pH).
- This stimulates the entry of potassium ions into the cell through potassium channels, decreasing the water potential inside the cell.
- The decrease in pH also creates the optimum conditions for proteins known as expansins to become activated and to weaken the cell wall, temporarily disrupting the hydrogen bonding between cellulose microfibrils and between these and other cell wall polysaccharides.
- This causes a loosening of the cell wall.
- Water entering the cell by osmosis down a water potential gradient will cause an increase in turgor pressure and the loosening of the cell wall means that during active cell growth its protoplast can expand, causing elongation of the cell.

Role of gibberellins in the germination of barley seeds

Once plant seeds are formed they often remain dormant for some time before they germinate. This allows them to overcome adverse conditions like the cold temperatures of winter and allows time for them to be dispersed to new regions by wind or animals. This dormancy is, in part, due to the very low water content – between 5 and 10% – of most seeds. What then breaks dormancy and starts the process of germination? To answer this question, we need first to look at the structure of a typical endospermous seed such as barley. These seeds are made up of:

- **pericarp and testa** – an outer tough, protective layer made up of the testa (seed coat) and pericarp (fruit coat) fused together
- **aleurone layer** – a protein-rich layer just beneath the testa
- **endosperm** – a large region of stored starch that provides an energy source for the growing embryo
- **scutellum** – a modified form of the single cotyledon (seed leaf) of the seed
- **embryo** – the result of **mitotic** division of the zygote, this will develop into the new plant.

The process of germination typically requires the presence of water, oxygen and a favourable temperature. The stages of germination of a barley seed are as follows (the numbers refer to those in the summary of the process in Figure 3):

1. Water softens the pericarp and testa covering and enters the rest of the seed.
2. The water stimulates the embryo to produce **gibberellin**.
3. The gibberellin diffuses into the cells of the aleurone layer, where it causes the breakdown of DELLA proteins. These are proteins that bind to substances known as transcription factors (16.3b) that promote transcription. When DELLA proteins are broken down, transcription can proceed. **Transcription** of the genes coding for digestive enzymes produces mRNA for translation of these proteins. The protein store in the aleurone layer provides amino acids for the synthesis of α-amylase and other enzymes.
4. The α-amylase and other enzymes diffuse into the endosperm.
5. α-amylase **hydrolyses** the starch in the endosperm into maltose, which in turn is hydrolysed by maltase to glucose.
6. The glucose diffuses, via the scutellum, into the embryo where it is used to provide the ATP (from respiratory breakdown) and raw material (e.g. cellulose) needed for germination and growth.

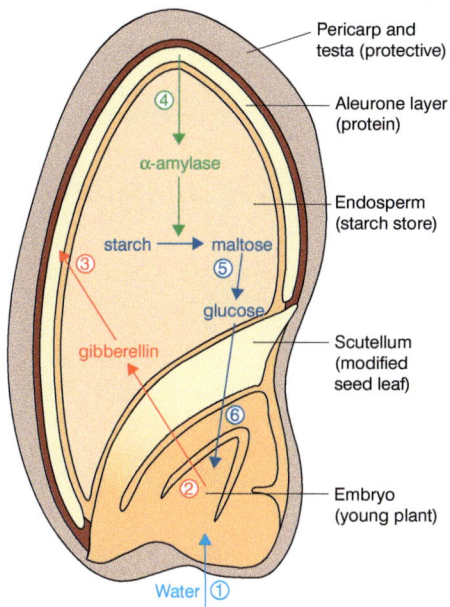

Figure 3 *Structure of a barley seed and the role of gibberellin in its germination*

Summary test 15.2a

The Venus fly trap has modified leaves which are leaf **(1)** that have sensory receptors known as **(2)**. The mechanical stimulus is converted to **(3)** energy and causes depolarisation. When two of these are touched in a short time, an **(4)** spreads to **(5)** and this causes water to enter the cells, making them **(6)** and causing the two parts of the modified leaf to become **(7)** and close the trap. Auxin causes cell **(8)** by stimulating the pumping out of **(9)** into the cell wall, This makes the cell wall **(10)**. Proteins known as **(11)** cause cell wall loosening and when the plant takes in water there is an increase in **(12)** pressure, which causes the cell to expand lengthways. **(13)** is a plant hormone involved in breaking dormancy. It is produced by the **(14)** and diffuses to cells of the **(15)**, where it causes the breakdown of **(16)** and leads to production of the enzyme **(17)** and other enzymes that can diffuse to the **(18)** and break down stores to be used for germination.

Launch additional digital resources for the chapter

15 Exam-style questions

1 Figure 1 is a diagram of a neuromuscular junction.

Figure 1

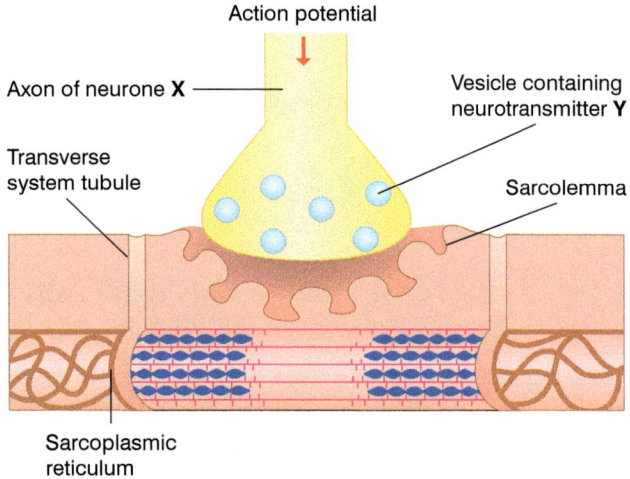

a Name neurone **X** and neurotransmitter **Y**.   *(2 marks)*

b Outline how an action potential arriving at neurone **X** can result in the depolarisation of the sarcolemma.   *(5 marks)*

c Describe the roles of transverse system tubules and sarcoplasmic reticulum when the sarcolemma is

   i depolarised   *(3 marks)*

   ii repolarised.   *(3 marks)*

d A type of anaerobic bacteria, *Clostridium botulinum*, may grow in contaminated canned foods. Poison is released from ingested bacteria that affects the neuromuscular junction, resulting in muscle paralysis (loss of muscle function). Eventually this causes death due to respiratory failure (loss of lung function).

   i Describe **one** mechanism by which the poison may cause muscle paralysis.   *(2 marks)*

   ii Explain how the poison can cause respiratory failure and lead to death.   *(4 marks)*

(Total 19 marks)

2 Figure 2 shows a taste bud on a human tongue. It contains chemoreceptor cells that are able to detect chemicals in food.

Figure 2

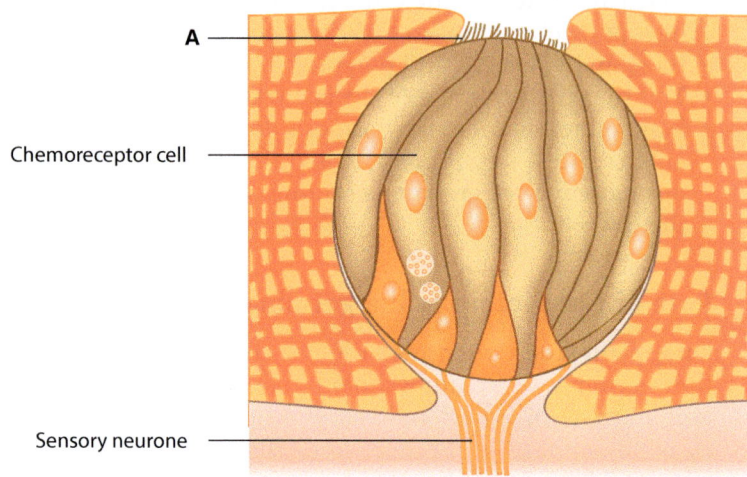

a Identify structure **A**.   *(1 mark)*

b Outline the sequence of events that occur in the **chemoreceptor** cell when food that is high in salt (sodium chloride) comes into contact with it.   *(5 marks)*

c Figure 3 shows the changes in the membrane potential of a sensory neurone when chemoreceptor cells are stimulated with different concentrations of sodium chloride solutions, **A** and **B**.

Figure 3

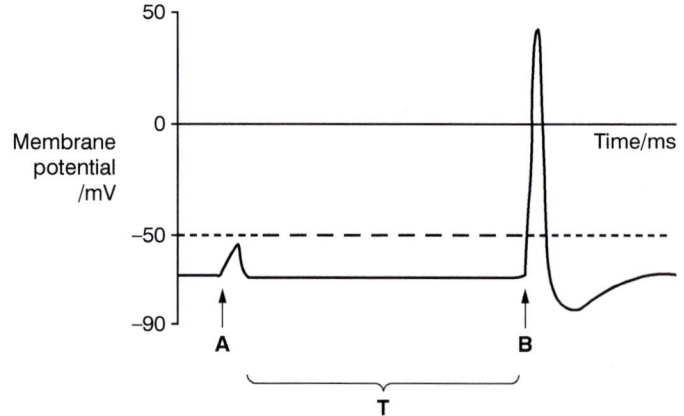

i State whether the following voltage-gated channels will open or close during **T**.

Na$^+$ channels ....

K$^+$ channels .... *(1 mark)*

ii Name the ions that move out of the membrane through leak channels during **T**. *(1 mark)*

iii Explain the difference in the effects of **A** and **B** on membrane potential. *(3 marks)*

(Total 11 marks)

15 Practice questions

3 The table below shows the speeds by which different axons conduct action potentials.

Axon	Myelin	Axon diameter /μm	Transmission speed / m s^{-1}
Human motor axon to leg muscle	Yes	20	120
Human sensory axon from skin pressure receptor	Yes	10	50
Squid giant axon	No	500	25
Human motor axon to internal organ	No	1	2

a Using data from the table, describe the effect of axon diameter on the speed of conductance of an action potential.

b The data show that a myelinated axon conducts an action potential faster than an unmyelinated one. Explain why this is so.

c What is the name of the cells whose membranes make up the myelin sheath around some types of axon?

d State whether the presence of myelin or the diameter of the axon has the greater influence on the speed of conductance of an action potential. Use information from the table to explain your answer

e The squid is an ectothermic animal. This means that its body temperature fluctuates with the temperature of the waters in which it lives. Suggest how this might affect the speed with which a squid conducts action potentials along its axon.

4 a Suggest a reason why there are numerous mitochondria in the sarcoplasm of muscle.

b If we cut across a myofibril at certain points, we see only thick myosin filaments. If we cut at a different point we see only thin actin filaments. At yet other points we see both types of filament. Explain why.

c How is the shape of the myosin filament adapted to its role in muscle contraction?

d During the contraction of a muscle sarcomere, a single actin filament moved 0.8 μm. If the hydrolysis of a single ATP molecule provides enough energy to move an actin filament 40 nm, how many ATP molecules were needed to move the actin filament 0.8 μm? Show your working.

e Dead cells can no longer produce ATP. Soon after death muscles contract, making the body stiff – a state known as rigor mortis. From your knowledge of muscle contraction, explain why rigor mortis occurs after death.

5 The Venus fly trap is a plant that captures and digests small insects. To do so it uses touch-sensitive hairs on its leaves. Describe how an insect touching the hairs can result in the rapid closure of the leaves around it.

16.1 Passage of information from parents to offspring

a. The role of meiosis

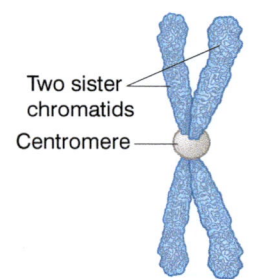

Two sister chromatids

Centromere

Figure 1 *Structure of a chromosome after DNA replication*

Table 1 *Differences between mitosis and meiosis*

Mitosis	Meiosis
A single division of the nucleus	A double division of the nucleus
The number of chromosomes remains the same	The number of chromosomes is halved
Homologous chromosomes do not associate	Homologous chromosomes associate and form bivalents
Chiasmata are never formed	Chiasmata are formed
Crossing over never occurs	Crossing over occurs
Daughter cells are genetically identical to parent cells (if no mutations)	Daughter cells are genetically different from parental ones
Two daughter cells	Four daughter cells
Daughter cells have the same number of chromosome sets as the parents	Daughter cells have half the number of chromosome sets as the parents

Mitosis and meiosis

In eukaryotes, there are two types of cell division, mitosis (5.2a) and meiosis (Table 1). Cell division by mitosis is important in asexual reproduction, growth by increase in cell numbers, replacement of cells and repair of tissue (5.1b). Cell division by meiosis is the cell division that is involved in the production of gametes (gametogenesis) in sexually reproducing organisms.

Diploid and haploid

Most organisms that reproduce by sexual reproduction have two or more complete sets of chromosomes. The number of chromosome sets, known as the ploidy, and the number of chromosomes per set is constant for each particular species.

An organism with two sets of chromosomes is said to have the diploid, or 2n, number of chromosomes. The haploid (half the diploid) number of chromosomes occurs in the gametes of sexually reproducing organisms: egg or ovum in females; sperm (animals) and pollen (plants) in males. Gametes are produced from cells known as germ cells. Other body cells are known as somatic cells. The haploid number, or n, is the number of chromosomes in one complete set of chromosomes. This one set will contain one copy of all the genes for that particular species of organism.

for humans, *Homo sapiens*, 2n = 46, n = 23

for onion, *Allium cepa*, 2n = 16, n = 8

The need for a reduction division in meiosis

In sexual reproduction, two gametes fuse to form a zygote, which will become the new individual. If gametes are produced with the same number of chromosomes as somatic cells, at fertilisation, the zygote will have twice the number of chromosome sets and so double the number of chromosomes as the cells of the parents. This changes the ploidy, which is constant for any one species.

For example, for diploid (2n) parents producing diploid gametes, 2n + 2n = 4n, will give a zygote with four chromosome sets, or tetraploid (see 17.3b) and this means that the species is not being continued. To keep the number of chromosomes and ploidy constant for the species, the diploid parents must produce haploid gametes with only one set of chromosomes, hence half the number. This means that at fertilisation, when the nucleus of the male gamete fuses with the nucleus of the female gamete, the normal diploid number is restored in the zygote.

Homologous chromosomes

Fertilisation brings together two sets of chromosomes to produce the diploid individual. The nuclei of the somatic cells will therefore have a maternal set of chromosomes and a paternal set of chromosomes. It is possible to match chromosomes in a maternal set with those in the paternal set. Figure 1 shows a generalised chromosome as it would appear during the first stages of cell division (after replication each chromosome is composed of two identical chromatids). Figure 2 shows all 46 human chromosomes. It is not possible to say whether a chromosome is of paternal or maternal origin. However, these chromosomes can be matched in pairs to produce an organised karyotype (see 5.1a). The pair of sex chromosomes (see 16.2e) are denoted pair 23. For the other 22 pairs of chromosomes, the largest pair is pair number 1 and chromosome pair 22 is the smallest.

A matching pair of chromosomes is termed a homologous pair. Each pair:

- has the same genes in the same positions (loci) on the chromosome, but not necessarily the same forms (alleles) of the gene
- is the same length and overall size
- has the centromere in the same position
- has one chromosome of maternal origin and one chromosome of paternal origin
- has the same banding pattern (see Figure 2)
- will come together and pair up in prophase I of meiosis.

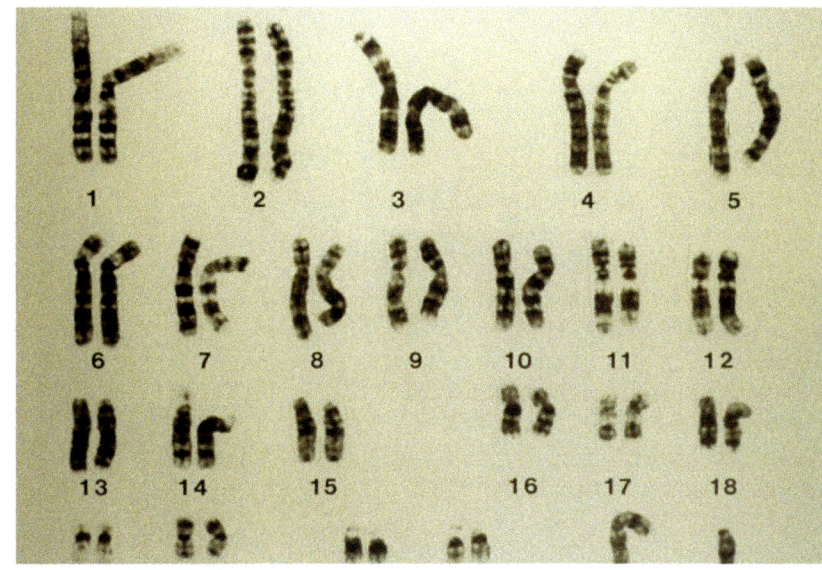

Figure 2 *Human chromosomes: photomicrograph of a male karyotype*

If the sex chromosomes are different, as in XY in males, then they will be of different sizes and have a different genetic composition. They still form a homologous pair at meiosis. The events of meiosis are explained in 16.1b.

The principles behind meiosis

Meiosis is described as a reduction division, but the halving of the chromosome number is not a random process. It is an organised sequence of events that results in daughter cells that each have one complete set of chromosomes.

- Cell division by meiosis requires two divisions of the nucleus to produce four daughter cells.
- The four daughter cells have half the number of chromosomes of the parent.
- Each daughter cell is genetically different (see 16.1c).
- The reduction in chromosome number occurs in the first division when homologous chromosomes pair up and then separate (segregate) so that each homologue (each member of a pair) ends up in a different daughter cell.
- The second division results in sister chromatids of each chromosome segregating so that each daughter cell has a full set of (daughter) chromosomes that now have only one DNA molecule per chromosome.

Remember

In diploid organisms, only the reproductive cells, the gametes, will have one set of chromosomes, or the haploid (n) number. These cells have been produced to fertilise with a gamete from another individual to form a diploid zygote. The nucleus of somatic cells has the diploid (2n) number of chromosomes.

Extension

Human chromosome pair number 21

Chromosome pair number 21 is actually smaller than pair 22. This was an original error discovered after Down syndrome, a condition where individuals have three of chromosome 21 (a chromosomal mutation) was named trisomy 21. To keep the name of the conditon as trisomy 21, the chromosome pair number has been kept as 21 (see 6.2d Extension).

Summary test 16.1a

Organisms that have two sets of chromosome in their **(1)** (non-reproductive) cells are said to have a **(2)** number of chromosomes. The products of meiosis, the **(3)** have a **(4)** number so that at **(5)** the original parental number of chromosomes is **(6)**. If an organism has two sets of chromosomes, the chromosomes can form **(7)** pairs. These have features in common. They have the same length and same position of **(8)**. They have the same genes in the same **(9)** on the chromosome and the same **(10)** pattern. One chromosome has a **(11)** origin and the other a paternal origin. In meiosis there are two divisions of the **(12)** and **(13)** daughter cells are produced. The first division is a **(14)** division where the chromosome number is **(15)**. Meiosis also results in **(16)** different cells.

These pages help you to:

- describe the behaviour of chromosomes in plant and animal cells during meiosis, to include the names of the main stages of meiosis (16.1.4)
- describe the associated behaviour of the nuclear envelope, the cell surface membrane and the spindle during meiosis (16.1.4)
- identify the main stages of meiosis (16.1.5)
- interpret photomicrographs and diagrams of cells in different stages of meiosis (16.1.5)

You will also:

- read about nondisjunction, aneuploidy and polyploidy.

The stages of meiosis (**reduction division**) are described in Figure 1. The parent cell has two sets of chromosomes (diploid). For convenience, only four chromosomes are shown, two in each set.

> **Remember**
>
> For the formation of the spindle, the cells of higher plants do not have centrioles, but they do have MTOCs (microtubule organising centres) that carry out the same function.

Interphase

In late interphase (S phase), before meiosis, DNA replicates. The early interphase chromosome is a single structure with one DNA molecule – the chromosome before meiosis has two identical chromatids each with a DNA molecule. In animal cells the pair of centrioles replicates.

Prophase I

The chromosomes shorten and fatten (condensation) and come together in their homologous pairs to form bivalents. The chromatids wrap around one another and non-sister chromatids of homologous chromosomes attach at points called chiasmata. The chromatids may break at these points and swap similar sections of chromatids with one another in a process called crossing over. Finally the nucleolus disappears and the nuclear envelope disassembles. The centromeres are attached to spindle fibres.

Metaphase I

With centromeres attached to the fully formed spindle, the bivalents arrange themselves randomly on the equator of the cell with each of a pair of homologous chromosomes facing opposite poles.

Anaphase I

One of each pair of homologous chromosomes is pulled by the contraction of spindle fibres to opposite poles.

Telophase I and cytokinesis

In animal cells a cleavage furrow forms. Microtubules pull two sides of the cell surface membrane together so that the cell becomes narrower towards its centre until the opposite parts of the membrane fuse to give two separate cells. In plant cells, a cell plate forms. In most animal cells a nuclear envelope re-forms around the chromosomes at each pole, but in most plant cells there is no telophase I and the cell goes directly into prophase II.

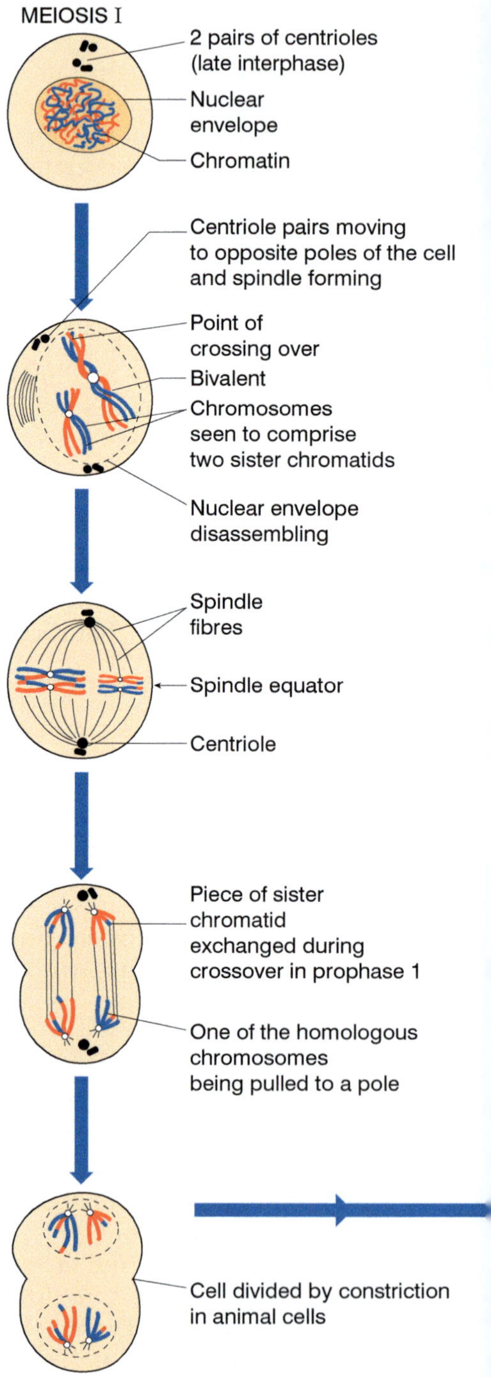

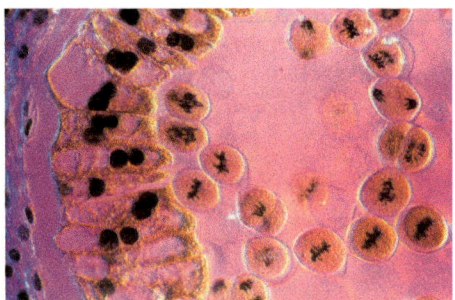

Figure 2 *Photomicrograph of meiosis in bluebell anther cells. In the right half of the image, cells mostly in prophase I, metaphase I and anaphase I of meiosis can be seen (2n = 16)*

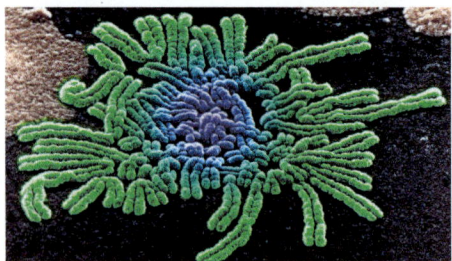

Figure 3 *Colourised scanning electron micrograph of chromosomes during metaphase I of meiosis. The chromosomes are grouped together at the equator of the cell. This is a semi polar view rather that the equatorial view shown in Figure 1*

MEIOSIS I

- 2 pairs of centrioles (late interphase)
- Nuclear envelope
- Chromatin

- Centriole pairs moving to opposite poles of the cell and spindle forming
- Point of crossing over
- Bivalent
- Chromosomes seen to comprise two sister chromatids
- Nuclear envelope disassembling

- Spindle fibres
- Spindle equator
- Centriole

- Piece of sister chromatid exchanged during crossover in prophase 1
- One of the homologous chromosomes being pulled to a pole

- Cell divided by constriction in animal cells

Figure 1 *Stages of meiosis in an animal cell*

The process of meiosis

Meiosis has two nuclear divisions that normally occur immediately one after the other:

- **The first meiotic division (meiosis I)** is separated for convenience into four stages – prophase I, metaphase I, anaphase I and telophase I. Unlike prophase of mitosis, in prophase I of meiosis, homologous pairs come together to form a **bivalent** in a process called **synapsis**. **Crossing over** occurs (see 16.1c).
- **The second meiotic division (meiosis II)** is basically a mitotic division: no chiasmata are formed, individual chromosomes line up at the spindle equator, centromeres

split and sister chromatids separate and move to opposite poles. The four stages – prophase II, metaphase II, anaphase II and telophase II – occur simultaneously in the two daughter cells formed in meiosis I. At the end of this second meiotic division four daughter cells are formed.

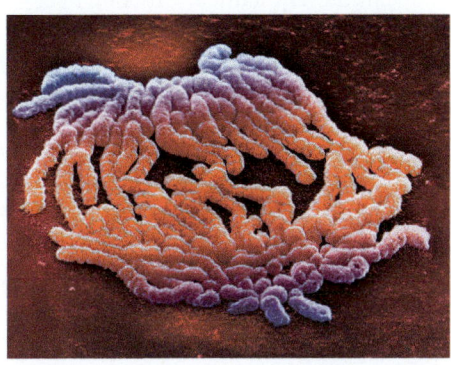

Figure 4 *Colourised scanning electron micrograph of chromosomes during anaphase I of meiosis. The chromosomes are seen pulling apart towards the poles of the cell. The view is from the same angle as in Figure 3*

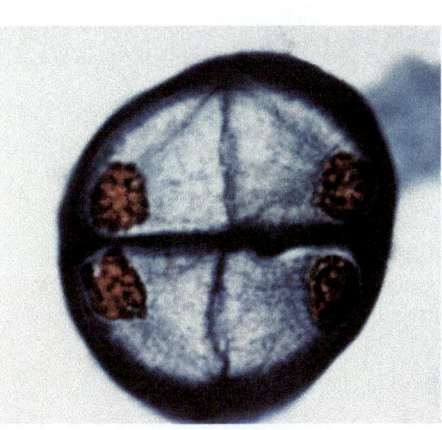

Figure 5 *Photomicrograph of anther of Lilium (lily) showing telophase II stage of meiosis in a pollen mother cell*

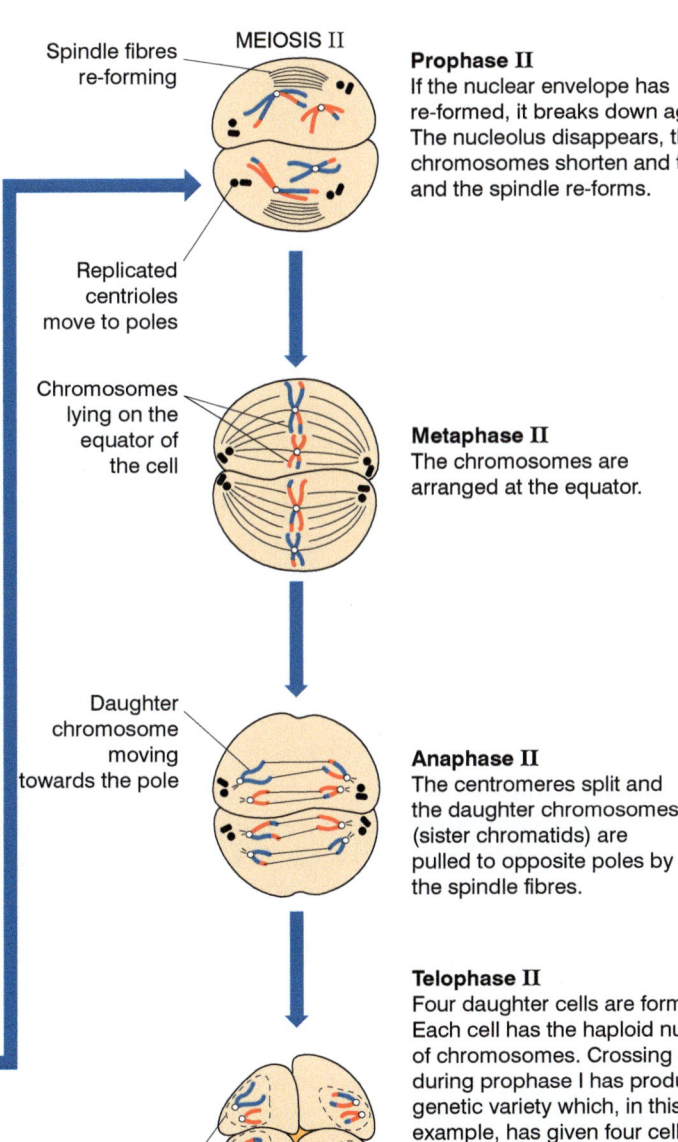

MEIOSIS II

Spindle fibres re-forming

Prophase II
If the nuclear envelope has re-formed, it breaks down again. The nucleolus disappears, the chromosomes shorten and thicken and the spindle re-forms.

Replicated centrioles move to poles

Chromosomes lying on the equator of the cell

Metaphase II
The chromosomes are arranged at the equator.

Daughter chromosome moving towards the pole

Anaphase II
The centromeres split and the daughter chromosomes (sister chromatids) are pulled to opposite poles by the spindle fibres.

Telophase II
Four daughter cells are formed. Each cell has the haploid number of chromosomes. Crossing over during prophase I has produced genetic variety which, in this example, has given four cells of different genetic composition.

Nuclear envelope re-forming

In early prophase I bivalents cannot be seen. After synapsis, the formation of bivalents means that only half the number of separate structures is visible using a microscope. These appear densely stained. Crossing over cannot be seen, but chiasmata are visible in late prophase I.

Extension

Unequal cytoplasmic division in meiosis

The division of the cytoplasm in meiosis is not always equal. For example, in oogenesis (formation of the egg) in humans, during cytokinesis in the first meiotic division most of the cytoplasm (including the organelles) are moved into one of the two daughter cells. In the second meiotic division of this larger cell, the same happens again at cytokinesis and the resulting larger cell will be the egg cell. The other smaller cells are known as polar bodies and are non-functional. In spermatogenesis (formation of the sperm), in both meiotic divisions the cytoplasm is shared out equally and all four cells are functional. This difference makes sure that there are many sperm to increase the chance of fertilising one egg cell.

Summary test 16.1b

By the end of **(1)** of meiosis, the **(2)** is fully formed. During this stage homologous pairs form **(3)** so that **(4)** the number of original separate structures can be seen. **(5)** occurs between sections of **(6)** of homologous pairs. Towards the end of this stage, homologues can still be seen to be joined at points called **(7)**. Each homologous pair orientates at the **(8)** in metaphase I. Homologues separate at the **(9)** stage and at the end of meiosis 1 there is a **(10)** number of chromosomes in each cell. The second division of meiosis is like a **(11)** division. At metaphase II, **(12)** split and **(13)**, now called daughter chromosomes, are pulled to opposite **(14)**.

Extension

Aneuploidy and polyploidy

Aneuploidy

On rare occasions, homologues do not separate during anaphase I of meiosis or chromosomes do not separate into two sister chromatids during anaphase II of meiosis. This process is known as nondisjunction and so can result in one extra, or one less chromosome in the gamete formed. At fertilisation, the zygote will have one extra, or one less chromosome than the normal diploid number (a condition known as aneuploidy). One extra chromosome is known as trisomy (as in Trisomy 21 outlined in 16.1a Extension) and one less chromosome is known as monosomy.

Polyploidy

On rare occasions, errors occur during the formation of gametes, and a diploid parent may produce a diploid gamete. If this fuses with another (rare event) diploid gamete, a viable (able to survive) polyploid (in this case tetraploid) zygote results and a new species is formed. In evolutionary history, this has occurred far more frequently in plants than in animals. There are many examples of plant and animal species that are polyploids, with more than two complete sets of chromosomes. Most species of wheat are tetraploids (4n) or hexaploids (6n).

Terminology in meiosis

It is important when giving an account of meiosis that the terminology is used in the correct way. The following may be helpful in becoming more confident in using terminology associated with this process:

Meiosis I and meiosis II

When describing stages of meiosis it is important to state whether it is meiosis I or meiosis II, because very different events occur in these divisions.

Centrioles and MTOC

Centrioles, structures that organise microtubules to form spindle fibres, are not seen in higher plants, so when describing the formation of the spindle the term 'microtubule organising centre' or MTOC is appropriate. In animal cells, the spindle forms from the centrioles, so this term can be used.

Microtubules, spindle fibres, spindle

Microtubules are used to make spindle fibres. These fibres form a three-dimensional structure called a spindle.

Chromatids and chromosomes

Because DNA replication has occurred, a chromosome at the start of meiosis I has two identical DNA molecules – one for each of the sister chromatids. During meiosis I the sister chromatids of a chromosome remain joined together at the centromere. During meiosis II, when the centromere divides at anaphase II, the separating sister chromatids may now be termed daughter chromosomes. This is because they will be the chromosomes of the new cells to be formed. Each chromosome in the new cell will comprise one DNA molecule.

Homologous chromosomes, homologous pair and bivalent

When two homologous chromosomes join at synapsis, they form a single homologous pair. The complete structure is called a bivalent (singular). Making reference to bivalents (plural) implies two or more homologous pairs.

Meiosis halves the number of chromosomes to form cells such as gametes and makes sure that the diploid number is maintained when haploid gametes fuse. Meiosis also produces genetic variation among offspring, allowing an organism to adapt and survive in a changing world. Meiosis brings about this variation in three main ways: genetic recombination by crossing over, random orientation (independent assortment) of homologous chromosomes at metaphase I, and production of haploid gametes that fuse randomly at fertilisation.

Genetic recombination by crossing over

We saw in 16.1b that during meiosis I each chromosome synapses with its homologous partner. The following events (Figure 1) then take place.

- The chromatids of each pair become twisted around one another.
- During this twisting process tensions are created and portions of the chromatids break off.
- These broken portions then rejoin with the non-sister chromatids of the homologous partner. The points where crossing over occurs are called chiasmata.
- Generally equivalent portions of homologous chromosomes are exchanged and genetic combinations of maternal and paternal alleles (forms or versions of a gene) are produced.

The effect of this recombination on the cells produced at the end of meiosis is shown in Figure 2. Where there is no recombination by crossing over only two different types of cell are produced. However, where recombination does occur there are four different cell types. Recombination by crossing over therefore increases genetic variety.

These pages help you to:

- explain how genetically different gametes are produced from crossing over and random orientation (independent assortment) of pairs of homologous chromosomes and sister chromatids during meiosis (16.1.6)
- explain that the random fusion of gametes at fertilisation produces genetically different individuals (16.1.7)

You will also:

- understand that separation of chromosomes and chromatids also separates alleles of a gene

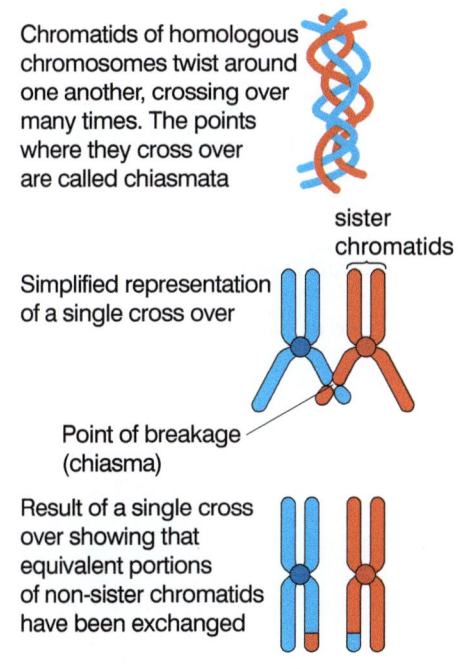

Chromatids of homologous chromosomes twist around one another, crossing over many times. The points where they cross over are called chiasmata

sister chromatids

Simplified representation of a single cross over

Point of breakage (chiasma)

Result of a single cross over showing that equivalent portions of non-sister chromatids have been exchanged

Figure 1 *Crossing over*

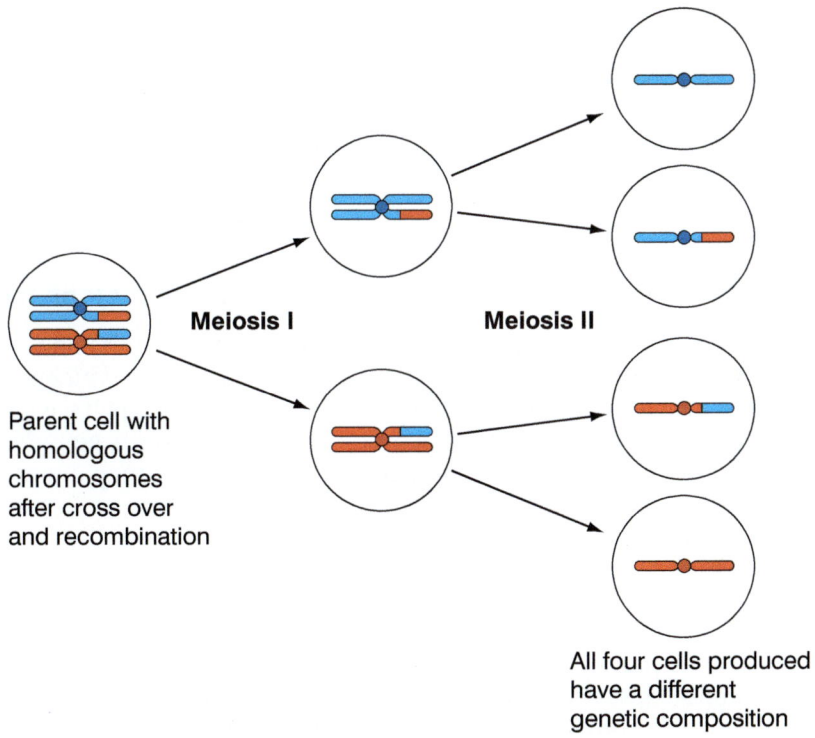

Meiosis I   Meiosis II

Parent cell with homologous chromosomes after cross over and recombination

All four cells produced have a different genetic composition

Figure 2 *Genetic variation as a result of recombination by crossing over*

> ### Remember
>
> The two chromatids that make up a single chromosome are called **sister chromatids**. Before meiosis these are genetically identical.

Consider two different genes on separate, non-homologous chromosomes. One gene is for stem length and has two alleles, short and tall. The other gene is for flower position and has two alleles, terminal flower and axial flower. The separation of chromosomes at anaphase I and the separation of sister chromatids at anaphase II also segregates (separates) alleles of a gene into different cells.

In **arrangement 1**, the two pairs of homologous chromosomes orientate themselves on the equator in such a way that the chromosome carrying the allele for tall stem and the one carrying the allele for terminal flowers migrate to the same pole. The alleles for short stems and axial flowers migrate to the opposite pole. Cell ❶ therefore carries the alleles for tall stems and terminal flowers while cell ❷ carries the ones for short stems and axial flowers.

In **arrangement 2**, the left-hand homologous pair of chromosomes is shown orientated the opposite way around. As this orientation is random, this arrangement is equally as likely as the first one. The result of this different arrangement is that cell ❸ carries the alleles for short stems and terminal flowers, whereas cell ❹ carries ones for tall stems and axial flowers.

All four resultant cells are different from one another. With more homologous pairs the number of possible combinations becomes enormous. In pea plants with 7 pairs, this is 2^7 combinations; a human, with 23 such pairs, has the potential for $2^{23} = 8\,388\,608$ combinations.

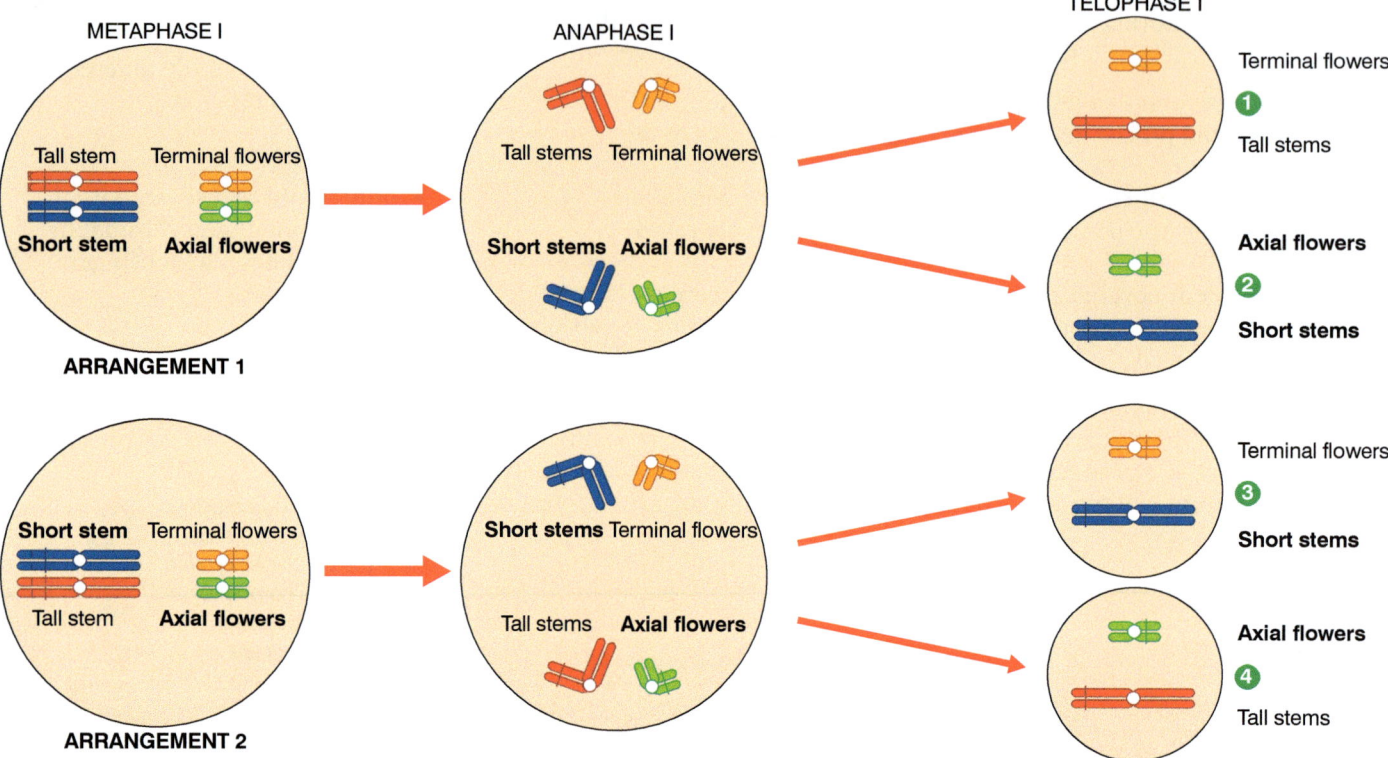

Figure 3 *How random orientation of homologous pairs during metaphase I contributes to genetic variation in gametes and hence the offspring*

Random orientation of homologous chromosomes at metaphase I

When the pairs of homologous chromosomes arrange themselves on the equator of the spindle during metaphase I of meiosis, they do so independently of each other and randomly. For example, if two homologous pairs, each consisting of a maternal and paternal chromosome, come to the equator and orientate randomly, in one cell both maternal chromosomes may move to one pole and both paternal chromosomes to the other. In another cell, a maternal chromosome from one pair and the paternal chromosome from the other pair may end up in the same cell. Although each one of a pair has the same genes, they may differ in the alleles that they possess. Random orientation produces new genetic combinations. A simple example is shown in Figure 3. As each homologous pair can orientate in two different ways at the spindle equator, and as the homologous pairs orientate independently of each other, the total number of possible combinations is 2^n, where n is the haploid number.

The situation shown in Figure 3 does not take into account crossing over. If crossing over has occurred, each of the chromosomes shown in telophase I would be composed of sister chromatids that are genetically different.

This means that the combined effect of crossing over and random orientation will produce a huge number of genetic combinations in the gametes formed.

Remember that in Figure 3, the cells shown in telophase I will continue to the second division of meiosis. This means that arrangement 1 and arrangement 2 will each complete meiosis with four genetically different haploid cells.

Production of haploid gametes that fuse randomly at fertilisation

The haploid gametes produced by meiosis must fuse to restore the diploid state. Each parent will produce genetically different gametes. Fusion (fertilisation) will be random – any one of the different gametes of one parent will fuse randomly with any one of the other parent. This will produce genetic variation. If many offspring are produced, random fusion will result in many genetically different individuals.

Summary test 16.1c

Genetic recombination occurs during the **(1)** stage of meiosis in an event known as **(2)**. Here, **(3)** occur in the chromatids and portions of **(4)** chromatids are swapped. This means that there are new combinations of alleles and so leads to genetic **(5)**. At the **(6)** stage of meiosis, homologous chromosome pairs **(7)** themselves **(8)** and independently of other pairs in a process known as **(9)**. Depending on the arrangement, there will be different combinations of **(10)** of different genes in the daughter cells. Random **(11)** of gametes at fertilisation also produces variety in the offpsring.

Remember

Genes are on chromosomes. Chromosomes of a homologous pair may have different alleles. The separation of chromosomes at anaphase I and the separation of sister chromatids at anaphase II also segregates (separates) alleles of a gene into different cells.

The role of genes in determining the phenotype

a. Genetic terminology

These pages help you to:

- understand and learn definitions of the terms
  – phenotype, genotype
  – gene, locus, allele
  – homozygous and heterozygous
  – dominant, recessive, codominant (16.2.1)

You will also:

- understand what is meant by multiple alleles and hemizygous

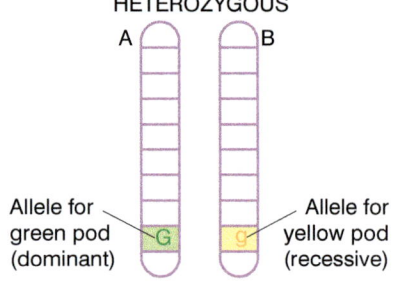

HOMOZYGOUS DOMINANT

Chromosome A of homologous pair

Chromosome B of homologous pair

Both alleles for green pod (dominant)

Gene for pod colour

Homologous chromosomes

HETEROZYGOUS

A   B

Allele for green pod (dominant)

Allele for yellow pod (recessive)

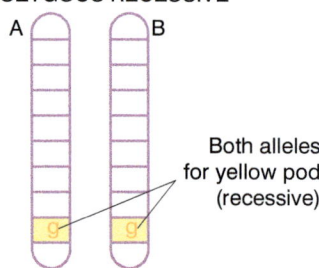

HOMOZYGOUS RECESSIVE

A   B

Both alleles for yellow pod (recessive)

Figure 1 *Pair of homologous chromosomes showing different possible pairings of dominant and recessive alleles*

Remember

There are also genes that are transcribed to produce the tRNA and rRNA molecules needed by the cell – see 16.3a.

It took the re-discovery, at the beginning of the last century, of the work of a scientist and monk called Gregor Mendel (1822–1884) to establish the basic laws by which characteristics are inherited.

Genotype and phenotype

- **Genotype** is the genetic make-up of an organism. It describes all the alleles that an organism contains. The term genotype is also used when referring to a particular gene, to describe the combination of alleles possessed by an individual for that gene.
- The genotype sets the limits within which the characteristics of an individual may vary. It may determine that a human baby could grow to be 1.8 m tall, but the actual height this individual reaches is affected by other factors such as diet. A lack of an element such as calcium (for bone development) or iodine (for production of the hormone thyroxine) at a particular stage of development could mean that the individual never reaches his/her potential maximum height. Any change to the genotype as a result of a change to the DNA is called a **mutation** and may be inherited if it occurs in the gametes.
- **Phenotype** is the observable characteristics of an organism. It is the result of the interaction between the genotype and the environment, which can modify an organism's appearance (it can be used to describe the whole organism or the observable effect of a specific gene).

Genes and alleles

- **A gene** is a length of DNA, i.e. a sequence of DNA nucleotides. A specific gene carries coded information for the synthesis of a particular polypeptide. The polypeptide coded for by a gene may form a functioning protein, such as an enzyme, or may be part of a protein, such as an antibody or haemoglobin. Some genes may determine a single characteristic, such as blood type in the ABO blood grouping system, whereas some genes may be enzymes in biochemical pathways that result in a particular characteristic. **The locus** is the position of a gene on a chromosome. In a diploid organism, the alleles of a gene occupy the same locus on homologous chromosomes. The plural of locus is loci.
- **An allele** is one of the different forms of a gene. Alleles of the same gene have the same locus. The sequences of different alleles of a gene will differ in one or a few nucleotides. In pea plants, for example, there is a gene for the colour of the seed pod. This gene has two different forms, or alleles – an allele for a green pod and another allele for a yellow pod. The gene is the same characteristic, colour of pea pod, but the two different alleles result in different colours.

Homozygous and heterozygous

Only one allele of a gene can occur at the locus of any one chromosome. However, in sexually reproducing organisms the chromosomes occur in homologous pairs (16.1b). If the allele on each of the chromosomes is the same then the organism is said to be **homozygous** for the characteristic. If the two alleles are different then the organism is said to be **heterozygous** for the characteristic.

Dominance, recessiveness and codominance

A dominant allele is an allele that is expressed in the phenotype of a heterozygote. A dominant allele masks the effect of the recessive allele so only one copy of the dominant allele is required for it to show its effect.

A recessive allele is an allele that has its effect masked by a dominant allele. In a diploid organism two copies of the recessive allele are required for it to show its effect. A recessive allele will only show in the phenotypes of individuals that have a homozygous genotype. For instance, in our example, pea plants that are heterozygous for pod colour will all have green pods. The green pod allele is dominant and the yellow pod allele is recessive, so only green pod is observed in the phenotype. A homozygous organism with two dominant alleles is called **homozygous dominant**, whereas one with two recessive alleles is called **homozygous recessive**. These different genetic types are shown in Figure 1, using green pod as a dominant allele and yellow pod as a recessive allele.

When there is only one copy of a gene in a diploid organism (a combination known as hemizygous), a single recessive allele will show its effect as there is no dominant allele to mask it, e.g. the Y chromosome of males (XY) lacks the genes of the X chromosome.

Codominance and multiple alleles

In some cases, two alleles both contribute to the phenotype, in which case they are referred to as **codominant**. In this situation when both alleles occur together, the phenotype is either a blend of both features, e.g. flower petal colour in snapdragons (*Antirrhinum*) where pink flowers result from an allele for red colour and an allele for white colour, or both features are represented (e.g. the presence of both A and B antigens in blood group AB).

Sometimes a gene of an organism has more than two possible alleles. The organism is said to have **multiple alleles** for that gene. However, as there are always only two chromosomes in a homologous pair, it follows that only two of the three or more alleles in existence can be present in a single organism. Multiple alleles occur in the human ABO blood grouping system (16.2d).

Figure 2 summarises the different terms used in genetics.

Summary test 16.2a

The genetic composition of an organism is the **(1)** and any change to it is termed **(2)**. The actual appearance of an organism is termed the **(3)**. When applied to a particular gene, the term **(1)** refers to the combination of **(4)** possessed by an individual. A gene is a sequence of **(5)** along a piece of DNA that codes for a particular **(6)**. Each gene has two or more different forms called alleles. If the two alleles on a homologous pair of chromosomes are the same, they are termed **(7)**, but if they are different, they are termed **(8)**. An allele that is not apparent in the phenotype when paired with a dominant allele is termed **(9)**. When both alleles contribute to the phenotype they are termed **(10)**.

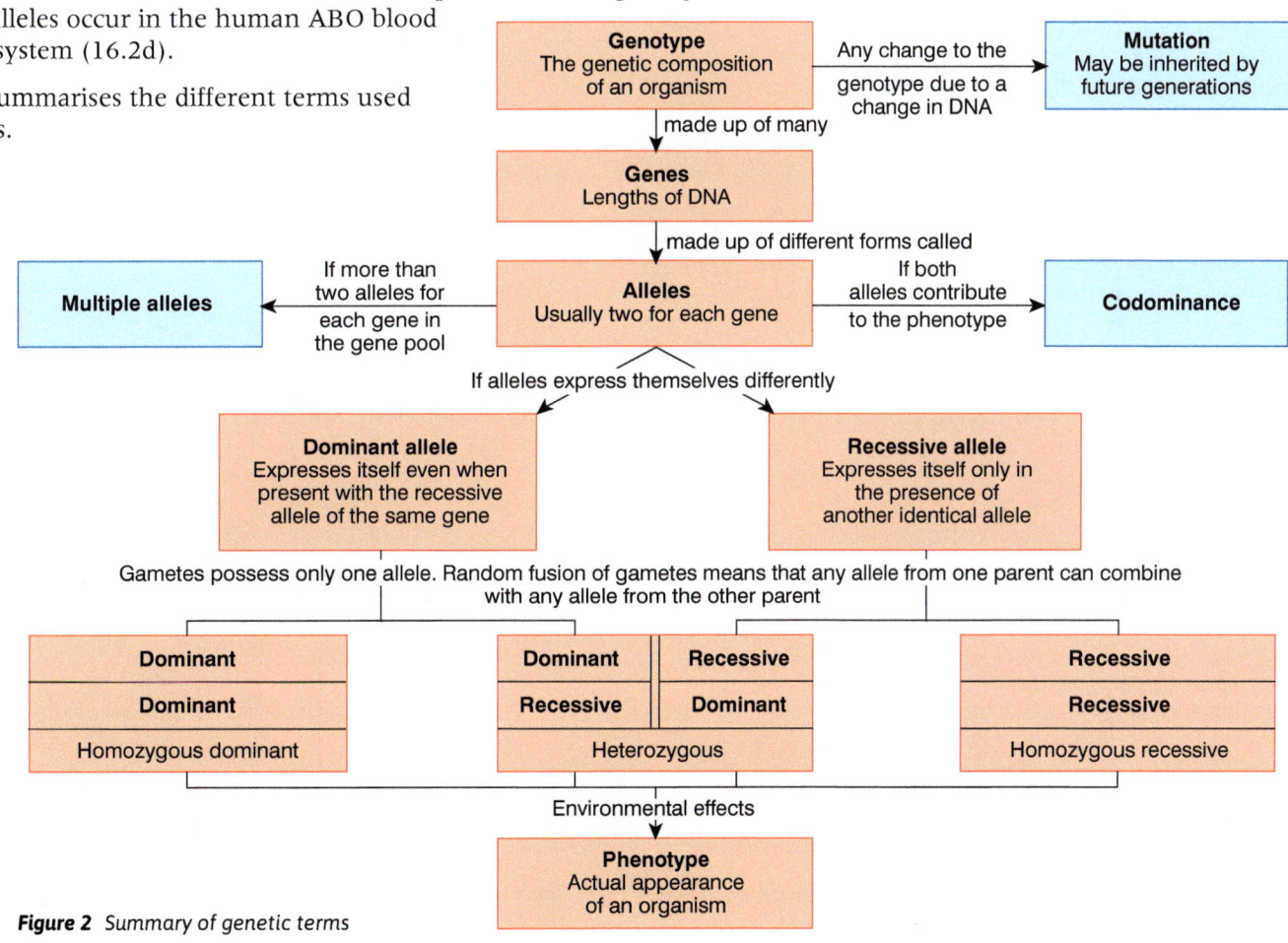

Figure 2 *Summary of genetic terms*

These pages help you to:

- interpret and construct genetic diagrams, including Punnett squares, to explain and predict the results of monohybrid crosses involving dominance and recessiveness (16.2.2)
- explain the terms F_1 and F_2 (16.2.1)

You will also:

- read about the work of Gregor Mendel

Monohybrid inheritance is the inheritance of a single gene. A characteristic, or trait, is any feature that is measured, for example, blood group type or flower colour.

Inheritance of pod colour in peas

Pod colour in peas is known to be controlled by a single gene. If pea plants with green pods are bred repeatedly with each other so that they always produce plants with green pods, they are said to be **pure breeding** for the characteristic of green pods. Pure breeding strains can be bred for almost any characteristic. What it means is that the organisms are homozygous (i.e. they have two **alleles** that are the same) for that particular gene.

If these pure breeding green-pod plants are then crossed with pure breeding yellow-pod plants, all the offspring, known as the **first filial** or **F_1 generation**, turn out to

produce green pods. This means that the allele for green pods is dominant to the allele for yellow pods, which is therefore recessive. This cross is shown in Figure 1.

When the heterozygous plants (Gg) of the F_1 generation are crossed with one another (= F_1 intercross), the offspring (known as the **second filial or F_2 generation**) are always in an approximate ratio of 3 plants with green pods to each 1 plant with yellow pods. This cross is shown in Figure 2. Notice that the green pod phenotype contains heterozyous genotypes and homozygous dominant genotypes in the ratio two to one. Only the genotype of the yellow pods can be deduced from the phenotype.

These observed facts led to the formation of the **law of segregation**, sometimes called Mendel's first law, which states: **In diploid organisms, characteristics are determined by alleles that occur in pairs. Only one of each pair of alleles can be present in a single gamete.**

Representing genetic crosses

Genetic crosses are usually represented in a standard form of shorthand (Table 1). Although you may occasionally come across some minor variations to this scheme, that outlined in Table 1 is the one normally used. Always carry out the procedures completely. Do not be tempted to miss out stages or explanations. To get full credit for your efforts and to avoid errors, construct genetic crosses so that they are easy to follow and all the information is written down.

> **Remember**
>
> The term F_1 should be used only for the offspring of crosses in which the original parents are homozygous, whereas the term F_2 should be used only for the offspring resulting from crossing the F_1 individuals.

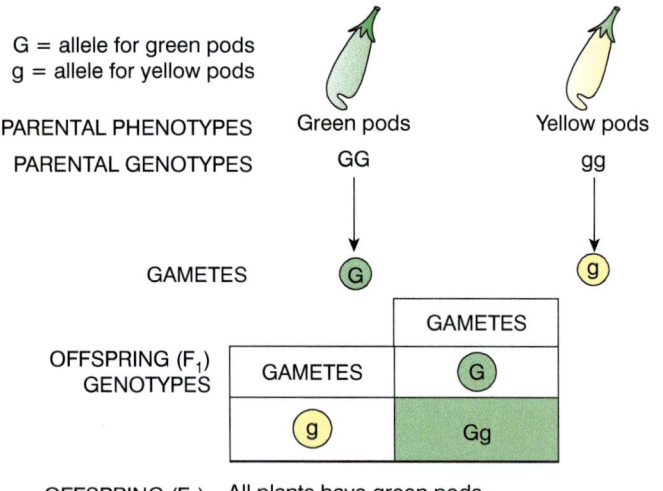

Figure 1 Cross between a pea plant that is pure breeding for green pods and one that is pure breeding for yellow pods

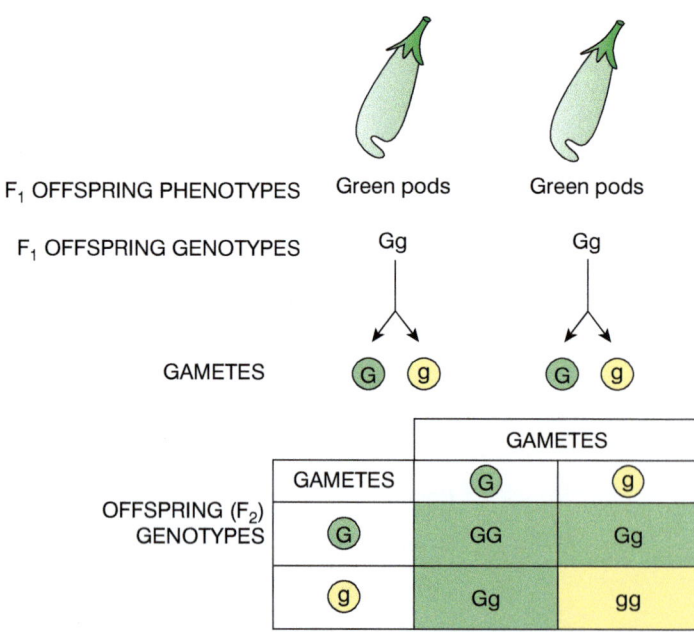

Figure 2 F_1 intercross between pea plants that are heterozygous for green pods

Table 1 *Representing genetic crosses*

Instruction	Reason/notes	Example
Choose a single letter to represent each characteristic	An easy form of shorthand. (In some genetic crosses, e.g. in *Drosophila*, there are set symbols, some of which use two letters)	–
Choose the first letter of one of the contrasting features	When more than one gene and its characteristic is considered at one time such a logical choice means it is easy to identify which letter refers to which gene	Choose G (green) or Y (yellow) for the gene for pea pod colour Choose R (round) or W (wrinkled) for the gene for pea seed shape
If possible, choose the letter in which the upper and lower case forms differ in shape as well as size. It is often helpful to choose the letter of the alphabet that represents the dominant allele	If the upper and lower case forms differ it is almost impossible to confuse them, regardless of their size	Choose G because green is the dominant allele and the upper case form (G) differs in shape from the lower case form (g). Choose R because round is the dominant allele (and R and r look very different)
Let the upper case letter represent the dominant feature and the lower case letter the recessive one. Never use two different letters where one characteristic is dominant	The dominant and recessive feature can easily be identified. Do not use two different letters as this indicates codominance	Let G = green allele and g = yellow allele Do *not* use G for green and Y for yellow Let R = round allele and r = wrinkled allele
Where a feature is compared to 'normal', as in human genetic conditions, then the letter of the alphabet can be used to represent the condition	Otherwise N for normal would be used, which gives no information about the feature and would be a problem when handling crosses with two genes, each with a dominant normal allele	In the gene coding for an enzyme involved in the production of the dark pigment melanin let A = normal dominant allele a = recessive allele for albinism (see 16.2g)
Represent the parents with the appropriate pairs of letters. Use the label 'parental' with 'genotypes' or 'phenotypes' and state their phenotypes	This makes it clear to the reader what the symbols refer to	Parental phenotypes Green pod Yellow pod Parental genotypes GG × gg
State the gamete types produced by each parent. Label them clearly, and encircle them. Only write the different types of gametes produced (e.g. for green pod do not write two encircled Gs)	This explains why the gametes only possess one of the two parental alleles. Encircling them reinforces the idea that they are separate and writing each type once only shows the **different** gametes present	Gametes Ⓖ ⓖ
Use a type of chequerboard or matrix, called a **Punnett square**, to show the results of the random crossing of the gametes. Only label which parents are male and which are female if instructed to do so or if it is a sex-linked cross involving the use of X and Y (see 16.2f)	This method is less prone to error than drawing lines between the gametes and the offspring. Labelling the sexes is only important when considering sex-linked crosses	GAMETES Ⓖ Ⓖ GAMETES ⓖ Gg Gg ⓖ Gg Gg
State the phenotypes of each different genotype and indicate the numbers of each type. Always put the higher case (dominant) letter first when writing out the genotype	Always putting the dominant feature first can reduce errors in cases where it is not possible to avoid using symbols with the upper and lower case letters of the same shape	All offspring are plants producing green pods (Gg)

Summary test 16.2b

When representing a genetic cross, there is a standard form of shorthand that is normally used. Where the allele for one characteristic is dominant to the allele for another, it is normal to use an **(1)** case letter to represent the dominant allele and a **(2)** case letter to represent the **(3)** allele. Where gametes are involved, the letter for the allele should be written and then **(4)**. To show all the possible outcomes of different gametes fusing, a type of chequerboard called a **(5)** is used. The inheritance of a single gene is known as **(6)** inheritance. One example is a cross between pea plants with yellow seed pods and ones with green pods. The first generation of plants produced is called the **(7)** generation and all have pods coloured **(8)**. When these offspring are crossed with one another the next generation, called the **(9)** generation, has a ratio of three **(10)** coloured pods to one **(11)** pod.

These pages help you to:

- explain the test cross (16.2.1)
- interpret and construct genetic diagrams to explain and predict the results of monohybrid test crosses (16.2.4)

You will also:

- understand why actual results of genetic crosses are rarely the same as predicted crosses

In a monohybrid cross, an organism whose phenotype displays a dominant characteristic may possess either of two **genotypes**:

- two dominant **alleles** (homozygous dominant)
- one dominant allele and one recessive allele (heterozygous).

A **test cross** is a cross to determine the genotype of a individual. It is carried out between an individual with the unknown genotype and an individual having the homozygous recessive genotype.

Carrying out a test cross

To look at how we carry out a test cross, let us use the example in 16.2b of pea plants with different seed pod colours. Suppose we have a plant from the F_2 generation that produces green seed pods. This plant has two possible genotypes with respect to pod colour:

- homozygous dominant (GG)
- heterozygous (Gg).

To discover its actual genotype, we cross the plant with an organism displaying the recessive **phenotype** of the same characteristic, i.e. in our case with a pea plant producing yellow pods (gg). Figure 1 shows that:

- if the organism is homozygous dominant (GG), then all the offspring will be heterozygous (Gg) and will show the dominant feature (green pods)

- if the organism is heterozygous (Gg), then it would be expected that half the offspring would be heterozygous (Gg) and show the dominant feature (green pods) while half the offspring would be homozygous recessive (gg) and show the recessive feature (yellow pods). There is a 1:1 of green to yellow pods.

The test cross is so called because it 'tests' the unknown genotype of a dominant characteristic. Is the test cross foolproof? The answer is 'yes and no':

- **Yes**, if any single offspring displays the recessive characteristic (in our case yellow pods). This plant is homozygous recessive and must have obtained one recessive allele from each parent. Our unknown parental genotype must therefore have a recessive allele and be heterozygous (in our case Gg). Assuming no mutations, we can say with absolute certainty that our unknown genotype is heterozygous (Gg).

- **No**, if all the offspring display the dominant characteristic (in our case green pods). While the likelihood is that the unknown genotype is homozygous dominant (in our case GG), we cannot completely discount the possibility that it could be heterozygous (Gg). This is because the gametes produced from our parent of unknown genotype contain alleles of two types, either dominant (G) or recessive (g). It is a matter of chance which of these gametes fuses with those from our recessive parent – all these gametes have a recessive allele (g). It is just possible that in every case it is the gametes with the dominant allele that fuse and so all the offspring show the dominant characteristic. Provided the sample

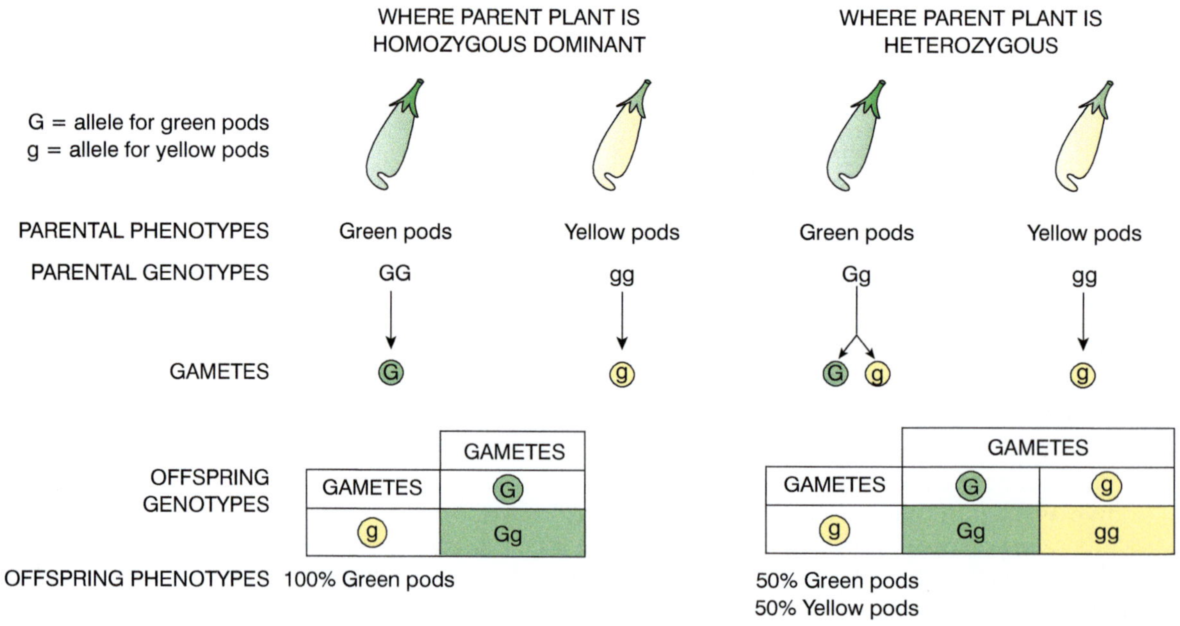

G = allele for green pods
g = allele for yellow pods

	WHERE PARENT PLANT IS HOMOZYGOUS DOMINANT		WHERE PARENT PLANT IS HETEROZYGOUS	
PARENTAL PHENOTYPES	Green pods	Yellow pods	Green pods	Yellow pods
PARENTAL GENOTYPES	GG	gg	Gg	gg
GAMETES	G	g	G g	g

OFFSPRING GENOTYPES

GAMETES	GAMETES	
		G
g		Gg

OFFSPRING PHENOTYPES 100% Green pods

GAMETES	GAMETES	
	G	g
g	Gg	gg

50% Green pods
50% Yellow pods

Figure 1 *The test cross*

of offspring is large enough, however, we can be reasonably sure that the unknown genotype is homozygous dominant.

Why actual results of genetic crosses are rarely the same as the predicted results

If you look at Table 1, you will see the results that Gregor Mendel actually obtained in his experiments. Our knowledge of genetics tells us that for each cross we would expect that, in the F_2 generation, there would be three offspring showing the dominant feature to every one showing the recessive feature. However, in no case did Mendel obtain an exact 3:1 ratio. The same is true of almost any genetic cross. These differences are due to statistical error.

Imagine tossing a coin 20 times. In theory you would expect it to come down heads on 10 occasions and tails on 10 occasions. In practice it rarely does – try it. This is because each toss of the coin is an independent event that is not affected by what went before. If the coin has come down heads 9 times out of 19 tosses, there is still a 50% chance it will come down tails, rather than the head needed to complete the 1:1 ratio. The coin does not 'know' it is expected to come down heads.

The same is true of gametes. It is chance that determines which ones fuse with which. In our cross between the heterozygote (Gg) and the homozygous recessive (gg), all the gametes of the homozygous parent are recessive (g), whereas the heterozygote parent produces gametes

of which half are dominant (G) and half are recessive (g). If it is the dominant gamete that meets the recessive one, plants with green pods are produced (Gg). If it is the recessive gamete, the plants have yellow pods. The larger the sample, the more likely are the actual results to match the theoretical ones. It is therefore important to use large numbers of organisms in genetic crosses if representative results are to be obtained. It is no coincidence that the two ratios nearest to the theoretical value of 3:1 in Mendel's experiments were those with the largest sample size, whereas the ratio furthest from the theoretical value had the smallest sample size (Table 1).

Summary test 16.2c

Suppose the appearance, otherwise known as the **(1)**, of an organism displays a feature that is determined by a dominant allele. This organism may have a genotype that is either **(2)** or **(3)** for this feature. To determine which genotype it has we can carry out a **(4)** cross. To do this we cross our organism of unknown genotype with an organism of the same species that has a genotype that is **(5)** for the feature. The gametes of this organism will all contain recessive **(6)** for this feature. If some of the resultant offspring from the cross show the recessive feature, then the unknown genotype must have been **(7)**. If, however, all the resultant offspring show only the dominant feature, then it is most probable that the unknown genotype was **(8)**. This becomes increasingly probable when the number of offspring is **(9)**.

Table 1 *Actual results of Mendel's crosses in pea plants*

Characteristic	F_2 results		Ratio
Cotyledon colour	6020 yellow	2001 green	3.01:1
Seed type	5474 smooth	1850 wrinkled	2.96:1
Pod type	882 inflated	299 constricted	2.95:1
Flower position	651 axial	207 terminal	3.14:1
Petal colour	705 purple	224 white	3.15:1
Stem height	787 long	277 short	2.84:1
Pod colour	428 green	152 yellow	2.82:1

These pages help you to:

- interpret and construct genetic diagrams, including Punnett squares, to explain and predict the results of monohybrid crosses that involve
  - codominance
  - multiple alleles (16.2.2)

You will also:

- understand how to give symbols for codominant alleles in a genetic diagram

We have looked at the straightforward situations in which there were two possible **alleles** at each **locus** on a chromosome, one of which was dominant and the other recessive. We shall now look at situations in which both alleles contribute to the phenotype, called **codominance**, and where there are more than two alleles, **multiple alleles**, of which only two may be present at the loci of the **homologous chromosomes** of an individual.

Codominance

Codominance occurs when both alleles of a gene are expressed in the phenotype. One example occurs in the snapdragon plant, in which one allele codes for an enzyme that catalyses the formation of a red pigment (anthocyanin) in flowers. The other allele codes for an altered enzyme that lacks this catalytic activity and so does not produce the pigment. In plants that are homozygous for this second allele, no pigment is made and the flowers are white. Heterozygous plants, with their single allele for the functional enzyme, produce just enough red pigment to produce pink flowers. If a snapdragon with red flowers is crossed with one with white flowers, the resulting seeds give rise to plants with pink flowers.

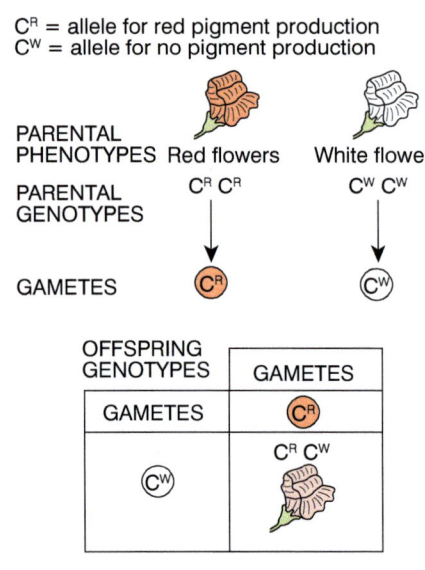

C^R = allele for red pigment production
C^W = allele for no pigment production

Figure 1 *Cross between snapdragons with red flowers and ones with white flowers*

Note that we cannot use upper and lower case letters for the alleles, as this would imply that one (the upper case) was dominant to the other (the lower case). We therefore use different letters – R for red and W for white – and use these as superscripts on a letter that represents the gene, in this case C for colour. Hence the allele for red pigment is written as C^R and the allele for no pigment as C^W. Figure 1 shows a cross between a red and a white snapdragon and Figure 2 a cross between the pink-flowered plants that result.

Figure 1 shows that codominance produces a novel (new) phenotype when pure breeding (homozygous) parents are crossed. The phenotype of the offspring does not resemble either parent. This means that when the offspring are crossed, there will not be the normal F_2 phenotypic ratio of 3:1. The phenotypic ratio of 1:2:1 is also the genotypic ratio. Some examples of codominance produce a phenotype that has both of the homozygous parental phenotypes showing. For example, the AB blood group in the ABO blood grouping system discussed in the multiple alleles section is a result of an allele for blood group A and an allele for blood group B. There is no blend (mix) as in the snapdragon example.

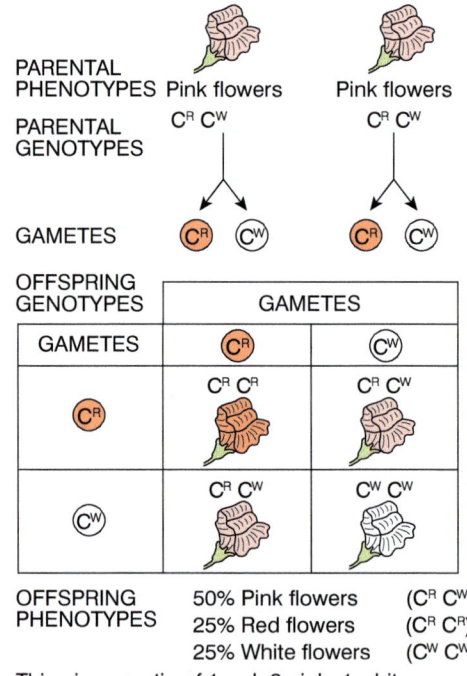

This gives a ratio of 1 red: 2 pink: 1 white

Figure 2 *Cross between two snapdragons with pink flowers*

Multiple alleles

Sometimes a gene has more than two alleles, i.e. it has **multiple alleles**. The inheritance of the human

ABO blood groups is an example. There are three alleles associated with the *ABO* gene (I), which lead to the production of different **antigens** on the surface membrane of red blood cells:

- **allele I^A** leads to the production of antigen A
- **allele I^B** leads to the production of antigen B
- **allele I^o** does not lead to the production of any antigens.

Although there are three alleles, only two can be present in an individual at any one time, as there are only two homologous chromosomes and therefore only two gene loci. The alleles I^A and I^B are codominant, whereas the allele I^o is recessive to both. The possible **genotypes** for the four blood groups are shown in Table 1. There are obviously many different possible crosses between different blood groups, but two of the most interesting are:

- A cross between an individual of blood group O and one of blood group AB, rather than producing individuals of either of the parental blood groups, produces only individuals of the other two groups, A and B. Figure 3 shows the predicted ratio of phenotypes in the offspring, which is 1:1 (blood group A to blood group B).
- When certain individuals of blood group A are crossed with certain individuals of blood group B, their children may have any of the four blood groups. Figure 4 shows that there is a predicted ratio of 1:1:1:1 in the offspring.

Table 1 Possible genotypes of blood groups in the ABO system

Blood group	Possible genotype
A	$I^A I^A$ or $I^A I^o$
B	$I^B I^B$ or $I^B I^o$
AB	$I^A I^B$
O	$I^o I^o$

Coat colour in rabbits is complex. There are five main genes involved and a variety of coat colours has been produced in rabbit breeding. Multiple alleles at the C-locus demonstrate a hierarchy of dominance and also examples of codominance. Table 2 shows alleles of the C-locus and their symbols. Table 3 shows the different phenotypes obtained with different genotypes.

In Table 3, we can see that the agouti coat allele is dominant to all other alleles. The chinchilla allele is codominant to the Himalayan and albino alleles as a mixed colour phenotype, light grey, has been obtained in the heterozygous condition. The Himalayan allele is dominant to the albino coat allele.

Table 2 The C-locus alleles in rabbit coat colour

Alleles	Allele symbol
Agouti coat	C^A
Chinchilla coat	C^{Ch}
Himalayan coat	C^H
Albino coat	C^a

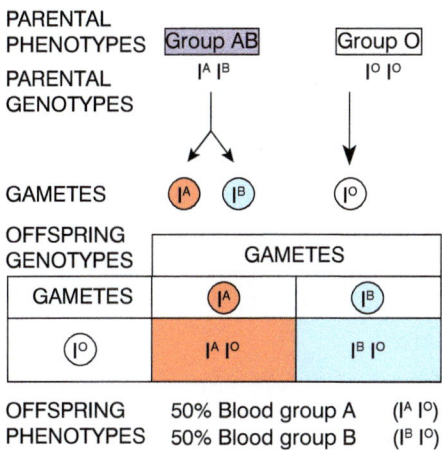

Figure 3 Cross between an individual of blood group AB and one of blood group O

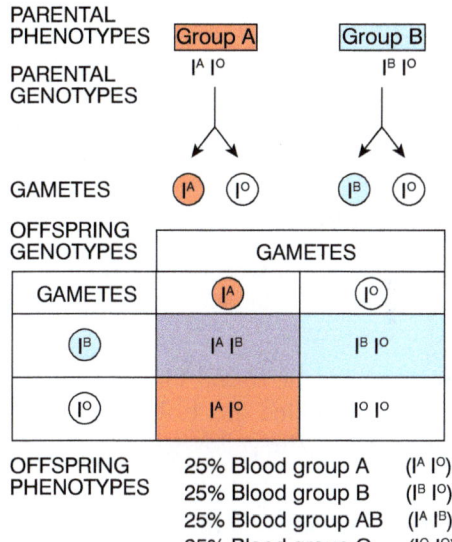

Figure 4 Cross between heterozygous individuals of blood group A and blood group B

Table 3 Rabbit coat colour phenotypes obtained with different genotypes

Genotypes	Phenotypes
$C^A C^A$ / $C^A C^{Ch}$ / $C^A C^H$ / $C^A C^a$	Agouti coat
$C^{Ch} C^{Ch}$	Chinchilla coat
$C^{Ch} C^H$ / $C^{Ch} C^a$	Light grey coat
$C^H C^H$ / $C^H C^a$	Himalayan coat
$C^a C^a$	Albino coat

Summary test 16.2d

Codominance is shown in a **(1)** genotype. This genotype produces a **(2)** that is different to that of both parents. If pure breeding parents are crossed **(3)**% of the offspring will have the new feature. If these offspring are crossed then the ratio that will be obtained is **(4)** and there will be **(5)**% codominant offspring. In **(6)** alleles, a gene has more than two alleles. In the ABO blood system the I^o allele is **(7)** to the I^A and I^B alleles.

These pages help you to:

- interpret and construct genetic diagrams, including Punnett squares, to explain and predict the results of dihybrid crosses that involve dominance and recessiveness (16.2.2)
- interpret and construct genetic diagrams to explain and predict the results of dihybrid test crosses (16.2.4)

You will also:

- become familiar with one of Gregor Mendel's experiments

In 16.2b we saw how a single characteristic controlled by one gene is passed on from one generation to the next (monohybrid inheritance). In practice, many thousands of characteristics are inherited together. In this topic we shall look at how two characteristics, determined by two **genes** located on non-homologous chromosomes, are inherited. This is referred to as **dihybrid inheritance**.

An example of dihybrid inheritance

In one of his experiments, Gregor Mendel investigated the inheritance of two characteristics of a pea plant at the same time. These were:

- **seed shape** – where the round shape allele, R, is dominant to the wrinkled shape allele
- **seed colour** – where the yellow-coloured seed allele, Y, is dominant to the green-coloured allele, y.

He carried out a cross between the following two pure breeding types of plants:

- one producing round-shaped, yellow-coloured seeds (both dominant features)
- one producing wrinkled-shaped, green-coloured seeds (both recessive features).

Figure 1 shows a cross he carried out between pure breeding plants producing round-shaped, yellow-coloured

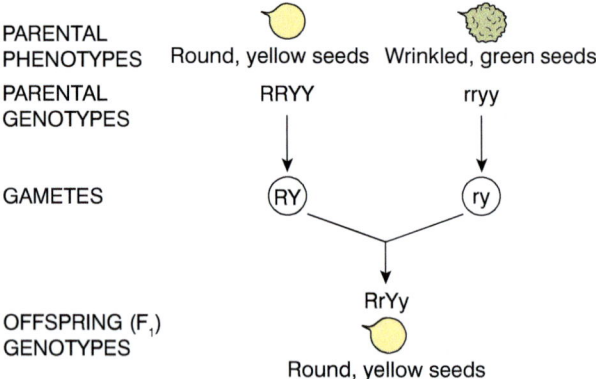

Figure 1 *Genetic explanation of Mendel's cross between a pure breeding plant for round, yellow seeds and a pure breeding one for wrinkled, green seeds*

> **Remember**
>
> Here yellow is a dominant allele. The two letters need to be clearly identified as upper (Y) or lower (y) case, for example the lower case y could have a curly tail.

seeds (both dominant features) and pure breeding plants producing wrinkled-shaped, green-coloured seeds (both recessive features).

In the F_1 generation Mendel obtained plants all of which produced round-shaped, yellow-coloured seeds, i.e. both dominant features (Figure 1). He then raised the plants from these seeds and crossed them with one another to obtain the F_2 results shown in Table 1. Figure 2 summarises this cross.

Table 1 *Results obtained by Gregor Mendel when he crossed F_1 generation plants (round shaped, yellow coloured seeds) with each other*

Appearance of seeds	Condition	Number produced
Round Yellow	Dominant Dominant	315
Round Green	Dominant Recessive	108
Wrinkled Yellow	Recessive Dominant	101
Wrinkled Green	Recessive Recessive	32

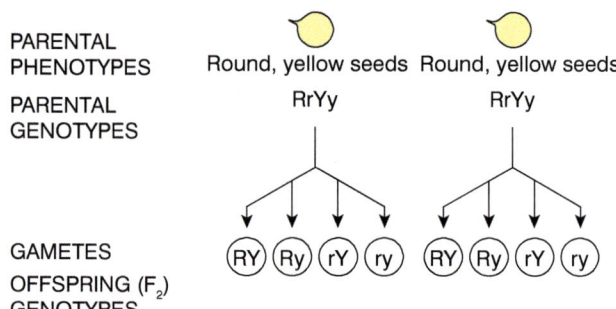

	GAMETES			
GAMETES	RY	Ry	rY	ry
RY	RRYY	RRYy	RrYY	RrYy
Ry	RRYy	RRyy	RrYy	Rryy
rY	RrYY	RrYy	rrYY	rrYy
ry	RrYy	Rryy	rrYy	rryy

OFFSPRING (F_2) PHENOTYPES
- 9 Round, yellow seeds
- 3 Round, green seeds
- 3 Wrinkled, yellow seeds
- 1 Wrinkled, green seed

Figure 2 *Genetic explanation of Mendel's intercross between plants of the F_1 generation*

Remember

Be prepared to give predicted results in terms of ratios, percentages and decimal proportions as well as in fractions. e.g. 1/2 and 1/2 is 1:1 or 50% and 50% or 0.5 and 0.5.

From Figure 2 it can be seen that the plants of the F_1 generation produce four types of gamete (RY, Ry, rY, ry). This is because the gene for seed colour and the gene for seed shape are on non-homologous chromosomes. As the homologous pairs arrange themselves randomly on the equator during meiosis (16.1c), any one of the two **alleles** of the gene for seed colour (Y and y) can combine with any one of the alleles for seed shape (R and r). Fertilisation is also random, so that any of the four types of gamete (with respect to seed colour and seed shape) of one plant can combine with any of the four types from the other plant.

The theoretical ratio produced of 9:3:3:1 is close enough, allowing for statistical error (16.2c), to Mendel's observed results of 315:108:101:32. Mendel's observations led him to formulate his **law of independent assortment** which, written in today's biological language states: **For genes that are on separate, non-homologous chromosomes, each member of a pair of alleles may combine randomly with either of another pair.**

Dihybrid test cross

It is possible to perform a dihybrid test cross (see 16.2c). Here the unknown genotype is crossed with an individual with a double homozygous recessive genotype.

In our example, a plant that produces round, yellow seeds (i.e. has both dominant alleles) has four possible genotypes:

RRYY; RrYY; RRYy; RrYy.

To find out the actual genotype of this plant, it can be crossed with one displaying the recessive characteristic for both seed colour and seed shape, i.e. a plant producing wrinkled, green seeds. This plant has only one possible genotype – rryy – and therefore all its gametes are ry with

respect to these features. The outcome of each of the four crosses is shown in Table 2. The unknown genotypes may be identified from examining the seeds produced by the offspring of each cross. The presence of even one plant producing wrinkled green seeds (rryy) indicates that the unknown genotype can only have been RrYy. Note that a ratio of 1:1:1:1 is obtained for this double heterozygote. To identify the other possible genotypes it is necessary to count a large sample of seeds – say in excess of 100 – and check the ratios of each type against the table of theoretical ratios. There is a statistical test called the **chi-squared (χ^2) test** that allows us to test the statistical validity of our results. Its use is explained in 16.2h.

Table 2 Dihybrid test cross

Possible genotypes of plant producing round, yellow seeds	Possible gametes	Genotypes of offspring crossed with plant producing wrinkled, green seeds (gamete = (ry))	Phenotype (type of seeds produced)
RRYY	(RY)	RrYy	All round and yellow
RrYY	(RY)	RrYy	$\frac{1}{2}$ round and yellow
	(rY)	rrYy	$\frac{1}{2}$ wrinkled and yellow
RRYy	(RY)	RrYy	$\frac{1}{2}$ round and yellow
	(Ry)	Rryy	$\frac{1}{2}$ round and green
RrYy	(RY)	RrYy	$\frac{1}{4}$ round and yellow
	(Ry)	Rryy	$\frac{1}{4}$ round and green
	(rY)	rrYy	$\frac{1}{4}$ wrinkled and yellow
	(ry)	rryy	$\frac{1}{4}$ wrinkled and green

Summary test 16.2e

The inheritance of two characteristics, determined by two genes located on non-homologous chromosomes is referred to as **(1)** inheritance. Mendel investigated two characteristics, seed shape, where the round shape allele is **(2)** to the wrinkled shape allele which is **(3)**, and seed colour where the green allele is **(4)** and the yellow allele is **(5)**. In a cross between a plant producing round-shaped, yellow-coloured seeds (genotype RRYY) and one producing wrinkled-shaped, green-coloured seeds (rryy), all the offspring produced seeds that were **(6)** in shape and **(7)** in colour. Each plant could produce four types of gametes depending on the **(8)** of the two genes that they possess. These four types are represented as **(9)**, **(10)**, **(11)** and **(12)**. With random fusion of gametes, the offspring produce seeds, of which nine in every 16 are **(13)** in shape and **(14)** in colour, and only one in every 16 is **(15)** in shape and **(16)** in colour. If a plant that is heterozygous for seed shape and homozygous dominant for seed colour is crossed with a plant producing green, wrinkled seeds, the offspring produce either **(17)**-shaped and **(18)**-coloured seeds or **(19)**-shaped and **(20)**-coloured seeds.

These pages help you to:

- understand and define the term linkage (16.2.1)
- interpret and construct genetic diagrams, including Punnett squares, to explain and predict the results of
  - monohybrid crosses that involve sex linkage (16.2.2)
  - dihybrid crosses that involve autosomal linkage (16.2.3)

You will also:

- understand the role of sex chromosomes in the determination of sex
- understand what is meant by a pedigree chart

In humans, females (XX) are the **homogametic sex** as all gametes produced contain an X chromosome. Males (XY) are the **heterogametic sex** as the gametes produced contain either an X chromosome (50%) or the Y chromosome (50%). X and Y are called the sex chromosomes. All other chromosomes are termed **autosomes**.

Figure 2 shows sex determination in humans.

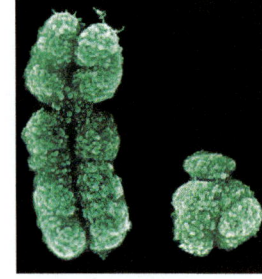

Figure 1 *Scanning electron micrograph of human X and Y chromosomes. There are some organisms where the sex chromosomes are known by different letters and where the same two sex chromosomes are for the male*

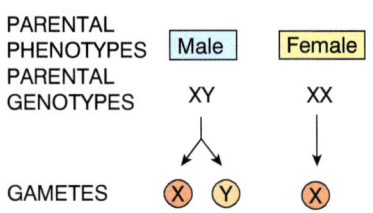

PARENTAL PHENOTYPES   Male   Female
PARENTAL GENOTYPES   XY   XX

GAMETES   X   Y   X

OFFSPRING GENOTYPES

	GAMETES	
GAMETES	X	Y
X	XX	XY

OFFSPRING PHENOTYPES
50% Male
50% Female

Figure 2 *Sex determination in humans*

Sex linkage

Any gene that is carried on either the X or Y chromosome is said to be **sex-linked**. Because of its small size (Figure 1), very few genes are carried on the Y chromosome in humans. Those that are, such as the *SRY* gene (sex-determining region on the Y chromosome), are only ever found in males. Gametes containing the Y chromosome will not have a copy of the genes located on the X chromosome, so in males (XY), a recessive allele located on a sex chromosome will show its effect.

One example of sex linkage in humans is a condition called **haemophilia**.

This is caused by a mutation in a recessive allele of the *F8* gene, located on the X chromosome (X-linked gene). The normal dominant allele codes for a blood clotting protein, **factor VIII**, but expression of the recessive allele produces a non-functioning protein (see 16.2i), so blood does not clot. Figure 3 shows the inheritance of haemophilia. H and h are shown linked to the X chromosome, with no allele on the Y chromosome.

Males obtain the Y chromosome from their father, so haemophilia is inherited from their mother. If the mothers are symptomless and phenotypically normal, they must be heterozygous $X^H X^h$. In Figure 3, a summary of the proportions of normal compared to haemophiliac would be 75% to 25%, or 3:1 (or 0.75 and 0.25). This ratio of 3:1 is the same as the F_2 for a monohybrid cross, but sex-linkage is indicated because there are no haemophiliac females.

H = allele for production of factor VIII (normal blood clotting)
h = allele for non-production of factor VIII (absence of blood clotting)

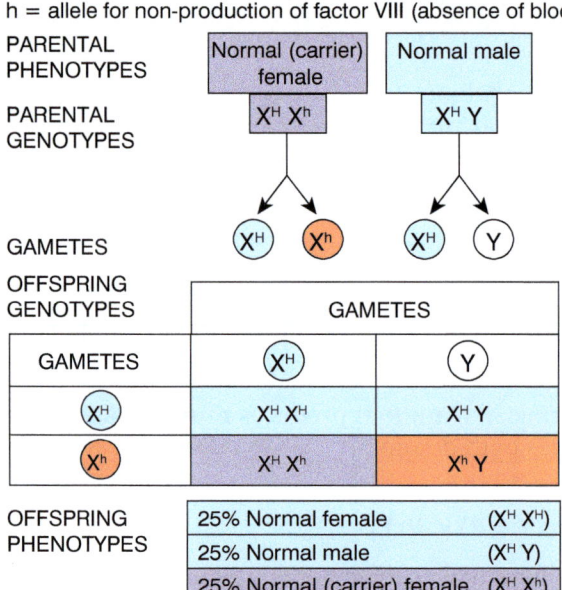

OFFSPRING PHENOTYPES

25% Normal female	($X^H X^H$)
25% Normal male	($X^H Y$)
25% Normal (carrier) female	($X^H X^h$)
25% Haemophiliac male	($X^h Y$)

Figure 3 *Inheritance of haemophilia from a carrier female*

Males pass the Y chromosome to their sons, so they pass the allele to their daughters, via the X chromosome. The daughters will be carriers of the disease if they have inherited a normal X chromosome (Figure 4). If their mother is a carrier ($X^H X^h$), then there is a 50% chance that the daughters will have the condition. In the very rare event that their mother also has the condition ($X^h X^h$), then all children will have haemophilia. In Figure 4, the outcome of the cross seems the same as a standard example of monohybrid inheritance, with the normal allele being dominant and all individuals being healthy. To confirm sex-linked inheritance, the results of a reciprocal cross are needed. A female with haemophilia (rare) and a normal male, would result in a very different ratio in the first generation, as all the female offspring would be normal (carriers) but all the male offspring would have haemophilia.

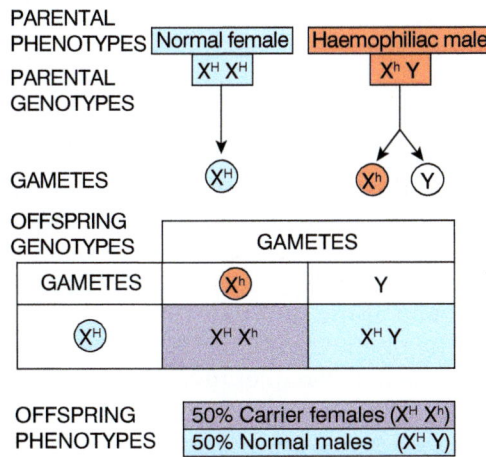

Figure 4 *Inheritance of the haemophiliac allele from a haemophiliac male*

Pedigree charts

One useful way to trace the inheritance of sex-linked characteristics is to use a pedigree chart. In these a male is represented by a square and a female by a circle. Shading indicates the phenotypic presence of a characteristic such as haemophilia. Half-shading represents a normal phenotype who carries the mutant allele. A sex-linked condition is suspected on pedigree charts where only males (or far more males) are seen to be affected over the generations, and where the fathers of all the affected males are healthy, without the condition.

Autosomal linkage

Any two genes that occur on the same chromosome are said to be **linked**. All the genes on a single chromosome form a **linkage group**. If genes are linked, there will be no random orientation of homologous pairs at meiosis I (16.2e). Figure 5 shows a genetic cross where there is no variation in the F_2, as all offspring resemble the parental phenotypes. We can deduce that the genes are so close together that they are always inherited together and no crossing over occurs.

If the genes are far enough apart, it is also possible to produce Ab and aB gametes in the F_1 from crossing over (recombination, see Figure 6). There will still be more AB and ab gametes produced by an individual, because far fewer cells will have a cross over event to produce all four gamete types. A Punnett square of the F_2 offspring will produce the same variety of genotypes as in a normal dihybrid cross but there will be more parental types than recombinant types and a ratio of 9:3:3:1 will not be obtained. The further apart the genes on the chromosome, the greater the chance of crossing over and the greater the proportion of recombinant types. Performing test crosses where linked genes are involved will also affect the ratios produced.

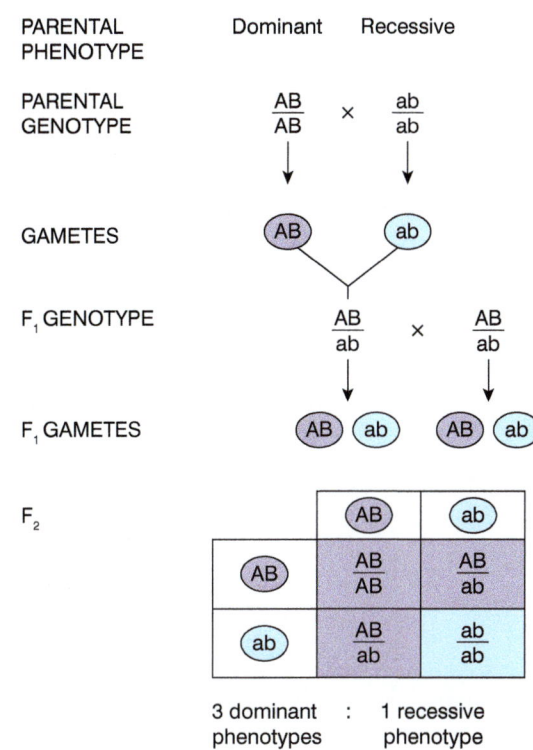

Figure 5 *Genetic cross with linked genes and no crossing over*

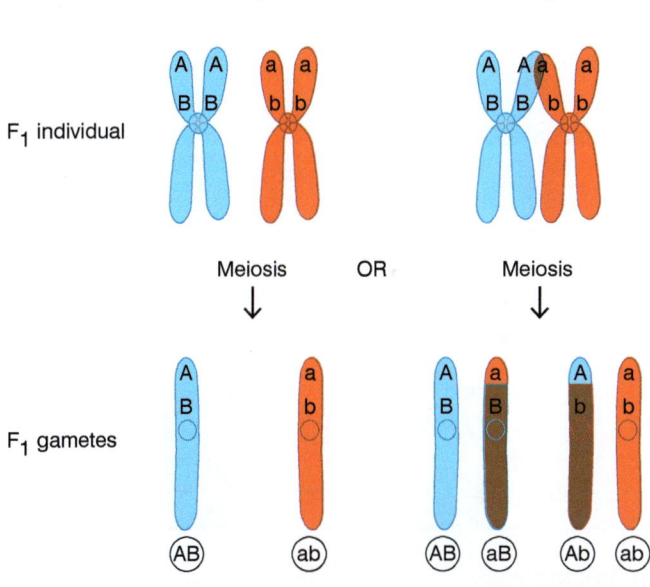

Figure 6 *Gamete formation in an individual involving two linked genes, with no crossing over (higher proportion) and some crossing over (smaller proportion).*

Summary test 16.2f

In a sex-linked disease, the faulty allele is located on the **(1)**. Males with the disease cannot pass this to their **(2)**, because they pass on their **(3)** chromosome. Females who are **(4)** have one faulty allele and are phenotypically normal. Genes located on the same chromosome are known as **(5)** genes. If they are very close, there will be no **(6)** at meiosis; in the F_2, only **(7)** offspring types occur and no **(8)** types. Here, a ratio of **(9)** is seen.

353

These pages help you to:

- interpret and construct genetic diagrams, including Punnett squares, to explain and predict the results of dihybrid crosses that involve epistasis (16.2.3)

You will also:

- read about complementary gene interaction

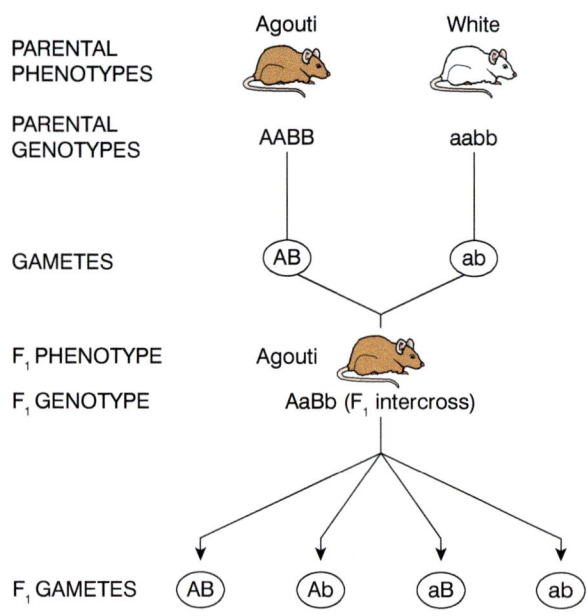

		GAMETES		
GAMETES	AB	Ab	aB	ab
AB	AABB	AABb	AaBB	AaBb
Ab	AABb	AAbb	AaBb	Aabb
aB	AaBB	AaBb	aaBB	aaBb
ab	AaBb	Aabb	aaBb	aabb

F₂ PHENOTYPES

9 Agouti   4 Albino   3 Black

Figure 1 *Epistatic gene interaction in mice*

Remember

Analysing F₂ ratios can help to work out gene interactions:

9:3:3:1 – no interaction.
9:4:3 – recessive epistasis
12:3:1 – dominant epistasis
9:7 – complementary gene action.

Inheritance involving a single gene with codominant alleles gives a 1:2:1 ratio in the F_2, compared to the standard 3:1 Mendelian ratio. Similarly, there are deviations from the 9:3:3:1 ratio of dihybrid crosses when autosomal linkage is involved. For example, when linkage is complete, a 3:1 ratio is obtained. Sex linkage gives different ratios in F_1 and F_2 ratios when a reciprocal cross is performed, and as the genes are on the X chromosome, the ratios of the phenotypes differ in males and females. Let us consider some examples involving gene interaction.

Epistasis

Epistasis describes a gene interaction where one gene interferes with the expression of another gene situated at a different locus. The epistatic gene suppresses or masks the action of the other gene, so that the normal phenotypic effects of that gene are not observed.

Coat colour in mice

An example of epistasis occurs in mice, where several genes determine coat colour. The brown to black pigment melanin is produced in many animals, including mice, as a basis for coat or skin colouring. Mice have over 50 genes involved in coat colour, so although melanin is produced, there is a huge variety in coat colour and pattern. Let us look at an example of epistasis involving two genes and mice that have agouti, black or white coat colour (Figure 2).

Gene A has two alleles, A and a. Individuals that are heterozygous or homozygous for the A allele (Aa, AA) have an agouti coat (black hairs with yellow banding, resulting in overall agouti). Individuals that are homozgous recessive (aa) have no yellow banding and appear black.

Gene B is an epistatic gene. If an individual is homozygous recessive for this gene, bb, then all mice will lack pigment and will be albino, with a white coat colour.

If an agouti mouse with the genotype AABB is crossed with an albino mouse with the genotype aabb, then the offspring are all agouti. If individuals from the F_1 generation are crossed to produce the F_2 generation the following ratio is produced:

- 9 agouti mice
- 4 albino mice
- 3 black mice.

The crosses are shown in Figure 1.

The explanation of the results is that the expression of gene A (distribution of melanin) is affected by the expression of gene B (production of melanin). If gene B is in the homozygous recessive state (bb), then no melanin is produced and the coat is white. In the absence

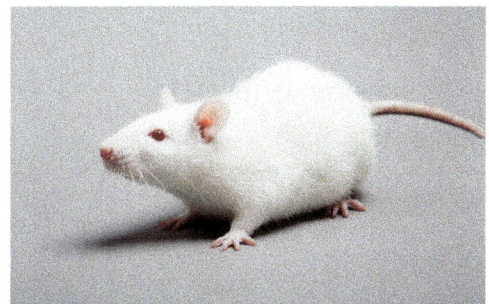

Figure 2 Agouti, black and albino mice

of melanin, gene A cannot be expressed. It makes no difference which alleles are present (AA, Aa or aa); if there is no pigment, then the hairs cannot be coloured or banded. Where a dominant allele B is present, melanin is produced. If this allele is present with a dominant allele A, then banding occurs and an agouti coat results. Where allele B is present with two recessive alleles a, the hairs, and hence the coat, are uniform black.

This is an example of recessive epistasis – in bb homozygotes the effect of the A gene is masked to produce the ratio of 9:4:3. If dominant epistasis was occurring, then the resulting F_2 would be 12 albino, 3 agouti and 1 black (that is, all genotypes with at least one B allele are albino).

Extension

Complementary gene interaction

There are other forms of gene interaction, such as when genes act in sequence by determining the enzymes in a biochemical pathway. An example occurs in maize (corn), *Zea mays*, where some varieties have purple seeds due to the presence of a pigment called anthocyanin in their seed coat. In the absence of the pigment, the seeds are white. The production of anthocyanin is controlled by two genes A and B.

If one pure breeding variety of white-seeded corn with the genotype AAbb is crossed with another pure breeding variety of white seeded corn with the genotype aaBB, all the offspring have purple seeds. A cross between two of the F_1 generation (AaBb) produces a ratio of 9 purple-seeded plants to 7 white-seeded plants.

Figure 3 shows the results of this F_1 intercross.

The production of anthocyanin involves a two-stage process that can be summarised as:

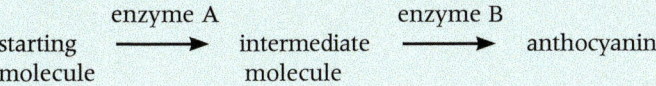

starting molecule $\xrightarrow{\text{enzyme A}}$ intermediate molecule $\xrightarrow{\text{enzyme B}}$ anthocyanin

The production of enzymes A and B is coded for by genes A and B, respectively. Dominant alleles of each gene code for a functional enzyme, whereas recessive alleles code for a non-functional enzyme. It follows that if the alleles of either gene are both recessive then that enzyme will be non-functional and the pathway cannot be completed. This affects the other gene in that, even if it is functional and produces its enzyme,

its effects cannot be expressed. This is because both enzymes need to function to make anthocyanin.

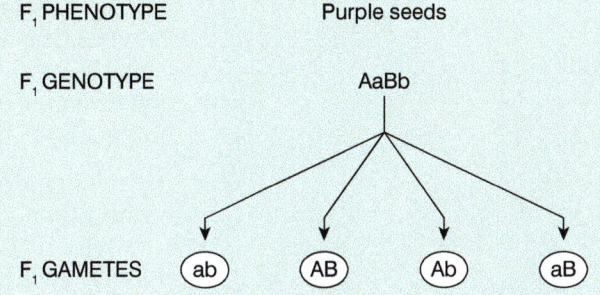

| F_1 PHENOTYPE | Purple seeds |
| F_1 GENOTYPE | AaBb |

F_1 GAMETES: ab   AB   Ab   aB

F_2 OFFSPRING

| | | GAMETES | | |
GAMETES	AB	Ab	aB	ab
AB	AABB	AABb	AaBB	AaBb
Ab	AABb	AAbb	AaBb	Aabb
aB	AaBB	AaBb	aaBB	aaBb
ab	AaBb	Aabb	aaBb	aabb

Figure 3 Results of the F_1 intercross

Summary test 16.2g

Using the example of epistatic gene interaction in mice in this topic, consider a cross between mouse X that is heterozygous for gene A (colour distribution) and homozygous recessive for gene B (melanin production) with mouse Y that is heterozygous for both genes. The colour of mouse X is **(1)**, whereas the colour of mouse Y is **(2)**. Of the eight genotypes produced from this cross the two genotypes that appear twice are **(3)** and **(4)**. The remaining four genotypes are **(5)**, **(6)**, **(7)** and **(8)**. The number of agouti mice in the F_2 generation is **(9)** and the number of albino mice is **(10)**.

These pages help you to:

- use the formula to perform the chi-squared test to test the significance of differences between observed and expected results (16.2.5)

You will also:

- be able to apply the principle of a null hypothesis to other situations

Figure 1 *The single characteristic of comb shape in domestic fowl is controlled by two unlinked genes*

If you toss a coin 100 times it would be reasonable to expect it to land heads on 50 occasions and tails on 50 occasions. In practice, it would be unusual if these exact results were obtained (try it if you like!). If it lands heads 55 times and tails only 45 times, does this mean that the coin is weighted or biased in some way, or is it purely a chance deviation from the expected result? How can we test which of these two options is correct?

What is the chi-squared test?

The chi-squared (χ²) test is used to test the null hypothesis. The null hypothesis is used to examine the results of scientific investigations and is based on the assumption that there will be no statistically significant difference between sets of observations, any difference being due to chance alone. In our coin tossing example, the null hypothesis would be that there is no significant difference between the number of times it lands heads and the number of times it lands tails. The chi-squared test is a means of testing whether any deviation between the observed and the expected numbers in an investigation is significant or not. It is a simple test that can be used only if certain criteria are met:

- the sample size must be relatively large, i.e. over 20
- the data must fall into discrete categories – i.e. there is discontinuous variation (17.1b)
- only raw counts and not percentages, rates, etc. can be used
- it is used to compare experimental results with theoretical ones, e.g. in genetic crosses with expected Mendelian ratios.

The formula is:

$$\text{chi squared} = \text{sum of } \frac{[\text{observed numbers (O)} - \text{expected numbers (E)}]^2}{\text{expected numbers (E)}}$$

summarised as:

$$\chi^2 = \sum \frac{[(O - E)]^2}{E}$$

The value obtained is then read off on a chi-squared distribution table (Table 1) to determine whether any deviation from the expected results is significant or not. To do this we need to know the number of **degrees of freedom**. This is simply the number of classes (categories) minus one, i.e. if a human can have blood group A or B or AB or O, there are 4 classes and 3 degrees of freedom in this case.

Table 1 *Part of a χ² table (based on Fisher)*

Degrees of freedom	Number of classes	χ²							
1	2	0.00	0.10	0.45	1.32	2.71	3.84	5.41	6.64
2	3	0.02	0.58	1.39	2.77	4.61	5.99	7.82	9.21
3	4	0.12	1.21	2.37	4.11	6.25	7.82	9.84	11.34
4	5	0.30	1.92	3.36	5.39	7.78	9.49	11.67	13.28
5	6	0.55	2.67	4.35	6.63	9.24	11.07	13.39	15.09
Probability that deviation is due to chance alone		0.99 (99%)	0.75 (75%)	0.50 (50%)	0.25 (25%)	0.10 (10%)	0.05 (5%)	0.02 (2%)	0.01 (1%)

← Accept null hypothesis
(Any difference is due to chance and not significant)

CRITICAL VALUE

Reject null hypothesis and therefore accept experimental hypothesis that 'any difference is not due to chance and is significant' →

of χ² at 0.05p level as this is the smallest value accepted by statisticians for results being due to chance

Calculating chi squared

Using our example of the coin tossed 100 times, we can calculate the chi-squared value:

Class (category)	Observed (O)	Expected (E)	O − E	(O − E)²	$\frac{(O − E)^2}{E}$
Heads	55	50	+5	25	0.5
Tails	45	50	−5	25	0.5
					Σ = 1.0

Therefore the value of $\chi^2 = 1.0$.

Using the chi-squared table

To find out whether this value of 1.0 is significant or not we use a chi-squared table, part of which is given in Table 1.

Instruction	Action
Decide on the number of **classes of results**	Two classes of results, 'heads' and 'tails'
Calculate the degrees of freedom	Number of classes minus one = 2 − 1 = 1
Read along the correct row on the χ^2 table for the calculated χ^2 value	Read along 1 degree of freedom row for calculated value of 1.0
Find the critical value for p = 0.05	The critical value at p = 0.05 is 3.84
Determine whether the calculated χ^2 value is lower or higher than the critical value at p = 0.05	The calculated value of 1.0 is lower than the critical value of 3.84 (1.0 lies between 0.45 (at p = 0.50) and 1.32 (at p = 0.25))
Lower than critical – accept the null hypothesis Higher than critical – reject the null hypothesis	Accept the null hypothesis
Make a statement about significance	• The deviation from the expected value of the numbers of heads and tails (from tossing the coin) is due to chance • The deviation is not significant

Had we obtained 60 heads and 40 tails, $X^2 = 4.0$, so this is greater than the critical value at 0.05. In which case the null hypothesis would be rejected and we would assume that the coin might be weighted or biased in some way.

Chi-squared test in genetics

The chi-squared test is especially useful in genetics. Let us consider a dihybrid F_1 cross for pea colour and shape (16.2e). Below are the expected F_2 phenotypic ratios and, in brackets, the actual numbers obtained for 320 plants:

9 round, yellow seeds (186)   3 wrinkled, yellow seeds (72)
3 round, green seeds (48)   1 wrinkled, green seeds (14)

The expected numbers for 320 plants would be 180:60:60:20. Could the observed variation be due to statistical chance or could some other factor be the reason for the differences? Our null hypothesis states that there is no significant difference between the observed and the expected results. Applying the chi-squared test:

Class (category)	Observed (O)	Expected (E)	O − E	(O − E)²	$\frac{(O − E)^2}{E}$
Round, yellow seeds	186	180	+6	36	0.2
Round, green seeds	48	60	−12	144	2.4
Wrinkled, yellow seeds	72	60	+12	144	2.4
Wrinkled, green seeds	14	20	−6	36	1.8
					Σ = 6.8

Here, there are four classes, so we look up our value of 6.8 on the row for 3 degrees of freedom in the chi-squared table (Table 1). Our value of 6.8 is lower than 7.82 at p = 0.05 (it falls between 0.1 and 0.05 probability). This tells us that any deviation from the expected can be accepted to be due to chance. Therefore we accept the null hypothesis and accept that the results are a 9:3:3:1 ratio.

In another experiment, domestic fowl with walnut combs were crossed with each other. The expected offspring ratio of comb types was 9 walnut, 3 rose, 3 pea and 1 single. In the event, the 160 offspring produced 103 walnut combs, 20 rose combs, 33 pea combs and 4 single combs (see Figure 1). The null hypothesis states that there is no significant difference between the observed and the expected results. Applying the chi-squared test:

Class (category)	Observed (O)	Expected (E)	O − E	(O − E)²	$\frac{(O − E)^2}{E}$
Walnut comb	103	90	+13	169	1.88
Rose comb	20	30	−10	100	3.33
Pea comb	33	30	+3	9	0.30
Single comb	4	10	−6	36	3.60
					Σ = 9.11

These results give us a chi-squared value of 9.11. There are four classes of results (walnut, rose, pea and single comb), so we must use the row for 3 degrees of freedom. The value of 9.11 lies between 7.82 and 9.84, which is equivalent to a probability of between 0.05 and 0.02 that the deviation is due to chance alone. This deviation is significant and we must reject the null hypothesis. Instead we must investigate what may be causing this deviation.

Summary test 16.2h

In genetic crosses, observed results may deviate from **(1)** results. We can use the chi-squared test to see if these deviations are **(2)**, that is, if they are due to **(3)** effects or not. After calculating the chi-squared value we use a look-up table. The number of **(4)** is the number of **(5)** minus one. The calculated value of chi-squared is checked against the **(6)** value at the p = **(7)** level. Any value **(8)** than this is said to be significant and so the **(9)** can be rejected.

These pages help you to:

- explain the relationship between genes, proteins and phenotype with respect to the:
  - *TYR* gene, tyrosinase and albinism
  - *HBB* gene, haemoglobin and sickle cell anaemia
  - *F8* gene, factor VIII and haemophilia (16.2.6)

You will also:

- read about the *F9* gene

A = allele for tyrosinase production

a = allele causing absence of tyrosinase

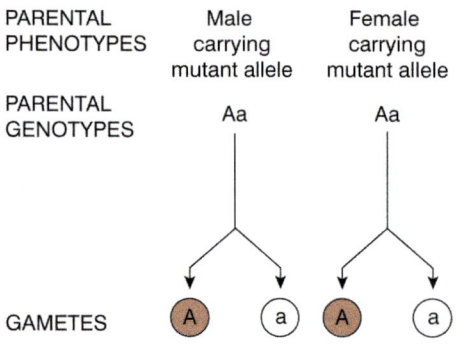

PARENTAL PHENOTYPES	Male carrying mutant allele	Female carrying mutant allele
PARENTAL GENOTYPES	Aa	Aa
GAMETES	A a	A a

	GAMETES	
GAMETES	A	a
A	AA	Aa
a	Aa	aa

75% individuals with melanin (AA, Aa)

25% individuals without melanin (aa) (have albinism)

Figure 1 *Cross between two parents that are carriers of the recessive allele (heterozygotes) for the TYR gene*

Extension

The *F9* gene

The *F9* gene is also located on the X chromosome. It codes for a coagulation factor protein involved in blood clotting. Mutations in the *F9* gene will cause the disease haemophilia B.

We have looked at different types of mutation and how they occur in 6.2d. Let us now consider the effects of recessive mutations on the phenotype in humans, by considering the examples albinism, **sickle cell anaemia** and haemophilia.

Albinism

Albinism is an autosomal recessive condition that is an example of the relationship between genes, enzymes and phenotype. The *TYR* gene codes for the enzyme tyrosinase, which catalyses the hydroxylation of the amino acid tyrosine to form a chemical known as DOPA. It also then catalyses the oxidation of DOPA to form dopaquinone, from which the dark pigment melanin is synthesised (in specialised cells known as melanocytes). Individuals that produce melanin in this way have a phenotype that includes coloured irises of the eyes, as well as hair and skin that are varying degrees of brown and black.

A number of different mutations of the *TYR* gene, located on chromosome 11, have been identified. Most of these result in the production of a non-functioning enzyme. In the absence of the enzyme no melanin is produced and the phenotype is pale skin, white hair and eyes that appear pink because the red retina is visible through the almost transparent iris. An individual with albinism is homozygous recessive and has inherited a recessive allele from both parents. This may be either when the two parents are heterozygous for the condition, or one is heterozygous and the other has albinism (is homozygous recessive). Figure 1 shows how an albino results from a cross between parents who are each heterozygous for the condition.

Haemophilia

There are a number of causes of haemophilia. Haemophilia A is a sex-linked recessive disorder caused by a mutation in the *F8* gene located on the X chromosome. The normal allele codes for a protein that has a role in blood clotting known as coagulation factor VIII, or factor VIII. The protein is synthesised in liver cells and is released in an inactive form into the circulation. Blood vessel injury triggers a complex sequence of events known as a coagulation cascade. This involves blood platelets, plasma proteins and coagulation factor proteins such as factor VIII. A lack of factor VIII prevents the activation of the enzyme thrombin, which catalyses the formation of the insoluble protein fibrin, a component of the blood clot. As this is a sex-linked disease, mostly males are affected.

There have been many different mutations reported in the *F8* gene that can cause haemophilia A. The most common (approximately 90%) are base substitution mutations. Depending on the substitution, these mutations will result in a change in a single amino acid (missense mutations), or if the change in the mRNA codon is to a STOP codon, a shortened protein (nonsense mutation). The range of severity of disease varies with different mutations. For example, a protein may be produced that has some function if the amino acid change does not cause a greatly altered tertiary structure. In these cases, the disease will be less severe. Severe haemophilia has been associated with shortened proteins (from nonsense mutations) that may not be folded or released from the cell into the circulation. Mutations associated with insertions or deletions (see 6.2d) result in severe haemophilia.

The blood clotting time for individuals with haemophilia is greatly increased, and so abnormal bleeding occurs after events like injury, dental treatment or surgery. With the more severe forms, there can be slow and continued internal bleeding, especially in the joints or muscles. The disease can be life-threatening, although it is now controlled by treatment, for example, with factor VIII produced using recombinant gene technology. This means that people with haemophilia can lead near-normal lives.

Sickle cell anaemia

Sickle cell anaemia, an autosomal disorder, shows how the smallest of mutations can have a very large effect on the phenotype. The disease can be very severe and is life-threatening. It is the result of a single base substitution mutation in chromosome 11 in the *HBB* gene coding for the β-globin polypeptide (β chain) of the globular protein molecule, haemoglobin. It results in normal haemoglobin-A (HbA) being replaced with sickle cell haemoglobin (haemoglobin-S or HbS). Figure 2 outlines how a single base substitution leads to sickle cell anaemia.

- The 6th DNA triplet is changed, with a thymine replacing an adenine:
  – on the non-template strand GTG replaces normal GAG
  – on the template (transcribed) strand CAC replaces normal CTC.
- The 6th codon of mRNA transcript has the codon GUG, for valine, rather than GAG, for glutamic acid
- The sixth amino acid of the β chain now has valine, which has a hydrophobic R-group instead of glutamic acid, which has a polar R-group. This minor change in the primary structure of the β-chain changes the tertiary and quaternary structure of the haemoglobin molecule.
- The change causes the loss of the globular shape of haemoglobin and it becomes less soluble.
- This produces a molecule of haemoglobin-S that has a 'sticky patch', so that when the haemoglobin molecules are not carrying oxygen (i.e. at low oxygen concentrations) they tend to adhere to one another by their sticky patches and form long fibres within the red blood cells. The affinity of haemoglobin for oxygen is greatly reduced.
- These fibres distort the red blood cells, making them less flexible and sickle (crescent) shaped.

Stage 5 in Figure 2 outlines the effect of the sickling of red blood cells on the health of the person.

- If sickle cells block capillaries, the supply of oxygen to tissues and organs is reduced. The blockages caused by sickle cells can cause pain.
- Sickle cells have a short life span of 10–20 days compared to the lifespan of normal red blood cells of 120 days, and large-scale removal can result in anaemia (haemolytic crisis). The lack of red blood cells in anaemia causes tiredness and inactivity as there is not enough oxygen transported to body tissues.

The three different genotypes result in three different phenotypes: Hb^A Hb^A (normal); Hb^S Hb^S (sickle cell anaemia); Hb^A Hb^S (sickle cell trait). This is an example of codominance. Heterozygous indiviuals are generally symptomless except when the oxygen concentration of their blood is low, e.g. in exercising muscles, when the abnormal haemoglobin makes the red blood cells sickle shaped and less able to carry oxygen, leading to tiredness.

Summary test 16.2i

Sickle cell anaemia is caused by a mutation in the **(1)** gene coding for the **(2)** chain of haemoglobin. It is caused by a **(3)** mutation and results in the amino acid **(4)**, which has a hydrophobic R-group, replacing **(5)**. Haemoglobin loses its **(6)** shape and becomes **(7)** in low oxygen tensions. This causes red blood cells to become **(8)** and reduces the quantity of **(9)** that can be transported. The **(10)** gene codes for the enzyme **(11)**, which is important in the manufacture of the pigment **(12)**. Homozygous **(13)** individuals that lack this enzyme have a condition known as **(14)**. The disease known as **(15)** is a **(16)**-linked disease caused by a mutation in the *F8* gene. This results in a lack of ability of **(17)**.

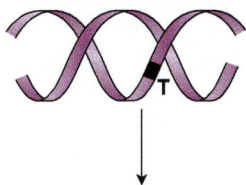

1. The *HBB* gene coding for the chain has a mutation where the base thymine replaces adenine on its non-template strand

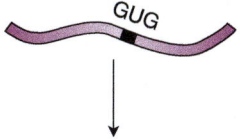

2. The mRNA produced has the triplet codon GUG (for amino acid valine) rather than GAG (for amino acid glutamic acid)

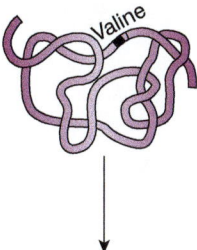

3. The β-globin polypeptide chain produced has one glutamic acid replaced by a valine

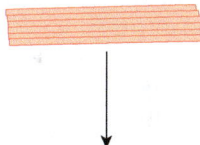

4. The haemoglobin molecules containing the abnormal β chains become sticky and clump to form long fibres when the oxygen level of the blood is low. This haemoglobin is called haemoglobin-S

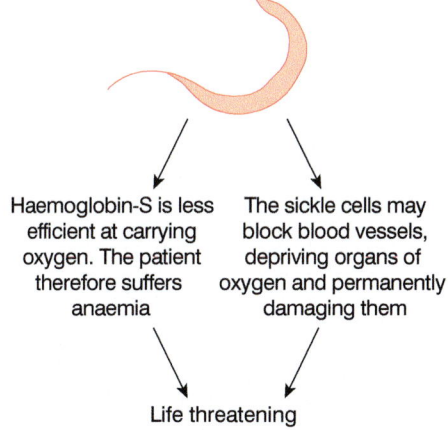

5. The haemoglobin-S molecules within the red blood cell causes the shape of the cell to become crescent (sickle) shaped

Haemoglobin-S is less efficient at carrying oxygen. The patient therefore suffers anaemia

The sickle cells may block blood vessels, depriving organs of oxygen and permanently damaging them

Life threatening

Figure 2 *How a single substitution mutation results in sickle cell anaemia*

These pages help you to:

- explain the relationship between genes, proteins and phenotype with respect to the *HTT* gene, huntingtin and Huntington's disease (16.2.6)
- explain the role of gibberellin in stem elongation (16.2.7)
- explain the role of the Le/le alleles in the gibberellin synthesis pathway (16.2.7)

You will also:

- read about the huntingtin protein

We have seen in 16.2i examples of the relationship between genes, proteins and phenotypes. Sickle cell anaemia involves a mutation to produce a codominant allele. The diseases albinism and haemophilia involve mutations to produce recessive alleles. A number of diseases, such as haemophilia, occur on the large X chromosome (which has over 1400 genes). Here the effect of the recessive allele is not masked by the dominant allele because of the lack of genes on the small Y chromosome. On these pages, we will look at two very different examples of the relationship between genes, proteins and phenotypes: a disease in humans caused by a dominant allele and one of the characteristics (traits) described by Gregor Mendel in his 1866 publication 'Experiments in plant hybridisation'.

Huntington's disease

Although most hereditary diseases are caused by recessive alleles, not all of them are. Huntington's disease is a rare disease caused by a dominant allele. Everyone who inherits this allele will be affected by the disease. Dominant mutant alleles do not normally last in human populations because the disadvantages caused often prevent individuals surviving long enough to reproduce and so pass on the allele to their offspring. The effects of Huntington's disease, a progressive deterioration of cells within the brain, is not usually apparent until individuals are over 30 years old. Because the disease affects brain tissue, symptoms are associated with brain function. Disorders associated with motor functions (movement), behaviour, and cognition (thinking and processing information) are common. Some people with the dominant allele will have children before the symptoms develop, so the allele can therefore be passed on before this life-limiting disease develops.

Remember

In Figure 3, note that the symbols X and Y should not be used in the genetic diagram because this is not a sex-linked disease. The references to 'father' and 'mother' are used as an example only and the diagram would be the same if the mother has the disease and the father is normal.

Extension

Huntingtin

Much research has been carried out on the huntingtin protein, whose exact functions are unknown. The protein is expressed widely throughout the body and appears to have many intracellular functions. It is involved in the cytoskeleton (1.2e) such as in the movement of vesicles, and in coordinating cytoskeletal structures in cell division. It has also been linked to the formation of cilia, the regulation of transcription and autophagy (the breakdown, for example, of worn out organelles or misfolded proteins).

The huntingtin gene, *HTT*, on chromosome 4, an autosome, codes for a very large protein of 3144 amino acids known as huntingtin (see Extension). Mutations in this gene result in many repeats of the sequence CAG, which results in a protein with many repeats of the amino acid glutamine. Unaffected people have 9 to 35 repeats. People with the mutation have an abnormally long stretch of the repeats, varying up to 120 repeats. Individuals with 36 to 39 repeats have a later onset of the disease and less severe symptoms than those with 40 or more repeats. Generally, the onset of the disease is earlier and the severity of the symptoms greater the more repeats there are.

As Figure 3 shows, a person who is heterozygous for Huntington's disease has a 50% chance of passing the dominant allele to his or her children, even if the other parent does not have the disease. Almost all people with Huntington's disease have the heterozygous genotype. People with the homozygous genotype, HH, have been reported, but these are rare cases.

Let allele for Huntington's disease = H
Let allele for normal condition = h

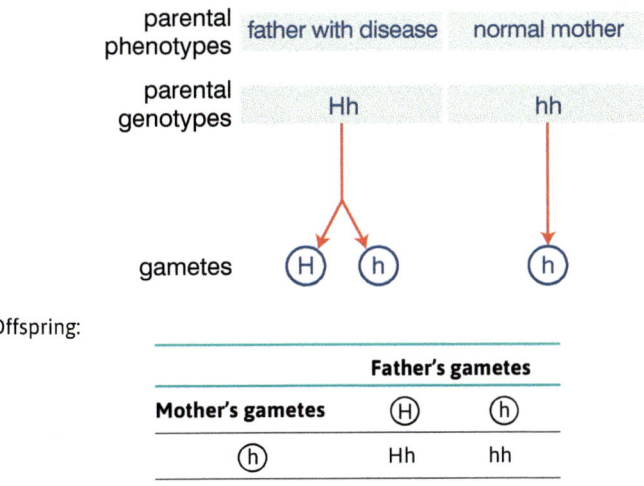

Half (50%) of offspring will have Huntington's disease (Hh).
Half (50%) of offspring will be normal (hh).

Figure 3 *Cross between one parent with Huntington's disease and the other without the disease*

Gibberellin

Gregor Mendel's experiments on pea *(Pisum sativum)* plants included a trait that he described as 'difference in the length of the stem'. He carried out genetic crosses and concluded that tall stem was dominant to dwarf (short) stem. It is now known that the dwarf phenotype is due to a mutation in the **Le** gene (length), which produces a recessive allele, *le*, and that the plant hormone gibberellin controls stem elongation.

There are many different gibberellins. The *Le* gene codes for an enzyme, GA 3β-hydroxylase, that catalyses the last step in the biochemical pathway for the synthesis of GA_1 (from GA_{20}). GA_1 is the main gibberellin involved in stem elongation in plants. The recessive allele, *le*, codes for a non-functioning enzyme.

The *Le* gene is expressed in germinating seedlings and in the stems of growing plants. Plants that are homozygous dominant (LeLe) or heterozygous (Lele) have normal tall stems. Plants that are homozygous recessive (lele) have dwarf stems. These have a shorter internode distance (the distance between the locations where leaves develop). If the gibberellin is added to certain genetic dwarf varieties of plant, the plants grow to normal size.

Gibberellin can be described as a growth promoter. Within the cell, gibberellin binds to an intracellular receptor and this triggers a sequence of events that lead to stem elongation. This is further described in 16.3b. Gibberellin is also known to affect the cell wall so that it becomes more extensible (able to extend), so that an increase in turgor pressure will help the cells in the stem to elongate, but the exact way in which it functions is not known.

Summary test 16.2j

Huntington's disease is caused by a **(1)** allele in a gene coding for the **(2)** protein. The mutated allele has a longer stretch of a repeat region of the sequence **(3)**. People with the **(4)** genotype do not develop the disease. Phenotypically, Huntington's disease causes deterioration of motor, **(5)** and **(6)** functions. The **(7)** gene codes for an enzyme, **(8)** involved in the **(9)** synthesis pathway. This plant hormone is involved in **(10)** and the non-functioning enzyme in homozygous **(11)** individuals results in **(12)** plants.

Gene control

These pages help you to:

- describe the difference between structural genes and regulatory genes (16.3.1)
- describe the difference between repressible enzymes and inducible enzymes (16.3.1)
- explain genetic control of protein production in a prokaryote using the lac operon (16.3.3)

You will also:

- consolidate your knowledge of protein synthesis

Some proteins are needed continually by the cell and so the polypeptides of which they are made are produced continuously. Many of these proteins are enzymes. Other proteins are only required in certain circumstances and it is a waste of materials and energy to produce them all the time.

- **Repressible enzymes** are normally produced continuously because the gene that codes for them is always expressed (switched on). They are usually involved in anabolic pathways and the synthesis of products essential for the cell. However, their production can be decreased as the concentration of certain substances, such as the products of the reaction they catalyse, increases. The product may bind to an allosteric site of an inactive repressor protein (see **regulatory genes** on this page). The activated repressor then binds to the operator (see **lac operon**) and prevents RNA polymerase binding or progressing along the DNA. As this binding is temporary, when the product is used up in the cell, the situation reverses and transcription proceeds.
- **Inducible enzymes** are produced only when the gene that codes for them is switched on as a result of the presence of a specific molecule, such as the substrate of the enzyme. Examples of inducible enzymes are those produced in the lac operon.

Structural genes and regulatory genes

A structural gene codes for synthesis of a polypeptide that will become a protein or form part of a functioning protein. The protein products may be structural or metabolic, such as enzymes. Expression of these genes involves mRNA synthesis. There are also structural genes that are transcribed to synthesise tRNA and rRNA molecules.

Regulatory genes

Regulatory genes are involved in the control of gene expression. A regulatory gene codes for a protein that controls transcription (see transcription factors in 16.3b). The protein product of a regulatory gene can bind to DNA, such as the repressor protein of the lac operon *lacI* gene. Repressor proteins can bind to the promoter regions of DNA or other regions involved in regulation of gene expression.

Control of protein synthesis in bacteria

Under normal circumstances the bacterium *Escherichia coli* absorbs and respires glucose as its main respiratory substrate. If, however, it is grown on a medium in which lactose is present it is able to produce three enzymes:

- β-galactosidase – the enzyme that hydrolyses lactose to glucose and galactose. It also catalyses the conversion of lactose to allolactose, which is the molecule that binds to the repressor protein: coded for by gene *lac Z*
- lactose permease – a membrane transport protein for the uptake of lactose: coded for by gene *lac Y*
- transacetylase – an enzyme thought to have a role in sugar metabolism and detoxification: coded for by gene *lac A*.

As lactose is not always available, it is far better to express the genes that code for these enzymes only when they are needed, i.e. when lactose is available. How then is *E. coli* able to do this?

The lac operon

The lac operon is a length of DNA within which there are genes coding for the production of β-galactosidase, lactose permease and transacetylase (Figure 1). The operon is made up of a number of parts.

- **The structural genes** comprise the length of DNA with the sequence of nucleotides coding for the three enzymes.
- **The operator** is a portion of DNA lying next to the structural genes that effectively switches them on and off.
- **The promoter** is a portion of DNA to which the enzyme RNA polymerase becomes attached to begin the process of **transcription** of DNA to form mRNA from the structural genes. The promoter is adjacent to the operator.
- **The regulatory gene**, *lacI*, is a portion of the DNA that is not part of the lac operon and is situated some distance from it (Figure 1). It codes for a protein called the repressor protein.

The following account of how *E. coli* controls the production of the three enzymes is also shown in Figure 1.

- The repressor protein has two different binding sites:
  - one that binds to lactose (allolactose)
  - one that binds to the operator.
- If there is no lactose present in the medium on which *E. coli* is growing, the repressor protein will bind to the operator.

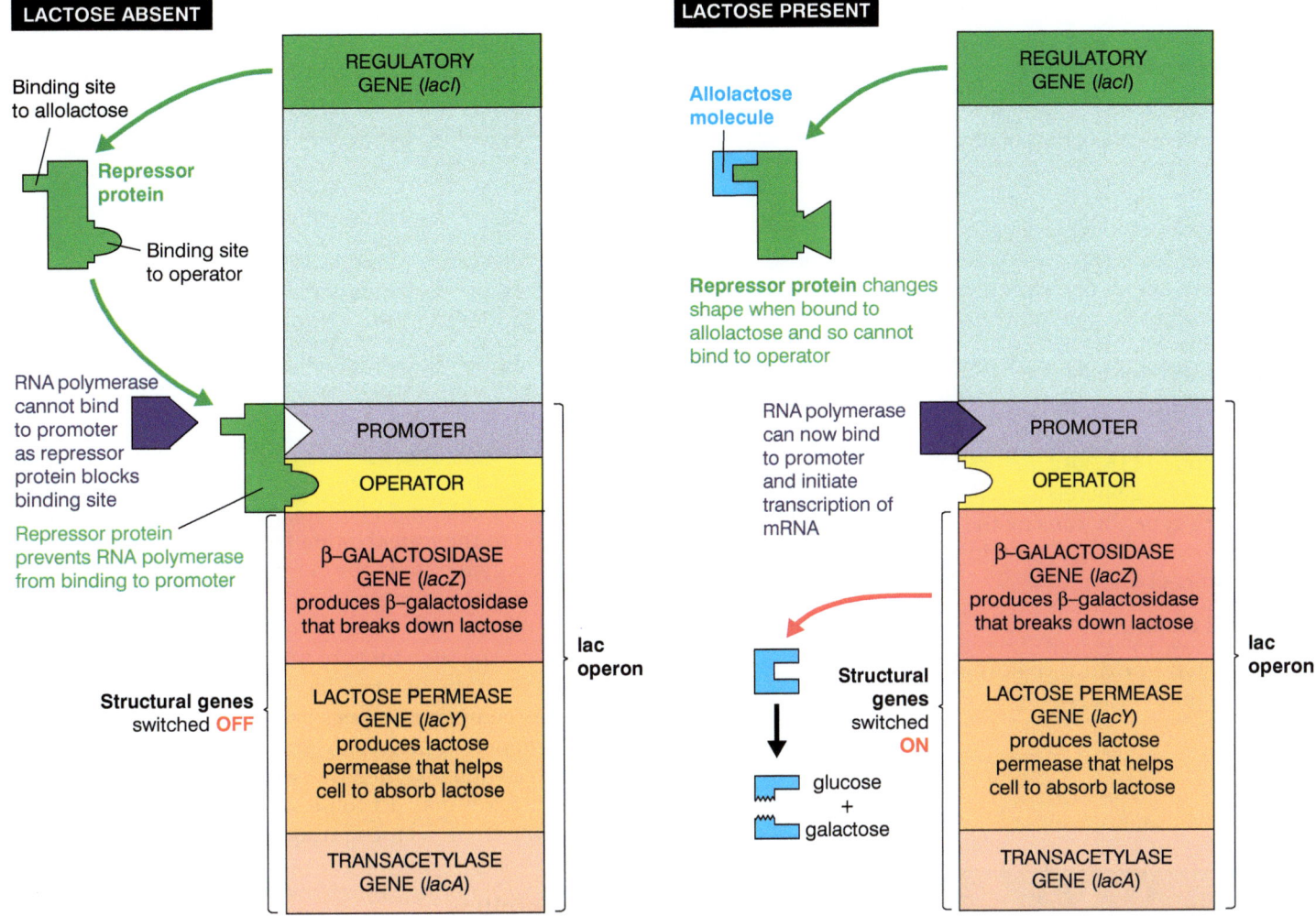

Figure 1 *Functioning of the lac operon in E. coli*

- Because the operator and promoter are close together, the repressor protein covers part of the promoter when it binds to the operator. This blocks the site on the promoter to which RNA polymerase normally attaches.
- RNA polymerase cannot attach to the promoter and therefore cannot express (switch on) the structural genes that code for the three enzymes.
- mRNA cannot be made so β-galactosidase, lactose permease and transacetylase cannot be synthesised, i.e. their production stops.
- If lactose is added to the medium on which *E. coli* is growing, it is converted to allolactose, which binds to its site on the repressor protein (there is a very small quantity of β-galactosidase present to convert lactose to allolactose). Allolactose acts as an inducer.
- As a result of this binding of allolactose, the repressor protein changes shape in such a way that it can no longer use its other binding site to attach to the operator.
- With no repressor protein to block the promoter, RNA polymerase can now attach to the promoter and begin the transcription of the structural genes and form mRNA.
- At the ribosomes, this mRNA acts as a template for the assembly of the amino acids needed to synthesise β-galactosidase, lactose permease and transacetylase.
- Lactose permease helps *E. coli* to absorb lactose rapidly from the medium and this is hydrolysed by β-galactosidase to glucose and galactose – the glucose being used as a respiratory substrate.

Summary test 16.3a

In terms of production there are two types of enzyme, inducible and **(1)**. The enzymes of the lac operon are **(2)** enzymes. Regulatory genes such as *lacI* code for **(3)** proteins that help to control **(4)**. In the lac operon, in the absence of lactose this protein binds to the **(5)** and prevents **(6)** enzyme from binding to the **(7)**. When lactose is present, some is converted to **(8)**, which binds to another site on the repressor and so the protein no longer blocks the synthesis of **(9)**, which, when produced, is able to bind to ribosomes for the synthesis of the lac enzymes, **(10)**, **(11)** and **(12)**.

These pages help you to:

- understand that transcription factors are proteins that bind to DNA (16.3.3)
- explain how transcription factors are involved in the control of gene expression in eukaryotes by decreasing or increasing the rate of transcription (16.3.3)
- understand that DELLA protein repressors normally inhibit factors that promote transcription (16.3.4)
- explain how gibberellin activates genes by causing the breakdown of DELLA protein repressors (16.3.4)

You will also:

- read about nuclear receptors as transcription factors

Extension

Gibberellins

Gibberellins are a group of over 90 plant hormones (plant growth regulators) found not only in flowering plants but also in fungi, algae and some bacteria. They are thought to be made in developing seeds and apical portions of stems and roots.

We saw in 16.3a how genes can be switched on and off to control protein, especially enzyme synthesis in prokaryotes. Let us now investigate some ways in which cells regulate gene expression in eukaryotes using **transcription factors**.

Transcription factors

RNA polymerase in eukaryotic cells cannot bind to DNA and initiate transcription without the presence of specific molecules, known as transcription factors. These are produced in the cytoplasm and move into the nucleus. Most transcription factors are proteins. Different transcription factors have different roles but they are all involved in the control of gene expression (switching genes on or off).

- Some transcription factors bind to specific regions of DNA. These sites may be within the promoter region or at other sites known as enhancer regions that also have a role in initiating transcription.
- Other transcription factors bind to the transcription factors attached to the DNA to form a complex. RNA polymerase binds to this complex to form a transcription initiation complex and so transcription of the structural genes can begin.
- Messenger RNA is produced and the sequences of nucleotides it carries are translated at the ribosomes to form the polypeptide.
- The formation of many of these complexes, especially in higher eukaryotes, requires the presence of many different molecules. If a specific factor is missing to complete the formation of the complex, then transcription will not proceed.
- Some transcription factor complexes may act to prevent RNA polymerase binding or progressing along the DNA, so preventing gene expression.

Activation of genes by gibberellins

In 15.2a, we looked at some of the effects of **plant growth regulators** called gibberellins on germination. In 16.2j, we saw that gibberellins have an important role in stem elongation. Let us now examine how gibberellins have their effect by activating genes.

We saw that gibberellins promote the germination of seeds such as barley and the increase in length of stems during plant growth. Present in plant cells are substances called **DELLA** proteins. DELLA proteins bind to transcription factors, preventing them from initiating the expression of genes associated with proteins involved in growth. In this way, DELLA proteins act as inhibitors of cell growth and therefore maintain dormancy by inhibiting seed germination or maintain control of growth. By causing the breakdown of these DELLA proteins, gibberellins are able to stimulate germination and stem elongation. The process by which gibberellins activate genes is as follows.

- Gibberellin binds to a specific receptor within the cell known as GID1.
- The gibberellin–receptor complex binds to DELLA proteins.
- This binding leads to small protein molecules, known as ubiquitins, attaching to the complex.
- Ubiquitin attachment 'marks' the DELLA proteins for breakdown by a large enzyme complex known as a proteasome.
- The transcription factors are now free to bind to DNA and allow RNA polymerase to bind for transcription.
- Proteins and enzymes involved in the germination process or in the stem elongation process can be synthesised from the mRNA formed.

Extension

The oestrogen receptor as a transcription factor

Extracellular factors can be involved in the control of gene expression by transcription factors. One example is the hormone oestrogen (see Figure 1):

- Once inside the cytoplasm of a cell, oestrogen enters the nucleus and binds to a complementary site in an oestrogen receptor molecule (ER). The ER is a transcription factor.
- Binding of oestrogen to ER causes attached proteins (heat-shock proteins) to dissociate and the shape of the receptor to change.
- This change of shape and the removal of the heat-shock proteins allows the oestrogen-ER complex to bind to DNA.
- Together with other factors, a transcription initiation complex is formed and transcription begins.
- The genes that are expressed as a result of the activation of the transcription factor ER are those associated with proteins involved in growth.

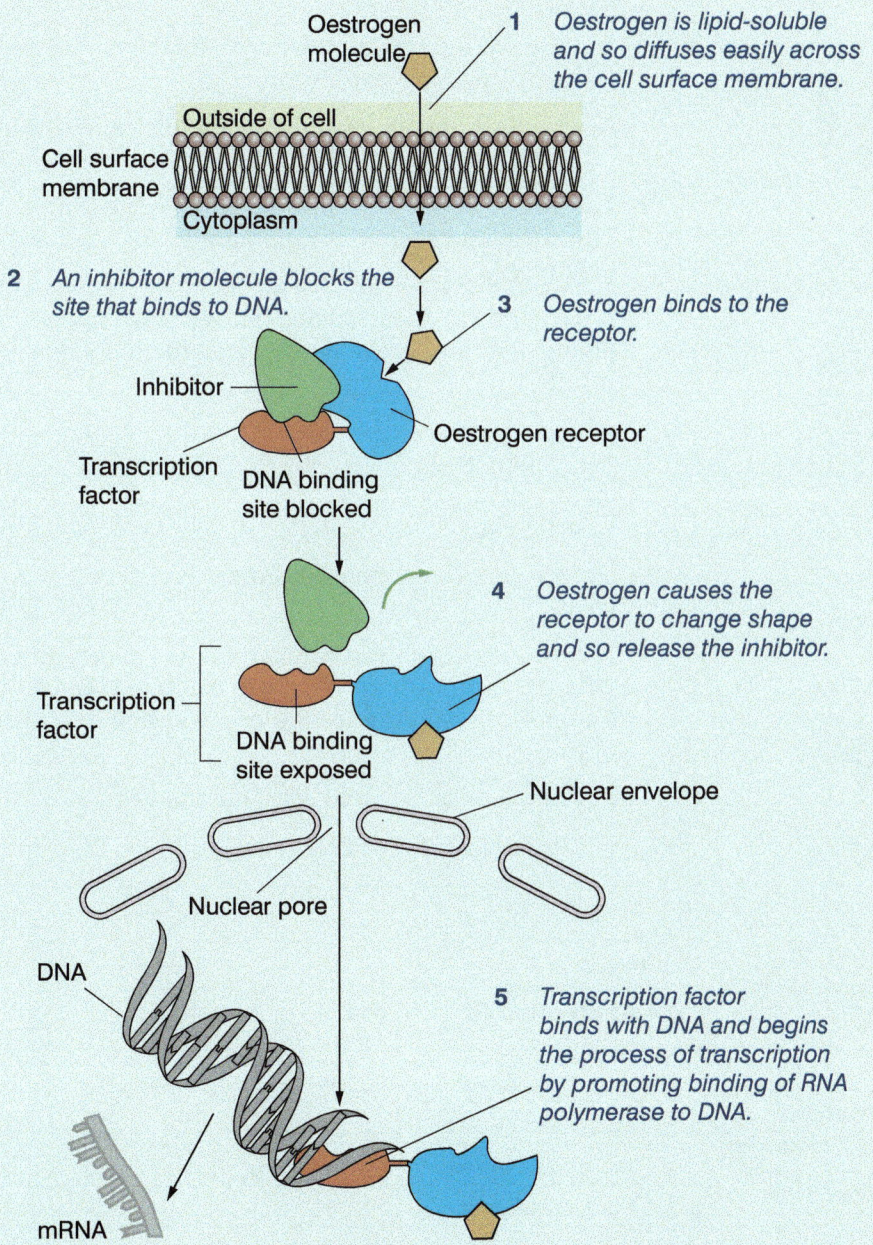

1 Oestrogen is lipid-soluble and so diffuses easily across the cell surface membrane.

Oestrogen molecule

Outside of cell

Cell surface membrane

Cytoplasm

2 An inhibitor molecule blocks the site that binds to DNA.

3 Oestrogen binds to the receptor.

Inhibitor

Oestrogen receptor

Transcription factor

DNA binding site blocked

4 Oestrogen causes the receptor to change shape and so release the inhibitor.

Transcription factor

DNA binding site exposed

Nuclear envelope

Nuclear pore

DNA

5 Transcription factor binds with DNA and begins the process of transcription by promoting binding of RNA polymerase to DNA.

mRNA

Figure 1 *The effect of oestrogen on gene transcription*

Summary test 16.3b

For a gene to produce mRNA it needs to be stimulated by specific molecules that move into the **(1)**. These molecules are called transcription factors. They bind to a specific region of **(2)**. If one or more factors that make up a transcription initiation complex is missing then RNA polymerase cannot proceed and the gene is switched **(3)**. Transcription factors may also act to prevent **(4)** binding and so prevent gene **(5)**. This means that **(6)** is not synthesised and so the process of **(7)** does not occur at the ribosomes for polypeptide synthesis. In plants, genes may be activated by plant growth factors called **(8)** that combine with, and cause the breakdown of, **(9)** proteins. These proteins **(10)** transcription factors and so their breakdown allows transcription to take place.

16 Exam-style questions

1 Figure 1 shows electron micrographs of a cell in the anther of a lily, *Lilium glandiforum*, at various stages of meiosis, **A** to **F**.

Figure 1

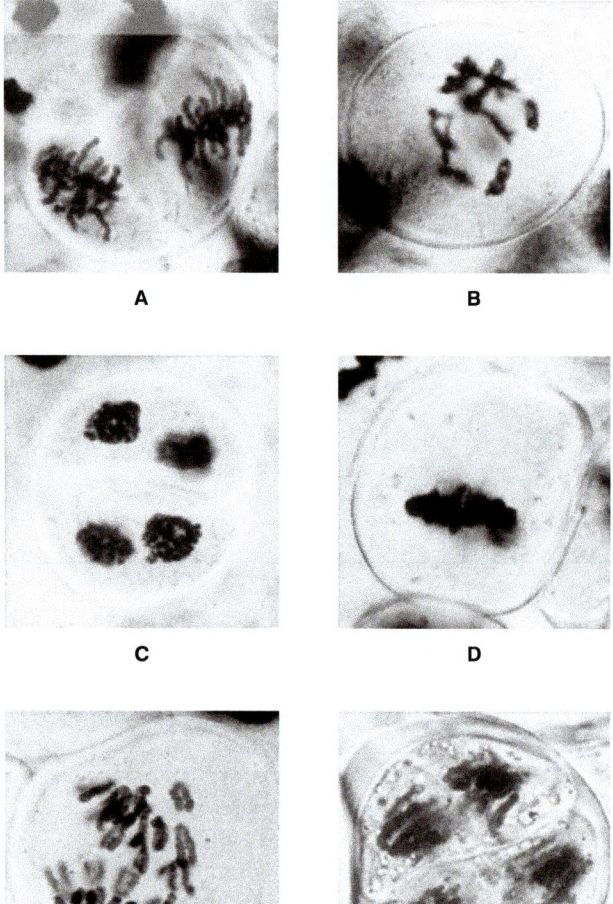

A

B

C

D

E

F

a List the letters shown in Figure 1 in the order in which these stages occur during a meiotic cell cycle. The first and last stages have been entered for you.

B .... **C** *(2 marks)*

b Describe how a process that occurs in B produces genetically different gametes. *(3 marks)*

(Total 5 marks)

2 The height of garden pea plants, *Pisum sativum*, is controlled by a gene that has two alleles.

- The dominant allele, *Le*, results in tall plants.

- The recessive allele, *le*, results in dwarf plants.

The proteins that are subsequently produced from transcription of *Le* or *le* alleles affect gibberellin synthesis. Gibberellin is a plant growth hormone that promotes the expression of genes involved in stem elongation. These genes are also regulated by transcription factors.

a i Describe the role of transcription factors in regulating gene expression. *(3 marks)*

ii Explain how the expression of *le* alleles results in dwarf plants. *(4 marks)*

b The colour of pea pods may be green or yellow. The allele for green, G is dominant to the allele for yellow, g.

A dihybrid cross was carried out with two tall pea plants that have green pods, giving the following results:

tall, green pods	49
tall, yellow pods	17
dwarf, green pods	10
dawrf, yellow pods	4

Draw a genetic diagram to show this dihybrid cross. *(5 marks)*

c A chi-squared (χ^2) test was carried out to determine whether or not the results of the cross in **b** were significantly different from those expected for crosses of this type.

i Complete Table 1 and calculate the value of χ^2.

The formula for calculating χ^2 is:

$$\chi^2 = \Sigma \frac{(O-E)^2}{E}$$

Table 1

offspring phenotype	observed number (O)	expected number (E)	$\frac{(O-E)^2}{E}$
tall, green pea pods	49		
tall, yellow pea pods	17		
dwarf, green pea pods	10		
dwarf, yellow pea pods	4		
		$\chi^2 =$	

(3 marks)

ii Table 2 shows some critical values for χ^2 at different probabilities.

Table 2

degrees of freedom	probability						
	0.50	0.20	0.10	0.05	0.02	0.01	0.001
3	2.37	4.64	6.25	7.82	9.84	11.34	16.27

Using Table 2, explain whether or not the χ^2 calculated in Table 1 is significant. *(1 mark)*

(Total 16 marks)

3 Normal fruit flies, *Drosophila melanogaster* have red eyes and long wings. Some flies may have brown eyes and may have vestigial (short, non-functional) wings. These variations are coded by two genes:

- red eyes, coded by the dominant allele of R/r
- long wings, coded by the dominant allele of N/n.

A normal fly that is heterozygous for both genes is crossed with a fly that has brown eyes and vestigial wings, giving the following results:

long wings, red eyes	24
vestigial wings, red eyes	189
long wings, brown eyes	195
vestigal wings, brown eyes	22

a Explain why the results suggest that these genes are linked. *(2 marks)*

b In Figure 2, sketch the positions of the alleles for eye colour and wing shape in the normal fly that was used in the cross. *(2 marks)*

(Total 4 marks)

Figure 2

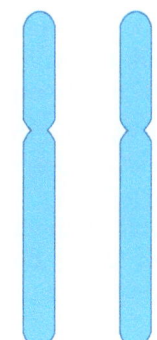

16 Practice questions

4 In humans, Huntington's disease is caused by a dominant, mutant allele. Draw a genetic diagram to show the possible genotypes and phenotypes of the offspring produced by a man with one allele for the disease and a woman who does not have any alleles for the disease.

5 In cocker spaniels, black coat colour is the result of a dominant allele and red coat colour is the result of a corresponding recessive allele.

a Draw a genetic diagram to show a cross between a pure breeding bitch (female) with a black coat and a pure breeding dog (male) with a red coat.

b If a dog and a bitch from this first cross are mated, what is the probability that any one of the offspring will have a red coat? Use a genetic diagram to show your working.

6 In shorthorn cattle there is a gene C that determines coat colour. The gene has two alleles:

- the allele C^W produces a white coat when homozygous
- the allele C^R produces a red coat when homozygous.

In the heterozygous state the coat is light red, a colour also known as roan. The roan coat is a mixture of all white hairs and all red hairs. As each hair is either all red or all white, the C^W and C^R alleles are codominant.

The gene for coat colour is **not** sex-linked.

a Draw a genetic diagram to show the possible genotypes and phenotypes of a cross between a bull with a white coat and a cow with a roan coat.

b In each of the following crosses between shorthorn cattle what is the percentage of offspring with a roan coat?
  i red coat × white coat
  ii red coat × roan coat
  iii white coat × roan coat
  iv roan coat × roan coat.

7 A man claims not to be the father of a child. The man is blood group O while the mother of the child is blood group A and the child is blood group AB. State, with your reasons, whether you think the man could be the father of the child.

8 In some breeds of domestic fowl, the gene controlling feather shape has two alleles that are codominant. The allele A^S when homozygous produces straight feathers. The allele A^F when homozygous produces frizzled feathers. The heterozygote for feather shape gives mildly frizzled feathers. Draw a genetic diagram to show the genotypes and phenotypes resulting from a cross between a mildly frizzled cockerel and a frizzled hen. The gene for feather shape is **not** sex-linked.

17.1 Variation

These pages help you to:

- explain that phenotypic variation is due to genetic factors or environmental factors or a combination of genetic and environmental factors (17.1.1)
- describe examples to show how environmental factors contribute to phenotypic variation (17.1.1)

You will also:

- practise interpreting experimental results

Figure 1 *Siamese cats have dark fur at the extremities of their bodies as a result of an enzyme involved in melanin production that only functions at lower temperatures*

Figure 2 *The Arctic fox produces darker pigmentation when the temperature is warmer, giving rise to the grey-brown summer coat. In colder conditions, no pigmentation occurs, giving rise to the white winter coat that camouflages it better against its snowy background*

a. Contribution of the environment to phenotypic variation

In some cases, the variation shown in the phenotype of individuals for any particular characteristic reflects their genotype completely. For example, the expression of the ABO blood group gene to give the four different blood group types, A, B, AB and O, cannot be modified by the environment. At the other extreme, individuals with identical DNA, such as plants produced asexually by vegetative propagation (5.1b), may grow so that there is a very wide range of size of plants, depending on environmental factors such as availability of water and light intensity. Here, we will look at some examples of how the environment can contribute to the overall variation seen in the phenotype of organisms.

How the environment may affect the phenotype

The **alleles** that make up the genotype of an organism provide a blueprint that determines the limits within which the organism will develop. The degree to which an allele is expressed often depends on the environment. Examples include:

- The **recessive** c^s allele in Siamese cats and the equivalent c^h alelle in Himalayan rabbits code for a heat sensitive form of the enzyme tyrosinase (16.2i). This enzyme is involved in the production of the dark pigment, melanin. The c^s/c^h form of the enzyme does not function at temperatures above 33 °C. Over much of the body surface of Siamese cats and Himalayan rabbits the temperature is above 33 °C and so the enzyme is inactive and no melanin is produced during development. The fur in these regions is therefore light in colour. At the extremities such as the tips of the tail, ears, feet and nose, the temperature is usually below 33 °C and so the heat sensitive form of tyrosinase is active and melanin is produced. These regions are therefore much darker in colour (Figure 1).

- Arctic foxes (Figure 2) have the alleles to make fur pigments and so produce dark coats. These pigments are, however, produced only in warm temperatures. They are therefore not produced as the colder temperatures of winter approach and the surface hairs are slowly replaced by white ones. By the time the winter snows cover the ground, the Arctic fox is completely white and better camouflaged and therefore more able to capture its prey.

- A small Californian plant, *Potentilla glandulosa*, has a number of genetic forms, each adapted to growing at different altitudes. Experiments were carried out as follows:
  - plants of *Potentilla* were collected from three altitudes – their original locations, high (3050 m), medium (1400 m) and low (30 m) altitude
  - using cuttings, clones (identical genotypes) were produced for each of the three different genetic forms
  - these cloned plants were grown at each altitude (high, medium and low)
  - this means that, for each of the three genetic forms, genetically identical plants were grown in three different environments.

The results are illustrated in Figure 3 and show that plants with identical genotypes differ in phenotype (height, number of leaves, overall size and shape) and even survival rate, according to the environment in which they live.

- The height of humans is determined by the range of alleles for height that each of us inherits from our parents. However, even if our alleles allow us to grow tall, our diet will influence whether we do so. For example, a lack of calcium, phosphate or poor overall nutrition especially at critical growth

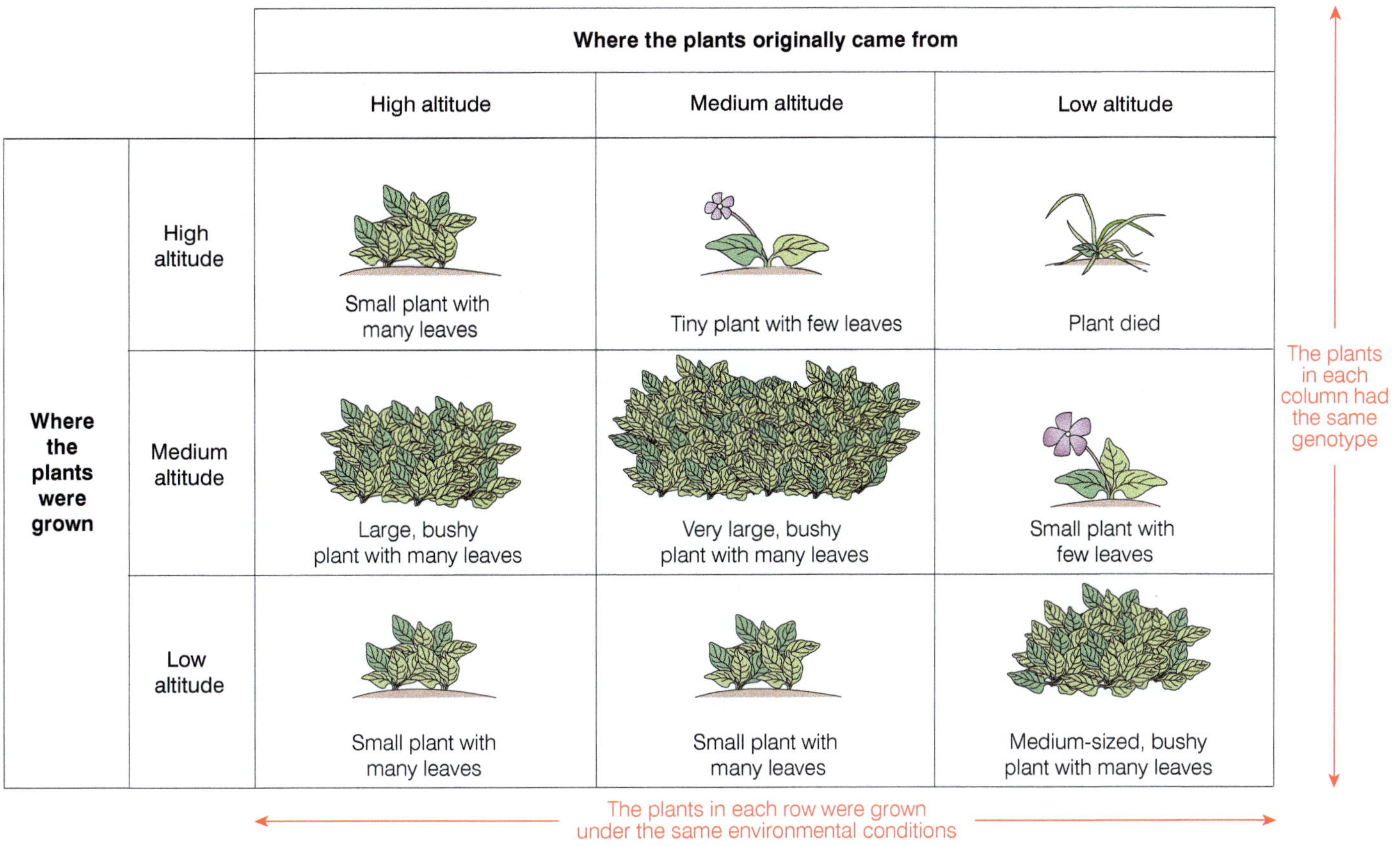

		High altitude	Medium altitude	Low altitude
Where the plants were grown	High altitude	Small plant with many leaves	Tiny plant with few leaves	Plant died
	Medium altitude	Large, bushy plant with many leaves	Very large, bushy plant with many leaves	Small plant with few leaves
	Low altitude	Small plant with many leaves	Small plant with many leaves	Medium-sized, bushy plant with many leaves

The plants in each column had the same genotype

The plants in each row were grown under the same environmental conditions

Figure 3 *Effect of environment on phenotype – growing genetically identical* Potentilla glandulosa *at different altitudes*

periods (early years and adolescence) may prevent maximum bone and body growth and so we fail to realise our full potential height.

- A set of plants grown in a soil deficient in nitrogen will develop far less **biomass** than another genetically identical set grown in soils with a plentiful supply of nitrogen.
- The environment may induce a mutation which affects the phenotype. For example, ultraviolet radiation from the sun or tanning lamps can disrupt DNA replication and lead to the production of melanomas on the skin. Melanomas are a form of skin cancer which cause changes to the appearance and patterning of moles on the skin.

The effect of the environment on the phenotype is greater for those characteristics that are determined by more than one gene – polygenes (see 17.1b). The genotype determines the range of possible phenotypes, but the environment often determines where within that range the actual appearance of an organism lies.

Extension

Further proof!

How can we be sure that the dark extremities of Siamese cats are the result of the temperature at which fur develops, rather than simply being genetically determined? A couple of observations:

- If a veterinary surgeon removes some dark fur from the tail of a Siamese cat during treatment and keeps the cat in a warmer than usual environment, the new fur that develops is light in colour.
- When light fur is removed from the back of a Siamese cat during treatment and the cat is kept at a lower than normal temperature, then new growth of fur is black.

If fur colour is determined only by genes, with no environmental influence, then in both cases the new fur would have matched the original colour.

Summary test 17.1a

The phenotype of an organism is the result of the effect of the **(1)** and the organism's **(2)**. For example, in Siamese cats there is a heat sensitive form of the **(3)** called tyrosinase that is involved in the production of the pigment known as **(4)**. The production of this heat sensitive form of tyrosinase is controlled by an **(5)** represented by c^s. This form of the enzyme is inactive at temperatures **(6)** 33°C. Body temperatures below this normally occur at the **(7)** of the body and so in these regions the pigment is produced and the fur is coloured **(8)**. If genetically identical forms of the plant *Potentilla glandulosa* are grown at different **(9)** their phenotype differs in **(10)** and **(11)** due to the different environments they experience. It is clear therefore that the **(12)** of an organism determines the **(13)** of possible phenotypes, but it is the **(14)** that influences its final appearance.

369

These pages help you to:

- explain, with examples, that genetic factors and environmental factors can contribute to phenotypic variation (17.1.1)
- describe the features of continuous variation and discontinuous variation (17.1.2)
- understand the genetic basis of discontinuous variation and continuous variation (17.1.3)

You will also:

- review meiosis as a source of genetic variation

Table 1 *Frequency of heights in a sample of humans (measured to the nearest 2 cm)*

Height/cm	Frequency
140	0
144	1
148	23
152	90
156	261
160	393
164	440
168	413
172	177
176	63
180	17
184	4
188	1
190	0
192	0

Remember

The genetic basis of discontinuous variation is the presence of one or a few genes, producing discrete (distinct) groups.

The genetic basis of continuous variation is often the presence of many genes (polygenes) that have an additive effect, to give a range that produces a normal distribution of phenotypes. There are no distinct groups.

Every one of the billions of organisms on planet Earth is unique. Even monozygotic twins, although genetically identical, vary as a result of their different environmental experiences. The phenotypic variation shown within a species for a particular characteristic can be quantified. There are two main types of variation: **continuous variation** and **discontinuous variation**.

Continuous variation

Some characteristics of organisms appear to have a graded effect and the phenotypes do not appear to fall into distinct classes. In humans, two examples are height and mass. Characteristics that display this type of variation are not controlled by a single gene, but by many genes (polygenes). These genes have an additive effect, each contributing in some way, and to a different extent, to the overall phenotype produced.

Environmental factors play a major role in determining where on the continuum an organism lies. For example, individuals who are genetically predetermined to be the same height grow to different heights as a result of variations in environmental factors, such as diet.

This type of variation is the product of polygenes and the environment. Table 1 shows the number of people in a particular sample (frequency) with various heights. If we take these data and plot them on a graph, we obtain a bell-shaped curve known as a normal distribution curve (Figure 1).

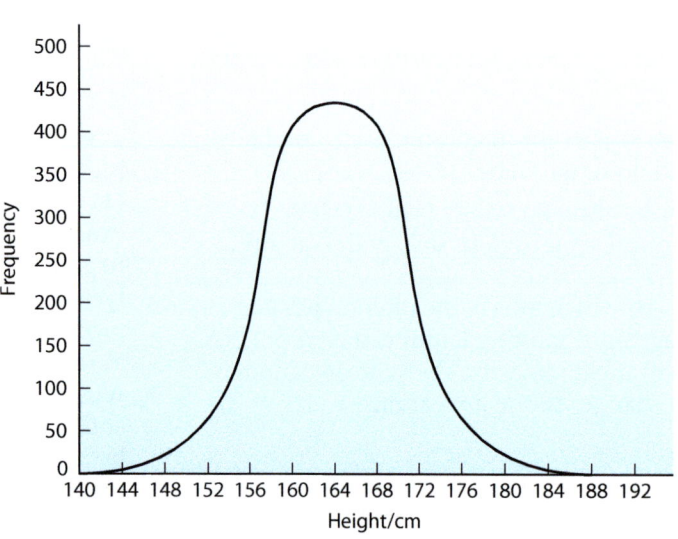

Figure 1 *Graph of frequency against height for a sample of humans*

Discontinuous variation

Some characteristics in organisms fit into a few distinct forms; there are no intermediate types, or at least there is very little overlap between groups. This is called discontinuous variation. In the ABO blood grouping system (16.2d), for example, there are four distinct groups: A, B, AB and O (Figure 2). A characteristic displaying discontinuous variation is usually controlled by a few genes or often just a single gene – in the case of blood groups the *I* gene or in the *Le/le* gene which produces tall or dwarf plants. Discontinuous variation can be represented on bar charts or pie graphs. Environmental factors have little influence on discontinuous variation.

As features showing discontinuous variation are often controlled by a single gene and gene mutations normally affect a single gene, it follows that many human diseases that result from gene mutations show discontinuous variation. Examples include albinism, sickle cell anaemia, haemophilia and Huntington's disease, which were discussed in 16.2i and 16.2j.

Measuring variation within a species or population

The overall phenotypic variation, V, shown for a characteristic or trait can be summarised:

$$V_{\text{(phenotypic/observable)}} = V_{\text{G (genetic/inherited)}} + V_{\text{E (environmental)}}$$

To measure the contribution made by environmental variation, V_G must be equal to zero. We saw in 17.1a that this was achieved with the *Potentilla* plants grown at different altitudes by taking cuttings to obtain identical genotypes. In humans, monozygotic (identical) twin studies are carried out as these twins have identical DNA.

V_G can be investigated by keeping any environmental factors constant. For example, the different genetic forms of *Potentilla* (17.1a) were all grown in the same garden plot, so that temperature, water availability, light intensity and duration, and soil factors were all the same.

The same feature can be described as discontinuous or continuous, depending on exactly what is to be studied. For example, a population of pea plants shows discontinuous variation in stem length, as there are just two groups, tall and dwarf, with a single gene controlling the feature. However, in these groups, the effect of environmental factors will be evident as there will be a wide range of variation in stem length within each group. For example, interaction of the tall genotype with environmental factors that affect growth will give a normal distribution curve such as that in Figure 1. This is described as continuous variation.

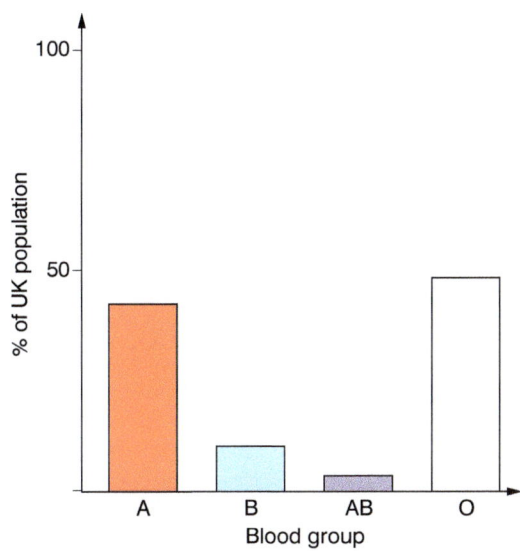

Figure 2 *Discontinuous variation illustrated by the percentage of the UK population with blood groups A, B, AB and O*

Causes of variation – genetic differences

Genetic variation is the result of the genotype of each individual, in other words the genes they possess and the forms of allele of each gene that are present. This genetic make-up varies from generation to generation as a result of:

- **Mutations** – a change in sequence of bases in DNA is called a **gene mutation** (6.2d). While mutations in body cells are not passed on to the next generation, those in reproductive tissues (testes and ovaries in animals and anthers and ovaries in flowering plants) may be inherited. In organisms that are asexually reproducing, mutations are the only source of genetic variation. Mutations can also be chromosomal, such as an addition or loss of one chromosome, or rearrangements of chromosomes, for example a section of a chromosome removed and added to a different chromosome.
- **Crossing over** and the consequent formation of recombinants during prophase I of meiosis (16.1c) leads to equivalent sections of non-sister chromatids being exchanged and therefore separates alleles of linked genes that would otherwise be inherited together.
- **Random orientation of pairs of homologous chromosomes** at metaphase I of meiosis (16.1c) results in daughter cells that are genetically different. This is because the chromosome set they have received is the result of a random alignment of homologous pairs at the spindle equator. The greater the haploid number, the greater the number of different possible combinations.
- **Random mating between individuals within a species** – which pair of organisms of a species that mate, and hence which two genotypes combine, is largely a matter of chance, although in some animals (especially humans) there may be an element of choice involved.
- **Random fusion of gametes at fertilisation**. When mating takes place, which gamete fuses with which at fertilisation is random.

Causes of variation – environmental influences

Environmental influences affect the way a genotype is expressed and result in different phenotypes (17.1a). The effect of the environment is usually greater where many genes (polygenes) affect a characteristic. Climatic factors (e.g. temperature, availability of water and sunlight) lead to variation, as do pH and quantity and type of nutrients. The environment may also influence genetic variation by, for example, affecting the rate of mutation. It may also switch genes on and off.

These pages help you to:

- understand how to calculate the mean and sample standard deviation as part of the *t*-test to compare the means of two different samples (17.1.4)

You will also:

- understand when to use the *t*-test

The *t*-test is used to find out if the difference between the mean of two sets of continuous data is significant or if it is purely due to chance. The *t*-test is used if:

- the data that have been collected are continuous
- the data are from a population that is normally distributed
- the standard deviations are approximately the same
- each of the two samples has fewer than 30 values.

The equation for the *t*-test is in two parts that are expressed as:

$$t = \frac{\bar{x}_1 - \bar{x}_2}{\sqrt{\dfrac{s_1^2}{n_1} + \dfrac{s_2^2}{n_2}}}$$

and

$$v = n_1 + n_2 - 2$$

where:

$\bar{x}$ = mean value
s = sample standard deviation
n = sample size (number of observations)
v = degrees of freedom

The *t*-test makes use of the **mean** and **standard deviation**, so let us begin by looking at these.

Mean and standard deviation

A normal distribution curve always has the same basic shape (Figure 1). It differs in two measurements: its maximum height and its width.

- The **mean** is the measurement at the maximum height of the curve. The mean of a sample of data provides an average value and useful information when comparing one sample with another. It does not, however, provide any information about the range of values within that sample. For example, the mean number of children in a sample of eight families may be 2. However, this could be made up of eight families each with two children or six families with no children and two families with eight children each.
- The sample **standard deviation** (*s*) is a measure of the width of the curve. It gives an indication of the range of values either side of the mean. A standard deviation is the distance from the mean to the point where the curve changes from being convex to concave (the point of inflexion). Of all the measurements, 68% lie within this range. Increasing this width to almost two (actually 1.96) standard deviations takes in 95% of all measurements. These measurements are shown in Figure 1.

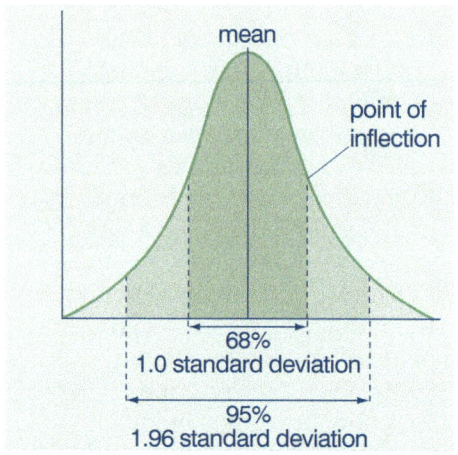

Figure 1 *The normal distribution curve, showing values for standard deviation*

Calculating the standard deviation

At first sight, the formula for standard deviation can look complex:

$$\text{standard deviation} = \sqrt{\frac{\sum (x - \bar{x})^2}{n - 1}}$$

where:

$\sum$ = the sum of

x = measured value (from the sample)

$\bar{x}$ = mean value

n = sample size (number of observations in the sample)

However, it is straightforward to calculate and less daunting if you take it step by step. The following very simple example, using the six measured values (x) 4, 1, 2, 3, 5 and 0, illustrates each step in the process.

Step 1 Calculate the mean value ($\bar{x}$), i.e. $4 + 1 + 2 + 3 + 5 + 0 = 15$

$$15 \div 6 = 2.5.$$

Step 2 Subtract the mean value (2.5) from each of the measured values ($x - \bar{x}$). This gives: +1.5, −1.5, −0.5, +0.5, +2.5, −2.5.

Step 3 As some of these numbers are negative, we need to make them positive. To do this, square **all** the numbers ($x - \bar{x})^2$. Remember to square all the numbers and not just the negative ones. This gives: 2.25, 2.25, 0.25, 0.25, 6.25, 6.25.

Step 4 Add all these squared numbers together:

$$\sum(x - \bar{x})^2 = 17.5$$

Step 5 Divide this number by the original number of measurements less one, i.e. 5:

$$\frac{\sum(x - \bar{x})^2}{n - 1} = \frac{17.5}{5} = 3.5$$

Step 6 As all the numbers have been squared, the final step is to take the square root in order to get back to the same units as the mean:

$$\sqrt{\frac{\sum(x - \bar{x})^2}{n - 1}} = \sqrt{3.5} = 1.87$$

Significant figures

You will need to use a calculator to find the value of standard deviations, as it will considerably speed up your calculation. In doing so you will often find the calculator gives a long figure running to many decimal places. In our calculation, for example, the calculation $\sqrt{3.5}$ produces the answer 1.870828693. Clearly the significance of the latter digits is less than the earlier ones. It is normal to reduce these figures to a certain number of significant figures. In our case we have rounded down the answer to three significant figures, namely 1.87. We did this because we calculated our square values to be 2.25, 0.25, 6.25, etc. As these had three significant figures, we used the same number in our final calculation.

Summary test 17.1c

The t-test can be used to compare the **(1)** of two different samples to see if any differences are **(2)**. The test can be carried out if the sample sizes are less than **(3)** and the collected measurements are **(4)**. The data should be **(5)** distributed. The **(6)**, or s measures the extent to which the data is spread about the **(7)**. **(8)**% of measurements fall within 1.96 SD.

These pages help you to:

- use a provided formula to carry out the *t*-test to compare the means of two different samples (17.1.4)

You will also:

- consolidate your understanding of the null hypothesis in statistical tests

Table 1 *Yield of wheat for fertilisers A and B*

Number of tonnes of wheat per plot		
Fertiliser A	**Fertiliser B**	
5	4	
9	3	
11	6	
9	7	
10	5	
7	3	
5	3	
8	5	
64	36	**Total**
8	8	**Number of plots**
8	4.5	**Mean**

To demonstrate how the *t*-test works, let us consider a worked example. A farmer, who has been using fertiliser B on her wheat crops, has been told by a supplier that she will get a better crop yield if she uses fertiliser A. The farmer decides to plan and carry out an experiment to test her prediction that fertiliser A will give a better yield than fertiliser B. She divides her fields into 16 plots, eight of which she treats with fertiliser A and eight with fertiliser B. The number of tonnes of wheat obtained from each plot is given in Table 1.

The farmer decided that the *t*-test was the most appropriate statistical test to use to see whether the hypothesis could be supported or not. This was because:

- the data collected was continuous
- the data was from a population that is normally distributed
- the standard deviations were approximately the same
- each of the two samples, fertiliser A and fertiliser B were used on 8 plots which is fewer than 30 values.

The first stage of the *t*-test is to calculate the standard deviation for each sample. To do this we must calculate:

- the mean of each sample
- the deviation of each reading from the mean
- the square of this deviation and the sum of the squares.

All these values are calculated and shown in Table 2.

Table 2 *Calculating the standard deviation for each sample*

Fertiliser A			Fertiliser B		
Observation (x)	**Deviation from the mean $(x - \bar{x}_1)$**	**Square of the deviation $(x - \bar{x}_1)^2$**	**Observation (x)**	**Deviation from the mean $(x - \bar{x}_2)$**	**Square of the deviation $(x - \bar{x}_2)^2$**
5	−3	9	4	−0.5	0.25
9	+1	1	3	−1.5	2.25
11	+3	9	6	+1.5	2.25
9	+1	1	7	+2.5	6.25
10	+2	4	5	+0.5	0.25
7	−1	1	3	−1.5	2.25
5	−3	9	3	−1.5	2.25
8	0	0	5	+0.5	0.25
Sum of squares of deviation:		34	Sum of squares of deviation:		16
Standard deviation $\sqrt{\dfrac{\Sigma(x - \bar{x}_1)^2}{n-1}}$		$\sqrt{\dfrac{34}{7}} = 2.20$	Standard deviation $\sqrt{\dfrac{\Sigma(x - \bar{x}_2)^2}{n-1}}$		$\sqrt{\dfrac{16}{7}} = 1.51$

We can now substitute the calculated values in the *t*-test equation as follows:

$$t = \frac{\bar{x}_1 - \bar{x}_2}{\sqrt{\dfrac{s_1^2}{n_1} + \dfrac{s_2^2}{n_2}}} = \frac{8 - 4.5}{\sqrt{\dfrac{2.20^2}{8} + \dfrac{1.51^2}{8}}} = \frac{3.5}{\sqrt{\dfrac{4.84}{8} + \dfrac{2.28}{8}}}$$

$$= \frac{3.5}{\sqrt{0.61 + 0.29}}$$

$$= \frac{3.5}{\sqrt{0.9}} = \frac{3.5}{0.95} = \mathbf{3.68}$$

Finally, to discover if our value of 3.68 indicates whether the different readings are significant, or merely due to chance, we need to look up 3.68 on a statistical table called the *t*-table, part of which is reproduced as Table 3. To do this we need to know the degrees of freedom. This is calculated according to the formula:

Degrees of freedom $(v) = (n_1 + n_2) - 2$

In our example $\quad v = (8 + 8) - 2$

$$= 14$$

We now find that looking along the row for 14 degrees of freedom, the critical value for *t* at the $p = 0.05$ significance level is 2.15. Our value of 3.68 lies between 2.98 and 4.14, which corresponds to a probability value of between 0.01 and 0.001. These values refer to the probability that chance alone is the reason for the difference between our two sets of data. In our example, the probability that the different wheat yields when using our fertilisers was pure chance was between one in a hundred ($p = 0.01$) and one in a thousand ($p = 0.001$). Assuming all other factors in the experiment were constant, it can be stated that, at the 1% confidence level, there is a difference in the yields from the use of the two different fertilisers, and that the differences are not due to chance effects.

The null hypothesis

The prediction made by the farmer was that fertiliser A will give a better yield than fertiliser B. The results she obtained appeared to agree with her prediction. Carrying out the *t*-test will help to confirm her observation and give statistical support to the prediction.

The null hypothesis for this experiment was that: 'There is no significant difference between the mean yield of the two groups of wheat treated with different fertilisers and any difference is due to chance effects.'

Based on the prediction made by the farmer, the alternate hypothesis states that: 'There is a significant difference between the mean yield of the two groups of wheat treated with different fertilisers.'

In this experiment, the calculated value of *t* was higher than the critical value at $p = 0.05$. In fact, it was higher than the critical value at $p = 0.01$.

This means that we can reject the null hypothesis.

Carrying out this statistical test means that we can place more confidence in our conclusions about the greater effectiveness of fertiliser A in improving crop yield compared to fertiliser B. However, we have to examine whether the farmer has made every effort to minimise the effect of variables that may affect the results. For example, if the plots containing the wheat plants with fertiliser A had more water, or greater access to light, this could explain the higher crop yield. This shows the importance of standardising variables when planning experiments.

Table 3 *The t-table*

Degrees of freedom	Value of t			
1	6.31	12.71	63.66	636.62
2	2.92	4.30	9.93	31.60
3	2.35	3.18	5.84	12.94
4	2.13	2.78	4.60	8.61
5	2.02	2.57	4.03	6.86
6	1.94	2.45	3.71	5.96
7	1.90	2.37	3.50	5.41
8	1.86	2.31	3.36	5.04
9	1.83	2.26	3.25	4.78
10	1.81	2.23	3.17	4.59
11	1.80	2.20	3.11	4.44
12	1.78	2.18	3.06	4.32
13	1.77	2.16	3.01	4.22
14	1.76	2.15	2.98	4.14
15	1.75	2.13	2.95	4.07
16	1.75	2.12	2.92	4.02
17	1.74	2.11	2.90	3.97
18	1.73	2.10	2.88	3.92
19	1.73	2.09	2.86	3.88
20	1.73	2.09	2.85	3.85
21	1.72	2.08	2.83	3.82
22	1.72	2.07	2.82	3.79
23	1.71	2.07	2.81	3.77
24	1.71	2.06	2.80	3.75
25	1.71	2.06	2.79	3.73
26	1.71	2.06	2.78	3.71
27	1.70	2.05	2.77	3.69
28	1.70	2.05	2.76	3.67
29	1.70	2.05	2.76	3.66
30	1.70	2.04	2.75	3.65
40	1.68	2.02	2.70	3.55
60	1.67	2.00	2.66	3.46
Probability that chance produced this value of t	0.1	0.05	0.01	0.001
Confidence level	10%	5%	1%	0.1%

Summary test 17.1d

The *t*-test first involves calculating a **(1)** for each of the two samples and then calculating the standard **(2)** for each sample. With these we can calculate a value of *t*. The equation, **(3)** is used to work out the number of degrees of freedom, *v*. In the *t*-test table, if the value of *t* is greater than the **(4)** value given at $p =$ **(5)** for the calculated degrees of freedom, then we can **(6)** the null hypothesis.

These pages help you to:

- explain natural selection in terms of:
  - populations have the capacity to produce many offspring that compete for resources
  - in the 'struggle for existence', individuals that are best adapted are most likely to survive
  - individuals that survive can reproduce and pass on their alleles to the next generation (17.2.1)

You will also:

- consider population growth curves

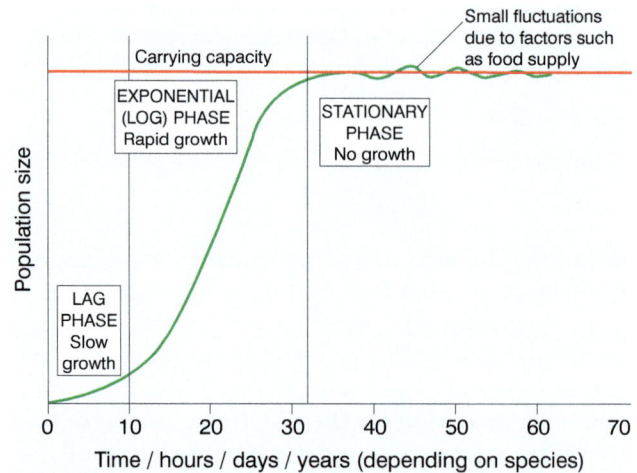

Figure 1 *Typical population growth curve starting with a small initial population. A point is reached where factors such as lack of food cause the population to plateau (level out). The population is said to have reached its carrying capacity*

The principles of natural selection

Charles Darwin and Alfred Wallace in 1858 independently developed the theory of evolution by natural selection based on the following principles:

- All organisms produce more offspring than can be supported by the supply of food, light, space, etc.
- Despite the over-production of offspring, most **populations** remain relatively constant in size.
- There must therefore be competition between members of a species to be the ones that survive = intraspecific competition, with individuals competing for resources such as food, breeding sites, space, light and water.
- Within any population of a species there will be a wide variety of genetically different organisms (17.1a).
- Some of these individuals will possess **alleles** that make them better adapted to survive (fitter) and so more likely to breed.
- Only those individuals that do survive and breed will pass on their alleles to the next generation.
- The advantageous alleles that gave these individuals the edge in the struggle to survive and reproduce are therefore likely to be passed on to the next generation.
- Over many generations, the individuals with beneficial alleles are more likely to survive to reproduce (breed) and therefore increase in number compared to the individuals with less favourable alleles.
- The frequency of favourable alleles in the population will increase over time. Any environmental factor that acts to give a difference in survival (differential survival) between individuals with different adaptations is known as a selection pressure (see 17.2b).

Over-production of offspring

Darwin appreciated that all species have the potential to increase their numbers exponentially. He realised that, in nature, populations rarely, if ever, increased in size at such a rate (Figure 1). He rightly concluded that the death rate of even the most slow-breeding species must be extremely high. For most species, the rate of reproduction and the production of offspring is high, but only a very small proportion survive. The reason why reproductive rates are high is because a species cannot control factors such as the climate, rate of predation, or availability of food. Therefore to ensure a sufficiently large population survives to breed and produce the next generation, each species must produce vast numbers of offspring. This is to compensate for considerable death rates from, for example, predation, lack of food (including light in plants) and water, extremes of temperature, or natural disasters such as earthquake and fire, disease.

> **Remember**
>
> If an environmental change is great enough, there may be no phenotype suited to the new conditions, in which case the population will die out.

How organisms over-produce depends on the species in question and its means of reproduction. Some examples include:

- A bacterium can divide by binary fission about every 20 minutes when conditions are favourable. A single bacterium could theoretically give rise to 4×10^{21} cells in just 24 hours.

- Some fungi can produce over 500 000 spores each minute at the peak of production. Each spore has the potential to develop a new fungal **mycelium**.
- Higher plants can spread rapidly by **vegetative propagation**, e.g. the production of bulbs, rhizomes, runners, etc.
- Flowering plants produce vast amounts of pollen from their anthers. These can fertilise the many ovules in plants of the same species, leading to the production, in some cases, of millions of seeds from a single plant.
- Animals produce vast numbers of sperm, and sometimes large numbers of eggs also. A female oyster, for example, can produce 100 million eggs in a year and the male oyster produces many more times this number of sperm.
- Many organisms, e.g. birds such as blue tits and mammals like the rabbit, produce several clutches/litters every year, each of which comprises several offspring.

Remember

- A population contains individuals that all belong to the same species.
- Intraspecific competition describes competition between members of the same species.
- Interspecific competition describes competition between different species.

Intraspecific competition

The importance of over-production to natural selection lies in the fact that, where there are too many offspring for the available resources, there is competition amongst individuals of the same species (**intraspecific competition**) for the limited resources available. The greater the numbers, the greater this competition and the more individuals will die in the struggle to survive. These deaths are, however, not random. Those individuals best suited to the conditions (have adaptations that make them better able to hide from or escape predators, better able to obtain light or catch prey or better able to resist disease) will be more likely to survive (differential survival) than those less well adapted. This means that the selection pressure acts **against** those less well adapted and acts **for** those that are better adapted. These individuals will be more likely to reproduce (differential reproduction) and so pass on these favourable characteristics, via their alleles, to the next generation, which will therefore be slightly different from the previous one – i.e. the species will have changed over time to be better adapted to the current conditions. This selection process, however, depends on individuals of a species being genetically different from one another.

Variation and natural selection

If an organism can survive in the conditions in which it lives, you may wonder why it doesn't produce offspring that are identical to itself. These will, after all, be equally capable of survival in these conditions, whereas variation may produce individuals that are less suited. However, conditions change over time and having a wide range of different individuals in the population means that some will have the combination of alleles needed to survive in almost any set of new circumstances. Populations showing little individual variation are vulnerable to new diseases and climate changes. It is also important that a species adapts to changes resulting from changes to the allele frequencies within other species. If, for example, rabbits in a particular region have alleles as a result of mutation that allow them to run faster, then foxes and other predators will be less able to catch them. The foxes will therefore have less food, unless they in turn develop greater speed as a result of new adaptations occurring from mutation.

Mutations occur in populations that are neutral in their effect. These may become beneficial in a changing environment. A species cannot predict future changes; it does not know whether the climate will become wetter/drier, warmer/colder or how its prey or predator populations will change, or what new disease agent may occur. However, the larger a population is, and the more genetically varied the organisms within it, the greater the chance that one or more individuals will have the genetic characteristics that give them an advantage in the struggle for survival. These individuals will therefore be more likely to breed and pass their more advantageous alleles on to future generations. Variation therefore provides the potential for a species to evolve and so adapt to new circumstances.

Summary test 17.2a

The theory of natural selection by survival of the fittest was developed independently by Charles Darwin and **(1)**. It is based on the principles that all organisms produce **(2)** offspring than can be supported by the food, light and space available for them. However, the size of most populations is **(3)** as a result of competition between members of each species for the limited resources available. This type of competition is called **(4)**. Within any population there will be many types of **(5)** different individuals. Those individuals with **(6)** that better suit them to the existing conditions are more likely to survive and so more likely to **(7)** and have offspring and pass on **(8)** for advantageous characteristics to the next generation. Over time, if **(9)** do not change and if the same **(10)** pressures are acting, the frequency of these alleles will increase in the **(11)**.

377

These pages help you to:

- explain how environmental factors can act as stabilising, disruptive and directional forces of natural selection (17.2.2)
- explain how selection may affect allele frequencies in populations (17.2.3)

You will also:

- be able to give examples of selection pressures
- be able to give examples of the three types of natural selection

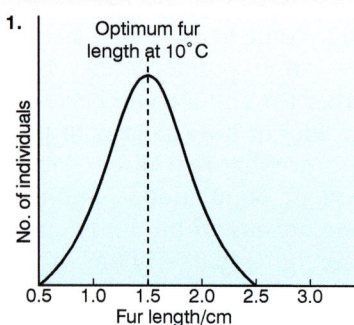

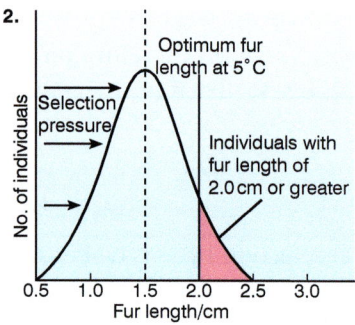

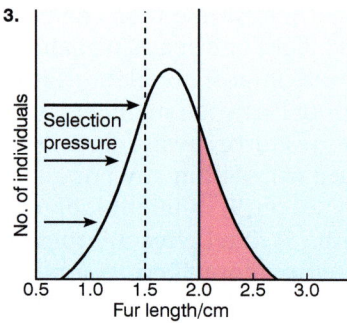

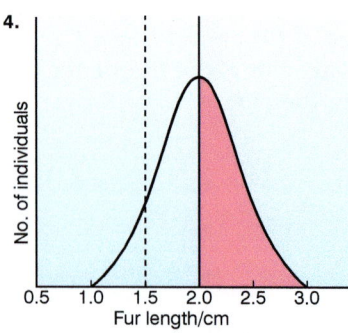

Any environmental factor that acts on a characteristic that shows variation in a population, and results in differential survival, is a selection pressure. Every organism faces a process of selection, based upon the organism's suitability for survival under the conditions that exist at the time. Common selection pressures that act on, and limit, populations include: competition for resources that may be in short supply (e.g. food, water, mates, space to live, breed and rear young); climatic factors (e.g. temperature, rainfall, wind, water currents, light intensity); predation; and disease.

Types of natural selection

A **gene pool** is the total of all the alleles of all the genes of all individuals within a particular population at a given time. Selection pressures act on phenotypes within a population, but in doing so they can also cause changes to the frequency of alleles in the gene pool over time.

There are three main types of selection:

- Selection that changes the characteristics of a population by favouring individuals that vary in one direction from the mean of the population = **directional selection**.
- Selection that preserves the characteristics of a population by favouring average individuals (those at or near the mean of the population) = **stabilising selection**.
- Selection that changes the characteristics of a population by favouring individuals at the extremes rather than those around the mean of the population = **disruptive selection**. Figures 1, 2 and 3 use a theoretical example of fur length in a particular mammalian species.

Directional selection

Within a population there will be a range of individuals in respect of any one characteristic, such as fur length. The continuous variation amongst these individuals forms a normal distribution curve which has a mean that represents the optimum value for the characteristic under the existing conditions. If the environmental conditions change, so will the optimum value needed for survival. Some individuals, either to the left or the right of the mean, will possess a phenotype with the new optimum for the characteristic and so there will be a selection pressure moving the mean to either the left or the right of its original position. Directional selection therefore results in one extreme of a range of variation being selected against in favour of the other extreme. Antibiotic resistance in bacteria (17.2c) is an example of directional selection.

Stabilising selection

Stabilising selection tends to eliminate the extremes of the **phenotype** range within a population and with it the opportunity for evolutionary change. It arises

Figure 1 *Directional selection*

1.	When the average environmental temperature is 10 °C, the optimum fur length is 1.5 cm. This then represents the mean fur length of the population.
2.	A few individuals in the population already have a fur length of 2.0 cm or greater. If the average environmental temperature falls to 5 °C, these individuals are better insulated and so are more likely to survive to breed. There is a selection pressure favouring individuals with longer fur.
3.	The selection pressure causes a shift in the mean fur length towards longer fur over a number of generations. The selection pressure continues.
4.	Over further generations the shift in the mean fur length continues until it reaches 2.0 cm – the optimum length for the average environmental temperature of 5 °C. The selection pressure now stops provided the environmental temperature stays the same.

where the environmental conditions are constant. Figure 2 shows that in years when the environmental temperatures are hotter than usual, the individuals with shorter fur length will be at an advantage because they can lose body heat more rapidly. In colder years the opposite is true and those with longer fur length will survive better as they are better insulated. Therefore, if the environment fluctuates from year to year, both extremes will survive because each will have some years when it can thrive at the expense of the other. If, the environmental temperature is constantly 10 °C, individuals at the extremes will never be at an advantage and will be selected against in favour of those with average fur length. The mean will remain the same, but there will be fewer individuals at either extreme (Figure 2). An actual example of stabilising selection is the body mass of human children at birth. Babies born with a body mass greater or less than the optimum of 3.2 kg have a higher mortality rate.

Disruptive selection

Disruptive selection is the opposite of stabilising selection. It favours the two extreme phenotypes and does not favour the intermediate phenotype. It is the least common form of selection, but is most important in bringing about evolutionary change. In our example this might occur if the temperature alternated between 5 °C in winter (favouring long fur length) and 15 °C in summer (favouring short fur length). This could lead at some time in the future to two separate species of the mammal – one with long fur and active in winter, the other with short fur and active in summer (Figure 3). Another example is coho salmon, where large males and small males have a selective advantage over intermediate-sized males in passing on their alleles to the next generation. The small males are able to sneak up to the females in the spawning grounds. The large males are fierce competitors. This leaves intermediate-sized males at a disadvantage and they will be less likely to pass on their alleles.

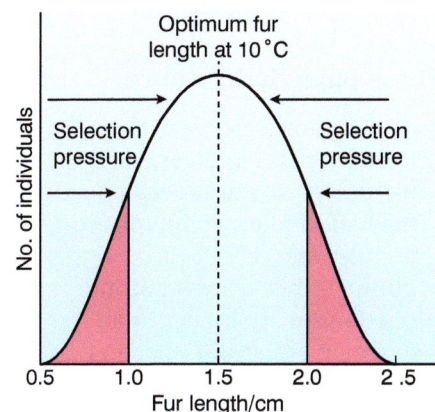

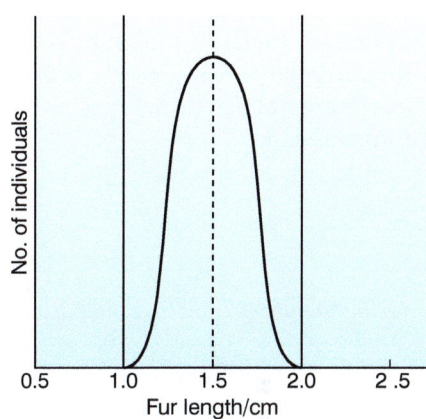

1. Initially there is a wide range of fur lengths about the mean of 1.5 cm. The fur lengths of less than 1.0 cm or greater than 2.0 cm in individuals are maintained by rapid breeding in years when the average temperature is much warmer or colder than normal.

2. When the average environmental temperature is consistently around 10 °C with little annual variation, individuals with very long or very short hair are eliminated from the population over a number of generations.

Figure 2 *Stabilising selection*

Summary test 17.2b

Natural selection that acts over time to remove extreme **(1)** is known as **(2)**. This occurs when environmental conditions are **(3)**. If intermediate phenotypes are selected against, this is known as **(4)** selection. The type of natural selection occurring where phenotypes to the right or left of the optimum (mean) are selected for is known as **(5)**. **(6)** selection is least likely to lead to the formation of new species. With **(7)** selection, the mean does not change from the original population mean.

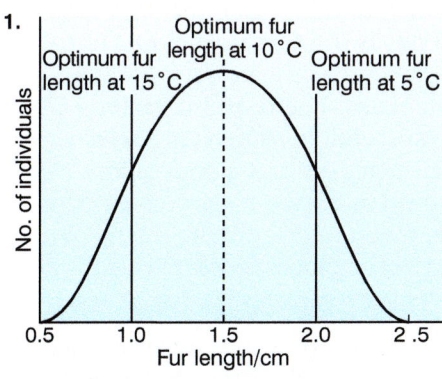

1. When there is a wide range of temperatures throughout the year, there is continuous variation in fur length around a mean of 1.5 cm.

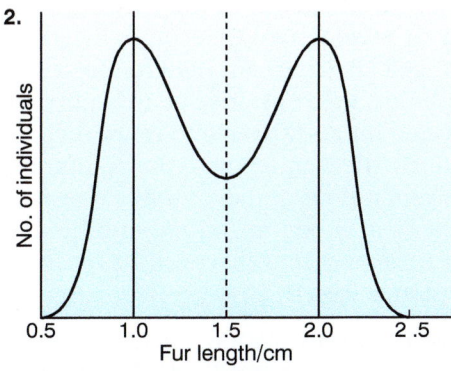

2. Where the summer temperature is static around 15 °C and the winter temperature is static around 5 °C, individuals with two distinct fur lengths predominate: 1.0 cm types which are active in summer and 2.0 cm types which are active in winter.

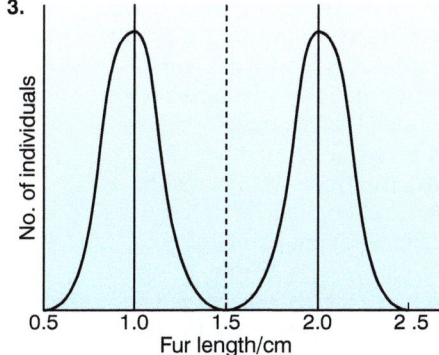

3. After many generations two distinct sub-populations are formed.

Figure 3 *Disruptive selection*

These pages help you to:

- explain how selection, the founder effect and genetic drift, including the bottleneck effect, may affect allele frequencies in populations (17.2.3)
- outline how bacteria become resistant to antibiotics as an example of natural selection (17.2.4)

You will also:

- understand what is meant by heterozygote advantage
- learn more about horizontal transmission

Remember

Mutations are rare, but because there are so many bacteria and because they have a short generation time, it is no surprise that mutations that give bacteria resistance to antibiotics can occur.

Extension

Horizontal gene transmission

There are three different modes of horizontal transmission:

- **Conjugation** – involves physical contact between bacteria. A conjugation tube is formed and a copy of DNA passes across from one donor bacterium to a recipient. Plasmids are frequently successfully passed across as they are small.
- **Transformation** – when bacteria die, the plasmids that are released can be taken up by other bacteria.
- **Transduction** – by viruses that infect bacteria (bacteriophages). When new viral particles are assembled, the gene for resistance can be accidentally packaged and the genes are transferred when the viruses infect other bacterial cells. Frequently, the virus does not damage the bacterial cell, allowing it to survive.

In theory, any sexually mature individual in a **population** is capable of breeding with any other. This means that the **alleles** of any individual organism may combine with the alleles of any other individual in the population.

Before looking at allele frequencies, we need to understand what is meant by a 'population'. A population is a group of organisms of the same species that occupies a particular space at a particular time and may potentially interbreed.

Any species may exist as one or more populations. More information on populations is given in Chapter 18.

All the alleles of all the genes of all the individuals in a population at any one time is known as the gene pool. The number of times an allele occurs within the gene pool (see 17.2b) is referred to as the allele frequency.

There are a number of different processes that can affect allele frequencies and diversity in the gene pool (17.2b) of populations. However, the extent of the effect of each of these is different within different populations. In a stable population in unchanging conditions, the main force acting on allele frequencies is the process of genetic drift. This may have a relatively small effect or cause dramatic changes, as in the bottleneck effect and founder effect, discussed here.

Antibiotic resistance in bacteria

Natural selection leads to an increase in the frequency of advantageous alleles in a population. It is a process that occurs for all species. The development of antibiotic resistance in bacteria is a well-known example of directional selection.

Soon after the discovery of antibiotics, it was observed that some antibiotics no longer killed bacteria as effectively as before. These populations of bacteria had become resistant to the antibiotics (10.2a) as a result of chance mutations. Genes with mutations that conferred antibiotic resistance are commonly located on plasmids (1.2f), which can replicate within the bacterial cell.

Let us consider two people, R and S, who are prescribed a course of an antibiotic for a bacterial infection. This rapidly kills the most susceptible bacteria and R and S soon feel better. S finishes the course and all the bacteria are destroyed. R stops taking the antibiotics, leaving a reservoir of bacteria in the body that can divide for a number of generations, increasing the chance of a mutation in a bacterium which gives it resistance to the antibiotic. This is not advantageous in the absence of the antibiotic. However, the population gets to a size where R becomes ill again and needs the same antibiotic. In this changed environment, where the selection pressure is the presence of the antibiotic, the resistance gene is now advantageous. The resistant bacteria are selected for and survive to reproduce, while susceptible bacteria are selected against. The frequency of the resistance gene increases in the population over the generations and eventually a resistant strain of bacteria is produced. The bacteria may be transmitted to other people, who now cannot be treated with the antibiotic. In this way, R has contributed to the global problem of antibiotic resistance (see 10.2a).

In vertical transmission, bacteria are also able to pass on genes for resistance to the two new cells produced during asexual reproduction (a process known as binary fission). In horizontal transmission, the gene for resistance passes across to other bacteria (see Extension) of the same or other species.

Genetic drift

Genetic drift describes a situation where the frequency of alleles in the gene pool may fluctuate over time due to random events. Changes to the gene pool are as a result of chance and cannot be predicted. For example, over one or a few generations, from random fusion or random mating or other chance events, there could be a slight decrease in the frequency of an allele, but in the next one or in a few generations this might increase again and so overall the frequency appears to remain the same.

Genetic drift has a greater impact in small populations than large ones, because there is a greater chance that an allele will be lost from a population, which will reduce variation. Overall, the effect of genetic drift over a large number of generations is a loss of alleles.

Changes to the gene pool caused by genetic drift are usually not extreme enough to cause a large effect from one generation to the next. However, the bottleneck effect and the founder effect are two examples of genetic drift where the gene pool can change markedly in a short time.

The bottleneck effect

Sometimes a large decrease in genetic diversity is seen in populations that also have a sudden decrease in population numbers. For example, fire or a natural disaster such as an earthquake can lead to only a small group of survivors and a gene pool that does not reflect the same variety of the original gene pool.

Some animal species have experienced a population bottleneck because humans have hunted them to near extinction in the past. The few individuals remaining have a limited gene pool compared to the larger original population. **Conservation** efforts can help numbers to recover, but because there is a limited gene pool, an increase in numbers does not mean an increase in genetic diversity (see Extension).

The founder effect

The founder effect occurs when just a few individuals from a population colonise a new region. These few individuals will carry with them only a small fraction of the alleles of the population as a whole. This means that the gene pool of the founder population may not be representative of the gene pool of the larger population. The new population that develops from the few colonisers will therefore show less genetic diversity than the population from which they came.

The founder effect often takes place when new volcanic islands rise up out of the sea. The few individuals that colonise these barren islands give rise to populations that are genetically distinct from the populations they left behind. The new population may, in time, develop into a separate species. As these species have lower genetic diversity they are less able to adapt to changing conditions than the original population. Darwin's finches are a well-known example of the founder effect (see 17.3c).

Extension

An example of a genetic bottleneck effect

Genetic analysis and computer modelling show that the Florida panther, *Puma concolor coryi*, (Figure 1) has a third of the genetic diversity of Florida panthers living in the 19th century. This is because of a severe bottleneck effect. This occurred as a result of human effects, mainly by loss of habitat and from conflicts resulting in the death of puma. These caused the decline of the population in the 1970s to lower than 30 individuals. The population in the wild has since recovered to about 120 individuals, but these pumas are still under threat from habitat loss and human disturbance.

Figure 1 *The Florida panther, Puma concolor coryi*

Extension

Sickle cell anaemia and malaria

Sickle cell anaemia (Figure 2) is a disease that occurs throughout the world, mainly in people from sub-Saharan Africa, India, Saudi Arabia and Mediterranean countries. Selection acts against individuals with the sickle cell anaemia phenotype (16.2i). In many countries where the disease is most common, the lack of access to medical treatment means that many children die before they are 5 years old, and so do not pass on the recessive allele (Hb^S) to the next generation. Therefore, it would be

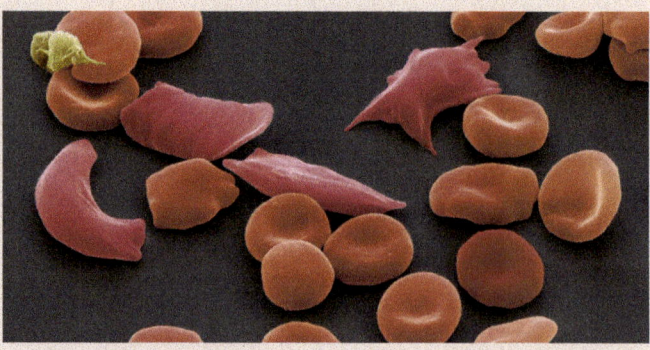

Figure 2 Scanning electron micrograph of red blood cells in sickle cell anaemia. The sickle shaped cells (pink) are the result of a single base substitution in the DNA that codes for the beta-globin chain of haemoglobin.

expected that the frequency of Hb^S would decrease in these populations. However, the malarial parasite, *Plasmodium falciparum*, is less able to survive in red blood cells containing haemoglobin-S (Hb-S), which means that in areas where malaria is endemic, individuals with the sickle cell trait phenotype (genotype Hb^{A}Hb^S) have a greater chance of survival than individuals with the normal haemoglobin-A phenotype (genotype Hb^{A}Hb^A) (Figure 3). This is known as heterozygote advantage and is a mechanism that maintains the frequency of the recessive allele in the population. If both parents have the sickle cell trait phenotype, they could have children with sickle cell anaemia.

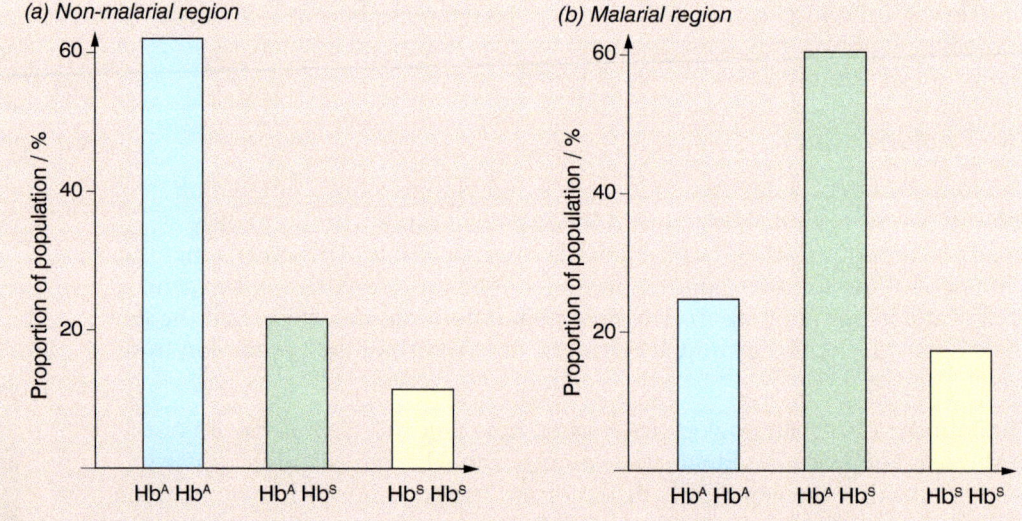

Figure 3 Distribution of the sickle cell allele in a non-malarial and a malarial population

Remember

Environmental factors do **not** affect the probability of a **particular** mutant allele occurring, they simply affect the frequency of a mutant allele that is already present in the gene pool. Some environmental factors may influence the overall **mutation** rate (such as ionising radiations, 6.2d), but this is a **general** and **random** process rather than one that affects a specific allele in a specific way.

Extension

Industrial melanism, an example of natural selection and changes in allele frequencies

Some species of organisms have two or more distinct forms or morphs. These different forms are genetically distinct but exist within the same interbreeding population. This situation is called **polymorphism** ('poly' = many; 'morph' = form). One example is the peppered moth (*Biston betularia*) in England. The original form of the moth is light coloured. It is well camouflaged when resting on lichen-covered trees and rocks. In rural areas, the majority of moths are light coloured. Melanic (black) forms of the moth that arose by mutation are easily seen and eaten by predators (insect-eating birds). With increased industrialisation (in the middle of the nineteenth century), pollution killed the lichen on the trees, and rocks, and buildings were covered by black

Figure 4 *Industrial melanism in the peppered moth (Biston betularia). Against a natural background (above) the dark melanic form is far more visible and more readily predated on by birds. Natural selection favours the light form in rural areas. In polluted areas, however, the melanic form is better camouflaged and this selective advantage leads to this form being favoured by natural selection.*

soot (particles from industrial smoke). In the populations of moths in these areas, light moths were no longer well camouflaged and the now better camouflaged melanic form increased in numbers. Over the generations, the frequency of the melanic form in these populations rapidly increased (Figure 4).

This is an example of how a change in the environment can rapidly alter the allele frequency in populations. Here the variation that exists is the light and dark forms, and the selection pressure exerted is predation by birds. The moths are still members of the same species and can interbreed. To become two distinct species, the two populations would need to become reproductively isolated from one another (17.3a).

Extension

A word from Darwin

Darwin did not know about alleles, but his observations about biological variation, the struggle for existence, and survival of the fittest are the basis for our understanding of changes in allele frequencies in populations. In 1844, Darwin wrote:

'Now can it be doubted, from the struggle each individual has to obtain subsistence, that any minute variation in structure, habits, or instincts, adapting that individual better to the new conditions, would tell upon its vigour and health? In the struggle it would have a better *chance* of surviving; and those of its offspring which inherited the variation, be it ever so slight, would have a better *chance*'.

Summary test 17.2c

Natural selection and genetic drift are two mechanisms that can cause changes to allele frequencies and to the **(1)** of populations. In natural selection, phenotypes with **(2)** alleles are selected for. These phenotypes will survive to **(3)** and pass on these alleles to the next generation. Genetic drift is a **(4)** process and so changes over generations cannot be **(5)**. The **(6)** effect is caused when there is a rapid decline in the size of a population and this is accompanied by a decrease in **(7)**. The **(8)** effect describes a situation where a new population is formed by a few individuals that have been separated from the main population.

These pages help you to:

- state the conditions when the Hardy–Weinberg principle can be applied (17.2.5)
- use the two provided equations of the Hardy–Weinberg principle to calculate allele and genotype frequencies in populations (17.2.5)

You will also:

- read about some aspects of population genetics

Extension

Population genetics

Population genetics is the study of the genetic composition of populations. Studying changes to the gene pools of populations is a key aspect of population genetics as it provides us with information about evolutionary change. There are a number of factors that cause these changes: natural selection, genetic drift, migration, immigration and emigration. In some species, such as in humans, there is also non-random mating, which will have an affect on allele frequencies. In non-random mating, individuals show a sexual preference for a particular phenotype.

Remember

Recessive and dominant has nothing to do with whether an allele is harmful or beneficial. People with type O blood group have two recessive alleles for the *I* gene ($I^O I^O$). As it is the most common blood group it can hardly be harmful. Also, Huntington's disease is a life-limiting condition due to a dominant allele.

Remember

All the alleles of all the genes of all the individuals in a population at any one time is known as the gene pool. The number of times an allele occurs within the gene pool is referred to as the allele frequency.

Let us look at how allele frequency can vary within a gene pool by considering just one gene that has two alleles, one of which is dominant and the other recessive. An example is the gene responsible for cystic fibrosis, a disease in humans in which the mucus produced by affected individuals is thicker than usual (see 19.2b). The gene has a dominant allele (F) that leads to normal mucus production and a recessive allele (f) that leads to the production of thicker mucus and hence cystic fibrosis. Any individual human has two of these alleles in every one of their cells, one on each of the pair of homologous chromosomes on which the gene is found. As these alleles are the same in every cell, we only count one pair of alleles, per gene, per individual when considering a gene pool. If there are 10 000 people in a population, there will be twice as many (20 000) alleles in the gene pool of this gene.

The pair of alleles of the cystic fibrosis gene has three different possible combinations, namely homozygous dominant (FF), homozygous recessive (ff) and heterozygous (Ff). When we look at genotype frequencies, however, it is important to appreciate that the heterozygous combination can exist in two different arrangements, namely Ff and fF (it is just convention that we put the dominant allele first in all cases). This is because the male parent may contribute either F or f as gametes and the female parent also F or f.

In any population, the total number of alleles is taken to be 1.0. In our population of 10 000 people, if everyone had the genotype FF, then the frequency of the dominant allele (F) would be 1.0 and the frequency of the recessive allele (f) would be 0.0. If everyone was heterozygous Ff, the frequency of the dominant allele (F) would be 0.5 and the frequency of the recessive allele (f) would be 0.5. Of course, in practice, the population is not made up of one genotype, but a mixture of all three, the proportions of which vary from population to population. How then can we work out the allele frequency of these mixed populations?

The Hardy–Weinberg principle

The Hardy–Weinberg principle provides a mathematical equation that can be used to calculate the frequencies of the alleles of a particular gene in a population. The principle predicts that the proportion of dominant and recessive alleles of any gene in a population remains the same from one generation to the next provided that five conditions are met:

- no mutations occur
- the population is isolated, i.e. there is no flow of alleles into or out of the population
- there is no selection, i.e. all alleles are equally likely to pass to the next generation
- the population is large – large populations reduce the effect that chance events will have on allele frequencies
- mating within the population is random.

Although these conditions are probably never totally met in a natural population, the Hardy–Weinberg principle is still useful when studying allele and genotype frequencies to give us an estimate of these frequencies.

To help us understand the principle, let us consider a gene that has two alleles, a dominant allele A and a recessive allele a.

Let the frequency of allele A = p.
Let the frequency of allele a = q.

The first equation we can write is:

$$p + q = 1.0$$

because there are only two alleles and so the frequency of one plus the other must be 1.0 (100%).

A genotype results from the fertilisation of the male and female gamete. Table 1 shows the outcome of random fertilisation of gametes from heterozygous parents.

Table 1 *Results obtained from the random fusion of gametes of two heterozygous parents*

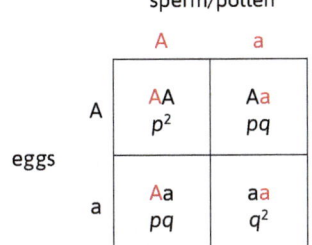

The probability of 'taking' an A gamete from the pool = p

The probability of 'taking' an a gamete from the pool = q

(male A × female A) = $p × p = p^2$
(male a × female a) = $q × q = q^2$
(male A × female a) = $p × q = pq$
(male a × female A) = $q × p = pq$

Therefore we can state that:

AA + Aa + aA + aa = 1.0   or, expressing this as genotype frequencies:

$$p^2 + 2pq + q^2 = 1.0 \text{ (Hardy–Weinberg equation)}$$

We can now use these equations to determine the frequency of any allele in a population and to calculate the frequency of the heterozygous genotype in a population. For example, suppose that a particular characteristic is the result of a recessive allele a, and we know that one person in 25 000 displays the characteristic.

- The characteristic, being recessive, will only be observed in individuals who have two recessive alleles aa.
- The frequency of aa must be 1/25 000 or 0.00004.
- The frequency of aa is q^2.
- If $q^2 = 0.00004$, then $q = \sqrt{0.00004}$ or 0.0063 approx.
- We know that the frequency of both alleles A and a is $p + q$ and is equal to 1.0.
- If $p + q = 1.0$, and $q = 0.0063$ then, $p = 1.0 − 0.0063 = 0.9937$, i.e. the frequency of allele A = 0.9937.
- We can now calculate the frequency of the heterozygous individuals in the population.
- From the Hardy–Weinberg equation we know that the frequency of the heterozygotes is $2pq$.
- In this case $2pq = (2 × 0.9937 × 0.0063) = 0.0125$.
- In other words, 125 individuals in 10 000 carry the recessive allele for the characteristic. This is the equivalent of 313 in our population of 25 000.
- These individuals act as a reservoir of recessive alleles in the population, although they do not express the allele in their phenotype.

These pages help you to:

- describe the principles of selective breeding (artificial selection) (17.2.6)
- outline the improvement of milk yield of dairy cattle as an example of selective breeding (17.2.7)

You will also:

- learn about artificial insemination and embryo transplantation

Selective breeding, also known as artificial selection, involves identifying individuals with the desired characteristics and using them to parent the next generation. Offspring that do not exhibit (show) the desired characteristic are not allowed to survive, or at least prevented from breeding. In this way the **gene pool** is deliberately restricted to a number of desired alleles and this smaller gene pool means that the genetic variation within the **population** is reduced. Over many generations, this leads to all individuals within a population possessing the desired qualities. Some differences between selective breeding and natural selection are given in Table 1.

Table 1 *Differences between selective breeding and natural selection*

Selective breeding	Natural selection
Selection pressure exerted by humans	Selection pressure exerted by environmental factors
Genetic diversity is lowered	Genetic diversity remains high
Does not lead to new species forming	May lead to new species forming
Inbreeding is common, leading to loss of hybrid vigour in offspring	Outbreeding is common, leading to hybrid vigour
Proportion of heterozygotes in the population is reduced	Proportion of heterozygotes in the population remains high
Genetic isolation mechanisms do not operate	Genetic isolation mechanisms operate

Carrying out selective breeding

There are two main methods of carrying out selective breeding:

- **Outbreeding** involves the breeding of unrelated individuals. This may be used to try to combine two different desirable characteristics each possessed by separate individuals, for example by crossing a crop plant that gives an excellent yield with one resistant to disease in the expectation of a plant with a high yield and disease resistance. Outbreeding by crossing two individuals from different inbred strains can frequently produce more hardy (tougher) organisms that are genetically superior to their parents and have a higher chance of survival. This is known as **hybrid vigour**.
- **Inbreeding** is used to keep, as far as possible, a desirable characteristic that has arisen by chance **mutation**. By breeding the individual with close relatives, the chances of the offspring showing the desired characteristic are greater. There are harmful effects with inbreeding. For example, there is loss of hybrid vigour, with the population being weakened over generations by a lack of diversity and reduced fertility. This is known as inbreeding depression. There is also an increased danger of a harmful recessive allele expressing itself, because there is a greater risk of a **homozygous recessive** individual arising. As a result, inbreeding is not carried out indefinitely and outbreeding may be needed to make the population stronger and healthier.

Figure 1 *Domesticated milking cow*

Figure 2 *Wild cow (Bos sp.)*

Selective breeding for increased milk production in dairy cows

Although the primary focus is to breed cattle that produce an increased volume of milk, there are a number of other characteristics that are desirable in these cattle. Selective breeding in modern-day cattle will therefore also consider factors such as:

- high volume of milk produced each day
- length of milking (lactation) period – can obtain the same quantity of milk by housing and feeding fewer cows, which reduces costs

- high protein and fat content of milk for the particular breed of cattle concerned (different breeds have different protein and fat contents)
- type of udder, e.g. degree of support, length, shape and angle of teats (important for use of the milking machine)
- quantity and type of feed required
- disease resistance, e.g. to mastitis – this is inflammation of the udder, a common disease in dairy cattle
- good temperament (e.g. calm, cooperative and can cope with a long length of time attached to milking machine).

The selective breeding process is outlined as follows:

- Selecting a suitable cow and bull by consulting the pedigree records of each and through progeny testing.
- Collection of sperm from the selected bull and storing by freezing.
- Detection of when the cow is in **oestrus** by observing changes in her behaviour, e.g. increasing restlessness, mounting other cows and being mounted by them, feeding less.
- Artificially inseminating the defrosted semen into the cow.
- Checking that fertilisation has occurred and that the cow is in calf.

An alternative to artificial insemination is the use of embryo transplantation (see Extension).

Although selective breeding has improved milk production in dairy cattle, it has also created issues. Two of the main problems are a decrease in fertility, and a greater susceptibility to metabolic disorders.

Progeny testing

Progeny testing involves the maintenance of detailed data on all the offspring (progeny) of a particular organism. In the case of dairy cattle this might include growth rate of the calves, body size, amount of body fat, milk yield, quality of milk, length of lactation period, lifespan and veterinary history. The data produced are extremely useful in selecting the correct animal for any particular set of desired characteristics, based upon the offspring it has already produced.

Summary test 17.2e

Selective breeding is also known as **(1)** and differs from natural selection in that genetic diversity is **(2)** and the proportion of **(3)** in the population is reduced. The two main methods of carrying out selective breeding are **(4)** and **(5)**. The process can be used with dairy herds to increase milk production and begins with the selection of a suitable bull and cow by consulting the **(6)** records of each and the checking of data on the offspring each have produced – a process called **(7)**. Semen is then collected from the chosen bull and inserted into the **(8)** of the chosen cow by a technique known as **(9)**. Alternatively, ova may be removed from the cow and fertilised in the laboratory before being returned to the donor cow. This process is known as **(10)**.

Extension

Artificial insemination and embryo transplantation

Artificial insemination (AI) is the collection of semen and its introduction into the vagina or uterus by artificial means. Some of the advantages of AI over natural selection include:

- Specific characteristics required in the offspring can be selected.
- Cattle do not need to be transported for mating to occur – the semen can be frozen and transported.
- Frozen semen can be kept for years, often long after the death of the donor bull.
- The costs of keeping bulls are reduced or eliminated altogether.
- The rate of conception is greater.
- The risk of contracting a sexually transmitted disease is reduced.

One disadvantage of artificial insemination is that the semen of one male can be used to inseminate many hundreds of females and there is less genetic diversity amongst offspring than where natural processes are used.

Embryo transplantation involves fertilising ova in the laboratory before implanting the developing embryos into the uterus of the natural or a surrogate mother.

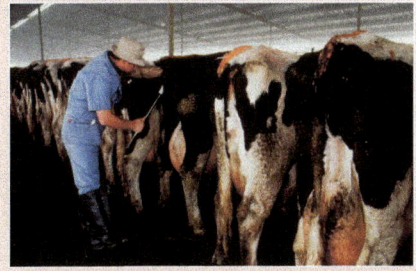

Figure 3 *Artificial insemination of cattle*

These pages help you to:

- outline the introduction of disease resistance in varieties of wheat and rice as examples of selective breeding (17.2.7)
- know about inbreeding and hybridisation in maize to produce vigorous, uniform varieties (17.2.7)

You will also:

- read about selective breeding to produce dwarf varieties

Figure 1 *Wheat plants infected with a fungal disease known as brown rust* (Puccinia recondita)

Extension

Using genetic markers in selective breeding

Marker-assisted selection (MAS) can be used in plant breeding to reduce the time taken to produce a new plant breed (e.g. from 25 years to 10 years). A gene marker is a sequence of nucleotides located very close to the nucleotide sequence of the desired gene. The marker is inherited with the gene, so identification of the marker indicates that the desired gene is likely to be present, and narrows down the area of DNA to be analysed to confirm the presence of the desired gene.

To supply the food required to satisfy the increasing demands of an expanding world population, crops need to be constantly improved so they yield more. One major loss of yield is due to crop diseases. Toxins (mycotoxins) produced as a result of some fungal diseases may be harmful to humans when they eat crop products. Although many of these diseases can be managed by pesticides, selectively breeding resistant varieties is a more ecologically sound and sustainable way of achieving control of disease. The main stages in selective breeding are:

- to decide which characteristics are desirable
- to select the parents that show these characteristics
- to choose the offspring that most clearly display these characteristics and use them to breed the next generation
- to repeat the process continuously.

Let us now consider some examples of how selective breeding is used to improve crops.

Introduction of disease resistance to varieties of wheat

Diseases of wheat, *Triticum aestivum*, such as rusts (Figure 1) and mildews caused by fungal pathogens, are a major factor in reducing crop yields. The more resistant a variety of wheat is to disease, the greater the potential yield. Farmers have always selected those plants that were most productive and, in doing so, will have selected disease-resistant varieties along with other favourable features.

More recently, scientists have deliberately crossed wheat plants known to be disease resistant with others that were known to be high yielding. Initially they targeted resistance to particular diseases but soon chance mutations led to the **pathogen** developing resistance to the disease, leaving the wheat vulnerable once again. Attention has since turned to selecting varieties of wheat with features that give more general resistance to most diseases rather than just to a specific one.

Modern breeders can now use computers to search through the entire DNA of an organism in a process known as genome scanning. They can scan the genome of wheat plants and detect regions that differ between disease-resistant ones and those that are not resistant. They can then use gene markers (see Extension) to test new varieties of wheat for those genes that give disease resistance. This allows them to select plants more quickly than growing large numbers to maturity to see whether they have inherited the desired resistance.

Introduction of disease resistance to varieties of rice

The fungal disease known as blast is among the most widespread and damaging diseases of Asian rice, *Oryza sativa*, and can cause more than 50% losses in yield. Selection of varieties of rice that are resistant to blast has followed the same pattern as selecting disease-resistant varieties of wheat. Breeders screen and breed for resistance to blast, along with other desired traits that will suit various ecosystems. Selected plants showing resistance to blast are grown and F_1 seeds are increased to produce the F_2 generation. Starting from the F_2, breeders evaluate the lines for blast resistance. Selection for blast resistance, along with other desired traits, such as high yield, begins at the F_2 generation and continues for a number of generations.

Gene markers are also used to speed up the selection process. 'Tetep', a rice cultivar from Vietnam, has several genes that give resistance to blast. These have been tagged with markers linked to the genes. These markers are then used to look for the same genes in plants used in breeding experiments, so that they can be selected.

Another disease affecting Asian rice is bacterial blight disease. African rice, *Oryza glaberrima*, is known for its resistance to blast and to bacterial blight disease. Crop improvement by carrying out interspecific crosses (*O. sativa* × *O. glaberrima*) is another way of producing disease-resistant Asian rice. Here, varieties can be screened for the best resistance to disease and the ability to grow in a wide range of environments. Desirable features of disease resistance include long-term resistance and resistance in seeds.

Inbreeding and hybridisation in maize

For generations, humans have selectively bred organisms in order to obtain varieties that produce characteristics they find beneficial. They largely do this by cross fertilising two closely related individuals displaying the desired characteristic. These individuals will have similar genotypes and leads to homozygosity and reduced genetic variation. This is called **inbreeding** and was discussed in 17.2e. We also saw that crossing two individuals from different inbred strains (outbreeding) can produce organisms that are genetically superior to their parents. This is known as **hybrid vigour** and leads to increased heterozygosity.

Hybridisation is combining the genes of different varieties or species of organism to produce a **hybrid**.

Up to the beginning of the twentieth century, in maize, *Zea mays*, inbreeding to produce greater yields was common. The yield from these inbred varieties gradually declined, probably due to an increase in the frequency of harmful recessive alleles. Then scientists crossed two different inbred varieties (Southern Dent and Northern Flint) to produce a hybrid that increased yields up to four times. Since that time many hybrid varieties of maize have been developed. These produce the taller, more resistant and higher yielding plants that are grown today.

The new genetic variety within hybrids is clearly beneficial to farmers. The problems associated with inbreeding depression do not occur (see 17.2e). It has a disadvantage, however, in

that crosses between numbers of different strains produces variety between individual plants. Farmers prefer uniformity (Figure 2) because similar plants are easier to harvest and produce a more uniform crop which is easier to sell.

To overcome this, companies now produce different strains of maize where each one is the result of a single cross. The farmer can then choose a strain knowing that all the seed purchased will produce F_1 plants that have the same genotype. These will provide uniformity while still showing hybrid vigour. With numerous F_1 strains available, different farmers can choose the one most suitable for their particular circumstances. Some may select drought-resistant varieties, others, ones that thrive (grow) best on a clay soil and yet others ones that are resistant to a particular pest found in their region. It follows that farmers no longer keep their own seed to sow because the plants produced would not breed true for the characteristic they want. Instead they purchase fresh F_1 seeds from commercial suppliers every year.

Figure 2 *Field of hybrid maize plants showing the uniformity preferred by farmers*

Summary test 17.2f

Selective breeding to create disease resistance in wheat is used to increase (**1**). To improve varieties, breeders scan the (**2**) of wheat plants to detect differences between resistant and non-resistant varieties. Gene markers can then be used to test new varieties for genes that give resistance. A similar technique is used to select varieties of (**3**) that are resistant to a disease called blast. In the past, selective breeding in maize involved the process of (**4**) to increase crop yield. Here, (**5**) individuals with very similar (**6**) were crossed. Over time, (**7**) occurred – fertility and crop yield of these varieties had decreased. A change of method to a process known as (**8**) increased yield. Two different (**9**) varieties were crossed to produce superior individuals known as hybrids, which give higher yield, are (**10**) and more (**11**) to disease. To overcome the problems of producing (**12**) with this method, farmers can buy F_2 seeds that will have the same genotype and (**13**) when grown.

Figure 1 *Charles Darwin*

Figure 2 *Alfred Russel Wallace*

Evolution

Evidence from fossils shows that organisms have changed over time, or evolved. New species form, over time, from species that already exist (pre-existing species). The gene pool of each population is unique, and changes to gene pools from generation to generation can therefore lead to new species.

Some species become extinct as new species form. Some species form as a result of a population bottleneck or the founder effect (see genetic drift in 17.2c).

The theory of evolution

The theory of evolution has been developed to explain how species have formed, and how organisms change over time. The theory also helps to explain the biodiversity (see Chapter 18) that we have on Earth. The main features of the theory, together with some further explanation, are listed below.

- Species have evolved over time through a process of change from pre-existing species.
  - The formation of new species, which is discussed in more detail in 17.3b, is known as speciation.
  - Because changes occur in small stages and over many generations, evolutionary change is gradual.
  - An evolutionary timescale can be as long as many thousands, or hundreds of thousands, of years.
  - Evolution and speciation will generally occur more slowly in organisms that have long generation times.
- There is variation within a population (17.1a and 17.1b).
  - Variation results from mutation (6.2d), which introduces new alleles into the gene pool of a population.
  - Mutations that occur during gamete formation can be inherited and passed to future generations.
  - In sexually reproducing organisms, variation occurs as a result of random assortment and recombination of genes at meiosis, and of random fusion of gametes at fertilisation (16.1c).
- Nearly all species produce more offspring than can be supported by the available resources (17.2a).
  - The size of most populations remains relatively stable.
  - Within a population, there is competition for resources that are in short supply (struggle for existence).
- Natural selection (17.2a) is a mechanism proposed in 1858 by Charles Darwin (Figure 1) and Alfred Russel Wallace (Figure 2) to explain how evolution can occur.
- Natural selection acts because there is biological variation within the population – those with adaptations that confer a survival advantage are more likely to survive and pass on their alleles to the next generation.
  - Over time, natural selection leads to changes in the gene pool of populations.
- Organisms are descended from a common ancestor.
  - The 'Tree of Life' represents a pathway, in which branching shows speciation. German zoologist Ernst Haeckel was known for his early versions of the Tree of Life.
  - The more recently separated two species are, the more closely related they are.

DNA sequence data and evolutionary relationships

The theory of evolution includes the concept that species form from pre-existing species. In 17.3b we will see how speciation can occur. As changes occur over millions of years, how can we determine which organisms are closely related? One method is to compare the DNA of different species.

Phylogenetics is the study of evolutionary relationships between organisms. One method used to work out evolutionary relationships is to compare the genomes of species to look for similarities and differences between them. The entire genome of an organism consists of the DNA found in the nucleus, nuclear DNA, as well as mitochondrial DNA (mtDNA). Plants also have the DNA that is found in their chloroplasts.

Using DNA sequence data in studies of evolutionary relationships involves comparing the sequence of nucleotide bases in DNA for particular genes, or comparing information for whole genomes. As more species have their genome or part of their genome sequenced, it means that the quantity of data collected so far is vast (extremely large). Evolutionary biologists can now process and analyse data using advanced techniques in information technology and the results of these analyses are making important contributions to constructing phylogenetic trees.

Changes to the nucleotide sequence in DNA occurs by mutation and over evolutionary time the number of inherited mutations build up. This means that more closely related species will share more mutations than distantly related species. In addition to base substitution mutations, there will be insertion and deletion mutations, which will change the length of the section of genome that is being studied. Clearly, making large-scale comparisons of nuclear DNA between species has only become possible for evolutionary biologists with the help of information technology.

The DNA found in mitochondria is made up of relatively few genes. The nucleotide bases of these genes can be sequenced to reveal patterns that are recognisable in different species. Mitochondrial DNA is only inherited along the female line and so remains relatively unchanged from generation to generation, as no meiosis occurs to introduce variety. The only change to mitochondrial DNA is by mutations, which are very rare. However, assuming very occasional mutations, the patterns of nucleotide bases will change over time, although very slowly. If we compare the mitochondrial DNA of two species, then the more similar their nucleotide base patterns are, the more closely they are related.

Summary test 17.3a

The theory of (1) suggests that new species form from (2) species and that this involves changes to the (3) over many (4). The main mechanism to explain this theory is (5), where environmental factors known as (6) act to increase the frequency of (7) that produce phenotypes that are (8) to the environmental conditions at the time. Biologists have built up a (9) to show how species have evolved from a common (10). In phylogenetics, biologists study (11). One method to do this is to use (12) data to compare genomes or parts of genomes and look for changes owing to (13) that have occurred over (14) time. The more (15) species will have fewer differences between them.

Remember

Antibiotic resistance in bacteria is an example of a very short evolutionary timescale. The time taken for a large number of generations is not long in bacteria, given that many species can have generation times as short as 15 to 20 minutes. As we have seen in 17.2c, the mechanism leading to evolution is directional selection.

Extension

Scientific theories in biology

These are ideas that have been proposed to explain biological phenomena. A theory is supported by much evidence from observation and experimentation. It becomes more widely accepted if further evidence supports it, and, as with the theory of evolution, it can be challenged and developed as more scientific discoveries are made. It is rejected if convincing evidence emerges that does not support it. There are many examples in biology where two or more theories have been proposed for the same phenomenon because there is not yet enough evidence for one particular theory to be widely accepted.

Extension

The Earth BioGenome project (EBG)

In a 'sequencing of life' project, EBG aims to sequence the genomes of all eukaryotic species over a ten-year period. Two of the goals of the project are to better understand evolutionary relationships and processes. Information such as this would help to confirm or make modifications to the current constructions of the Tree of Life.

Speciation is the evolution of new species from pre-existing species. A **species** is a group of individuals that have a common ancestry and so share the same set of **genes** and are capable of breeding with one another to produce fertile offspring. In other words, members of a species are **reproductively isolated**.

It is through the process of speciation that evolutionary change has taken place over millions of years. This has resulted in great diversity of forms amongst organisms, past and present.

How new species are formed

The formation of new species can occur in two different ways:

- **Cross fertilisation between individuals of two different species** that leads to the formation of a hybrid. This is thought to have occurred in the production of modern wheat plants (hexaploids, 6n) from a chance hybridisation of emmer wheat (a tetraploid, 4n, species of wheat) and a goat grass (diploid, 2n). This is an example of a new species forming as a result of a change in ploidy: 4n + 2n = 6n.
- **Reproductive isolation followed by genetic change due to natural selection**. Within a population of any species, there are groups of individuals that breed with one another. These breeding subpopulations are called **demes**. Although individuals tend to breed only with others in the same deme, they are capable of breeding with individuals in other demes. In other words, the population has a single **gene pool**. Suppose, however, that the demes become isolated in some way and each undergoes different mutations and becomes genetically different. Each deme will then adapt to the different environmental influences it is subjected to. This is known as adaptive radiation and results in changes to the **allele** frequencies in each population and in the various **phenotypes** present. Genetic drift may also occur to increase the genetic differences. As a result of these genetic differences it may be that, even if the species were no longer physically isolated from one another, they would be unable to interbreed successfully. Each group would now be a different species, each with its own gene pool. This type of speciation has two main forms, **allopatric speciation** and **sympatric speciation**.

Allopatric speciation by geographical separation

Allopatric describes the form of speciation where two populations become **geographically isolated**. Geographical isolation may be the result of any physical barrier between two populations which prevents them interbreeding. These barriers include oceans, rivers, mountain ranges and deserts. What proves a barrier to one species may be no problem to another. While an ocean may isolate populations of goats, it can be crossed by many birds and for marine fish it is their mode of getting from place to place. A tiny stream may be a barrier to snails, whereas the whole of the Pacific Ocean fails to separate populations of certain birds. If environmental conditions either side of the barrier vary, then natural selection will influence the two populations differently and each will adapt in order to survive in their local conditions. These changes take many hundreds or even thousands of generations, but in the end lead to reproductive isolation and the formation of separate species. Figure 1 shows how speciation might occur when two populations of a forest-living species become geographically isolated by a region of arid grassland.

Sympatric speciation

Sympatric describes the form of speciation that results from reproductive isolation even though individuals in a population live in the same area. There are various forms of isolation that lead to sympatric speciation and two examples of these are ecological isolation and behavioural isolation.

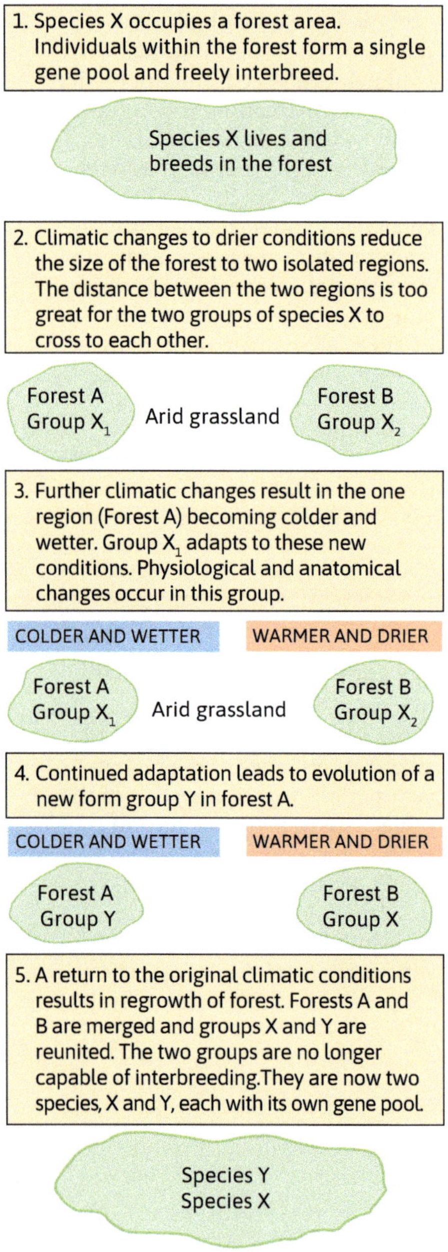

These pages help you to:

- explain how speciation may occur as a result of genetic isolation by:
  - geographical separation (allopatric speciation)
  - ecological and behavioural separation (sympatric speciation) (17.3.3)

You will also:

- read about pre- and post-zygotic isolating mechanisms

1. Species X occupies a forest area. Individuals within the forest form a single gene pool and freely interbreed.

Species X lives and breeds in the forest

2. Climatic changes to drier conditions reduce the size of the forest to two isolated regions. The distance between the two regions is too great for the two groups of species X to cross to each other.

Forest A Group X_1 Arid grassland   Forest B Group X_2

3. Further climatic changes result in the one region (Forest A) becoming colder and wetter. Group X_1 adapts to these new conditions. Physiological and anatomical changes occur in this group.

COLDER AND WETTER   WARMER AND DRIER

Forest A Group X_1 Arid grassland   Forest B Group X_2

4. Continued adaptation leads to evolution of a new form group Y in forest A.

COLDER AND WETTER   WARMER AND DRIER

Forest A Group Y   Forest B Group X

5. A return to the original climatic conditions results in regrowth of forest. Forests A and B are merged and groups X and Y are reunited. The two groups are no longer capable of interbreeding. They are now two species, X and Y, each with its own gene pool.

Species Y Species X

Figure 1 *Speciation as a result of geographical isolation*

In **ecological isolation**, members of the population living in one area form subpopulations that may live in different microhabitats, experiencing different microclimates and differences in available food resources. Individuals rarely move out of their small area and over time changes occur so that interbreeding becomes no longer possible.

In **behavioural isolation**, changes to behaviour, usually in mating rituals and in courtship behaviour, can bring about reproductive isolation. Mutations occurring in subpopulations may result in differences in morphology, for example changes in colours that are associated with attracting mates, or differences in courtship behaviour. Only members within the subpopulation respond to these changes during courtship and mating, so that eventually groups are so different that interbreeding no longer occurs.

The role of pre-zygotic and post-zygotic isolation mechanisms in the evolution of new species

The formation of new species requires time for the gene pools of the reproductively isolated populations to become so different that interbreeding is no longer possible (or if it is possible, no fertile offspring are produced). Two types of mechanism may operate to ensure that groups remain reproductively isolated: pre-zygotic mechanisms and post-zygotic mechanisms. Three types of pre-zygotic mechanism, geographical, ecological and behavioural have already been described.

- **Pre-zygotic mechanisms** – occur before mating takes place and prevent the exchange of gametes. They are more efficient than post-mating mechanisms in bringing about speciation.
- **Post-zygotic mechanisms** – occur after mating has taken place and in some way prevent the development of zygotes into offspring. As a result of different mutations occurring within the subpopulations, viable offspring can no longer be produced when individuals from the two groups mate.

Summary test 17.3b

The evolution of new species from existing ones is known as **(1)**. A species is a population of organisms that is **(2)** isolated from other populations. New species may arise when a breeding subunit, called a **(3)**, of a population becomes isolated in some way. The isolated subunit may become genetically different as it adapts to different environmental conditions. This process is called **(4)** and results in changes to **(5)** and phenotypes of the two populations. In time the two populations may become so changed that they are unable to interbreed, at which point they have become different **(6)**. There are two main types of speciation: **(7)** speciation occurs when two populations become geographically isolated, e.g. by rivers, oceans or mountain ranges. Where the two populations become reproductively isolated but are not geographically isolated, this is known as **(8)** speciation. Mechanisms to maintain reproductive isolation in the formation of new species can be divided into **(9)** and **(10)** mechanisms.

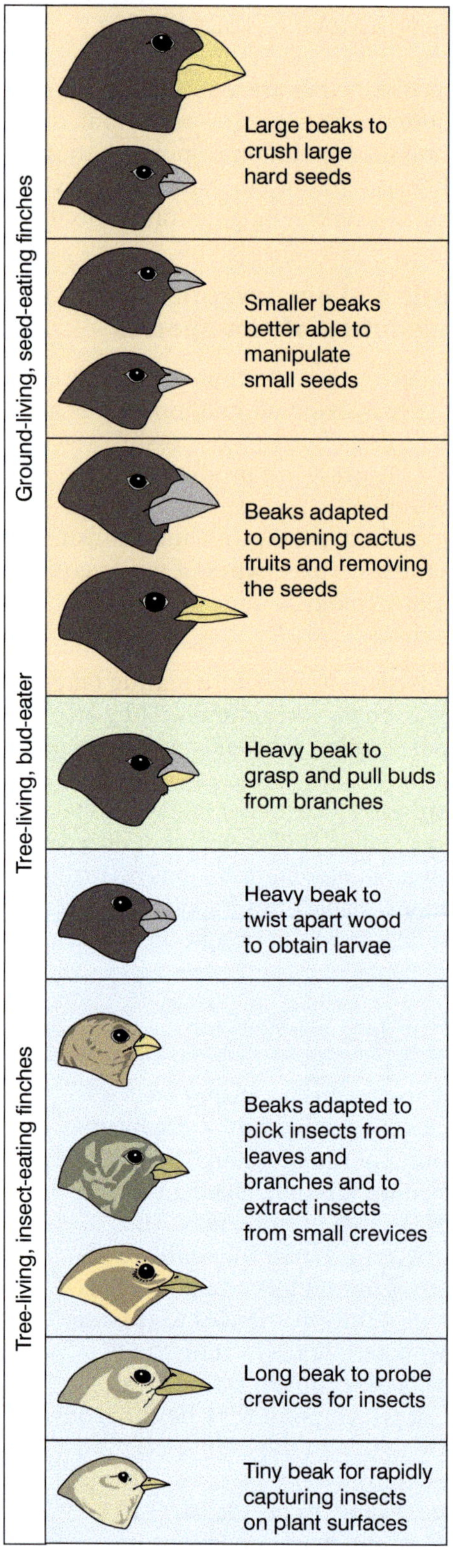

Figure 1 *Adaptive radiation amongst the thirteen species of Galapagos (Darwin's) finches*

An organism is considered to be adapted to a particular environment if it survives and reproduces better than other organisms in that environment. Adaptation is a relative term that compares performance both within and between species.

Adaptation and speciation

Adaptation and speciation are often related. As species adapt to different environments, they will develop differences that may lead to reproductive isolation and therefore speciation. For example, the male *Anolis* lizards of the Caribbean court females by extending a colourful flap of skin under their throat called a dewlap. There is considerable variation in the colour of these dewlaps. Some are easier to see in open **habitats**, others in shaded areas. As lizards occupy new habitats, there is selection pressure favouring the dewlaps that are most conspicuous, e.g. light coloured ones in a dark shaded forest. This adaptive change in dewlap colour means that the male may only be attractive to females stimulated by lighter dewlaps and not to ones attracted by darker dewlaps, i.e. they have become reproductively isolated and hence form a separate species.

Adaptive radiation and the founder effect – Darwin's finches

While visiting the Galapagos Islands during his voyage on the HMS *Beagle*, Darwin was greatly interested by the range of different beaks displayed by the 13 species of finches found there and in particular how each was adapted to obtaining different food. It is generally accepted that this variety of beaks arose as a result of what is called **adaptive radiation**. This process occurred as follows:

- The Galapagos Islands are geographically isolated, being some 1000 km from Ecuador, the nearest country on the South American mainland.
- By some means, e.g. blown by gales, or carried on a boat or vegetation, some seed-eating finches made the improbable journey from the mainland to one of the volcanic Galapagos Islands (the founder effect).
- This single ancestral species found few competitors on this sparsely colonised (very few other organisms) island, and so flourished.
- As with all species, **mutations** occurred, leading to natural selection favouring those individuals that were better suited to some of the many **ecological niches** available on the island. In particular, changes in beak shape allowed them to exploit (make use of) new food sources.
- The adaptations to these niches meant that these finches were now different from the ancestral ones on the mainland.
- Some finches spread to other islands in the Galapagos, although the island groups were some distance apart and so were geographically isolated.
- These new arrivals survived well because there was little competition.
- Mutations again led to increased variety and natural selection favoured those changes of beak that allowed some types to use new and different varieties of food.
- The geographical isolation of the islands from the mainland, and from each other, meant that the finches on each island group were reproductively isolated and so, in time, became separate species. Even where they returned to former islands or the mainland, they could not breed successfully with populations that had remained there.
- Even on a single island group, the adaptations to different niches led to reproductive isolation and speciation.

The range of beak adaptations to suit different food sources among Galapagos finches is shown in Figure 1.

Other examples of structural adaptations to different environments

As heat is lost and gained through the body surface it follows that, the larger the body surface area is compared with the body volume, the faster will be the rate of exchange. In general, animals in cold environments have a smaller surface area to volume ratio than their relatives living in warmer climates. Mammals are **endotherms**; they gain their heat from the metabolic activities taking place inside their bodies in order to maintain a more or less constant body temperature. Those living in cold climates, such as an Arctic fox, have a smaller body surface area to volume ratio than their relations, such as the fennec fox, that live in warm conditions. This is largely achieved through the size of their ears – Arctic foxes have very short external ears that reduce heat loss. Fennec foxes, by contrast, have very large external ears, enabling them to lose heat, especially during and after exertion (Figure 2).

For plants, the ability to withstand a shortage of water is very important. Plants transpire and so lose water continuously. If water is in short supply they must reduce **transpiration** if they are to survive. Structural adaptations to reduce transpiration (see also 7.2c) are known as **xeromorphic** features and include:

- a thick waxy **cuticle** on leaves
- leaves that roll and trap moist air within the leaf
- hairy leaves that trap moist air next to the surface
- **stomata** in grooves or pits that reduce the diffusion gradient
- leaves reduced in size that give a small surface area to volume ratio
- leaves absent and photosynthesis carried out by stems as these have fewer stomata
- succulent leaves and stems that store water
- extensive root systems that collect water quickly when it is available.

Examples of physiological adaptations to different environments

Desert-living animals need to survive water shortage. In the case of the kangaroo rat, a desert rodent, the kidney shows a range of physiological adaptations designed to conserve water by producing concentrated urine. It oxidises fat rather than carbohydrate, which yields almost twice as much water, but it is still crucial to keep water losses to a minimum. Kangaroo rats reduce evaporation from the lungs, do not sweat and produce very dry faeces, as well as reducing water loss when removing waste products through the kidney. They produce urine that is four times more concentrated than that of humans (24% urea as opposed to a maximum of 6% in humans) and seventeen times more concentrated than their own blood. This is achieved by having an extremely long loop of Henlé (14.1c) that is important in creating a **counter-current system** involved in the reabsorption of water back into the blood stream. Reabsorption of water is aided by the unusually high levels of ADH (14.1f) in the blood.

Figure 2 *Arctic fox (top), living in a colder environment, has much shorter ears than the fennec fox (below) that lives in a warmer climate*

Summary test 17.3c

When visiting the Galapagos Islands, Darwin observed the variety of beaks of finches. A single ancestral species is thought to have initially inhabited the Islands. As a result of **(1)** in the genes of this species, new varieties of finches occurred. Some of the new individuals were better suited to the different **(2)** available on the Islands. Over time these varieties became **(3)** leading to differences in their gene pools and each became a separate **(4)**. Adaptive radiation produces organisms with characteristics that suit them to different environments. For example, plants in dry regions develop **(5)** features to reduce transpiration. These include a thick waxy **(6)** on leaves, extensive **(7)** systems and **(8)** that are reduced in number located only in pits or grooves. Mammals like the kangaroo rat that live in dry regions have extremely long **(9)** in their kidneys that help to produce very concentrated **(10)**.

395

17 Exam-style and practice questions

 Launch additional digital resources for the chapter

17 Exam-style questions

1 Figures 1a and b show a grey-cheeked thrush, *Catharus minimus*, and Bicknell's thrush, *Catharus bicknelli*, respectively. The birds look very similar to each other and both breed in the boreal forests (coniferous forests) of Canada.

Figure 1a

Figure 1b

Scientists recently classified these birds as separate species based on a few studies. One of the studies involved measuring morphological (physical) characteristics, like culmen (upper part of the beak) length.

Table 1 shows the culmen length of birds sampled from different parts of Canada.

Table 1

Area	Number of samples		Culmen length ± s / mm	
	Males	Females	Males	Females
Newfoundland	30	15	13.2 ± 0.1	13.1 ± 0.2
New Brunswick	22	13	12.7 ± 0.1	12.6 ± 0.1

s = standard deviation

a The scientists used a *t*-test to find out if the difference in culmen lengths was significant.
   i State why a *t*-test can be used for this data.   *(1 mark)*

Table 2 shows the probability values of *t*.

Table 2

degrees of freedom	20	22	24	26	28	30	40	50
probability 0.05	2.09	2.07	2.06	2.06	2.05	2.04	2.02	2.01

   ii The scientists concluded that the difference in both male and female culmen lengths was significant. Explain why they made that conclusion.   *(2 marks)*

b Suggest **two** characteristics, other than morphology, that could be researched to identify differences between the birds.   *(2 marks)*

Figure 2 shows their distribution in some parts of Canada.

Figure 2

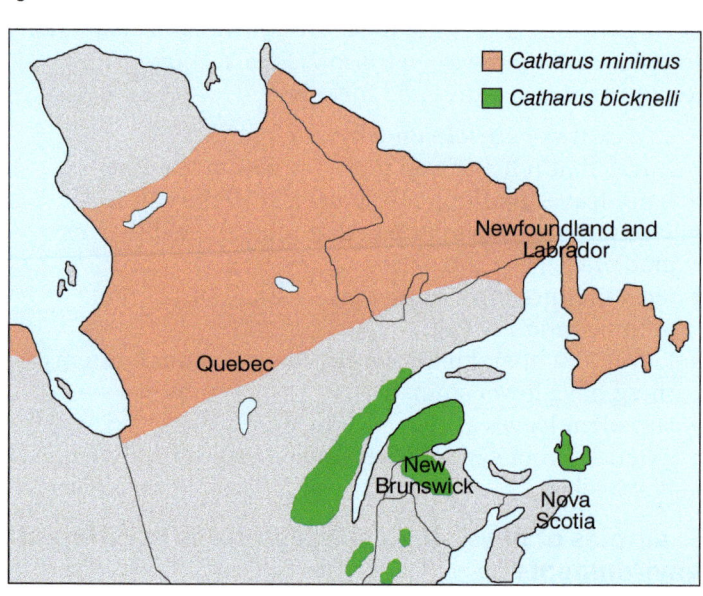

c Scientists believe that *C. minimus* and *C. bicknelli* evolved from the same ancestral species during the Ice Age.

Glacier ice sheets formed during the Ice Age became geological barriers between the bird populations.

Explain how these two species were established.

(4 marks)

(Total 9 marks)

2 Bacterial blight is a disease that affects rice, *Oryza sativa*. Rice plants that have at least one copy of the dominant allele *Xa7*, will be resistant against bacterial blight.

314 rice plants from a particular field were tested for the blight resistance. 87 did not show resistance against the blight.

a Using the Hardy–Weinberg principle, calculate the frequency of allele *Xa7*. The equations are shown below:

$$p + q = 1$$
$$p^2 + 2pq + q^2 = 1$$

Show your working. *(3 marks)*

b Outline how selective breeding can improve blight resistance in rice crops. *(3 marks)*

(Total 6 marks)

17 Practice questions

3 a What is natural selection?

b State the differences between directional and stabilising selection.

c A severe cold period in 1996 killed over 50% of swallows (a type of bird) living on cliffs in Nebraska. Biologists collected nearly 2000 dead swallows from beneath the cliffs and captured around 1000 living ones. By measuring the body mass of the birds, they found that birds with larger than average body mass survived the cold spell better than ones with smaller than average body mass. State, giving your reasons, which type of selection was taking place here.

4 A type of bird known as a cuckoo lays its eggs in the nests of other birds. The host birds will often raise these parasite chicks alongside their own. In many valleys in southern Spain, great cuckoos and common magpies have lived together for hundreds of years. In some valleys, however, magpies have been around for centuries but cuckoos have only recently arrived.

Scientists placed artificial cuckoo eggs into magpie nests in both types of valley. Where cuckoos and magpies had lived together for a long period, 78% of the magpies removed the cuckoo eggs from their nests. Where cuckoos had only recently colonised the valleys, only 14% of the magpies removed the cuckoo eggs.

It would appear that, in the valleys where cuckoos are well established, selection has favoured those magpies that removed the cuckoo eggs.

a Suggest one advantage to the magpies of removing cuckoo eggs from their nest.

b Explain how removing cuckoo eggs increases the probability of the alleles for this type of behaviour in magpies being passed on to subsequent generations.

c Suggest why this form of behaviour is not shown by magpies in those valleys where cuckoos have only recently arrived.

d State, with your reasons, which type of selection is taking place here.

5 Each of statements **A** to **G** is an explanation for an observation in Table 3. Match each explanation to its observation, using the letters **A** to **G**.

a Competition for resources in short supply is occurring

b Some individuals have adaptations better suited to the selection pressures

c Environmental conditions change so that selection pressures change

d Selection acts to remove the extremes of the range of phenotypes

e Selection acts to favour the extremes of the range of phenotypes

f Genetic drift is occurring in a population

g A bottleneck effect has occurred in a population

Table 3

Observation	Explanation
1 Over time, a population experiences stabilising selection for a characteristic	
2 The frequency of alleles in a gene pool fluctuates over time owing to chance effects	
3 Population size remains constant even though there is over-production of offspring	
4 Over time, a population experiences disruptive selection for a characteristic	
5 There is a sudden decrease in population numbers and a loss of genetic diversity occurs	
6 Neutral mutations existing in a population become advantageous	
7 In a population some phenotypes are more likely to survive than other phenotypes	

18 Classification, biodiversity and conservation

18.1 Classification

a. Taxonomy and the species concept

These pages help you to:

- discuss the meaning of the term species, by considering the:
  - biological species concept
  - morphological species concept
  - ecological species concept (18.1.1)
- describe the classification of organisms in the Eukarya domain into the taxonomic hierarchy of kingdom, phylum, class, order, family, genus and species (18.1.4)

You will also:

- understand what is meant by the binomial system
- see examples of the classification of organisms

The concept of a species

A species is the basic and natural unit of classification. In 17.3b, we saw that members of a species have common ancestry as they are descendants by adaptation of pre-existing species. We also saw that different species have different gene pools and are reproductively isolated. As there are millions of different species, it is not easy to find a definition that will fit all. Three of the main concepts of a species are:

- the biological species concept
- the morphological species concept
- the ecological species concept.

The biological species concept (BSC)

This concept is based on the idea that only members of the same species **are capable of breeding** to produce living offspring **which themselves are fertile** and so can successfully produce more offspring. That is, a species is reproductively isolated from other species. Reproductive isolation is not the same as geographical isolation. A population of one species can live in the same area as a population of a different species, but only members of the same population breed successfully with each other to have fertile offspring. Two populations can be geographically separated, but if individuals from each population come together and can interbreed to produce fertile offspring, then they are all members of the same species. A disadvantage of the BSC is that it only applies to sexually reproducing organisms.

The morphological species concept (MSC)

The MSC applies to sexually and asexually reproducing organisms. It is based on members of the same species sharing the same distinctive morphological characteristics. Features such as body form (shape) and size and more detailed structural characteristics are used to distinguish between different species. The MSC has been used extensively to classify fossil species, but relies on scientists agreeing the key features that define a species. There are many examples where closely related species are morphologically the same, but other identifying factors, such as behaviour and DNA analysis, show they are different species.

Extension

When is a species not a species?

A horse and a donkey are different species but are capable of mating and producing offspring – known as mules. Mules are infertile hybrids, i.e. they can almost never produce offspring when mated with each other. There is some evidence that a few female mules are fertile, although this is extremely rare. Why then are mules infertile? A horse has 64 chromosomes (32 pairs) and a donkey has 62 chromosomes (31 pairs). The gametes of a horse and a donkey therefore have 32 and 31 respectively. On fusion of the gametes of a horse and a donkey, the offspring (the mule) has 63 chromosomes and you cannot exactly match up 63 chromosomes into pairs. However, mitosis can take place and therefore a mule grows and develops normally, but because the chromosomes cannot form homologous pairs at prophase I, meiosis cannot occur. As this is how gametes are formed, a mule cannot produce gametes and is therefore infertile.

Subspecies

There is no agreed definition of a subspecies, that is, a subdivision of a species. Different subspecies of a species are generally geographically separated and have some morphological differences. An example of this is *Canis lupus*, the grey wolf, which has a number of subspecies. Figures 1 and 2 show two of these: the Arctic wolf and the Mexican wolf.

Figure 1 *The Arctic wolf, Canis lupus arctos, a subspecies of the grey wolf, Canis lupus*

Figure 2 *The Mexican wolf, Canis lupus baileyi, a subspecies of Canis lupis*

Members of the same subspecies will be genetically more similar to each other than to members of another subspecies. However, for any one species, individuals from one subspecies still have the potential to interbreed with individuals of another subspecies to produce fertile offspring. Some subspecies are considered to be nearly at the point of forming a new species, and these will be more genetically distinct than recently formed subspecies, and they may be partially reproductively isolated.

The ecological species concept (ESC)

This concept considers that individuals of the same species **occupy the same ecological niche** (18.2a), to the exclusion of other species. Two species cannot occupy identical niches. Individuals of the same species share the same ecological role in the community (see 18.2b for a definition of community), which means they live in the same set of environmental conditions and so need the same resources for life and have the same interactions with other species.

Naming species – the binomial system

Organisms are identified by their species name, which consists of two parts and so the system is called the **binomial system**. Its features include:

- It is a universal system based upon Latin/Greek names.
- The first part of the species name is the generic part and indicates the genus to which the organism belongs.
- The second, or **specific** part, indicates the species to which the organism belongs.

There are a number of rules that are applied to the use of the binomial system in scientific writing:

- The names are printed in italics or, if hand written, they are underlined to show they are scientific names. Scientific names are printed in italics for emphasis. (Conversely, if a piece of text is already in italics, then the scientific names will appear in roman type – that is, 'upright' text.) In a hand-written document, scientific names are often underlined.
- The first letter of the generic name is in upper case (capitals), but the specific name is not.
- If the specific name is not known, it can be written as sp., e.g. *Triticum* sp.
- When referring to all members of a genus, the specific name is written as the plural, spp., e.g. all members of the genus *Amoeba* is written as *Amoeba* spp.
- If the generic name has already been used, it can be abbreviated in later text to the first letter, e.g. the creeping buttercup *Ranunculus repens* can be written as *R. repens*.
- Subspecies are often given a three-part name (trinomial name), such as the Arctic wolf *Canis lupus arctos* and the Mexican wolf *C. l. baileyi* (i.e. *Canis lupus baileyi* – note the same convention of abbreviating).

Remember

A useful mnemonic for remembering the order of these taxonomic ranks is 'Delicious King Prawn Curry Or Fat Greasy Sausages' (Domain, Kingdom, Phylum, Class, Order, Family, Genus, Species).

Extension

The changing world of taxonomy

Taxonomists are continually making changes as more information is gathered about a species or one of the taxonomic ranks in a hierarchy. Evidence from molecular analyses may help to confirm a classification or may show that re-classification is required. Some of the changes are in the names assigned to taxonomic ranks, while others involve movement of a taxonomic group to another area (for example, moving a species of insect to a different genus), or dividing a taxonomic group into two.

Summary test 18.1a

The species concept that can only be used for sexually reproducing organisms is the **(1)**. It is based on the idea that species are **(2)** isolated and that only members of a species can breed to produce **(3)** offspring. A definition of species based on distinct body form and structural features is known as the **(4)**. A species can also be defined by having a specific **(5)** role that is not shared by other species – different species cannot occupy the same **(6)**. This is known as the **(7)** concept. A **(8)** is a group of organisms that can be placed into a hierarchical order of classification. In the domain Eukarya, the largest group is the **(9)**. Related families belong to the same **(10)** and a family can be divided into **(11)**.

In practice, scientists may use the ideas from more than one species concept to help them identify a species. Depending on the type of organisms studied, they can also compare physiological, biochemical, immunological and behavioural characteristics. Species are not fixed forever, but change and evolve over time. Within an individual species there can be considerable variation amongst individuals. All dogs, for example, belong to the same species, but artificial selection has led to a variety of different breeds.

Grouping species together – the principles of classification

Around 1.9 million different **eukaryotic** species have been identified and named, and yet this represents only a small proportion of the total thought to exist on Earth. There are probably at least another 10 to 15 million eukaryotic species either undiscovered or yet to be named. It makes sense to organise these species into manageable groups, and allow better communication between scientists. The grouping of organisms is known as **classification**, while the study of biological classification is called **taxonomy**. There are two basic types of biological classification:

- **Artificial classification** divides organisms according to differences that are useful at the time. Such features may include colour, size, number of legs, leaf shape, etc. These are described as **analogous** features where they have the same function but do not have the same evolutionary origins. For example, the wings of butterflies and birds are both used for flight but they originated in different ways.
- **Phylogenetic (natural) classification** is more widely used in biology and:
  - is based upon the evolutionary relationships between organisms and their evolutionary descent (**phylogeny**)
  - classifies species into groups using shared features derived from their ancestors
  - is arranged in a **hierarchy** in which groups are contained within larger groups with no overlap.

Relationships in a phylogenetic classification are partly based upon **homologous** characteristics rather than analogous ones. Homologous characteristics have similar evolutionary origins regardless of their functions in the adult of a species. For example, the wing of a bird, the arm of a human and the front leg of a horse all have the same basic structure and similar evolutionary origins and are therefore homologous.

Organising the groups of species – taxonomy

Each group within a phylogenetic biological classification is called a **taxon**. Taxonomy is the study of these groups, which allows them to be placed in a hierarchical order, known as **taxonomic ranks**, based upon the evolutionary line of descent of the group members.

Organisms are placed into one of the three domains. Within the domain Eukarya (see 18.1b) the largest groups are known as kingdoms, which are then divided into phyla. Organisms in each phylum have a body plan radically different from organisms in any other phylum. Diversity within each phylum allows it to be divided into classes. Each class is divided into orders of organisms that have additional features in common. Each order is divided into families and at this level the differences are less obvious. Each family is divided into genera and each genus (singular) into species.

b. Domains and kingdoms

The main characteristics of the three domains of living organisms are listed below.

Bacteria (Figure 1) are a group of single-celled prokaryotes with the following features:

- the absence of double-membrane-bound organelles such as nuclei or mitochondria
- unicellular, although cells may occur in chains or clusters
- ribosomes are smaller (70S) than in eukaryotic cells
- cell walls are present and made of peptidoglycan (murein) but never **chitin** or cellulose
- single loop (circular) of naked DNA made up of nucleic acids but no **histones**
- small in size – typically 0.5–5.0 µm in length.

Archaea (Figure 2) are a group of single-celled prokaryotes that were originally classified as bacteria, which they resemble in appearance. Now they form their own group as they have some unique features and also share some features with Bacteria and Eukarya:

- they have a wide range of morphologies, varying in shape and can be single celled, form filaments or group together
- they are found in a wide range of habitats and are common in extremes of temperature and salinity (extremophiles)
- they do not have membrane-bound organelles and have circular DNA, although often much smaller than in bacteria, and they also have plasmids
- the promoter region (19.1d) of the DNA and the RNA polymerase is more similar to those of eukaryotic cells than those of bacterial cells
- they have 70S ribosomes but the ribosome structure is different to that of bacterial ribosomes and shows a very similar response to eukaryotic 80S ribosomes to antibiotics
- their genes and protein synthesis are more similar to eukaryotes
- their membranes contain very different lipids to bacterial and eukaryotic membranes. Although archaeans may have some phospholipids as in bacterial and eukaryotic cells, the highest proportion of phosphate-containing lipids are ether lipids; here, glycerol is attached by highly resistant ether bonds to branched chains called alkyl chains
- there is no peptidoglycan in their cell walls and there is more variety in composition than found in bacterial cells.

Eukarya are a group of organisms made up of one or more eukaryotic cells. Their features are:

- their cells have chromosomes composed of linear DNA complexed with histone proteins and their chromosomes are enclosed in a double-membrane (nuclear envelope)
- their cells possess both single (e.g. ER, Golgi body) and double (e.g. mitochondria, chloroplasts) membrane-bound organelles
- not all possess cells with a cell wall, but where they do it contains no peptidoglycan, e.g. cellulose in plant cells and photosynthetic prokarotyes, and chitin in most fungi
- ribosomes are larger (80S) than in bacterial and archaean cells (with 70S ribosomes in mitochondria and chloroplasts).

These pages help you to:

- describe the classification of organisms into the Archaea, Bacteria and Eukarya domains (18.1.2)
- understand that, although Archaea and Bacteria are prokaryotes, the main differences between them are in membrane lipids, ribosomal RNA and the composition of cell walls (18.1.3)
- outline the characteristic features of the Protoctista, Fungi, Plantae and Animalia kingdoms (18.1.5)
- explain that viruses can be classified according to the type of nucleic acid (RNA or DNA) they have and whether this is single stranded or double stranded (18.1.6)

You will also:

- review features of prokaryotes, eukaryotes and viruses

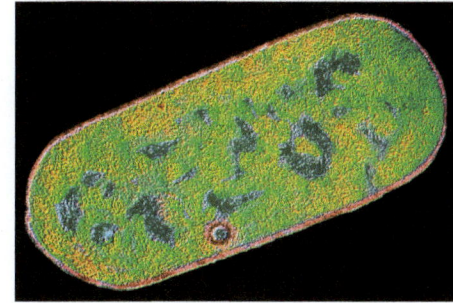

Figure 1 An example of a bacterium is Clostridium perfringens, *which causes blood poisoning and gas gangrene in humans*

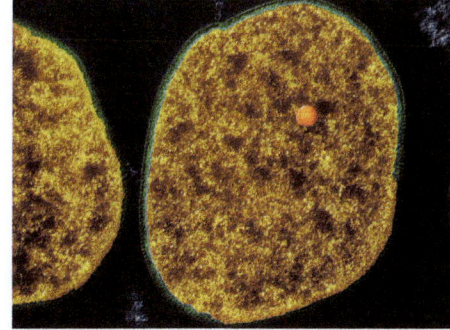

Figure 2 An example of an archaean is Sulfolobus. *This organism is an extremophile, found living in hot springs. It grows well in acidic and high sulfur environment conditions*

Viruses

Viruses are simple structures comprising a nucleic acid core surrounded by a protein coat known as a capsid. The capsid is composed of subunits known as capsomeres. Some viruses also have an outer envelope (see 1.2f). They are not included in the three-domain system because they are not usually considered to be living organisms. They do not fit into the key concept that cells are the units of life and that living organisms are composed of one or more cells. They do not have their own metabolism and therefore need a host cell to make new products and to reproduce. Viruses can, however, be classified into different types, for example on the basis of their nucleic acid as they have only DNA or only RNA as their genetic material. A simple system groups them into four categories depending whether they possess DNA or RNA and whether this is single or double stranded.

Kingdoms of the Eukarya

Protoctista

The Protoctista are an extremely varied group of organisms with little in common except that they are unicellular or made up of groups of similar cells and they are **eukaryotic**. The group includes algae, which are photosynthetic organisms, *Amoeba* spp. (Figure 3) and *Plasmodium* spp. (10.1e). Many protoctists share features with other kingdoms and were at one time classified in those kingdoms. However, as each kingdom became more clearly defined it meant that some organisms were reclassified into the Protoctista.

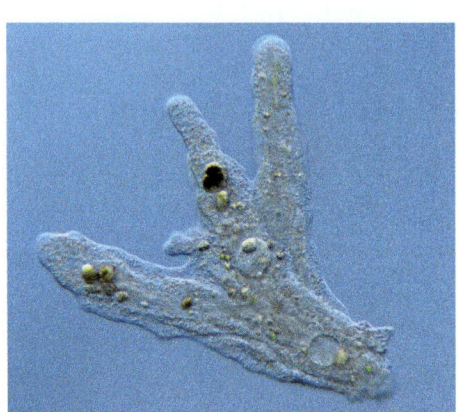

Figure 3 *The unicellular organism* Amoeba proteus *belongs to the kingdom Protoctista*

The distinguishing features of the Protoctista are:

- eukaryotic cells, i.e. they have linear DNA complexed with histone protein and they have double-membrane-bound organelles such as a nucleus and mitochondria
- the majority are unicellular or groups of similar cells
- some are multicellular, but less complex than plants and animals; most form groups of similar cells although the macroscopic marine algae, known commonly as seaweeds, can have relatively complex morphologies with tissues specialised for particular functions.

Fungi

The Fungi are a large group of organisms that were once classified as plants but are now allocated to a kingdom in their own right. The group includes moulds (Figure 4), yeasts, mushrooms and toadstools.

The distinguishing features of the Fungi are:

- they are eukaryotic organisms
- absence of chlorophyll and therefore they do not photosynthesise but feed **heterotrophically** by absorbing their food, either as saprophytes (decomposers) or as parasites (living in or on other living organisms)
- cell walls usually made of chitin and never of cellulose
- some are unicellular (e.g. yeasts) but most are made up of thread-like **hyphae** that collectively form a **mycelium**
- carbohydrate is stored as glycogen
- they reproduce sexually and/or asexually by means of spores that lack a flagellum.

Figure 4 *The green mould growing on this lemon is* Penicillium sp, *which belongs to the kingdom Fungi*

Plantae

The Plantae is a diverse group that ranges in size from liverworts, a few millimetres across, to giant redwood trees over 120 metres high. The group includes liverworts, mosses, ferns, coniferous trees and flowering plants.

The distinguishing features of the Plantae are:

- they are eukaryotic organisms
- they are multicellular organisms with a higher level of complexity than multicellular protoctists or fungi – for example, organs for photosynthesis (leaf) and in ferns and seed-producing plants, specialised vascular tissues (xylem and phloem)
- they possess chlorophyll and other pigments and therefore feed **autotrophically** by photosynthesis
- they possess cells with cell walls that are composed of cellulose
- carbohydrate is stored as starch
- they show alternation of generations (a life cycle of two generations) – a multicellular haploid gametophyte generation (produces gametes) and a multicellular diploid sporophyte generation (produces spores by meiosis).

Figure 5 Lathyrus odoratus (*sweet pea*)

Animalia

The Animalia show the greatest diversity of form of any of the kingdoms. Much of this diversity is a result of their ability to move from place to place, which has led to the evolution of a wide range of different methods of locomotion.

The distinguishing features of the Animalia are:

- they are eukaryotic organisms
- they are multicellular organisms that have a high level of cellular organisation (specialised tissues and organs)
- their cells do not possess chlorophyll and therefore feed heterotrophically
- their cells do not possess cell walls
- carbohydrate is stored as glycogen
- can respond to stimuli in a coordinated way, with most having a nervous system
- they have fibres that can contract so that they able to move from one location to another (locomotion) or have the ability to move parts of their body

An example of an organism belonging to each of the kingdoms in the domain Eukarya is shown in Figures 3, 4, 5 and 6. The hierarchical classification (18.1a) of each organism is given in Table 1.

Figure 6 Panthera tigris (*tiger*)

Extension

Table 1 *Classification of four organisms into the main taxonomic ranks*

Common name / Rank	Amoeba	Green mould	Sweet pea	Tiger
Kingdom	Protoctista	Fungi	Plantae	Animalia
Phylum	Amoebozoa	Ascomycota	Angiospermophyta	Chordata
Class	Tubulinea	Eurotiomycetes	Dicotyledonae	Mammalia
Order	Tubulinida	Eurotiales	Rosales	Carnivora
Family	Amoebidae	Trichocomaceae	Fabaceae	Felidae
Genus	Amoeba	Penicillium	Lathyrus	Panthera
Species	Amoeba proteus	Penicillium digitatum	Lathyrus odoratus	Panthera tigris

Summary test 18.1b

The Protoctista are a very varied group of organisms that possess membrane-bound organelles and are therefore known as **(1)** cells. The Fungi comprise organisms that feed **(2)**. Most are made up of thread-like **(3)** that collectively form a **(4)** and have cell walls containing **(5)**. Plants are multicellular organisms that possess **(6)** and other pigments. They feed **(7)** by photosynthesis, most have cell walls made of **(8)** and store carbohydrate as **(9)**. Animals store carbohydrate as **(10)** and most possess a **(11)** that allows them to coordinate activities.

Biodiversity
a. Biodiversity at different levels

These pages help you to:

- define the terms ecosystem and niche (18.2.1)
- understand that biodiversity can be assessed at different levels (18.2.2)
- explain what is meant by:
  - ecosystem and habitat diversity
  - species diversity
  - genetic diversity (18.2.2)

You will also:

- understand what is meant by a keystone species

Figure 1 *In a tropical rainforest there is high species diversity*

Remember

Organisms are found in places where local conditions fall within the range that their adaptations can cope with.

Extension

Keystone species

A keystone species maintains the stability and biodiversity of its ecosystem. The species has a role within the ecosystem that is out of proportion to its abundance and its presence is critical to the survival of other species. The loss of a keystone species from an ecosystem can greatly affect the flow of energy through the ecosystem (see 18.2b) and can lead to the loss of other species or the invasion of the ecosystem by alien (non-native) species. Examples of keystone species are sea otters in the kelp forest (see 13.1a) ecosystem and African elephants in the savannah (mix of grassland and woodland) ecosystem.

Biodiversity is the general term used to describe variety in the living world. It refers to the number and variety of living organisms in a particular area and can be considered at a number of different levels: genetic diversity, species diversity and ecosystem diversity. Before we look at these levels of biodiversity, it is useful to have an understanding of what is meant by the two terms ecosystem and niche. See also 18.2b for further explanations of the ecological terms population, **community**, habitat and biosphere.

Ecosystem

An ecosystem is made up of all the interacting **biotic** (living) and abiotic (non-living) components in a specific area. Ecosystems are more or less self-contained functional units. An ecosystem contains a community of organisms (see 18.2b). Within an ecosystem, there are two major processes to consider:

- the flow of energy through the system
- the cycling of nutrients such as carbon and nitrogen in the system.

In theory, the biosphere (18.2b) can be considered as a single ecosystem because energy flows through it and nutrients are recycled within it. In practice, there are much smaller units that are more or less self-contained in terms of energy and nutrients. A fresh-water pond, for example, has its own community of plants to collect the necessary sunlight energy to supply the organisms within it. Nutrients such as nitrates and phosphates are recycled within the pond, with little or no loss or gain between it and other ecosystems. An example of a much larger ecosystem is a tropical rainforest (Figure 1). Within each ecosystem, there are a number of interacting populations known as a community.

Niche

An ecological niche is all of the ranges of environmental conditions and resources required for an organism to survive, reproduce and maintain a viable population. It is also sometimes referred to as the ecological or functional role of a species within its community. This includes a description of where the population lives and how it obtains its energy, that is, its position in a food web (see 18.2b). Some species may appear very similar, but their nesting habits or other aspects of their behaviour will be different, or they may show different levels of tolerance to, e.g. a pollutant or a shortage of oxygen or nitrates. Any differences in niche, however small, limit competition between species. No two species occupy exactly the same niche.

Genetic diversity

Organisms of the same species can show considerable genetic diversity; although they share the same genes, they will each have their own combinations of alleles. Even within a species, different populations may show differences in their genetic diversity. This may be because of the different selection pressures acting on the populations or the effects of humans (which often leads to a loss of genetic diversity). If a population of a particular species becomes locally extinct, then it is also possible that overall genetic diversity of the species decreases.

Species diversity

One measure of biodiversity is species diversity. It may be measured within a community (a group of interacting populations in a defined area; see 18.2b), or it may be measured in a larger area such as a desert, which has a number of different communities. Species diversity has also been compared between different countries and not surprisingly countries with tropical rainforests (Figure 1), such as Brazil, come out at the top. Species diversity in a community has two components:

- the number of different species in a given area, which is known as **species richness**
- the proportion of the community that any individual species makes up, which is known as **relative abundance** or species evenness.

Two communities may have the same number of species but differ markedly in the proportion of the community that each species makes up. A natural grassland and a field of wheat may both have 25 species and the same total number of organisms. However, in the grassland all 25 might be equally abundant whereas in the wheat field over 95% of the plants may be a single species of wheat. The community with one or two dominant species is considered to have a lower species diversity.

Ecosystem and habitat diversity

The variety of ecosystems on the Earth can also be assessed. Ecosystem loss has a major impact on total biodiversity as habitats and communities are lost, and this is accompanied by local extinction of species. The variety of habitats, the places where organisms live (18.2b), is a measure of biodiversity. High species diversity within an ecosystem means a high diversity of habitats.

The different levels of biodiversity can be described separately, but cannot be considered in isolation. Biodiversity is a measure of how well an ecosystem functions. The higher the species diversity, the more stable an ecosystem usually is and the less it is affected by climate change. For example, if there is a drought, a community with a high species diversity is much more likely to have at least one species able to tolerate drought than a community with a low species diversity. At least some members are therefore likely to survive the drought and maintain the community.

In extreme environments such as the sub-arctic tundra (Figure 2) and hot deserts (Figure 3), only a few species have the necessary adaptations to survive the harsh conditions. The species diversity is therefore normally low. This usually results in an unstable ecosystem in which communities are dominated by climatic factors rather than by the organisms within the community. In less hostile environments like a tropical rainforest, the species diversity is normally high. This usually results in a stable ecosystem in which communities are dominated by living organisms rather than climate.

The biodiversity of a tropical rainforest is high because there is:

- the largest productivity (see 18.2b) of all terrestrial communities, which allows it to support a large variety of organisms
- a large number of species – up to 500 species of tree in each square kilometre
- high genetic diversity between these species
- many different habitats and niches
- constant biological activity throughout the year, which means that shelter and the leaves, flowers and fruits that provide animals with food are always available.

Ecosystems with a high diversity are likely to have complex food webs and a high level of nutrient recycling.

Figure 2 In the sub-arctic tundra there is low species diversity

Figure 3 In harsh environments, like this hot desert in Jordan, only a few species are adapted to survive the extreme conditions and therefore species diversity is low

Summary test 18.2a

Species diversity refers to the number of different species and the number of **(1)** of each species within a **(2)**. Ecosystem diversity includes the range of **(3)** within a particular area. The variety of different alleles possessed by individuals of any one species is called **(4)** diversity. An ecosystem with a high species diversity is more **(5)** than one with a low species diversity and is therefore less affected if there is a **(6)** change. An example of an ecosystem with a high species diversity is a **(7)** whereas one with a low species diversity is **(8)**. It is important to maintain biodiversity for ecological reasons because it helps to recycle **(9)**. An ecosystem is a **(10)** functioning unit in a defined, specific **(11)**, where living, or **(12)** components interact with each other and with non-living, or **(13)** components. A **(14)** defines the ecological or functional **(15)** of a species within the ecosystem.

Table 1 *Net primary production in different ecosystems*

Ecosystem	Mean NPP / kJ m^{-2} yr^{-1}
Desert	260
Ocean	4700
Temperate grassland	15 000
Intensive agriculture	30 000
Tropical rainforest	40 000

Some ecological terms

Community

A community is defined as **all the populations** of different organisms living and interacting in a **particular place** at the **same time**. Within a tropical rainforest, a community might include a large range of organisms such as banana trees, insects, macaws, monkeys, iguanas, jaguars, woodlice, fungi and bacteria.

Populations

A population is all of the organisms of the **same species** that occupy the **same place** at the **same time** and that have the chance to **interbreed** with one another. The boundaries of a population are difficult to define, except perhaps within a small pond.

Habitat

A habitat is the place where an organism lives. The habitat is the particular location that can be defined by physical features, such as a freshwater stream, or by the main producer in the area, such as an oak forest. Within an ecosystem there are many habitats. For example, in our tropical rainforest, the leaf canopy of the trees may be a habitat for macaws while a decaying log is the habitat for woodlice. A river flowing through the forest provides a very different habitat, within which aquatic plants and fish live. For a caiman (in the same family as the alligators), the river and banks are its habitat. Within each habitat there are smaller units, each with its own microclimate. These are called microhabitats.

Ecology is the study of the inter-relationships between organisms and their environment. The term **environment** refers to the conditions that surround an organism. These include both non-living (**abiotic**) and living (**biotic**) components. Ecology is a complex area of study which incorporates not only most aspects of biology but also elements of physics, chemistry, geography and geology. It is, in effect, the study of the life-supporting layer of land, air and water that surrounds the Earth, called the **biosphere**.

The organisms found in most **ecosystems**, rely on a source of energy to carry out all their activities. The initial source of this energy is sunlight, which is converted to chemical energy by **producers** (mostly photosynthetic organisms) and then passed as food from one animal (**consumer**) to another in a food chain or food web.

- **Gross primary productivity (GPP)** is the rate of production of complex organic molecules in a given area and in a given time.
- **Net primary productivity (NPP)** takes into account energy lost via respiration by the producer, so it is a measure of the quantity available to be eaten by consumers. Table 1 shows the mean NPP for a number of different ecosystems.

Consumers

Animals are consumers as they can only gain energy and nutrients by eating other organisms. In terms of energy or trophic levels, the herbivores are known as primary consumers as they eat plants, which are the (primary) producers. A carnivore that directly eats a primary consumer is known as a secondary consumer. Tertiary and quaternary consumers are carnivores. The carnivore at the end of the food chain is known as a top carnivore.

Decomposers and detritivores

When producers and consumers die, some energy is 'locked up' in the complex organic molecules of which they are made. This energy is used by a group of organisms that break down these complex materials into simple components again. In doing so, they also release valuable minerals and elements in a form that can be absorbed by plants and so contribute to recycling. The majority of this work is carried out by saprobiotic fungi and bacteria called **decomposers** and, to a lesser extent, breakdown is carried out by certain animals, such as woodlice and earthworms, called **detritivores**.

Food chains and webs

The term **food chain** describes a feeding relationship in which plants are eaten by herbivores, which are in turn eaten by carnivores. Each stage in this chain is referred to as a **trophic level**. The first trophic level is represented by producers, the second by herbivores, and all subsequent ones by carnivores. The longest food chains usually have no more than four or five trophic levels and the arrows represent the **direction of energy flow**.

coconut palm → herbivorous insect → tree frog → jaguar
producer   primary   secondary   tertiary
                    consumer   consumer   consumer

Food chains in aquatic ecosystems are often longer than in terrestrial ecosystems as less energy is lost at each trophic level.

In reality, most animals do not rely upon a single food source and, within a single **ecosystem**, many food chains will be linked together to form a **food web**. For example, in a tropical rainforest food chains can be linked to form the web shown in Figure 1. Notice here that the jaguar is feeding as a tertiary consumer and a secondary consumer.

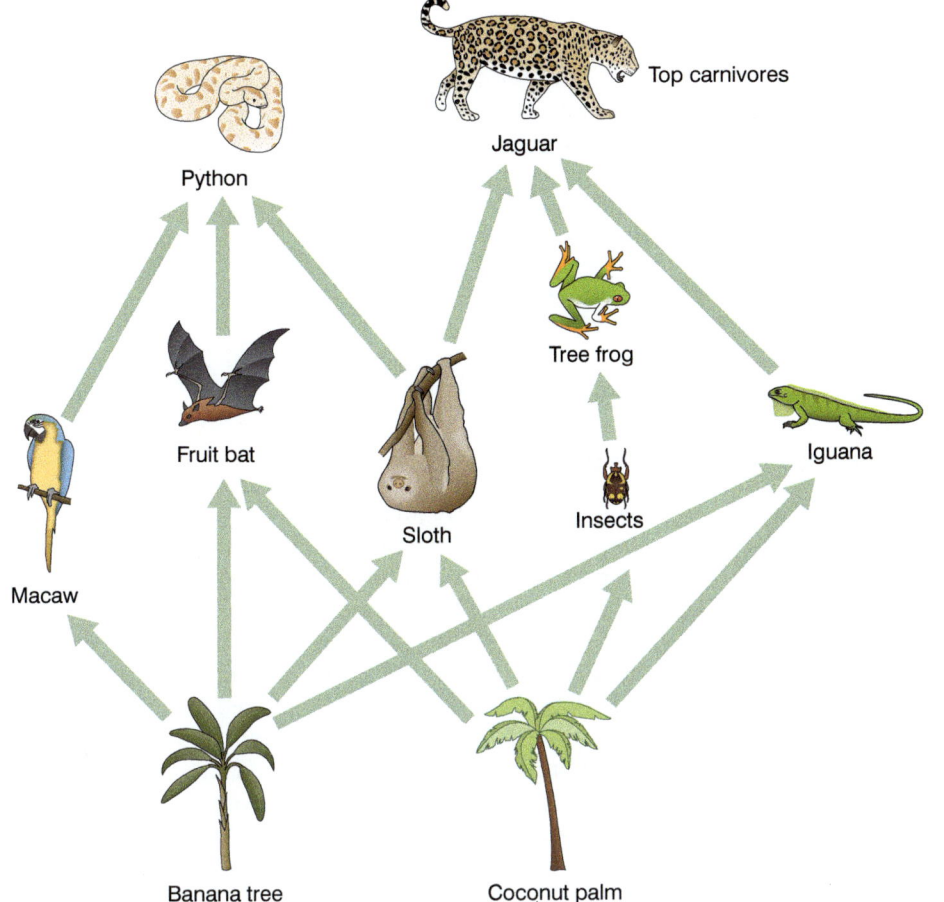

Figure 1 *Part of a simplified tropical rainforest food web (some arrows have been omitted for simplicity)*

Energy losses in food chains and webs

Plants normally convert between 1% and 3% of the Sun's energy available to them into organic matter. Losses occur in a number of ways. For example:

- Over 90% of solar energy is reflected back into space by clouds and dust or absorbed by the atmosphere and re-radiated.
- Not all wavelengths of light can be absorbed and used for photosynthesis.
- Light may not fall on a chlorophyll molecule.
- Low carbon dioxide levels may limit the rate of photosynthesis.

Plants then lose 20–50% of their **gross primary production** via respiration, and only about 10% of the **net primary production** of plants is used by primary consumers for growth. This low percentage is the result of the following:

- Some of the plant is not eaten or is not digested (egestion).
- Some of the energy is lost in excretory materials (e.g. urine).
- Some energy losses occur in respiration and heat loss to the environment.
- Energy stored at each level decreases as one moves up a food chain.

Tropical rainforests

Tropical rainforests have been estimated to contain 50% of the world's standing timber. They represent a huge store for carbon and sink for carbon dioxide and their destruction may increase atmospheric concentrations of carbon dioxide by 50%. They conserve soil nutrients and prevent large-scale erosion in regions of high rainfall. They contain a large gene pool of plant resources and their potential for the production of food, fibre and pharmaceutical products is not known. At present rates of destruction, there will be no tropical rainforests left by the end of this century.

Attempts to exploit the forest on a large scale has had a very damaging effect. The scale of the problem is huge. For example, in the rainforests of Brazil and other countries of the Amazon basin, the forest has been cleared for rubber plantations, timber extraction, planting of cash crops like cocoa, coffee and oil palm, extraction of minerals, especially bauxite, and for pulp and paper manufacture. The consequences of deforestation have been soil infertility, floods, soil erosion and increased sediment in rivers. However, some areas are being set aside as reserves and some attempts have been made at replanting.

Summary test 18.2b

The study of the inter-relationships between organisms and their environment is called **(1)**. The layer of land, air and water that surrounds the Earth is called the **(2)**. Food chains and **(3)** show how energy flows through ecosystems. The number of **(4)** levels are limited because energy is lost at each level. Within each ecosystem are groups of organisms, called a **(5)**, which live and interact in a particular place at the same time. A group of interbreeding organisms occupying the same place at the same time is called a **(6)**, and the place where they live is known as a **(7)**.

These pages help you to:

- explain the importance of random sampling in determining the biodiversity of an area (18.2.3)
- describe how to use frame quadrats, line transects and belt transects to assess the distribution and abundance of organisms in an area (18.2.4)
- describe how to carry out mark-release-recapture and estimate the abundance of organisms using the provided formula for the Lincoln index (18.2.4)

You will also:

- be able to judge which techniques to use when assessing distribution and abundance of organisms

0.5 metre (internal dimension)

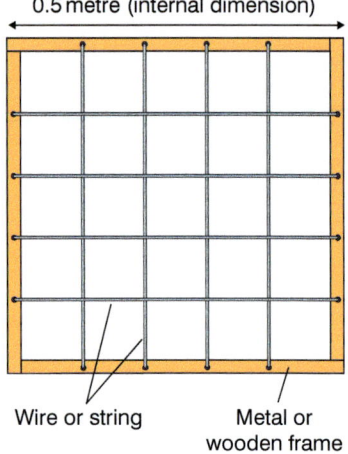

Wire or string   Metal or wooden frame

Figure 1 *A frame quadrat*

It is often necessary to measure the numbers of individuals of each species (abundance) in particular habitats. As it is virtually impossible to identify and count every organism, only small samples of the **ecosystem** are usually studied in detail. Provided these are representative of an area as a whole, any conclusion drawn from the findings will be valid. There are a number of sampling techniques including:

- random sampling using frame quadrats (Figures 1 and 2)
- systematic sampling along transects.

These techniques can also be used to assess the distribution of each species, that is, where a species occurs within an area.

Random sampling using frame quadrats

A quadrat is a sturdily built square frame (Figure 1) divided by string or wire into equally sized subdivisions. Some can be folded to make them more compact for storage and transport. The size of quadrat used will depend on the size of the plants or animals being counted. Suppose we wish to investigate the effects of grazing animals on the species of plants growing in a field. We would choose two fields as close together as possible to minimise soil, climatic and other **abiotic** differences. One field should be regularly grazed by animals such as sheep, whereas the other should not have been grazed for many years. We would take random samples at many sites on each field by placing the quadrat on the ground and recording the name and abundance of each species found within the area of the quadrat. To get a truly random sample we need to use a method where there is no personal bias (for example avoiding a muddy wet area in preference for a dry area).

For our grazed field, and then repeated for our ungrazed field, an unbiased form of random sampling method is to:

- lay out two long tape measures at right angles, along two sides of the study area
- use random numbers from a table or generated on a computer or certain types of calculator (or use a phone app), obtain a series of coordinates
- place a quadrat at the intersection of each pair of coordinates and record the species within it.

Abundance can be measured in a number of ways, depending on the size of the species being counted and the habitat.

- **Species density**: calculated by counting the number of times an individual of a particular species occurs within all the quadrats used and calculating the mean number of individuals per unit area, e.g. 12 per square metre. This method can be time-consuming where individuals of a species are very small, and it is often difficult to judge where one plant ends and the next begins.
- **Frequency of occurrence**: the likelihood of a particular species occurring in a quadrat. If, for example, a species occurs in 15 out of 30 quadrats, the frequency of occurrence is 50%. This method is useful where a species, e.g. grass, is hard to count, but it ignores the density and distribution of a species.
- **Percentage cover**: an estimate of the area within a quadrat that a particular plant species covers. It is useful where a species is particularly abundant or is difficult to count. It is less useful where organisms, more probably plants, occur in several overlapping layers.
- **Abundance scales**: specific measures that give the relative abundance of a particular species. The scales vary from one species to the next. One such scale lists organisms as abundant, common, frequent, occasional or rare (ACFOR scale). The process is simple and easy to use but subjective – investigators often give different values for the same sample quadrat.

To obtain reliable results, the sample size should be large, i.e. many quadrats are used and a mean is obtained. A larger number of samples gives a more representative result of the field than a small number of samples.

Systematic sampling along transects

It is sometimes more informative to measure the abundance and distribution of a species in a systematic rather than a random manner. For example, the distribution of organisms on a tidal seashore is determined by the relative periods of time they spend under water and time they spend exposed to the air, i.e. by their vertical height up the shore. In these circumstances more useful data are obtained using a transect, of which there are two main types:

- **line transect**: a string or tape stretched across the ground in a straight line; any organism over which the line passes is recorded
- **belt transect**: a strip, usually a metre wide, marked by putting a second line transect parallel to the first; the species occurring within the belt between the lines are recorded. Alternatively, a metre-square frame quadrat can be laid alongside a single line transect and the species within it recorded. The quadrat is then moved its own length along the line and the process repeated.

Both line and belt transects are of two types:

- **continuous transect**: in which sampling takes place over a relatively short distance and therefore takes place from one end of the line/belt to the other
- **interrupted (ladder) transect**: in which a much larger distance is involved and therefore it is only practical to take samples at intervals, e.g. every 10 metres, along the line/belt.

Mark-release-recapture techniques

The methods of measuring abundance described work well with plant communities but not with most animals as they are mobile and move away when approached. They are often hidden and difficult to find and identify. To estimate the abundance of most animals requires an altogether different technique.

A known number of animals are caught, marked in some way, and then released back into the community. Some time later, a given number of individuals are collected randomly and the number of marked individuals is recorded. The size of the population is then calculated using the Lincoln index as follows:

$$\text{Estimated size of population} = \frac{n_1 \times n_2}{m_2}$$

where n_1 = total number of individuals captured in the first sample

n_2 = total number of individuals (both marked and unmarked) captured in the second sample

m_2 = number of marked individuals recaptured in the second sample.

This technique makes a number of assumptions:

- the proportion of marked to unmarked individuals in the second sample is the same as the proportion of marked to unmarked individuals in the population
- the marked individuals released from the first sample distribute themselves evenly among the remainder of the population and have sufficient time to do so
- the population has a definite boundary so that there is no immigration into or emigration out of it
- there are few, if any, deaths and 'births' within the population
- the method of marking used is not toxic to the individual, or make the individual more conspicuous (easily seen) and so more liable to predation
- the mark or label is not lost or rubbed off during the investigation.

Figure 2 *Ecology student using a quadrat*

Summary test 18.2c

We can measure the abundance of a species within a frame quadrat by counting the number of times individuals belonging to that species occur – known as the **(1)** of a species. Where a species is very **(2)** it is preferable to measure its percentage **(3)** within the quadrat. Systematic, rather than random, sampling is preferable in places such as a **(4)**. Here a transect is used. Sampling along a transect may be continuous or at intervals, in which case it is known as an **(5)** transect. To estimate the abundance of animals we use the **(6)** technique. Using this technique an ecologist collected and marked 100 individuals of a species. A week later she collected 80 individuals of which five were marked. The estimated size of this population is therefore **(7)**.

These pages help you to:

- use a provided formula for Spearman's rank correlation to analyse the relationship between two variables, including how biotic and abiotic factors affect the distribution and abundance of species (18.2.5)

You will also:

- consolidate your understanding of the null hypothesis in statistical tests

To make sense of the data that we collect from ecological studies we often need to analyse it. There are a number of statistical tests that can be used to analyse data. Some of these allow us to determine whether or not there is a relationship between two sets of data. We have already looked at one such test, the *t*-test (17.1c and 17.1d). We will now look at others.

Spearman's rank correlation

Spearman's rank correlation measures the relationship between two sets of **ranked** data. There are some criteria that must be met for the test to be valid.

- Ordinal data are used or any data that have been collected can be converted to an ordinal scale using ranking. Ordinal data are data that have two or more categories that can be ordered or ranked.
- The data points within samples must be independent of one another.
- A scatter diagram indicates that there is a relationship whereby as the value of one increases, so does the value of the other variable **or** as the value of one increases, the value of the other variable decreases.
- All individuals must be selected at random from a population.
- Each individual must have an equal chance of being selected.
- More than five paired observations are needed, but 10 to 30 are ideal.

The Spearman's correlation coefficient is represented by the Greek letter rho (ρ) or r_s and the equation is:

$$r_s = 1 - \left(\frac{6 \times \sum D^2}{n^3 - n} \right)$$

$\sum$ = sum of
D = difference between each pair of ranked measurements
n = number of pairs of items in the sample

The best way to explain how this equation operates is to work through a particular example.

An ecologist is trying to determine whether the number of plants (a biotic factor) found at different sites in a woodland is related to the light intensity (an abiotic factor) at each site. He uses random quadrats to count the number of plants and a light meter to measure light intensity. His results are shown in Table 1.

The first stage of the analysis is to rank the two sets of data from highest to lowest. For the number of plants this is straightforward, but for light intensity there are two identical values. For example, the value of 7000 is sixth in rank but there are two of these values. In other words rank 6 and rank 7 are both 7000. We therefore average the two ranks ($6 + 7 = 13 \div 2 = 6.5$) and give each the value of 6.5. **Remember that as ranks 6 and 7 have both been used, the next rank value is 8**. Table 2 shows the rank values for our data.

The second stage of the analysis is to calculate the difference (*D*) between the two sets of rank values by taking the second value away from the first. Some values of *D* will be negative, but as the next stage is to square these values (*D*²) then they all become positive. Finally we add all the values of D^2 to give a total of 31.50. See Table 2.

Table 1

Quadrat number	Number of plants	Light intensity/lux
1	40	9000
2	12	7000
3	8	2000
4	27	8000
5	24	7000
6	21	6000
7	25	5000
8	60	15000
9	18	3000
10	64	19000
11	19	4000
12	70	22000

Table 2

Quadrat number	Number of plants	Rank order of plant numbers	Light intensity/ lux	Rank order of light intensity	Difference (D)	D^2
1	40	4	9000	4	0.0	0.00
2	12	11	7000	6.5	4.5	20.25
3	8	12	2000	12	0.0	0.00
4	27	5	8000	5	0.0	0.00
5	24	7	7000	6.5	0.5	0.25
6	21	8	6000	8	0.0	0.00
7	25	6	5000	9	−3.0	9.00
8	60	3	15000	3	0.0	0.00
9	18	10	3000	11	−1.0	1.00
10	64	2	19000	2	0.0	0.00
11	19	9	4000	10	−1.0	1.00
12	70	1	22000	1	0.0	0.00
					Total	**31.50**

The third stage of the analysis is calculate a correlation coefficient and assess whether there is a significant correlation between the two factors. We now substitute the values of n and D^2 in the Spearman's rank correlation equation as follows:

$$r_s = 1 - \left(\frac{6 \times 31.5}{1728 - 12} \right)$$

$$= 1 - 0.1101$$

$$= 0.8899$$

The correlation coefficient will range in value from −1.0 to +1.0. The value of 0.890 (to three decimal places), which is close to +1, gives an indication that there is a relationship between light intensity and the number of plants at the selected sites. To obtain a more accurate measure of the strength of the relationship, it is necessary to look up the coefficient in critical value tables. This will provide a level of significance for the relationship. Table 3 shows a small, but relevant, part of the critical values table for the Spearman's rank correlation coefficient. In this table, with $n = 12$ (the number of quadrats used), the calculated value of r exceeds the critical value of 0.591 at the 0.05 probability level (and exceeds 0.777 at $p = 0.01$). The null hypothesis states that there is no correlation between light intensity and the number of plants and as light intensity increases, the rank of number of plants does not increase or decrease. As a probability level of 0.05 or lower is considered acceptable, the null hypothesis can be rejected and it can be stated that there is a significant correlation between the two factors: as light intensity increases, so does the number of plants.

Table 3

n	p = 0.05 level	p = 0.01 level
12	0.591	0.777
14	0.544	0.715
16	0.506	0.665
18	0.475	0.625
20	0.450	0.591

Summary test 18.2d

The Spearman's rank **(1)** measures the relationship between two sets of ranked data. It can be used if data collected is **(2)** or can be converted to an **(2)** scale using ranking. Individuals must be selected **(3)** from a population and each individual must have an **(4)** of selection. To perform the analysis more than **(5)** paired observations are needed. An r_s value of −1 indicates perfect **(6)** and a value of 0 indicates **(7)**. If a statistically significant correlation is found, then the **(8)** can be rejected.

These pages help you to:

- use a provided formula for Pearson's linear correlation to analyse the relationship between two variables, including how biotic and abiotic factors affect the distribution and abundance of species (18.2.5)
- learn how to interpret values of *D* for Simpson's diversity index (18.2.6)

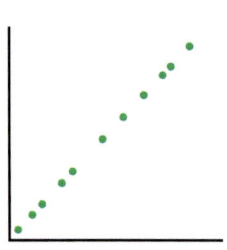

r = 1
Data lie on a perfect straight line with a positive slope

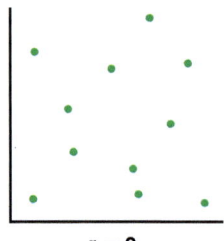

r = 0
No linear relationship between the variables

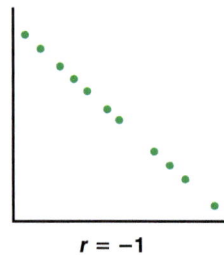

r = −1
Data lie on a perfect straight line with a negative slope

Figure 1 *Values of Pearson's correlations coefficients*

Pearson's linear correlation

Pearson's linear correlation is used to investigate the relationship between two quantitative, continuous variables, for example, age and blood pressure or percentage cover of a plant species (a biotic factor) and the percentage of organic matter in the soil (an abiotic factor) in different locations. Pearson's correlation coefficient (*r*) is a measure of the strength of the association between the two variables. It measures continuous variables rather than the categorical ones needed for Spearman's rank correlation. Again we need to satisfy some criteria.

- The data collected must be continuous.
- A scatter diagram indicates a linear relationship.
- The data collected must be normally distributed.
- There are at least five paired observations, but 10 or more are ideal.

There are a number of different ways of expressing the Pearson's correlation coefficient equation. One is:

$$r = \frac{\sum xy - n\bar{x}\bar{y}}{(n-1)\, s_x s_y}$$

where $\sum$ = sum of
n = number of observations
x and y = observations
$\bar{x}$ and $\bar{y}$ = mean of observations
s = standard deviation

The values obtained for the Pearson's correlation coefficient lie between −1 and +1. As with the Spearman's rank correlation, a table of critical values for Pearson's linear correlation can be used to assess whether there is a signficant relationship between the two variables at the $p = 0.05$ level.

For both Spearman's rank correlation and Pearson's linear correlation, the coefficient tells us two things about the linear relationship between our two variables.

- **Strength** – the larger the value the stronger the relationship; 0.0 indicates the absence of a relationship, whereas 1.0 is a perfect relationship.
- **Direction** – The sign (+ or −) indicates the direction of the relationship; the coefficient is positive if both variables increase or decrease together; the coefficient is negative if one variable increases while the other decreases.

These relationships are shown in Figure 1.

> **Remember**
>
> The Spearman's rank correlation and the Pearson's linear correlation only indicate a correlation. They do not imply a causative relationship.

Measuring species diversity

Consider the data shown in Table 1 about two habitats. The final two rows don't tell us much about the differences between the two habitats because in both cases the total number of species and the total number of individuals are identical. However, if we measure the species diversity we get a different picture of the biodiversity of the two different areas.

Table 1 *Number and types of species found in two habitats within the same ecosystem*

Species found	Numbers (n) found in habitat X	Numbers (n) found in habitat Y
A	10	3
B	10	5
C	10	2
D	10	36
E	10	4
No. species	5	5
Total no. all individuals (N)	50	50

One way of measuring species diversity is to use the Simpson's index of diversity using the formula:

$$D = 1 - \left(\Sigma \left(\frac{n}{N} \right)^2 \right)$$

where D = species diversity index

N = total number of all individuals of all types present in the sample

n = total number of individuals of each type present in the sample

Σ = the sum of

Although 'type' is often species, the diversity index can also be calculated for other taxonomic ranks, such as genera and families.

Calculation of the diversity index for habitat X:

$$D = 1 - \left(\left(\frac{10}{50} \right)^2 + \left(\frac{10}{50} \right)^2 + \left(\frac{10}{50} \right)^2 + \left(\frac{10}{50} \right)^2 + \left(\frac{10}{50} \right)^2 \right)$$

$$D = 1 - (0.2^2 + 0.2^2 + 0.2^2 + 0.2^2 + 0.2^2)$$

$$D = 1 - (0.04 + 0.04 + 0.04 + 0.04 + 0.04)$$

$$D = 1 - 0.2$$

$$D = \mathbf{0.8}$$

Calculation of the diversity index for habitat Y:

$$D = 1 - \left(\left(\frac{3}{50} \right)^2 + \left(\frac{5}{50} \right)^2 + \left(\frac{2}{50} \right)^2 + \left(\frac{36}{50} \right)^2 + \left(\frac{4}{50} \right)^2 \right)$$

$$D = 1 - (0.06^2 + 0.10^2 + 0.04^2 + 0.72^2 + 0.08^2)$$

$$D = 1 - (0.0036 + 0.0100 + 0.0016 + 0.5184 + 0.0064)$$

$$D = 1 - 0.54$$

$$D = \mathbf{0.46}$$

The higher the value D the greater the species diversity. So in this case, although both habitats have the same total number of species and the same total number of individuals, the species diversity of habitat X is greater (0.8) than that of habitat Y (0.46).

The value of D obtained will be between 0 and 1. Complete species diversity will be equal to 1 and no species diversity will be equal to 0.

Remember

Calculating a species diversity index provides a number that makes it easier to compare the variety in different habitats. It would be much harder, and less precise, if we had to rely on descriptions of different habitats to make these comparisons.

Extension

Interpreting values of D

Values of D obtained using Simpson's index of diversity may be used to compare species diversity in different areas or it could be used to see how diversity changes over time for a particular area. If the D value for an area decreases over time, then this could indicate a change in environmental conditions, such as the effects of climate change, pollution or the introduction of an alien species that begins to dominate an area. The success of efforts to combat this loss of diversity can be gauged by an increased value of D at some time in the future. When comparing two different areas, a low species diversity could indicate that the environment is very extreme and there are only a few species that are well adapted to the harsher conditions, whereas an area with a high species diversity indicates that the ecosystem is more complex and can support a greater number of organisms and a greater variety of species.

Summary test 18.2e

To investigate the relationship between two quantitative **(1)** variables, Pearson's **(2)** correlation can be used. There must be at least **(3)** paired observations but **(4)** or more are preferable. A **(5)** correlation indicates that as one variable increases, the other variable decreases. In **(6)** index of diversity two different areas can be compared. If area **X** has a value $D = 0.8$ and area **Y** has a value of $D = 0.7$, then this indicates that area **Y** has a **(7)** than area **X**.

Conservation
a. Why species become extinct

Figure 1 *Deforestation in Indonesian Borneo. Deforestation affects biodiversity, soils and drainage basins.*

Figure 2 *This photo shows Martha, believed to have been the last passenger pigeon. She died in the Cincinnati Zoological Park in 1914.*

Extinction is a normal part of natural selection and is a natural process. More than 99% of species known from fossil records are extinct. However, the current rate of extinction is alarmingly high and there is an accelerating pace of species extinctions and habitat losses as a consequence of human activities. There is often conflict between the needs of a country to produce sufficient food to feed its inhabitants and the need to conserve habitats and wildlife. Let us investigate some of the reasons for this high extinction rate.

Habitat loss and degradation

Humans exploit many natural habitats, destroying them in the process. Examples include:

- Deforestation (timber cutting and its removal) (Figure 1) destroys forests and endangers species such as the orangutan.
- Industrial and agricultural developments threaten many plant species of the Amazon rainforest.
- Clearing of river banks destroys the natural habitat of the otter and beaver.
- Modern farming methods remove trees and hedgerows as well as drain wetlands. These practices endanger the species that live and breed there. In Central America, for example, a traditional coffee plantation has coffee bushes grown in the shade beneath large trees. The canopy of these trees supports a diverse variety of species and the crop requires few pesticides. To increase productivity, modern coffee plantations use varieties of coffee that require full sun. To accommodate these, the trees are removed, with consequent loss of biodiversity, and large applications of pesticides are needed to control pests.

The condition of a habitat can be made worse by many human activities. This may result in a habitat that can no longer support the variety of species as previously and local extinctions may occur. If a species exists only in that area, then species extinction occurs. Habitat degradation is common after pollution incidents (see Extension box), or the excessive removal of particular plant or animals species, for example for use in traditional medicine or because the organisms are seen as dangerous. Hillsides can be destabilised by mining and industrial waste and seabeds can be damaged by trawling. A habitat can be degraded by natural means, such as fire or volcanic ash. A habitat that is severely degraded will no longer be able to support a community.

Competition from humans and their animals

The human population now exceeds 7 billion, putting ever-increasing pressure on land-use. As more and more land is taken up for building, industry and farming, there is more intense competition amongst wildlife for food, shelter and breeding sites in the remaining natural habitats. Interspecific competition has always led to extinctions. Species compete with each other for food, territory and nesting sites, but the competition some species face from humans has accelerated the process. Where a species is restricted to a small area, e.g. the giant tortoises in the Galapagos Islands, they are often unable to compete with the influx of humans and their animals. Because their habitat is restricted, in this case by water, they cannot escape. Humans often introduce new species that out-compete native ones. Almost half of all small- to medium-sized Australian marsupials have been exterminated by competition with introduced rabbits and predation by introduced foxes and cats.

Hunting, poaching and fishing

Humans hunt tigers for sport, crocodiles and foxes for their skins, oryx as trophies, elephants for ivory, whales for oil and rhinoceros for their horn.

Other organisms are collected for the pet trade, e.g. tamarins and parrots; and for research purposes, e.g. frogs. These are in addition to the numerous species hunted purely as food. These activities have led to the loss of species such as the passenger pigeon. Thought to have once been the most abundant bird on the planet, the passenger pigeon (Figure 2) was hunted for food and sport. In addition, its woodland habitat was destroyed to make room for agriculture. These combined effects led to its extinction, the last survivor dying in a zoo in 1914.

Other species, such as the black rhinoceros, have been brought to the brink (edge) of extinction.

Climate change

The emission of **greenhouse gases** when fossil fuels are burned has led to global warming. This has caused changes in the weather patterns with consequent changes to habitats. The abundance and distribution of individual species around the globe has been affected as a result of areas becoming wetter or drier, warmer or colder. The death of the last golden toad in Central America in 1999 is an example of a species probably made extinct by climate change. Rising sea levels are beginning to create problems for many coastal ecosystems. Throughout the tropics, a stress response to rising ocean temperatures has caused the breakdown of the very close beneficial relationship between coral and a group of unicellular algae (zooxanthellae). This is known as coral bleaching. This has meant that the coral have lost up to 90% of their energy source and many have not survived. The coral ecosystem is important for many other aquatic species and large-scale loss of coral species threatens others. Rises in sea level as a result of global warming could result in the loss of nesting sites for turtles and their possible extinction. The climate is also becoming more unpredictable, and extreme – often devastating – events are becoming more frequent. All these changes threaten biodiversity.

Figure 3 *A pelican coated in oil from the Deepwater Horizon oil spill in the Gulf of Mexico in 2010. The survival of species like these can be threatened by pollution of this kind.*

Extension

Other causes of extinction
Habitat fragmentation

As natural habitats are destroyed, those remaining become increasingly fragmented (broken up) and isolated. Habitat fragmentation occurs, for example, when housing estates, industrial areas or roads are built. These patches often cannot support a species. For example, when the Central American tropical rainforest becomes fragmented, species such as the spider monkey and the tufted capuchin, which have large ranges, are the first to disappear.

Elimination of organisms considered dangerous
Many species are persecuted because they carry diseases of domesticated species, e.g. badgers (tuberculosis of cattle) and eland (various cattle diseases). Others, such as crocodiles and the big cats are seen as a direct threat to human life and are removed to make people feel more secure.

Pollution
Oil pollution, such as the 2010 Deepwater Horizon oil spill in the Gulf of Mexico (Figure 3), threatens some rare species of sea birds as well as turtles and the dwarf seahorse. The build-up of certain insecticides along food chains endangers predatory birds like the peregrine falcon and the golden eagle.

Wars
Conflicts around the globe lead to the destruction of habitats and the death of other organisms as well as humans.

Summary test 18.3a

Many human activities threaten species. Some human activities destroy habitats. These include the clearing of **(1)**, which threatens otters, **(2)**, which is timber cutting and removal, which threatens the orangutan, and habitat **(3)**, which is the decrease in condition of a habitat as a result of pollution or other damaging events. The introduction of **(4)** to Australia led to the extinction of many native marsupials as they competed for similar food. As more land is used by humans, this increases **(5)** for resources for wildlife. Animals can also become exinct as a result of **(6)** by humans for sport or to sell animal parts. Changes to weather patterns have been caused by **(7)** and rising sea levels threaten **(8)** ecosystems. The loss of zooxanthellae can lead to **(9)** bleaching and its loss, together with the loss of other species.

These pages help you to:

- outline reasons for the need to maintain biodiversity (18.3.2)
- outline the role in conservation of the IUCN and CITES (18.3.6)

You will also:

- learn about the World Wide Fund for Nature
- read about the change in extinction rates

Figure 1 *Costa Rica has done much to restore the loss of rainforest, which has led to a growing ecotourism industry.*

Conservation is the protection, maintenance and management of the Earth's natural resources in such a way that maximum use can be made of them in the future. This involves active intervention by humans to maintain ecosystems and biodiversity. It is a dynamic process that involves:

- carefully managing existing resources
- restoring habitats already damaged by humans
- restoring biodiversity in areas where human action has reduced it.

Importance of maintaining biodiversity

The world possesses a rich diversity of species and ecosystems that are of great potential value to humankind. It is important to maintain this rich biodiversity for a number of reasons:

- **Ecological importance** – high biodiversity helps with the recycling of nutrients, in the formation and protection of soils and in the maintenance of ecosystems. By retaining water and minerals, soil can support stable plant growth and can help prevent natural disasters such as floods and **desertification**. High biodiversity also increases the stability of ecosystems and therefore allows them to recover more easily from unpredictable events, e.g. fires and drought.
- **Economic importance** – a high biodiversity means that there is a larger variety of species that can provide a larger variety of useful materials and a larger genetic diversity, which is essential to adapt to a changing world. These include food, fibres for clothing, medicines, and timber for construction. Most of the world's food comes from a small number of plant species, many of which have been inbred to improve yields. Wild strains possess a **gene pool** that may be required in the future to further improve yields or introduce disease resistance. Around half of all medicines, e.g. aspirin, used today have active ingredients extracted from living organisms. Conserving biodiversity helps safeguard our future supply of food and medicines. In addition, areas of high biodiversity have considerable potential for tourism. In Costa Rica, for example, 12% of its land area, including much of its tropical rainforests and cloud forests, has been placed under protection (Figure 1). These regions attract three million visitors a year and produce an income of around three billion dollars (Figure 2). The prevention of natural disasters mentioned in ecological importance also has an economic benefit. Maintaining the diversity of organisms in a habitat is important as species may have economic importance outside their habitat, e.g. pollinating insects.
- **Ethical, cultural and social importance** – a high biodiversity is necessary to safeguard future resources and to maintain a diversity of genes. It allows the indigenous (native) population to maintain its own cultural values and way of life, as well as providing the opportunity for ecotourism and recreation. It also permits research to be carried out and for others to learn about the vast range of organisms on the planet. Many people feel that humans have a responsibility to conserve biodiversity, not just for ecological and economic reasons, but also for its aesthetic value. Imagine how less fulfilling life would be without the beauty of flowers and other wildlife.

Legal protection for endangered species

In many countries it is illegal to collect or kill certain species, e.g. the koala in Australia. The **Convention on International Trade in Endangered Species of Wild Fauna and Flora (CITES)** came into force in 1975. Its aim is to prevent international trade from threatening the survival of certain endangered species. The freely available CITES appendices contains a list of these species and notes about products obtained from some species. Some 5000 species of animals and 30 000 species of plants are protected against overexploitation through international trade. Although participation is voluntary, it is legally binding on those countries that choose to sign up. CITES provides a framework for each country to adopt its own legislation and to implement it. Most of these countries have very strict laws banning the import or export of endangered plants and animals and their products.

The International Union for Conservation of Nature (IUCN) is a global organisation for nature conservation and the sustainable use of natural resources. The IUCN works with other organisations and governments around the world to improve efforts to conserve species. The IUCN Red List of Threatened Species™ assesses the conservation status of animal, plant and fungal species. The risk of extinction is evaluated using scientific data for the species on the list: in 2019 more than 30 000 species had been assessed as threatened with extinction, out of a total of more than 112 400 species assessed. The list is the most important resource to indicate the health of global biodiversity. There are nine categories: Not Evaluated, Data Deficient (not enough information to make an assessment), Least Concern, Near Threatened, Vulnerable, Endangered, Critically Endangered, Extinct in the Wild, and Extinct.

The IUCN Red List data is used by many different groups, such as CITES, to allow international agreements to be made about protection of species. The list is used by members of the World Bank Group, so that they can be informed about the status of biodiversity in areas and help make decisions about how to minimise risk to biodiversity when introducing large-scale infrastructure and about providing financial support for sustainable development. Governments can use the IUCN Red List for policy-making decisions for National parks or when considering whether to create protected areas. Zoos, educational institutions, scientists and the media can inform the public and students and make them more aware of the risks to biodiversity and the actions that can be taken to help conserve species.

Figure 2 *Apart from the aesthetic value of maintaining biodiversity, countries such as Costa Rica have benefited from a growing ecotourism industry by conserving rainforests for visitors to enjoy.*

Summary test 18.3b

The aim of conservation is to **(1)**, maintain and manage the **(2)** of the Earth so that maximum use can be made of them in the future. High diversity increases the **(3)** of ecosystems, which helps to prevent soil **(4)** and the formation of deserts from fertile land, known as **(5)**. Wild strains of crops have a **(6)** which may be needed in the future to improve yields. Conserving biodiversity helps to safeguard the source of future **(7)**, such as aspirin, and can increase the economic status of countries by attracting visitors for the **(8)** industry. Maintaining biodiversity is also important for ethical, **(9)** and social reasons. The aim of **(10)** is to prevent international trade of endangered species. The IUCN evaluates the conservation status of plant, animal and **(11)** species and publishes the **(12)**, which has **(13)** categories of conservation status. The category before 'Extinct in the Wild' is **(14)**, and this category lists those organisms that are most at risk from extinction.

Extension

WWF

Non-governmental organisations such as the **World Wide Fund for Nature (WWF)** also have a role to play. WWF works on conserving, preserving and restoring the environment. It is the world's largest independent conservation organisation, supporting around 1300 conservation and environmental projects. Its aim is to stop the degradation of the planet's natural environment and to build a future in which humans live in harmony with nature. Its work concentrates on the conservation of the oceans and coasts, forests, and freshwater ecosystems, as these contain most of the world's biodiversity. It is also concerned with endangered species, pollution and climate change.

These pages help you to:

- outline the roles of zoos, botanic gardens, national parks and marine parks (conserved areas), 'frozen zoos' and seed banks, in the conservation of endangered species (18.3.3)

You will also:

- learn about other methods of protecting species

Figure 1 *Giant panda at Chengdu Research Base of Giant Panda Breeding in China. The base carries out a captive breeding programme and reintroduces this endangered species back into the wild.*

Figure 2 *African elephant herd in the Amboseli National Park, Kenya. National reserves like these help in the conservation of endangered species.*

A species is considered endangered when it is facing a very high risk of extinction in the near future. The three relevant categories in the IUCN Red List of Threatened Species™ are Endangered, Critically Endangered, and Extinct in the Wild. Some non-governmental organisations (NGOs) play a major role in protecting and conserving endangered species. These organisations complement the work of governments. They can often work more quickly than governments to bring about cooperation between countries for the conservation of endangered species and for the preservation of habitats (leaving habitats undisturbed by humans). Their role also includes trying to find a balance between the needs of local people and the need to protect endangered species.

Development of conserved areas: national parks and marine parks

National parks, marine parks and nature reserves are habitats legally safeguarded and patrolled by wardens. They may preserve a vulnerable food source, e.g. in China areas of bamboo forest are protected to help conserve the giant panda (Figure 1). In Africa, game parks help to protect endangered species such as the African elephant (Figure 2). Efforts are being made to conserve the decreasing areas of tropical rainforest in Central America and elsewhere. Planning authorities have greater powers to control developments and activities within these areas. Nest sites and the young can be monitored and protected to help ensure they mature to adulthood and have the opportunity to breed.

The importance of conserving the biodiversity of the seas is being increasingly appreciated. As a result, more and more **marine parks** (Figure 3) are being designated by governments throughout the world. Areas of the sea are set aside to preserve a specific habitat and ensure that the ecosystem is sustained for the organisms that live there. Coral reefs are one of the most biodiverse habitats on the planet, and yet they are especially vulnerable because:

- Climate change is raising the temperature of the seas and increasing their carbon dioxide concentration.
- More dissolved carbon dioxide decreases the pH of the seas, which causes the skeletons of corals to dissolve and the reef to break up.
- Rising sea levels and pollution by oil and sewage are killing species that live on them.
- The loss of photosynthetic algae (zooxanthellae) decreases their energy source (see 18.2b).
- Intensive fishing and disturbance from tourists diving and snorkelling on them also threaten their fragile ecology.

The status of a marine park allows fishing and diving to be restricted and special measures taken to avoid pollution. Two of the largest marine parks are the Great Barrier Reef Marine Park in Australia and the Chagos Marine Park in the Indian Ocean.

Zoos and botanical gardens

Botanic gardens and zoos serve as safe locations for plants and animals that could become or are already extinct in the wild, to survive, reproduce and so pass on their DNA. Botanic gardens are also a source of disease-free seeds. The scientists that work in zoos and botanic gardens have most expertise in conservation. They carry out research to improve understanding and knowledge of conservation and of techniques for long-term storage of seeds, embryos and sperm. They are also able to use their knowledge in the natural environment to help conserve animals and plants, including threatened trees located in natural habitats. Members of the public learn more about threatened species by visiting zoos and botanic gardens, and greater public support is critical to the success of conservation efforts. Endangered species may be bred in the protected environment of a zoo and when numbers have been sufficiently increased they may be reintroduced into the wild. One species conserved in this way has been the Hawaiian Goose or Nene. Its population in the wild fell to around 20 pairs before being supplemented by thousands of birds bred in captivity and released in Hawaii. Captive breeding programmes have the following advantages:

- There is less need to capture wild animals and remove plants from their natural habitats to supply zoos and botanical gardens.
- Natural populations can be maintained or increased by reintroduction of individuals bred in captivity.
- Breeding success is improved by techniques such as *in-vitro* fertilisation (IVF) and monitoring mothers during the gestation period (antenatal and postnatal care).

Captive breeding is not without its problems however. These include:

- Inbreeding leading to a gene pool that is small and offspring that may be weak with the potential for genetic defects.
- When reintroduced into the wild, captively bred individuals may not adapt to their new circumstances. They may have problems feeding, mating and be more prone to disease and more vulnerable to predators.
- Introducing pathogens and diseases that have been acquired in captivity, into the wild population.
- Captivity is an unnatural state for wild animals. They often become stressed which makes them unable to mate and makes them more vulnerable to disease.

Figure 3 *A ranger collecting freshly laid eggs from a hawksbill turtle at Turtle Island Marine Park, Sabah, Malaysia. The eggs are relocated to an artificial nest in a hatchery as soon as they are laid to protect them from being dug up by other turtles or monitor lizards. The loss of nesting beaches and the effects of hunting and pollution have endangered some turtle species.*

Extension

Other methods of protection
- **Education** – It is important to educate people in ways of preventing habitat destruction and encouraging conservation.
- **A ban on hunting and fishing coupled with commercial farming** – Legislation to control hunting and fishing of endangered species helps maintain their numbers.
- **Removal of animals from threatened areas** – Organisms in habitats threatened by humans, or by natural disasters such as floods, may be removed and resettled in more secure habitats.
- **Control of introduced species** – Organisms introduced into a country by humans often require strict control if they are not to out-compete the indigenous species.
- **Ecological study of threatened habitats** – Careful analysis of all natural habitats is essential if they are to be managed in a way that permits conservation of a maximum number of species.
- **Pollution control** – Measures to control pollution such as smoke emissions, oil spillage, over-use of pesticides, fertiliser run-off, etc. help to prevent habitat and species destruction.
- **Recycling** – The more material that is recycled, the less need there is to obtain that material from natural sources, e.g. through mining.

Summary test 18.3c

National parks and marine parks are examples of **(1)** areas. They can be protected and patrolled by **(2)**. Zoos and botanic gardens are places that have scientists that carry out **(3)** into conservation. They are also places where the public can be **(4)** about the need to conserve plants and animals. Zoos can carry out **(5)** programmes, with the aim of reintroducing animals into the wild. They can also cryopreserve ova, sperm and **(6)** in what are called **(7)**. Seeds can be preserved in **(8)**. Some are cryopreserved and others can have their **(9)** content reduced before storing at **(10)** °C in **(11)** chambers. They can be removed for research, or can be checked for **(12)** and **(13)** when necessary.

Establishing seed, embryo and sperm banks

Zoos and botanic gardens can store the DNA of species of animals and plants in gene banks.

In addition to captive-breeding programmes, zoos often 'freeze' (cryopreservation) ova, sperm and embryos ('**frozen zoos**') for later use when natural habitats become available and finances permit. Long-term storage is also useful as an insurance against epidemics and natural disasters.

Reproductive tissue from deceased animals can be frozen to preserve genetic diversity. The use of frozen sperm has the advantage of being less stressful to animals than transporting them over large distances for breeding. Using embryo transfer and surrogacy (see 18.3d), these 'frozen genes' can be later used to yield additional individuals of endangered species.

In the same way, plant species may be protected in botanical gardens, either as adult individuals or their genetic material temporarily preserved in **seed banks**. The Millennium Seed Bank partnership at Kew Gardens in England has already banked 92 500 seed collections from over 40 000 plant species, the world's largest collection. Seeds from plants and regions most at risk from climate change and other human activities have been targeted. As well as serving to conserve endangered species, the seed banks are an insurance against biodiversity loss, climate change, plant disease and can act as a store of seeds of important food crops.

Seeds, embryos and tissues are stored at −80 °C using solid carbon dioxide or −196 °C using liquid nitrogen (cryopreservation). Some seeds can have their moisture content reduced to around 4–6% (of fresh weight), before they are stored in deep-freeze chambers at −18 to −20 °C, to prevent germination. Others need to be cryopreserved. The seeds are regularly restocked and tested for viability (can germinate). The advantages of seed banks are that the samples are small so less space is required, maintenance is simple and relatively inexpensive and the samples can last for a very long time.

Extension

The humpback whale, *Megaptera novaeangliae*

Introduction

The humpback whale (Figure 4) is considered to be one example where conservation action has saved a species from becoming extinct. The whales are filter feeders and their diet is mainly krill (small crustacea), plankton (small aquatic organisms) and small fish. They have a structure known as a baleen which filters seawater to extract the food. The main component of baleen is a hard protein known as keratin (the same protein found in our skin, hair and nails). The whales are distributed globally, feeding in summer in cooler, temperate waters and migrating in winter to warmer subtropical and tropical waters for mating and breeding. Because summer in the northern hemisphere is winter in the southern hemisphere, breeding in warmer waters for northern hemisphere humpback whale populations will be at totally different times for southern hemisphere populations. The migratory patterns of some individuals does not always follow the general pattern, and there is still much to be learned about the species.

Figure 4 *Humpback whale*

The decline (decrease) in numbers of the humpback whale

In the 18th, 19th and first half of the 20th century, whales were hunted globally, particularly in the southern hemisphere. In this time, it is estimated that at least 3 000 000 humpback whales were killed and many populations had decreased so severely that they became almost extinct. The main reason for hunting whales was to obtain whale oil, derived from whale blubber (fat), that could be used in oil lamps, for engineering oil, and for the production of soaps, cooking oil and in margarine. Baleen (also known as whalebone), because of its strength and flexibility, was used to make a wide range of products, such as door and knife handles, combs, umbrellas and brushes. Today, these items would be made of synthetic materials.

Conservation measures and their consequences

Unlike many other species, humpback whales cannot be kept in zoos or small marine enclosures and so must be protected in the wild. In 1966 the whales were given legal protection from commercial whaling by the International Whaling Commission (IWC). Illegal hunting, which continued until 1972, was the main reason why numbers of the whales decreased further after 1966. Some whales were also killed legally for scientific research and others were killed in collisions with ships and or by becoming tangled in nets. Even with protection, noise and vibration disturbance from ships is also known to affect mating behaviour and the health of whales is affected by aquatic pollutants.

Because countries have worked together to enforce the legal protection given to the humpback whale, numbers have gradually increased. Australia and New Zealand have programmes to disentangle whales that are caught in fishing lines and nets. There are now designated sanctuaries (areas of safety from hunting) in breeding and feeding areas of the humpback whale. The IWC established the Indian Ocean Sanctuary and the Southern Ocean Sanctuary around Antarctica and different countries have also set up marine sanctuaries and conservation areas in waters along their coastlines. Although there are still some populations that are considered threatened or endangered, there are now many populations that have made a strong recovery and in 2018 the species was categorised on the IUCN Red List of Threatened Species as 'least concern'. This shows that if the correct measures are taken, conservation efforts to save a species from extinction can be successful.

Although some of the population sizes of humpback whales in many areas have increased, this does not always mean that the populations have the same genetic diversity as previously. During a short time period of intensive hunting, population bottlenecks will have occurred (see 17.2c).

In some areas, the numbers of whales have now increased to a point where concern has been expressed that fish numbers will decrease, as these also feed on the same main food source of whales. Indeed, since the ban on whale hunting, some opposition to the protection given to the whales has come from Japan, who argue that a proportion of whales should be killed to protect decreasing fish stocks.

The western South Atlantic humpback whale population – an example of successful conservation

Research and modelling on western South Atlantic (WSA) humpback whales showed that the whale population became almost extinct. An estimated 40 000 to 60 000 whales were killed between the early 1800s and the introduction of protection, with an estimated 27 000 whales in 1830 to 450 in the mid 1950s. A report in 2019 suggests that the population has recovered well and the current population size is estimated to be at 93% of the original population before intense whale hunting began in the early 1800s. Figure 5 shows estimates of the size of the WSA population of humpback whale in the time period from 1830 to 2019, and also shows a projection of numbers to 2030. In addition, the annual number of whales caught in the same time period is shown.

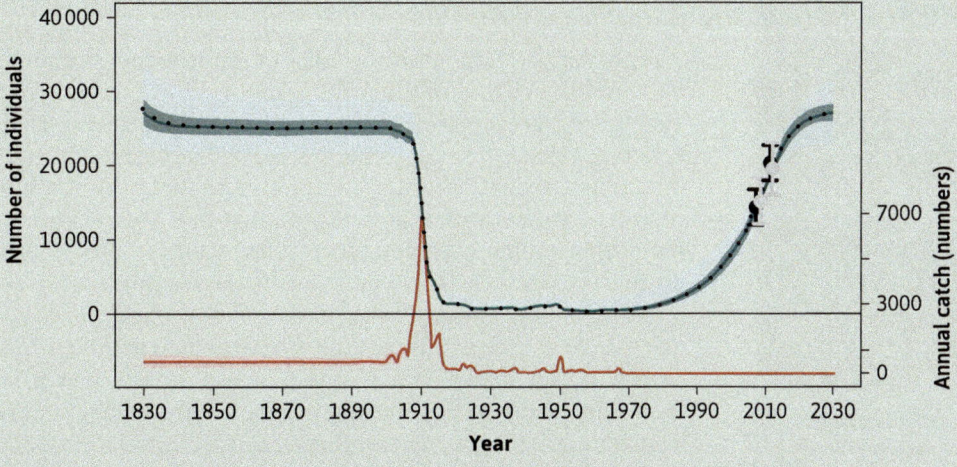

Figure 5 *Graph showing changes in the population size of the WSA population of humpback whale and corresponding annual catch sizes (Source published by the Royal Society, 2019, reprinted under the terms of the Creative Commons Attribution License CC-BY 4.0)*

A consequence of the recovery of the WSA population of humpback whale may be that a large quantity of krill will be removed by the whales and, in the aquatic communities, where the whales feed, there will be considerable changes in the community and hence the ecosystem as a whole.

These pages help you to:

- describe IVF, embryo transfer and surrogacy as methods of assisted reproduction used in the conservation of endangered mammals (18.3.4)
- explain reasons for controlling invasive alien species (18.3.5)

You will also:

- learn about the role of artificial insemination, culling and contraceptives in conservation

Figure 1 *The numbers of black rhinoceros (Diceros bicornis) have been increased using assisted reproduction*

Assisted reproduction in mammals

When the population of a species becomes so low that it is threatened with extinction, it is sometimes necessary to assist the natural reproductive process in order to build up its numbers again. One problem is that a small population has a limited **gene pool** and so a priority is to maintain or increase genetic diversity and to avoid inbreeding, which causes poor fertility and increased susceptibility to disease.

To be successful, information on an mammal's reproductive cycle is required. As this is controlled by hormones, it is important to know when each hormone is being produced. At one time this would have required taking blood samples from anaesthetised animals, but new techniques allow us to measure hormone levels in faeces, and in urine, removing the need to ever touch the animal. Useful information can be obtained about the time of ovulation, whether an animal is pregnant and, if so, the likely time of birth. Mammals whose reproduction is assisted in this way include the cheetah, snow leopard, ocelot and black rhinoceros (Figure 1). The techniques employed are often the ones used to improve human fertility, including:

- ***In-vitro* fertilisation** – involves female mammals being treated with gonadotrophins, which are hormones that stimulate the maturation of oocytes for fertilisation by sperm. These mature oocytes are then collected by using ultrasound to guide a needle to the ovaries and to collect the oocytes by 'sucking' them into the needle (aspiration). The oocytes are then fertilised in the laboratory by sperm, either frozen or fresh, from a genetically different male donor. The embryos can then be transplanted back into the donor female or into a surrogate mother, or they can be frozen until a suitable recipient becomes available. This technique has been successfully used to produce offspring of the endangered black rhinoceros.
- **Embryo transfer** – involves the collection of pre-implantation embryos from a donor female. The embryos may be transferred immediately or can be frozen to store for a period of time. If the embryos are to be kept for a long time, they may be cryopreserved. Frozen embryos can be transported long distances. When required they can be thawed and transferred into the reproductive tract of a surrogate mother (recipient female of the same or closely related species). The donor female must be healthy. The process may involve treating the donor female with gonadotrophins to stimulate the production of a number of oocytes, followed by artificial insemination (see Extension) to allow fertilisation and the resulting embryos to implant. Embryos can be checked using a microscope to make sure they are suitable for implantation. The embryos are usually removed by flushing the uterus with a solution designed to provide the best possible conditions for the survival of the embryos. Embryo transfer allows a greater number of offspring to be produced than would occur normally in nature.

Extension

Artificial insemination – where sperm are introduced into the vagina of a female by artificial means. Sperm from a male that is genetically different from the female is usually chosen to increase genetic diversity. Essential to this is the large genetic database that has been assembled, detailing the genome of a large number of individuals. To improve the chances of success, semen can be screened to select the most fertile, disease-free sperm, and insemination can be carried out around the time of female ovulation as determined by hormone analysis. Artificial insemination has been successful in many animals, including koalas, wallabies and giant pandas.

Extension

Preventing over-population by culling and contraception

It may seem odd, but sometimes the best way of conserving a species is to limit its population. There is a limit on how many individuals of a species a particular habitat can support. If this is exceeded, then a shortage of food and breeding territories may threaten the welfare of the species as a whole. Over-population of one species might threaten the welfare of another. In these circumstances it is better to cull some of the population to allow the remainder the best conditions in which to thrive. Culling is usually selective and involves killing the physically weaker, or genetically damaged, individuals in order to improve the quality of the remaining stock.

Contraception takes time to reduce the population and a relatively high proportion of females must be made infertile for it to be effective.

Culling and the use of contraceptives are also a means of controlling non-protected species that compete with protected ones for food, water and territories or spread disease. By controlling the populations of these competitors, there is less disease and more resources to allow the populations of protected species to recover.

- **Surrogacy** – where the embryo of one individual is implanted into the uterus of another. Here it develops and is carried by the surrogate mother until birth. It is used to simultaneously raise many embryos produced by artificial insemination.

Control of alien species

Some non-native, or alien, species have been introduced into new areas unintentionally (by accident), for example, arriving in ship containers or brought back unknowingly by tourists. Others, however have been introduced for beneficial purposes or for pleasure (e.g. for food, for biological pest control, as pets, for zoos, as attractive garden plants).

The introduction of non-native species into a new area can create major problems. There are often no natural predators, or grazing animals, to control their populations, which therefore expand rapidly. They can aggressively outcompete the native species and so present a serious threat to biodiversity and a major cause of extinction globally. In Europe, the red squirrel populations are on the brink of extinction in the UK and Italy, following the introduction of the larger American grey squirrel. The American grey squirrel damages trees, with huge consequences for the timber industry. Dutch elm disease is caused by an introduced fungus and has vastly reduced elm trees in the forests of central Europe. Japanese knotweed is a particularly invasive non-native plant in some parts of the world. It competitively eliminates native species but is found to support 40% fewer insect species. This damages habitats and reduces food supply for insect-eating animals. It is essential to control alien species to prevent them from disrupting habitats and causing the individual problems mentioned above.

Herbicides may be used to remove alien plant species, or mechanical methods such as mowing, cutting or digging, or even hand pulling. Biological control methods, such as viral or bacterial pathogens to kill plants or animal alien species can also be used. Many countries now have strict regulations about the use of biological control methods so that there is no threat to domestic or native species, or to agriculture. Poison bait or traps may be used to control alien animal species.

Summary test 18.3d

One method of conservation is (1) reproduction. This takes a number of forms, including (2), where females can be treated with hormones known as (3) and the mature (4) are removed from a female and (5) by sperm in a laboratory. The (6) are placed back into the donor female or into another female. In a process known as (7), pre-implantation embryos are collected from a donor female. These are transferred into another female known as the (8), who carries the developing embryo until birth. Another method of conserving species is to control non-native or (9) species that have been introduced into a new area. These species can create problems as they (10) the native species because there are no natural (11) to control their numbers.

$$\boxed{\text{Launch additional digital resources for the chapter}}$$

18 Exam-style questions

1 Figure 1 shows the graceful sun-moth, *Synemon gratiosa* that is restricted to the coastal dunes of Western Australia.

Figure 1

A species of mat-rush (large grass-like plant), *Lomandra maritima* grows abundantly in Western Australia.

A study investigated the relationship between the percentage cover of mat-rush and number of graceful sun-moths.

To do this, a Spearman's rank correlation (r_s) was carried out using the data in Table 1.

a The formula for Spearman's rank correlation is:

$$r_s = 1 - \left(\frac{6 \times \Sigma D^2}{n^3 - n} \right)$$

n = number of pairs of items in the sample
D = difference between each pair of ranked measurements.

i Complete Table 1 to show how the values for D^2 were calculated. *(2 marks)*

ii Calculate the value of r_s. Give your answer to **two** decimal places. *(2 marks)*

b Table 2 shows the critical values of r_s at the 0.05 probability level.

Table 2

n	5	6	7	8	9	10	11	12
critical value of r_s	1.00	0.89	0.79	0.76	0.68	0.65	0.60	0.54

Using Table 2, explain whether or not the r_s calculated is significant. *(1 mark)*

(Total 5 marks)

2 A group of scientists wanted to assess the biodiversity of a river using Simpson's Index of Biodiversity (D):

$$D = 1 - \left(\Sigma \left(\frac{n}{N} \right)^2 \right)$$

n = number of individuals of each species present in the sample

N = total number of all individuals of all species

Samples of aquatic insects were collected from the river. The main groups of insects present were identified and counted.

Table 3 shows the results.

Table 1

Sampling site	Percentage cover of mat-rush	Rank of percentage cover of mat-rush	Number of graceful sun-moth	Rank of number of graceful sun-moth	Difference in rank, D	D²
1	77.5	8	15			1
2	54.5	5	13			0
3	44.1	4	8			4
4	74.2	7	20			1
5	58.7	6	14			0
6	22.7	1	9			6.25
7	33.9	3	5			4
8	31.7	2	9			2.25

Table 3

Insect group	Number present in sampling site	$\frac{n}{N}$	$\left(\frac{n}{N}\right)^2$
Dragonfly	1194		
Beetle	315		
Water scorpion	530		
Pond skater	772		
Total	2811		

a Calculate Simpson's Index of Diversity by completing Table 3 in the spaces provided.

Show all working to **three** decimal places. *(3 marks)*

b Explain what this value shows about the diversity at that site. *(2 marks)*

(Total 5 marks)

18 Practice questions

3 a State four features that are shared by members of the same species.

b State the main features of a phylogenetic (natural) system of classification.

c *Rana temporaria* is the frog commonly found in Britain. The incomplete table below shows some of its classification. Give the name for each of the blanks in the table represented by the numbers 1–7.

Kingdom	Animalia
1	Chordata
2	Amphibia
3	Anura
4	Ranidae
Genus	5
6	7

4 Scientists believe that the production of greenhouse gases by human activities is contributing to climate change.

a Explain why an increase in greenhouse gases is more likely to result in damage to communities with a low species diversity than ones with a high species diversity.

b The figure below shows the effect of environmental change on the stability and the functioning of ecosystems.

Key
— Community with low species diversity
— Community with high species diversity
— Environmental change

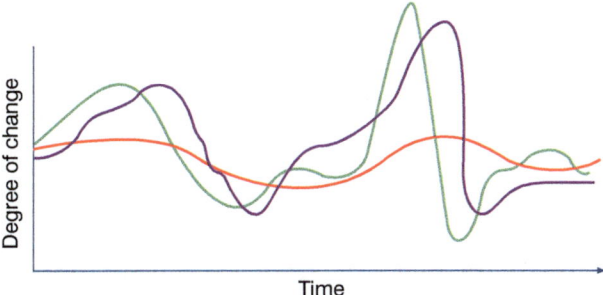

i Describe the relationship between environmental change and the community with low species diversity.

ii Explain the different responses to environmental change between communities with low and high species diversity.

5 Outline the difference between habitat loss and habitat degradation.

Use examples to help your answer.

6 Discuss the balance between maintaining biodiversity and encouraging ecotourism.

7 Outline four ways in which botanical gardens can contribute to conservation of threatened or endangered plant species.

19 Genetic technology

19.1 Principles of genetic technology

These pages help you to:

- define the term recombinant DNA (19.1.1)
- understand that genetic engineering involves the deliberate manipulation of genetic material to modify specific characteristics of an organism (19.1.2)
- explain that genetic engineering may involve transferring a gene into an organism so that the gene is expressed (19.1.2)
- explain that genes to be transferred into an organism may be extracted from the DNA of a donor organism or synthesised
  - from the mRNA of a donor organism
  - chemically from nucleotides (19.1.3)
- explain the roles of restriction endonucleases, DNA polymerase and reverse transcriptase in obtaining genes for transfer into an organism (19.1.4)
- describe and explain how gel electrophoresis is used to separate DNA fragments of different lengths (19.1.9)

You will also:

- understand the roles of reverse transcriptase in viruses and restriction endonucleases in bacteria
- read about other uses of electrophoresis

Remember

Genetic engineering is also known as genetic manipulation, genetic technology and recombinant DNA techology.

a. Obtaining genes for genetic engineering; gel electrophoresis

One of the most important scientific advances since the discovery of the structure of DNA in 1953 has been the development of gene technology. In a branch of biology known as **genetic engineering**, techniques have been devised that allow the synthesis of genes, the removal and alteration of genes, and the transfer of genes from organism to organism. The deliberate manipulation of DNA in genetic engineering results in an organism that has specifically altered characteristics: this may be from a direct alteration of its genes, or by transferring into it genes from another organism. As a result, the affected cells of the organism make a different product during protein synthesis.

Gel electrophoresis is a technique that is able to separate and identify fragments of DNA, useful in genetic engineering and in DNA forensics.

Recombinant DNA

When DNA from two different sources is joined together, the novel DNA that is formed is known as **recombinant DNA**. Genetic engineering always involves the formation of recombinant DNA. An organism containing recombinant DNA is known as a **genetically modified organism (GMO)**. Where the DNA has been transferred into another organism for a protein product to be synthesised and harvested, the organism may be termed the **recombinant host**. Sometimes the introduced DNA is termed 'foreign DNA' or 'foreign gene'.

Outline of genetic engineering

Techniques have been developed to produce large quantities of 'pure' proteins by isolating genes, **cloning** them and transferring them into host organisms. These host organisms are frequently microorganisms, such as non-pathogenic bacteria, that are used for the continuous production of a desired protein. The process of making a protein using genetic engineering has a number of stages:

- **obtaining a gene** coding for the desired protein
- **cloning** (making many genetically identical copies) of the DNA using DNA polymerase
- **transformation** – the transfer of DNA into suitable host cells using an appropriate method such as a plasmid vector (19.1c). DNA transferred to the host may contain additional nucleotide sequences necessary for transcription.
- **identification** of host cells that have successfully taken up the gene by use of **gene markers**
- **large-scale production** of the population of host cells.

Obtaining the desired gene

The required gene may consist of a sequence of a few hundred bases among, for example, the many millions in human DNA. It must be identified and extracted for use, or must be synthesised. Genes can be synthesised by using mRNA as a template or by using a combination of chemical and molecular biology methods.

Reverse transcriptase

This catalyses a reaction where DNA is produced from RNA (the reverse of transcription). This enzyme can be used in genetic engineering to synthesise the DNA required from messenger RNA. The process of using **reverse transcriptase** to synthesise a gene is described and shown in Figure 1.

- The DNA produced by reverse transcription is known as **complementary DNA (cDNA)** because it is made up of the nucleotides that are complementary to the mRNA.
- Nucleotides can be added to the ends of the DNA to produce 'sticky ends' (see page 428) for the next step of the process.

The advantage of synthesising genes in this way is that it is much easier to extract the specific mRNA and the mRNA is present in many copies (unlike the gene). Also the host cells used may be bacteria and they may not have the metabolic capability of processing RNA transcripts that contain non-coding portions of DNA (introns).

Extension

Retroviruses

Retroviruses are a group of RNA viruses, the best known of which is the human immunodeficiency virus (HIV). Retroviruses have an enzyme called reverse transcriptase. When HIV has entered a host cell, it can synthesise DNA from its RNA using this enzyme. The DNA can then integrate into the DNA of the host cell. The enzyme is also known as RNA-dependent DNA polymerase.

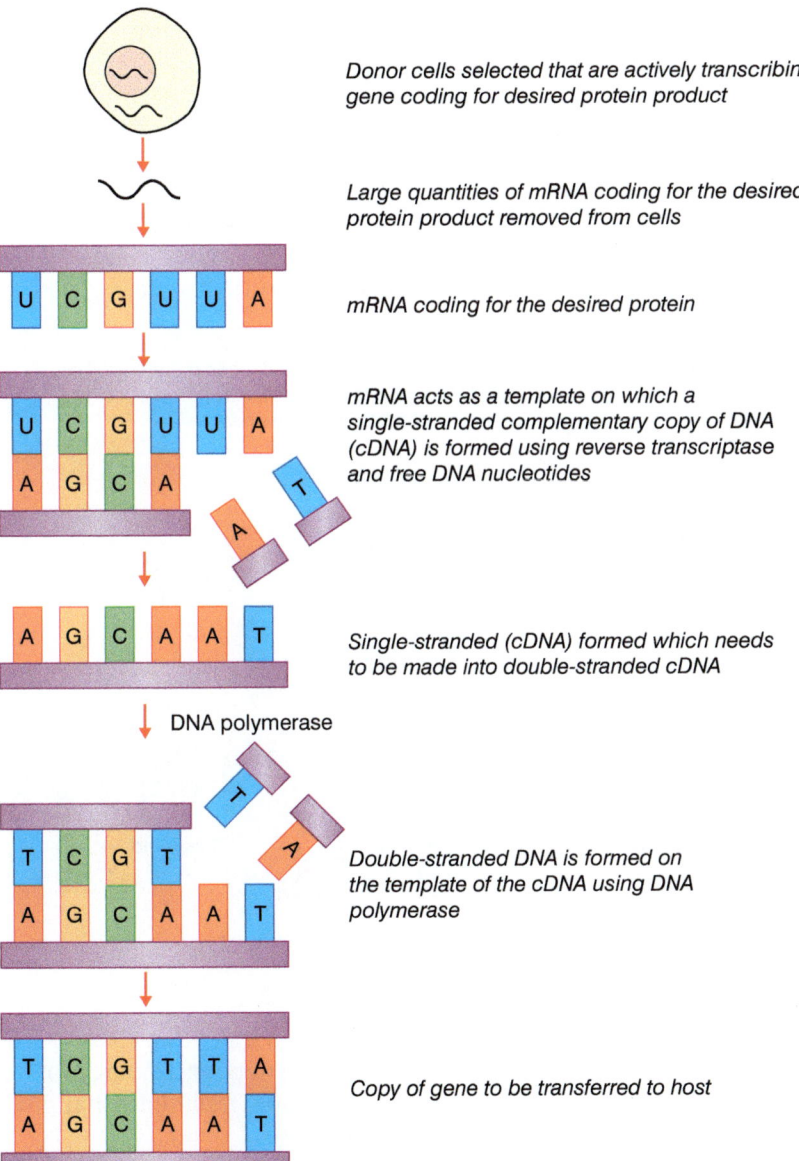

Donor cells selected that are actively transcribing gene coding for desired protein product

Large quantities of mRNA coding for the desired protein product removed from cells

mRNA coding for the desired protein

mRNA acts as a template on which a single-stranded complementary copy of DNA (cDNA) is formed using reverse transcriptase and free DNA nucleotides

Single-stranded (cDNA) formed which needs to be made into double-stranded cDNA

DNA polymerase

Double-stranded DNA is formed on the template of the cDNA using DNA polymerase

Copy of gene to be transferred to host

Figure 1 Using reverse transcriptase to synthesise a gene

Remember

Each restriction endonuclease recognises and cuts DNA at a specific sequence of bases. These sequences occur in the DNA of all species of organisms – but not in the same places!

Extension

Bacterial defence against viruses

In nature, restriction endonuclease enzymes are produced by some bacteria to defend themselves against bacteriophages, which are viruses that infect bacteria. The restriction endonucleases cut up viral DNA, so preventing viral replication and damage to the bacteria cell.

Chemically synthesising a gene from nucleotides

If the amino acid sequence of the desired protein product is known, it is possible to synthesise an artificial gene. The genetic code tells us which sequence of three bases will code for a particular amino acid. A sequence of nucleotides can be determined that will allow the production of a gene that codes for the protein. The synthesis of a gene with this method does not need a DNA or mRNA template. Short nucleotide sequences are built up that can then be joined to produce the complete nucleotide sequence.

Restriction endonucleases

Desired genes can be 'cut' out of a long DNA sequence using enzymes that cleave (cut) DNA in particular places. These enzymes are called restriction endonucleases.

Many types of restriction endonucleases exist. Each one cuts a DNA double strand at a specific sequence of bases called a recognition sequence. Sometimes this cut occurs between two opposite base pairs. This leaves two straight edges known as blunt ends. For example, one restriction endonuclease cuts in the middle of a base recognition sequence GTTAAC (Figure 2a). Other restriction endonucleases cut DNA in a staggered fashion. This leaves an uneven cut in which each strand of the DNA has exposed, unpaired bases. An example is a restriction endonuclease that recognises a six-base pair (six bp) AAGCTT, as shown in Figure 2b. In this figure, look at the sequence of unpaired bases that remain. If you read both the four unpaired bases at each end from left to right, the two sequences are opposites of one another, i.e. they are a **palindrome**. The recognition sequence is referred to as a six bp palindromic sequence. This feature is typical of the way restriction endonucleases cut DNA to leave 'sticky ends'. We shall look at the importance of these 'sticky ends' later.

a HpaI *restriction endonuclease has a recognition site GTTAAC, which produces a straight cut and therefore blunt ends:*

b HindIII *restriction endonuclease has the recognition site AAGCTT, which produces a staggered cut and therefore 'sticky ends':*

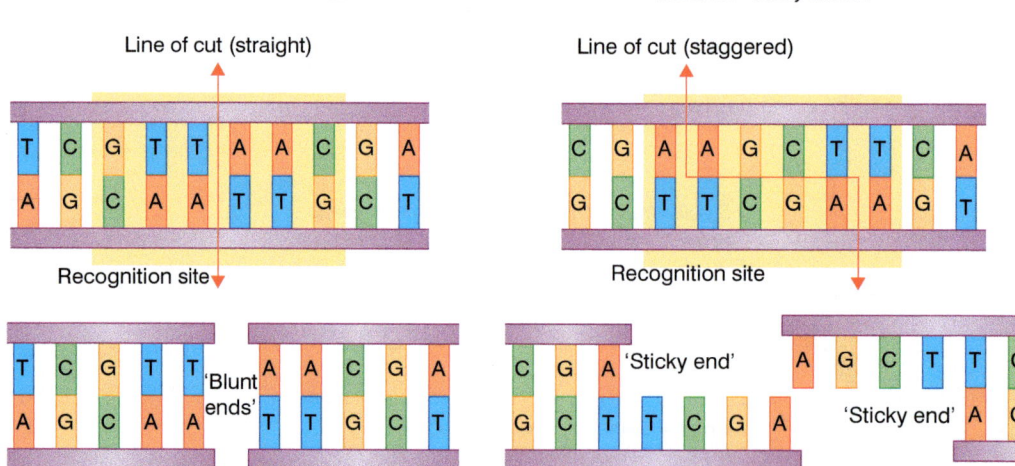

Figure 2 *Action of restriction endonucleases*

Gel electrophoresis

Gel electrophoresis is a technique that can be used to separate molecules based on their charge and their size. It is commonly used in genetic technology to separate fragments of DNA of varying lengths, for example fragments that have been obtained after digestion by restriction endonucleases.

The gel that is often used in gel electrophoresis is known as agarose.

The DNA fragments are loaded into wells cut into an agarose gel at the cathode (negative) end of the gel. Figure 3 shows that the loaded wells appear blue. This is because a loading dye has been added. This makes the samples denser

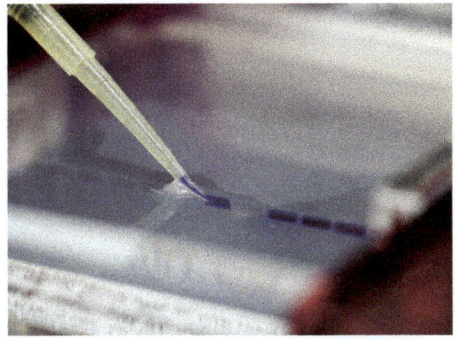

Figure 3 *Samples of DNA being loaded onto an agarose gel for electrophoresis*

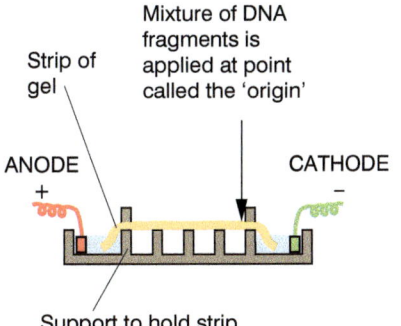

Strip of gel

Mixture of DNA fragments is applied at point called the 'origin'

ANODE +

CATHODE −

Support to hold strip

Figure 4 *Apparatus for carrying out electrophoresis*

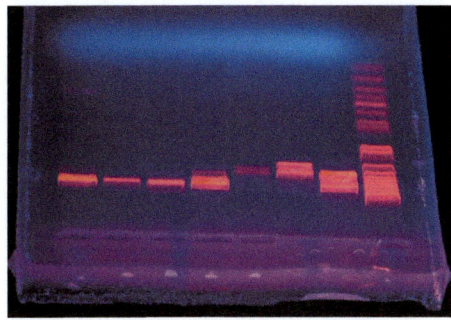

Figure 5 *DNA fragments separated by gel electrophoresis and stained. They can be seen when the gel is placed under UV light. The lane on the far right is a DNA ladder and the other seven lanes represent different DNA samples*

to make sure they sink into the wells. The dye runs through the gel at a standard rate to help follow the progress of the electrophoresis. A DC (direct current) voltage is applied across the gel (Figure 4) to create an electric field. The sugar–phosphate backbone of DNA, owing to its phosphate groups, has an overall negative charge. The fragments move through the gel towards the anode (positive end) as they are negatively charged. Because of the resistance of the gel, they move at different rates depending on their mass and, to a lesser extent, their shape. The larger the fragments, the more slowly they move. Over a fixed period, therefore, the smaller pieces move further than the larger ones. In this way, fragments of DNA of different lengths are separated. Electrophoresis of DNA is usually only on the basis of size as the gel is placed into the tank which contains a buffer so that all fragments have the same charge. One well can be filled with a DNA mixture containing known fragment sizes. This forms a pattern known as a DNA ladder and can serve as a standard against which the experimental DNA fragments can be compared. DNA lengths are stated as numbers of base pairs (bp). A thousand base pairs = kb. Gel electrophoresis can separate fragments from approximately 100 bp to 25 kb. DNA is colourless, so a dye that binds to DNA is used to locate the position of the fragments. One of the most common dyes used is ethidium bromide. The bands of DNA can be seen when the gel is placed under UV light (Figure 5). As well as locating the fragments, the intensity of fluorescence indicates the quantity of DNA.

Extension

Uses of gel electrophoresis

By altering the composition of the gel (gives different pore sizes), the time the electrophoresis is run for and the voltage applied, gel electophoresis can be adapted for the separation of many different mixtures of macromolecules.

DNA fingerprinting is one use of gel electrophoresis. Here PCR (19.1b) is used to increase the quantity of DNA before electrophoresis (with some DNA kept for future testing). After electrophoresis, a procedure known as southern blotting is carried out to obtain a visual DNA fingerprint. RNA can also be separated by electrophoresis, for example different mRNA molecules will be of different lengths as the genes from which they were transcribed are of different lengths.

Gel electrophoresis is used to separate not just DNA fragments, but also proteins. Proteins can be separated on the basis of size and charge. They can be treated so that they lose their tertiary structure and form linear molecules. They can then be separated on the basis of overall charge (on the basis of their different R groups). The beta-globin polypeptides for normal and for sickle cell haemoglobin can be identified by carrying out electrophoresis against known marker molecules.

We can also use gel electrophoresis to distinguish between different alleles of a gene. As the two alleles differ slightly in DNA sequence, it is also likely that they will differ in one or more restriction sites. If so, each will produce different sized fragments when cut by the same restriction enzyme. Gel electrophoresis can then be used to separate the different sized fragments from the two alleles. Different band patterns will therefore be produced, allowing us to distinguish the two alleles.

Summary test 19.1a

Joining together DNA from two different sources produces novel DNA known as **(1)**. When a gene is transferred into a host organism, the host is known as a **(2)**. The host will have altered **(3)** and with the new gene will produce a **(4)** product. Genes can be cut out of donor cells using the enzyme **(5)** or can be made completely synthetically by producing shorter **(6)** sequences that are joined to make the longer length of DNA. **(7)** can be extracted from cells where the gene is being actively **(8)** and using the enzyme **(9)** a single-stranded copy of DNA, known as **(10)** can be made, and then converted into double-stranded DNA using the enzyme **(11)**. Gel electrophoresis can separate DNA fragments on the basis of **(12)**. The DNA samples are loaded into **(13)** on an **(14)** gel and a **(15)** voltage is applied to create an **(16)**. The DNA is **(17)** charged because of the **(18)** groups. A **(19)** is used to make all the DNA the same charge. The fragments move towards the **(20)**, with the **(21)** fragments moving slower than the **(22)** fragments. A known mixture of DNA fragments can be added to create a DNA **(23)**. The DNA needs to be stained and visualised using **(24)** light.

These pages help you to:

- describe and explain the steps involved in the polymerase chain reaction (PCR) to clone and amplify DNA (19.1.8)
- understand the role of *Taq* polymerase in the PCR (19.1.8)

You will also:

- find out who invented PCR
- appreciate the use of PCR in forensic research

> **Remember**
>
> DNA polymerase causes nucleotides to join together as a strand. It does **not** cause complementary bases to join together.

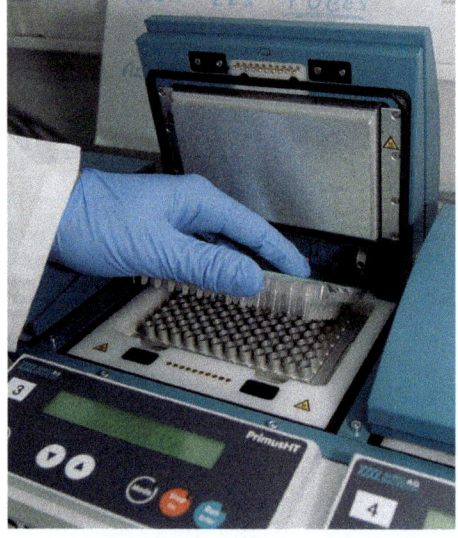

Figure 1 *Thermocycler – a machine that carries out the polymerase chain reaction (PCR)*

> **Remember**
>
> The polymerase chain reaction is **not** the same as semi-conservative replication of DNA in cells.

Once the required fragment containing the gene is extracted and synthesised, the many identical DNA fragments are created for use in the next step. This is known as DNA cloning and one means of carrying it out is to use the polymerase chain reaction.

Polymerase chain reaction

The **polymerase chain reaction (PCR)** is an automated process, making it both rapid and efficient. It requires the following:

- **The DNA fragment** to be copied.
- *Taq* **polymerase** – DNA polymerase obtained from the bacterium *Thermus aquaticus*, after which it is named. The bacterium lives in hot springs, and so the remarkable feature of *Taq* polymerase is that it is very tolerant to heat (it is thermostable) and does not denature at the high temperatures of the polymerase chain reaction, so that it can be used throughout the many cycles of replication that take place. DNA polymerase is an enzyme capable of joining together tens of thousands of **nucleotides** in a matter of minutes.
- **Primers** – short sequences of nucleotides that have a set of bases complementary to those at one end of each of the two DNA fragments.
- **Nucleotides** – which contain each of the four bases found in DNA. They are nucleotide triphosphates (dNTPs) as energy is required for the synthesis of the phosphodiester bonds.
- **Thermocycler** – a computer-controlled machine that varies temperatures precisely over a period of time (Figure 1).

The polymerase chain reaction is illustrated in Figure 2 and is carried out in three stages:

- **Separation of the DNA strands (double helix)** – the mixture containing DNA fragments, primers, dNTPs and *Taq* polymerase is placed in a vessel in the thermocycler. The temperature is increased to 95 °C causing the two strands of the DNA fragments to separate as hydrogen bonds are broken.
- **Annealing of the primers** – the mixture is cooled to 55 °C causing the primers to join (anneal) to their complementary bases at the end of the DNA fragment. The primers provide the starting sequences for *Taq* polymerase to begin DNA copying because *Taq* polymerase can only attach nucleotides to the end of an existing chain. Primers also prevent the two separate strands from simply rejoining.
- **Synthesis of DNA** – the temperature is increased to 72 °C. This is the optimum temperature for the *Taq* polymerase to add complementary nucleotides along each of the separated DNA strands. It begins at the primer on both strands and adds the nucleotides in sequence until it reaches the end of the chain.

Because both separated strands are copied simultaneously (at the same time) there are now two copies of the original fragment. Once the two DNA strands are completed, the process is repeated by carrying out the temperature cycle again. This gives four molecules, and so on, until millions of copies have been made. This is known as **DNA amplification**. The complete cycle takes around two minutes. After only 30 cycles, over a billion copies of the DNA can be made and generally 25 to 35 cycles are sufficient (enough). There is a limit to the number of cycles that can be carried out because the enzyme will eventually be degraded. The ability to amplify DNA using the polymerase chain reaction has revolutionised many aspects of science and medicine.

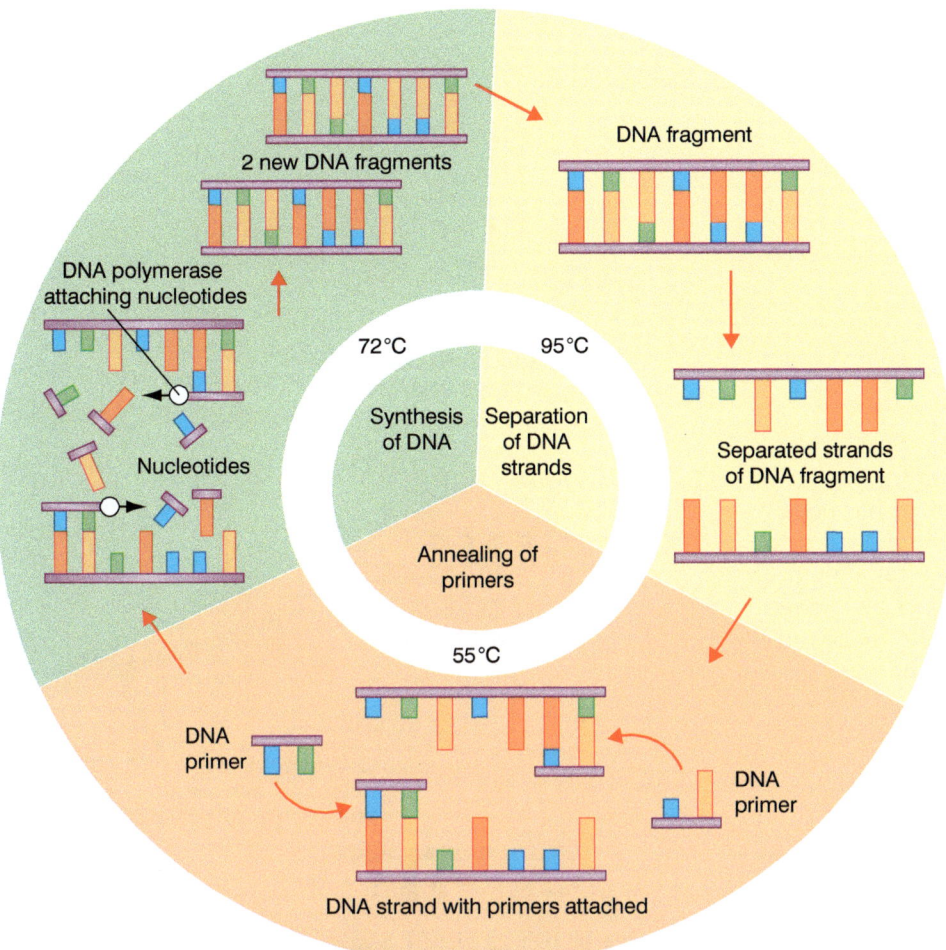

Figure 2 *The polymerase chain reaction showing a single cycle*

Advantages of PCR for DNA and gene cloning

The advantages of this type of DNA cloning are that it:

- **is extremely rapid**. Within a matter of hours many billions of copies of a gene or of a length of DNA can be made. This is particularly valuable where only a minute amount of DNA is available, for example following extraction from donor cells for a genetic engineering procedure or at the scene of a crime. Crime-scene DNA can quickly be increased using the polymerase chain reaction and so valuable time is not lost before forensic analysis and matching can take place.
- **does not require living cells**. All that is required is a base sequence of DNA that needs amplification. No complex culturing techniques are needed, which require time and effort.

Extension

The use of PCR in forensic medicine and criminal investigations

The DNA to be analysed in forensic medicine and from crime scenes can come from very small original samples.

Using the polymerase chain reaction, millions of copies of the DNA can be produced so that there is enough for DNA fingerprinting to be carried out and for samples to be kept for future testing. The procedure must be carried out to very strict guidelines to avoid contamination of the samples.

Even the most minute sample of DNA from a single hair or a speck of blood can now be multiplied to allow forensic examination and accurate cross-matching.

Extension

The discovery of PCR

The biochemist Kary Mullis invented the polymerase chain reaction and patented it in 1983. His invention used some ideas from the development of DNA sequencing carried out in 1975 by the biochemist Frederick Sanger. Before PCR, a common method to obtain identical copies of DNA involved using bacteria. The gene that needed to be copied was inserted into a plasmid, which was then introduced into bacterial cells. Plasmids replicate independently inside host bacterial cells, using the semi-conservative method for DNA replication. The bacterial cells grow and divide and so this also increased the number of identical copies of the gene. This was a much slower and more time-consuming method than the polymerase chain reaction.

Summary test 19.1b

The polymerase chain reaction (PCR) is both rapid and efficient because it is an **(1)** process. PCR begins with DNA fragments, *Taq* polymerase, dNTPs and primers being placed in a machine called a **(2)**. The temperature of the mixture is then increased to **(3)** which causes the strands of the two DNA fragments to **(4)**. The temperature of the mixture is then changed to **(5)** which makes the primers join to their **(6)** at the end of the DNA fragment. The primers also prevent the strands **(7)**. Finally the temperature is changed to **(8)** which allows *Taq* polymerase to add **(9)** to each of the separated DNA strands. The complete cycle takes around **(10)** minutes.

These pages help you to:

- explain the roles of restriction endonucleases, DNA ligase and plasmids in the transfer of a gene into an organism (19.1.4)

You will also:

- understand why plasmids are ideal vectors in genetic engineering

Once the required fragment of DNA containing the gene has been cut from the rest of the DNA or has been synthesised, the next task is to transfer it to the host cell. One method for doing this is to join it into a carrying unit, known as a **vector**. Before we look at how this is carried out, let us first consider the importance of the 'sticky ends' left when DNA is cut by **restriction endonucleases** (restriction enzymes).

Importance of 'sticky ends' and DNA ligase

The sequences of DNA that are cut by specific restriction endonucleases are called recognition sites. Where the recognition site is cut in a staggered fashion, the cut ends of the DNA double strand are left with a single strand that is a few **nucleotide** bases long (19.1a). The nucleotides on the single strand at one side of the cut are obviously complementary to those at the other side, because they were previously paired together.

If the same restriction endonuclease is used to cut DNA, then all the fragments produced will have bases that are complementary to one another. This means that the single-stranded end of any one fragment can be joined (stuck) to the single-stranded end of any other. In other words their ends are 'sticky'. Once the complementary bases of two 'sticky ends' have paired up and hydrogen bonds have formed, an enzyme called **DNA ligase** is used to join the phosphate-sugar framework of the two sections of DNA and so unite them as one.

'Sticky ends' have considerable importance because, provided the same restriction endonuclease is used, we can combine the DNA by phosphodiester bonds of any organism with that of any other organism (Figure 1). They have a number of recognition sites so that different restriction endonucleases may be used.

Inserting DNA into a plasmid vector

There are different types of vector but when the host cell is a bacterium, the most commonly used is the **plasmid**. In addition to carrying the required gene, an additional

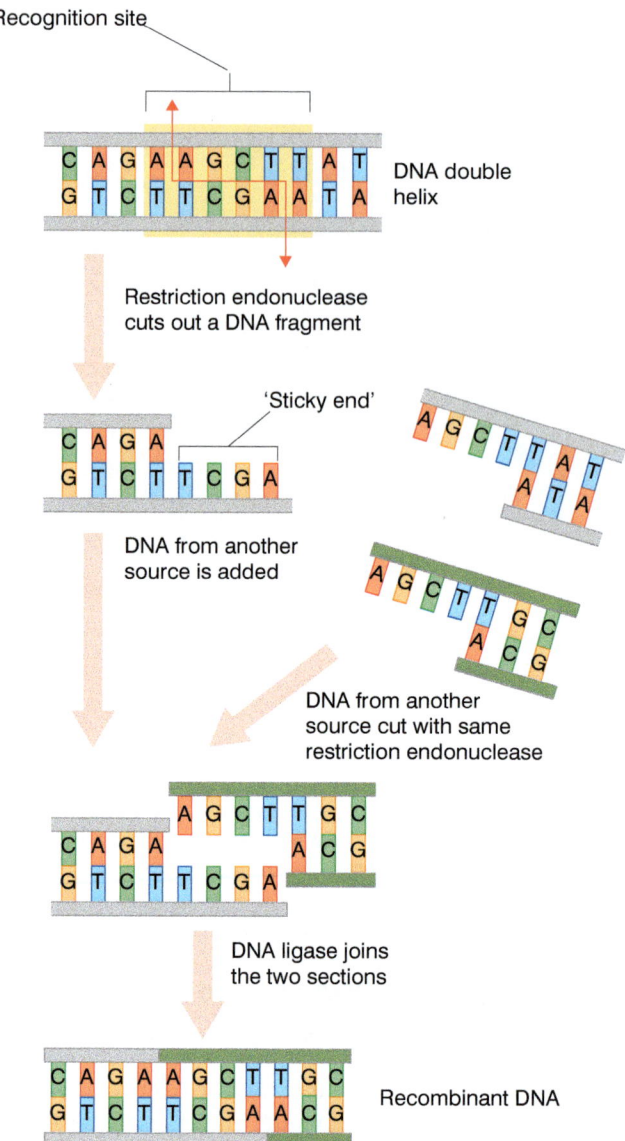

Figure 1 *The use of 'sticky ends' to combine DNA from different sources*

'marker' gene can be added to the plasmid (Figure 3). One type that can be used is a marker gene coding for fluorescent products, such as the gene coding for GFP, green fluorescent protein (see 19.1d).

The same restriction endonuclease is used as the one that cut out the DNA fragment. This ensures that the 'sticky ends' of the opened-up plasmid are complementary to the 'sticky ends' of the DNA fragment. When the DNA fragments are mixed with the opened-up plasmids, they may become incorporated into them. Where they are incorporated, the join is made permanent using the enzyme DNA ligase. These plasmids now have recombinant DNA and are termed recombinant plasmids. These events are summarised in Figure 2.

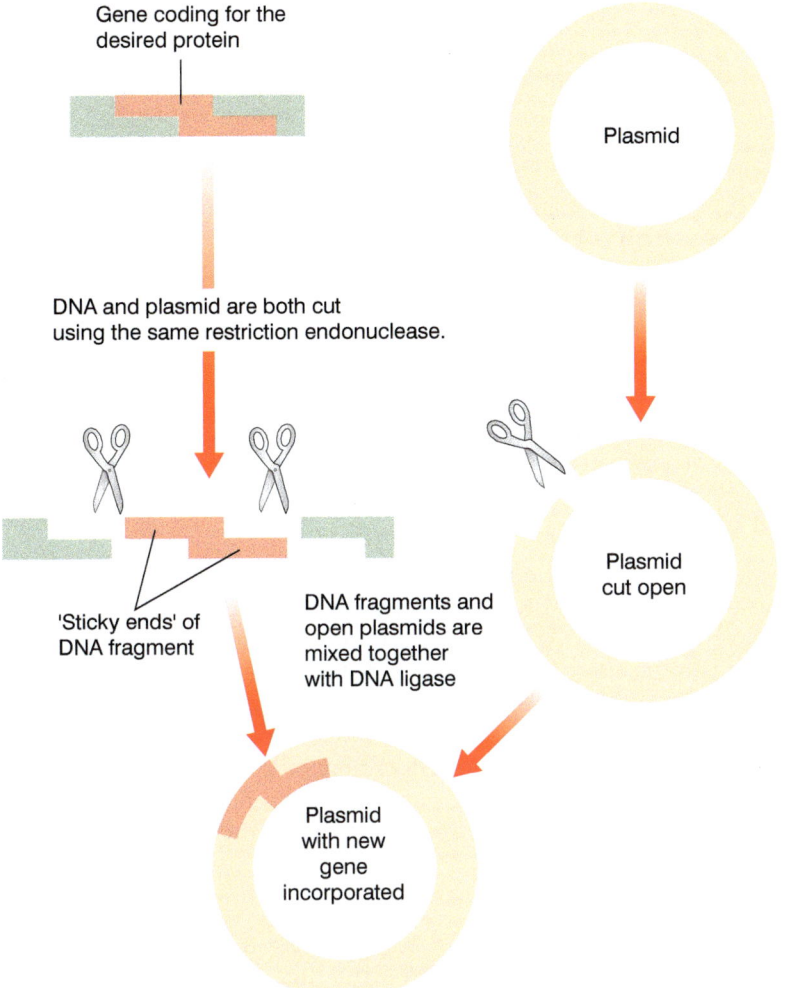

Figure 2 *Inserting a gene into a plasmid vector*

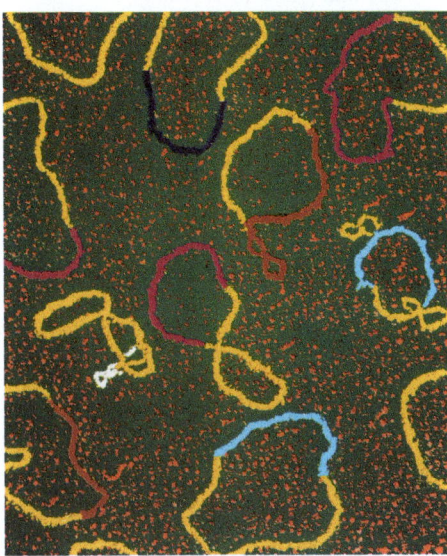

Figure 3 *Colourised TEM of genetically engineered DNA plasmids from the bacterium Escherichia coli. The plasmids (yellow) have had different gene sequences (various colours) inserted into them.*

In the early days of genetic technology, plasmids needed to be removed from bacteria by the molecular biologists carrying out genetic engineering. Today, it is possible to obtain from commercial suppliers a very wide range of specifically constructed plasmids for use as vectors. For example, plasmid vectors can be obtained that already have a marker gene, such as the GFP gene, added to them.

Extension

Properties of plasmids that make them suitable for use in gene cloning

- They are small and so do not contribute much additional DNA to the host cell. It is also easier to get small pieces of DNA into a bacterium.
- They replicate rapidly in the host cell and independently of the host cell. Replication produces genetically identical copies (gene cloning occurs).
- They are easily taken up by bacterial cells.
- It is easy to determine their DNA sequence, making it easier to use recombinant DNA techniques.
- They have a number of recognition sites so that different restriction endonucleases may be used.
- They are easily manipulated. For example, as they do not carry genes essential to survival, unnecessary genetic material can be removed to decrease the size of the plasmid for easier uptake by the host.
- If there are no other marker genes that can be used, then some plasmids possess natural marker genes for antibiotic resistance.

Summary test 19.1c

Plasmids are small **(1)** DNA molecules found in **(2)** cells. They can be cut open by restriction **(3)** that cut at specific sequences of DNA called **(4)**. Where the cut is staggered the ends of the DNA double strand are known as **(5)**. The same **(6)** is used to cut out the desired gene from the donor. The genes and cut plasmids are mixed with an enzyme known as **(7)**. The gene inserts into the plasmid and the **(8)** backbone is sealed using the enzyme. The plasmid is called a **(9)** plasmid and it is used as a **(10)** to transfer the gene into the host.

These pages help you to:

- understand why a promoter may have to be transferred into an organism as well as the desired gene (19.1.5)
- explain how gene expression may be confirmed by using marker genes coding for fluorescent products (19.1.6)

You will also:

- learn about other methods for transferring genes into cells

Remember

A genetically modified organism can also be called a transgenic organism.

Extension

Antibiotic resistance markers

Some plasmids carry genes for resistance to one or more antibiotics. An example is the R-plasmid, which carries genes for resistance to the two antibiotics, ampicillin and tetracycline.

The gene to be transferred is inserted within one of these two resistance genes, for example ampicillin, so disabling that gene. The bacteria can be screened and checked for their different abilities to grow in the presence of antibiotics:

- Bacteria that have not been transformed (that is, have not taken up a plasmid) will die when cultured in a medium containing one or both antibiotics.
- Bacteria containing the original plasmid will grow on a medium containing both antibiotics.
- Successfully transformed bacteria grow only on a medium containing tetracycline as they have lost their resistance to ampicillin. It is these bacteria that can be selected for large-scale culture.

After preparation of the DNA that is to be transferred, the next step is to find a method to insert the DNA into the host. Host cells may be: bacteria, unicellular fungi, such as yeast cells, plant cells or animal cells. In many cases, the transferred DNA consists of the gene together with other sequences of DNA needed to stimulate transcription of the gene. Marker genes may also be needed to determine which cells have successfully taken up the gene.

Once in the host cell, the desired outcome is that:

- the transferred DNA will incorporate into the host cell genome
- the host cell will start transcribing the DNA nucleotide sequence of the gene to produce mRNA
- the cell will synthesise the desired protein product
- the characteristics of the host organism are altered.

Promoters and other control sequences

The promoter is located close to the nucleotide sequence of the gene to be transcribed and is required so that RNA polymerase can bind and transcription can begin. Some promoters, called inducible promoters, can be triggered to start the process in response to a stimulus such as heat or a specific chemical, e.g. lactose (16.3b). Without the promoter, the gene would have to be inserted near an existing promoter, which would be difficult and could disrupt expression of the gene. Other control sequences may be required, such as those coding for transcription factors that are not present in the host cell or those responsible for the termination of transcription. The promoter and the other control sequences are therefore used to:

- control where the gene is located
- begin the process of transcription of the gene (switches on the gene)
- allow binding of RNA polymerase for mRNA formation
- allow binding of transcription factors
- determine the level of gene expression
- terminate transcription.

Transformation of host cells

This process of adding DNA to a bacterial cell is called **transformation**, and involves the plasmid vectors and bacterial cells being mixed in a medium containing calcium ions. The temperature of the medium is increased. These conditions appear to increase the uptake of plasmids through the bacterial cell wall and cell surface membrane. Only a small proportion of bacterial cells will actually contain the transferred DNA. There are two main reasons for this.

- Only a few bacterial cells (as few as 1%) take up the plasmids when the two are mixed together.
- Some plasmids will have closed up again in the preparation of the vector without incorporating the DNA fragment and so will not be recombinant plasmids.

Marker genes

The task now is to identify which bacterial cells contain the transferred DNA. This can be done using **marker genes**. There are a number of different ways in which this can be achieved. They all involve using a separate gene on the plasmid that contains the gene that we want. This second gene is easily identifiable for one reason or another. For example, genes that code for proteins that fluoresce (fluorescent proteins) when they absorb light can be used. Marker genes coding for enzymes that catalyse reactions that involve a colour change can also be used reliably to identify successfully transformed cells. Historically, for bacterial host cells, genes giving resistance to antibiotics have been used extensively as markers (see Extension), but these are now much less common choices.

The use of antibiotic resistance markers risks spreading resistance to other bacteria, for example, by uptake of plasmids released when bacterial cells die, or by conjugation. This is undesirable because it makes antibiotics less effective at treating diseases. For these reasons, their use is now rare.

Fluorescent markers

A more recent and more rapid method of screening and identifying the host cells which contain the transferred DNA is to use a gene that codes for a fluorescent protein as a marker. This is transferred into the plasmid vector with the DNA. An example is the *GFP* gene obtained from a jellyfish (see Figure 1), which codes for the production of a green fluorescent protein (GFP). When this protein is present, it fluoresces green under blue to ultraviolet (UV) light, so it is easily detected. GFP does not require any other molecules for fluorescence, which makes the use of the *GFP* gene an ideal marker gene. In addition, the gene can be transferred into prokaryotic and eukaryotic hosts and the protein will be expressed. It appears to have no harmful effects on the host organism.

The gene can be inserted downstream from the promoter region, so that both the marker and the required genes are transcribed together. This produces the desired protein product with a short 'marker' protein attached. In this way, recombinant host cells are easily identified. The proteins produced in this way do not have their function affected by the presence of GFP.

The *GFP* gene has also been described as a reporter gene, because the fluorescence is only produced if the host cell has also successfully transcribed and translated the transferred gene. It serves to report that gene expression is occurring.

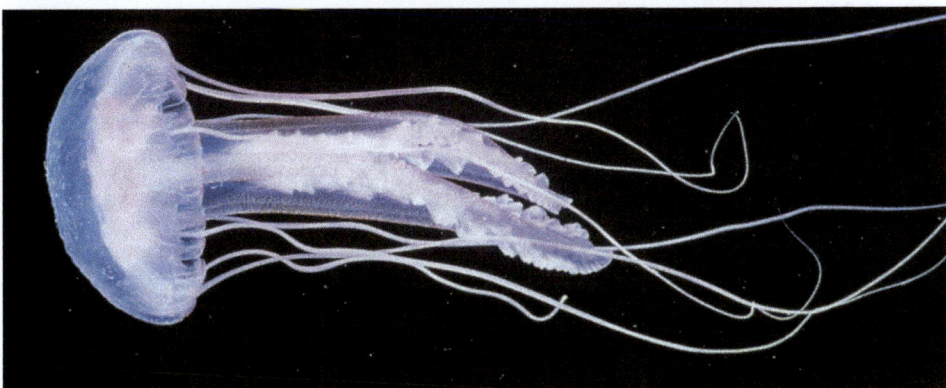

Figure 1 *The gene in this jellyfish, which produces a green fluorescent protein, can be transferred together with the required gene into other organisms and used as a fluorescent marker. The GFP gene was first isolated from the jellyfish* Aequorea victoria.

Summary test 19.1d

To help the uptake of (**1**) plasmids into bacterial cells, (**2**) ions are added to the medium and the temperature increased. A bacterial cell that can take up plasmids is described as (**3**). When transferring the gene into the host cell, other DNA (**4**) may also be required, for example promoters and (**5**) genes (to screen for successful recombinant hosts). An example is the (**6**) gene which produces a (**7**) fluorescent protein when (**8**) light is absorbed. The promoter is necessary for (**9**) enzyme to bind to the DNA and for the process of (**10**) to begin.

Transferring genes into plant cells

Using *Agrobacterium tumefaciens* as a vector

Agrobacterium tumefaciens is a soil bacterium that can cause a disease in plants known as crown gall disease. It contains a plasmid known as a Ti (tumour-inducing) plasmid that can be removed and genetically modified to contain a gene from a donor, plus other required DNA sections. The recombinant Ti plasmids are taken up by *A. tumefaciens* to produce a recombinant bacterium that can act as a vector. The modified Ti plasmids have their disease-causing sections removed but still contain the necessary genes for the bacterium to attach to plant cells and insert part of the plasmid into the plant cell to be transformed.

Gene guns for direct gene transfer into plant cells

Tiny gold or tungsten pellets can be coated with copies of the gene and associated DNA. A special gun, known as a gene gun, is used to fire the pellets, and these are prevented from leaving the gun by hitting a mesh plate. There is enough propulsive force for the DNA coating the pellet to enter the plant cell to reach the nucleus. The technique is also known as biolistics (for 'biological ballistics'). This method can also be used for animal cells.

Extension

Transferring genes into animal cells

Electroporation

Direct gene transfer occurs in electroporation. The suspension containing the animal cells is conductive and a short electrical pulse is used to create tiny temporary gaps in the phospholipid bilayer of the cell surface membrane. DNA, which is a charged molecule, is able to enter the cells at the same time.

Viral vectors

Viruses that infect particular animal cells can be modified so that they can infect and insert DNA into cells but are unable to replicate within the cell and cause damage. The gene to be transferred and other necessary DNA is carried by the virus to the host cell.

These pages help you to:

- explain that gene editing is a form of genetic engineering involving the insertion, deletion or replacement of DNA at specific sites in the genome (19.1.7)
- outline how microarrays are used in the analysis of genomes (19.1.10)
- outline how microarrays are used in detecting mRNA in studies of gene expression (19.1.10)

You will also:

- learn more about specific gene editing methods

Extension

CRISPR, ZFN and TALEN

CRISPR stands for Clustered Regularly Interspaced Short Palindromic Repeats.

ZFN stands for zinc-finger nucleases.

TALEN stands for transcription activator-like effector nucleases.

The CRISPR-Cas9 is based on a naturally-occurring defence system in prokaryotes (archaea and bacteria). The bacteria use sections of DNA from bacteriophages (viruses that infect bacteria) to form lengths of DNA known as CRISPR arrays. If the same type of virus infects the cell, the bacteria transcribe the DNA and produce RNA which is linked to a Cas9 enzyme. This system recognises and binds to complementary viral nucleic acid and cut it to destroy the viral genome.

The CRISPR-CPF1 system is similar to CRISPR-Cas9 but is smaller and more easily introduced into cells. The cuts to the DNA are staggered, so it is more efficient than CRISPR-Cas9 if sections of DNA are to be added.

Remember

Gene mutations involve changes to one or a few nucleotides in the sequence of nucleotides that make up a gene.

So far, we have considered how we are able to alter the characteristics of an organism. We can do this by the transfer into the organism of a gene that has been removed from another organism or synthesised from mRNA, or synthesised artificially by chemical methods. The genetically modified organisms are able to produce a protein product that could not be previously produced. Now let us look at a type of genetic engineering that involves the modification of genes that are already present in an organism.

Gene editing

With gene editing, DNA is added, or removed, or altered at particular locations in the genome. This may modify the function of the genes. This contrasts with the genetic engineering technique of adding a complete gene that may insert into the genome in any location. The effect of gene editing is permanent within the cells where it has been carried out, but unless this is in gametes, its effects will not be inherited by the next generation.

Gene editing involves using specific enzymes that cut the double-stranded DNA at precise locations. The enzymes need to be engineered in some way so that the target region can be exactly identified for cutting. ZFNs or TALEN are engineered proteins with a DNA-binding region that recognises and binds to a precise DNA location and a nuclease region to cut the DNA. Alternatively, an endonuclease enzyme can be linked to a short 20-nucleotide length of RNA, known as guide RNA. The sequence of RNA nucleotides, which is a non-coding section, is complementary to the DNA section to be modified. This type of gene editing is known in short as CRISPR, an example of which is the CRISPR-Cas9 system. Cas9 protein is an endonuclease that cleaves the double-stranded DNA.

The technology behind gene editing allows manipulation of DNA and involves precise changes to the sequence of DNA. The CRISPR-Cas9 system of gene editing, developed in 2009, has proved to be accurate and fast, with the ability to target more than one gene. The technique costs less than other gene editing methods. Many thousands of guide RNA sequences are available for use by scientists.

One of the aims of gene editing technology is to correct mutations that cause disease in humans or could potentially cause disease. The most obvious genetic diseases for gene editing will be those involving a single gene, such as cystic fibrosis or sickle cell anaemia. In some cases, it may be possible to repair the section of mutated DNA by cutting out the section and replacing it with the correct sequence to allow the gene to function normally. Another aim is to prevent expression of a mutation associated with the production of a protein that in some way does harm. With gene editing, endonuclease action will cut within the DNA sequence. The cell repair mechanism repairs cuts but in doing so will insert or delete DNA nucleotides. These alter the sequence so that synthesis of the mRNA needed for translation is prevented and the harmful protein is not produced.

Microarrays

DNA microarrays are used to investigate gene expression. They have the following features:

- Thousands of spots are arranged in rows and columns on a solid surface of glass, plastic or silicon known as a microarray chip.
- Microarrays can be the size of a microscope slide, or even smaller.
- Each spot on a microarray contains multiple copies of a short length of single-stranded DNA.

- The DNA sequence on each spot is unique and known as a probe.
- Each spot represents a single gene or a sequence from part of a gene and is complementary to the DNA, or alleles, or genes that are being analysed.
- The exact location and sequence of each spot is recorded in a computer database. Figure 1 shows a prepared microarray being placed in a machine for analysis.

Using DNA microarrays, scientists can carry out an analysis on thousands of genes simultaneously. This has a number of uses including:

- **Gene expression profiling** – At any given moment, a human cell has some combination of its 21 000 genes being expressed (switched on) and so will produce mRNA, and others are not expressed (switched off). The pattern of gene expression at any one time is called the **gene profile**. One way to determine which genes are being expressed in the cells of an organism and which are not is to start with a DNA microarray that is spotted with **DNA probes** that represent specific gene coding regions. The DNA sequences that are to be used as probes can be obtained commercially.
  - All the mRNA in the cell to be tested is extracted.
  - This mRNA is then converted into single-stranded complementary DNA (cDNA) using reverse transcriptase.
  - The cDNA is labelled using fluorescent tags of a particular colour, for example red.
  - The mixture of mRNA and cDNA is treated so that any mRNA is broken down.
  - The purified cDNA is then added to the microarray.
  - Where a gene is being expressed, the cDNA with complementary bases to that gene will hybridise (bind) with the complementary DNA probe. Where the gene is not being expressed, no cDNA will hybridise.
  - The microarray can be scanned by lasers to produce fluorescent spots, in this case red fluorescence, that can be detected and are analysed to show exactly which genes have attached to cDNA and are therefore being expressed.
  - The intensity of the fluorescence can also be recorded to show the level of gene expression that is occurring. The higher the intensity, the more mRNA is produced and the more active the gene.

This technique is particularly useful in comparing gene expression in healthy and diseased tissue. Here, mRNA from diseased cells is converted into cDNA that will have a different fluorescence colour (e.g. red) than the cDNA produced from mRNA extracted from healthy cells (e.g. green). Spots that only fluoresce red show that the diseased state causes particular genes to switch on. If there are some spots that are only green, then the diseased state has led to those genes being switched off. Yellow spots indicate that genes are active for both the diseased and normal states (red + green = yellow) (Figure 2).

- **Genome analysis** – Microarrays can allow the quick and efficient comparison of two closely related genomes. Each spot on the microarray surface contains a DNA probe that represents the genes being compared. Thousands of genes can be compared using one microarray. In a genome analysis, the DNA from the two sources to be compared is isolated. For each DNA source, the DNA is denatured to obtain single-stranded DNA, and then cut into smaller fragments. The two different DNAs are coloured with different fluorescent tags before adding to the microarray chip. Hybridisation of the two samples with the DNA on the microarray takes place and if only a particular set of alleles or genes is being compared, any DNA fragments that have not hybridised can be washed off. Fluorescence patterns of each sample are compared. As the DNA probes have been arranged in an ordered way and the details of each probe is known, the genes contained within each of the two different genomes can be identified. Differences may indicate gains or losses of genetic material, for instance due to mutation. This method can be used to determine abnormal DNA sequences, which may indicate disease.

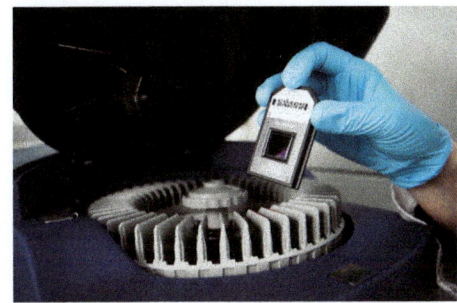

Figure 1 *Prepared microarray being placed into an analyser machine*

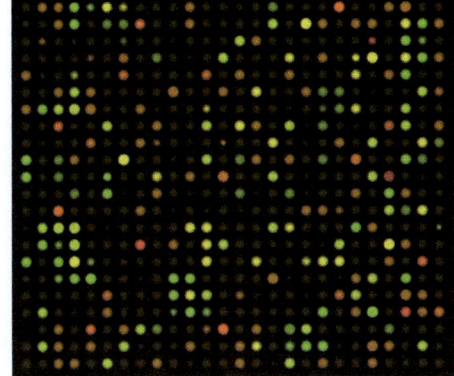

Figure 2 *A microarray*

Summary test 19.1e

Gene editing involves the removal, modification or **(1)** of DNA in a precise location within a **(2)**. Gene editing involves the use of **(3)** enzymes that cut the DNA at a precise location. In the CRISPR-Cas9 system, the location to be cut is identified by **(4)** molecules that have a **(5)** sequence to the location. These molecules have **(6)** attached to them. Another example of a gene editing system is **(7)**: these molecules contain a **(8)** region to identify the correct location to cut. A microarray chip can contain thousands of unique **(9)**. In detecting gene expression, **(10)** is collected from cells and **(11)**-stranded **(12)** DNA is made using the enzyme **(13)**. The DNA is labelled with a **(14)** to identify which genes are being expressed. A **(15)** is used to detect expression and a high level of expression is shown by a **(16)**. A microarray can also be used to compare genomes from two different sources. The DNA is **(17)** and then cut into fragments before labelling.

These pages help you to:

- outline the benefits of using databases that provide information about nucleotide sequences of genes and genomes, amino acid sequences of proteins and protein structures (19.1.11)

You will also:

- read about the importance of sequencing DNA of pathogens such as *Plasmodium*

Remember

DNA sequencing is an example of the use of bioinformatics. It is routinely done by automatic machines and the data produced analysed by computers.

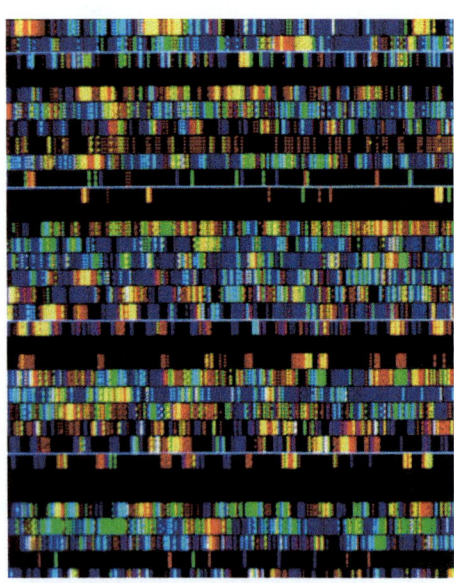

Figure 1 *Computer screen display of a DNA sequence. Each coloured band represents one of the four nucleotide bases.*

Biological databases

Biological databases contain large quantities of organised biological information that can be accessed and used by scientists. The databases are associated with bioinformatics, which is the science of collecting, organising, storing and analysing complex biological data using computers. It also uses algorithms (mathematical formulae) to analyse and interpret biological data. Biological databases are freely available and information can be shared. Because of the use of computers, databases can also be linked. Researchers continually add information to the databases so that information is accumulating (building up) at an enormous rate. This information can be retrieved and analysed or compared to new information to look for patterns.

There is minimal cost involved in adding information to biological databases and because of the internet, information can be uploaded soon after it becomes available. The databases have search tools to speed up information gathering and to look for patterns (data mining). Before bioinformatics, information gathering occurred at a much slower rate and progress in research was slower. The most inspiring features of these freely available databases is that information is available at no cost to the user and that scientists around the world are working cooperatively to share biological information.

In addition to nucleic acid, genome and protein databases, there are biological databases that store and organise information about phenotypes and about therapeutic (medicinal) drugs. The Extension box about *Plasmodium* is an example of how information taken from the different databases can be used in a meaningful way to make progress in treating disease.

Nucleic acid and genome databases

One particular use of bioinformatics and databases is in the sequencing of DNA (Figure 1). When you consider that the human genome consists of over 3 billion base pairs organised into 21 000 genes, sequencing every one of those bases is a huge task. Without the use of bioinformatics it is unlikely that we would have achieved success for many years to come. The sequencing of the human genome (the Human Genome Project) took just 13 years. The medical advances that have been made as a result of sequencing the human genome are many. For example, over 1.4 million single nucleotide polymorphisms (SNPs) have been found in the human genome. SNPs are single-base variations in the genome that may be associated with disease and other disorders. Medical screening of individuals has allowed quick identification of potential medical problems and for treatment to be given at a much earlier stage. Sequencing the DNA of different organisms has also made it possible to establish the evolutionary links between species.

Much of the information about genome sequences that is stored in databases has been obtained from microarray analyses (19.1e). In addition to providing information about the species for which genomes are stored, the databases are used extensively in phylogenetic (evolutionary) studies. Nucleic acid sequence databases are frequently used to look for similarities between a newly sequenced section of nucleic acid and one existing on the database. Information about DNA and RNA nucleotide sequences is available, as well as the proteins that are associated with the sequences. Three different computerised database organisations, DNA Data Bank of Japan (DDBJ), GenBank (USA) and the European Nucleotide Archive (ENA) (UK) work cooperatively to share information and agree a common format for searching and for presenting information.

Protein databases

There are also biological databases that store information about the amino acid sequences of proteins (protein sequences) (Figure 2), about protein structure and protein function. When researchers are studying a new protein, they can quickly check databases to determine any structural or functional relationships that exist with analysed proteins coded for within the same genome, or to check for relationships between different species. Phylogenetic (evolutionary) information can also be obtained. Imagine the time that would be needed to check through scientific papers, or search through information held on CDs containing results of research.

There are many different protein databases, some holding vast quantities of information, and others containing information about specific proteins that are shared by researchers specialising in that particular area. One of the most widely used protein sequence databases is known as Uniprot.

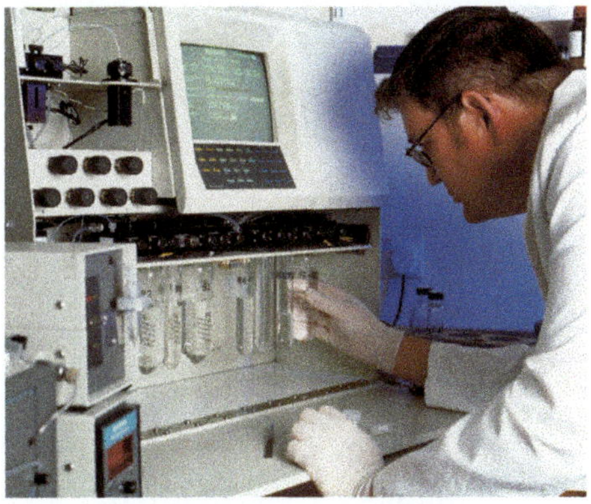

Figure 2 *An automated microsequencer machine to analyse amino acid sequences of samples of protein*

Extension

Plasmodium

The sequencing of the DNA of parasites such as *Plasmodium falciparum*, which causes malaria (10.1e), has given us an insight into its metabolism. Knowledge of the proteins and other substances it produces will be invaluable in helping us to develop a cure for this disease. As a eukaryote, *Plasmodium* is known to have many antigens, and that different antigens are produced at different stages of the life cycle. Knowledge of the protein structure of these antigens, the amino acid sequences and the genes that code for them, will help researchers develop vaccines and therapeutic drugs. There is also the potential to develop genetically engineered *Plasmodium* for use in vaccines. Again, only the power of bioinformatics has allowed us to sequence all 5300 genes on *Plasmodium's* 14 chromosomes in such a short period.

Summary test 19.1f

Biological databases are an important part of the science of **(1)**, which uses computer technology to collect and **(2)** complex biological data. Examples of biological data bases are those that store information about DNA and protein **(3)**. Because of the **(4)**, information can be uploaded soon after it becomes available. The databases have **(5)** to speed up information gathering and to look for patterns, a process known as **(6)**.

Genetic technology applied to medicine
a. Treating disease with recombinant proteins

These pages help you to:

- explain the advantages of using recombinant human proteins to treat disease:
  - diabetes type I using insulin
  - haemophilia using factor VIII
  - severe combined immunodeficiency using adenosine deaminase (19.2.1)

You will also:

- understand the global need for insulin

Extension

The need for insulin

People with type 1 diabetes need to have regular injections of insulin to control their blood glucose levels. Many people with type II diabetes are able to manage their condition with a controlled diet, exercise and anti-diabetes medication. Weight loss can also help. However, a proportion of people with type II diabetes, particularly adults that have had the disease for some time, cannot control their blood glucose levels with the treatment advice and they require insulin injections.

An in-depth study in 2019 estimated the number of people (aged between 20 to 79) with diabetes worldwide to be 463 million (95% confidence interval: 369–601 million), which is 9.3% of the adult population. Of these, it is estimated that only 1 in 2 people know that they have the disease. The projection for 2030 is an estimated 578 million people. With improved diagnosis and the estimated increase in the disease, the need for insulin is great and highlights the importance of obtaining enough insulin by recombinant DNA technology.

In the past few topics we have seen how we can use recombinant DNA (genetic) technology to introduce a gene that codes for a particular protein into bacteria. The technique can be used to produce human proteins necessary to treat a variety of disorders. These proteins are known as recombinant proteins.

Insulin

There are three forms of diabetes mellitus:

- **Type I (insulin dependent)** is due to the body being unable to produce insulin. It normally begins in childhood and is therefore also called juvenile-onset diabetes. It is thought to be the result of an **autoimmune response** where the body's immune system attacks its own cells – in this case the β-cells of the **islets of Langerhans**.
- **Type II (insulin independent)** is due to the **glycoprotein** receptors on the body cells losing their responsiveness to insulin. Many people also have impaired (reduced) production of insulin from the β-cells of the pancreas. Type II diabetes mainly develops in adulthood.
- **Gestational diabetes** is a temporary condition that develops in some women during pregnancy. A proportion will need insulin injections during this time.

Type I diabetes is treated by injections of insulin (Figure 1). It cannot be taken by mouth because, being a protein, it would be digested in the alimentary canal. It is therefore injected. Many people with Type II diabetes also need to be treated with insulin (see Extension).

Through the use of recombinant DNA technology, people with Type I diabetes can use insulin produced by genetically engineered bacteria. Before this technology, the only source of insulin extraction was from the pancreases of animals such as cows and pigs.

Genetically engineered insulin has a number of advantages over that extracted from animals when it comes to treating diabetes:

- It is more effective because it is an **exact** copy of human insulin, whereas animal insulin has slight differences.
- It is more rapid in its action because it is identical to human insulin.
- There is no immune response, whereas animal insulin, with its slight differences, can sometimes stimulate an immune reaction.
- There is no risk of infection being transferred with the insulin. Animal insulin can transfer certain diseases.
- Some patients develop tolerance to animal insulin and become less sensitive to it, requiring them to have increasingly large doses to achieve the same effect. This is less of a problem with genetically engineered insulin.
- It is cheaper to produce in large volumes than extracting and purifying animal insulin. For example, the costs of feed, large space required and heating are much greater when rearing animals compared with culturing bacteria in a fermenter.
- It has fewer ethical and moral objections because animals are not involved in its production. While the animals from which insulin was extracted were killed primarily for food (insulin being purely a by-product), many vegetarians and others were unhappy using an animal product in this way.

For some people, genetically engineered insulin has not proved to be better than animal insulin. Some have found that their response is better and they have experienced fewer side effects with animal insulin.

Factor VIII

Factor VIII is also known as anti-haemophilic factor (AHF). It is essential in the process of blood clotting. A recessive mutation in the X chromosome-linked gene coding for factor VIII leads to the disorder known as haemophilia (16.2f). Factor VIII is a protein that circulates in the bloodstream in an inactive form. When injury occurs it is activated and leads, by a series of reactions, to clotting of blood. Haemophiliacs required factor VIII extracted from blood donations to allow them to lead normal lives. In 1984 the genes that control the production of factor VIII were isolated and six years later it was produced using recombinant DNA techniques. Factor VIII is produced by recombinant mammalian cells in large-scale fermenter cultures, then purified and freeze dried for storage.

The advantages of producing factor VIII by recombinant DNA techniques is that it overcomes most of the problems that come with obtaining it from blood donations. For example extracting factor VIII from blood is difficult as it needs many donations to obtain just a small amount of factor VIII. There is also a risk that the factor VIII extracted could be contaminated and transfer disease from the donor. Recombinant DNA techniques produce far more factor VIII, more easily and without the risk of disease or contamination. They also overcome any ethical objections that people may have to extracting and transferring human material from one person to another.

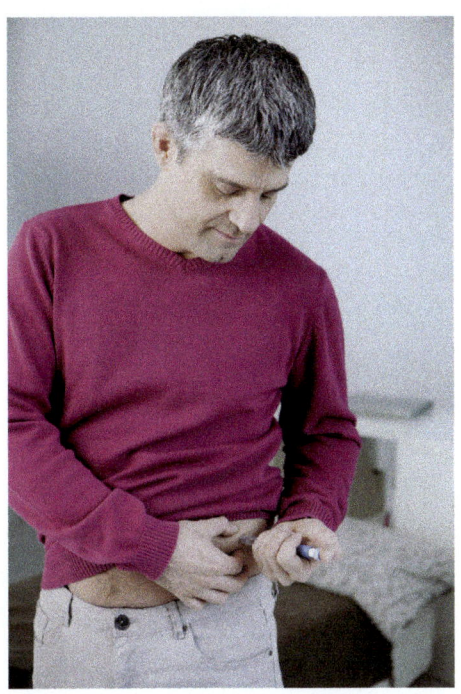

Figure 1 *A person with diabetes injecting insulin*

Adenosine deaminase

The enzyme adenosine deaminase (ADA) is coded for by the *ADA* gene. It is made in all cells, but the highest levels of adenosine deaminase are found in lymphocytes. The function of the enzyme is to break down a molecule called deoxyadenosine, which is formed when DNA is broken down. Deoxyadenosine is toxic and so without the enzyme adenosine deaminase it builds up and interferes with the development and maintenance of lymphocytes. There are more than 70 mutations of the *ADA* gene, most involving a single amino acid change in the enzyme. This is an autosomal recessive mutation. The lack of the enzyme leads to a very rare condition, which usually appears in childhood, called **severe combined immunodeficiency (SCID)** where the person does not show a T-lymphocyte (cell-mediated) response (11.1c) and is also not able to produce antibodies in a B-lymphocyte (humoral) response. This leaves the person very susceptible to infectious diseases as an immune response cannot be stimulated (11.1b). Recombinant DNA techniques can be used to introduce the normal *ADA* gene into bacterial cells which are then cultured. The adenosine deaminase produced by the recombinant bacteria is harvested and can be administered to the person with SCID. This is known as enzyme replacement therapy. Another type of SCID (there are 14 known different types) is discussed in 19.2c (gene therapy).

The advantage of using recombinant DNA techniques to treat SCID is that it provides an effective treatment. Previously, treatment with ADA extracted from domesticated cattle (bovine ADA) had varied success. Another advantage of using recombinant protein is that it has a longer shelf-life. Using recombinant protein means that animals (cows) do not have to be fed and sheltered and the difficulties in extraction of the enzyme are avoided. In addition, not using animals is more ethically and culturally acceptable for many people.

Summary test 19.2a

There are three forms of diabetes mellitus. Type I is also called **(1)** diabetes and may result from the body's white blood cells attacking the **(2)** cells found in the **(3)**. This form of self-attack is known as an **(4)** response. Type I diabetes can be treated by injections of insulin. Insulin cannot be taken by mouth because it is a **(5)** and would therefore be digested. Genetically engineered insulin is preferable to that extracted from animals because it is an **(6)** copy of human insulin and so is more **(7)** in its action and does not induce an **(8)** response. There is no risk of **(9)** being transferred, it is **(10)** to produce in large quantities and there is less risk of **(11)** to insulin developing. As animals are not involved in its production, it is **(12)** more acceptable. Two other proteins produced using gene technology are Factor VIII, used to treat **(13)**, and **(14)**, used to treat severe combined immunodeficiency (SCID). Before the production of these recombinant proteins, Factor VIII was obtained from **(15)**, and many are needed to obtain just a small quantity. The protein for SCID was obtained from **(16)**, which was not always as effective as the recombinant protein for increasing the response of the **(17)** system and preventing infections.

These pages help you to:

- outline the advantages of genetic screening, using the examples of breast cancer (BRCA1 and BRCA2), Huntington's disease and cystic fibrosis (19.2.2)

You will also:

- understand the importance of genetic counselling

Genetic techniques can determine whether a person has a genetic condition, is likely to develop a disease that has a genetic basis, or is a carrier of a genetic condition. They can also determine for some genetic conditions whether an embryo or fetus will have a genetic disorder. The process by which this is done is called **genetic screening** or **genetic testing**. It is also carried out on children and adults for the reasons discussed in this section.

Many genetic disorders are the result of **gene mutations**. We saw in 6.2d that gene mutations may occur if the sequence of **nucleotides** in DNA are changed, either by substitution or deletion or insertion. If the mutation results in a **dominant allele**, all individuals will have the genetic disorder as in Huntington's disease. If the allele is **recessive**, as in cystic fibrosis, it will only appear in those individuals that have two recessive alleles, i.e. are **homozygous** recessive. Individuals that are **heterozygous** will not display symptoms of the disease but will carry one copy of the mutant allele. They have the capacity to pass the disease to their offspring if the other parent is also heterozygous or homozygous recessive.

It is important to screen individuals who may carry a mutant allele. These individuals will often have a family history of the disease. Screening can determine the probabilities of a couple having offspring with a genetic disorder. Using family history and the results of screening tests, potential parents can obtain advice from a genetic counsellor about the implications if they choose to have children.

Genetic screening for a gene mutation has a number of advantages:

- Test results, even where a mutation is found, can provide relief from uncertainty.
- On the basis of test results, individuals and families can make informed decisions about what to do.
- A negative result may remove the need for unnecessary checkups and screening tests.
- A positive result can lead to individuals taking preventative measures and/or continuing to monitor the situation and/or seeking treatment.
- Some test results may assist people to make decisions about whether or not to have children.
- Screening of newborn babies can identify genetic disorders early so treatment can be started as soon as possible.

Genetic screening can be used for a wide variety of genetic disorders including:

- **Breast cancer** – The risk of developing breast cancer is greatly increased if a woman or man (men can get breast cancer too although it is much rarer) inherits a mutation in the *BRCA1* gene or the *BRCA2* gene. They may also be at increased risk of other forms of cancer. *BRCA1* and *BRCA2* genes produce tumour suppressor proteins, which help to repair damaged DNA. Mutation of either of these genes can mean that the tumour-suppressor proteins are not produced or do not function correctly. As a result, damage to DNA may not be properly repaired. Cells are therefore more likely to develop genetic changes that can lead to cancer.

  Genetic tests, involving taking DNA from a blood or saliva sample, can check for mutations in the *BRCA1* and *BRCA2* genes. These are targeted at people whose family history suggests the likely presence of a harmful mutation in one of these genes. If a harmful *BRCA1* or *BRCA2* mutation is found, several options are available to help a person manage their cancer risk. Some women have chosen to have a total mastectomy (both breasts removed): this is an example of preventive action. Others are aware that more frequent checks for abnormalities may help to spot early signs of cancer.

- **Huntington's disease** is a progressive disorder of the central nervous system caused by a dominant allele (16.2j). A child who has one unaffected parent and one who has a dominant allele for Huntington's (heterozygote) has a 50% chance of inheriting the dominant allele and in these cases will develop the disease. However, as the symptoms only arise later in life, it is normal to wait until a child is 18 years old before carrying out a genetic test. If they have inherited the mutant gene, they will develop Huntington's, although it is not possible to know at what age. As there is no cure for the condition, some people choose not to have the test. Of those asking to be tested, some use the results to help them decide whether or not to have children. Some also feel that it gives them the choice to better plan their lives and makes sure that when symptoms appear, doctors can begin prompt treatment to manage the symptoms, as they already have a diagnosis.

- **Cystic fibrosis** is the most common genetic disorder among the white population of Europe and North America, with around 1 in every 20 000 people having the disease. Of these, 70% of cases are caused by a mutant **recessive allele** in which three DNA bases, adenine–adenine–adenine are missing. This form is therefore an example of a deletion **mutation**. Other types of mutation can lead to the same condition. The normal allele of the *CFTR* gene (cystic fibrosis transmembrane conductance regulator) gene produces a protein of some 1480 amino acids. The deletion results in a single amino acid being left out of the protein and it is unable to perform its role of transporting chloride ions across epithelial membranes. CFTR is a unique transport protein that requires ATP to transport chloride ions out of epithelial cells. Part of the protein forms a channel through which chloride ions pass (not to be confused with channel proteins and facilitated diffusion). In this way, epithelial membranes are kept moist as a watery mucus is produced.

In a person with cystic fibrosis, the defective gene means that the protein is either not made or does not function normally, depending on which type of mutation the person has. The epithelial membranes produce mucus that is viscous and sticky. Cystic fibrosis causes mucus congestion and breathing difficulties (Figure 1). The life expectancy for people with the disease has increased considerably in recent years, and in a number of countries, with treatment, the average life expectancy is in the mid 40s. However, this is expected to increase as new treatments appear.

As cystic fibrosis is caused by a recessive allele, it is possible that two normal parents could have a child who has the disease. Where there is a history of the disease in both families, the parents may choose to be genetically screened to see whether they carry the allele. A genetic test checks for the mutant allele by either analysing a saliva sample taken from inside the cheek or analysing a blood sample. Testing couples to determine if they are carriers of cystic fibrosis helps them to make decisions about whether to have children or not. In some cases couples may opt to go through IVF and have embryos checked before implantation.

A test can be carried out on a woman when she is pregnant to see if her embryo has cystic fibrosis. The test uses chorionic villus sampling. Antenatal testing for cystic fibrosis is usually only offered to mothers who are thought to be at high risk of having a child with the disease, such as women with a family history of the condition. Parents are then faced with difficult choices about whether to continue with a pregnancy.

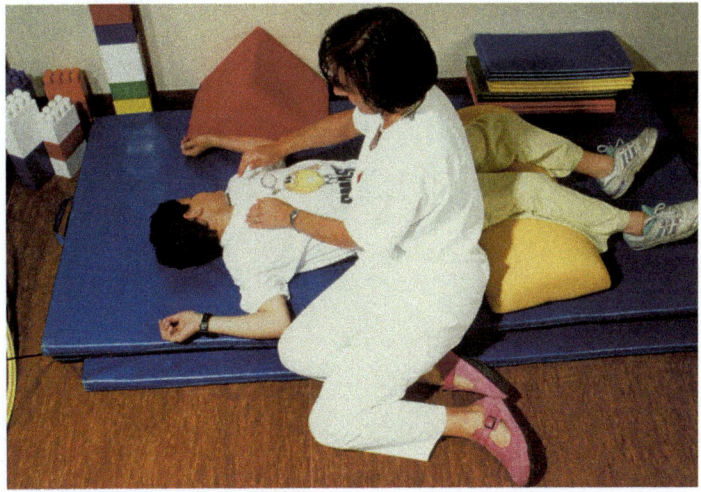

Figure 1 *Physiotherapist treating a young cystic fibrosis patient*

Summary test 19.2b

Before a person or a couple decide to be screened for a genetic condition, it is important that they first have **(1)** where they can get **(2)** advice. Genetic screening can be carried out on an embryo or **(3)** as well as on children and adults. Many people find that the results of genetic screening provide them with relief from **(4)** and helps them to make **(5)** about what to do. In breast cancer screening, checks are made on mutations in two genes, **(6),** which code for **(7)** proteins. People with a mutation in one or both of these genes may decide to carry out preventive measures such as total **(8)** or more frequent checks for **(9)**. In Huntington's disease, some people ask to be screened to help them decide whether to have children, because if they are heterozygous for the condition, there is a **(10)** chance that their children will also have the condition. Cystic fibrosis is an autosomal **(11)** condition which causes **(12)** difficulties and **(13)** congestion. A test can be carried out to see if a person is a heterozygote, or a **(14)** of the disease. If, in a couple, both are heterozygous, they may choose to go through an **(15)** procedure and for their **(16)** to be tested before implantation.

Genetic counselling

Genetic screening goes hand in hand with genetic counselling. Here, expert advice is provided to enable individuals to understand the results and implications of the screening and so make appropriate decisions.

Genetic counselling is normally recommended before and after any genetic test to:

- explain how the test is carried out and its technical accuracy
- discuss whether genetic testing is appropriate
- explain the medical implications of a positive or a negative test result
- point out the possibility that a test result might not be conclusive
- discuss psychological risks and benefits of genetic test results
- explain the risk of passing a mutation to children.

Genetic counselling involves giving advice and information to allow others to make personal decisions about themselves or their offspring. An important aspect of genetic counselling is to research the family history of inherited disease and to advise parents on the likelihood of it arising in their children.

Counselling can also inform them of the symptoms of the disease and any emotional, psychological, medical, social and economic consequences of disease. This may include the likely cost of any care that an affected person might need, the life expectancy of the person and how this might be extended using drugs or gene therapy. On the basis of this advice the couple can be helped to make difficult decisions such as: not to have children at all, to adopt, to continue and have children, to use artificial insemination with a surrogate mother (if the female is affected), to use a sperm donation from an unaffected male (if the male is affected). If conception has already occurred, the couple can decide whether to have a termination. Counselling can also make them aware of any further medical tests that might produce a more accurate prediction of whether their children will have the condition.

Genetic counselling is closely linked to genetic screening and the results provide the genetic counsellor with the basis for an informed discussion. For example, screening for cancer can help to detect:

- Oncogene mutations that can determine the type of cancer the patient has and hence the most effective drug or radiotherapy to use.
- Gene changes that predict which patients are more likely to benefit from certain treatments and have the best chance of survival. For example, the drug herceptin is most effective at treating certain types of breast cancer.
- A single cancer cell amongst millions of normal cells and so identify patients at risk of relapse from certain forms of leukaemia.

The information provided by the screening can help a counsellor to discuss with the patient the best course of treatment and their prospects of survival.

As our knowledge of the causes of genetic diseases has increased and as genetic techniques have improved, the potential to treat or partially cure these diseases by **gene therapy** has increased. In gene therapy, the length of DNA which has the sequence of nucleotides corresponding to the normal allele, is frequently called the healthy gene or the normal gene. The aim is to add the normal allele to target cells, so that the allele can be expressed to produce the functioning protein and so mask the effect of the defective allele. The best candidates for gene therapy at the moment are those diseases caused by recessive mutations in single genes and which are not associated with environmental influences, such as SCID and the inherited eye condition known as Leber's congenital amaurosis (LCA). Gene therapy for these diseases is known as somatic-cell gene therapy as it targets just the affected tissues, such as lymphocytes or cells in the retina of the eye, and the additional allele is therefore not present in sperm or eggs, and so not passed on to future generations.

Delivering the cloned *normal* alleles

The aim of somatic-cell gene therapy is to introduce cloned normal alleles into the DNA of the target cells and for the allele to become integrated into the target cell genome so that transcription can occur. The successful delivery of the normal allele in SCID and LCA is by using viral vectors.

Some viruses can be used in gene therapy to deliver the normal alleles to target cells. The viruses are cultured in mammalian tissue and are modified to carry DNA containing the normal allele. The ability to infect a cell is retained so that the normal allele will be delivered into the cell. Examples of viral vectors are retroviruses, which is used in SCID and adeno-associated virus (AAV) (Figure 1 on page 447), used in LCA. The viruses need to be:

- large enough to carry the normal allele
- able to reach and attach to the target cell
- able to inject the allele into the cell or enter the cell and release the allele
- harmless and unable to cause disease in humans.

There are a number of non-viral methods of delivering alleles to target cells that have been developed or are being trialled.

Liposomes can be used in gene therapy. These are vesicles with an outer phospholipid bilayer and the normal allele contained within the centre of the vesicle. The liposomes can pass through the phospholipid bilayer of the cell surface membrane of the target cell to deliver the normal allele. Depending on the location of target cells, liposomes may enter through the skin (e.g. as part of a gel), breathed into the lungs via a nebuliser, as a nasal spray, be taken orally, and injected to specific areas. The liposomes can pass through mucous membranes to enter the body.

Other methods of delivering the normal allele include using electroporation and gene guns (see 19.1d Extension).

Challenges in choosing appropriate vectors

There is no perfect method for delivering cloned genes; each has its advantages and disadvantages. There is also always a concern that the DNA containing the normal allele will integrate into the target cell genome in a location that triggers a cell response leading to a cancerous cell.

These pages help you to:

- outline how the genetic diseases severe combined immunodeficiency (SCID) and inherited eye diseases can be treated with gene therapy (19.2.3)
- discuss the social and ethical considerations of using genetic screening and gene therapy in medicine (19.2.4)

You will also:

- learn about the different types of gene therapy and methods of delivery

---

Extension

Germ-line gene therapy

This is where the defective gene is replaced or supplemented in the fertilised egg. This makes sure that all cells of the organism will develop normally, as will all the cells of their offspring. This is therefore a much more permanent solution, than somatic-cell gene therapy, affecting future generations. However, the moral and ethical issues of manipulating such a long-term genetic change mean that the process is prohibited in most countries.

Remember

Adding a normal allele to a cell with a defective allele is sometimes called gene supplementation therapy. With the development of gene editing techniques (19.1e), gene replacement may be possible in the treatment of inherited diseases.

Gene supplementation **does not involve replacing** a gene, it simply introduces a dominant allele so that it is present with the existing recessive ones. The dominant allele therefore masks the effect of the recessive ones.

Remember

Inserting a functional allele does not remove the defective alleles – it just means that cells produce both functional and non-functional proteins at the same time.

Extension

Stem cell transplantation

Enzyme replacement therapy (19.2a) is a lifelong treatment for ADA-deficient SCID and not a cure. However, a bone marrow transplant (haematopoietic stem cell transplantation) can result in a cure or partial cure for ADA-deficient SCID and for SCID-X and is the first choice of treatment if a donor is found. A very good match of donor tissue is needed to avoid rejection and there is more success if it is carried out at a very early age. The aim is for the transplanted stem cells to produce healthy lymphocytes.

Remember

In gene therapy, a transduced cell is one that has been genetically modified by a virus. The virus acts as a vector to introduce a normal 'healthy' allele into the cells of the person with the disease.

Gene therapy uses defective stem cells from the child with SCID and modifies these by adding the normal allele – a stem cell transplant is different because it uses healthy cells from a donor.

Remember

Only boys have been reported to have SCID-X. The only way for a girl to have SCID-X is for her father to have the condition and the mother to carry the mutation. Given that this is such a rare condition, the chances of this situation occurring are very low. Also, before stem cell transplantation a boy with the disease would not have survived unless he was kept in the sterile environment of an isolation tent or 'bubble'.

The advantages of viral vectors are that they are very good at targeting and entering cells and can be targeted at specific types of cell. They can also be modified so that they do not replicate and destroy cells. They have the disadvantage that they can carry a limited amount of genetic material, and therefore some genes may be too big to fit into some viruses. They can also cause immune responses in patients, making them ill. In addition the immune system may block the virus from delivering the gene to the patient's cells, or it may kill the cells once the gene has been delivered.

The advantage of using liposomes is that they can carry larger genes, and rarely trigger an immune response. The disadvantage is that they are much less efficient than viruses at getting genes into cells.

Treatment of severe combined immunodeficiency (SCID) using gene therapy

SCID is a rare, inherited disease. There are a number of different types of SCID. In all types, there is a lack of functioning T-lymphocytes. Immune responses to infection cannot occur so every infection is life-threatening. In ADA-deficient SCID (see 19.2a) B-lymphocytes also do not function. The most common type of SCID is known as SCID-X, a sex-liked (X-linked) disease. Here, a mutation in the *IL2RG* gene leads to defective cytokine receptors in T-lymphocytes. The cells cannot develop and so do not function to stimulate a response in the B-lymphocytes that may be present.

Following clinical trials, approval was given in Europe in 2016 for a gene therapy treatment, Strimvelis, for children with ADA-deficient SCID who did not have a suitable match for a stem cell transplant:

- The child with SCID is given a drug to increase the number of haematopoietic stem cells in the bone marrow. These are stem cells that are able to divide and form blood cells.
- Tissue from the bone marrow is removed and purified to obtain the stem cells that will be genetically modified.
- A normal 'healthy' allele of the *ADA* gene is incorporated into a retrovirus known as gamma-retrovirus to create a viral vector.
- When cultured together in the laboratory, the viral vector infects the stem cells so that the allele is introduced into the cells.
- The allele becomes integrated into the genome of the stem cells, which are now known as transduced haematopoietic stem cells (stem cells genetically modified by viruses).
- The child is given a low dose of a chemotherapy drug that kills remaining stem cells so that space is created in the bone marrow for the transduced stem cells.
- The transduced stem cells are infused (injected) back into the child's body and enter the bone marrow, where they are able to divide and produce lymphocytes that express the enzyme ADA.

The advantage of using genetically modified stem cells is their ability to divide to increase the supply of lymphocytes that have the functioning copy of the *ADA* gene. A similar gene therapy treatment has been used successfully in trials for children with SCID-X. Here the viral vector contains the normal allele of the *IL2RG* gene, so that the transduced haematopoietic stem cells can form T-lymphocytes with active cytokine receptors, and the T-lymphocytes are able to stimulate the B-lymphocytes.

Other features of gene therapy for SCID include:

- the cells that are transduced to produce genetically modified stem cells are taken from the child's body so that there is an exact match and no problems of rejection
- the gamma-retrovirus vector is able to infect cells but does not harm human cells
- the normal alleles of the genes (*ADA* or *IL2RG*) are small and so can be packaged into the viral vector.

Treatment of Leber's congenital amaurosis

Leber's congenital amaurosis (LCA) is a rare inherited eye disease that affects around 1 in 80 000 of the population. People with LCA have impaired (poor) vision at birth and this condition degenerates over time, leading to blindness. It is the result of an autosomal recessive mutation thought to be caused by abnormal development of photoreceptor cells in the eye. In 2008, a young man with this form of genetic blindness had his sight partially restored using gene therapy. In this case, the vector used was adeno associated virus (AAV) carrying a normal copy of the *RPE65* gene, which codes for an enzyme involved in visual pigment formation. AAV is a very small non-enveloped virus that is a good choice as a viral vector for gene therapy. It is not known to cause disease in humans, and infection only causes a mild immune response. Also, it can integrate its DNA into a direct location within the genome of the cell, avoiding the concern that integration of DNA into the wrong location may trigger off responses in the cell that lead to uncontrolled growth and cancer. Since the first treatment, others have been given this gene therapy with some success in improving vision. The AAV-vector is known as the drug voretigene neparvovec. The drug is delivered by direct injection into an area, known as the subretinal space, close to the defective cells of the retina. As this is a relatively new treatment, it is not known how long these improvements will last for after therapy. There are a number of other similar inherited eye diseases that may also be treated by this type of gene therapy.

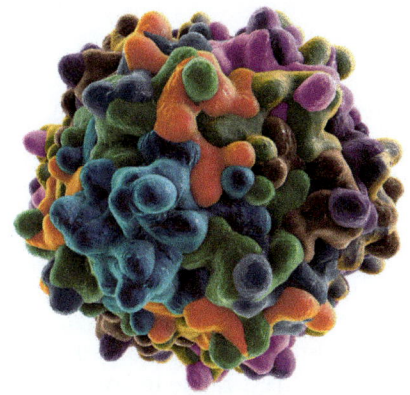

Figure 1 *Computer illustration of adeno-associated virus (AAV) used in gene therapy*

Social and ethical considerations of genetic testing and gene therapy

As with many scientific applications, the use of genetic testing (Topic 19.2b) and gene therapy brings risks and benefits, and raises ethical and social issues:

- Do disabilities need to be cured or prevented, or are they just part of the genetic variety that makes up all species?
- Who decides what is normal and what is a disability? While serious diseases are clearly disabling, there are many other conditions that some individuals consider disabling. These might include being very tall or short, having a particular hair colour, skin colour, body shape, birthmark, etc. Are these candidates for gene therapy?
- Gene therapy research and treatment is very expensive. Could the money be better spent on more proven treatments, where success is guaranteed?
- Germ-line therapy would be very effective, but what might be the long-term consequences of introducing heritable genes into the population? Could it lead to selection of one race in favour of another **(eugenics)**?
- Could the use of gene therapy make people less accepting of those who are different?
- Should gene therapy be used to enhance basic human traits such as height, intelligence, or athletic ability? How long before there are genetic tests for these traits, so that we can choose the features of our offspring? Genetic testing involves similar selection when parents choose whether or not to have a child with a disorder.
- Should people undergoing in-vitro fertilisation (IVF) have the right to genetically screen the eggs and sperm? Should they be able to pre-select the ones they use? Should a biopsy be carried out on the in-vitro embryo to screen for genetic disorders before it is implanted in the uterus?
- Should genetic testing of embryos in the uterus be carried out routinely? Should parents have the choice of a therapeutic abortion if there is some genetic abnormality?
- Who should know about the results of a genetic test? Would employers choose to not employ someone with a genetic disorder? Would insurance premiums rise for that individual?
- Is it reasonable to carry out a genetic test for a disease for which there is no known cure?

Summary test 19.2c

SCID, which stands for **(1)** is an inherited disease that can be treated with gene therapy. The treatment involves the removal of **(2)** from the **(3)** of the child with SCID, and **(4)** these using a genetically modified viral **(5)**, which is a **(6)** carrying the normal allele for the **(7)** gene or, with SCID-X, the **(8)** gene. The virus infects the cells and these are replaced back into the child. As they are dividing cells, the new **(9)** and **(10)** lymphocytes formed are healthy. Inherited eye diseases can also be treated with gene therapy. One such disease, LCA is caused by a **(11)** mutation and is a degenerative disease that leads to **(12)**. The viral vector here is an **(13)**, containing the normal allele for the **(14)** gene.

Genetically modified organisms in agriculture
a. Soybean, cotton, and salmon

Recombinant DNA technology produces genetically modified organisms (GMOs) that have some added feature that makes them of increased benefit to humans. GMOs used in agriculture can lead to a greatly improved yield to help supply the increasing global demand for food.

Agricultural pests are plants and animals that are harmful to the production of agricultural products. Pesticides are chemicals that kill pests. Farmers apply herbicides (pesticide for weeds) and insecticides (pesticide for insect pests) when the commercial gain from an increased yield outweighs the cost of buying and applying the chemical.

Herbicide resistance in soybean plants and resistance to insect pests in cotton plants are two examples of GM crops produced to improve crop yield. Scientists have also produced GM salmon, an important food source, which is larger in size than non-GM salmon. In addition to environmental and economic implications, there are social and ethical implications of using GMOs in food production and some of these will be discussed here.

Herbicide resistance in soybean

The soybean plant, *Glycine max* (Figure 1), is a plant native to southeast Asia, and a member of the pea family (see Extension). It is one of the world's most important crops, valuable for the high oil and protein content of soybean seeds. The five largest producers of soybean are (in order) the United States, Brazil, Argentina, China and India. Soybean has a very wide range of uses. Soybean seeds are a nutritious food source for humans, for example, soybean oil, soybean milk and tofu. Soybean meal is a good livestock food. Soybean is also produced as a source of biofuel.

Figure 1 *Maturing soybean plants in a soybean field*

Farmers have used broad spectrum post-emergence herbicides (herbicides that are applied after the soybean plant has germinated and can kill broad-leaved and grass weeds) since the 1980s to control weeds. This has allowed rows of plants to be grown closer together, as tillage (turning over soil) for weed control is not needed and larger areas can be managed because herbicide application takes less time. The main problem for farmers is financial, as there is a loss of crop owing to the effect of herbicides on soybean plants as well as the potential for reduced quality of crop.

The development of genetically modified (GM) soybean varieties that are resistant to these broad-spectrum, post-emergence herbicides increases the total yield of soybean crops and so has social benefits as it contributes to the growing global demand for food. This is because the herbicide can be used effectively to kill weeds without harming soybean plants, as well as reduce competition for soil water, mineral ions, space and light. Clearly this is of considerable benefit to the farmer, who can spray whole fields with the herbicide rather than having to specifically target the weeds – a difficult and expensive task. With the weeds eliminated, the yield of the crops is substantially improved.

Currently there are genetically modified soybean varieties that are resistant to one of the four different herbicides, 2.4-D, dicamba, glyphosate and glufosinate. The gene coding for herbicide resistance can be transferred into soybean plant tissue using a gene gun delivery method or *Agrobacterium tumefaciens* (19.1d).

The use of genetically modified plants has great social and ethical benefits but, together with the herbicide, may potentially have the following detrimental effects:

- The development of herbicide resistance in weeds could lead to increased doses of the herbicide being necessary to produce the same effect. This may present environmental or human health risks.
- Spread of herbicide resistance from soybean weeds. As we have seen in 17.3b, hybridisation between plants can occur naturally. This could lead to genes for herbicide resistance being spread to other species. If the gene were to be transferred to weeds, this would make the specific herbicide ineffective as a weed killer.
- The removal of the weeds by the herbicide reduces biodiversity. These weeds form part of the food chain for animals such as insects and birds. The population of these other species could be reduced or they might disappear altogether. Apart from the ecological effects, there is an ethical advantage in protecting and maintaining biodiversity.
- The herbicide-resistant varieties of plants are usually patented by companies. These companies often also produce the particular herbicide to which the new variety is resistant. The two are therefore sold as a pair. The company has a monopoly on both products, leaving no room for commercial competition. This leads to higher charges for the farmer, which leads to high charges for the consumer.

Extension

Legumes

Members of the pea family, such as beans, peas, peanuts, lentils and soybean are legumes. These plants have nodules in their roots that contain **nitrogen-fixing bacteria**. The bacteria are able to convert atmospheric nitrogen into a form useable by plants, such as ammonia and nitrates. The advantages of growing leguminous crops is that they increase the fertility of the soil.

Insect resistance in cotton

Cotton is an important crop worldwide. It is grown for its fibre, which is used in textiles that are made into furnishings and clothes. Other products from cotton include oil and livestock feed. Although the main aim of cotton production is for the fibre, when cotton plants are harvested, cotton seeds are also obtained. Cottonseed is valuable as livestock feed, particularly in dairy cattle, as it has a high fat content (20% of dry mass) as an energy source, a high protein content (23%), and high fibre content (24%). In dairy cattle, cottonseed as part of livestock feed can increase milk yield.

Cotton crops can be attacked by insects, therefore reducing yields. Cotton boll weevils and caterpillars feed within the fruits of cotton plants with devastating effects (Figure 2). Indeed cotton has such a range of insect pests that more insecticides are sprayed on it per hectare than on any other crop – often 10–15 sprayings a season and, in extreme cases, up to 30 sprayings.

At the beginning of the twentieth century a soil bacterium, *Bacillus thuringiensis* (Bt) was found to produce a toxin with insecticidal properties that killed certain caterpillars. The bacteria were used to produce a range of different insecticides, which were then sprayed on crops to control a variety of insect larvae.

In the 1990s, the gene for the Bt toxin was isolated and transferred into potato, maize and cotton plants. The genetically modified plants produce their own Bt toxin, which kills insect larvae that feed on it. The advantages of Bt cotton plants include:

- There is less environmental impact because only insects feeding on the plant are killed. Spraying crops with insecticides kills most insects, including beneficial ones such as pollinating butterflies and bees. This decreases biodiversity.
- The plant produces sufficient Bt toxin to be effective in killing insect larval pests that eat it.
- It is more economic as the use of conventional insecticides is much reduced.
- Control of pests is easier, especially for smaller farmers, because less specialist knowledge and equipment is required than when spraying insecticides.

Some potentially detrimental effects include:

- The possible transfer of the Bt toxin gene to related species through hybridisation cannot be ruled out.
- There have been concerns that the Bt toxin could be exuded (released) from the roots of Bt plants or remain in the parts of the plants not harvested. The Bt toxin could then adversely affect soil organisms.
- There are similar concerns that the Bt toxin may be harmful to animals that eat the GM cottonseed.
- Genetically modified seeds cost more than non-GM seeds. These extra costs need to be weighed against the considerable costs of spraying insecticides.
- Insects may become resistant to the Bt toxin, making Bt cotton vulnerable to insect attack. Again this needs to be weighed against the use of less insecticide, which reduces the chance of resistance developing in the first place.

Genetically modified salmon

GM salmon have been developed for their ability to grow two to four times faster than other farmed salmon. The GM Atlantic salmon, called AquAdvantage, include a growth hormone-regulating gene from the Chinook salmon as well as a promoter gene from an ocean pout fish. The GM salmon have the potential to grow to market size in half the time (18 months rather than 3 years), because the genes increase the amount of growth hormone

Figure 2 *Cotton boll severely damaged by a boll weevil. Damage like this can be prevented by sowing insect-resistant varieties of cotton plants.*

in the blood and allow the fish to grow throughout the year rather than just in spring and summer as with conventional salmon. The fish have a similar nutritional quality to traditional Atlantic salmon.

Some describe GM salmon as unnatural and believe that it is not ethical to genetically modify animals, particularly for food. Others argue that society has an ethical obligation to help feed the world and so have no objections to science increasing food availability by producing GMOs. GM salmon are bred to be sterile, but there are concerns that some GM salmon may be fertile and could interbreed with wild salmon, affecting the wild salmon industry.

Summary test 19.3a

Herbicide resistance in soybean plants allows farmers to apply **(1)** broad spectrum herbicides to kill **(2)** and so reduce **(3)** for water and other resources. This produces a greater yield of crop, with soybeans being a rich source of **(4)** and **(5)**. Bt-resistant cotton plants have a gene that allows the plants to produce a **(6)** that kills insect pests. Less **(7)** needs to be applied and this prevents the loss of beneficial insects, such as **(8)**, that are important pollinators of plant crops. Improved cotton yield means more **(9)** feedstock for domestic livestock such a dairy cattle, leading to greater milk production and higher **(10)** of milk. GM salmon contain a **(11)** gene from the **(12)**, and a **(13)** from the ocean pout. The increased food production from this fish is because it grows to market size in **(14)** compared with 36 months of other farmed salmon.

Figure 3 *Genetically engineered salmon, swimming inside breeding tank*

Figure 4 *A facility manager holding one of the last batch of conventional Atlantic salmon raised at a commercial fish farm in the US*

These pages help you to:

- discuss the ethical and social implications of using genetically modified organisms (GMOs) in food production (19.3.2)

You will also:

- understand what is meant by pharming

Gene technology undoubtedly brings many benefits to humankind, but it is not without its risks. Let us consider these benefits and risks and evaluate the ethical and social issues associated with the use of gene technology.

Genetically modified crops can be engineered to have economic and environmental advantages. These include making plants more tolerant to environmental extremes, e.g. able to survive drought, cold, heat, salt or polluted soils, etc. This permits crops to be grown commercially in places where they are not at present. Growing of genetically modified plants, such as salt-tolerant tomato plants, could bring land back into productivity. Other examples include producing genetically modified forms of crop plants that are resistant to herbicides, such as the soybean plant (see 19.3a). This allows weeds competing for light, water and nutrients to be killed by the herbicide but with minimum effect on the crop. This gives greater yields. Another example of such a crop treated in this way is maize (Figure 1). In a world where millions lack a basic nutritious diet, can we ethically oppose the use of such crop plants?

Genetically modified crops can help prevent certain diseases. Rice can have a gene for vitamin A production added. This rice, when fed to people with vitamin A deficiency, can give better health, help prevent ear infections and prevent one form of blindness. Can we ethically justify not developing more vitamin A enriched crops when 140 million children worldwide are at risk from vitamin A deficiency?

Genetically modified animals that have resistance to disease or produce a greater yield have also been developed. An example is genetically modified salmon that grow at a much faster rate and so provide more food more quickly, as described in 19.3a.

Table 1 summarises some of the main benefits and concerns of GM crop production. Against the benefits of gene technology, must be weighed the risks – both real and potential. These include the following.

Table 1 *Summary of the benefits and concerns surrounding GM crops*

BENEFITS

- Crop yields can be improved reducing hunger and starvation
- Production is cheaper leading to less expensive food
- Quality of food is improved (more nutrients)
- Unproductive land can be farmed using GM varieties engineered to suit extreme conditions
- Some deficiency diseases can be prevented leading to better health
- Produce can be stored and transported without spoiling
- Less insecticide is needed, reducing the ecological damage they cause

CONCERNS

- Cost of GM seeds is high and farmers cannot use their own seed
- Global companies become more powerful
- Engineered genes may spread to other species through hybridisation
- GM crops may be difficult to sell due to consumer concerns
- GM varieties may be genetically unstable
- There are no long-term studies on the effects to human health
- Biodiversity may be reduced, e.g. more herbicide may be used and remain in the soil to affect non-GM crops grown the next season *or* traditional crop varieties may no longer be grown, leading to loss of genetic diversity
- Risk of cross-pollination with organic crops
- Cross-pollination with wild plants and the production of more resistant weeds (superweeds)
- Lack of labelling of food will not allow the public to choose what foods they eat

Figure 1 *This maize has been genetically modified to be herbicide resistant. When the crop is treated with herbicide the maize is unaffected, but weeds are killed. This aims to increase the yield of such crops by reducing competition from weeds.*

- It is impossible to predict with complete accuracy what the ecological consequences will be of releasing genetically engineered organisms into the environment. The delicate balance that exists in any habitat may be irreversibly damaged by the introduction of organisms with engineered genes. This could have social implications should a genetically modified organism out-compete other crop plants to the point that the overall production of food was reduced. This might lead to widespread famine.

- A modified gene may pass from the organism it was placed in, to a completely different one. We know, for example, that viruses can transfer genes from one organism to another. What if a virus were to transfer genes for herbicide resistance and vigorous growth from a crop plant to a weed that competed with the crop plant? What if the same gene were transferred by pollen to other plants? How would we then be able to control this weed?

- Any manipulation of the DNA of a cell will have consequences for the metabolic pathways within that cell. We cannot be sure until after the event what unpredictable by-products of the change might be produced. Could these lead to metabolic malfunctions, cause cancer, or create a new form of disease?

- Genetically modified bacteria sometimes have antibiotic resistance marker genes that have been added. These bacteria can spread antibiotic resistance to harmful bacteria, making certain diseases harder to treat.

- All genes mutate. What then, might be the consequences of our engineered gene mutating?

- An important ethical issue is what might be the long-term consequences of introducing new gene combinations? We cannot be certain of the effects on the future evolution of organisms. Will the artificial selection of 'desired' genes reduce the genetic variety that is so essential to evolution?

- What might be the social and economic consequences of developing plants and animals to grow in new regions? Developing bananas that can grow in Europe could have disastrous consequences for the Caribbean economies that rely heavily on this crop for their income.

- What will be the consequences of the ability to manipulate genes getting into the wrong hands? Will some individuals, groups or governments use this power to achieve political goals, control opposition or gain overall power?

- Is it ethically right to interfere with genes at all? Should we let nature take its own course in its own time?

- Is it right that an individual or company can patent, and therefore effectively own, a gene? What are the ethical implications of individuals owning a gene that can prevent famine by increasing crop yields? Could they hold large populations to ransom?

It is inevitable that we remain inquisitive about the world in which we live, and that we will seek to try to improve the conditions in which we live. Genetic research is bound to continue, but the challenge will be to develop the safeguards and ethical guidelines that will allow genetic engineering to be used in a safe and effective manner.

Extension

Pharming

Pharming is a term used to describe the genetic modification of a plant or animal so that it contains a gene that, when expressed, produces a pharmaceutical product.

- Genetically modified plants can be transformed to produce a specific substance in a particular organ of the plant. These organs can then be harvested and the desired substance extracted. If a drug is involved, the process is called plant pharming. One promising application of this technique is in the production of plants that manufacture antibodies to a particular disease, or manufacture **antigens** which, when injected into humans, induce natural **antibody** production.

- Animal pharming is also possible. For example, transgenic (genetically modifed) goats have been produced that are able to synthesise milk containing an anticoagulant plasma protein called antithrombin.

Summary test 19.3b

Genetically modified plants can be produced that are more tolerant to environmental extremes such as drought, heat, **(1)** or **(2)**, and so can grow in places where crops are not able to grow. By growing crops that are **(3)** resistant, weeds can be killed, leading to greater **(4)**. **(5)** plants can be genetically modified to produce vitamin **(6)** to help supplement the diet of children and prevent illness, potential hearing loss and **(7)**. There is the possibility that a **(8)** may transfer genes from a GM plant to a non-GM plant, or that **(9)** may be transferred to produce superweeds. The insertion of genes into plants may cause **(10)** malfunctions. Some GMOs have been produced using bacteria with **(11)** markers and there is the potential for this to spread to **(12)** bacteria and make diseases harder to treat. There are concerns that companies could **(13)** a GM organism and effectively own the novel DNA that is the organism's **(14)**.

Launch additional digital resources for the chapter

19 Exam-style questions

1   The soil bacterium *Bacillus thuringiensis* produces Cry-proteins that are toxic to insects.

Cotton plants can be genetically modified to produce Cry-proteins for combating bollworm pests.

a   To genetically modify cotton plants, a recombinant DNA containing Cry-protein gene is made first.

i   Define the term *recombinant DNA*.   *(1 mark)*

ii   Complete Table 1 to show the role of each enzyme in producing recombinant DNA.   *(4 marks)*

Table 1

enzyme	role
reverse transcriptase	
DNA polymerase	
restriction enzyme	
DNA ligase	

iii   The recombinant DNA also contains CaMV 35S promoter taken from cauliflower mosaic virus.

Explain why the viral DNA is included in recombinant DNA.   *(2 marks)*

b   State **two** benefits of modifying cotton plants to produce Cry-proteins.   *(2 marks)*

c   State **two** possible risks of modifying cotton plants to produce Cry-proteins.   *(2 marks)*

(Total 11 marks)

2   Severe combined immunodeficiency and some inherited eye diseases can be treated with gene therapy. A disease known as cystic fibrosis (CF) has also been treated with gene therapy, with limited success.

Cystic fibrosis is an autosomal recessive genetic disease, caused by a mutation of the cystic fibrosis transmembrane regulator (CFTR) gene. The most common mutation results in the loss of one amino acid in the CFTR protein. Faulty CFTRs cause abnormal production of thick mucus in the lungs and other parts of the body.

Treatment of cystic fibrosis with gene therapy involves using liposomes (vesicles with an outer phospholipid bilayer). Liposomes containing normal CFTR alleles are administered into the noses of CF patients through an aerosol spray.

a   Suggest why gene therapy may be effective in treating CF.   *(2 marks)*

b   A clinical trial was conducted to test the effectiveness of this treatment on 115 CF patients.

* First, a pulmonary function test was performed on each patient to measure percentage forced expiratory volume in one second ($\%FEV_1$). FEV_1 is the maximum volume of air exhaled in the first second of a forced expiration from a position of full inspiration. This was recorded as the baseline value.
* The patients were assigned to two groups using a computer-based randomisation system.
* One group was treated with pGM169/GL67A (CFTR allele–liposome complex). The spray was administered once a month for a year.
* The other group was treated with saline (salt) solution instead. Neither of the groups knew whether they were being given pGM169/GL67A or saline solution.
* The FEV_1 was measured again at the end of the trial. The percentage change in FEV_1 compared to the base line was calculated for each individual.

Table 2 shows the results of this trial. An improvement in pulmonary function is represented by positive values.

Table 2

Type of treatment	Number of patients	Mean percentage change in $FEV_1 \pm S_M$	95% confidence intervals / %
pGM169/GL67A	61	−0.4 ± 1.3	−3.0 to +2.2
saline solution	54	−4.0 ± 1.3	

S_M = standard error

i   State the reason for having one group treated with saline solution.   *(1 mark)*

ii   Using the formula below, calculate the 95% confidence intervals (CI) for saline solution. Show your working.   *(2 marks)*

95% CI = mean ± 2 S_M

iii   State **one** way in which the data shows that pGM169/GL67A is effective in treating CF and **one** way in which it does not.   *(2 marks)*

c   Another form of mutation is a base substitution that produces a stop codon within the CFTR gene.

A drug called PTC124 allows translation to continue through the stop codon. This drug is taken orally and can be taken up into cells all over the body.

Suggest the advantages of PTC124 over the pGM169/GL67A treatment. *(2 marks)*

d A company based in Germany recently developed a microarray containing DNA probes for 25 different mutations associated with CF.

   i Outline how a microarray enables the detection of specific CFTR alleles. *(5 marks)*

   ii Suggest why such analysis is useful in treating CF. *(1 mark)*

(Total 15 marks)

19 Practice questions

3 Outline the steps that are involved in the genetic modification of a host bacterial cell using a plasmid as a vector.

4 a What is the role of a vector in genetic engineering?

  b In some genetic engineering procedures, the *GFP* gene, which codes for a green fluorescent protein, is added to the vector. This gene is termed a marker gene.

    Explain why marker genes are necessary in genetic engineering.

  c Explain how marker genes coding for fluorescent products are used to confirm gene expression.

5 Factor VIII is a protein essential in the blood clotting process. A person who does not produce Factor VIII will have a disease known as haemophilia. If untreated the person will continue to bleed when injured. In the past haemophilia was treated by extracting Factor VII from blood donations. Now, Factor VII can be produced using recombinant DNA techniques.

  a Recombinant mammalian cells are used to produce Factor VIII, rather than recombinant bacteria. One reason for this is that mammalian cells have better systems for post-translation modification (protein folding and further modification after translation).

    Suggest why post-translational modification is necessary in the production of Factor VIII.

  b State one advantage of using recombinant Factor VIII produced by genetic engineering techniques rather than using Factor VIII extracted from blood donations.

6 Some family tree tracing websites offer genetic screening tests to give users more detailed ancestry information. These results can include identifying genes in their genome that indicate a person has an increased chance of developing a genetic disease.

a Give three reasons why someone should seek genetic counselling **before** undertaking a genetic screening test.

b Give two reasons why someone might like to know about a genetic disease they are likely to develop.

Summary-test answers

Chapter 1

Summary test 1.1a
1. nanometre
2. nm
3. multiply
4. metre
5. ×100

Summary test 1.1b
1. light
2. temporary
3. stains
4. cover slip
5. forceps
6. air bubbles

Summary test 1.1c
1. nucleoli
2. tonoplast
3. cytoplasm/cytosol
4. cell surface membrane/plasma membrane
5. squamous epithelial
6. smear

Summary test 1.1d
1. light
2. eyepiece
3. micrometer
4. calibrated
5. 20
6. 3000

Summary test 1.1e
1. 200
2. shorter
3. nm
4. resolution
5. air
6. vacuum
7. scanning
8. three-dimensional/3D
9. thin
10. transmission

Summary test 1.1f
1. bigger/larger
2. resolution
3. micrographs
4. detail
5. light
6. artefacts

Summary test 1.2a
1. units
2. multicellular
3. unicellular
4. labour
5. specialised
6. eukaryotic
7. prokaryotic
8. nuclear envelope

Summary test 1.2b
1. smooth
2. microtubules
3. microvilli
4. chloroplasts
5. glycogen
6. plasmodesmata

Summary test 1.2c
1. nuclear envelope
2. DNA
3. nuclear pores
4. nucleolus
5. ribosomal
6. ribosomes
7. photosynthesis
8. grana
9. chlorophyll
10. aerobic
11. (mitochondrial) matrix
12. inner
13. cristae

Summary test 1.2d
1. 80S ribosomes
2. external/cytosol facing
3. lumen
4. lipids/cholesterol
5. tubular
6. cisternae
7. vesicles
8. Golgi
9. modified
10. Golgi vesicles
11. acid hydrolases
12. lysosomes
13. breakdown/hydrolyse/digest
14. organelles

Summary test 1.2e
1. barrier
2. partially
3. microvilli
4. absorption
5. 9 + 2
6. two
7. spindle
8. tonoplast
9. plasmodesmata
10. (cell) lysis

Summary test 1.2f
1. bacteria
2. circular
3. nuclear envelope
4. 70S/smaller
5. peptidoglycan/murein
6. non-cellular/acellular
7. RNA
8. capsid
9. capsomeres
10. envelope

Chapter 2

Summary test 2.1a
1. macromolecules
2. subunits/monomers
3. polypeptide
4. covalent/peptide
5. condensation
6. anabolism
7. hydrolysis
8. water

Summary test 2.1b
1. iodine (in potassium iodide)
2. orange
3. blue-black
4. non-reducing sugar
5. hydrochloric acid
6. precipitate
7. semi-quantitative
8. biuret
9. lilac/purple
10. ethanol/alcohol
11. emulsion

Summary test 2.2a
1. monomers
2. hexose
3. condensation
4. fructose
5. maltose
6. reducing

7 non-reducing
8 glycosidic
9 hydrolysis

Summary test 2.2b
1 alpha
2 glycosidic
3 amylose
4 helical
5 animal
6 energy
7 insoluble
8 branched
9 α-1,6
10 muscle
11 compact

Summary test 2.2c
1 β-glucose
2 1,4 glycosidic
3 hydrogen bonds
4 microfibrils
5 structural / support
6 hydrophilic
7 insoluble

Summary test 2.2d
1 triglycerides
2 glycerol
3 polyunsaturated
4 2
5 hydrophobic
6 hydrogen
7 energy

Summary test 2.3a
1 –COOH
2 amino
3 amphoteric
4 condensation
5 peptide
6 primary
7 hydrogen
8 α-helix
9 β-pleated sheet

Summary test 2.3b
1 amino acids
2 polypeptide
3 hydrogen bonds
4 –CO
5 amino acid
6 sulfur
7 a disulfide bond
8 ionic (bonds)
9 hydrophobic interactions
10 prosthetic

Summary test 2.3c
1 globular
2 fibrous
3 glycine–proline–alanine
4 tendons
5 strength/flexibility
6 strength/flexibility
7 4
8 haem
9 Fe^{2+} / ferrous ion

Summary test 2.4a
1 dipolar
2 electrons
3 hydrogen bonds
4 specific heat capacity
5 latent heat of vaporization

Chapter 3

Summary test 3.1a
1 catalysts
2 globular
3 active site
4 activation energy
5 substrate
6 products
7 lock and key
8 induced fit

Summary test 3.1b
1 time course
2 disappearance
3 product
4 maltose
5 starch
6 hydrogen peroxide
7 dependent
8 time / s
9 initial
10 amylase
11 iodine in potassium iodide / I in KI
12 end point

Summary test 3.1c
1 colorimeter
2 quantitative
3 cuvette
4 sensor
5 transmittance (transmission)
6 absorbed

Summary test 3.2a
1 increase
2 active site
3 denatured
4 37°C

5 2
6 salivary amylase
7 hydrogen ions
8 ionic
9 shape
10 electrons

Summary test 3.2b
1 initial rate of reaction
2 increases
3 active sites
4 halved
5 be constant
6 Michaelis–Menten
7 affinity

Summary test 3.2c
1 substrate
2 enzyme–substrate complex
3 V_{max}
4 affinity
5 allosteric site
6 shape/conformation
7 complementary

Summary test 3.2d
1 alginate
2 syringe
3 calcium chloride
4 contaminated
5 re-used
6 pH
7 downstream processing

Chapter 4

Summary test 4.1a
1 bilayer
2 hydrophilic
3 hydrophobic
4 intrinsic / integral
5 extrinsic / peripheral
6 cholesterol/glycolipids/ glycoproteins
7 cholesterol/glycolipids/ glycoproteins
8 cholesterol/glycolipids/ glycoproteins

Summary test 4.1b
1 bilayer
2 ions
3 hydrophobic
4 water
5 carrier
6 cholesterol
7 unsaturated

8 glycoproteins
9 recognition
10 ligands
11 receptors
12 target

Summary test 4.2a

1 higher / greater
2 lower / less
3 kinetic
4 passive
5 less / reduced / lower
6 less / reduced / lower
7 more / greater / higher
8 channel
9 ion
10 binding site
11 conformational

Summary test 4.2b

1 water
2 selectively permeable
3 pressure
4 zero
5 lower / more negative
6 B
7 passive

Summary test 4.2c

1 higher / less negative
2 (solute) concentration / water potential
3 osmosis
4 protoplast
5 (cellulose) cell wall
6 higher / less negative
7 plasmolysis

Summary test 4.2d

1 minutes
2 zero / no
3 mass
4 water potential
5 dialysis / Visking
6 water potential gradient
7 swollen / full
8 glucose
9 (passive / simple) diffusion
10 Benedict's
11 iodine (in potassium iodide)
12 orange

Summary test 4.2e

- diffusion
- pH
- hydrochloric acid
- longer
- surface area to volume ratio / SA:V

- reliability
- random
- volume
- π r h

Summary test 4.2f

1 against
2 ATP
3 mitochondria
4 respiratory
5 cytosis
6 endocytosis
7 exocytosis
8 phagocytosis
9 pinocytosis

Chapter 5

Summary test 5.1a

1 sister chromatids
2 centromere
3 histone
4 telomeres
5 genes / genetic information
6 shortening / being degraded
7 cell cycle
8 cytokinesis
9 organelles
10 S phase
11 G1 and G2
12 four

Summary test 5.1b

1 mutation
2 red blood
3 growth (in multicellular organisms); tissue repair; asexual reproduction
4 growth (in multicellular organisms); tissue repair; asexual reproduction
5 growth (in multicellular organisms); tissue repair; asexual reproduction
6 stem cells
7 tumour

Summary test 5.2a

1 interphase
2 prophase
3 centrioles
4 poles
5 spindle apparatus
6 nuclear envelope
7 nucleolus
8 metaphase
9 equator
10 anaphase

11 centromere
12 chromatids / daughter chromosomes
13 telophase

Summary test 5.2b

1 meristem / meristematic
2 DNA
3 root cap
4 interphase
5 objective lens
6 annotations
7 proportion
8 the spindle/ spindle fibres / microtubules
9 eyepiece graticule

Chapter 6

Summary test 6.1a

1 nitrogen/phosphorus
2 nitrogen/phosphorus
3 pentose
4 five
5 ribose/deoxyribose
6 ribose/deoxyribose
7 pyrimidines
8 cytosine; uracil
9 cytosine; uracil
10 purines
11 5
12 guanine; adenine
13 guanine; adenine
14 thymine
15 ribosomal RNA
16 transfer RNA
17 messenger RNA

Summary test 6.1b

1 pentose
2 deoxyribose
3 phosphate
4 adenine
5 cytosine
6 antiparallel
7 double helix

Summary test 6.1c

1 polynucleotide
2 hydrogen
3 replication forks
4 DNA polymerase
5 complementary
6 leading
7 Okazaki fragments
8 lagging strand
9 DNA ligase
10 semi-conservative

Summary test 6.1d

1 ^{14}N
2 ^{15}N
3 isotope
4 control
5 centrifuged
6 light; hybrid
7 light; hybrid
8 light
9 hybrid
10 semi-conservative

Summary test 6.2a

1 gene
2 three
3 codon
4 3.2 billion (3.2×10^9)
5 degenerate
6 non-overlapping
7 stop
8 Tyr (tyrosine)
9 ATA; ATG (complementary to UAU and UAC on mRNA)
10 ATA; ATG (complementary to UAU and UAC on mRNA)

Summary test 6.2b

1 template / transcribed
2 primary transcript
3 mRNA
4 RNA polymerase
5 hydrogen
6 activated
7 uracil
8 guanine
9 single
10 guanine
11 adenine
12 introns
13 exons
14 mRNA
15 nuclear pore

Summary test 6.2c

1 translation
2 phosphates
3 amino-acyl tRNA
4 ribosome
5 anticodon
6 peptide
7 STOP

Summary test 6.2d

1 alleles
2 nucleotides
3 insertion
4 substitution
5 substitution
6 deletion

7 insertion
8 mis-sense
9 silent
10 nonsense

Chapter 7

Summary test 7.1a

1 water
2 roots
3 photosynthates / assimilates
4 phloem (sieve tubes)
5 vascular
6 stem
7 ring pattern
8 (non-)woody
9 embryonic leaves / seed leaves / dicotyledons

Summary test 7.1b

1 organs
2 epidermis
3 cuticle
4 parenchyma
5 storage
6 in the centre / centrally
7 xylem
8 phloem

Summary test 7.1c

1 dicotyledonous
2 lamina/ blade
3 vein
4 side veins
5 epidermis
6 spongy mesophyll
7 intercellular air spaces
8 palisade mesophyll
9 xylem

Summary test 7.1d

1 vessels
2 lignin
3 annular; reticulate; spiral
4 annular; reticulate; spiral
5 annular; reticulate; spiral
6 lumen
7 pits
8 sclerenchyma (fibres)
9 elongate / long
10 tube
11 hollow / empty
12 cytoplasm
13 end walls
14 resistance
15 lignified / lignin
16 inward collapse

Summary test 7.1e

1 sucrose; amino acids; plant hormones
2 sucrose; amino acids; plant hormones (*any two*)
3 storage
4 sieve plates
5 phloem-protein
6 nucleus; Golgi body; ribosome; large vacuole; RER; SER
7 nucleus; Golgi body; ribosome; large vacuole; RER; SER
8 nucleus; Golgi body; ribosome; large vacuole; RER; SER (*any three*)
9 companion cells
10 plasmodesmata

Summary test 7.2a

1 root hairs
2 lower (more negative)
3 apoplast
4 symplast
5 plasmodesmata
6 endodermis
7 Casparian strip
8 suberin
9 protoplast
10 mineral
11 decreases/lowers

Summary test 7.2b

1 evaporates
2 stomata
3 guard cells
4 lower / more negative
5 water potential
6 cohesion
7 cellulose
8 adhesion

Summary test 7.2c

1 sand dunes; salt marshes; areas where ground is frozen for much of the year
2 sand dunes; salt marshes; areas where ground is frozen for much of the year (*any two*)
3 cuticle
4 trichomes (hairy leaves); stomata in pits or grooves; leaves that roll up/curl
5 trichomes (hairy leaves); stomata in pits or grooves; leaves that roll up/curl
6 trichomes (hairy leaves); stomata in pits or grooves; leaves that roll up/curl

Summary test 7.2d
1 phloem
2 sources
3 sinks
4 mass flow
5 companion cell
6 apoplast / cell wall
7 cotransport
8 lower / more negative
9 xylem
10 higher / less negative
11 osmosis
12 hydrostatic

Chapter 8

Summary test 8.1a
1 double
2 heart
3 systemic
4 (blood) vessels
5 arterioles
6 venules
7 endothelium
8 diffusion
9 red blood
10 aorta
11 oxygenated
12 lungs

Summary test 8.1b
1 tunica adventitia/externa
2 collagen
3 tunica intima
4 endothelial
5 arteries
6 veins
7 smooth
8 aorta / pulmonary artery
9 valves
10 vein

Summary test 8.1c
1 plasma
2 red (blood) cells
3 7–8 μm
4 120 days
5 haemoglobin
6 oxygen
7 white (blood) cells
8 phagocytes
9 macrophages
10 (multi-)lobed
11 neutrophil
12 kidney-shaped / bean-shaped
13 spherical
14 neutrophils

Summary test 8.1d
1 plasma
2 hydrostatic
3 arterial
4 ultrafiltration
5 90%
6 solvent
7 dissolve
8 urea
9 high specific heat capacity

Summary test 8.2a
1 respiratory pigment
2 red blood cells
3 four
4 iron (Fe^{2+})
5 polypeptides
6 four
7 tension / partial pressure
8 oxygen dissociation curve
9 allosteric
10 first
11 large
12 saturation
13 affinity

Summary test 8.2b
1 aerobic respiration
2 carbaminohaemoglobin
3 hydrogen
4 10
5 5
6 plasma
7 85
8 hydrogencarbonate ions
9 carbonic acid
10 carbonic anhydrase
11 haemoglobinic acid
12 buffer
13 Bohr effect

Summary test 8.3a
1 atria
2 ventricles
3 left atrioventricular / bicuspid / mitral
4 right atrioventricular / tricuspid
5 pulmonary veins
6 left atrium
7 aorta

Summary test 8.3b
1 70
2 diastole
3 atrial systole
4 atrioventricular
5 ventricles
6 semilunar

7 pulmonary artery
8 aorta

Summary test 8.3c
1 myogenic
2 sinoatrial node
3 right atrium
4 atria
5 atrioventricular node
6 Purkyne tissue

Chapter 9

Summary test 9.1a
1 C
2 goblet
3 bacteria; pollen; dust
4 bacteria; pollen; dust (any two)
5 cilia
6 bronchioles
7 smooth muscle
8 elastic fibres

Summary test 9.1b
1 bronchus / bronchi
2 collagen
3 contracts
4 bronchioles
5 mucous glands
6 sticky
7 cilia

Summary test 9.1c
1 100–300 μm
2 squamous epithelium
3 0.1–0.5 μm
4 thin
5 surface area
6 pulmonary
7 slowed; flattened
8 slowed; flattened

Summary test 9.1d
1 bronchioles
2 cartilage
3 bronchus / bronchi
4 bronchiole
5 alveoli
6 goblet cells

Chapter 10

Summary test 10.1a
1 pathogen
2 protoctists
3 viruses
4 bacterium
5 *Vibrio cholerae*

6 malaria
7 eukaryotic
8 tuberculosis / TB
9 virus

Summary test 10.1b

1 HIV-positive
2 opportunistic
3 immune
4 human immunodeficiency virus
5 ART/antiretroviral therapy
6 transmission
7 any three of: drug abusers sharing contaminated needles / sexual intercourse / transfusion of contaminated blood / mother to child during breastfeeding or in breastmilk / mother to child during birth /mother to child across the placenta
8 see 7
9 see 7

Summary test 10.1c

1 *Mycobacterium tuberculosis*
2 *Mycobacterium bovis*
3 air
4 inhales / breathes in / inspires
5 latent
6 over-crowded
7 HIV positive
8 Bacille-Calmette-Guerin / BCG
9 6–9
10 (multi-drug) resistant / MDR

Summary test 10.1d

1 *Vibrio cholerae*
2 faecal–oral
3 faeces / diarrhoea
4 water
5 glucose / sugar
6 oral rehydration solution (ORS)
7 vaccination
8 hygiene
9 treated / boiled / bottled / piped
10 (contaminated) sewage

Summary test 10.1e

1 Protoctista (protoctistan)
2 *Anopheles*
3 vector
4 blood
5 anticoagulant
6 larva / pupa
7 insecticide; oil
8 insecticide; oil
9 fish; bacteria (*Bacillus thuringiensis*)

10 fish; bacteria (*Bacillus thuringiensis*)
11 nets
12 insect repellent
13 indoor residual spraying
14 prophylactic

Summary test 10.2a

1 autolysins
2 stretch / expand
3 peptidoglycan (murein)
4 transpeptidase enzymes
5 peptide
6 osmotic lysis
7 penicillinase
8 mutation
9 plasmids
10 vertical transmission
11 horizontal transmission

Chapter 11

Summary test 11.1a

1 self
2 non-self
3 protein
4 phagocytosis
5 macrophages; neutrophils
6 macrophages; neutrophils
7 non-specific
8 receptors
9 phagosome / phagocytic vacuole
10 lysosomes

Summary test 11.1b

1 primary immune
2 activated / stimulated
3 macrophages
4 antigen-presenting
5 clonal expansion
6 plasma
7 antibodies
8 antibody-antigen
9 memory
10 immunity
11 secondary immune

Summary test 11.1c

1 viruses
2 cell-mediated
3 T-helper
4 cytokines
5 macrophages
6 phagocytosis
7 B-cells
8 plasma
9 T-killer (T-cytotoxic)

Summary test 11.2a

1 B
2 hybridoma
3 clone
4 diagnosing
5 herceptin
6 cytotoxic
7 globular
8 heavy
9 light
10 disulfide bonds
11 Fab
12 variable
13 hinge
14 phagocytes
15 phagocytosis

Summary test 11.2b

1 natural
2 passive
3 vaccination
4 natural passive
5 artificial active
6 artificial passive

Summary test 11.2c

1 protection/immunity
2 herd immunity
3 side-effects / allergic effects
4 freeze-dried
5 during war /during natural disasters / when vaccination programmes break down
6 malnourished
7 boosters

Chapter 12

Summary test 12.1a

1 work
2 kinetic
3 potential
4 anabolic
5 active transport
6 (high) body temperature
7 activation
8 light / sunlight / solar
9 organic
10 photosynthesis
11 respiration
12 ATP

Summary test 12.1b

1 adenosine triphosphate
2 universal
3 hydrolysed
4 30.5

5 small
6 water-soluble
7 turnover
8 reversible
9 store
10 phosphate
11 substrate-linked
12 chemiosmosis
13 electrochemical / proton / hydrogen ion
14 oxidative
15 photophosphorylation

Summary test 12.1c
1 respirometer
2 time (period)
3 soda lime
4 ratio
5 respiratory quotient / RQ
6 1.0
7 0.7
8 respiration in anaerobic conditions (anaerobic respiration)

Summary test 12.2a
1 cytoplasm
2 glucose
3 phosphate
4 ATP
5 fructose 1,6–bisphosphate
6 triose phosphate
7 hydrogen
8 NAD⁺ (nicotinamide adenine dinucleotide)
9 pyruvate
10 ATP

Summary test 12.2b
1 glycolysis
2 matrix
3 active transport
4 decarboxylation
5 dehydrogenation
6 acetyl coenzyme A
7 fatty acids
8 oxaloacetate
9 citrate
10 nicotinamide adenine dinucleotide (NAD⁺)

Summary test 12.2c
1 NAD
2 atoms
3 inner
4 energetic
5 electron transport chain
6 energy
7 intermembrane space
8 gradient

9 ATP synthase complex
10 energy
11 phosphorylation
12 oxygen
13 final
14 water

Summary test 12.2d
1 envelope
2 cristae
3 surface area
4 electron transport chain
5 ATP synthase
6 protons / hydrogen ions
7 electrochemical/proton
8 chemiosmosis / oxidative phosphorylation
9 matrix
10 enzymes
11 Krebs

Summary test 12.2e
1 two
2 lactate
3 lactate dehydrogenase
4 alcoholic
5 ethanal
6 carbon dioxide
7 NAD
8 Krebs
9 adapted
10 aerenchyma
11 oxygen
12 stem elongation / growth
13 ethene / ethylene
14 alcoholic fermentation

Summary test 12.2f
1 glucose
2 DCPIP
3 methylene blue
4 blue
5 colourless
6 reduced
7 1/*t*
8 digital / electronic water bath
9 temperature
10 substrate concentration
11 time taken to change from blue to colourless
12 respirometer

Chapter 13

Summary test 13.1a
1 $C_6H_{12}O_6$
2 carbon dioxide
3 sunlight / light / solar

4 light-dependent
5 reduced NADP
6 coenzyme
7 oxygen
8 (aerobic) respiration
9 Light-independent
10 carbon dioxide

Summary test 13.1b
1 palisade (mesophyll)
2 stomata
3 xylem
4 phloem
5 sugars / sucrose / assimilates / photosynthates / amino acids
6 envelope
7 small circular DNA; ribosomes
8 small circular DNA; ribosomes
9 stroma
10 light-independent
11 starch
12 thylakoids
13 grana
14 light-dependent
15 pigments
16 carriers
17 ATP synthase

Summary test 13.1c
1 chromatography
2 solvent
3 carotene
4 solvent front
5 distance travelled / migrated / moved
6 R_f
7 reference

Summary test 13.1d
1 magnesium
2 carotene
3 xanthophyll
4 special pair
5 accessory
6 energy
7 700
8 680

Summary test 13.1e
1 photolysis
2 oxygen-evolving complex
3 electrons
4 oxygen
5 photoactivation
6 higher
7 electron transport chain
8 ATP
9 non-cyclic
10 NADP

Summary test 13.1f

1 Calvin
2 ribulose bisphosphate (RuBP)
3 glycerate 3-phosphate (GP)
4 ATP; reduced NADP (NADPH + H$^+$)
5 ATP; reduced NADP (NADPH + H$^+$)
6 light-dependent
7 triose phosphate
8 glucose
9 starch
10 lipids
11 regenerated / recycled
12 ATP
13 GP / glycerate 3-phosphate

Summary test 13.2a

1 limiting factor
2 carbon dioxide
3 oxygen
4 light compensation point
5 0.04
6 0.1
7 linearly
8 light intensity
9 plateaus / becomes constant

Summary test 13.2b

1 light-dependent
2 methylene blue
3 redox
4 electron / hydrogen
5 NADP
6 blue-green
7 green
8 wavelengths
9 intensities

Summary test 13.2c

1 aquatic
2 oxygen
3 time
4 photosynthometer
5 distance
6 $1/d^2$
7 sodium hydrogen carbonate solution

Chapter 14

Summary test 14.1a

1 internal / cellular
2 changes / fluctuations
3 stimulus
4 receptor
5 control centre
6 effectors

7 glands
8 set-point / norm
9 negative feedback
10 endocrine

Summary test 14.1b

1 excretion
2 urea
3 amino
4 amino acids
5 toxic
6 liver
7 (fibrous) capsule
8 cortex
9 medulla
10 nephrons
11 renal artery
12 ureter

Summary test 14.1c

1 Bowman's (renal) capsule
2 glomerulus
3 afferent
4 podocytes
5 proximal
6 cuboid
7 microvilli
8 loop of Henlé
9 distal
10 collecting duct
11 peritubular

Summary test 14.1d

1 ultrafiltration
2 glomerulus
3 efferent
4 afferent
5 glomerular
6 urea
7 proximal convoluted tubule
8 selective reabsorption
9 sodium
10 facilitated diffusion
11 peritubular
12 concentration gradient
13 sodium–potassium
14 mitochondria
15 microvilli

Summary test 14.1e

1 osmoregulation
2 volume
3 solutes
4 glucose
5 loop of Henlé
6 collecting duct
7 lower
8 sodium
9 chloride

Summary test 14.1f

1 homeostatic (accept also negative feedback)
2 antidiuretic
3 collecting duct
4 sweating
5 decrease / become lower
6 hypothalamus
7 posterior pituitary
8 blood / circulatory system
9 permeability
10 urea
11 thirst
12 increases / rises
13 negative feedback

Summary test 14.1g

1 blood
2 target
3 permanent
4 steroids
5 complementary / specific
6 insulin
7 islets of Langerhans
8 α (alpha)
9 G-protein-coupled receptor
10 conformational
11 G-protein
12 adenylyl cyclase
13 cAMP / cyclic AMP
14 second
15 protein kinase A
16 enzyme cascade
17 amplification
18 phosphorylation
19 glycogen
20 glucose

Summary test 14.1h

1 respiratory substrate
2 90–100
3 homeostasis
4 brain
5 osmotic
6 carbohydrates
7 glycogen
8 muscle
9 amino acids
10 gluconeogenesis
11 glycogen
12 respiration
13 endocrine
14 islets of Langerhans
15 smaller
16 insulin
17 lower / reduce / fall/decrease
18 glucagon
19 antagonistically

20 (skeletal) muscle
21 specific transport proteins /
transporters / GLUT4 transporters
22 respiration / formation of glycogen
or glycogenesis
23 respiration / formation of glycogen
or glycogenesis
24 concentration

Summary test 14.1i
1 oxygen
2 glucose oxidase
3 gluconic acid
4 test strip
5 hydrogen donor
6 peroxidase
7 semi-quantitative
8 biosensors
9 blood
10 immobilised
11 biological recognition layer
12 diffuses

Summary test 14.2a
1 carbon dioxide; water vapour
2 carbon dioxide; water vapour
3 ATP synthase
4 chloroplasts
5 active transport
6 potassium (K^+)
7 solute
8 reduces/decreases/becomes more
negative
9 turgid
10 stress hormone
11 calcium

Chapter 15

Summary test 15.1a
1 response
2 sensory receptor
3 effector
4 electrical
5 impulses
6 endocrine
7 chemical
8 short
9 long-term / permanent / irreversible
10 target
11 receptors
12 peptide / shorter-chain amino acid
13 water
14 (neurosecretory cells of the)
hypothalamus
15 (islets of Langerhans of the) pancreas
16 ductless

Summary test 15.1b
1 cell body
2 Nissl's granules
3 axon
4 myelin sheath
5 Schwann
6 dendrites
7 sensory receptors
8 central nervous
9 motor / effector
10 muscles
11 intermediate / relay

Summary test 15.1c
1 perception
2 dissolved chemicals
3 receptor
4 transducers
5 generator
6 action potential
7 all or nothing
8 specific
9 sodium
10 channel proteins / ion
channels / ion channel proteins
11 microvilli
12 depolarise
13 calcium
14 vesicles
15 sensory
16 neurotransmitter

Summary test 15.1d
1 electrical
2 −50 to −90
3 −65
4 polarised
5 positively
6 40
7 depolarised
8 sodium
9 potassium
10 absolute
11 relative
12 stimulus
13 frequency

Summary test 15.1e
1 myelinated
2 Schwann
3 insulates
4 depolarisation
5 Ranvier
6 local circuits
7 saltatory
8 transmission

Summary test 15.1f
1 dendrite
2 cleft
3 20–30
4 presynaptic
5 neurotransmitter
6 synaptic vesicles
7 postsynaptic
8 unidirectional

Summary test 15.1g
1 calcium
2 synaptic vesicles
3 exocytosis
4 synaptic cleft
5 sodium
6 diffusion
7 excitatory postsynaptic
8 action potential

Summary test 15.1h
1 muscle fibre
2 multinucleate
3 protein
4 actin
5 sarcomere
6 Z
7 I
8 A
9 motor / effector
10 neuromuscular junction / motor
end plate
11 neurotransmitter / acetylcholine
12 postsynaptic
membrane / sarcolemma

Summary test 15.1i
1 A-band
2 myosin
3 actin
4 head
5 filament
6 globular
7 actin
8 troponin

Summary test 15.1j
1 pumped / actively transported
2 sarcoplasmic reticulum
3 presynaptic / motor neurone
4 neuromuscular
5 acetylcholine / neurotransmitter
6 transverse system/T
7 sarcoplasmic reticulum
8 troponin
9 tropomyosin
10 myosin
11 ATP

Summary test 15.2

1 lobes
2 trigger hairs / trigger hair cells / hair cells
3 electrical
4 action potential
5 hinge cells / midrib cells
6 turgid
7 concave
8 elongation
9 hydrogen ions
10 acidic / acidified / have a decreased pH
11 expansins
12 turgor
13 gibberellin
14 embryo
15 aleurone layer
16 DELLA proteins
17 α-amylase
18 endosperm

Chapter 16

Summary test 16.1a

1 somatic
2 diploid
3 gametes
4 haploid
5 fertilisation
6 restored
7 homologous
8 centromere
9 positions / loci
10 banding
11 maternal
12 nucleus
13 four
14 reduction
15 halved
16 genetically

Summary test 16.1b

1 prophase I
2 spindle
3 bivalents
4 half
5 crossing over / crossover
6 non-sister chromatids
7 chiasmata
8 spindle equator / equator / metaphase plate
9 anaphase I
10 haploid
11 mitotic
12 centromeres

13 sister chromatids
14 poles

Summary test 16.1c

1 prophase I
2 crossing over
3 breaks
4 non-sister
5 variation
6 metaphase I
7 orientate / arrange
8 randomly
9 random orientation / random assortment / independent assortment
10 alleles
11 fusion / fertilisation

Summary test 16.2a

1 genotype
2 mutation
3 phenotype
4 alleles
5 nucleotides
6 polypeptide
7 homozygous
8 heterozygous
9 recessive
10 codominant

Summary test 16.2b

1 upper
2 lower
3 recessive
4 encircled / put in a circle
5 Punnett square
6 monohybrid
7 first filial / F_1
8 green
9 second filial / F_2
10 green
11 yellow

Summary test 16.2c

1 phenotype
2 heterozygous; homozygous dominant
3 heterozygous; homozygous dominant
4 test
5 homozygous recessive
6 alleles
7 heterozygous
8 homozygous dominant
9 large / greater

Summary test 16.2d

1 heterozygous
2 phenotype

3 100
4 1:2:1
5 50%
6 multiple
7 recessive

Summary test 16.2e

1 dihybrid
2 dominant
3 recessive
4 recessive
5 dominant
6 round
7 yellow
8 alleles
9
10
11
12 (RY); (Ry); (rY); (ry)
(correct 4 gametes in any order)
13 round
14 yellow
15 wrinkled
16 green
17 round
18 yellow
19 wrinkled
20 yellow

Summary test 16.2f

1 X chromosome
2 sons
3 Y
4 carriers
5 linked
6 crossing over / cross over events / recombination
7 parental
8 recombinant
9 3:1

Summary test 16.2g

1 white/albino
2 agouti
3 AaBb; Aabb
4 AaBb; Aabb (correct 2 genotypes in any order)
5 AABb; AAbb; aaBb; aabb
6 AABb; AAbb; aaBb; aabb
7 AABb; AAbb; aaBb; aabb

8 AABb; AAbb; aaBb; aabb (correct 4 genotypes in any order)

9 3

10 4

Summary test 16.2h

1 expected
2 significant
3 chance
4 degrees of freedom
5 classes
6 critical
7 0.05
8 higher
9 null hypothesis

Summary test 16.2i

1 *HBB*
2 β-globin
3 base substitution
4 valine
5 glutamic acid
6 globular
7 sticky / fibrous
8 sickle shaped / crescent shaped
9 oxygen
10 *TYR*
11 tyrosinase
12 melanin
13 recessive
14 albinism
15 haemophilia (A)
16 sex- / X-
17 blood to clot

Summary test 16.2j

1 dominant
2 huntingtin
3 CAG
4 homozygous recessive
5 cognitive
6 behavioural
7 *Le/le* or *Le*
8 GA 3β-hydroxylase
9 gibberellin
10 stem elongation
11 recessive
12 dwarf / short

Summary test 16.3a

1 repressible
2 inducible
3 repressor
4 transcription / gene expression
5 promoter
6 RNA polymerase
7 operator
8 allolactose
9 mRNA

10 β-galactosidase; lactose permease; transacetylase
11 β-galactosidase; lactose permease; transacetylase
12 β-galactosidase; lactose permease; transacetylase

Summary test 16.3b

1 nucleus
2 DNA
3 off
4 RNA polymerase
5 transcription/expression
6 mRNA
7 translation
8 gibberellins
9 DELLA
10 inhibit

Chapter 17

Summary test 17.1a

1 environment
2 genotype
3 enzyme
4 melanin
5 (recessive) allele
6 above
7 extremities / tips / any suitable example
8 black / dark
9 altitude
10 height / number of leaves / overall size / shape / survival rate (*any two*)
11 height / number of leaves / overall size / shape / survival rate (*any two*)
12 genotype
13 range / extent / limit
14 environment

Summary test 17.1b

1 height; mass
2 height; mass
3 normal distribution curve
4 polygenes
5 environment
6 one / a single
7 blood groups / albinism / sickle cell anaemia / Huntington's disease / haemophilia
8 mutation
9 prophase I
10 recombinants
11 random orientation / independent assortment

12 metaphase I
13 mating
14 species
15 fusion / fertilisation

Summary test 17.1c

1 mean
2 significant
3 30
4 continuous
5 normally
6 standard deviation
7 mean
8 95

Summary test 17.1d

1 mean
2 deviation
3 $v = (n_1 + n_2) - 2$
4 critical
5 0.05
6 reject

Summary test 17.2a

1 Alfred Wallace
2 more
3 constant / stable
4 intraspecific (competition)
5 genetically
6 adaptations
7 reproduce / breed
8 alleles
9 conditions
10 selection
11 population

Summary test 17.2b

1 phenotypes
2 stabilising selection
3 constant
4 disruptive
5 directional
6 stabilising
7 stabilising

Summary test 17.2c

1 gene pools
2 advantageous / beneficial
3 reproduce / breed
4 random / chance
5 predicted / calculated
6 bottleneck
7 genetic diversity / size of gene pool / genetic variation
8 founder

Summary test 17.2d

1 gene pool
2 frequency
3 Hardy–Weinberg

4 isolated/large
5 isolated/large
6 selection/mutations
7 selection/mutations
8 random
9 10.9% / 0.109
   ($p + q = 1.0$ and $p = 0.942$
   Therefore $q = 1.0 - 0.942 = 0.058$
   Frequency of the heterozygous
   genotype = $2pq$
   = $2 \times 0.942 \times 0.058$
   = 0.109
   As a %, $0.109 \times 100 = 10.9\%$)

Summary test 17.2e
1 artificial selection
2 lowered / less / reduced
3 heterozygotes
4 inbreeding / outbreeding
5 inbreeding / outbreeding
6 pedigree
7 progeny testing
8 vagina/uterus
9 artificial insemination
10 embryo transplantation

Summary test 17.2f
1 crop yield
2 genome
3 rice
4 inbreeding
5 closely related
6 genotypes
7 inbreeding depression
8 hybridisation
9 inbred
10 taller
11 resistant
12 variety
13 phenotype/uniformity

Summary test 17.3a
1 evolution
2 pre-existing
3 gene pool(s)
4 generations
5 natural selection
6 selection pressures
7 alleles
8 adapted / suited
9 Tree of Life
10 ancestor
11 evolutionary relationships
12 DNA sequence
13 mutations
14 evolutionary
15 closely related

Summary test 17.3b
1 speciation
2 reproductively
3 deme
4 adaptive radiation
5 allele frequencies
6 species
7 allopatric
8 sympatric
9 prezygotic; postzygotic
10 prezygotic; postzygotic

Summary test 17.3c
1 mutations
2 (ecological) niches
3 reproductively isolated
4 species
5 xeromorphic
6 cuticle
7 root
8 stomata
9 loops of Henlé
10 urine

Chapter 18

Summary test 18.1a
1 biological species concept
2 reproductively
3 fertile
4 morphological species concept
5 ecological
6 (ecological) niche
7 ecological species
8 taxon
9 kingdom
10 order
11 genera

Summary test 18.1b
1 eukaryotic
2 heterotrophically
3 hyphae
4 mycelium
5 chitin
6 chlorophyll
7 autotrophically
8 cellulose
9 starch
10 glycogen
11 nervous system

Summary test 18.2a
1 individuals
2 community
3 habitats
4 genetic

5 stable
6 climatic
7 tropical rain forest
8 arctic tundra / hot desert
9 mineral nutrients
10 self-contained
11 area
12 biotic
13 abiotic
14 niche
15 role

Summary test 18.2b
1 ecology
2 biosphere
3 food webs
4 trophic
5 community
6 population
7 habitat

Summary test 18.2c
1 density
2 abundant/common/frequent
3 cover
4 seashore
5 interrupted/ladder
6 mark–release–recapture
7 1600 ($100 \times 80 \div 5$)

Summary test 18.2d
1 correlation
2 ordinal
3 at random / randomly
4 equal chance
5 five
6 negative correlation
7 no correlation
8 null hypothesis

Summary test 18.2e
1 continuous
2 linear
3 five
4 ten
5 negative
6 Simpson's
7 lower species diversity

Summary test 18.3a
1 river banks
2 deforestation
3 degradation
4 rabbits
5 competition
6 hunting
7 climate change / global warming
8 coastal
9 coral

Summary test 18.3b

1 protect
2 natural resources
3 stability
4 erosion
5 desertification
6 gene pool
7 medicines
8 ecotourism
9 cultural
10 CITES / Convention on International Trade in Endangered Species of Wild Fauna and Flora
11 fungal
12 The IUCN Red List of Threatened Species™
13 nine
14 Critically Endangered

Summary test 18.3c

1 conserved
2 wardens
3 research
4 educated / taught / informed
5 captive breeding
6 embryos
7 frozen zoos
8 seed banks
9 moisture
10 −18 to −20
11 deep-freeze
12 viability
13 restocked

Summary test 18.3d

1 assisted
2 IVF / in vitro fertilisation
3 gonadotrophins
4 oocytes
5 fertilised
6 embryos
7 embryo transfer
8 surrogate / surrogate mother
9 alien
10 outcompete
11 predators

Chapter 19

Summary test 19.1a

1 recombinant DNA
2 genetically modified organism
3 characteristics
4 protein
5 restriction endonuclease
6 nucleotide / oligonucleotide
7 messenger RNA / mRNA

8 transcribed
9 reverse transcriptase
10 complementary DNA / cDNA
11 DNA polymerase
12 size
13 wells
14 agarose
15 DC / direct current
16 electric field
17 negatively
18 phosphate
19 buffer
20 anode
21 larger / longer
22 smaller / shorter
23 ladder
24 UV / ultraviolet

Summary test 19.1b

1 automated
2 thermocycler
3 95°C
4 separate
5 55°C
6 complementary bases
7 rejoining
8 72°C
9 (complementary) nucleotides
10 2

Summary test 19.1c

1 circular
2 bacterial
3 endonucleases / enzymes
4 recognition sites
5 sticky ends
6 enzyme / restriction enzyme / restriction endonuclease
7 (DNA) ligase
8 sugar–phosphate
9 recombinant
10 vector

Summary test 19.1d

1 recombinant
2 calcium
3 competent
4 sequences / lengths / sections
5 marker
6 *GFP* / green fluorescent protein
7 green
8 blue / UV / ultraviolet
9 RNA polymerase
10 transcription

Summary test 19.1e

1 addition
2 genome
3 endonuclease / nuclease

4 RNA
5 complementary
6 Cas9 / endonuclease / nuclease / the cutting protein
7 TALEN / ZFN
8 DNA-binding
9 DNA probes
10 mRNA
11 single
12 complementary
13 reverse transcriptase
14 fluorescent tag / fluorescent dye
15 laser scan
16 high intensity of fluorescence
17 denatured

Summary test 19.1f

1 bioinformatics
2 analyse / organise
3 sequences
4 internet
5 search tools
6 data mining

Summary test 19.2a

1 insulin dependent
2 β
3 islets of Langerhans / pancreas
4 autoimmune
5 protein
6 exact / identical
7 rapid
8 immune / allergic
9 infections / diseases
10 cheaper
11 tolerance / insensitivity
12 ethically / morally / socially
13 haemophilia
14 adenosine deaminase
15 blood donations
16 cows / bovine sources
17 immune

Summary test 19.2b

1 genetic counselling
2 expert
3 foetus / fetus
4 not knowing / uncertainty
5 decisions / choices
6 *BRCA1* and *BRCA2*
7 tumour suppressor proteins
8 mastectomy
9 abnormalities / lumps / tumorous growths
10 1 in 2 / 50% / 0.5
11 recessive
12 breathing
13 mucus

14 carrier

15 IVF / in vitro fertilisation

16 embryos

Summary test 19.2c

1 severe combined immunodeficiency disease

2 stem cells

3 bone marrow

4 transforming / genetically modifying

5 vector

6 retrovirus

7 *ADA*

8 *IL2RG*

9 B-

10 T-

11 recessive

12 blindness

13 adeno-associated virus

14 *RPE65*

Summary test 19.3a

1 post-emergence

2 weeds

3 competition

4 oil

5 protein

6 toxin

7 insecticide / pesticide

8 bees

9 cottonseed

10 quality

11 growth-regulating

12 Chinook salmon

13 promoter

14 18 months / half the time

Summary test 19.3b

1 cold / salt / polluted soil (*any one*)

2 cold / salt / polluted soil (*any one*)

3 herbicide

4 yield / productivity

5 rice

6 A

7 blindness

8 virus

9 pollen

10 metabolic

11 antibiotic resistance

12 pathogenic / disease-causing / harmful

13 patent

14 genome

Glossary

abiotic an ecological factor that makes up part of the non-biological environment of an organism. Examples include temperature, pH, rainfall and humidity. See also *biotic*.

absorption spectrum a graph that results from plotting the degree of absorption of light of different wavelengths by a pigment such as chlorophyll.

acetylcholine one of a group of chemicals, called *neurotransmitters*, released an *axon*. It diffuses across the gap (*synapse*) between adjacent neurones and so passes an impulse from one neurone to the next.

action potential change that occurs in the electrical charge across the membrane of an *axon* when it is stimulated and a nerve impulse passes.

action spectrum graph displaying the proportion of each wavelength of light that is used in a process such as photosynthesis.

actin filamentous protein which is involved in contraction within cells, especially muscle cells. See also *myosin*.

activation energy energy required to bring about a reaction. The activation energy is lowered by the presence of enzymes.

active immunity protection from infection, so that the person does not become ill: it results from an immune response involving the production of memory cells to give long-term protection.

active site a group of amino acids that makes up the region of an enzyme into which the substrate fits in order to catalyse a reaction.

active transport movement of a substance from a region where it is in a low concentration to a region where it is in a high concentration. The process requires the expenditure of energy.

adenosine triphosphate (ATP) an activated *nucleotide* found in all living cells that acts as an energy carrier. The *hydrolysis* of ATP leads to the formation of adenosine diphosphate (ADP) and inorganic phosphate, with the release of energy.

adhesion attraction between the molecules of different types such as between water molecules and cellulose molecules. See also *cohesion*.

adipose tissue a form of connective tissue that is made up of cells storing large amounts of fat.

adrenaline a hormone produced by the adrenal glands in times of stress that prepares the body for an emergency.

aerobic connected with the presence of free oxygen. Aerobic respiration requires free oxygen to release energy from glucose and other foods. See also *anaerobic*.

aleurone layer protein-rich layer beneath the testa of a cereal seed that makes amylase during germination.

allele one of a number of alternative *nucleotide* sequences at a single gene *locus*. For example, the gene for the shape of pea seeds has two alleles, one for 'round' and one for 'wrinkled'.

allergen a normally harmless substance that causes the immune system to produce an immune response.

allopatric speciation the formation of a new species as a result of *populations* of a parent species becoming geographically isolated. See also *sympatric speciation*.

anabolism an energy-requiring process of metabolism in which small molecules are combined to make larger ones.

anaerobic connected with the absence of free oxygen. Anaerobic respiration releases energy from glucose or other foods without the presence of free oxygen. See also *aerobic*.

anion negatively charged *ion* that is attracted to the anode during electrolysis. See also *cation*.

antibiotic a substance produced by one kind of microorganism that inhibits the growth of, or kills, another.

antibiotic resistance the development in microorganisms of mechanisms that prevent *antibiotics* from killing them.

antibody a *glycoprotein* produced by a plasma cell in response to the presence of the appropriate *antigen*.

antidiuretic hormone (ADH) a hormone produced by the *hypothalamus* that passes to the posterior *pituitary gland* from where it is secreted. ADH reduces the amount of water in urine by increasing water reabsorption in the kidneys.

antigen a molecule that is recognised by the body as *non-self* and triggers an *immune response*.

antioxidant chemical which reduces or prevents *oxidation*. Often used as an additive to prolong the shelf-life of certain foods.

apoplast pathway route through the cell walls and intercellular spaces of plants by which water and dissolved substances are transported. See also *symplast pathway*.

aquaporin integral protein that forms a water channel in cell surface membranes. It selectively conducts water molecules through the membrane while preventing ions and other solutes from doing so.

artefact feature that is not naturally present but produced during preparation of a section.

artificial immunity protection against infection, where the person does not become ill, acquired as a result of the deliberate exposure of the body to *antibodies* or *antigens* in non-natural circumstances, e.g. *vaccination*.

ATP see *adenosine triphosphate*.

atrioventricular node (AV node) area of muscle between the atria and ventricles of the heart that plays an important role in coordinating the heartbeat.

autosome a *chromosome* that is not a sex chromosome.

autotrophic nutrition form of feeding in which an organism uses energy from light or chemicals to build up complex organic molecules from simple inorganic substances. See also *heterotrophic nutrition*.

auxin a *plant growth regulator* that affects plant growth by stimulating cell division and enlargement.

axon a process extending from a *neurone* that conducts *action potentials* away from the cell body.

Benedict's test a simple biochemical reaction to detect the presence of reducing sugars.

biodiversity the range and variety of living organisms within a particular region. The term can also be applied to ecosystems, habitats, and genetic variation within species.

biomass the total mass of living material, normally measured in a specific area over a given period of time.

biosensor a device that uses biological molecules to measure the levels of certain chemicals.

biosphere the life-supporting layer of land, air and water that surrounds the Earth.

biotic an ecological factor that makes up part of the living environment of an organism. Examples include food availability, competition and predation. See also *abiotic*.

Biuret test a simple biochemical reaction to detect the presence of protein.

B lymphocyte type of white blood cell that is produced and matures within the bone marrow. B lymphocytes produce *antibodies* as part of their role in *immunity*. See also *T lymphocyte*.

Bohr effect the reduced affinity of *haemoglobin* for oxygen in the presence of carbon dioxide.

Bowman's capsule see *renal capsule*.

buffer solution with the ability to absorb hydrogen *ions* and which therefore does not significantly change its pH when moderate amounts of acid or alkali are added.

Calvin cycle a biochemical pathway that forms part of the *light independent reaction* of photosynthesis during which carbon dioxide is reduced to form carbohydrate.

cambium dividing layer of cells in higher plants, parallel to the surface of stems and roots, which produces new cells leading to an increase in their diameter.

cancer a disease resulting from *mutations* that leads to uncontrolled cell division and the eventual formation of a group of abnormal cells called a tumour, from which cells may break away (*metastasis*) and form secondary tumours elsewhere in the body.

cardiac cycle a continuous series of events which make up a single heartbeat.

cardiac muscle type of muscle found only in the heart that can contract and relax continuously throughout life without stimulation by nerve impulses. See also *smooth muscle*.

cardiac output the total volume of blood which the heart can pump each minute. It is calculated as the volume of blood pumped at each beat (*stroke volume*) multiplied by the number of heart beats per minute (heart rate).

carrier protein (carrier molecule) a protein that helps to transport molecules across the plasma membrane.

cartilage flexible supporting tissue found at the end of bones and between vertebrae, where it cushions the shocks and jolts that occur during movement.

Casparian strip a distinctive band of suberin around the endodermal cells of a plant root which prevents water passing into *xylem vessels* via the cell walls. The water is forced through the living part (protoplast) of the endodermal cells.

catabolism chemical reactions of metabolism involving the breakdown of large molecules.

cation positively charged *ion* which is attracted to the cathode during electrolysis. See also *anion*.

cell signalling the means by which cells interact with the environment or with the cells around them.

cellular material includes whole organisms, organs, tissues or individual cells.

centrifugation process of separating out particles of different sizes and densities by spinning them at high speed in a centrifuge.

channel protein water-filled channel in protein molecules of the cell surface membrane for the diffusion of water-soluble ions.

chemiosmosis the synthesis of *ATP* in mitochondria and chloroplasts using energy that is stored as a hydrogen *ion* concentration gradient across a membrane.

chitin tough, nitrogen-containing polysaccharide that forms the walls of fungi and the exoskeleton of insects.

chloride shift the movement of negatively charged chloride *ions* from the plasma into red blood cells to replace the loss of negatively charged hydrogencarbonate ions during the transport of carbon dioxide. In this way the overall electrochemical neutrality of the red blood cells is maintained.

cholesterol lipid occurring in large quantities in the brain, spinal cord and liver. It is an intermediate in the formation of vitamin D and steroid hormones.

chromatid one of the two identical structures formed after DNA replication in late interphase, joined at the centromere to make the chromosome that becomes visible during prophase of mitosis and meiosis.

chromatin the diffuse material that comprises chromosomes in their decondensed state. It consists of DNA and proteins, especially *histones*.

chromatography technique by which substances in a mixture are separated according to their different solubilities in a solvent.

chromosome a cell structure made of linear DNA complexed with histone proteins by which hereditary information is physically passed from one generation to the next.

cilium (plural **cilia**) short projection from the surface of a *eukaryotic cell* that has an internal 9 + 2 arrangement of microtubules.

clone a group of genetically identical organisms formed from a single parent as the result of asexual reproduction or by artificial means.

cloning the act of propagating (an organism or cell) as a clone.

codominance condition in which both alleles for one gene in a *heterozygous* organism are expressed and so contribute to the *phenotype*.

codon a sequence of three adjacent *nucleotides* in mRNA that codes for one amino acid.

cohesion attraction between molecules of the same type. It is important in the movement of water up the plant. See also *adhesion*.

collagen fibrous protein that is the main constituent of connective tissues such as *tendons, cartilage* and bone.

collenchyma plant tissue which has cell walls thickened by cellulose especially in the corners. It provides mechanical support, especially in young stems and leaves.

colloidal describes a mixture consisting of microscopic particles evenly dispersed throughout another substance.

community all the *populations* of different species within a particular area at a given time.

complementary DNA DNA which is made from messenger RNA using the enzyme *reverse transcriptase* in a process which is the reverse of normal *transcription*.

condensation reaction chemical process in which two molecules combine to form a more complex one with the elimination of a simple substance, usually water. Many biological *polymers*, such as polysaccharides and polypeptides, are formed by *condensation reactions*. See also *hydrolysis*.

conjugation the transfer of DNA from one cell to another by means of a thin tube between the two.

conservation method of maintaining *ecosystems* and the living organisms that occupy them. It requires planning and organisation to make best use of resources while preserving the natural landscape and wildlife.

consumer *heterotrophic* organism that obtains energy by eating or decomposing other organisms. Herbivores feed on plants and are known as primary consumers and carnivores feeding on herbivores are known as secondary consumers. See also *producer*.

continuous variation variation in which measurements of any one characteristic do not fall into distinct categories, but rather there are gradations from one extreme to the other, e.g. height in humans. See also *discontinuous variation*.

cotyledon an embryonic leaf found in the seed of a plant.

counter-current system a mechanism by which the efficiency of exchange between two substances is increased by having them flowing in opposite directions.

covalent bond type of chemical bond in which two atoms share a pair of *electrons*, one from each atom.

crossing over the process whereby a *chromatid* breaks during *meiosis* I and rejoins to the chromatid of its *homologous chromosome* so that their *alleles* are exchanged.

cuticle exposed non-cellular outer layer of certain animals and the leaves of plants. It is waxy and therefore helps to reduce water loss.

cystic fibrosis inherited *disease* in which the body produces abnormally thick mucus that obstructs breathing passages and prevents secretion of pancreatic enzymes. It is a *recessive* condition that leads to production of a non-functioning membrane protein needed to transport chloride *ions*.

cytokines chemicals secreted by T helper cells that stimulate an *immune response* in other white blood cells.

deamination removal of an amino group ($-NH_2$) from a compound, particularly an amino acid.

decomposer a saprobiontic organism that breaks down the organic matter of dead organisms and waste products to form water, carbon dioxide and inorganic *ions*.

denaturation permanent changes due to the breaking of one or more types of bond that maintain the three-dimensional structure of a protein as a result of factors such as changes in temperature or pH.

denatured see *denaturation*.

dendrite a process, usually branched, extending from the cell body of a *neurone* that conducts impulses toward the cell body.

depolarisation temporary reversal of charges on the axon membrane of a *neurone* that takes place when a nerve impulse is transmitted.

desertification process by which a desert slowly spreads into neighbouring areas of semi desert.

diabetes metabolic disorder in which there is abnormal thirst and the production of large amounts of urine. Diabetes mellitus is caused by a reduction or absence of insulin production by the pancreas or insensitivity of insulin receptors on cells, leading to changes in the blood glucose level.

diastole the stage in the *cardiac cycle* when the heart muscle relaxes. See also *systole*.

dicotyledonous plants any member of the class of flowering plants called Dicotyledonae. Their features include: having two seed leaves (cotyledons), broad leaves, flower parts in rings of four or five, and vascular tissue arranged in a ring in stems. See also *monocotyledonous plants*.

diffusion the net movement of molecules or ions from a region where they are in high concentration to one where their concentration is lower.

diploid a term applied to *eukaryotic* cells in which the nucleus contains two sets of *chromosomes*. See also *haploid*.

directional selection selection that operates towards one extreme in a range of variation.

disease an abnormal condition affecting an organism and reducing the effectiveness of its functions.

discontinuous variation variation shown when different forms or phenotypes for any one characteristic fall into distinct categories, e.g. blood groups in humans. See also *continuous variation*.

disulfide bonds S–S bonds between two cysteine amino acids that are important in maintaining the structure of proteins.

DNA probe a single strand of DNA used to identify a particular *gene*.

DNA helicase enzyme that acts on a specific region of the DNA molecule to break the *hydrogen bonds* between the bases causing the two strands to separate and expose the *nucleotide* bases in that region.

DNA replication the process in which the double helix of a DNA molecule unwinds and each strand acts as a template on which a new strand is constructed.

dominant allele an *allele* that is always expressed in the *phenotype* of an organism even when present with an allele that is *recessive* to it.

ecological niche role of a species within its *community*. It includes what the species is like, where it occurs, how it behaves, its interactions with other species and how it responds to the *abiotic* environment.

ecology study of the interrelationships of organisms with each other and their environment.

ecosystem all the living (*biotic*) and non-living (*abiotic*) components of a particular area interacting together to make one functional unit.

electron negatively charged sub-atomic particle that orbits the positively charged nucleus of all atoms. See also *proton*.

element one of just over 100 substances that cannot be split into simpler substances by chemical means.

emulsion test a test for lipids.

endemic describes any *disease* that occurs regularly in a particular region or amongst a particular *population*. See also *epidemic* and *pandemic*.

endocrine gland a gland with cells which secrete a hormone into the blood at a distance from the hormone's target organ.

endocytosis the inward transport of large molecules through the cell surface membrane. See also *exocytosis*.

endergonic a chemical reaction in which the products contain more energy than the reactants so that, if the reaction is to proceed, free energy must be provided from outside. See also *exergonic*.

endosperm a storage tissue found in the seeds of plants such as cereals.

endotherm an animal which uses physiological processes to maintain its body temperature at a more or less constant level. Birds and mammals are endotherms.

environment the external conditions, resources and stimuli with which organisms interact.

epidemic describes any disease that rapidly spreads through a population to affect a large number of individuals. See also *endemic* and *pandemic*.

epidemiology the study of the spread of disease and the factors that affect this spread.

epidermis the outermost layer of cells in a multicellular organism.

epithelial cells cells covering the external and internal surfaces of animals.

essential amino acid an amino acid that cannot be synthesised by the human body and which must therefore be included in the diet.

eugenics human improvement by the controlling the production of offspring.

eukaryote an organism whose cells have a membrane-bound nucleus that contains *chromosomes*. The cells also possess a variety of other membranous organelles such as mitochondria and endoplasmic reticulum. See also *prokaryote*.

excretion the removal of metabolic waste products from the body.

exergonic a chemical reaction in which the products contain less free energy than the reactants and so free energy is released during the reaction. See also *endergonic*.

exocytosis the bulk transport of materials out of cells by cytoplasmic vesicles fusing with the cell surface membrane and releasing their contents to the outside. See also *endocytosis*.

facilitated diffusion diffusion down a concentration gradient through cell membranes using specific protein carrier channels.

flagellum (plural **flagella**) long, whip-like extension of a cell used as a means of locomotion.

gel electrophoresis technique for separating a mixture of charged particles in a gel, by applying a voltage across the fluid. It is used in the analysis of mixtures of substances, especially proteins.

gene sequence of *nucleotides* on a DNA molecule coding for a specific polypeptide. It is now known that some genes may code for more than one polypeptide.

gene marker a gene used as a label in genetic engineering because its effects can be easily recognised.

gene pool total number of *alleles* in a particular *population* at a specific time.

gene technology general term that covers the processes by which *genes* are manipulated, altered or transferred from organism to organism. Also known as *genetic engineering*.

gene therapy a mechanism by which genetic *diseases* such as *cystic fibrosis* may be cured or treated by masking the effect of the defective *gene* by inserting a functional gene.

generator potential *depolarisation* of the membrane of a receptor cell as a result of a stimulus.

genetically modified organism (GMO) organism that has had its DNA altered as a result of *gene technology*.

genetic engineering see *gene technology*.

genome all of the genetic material of an organism.

genotype the genetic composition of an organism.

global warming the recent increase in average temperatures at the Earth's surface, thought to be the result of the increased production of *greenhouse gases* such as carbon dioxide and methane. These gases help to trap solar radiation at or near the Earth's surface.

gibberellins *plant growth regulators* that stimulate cell division, stem elongation and germination.

glomerulus a cluster of blood capillaries enclosed by the *renal (Bowman's) capsule* in the kidney.

glucagon a hormone produced by α cells of the *islets of Langerhans* in the pancreas that increases blood glucose levels by initiating the breakdown of glycogen to glucose.

glycolysis first part of cellular respiration in which glucose is broken down anaerobically in the cytoplasm to two molecules of pyruvate.

glycoprotein substance made up of a carbohydrate molecule and a protein molecule. Part of the cell surface membrane and certain hormones are glycoproteins.

goblet cell mucus-producing cell found in the epithelium of the intestines and bronchi, so called because its shape resembles a wine glass or goblet.

granum (plural **grana**) a stack of *thylakoids* in a chloroplast that resembles a pile of coins.

greenhouse gases gases such as methane and carbon dioxide which in the atmosphere cause more heat energy to be trapped, so raising the temperature at the Earth's surface.

gross primary production the total energy production in the form of *biomass* made by *producers* (plants) during photosynthesis. It is normally expressed as the biomass per unit area in unit time. See also *net primary production*.

guard cell one of a pair of cells that surround a *stoma* in plant leaves and control its opening and closing.

habitat the place where an organism normally lives and which is characterised by physical conditions and the types of other organisms present.

haemoglobin globular protein in mammalian blood that readily combines with oxygen to transport it around the body. It comprises four polypeptide chains around an iron-containing haem group. See also *myoglobin*.

haploid term referring to *eukaryotic* cells that contain only a single copy of each *homologous chromosome* e.g. the sex cells or gametes.

health a person's mental or physical condition.

herbaceous term applied to non-woody plants.

heterotrophic nutrition form of feeding in which the organism consumes complex organic material. See also *autotrophic nutrition*.

heterozygous condition in which the *alleles* at a particular *gene locus* of a *diploid* cell are different.

histones proteins associated with the DNA in *chromosomes*. Their function is to condense *chromatin* and coil the chromosomes during cell division.

homeostasis the maintenance of a more or less constant internal environment despite fluctuations in the external environment and involving negative feedback mechanisms.

homologous chromosomes a pair of *chromosomes*, one maternal and one paternal, that have the same gene loci and therefore determine the same features. They are not necessarily identical, however, as individual *alleles* of the same *gene* may vary, e.g. one chromosome may carry the allele for normal haemoglobin (*HbA*), the other the allele for sickle cell haemoglobin (*HbS*). Homologous chromosomes are capable of pairing during *meiosis* I.

homozygous condition in which the *alleles* at a particular *gene locus* of a *diploid* cell are identical.

homozygous dominant describes a homozygous organism with two dominant alleles.

homozygous recessive describes a homozygous organism with two recessive alleles.

human genome all of the DNA sequences on the *chromosomes* of a single human cell.

hydrogen bond chemical bond formed between the positive charge on a hydrogen atom and the negative charge on another atom of an adjacent molecule, e.g. between the hydrogen atom of one water molecule and the oxygen atom of an adjacent water molecule.

hydrolysis the breaking down of large molecules into smaller ones by the addition of water molecules. See also *condensation reaction*.

hypertonic a solution that has a higher solute concentration, and therefore a lower water potential, than another solution. See also *hypotonic*.

hyphae thread-like structures that make up the body mass of a fungus.

hypothalamus region of the brain adjoining the *pituitary gland* that acts as the control centre for the *autonomic nervous system* and regulates body temperature, fluid balance, thirst, hunger and sexual activity.

hypotonic a solution that has a lower solute concentration, and therefore a higher water potential, than another solution. See also *hypertonic*.

immune response the complex series of reactions of the body to an *antigen* by which the body protects itself from infection.

immunisation an artificial means of producing *immunity*, either by injection of *antibodies* (passive immunity) or by inducing the body to produce its own antibodies (active immunity).

immunity the means by which the body protects itself from infection.

incidence the number of new cases of a *disease* in a *population* in a given time, e.g. in one month or one year.

industrial melanism the evolutionary process in which the frequency of organisms that are initially light coloured becomes less, and the frequency of those that are dark increases, as a result of natural selection in areas blackened by pollution.

infectious disease *disease* caused by a *pathogen* that can be transmitted from one organism to another.

insulin a hormone, produced by the β cells of the *islets of Langerhans* in the pancreas, that decreases blood glucose levels by, amongst other things, increasing the conversion of glucose to glycogen.

intraspecific competition competition between organisms of the same species.

intrinsic proteins proteins of the cell surface membrane that completely or partially span the *phospholipid* bilayer from one side to the other.

introns portions of DNA within a *gene* that do not code for a polypeptide. The introns are removed from messenger RNA after *transcription*.

ion an atom or group of atoms that have lost or gained one or more *electrons*. Ions therefore have either a positive or negative charge. See also *anion* and *cation*.

ion channel a passage across a cell surface membrane made up of a protein that spans the membranes: some open and close to allow *ions* to pass in and out of the cell.

islets of Langerhans groups of cells in the pancreas comprising large α cells that produce the hormone *glucagon*, and small β cells that produce the hormone *insulin*.

isotonic solutions that possess the same concentration of solutes and therefore have the same *water potential*.

isotope variations of a chemical element that have the same number of *protons* and *electrons* but different numbers of neutrons. While their chemical properties are similar they differ in mass. One example is carbon which has a relative atomic mass of 12 and an isotope with a relative atomic mass of 14.

kinetic energy energy that an object possesses due to its motion.

Krebs cycle series of biochemical reactions in most *eukaryotic* cells by which energy is obtained through the oxidation of acetyl coenzyme A produced from the breakdown of glucose.

leach process in which chemicals are removed from soil by being dissolved in rainwater and washed away.

light dependent reaction stage of photosynthesis in which light energy is required to produce ATP and reduced NADP.

light independent reaction stage of photosynthesis which does not require light energy directly but does need the products of the *light dependent reaction* to reduce carbon dioxide and so form carbohydrate.

lignin a complex, non-carbohydrate polymer associated with cellulose in plant cell walls. Lignin makes the cell walls stronger, allowing them to resist tension and compression. It also makes them more waterproof.

link reaction the process linking *glycolysis* with *Krebs cycle* in which pyruvate is dehydrogenated and decarboxylated to form acetyl coenzyme A in the matrix of the mitochondria.

locus the position of a *gene* on a *chromosome*.

loop of Henlé the portion of a *nephron* that forms a hairpin loop which extends into the medulla of the kidney. It has a role in the reabsorption of water.

lumen the hollow cavity inside a tubular structure such as the gut or a *xylem vessel*.

lymph a slightly milky fluid found in lymph vessels and made up of *tissue fluid*, fats and *lymphocytes*.

lymphocytes type of white blood cell responsible for the *immune response*. They become activated in the presence of *antigens*. There are two types: *B lymphocytes* and *T lymphocytes*.

lysis the breakdown of a cell or compound.

magnification the size of the image of an object compared to the actual size.

meiosis the type of nuclear division in which the number of *chromosomes* is halved. In a cell with two sets of chromosomes (diploid), meiosis results in daughter cells, each with one set of chromosomes (haploid).

memory cells type of *lymphocyte* that circulates in the blood and *tissue fluid* long after the original *antigen* that caused them to develop has gone. They are reactivated when the same antigen returns, triggering an immediate secondary *immune response*.

mesophyll tissue found between the two layers of *epidermis* in a plant leaf comprising an upper layer of *palisade* cells and a lower layer of *spongy* cells.

messenger RNA form of ribonucleic acid that carries the information held by DNA, in the form of a nucleotide sequence, from the nucleus to the ribosomes in the cytoplasm, where it acts as a template on which polypeptides are assembled.

metabolism all the chemical processes that take place in living organisms.

mitosis the type of nuclear division in which the daughter cells have the same number of *chromosomes* as the parent cell.

mitotic to do with mitosis. See *mitosis*.

monocotyledonous plant any member of the class of flowering plants called Monocotyledonae. Their features include having a single seed leaf (cotyledon) and leaves that are parallel veined. See also *dicotyledonous plants*.

morbidity rate a measure of the frequency or proportion with which a disease appears in a population.

mortality rate a measure of the number of deaths in a given area or period, or from a particular cause.

motor neurone *neurone* that transmits *action potentials* from the central nervous system to an effector such as a muscle or gland.

multiple alleles term used to describe a *gene* that has more than two possible *alleles*.

mutagen any agent that induces a *mutation*.

mutation a permanent change in the amount or arrangement of a cell's DNA. A gene mutation is a change in the sequence of nucleotides that may result in an altered polypeptide.

mycelium a mass of fungal hyphae.

myelin a fatty substance that surrounds *axons* and *dendrites* in certain *neurones*.

myocardial infarction otherwise known as a heart attack, results from the interruption of the blood supply to the heart muscle causing damage to an area of the heart with consequent disruption to its function.

myoglobin red-coloured pigment found in muscle and used to store oxygen. See also *haemoglobin*.

myosin the thick filamentous protein found in skeletal muscle.

NAD (nicotinamide adenine dinucleotide) a molecule that carries high energy *electrons* and hydrogen ions from oxidised molecules to pathways that produce *ATP* during *aerobic* respiration.

natural immunity protection against infection so that the person does not become ill: it is provided by the transfer of antibodies from a mother to her fetus or through breastfeeding or is acquired as a result of having an infection.

negative feedback a series of changes, important in *homeostasis*, that result in a substance being restored to its normal level. See also *positive feedback*.

nephron basic functional unit of the mammalian kidney responsible for the formation of urine.

net primary production the rate at which material produced during photosynthesis is built up in a plant. Also known as the net assimilation rate, it is the *gross primary production* less the 20% or so used by the plant in processes such as respiration.

neuromuscular junction a *synapse* that occurs between a *neurone* and a muscle.

neurone a nerve cell, comprising a cell body, *axon* and *dendrites*, that is adapted to conduct *action potentials*.

neurotransmitter one of a number of chemicals that are involved in communication between adjacent nerve cells or between nerve cells and muscles. Two important examples are *acetylcholine* and noradrenaline.

neutron uncharged sub-atomic particle that occurs in the nucleus of an atom.

niche the functional role or place of a *species* within an *ecosystem*. It includes all of the ranges of environmental conditions and resources required for an organism to survive, reproduce and maintain a viable *population*.

nitrogen-fixing bacteria group of microorganisms that incorporate atmospheric nitrogen into nitrogen-containing compounds using the enzyme nitrogenase. They may be either free-living or act in conjunction with leguminous plants.

node of Ranvier a gap in the *myelin* sheath that surrounds the *axon* of a *neurone*.

non-infectious disease disease that is not caused by a *pathogen* e.g. genetic diseases.

non-self substances (usually proteins) that are not recognised by the immune system and can therefore trigger an *immune response* in the body.

nucleotides complex chemicals made up of an organic base, a sugar and a phosphate. They are the basic units of which the nucleic acids DNA and RNA are made.

oestrus the period in the oestrous cycle immediately after ovulation when the female is most fertile.

operator portion of DNA next to structural *genes* of an operon that switches them on or off.

operon a group of *genes* that codes for one or more proteins and controls its/their production.

oral rehydration therapy (ORT) means of treating dehydration, involving giving, by mouth, a balanced solution of salts and glucose that stimulates the gut to re-absorb water.

osmosis the passage of water from a region where it is at a higher water potential to a region where its water potential is lower, through a partially permeable membrane.

osmotic connected with the process of osmosis. see *osmosis*.

outbreak the sudden start of something unpleasant, especially violence or a disease.

oxidation chemical reaction involving the loss of *electrons*.

oxidative phosphorylation the formation of *ATP* in the electron transport system of *aerobic* respiration.

oxygen debt the quantity of oxygen needed to oxidise the lactate that accumulates during *anaerobic* respiration.

oxyhaemoglobin the name of a molecule that is formed when haemoglobin combines with oxygen, which changes colour from purple to bright red.

palisade a layer of long cells between two thin surface layers of a leaf that contains a lot of chloroplasts.

palisade mesophyll cells long, narrow cells, packed with chloroplasts, that are found in the upper region of a leaf and which carry out photosynthesis. See also *spongy mesophyll*.

pandemic describes any *disease* that spreads over vast areas of the world, e.g. HIV/AIDS. See also *endemic* and *epidemic*.

parasite an organism that lives on or in a host organism. The parasite gains a nutritional advantage and the host is harmed in some way.

passive immunity protection from infection so that the person does not become ill: it is acquired from the introduction of *antibodies* from another individual, rather than an individual's own immune system, e.g. across the placenta or in the mother's milk. It is usually short-lived.

pathogen any biological agent that causes disease.

phagocytosis form of endocytosis by which cells transport large particles across the cell surface membrane into the cell.

phenotype the physical, detectable expression of the particular *alleles* of an organism resulting from both its *genotype* and the effects of the environment.

phospholipid lipid molecule in which one of the three fatty acid molecules is replaced by a phosphate group, attached to a simple organic molecule such as choline. Phospholipids are important in the structure and functioning of the plasma membranes.

photolysis splitting of a water molecule by light such as occurs during the *light dependent reaction* of photosynthesis.

photomicrograph a photograph of the image seen using a light microscope.

photon 'particle' of light with a quantum of energy.

photosystem an organised group of chlorophyll and other pigment molecules situated in the *thylakoids* of chloroplasts that traps *photons* of light in a process called light harvesting.

pinocytosis form of *endocytosis* by which cells take up liquids from their environment.

pituitary gland master gland of the endocrine (hormone) system situated at the base of the brain.

plant growth regulator (plant hormone) chemicals produced by plants in tiny quantities that affect their growth or development. Examples include *auxins*, *gibberellins*, and *ethene*.

plasmid a small circular piece of DNA found in bacterial cells and often used as a *vector* in *gene technology*.

plasmodesmata fine strands of cytoplasm that extend through pores in adjacent cell walls and connect the cytoplasm of one cell with another.

platelets cells found in blood which play an important role in blood clotting.

podocyte cell from the inner lining of the *renal capsule* that has many processes and is adapted to help *ultrafiltration*.

polymer large molecule made up of repeating sub-units.

polymerase chain reaction (PCR) process of making many copies of a specific sequence of DNA or part of a *gene*. It is used extensively in *gene technology* and genetic fingerprinting.

polymerisation production of large molecules called polymers that are made of numerous similar sub-units.

polymerised see *polymerisation*.

polyploidy the possession of three or more sets of *chromosomes*.

polyunsaturated fatty acid (PUFA) fatty acid that possesses carbon chains with many double bonds.

population all the organisms of a particular species that occur in the same place at the same time.

positive feedback process which results in a substance that departs from its normal level becoming further from its norm. See also *negative feedback*.

prevalence the number of people in a *population* who have a particular *disease* at a particular time.

producer an *autotrophic* organism that synthesises organic molecules from simple inorganic ones such as carbon dioxide and water. Most producers are photosynthetic and form the first *trophic level* of a food chain. See also *consumer*.

prokaryote an organism belonging to the kingdom Prokaryotae that is characterised by having cells less than 5 μm in diameter which lack a nucleus and double membrane-bound organelles. Examples include bacteria and blue-green bacteria. See also *eukaryote*.

promoter the portion of an *operon* to which *RNA polymerase* attaches to begin the *transcription* of mRNA from the structural *genes*.

protoctist an organism belonging to the kingdom Protoctista, many of which are single celled *eukaryotes* such as certain algae and *protozoa*.

proton positively charged sub-atomic particle found in the nucleus of the atom. See also *electron*.

protoplast the living portion of a plant cell, i.e. the nucleus and cytoplasm along with the organelles it contains.

protozoa a sub-group of the kingdom *Protoctista* made up of single-celled organisms such as *Amoeba* and *Plasmodium*.

Purkyne tissue a region of specialist heart muscle that conducts a wave of excitation that causes contraction of the ventricles.

reaction centre a molecule of chlorophyll *a* that collects light energy that has been absorbed from the surrounding accessory pigments in the *photosystem*.

recessive the condition in which the effect of an *allele* is apparent in the *phenotype* of a *diploid* organism only in the presence of another identical allele. See also *dominant*.

reduction division see *meiosis*.

reflex arc the nerve pathway in the body taken by an *action potential* that leads to a rapid, involuntary response to a stimulus.

477

refractory period period during which the membrane of a *neurone* cannot be *depolarised* and no new *action potential* can be initiated.

renal capsule the cup-shaped portion at the start of a *nephron* that encloses the *glomerulus*.

repolarisation return of the *resting potential* in a *neurone* after an *action potential*.

resolution ability of a microscope to distinguish two objects as separate from each other.

respiratory quotient (RQ) a measure of the ratio of carbon dioxide given out by an organism to the oxygen taken in over a certain period.

resting potential the difference in electrical charge maintained across the cell membrane of an *axon* when not stimulated.

restriction endonucleases a group of enzymes that are able to cut DNA into shorter lengths at specific points. Found naturally in certain bacteria, they are important in *gene technology*.

reverse transcriptase enzyme capable of producing a DNA molecule from the corresponding *messenger RNA*. Found in many viruses, reverse transcriptase is used in *gene technology*.

RNA polymerase enzyme that joins together RNA *nucleotides* to form messenger RNA during *transcription*.

saltatory conduction propagation of an nerve impulse along a *myelinated dendron* or *axon* in which the *action potential* jumps from *node of Ranvier* to node of Ranvier.

sarcomere a section of myofibril between two Z-lines that forms the basic unit of striated muscle.

Schwann cell cell around a *neurone* whose cell surface membrane wraps around the *dendron* or *axon* to form the *myelin* sheath.

sclerenchyma (fibre) plant tissue whose cells have become rigid due to the presence of cell walls thickened with *lignin*. The cells are dead and function to provide support to the plant.

selection process that results in the best adapted individuals in a *population* surviving to breed and so pass their favourable *alleles* to the next generation.

self substances that are the product of the body's own *genes* and therefore do not trigger an *immune response* in that body.

semi-conservative replication the means by which DNA makes exact copies of itself by unwinding the double helix so that each strand acts as a template for the next. The new copies therefore possess one original and one new strand of DNA.

sensory neurone a *neurone* that transmits an *action potential* from a sensory receptor to the central nervous system.

serum clear liquid that is left after blood has clotted and the clot has been removed. It is therefore blood plasma without the clotting factors.

sickle cell anaemia inherited blood disorder in which abnormal *haemoglobin* leads to red cells becoming sickle-shaped and less able to carry oxygen.

sieve plate the perforated end wall of the phloem component called the sieve tube element.

sieve tube elements part of phloem tissue, elongate cells that join end to end to form tube-like structures for the transport of dissolved organic substances.

sinoatrial node (SAN) an area of *cardiac muscle* in the right atrium that controls and coordinates the contraction of the heart. Also known as the pacemaker.

smooth muscle also known as involuntary or unstriated muscle, smooth muscle is not under conscious control.

sodium–potassium pump carrier proteins across cell surface membranes that use *ATP* to move sodium *ions* out of the cell in exchange for potassium ions that move in.

speciation the evolution of two or more *species* from existing ones.

species a group of reproductively-isolated organisms which interbreed to produce fertile offspring.

spongy mesophyll cells irregularly shaped photosynthetic cells in the lower section of the leaf, below the palisade mesophyll layer. They have many air-spaces between them and are important in exchanging gases between the atmosphere and the rest of the leaf. See also *palisade mesophyll cells*.

stabilising selection selection that tends to eliminate the extremes of the *phenotype* range within a *population*. It occurs when environmental conditions are constant.

stem cells undifferentiated cells that can divide by mitosis to form new stem cells and can form specialised cells during development.

steroid a lipid, of which cholesterol is an example, that does not contain fatty acids.

stoma (plural stomata) pore, mostly in the lower epidermis of a leaf, through which gases diffuse in and out of the leaf.

stroke volume the volume of blood pumped at each ventricular contraction of the heart.

stroma fluid matrix of a chloroplast where the *light independent reaction* of photosynthesis takes place.

subcellular detail detail within the cell.

suberin a waxy, waterproof substance found in certain plant cell walls like endodermal cells of a root.

sympatric speciation the formation of new *species* that occurs when organisms that are living together become reproductively isolated, e.g. different *populations* may have different breeding seasons. See also *allopatric speciation*.

symplast pathway route through the cytoplasm, vacuoles and *plasmodesmata* of plant cells by which water and dissolved substances are transported. See also *apoplast pathway*.

synapse a junction between *neurones* in which they do not touch but have a narrow gap, the synaptic cleft, across which a *neurotransmitter* can pass.

systole the stage in the *cardiac cycle* in which the heart muscle contracts. It occurs in two stages: atrial systole when the atria contract and ventricular systole when the ventricles contact. See also *diastole*.

telomere ends of chromosomes (and *chromatids*) where a sequence of *nucleotides* is repeated many times.

tendons tough, flexible connective tissue that joins muscle to bone.

threshold level/value the minimum intensity that a stimulus must reach in order to trigger an *action potential* in a *neurone*.

thylakoid flattened membranous sac in a chloroplast that contains chlorophyll and the associated molecules needed for the *light dependent reaction* of photosynthesis.

tissue of cells of one (e.g. squamous epithelium) or a few types (e.g. phloem), specialised to perform a particular function.

tissue fluid fluid that surrounds the cells of the body. Its composition is similar to that of blood plasma except that it lacks some of the larger proteins, in particular those that cause the blood to clot. It supplies nutrients to the cells and removes waste products.

T lymphocyte type of white blood cell that is produced in the bone marrow but matures in the thymus gland. T lymphocytes coordinate the immune response and kill infected cells. See also *B lymphocyte*.

transcription the formation of *messenger RNA* molecules from the DNA that makes up a particular *gene*. It is the first part of protein synthesis.

transduction the process by which one form of energy is converted into another. In microbiology, the natural process by which genetic material is transferred between one host cell and another by a virus.

translation process whereby the code on a section of messenger RNA is converted to a particular sequence of amino acids that will go on to make a polypeptide and ultimately a protein.

translocation process where the information in the nucleotide sequence of a messenger RNA molecule is converted to a particular sequence of amino acids on a polypeptide chain: processing after translation forms the functioning protein.

transpiration the loss of water vapour from the aerial parts of a plant, usually the leaves: evaporation from the surfaces of mesophyll cells is followed by diffusion out of water vapour to the atmosphere down the water potential gradient.

triglyceride an individual fat or oil molecule made up of a glycerol molecule and three fatty acids.

trophic level the position of an organism in a food chain. See also *producer* and *consumer*.

tumour a swelling in an organism that is made up of cells which continue to divide in an abnormal way.

tumour suppressor genes *genes* that code for proteins that repress the cell cycle.

ultrafiltration filtration under pressure. A term applied to the first stage of urine formation in the kidney.

ultrastructure detail of the cell that can be seen using an electron microscope.

undifferentiated a term for describing stem cells, which can divide to produce some offspring cells that continue as stem cells and some cells that are designed to differentiate (meaning to become specialised).

urea organic molecule, $CO(NH_2)_2$, that is the main nitrogenous excretory product in mammals.

uric acid an almost insoluble compound which is a breakdown product of nitrogenous metabolism. It is the main excretory product in birds, reptiles, and insects.

vaccination the introduction of a vaccine containing appropriate *disease antigens* or *antibodies* into the body, by injection or mouth, in order to induce *artificial immunity*.

vascular bundle a strand of conducting vessels in the stem or leaves of a plant, typically with phloem on the outside and xylem on the inside.

vasoconstriction narrowing of the internal diameter of blood vessels. See also *vasodilation*.

vasodilation widening of the internal diameter of blood vessels. See also *vasoconstriction*.

vector a carrier. The term may refer to something such as a *plasmid*, which carries DNA into a cell, or to an organism that carries a parasite to its primary host.

vegetative propagation form of asexual reproduction in higher plants involving the separation of a piece of the original plant (stem, root or leaf), which then develops into a separate plant.

virulence a measure of how virulent something is - see *virulent*.

virulent able to cause disease or cause harm. The term is applied to a *disease* that spreads rapidly through a population.

voltage-gated channel channel protein across a cell surface membrane that opens and closes according to changes in the electrical potential across the membrane.

water potential the tendency of water to move from one area to another. It is a measure of potential energy and is expressed in units of pressure. The greater the number of water molecules present, the higher (less negative) the water potential. Pure water has a water potential of zero.

World Health Organization (WHO) a specialised agency of the United Nations concerned with global public health.

xerophyte a plant adapted to living in dry conditions. See also *hydrophyte*.

xylem vessel an tracheary element of xylem made up of a series of cells arranged in a way that enables water and mineral conduction.

Index